W9-AKX-665

Professional SQL Server® 2008 Integration Services

Professional
SQL Server® 2008
Integration Services

Professional
SQL Server® 2008
Integration Services

Brian Knight
Erik Veerman
Grant Dickinson
Douglas Hinson
Darren Herbold

WILEY

Wiley Publishing, Inc.

Professional SQL Server® 2008 Integration Services

Published by
Wiley Publishing, Inc.
10475 Crosspoint Boulevard
Indianapolis, IN 46256
www.wiley.com

Copyright © 2008 by Wiley Publishing, Inc., Indianapolis, Indiana

Published simultaneously in Canada

ISBN: 978-0-470-24795-2

Manufactured in the United States of America

10 9 8 7 6 5 4 3 2 1

Library of Congress Cataloging-in-Publication Data

> Professional Microsoft SQL server 2008 integration services / Brian Knight . . . [et al.].
> p. cm.
> Includes index.
> ISBN 978-0-470-24795-2 (paper/website)
> 1. SQL server. 2. Database management. I. Knight, Brian.
> QA76.9.D3P7662 2008
> 005.75'85—dc22

2008025018

No part of this publication may be reproduced, stored in a retrieval system or transmitted in any form or by any means, electronic, mechanical, photocopying, recording, scanning or otherwise, except as permitted under Sections 107 or 108 of the 1976 United States Copyright Act, without either the prior written permission of the Publisher, or authorization through payment of the appropriate per-copy fee to the Copyright Clearance Center, 222 Rosewood Drive, Danvers, MA 01923, (978) 750-8400, fax (978) 646-8600. Requests to the Publisher for permission should be addressed to the Legal Department, Wiley Publishing, Inc., 10475 Crosspoint Blvd., Indianapolis, IN 46256, (317) 572-3447, fax (317) 572-4355, or online at http://www.wiley.com/go/permissions.

Limit of Liability/Disclaimer of Warranty: The publisher and the author make no representations or warranties with respect to the accuracy or completeness of the contents of this work and specifically disclaim all warranties, including without limitation warranties of fitness for a particular purpose. No warranty may be created or extended by sales or promotional materials. The advice and strategies contained herein may not be suitable for every situation. This work is sold with the understanding that the publisher is not engaged in rendering legal, accounting, or other professional services. If professional assistance is required, the services of a competent professional person should be sought. Neither the publisher nor the author shall be liable for damages arising herefrom. The fact that an organization or Website is referred to in this work as a citation and/or a potential source of further information does not mean that the author or the publisher endorses the information the organization or Website may provide or recommendations it may make. Further, readers should be aware that Internet Websites listed in this work may have changed or disappeared between when this work was written and when it is read.

For general information on our other products and services or to obtain technical support, please contact our Customer Care Department within the U.S. at (800) 762-2974, outside the U.S. at (317) 572-3993 or fax (317) 572-4002.

Trademarks: Wiley and the Wiley logo, Wrox, the Wrox logo, Wrox Programmer to Programmer, and related trade dress are trademarks or registered trademarks of John Wiley & Sons, Inc. and/or its affiliates, in the United States and other countries, and may not be used without written permission. Microsoft and SQL Server are registered trademarks of Microsoft Corporation in the United States and/or other countries. All other trademarks are the property of their respective owners. Wiley Publishing, Inc. is not associated with any product or vendor mentioned in this book.

Wiley also publishes its books in a variety of electronic formats. Some content that appears in print may not be available in electronic books.

About the Authors

Brian Knight, SQL Server MVP, MCSE, MCDBA, is the co-founder of SQLServerCentral.com and JumpstartTV.com. Brian is a Principal Consultant and owner of Pragmatic Works. He runs the local SQL Server users' group in Jacksonville (JSSUG) and was on the Board of Directors of the Professional Association for SQL Server (PASS). Brian is a contributing columnist for SQL Server Standard and also maintains a regular column for the database website SQLServerCentral.com and does regular webcasts at Jumpstart TV. He has authored nine SQL Server books during the past 10 years. Brian has spoken at conferences like PASS, SQL Connections, and TechEd, and many Code Camps. You can find his blog at http://www.pragmaticworks.com. Brian spends weekends practicing to be a professional cage fighter and practicing for next season's *American Idol*.

Erik Veerman is a Mentor for Solid Quality Mentors focusing on training, mentoring, and architecting solutions on the SQL Server BI platform. His industry recognition includes Microsoft's Worldwide BI Solution of the Year and *SQL Server Magazine's* Innovator Cup winner. Erik has designed dozens of BI solutions across a broad business spectrum — telecommunications, marketing, retail, commercial real estate, finance, supply chain, and information technology. His experience with high-volume multi-terabyte environments and SQL Server 64-bit has enabled clients to scale their Microsoft-based BI solutions for optimal potential. As an expert in OLAP design, ETL processing, and dimensional modeling, Erik is a presenter, author, and instructor. He led the ETL architecture and design for the first production implementation of Integration Services (SSIS) and helped drive the ETL standards and best practices for SSIS on Microsoft's SQL Server 2005 reference initiative, Project REAL. Erik is also co-author of *Professional SQL Server 2005 Integration Services* and *Expert SQL Server 2005 Integration Services*, and lead author for the MS Press Training Kit *SQL Server 2005 Business Intelligence Implementation and Maintenance*. As a resident of Atlanta, GA, Erik participates in the local Atlanta SQL Server User's Group, a PASS chapter.

Grant Dickinson is a Program Manager at Microsoft, focusing on designing technologies that enable customers and partners to create innovative and scalable Business Intelligence solutions. Grant has helped qualify, architect, and implement BI solutions across a broad range of industries, including a solution that was once one of the largest Microsoft-based data warehouses in the world. He has designed and provided expertise into product features across the Microsoft BI stack, including technologies in SSIS, SQL Server, and Office. Grant helped develop the Microsoft best-practices ETL reference implementation, Project REAL, and has spoken at conferences around the world. Grant is currently focused on data quality and stewardship in the Master Data Management space. Grant was born in Zimbabwe and spent much of his youth in Southern Africa. He gained a BSc Computer Science at the University of the Witwatersrand in Johannesburg, and today he lives in Seattle with his wife and family.

Douglas Hinson splits his time between database and software development for financial applications in the logistics and insurance industries. Douglas specializes in conceptualizing, reengineering, and developing back-end solutions that connect business operational and financial functions. As a result, he has an extensive background in SQL Server and financial applications, and fits in some technical writing on the side. He has coauthored several Wrox books, including *SQL Server 2005 Performance Tuning*, *SQL Server 2005 CLR Programming*, and the previous edition of this book, *SQL Server 2005 Integration Services*.

About the Authors

Darren Herbold, MCDBA, MCSE is a dedicated consultant who is passionate about delivering business value to his clients. A principal consultant at Pragmatic Works Consulting (www.PragmaticWorks.com) and a graduate from Florida State University, he has expertise in Business Intelligence, Database Administration, and .NET Software Development. His main focus is on the SQL Server stack, where he delivers training, mentoring, and develops Data Warehouse, ETL, and Reporting solutions for his clients. He has developed a robust .NET application development framework and a code-generation tool that saves clients an average of 30 to 40 percent off of development time. Darren has also created BI and software solutions for clients such as Microsoft, Post Properties, and the University of South Florida. Visit his blog at: http://pragmaticworks.com/community/blogs/.

Credits

Executive Editor
Bob Elliott

Development Editor
Brian MacDonald

Technical Editors
Douglas Laudenschlager
Carla Sabotta
Michael A. Entin
Ranjeeta Nanda
Ritu Kothari
Feng Guo
Neal Graves
Devin Knight

Production Editor
Kathleen Wisor

Copy Editor
Kim Cofer

Editorial Manager
Mary Beth Wakefield

Production Manager
Tim Tate

Vice President and Executive Group Publisher
Richard Swadley

Vice President and Executive Publisher
Joseph B. Wikert

Project Coordinator, Cover
Lynsey Stanford

Proofreader
Nancy Carrasco

Indexer
Melanie Belkin

Acknowledgments

As always, I must thank my wife and best friend for supporting me for the past 10 years of marriage. I've been fortunate to have found a woman who doesn't fall asleep immediately when copyediting my technical writing. Thanks to my three children: Colton, Liam, and Camille for allowing their daddy to be distracted sometimes with this book when they wanted to play. Thanks also to all the wonderful co-authors, who truly made this book possible. Once again, I must thank the Pepsi Cola Company for inventing Mountain Dew, which drove the late night writing. Lastly, thanks to my sensei and song writer Sensei Yoshi, who has helped me win my first cage fighting match and is preparing me for next year's *American Idol*.

—*Brian Knight*

First of all, I'd like to thank my kids, Meg, Nate, Kate, and Caleb, for being patient with me through the sometimes tiresome process of writing. And of course, my wife, Amy, is amazing! Also thanks to Brian Knight and the other authors who helped make this book so valuable. And thanks to Andy Leonard for his help. There's no one better at knowing how SSIS integrates with Visual Studio Team System. Thanks go to the producers of coffee beans, because without caffeine, I honestly don't know if my contribution to this book would have been worth anything!

—*Erik Veerman*

To my beautiful Heidi, thank you for your support, encouragement, and understanding, and for being the best wife and friend I could ask for. Jessica and Anna, my two wonderful little girls, I thank God every day that we have the gift of you in our lives. I cherish the times when you two sat on my lap while I (ungainly) authored this book, waiting for me to finish so we could go and play outside. You are so little but you give so much. Bruce, you are a brother and uncle-extraordinaire. Dad, Mom, Mae, Pai (and the whole fandamily); though we are spread around the world, your legacy keeps our faith, values, and family strong. Hatch, Dives, Cyril, Neil, Len, Dave, Donald, Erik, and Henk, thanks for your friendship, mentorship, and passion during these years in Microsoft. Finally, my gratitude to Brian; it's been fun presenting and writing with you — good job on another great book!

—*Grant Dickinson*

Thanks to God for the blessing of being able to do what I love for a living. To my beautiful wife, Misty, thank you for being so supportive and understanding during this project, as always. Kyle and Mariah, thanks for being so patient with your Dad while he was putting this project together. A big thanks to the Wrox and Microsoft Tech editors and our Jacksonville area SQL Server guru, Brian Knight, who has come through again with a great cast of authors and a reworked, well-crafted guide to SQL Server Integrated Services 2008.

—*Douglas Hinson*

Acknowledgments

I'd first like to thank my beautiful wife, Ashley, and my wonderful children, Sydney and Kiley, for all their patience and support during this process. I want to also thank Brian Knight for giving me the awesome opportunity to be involved in this project. He's been a fantastic mentor, friend, and overall great guy. Mt. Dew played a pivotal role in this too, for obvious reasons. I also would like to thank all the great folks at KBX Boxing Gym in Alpharetta for teaching me to dig deep when I would much rather vomit and pass out. Go Krav Maga! Lastly, I want to thank the fine staff at Wiley Publishing for their support and guidance in this endeavor.

—*Darren Herbold*

Professional
SQL Server® 2008
Integration Services

Contents

Contents

Contents

Contents

Contents

Contents

Contents

Contents

Contents

Contents

Introduction

SQL Server Integration Services (SSIS) was released to the market in SQL Server 2005 and took the Extract Transform Load (ETL) market by surprise. In SQL Server 2008, SSIS has focused on maturing the product and improving the product's scalability and performance by an astonishing 70% in some cases. If you're new to SSIS, you've picked a fantastic field to become involved in! The one consistent skill needed in today's technical job market is ETL. If a company wants to establish a partnership with another company, they'll need to communicate data back and forth between the two companies. If your company wants to launch new products, they'll need a way to integrate those products into their website and catalog. All of these types of tasks are going to require the skillset you are developing and will learn in this book.

Companies that had never used SQL Server before are now allowing it in their environment because SSIS is such an easy-to-use and cost-effective way to move data. SSIS competes with the largest ETL tools on the market, like Data Stage and Ab Initio, at a tiny fraction of the price. SQL Server 2008 now offers more components that you use to make your life even easier and the performance scales to a level never seen on the SQL Server platform.

The best thing about SSIS is its price tag: free with your SQL Server purchase. Many ETL vendors charge hundreds of thousands of dollars for what you will see in this book. SSIS is also a great platform for you to expand and integrate into, which many ETL vendors do not offer. Once you get past the initial learning curve, you'll be amazed with the power of the tool, and it can take weeks off your time to market.

Who This Book Is For

Having used SSIS since the beta stages of SQL Server 2005 and through its evolution into its current form, the idea of writing this book was quite compelling. If you've never used SSIS before, we spend the first chapters focusing on lowering your learning curve on this product. If you've used SSIS in the past, we've added quite a bit of new content that is specific to SQL Server 2008 and to take your skills to the next level. If you're an SSIS 2005 user, luckily, this is an incremental release, and you won't have to completely relearn your skills.

This book is intended for developers, DBAs, and casual users who hope to use SSIS for transforming data, creating a workflow, or maintaining their SQL Server. This book is a *professional* book, meaning that the authors assume that you know the basics of how to query a SQL Server and have some rudimentary programming skills. Not much programming skill will be needed or assumed, but it will help with your advancement. No skills in the prior release of SSIS (called DTS then) are required, but we do reference it throughout the book when we call attention to feature enhancements.

What This Book Covers

Whether you're new to SSIS or an experienced SSIS developer, there's something for you in this book. This book takes you from the architecture and basics of SSIS all the way through to developing hard-core SSIS solutions to solve many of the industry's common business scenarios. The book is tutorial based, meaning that it teaches you through simple examples.

By the time you've completed this book, you'll know how to load and synchronize database systems using SSIS by using some of the new SQL Server 2008 features. You'll also know how to load data warehouses, which is a very hot and specialized skill. Even in warehousing, you'll find features in the new 2008 release that you'll wonder how you lived without!

How This Book Is Structured

After discussing the architecture of SSIS, we'll start with the basics by introducing the fundamental concepts of SSIS: The Data Flow and Control Flow. We'll then build through the various other features, including the warehousing and scripting, and proceed to advanced topics like programming and extending the engine. We'll conclude with a case study that helps to tie everything together. SSIS is a very feature-rich product, and it took a lot to cover the product.

Chapter 1, "Welcome to SQL Server Integration Services," introduces the concepts that we're going to discuss throughout the remainder of this book. We talk about the SSIS architecture and give a brief overview of what you can do with SSIS.

Chapter 2, "The SSIS Tools," shows you how to quickly learn how to import and export data by using the Import and Export Wizard and then takes you on a tour of the Business Intelligence Development Studio (BIDS).

Chapter 3, "SSIS Tasks," goes into each of the tasks that are available to you in SSIS. These tasks are the building blocks for your SSIS workflow and are much like Lego block programming.

Chapter 4, "Containers," covers how to use containers to do looping in SSIS and describes how to configure each of the basic transforms.

Chapter 5, "The Data Flow," dives into the data flow components in SSIS. These components are where typical ETL developers will spend 75% of their time when loading a database.

Chapter 6, "Using Expressions and Variables," instructs you how to use the obscure expression language in SSIS by showing you many example use cases and how to solve them through the language.

Chapter 7, "Joining Data," focuses on how to join systems together, whether those systems are two flat files or database platforms. Much of the chapter is spent showing the Lookup Component, which is where much of the work into SSIS 2008 went.

Now that you know how to configure most of the tasks and transforms, Chapter 8, "Creating an End-to-End Package," puts it all together with a large example that lets you try out your SSIS experience.

Chapter 9, "Scripting in SSIS," shows you some of the ways you can use the Script Task in SSIS.

Chapter 10, "Loading a Data Warehouse," covers how to load a data warehouse from the ground up through example. Even smaller companies now are finding that to compete they need to make their data work for them by employing a data warehouse. We show how to load dimension and fact tables in this chapter and some of the common issues.

Chapter 11, "Using the Relational Engine" focuses on how to synchronize systems incrementally. Generally, it's too inefficient to completely purge and load a system daily or monthly. This chapter shows you some of the new SQL Server 2008 features like Change Data Capture that help you make this synchronization a smooth process.

Sometimes you connect to systems other than SQL Server. Chapter 12, "Accessing Heterogeneous Data," shows you how to connect to systems other than SQL Server like Excel, XML, and Web services.

Chapter 13, "Reliability and Scalability" demonstrates how to scale SSIS and make it more reliable. You can use the features in this chapter to show you how to make the package restartable if a problem occurs.

Chapter 14, "Understanding and Tuning the Data Flow Engine," explains the architecture of the SSIS Data Flow engine in detail and how to tune your SSIS packages for maximum efficiency.

Chapter 15, "Source Control and Software Development Life Cycle," introduces a software development life cycle methodology to you. It speaks to how SSIS can integrate with Visual Studio Team System.

Chapter 16, "DTS 2000 Migration" shows how to migrate DTS 2000 packages to SSIS and if necessary, how to run DTS 2000 packages under SSIS. It also discusses third-party management to convert packages.

Chapter 17, "Error and Event Handling," discusses how to handle problems with SSIS with error and event handling.

Chapter 18, "Programming and Extending SSIS," shows the SSIS object model and how to use it to extend SSIS. The chapter goes through creating your own task, and then Chapter 19, "Adding a User Interface to Your Component," adds a user interface to the discussion.

Chapter 20, "External Management and WMI Task Implementation," walks through creating an application that interfaces with the SSIS to manage the environment. It also discusses the WMI set of tasks.

Chapter 21, "Using SSIS with External Applications," teaches you how to expose the SSIS Data Flow to other programs like InfoPath and your own .NET applications.

Chapter 22, "Administering SSIS," shows you how to deploy and administer the packages that you've worked so hard to develop. We cover the SSIS service, how to run packages and schedule packages and some of the challenges you'll see with 64-bit systems.

Chapter 23 is a programmatic case study that creates three SSIS packages for a banking application.

What You Need to Use This Book

To follow this book, you will only need to have SQL Server 2008 and the Integration Services component installed. You'll need a machine that can support the minimum hardware requirements to run SQL Server 2008. You'll also want to have the AdventureWorks2008 and AdventureWorksDW2008 databases installed. Instructions for accessing these databases can be found in the ReadMe file on this book's Web site.

Conventions

To help you get the most from the text and keep track of what's happening, we've used a number of conventions throughout the book:

- ❑ We *highlight* new terms and important words when we introduce them.
- ❑ We show keyboard strokes like this: Ctrl+A.
- ❑ We show filenames, URLs, and code within the text like so: `persistence.properties`.
- ❑ We present code in two different ways:

```
In code examples we highlight new and important code with a gray background.
```

```
The gray highlighting is not used for code that's less important in the present
context or that has been shown before.
```

Source Code

As you work through the examples in this book, you may choose either to type in all the code manually or to use the source code files that accompany the book. All of the source code used in this book is available for download at `http://www.wrox.com`. Once at the site, simply locate the book's title (either by using the Search box or by using one of the title lists) and click the Download Code link on the book's detail page to obtain all the source code for the book.

Because many books have similar titles, you may find it easiest to search by ISBN; this book's ISBN is 978-0-470-24795-2.

Once you download the code, just decompress it with your favorite compression tool. Alternatively, you can go to the main Wrox code download page at `www.wrox.com/dynamic/books/download.aspx` to see the code available for this book and all other Wrox books.

Errata

We make every effort to ensure that there are no errors in the text or in the code. However, no one is perfect, and mistakes do occur. If you find an error in one of our books, like a spelling mistake or faulty piece of code, we would be very grateful for your feedback. By sending in errata, you may save another reader hours of frustration, and at the same time you will be helping us provide even higher-quality information.

To find the errata page for this book, go to http://www.wrox.com and locate the title using the Search box or one of the title lists. Then, on the book details page, click the Book Errata link. On this page you can view all errata that has been submitted for this book and posted by Wrox editors. A complete book list including links to each book's errata is also available at www.wrox.com/misc-pages/booklist.shtml.

If you don't spot "your" error on the Book Errata page, go to www.wrox.com/contact/techsupport.shtml and complete the form there to send us the error you have found. We'll check the information and, if appropriate, post a message to the book's errata page and fix the problem in subsequent editions of the book.

p2p.wrox.com

For author and peer discussion, join the P2P forums at p2p.wrox.com. The forums are a Web-based system for you to post messages relating to Wrox books and related technologies and to interact with other readers and technology users. The forums offer a subscription feature to e-mail you topics of interest of your choosing when new posts are made to the forums. Wrox authors, editors, other industry experts, and your fellow readers are present on these forums.

At http://p2p.wrox.com you will find a number of different forums that will help you, not only as you read this book, but also as you develop your own applications. To join the forums, just follow these steps:

1. Go to p2p.wrox.com and click the Register link.

2. Read the terms of use and click Agree.

3. Complete the required information to join as well as any optional information you wish to provide and click Submit.

4. You will receive an e-mail with information describing how to verify your account and complete the joining process.

    You can read messages in the forums without joining P2P, but in order to post your own messages, you must join.

Once you join, you can post new messages and respond to messages other users post. You can read messages at any time on the Web. If you would like to have new messages from a particular forum e-mailed to you, click the Subscribe to this Forum icon by the forum name in the forum listing.

For more information about how to use the Wrox P2P, be sure to read the P2P FAQs for answers to questions about how the forum software works, as well as many common questions specific to P2P and Wrox books. To read the FAQs, click the FAQ link on any P2P page.

1

Welcome to SQL Server Integration Services

SQL Server Integration Services (SSIS) is the anchor in a trilogy of products that make up the Microsoft SQL Server Business Intelligence (BI) platform. SSIS along with Analysis Services and Reporting Services round out a platform that clearly puts Microsoft on the map in the enterprise Business Intelligence arena. In its simplest form, SSIS is an enterprise-level extract, transform, and load (ETL) development tool. However, SSIS is not just a fancy wrapper around an import wizard. In a drag-and-drop development environment, ETL developers can snap together intricate workflows and out-of-the-box data-cleansing flows that rival custom coding and expensive third-party tools. For your edge cases, the model is easily extensible and custom components can be developed in .NET languages to simply snap into the framework. However, custom coding most likely will not even be necessary. With the latest version of SSIS, novice developers can use the embedded Visual Studio Tools for Applications (VSTA) development environment to custom code workflow tasks and data pipeline transformations in VB or C# .NET languages.

When we put together the first edition of this book, we were blown away by the new architecture and capabilities of SSIS. SSIS was a big change from the Data Transformation Services (DTS) product that it replaced and there has been much to learn. Since the first edition of SSIS, we have collectively racked up many years of experience converting older DTS packages and mindsets over to using SSIS, and trust us when we say that no one who's made the change is asking to go back. We've learned some things, too. If you run into an issue getting up and running, converting older packages, or creating new ones, we've probably run into that issue too and have a solution for you here in this book. This book is a new edition and a whole new book. Nothing was sacred in this rewrite because we really dug in to put the last few years of experience working with this product back into these pages. We think the result is worth it and this edition will make your experience with SSIS a more productive one. This chapter starts from the beginning and provides an overview of SSIS, describes where it fits within the BI product platform, and ETL development in general.

SQL Server SSIS Historical Overview

In SQL Server 7.0, Microsoft had a small team of developers work on a much understated feature of SQL Server called Data Transformation Services (DTS). DTS was the backbone of the Import/Export Wizard, and the DTS's primary purpose was to transform data from almost any OLE DB–compliant Data Source to another destination. It also had the ability to execute programs and run scripts, making workflow a minor feature.

By the time that SQL Server 2000 was released, DTS had a strong following of DBAs and maybe a few developers. Microsoft included in the release new features like the Dynamic Properties Task that enabled you to alter the package dynamically at runtime. Even though DTS utilized extensive logging along with simple and complex multiphase data pumps, usability studies still showed that developers had to create elaborate scripts to extend DTS to get what they wanted done. A typical use case was enabling DTS to load data conditionally based on the existence of a file. To accomplish this in DTS, you would have had to use the ActiveX Script Task to code a solution using the file system object in VBScript. The problem here was that DTS simply lacked some of the common components to support typical ETL processes. Although it was powerful if you knew how to write scripting code, most DBAs just didn't have this type of scripting experience (or time).

After five years, Microsoft released the much touted SQL Server 2005, and SSIS, which is no longer an understated feature like DTS. With the 2008 release, SSIS is now one of the main business intelligence (BI) platform foundations. SSIS has moved so far up in importance that it now has its own service along with the new name. This is entirely appropriate because so much has been added to SSIS. Microsoft made a huge investment in usability, adding the first set of ETL tool-based components and upping the ante again with this latest version. If what you need to do isn't readily available, you now have the full .NET library with VB and C# programming languages to add your own custom coding to message data or manage the ETL process. However, you'll be surprised how rarely you'll need to drop into a coding environment. In fact, as you dig into the toolset, you'll find that things you may have needed to hand-code in a Script Task are simply part of the out-of-the-box components.

What's New in SSIS

SSIS is now in its second edition. If you are brand new to SSIS, everything will be new, but even if you are already using SSIS each version just keeps getting better. This latest version of SSIS includes enhancements for performance and scalability, upgrades to handle new TSQL capabilities, and the addition of new components, including the long-awaited ability to use C# in the scripting tasks. We'll hit the highlights here.

The data pipeline has been overhauled so that it scales to better use the multiple, dual, and quad-core processor improvements. The Lookup Component that performs foreign key resolutions has also been redesigned to allow for persistence of lookup cache that screams when you tune them for dimension tables. Underneath SSIS now allows new TSQL extensions for multiple data manipulation language (DML) operations like the MERGE statement.

If you are looking for the latest toys, this version of SSIS has added new workflow components to control the cache window maintenance, to generate TSQL traces, or reset row count variables. In the Data Flows, there are new ADO Sources and Destinations to add to the OLE Sources and Destinations that were part of the first version.

Lastly, there has been a major improvement to the development environment from the previous versions with the removal of the cobbled-together Visual Basic for Applications (VBA) implementation. The VBA environment was only intended as a temporary implementation to allow custom scripting within your ETL processes, evidenced by the clunky integration and that you were limited to VB.NET only. Now the Script Tasks and Components use an embedded version of the Microsoft Visual Studio 2008 Tools for Applications (VSTA) environment that supports both VB and C# .NET programming languages. In addition, you can now add web references to your ETL processes without having to code your own wrappers to web services to make use of existing business logic or data sources. We'll touch on all of these improvements as you read through this book and explore the examples, but first let's get started.

Getting Started

Most of this book will assume that you know nothing about the past releases of SQL Server DTS and will start with a fresh look at SQL Server SSIS. After all, when you dive into the new features, you'll realize how little knowing anything about the old release actually helps you when learning this one. However, if you don't come from the world of DTS, it's hard for us not to throw in a few analogies here and there to get these folks also up to speed on SSIS. The learning curve can be considered steep at first, but once you figure out the basics, you'll be creating what would have been complex packages in DTS in no time. To get an idea of how easy SSIS is to use, look at a tool that is a staple in the ETL world, the Import and Export Wizard.

Import and Export Wizard

If you need to move data quickly from almost any OLE DB–compliant Data Source to a destination, you can use the SSIS Import and Export Wizard (shown in Figure 1-1). In fact, many SSIS packages are born this way. The wizard is a quick way to move the data, perform very light transformations of data, and all versions except Express allow you to persist the logic of the data movement into a package. The basic concept of an import/export wizard has not changed substantially from the days of DTS. You still have the option of checking all the tables you'd like to transfer. However, you also get the option now of encapsulating the entire transfer of data into a single transaction.

Where do you find the wizard? It depends. If you just need to perform a quick import or export, access the wizard directly from the Start menu by navigating to Start ⇨ Microsoft SQL Server 2008 ⇨ Import and Export Data. The other option is to open up a project in the SSIS development environment and select the menu option Project ⇨ SSIS Import and Export Wizard. We cover this in detail in Chapter 2. Before we get into all the mechanics for that, Figure 1-1 shows an example of the wizard fully loaded and ready to move some data.

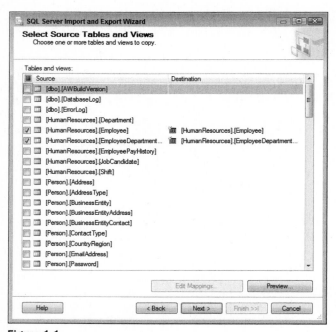

Figure 1-1

The Business Intelligence Development Studio

The Business Intelligence Development Studio (BIDS) is the central environment that you'll spend most of your time in as an SSIS developer. BIDS is just a specialized use of the familiar Visual Studio development environment that can host many different project types from Console applications to Class Libraries and Windows applications. Although you may see many project types, BIDS actually only contains project templates for Analysis Services, Integration Services, Report Server, and Report Model Projects. SSIS in particular uses a business-intelligence project type called an Integration Services project that provides development design surfaces with a completely ETL-based set of tools in the Toolbox window. Get your first look at the development environment in Figure 1-2.

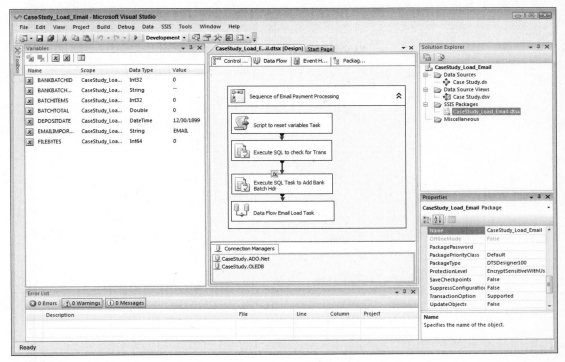

Figure 1-2

Though this development environment is similar to the legacy DTS Designer, the approach is completely different. Most importantly, this is a collaborative development environment just like any Visual Studio development effort with full source code management, version control, and multi-user project management. In fact, SSIS was not developed in the context of a SQL Server instance like the DTS Designer, and you don't get to the SSIS IDE from within a particular SQL Server instance. SSIS solutions are developed just like all other .NET development solutions, including being persisted to files — in this case, XML file-based structures. You can even develop within the BIDS environment without a connection to a SQL Server instance using the off-line mode. Once your solution is complete, it can be built and deployed to one or multiple target SQL servers. These changes are crucial to establishing the discipline and best practices of existing .NET development methodologies as you develop business intelligence solutions. We'll discuss this BIDS development interface in more detail later.

Architecture

Microsoft has truly established SSIS in SQL Server as a major player in the extraction, transformation, and loading (ETL) market. Not only is SSIS technology a complete code rewrite from SQL Server 2000 DTS, but now it rivals other third-party ETL tools costing hundreds or thousands of dollars based on how you scale the software — and it comes free with the purchase of SQL Server 2005 and later versions. Free is great, but it can take you only so far if the feature set is minimal, or if the toolset has limited usability, scalability, or enterprise performance limitations. But SSIS is for real, satisfying these typical

ETL requirements with a new architecture that has expanded dramatically, as you can see in Figure 1-3. The SSIS architecture consists of four main components:

❑ The SSIS Service

❑ The SSIS runtime engine and the runtime executables

❑ The SSIS Data Flow engine and the Data Flow Components

❑ The SSIS clients

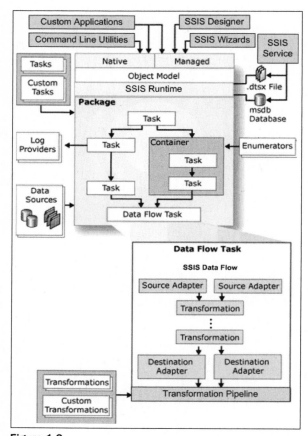

Figure 1-3

The SSIS Service handles the operational aspects of SSIS. It is a Windows service installed when you install the SSIS Component of SQL Server. It tracks the execution of packages (a collection of work items) and helps with the storage of the packages. Don't worry; we'll get to explaining what packages are shortly. The SSIS Service is turned on by default and is set to automatic. You don't need the SSIS service to be on to run SSIS packages, but if the service is stopped, the default behavior is for all the SSIS packages that are currently running to also stop. (You can configure this service differently in the service configuration if this is not the behavior you require.)

The SSIS runtime engine and its complementary programs actually run your SSIS packages. The engine saves the layout of your packages and manages the logging, debugging, configuration, connections, and transactions. Additionally, it manages handling your events when they are raised within your package. The runtime executables provide the following functionality, which you'll explore in more detail later in this chapter:

- ❑ **Containers:** Provide structure and scope to your package.

- ❑ **Tasks:** Provide the functionality to your package.

- ❑ **Event handlers:** Respond to raised events in your package.

- ❑ **Precedence constraints:** Provide ordinal relationship between various items in your package.

In Chapter 3, you'll spend a lot of time in each of these architectural sections, but the next few sections provide a nice overview for the ones that are the most important.

Packages

A core component of SSIS and DTS is the notion of a *package*. A package best parallels an executable program that maintains workflow and business logic. Essentially, a package is a collection of tasks snapped together to execute in an orderly fashion. Precedence constraints are used to connect the tasks together and manage the order in which tasks will execute, based on what happens in each task or specialized rules. The package is compiled into a .DTSX file that is actually an XML-structured file with collections of properties. Just like other .NET solutions, the file-based code is marked up using the development environment and can then be saved and compiled for deployment to a SQL Server as a file in the file system or can be saved into the msdb database metadata. The package XML structure stripped down to the basic elements looks like this:

```
<?xml version="1.0"?>
<DTS:Executable xmlns:DTS="www.microsoft.com/SqlServer/Dts"
DTS:ExecutableType="MSDTS.Package.2">
<DTS:ConnectionManager></DTS:ConnectionManager>
<DTS:PackageVariable></DTS:PackageVariable>
<DTS:Executable></DTS:Executable>
<DTS:Executable DTS:ExecutableType="DTS.Pipeline.2">
    <components>
        <component></component>
    </components>
</DTS:Executable>
<DTS:EventHandler></DTS:EventHandler>
<DTS:PrecedenceConstraint></DTS:PrecedenceConstraint>
<DTS:Executable>
```

Here you can see the package collections of connections, package variables, executables, and precedence constraints. The specific executable named DTS.Pipeline.2 is a special task type that allows for transformation of a data stream or pipeline that we'll discover later. The point here is that the SSIS package is an XML-structured file much like .RDL files are to Reporting Services. Of course, there is much more to packages than that, but you'll explore the other elements of packages, like event handlers, later in this chapter.

Tasks

A *task* can best be described as an individual unit of work. In the previous XML package snippet these are the `<DTS:Executable>` nodes. Tasks provide functionality to your package, in much the same way that a method does in a programming language. However, in SSIS, you aren't coding the methods; rather, you are dragging and dropping them onto a design surface and configuring them. You can also develop your own tasks, but here are the current ETL Tasks available to you out-of-the-box:

❑ **ActiveX Script Task:** Executes an ActiveX script in your SSIS package. This task is only to facilitate conversion of legacy DTS packages that use this deprecated scripting method.

❑ **Analysis Services Execute DDL Task:** Executes a DDL Task in Analysis Services. For example, this can create, drop, or alter a cube (Enterprise and Developer Editions only).

❑ **Analysis Services Processing Task:** This task processes a SQL Server Analysis Services cube, dimension, or mining model.

❑ **Bulk Insert Task:** Loads data into a table by using the `BULK INSERT SQL` command.

❑ **Data Flow Task:** This very specialized task loads and transforms data into an OLE DB, and now, optionally, an ADO.NET Destination.

❑ **Data Mining Query Task:** Allows you to run predictive queries against your Analysis Services data-mining models.

❑ **Data Profiling Task:** This exciting new task allows for the examination of data to replace your ad-hoc data profiling techniques.

❑ **Execute DTS 2000 Package Task:** Exposes legacy SQL Server 2000 DTS packages to your SSIS package.

❑ **Execute Package Task:** Allows you to execute a package from within a package, making your SSIS packages modular.

❑ **Execute Process Task:** Executes a program external to your package, such as one to split your extract file into many files before processing the individual files.

❑ **Execute SQL Task:** Executes a SQL statement or stored procedure.

❑ **File System Task:** This task can handle directory operations such as creating, renaming, or deleting a directory. It can also manage file operations such as moving, copying, or deleting files.

❑ **FTP Task:** Sends or receives files from an FTP site.

❑ **Message Queue Task:** Sends or receives messages from a Microsoft Message Queue (MSMQ).

❑ **Script Task:** This task allows you to perform more .NET-based scripting in the Visual Studio Tools for Applications programming environment.

❑ **Send Mail Task:** Sends a mail message through SMTP.

❑ **Web Service Task:** Executes a method on a Web service.

❑ **WMI Data Reader Task:** This task can run WQL queries against the Windows Management Instrumentation. This allows you to read the event log, get a list of applications that are installed, or determine hardware that is installed, to name a few examples.

❏ **WMI Event Watcher Task:** This task empowers SSIS to wait for and respond to certain WMI events that occur in the operating system.

❏ **XML Task:** Parses or processes an XML file. It can merge, split, or reformat an XML file.

There is also a whole set of tasks that are DBA-oriented, allowing you to create packages that can be used to maintain your SQL Server environment. These tasks perform functions such as transferring your SQL Server databases, backing up your database, or shrinking the database. Each of the tasks available to you is described in Chapter 3 in much more detail, and you will see them in other examples throughout the book. Tasks are extensible, and you can create your own custom tasks in .NET if you need a workflow item that doesn't exist or if you have a common scripting function that can benefit from reuse in your package development. We cover this topic in Chapter 18, "Programming and Extending SSIS."

Data Source Elements

The core strength of SSIS is its capability to extract data, transform it, and write it out to an alternative destination. Data sources are the conduit for these data pipelines and are represented by connections that can be used by sources or destinations once they've been defined. A data source uses connections that are OLE DB–compliant and with SSIS 2008 this now includes ADO.NET Data Sources, such as SQL Server, Oracle, DB2, or even nontraditional Data Sources, such as Analysis Services and Outlook. The data sources can be localized to a single SSIS package or shared across multiple packages in BIDS.

All the characteristics of the connection are defined in the Connection Manager. The Connection Manager dialog box options vary based on the type of connection you're trying to configure. Figure 1-4 shows you what a typical connection to SQL Server would look like.

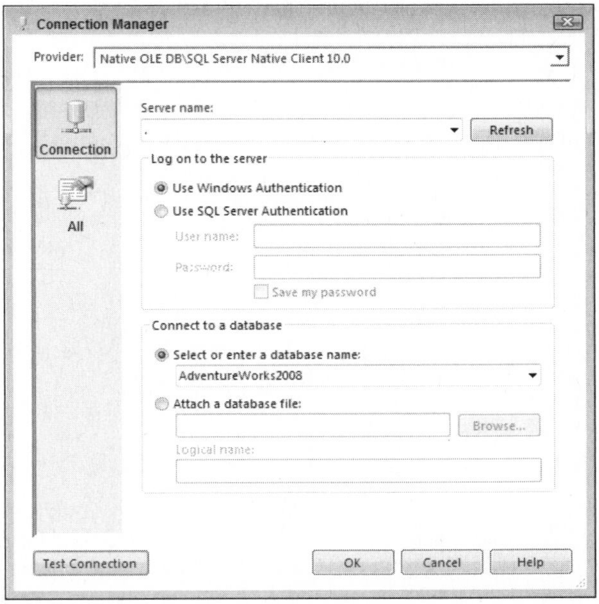

Figure 1-4

Connection Managers are used to centralize connection strings to data sources and abstract them from the SSIS packages themselves. In fact, the connections created by a Connection Manager are typically created in the registry of a machine and not stored in the package itself — although you can encrypt this information and store it. This allows you to deploy the SSIS package with a configuration file (which we'll describe later) that can set the full value of the connection properties at runtime. One nice thing is that you can even configure the connection offline and completely design an SSIS package without connecting to the server until you are ready to test. SSIS will not use the connection until you begin to instantiate it in the package. This provides the ultimate in lightweight development portability for SSIS.

Data Source Views

Data source views (DSVs) are handy abstract concepts that you can use in SSIS and other SQL Server projects. This feature allows you to create logical views of your business data. These views are a combination of tables, views, stored procedures, and queries that can be shared across your project and leveraged in Analysis Services and Report Builder projects.

This is especially useful in large complex data models that are prevalent in ERP systems like Siebel or SAP. These systems have column names like ER328F2 to make the data model flexible for nearly any environment. However, this complex naming convention creates difficulties for the typical business user or developer, impeding productivity that a simple readable name would eliminate. A DSV can be used to map such columns to entities like LastPaymentDate to increase readability of the model. DSVs can also be used to map the relationships between the tables that don't necessarily exist in the physical model.

Another common use of DSVs is to segment large sections of the data model into more security- or functional-based chunks. DSVs provide an abstraction that transcends schema or even data source separation. Take, for example, a DSV from the AdventureWorks Human Resource model as shown in Figure 1-5. As you can see in this figure, not only has the DSV unified the different schemas, but a friendly name has also been assigned to rename the Birth Date column in the Employee entity to DOB.

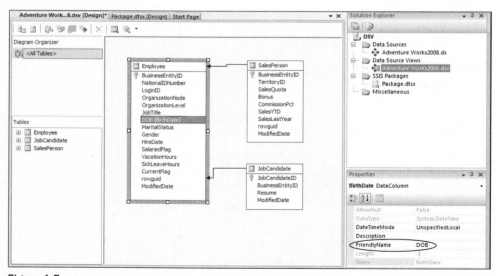

Figure 1-5

DSVs are used just like Connection Managers. However, there are a few key differences to remember when using them. Like data sources, DSVs allow you to define the connection logic once and reuse it across your SSIS packages. However, unlike connections, DSV structures are stored once, and then are disconnected from the real source. This means that the underlying structure of the DSVs may change, but the DSVs are not automatically refreshed. This can cause some problems during execution; if you were to change the Employee table in a connection to a DSV for Human Resources, the DSV would not pick up the change. On the other hand, if your model does not change often, this type of caching is a huge benefit in your development of SSIS packages. The DSVs provide the disconnected capabilities to allow development of SSIS packages to continue against cached metadata. DSVs also provide a side advantage in speeding up package development. Because DSVs are most likely defined as a subset of the actual Data Source, your SSIS connection dialog boxes will connect, realize data, and subsequently load much faster.

Precedence Constraints

Precedence constraints direct the tasks to execute in a given order. In fact, precedence constraints are the connectors that not only link tasks together but define the workflow of your SSIS package. Constraints control the execution of the two linked tasks by executing the destination task based upon the final state of the prior task and business rules that are defined using special expressions. The expression language embedded in SSIS essentially replaces the need to control workflow using script-based methodologies that enabled and disabled tasks, as was used in the DTS legacy solution. With expressions, you can direct the workflow of your SSIS package based on all manner of given conditions. We'll go into many examples of using these constraints throughout this book.

To set up a precedence constraint between two tasks, the constraint value must be set, and optionally you can set an expression. The next sections give a quick overview of the differences between the two.

Constraint Value

Constraint values define how the package will react when the prior task of two linked tasks completes an execution. The choices define whether the destination task of two linked tasks should execute based solely on how the prior task completes. There are three types of constraint values:

- ❑ **Success:** A task that's chained to another task with this constraint will execute only if the prior task completes successfully. These precedence constraints are colored green.

- ❑ **Completion:** A task that's chained to another task with this constraint will execute if the prior task completes. Whether the prior task succeeds or fails is inconsequential. These precedence constraints are colored blue.

- ❑ **Failure:** A task that's chained to another task with this constraint will execute only if the prior task fails to complete. This type of constraint is usually used to notify an operator of a failed event or write bad records to an exception queue. These precedence constraints are colored red.

Conditional Expressions

The conditional expression options that you can apply to a precedence constraint allow you to mix in a dynamically realized expression with the constraint value to determine the package workflow between two or more linked tasks. An *expression* allows you to evaluate whether certain conditions have been met before the task is executed and the path followed. The *constraint* evaluates only the success or failure of the previous task to determine whether the next step will be executed. The SSIS developer can set the conditions by using evaluation operators. Once you create a precedence constraint, you can set the Evaluation Option property to any one of the following options:

❑ **Constraint:** This is the default setting and specifies that only the constraint will be followed in the workflow.

❑ **Expression:** This option gives you the ability to write an expression (much like VB.NET) that allows you to control the workflow based on conditions that you specify.

❑ **ExpressionAndConstraint:** Specifies that both the expression and the constraint must be met before proceeding.

❑ **ExpressionOrConstraint:** Specifies that either the expression or the constraint can be met before proceeding.

In Figure 1-6, you can see an example that contains three tasks. In this example, the package first attempts the copying of files using the File System Task. If this prior task is successful and meets the expression criteria for a good file to transfer, the package will divert to the Data Flow Task to transform the files. However, if the first step fails, a message will be sent to the user using the Send Mail Task. You can also see in the graphic a small *fx* icon above the Data Flow Task and on the precedence constraint. This is the graphical representation for a conditional expression and visually informs that this task will not execute unless an expression has also been met. The expression can check anything, such as looking at a checksum, before running the Data Flow Task.

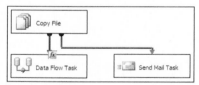

Figure 1-6

Containers

Containers are a core unit in the SSIS architecture to group tasks together logically into units of work. Besides providing visual consistency, containers allow you to define variables and event handlers (these are discussed in a moment) within the scope of the container instead of the package. There are four types of containers in SSIS:

❑ **Task Host Container:** The core type of container implements the basic interface to which every task implicitly belongs by default. The SSIS architecture extends variables and event handlers to the task through the Task Host Container.

The Task Host Container is not a visible element that you'll find in the Toolbox, but is an abstract concept like an interface.

❑ **Sequence Container:** Allows you to group tasks into logical subject areas. Within the development environment, you can then collapse or expand this container for usability. This is similar to the region concept in .NET coding.

❑ **For Loop Container:** Loops through a series of tasks for a given amount of time or using an iterator until a condition is met.

❑ **Foreach Loop Container:** Loops through a series of files or records in a data set, and then executes the tasks in the container for each record in the collection.

Containers are so integral to SSIS development that you'll find Chapter 4 is devoted to them. As you read through this book, we'll give you many real-world examples of using each of these types of containers for typical ETL development tasks.

Variables

Variables are another vital component of the SSIS architecture. In legacy DTS ETL development, global variables could be defined either by the Dynamic Property Task or by hand in the Active X Task, but they could only store static values. SSIS variables can be set to evaluate to an expression at runtime, removing much of the need to push values into the variables. However, you still can do this with the Scripting Tasks and Transforms, and as always, the configuration processes can set these variables. Variables in SSIS have become the method of exchange between many tasks and transforms, making the scoping of variables much more important. SSIS variables exist within a scope in the package. The default is to create variables at a package scope, but they can be scoped to different levels within a package as mentioned earlier in the "Containers" section.

Using variables allows you to configure a package dynamically at runtime. Without variables, each time you wanted to deploy a package from development to production, you'd have to open the package and change all the hard-coded connection settings to point to the new environment. A best practice is to set up SSIS packages using variables, so that you can just change the variables at deployment time, and anything that uses those variables will adjust.

Data Flow Elements

You learned earlier that the Data Flow Task is simply another executable task in the package. The Data Flow replaces the simple black arrow data pump that you may be familiar with from legacy DTS packages. If this is not familiar, this arrow describes what the Data Flow does, wonderfully. The Data Flow Task is the pumping mechanism that moves data from source to destination. However, in the case of SSIS, you have much more control of what happens from start to finish. In fact, you have a set of out-of-the box transformation components that you snap together to clean and manipulate the data while it is in the data pipeline.

One confusing thing for new SSIS developers is that once you drag and drop a Data Flow Task in the Control Flow, it spawns a new Data Flow design surface with its own new tab in the BIDS user interface. Each Data Flow Task has its own design surface that you can access by double-clicking the Data Flow Task or by clicking the Data Flow tab and selecting Data Flow Task from the drop-down list. Just as the Controller Flow handles the main workflow of the package, the Data Flow handles the transformation of data. Almost anything that manipulates data falls into the Data Flow category. As data moves through each step of the Data Flow, the data changes, based on what the transform does. For example, in Figure 1-7, a new column is derived using the Derived Column Transform, and that new column is then available to subsequent transformations or to the destination.

In this section, each of the sources, destinations, and transformations are covered from an overview perspective. These areas are covered in much more detail in later chapters.

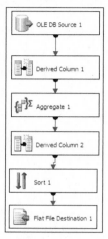

Figure 1-7

Sources

A *source* is a component that you add to the Data Flow design surface to specify the location of the source data that is to feed into the data pump. Sources are configured to use Connection Managers to allow for the ability to reuse connections throughout your package. Six sources can be used out-of-the-box with SSIS:

- ❏ **OLE DB Source:** Connects to nearly any OLE DB Data Source, such as SQL Server, Access, Oracle, or DB2, to name just a few.

- ❏ **Excel Source:** Specializes in receiving data from Excel spreadsheets. This source also makes it easy to run SQL queries against your Excel spreadsheet to narrow the scope of the data that you wish to pass through the flow.

- ❏ **Flat File Source:** Connects to a delimited or fixed-width file.

- ❏ **Raw File Source:** Produces a specialized binary file format for data that is in transit and is especially quick to read by SSIS.

- ❏ **Xml Source:** Can retrieve data from an XML document.

- ❏ **ADO.NET Source:** This source is just like the OLE DB Source but only for ADO.NET-based sources. The internal implementation uses an ADO.NET DataReader as the source. The ADO .NET connection is much like the one you see in the .NET Framework when handcoding a connection and retrieval from a database.

Sources can also be hand coded using two methods. One method is to use the Script Component to create a source stream using the existing .NET libraries. This method is more practical for single-use applications. If you need to reuse a custom source, you can develop one by extending the SSIS object model.

Destinations

Inside the Data Flow, destinations consume the data after the data pipe leaves the last transformation components. The flexible architecture can send the data to nearly any OLE DB–compliant, flat-file, or ADO.NET Data Source. Like sources, destinations are also managed through the Connection Manager. The following destinations are available to you in SSIS:

❑ **Data Mining Model Training:** Trains an Analysis Services mining model by passing in data from the Data Flow to the destination.

❑ **ADO.NET Destination:** Exposes data to other external processes, such as Reporting Services or your own .NET application. It also uses the ADO.NET DataReader interface similar to the ADO .NET Source to consume the data.

❑ **Data Reader Destination:** Allows the ADO.NET DataReader interface to consume data similar to the ADO.NET Destination.

❑ **Dimension Processing:** Loads and processes an Analysis Services dimension. It can perform a full, update, or incremental refresh of the dimension.

❑ **Excel Destination:** Outputs data from the Data Flow to an Excel spreadsheet.

❑ **Flat File Destination:** Enables you to write data to a comma-delimited or fixed-width file.

❑ **OLE DB Destination:** Outputs data to an OLE DB data connection like SQL Server, Oracle, or Access.

❑ **Partition Processing:** Enables you to perform incremental, full, or update processing of an Analysis Services partition.

❑ **Raw File Destination:** Outputs data in a binary format that can be used later as a Raw File Source. Is usually used as an intermediate persistence mechanism.

❑ **Recordset Destination:** Writes the records to an ADO record set.

❑ **SQL Server Destination:** The destination that you use to write data to SQL Server most efficiently.

❑ **SQL Server Compact Edition Destination:** Inserts data into a SQL Server running on a Pocket PC.

Transformations

Transformations are key components within the Data Flow that allow changes to the data in the data pipe. You can use transformations to split, divert, and remerge data in the data pipe. Data can also be validated, cleansed, and rejected using specific rules. For example, you may want your dimension data to be sorted and validated. This can be simply accomplished by dropping a Sort and a Lookup Transformation onto the Data Flow design surface and configuring them.

Transform Components in the SSIS Data Flow affect data in the data pipe in-memory. This is not always the panacea for ETL processing, especially under high-volume data processing. However, the latest version of SSIS has changed the way the Data Flow Task breaks down the execution tree for the transforms to take full advantage of asynchronous processing and parallelism to get the most from multi-processor machines. Here's a complete list of transforms:

- ❑ **Aggregate:** Aggregates data from transform or source.

- ❑ **Audit:** Exposes auditing information from the package to the data pipe, such as when the package was run and by whom.

- ❑ **Character Map:** Makes common string data changes for you, such as changing data from lowercase to uppercase.

- ❑ **Conditional Split:** Splits the data based on certain conditions being met. For example, this transformation could be instructed to send data down a different path if the State column is equal to Florida.

- ❑ **Copy Column:** Adds a copy of a column to the transformation output. You can later transform the copy, keeping the original for auditing purposes.

- ❑ **Data Conversion:** Converts a column's data type to another data type.

- ❑ **Data Mining Query:** Performs a data-mining query against Analysis Services.

- ❑ **Derived Column:** Creates a new derived column calculated from an expression.

- ❑ **Export Column:** Exports a column from the Data Flow to the file system. For example, you can use this transformation to write a column that contains an image to a file.

- ❑ **Fuzzy Grouping:** Performs data cleansing by finding rows that are likely duplicates.

- ❑ **Fuzzy Lookup:** Matches and standardizes data based on fuzzy logic. For example, this can transform the name Jon to John.

- ❑ **Import Column:** Reads data from a file and adds it into a Data Flow.

- ❑ **Lookup:** Performs a lookup on data to be used later in a transformation. For example, you can use this transformation to look up a city based on the zip code.

- ❑ **Merge:** Merges two sorted data sets into a single data set in a Data Flow.

- ❑ **Merge Join:** Merges two data sets into a single data set using a join function.

- ❑ **Multicast:** Sends a copy of the data to an additional path in the workflow.

- ❑ **OLE DB Command:** Executes an OLE DB command for each row in the Data Flow.

- ❑ **Percentage Sampling:** Captures a sampling of the data from the Data Flow by using a percentage of the total rows in the Data Flow.

- ❑ **Pivot:** Pivots the data on a column into a more non-relational form. *Pivoting* a table means that you can slice the data in multiple ways, much like in OLAP and Excel.

- ❑ **Row Count:** Stores the row count from the Data Flow into a variable.

❏ **Row Sampling:** Captures a sampling of the data from the Data Flow by using a row count of the total rows in the Data Flow.

❏ **Script Component:** Uses a script to transform the data. For example, you can use this to apply specialized business logic to your Data Flow.

❏ **Slowly Changing Dimension:** Coordinates the conditional insert or update of data in a slowly changing dimension.

❏ **Sort:** Sorts the data in the Data Flow by a given column.

❏ **Term Extraction:** Looks up a noun or adjective in text data.

❏ **Term Lookup:** Looks up terms extracted from text and references the value from a reference table.

❏ **Union All:** Merges multiple data sets into a single data set.

❏ **Unpivot:** Unpivots the data from a non-normalized format to a relational format.

Error Handling and Logging

In SSIS, there are several places that you can control error handling, and they depend on whether you are handling task or Data Flow errors. For task errors, package events are exposed in the user interface, with each event having the possibility of its own event handler design surface. This *design surface* is yet another area where you can define workflow along with the task and Data Flow surfaces you've already learned about. The event-handler design surface in SSIS is where you can specify a series of tasks to be performed if a given event happens for a task in the task flow. There are event handlers to help you develop packages that can self-fix problems. For example, the OnError error handler triggers an event whenever an error occurs anywhere in scope. The scope can be the entire package or an individual container. Event handlers are represented as a workflow, much like any other workflow in SSIS. An ideal use for event handlers would be to notify an operator if any component fails inside the package. You learn much more about event handlers in Chapter 17. You can also use the precedence constraints directly on the task flow design surface to direct workflow when a proceeding task fails to complete or evaluates to an expression that forces the workflow change.

An ultimate error within a Data Flow Task can be captured and handled with an error handler, but for finer control within the data pipe itself, each transformation must be configured to define the action that should be taken if a specific error occurs while processing the data. You can define whether the entire data transformation should fail and exit upon an error, or that only the bad rows should be redirected to a failed Data Flow branch. You can also choose to ignore any errors. The error handler shown in Figure 1-8 defines that if an error occurs during the Derived Column Transformation, the error rows will be output to a new error data stream. You can then use that outputted information to write to an output log or a destination connection as seen in Figure 1-8.

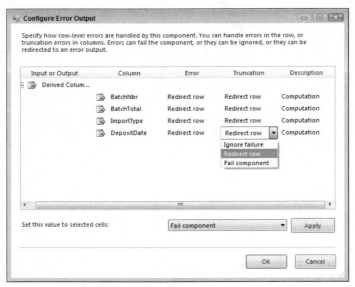

Figure 1-8

The On Failure error data stream can be seen in Figure 1-9 as a red line connecting the transform Derived Column Task to a Script Component Destination. The green lines show the normal happy path for the Data Flow through the data pipeline.

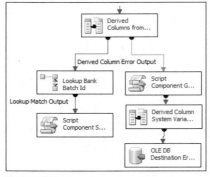

Figure 1-9

Logging has also been improved in SSIS. It is now at a much finer detail than what was available in the legacy DTS. More than a dozen events can be simply selected within each task or package for logging. You can enable partial logging for one task and enable much more detailed logging for billing tasks. Some of the examples of events that can be monitored are: `OnError`, `OnPostValidate`, `OnProgress`, and `OnWarning`, to name just a few. The logs can be written to nearly any connection: SQL Profiler, text files, SQL Server, the Windows Event log, or an XML file. We go through some examples of this in Chapter 17.

Editions of SQL Server

The available features in SSIS and SQL Server vary widely based on what edition of SQL Server you're using. As you can imagine, the more high-end the edition of SQL Server, the more features are available. In order from high-end to low-end, the following SQL Server editions are available:

❑ **SQL Server Enterprise Edition:** This edition of SQL Server is for large enterprises that need higher availability and more advanced features in SQL Server and business intelligence. For example, there is no limit on processors or RAM in this edition. You're bound only by the number of processors and amount of RAM that the OS can handle. Microsoft will also continue to support Developer Edition, which lets developers develop SQL Server solutions at a much reduced price.

❑ **SQL Server Standard Edition:** This edition of SQL Server now has a lot more value than ever before. For example, you can now create a highly available system in Standard Edition by using clustering, database mirroring, and integrated 64-bit support. These features were available only in Enterprise Edition in SQL Server 2000 and caused many businesses to purchase Enterprise Edition when Standard Edition was probably sufficient for them. Like Enterprise Edition in SQL Server 2005, it also offers unlimited RAM. Thus, you can scale it as high as your physical hardware and OS will allow. However, there is a cap of four processors with this edition.

❑ **SQL Server Workgroup Edition:** This new edition is designed for small and medium-sized businesses that need a database server with limited business intelligence and Reporting Services. Workgroup Edition supports up to two processors with unlimited database size. In SQL Server 2008 Workgroup Edition, the limit is 3 GB of RAM.

❑ **SQL Server 2008 Compact Edition:** This version was formally called the Express Edition and is the equivalent of Desktop Edition (MSDE) in SQL Server 2000 but with several enhancements. For example, MSDE never offered any type of management tool, and this is now included. Also included are the Import and Export Wizard, and a series of other enhancements. This remains a free addition of SQL Server for small applications. It has a database size limit of 4 GB. Most important, the query governor has been removed from this edition, allowing for more people to query the instance at the same time.

As for SSIS, you'll have to use at least the Standard Edition to receive the bulk of the SSIS features. In the Express and Workgroup Editions, only the Import and Export Wizard is available to you. You'll have to upgrade to the Enterprise or Developer Edition to see some features in SSIS. For example, the following advanced transformations are available only with the Enterprise Edition:

❑ Analysis Services Partition Processing Destination

❑ Analysis Services Dimension Processing Destination

❑ Data Mining Training Destination

❑ Data Mining Query Component

❑ Fuzzy Grouping

❑ Fuzzy Lookup

❑ Term Extraction

❑ Term Lookup

Half of these transformations are used in servicing Analysis Services. To continue that theme, one task is available only in Enterprise Edition — the Data Mining Query Task.

Summary

In this chapter, you were introduced to the historical legacy and the exciting new capabilities of the SQL Server Integration Services (SSIS) platform. We looked at where SSIS fits into the Business Intelligence roadmap for SQL Server, and then dove into an overview of the SSIS architecture. Within the architecture we stayed up at 20,000 feet to make sure you have a good understanding of how SSIS works and the core parts of the architecture. We talked about the core components of tasks, Data Flows, transformations, event handlers, containers, and variables — all crucial concepts that you'll be dealing with daily in SSIS. Packages are executable programs in SSIS that are a collection of tasks. Tasks are individual units of work that are chained together with precedence constraints. Lastly, transformations are the Data Flow items that change the data to the form you request, such as sorting the data.

In the next chapter, you look at some of the tools and wizards you have at your disposal to expedite tasks in SSIS. In Chapter 3, we do a deep dive into the various tasks in the Toolbox menu that you can use to create SSIS workflows, then move on to containers in the following chapter. In Chapter 4, we circle back into the Data Flow Task and examine the data components that are available to use within the data pipeline to perform the transform in ETL.

The SSIS Tools

As with any Microsoft product, SQL Server ships with a myriad of wizards and tools to make your life easier and reduce your time to market. In this chapter you learn about some of the tools that are available to you and how to create your first basic package. These wizards make transporting data and deploying your packages much easier and can save you hours of work in the long run. We start the discussion with the Import and Export Wizard, which allows you to create a package for importing or exporting data quickly. As a matter of fact, you may run this tool in your day-to-day work without even knowing that SSIS is the back-end for the wizard. The latter part of this chapter explores other tools that are available to you, such as Business Intelligence Development Studio.

Import and Export Wizard

The Import and Export Wizard is the easiest method to move data from sources like Oracle, DB2, SQL Server, and text files to nearly any destination and is available across all the versions of SQL Server; even those that don't have SSIS. This wizard uses SSIS as a framework and can optionally save a package as its output prior to executing. The package it produces may not be the most elegant, but it can take a lot of the hard work of a package development and provide the building blocks that are necessary for you to build the remainder of the package. Oftentimes as an SSIS developer, you'll want to relegate the grunt work and heavy lifting to the wizard, and then do the more complex coding yourself.

As with any of the SSIS tools, there are numerous ways to open the tool. To open the Import and Export Wizard, right-click the database you want to import data from or export data to in SQL Server Management Studio and select Tasks ⇨ Import Data (or Export Data based on what task you're performing). You can also open the wizard by right-clicking SSIS Packages in BIDS and selecting SSIS Import and Export Wizard. Another common way to open it is from the Start menu under SQL Server 2008, and it's called Import and Export Data. The last way to open the wizard is by typing **dtswizard.exe** at the command line or Run prompt. No matter whether you need to import or export the data, the first few screens in the wizard will look very similar.

Once the wizard comes up, you'll see the typical Microsoft wizard welcome screen. Click Next to begin specifying the source connection. If you had opened the wizard from Management Studio by selecting Export Data, this screen would be pre-populated. In this screen you'll specify where your data is coming from in the Source drop-down box. Once you select the source, the rest of the options on the dialog box may vary based on the type of connection. The default source is SQL Native Client, and it looks like Figure 2-1. You have OLE DB sources like SQL Server, Oracle, and Access available out-of-the-box. You can also use text files, Excel files, and XML files. After selecting the source, you'll have to fill in the provider-specific information.

For SQL Server, you must enter the server name, as well as the user name and password you'd like to use. If you're going to connect with your Windows account, simply select Use Windows Authentication. Windows Authentication will pass your Windows local or domain credentials into the data source. Lastly, choose a database that you'd like to connect to. For most of the examples in this book, you'll use the AdventureWorks2008 database. This database can be downloaded as an optional installation on CodePlex.com.

> Additional sources such as Sybase and DB2 can also become available if you install the vendor's OLE DB providers. You can download the OLE DB Provider for DB2 for free if you're using Enterprise Edition by going to the SQL Server 2008 Feature Pack on the Microsoft website.

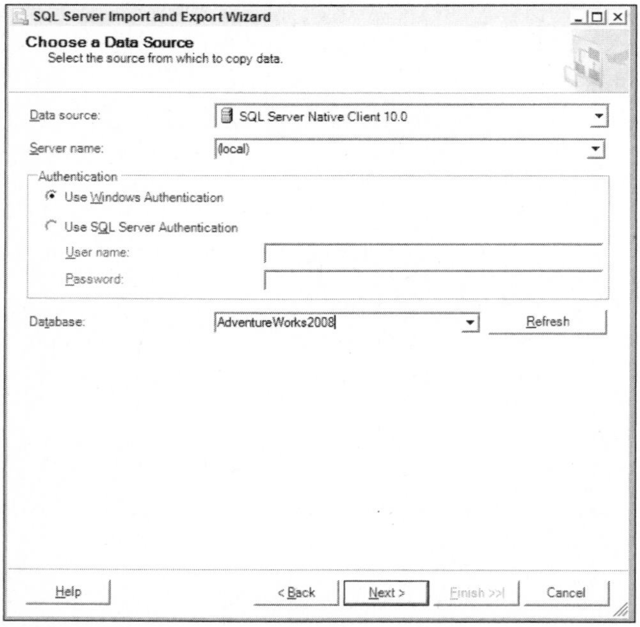

Figure 2-1

After you click Next, you'll be taken to the next screen in the wizard, where you specify the destination for your data. The properties for this screen are exactly identical to those for the previous screen with the exception of the database. Select TempDB from the Database drop-down box. This will just create and load the tables into a temporary space, which will disappear once you restart your instance of SQL Server. Click Next again to be taken to the Specify Table Copy or Query screen (see Figure 2-2). On the next screen, if you select "Copy data from one or more tables or views," you can simply check the tables you want. If you select "Write a query to specify the data to transfer," you'll be able to write an ad hoc query (after clicking Next) of where to select the data from, or what stored procedure to use to retrieve your data.

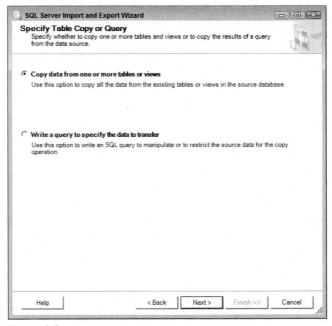

Figure 2-2

For the purpose of this example, select "Copy data from one or more tables or views" and click Next. This takes you to the screen where you can check the tables or views that you'd like to transfer to the destination (see Figure 2-3). For this tutorial, check some of the tables that belong to the HumanResources schema, other than the Employee table, in the AdventureWorks2008 database.

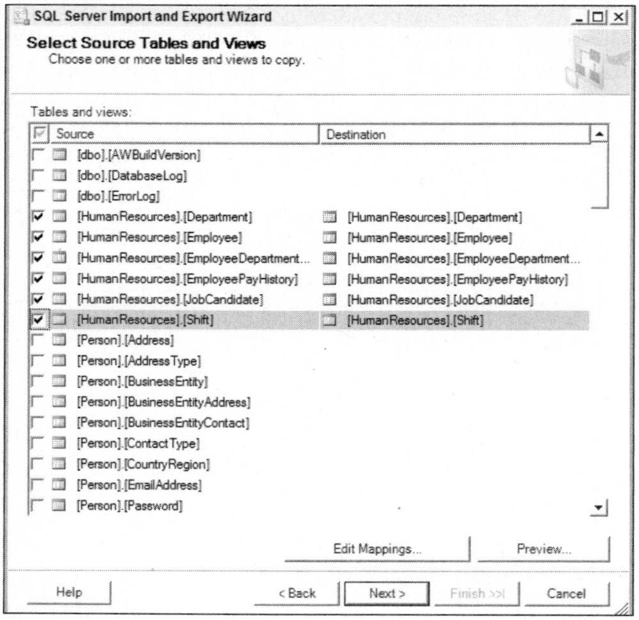

Figure 2-3

If you wish, you can click the Edit buttons to go to the Column Mappings dialog box for each table (see Figure 2-4). Here you can change the mapping between each source and destination column. For example, if you want the DepartmentID column to go to the DepartmentID2 column on the destination, simply select the Destination cell for the DepartmentID column and point it to the new column, or select <ignore> to ignore the column altogether.

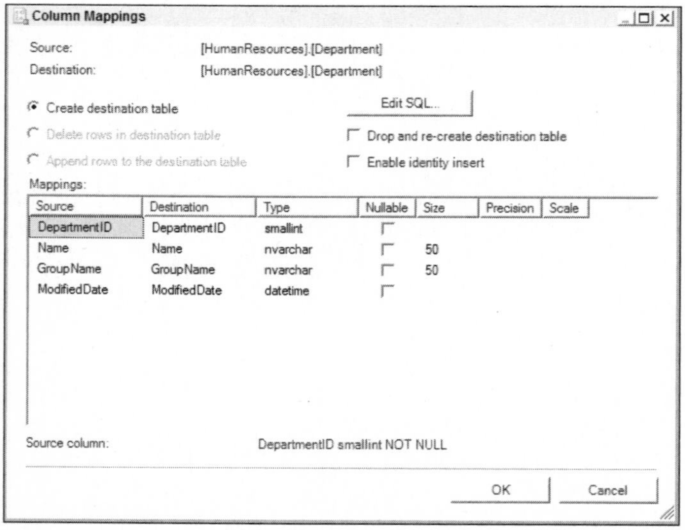

Figure 2-4

Notice that because you're moving the data to a new database that doesn't have the Department table already there, the "Create destination table" option is one of the few options enabled by default. This will create the Department table on the destination before populating it with data from the source. If the table did already exist, you could select that all the rows in the destination table will be deleted before populating it. The default setting, if you already have the table there, is to append the data from the source to the destination. You can also specify that you want the table to be dropped and re-created. The Edit SQL option allows you to specify the schema for the destination table that will be created. Keep in mind that this import or export process can be rerun later over and over again if you save the package.

Finally, you can enable the "identity insert" option if the table you're going to move data into has an identity column. If the table did have an identity column in it, the wizard would automatically enable this option. If you don't have the option enabled and you try to move data into an identity column, the wizard will fail to execute.

For the purpose of this example, don't change any of the settings in this screen. Click OK to apply the settings from the Column Mappings dialog box and Next to proceed to the Save and Execute Package screen. If there were any mapping errors or warnings from this previous screen, you'll be taken to the Review Data Type Mapping screen, where you'll be able to specify how you want to handle data conversion errors.

If no errors were seen, you will be taken to the Save and Execute Package screen. Here you can specify whether you want the package to execute only once, or whether you'd like to save the package off for later use. As you saw earlier, you don't necessarily have to execute the package here. You can uncheck Execute Immediately and just save the package for later modification and execution. In this example, set the wizard to Execute Immediately, Save the SSIS Package and the File System option. This collection of options is going to execute the package and also save the package as a .dtsx file to your computer. You learn more about where to save your SSIS packages later in this chapter.

You're also asked in this screen how you wish to protect the sensitive data in your package. SSIS packages are essentially large XML files behind the scenes, and encryption of the sensitive data, such as passwords, is critical to ensuring that no one sees that information by opening up the XML manually. Again, you learn more about this later in this chapter, so for the time being, change the Package Protection Level property to "Encrypt sensitive data with password" to protect your sensitive data with a password, and give the dialog box a password (as shown in Figure 2-5).

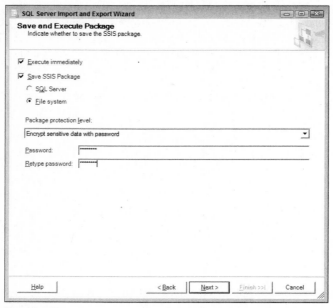

Figure 2-5

You will then be taken to the Save SSIS Package screen, where you can type the name of the package and the location to which you'd like to save the package. Optionally, you can add a description to the package. This helps you later operationally when you need to identify the purpose of the package (see Figure 2-6).

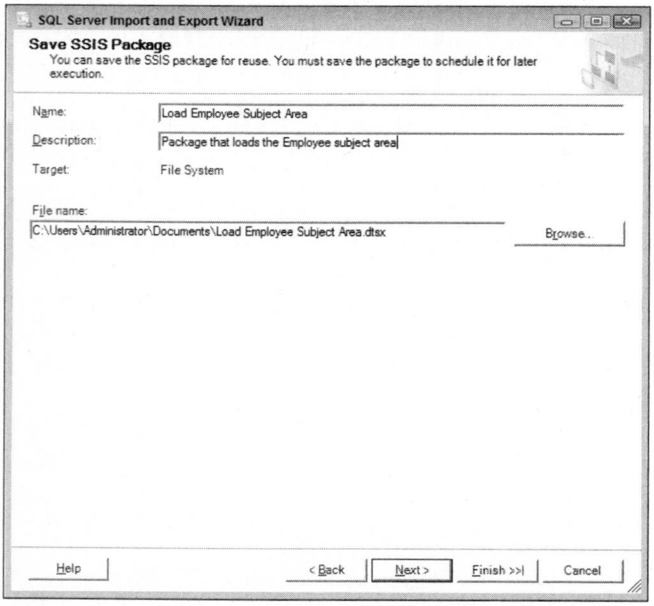

Figure 2-6

Click Next and confirm what tasks you wish the wizard to perform. The package will then execute when you click Finish, and you'll see the page in Figure 2-7. Any errors will be displayed in the Message column. You can also see how many rows were copied over in this column. You can also double-click an entry that failed to see why it failed.

Figure 2-7

After the wizard executes, the package can be found in the location that you have specified, but the default is in the My Documents directory. You can open the package that executed in BIDS if you'd like, by creating a project in BIDS and dragging the package into the project. You will not be able to edit the package without a BIDS project to contain the package. We discuss how to do this in detail in the "Business Intelligence Development Studio" section later in this chapter. You can see the Control Flow tab for the package in Figure 2-8. There is a Control Flow tab that contains the task that prepares the environment, such as creating the tables. Then, the tables are loaded, and then the same steps occur for the children tables. So as you can see, referential integrity is completely maintained by the Import and Export Wizard.

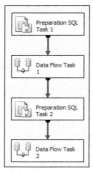

Figure 2-8

You'll also see in the package that there are only two connections: one for the destination and another for the source shown in the Connection Manager pane in BIDS. Even though it's a shared connection, each transformation runs in parallel, which is a marked improvement from SQL Server 2000, where this would be a serial operation when using a single connection.

Business Intelligence Development Studio

The Business Intelligence Development Studio (BIDS) is where you'll spend most of your time as an SSIS developer. It is where you create and deploy your SSIS projects.

BIDS uses a light version of Visual Studio 2008. If you have the full version of Visual Studio 2008 and SQL Server 2008 installed, you can create business intelligence projects there as well in the full interface, but as far as SSIS is concerned, there's no value in using the full version of Visual Studio. Either way, the user experience is the same. In SQL Server 2008, the SSIS development environment is detached from SQL Server, so you can develop your SSIS solution offline, and then deploy it to wherever you'd like in a single click.

You'll find BIDS in the root of the Microsoft SQL Server 2008 program group from the Start menu. Once you start BIDS, you'll be taken to the Start Page, an example of which is shown in Figure 2-9, before you open or create your first project. You can open more windows (you learn about these various windows in a moment) by clicking their corresponding icon in the upper-right corner or under the View menu.

The Start Page contains key information about your BIDS environment, such as the last few projects that you had open under the Recent Projects box. You can also see the latest MSDN news under the Get News from Microsoft box.

The nicest thing about SSIS development in the Visual Studio environment is that it gives you full access to the Visual Studio feature set, such as debugging, automatic integration with Source Safe, and integrated help. It is a familiar environment for developers and makes deployments easy.

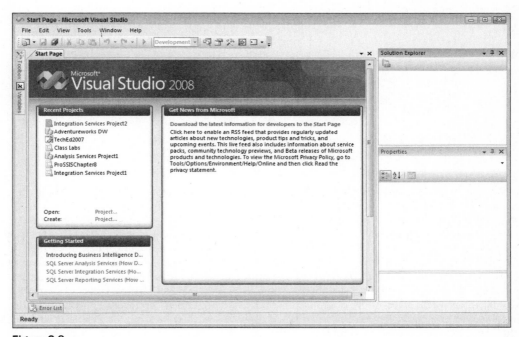

Figure 2-9

To start a new SSIS project, you will first need to open BIDS and select File ⇨ New ⇨ Project. You'll notice a series of new templates (shown in Figure 2-10) in your template list now that you've installed SQL Server 2008. Select Integration Services Project, and name your project and solution whatever you'd like. There is another type of SSIS project called the Integration Services Connections that can be seen in Figure 2-10 that is solely meant for creating a shell of a package with the necessary connections but nothing more.

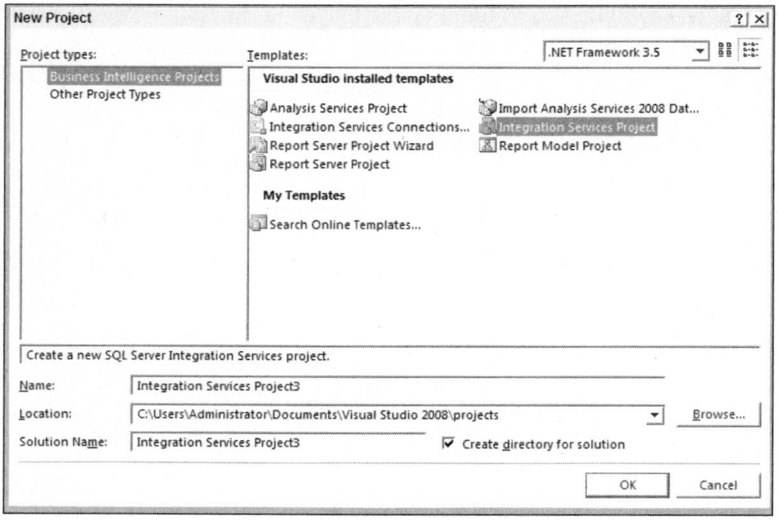

Figure 2-10

As you can see in Figure 2-10, BIDS incorporates the concept of solutions and projects. *Solutions* are containers for lots of projects or just a single project in most cases. Solutions can hold any type of Visual Studio project like Reporting Services and a project for SSIS all in the same container. You would typically want to align projects into the same solution that fit a business project that you're trying to develop for. For example, you may have a business project that you've been assigned to for the creation of a data warehouse. That warehouse project would probably have ETL, Management Studio scripts, and Reporting Services reports. You could place all of these into a single solution so you could manage them from a unified interface. You'll notice that once you begin work in Visual Studio, if your solution contains only a single project, the solution will be hidden by default. If you want to always see the solution name, go to Tools ⇨ Options and check Always Show Solution from the Projects and Solutions group. Once the second project is added to it, you'll see the solution and both projects under the solution.

Creating Your First Package

Before you jump into the fundamentals of the toolset, you should exercise some of the BIDS features by creating a very basic package. If you don't understand some of this, don't worry yet. It will make much more sense later in this chapter and in Chapter 3. This quick example shows you how to configure a task and how to chain tasks together with precedence constraints.

Start by opening BIDS by selecting Start ⇨ Programs ⇨ Microsoft SQL Server 2008 ⇨ SQL Server Business Intelligence Development Studio. Once BIDS is open, select New ⇨ Project from the File menu. Under the Business Intelligence Project Type on the left, select Integration Services Project. Call the project "Basic Package" for the Name option, and then click OK.

In the Solution Explorer to the right of BIDS, you'll see that an empty package called `Package.dtsx` was created. On the left of BIDS is your Toolbox, which contains all of the work items that you can apply in whatever tab you're in. In the Toolbox, drag the Execute Process task over to the empty design pane in the middle. Double-click the task to configure it. This opens the editor for the given task, transformation, or data connection you wish to configure. Name the task Notepad, and you can optionally enter a description in the General page. Select the Process page in the left pane of the task editor, and for the Executable option, select `Notepad.exe`. Click OK to exit the editor.

Drag another Execute Process task over and double-click it to open the editor again. Name this task Calc. In the Process page, type **calc.exe** for the Executable option. Click OK to exit the editor. Click the first Notepad task and you'll see a green arrow pointing downward from the task. This is a precedence constraint, which was mentioned in Chapter 1. Left-click the arrow and drag it onto the Calc task. These tasks are now connected, and the Calc task will not execute until the first task succeeds.

Click the Save icon to save the package. Select Debug ⇨ Start Debugging or hit F5. This will execute the package. You should first see Notepad open, and once you close Notepad, the Windows calculator will open (as shown in Figure 2-11). Once you close the calculator, the package will complete. The two tasks should also show as green in color, which means they successfully executed. You can click the Stop button or select Debug ⇨ Stop Debugging to complete the package's execution.

Congratulations, you have created your first package. Granted, this package will never be used in a production environment, but it does show you the basic concepts in SSIS. It's important to note that you will not develop packages that have interactive windows like this. If you were to execute this in production, it would wait for a user's interaction to close the window before the package would complete. The concepts you were introduced to here are described in greater detail in each upcoming chapter, and now you'll learn about the features that are available to you in BIDS.

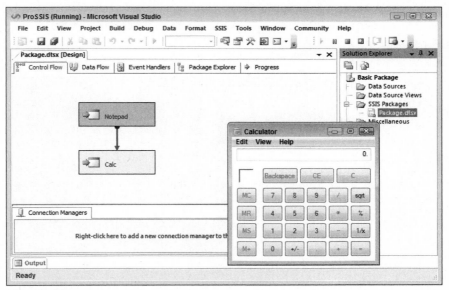

Figure 2-11

The Solution Explorer Window

The Solution Explorer window is where you can find all of your created SSIS packages, shared connections, data source views, and any other miscellaneous files needed for the project, such as installation documents. As we mentioned earlier, a solution is a container that holds a series of projects. Each project holds a myriad of objects for whatever type of project you're working in. For SSIS, it will hold your packages, data source views, and shared connections. Once you create a solution, you can store many projects inside of it. For example, you may have a solution that has your VB.NET application and all the SSIS packages that support that application. In this example, you would probably have two projects: one for VB and another for SSIS.

After creating a new project, your Solution Explorer window will contain a series of empty folders. Figure 2-12 shows you a partially filled Solution Explorer. In this screenshot, there's a solution named ProSSIS with two projects: SSAS Sample Project and SSIS Sample Project. Inside that project, there are two SSIS packages.

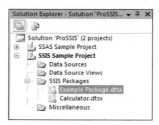

Figure 2-12

To create a new project inside an existing open solution, right-click the solution name in the Solution Explorer window and select Add ⇨ New Project. To create a new item to your project in the folder, right-click the folder that holds the type of item that you wish to add and select New Data Source, New Data Source View, or New SSIS Package. You can also drag files or copy and paste files into the project that are of a similar type, like .dtsx files.

If you look into the directory that contains your solution and project files, you'll see all the files that are represented in the Solution Explorer window. Some of the base files you may see will have the following extensions:

❑　.dtsx : An SSIS package, which uses its legacy extension from the early beta cycles of SQL Server 2008 when SSIS was still called DTS

❑　.ds : A shared data source file

❑　.dsv : A data source view

- ❏ `.sln`: A solution file that contains one or more projects

- ❏ `.dtproj`: An SSIS project file

If you copy any file that does not match the `.ds`, `.dtsx`, or `.dsv` extension, it will be placed in the Miscellaneous folder. This folder is used to hold any files that describe the installation of the package, like Word documents or requirements documents. Anything you'd like can go into that folder, and it can potentially all be checked into a source control system like Source Safe with the code. We discuss more about source control systems in Chapter 15, "Source Control and Software Development Life Cycle."

The Toolbox

The Toolbox contains all the items that you can use in the particular tab's design pane at any given point in time. For example, the Control Flow tab has a list of tasks (a partial list can be seen in Figure 2-13). This list may grow based on what custom tasks are installed. The list will be completely different when you're in a different tab, such as the Data Flow tab. All the tasks you see in Figure 2-13 are covered in Chapter 3 in much more detail.

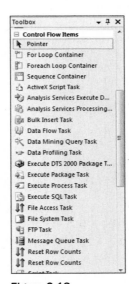

Figure 2-13

The Toolbox is organized into tabs such as Maintenance Tasks and Control Flow Items. These tabs can be collapsed and expanded for usability. As you use the Toolbox, you may want to customize your view by removing tasks or tabs from the default view. You can remove or customize the list of items in your Toolbox by right-clicking an item and selecting Choose Items. This takes you to the Choose Toolbox Items dialog box shown in Figure 2-14, and may take a few seconds to open. To customize the list that you see when you're in the Control Flow tab, select the SSIS Control Flow Items tab, and check the tasks you'd like to see. After you install a custom component, you'll need to come back to this screen again to check the component that you installed to add it to your Toolbox.

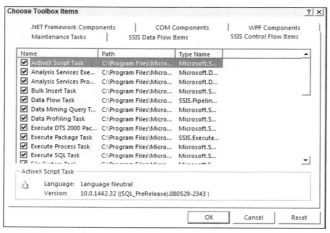

Figure 2-14

If you right-click a particular task, you'll get a menu that will let you customize your view by adding or removing tabs and adding, renaming, or removing items. You can also change the order in which the items or tabs appear, just by clicking and dragging from the source to the destination or by right-clicking and selecting Sort Alphabetically. You can also reset the Toolbox at any time by right-clicking in the Toolbox and selecting Reset Toolbox. This will remove all non-default items and custom tasks that you may have installed from the Toolbox.

The Properties Windows

The Properties window (shown in Figure 2-15) is where you can customize almost any item that you have selected. For example, if you select a task in the design pane, you'll receive a list of properties to configure, such as the task's name and what query it's going to use. The view will vary widely based on what item you have selected. Figure 2-15 shows the properties of the Execute Process task you created in an earlier section of this chapter.

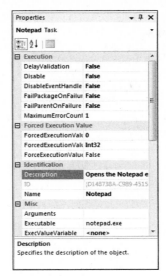

Figure 2-15

Most tasks can be configured through the user interface of the tasks or by going to the Properties pane when the task is selected. To edit the properties for the package, simply select the design pane in the background. If the Properties pane ever gets closed, you can press F4 to reopen it or select the Properties Window button under View.

Navigation Pane

One of the nice usability features that have been added in BIDS is the ability to navigate quickly through the package by using the navigation pane (as shown in Figure 2-16) in the bottom-right corner of the package. The pane is visible only when your package is more than one screen in size, and it allows you to quickly navigate through the package. To access the pane, left-click and hold on the cross-arrow in the bottom-right corner of the screen. You can then scroll up and down a large package with ease.

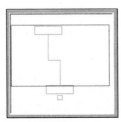

Figure 2-16

Other Windows

At design time, the BIDS has several other windows that you can choose to dock, undock, show, hide, or auto-hide based on your needs, or what stage you are at in development. These supplementary windows include the following:

- ❑ **Error List window:** Shows errors and warnings that have been detected in the package. Double-clicking an entry in this window will open the editor of the object causing the error.

- ❑ **Output window:** Shows the results from when you build or execute a package in the BIDS environment. For example, the Output window will show any errors that occur during building or deploying or during runtime.

- ❑ **Task List window:** Shows tasks that a developer can create for descriptive purpose or as a follow-up for later development.

As you begin to test your packages, you will want to execute them inside of the BIDS. This will shift the mode into runtime, and no editing will be allowed until the package has completed execution. During runtime, the following windows will also appear:

- ❑ **Call Stack window:** Shows the names of functions or tasks on the stack.

- ❑ **Breakpoints window:** Shows all of the breakpoints set in the current project.

- ❑ **Command window:** Used to execute commands or aliases directly in the BIDS.

- ❑ **Immediate window:** Used to debug and evaluate expressions, execute statements, and print variable values.

- ❑ **Autos window:** Displays variables used in the current statement and the previous statement.

- ❑ **Locals window:** Shows all of the local variables in the current scope.

- ❑ **Watch windows:** Allow you to add specific variables to the window that can be viewed as package execution takes place. You can also directly modify, and read/write variables in this window.

You learn more about all of these windows in much more detail in later chapters.

The SSIS Package Designer

The SSIS Package Designer contains the design panes that you'll use to create an SSIS package. The tool contains all the items you need to move data or create a workflow with minimal or no code. The great thing about SSIS is that it is like programming with building blocks. The Package Designer contains four tabs: Control Flow, Data Flow, Event Handlers, and Package Explorer. One additional tab, Progress, also appears when you execute packages. This Progress tab also is renamed to Execution Results after the package stops running and you click Stop.

In this chapter, you mainly explore the Control Flow tab, and we'll spend the bulk of the next chapter really diving into the details about this tab. Unlike SQL Server 2000 DTS, where control and Data Flows were intermingled, Control Flow and Data Flow editors are completely separated by these tabs. This usability feature gives you greater control when creating and editing packages. The task that binds the

Control Flow and Data Flow together is the Data Flow Task, which you study in depth over the next two chapters.

The difference between the Control Flow and Data Flow tabs is one of the largest learning curves for a new SSIS developer. The easiest way to keep them straight is to think of the Data Flow tab as simply a way to configure the Data Flow task. This separation gives you a huge amount of power when configuring the task. The other way to differentiate the two tabs is that the Control Flow tab handles the workflow of the package and ties the tasks together, and the Data Flow tab handles a data load.

Control Flow

The Control Flow is most similar to SQL Server 2000 DTS, because it contains most of the tasks you're used to in SQL Server 2000. It contains the workflow parts of the package, which include the tasks, containers, and precedence constraints. SSIS has introduced the new concept of containers, which was briefly discussed in Chapter 1 and is covered in detail in Chapter 4. In the Control Flow tab, you can click and drag a task from the Toolbox into the Control Flow design pane. Once you have a task created, you can double-click the task to configure it. Until the task is configured, you may see a yellow warning or red error indicator on the task.

After you configure the task, you can link it to other tasks by using precedence constraints. Once you click the task, you'll notice a green arrow pointing down from the task, as shown in Figure 2-17.

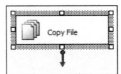

Figure 2-17

To create an On Success precedence constraint, click the green arrow coming out of the task and drag it to the task you wish to link to the first task. In Figure 2-18, you can see the On Success precedence constraint between a File System task called Copy File and a Data Flow task called Load Data. You can also see an On Failure constraint, which is represented as a red arrow between the File System task and the Send Mail task. This type of Control Flow may send a message to an operator in the event that the task named Copy File fails. After the Copy File task succeeds, the Load Data task will execute.

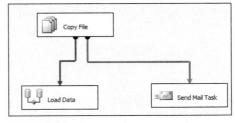

Figure 2-18

When you click a source or a transformation in the Data Flow tab, you'll also see a red arrow pointing down, enabling you to quickly direct your bad data to a separate output. So if you run a formula that returns an error in the Data Flow, that single row could be outputted to a different table, and then all other rows could continue down the proper path.

In the Control Flow, though, you'll need to use a different approach. If you'd like the next task to execute only if the first task has failed, create a precedence constraint as was shown earlier for the On Success constraint. After the constraint is created, double-click the constraint arrow and you'll be taken to the Precedence Constraint Editor (shown in Figure 2-19).

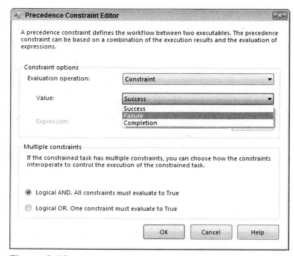

Figure 2-19

In this editor, you can set what type of constraint you'll be using in the Value drop-down field: Success, Failure, or Completion. In SSIS, you have the option of adding a logical AND or OR when a task has multiple constraints. In the Precedence Constraint Editor in SSIS 2008, you can configure the task to execute only if the group of predecessor tasks has completed (AND), or if any one of the predecessor tasks has completed (OR). If a constraint is a logical AND, the precedence constraint line is solid. If it is set to OR, the line is dotted. This is useful if you want to be notified if any one of the tasks fails by using the logical OR constraint.

In the Evaluation Operation drop-down box, you can edit how the task will be evaluated.

❑ **Constraint:** Evaluates the success, failure, or completion of the predecessor task or tasks.

❑ **Expression:** Evaluates the success of a customized condition that is programmed using an expression.

❑ **Expression and Constraint:** Evaluates both the expression and the constraint before moving to the next task.

❑ **Expression or Constraint:** Determines if either the expression or the constraint has been successfully met before moving to the next task.

If you select Expression or one of its variants as your option, you'll be able to type an expression in the Expression box. An expression is usually used to evaluate a variable before proceeding to the next task. For example, if you want to ensure that `InputFileVariable` variable is equal to `Variable2` variable, you would use the following syntax in the Expression box:

```
@InputFileVariable == @Variable2
```

You can also single-click the constraint and use the Properties window to the right to set these properties, if you prefer not to use the editor.

Task Grouping

A very nice usability feature in SSIS is the ability to group tasks logically in *containers*. For example, if you have a group of tasks that create and purge the staging environment, you can group them together so that your package is not cluttered visually. For example, in Figure 2-20 there are two tasks to load data and send a message. To group them, select both tasks by clicking one task and holding the Ctrl key down while you select the second task. Then, right-click the tasks and select Group.

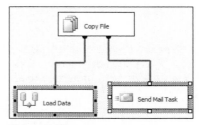

Figure 2-20

Once you have the two tasks grouped, you'll see a box container around the tasks. This container will be called Group by default. To rename the group, simply double-click the container and type the new name over the old one. You can also collapse the group so that your package isn't cluttered. To do this, just click the arrows that are pointing downward in the group. Once collapsed, your grouping will look like Figure 2-21. You can also ungroup the tasks by right-clicking the group and selecting Ungroup.

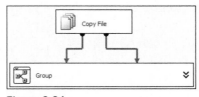

Figure 2-21

We discuss more about containers in Chapter 4.

Annotation

Annotation is a key part of any package that a good developer never wants to leave out. An *annotation* is a comment that you place in your package to help others and yourself understand what is happening in the package. To add an annotation, right-click where you'd like to place the comment, select Add Annotation, and begin typing. You can resize the box as well as add a carriage return by pressing Ctrl+Enter. It is a good idea to always add an annotation to your package that shows the title and version your package is on. Most SSIS developers like to also put a version history annotation note in the package, so that they can see what's changed in the package between releases and who performed the change. You can see an example of this in Figure 2-22. You can also right-click the text to change the color of the annotation or bold it.

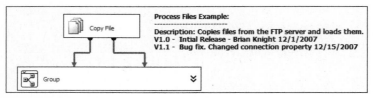

Figure 2-22

Connection Managers

You may have already noticed that there is a Connection Managers tab at the bottom of your Package Designer pane. This tab contains a list of connections that both Control Flow and Data Flow Tasks can use. Whether the connection is an FTP address or a connection to an Analysis Services server, you'll see a reference to it here. These connections can be referenced as either sources or targets in any of the operations and can connect to relational or Analysis Services databases, flat files, or other data sources.

When you create a new package, there are no connections defined. You can create connections by right-clicking in the Connections area and choosing the appropriate data connection type. Once the connection is created, you can rename it to fit your naming conventions or to better describe what is contained in the connection. Even if you have a shared connection defined for your project, it won't be usable in the package until you add it to the Connection Managers tab. Nearly any task or transformation that uses data or references a file will require a Connection Manager. There are very few exceptions, such as the Raw File destination and XML source, that allow you to define your connection inline. Figure 2-23 shows a few connections: two to a relational database (AdventureWorksDW2008), an SMTP reference, and several flat files.

Notice that there are two Connection Managers that refer to the AdventureWorksDW2008 database. The one with a database icon is a local Connection Manager that can only be seen inside a single package. The Connection Manager with the arrows coming out of it is referencing a shared connection, which can be used anywhere in the project.

Figure 2-23

Variables

Variables are a powerful piece of the SSIS architecture; they allow you to dynamically control the package at runtime, much like you do in any .NET language. There are two types of variables: system and user. *System variables* are ones that are built into SSIS, such as a package name or the package's start time; whereas *user variables* are created by the SSIS developer. Variables can also have varying scope, with the default scope being the entire package. They can also be set to be in scope of a container, task, or event handler inside the package.

One of the optional design-time windows can display a list of variables. To access the Variables window, right-click in the design pane and select Variables. The Variables window (shown in Figure 2-24) will appear where the Toolbox was, and you can toggle between the two windows by selecting the corresponding tab below the window. By default, you will see only the user variables; to see the system variables as well, select the Show System Variables icon in the top of the window. To add a new variable, click the Add Variable icon in the Variables window and type the name.

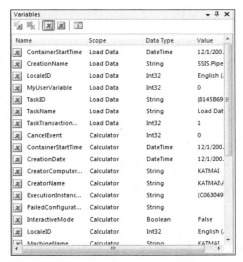

Figure 2-24

When you click the Add Variable icon, whatever task or container you select at the time will be the scope for the variable. Once the scope is set for the variable, it cannot be changed, so be sure to set it to the right scope the first time. You can also click the Choose Variable Columns button in order to see more columns in the pane other than the name, scope, data type, and value. Some of the additional columns you can see are the namespace and raise event on variable change properties. Lastly, you can select a variable and go to the Properties pane to see extended properties on the variable. We discuss these properties in more depth Chapter 3.

You'll find yourself using system variables throughout your package habitually for auditing or error handling. Some of the system variables that are in the scope of a package that you may find interesting for auditing purposes are listed in the following table.

Variable Name	Data Type	Description
CreationDate	DateTime	The date when the package was created.
InteractiveMode	Boolean	Indicates how the package was executed. If the package was executed from BIDS, this would be set to true. If it was executed as a job, it would be set to false.
MachineName	String	The computer where the package is running.
PackageID	String	The globally unique identifier (GUID) for the package.
PackageName	String	The name of the package.
StartTime	DateTime	The time when the package started.
UserName	String	The user that started the package.
VersionBuild	Int32	The version of the package.

Variables are discussed in greater detail in each chapter. For a full list of system variables, please refer to Books Online under "System Variables."

Data Flow

Most of your time in SSIS is spent in the Data Flow tab. When you create a Data Flow task in the Control Flow, a subsequent Data Flow is created in the Data Flow tab. You can expand the Data Flow by double-clicking the task or by going to the Data Flow tab and selecting the appropriate Data Flow task from the top drop-down box (shown in Figure 2-25). The Data Flow key components are sources, destinations, transformations (which appear in the Toolbox), and paths. The green and red arrows that were the precedence constraints in the Control Flow tab are now called *paths*.

When you first start defining the Data Flow, you will create a source to a data source, and then a destination to go to. The transformations (also known as transforms throughout this book) modify the data before it is written to the destination. As the data flows through the path from transform to transform, the data changes based on what transform you have selected. This entire process is covered in much more detail in Chapter 5.

Figure 2-25

Event Handlers

The Event Handlers tab allows you to create workflows to handle errors, warnings, or completion in tasks, containers, or packages. For example, if you want to trap any errors and have them emailed to you, you could create an OnError event handler that is scoped to the entire package and configure it to send a message out to an operator, as shown in Figure 2-26.

Figure 2-26

You can configure the event handler scope under the Executable drop-down box. An executable can be a package, Foreach Loop container, For Loop container, Sequence container, or a task. In the Event Handler box, you can specify the event you wish to monitor for. The events you can select are in the following table:

Event	When Event Is Raised
OnError	When an error occurs
OnExecStatusChanged	When an executable's status changes
OnInformation	When an informational event is raised during the validation and execution of an executable
OnPostExecute	When an executable completes
OnPostValidate	When an executable's validation is complete
OnPreExecute	Before an executable runs
OnPreValidate	Before an executable's validation begins
OnProgress	When measurable progress has happened on an executable
OnQueryCancel	When a query has been instructed to cancel
OnTaskFailed	When a task fails
OnVariableValueChanged	When a variable is changed at runtime
OnWarning	When a warning occurs in your package

Event handlers are critically important to developing a package that is "self-healing" and can correct its own problems. The key events to trap are the `OnError`, `OnWarning`, `OnPreExecute`, and `OnPostExecute`. You learn more about event handlers in Chapter 17.

Package Explorer

The final tab in the SSIS Package Designer is the Package Explorer tab. This tab consolidates all the design panes into a single view. The Package Explorer tab (shown in Figure 2-27) lists all the tasks, connections, containers, event handlers, variables, and transforms in your package, and you can double-click any item here to configure it easily. You can also modify the properties for the item in the right Properties window after selecting the item you wish to modify.

Figure 2-27

This tab is useful if you have a task that is throwing an error and you can't find it to remove or fix it. This problem happens sometimes when you have tasks that accidentally fall behind a container or another task.

Executing a Package

When you want to execute a package, you can click the Play icon on the toolbar, press F5, or choose Debug ⇨ Start. You can also execute packages by right-clicking the package in Solution Explorer and selecting Execute Package. This technique may be a better habit to get into because clicking the Play button will initiate a build, and if some properties are selected, which we'll discuss later, it will cause each package to open prior to your package execution. This puts the design environment into execution mode, opens several new windows, enables several new menu and toolbar items, and begins to execute the package. When the package finishes running, BIDS doesn't immediately go back to design mode, but rather stays in execution mode to allow you to inspect any runtime variables or to view any execution output. This also means that you can't make any changes to the objects within the package, but you can modify variables and objects' read/write properties. You may already be familiar with this concept from executing .NET projects.

To get back to design mode, you must click the Stop icon on the debugging toolbar, press Shift+F5, or choose Debug ⇨ Stop Debugging.

Package Installation Wizard

Another wizard that you may see and use regularly is the Package Installation Wizard, which walks you through installing your SSIS project onto a new server. You may receive a .SSISDeploymentManifest file from a vendor or from a developer to run. If you double-click the file ProSSISChapter5 .SSISDeploymentManifest, for example, it will launch the Package Installation Wizard to install the SSIS project called ProSSISChapter5 into a new environment.

After the wizard's introduction screen, you must choose whether you'd like the wizard to install the packages onto the SQL Server (msdb database) or install them as files on the server. If you select files, you will be prompted for the location in which you'd like them placed. If you select SQL Server, you'll be prompted for the SQL Server onto which you'd like to install the package.

This wizard is covered in greater detail in Chapter 21 when deployments are discussed. Until then, you can create a manifest file yourself by right-clicking a project, properties, and selecting True for the CreateDeploymentUtility option in the Deployment Utility page. After you do this, you'll have to build the project from the Build menu in BIDS.

Management Studio

In SSIS, there is delineation between the SSIS developer and administrator. Management Studio is where the administrator will do most of his work, executing, securing, and updating packages. From the Management Studio interface the administrator will not be able to design packages, however. This function is reserved for BIDS only.

You can open SQL Server Management Studio under the Microsoft SQL Server 2008 program group on the Start menu. Then, in the Object Browser pane (can be opened from the View menu if it's closed) select Connect ⇨ Integration Services. Type your SSIS server name and click Connect. Unlike SQL Server, SSIS contains only a single instance per server or cluster. If you receive an error, you may want to jump ahead to Chapter 21 on how to correct connectivity issues.

From the Object Explorer shown in Figure 2-28, you'll be able to see which packages are running and kill rogue packages. You'll also be able to execute packages by right-clicking a package in the Stored Packages tree and selecting Execute Package. You can right-click nearly any folder to read reports about your packages or who is executing packages.

Figure 2-28

In Chapter 22, we discuss administration of your SSIS packages.

Summary

This chapter's goal was to get you acclimated with the main SSIS wizards and core tools. The Import and Export Wizard is a quick way to create a package that does a simple import or export of data. The wizard can produce a package that can be run multiple times. The Package Installation Wizard is a method to deploy your SSIS project after its development is complete.

You were then taken on a tour of the Business Intelligence Development Studio (BIDS), which is where you'll be spending most of your time as you develop packages. You looked at the key parts of the interface and learned how to create your first simple package. Don't worry if you didn't understand all the components of SSIS yet. Now that you have the core understanding, we'll dive deeper into SSIS to talk about each component.

Now that you've gotten your feet wet, it's time to see the real power of SSIS, which lies in the multitude of tasks you can use in your packages. You learn about some of the more common ones in Chapter 3 and containers in Chapter 4.

3

SSIS Tasks

SSIS *tasks* are the foundation for the Control Flow in SSIS. When you are on the Control Flow design surface in BIDS, the toolbar is populated with a set of Tasks components that can be snapped together to represent a logical or control workflow for your package. What you might not know is that tasks may also be used to define Control Flows in response to an event raised somewhere in the package. In either case, using Task components to map out the logical sequence of actions for a package is probably the most similar aspect that SSIS has to the legacy DTS product.

A *task* is a discrete unit of work that can perform typical actions required by an ETL process from moving a file and preparing data sources to sending email confirmations when everything is complete. This is most evident in the fact that the Data Flow is tied to the controller flow with a specific Data Flow task. More advanced tasks enable you to perform actions like executing SQL commands, sending mail, running ActiveX scripts, and accessing Web services. If you look at the toolbar, you'll see there is a large list of tasks that you can use out-of-the-box for ETL package development and a few that are more enterprise application integration (EAI) related. Most of the tasks are covered in this chapter, however some in less detail, since they are covered in other chapters. The exception will be the Looping and Sequence Containers, which are covered separately in Chapter 4. This chapter introduces you to most of the tasks you'll be using on a frequent basis and gives you some examples of how to use them. This will all be reinforced as you read through the rest of the book, because each of these tasks will be used in at least one further example in later chapters.

SSIS Task Objects

Tasks are component-based small units of work that can be sequenced in an SSIS package Control or event handler Flow. To add a task to a flow, click and drag it from the Toolbox onto the design surface. You can then double-click the task to configure it. You may immediately see a red or yellow warning on the task until you configure any required properties. Setup requirements vary depending upon the task. You may need to provide a database connection, external mail server connection, or the name of an external package to complete the configuration of the task itself. SSIS is quite helpful in this regard. If you hover over the task, a tooltip help window like that shown in Figure 3-1 will provide the details for what needs to be configured for the task to work.

Figure 3-1

This Execute SQL Task just needs a valid Connection Manager to an RDBMS (Relational Database Management Systems) or Excel data source to be configured. To do this you need to use the Task Editor.

Using the Task Editor

To configure a task you need to access the Task Editor. You can do this by double-clicking directly on the task in the Control Flow design surface or by right-clicking the task and selecting the Edit option in the pop-up menu. In either case, generally you'll see a task editor dialog appear. (We say generally, because not all tasks have a task editor to configure.) The task editor provides a specialized interface that allows for the configuration of the properties of the task. Each task has different property and setup requirements, but the task editor always employs a consistent design that makes it easy to follow. Figure 3-2 is a sample of a typical Task Editor dialog to help get you oriented.

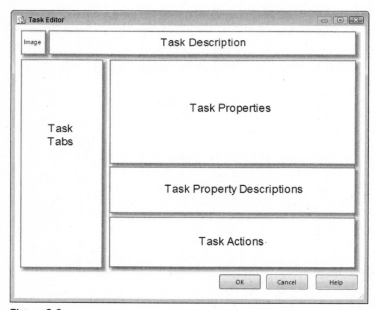

Figure 3-2

Each task editor contains a unique image and a description of the task in the top section of the dialog. Moving clockwise, the Task Properties section of the dialog lists a set of properties for configuration. The nature and type of the properties displayed depend upon the selection in the Task Tabs section. The Task Tabs section provides a listing of selectable options that drive the properties in the Task Properties section. If you select a specific property in the Task Properties section, you'll see a description of the property in the section below. Finally, the Task Actions section may contain actionable buttons for specific actions that you can take for the selection in the Task Tabs section.

Familiarizing yourself with this dialog will make configuring new tasks much easier. In the latest version of SSIS, there have been some improvements to make this UI even more consistent. All of these touches help make SSIS a more usable, trainable tool for ETL development. For example, the Script Task and Script Transform Editors now both use an Edit Script caption on their respective actionable buttons, and all Task Editors now include the Expressions tab, which is discussed next.

The Task Editor Expressions Tab

SSIS uses a new concept of setting the value of most task properties to a dynamic expression that is realized at runtime. This way, you can dynamically configure packages at runtime, replacing the Dynamic Properties Task and scripting-based configuration of the legacy DTS object model. Common to all the tasks is an Expressions tab in each of the editors that expose the properties that you can set dynamically at runtime with an expression. The expression can be a constant value, an expression, or an SSIS variable that is either a scalar constant or an expression. With this capability, you could read a series of variables from a configuration file (these are discussed later) and then dynamically set properties in an Execute Process Task or any other SSIS task. We provide many examples of using the expressions throughout this book. We've also added a variables and expressions chapter (Chapter 6) to this new edition for a complete explanation of how to use variables and expressions in SSIS.

For a basic understanding of this common tab within each task, click the ellipsis (. . .) button next to the Expressions option in the Expressions tab of any of the task editors. This will take you to the Property Expressions Editor, shown in Figure 3-3, where you can manage setting properties within a task directly by providing the actual expression or indirectly by providing the variable that evaluates to the result of an expression. To create a new one, select the property you wish to set from the Property column and then type the expression into the Expression column. Optionally, you can also select the ellipsis button in the Expression column to open the Expression Builder to create an expression using a visual UI. You'll see this capability in most of the SSIS tasks.

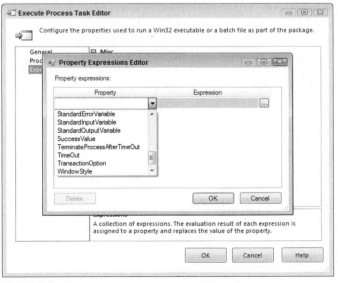

Figure 3-3

Now that you've looked at the how to add and configure individual tasks in the SSIS package Control Flow, let's look at how to connect them together and establish precedence constraints between them.

Execution Results

Every task must return an execution result of either Cancelled, Failure, or Success. In addition, the Completion result is always returned once the task has completed. This execution result provides the foundation for connecting tasks together to design the Control Flow of a package. Setting precedence between two tasks can be as simple as dragging and dropping the colored arrows between two tasks. Alternatively, you can right click the preceding task and select the pop-up menu option Add Precedence Constraint to create a new precedence constraint to the next task as seen in Figure 3-4. (The options available in the To: drop-down list depend upon the tasks that are available in your package. The options in Figure 3-4 represent the tasks available in the blown out example in Figure 3-5.)

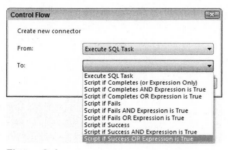

Figure 3-4

In the SSIS object model, the named execution results are enforced by the `IDTSTaskHost100` interface. This just means that every task is required to have the same execution results structure. In BIDS, you'll interact with this property with three colored arrows that appear on the task in the design surface. These arrows are used to connect a preceding task to the next task in the Control Flow. A blue arrow indicates that the next task in the Control Flow will execute upon completion of the preceding task. A green arrow requires that the preceding task completes successfully; the red arrow executes the next task if the proceeding task fails. You can review Chapter 2 if you need more information about task Control Flow, or review how Figure 3-5 demonstrates the available possibilities for constraints between SSIS tasks.

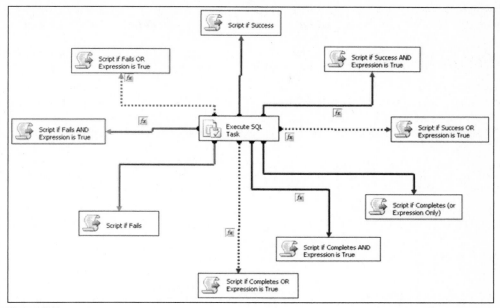

Figure 3-5

Notice the visual differences in each of the constraints between these tasks. If the constraint involves an expression, you'll see the tiny graphic with the *fx* designation. Not only do you see colors to indicate what type of result the preceding task must provide to complete the precedence constraint, but the dotted lines provide an indicator that an OR condition is also being employed. It is extremely helpful to be able to simply look at the Control Flow in your package and know what type of constraint it is and whether the constraint involves an expression. Along with the Execution Results, tasks also implement a set of properties that are common across every package. Now, let's examine these in detail.

Common Properties

No matter what task you use in your packages, there is a standard set of properties exposed in the design interface of the task. Many of the same properties have been carried over from the legacy DTS product, but most are new and complete the vision of an enterprise-ready ETL tool. Here is a list of the properties that you will use (listed alphabetically):

❑ **Disable:** If set to true, the task is disabled and will not execute. This is helpful if you are testing a package and want to disable the execution of a task temporarily.

❑ **DelayValidation:** If set to true, SSIS will not validate any of the properties set in the task until runtime. This is useful if you are operating in a disconnected mode, and you want to enter a value for production that cannot be validated until the package is deployed, or if you are dynamically setting the properties using expressions (more about these later). The default value for this property is false.

❏ **Description:** The description of what the instance of the task does. The default name for this is <task name>, or if you have multiple tasks of the same type, it would read <task name 1> (where the number 1 increments). This property does not have to be unique and is optional. If you do provide detail here, it will display in the tooltip when hovering over the task object. For consistency, the property should accurately describe what the task does for people who may be monitoring the package in your operations group.

❏ **ExecValueVariable:** Contains the name of the custom variable that will store the output of the task's execution. The default value of this property is <none>, which means that the execution output is not stored. This variable provides for exciting workflow possibilities because it gives the task an ability to expose information relating to the results of the internal actions within the task. An Execute SQL Task can return the number of rows updated, or the WMI Task can return a filename for a file recently dropped into a folder. Other tasks can now be triggered as a result of precedence being defined based on the value of the variable named in this property.

❏ **FailPackageOnFailure:** If set to true, the entire package will fail if the individual task fails. Typically, you want to control what happens to a package if a task fails with a custom error handler or Control Flow. Therefore, by default, this property is set to false.

❏ **FailParentOnFailure:** If set to true, the task's parent will fail if the individual task reports an error. The task's parent can be a package or container. You'll read more about containers later.

❏ **ID:** This is read-only, automatically generated unique ID that is associated to an instance of a task. The ID is in GUID format and looks like this: {BK4FH3I-RDN3-I8RF-KU3F-JF83AFJRLS}.

❏ **IsolationLevel:** Specifies the isolation level of the transaction, if transactions are enabled in the TransactionMode property. The values are Chaos, ReadCommitted, ReadUncommitted, RepeatableRead, Serializable, Unspecified, and Snapshot. The default value of this property is Serializable. These options correspond with standard SQL Server transaction types.

❏ **LoggingMode:** Specifies the type of logging that will be performed for this task. The values are UseParentSetting, Enabled, and Disabled. The default value of this property is UseParentSetting, which tells the task to use the logging mechanism for the package or container.

❏ **Name:** The name associated with the task. The default name for this is <task name>, or if you have multiple tasks of the same type, it would read <task name 1> (where the number 1 increments). As an SSIS designer, you should probably change this name to make it more readable to an operator at runtime, but it must be unique inside your package.

❏ **TransactionOption:** Specifies the transaction attribute for the task. The values are NotSupported, Supported, and Required. The default value of this property is Supported, which enables the option for you to use transactions in your task.

Now that you've got a good idea about what tasks are, let's dive into putting these new tools to work on some real-world problems. Do you need to retrieve settings from stored procedure output parameters? Call a Web service for some data? You'll look at these and other advanced implementations of some of the tasks throughout the rest of the chapter. We've put the tasks into functional groupings that give them some relativity to your typical ETL processes.

Looping and Sequence Tasks

First up in the Toolbox are three container tasks: For Loop, Foreach, and Sequence. These are all Control Flow Tasks that simplify the process of repeated processing of a set of logic. In legacy DTS, looping constructs were not intuitive. If you wanted this type of Control Flow logic, you had to set properties on the tasks directly using code in the ActiveX Scripting Tasks. To achieve the same thing in SSIS, you only need to add one of these containers to your Control Flow and define what is being used to enumerate the loop. Again, these containers are covered in detail in Chapter 4, so we'll only mention them here.

Scripting Tasks

Scripting Tasks are extremely useful to perform functions that may not be fully supported within a provided drag-and-drop control, but may not require full custom task development. SSIS has two script tasks, the ActiveX Task and the Script Task.

ActiveX Script Task

This task exists solely for the purposes of backwards compatibility during the conversion of legacy DTS packages. If you aren't converting DTS packages, you can probably skip learning about this task, since it will eventually not be supported. If fact, you can't run this Task on 64-bit computers and you'll need the DTS 2000 runtime to run on any machine after SQL Server 2008. However, if you convert a legacy DTS package, you may find your ActiveX scripting code in this task container; and there's a good chance that you won't be able to run it. ActiveX script in the legacy DTS packages was largely used to traverse the package model directly. Unfortunately, this direct type of code-based action is not supported in SSIS. If you can get the code to run, you'll want to pull this functionality out into the newer Script Task, because the ActiveX Task is not intended for future use. Here's an example of something that won't convert from DTS:

```
[VB Script]
Function Main()
        Dim oPkg
        Dim oConn

        Set oPkg = DTSGlobalVariables.Parent
        Set oConn = oPkg.Connections("Test File")
        msgbox oConn.ConnectionString
End Function
```

Scripts like this were often used to set the value of the flat file connection to the next file in a directory or to retrieve the current value of the connection, as in this case. If you put this code into the SSIS ActiveX Task and run it, you'll get this error:

```
Error: 0xc0348006 at ActiveX Retrieve File from Connection, ActiveX
Script Task: Retrieving the file name for a component failed with error
code 0x000F2E6C.
```

If you correctly determined that the connection collection doesn't exist at the same place in the model, don't also assume that you could attempt to use the new syntax to access a connection starting at the static DTS object.

```
[VB.Net] - Doesn't work in ActiveX Task
mySqlConn = _
  DirectCast(Dts.Connections("local.aw").AcquireConnection(Dts.Transaction), _
  SqlClient.SqlConnection)
```

The new way won't work either because VBScript doesn't know this syntax. VBScript will also not be able to interpret a modified VBScript version of this VB.NET code. The problem is that SSIS simply does not allow direct access to the package object model. This was a common coding activity in the older DTS packages, so you'll find that many things that used to work will need to be converted into existing SSIS tasks or re-coded in the new Script Tasks.

However, there is one exception to this rule and that is for scripts and functions that only interact with the global variable collection. Examples of these scripts are those that you may have for generating new filenames or doing odd tasks that don't involve the object model. These will convert into SSIS just fine. Here is an example of a legacy DTS script that checks to see if a specific file provided by a variable named MyFile in the variables collection exists:

```
[VB Script]
Function Main()
  Dim objFSys
  Dim objFStream
  Dim strFile

  strFile = DtsGlobalVariables("User::MyFile")
  Set objFSys = CreateObject("Scripting.FileSystemObject")
        Set objFStream = objFSys.OpenTextFile(strFile, 1, 0)
  sLine =  objFStream.ReadLine

  if trim(sLine)  = "" or err.number <> 0 then
    Main = DTSTaskExecResult_Failure
  else
                              MsgBox "File " + strFile + " exists"
    Main = DTSTaskExecResult_Success
  end if

  objFStream.Close
        Set objFStream = Nothing
  set objFSys = nothing
End Function
```

If you copy this into an ActiveX Script Task and set the EntryMethod property to point to the Main() function, you can run this successfully and the full file path provided for the variable MyFile will be checked for a file existence. Obviously, you can find better ways to do this and we'll show you how.

Script Task (.NET)

The Script Task allows you to access the Microsoft Visual Studio Tools for Applications (VSTA) environment to write and execute scripts using the VB and C# languages. The VSTA environment is new in the latest version of SSIS and replaces the Visual Studio for Applications (VSA) environment from the 2005 version. Scripting now is almost a misnomer because the latest SSIS edition solidifies the connection to the full .NET libraries for both VB and C#. The latest addition to SSIS of the VSTA environment and the Script Task in general also offer these extra functional advantages:

❏   A coding environment with the advantage of IntelliSense

❏   An integrated Visual Studio design environment within SSIS

❏   An easy-to-use methodology for passing parameters into the script

❏   The ability to add breakpoints into your code for testing and debugging purposes (for only one Script Task per package)

❏   The automatic compiling of your script into binary format for a speed advantage (This was configurable in earlier releases of SSIS.)

The Script Task is configured through the Script tab in the Script Task Editor (shown in Figure 3-6). The ScriptLanguage property is where you select the .NET language you'd like to use in the task. Notice that the default language is set to C#, so if you are coding in VB.NET, don't whiz through these settings when setting up your Script Tasks. If you have done any SSIS development with the previous versions, you'll also notice that the PreCompileScriptIntoBinaryCode property has been permanently removed. The result is that all scripting code will automatically compile and persist into the package. This speeds up and reduces runtime errors in the task significantly.

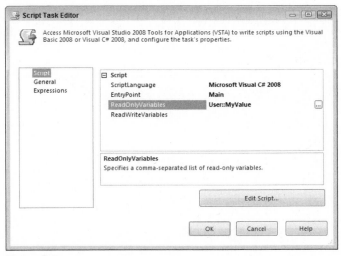

Figure 3-6

The EntryPoint property allows you to provide an alternative function to call initially when the ScriptMain class is instantiated. Typically, you'll leave this set to the default `Main()` function. The ReadOnlyVariables and ReadWriteVariables properties allow you to pass SSIS variables into the script as a listing of variable names separated by commas. The typing out of the variable names was a little unconventional in the earlier versions of SSIS, but the latest version provides the capability of browsing to the variable collection and selecting the variables. Having these variables provides a significant advantage when coding. You only need to refer to them by ordinal position or by name in the Variable collection to be able to access their values without worrying about locking, unlocking, or blocking variables during read and write actions. Just make sure you have the variables you wish to write back to in the ReadWriteVariables property, or you'll get an error in the script. There are also alternative methods for altering variables that aren't provided in these collections during set up that are demonstrated in Chapter 9 on scripting.

When you click the actionable Edit Script button, the Visual Studio Tools for Applications environment opens to allow coding directly in the class `ScriptMain`. In this IDE, you have access to all the advanced debugging tactics, breakpoints, and IntelliSense found in the Visual Studio environment. If you create a package with a variable named `myValue` containing the string `"Hello World"`, and set up the Script Task like Figure 3-7, the following example shows you how to write code that uses the passed-in `myValue` variable:

```
C#
public void Main()
{
    if(Dts.Variables.Contains("User::MyValue"))
    {
        System.Windows.Forms.MessageBox.Show("MyValue=" + Dts.Variables
["User::MyValue"].Value.ToString());
    }

    Dts.TaskResult = (int)ScriptResults.Success;
}

VB
Public Sub Main()
    If Dts.Variables.Contains("User::MyValue") = True Then
        System.Windows.Forms.MessageBox.Show("myValue=" & Dts.Variables
("User::MyValue").Value.ToString())
    End If

    Dts.TaskResult = ScriptResults.Success
End Sub
```

First, the script checks for the existence of the variable, and then pops up a message box with the famous message "Hello World" as you see in Figure 3-7.

Figure 3-7

This is just a very simple example of the Script Task in action. We've created an entire chapter to dive into the details and specific use cases for both the Script Task and the Data Flow version called the Script Component, so go read Chapter 9 for more information.

Analysis Services Tasks

The Analysis Services tasks are provided in the SSIS environment to deal with generating and updating cubes and working with data mining projects in SQL Server only. There are three tasks that can be used for Analysis Services in SSIS: the Analysis Services Execute DDL Task, Processing Task, and Data Mining Task. To review the tasks in this section, you'll need to have installed the sample Analysis Services databases from Microsoft SQL Server.

Analysis Services Execute DDL Task

The SQL Server Analysis Services Execute DDL Task is the Analysis Services equivalent of the Execute SQL Task, but limited in scope to issuing Data Definition Language statements. The task simply executes a DDL statement against an Analysis Services system. Typically, you would use DDL statements to create a cube, a dimension, or any other online analytical processing (OLAP) object.

To configure the task, go to the DDL tab and select the Connection Manager that you wish to execute the DDL statement against in the Connection option. Then in the SourceType property, select whether the DDL statement will be directly inputted, pulled from a file, or pulled from a variable option. Essentially the source type option determines whether you need to key in the DDL statement directly, provide a variable, or point to a file where the DDL statement is stored. Figure 3-8 shows an example of the DDL being directly entered into the SourceDirect property.

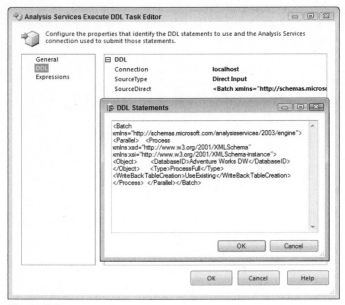

Figure 3-8

The Analysis Services DDL statement shown in this example from the SQL Server Books Online would be used to resubmit against the AdventureWorks2008 data to regenerate the warehouse cube. Note that this task can only be used to submit DDL statements. If you wish to query cubes to retrieve data, you need to use the Analysis Services Processing or Data Mining Tasks.

Analysis Services Processing Task

The SQL Server Analysis Services Processing Task takes care of the processing of Analysis Services objects. If you are familiar with using the Analysis Service projects in BIDS, then you'll be familiar with the task of processing a cube, dimension, or mining object. The configuration of the task is done in the Analysis Services Processing Task Editor in the Processing Settings tab. First, select the Analysis Services Connection Manager that you wish to process. Next, click the Add button and select the Analysis Services objects you'd like to process. After clicking OK, you'll be taken back to the Processing Settings tab, where you can change the type of processing you will be performing. To do this, right-click each object and select the process option you'd like. The option varies based on the type of object.

If you click Impact Analysis, analysis is performed on the selected objects, showing you the objects that will be affected by the processing. The Change Settings button lets you configure the batch settings for the task. For example, here you can change whether you want the objects to be processed in sequential order or in parallel and how you want errors handled.

To get a feel for how this SSIS task works, you'll need to download and install the AdventureWorksDW2008 database. Create an Analysis Services project to connect to the database and create a data source view with all the dimension tables. Then create a cube that uses the Employee dimension and select all the defaults to build the cube. Right-click the cube and select the process option to create the cube in the Analysis Services server. In SSIS, you can process the same cube using the

Analysis Services Processing Task. Connect to the same Analysis Services server, and in the Processing Settings tab select the Employee Cube and the Sales Territory dimension to process. The Task Editor should look like Figure 3-9.

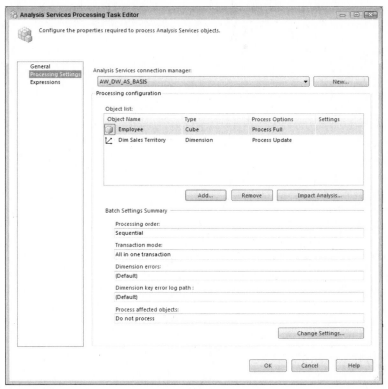

Figure 3-9

The Analysis Services Processing Task can then be run to reprocess the existing dimension and employee cube. These SSIS tasks allow the possibilities to periodically update your warehouse structures based on events that can be processed using an event captured by the Message Queue Task, which we cover later.

Data Mining Query Task

The Data Mining Query Task is an evolution of its SQL Server 2000 predecessor. The Data Mining Query Task allows you to run predictive queries against your Analysis Services data-mining models and output the results to a data source. The Data Mining Query Task is more similar to the Analysis Service Execute DDL Task in that you can execute subsequent mining queries against a processed mining model in Analysis Server. The Task Editor allows configuration to a source Analysis Services server and can output the results in any ADO.NET or OLE DB data source. An example of the Data Mining Task configured to run a mining query against a predefined Employee Dimensional Mining model can be seen in Figure 3-10.

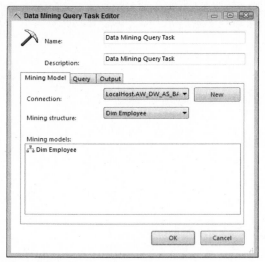

Figure 3-10

This task would be used to run predictive queries based on built-in prediction models in Analysis Services. The query uses a Data Mining Extension to TSQL called DMX. If you are not fluent in DMX, don't worry, the Query tab in this task will walk you through building one. However, first you need a mining structure to query against. In the Analysis Service server, a deployed data mining model would look like the highlighted Employee dimension in Figure 3-11.

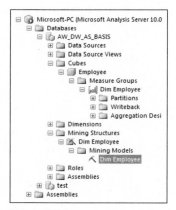

Figure 3-11

The results of the prediction query can be set to return single or multi-row results and can be saved to table structures for further analysis. These results can be useful for additional SSIS packages that can integrate the predictive results into further Data Flows. But before we can step any further into these capabilities, let's first go over the Data Flow Task itself.

Data Flow Task

If you are familiar with SQL Server 2000 DTS, you won't recognize the Data Flow Task in SSIS. In legacy DTS, there was a dark arrow called the Transform Data Task that connected an input source with a destination. Within this object you could build ActiveX-based transformations to apply at a column level as the data flowed through the data task. In contrast, the SSIS Data Flow Task can be selected directly from the BIDS Toolbox, and then the source and destinations are defined within the task. However, this comparison isn't even close. The Data Flow Task doesn't stop at being simply a mapping transform for input and output columns. This task has its own design surface like the Control Flow, where you can arrange task-like components called transforms to manipulate data as it flows in a pipeline from the source to a destination. The Data Flow, as you can imagine, is the heart of SSIS, because it encapsulates all the data transformation aspects of ETL.

Where DTS could only process data in one stream, Data Flows can split the data in the pipeline based on a data element and handle each stream separately. In the case study in Chapter 23, you can find an example of a flat file that contains header and detail information. In the Data Flow, the header line of the file can be split off and examined separately from the detail lines. As the pipeline exits the data cleansing process, the streams can be sent to separate destinations or converged to a final combined destination. One thing that some may not realize is that you may have several different Data Flows within an SSIS package. For each of the Data Flow Tasks you add to the control surface, you'll have a corresponding Data Flow surface. Figure 3-12 shows an example of three Data Flow Tasks and how you'd navigate to each.

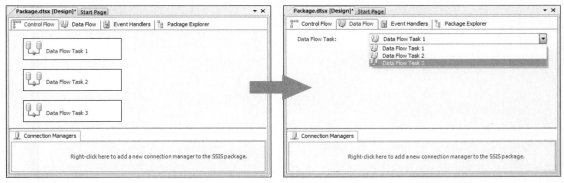

Figure 3-12

This task is so important and such a part of moving data in SSIS that we will leave the details until later in this book. It is covered separately in Chapter 5.

Data Preparation Tasks

Before processing data from other systems, you sometimes have to go and retrieve it or validate the content to determine your confidence level of the quality of the data. SSIS provides a set of tasks that can be used to retrieve data files using the files and folders available in the file system, or can reach out using FTP and Web Service protocols. This next section explores these tasks in SSIS.

Data Profiler

New to the latest version of SSIS is the Data Profiler Task that should really replace some of the script-based methods that have been devised since the introduction of DTS. Data profiling is the process of examining data and collecting metadata about the quality of the data, about frequency of statistical patterns, interdependencies, uniqueness, and redundancy. This type of analytical activity is important for the overall quality and health of an operational data store (ODS) or data warehouse. In fact, you've most likely been doing this activity whether or not you actually have a defined tool to perform the activity. Now instead of having a set of complicated queries or relying on a third-party product, you have a Data Profiler Task as part of the SSIS development environment.

The Data Profiler Task is located in the Task Toolbox, but you should probably not attempt to use the results to make an automated workflow decision in the SSIS package Control Flow. Rather it is more like an ad-hoc tool to be placed in a design-time package that will be run manually outside of a scheduled process. In fact, the task doesn't have built-in conditional workflow logic, but technically, you can use XPath queries on the results. Someone will probably come up with a way to parse through the output to attempt to drive a workflow based on some profiling results, but you need to be careful with this. The profiler can only report on statistics in the data; you still need to make judgments about these statistics. For example, a column may contain an overwhelming amount of NULL values, but the profiler doesn't know whether this scenario is a valid business scenario.

The structured output file that is produced by the Data Profiler Task can be viewed in a special Data Profiler Viewer that provides drill-downs back to the detail level. You can access this viewer by going to Start ⇨ Accessories ⇨ Run and typing **DataProfileViewer**. This will run the tool located in c:\ program files\microsoft SQL Server\100\DTS\binn. Once the tool is loaded, use the Open button to browse to the output file that will be generated by the Data Profiler Task. Figure 3-13 shows an example of an analysis of the Person.EmailAddress table in the AdventureWorks2008 database. You can see here that the majority of the email addresses in the table are between 26 and 29 characters long.

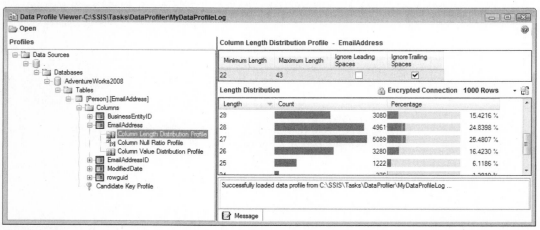

Figure 3-13

The task provides a set of defined profile request types that can be modified like the other tasks in specific properties. Here is an explanation of the different request types and how you can use them to profile your data:

- **Candidate Key Profile Request:** The profiling request will examine a column or set of columns to determine the likelihood of there being a unique candidate key for the dataset. Use this to determine if you've got duplicate key values or if it is possible to build a natural key with the data.

- **Column Length Distribution Profile:** This request allows you to analyze the statistical profile of all the data in a column with the percentage of incidence for each length. Use this to help you figure out if you've got your data column length settings set correctly or to look for bad data in attributes that are known to be one fixed size.

- **Column Null Ratio Profile Request:** This profiler looks at the ratio of NULL values in a column. Use this to determine whether you've got a data quality problem in your source system for critical data elements.

- **Column Pattern Profile Request:** This profiler allows you to apply regular expressions to a string column to determine the pass/fail ratio across all the rows. Use this profiler to evaluate business data using business formatting rules.

- **Column Statistics Profile Request:** This request can analyze all the rows and provide statistical information about the unique values across the entire source. This can help you find low incidence values that may indicate bad data. For example, a finding of only one color type in a set of 1 million rows may indicate that you've got a bad color attribute value.

- **Functional Dependency Profile Request:** This is one of two profiles that allow you to examine relationships between tables and columns to look for discrepancies within a known dependency. For example, you can use this request to find countries with incorrect currency codes.

- **Value Inclusion Profile Request:** This profile tests to see if the values in one column are all included in a separate lookup or dimension table. Use this request to test foreign key relationships.

There are two ways to activate these profiles. The first is to click the Quick Profile button on the Data Profiling Task Editor. This creates a set of profiles to run against the same table. You can also skip the quick profile option and create the profiles one by one. Either way you can navigate to the Profile Requests table to configure the request and add regular expressions or other parameter values to the task properties. Figure 3-14 is an example of the Data Profiling Task Editor with all the requests defined for the Person.StateProvince table.

Figure 3-14

For each profile request type, the lower section of the editor for the Request Properties will change to accept the configurable values. One thing to note is that the ConnectionManager property must be set to an ADO.NET-based Connection Manager like the one here connected to AdventureWorks2008. The oddity is that you must have this connection created prior to attempting to configure this task. This is a minor inconvenience to have such a powerful and welcome addition to the SSIS toolset rivaling the more expensive ETL tools.

File System Task

The File System Task is a configurable GUI component that performs file operations available in the System.IO.File .NET class. If you are converting from legacy DTS, this is an out-of-the box replacement for the VBScript utility classes that you use to write using the COM-based FileSystemObject. In either case, the File System Task can perform basic file operations such as:

❑ **Copy Directory:** Copies all files from one directory to another. Must provide the source and destination directories.

❑ **Copy File:** Copies a specific file. Must provide the source and destination filename.

❑ **Create Directory:** Creates a directory. Must provide the source directory name and indicate whether the task should fail if the destination directory already exists.

❑ **Delete Directory:** Deletes a directory. Must provide the source directory to delete.

❑ **Delete Directory Content:** Deletes all files in a source directory.

- ❏ **Delete File:** Deletes a specifically provided source file.

- ❏ **Move Directory:** Moves a provided source directory to a destination directory. Must indicate whether the task should fail if the destination directory already exists.

- ❏ **Move File:** Moves a specific provided source file to a destination. Must indicate whether the task should fail if the destination file already exists.

- ❏ **Rename File:** Moves a specific provided source file to a destination by changing the name. Must indicate whether the task should fail if the destination file already exists.

- ❏ **Set Attributes:** Sets Hidden, Read-Only, Archive, or System attributes on a provided source file.

One benefit that may not be apparent in these functional descriptions is that the creation of directory structures does not have to be made recursively. For example, you may create the path named `c:\ssis\tasks\my file system task\` using the Create Directory form of the File System Task by simply providing the path. You don't have to create each part of the directory separately like you did in the DTS legacy product. This capability really reduces the typical file operation coding to a simple configuration task for directory operations. However, don't assume that you can do the same with a file-level operation. If you attempt to rename a file from `c:\ssis\` to `c:\ssis\my archive\` and the folder `\my archive\` doesn't exist, you'll get an error that the path is not found.

Another feature of this task that may not be so apparent is that the task is written for a single operation. This is by design. If you need to iterate over a series of files or directories, the File System Task can be simply placed within a Looping or iterative task. By keeping the task granular and singularly focused, it is simplified and easily reused.

Most of the properties in this task are set in the General tab of the File System Task Editor. This tab is shown in Figure 3-15. The contents of this tab may vary widely based on what you set in the Operation property. These options correspond to specific file operations that the task can perform. Once the option is set, you may be prompted to complete other properties not shown in this figure.

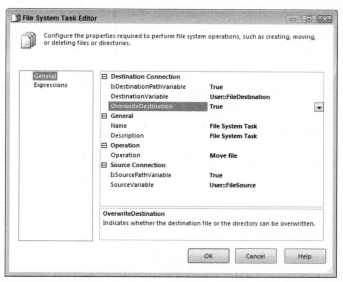

Figure 3-15

The Operation property in Figure 3-15 is set to "Move file," which should move a file from a working source path to an archive destination path. The IsDestinationPathVariable property allows you to specify whether the destination path will be set to an SSIS variable or using a Connection Manager. If this is set to true, the dynamic property DestinationVariable sets the destination path to a variable. If it's set to false, then the DestinationConnection option will be available for you to select the Connection Manager that contains your file or directory. These same properties exist for the source connection in the bottom of the tab. The OverwriteDestination option is set to false by default and specifies whether the task will overwrite the destination file or directory if it already exists. To get an idea of how you'd configure this task, let's look at an example.

Archiving a File

Consider a typical use of the File System Task for an ETL process from a mainframe system. To automate a nightly data load the process would look like this:

- ❏ A file or series of similar files would be generated from a mainframe or other source system and dumped to a network drive.

- ❏ An SSIS package would start on a schedule to poll a directory looking for files to process. If any files were found, they would be moved into a staging or working directory.

- ❏ The data would then be extracted out of the file(s).

- ❏ The file(s) would then be archived to another directory.

In legacy DTS packages, each of these steps would have required some coding in the ActiveX Script Task. You would have had to write one task in VBScript to poll the directory to see if the file had arrived. Another script would pick up the file and move it to another directory. The last script would archive the file. To make this worse, the ActiveX scripts had to use the code-and-paste method of code reuse to perform the same function in other packages. Typically, this would lead to various states of unfinished code that was better in some packages than others and most certainly a nightmare to maintain.

In SSIS, the File System Task can simplify the creation of a package to perform these ETL file-based requirements. We'll postpone the task of polling until later in this chapter when we get to the WMI Event Watcher Task. The iteration of files is also discussed later in detail in Chapter 4. However, you can use what you know about the File System Task to move the file to an archive directory. Create a package in `c:\ssis\Tasks\FileSystemTask\` or download the complete code from `www.wrox.com`. Create a subdirectory called `c:\ssis\Tasks\FileSystemTask\Archive\`. Create a dummy file called `myfile.txt` in `c:\ssis\Tasks\FileSystemTask\`.

Now add a File System Task into the Control Flow. Configure the task to look like Figure 3-15. In the new task, select the option <New Variable. . .> in the drop-down for the properties DestinationVariable and SourceVariable to create the new variables and provide their values. In the FileSource Variable, set the value to `c:\ssis\tasks\filesystemtask\myfile.txt`. In the FileDestination Variable, set the value to `c:\ssis\tasks\filesystemtask\archive\`. This configures the task to move the file `myfile.txt` to the archive directory.

Now run the SSIS package, and you'll see the file `myfile.txt` move into the archive directory. If you wanted to rename the file as you moved it to a date-based filename, you'll want to specify the full filename in the variable and use the Rename File option of the File System Task. Then you get the movement of the file and a new filename in one task. The filename can also be dynamically set using a variable as an expression. For examples of how you can rename this file using a dynamically generated name as you archive, see Chapters 6 and 23.

FTP Task

The SSIS FTP Task enables the use of the File Transfer Protocol (FTP) in your package development tasks. New to the SSIS version of the FTP Task is the ability to send files using the FTP protocol as well as retrieving files for ETL processing. Additionally, the SSIS FTP Task exposes more FTP command capability, allowing you to create or remove local and remote directories and files. Another change from the legacy DTS FTP Task is the ability to use FTP in Passive Mode. This solves the problem that DTS had in communicating with FTP servers where the firewalls filtered the incoming data port connection to the server.

The General tab in the FTP Task Editor is where you specify the FTP Connection Manager for the FTP site you wish to access. If you haven't specified one, select <New Connection . . .> under the FTPConnection property. This will open the FTP Connection Manager and allow you to configure the FTP connection. In Figure 3-16, the Server Name property contains the FTP address for the FTP server. The Server Port property is set to 21, which is the default port for most FTP sites. You can change this if you need to. The other important option to note here is the "Use passive mode" checkbox option that is new to SSIS.

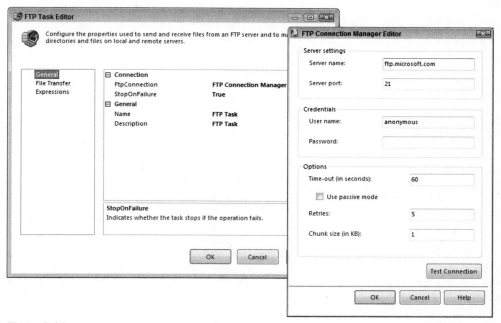

Figure 3-16

Once you have the FTP connection configured, move to the File Transfer tab. The IsRemotePathVariable and IsLocalPathVariable properties allow the paths to be set to an optional variable. Using variables allows you the option of setting these values dynamically at runtime. The RemotePath property sets the directory or files for the remote FTP system. Once the ftpConnection property from the General tab has been selected, you can browse to the actual remote file system to select the remote path or file by clicking the ellipsis in the Remote Path property. You'll see a dialog similar to Figure 3-17 for browsing the FTP remote paths.

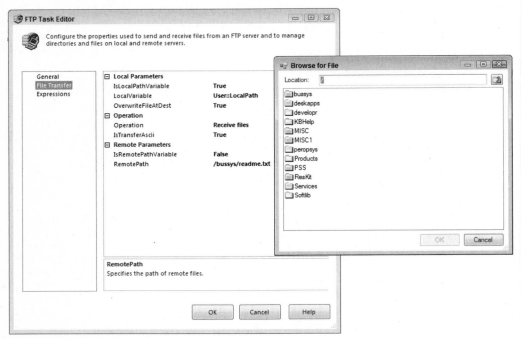

Figure 3-17

The LocalPath property is the Connection Manager that contains a directory on the SSIS side that is going to receive or send the files via FTP. The OverwriteFileAtDest option sets whether the file at the destination will be overwritten if a conflict exists. Like many FTP clients, you can set an option to transport the files in ASCII format by setting the IsTransferAscii option to true. If you set this option to false, the files will be transported in a default binary format. The most important option, of course, is the Operation option, which selects what type of action you'd like to perform. Let's try to set up an SSIS FTP Task to get a file from an FTP server like Microsoft.com.

Getting a File Using FTP

To build an SSIS package that can use FTP to retrieve a file from an FTP server, create a directory called c:\ssis\tasks\ftptask\ or copy the code from www.wrox.com. Then, create a new package in this folder and add an FTP Task to the Control Flow work surface.

Double-click the FTP Task to open the editor, and set it up similar to what was shown in Figure 3-17. For the FTPConnection drop-down box, select <New connection...>. This will open the FTP Connection Editor. Set the Server Name option to **ftp.microsoft.com** and click Test Connection. Click OK to go back to the FTP Task Editor.

Next, go to the File Transfer tab and click the ellipsis to browse to the /bussys/readme.txt folder on the remote path.

You may have to allow the FTP Task temporary access to bypass your firewall if you are using Windows Vista.

For the Local Path option, set the IsLocalPathVariable property to true and select <New Variable . . .> to create a new variable named LocalPath that is set to the value of c:\ssis\tasks_chapter\ftptask\. The Operation drop-down box should be set to Receive Files. For the OverwriteFileAtDest property, select True. The final task should look like Figure 3-17. If you run the package, you'll see that the file will be downloaded from the FTP site at Microsoft to your local file system. In a real-world scenario, you'd download the file, load it into a SQL Server, and then archive it. This complete scenario is discussed in detail in Chapter 8.

Web Service Task

The Web Service Task in SSIS is used to retrieve XML-based result sets by executing a method on a Web service. Just like the other tasks we've separated out into the Data Preparation Task category for this chapter, this task only retrieves the data; it doesn't yet address the need to navigate through the data, or extract sections of the resulting documents. Web services are a big part of advancing service-oriented architectures, and can be used in SSIS to provide real-time validation of data in your ETL processes or to maintain lookup or dimensional data.

The task requires the establishment of an HTTP Connection Manager to a specific HTTP endpoint on a website or to a specific WSDL file on a website. If the HTTP Connection Manager doesn't point to a WSDL file on the site, a local version must be provided. The WSDL file provides a standard XML-formatted list of available methods that can be called in the Web service. The WSDL file also provides information about what type of parameters can be provided and what results can be expected in return. Figure 3-18 provides a look at how you can configure the HTTP Connection Manager to access a Web service called USZIP at www.webservicex.net.

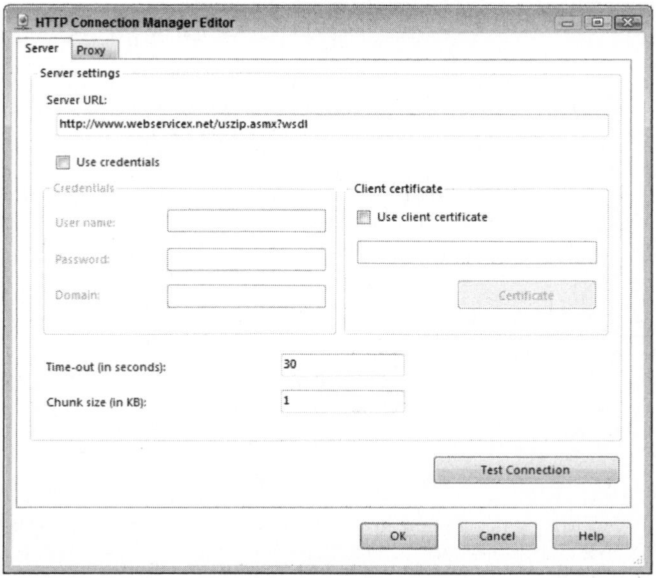

Figure 3-18

This is a simplistic HTTP Connection Manager setup. In this case, no special proxy, credentials, or certificate setup is required. If you are using secure, corporate Web services, this undoubtedly will not be the case. See Books Online if you need information on how to set up secure Web services.

The General tab on the Web Service Task is where you set the HttpConnection property of the task to the HTTP Connection Manager that you have already created or alternatively create at the same time by selecting the <New Connection. . .> option in the property. Note in Figure 3-19 that the value for the WSDL parameter file has been provided. This indicates to the Connection Manager that the definitions of the Web service can be obtained remotely. In this case, you are not required to provide a local version of the WSDL file as well. This property is only required if you don't provide the WSDL parameter in the Connection Manager. If this is the case, simply provide the local filename and click the Download WSDL button that you see in Figure 3-19 to have the task in design time reach out to the HTTP endpoint and retrieve a copy of the WSDL file for you.

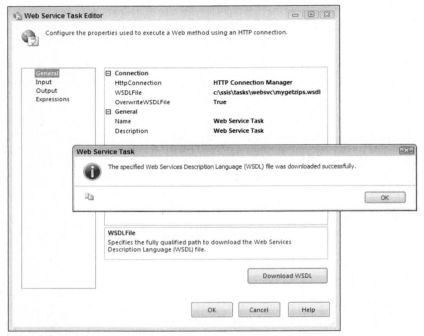

Figure 3-19

The next step is to define the input that you want to retrieve from the Web service. It makes sense that if you've defined the Web service in the General tab, you now need to specify the web method that you'll want to access for the input to the task. The Web Service Task makes this easy by using the WSDL file to provide a drop-down in the Input tab to allow for specific named method selection like you see in Figure 3-20.

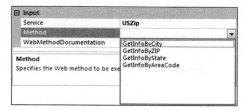

Figure 3-20

Once you select a web method like the GetInfoByAreaCode, the Web Service Task uses the WSDL to set up the interface for you to provide how the input parameters will be fed into the task. You can choose to set up hard-coded values as you see in Figure 3-21 or fill these parameters with variables.

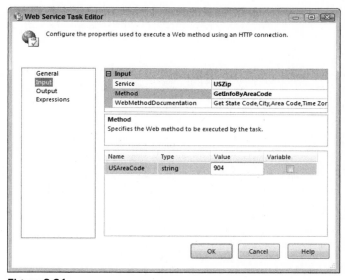

Figure 3-21

You can see here that all the named parameters, in this case only USAreaCode, are provided with the expected data types. If you selected the Variable option here, the Value column would morph into a drop-down list to allow the selection of a variable. Using variables allows you the flexibility to send something into the Web Service Task dynamically at runtime.

The remaining tab is the Output tab, shown in Figure 3-22. Here you have really only two options in this task. The resulting retrieval from the Web service method can be stored in a file or in a variable. The output is in XML format, so if you choose to save in a variable, select a data type of string. In this example, we'll set the OutputType property to a file connection, and then set the location of the file to a spot on the local file system.

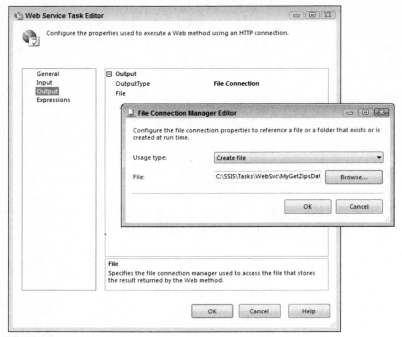

Figure 3-22

Running the Web Service Task using this configuration will result in calling the web method
GetInfoByZipCode on the Web service USZip and retrieving data into an XML file that looks like this:

```xml
<?xml version="1.0" encoding="utf-16"?>
<NewDataSet xmlns="">
  <Table>
    <CITY>Saint Augustine</CITY>
    <STATE>FL</STATE>
    <ZIP>32084</ZIP>
    <AREA_CODE>904</AREA_CODE>
    <TIME_ZONE>E</TIME_ZONE>
  </Table>
  <Table>
    <CITY>Jacksonville</CITY>
    <STATE>FL</STATE>
    <ZIP>32226</ZIP>
    <AREA_CODE>904</AREA_CODE>
    <TIME_ZONE>E</TIME_ZONE>
  </Table>
  <Table>
    <CITY>Macclenny</CITY>
    <STATE>FL</STATE>
    <ZIP>32063</ZIP>
    <AREA_CODE>904</AREA_CODE>
    <TIME_ZONE>E</TIME_ZONE>
  </Table>
</NewDataSet>
```

Retrieving data into a file is good, but using it in an SSIS package is even better. Let's look at an example of how you'd use the XML Task to retrieve this same ZIP Code data and use it in a Data Flow.

Retrieving Data Using the Web Service Task and XML Source Component

Set up a package in the directory `c:\SSIS\tasks_chapter\websvc\` or download the complete package from `www.wrox.com`. Drop a Web Service Task onto the control design surface and configure the task to use the GetInfoByZipCode on the Web service USZip as shown earlier in this section. However, instead of sending the output to the XML file, set the OutputType to store the results of the Web service method call to a variable named MyZipsByAreaCode. The variable should be set to the data type string to store the resulting XML data.

Now drop a Data Flow Task onto the Control Flow design surface and connect the Web Service Task to the Data Flow. In the Data Flow, drop an XML Source component on the design surface. If the XML Source contained schema information you could select the Use Inline Schema option, the Data Access Mode of XML data from Variable, and you'd be done. However, you've seen the data we are getting from the Web service, and there is no schema provided. You are going to have to generate an XML Schema Definition language file so that SSIS can predict and validate data types and lengths. Here's a little trick that will save you some time. To demonstrate the Web Service Task initially, you set the XML output to go to a file. This was not by accident. Having a concrete file gives you a basis to create an XSD, and you can do it right from the design-time XML Source component. Just provide the path to the physical XML file you downloaded earlier and click the Generate XSD button. Now you should have an XSD file that looks similar to this:

```xml
<?xml version="1.0"?>
<xs:schema attributeFormDefault="unqualified" elementFormDefault="qualified"
xmlns:xs="http://www.w3.org/2001/XMLSchema">
  <xs:element name="NewDataSet">
    <xs:complexType>
      <xs:sequence>
        <xs:element minOccurs="0" maxOccurs="unbounded" name="Table">
          <xs:complexType>
            <xs:sequence>
              <xs:element minOccurs="0" name="CITY" type="xs:string" />
              <xs:element minOccurs="0" name="STATE" type="xs:string" />
              <xs:element minOccurs="0" name="ZIP" type="xs:unsignedShort" />
              <xs:element minOccurs="0" name="AREA_CODE" type="xs:unsignedShort" />
              <xs:element minOccurs="0" name="TIME_ZONE" type="xs:string" />
            </xs:sequence>
          </xs:complexType>
        </xs:element>
      </xs:sequence>
    </xs:complexType>
  </xs:element>
</xs:schema>
```

You'll notice that the XSD generator is not perfect. It can only predict a data type based on what it sees in the data. Not to give the generator anthropomorphic qualities, but the ZIP and AREA_CODE data elements "look" like numeric values to the generator. You should always examine the XSD that is created and edit it accordingly. Change the sequence element lines for ZIP and AREA_CODE to look like this:

```
<xs:element minOccurs="0" name="ZIP" type="xs:string " />
<xs:element minOccurs="0" name="AREA_CODE" type=" xs:string" />
```

Now if you refresh the XML Source and select the Columns tab, as shown in Figure 3-23, you should be able to see the columns extracted from the physical XML file.

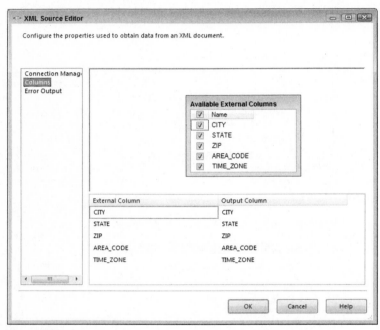

Figure 3-23

Now, it is just as easy to change back to retrieving this same data from a variable instead of having to save into a file from the task and picking it back up from a file in the Data Flow XML source. Since we know the data in the variable is in the same XML format, go back to the Connection Manager tab on the XML Source and reselect the Data Access Mode of XML data from Variable. Then select the variable MyZipsByAreaCode as the location of the XML data. The task will complain a bit, since you've changed the source and the lineages must be reset, but click OK, and now the columns will again look like Figure 3-23.

To complete the package, add an Excel Destination to dump the data into an Excel spreadsheet. Connect the output pipeline of the XML Source to the Excel Destination. Set the OLE DB Connection Manager to a new XLS file and click the New button to define the name of the Excel sheet. Click the Mappings tab in the Excel Destination Editor to map the output to the Excel sheet. The final Data Flow should look like Figure 3-24.

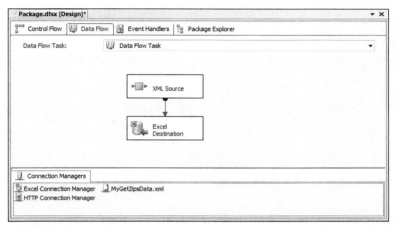

Figure 3-24

If you save and run the package it will download the XML file into a variable, and then export the columns and rows to an Excel spreadsheet. Hardly a robust example, but you should be able to see that the Web Service Task has made retrieving data from a Web service a very simple point-and-click task. However, the Web Service Task can only retrieve the results of a Web service call. You may find that you need to prepare, extract, or validate your XML files before running them through your ETL processes. This is where the XML task comes in.

XML Task

The XML Task is used when you need to validate, modify, extract, or even create files in an XML format. Earlier we used a Web Service Task to retrieve data in an XML-formatted Web service response. In terms of validating this type of XML result, the WSDL that you copy down locally is your contract with the Web service that will break if the XML contents of the results change. In other situations, you may be provided with XML data from a third-party source outside of a contractual relationship. In these cases, it is a good practice to validate the XML file against the schema definition before processing the file. This provides an opportunity to handle the issue programmatically.

If you look at the task in Figure 3-25, the editor looks simple. There are two tabs: only one for General configuration and the obligatory Expressions tab.

Figure 3-25

The current OperationType is set in this example to the Diff operation. The option is one of the more involved operations and requires two XML sources, one as the Input and the other as the Second Operand. However, these properties change based on the selection you make for the OperationType property. The options are:

- ❑ **Validate:** This option allows for the schema validation of an XML file against both Document Type Definition (DTD) or XML Schema Definition (XSD) binding control documents. You can use this option to ensure that a provided XML file adheres to your expected document format.

- ❑ **XSLT:** The Extensible Stylesheet Language Transformations (XSLT) are a subset of the XML language to allow for transformation of XML data. You might use this operation at the end of an ETL process to take resulting data and transform it to meet a presentation format.

- ❑ **XPATH:** This option XML Path Language allows the extraction of sections or specific nodes from the structure of the XML document. You would use this option if you want to extract data from the XML document prior to using the content. An example would be pulling out only the orders for a specific customer from an XML file.

- ❑ **Merge:** This option allows for the merging of two XML documents with the same structure. You might use this option to combine the results of two extracts from disparate systems into one document.

- ❑ **Diff:** This option uses difference algorithms to compare two XML documents to produce a third document called an XML Diffgram that contains the differences between the two. Use this option with another XML Task using the Patch option to produce a smaller subset of data to insert into your data store. An example use of this task is to extract only the prices that have changed from a new price sheet in XML format.

❑ **Patch:** This option applies the results of a Diff operation to an XML document to create a new XML document.

As you might expect, you can configure the task to use either a file source or a variable. The option to input the XML directly is also available, but not as practical. The best way to get an idea of how this task can be used is to demonstrate with a few examples. Therefore, we'll do this now.

Validating an XML File

First up is a basic use case of validating the internal schema format of an XML file. To make sure you are clear on what the XML Task does for you, the validation is not whether the XML file is properly formed, but contains the proper internal elements. If an XML file is malformed, simply attempting to load the XML file in the task will generate an error. However, if there is a missing node that is defined within the XSD contract, the XML Task Validation option will inform you that the XML file provided doesn't meet the conditions of the XSD validation. To set up an example, we'll borrow the information from the XML and XSD files in the Web Service Task example. If you recall we had an XSD that validated string node for City, State, Zip, Area_Code, and Time_Zone. (See the Web Service Task example to see the XSD format.) You can download this complete example at www.wrox.com.

We'll use three files to exercise this task. The first will be a valid XML file named MyGetZipsData.xml that looks like this:

```
<?xml version="1.0" encoding="utf-16"?>
<NewDataSet xmlns="">
  <Table>
    <CITY>Saint Augustine</CITY>
    <STATE>FL</STATE>
    <ZIP>32084</ZIP>
    <AREA_CODE>904</AREA_CODE>
    <TIME_ZONE>E</TIME_ZONE>
  </Table>
</NewDataSet>
```

The second file will be an invalid XML file named MyGetZipsData_Bad.xml. This file has an improperly named node <CITYZ> that doesn't match the XSD specification:

```
<?xml version="1.0" encoding="utf-16"?>
<NewDataSet xmlns="">
  <Table>
    <CITYZ>Saint Augustine</CITYZ>
    <STATE>FL</STATE>
    <ZIP>32084</ZIP>
    <AREA_CODE>904</AREA_CODE>
    <TIME_ZONE>E</TIME_ZONE>
  </Table>
</NewDataSet>
```

The last file is a malformed XML file named `MyGetZipsData_ReallyBad.xml`. This file has an empty `<Table>` node and is not a valid XML format:

```xml
<?xml version="1.0" encoding="utf-16"?>
<NewDataSet xmlns="">
  <Table></Table>
    <CITY>Saint Augustine</CITY>
    <STATE>FL</STATE>
    <ZIP>32084</ZIP>
    <AREA_CODE>904</AREA_CODE>
    <TIME_ZONE>E</TIME_ZONE>
  </Table>
</NewDataSet>
```

Create a package and add a new XML Task to the Control Flow surface. First, select the OperationType of Validate, set the Input Source Type to a new file connection, and browse to select the `MyGetZipsData.xml` file. Expand the OperationResult property in the Output section to configure an additional text file to capture the results of the validation. The result values are only true or false, so a simple text file is all you'll need to see how this works. Typically, you'd store the result in a variable, so you can test the results to determine the next action to take after validation. Set the OverwriteDestination property to True to allow the result to be overwritten in each run of the task.

In the Second Operand, you'll need to create another file connection to the XSD file that will be used for validation of the schema. Create another file connection that points to this XSD file. Finally, set the validation type to XSD, since we are using an XSD file to validate the XML. The editor at this point should look like Figure 3-26.

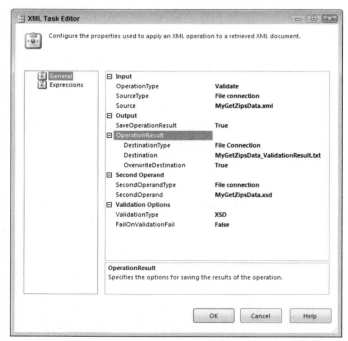

Figure 3-26

This completes the happy path use case. If you execute this task, it should execute successfully and the results file should contain the value of "true" to indicate the XML file contains the correct schema as defined by the XSD file. Now onto the true test: Change the source to a new connection for the MyGetZipsData_Bad.xml file. Execute the task again. This time although the task completes successfully, the result file contains the value of "false" to indicate a bad schema. This is really the whole point of the Validation option.

Finally, change the source to create a new connection to the poorly formatted XML file MyGetZipsData_ ReallyBad.xml to see what happens. You'll see that the task actually fails — even though the Validation options' FailOnValidationFail property is set to False. This is because the validation didn't fail — the loading of the XML file failed. The error message indicates the problem accurately:

```
[XML Task] Error: An error occurred with the following error message: "The
'NewDataSet' start tag on line 2 does not match the end tag of 'Table'. Line 9,
position 5.".
[XML Task] Error: An error occurred with the following error message: "Root element
is missing.".
```

Just be aware of the difference between validating the schema and validating the XML file itself when designing your package Control Flows and set up accordingly. You'll need to have a Control Flow for the failure of the task and for the successful completion with a failure result.

This is just one of the examples of how you can use the XML Task for SSIS development. There are obviously several other uses for this task that are highly legitimate and useful for preparing data to feed into your SSIS ETL package Data Flows. Let's now turn to another set of data preparation tasks that we've separated into their own category, since they deal specifically with retrieval and preparation of RDBMS data.

RDBMS Server Tasks

These tasks could also be considered Data Preparation Tasks as well, since they are responsible for bringing data sources into the ETL processes, but we've separated the Bulk Insert Task and the Execute SQL Task into this separate category because of the unique expectation of working with data from Relational Database Management Systems (RDBMS) like SQL Server, Oracle, and DB2. The exception is the Bulk Insert Task, which is a wrapper for the SQL Server bulk-copy-process.

Bulk Insert Task

The Bulk Insert Task allows you to insert data from a text or flat file into a SQL Server database table in the same high-octane manner as using a BULK INSERT statement or the bcp.exe command-line tool. In fact, the task is basically just a wizard to store the information needed to create and execute a bulk copying demand (BCP) command at runtime. If you aren't familiar with using BCP, then you can research the topic in detail in Books Online. The downside with the Bulk Insert Task is that it is strict in data format and precludes being able to work with data in a Data Flow within one action. This can be seen as a disadvantage in that it does not allow any transformations to occur to the data in flight, but not all ETL processes are efficiently modified in the Data Flow. In high-volume extracts, you may be better served to lay the initial extract down in a staging table and extract data in discrete chunks for processing within specific Data Flows. This tradeoff in functionality gives you have the fastest way to load data from a text file into a SQL Server database.

When you add a Bulk Insert Task to your Control Flow, open the Bulk Insert Task Editor to configure it. As in most tasks, the General tab allows you to name and describe the task. Make sure you name it something that describes its unit of work, like "Prepare Staging." This will help you later when you deploy the package and troubleshoot problems. The next tab called the Connection tab is the most important. This tab lets you specify the source and destination for the data. Select the destination from the Connection drop-down box in the Destination Connection group. Next, specify a destination table from the next drop-down box below the destination connection. While you're specifying connections, drop down to the bottom to specify the source connection's filename in the File drop-down box. Both the source and destination connections use the Connection Manager. If you haven't already created the shared connections, you'll be prompted to create them in either case by selecting <New Connection . . .>.

Both the source and the optional format file must be relative to the destination SQL Server, because the operation occurs there when a Bulk Insert Task is used. If you are using a network file location, use the UNC path (\\MachineName\ShareName\FileName.csv) to the source or format file.

After you specify the connections, you need to provide file specifications for the format of file you're importing. If you created the file using the BCP utility, you can use the -f option to create a format file as well. The Bulk Insert Task can then use the BCP format file to determine how the file is formatted, or you can select the column and row delimiters in the Format property of the task. The two options are Use File, which uses the BCP format (.fmt) file, or Specify, which allows you to select the file delimiters. The available delimiters are New Line ({CR}{LF}), Carriage Return ({CR}), Line Feed ({LF}), Semicolon (;), Comma (,), Tab, or Vertical Bar (|). Note that the defaults are for the row to be {CR}{LF} delimited and the column tab-delimited. Figure 3-27 shows how the Task Editor provides two different interfaces for these optional file specifications.

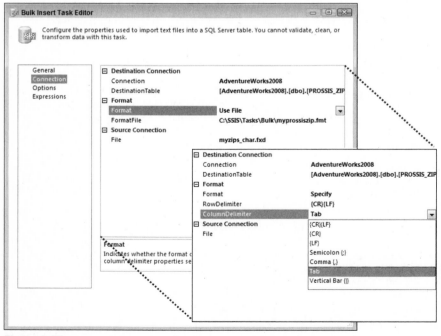

Figure 3-27

In the Options tab of the Bulk Insert Task Editor, you'll be able to use some lesser-known options. Here you can specify the code page for the source file. You will rarely want to change the code page from RAW, which is the default. Using RAW is the fastest data loading option because no code page conversion takes place. Other options include OEM, which you should use when copying from one SQL Server to another, ACP to convert non-Unicode data to the ANSI code page of the SQL Server you are loading the data into, or you can specify a specific code page mapping. The DataFileType option can specify what type of file the source file is. Options here include char, native, widechar, and widenative. Generally, files you receive will be the default char option, but in some cases, you may see a file with native format. A file (`myzips_native.txt`) in native format was created from SQL Server by using the `bcp.exe` program with the `-n` (native) switch and supplied with the download from `www.wrox.com`. You'll see how to import it later in an example.

In the Options tab, you can also specify the first and last row to copy if you'd like only a sampling of the rows. Commonly this is used to set the first row to two (2) when you want to skip a header row. The BatchSize option shows how many records will be written to SQL Server before committing the batch. If you have a BatchSize of 0 (the default), this means that all the records will be written to SQL Server in a single batch. If you have more than 100,000 records, then you may want to adjust this setting to 50,000 or adjust to a number based on how many you want to commit at a time. The adjustment may vary based on the width of your file. Figure 3-28 shows an example of the Bulk Insert Task Editor options.

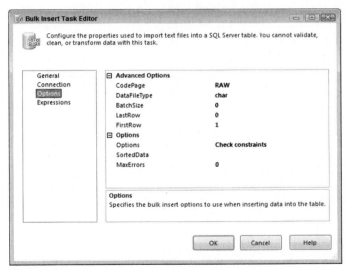

Figure 3-28

The Options drop-down box contains five options that you can turn off and on:

❑ **Check Constraints:** The option that checks table and column constraints before committing the record. This option is the only one turned on by default.

❑ **Keep Nulls:** By selecting this option, the Bulk Insert Task will replace any empty columns in the source file with NULLs in SQL Server.

❑ **Enable Identity Insert:** Enable this option if your destination table has an identity column that you're inserting into. Otherwise, you will receive an error.

❑ **Table Lock:** This option creates a SQL Server lock on the target table from insert and updates other than the records you're inserting. This option will speed up your process but may cause a production outage, since others will be blocked from modifying the table. If you check this option, SSIS will not have to compete for locks to insert massive amounts of data into the target table. Set this option only if you're certain that no other process will be competing with your task for table access.

❑ **Fire Triggers:** By default, the Bulk Insert Task will ignore triggers for maximum speed. By checking this option, the task will no longer ignore triggers and will fire the insert triggers for the table you're inserting into.

There are a few other options you can set in the Options tab. The SortedData option specifies what column you wish to sort by, while inserting the data. This option defaults to sort nothing, which means False. If you have a need to set this option, type the column name that you wish to sort. The MaxErrors option specifies how many errors are acceptable before the task is stopped with an error. Each row that does not insert is considered an error; by default, if a single row has a problem, the entire task fails.

> *The Bulk Insert Task does not log error-causing rows. If you want your bad records to be written to an error file or table, it's better to use the Data Flow Task.*

Using the Bulk Insert Task

Take time out briefly to exercise the Bulk Insert Task with a typical data load. First, create a new SSIS project called BulkInsert. Rename the package called Package.dtsx that's created with the project to BulkLoadZip.dtsx. If you haven't already downloaded the code files for this chapter from www.wrox.com, do so. Then extract the four files for this chapter named: myzips.csv, myzips_native.txt, zip5.xml, and zip5.fmt. Two of these files contain formatted data for all of the postal codes in the state of Florida. The other two are format files to help the BCP process read the files.

Create a table in the AdventureWorks2008 database using SQL Management Studio or the tool of your choice to store postal code information:

```
CREATE TABLE PROSSIS_ZIPCODE (
    ZipCode CHAR(5),
    State CHAR(2),
    ZipName VARCHAR(16)
)
```

Back in your empty SSIS solution, drag the Bulk Insert Task onto the Control Flow design pane. Notice that the task has a red icon on it telling you that the task hasn't been configured yet. Double-click the task to open the editor. In the General tab, provide the name "Load Zip Codes" for the Name option and "Loads zip codes from a flat file" for the description.

Click the Connection tab. From the Connection drop-down box, select <New connection . . .>. This will open the Configure OLE DB Connection Manager dialog box. You're going to create a connection to the AdventureWorks2008 database that can be reused throughout this chapter. Click New to add a new

Connection Manager. For the Server Name option, select the server that contains your AdventureWorks2008 database. For the database, select the AdventureWorks2008 database. Your final connection configuration should look like Figure 3-29, but your login information will vary based on your server's security configuration. Click OK to go back to the previous screen, and click OK again to go back to the Bulk Insert Task Editor.

Figure 3-29

You'll now see that the Connection Manager you just created has been transposed into the Connection drop-down box. Now you need to define the destination. For the DestinationTable option, select the [AdventureWorks2008].[dbo].[PROSSIS_ZIPCODE] table. For the first attempt, you'll import a comma-delimited version of the zip codes. This simulates importing a file that would have been dumped out of another SQL Server (with the same table name) using this `bcp` command:

```
bcp AdventureWorks2008.dbo.prossis_zipcode out c:\ssis\tasks\bulk\myzips.csv
-c -t, -T
```

Leave the remaining options set to the defaults. The RowDelimiter property option will be {CR}{LF} (a carriage return) and the ColumnDelimiter property should be set to comma delimited. For the File option, you will again select <New connection . . .> to create a new Connection Manager. This will open the File Connection Manager Editor. For the Usage Type, select Existing File. Then point to `myZips.csv` for the File option. Your final screen should look something like Figure 3-30.

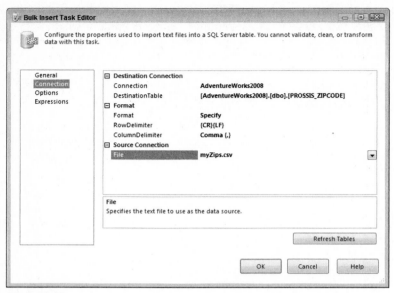

Figure 3-30

If you open the `myzips.csv` file, you'll notice that there is no header row with the column names before the data. If you had a column header and needed to skip it, go into the Options tab and change the FirstRow option to 2. This would start the import process on the second row, instead of the first that is the default.

You should be able to run the package now. When the package executes, the table will be populated with all the postal code from the import file. You should be able to verify this by selecting all the rows from the PROSSIS_ZIPS table.

To see how the Bulk Insert Task uses the BCP format file, go back to the Format property and change the option from Specify to Use File. Now the designer will change a bit, and you'll need to click into the FormatFile property and browse to the `zip5.fmt` file (also in code download). This format file was created by using the BCP command:

```
bcp AdventureWorks2008.dbo.prossis_zipcode format nul -c -t,
c:\ssis\tasks\bulk\zip5.fmt -T
```

Now rerun the package to re-import the data using the BCP format file. The data loads just as well. If you are using a BCP client 10.0 or greater, you can also load a file using an XML format file. To do this, add a connection to the `myzips_native.txt` file and set the format file to `zip5.xml`. The xml format file can be created using the BCP command:

```
bcp AdventureWorks2008.dbo.prossis_zipcode format nul -f
c:\ssis\tasks\bulk\zip5.xml -x -T -n
```

All these different methods are demonstrated in the download package for this chapter from
www.wrox.com. The point here is that the Bulk Insert Task is designed to be used to exchange highly
reliable sources of data — namely from one SQL Server to another. As you can see, the Bulk Insert Task is
a useful tool to load staging files quickly, but you may need to further process the file. One reason is that
this task provides no opportunity to divert the data into a transformation workflow to examine the
quality of the data. The other reason is that you have to import character-based data to avoid raising
errors during the loading process. The Bulk Insert Task has an all-or-nothing nature in its method of
error handling. If a single row fails to insert, then your task may fail (based on your setting for the
maximum number of allowed errors). These problems could be easily solved by using a Data Flow Task
if the data is unreliable or in smaller volumes.

Execute SQL Task

The Execute SQL Task is one of the most widely used tasks in SSIS for interacting with an RDBMS data
source. The Execute SQL Task is used for all sorts of things, like truncating staging data table prior to
importing, retrieving row counts to determine the next step in a workflow, or to call stored procedures to
perform business logic against sets of staged data. You'll also see the task used to retrieve information
from a database repository. This same task could also be found in the legacy DTS product, but the SSIS
version provides a better configuration editor and methods to map stored procedure parameters to read
back result and output values. In this section, it is simply easier to introduce you to all the possible ways
to configure this task by working through the different ways you can use the Execute SQL Task. You'll
work through how to execute parameterized SQL statements, batches of SQL statements, capturing
single row and multiple row results, and how to execute stored procedures.

Executing a Parameterized SQL Statement

The task can execute a SQL Task in two basic ways: by executing inline SQL statements, or by executing
stored procedures. The resulting action can also result in the need to perform one of two options: to
accept return values in parameters or in a result set. You can get an idea of how the task can be
configured to do these combinations in the General tab of the Execute SQL Task Editor shown in
Figure 3-31. In this figure, the Execute SQL Task is set to perform an Update operation on the Person.
Address table using an inline SQL statement with a variable-based parameter. This is the easiest use of
the Execute SQL Task because you don't need to configure the Result Set tab properties.

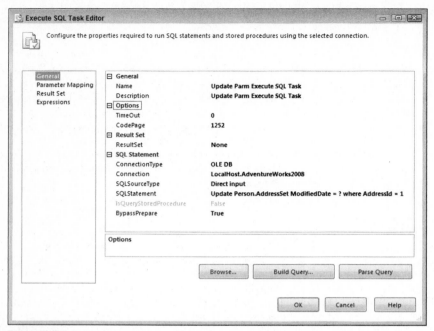

Figure 3-31

Notice in Figure 3-31 that the General tab contains the core properties of the task. Here the task is configured to point to an OLE DB connection. The other options for the ConnectionType include ODBC, ADO, ADO.NET, SQLMOBILE, and even EXCEL connections. The catch to all this connection flexibility is that the Execute SQL Task behaves differently depending upon the underlying data provider. For example, the SQLStatement property in Figure 3-31 shows a directly inputted TSQL statement with a question mark in the statement. The full statement is here:

```
Update Person.Address
  Set ModifiedDate = ?
  where AddressId = 1
```

This ? that indicates that a parameter is required is classic ODBC parameter marking and is used in most of the other providers; with the exception of the ADO.NET provider, which uses named parameters. This matters because in the task you need to configure the parameters to the SQL statement in the Parameters Mapping tab. The tab for this query would look like Figure 3-32.

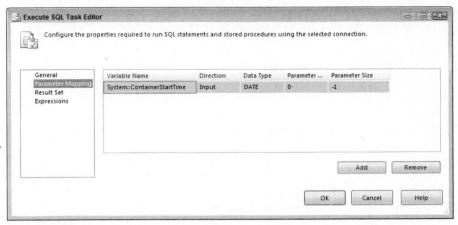

Figure 3-32

Here the parameter mapping collection maps the first parameter [ordinal position of zero (0)] to a system variable. When mapping parameters to connections and underlying providers use this table to set up this tab in the Task Editor:

If Using Connection of Type	Parameter Marker to Use	Parameter Name to Use
ADO	?	Param1, Param2, ...
ADO.NET	@<Real Param Name>	@<Real Param Name>
ODBC	?	1,2,3 (Note ordinal starts at 1)
OLEDB & EXCEL	?	0,1,2,3 (Note ordinal starts at 0)

Because we are using an OLE DB provider here, the parameter marker is ?, and the parameter is using the zero-based ordinal position. The other mapping you would have needed to do here is for the data type of the parameter. These data types will also change based on your underlying provider. SSIS is very specific about how you map data types, so you may need to experiment or check Books Online for the mapping equivalents for your parameters and provider. We'll go over many of the common issues in this regard throughout this section, but for this initial example, we mapped the System::ContainerStartTime to the OLE DB data type of DATE. At this point, the Execute SQL Task with this simple update statement could be executed and the ModifyDate would be updated in the database with a current datetime value.

A variation in this example is a case where the statement can be dynamically generated at runtime and simply fired into the Connection Manager. The SQLSourceType property on the General tab allows for three different types of SQL statement resolution: either directly input (as we did), via a variable, or from a file connection. Another way to build the SQL statement is to use the Build Query action button. This brings up a Query-By-Example (QBE) tool that helps you build a query by clicking the tables and establishing the relationships. The variable-based option is also straightforward. Typically, you'd define a variable that is resolved from an expression. Setting the SQLSourceType property in the Execute SQL

Task to Variable allows you to select the variable that will resolve to the SQL statement that you want the task to execute. The only thing you need to pay attention to here is that SSIS limits the size of a string to 4,000 characters.

> *Building inline Dynamic SQL statements with variables has a limitation of 4,000 characters.*

The other option of using a file connection warrants a little more discussion.

Executing a Batch of SQL Statements

If you use the File Connection option of the Execute SQL Task's SQLSourceType property, typically you are doing so to execute a batch of SQL statements. All you need to do is have the file that contains the batch of SQL statements available to the SSIS package during runtime. Set up a File Connection to point to the batch file you need to run. Make sure that your SQL batch follows a few rules. Some of these rules are typical SQL rules, like using a GO command between statements, but others are specific to the SSIS Execute SQL Task. Use these rules as a guide for executing a batch of SQL statements:

❑   Use GO statements between each distinct command. Note that some providers allow you to use the semicolon (;) as a command delimiter.

❑   If there are multiple parameterized statements in the batch, all parameters must match in type and order.

❑   Only one statement can return a result, and it must be the first statement.

❑   If the batch returns a result, the columns must match the same number and properly named result columns for the Execute SQL Task. If the two don't match and you have subsequent UPDATE or DELETE statements in the batch, these will execute even though the results don't bind, and you get an error. The batch is sent to SQL Server to execute and behaves the same way.

Returning results is something that we haven't explored in the Execute SQL Task, so let's look at some examples that do this in SSIS.

Capturing Singleton Results

On the General tab of the Execute SQL Task, you can set up the task to capture the type of result that you expect to have returned by configuring the ResultSet property. This property can be set to return nothing or None, a singleton result set, a multi-line result, or an XML-formatted string. Any other setting besides the selection of None will require the configuration of the Result Set tab on the editor. In the Result Set tab, you are defining the binding of returned values into a finite set of SSIS variables. For most data-type bindings, this is not an issue. You select the SSIS variable data type that most closely matches that of your provider. The issues that arise from this activity are caused by invalid casting that occurs as data in the Tabular Data Stream (TDS) from the underlying provider collide with the variable data types they are being assigned to. This casting happens internally within the Execute SQL Task and you don't have control over it like you would in a Script Task. Before you think that it is just a simple data-type-assignment issue, you need to understand that SSIS is the lowest common denominator when it comes to being able to bind to data types from all the possible data providers. For example, SSIS doesn't have a currency or decimal data type. The only thing close is the double data type. This is the type that must be used for real, numeric, current, decimal, float, and other similar data types.

Let's set up a simple inline SQL statement that will return a single row (or singleton result) to show both the normal cases and the exception cases for configuring the Execute SQL Task and handling these binding issues. First, we'll use a simple TSQL statement against the AdventureWorks2008 database that looks like this:

```
SELECT TOP 1
    CarrierTrackingNumber,
    LineTotal,
    OrderQty,
    UnitPrice
From Sales.SalesOrderDetail
```

We've chosen this odd result set because of the multiple data types in the SalesOrderDetail table. These data types provide an opportunity to highlight some of the solutions to difficulties with mapping these data types in the Execute SQL Task that we've been helping folks with since the first release of SSIS. Figure 3-33 shows the structure of the SalesOrderDetail table, where you can see we are pulling columns with nvarchar, smallint, money, and numeric data types.

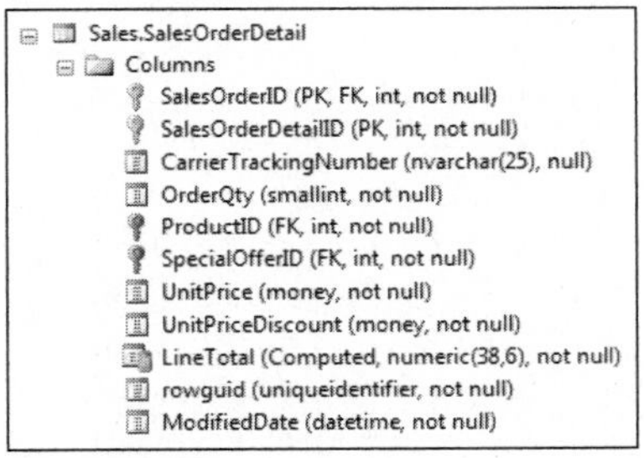

Figure 3-33

To capture these columns from this table, you need to create some variables in the package. Then these variables will be mapped one-for-one to the result columns. Some of the mappings are simple. The CarrierTrackingNumber can be easily mapped to a string variable data type. However, in the first release of SSIS, this didn't work that well, and you'd get TDS data stream errors. In this release, the mapping works for Nvarchar and Varchar data types. The OrderQty field that is using the smallint SQL Server data type will need to be mapped to an INT16 SSIS data type, or you will get an error like this.

```
[Execute SQL Task] Error: An error occurred while assigning a value to variable
"OrderQty": "The type of the value being assigned to variable "User::OrderQty"
differs from the current variable type. Variables may not change type during
execution. Variable types are strict, except for variables of type Object.".
```

The other two values for the SQL Server UnitPrice (money) and LineTotal (numeric) columns get more difficult. There really is no SSIS variable data type equivalent as you can see in Figure 3-34.

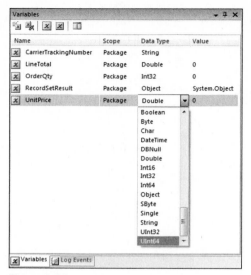

Figure 3-34

So what can you do? There are really only two options. The first is to capture these results in a string variable and cast them in a later Script Task, or depending upon your data you may be able to cast the results directly in the query. In both instances, you'll be casting in the SQL statement, but if you directly cast in the SQL statement, you avoid a later conversion task. You just need to pay attention to these casting operations, because it is possible to lose some significant figures depending upon the nature of your data. Because you can't directly set the value of the current money and numeric columns to a double, you have to explicitly cast these values in the SQL statement like this:

```
SELECT TOP 1
   CarrierTrackingNumber,
   Convert(float, LineTotal),
   OrderQty,
   Convert(float, UnitPrice)
From Sales.SalesOrderDetail
```

Converting to a float is not really a good option either because this is not a precise number, but it's the only option. Just make sure you understand your data and any casting issues that may result.

Now the parameters can simply be mapped in the Execute SQL Task Result Set tab, as shown in Figure 3-35.

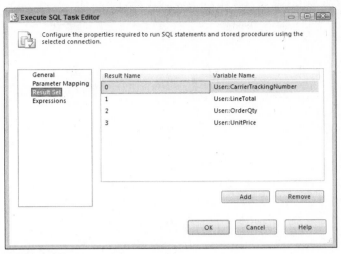

Figure 3-35

Notice in Figure 3-35 that the result names are provided by ordinal position. This is following the guide provided earlier for the OLE DB provider that uses ordinal positions. If you were using ADO.NET providers, then the result name could actually be the parameter name itself. Just use the Add and Remove buttons to put the result elements in order of how they will be returned, name them according to the provider requirements, get the right data types, and you'll be fine. If these are in the incorrect order, or if the data types can't be cast by the Execute SQL Task from the TDS data stream into the corresponding variable data type, you will get a binding error. This should give you a general guide to using the Execute SQL Task for capturing singleton results. Let's now look at capturing multiple row results.

Multi-Row Results

Typically, you capture multi-row results from a database as a recordset or as an XML file (particularly between SQL Server data sources) to use in either another Script Task for analysis or decision-making purposes, to provide an enumerator in a Foreach or Looping task, or to feed into a Data Flow Task for processing. Set up the SQLSourceType and SQLStatement properties to call either an inline SQL statement or a stored procedure. In either case, the Result Set tab will be set up to capture the results. The only change from capturing a singleton result is that you only need to capture the whole result into a variable instead of mapping each column. The data type you should use to capture the results depends upon what you are capturing. The XML file can be captured in either a string or object data type. The recordset can only be captured in a variable with object data type. An example of the Execute SQL Task configured to create an object data type to store the results of a selection of rows from the Sales. SalesOrderDetail table can be seen in Figure 3-36. Notice that the Result Set tab shows the capturing of these rows with the required zero-ordinal position.

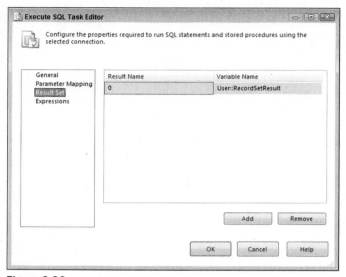

Figure 3-36

Once the recordset is stored as a variable, you can do things like "shred" the recordset. The term *shredding* means to iterate through the recordset one row at a time in a Foreach Loop operation. For each iteration, you can capture the variables from and perform an operation per row. Figure 3-37 shows how the Foreach Task would look using the variable-based recordset.

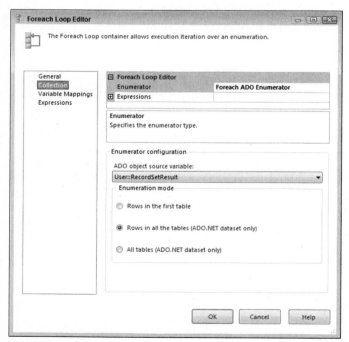

Figure 3-37

Another way to use the variable-based recordset is to use it to feed a data transform. To do this just create a Source Script Transform in a Data Flow and add to it the columns that you want to realize from the stored recordset and pass in the recordset variable. Then add code similar to this to turn the column data from the recordset into the output stream. (To save time and space only two columns are being realized in the recordset.)

```csharp
C#
public override void CreateNewOutputRows()
{
    System.Data.OleDb.OleDbDataAdapter oleDA =
            new System.Data.OleDb.OleDbDataAdapter();
    System.Data.DataTable dT = new System.Data.DataTable();

    oleDA.Fill(dT, Variables.RecordSetResult);
    foreach (DataRow dr in dT.Rows)
    {
        Output0Buffer.AddRow();
        //by Name
        Output0Buffer.CarrierTrackingNumber =
                dr["CarrierTrackingNumber"].ToString();
        //by Ordinal
        Output0Buffer.UnitPrice = System.Convert.ToDecimal(dr[6]);
    }
}
```

```vbnet
VB
Public Overrides Sub CreateNewOutputRows()
    Dim oleDA As New System.Data.OleDb.OleDbDataAdapter()
    Dim dT As New System.Data.DataTable()
    Dim row As System.Data.DataRow

    oleDA.Fill(dt, Variables.RecordSetResult)
    For Each row In dT.Rows
        Output0Buffer.AddRow()
        Output0Buffer.CarrierTrackingNumber = _
                row("CarrierTrackingNumber").ToString()
        Output0Buffer.UnitPrice = System.Convert.ToDecimal(row(6))
    Next
    End Sub
```

The XML version of capturing the result in a string is even easier. You don't need to use the Script Component to turn the XML string back into a source of data. Instead, use the out-of-the-box component called the XML Data source in the Data Flow that can accept a variable as the source of the data. (Go back and review the example on how to do this in the "Web Service Task" section of this chapter.) You can see that the Execute SQL Task is really quite useful at executing inline SQL statements and retrieving results, so now let's look at how you can use stored procedures as well in this task.

Executing a Stored Procedure

Another way to interact with an RDBMS is to execute stored procedures that can perform operations on a data source to return values, output parameters, or results. Set up the SSIS Execute SQL Task to execute stored procedures by providing the call to the proc name in the General tab's SQLStatement property. The catch is the same as before. Because the Execute SQL Task sits on top of several different data providers, you need to pay attention to the way each provider handles the stored procedure call. The following table provides a guide to how you should code the SQLStatement property in the Execute SQL Task:

If Using Connection Type	And IsQueryStoredProcedure	Code the SQL Statement Property Like This
OLEDB & EXCEL	N/A	`EXEC usp_StoredProc ?, ?`
ODBC	N/A	`{call usp_StoredProc (?, ?)}`
ADO	False	`EXEC usp_StoredProc ?, ?`
	True	`usp_StoredProc`
ADO.NET	False	`EXEC usp_StoredProc @Parm1, @Parm2`
	True	`usp_StoredProc @Parm1, @Parm2`

Following the earlier example where you used an inline SQL statement to update the modified date in the sales order detail, create a TSQL stored procedure that does the same thing like this:

```
CREATE PROCEDURE usp_UpdatePersonAddressModifyDate(
        @MODIFIED_DATE DATETIME
        )
AS
BEGIN
  Update Person.Address
  Set ModifiedDate = @MODIFIED_DATE
  where AddressId = 1
END
```

In the online downloads for this chapter, we've created a package that shows you how to call this procedure using both the OLE DB and ADO.NET Connection Managers. The Execute SQL Task should look like Figure 3-38 for the OLE DB connection.

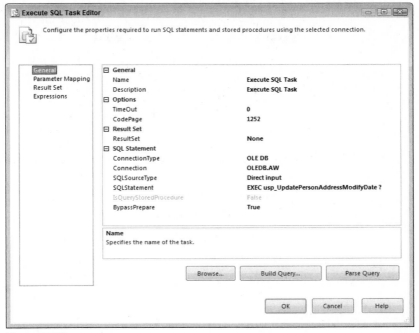

Figure 3-38

The SQLStatement property in Figure 3-38 is set up as prescribed earlier in the guide with the ? parameter markers for the one input parameter. Note also that the IsQueryStoredProcedure property is not enabled. You can't set this property for the OLE DB provider. However, this property would be enabled in the ADO.NET version of the Execute SQL Task to execute this same procedure. If you set the IsQueryStoredProcedure for the ADO.NET version to True, the SQLStatement property would also need to change. Remove the execute command and the parameter markers to look like this: `Usp_UpdatePersonAddressModifyDate`. In this mode, the Execute SQL Task will actually build the complete execution statement using the parameter listing that you'd provide in the Parameter Mapping tab of the Task Editor.

The Parameter Mapping tab of the Task Editor would vary based upon the underlying provider set on the Execute SQL Task as shown in Figure 3-39.

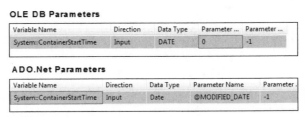

Figure 3-39

For brevity sake, Figure 3-39 just shows the differences in the parameter settings. You'll notice that the parameter names follow the same rules you used when applying parameters to inline SQL statements earlier in this chapter.

Retrieving Output Parameters from a Stored Procedure

Mapping input parameters for SQL statements is one thing, but there are some issues to consider when handling output parameters from stored procedures. The main thing to remember is that all retrieved output or return parameters have to be pushed into variables to have any downstream use. The variable types are defined within SSIS, and you have the same issues that we went over in the section "Capturing Singleton Results" for this task. In short, you have to be able to choose the correct variables when you bind the resulting provider output parameters to the SSIS variables, so that you can get a successful type conversion.

As an example, we'll duplicate the same type of SQL query we used earlier with the inline SQL statement to capture a singleton result, but we'll use a stored procedure object instead. Put this stored procedure in the AdventureWorks2008 database:

```
CREATE PROCEDURE usp_GetTop1SalesOrderDetail
 (
  @CARRIER_TRACKING_NUMBER nvarchar(25) OUTPUT,
  @LINE_TOTAL numeric(38,6) OUTPUT,
  @ORDER_QTY smallint OUTPUT,
  @UNIT_PRICE money OUTPUT
 )
AS
BEGIN
 SELECT TOP 1
  @CARRIER_TRACKING_NUMBER = CarrierTrackingNumber,
  @LINE_TOTAL = LineTotal,
  @ORDER_QTY = OrderQty,
  @UNIT_PRICE = UnitPrice
 From Sales.SalesOrderDetail
END
```

In this contrived example, the proc will provide four different output parameters that you can use to demonstrate how to set up the output parameter bindings. (Integer values are consistent and easy to map across almost all providers, so there is no need to demonstrate in this example.) One difference in returning singleton output parameters and a singleton row is that the General tab of the Execute SQL Task will set the ResultSet property to None since no row should be returned to capture. Instead, the Parameters in the Parameter Mapping tab will be set to the Direction of Output and the Data Types mapped based on the provider.

To get the defined SQL Server data type parameters to match to the SSIS variables, you'll need to setup the parameters with these mappings:

Parameter Name	SQL Server Data Type	SSIS Data Type
@CARRIER_TRACKING_NUMBER	nvarchar	string
@LINE_TOTAL	numeric	double
@ORDER_QTY	smallint	int16
@UNIT_PRICE	money	double

You'd think that you'd still have an issue with this binding, since if you recall, you attempted to return a single-row set from an inline SQL statement with these same data types and ended up with all types of binding and casting errors. You ended up having to change your inline statement to cast these values to get them to bind. You actually don't have to do this when binding to parameters, because this casting occurs outside of the tabular data stream. When binding parameters (as opposed to columns in a data stream), the numeric data type will bind directly to the `double`, and you will not get the error that you'd get if the same data was being bound from a rowset. We're not quite sure why this is the case, but it is a good thing that stored procedures don't have to be altered to use them in SSIS because of output parameter binding issues.

The remaining task to complete the parameter setup is to provide the correct placeholder for the parameter. Figure 3-40 is an example of the completed parameter setup for the procedure in OLE DB and ADO.NET connection contexts.

OLE DB Output Parameter Bindings

Variable Name	Direction	Data Type	Parameter ...	Parameter ..
User::CarrierTrackingNum...	Output	NVARCHAR	0	-1
User::LineTotal	Output	DOUBLE	1	-1
User::OrderQty	Output	SHORT	2	-1
User::UnitPrice	Output	DOUBLE	3	-1

ADO.Net Output Parameter Bindings

Variable Name	Direction	Data Type	Parameter Name	Parameter .
User::CarrierTracking...	Output	AnsiString	@CARRIER_TRACKING_...	-1
User::LineTotal	Output	Double	@LINE_TOTAL	-1
User::OrderQty	Output	Int16	@ORDER_QTY	-1
User::UnitPrice	Output	Double	@UNIT_PRICE	-1

Figure 3-40

So far, we've covered every scenario concerning binding to parameters and result sets. Stored procedures can also return multi-row results, but there is really no difference in how you will handle these rows from a stored procedure and an inline SQL statement. We covered multi-row scenarios earlier in this section on the Execute SQL Task. Now let's move away from tasks in the RDBMS world and into other tasks that involve other controlling external processes like other packages or applications in the operating system.

Workflow Tasks

So far, we've been focused on tasks that are occurring within the immediate realm of ETL processing. You've looked at tasks for creating control structures, preparing data, and performing RDBMS operations. Now let's look at being able to control other processes and applications in the operating system. Here we sidestep a bit from typical ETL definitions into things that can be more enterprise application integration (EAI) oriented. SSIS packages can also be organized to execute other packages or to call external programs that zip up files or send email alerts and even put messages directly into application queues for processing.

Execute Package Task

The Execute Package Task enables you to build SSIS solutions called *parent packages* that execute other packages called *child packages*. You'll find this capability an indispensable part of your SSIS development as your packages begin to grow. Separating packages into discrete functional workflows makes for shorter development and testing cycles and facilitates best development practices. Though the Execute Package Task has been around since the legacy DTS, several improvements have simplified the task. First, the child packages can be run as either in- or out-of-process executables. In the Package tab of the Task Editor (shown in Figure 3-41), you can see the new ExecuteOutOfProcess property, which if set to the default value of false, will execute the package in its own process and memory space. Another key difference is that the parent package no longer pushes parameters to the child package. Instead, the child package is aware of and can reach into the parent package to access parent-package-level configuration values.

The majority of the configurable properties are in the Package tab of the Execute Package Task Editor. The first option is to provide the location of the child package. The options here are File System and SQL Server. You can deploy an SSIS package in the File System Task as a `.dtsx` file, or within the msdb database of a SQL Server instance. If you select File System, you must first create a new Connection Manager connection to the package by selecting <New Connection . . .> from the Connection drop-down box. If the child package is located in a SQL Server, you'll need to provide the OLE DB Connection Manager for the SQL Server that holds your package. In either case, browse to and then select the child package within the connection to set the package to execute in the task, as shown in Figure 3-41.

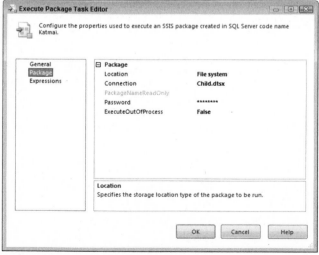

Figure 3-41

Setting Up Child Packages to Use Parent Variables

Once you start using parent and child package combinations with the Execute Package Task, it won't be long before the need arises to pass a common variable value at the parent level down into the child package. One such need occurs when you have child packages that need a foreign key passed down into them to use to build supporting data relationships. To demonstrate the concept of variable passing, first create a directory called ExecutePackage to store both a parent and a child package or download this entire parent/child example from www.wrox.com. In you are creating from scratch, first create the parent package, name the package parent, and then add a variable in the parent package called MYSTRING that is of the type string. Set the value of this variable to be "PARENT VALUE" without the quotes. Now create a child package, name it child, and close it. Reopen the parent package, and add an Execute Package Task that calls the child package using the File System option as explained earlier in this section. Finally add a Script Task after the Execute Package Task and connect the two. In the Script Task, add the following code to display the value of the parent variable:

```
C#
public void Main()
    {
        string myMsg = "In Parent Package: MYSTRING Value={0}";
        myMsg = string.Format(myMsg, Dts.Variables["MYSTRING"].Value.ToString());
        System.Windows.Forms.MessageBox.Show(myMsg);
        Dts.TaskResult = (int)ScriptResults.Success;
    }

VB
Public Sub Main()
    Dim myMsg As String = "In Parent Package: MYSTRING Value={0}"
    myMsg = String.Format(myMsg, Dts.Variables("MYSTRING").Value.ToString())
    System.Windows.Forms.MessageBox.Show(myMsg)
    Dts.TaskResult = ScriptResults.Success
End Sub
```

Now close the parent package and open up the child package. Add a new variable in the child package called PARENT_MYSTRING with an empty string for the value. To be able to reach into the parent and access the variables collection, you must first create a configuration for the child package. Do this by selecting the menu option SSIS ⇨ Package Configurations. (Sometimes you have to click around in different places on the Control Flow surface to see this option.) When the Package Configurations Organizer dialog appears (shown in the background in Figure 3-42), select the checkbox to enable package configurations, and then click the Add button to bring up the Package Configuration Wizard.

Figure 3-42

Click Next to be able to select the configuration settings. Figure 3-43 is a montage of the different sections of the configuration wizard. In the first panel, you need to select a configuration type of "Parent package variable." Then you need to specify the variables. You'll need the exact variable name here, and there will be no selection help. (Remember that variables are case-sensitive.) The second panel allows you to select the property of the child package that you wish to set using the variable value obtained from the parent. Here's where you could set the connection string in a child package level connection using a value in the parent package, or in this example, just set the value of the variable PARENT_MYSTRING. Notice that you have to open up the variable object and specifically point to the value property in the variable. Click Next to complete the wizard and save the configuration setting.

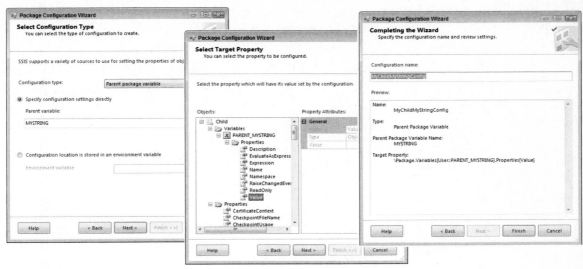

Figure 3-43

To verify that the child package now can see the value of the parent variable, drop a Script Task onto the control design surface. Set the read-only variable to PARENT_MYSTRING, and then within the Script Task, apply this code:

```
C#
public void Main()
    {
    string myMsg = "In Child Package: PARENT_MYSTRING Value={0}";
    myMsg = string.Format(myMsg,
                Dts.Variables["PARENT_MYSTRING"].Value.ToString());
    System.Windows.Forms.MessageBox.Show(myMsg);
    Dts.TaskResult = (int)ScriptResults.Success;
    }

VB
Public Sub Main()
    Dim myMsg As String = "In Child Package: PARENT_MYSTRING Value={0}"
    myMsg = String.Format(myMsg, _
        Dts.Variables("PARENT_MYSTRING").Value.ToString())
    System.Windows.Forms.MessageBox.Show(myMsg)
    Dts.TaskResult = ScriptResults.Success
End Sub
```

Now close the child package and reopen the parent package. You should now be able to run the parent package to see a dialog box once in the child package and then again in the parent package. Both instances report on the same variable value that you started out with in the parent package. Now that you've experienced passing variable values down into the child packages, let's look at changing the value of that variable for the parent down in the child package.

Changing Parent Variables in Child Packages

Using parent and child packages also requires the ability for the child package to perform some work and inform the parent package by passing variables back to the parent. You might think that you can just change the variable value in the child and the parent value will change. This depends on what you mean by the variable. If you change the new variable created in the child to hold the value of the parent variable, nothing in the parent will change. However, if you update the parent variable in a Script Task, the variable is global to both packages, and the value in the parent will change. To demonstrate how this works, replace the following code in the child package Script Task so that the parent variable is updated:

```
C#
public void Main()
    {
    string myMsg = "In Child Package: PARENT_MYSTRING Value={0}";
    myMsg = string.Format(myMsg,
            Dts.Variables["PARENT_MYSTRING "].Value.ToString());
    System.Windows.Forms.MessageBox.Show(myMsg);
    //Here we change the parent value
    Dts.Variables["MYSTRING"].Value = "CHILD VALUE";
    Dts.TaskResult = (int)ScriptResults.Success;
    }

VB
Public Sub Main()
    Dim myMsg As String = "In Child Package: PARENT_MYSTRING Value={0}"
    myMsg = String.Format(myMsg, _
                Dts.Variables("PARENT_MYSTRING ").Value.ToString())
    System.Windows.Forms.MessageBox.Show(myMsg)
    'Here we change the parent value
    Dts.Variable("MYSTRING").Value = "CHILD VALUE"
    Dts.TaskResult = ScriptResults.Success
End Sub
```

Now when you run the parent package, you'll see two messages: First the dialog will display the value of the parent package when it first goes into the child package. It should have the variable value "PARENT VALUE". When the second dialog in the Parent package executes, the variable in the parent has been changed to "CHILD VALUE".

This is just a simple example of how you can link packages together and share properties using the Package Configuration Wizard. There are many other ways you can use the configurations as well. We'll cover these options later in this book.

Execute Process Task

The Execute Process Task will execute a Windows or console application inside of the Controller Flow. You'll find great uses for this task to run command-line based programs and utilities prior to performing other ETL tasks. The most common example would have to be unzipping packed or encrypted data files with a command-line tool. The Execute Process Task has been improved on since SQL Server 2000, and now it is more robust in its error handling. For example, you may now store any errors resulting from the execution of the task into a variable that can be read later and logged. In addition, any output from the command file can also be written to a variable for logging purposes. Figure 3-44 is a sample of using the Execute Process Task to expand a compressed `customers.zip` file.

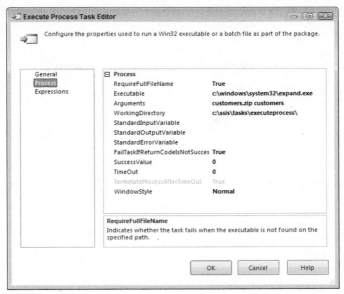

Figure 3-44

The Process tab in the Execute Process Task Editor contains most of the important configuration items for this task. The RequireFullFileName property tells the task whether it needs the full path to execute the command. If the file is not found at the full path or in the PATH environment variables of the machine, the task will fail. Typically, a full path is used only if you want to be explicit about the executable you want to run. However, if the file exists in the System32 directory, you wouldn't normally have to type the full path to the file because this path is automatically known to a typical Windows system.

The Executable property is the path and file name to the executable you'd like to run. Be careful not to provide any parameters or optional switches in this property that would be passed to the executable. Use the Arguments property to set these types of options separately. For example, Figure 3-44 shows that the task will execute expand.exe and pass in the cabinet from which you want to extract and where you'd like it to be extracted. The WorkingDirectory option contains the path from which the executable or command file will work.

The StandardInputVariable parameter is the variable you'd like to pass into the process as an argument. Use this property if you want to dynamically provide a parameter to the executable based on a variable. You can also capture the result of the execution by setting the property StandardOutputVariable to a variable. Any errors that occurred from the execution can be captured in the variable you provide in the StandardErrorVariable property. These variable values can be used to send back to a scripting component to log or can be used in a precedence constraint that checks the length of the variables to determine if you should go to the next task. This provides the logical functionality of looping back and trying again if the result of the execution of the expand.exe program was a sharing violation or another similar error. Another option for validating the task is the FailTaskIfReturnCodeIsNotSuccessValue property. The Execute Process Task will fail if the exit code passed from the program is different from the value provided in the SuccessValue option. The default value of 0 indicates that the task was successful in executing the process.

The Timeout property determines the number of seconds that must elapse before the program is considered a runaway process. A value of 0, which is the default, means the process can run for an infinite amount of time. This property is used in conjunction with the TerminateProcessAfterTimeOut property, which, if set to true, will terminate the process after the timeout has been surpassed. The last option is WindowStyle, which can set the executable to be run minimized, maximized, hidden, or normal. If this is set to any option other than hidden, the user will be able to see windows potentially pop up and may interact with them during runtime. Typically, you set these to hidden once the package is fully tested.

With the Execute Process Task, you can continue to use command-line or out-of-processes executables to organize work for ETL tasks. Now let's look at how SSIS can interact and integrate with your enterprise messaging bus.

Message Queue Task

The Message Queue Task allows you to send or receive messages from Microsoft Message Queuing (MSMQ) right out of the box. For integration with other messaging systems like IBM's MQ Series or Tibco's Rendezveus, you'll need to either code to a library within a Script Task, create a custom component, or execute TSQL statements to a SQL Server Service broker. Messaging architectures are created to ensure reliable communication between two disparate subsystems. A message can be a string, file, or variable. The main benefit to using this task is the ability to make packages communicate with each other at runtime. You can use this to scale out your packages, having multiple packages executing in parallel, with each loading a subset of the data, and then checking in with the parent package after they're at certain checkpoints. You can also use this task for enterprise-level information integration to do things like delivering dashboard-level information using XML files to an enterprise bus or distributing report content files across your network. Satellite offices or any other subscriber to those services could pull content from the queue for application-level processing.

The task is straightforward. In the General tab, shown in Figure 3-45, you specify the MSMQ Connection Manager under the MSMQConnection property. Then, you specify whether you'd like to send or receive a message under the Message option. In this tab, you can also select whether you'd like to use the legacy Windows 2000 version of MSMQ, which is by default set to false.

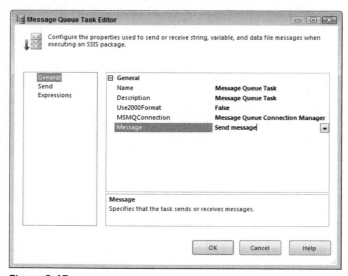

Figure 3-45

The bulk of the configuration is under the Send or Receive tab (the one you see varies based on the Message option you selected in the General tab). If you're on the Receive tab, you can configure the task to remove the message from the queue after it has been read. You can also set the timeout properties here, to control whether the task will produce an error if it experiences a timeout.

No matter whether you're sending or receiving messages, you'll be able to select what type of message you wish to send under the MessageType option. You can either send or receive a string message, a variable, or a data file. Additionally, if you're receiving a message, you can immediately convert the message you receive into a variable by selecting String Message to Variable and then specifying a variable in the Variable option.

Send Mail Task

The Send Mail Task provides a configurable SSIS task for sending out email messages via SMTP. In legacy DTS packages, you had to send messages out through MAPI, which meant installing Outlook on the server that the package was running on. That is now no longer a requirement. Most of the configuration options are set in the Mail (shown in Figure 3-46) of the Send Mail Task Editor. The SMTPConnection property is where you either create a new or select an existing SMTP Connection Manager.

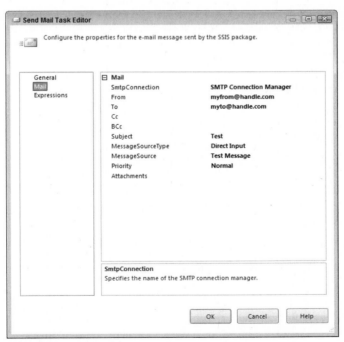

Figure 3-46

Most of the configuration options will depend upon your specific SMTP connection. One option that is of special interest is the MessageSourceType property, which specifies whether the message source will be provided from a file, a variable, or be directly inputted into the MessageSource property. Typically, the best practice is to use a variable-based approach to set the message source property. You can see an example of this in Chapter 23.

WMI Data Reader Task

Windows Management Instrumentation (WMI) is one of the best-kept secrets in Windows. WMI allows you to manage Windows servers and workstations through a scripting interface similar to running a TSQL query. The WMI Data Reader Task allows you to interface with this environment by writing WQL queries (the query language for WMI) against the server or workstation (to look at the Application Event Log, for example). The output of this query can be written to a file or variable for later consumption. The following are some applications for which you could use the WMI Data Reader Task:

❑ Read the event log looking for a given error.

❑ Query the list of applications that are running.

❑ Query to see how much RAM is available at package execution for debugging.

❑ Determine the amount of free space on a hard drive.

To get started, you first need to set up a WMI Connection Manager in the Connection Manager Editor. Connection requirements vary, but Figure 3-47 is an example of a WMI connection for a typical stand-alone workstation.

Figure 3-47

Notice here that the Use Windows Authentication option has been set. WMI typically requires some higher level of security authorization since you are able to query OS-level data. With a WMI connection, you can configure the WMI Data Reader Task Editor using the WMI Options tab shown in Figure 3-48.

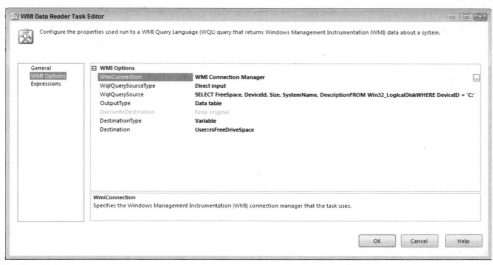

Figure 3-48

First, set the WMIConnection, and then determine whether the WMI query will be directly inputted, retrieved from a variable, or retrieved from a file, and set the WqlQuerySourceType. The WqlQuerySource is where you select the source for query that you wish to run against the connection. This may be a variable name, a text file name, or a hard-coded query itself.

The OutputType option is where you specify whether you want the output of the query to retrieve just the values from the query or also the column names with the values. The OverwriteDestination option sets whether you wish the destination to be overwritten each time it is run, or whether you want it to just append to any configured destination. If you save the output to an object variable, you can use some of the same technique of shredding a recordset that you learned earlier in the Execute SQL Task.

WQL queries look like SQL queries, and for all practical purposes they are, with the exception that you are getting back datasets from the operating systems. For example, the following query selects the free space, name, and a few other metrics about the C: drive:

```
SELECT FreeSpace, DeviceId, Size, SystemName, Description FROM Win32_LogicalDisk
WHERE DeviceID = 'C:'
```

The output of this type of query would look like this in a table:

```
Description, Local Fixed Disk
DeviceID, C:
FreeSpace, 32110985216
Size, 60003381248
SystemName, BKNIGHT
```

This example of a WQL query selects information written to the Application Event Log after a certain date and about the SQL Server and SSIS services:

```
SELECT * FROM Win32_NTLogEvent WHERE LogFile = 'Application' AND
(SourceName='SQLISService' OR SourceName='SQLISPackage') AND TimeGenerated >
'20050117'
```

The results would look like this:

```
0
BKNIGHT
12289
1073819649
3
System.String[]
Application
3738
SQLISPackage
20050430174924.000000-240
20050430174924.000000-240
information
BKNIGHT\Brian Knight
0
```

Typically, the WMI Data Reader Task is used in SQL Server administration packages to gather up operational type data from the SQL Server environments. However, the WMI Event Watcher Task has some interesting uses for ETL processes that you'll look at next.

WMI Event Watcher Task

The WMI Event Watcher Task empowers SSIS to wait for and respond to certain WMI events that occur in the operating system. The task operates in much the same way as the WMI Data Reader Task operates. The following are some of the useful things you can do with this task:

❑   Watch a directory for a certain file to be written.

❑   Wait for a given service to start.

❑   Wait for the memory of a server to reach a certain level before executing the rest of the package or before transferring files to the server.

❑   Watch for the CPU to be free.

To illustrate the last example of polling to determine when the CPU is less than 50% utilized, you could have the WMI Event Watcher Task look for an event with this WQL code:

```
SELECT * from __InstanceModificationEvent WITHIN 2 WHERE TargetInstance ISA
'Win32_Processor' and TargetInstance.LoadPercentage < 50
```

Let's now look at a direct application of this WMI Event Watcher Task to get a better idea of how to configure it and what it can do.

Polling a Directory for the Delivery of a File

One very practical use of the WMI Event Watcher for ETL processing is to provide a buffer between the times an SSIS job starts and the time a file is actually delivered to a folder location. If there is a window of variability in file delivery and an SSIS package starts on a one-time schedule, then it is possible to miss processing the file for the day. By using a WMI Event Watcher, you can set up your SSIS packages to poll a folder location for a set period until a file is detected. To set up a task to perform this automated action, open the task editor for the WMI Event Watcher and go to the WMI Options tab to review the options for this task. (See Figure 3-49.) You'll notice that this WMI Task is completely different from the WMI Data Reader Task.

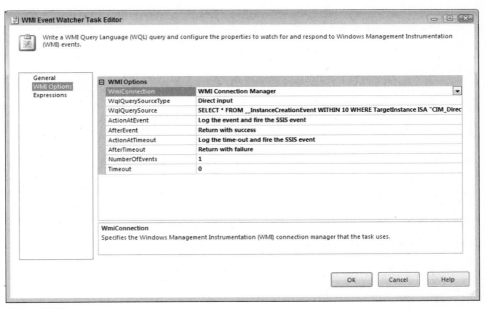

Figure 3-49

This WMI Event Watcher Task provides properties like the AfterEvent option to set whether the task should succeed, fail, or keep querying if the condition is met. You also need to provide an amount of time that the WMI Event Watcher stops watching by setting the Timeout property. The timeout value is in seconds. The default of zero (0) indicates that there is no timeout. Be very careful outside of your development activities with leaving this setting on zero (0). The WMI Event Watcher could leave your SSIS package running indefinitely.

You can also configure what will happen if a timeout occurs under the ActionAtTimeout and AfterTimeout settings. The NumberOfEvents option configures the number of events to watch for. You can use this setting to look for more than one file before you start processing.

The WqlQuerySource for the File Watcher Configuration for this WMI Task would look like this code:

```
SELECT * FROM __InstanceCreationEvent WITHIN 10
WHERE TargetInstance ISA "CIM_DirectoryContainsFile"
AND TargetInstance.GroupComponent = "Win32_Directory.Name=\"c:\\\\SSIS\""
```

If you run this task with no files in the `C:\ssis\` directory, the task will remain yellow as the watcher continuously waits for an event to be raised. If you copy a file into the directory, the task will turn green and complete successfully. This is a great addition that is less resource intensive than the legacy DTS version of iterating in a for loop until the file is found. As you can see, there are some major improvements in the capabilities of controlling workflow in SSIS.

SMO Administration Tasks

The last section of this chapter is reserved for a set of tasks that are convenient for copying or moving schema and data-level information. These tasks are similar to the Transfer SQL Objects tasks from DTS, and should be compatible if you transfer any packages using these tasks from DTS to SSIS. These tasks can do the following:

❑ Move or copy entire databases. This can be accomplished by detaching the database and moving the files (faster) or by moving the schema and content (slower).

❑ Transfer error messages from one server to another.

❑ Move or copy selected or entire SQL Agent jobs.

❑ Move or copy server-level or database-level logins.

❑ Move or copy objects such as tables, views, stored procedures, functions, defaults, user-defined data types, partition functions, partition schemas, schemas (or roles), SQL assemblies, user-defined aggregates, user-defined types, and XML schemas. These objects can be copied over by selecting all, by individually selecting each desired object types, or even by selecting individual objects themselves.

❑ Move or copy master stored procedures between two servers.

Transfer Database Task

The Transfer Database Task has, as you would expect, a source and destination connection and a database property. The other properties address how the transfer should take place. Figure 3-50 is an example of the Transfer Database Task filled out to copy a development database on the same server as a QA instance.

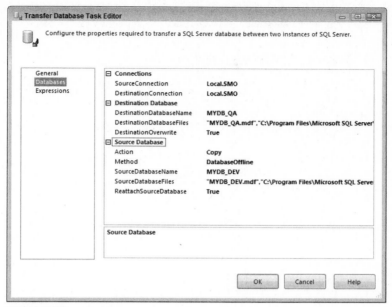

Figure 3-50

Notice that the destination and source are set to the same server. For this copy to work, the DestinationDatabaseFiles property has to be set to new mdf and ldf filenames. The property is set by default to the SourceDatabaseFiles property. To set the new destination database file names, click the ellipsis, and then change the Destination File or Destination Folder properties.

The Action property controls whether the task should copy or move the Source Database. The Method property controls whether the database should be copied while the source database is kept online, using SQL Server Management Objects (SMO), or by detaching the database, moving the files, and then reattaching the database. The DestinationOverwrite property controls whether the creation of the destination database should be allowed to overwrite. This includes deleting the database in the destination if it is found. This is useful in the case where you want to copy a database from production into a quality-control or production test environment, and the new database should replace any existing similar database. The last property is the ReattachSourceDatabase, which allows control over what action should be taken upon failure of the copy. Use this property if you have a package running on a schedule that takes a production database offline to copy it, and you need to guarantee that the database goes back online even if the copy fails.

What's really great about the Transfer Database Task is that the logins, roles, object permissions, and even the data can be transferred as well. This task may in some instances be too big of a hammer. You may find it more advantageous to just transfer specific sets of objects from one database to another. The next four tasks will give you these abilities.

Transfer Error Messages

If you are using custom error messages in the sys.messsages table, you need to remember to copy these over when you move a database from one server to another. In the past, you needed to code a cursor-based script to fire the sp_addmessage system stored procedure to move these messages around — and you needed to remember to do it. Now you can create a package that moves your database with the Transfer Database Task and add this Transfer Error Messages Task to move the messages as well.

One thing you'll find in this task that you'll see in the rest of the SMO administration tasks is the opportunity to select the specific things that you want to transfer. The properties ErrorMessagesList and ErrorMessageLanguagesList in the Messages tab, shown in Figure 3-51, are examples of this selective type UI. If you click the ellipsis, you'll get into a dialog where you can select specific messages to transfer.

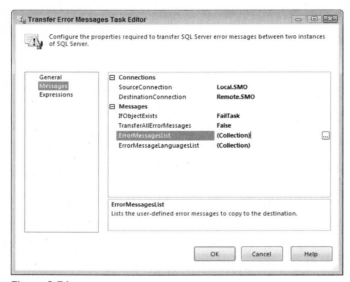

Figure 3-51

Generally, unless you are performing a one-off update, you should set the TransferAllErrorMessages property to True, and then set the IfObjectExists property to skip existing messages if they already exist in the destination database.

Transfer Logins Task

The Transfer Logins Task focuses only on the security aspects of your databases. Have you ever backed up and restored a database or used the SQL 2000 DTS to transfer logins only to find that the SIDs associated with the logins don't match? Now you can transfer the logins from one database and have them corrected at the destination.

Of course, you'll have your obligatory source and destination connection properties in this editor. You also have the choice to move logins from all databases or selected databases, or you can select individual logins to transfer. Make this choice in the LoginsToTransfer property; the default is SelectedLogIns. The partner properties to LoginsToTransfer are the LoginsList and DatabasesList. One will be activated based on your choice of logins to transfer. Figure 3-52 shows an example Transfer Logins Task Editor.

Two last properties to cover relate to what you want the transfer logins process to do if it encounters an existing login in the destination. If you want the login to be replaced, set the IfObjectExists property to Overwrite. Other options are to fail the task or to skip that login. The long-awaited option to resolve unmatched user security IDs is found in the property CopySids, and can be true or false.

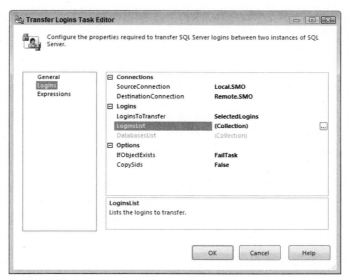

Figure 3-52

Transfer Master Stored Procedures Task

This task is used to transfer master stored procedures. If you need to transfer your own stored procedure, use the Transfer SQL Server Objects Task instead. To use this task, set the source and destination connections, and then set the property TransferAllStoredProcedures to true or false. If you set this property to false, you'll be able to select individual master stored procedures to transfer. The remaining property, IfObjectExists, allows you to select what action should take place if a transferring object exists in the destination. Again the choices are to Overwrite, FailTask, or Skip. Figure 3-53 is an example of a completed Transfer Master Stored Procedures Task Editor.

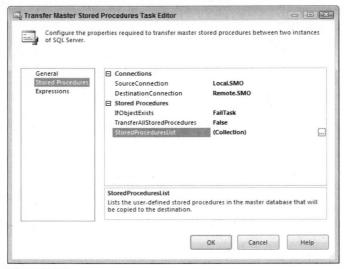

Figure 3-53

Transfer Jobs Task

This task allows you to transfer any of the existing SQL Server Agent jobs between SQL Server instances. Just like the other SMO tasks, you can either select to transfer all jobs to synchronize two instances, or use the task to selectively pick which jobs you want to move to another instance, as shown in Figure 3-54.

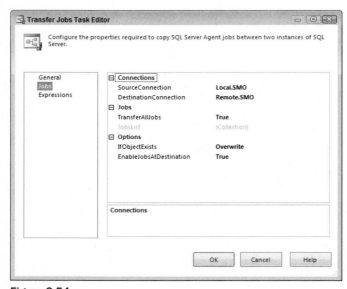

Figure 3-54

Transfer SQL Server Objects Task

The Transfer SQL Server Objects Task is the most flexible of the Transfer tasks. Within this task lies the ability to transfer all types of database objects. To use this task, set the properties to connect to a source and destination database; if the properties aren't visible, expand the Connection category. As you can see in Figure 3-55, there are many options available in this task. Some may be hidden until categories are expanded.

This task exists for those instances when selective object copying is needed. The selectivity is why this is not called the Transfer Database Task. You specifically have to set the property CopyData to true to get the bulk transfers of data. The property CopyAllObjects means that only the tables, views, stored procedures, defaults, rules, and UDFs will be transferred. If you want the table indexes, triggers, primary keys, foreign keys, full-text indexes, or extended properties, you'll have to select these individually. By expanding the ObjectsToCopy category, you'll expose properties that allow individual selections for tables, views, and other programmable objects. The security options give you some of the same abilities as the Transfer Database Task. You can transfer database users, roles, logins, and object-level permissions by selecting true for these properties.

The power lies in the complexity, since this task can be customized and used in packages to move only specific items, for example, during the promotion of objects from one environment to another, or to be less discriminate and copy all tables, views, and other database objects, with or without the data.

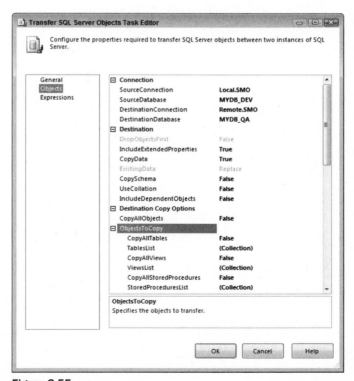

Figure 3-55

Summary

This chapter attempted to stick with the everyday nuts-and-bolts uses of the SSIS tasks. Throughout the chapter, you looked at each task, learned how to configure it, and were shown an example of the task in action. In fact, you saw a number of examples of how to use the tasks in real-world ETL and EAI applications. In the next chapter, you'll circle back to look at the Control Flow again to explore containers, which enable you to loop through tasks. In subsequent chapters, you'll come back to the Data Flow Task and dive deeper into configuring Data Flow and learn about all the transformations options that are available in this task.

Containers

In the last chapter, you read about tasks and how they interact in the Control Flow. There was one critical piece that was left out of that discussion. *Containers* are objects that help SSIS provide structure to one or more tasks. They can help you loop through a set of tasks until a criterion has been met or can help you group a set of tasks logically. Containers can also be nested, containing other containers. Containers are set in the Control Flow tab in the Package Designer. There are four types of containers in the Control Flow tab: Task Host, Sequence, For Loop, and Foreach Loop Containers.

Task Host Containers

The Task Host Container is the default container that single tasks fall into. You'll notice that this type of container is not in the Toolbox in Visual Studio, and is implicitly given to each task. In fact, even if you don't specify a container for a task, it will be placed in a Task Host Container. The SSIS architecture extends variables and event handlers to the task through the Task Host Container.

Sequence Containers

Sequence Containers handle the flow of a subset of a package and can help you divide a package into smaller, more manageable pieces. Some nice applications that you can use sequence containers for include the following:

❑   Grouping tasks so that you can disable a part of the package that's no longer needed

❑   Narrowing the scope of the variable to a container

❑   Managing the properties of multiple tasks in one step by setting the properties of the container

❑ Using one method to ensure that multiple tasks have to execute successfully before the next task executes

❑ Creating a transaction across a series of data-related tasks, but not on the entire package

❑ Creating event handlers on a single container, wherein you could send an email if anything inside one container fails and perhaps page if anything else fails

Sequence containers show up like any other task in your Control Flow tab. Once you drag and drop any container from your Toolbox onto the design pane, you just have to drag the tasks you'd like to use into the container. Figure 4-1 gives you an example of a Sequence Container. The container is a Sequence Container where two tasks must execute successfully before the task called "Run Script 3" will be executed. If you were to click the up-pointing arrows, the tasks inside the container will minimize.

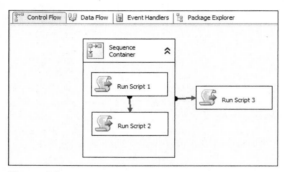

Figure 4-1

A container can be considered to be a miniature package. Inside the container, all task names must be unique, just like from within a package where there are no containers. You also cannot connect a task in one container to anything outside of the container. If you try to do this, you will receive the following error:

```
Cannot create connector.
Cannot connect executables from different containers.
```

Containers such as the Sequence Container can also be embedded in each other. As a best practice each of your SSIS packages should contain a series of containers to help organize the package and to make it easy to disable subject areas quickly. Each set of tables that you must load probably fits into a subject area, such as Accounting or HR. Each of these loads should be placed in its own Sequence Container. Additionally, you may want to create a Sequence Container for the preparation and cleanup stages of your package.

Groups

Groups are very similar to Sequence Containers with some very important differences. Groups are simply a collection of tasks and are not true containers. A key difference is that properties cannot be delegated through a container. Because of this, they don't have precedence constraints originating from them (only from the tasks). You also can't disable the entire group as in a Sequence Container. What they are good for is a quick compartmentalization of tasks for aesthetics.

To create a group, you highlight the tasks that you wish to place in the group, right-click, and select Group. To ungroup the tasks, right-click the group and select Ungroup. To add additional tasks into the group, simply drag the task into the group.

The same type of logic you saw in the Sequence Container earlier (Figure 4-1) can be seen in Figure 4-2. As you can see, the precedence constraint is originating from the task called "Run Script 2" to "Run Script 3".

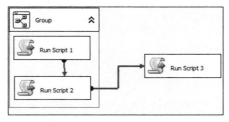

Figure 4-2

For Loop Container

The For Loop Container is a method to create looping in your package, similar to how you would loop in nearly any programming language. In this looping style, SSIS optionally initializes an expression and continues to evaluate it until the expression evaluates to false.

In the example in Figure 4-3, you can see that the Script Task called "Wait for File to Arrive" is continuously looped through until a condition is evaluated as false. Once the loop is broken, the Script Task is executed. Another real-world example would be to use a Message Queue Task inside the loop to continuously loop until a message arrives in the queue. Such a configuration would allow for scaling out your SSIS environment.

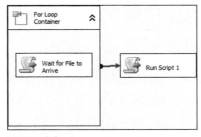

Figure 4-3

Let's try a simple example to demonstrate the functionality of the For Loop Container, where we'll use the container to loop over a series of tasks five times. Although this example is pretty rudimentary, you can plug whatever task you want in place of the Script Task.

1. Create a new SSIS project called Chapter 4, and change the name of the default package to `ForLoop.dtsx`.

2. Open the `ForLoop.dtsx` package, create a new variable, and call it `Counter`. You may have to open the Variable window if it isn't already open. To do this, right-click in the design pane and select Variables. Once the window is open, click the Add Variable button. Accept all the defaults for the variable (`int32`) and a default value of 0.

3. Drag the For Loop Container to the Control Flow and double-click it to open the editor. Set the `InitExpression` option to `@Counter = 0`. This will initialize the loop by setting the `Counter` variable to 0. Next, in the `EvalExpression` option, type `@Counter < 5` and `@Counter = @Counter + 1` for the `AssignExpression`. This means that the loop will iterate as long as the `Counter` variable is less than 5, and each time it loops, 1 will be added to the variable. The last step to configure the For Loop page is to type for the Name option "Iterate through a Script" (shown in Figure 4-4) and click OK.

Figure 4-4

4. Next, drag a Script Task into the For Loop Container and double-click the task to edit it. In the General tab, name the task "Pop Up the Iteration."

5. In the Script tab, set the `ReadOnlyVariables` (Figure 4-5) to `Counter` and select Microsoft Visual Basic 2008. Finally, click Edit Script to open the Visual Studio designer. By typing **Counter** for that option, you're going to pass in the `Counter` parameter to be used by the Script Task.

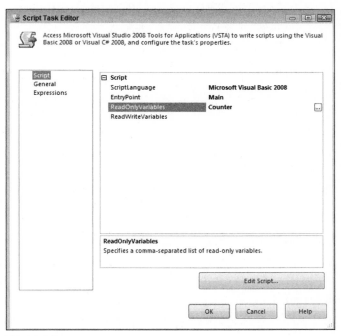

Figure 4-5

6. When you click Design Script, the Visual Studio 2008 design environment will open. Double-click `ScriptMain.vb` to open the script and replace the `Main()` subroutine with the following code. This code will read the variable and pop up a message box that tells you what the value of the `Counter` variable is.

```
Public Sub Main()
        '
        ' Add your code here
        '
        MsgBox(Dts.Variables("Counter").Value)
        Dts.TaskResult = ScriptResults.Success
End Sub
```

7. Save and exit the Visual Studio design environment, and click OK to exit the Script Task. When you execute the package, you should see results similar to Figure 4-6. You should see five pop-up boxes starting at iteration 0 and proceeding through iteration 4. Only one popup will appear at any given point. You'll see the Script Task go green and then back to yellow as it transitions between each iteration of the loop. After the loop is complete, the For Loop Container and the Script Task will both be green.

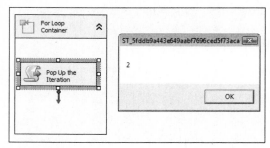

Figure 4-6

Foreach Loop Container

The Foreach Loop Container is a powerful looping mechanism that allows you to loop through a collection of objects. As you loop through the collection, the container will assign the value from the collection to a variable, which could later be used by tasks or connections inside or outside the container. You can also map the value to a variable. The type of objects that you will loop through can vary based on the enumerator you set in the editor in the Collection page. The behavior of the editor varies widely based on what you set for this option:

- ❑ **Foreach File Enumerator:** Performs an action for each file in a directory with a given file extension.

- ❑ **Foreach Item Enumerator:** Loops through a list of items that are set manually in the container.

- ❑ **Foreach ADO Enumerator:** Loops through a list of tables or rows in a table from an ADO record set.

- ❑ **Foreach ADO.NET Schema Rowset Enumerator:** Loops through an ADO.NET schema.

- ❑ **Foreach From Variable Enumerator:** Loops through an SSIS variable.

- ❑ **Foreach Nodelist Enumerator:** Loops through a node list in an XML document.

- ❑ **Foreach SMO Enumerator:** Enumerates a list of SQL Management Objects (SMO).

Foreach File Enumerator Example

In this example we'll use the most common type of enumerator, the Foreach File enumerator, to loop through a list of files and simulate some type of action that has occurred inside the container. This example has been simplified in an effort to just show the core functionality, but if you'd like a much more detailed example, turn to Chapter 8, which has an end-to-end example. For this example to work, you'll need a `C:\Projects\Pro SSIS 2008\Temp` folder and a `C:\Projects\Pro SSIS 2008\Temp\Archive` folder, which SSIS will be enumerating through.

To start, create a new package and string variable called `sFileName` with a default value of the word `default`. This variable will hold the name of the file that SSIS is working on during each iteration of the loop. Create the variable by right-clicking in the Package Designer area of the Control Flow tab and selecting Variables. Then, click the Add New Variable option, changing the data type to a String.

Next, drag over a Foreach Loop Container onto the Control Flow and double-click on the container to configure it, as shown in Figure 4-7. Set the Enumerator option to Foreach File Enumerator. Then, set the Folder property to `C:\Projects\Pro SSIS 2008\Temp` and leave the default Files property of `*.*`.

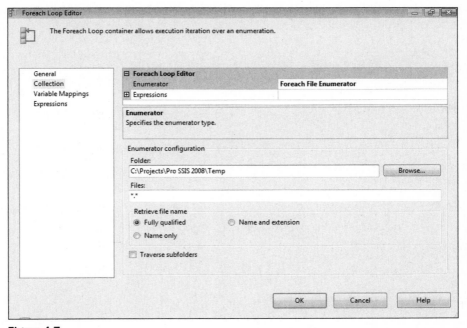

Figure 4-7

In the Variable Mappings page in the container, select the earlier created variable from the Variable drop-down box and then accept the default of 0 for the index, as shown in Figure 4-8. Click OK to save the settings and to get back to the Control Flow tab in the Package Designer.

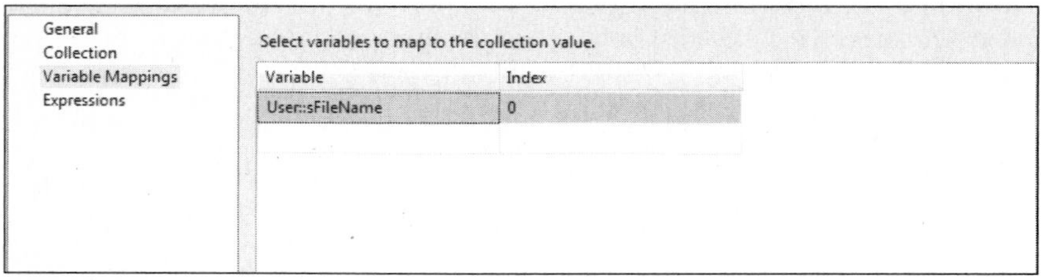

Figure 4-8

Drag over a new File System Task into the container's box. Double-click the new task to configure it. After setting the operation to Move File, you'll see the screen's properties change to resemble Figure 4-9 (once this example's step is complete). Select `<New Connection>` for the `DestinationConnection` property. When the Connection Manager dialog box opens, select Existing Folder and type `C:\Projects\Pro SSIS 2008\Temp\Archive` for the directory. Lastly, set the `IsSourcePathVariable` property to `True` and set the `SourceVariable` to `User::sFileName`.

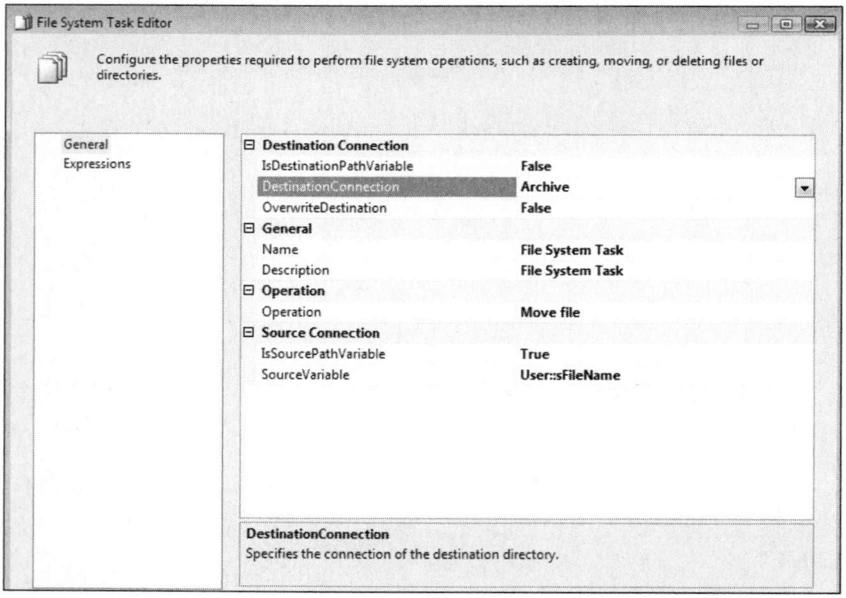

Figure 4-9

You're now ready to execute the package. Place any set of files you wish into the `C:\Projects\` `Pro SSIS 2008` folder and execute the package. During execution you'll see each file picked up and moved in Windows Explorer, and in the package you'll see what resembles Figure 4-10. If you had set the `OverwriteDestination` property to `True` in the File System Task, the file would have been overwritten if there was a conflict in duplicate file names.

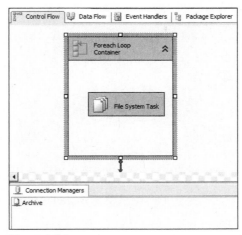

Figure 4-10

Foreach ADO Enumerator Example

The Foreach ADO Enumerator loops through a collection of records, and will execute anything inside the container for each row that is found. For example, if you had a table that contained metadata about your environment like the following table, you could loop over that table and reconfigure the package for each iteration of the loop. The first time through the loop, your Connection Managers would point to Client1, and retrieve their files from one directory. The next time, the Connection Managers would point to another client. Doing this could enable you to create a single package that would work for all of your partners.

Client	FTPLocation	ServerName	DatabaseName
Client1	C:\Client1\Pub	localhost	Client1DB
Client2	C:\Client2\Pub	localhost	Client2DB
Client3	C:\Client3\Pub	localhost	Client3DB

In this example, you will create a simple package that will simulate this type of example. The package will loop over a table, and then change the value for a variable for each row that is found. Inside the container, you will create a Script Task that will pop up the current variable's value.

To start the example, create a new package called `ForeachADOEnumerator.dtsx`. Create a new Connection Manager called `MasterConnection` that points to the master database on your development machine. Create two variables: one called `sDBName`, which is a string with no default, and the other called `objResults`, which is an object data type. Next, drag over an Execute SQL Task. You'll use the Execute SQL Task to populate the ADO recordset that is stored in a variable.

In the Execute SQL Task, point the `Connection` property to the `MasterConnection` Connection Manager. Change the `ResultSet` property to `Full Result Set`, which captures the results of the query run in this task to a result set in a variable. Type the following query for the `SQLStatement` property (as shown in Figure 4-11):

```
Select database_id, name from sys.databases
```

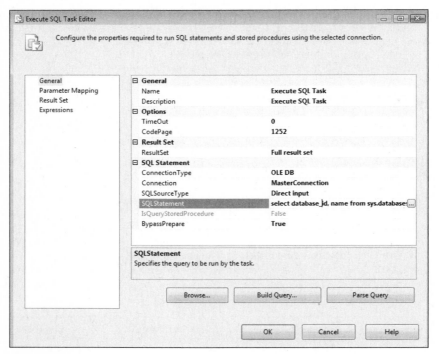

Figure 4-11

Still in the Execute SQL Task, go to the Result Set page and type **0** for the Result Name, as shown in Figure 4-12. This is the zero-based ordinal position for the result that you want to capture into a variable. If your previously typed query created multiple recordsets, then you could capture each here by giving their ordinal position. Map this recordset to a variable called `objResults` that is scoped to the package and an object data type. The object variable data type can store up to 2 GB of data in memory. If you do not select that option, the package will fail upon execution, because it is the only way to store a recordset in memory in SSIS.

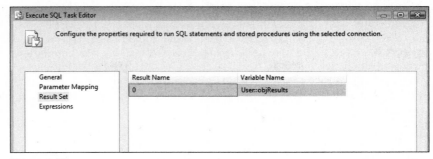

Figure 4-12

Back in the Control Flow tab, drag over a Foreach Loop Container and open it to configure the container, as shown in Figure 4-13. In the Collection page, select Foreach ADO Enumerator from the Enumerator drop-down box. Then, select the `objResults` variable from the ADO Object Source Variable drop-down box. This will tell the container that you wish to loop over the results stored in that variable.

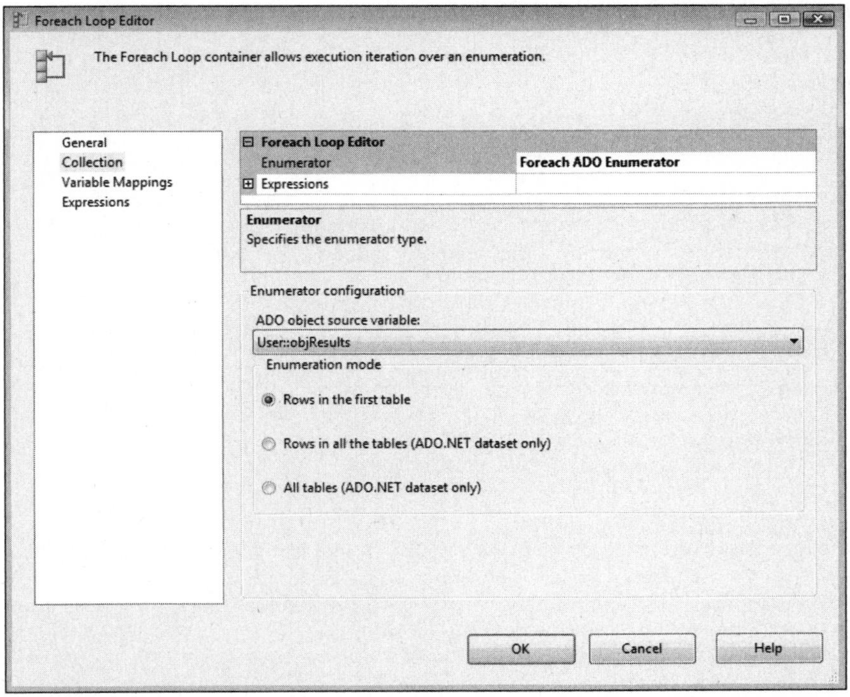

Figure 4-13

Go to the Variable Mappings page for the final configuration step of the container. Just like the Foreach File Enumerator, you must tell the container where you wish to map the value retrieved from the ADO result set. Your result set contains two columns: ID and Name from the `sys.databases` table. In this example, you want the second column, so select the `sDBName` variable by selecting the variable from the Variable drop-down box (shown in Figure 4-14) and type **1** for the Index. Typing **1** means you want the second column in the result set. The index starts at 0 and goes up by one for each column to the right. Because of this, be careful if you change the Execute SQL Task's query.

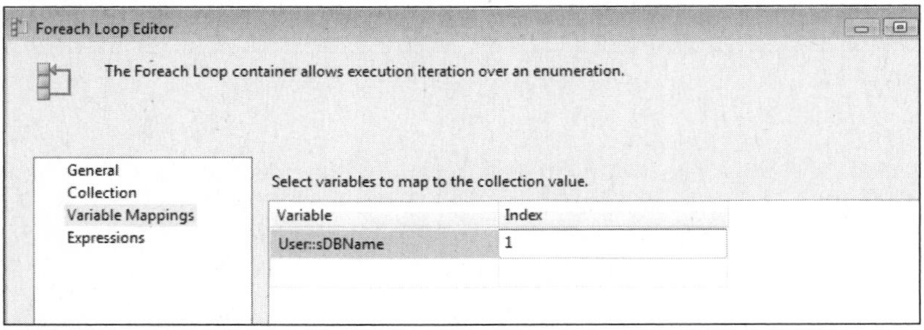

Figure 4-14

With the container now configured, drag over a Script Task into the container's box. In the Script tab of the Script Task, set the `ReadOnlyVariables` to `sDBName` and select Microsoft Visual Basic 2008. Finally, click Edit Script to open the Visual Studio designer. By typing **sDBName** for that option, you're going to pass in the `Counter` parameter to be used by the Script Task.

When you click Edit Script, the Visual Studio 2008 design environment will open. Double-click `ScriptMain.vb` to open the script and replace the `Main()` subroutine with the following code. This code will read the variable and pop up a message box that tells you what the value of the `sDBName` variable is.

```
Public Sub Main()
    '
    ' Add your code here
    '
    MsgBox(Dts.Variables("sDBName").Value)
    Dts.TaskResult = ScriptResults.Success
End Sub
```

Close the editor and task and execute the package. The final package should look like Figure 4-15, which pops up the value of the `sDBName` variable, showing you the current database. As you click OK to each popup, the next database name will display. This Script Task will obviously be replaced with a Data Flow Task to load the client's data in a less-contrived example.

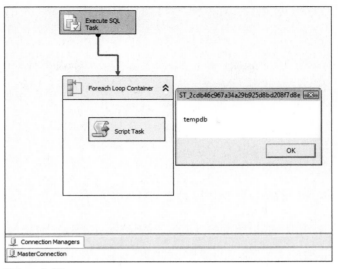

Figure 4-15

Summary

In this chapter, we've explored the four containers in SSIS: Task Host, For Loop, Foreach Loop, and the Sequence Containers. The For Loop Container will iterate through a loop until a requirement has been met. A Foreach Loop Container will loop through a collection of objects like files or records in a table. We covered one of the most common examples of looping through all the records in a table, but looping through files is also common and is covered in Chapter 8. Lastly, a Sequence Container helps you compartmentalize your various tasks into logical groupings. Each of the looping containers will execute all the items in the container for each time it iterates through the loop. Now that we have the basics out of the way of the Control Flow, the next chapter focuses on the Data Flow.

5

The Data Flow

In the last two chapters you were introduced to the Control Flow tab through tasks and containers. In this chapter, you'll continue along those lines with an exploration of the Data Flow tab, which is where you'll spend most of your time as an SSIS developer. The Data Flow Task is where the bulk of your data heavy lifting will occur in SSIS. This chapter walks you through how each transformation in the Data Flow Task can help you move and clean your data.

The Data Flow

One of the toughest concepts to understand for a new SSIS developer is the difference between the Control Flow and Data Flow tabs. Chapter 2 goes into this further, but just to restate a piece of that concept, the Control Flow tab controls the workflow of the package and the order of when each task will execute. Each task in the Control Flow has a user interface to configure the task with the exception of the Data Flow Task. The Data Flow Task is configured in the Data Flow tab. Once you drag a Data Flow Task over onto the Control Flow tab and double-click it to configure it, you're immediately taken to the Data Flow tab.

The Data Flow is made up of three components that will be discussed in this chapter: sources, transformations (also known as transforms), and destinations. These three components make up the fundamentals of ETL. Sources extract data out of flat files, OLE DB databases, and other locations. Transforms process the data once it has been pulled out, and destinations write the data to its final location.

Much of this ETL processing is done in memory, which is what gives SSIS its speed. It is much faster to apply business rules to your data in memory using a transform than have to constantly update a staging table. Because of this, though, your SSIS server will potentially need a large amount of memory based on the size of the file that you're processing.

Data Viewers

Data viewers are a very important feature in SSIS for debugging your data pump pipeline. They allow you to view data at points in time at runtime. If you place a data viewer before and after the Aggregate Transform, you can see the data flowing into the transform at runtime and what it looks like after the transform happens. Once you deploy your package and run it on the server as a job or with the service, the data viewers do not show because they are only a debug feature. Anytime the package is executed outside the designer, the data viewers won't show. There are four types of data viewers:

- **Grid:** Shows a snapshot of the data in grid format at that point in time.
- **Histogram:** Shows the distribution of numeric data in a histogram graph.
- **Scatter Plot:** Shows the distribution of numeric data using an x- and y-axis.
- **Column Chart:** Displays the occurrence count of discrete values in a selected column.

To place a data viewer in your pipeline, right-click one of the paths (red or green arrows leaving a transform or source) and select Data Viewers. The Configure "Data Flow Path Editor" dialog box will appear. Click Add to enter the Configure Data Viewer dialog box, and select the type of data viewer you wish to use and optionally give it a name if needed. You can go to the other tab that's named after the type of data viewer you're using to select what columns will be used in the data viewer.

Once you run the package, you'll see the data viewers open and populate with data when the package runs the transform that it's attached to. The package will not proceed until you click the > button. You can also copy the data into a viewer like Excel or Notepad for further investigation by clicking Copy Data. The data viewer will show up to 10,000 rows by default, so you may have to click the > button multiple times in order to go through all the data.

As you add more and more data viewers, you may want to remove them eventually to speed up your development execution. You can remove them by right-clicking the path that has the data viewer and selecting Data Viewers. You could then select the data viewer to remove and click Delete. You can also delete all the data viewers and breakpoints at one time by selecting Delete All Breakpoints from the Debug menu.

Sources

A *source* is where you specify the location of your source data. Most sources will point to the Connection Manager in SSIS. By pointing to the Connection Manager, you can reuse connections throughout your package, because you need only change the connection in one place. To reach the Data Flow tab, create a new Data Flow Task in the Control Flow tab. You can then drag the source from the Toolbox.

OLE DB Source

The OLE DB Source is the most common type of source, and it can point to any OLE DB–compliant Data Source such as SQL Server, Oracle, or DB2. To configure the OLE DB Source, double-click the source once you've added it to the design pane in the Data Flow tab. In the Connection Manager page of the OLE DB

Source Editor (Figure 5-1), select the Connection Manager of your OLE DB Source from the OLE DB Connection Manager drop-down box. You can also add a new Connection Manager in the editor by clicking the New button.

The "Data access mode" option sets how you wish to retrieve the data. Your options here are Table/View or SQL Command, or you can pull either from variables. Once you select the Data Access Mode, you will need the table or view, or you can type a query. It is a best practice for multiple reasons that will be mentioned momentarily to retrieve the data from a query. This query can also be a stored procedure. Additionally, you can pass a variable into the query by substituting a question mark (?) for where the parameter should be, then clicking the Parameters button. We'll discuss more about parameterization of your queries later in this chapter.

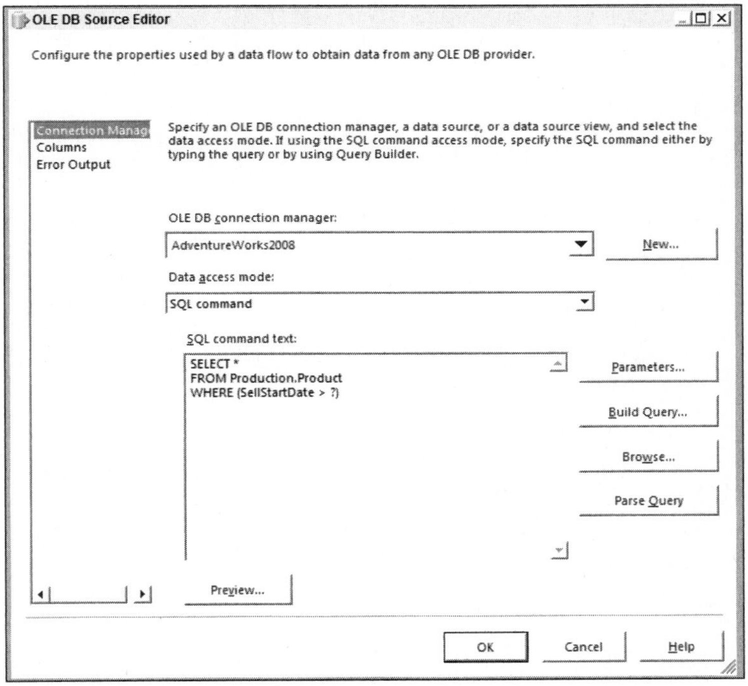

Figure 5-1

Like most sources, you can go to the Columns page to set columns that you wish to output to the Data Flow, as shown in Figure 5-2. Simply check the columns you wish to output, and you can then assign the name you wish to send down the Data Flow in the Output column. Select only the columns that you will want to use, because the smaller the dataset, the better performance you will receive.

This is where it's better from a performance perspective to have typed the query in the Connection Manager page versus selecting a table. Selecting a table to pull data from essentially selects all columns and all rows from the target table, transporting all of that data across the network. Then, going to the Columns page and unchecking the unnecessary columns applies a client-side filter on the data, which is not nearly as efficient as selecting only the necessary columns in the SQL query.

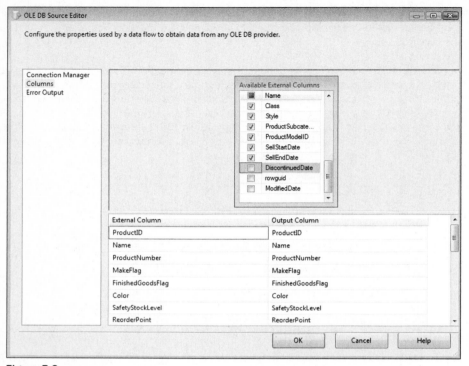

Figure 5-2

Optionally, you can go to the Error Output page (shown in Figure 5-3) and specify how you wish to handle rows that have errors. For example, you may wish to output any rows that have a data type conversion issue to a different path in the Data Flow. On each column, you can specify that if an error occurs, you wish the row to be ignored, be redirected, or fail. If you choose to ignore failures, the column for that row will be set to NULL. If you redirect the row, the row will be sent down the red path in the Data Flow coming out of the OLE DB Source.

The Truncation column specifies what to do if a data truncation occurs. A truncation error would occur, for example, if you try to place 200 characters of data into a column in the Data Flow that only supports 100. You have the same options available to you for Truncation as you do for the Error option.

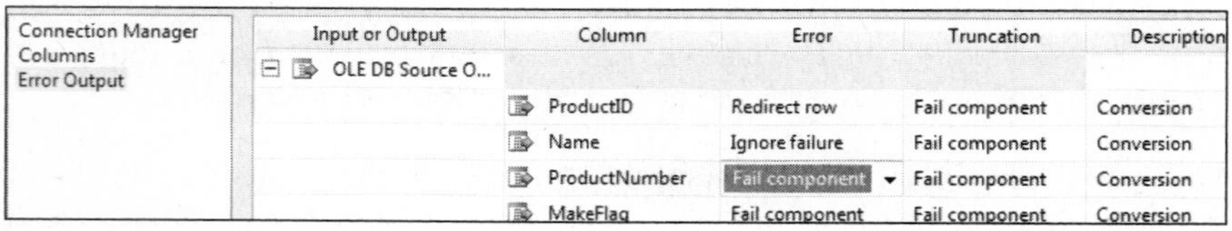

Connection Manager Columns Error Output	Input or Output	Column	Error	Truncation	Description
	⊟ 📷 OLE DB Source O...				
		📷 ProductID	Redirect row	Fail component	Conversion
		📷 Name	Ignore failure	Fail component	Conversion
		📷 ProductNumber	Fail component ▾	Fail component	Conversion
		📷 MakeFlag	Fail component	Fail component	Conversion

Figure 5-3

Excel Source

The Excel Source is a source that points to an Excel spreadsheet, just like it sounds. Once you point to an Excel Connection Manager (shown in Figure 5-4), you can select the sheet from the "Name of the Excel sheet" drop-down box, or you can run a query by changing the Data Access Mode. This source treats Excel just like a database, where an Excel sheet is the table and the workbook is the database.

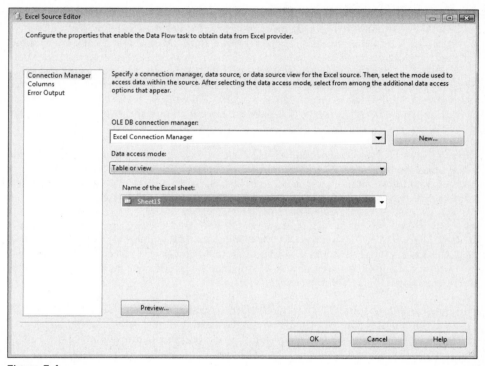

Figure 5-4

SSIS supports Excel data types, but it may not support them the way you wish by default. For example, the default format in Excel is General. If you right-click a column and select Format Cells, you'll find that most of your columns in your Excel spreadsheet have probably been set to General. SSIS translates this general format as a Unicode data type. In SQL Server, Unicode translates into nvarchar, which is probably not what you want. If you have a Unicode data type in SSIS and you try to insert into a varchar column, it will potentially fail. The answer is then to place a Data Conversion Transform between the source and the destination in order to change the Excel data types. You can read more about Data Conversion Transforms later in this chapter.

If you are connecting to an Excel 2007 spreadsheet or later, ensure that you select the proper Excel version when creating the Excel Connection Manager. You will not be able to connect to an Excel 2007 spreadsheet otherwise. Additionally the Excel driver is a 32 bit driver only and your packages will have to run in 32 bit mode when using Excel connectivity.

Flat File Source

The Flat File Source provides a Data Source for connections that are not relational. Flat File Sources are typically comma- or tab-delimited files, or they could be fixed-width or ragged-right. A fixed-width file is typically received from the mainframe, and it has fixed start and stop points for each column. This method makes for a fast load but takes longer at design-time for the developer to map each column. You specify a Flat File Source the same way you specify an OLE DB Source. Once you add it to your Data Flow pane, you point it to a Connection Manager connection that is a flat file or a multi-flat file. After that, you go to the Columns tab to specify what columns you want to be presented to the Data Flow. All the specifications for the flat file, such as delimiter type, were previously set in the Flat File Connection Manager.

In this example, you'll create a Connection Manager that points to a file called `FactSales.csv`, which you can download from this book's website at `www.wrox.com`. The file has a date column, a few string columns, integer columns, and a currency column. Because of its variety in data types, it presents an interesting case study to show how to configure a Flat File Connection Manager.

First, right-click in the Connection Manager area of the Package Designer and select New Flat File Connection Manager. This will open the Flat File Connection Manager Editor, which is seen in Figure 5-5. Name the Connection Manager Fact Sales and point it to wherever you placed the `FactSales.csv` file. Check the "Column names in the first data row" option, which specifies that the first row of the file contains a header row with the column names.

Another important option is the "Text qualifier" option. Although there isn't one for this file, sometimes your comma-delimited files may require that you have a text qualifier. A text qualifier places a character around each column of data to show that any comma delimiter inside that symbol should be ignored. For example, if you had the most common text qualifier of double-quotes around your data, a row may look like the following, where there are only three columns, even though the commas may indicate five:

```
"Knight,Brian", 123, "Jacksonville, FL"
```

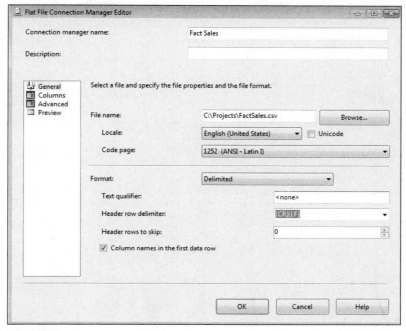

Figure 5-5

In the Columns page of the Connection Manager, you can specify what will delimit each column in the flat file if you chose a delimited file. The row delimiter specifies what will indicate a new row. The default option is a carriage return followed by a line feed. The Connection Manager's file will be automatically scanned to determine the column delimiter and as you can see in Figure 5-6, you want to use a tab delimiter for the example file.

Often, once you make a major change to your header delimiter or your text qualifier, you'll have to click the Reset Columns button. Doing so will requery the file in order to obtain the new column names. If you click this option, though, all of your metadata in the Advanced page will be re-created as well, and you may lose a sizable amount of work.

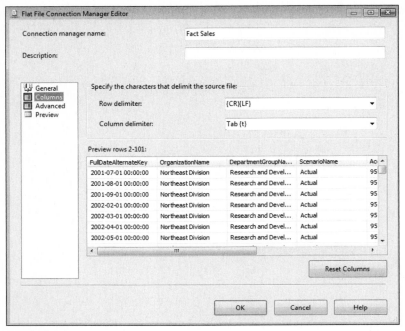

Figure 5-6

The Advanced page of the Connection Manager is the most important feature in the Connection Manager. In this tab, you specify the data type for each column in the flat file and the name of the column, as shown in Figure 5-7. This column name and data type will be later sent to the Data Flow. If you need to change the data types or names, you can always come back to the Connection Manager, but be aware that you'll need to open the Flat File Source again to refresh the metadata.

> *Making a change to the Connection Manager's data types or columns will require that you refresh any Data Flow Task using that Connection Manager. To do so, open the Flat File Source Editor, which will prompt you to refresh the metadata of the Data Flow. Answer yes to that question and the metadata will be corrected throughout the Data Flow.*

If you don't want to go to each column and specify the data type, you can click the Suggest Types button on this page to have SSIS scan the first 100 records (by default) in the file to guess the appropriate data types. Generally speaking, it does a bad job at guessing, but it's a great place to start if you have a lot of columns.

If you wish to do this manually, you can select each column, and then specify the data type for each column. You can also hold the Ctrl key or Shift key and select multiple columns at once and change the data types or column length for multiple columns all at the same time.

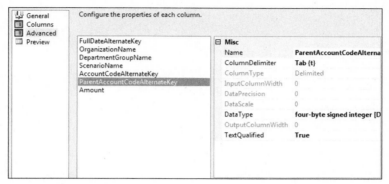

Figure 5-7

A Flat File Connection Manager will initially treat each column as a 50-character string by default. Leaving this default behavior will harm you when you have a truly integer column that you're trying to insert into SQL Server, or if your column contains more data than 50 characters of data. This Advanced page in the Connection Manager is the most important work you can do to ensure that all the data types for the columns are properly defined. You will also want to keep the data types as small as possible. If you have a zip code column, for example, that's only 9 digits in length, define it as a 9-character string. Doing this will save an additional 41 bytes in memory multiplied by however many rows you have.

A frustrating point with SSIS sometimes is how it deals with SQL Server data types. For example, a varchar maps in SSIS to a string column. It was made this way to translate well into the .NET development world and to make an agnostic product. The following table contains some of the common SQL Server data types and what they're going to map to in a Flat File Connection Manager.

SQL Server Data Type	Connection Manager Data Type
bigint	eight-byte signed integer [DT_I8]
binary	byte stream [DT_BYTES]
Bit	Boolean [DT_BOOL]
tinyint	single-byte unsigned integer [DT_UI1]
Datetime	database timestamp [DT_DBTIMESTAMP]
Decimal	numeric [DT_NUMERIC]
real	float [DT_R4]
Int	four-byte signed integer [DT_I4]
Image	image [DT_IMAGE]
Nvarchar or nchar	Unicode string [DT_WSTR]
Ntext	Unicode text stream [DT_NTEXT]
Numeric	numeric [DT_NUMERIC]
Smallint	two-byte signed integer [DT_I2]
Text	text stream [DT_TEXT]
Timestamp	byte stream [DT_BYTES]
Tinytint	single-byte unsigned integer [DT_UI1]
Uniqueidentifier	unique identifier [DT_GUID]
Varbinary	byte stream [DT_BYTES]
Varchar or char	string [DT_STR]
Xml	Unicode string [DT_WSTR]

FastParse Option

By default, there is a contract that SSIS issues between flat files and a Data Flow, which states that it must validate any numeric or date column. For example, if you have a flat file where a given column is set to a four-byte integer, every row must first go through a short validation routine to ensure it is truly an integer and no character data has passed through. On date columns, a quick check is done to ensure that every date is indeed a valid in-range date.

This process is fast but it does require approximately 20 to 30 percent more time to validate that contract. To set the property, go into the Data Flow Task where you're using a Flat File Source. Right-click the Flat File Source and select Show Advanced Editor. Once there, go to the Input and Output Properties and select any number or date column. In the right pane, change the Fast Parse property to True as shown in Figure 5-8.

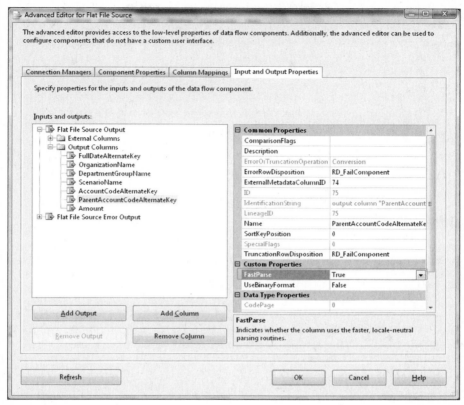

Figure 5-8

MultiFlatFile Connection Managers

If you know that you want to process a series of flat files in a Data Flow or refer to many files in the Control Flow, you can optionally use the MultiFlatFile or "multiple files Connection Manager." The Multiple Files Connection Manager refers to a list of files for copying, moving, or that may hold a series of SQL scripts to execute similar to the File Connection Manager. The Multiple Flat File Connection Manager gives you the same view as a Flat File Connection Manager but allows you to point to multiple files. In either case, you can point to a list of files by placing a vertical bar (|) between each filename:

```
C:\Projects\011305c.dat|C:\Projects\053105c.dat
```

The way the Multiple Flat File Connection Manager reacts in the Data Flow is by combining the total number of records from all the files that you have pointed to and appearing like a single merged file. Using this is a matter of personal preference in many cases compared to the Foreach Loop Containers. In either case, the metadata from the file must match in order to use them in the Data Flow. Most lean toward using For Loop Containers though, because it's easier to make them dynamic. With these Multiple File or Multiple Flat File Connection Managers, you'll have to parse your file list and add the vertical bar between them. In the Foreach Loop Containers case, it takes care of that for you.

Raw File Source

The Raw File Source is a specialized type of flat file that is optimized for quick usage from SSIS. A Raw File Source is created by a Raw File Destination (this will be discussed later in this chapter). You can't add columns to the Raw File Source, but you can remove unused columns from the source in much the same way you do in the other sources. Because the Raw File Source requires little translation, it can load data much faster than the Flat File Source, but the price of this is that you have little flexibility. Typically, you see raw files used to capture data at checkpoints to be used later in case of a package failure.

These sources are typically used for cross-package or cross-data flow communication. For example, if you have a Data Flow that takes four hours to run, you may wish to stage the data to a raw file halfway through the processing in case a problem occurs. Then, the second Data Flow Task would continue the remaining two hours of processing.

XML Source

The XML Source is a powerful SSIS source that can use a local or remote (via HTTP or UNC) XML file as the source. This Data Source is a bit different from the OLE DB Source in its configuration. First, you point to the XML file locally on your machine or at a UNC path. You can also point to a remote HTTP address for an XML file. This is useful for interaction with a vendor. This source is very useful when used in conjunction with the Web Service Task or the XML Task. Once you point the data item to an XML file, you must generate an XSD file (XML Schema Definition) by clicking the Generate XSD button or point to an existing XSD file. The schema definition can also be an in-line XML file, so you don't necessarily have to have an XSD file. The rest of the source resembles the other sources, where you can filter the columns you don't want to see down the chain.

ADO.NET Source

The ADO.NET Source allows you to make a .NET provider a source and allows you to make it available for consumption inside the package. The source uses an ADO.NET Connection Manager to connect to the provider. It is preferred for performance to use the OLE DB Source, but some providers may require that you use the ADO.NET Source. The source is identical in its interface appearance to the OLE DB Source, but it does require an ADO.NET Connection Manager.

Destinations

Inside the Data Flow, *destinations* accept the data from the Data Sources and from the transformations. The architecture can send the data to nearly any OLE DB–compliant Data Source, a flat file, or Analysis Services, to name just a few. Like sources, destinations are managed through the Connection Manager. The configuration difference between sources and destinations is that in destinations, you have a Mappings page (shown in Figure 5-9), where you specify how the inputted data from the Data Flow maps to the destination. As you can see in the Mappings page in this figure, the columns are automatically mapped based on column names but don't necessarily have to exactly be lined up. You can also choose to ignore given columns, such as when you're inserting into a table that has an identity column and don't wish to inherit the value from the source table.

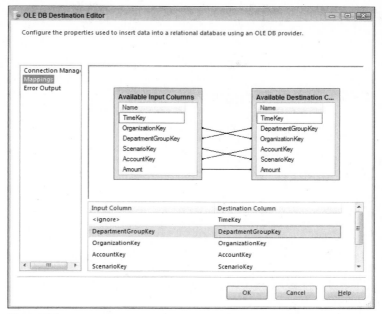

Figure 5-9

You won't be able to configure the destination until it is connected to the Data Flow. To do this, select the source or a transformation and drag the green arrow to the destination. If you want to output the bad data to a destination, you would drag the red arrow to that destination. If you try to configure the destination before attaching it to the transformation or source, you would see the error in Figure 5-10.

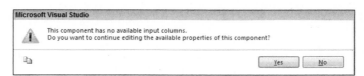

Figure 5-10

Data Mining Model Training

The Data Mining Model Training Destination can train an Analysis Services data mining model by passing it data from the Data Flow. You can train multiple mining models from a single destination and Data Flow. To use this destination, you would select an Analysis Services Connection Manager and the mining model. Analysis Services mining models are out of the scope of this book, and for more information on this, please see *Professional SQL Server Analysis Services 2008 with MDX* (Harinath 2009).

The data you pass into the Data Mining Model Training Destination must be presorted. To do this, you would use the Sort Transformation, which is discussed in the next section.

DataReader Destination

The DataReader Destination is a way of extending SSIS Data Flows to external packages or programs that can use the DataReader interface, such as a .NET application. When you configure this destination, you should make sure that the name of your destination is something that's easy to recognize later in your program, because you will be calling that name later. After you've configured the name and basic properties, check the columns you'd like outputted to the destination in the Input Columns tab.

Dimension and Partition Processing

The Dimension Processing Destination loads and processes an Analysis Services dimension. You have the option to perform full, incremental, or update processing. To configure the destination, select the Analysis Services Connection Manager that contains the dimension that you'd like to process on the Connection Manager page in the Dimension Processing Destination Editor. You will then see a list of dimensions and fact tables in the box. Select the dimension you'd like to load and process, and go to the Mappings page, where you'll map the data from the Data Flow to the selected dimension. Lastly, you can configure how you'd like to handle errors, such as unknown keys in the Advanced page. Generally, the default options are fine for this page unless you have special needs for error handling.

The Partition Processing Destination has identical options, but it processes an Analysis Services partition instead of a dimension.

Excel Destination

The Excel Destination (shown in Figure 5-11) is identical to the Excel Source, except that the destination accepts data instead of sending data. First, select the Excel Connection Manager from the Connection Manager page, and then specify which worksheet you wish to load data into.

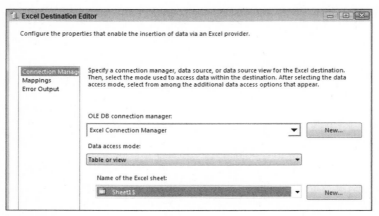

Figure 5-11

The big caveat with the Excel Destination is that unlike the Flat File Destination, an Excel spreadsheet must already exist with the sheet that you wish to copy data into. If the spreadsheet doesn't exist, you will receive an error. If you wish to work around this issue, you can create a blank spreadsheet to use as your template, and then use the File System Task to copy the file over.

Flat File Destination

The commonly used Flat File Destination sends data to a flat file, and can be fixed-width or delimited. The destination uses a Flat File Connection Manager. You can also add a custom header to the file by typing it into the Header option in the Connection Manager page. Lastly, you can specify on this page that the destination file will be overwritten each time the Data Flow is run.

OLE DB Destination

The most commonly used destination for you will probably be the OLE DB Destination (Figure 5-12). It can write data from the source or transformation to OLE DB–compliant Data Sources such as Oracle, DB2, Access, and SQL Server. It configures like any other destination and source, using OLE DB Connection Managers. A dynamic option it does have is the Data Access Mode. If you select Table or View - Fast Load, or its variable equivalent, you will have a number of options below, such as Table Lock. This Fast Load option is available only for SQL Server database instances.

A few options of note here are the Rows Per Batch option, which specifies how many rows are in each batch sent to the destination, and another option is the Maximum Insert Commit Size, which specifies how large the batch size will be prior to issuing a commit statement. The Table Lock option will place a lock on the destination table to speed up the load. As you can imagine, this will cause grief for your users if they're trying to read from the table at the same time. The other important option is Keep Identity. This option allows you to insert into a column that has the identity property set on it. Generally speaking, you can gain performance by setting the Max Insert Commit Size to a number like 10,000, but that number may vary based on how wide the columns are.

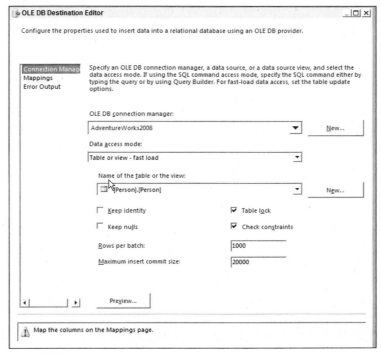

Figure 5-12

145

A common question is what is the difference between fast load and the normal load (table or view option) for the OLE DB Destination. The Fast Load option specifies that SSIS will load data in bulk into the OLE DB Destination's target table. Because this is a bulk operation, error handling via a redirection or ignoring of the data errors is not allowed. If you require this level of error handling, you need to turn off bulk loading of the data by selecting Table or View for the Data Access Mode option. Doing so will allow you to redirect your errors down the red line but will cause a slow down of the load by a factor of at least four.

Raw File Destination

The Raw File Destination is an especially speedy Data Destination that does not use a Connection Manager to configure. Instead, you point to the file on the server in the editor. This destination is written to typically as an intermediate point for partially transformed data. Once written to, other packages could read the data in by using the Raw File Source. The file is written in native format and so is very fast.

Recordset Destination

The Recordset Destination populates an ADO recordset that can be used outside the transformation. For example, you can populate the ADO recordset, and then a Script Task could read that recordset by reading a variable later in the Control Flow. This type of destination does not support an error output like some of the other destinations.

SQL Server and Mobile Destinations

The SQL Server Destination is the destination that is optimized for SQL Server. It gains its speed advantages by using the bulk insert features that are built into SQL Server. What's nice about this destination is that you can perform transformations earlier in the Data Flow and actually load data quickly in bulk into SQL Server after it has been transformed. Through the Advanced tab in the destination, you can configure the same features that are available in the bulk insert feature, such as executing triggers or locking the table. Note that this destination can be used only if the package is running on the same machine as SQL Server, because it uses an interface that's in-memory. Lastly, the SQL Server Mobile Destination is a destination that can direct data to a Pocket PC device.

Transformations

Transformations (the term *transform* will be used throughout this book) are key components to the Data Flow that transform the data to a desired format as you move from step to step. For example, you may wish a sampling of your data to be sorted and aggregated. Three transforms can accomplish this task for you: one to take a random sampling of the data, one to sort, and another to aggregate. The nicest thing about transforms in SSIS is that it is all done in-memory and it no longer requires elaborate scripting as in SQL Server 2000 DTS. As you add a transform, the data is altered and passed down the path in the Data Flow. Also, because this is done in-memory, you no longer have to create staging tables to perform most functions. When dealing with very large datasets, though, you may still choose to create staging tables.

You set up the transform by dragging it onto the Data Flow tab design area. Then, click the source or transform you'd like to connect it to, and drag the green arrow to the target transform or destination.

If you drag the red arrow, then rows that fail to transform will be directed to that target. After you have the transform connected, you can double-click it to configure the transform.

Synchronous versus Asynchronous Transformations

Transformations are broken into two main categories: synchronous and asynchronous. In SSIS, you want to ideally use all synchronous components. Synchronous transformations are components like the Derived Column and Data Conversion Transforms where rows flow into memory buffers in the transform and the same buffers come out. No rows are held and typically these transforms perform very quickly with minimal impact to your Data Flow.

There are two types of asynchronous transforms: fully blocking and partial blocking. Partial blocking transforms, such as the Union All Transform, create new memory buffers for the output of the transform than what come into the transform. Full blocking transforms, such as the Sort and Aggregate Transforms, do the same thing but cause a full block of the data. In order to sort the data, SSIS must first see every single row of the data. If you have a 100MB file, then you may require 200MB of RAM in order to process the Data Flow because of a fully blocking transform. These fully blocking transforms represent the single largest slowdown in SSIS and architecture decisions you must make. Chapter 14 covers this concept in much more breadth.

Aggregate

The Aggregate Transform allows you to aggregate data from the Data Flow to apply certain TSQL functions that are done in a GROUP BY statement like Average, Minimum, Maximum, and Count. For example, in Figure 5-13, you can see that the data is grouped together on the ProductID column and then the Quantity and ActualCost columns are summed. Lastly for every ProductID, the maximum TransactionDate is aggregated. This produces four new columns that can be consumed down the path, or future actions can be performed on them and the other columns are dropped at that time.

The Aggregate Transform is configured in the Aggregate Transformation Editor (see Figure 5-13). To configure it, first check the column that you wish to perform the action on. After you check the column, the input column will be filled below in the grid. Optionally, type an alias in the Output Alias column that you wish to give the column when it's outputted to the next transform or destination. For example, if the column now holds the total money per customer, you may change the name of the column that's outputted from InvoiceAmt to TotalCustomerSaleAmt. This will make it easier for you to recognize what the column is along the path of the data. The most important option is the Operation drop-down box. For this option, you can select the following:

❑   **Group By:** Breaks the dataset into groups by the column you specify.

❑   **Average:** Averages the selected column's numeric data.

❑   **Count:** Counts the records in a group.

❑   **Count Distinct:** Counts the distinct non-NULL values in a group.

❑   **Minimum:** Returns the minimum numeric value in the group.

❑   **Maximum:** Returns the maximum numeric value in the group.

❑   **Sum:** Returns sum of the selected column's numeric data in the group.

You can click the Advanced tab to see the options that allow you to configure multiple outputs from the transform. After you click Advanced, you can type a new Aggregation Name to create a new output. You will then be able to check the columns you'd like to aggregate again as if it were a new transform.

Figure 5-13

In the Advanced tab, the "Key scale" option sets an approximate number of keys. The option is set to Unspecified by default and optimizes the transform's cache to the appropriate level. For example, setting it to Low will optimize the transform to write 500,000 keys. Setting it to Medium will optimize it for 5,000,000 keys, and High will optimize the transform for 25,000,000 keys. You can also set the exact number of keys by using the "Number of keys" option.

The "Count distinct scale" option will optionally set the amount of distinct values that can be written by the transform. The default value is unspecified, but if you set it to Low, the transform will be optimized to write 500,000 distinct values. Setting the option to Medium will set it to 5,000,000 values, and High will optimize the transform to 25,000,000. The Auto Extend Factor specifies to what factor your memory can be extended by the transform. The default option is 25%, and you can specify other settings to keep your RAM from getting away from you.

Audit

The Audit Transform allows you to add auditing data to your Data Flow. In the age of HIPPA and Sarbanes-Oxley (SOX) audits, you often must be able to track who inserted the data into a table and when. This transform helps you with that function. For example, if you'd like to track what task inserted data into the table, you can add those columns to the Data Flow path with this transform.

The task is easy to configure. All other columns are passed through to the path as an output, and any auditing item you add will also be added to the path. Simply select the type of data you'd like to audit in the Audit Type column (shown in Figure 5-14), and then name the column that will be outputted to the flow. The following are some of the options you'll have available to you:

❑ **Execution Instance GUID:** The GUID that identifies the execution instance of the package

❑ **PackageID:** The unique ID for the package

❑ **PackageName:** The name of the package

❑ **VersionID:** The version GUID of the package

❑ **ExecutionStartTime:** The time the package began

❑ **MachineName:** The machine that the package ran on

❑ **UserName:** The user that started the package

❑ **TaskName:** The Data Flow Task name that holds the Audit Task

❑ **TaskID:** The unique identifier for the Data Flow Task that holds the Audit Task

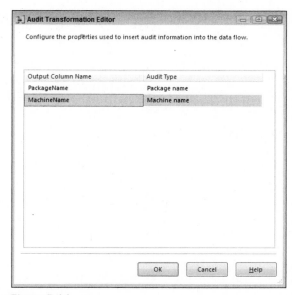

Figure 5-14

Cache Transform

The Cache Transform is a new transform to SQL Server 2008 that allows you to load a cache file on disk in the Data Flow. This cache file is later used for fast lookups in a Lookup Transform. The Cache Transform can be used to populate a cache file in the Data Flow as a transform, and then immediately used, or it can be used as a destination and then used by another package or Data Flow in the same package.

The cache file that's created allows you to perform lookups against large datasets that were previously not possible in the Lookup Transform. It also allows you to share the same lookup cache across many Data Flows. We cover this transform and the Lookup Transform much more in Chapter 7.

Character Map

The Character Map Transform (shown in Figure 5-15) performs common character translations in the flow. This simple transform can be configured in a single tab. To do so, check the columns you wish to transform. Then, select whether you want this modified column to be added as a new column or whether you want to update the original column. You can give the column a new name under the Output Alias column. Lastly, select the operation you wish to perform on the inputted column. The available operation types are as follows:

- ❑ **Byte Reversal:** Reverses the order of the bytes. For example, for the data 0x1234 0x9876, the result is 0x4321 0x6789. This uses the same behavior as LCMapString with the LCMAP_BYTEREV option.
- ❑ **Full Width:** Converts the half-width character type to full width.
- ❑ **Half Width:** Converts the full-width character type to half width.
- ❑ **Hiragana:** Converts the Katakana style of Japanese characters to Hiragana.
- ❑ **Katakana:** Converts the Hiragana style of Japanese characters to Katakana.
- ❑ **Linguistic Casing:** Applies the regional linguistic rules for casing.
- ❑ **Lowercase:** Changes all letters in the input to lowercase.
- ❑ **Traditional Chinese:** Converts the simplified Chinese characters to traditional Chinese.
- ❑ **Simplified Chinese:** Converts the traditional Chinese characters to simplified Chinese.
- ❑ **Uppercase:** Changes all letters in the input to uppercase.

In Figure 5-15, you can see that two columns are being transformed. Both columns will be transformed to uppercase. For the TaskName input, a new column is added, and the original is kept. The PackageName column is replaced in-line.

Figure 5-15

Conditional Split

The Conditional Split Transform is a fantastic way to add complex logic into your Data Flow. The transform allows you to send the data from a single data path to various outputs or paths based on conditions that use the SSIS expression language. For example, you could configure the transform to send all products with sales that have a quantity greater than 500 to one path, and products that have no sales down another path. Lastly, if neither condition is met, the sales would go down a third path, which is called "Small Sales," which essentially acts as an ELSE statement in TSQL. This exact situation is shown in Figure 5-16. You can drag and drop the column or code snippets from the tree above. After you complete the condition, you will need to name it something logical rather than the default name of Case 1. You'll use this case name later. You also can configure the Default Output Column Name, which will output any data that does not fit any case.

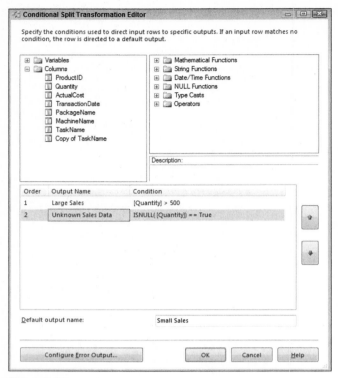

Figure 5-16

You can also conditionally read string data by using SSIS expressions like the following example, which reads the first letter of the City column:

```
SUBSTRING(City,1,1) == "F"
```

You can learn much more about the expression language in Chapter 6. Once you connect the transform to the next transform in the path or destination, you'll see a pop-up dialog box that lets you select which case you wish to flow down this path, as shown in Figure 5-17. In this figure, you can see three cases. The "Large Sales" condition can go down one path, "Unknown Sales Data" down another, and the default "Small Sales" down the last path. After you complete the configuration of the first case, you can create a path for each case in the conditional split.

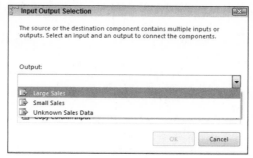

Figure 5-17

If our previous example was flushed out a bit more, your path may look like Figure 5-18, where the third data path, which had rows for the condition "Unknown Sales Data," would be just thrown away since it's not used.

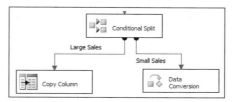

Figure 5-18

A much more detailed example is given in Chapter 8.

Copy Column

The Copy Column Transform is a very simple transformation that copies the output of a column to a clone of itself. This is useful if you wish to create a copy of a column before you perform some elaborate transformations. You could then keep the original value as your control subject and the copy as the modified column. To configure this transform, go to the Copy Column Transformation Editor and check the column you'd like to clone. Then assign a name to the new column.

Many transforms will allow you to transform the data from a column to a new column inherently.

Data Conversion

The Data Conversion Transform performs a similar function to the CONVERT or CAST functions in TSQL. The transform is configured in the Data Conversion Transformation Editor (Figure 5-19), where you would check each column that you wished to convert and then assign what you wish to convert it to under the Data Type column. The Output Alias is the column name you want to assign to the column after it is transformed. If you don't assign it a new name, it will show as Data Conversion: ColumnName later in the Data Flow.

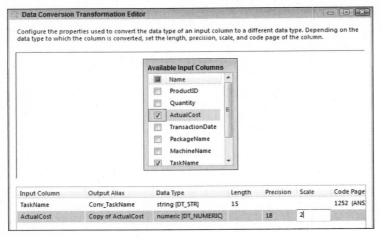

Figure 5-19

Data Mining Query

The Data Mining Query Transformation typically is used to fill in gaps in your data or predict a new column for your Data Flow. This transformation runs a data-mining query and adds the output to the Data Flow. It also can optionally add columns, such as the probability of a certain condition being true. A few great scenarios for this transformation would be the following:

❑ You could take columns, such as number of children, household income, and marital income, to predict a new column that states whether the person owns a house or not.

❑ You could predict what customers would want to buy based on their shopping cart items.

❑ You could fill in the blank holes in your data where customers didn't enter all the fields in a questionnaire.

The possibilities are endless with this.

Derived Column

The Derived Column Transform creates a new column that is derived from the output of another column. It is one of the most important transforms in your Data Flow arsenal. You may wish to use this transformation, for example, to multiply the quantity of orders by the cost of the order to derive the total cost of the order, as shown in Figure 5-20. You can also use it to find out the current date or to fill in the blanks in the data by using the ISNULL function. This is one of the top five transforms that you'll find yourself using to alleviate the need for TSQL scripting in the package.

To configure this transform, drag the column or variable into the Expression column as shown in Figure 5-20. Then add any functions to it. A list of functions can be found in the top-right corner of the Derive Column Transformation Editor. You must then specify, in the Derived Column drop-down box, if you want the output to replace an existing column in the Data Flow or to create a new column. As you see in Figure 5-20, the second derived column expression is doing an in-place update of the Quantity column. The expression states that if the Quantity column is null, then convert it to 0, otherwise, keep the existing data in the Quantity column. If you create a new column, specify the name in the Derived Column Name column.

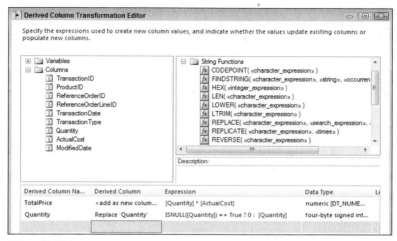

Figure 5-20

Export Column

The Export Column Transformation is a transformation that exports data to a file from the Data Flow. Unlike the other transformations, the Export Column Transform doesn't need a destination to create the file. To configure it, go to the Export Column Transformation Editor, which is shown in Figure 5-21. Select the column that contains the file from the Extract Column drop-down box. Select the column that contains the path and filename to send the files to in the File Path Column drop-down box.

The other options specify where the file will be overwritten or dropped. The Allow Append checkbox specifies whether the output will be appended to the existing file, if one exists. If you check Force Truncate, the existing file will be overwritten if it exists. The Write BOM option specifies whether a byte-order mark is written to the file if it is a DT_NTEXT or DT_WSTR data type.

If you do not check the Append or Truncate options and the file exists, the package will fail if the error is not handled. The following error is a subset of the complete error you'd receive:

```
Error: 0xC02090A6 at Data Flow Task, Export Column [61]: Opening the file
"wheel_small.gif" for writing failed. The file exists and cannot be
overwritten. If the AllowAppend property is FALSE and the ForceTruncate
property is set to FALSE, the existence of the file will cause this failure.
```

The Export Column Transformation Task is used to extract blob-type data from fields in a database and create files in their original formats to be stored in a file system or viewed by a format viewer, such as Microsoft Word or Microsoft Paint. The trick to understanding the Export Column Transformation is that it requires an input stream field that contains digitized document data and another field that can be used for a fully qualified path. The Export Column Transformation will convert the digitized data into a physical file on the file system for each row in the input stream using the fully qualified path.

In this example, you'll use existing data in the AdventureWorks2008 database to output some stored documents from the database back to file storage. The AdventureWorks2008 database has a table named [production].[document] that contains a file path and a field containing an embedded Microsoft Word document. Pull these documents out of the database and save them into a directory on the file system.

1. Create a directory with an easy name like `c:\exports\` that you can use when exporting these documents.

2. Create a new SSIS package named Export Column Example. Add a Data Flow Task to the Control Flow design surface.

3. On the Data Flow design surface, add an OLE DB Data Source configured to the AdventureWorks2008 database table [Production].[Document].

4. If you preview the data in this table, you'll notice that the FileName field in the table is a super-long file path. Modify that path so that it points to your directory `c:\exports\`.

5. Add a Derived Column Transformation Task to the Data Flow design surface. Connect the output of the OLE DB data to the task.

6. Create a Derived Column Name named NewFilePath. Use the Derived Column setting of <add as new column>. To derive a new filename, just use the primary key for the filename and add your path to it. To do this, set the expression to the following:

```
"c:\\exports\\" + (DT_WSTR,50)DocumentID + ".doc"
```

The \\ is required in the expressions editor instead of \ because of its use as an escape sequence.

7. Add an Export Column Transformation Task to the Data Flow design surface. Connect the output of the Derived Column Task to the Export Column Task. The Export Column Task will consume the input stream and separate all the fields into two usable categories: fields that can possibly be in digitized data formats, and fields that can possibly be used as filenames. Figure 5-21 is a graphic that has been created to show the contents of both categories for this example.

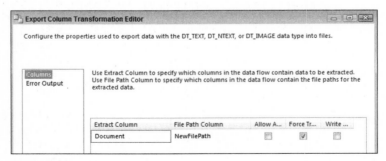

Figure 5-21

Notice that fields like the primary key [DocumentID] do not appear in either collection. This field doesn't contain embedded data, and it cannot be resolved to a filename.

8. Set the Extract Column equal to the [Document] field, since this contains the embedded MS Word object. Set the File Path Column equal to the field name [NewFilePath]. This field is the one that you derived in the Derived Column Task.

9. Check the Force Truncate option to rewrite the files if they exist. (This will allow you to run the package again without an error if the files already exist.)

10. Run the package and check the contents of the c:\exports\ directory. You should see a list of MS Word files in sequence from 1 to 9. Open one and you'll be able to read the document in MS Word.

Fuzzy Lookup

If you've done some work in the world of extract, transfer, and load processes (ETL), you've run into the proverbial crossroads of handling bad data. The test data is staged, but all attempts to retrieve a foreign key from a dimension table result in no matches for a number of rows. This is the crossroads of bad data. At this point, there are a finite set of options. You could create a set of hand-coded complex lookup functions using SQL Sound-Ex, full-text searching, or distance-based word calculation formulas. This strategy is time-consuming to create and test, complicated to implement, and dependent on language lexicon, and it isn't always consistent or reusable (not to mention that everyone from now on will be scared to alter the code for fear of breaking it). You could just give up and divert the row for manual processing by subject matter experts (that's a way to make some new friends). You could just add the new data to the lookup tables and retrieve the new keys. If you just add the data, the foreign key retrieval issue gets solved, but you could be adding an entry into the dimension table that will skew data-mining results downstream. This is what we like to call a *lazy-add*. This is a descriptive, not a technical, term. A lazy-add would import a misspelled job title like "prasedent" into the dimension table when there is already an entry of "president." It was added, but it was lazy.

The Fuzzy Lookup and Fuzzy Grouping Transformations add one more road to take at the crossroads of bad data. These transformations allow the addition of a step to the process that is easy to use, consistent, scalable, and reusable, and they will reduce your unmatched rows significantly — maybe even altogether. If you've already allowed bad data in your dimension tables, or you are just starting a new ETL process, you'll want to put the Fuzzy Grouping Transformation to work on your data to find data redundancy. This transformation can examine the contents of a suspect field in a staged or committed table and provide possible groupings of similar words based on provided tolerances. This matching information can then be used to clean up that table. Fuzzy Grouping is discussed later in this chapter.

If you are correcting data during an ETL process, use the Fuzzy Lookup Transformation — my suggestion is to do so *only* after attempting to perform a regular lookup on the field. This best practice is recommended because Fuzzy Lookups don't come cheap. Fuzzy Lookups build specialized indexes of the input stream and the reference data for comparison purposes. You can store them for efficiency, but these indexes can use up some disk space or can take up some memory if you choose to rebuild them on each run. Storing matches made by the Fuzzy Lookups over time in a translation or pre-dimension table is a great design. Regular Lookup Transforms can first be run against this translation table and then divert only those items in the Data Flow that can't be matched to a Fuzzy Lookup. This technique uses Lookup Transforms and translation tables to find matches using INNER JOINS. Fuzzy Lookups whittle the remaining unknowns down if similar matches can be found with a high level of confidence. Finally, if your last resort is to have the item diverted to a subject matter expert, you can save that decision into the translation table so that the ETL process can match it next time in the first iteration.

Using the Fuzzy Lookup Transformation requires an input stream of at least one field that is a string. Unlike the Term Lookup Transformation, which requires a NULL-terminated Unicode string, this transform just needs a DT_WSTR or DT_STR data type. Internally the transform has to be configured to connect to a reference table that will be used for comparison. The output to this transform will be a set of columns containing the following:

❑ **Input and Pass-Through Field Names and Values:** This column contains the name and value of the text input provided to the Fuzzy Lookup Transform Task or passed through during the lookup.

❑ **Reference Field Name and Value:** This column contains the name and value(s) of the matched results from the reference table.

❑ **Similarity:** This column contains a number between 0 and 1 representing similarity. Similarity is a threshold that you set when configuring the Fuzzy Lookup Task. The closer this number is to 1, the closer the two text fields must match.

❑ **Confidence:** This column contains a number between 0 and 1 representing confidence of the match relative to the set of matched results. Confidence is different from similarity, because it is not calculated by examining just one word against another but rather by comparing the chosen word match against all the other possible matches. Confidence gets better the more accurately your reference data represents your subject domain, and it can change based on the sample of the data coming into the ETL process.

The Fuzzy Lookup Transformation Editor has three configuration tabs.

❑ **Reference Table:** This tab (shown in Figure 5-22) sets up the OLE DB Connection to the source of the reference data. The Fuzzy Lookup takes this reference data and builds a token-based index (which is actually a table) out of it before it can begin to compare items. In this tab are the options to save that index or to use an existing index from a previous process. There is also an option to maintain the index, which will detect changes from run to run and keep the index current. Note that if you are processing large amounts of potential data, this index table can grow large.

❑ **Columns:** This tab allows mapping of the one text field in the input stream to the field in the reference table for comparison. Drag and drop a field from the Available Input Column onto the matching field in the Available Lookup Column. You can also click the two fields to be compared and right-click to create a relationship. Another neat feature is the ability to add the foreign key of the lookup table to the output stream. To do this, just click that field in the Available Input Columns.

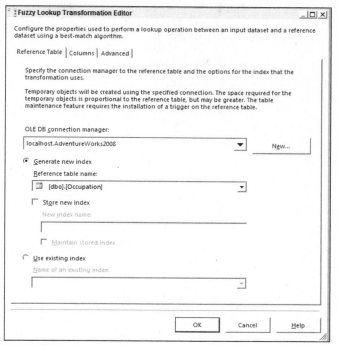

Figure 5-22

❑ **Advanced:** This tab contains the settings that control the fuzzy logic algorithms. You can set the maximum number of matches to output per incoming row. The default is set to 1, which means pull the best record out of the reference table if it meets the similarity threshold. Incrementing this setting higher than this may generate more results that you'll have to sift through, but it may be required if there are too many closely matching strings in your domain data. A slider controls the Similarity threshold. A recommendation is to start this setting at .75 when experimenting and move up or down as you review the results. This setting is normally decided based on a business person's review of the data, not the developer's review. If a row cannot be found that's similar enough, the columns that you checked in the Columns tab will be set to NULL. The token delimiters can also be set if, for example, you don't want the comparison process to break incoming strings up by a period (.) or spaces. The default for this setting is all common delimiters. See Figure 5-23 for an example of an Advanced tab.

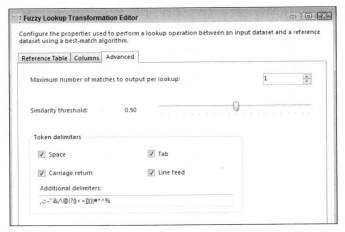

Figure 5-23

Back in the Reference Table tab (shown in Figure 5-22), there are a few additional settings that are of interest. The default option to set is the "Generate new index" option. By setting this, a table will be created on the reference table's Connection Manager each time the transform is run and that table will be populated with loads of data as was mentioned earlier in this section. The creation and loading of the table can be an expensive process. This table is removed after the transform is complete.

An alternative to that is to select the "Store new index" option, which will instantiate the table and not drop the table. You can then reuse that table from other Data Flows or packages and in additional days. As you can imagine though by doing this, your index table becomes stale soon after its creation. There are stored procedures you can run to refresh it in SQL, or you can click the "Maintain stored index" checkbox to create a trigger on the underlying reference table to automatically maintain the index table. This is available only with SQL Server reference tables and may slow down your insert, update, and delete statements to that table.

It's also important to not use Fuzzy Lookup as your primary Lookup Transform for lookups because of the slow down. You should always try an exact match using a Lookup Transform and then redirect non-matches to the Fuzzy Lookup if you need that level of lookup. Additionally, the Fuzzy Lookup Transform does require the Enterprise Edition of SQL Server 2008.

Although this transform neatly packages some highly complex logic in an easy-to-use component, the results won't be perfect. You'll need to spend some time experimenting with the configurable setting and monitoring the results. We'll show you an example of putting this transform to work.

You are going to create a quick demonstration of the Fuzzy Lookup Transform's capabilities by setting up a small table of occupation titles that will represent your dimension table. You will then import a set of person records that will require a lookup on the occupation to your dimension table. Not all will match, of course. The Fuzzy Lookup Transformation will be employed to find matches, and you will experiment with the settings to learn about its capabilities.

1. First copy the following data into a text file named `c:\Projects\FuzzyExample.txt`. This file can also be downloaded from `www.wrox.com`. This data will represent employee data that you are going to import. Notice that some of the occupation titles are cut off in the text file because of the positioning within the layout. Also notice that this file has an uneven right margin. Both of these issues are typical ETL situations that are especially painful.

```
EMPIDTITLE                    LNAME
00001EXECUTIVE VICE PRESIDENWASHINGTON
00002EXEC VICE PRES           PIZUR
00003EXECUTIVE VP             BROWN
00005EXEC VP                  MILLER
00006EXECUTIVE VICE PRASIDENSWAMI
00007FIELDS OPERATION MGR     SKY
00008FLDS OPS MGR             JEAN
00009FIELDS OPS MGR           GANDI
00010FIELDS OPERATIONS MANAGHINSON
00011BUSINESS OFFICE MANAGERBROWN
00012BUS OFFICE MANAGER       GREEN
00013BUS OFF MANAGER          GATES
00014BUS OFF MGR              HALE
00015BUS OFFICE MNGR          SMITH
00016BUS OFFICE MGR           AI
00017X-RAY TECHNOLOGIST       CHIN
00018XRAY TECHNOLOGIST        ABULA
00019XRAY TECH                HOGAN
00020X-RAY TECH               ROBERSON
```

2. Run the following SQL code in AdventureWorks2008 or in a database of your choice. This code will create your dimension table and add the accepted entries that will be used for reference purposes. Again, this file can be downloaded from `www.wrox.com`.

```
CREATE TABLE [Occupation](
  [OccupationID] [smallint] IDENTITY(1,1) NOT NULL,
  [OccupationLabel] [varchar] (50) NOT NULL
 CONSTRAINT [PK_Occupation_OccupationID] PRIMARY KEY CLUSTERED
(
  [OccupationID] ASC
) ON [PRIMARY]
) ON [PRIMARY]

GO

INSERT INTO [Occupation] Select 'EXEC VICE PRES'
INSERT INTO [Occupation] Select 'FIELDS OPS MGR'
INSERT INTO [Occupation] Select 'BUS OFFICE MGR'
INSERT INTO [Occupation] Select 'X-RAY TECH'
```

3. Create a new SSIS package and drop a Data Flow Task on the Control Flow design surface and click the Data Flow tab.

4.   Add a Flat File Connection to the Connection Manager. Name it "Employee Data," and then set the filename to `c:\projects\fuzzyexample.txt`. Set the Format property to Ragged Right. (By the way, for those of you who use flat files, the addition of the ability to process a ragged-right file is a welcome one.) Set the option to pull the column names from the first data row as shown in Figure 5-24.

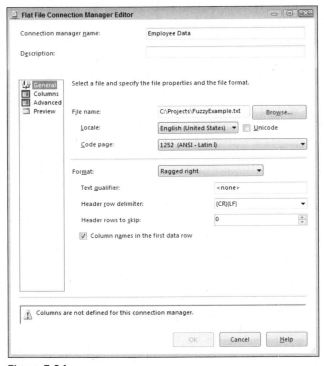

Figure 5-24

5.   Click the Columns tab and set the columns to break at positions 5 and 28. Click the Advanced tab and set the OuputColumnWidth property for the TITLE field to 50. Save the connection

6.   Add a Flat File Source to the Data Flow surface and configure it to use the Employee Data connection. Add an OLE DB Destination and configure it to point to the AdventureWorks2008 database or to the database of your choice.

7.   Add a Fuzzy Lookup Transform Task to the Data Flow design surface. Connect the output of the Flat File Source to the Fuzzy Lookup and the output of the Fuzzy Lookup to the OLE DB Destination.

8.   Open the Fuzzy Lookup Transformation Editor. Set the OLE DB Connection Manager in the Reference tab to use the AdventureWorks2008 database connection and the Occupation table. Set up the Columns tab connecting the input to the reference table columns as in Figure 5-22, and set up the Advanced tab with a Similarity threshold of 50 (.50).

9. Open the editor for the OLE DB Destination. Set the OLE DB connection to the AdventureWorks2008 database. Click New to create a new table to store the results. Change the table name in the DDL statement that is presented to you to create the [FuzzyResults] table. Click the Mappings tab, accept the defaults, and save.

10. Add a Data View of type grid to the Data Flow between the Fuzzy Lookup and the OLE DB Destination.

Run the package, and your results at the Data View should resemble those in Figure 5-25. Notice that the logic has matched most of the items at a 50% similarity threshold — and you have the foreign key OccupationID added to your input for free! Had you used a strict INNER JOIN or Lookup Transform, you would have made only four matches, a dismal 21% hit ratio. These items can be seen in the Fuzzy Lookup output where the values are 1 for similarity and confidence. A few of the columns are set to NULL now, and those are because the row like Executive VP wasn't 50% similar to the Exec Vice Pres value. You would typically send those NULL records with a conditional split to a table for manual inspection.

E...	TITLE	LNAME	OccupationLabel	OccupationID	_Similarity	_Confiden...	_Similarity...
0...	EXECUTIVE VICE PRESIDEN	WASHINGTON	EXEC VICE PRES	1	0.647...	0.8064223	0.6475845
0...	EXEC VICE PRES	PIZUR	EXEC VICE PRES	1	1	1	1
0...	EXECUTIVE VP	BROWN	NULL	NULL	0	0	0
0...	EXEC VP	MILLER	NULL	NULL	0	0	0
0...	EXECUTIVE VICE PRASIDEN	SWAMI	EXEC VICE PRES	1	0.532...	0.6813678	0.5326089
0...	FIELDS OPERATION MGR	SKY	FIELDS OPS MGR	2	0.545...	0.7460818	0.5453513
0...	FLDS OPS MGR	JEAN	FIELDS OPS MGR	2	0.852...	0.8694109	0.8527615
0...	FIELDS OPS MGR	GANDI	FIELDS OPS MGR	2	1	1	1
0...	FIELDS OPERATIONS MA...	HINSON	NULL	NULL	0	0	0
0...	BUSINESS OFFICE MANA...	BROWN	BUS OFFICE MGR	3	0.563...	0.9875	0.5635651
0...	BUS OFFICE MANAGER	GREEN	BUS OFFICE MGR	3	0.781...	0.7880174	0.7811869
0...	BUS OFF MANAGER	GATES	BUS OFFICE MGR	3	0.606...	0.9875	0.6061339
0...	BUS OFF MGR	HALE	BUS OFFICE MGR	3	0.799...	0.9130224	0.7993925
0...	BUS OFFICE MNGR	SMITH	BUS OFFICE MGR	3	0.918...	0.7897626	0.9182091
0...	BUS OFFICE MGR	AI	BUS OFFICE MGR	3	1	1	1
0...	X-RAY TECHNOLOGIST	CHIN	X-RAY TECH	4	0.782...	0.8982612	0.7820667
0...	XRAY TECHNOLOGIST	ABULA	X-RAY TECH	4	0.561...	0.5283869	0.5614583
0...	XRAY TECH	HOGAN	X-RAY TECH	4	0.903...	0.9875	0.9032399
0...	X-RAY TECH	ROBERSON	X-RAY TECH	4	1	1	1

Figure 5-25

Fuzzy Grouping

In the previous section, you learned about situations where bad data creep into your dimension tables. The blame was placed on the "lazy-add" ETL processes that add data to dimension tables to avoid rejecting rows when there are no natural key matches. Processes like these are responsible for state abbreviations like "XX," and entries that look to the human eye like duplicates but are stored as two separate entries. The occupation titles "X-Ray Tech" and "XRay Tech" are good examples of duplicates that humans can see but computers have a harder time with.

The Fuzzy Grouping Transformation can look through a list of similar text and group the results using the same logic as the Fuzzy Lookup. You can use these groupings in a transformation table to clean up source and destination data or to crunch fact tables into more meaningful results without altering the underlying data. The Fuzzy Group Transformation also expects an input stream of text. It also requires a connection to an OLE DB Data Source because it creates in that source a set of structures to use during the analysis of the input stream.

The Fuzzy Lookup Editor has three configuration tabs:

❑ **Connection Manager:** This tab sets the OLE DB connection that the transform will use to write the storage tables that it needs.

❑ **Columns:** This tab displays the Available Input Columns and allows the selection of any or all input columns for fuzzy grouping analysis. See Figure 5-26 for a completed Columns tab.

Each column selected will be analyzed and grouped into logical matches resulting in a new column representing that group match for each data row. Each column can also be selected for Pass-Through — meaning the data is not analyzed, but is available in the output stream. You can choose the names of any of the output columns: Group Output Alias, Output Alias, Clean Match, and Similarity Alias Score column.

The minimum similarity evaluation is available at the column level if you select more than one column.

The numerals option (which is not visible in Figure 5-26 but can be found by scrolling to the right) allows configuration of the significance of numbers in the input stream when grouping text logically. The options are to consider leading, trailing, leading and trailing, or neither leading nor trailing numbers significant. This option would need to be considered when comparing address or similar types of information.

Comparison flags are the same options to ignore or pay attention to case, kana type, nonspacing characters, character width, symbols, and punctuation.

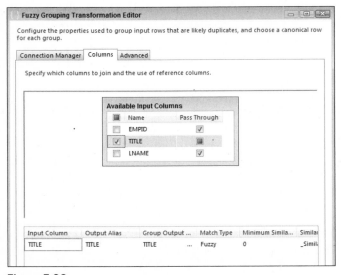

Figure 5-26

❑ **Advanced:** This tab contains the settings controlling the fuzzy logic algorithms that assign groupings to text in the input stream. You can set the names of the three additional fields that will be added automatically to the output of this transform. These fields are named _key_in, _key_out, and _score by default. A slider controls the Similarity threshold. A recommendation for this transform is to start this setting at 0.5 while experimenting and then move it up or down as you review the results. The token delimiters can also be set if, for example, you don't want the comparison process to break incoming strings up by a period (.) or spaces. The default for this setting is all common delimiters. See Figure 5-27 for a completed Advanced tab.

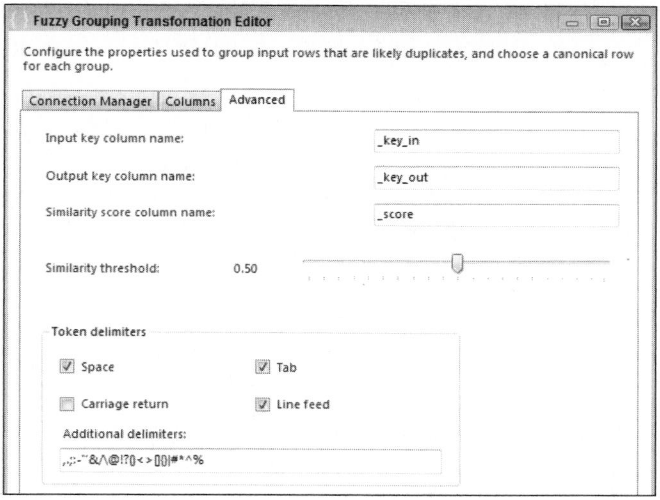

Figure 5-27

Suppose you are tasked with creating a brand-new occupations table using the employee occupations text file you imported in the Fuzzy Lookup example. Using only this data, you need to create a new employee occupations table with occupation titles that can serve as natural keys and that best represent this sample. You can use the Fuzzy Grouping Transform to develop the groupings for the dimension table, like this:

1. Create a new SSIS project named Fuzzy Grouping Example. Drop a Data Flow Task on the Control Flow design surface and click the Data Flow tab.

2. Add a Flat File Connection to the Connection Manager. Name it "Employee Data." Set the filename to c:\Projects\FuzzyExample.txt. (Use the FuzzyExample.txt file from the Fuzzy Lookup example.) Set the Format property to Ragged Right. Set the option to pull the column names from the first data row. Click the Columns tab and set the columns to break at positions 5 and 28. Click the Advanced tab and set the OuputColumnWidth property for the TITLE field to 50. Save the connection.

3. Add a Flat File Source to the Data Flow surface and configure it to use the Employee Data connection. Add an OLE DB Destination.

4. Add a Fuzzy Grouping Transform Task to the Data Flow design surface. Connect the output of the Flat File Source to the Fuzzy Lookup and the output of the Fuzzy Lookup to the OLE DB Destination.

5. Open the Fuzzy Grouping Editor and set the OLE DB Connection Manager to the AdventureWorks2008 connection.

6. In the Columns tab, select the Title column in the Available Input Columns. Accept the other defaults. Figure 5-26 is an example of a completed Columns tab for this example.

7. In the Advanced tab, set the Similarity threshold to .50. This will be your starting point for similarity comparisons as was shown in Figure 5-27.

8. Add an OLE DB Destination to the Data Flow design surface. Configure the destination to use the AdventureWorks2008 database or database of your choice. For the Name of Table or View, click the New button. Change the name of the table in the CREATE table statement to [FuzzyGrouping]. Click the Mappings tab to complete the task and save it.

9. Add a Data Viewer in the pipe between the Fuzzy Grouping Transform and the OLE DB Destination. Set the type to grid so that you can review the data at this point. Run the package. The output shown at multiple similarity thresholds would look similar to Figure 5-28.

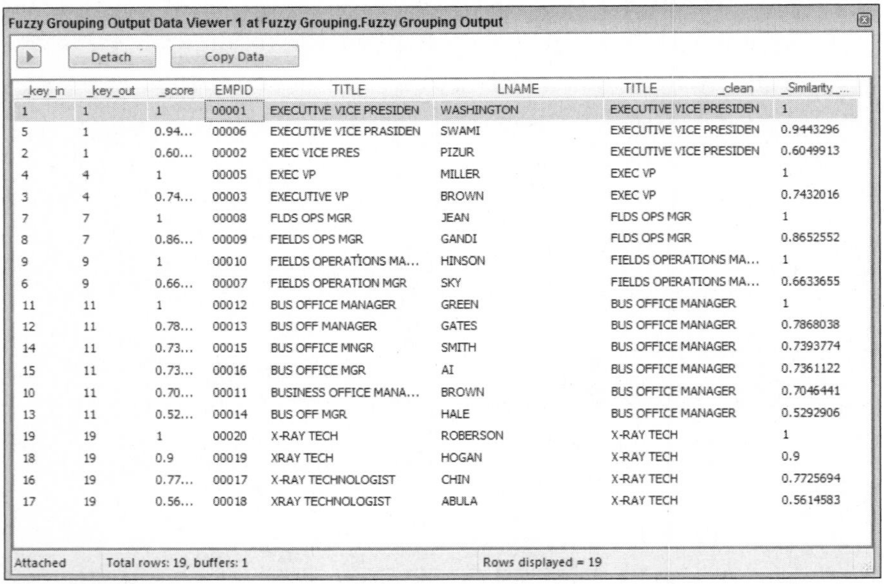

Fuzzy Grouping Output Data Viewer 1 at Fuzzy Grouping.Fuzzy Grouping Output

▶ Detach   Copy Data

_key_in	_key_out	_score	EMPID	TITLE	LNAME	TITLE	_clean	_Similarity_...
1	1	1	00001	EXECUTIVE VICE PRESIDEN	WASHINGTON	EXECUTIVE VICE PRESIDEN	1	
5	1	0.94...	00006	EXECUTIVE VICE PRASIDEN	SWAMI	EXECUTIVE VICE PRESIDEN	0.9443296	
2	1	0.60...	00002	EXEC VICE PRES	PIZUR	EXECUTIVE VICE PRESIDEN	0.6049913	
4	4	1	00005	EXEC VP	MILLER	EXEC VP	1	
3	4	0.74...	00003	EXECUTIVE VP	BROWN	EXEC VP	0.7432016	
7	7	1	00008	FLDS OPS MGR	JEAN	FLDS OPS MGR	1	
8	7	0.86...	00009	FIELDS OPS MGR	GANDI	FLDS OPS MGR	0.8652552	
9	9	1	00010	FIELDS OPERATIONS MA...	HINSON	FIELDS OPERATIONS MA...	1	
6	9	0.66...	00007	FIELDS OPERATION MGR	SKY	FIELDS OPERATIONS MA...	0.6633655	
11	11	1	00012	BUS OFFICE MANAGER	GREEN	BUS OFFICE MANAGER	1	
12	11	0.78...	00013	BUS OFF MANAGER	GATES	BUS OFFICE MANAGER	0.7868038	
14	11	0.73...	00015	BUS OFFICE MNGR	SMITH	BUS OFFICE MANAGER	0.7393774	
15	11	0.73...	00016	BUS OFFICE MGR	AI	BUS OFFICE MANAGER	0.7361122	
10	11	0.70...	00011	BUSINESS OFFICE MANA...	BROWN	BUS OFFICE MANAGER	0.7046441	
13	11	0.52...	00014	BUS OFF MGR	HALE	BUS OFFICE MANAGER	0.5292906	
19	19	1	00020	X-RAY TECH	ROBERSON	X-RAY TECH	1	
18	19	0.9	00019	XRAY TECH	HOGAN	X-RAY TECH	0.9	
16	19	0.77...	00017	X-RAY TECHNOLOGIST	CHIN	X-RAY TECH	0.7725694	
17	19	0.56...	00018	XRAY TECHNOLOGIST	ABULA	X-RAY TECH	0.5614583	

Attached   Total rows: 19, buffers: 1   Rows displayed = 19

Figure 5-28

Now you can look at these results and see more logical groupings and a few issues even at the lowest level of similarity. The title of "X-Ray Tech" is similar to the title "Xray Technologist." The title "Executive Vice Presiden" isn't really a complete title, and really should be grouped with "Exec VP." But this is pretty good for about five minutes of work.

To build a dimension table from this output, look at the two fields in the Data View named _key_in and _key_out. If these two values match, then the grouped value is the "best" representative candidate for the natural key in a dimension table. Separate the rows in the stream using a Conditional Split Transform where these two values match, and use an OLE Command Transform to insert the values in the dimension table. Remember that the more data, the better the grouping.

The output of the Fuzzy Grouping Transform is also a good basis for a translation table in your ETL processes. By saving both the original value and the Fuzzy Grouping value — with a little subject matter expert editing — you can use a Lookup Transform and this table to provide much-improved foreign key lookup results. You'll be able to improve on this idea with the Slowly Changing Dimension Transform later in the chapter.

Import Column

The Import Column Transform is a partner to the Export Column Transform. These transforms do the work of translating physical files from system file storage paths into database blob-type fields and vice versa. The trick to understanding the Import Column Transform is that its input source requires at least one column that is the fully qualified path to the file you are going to store in the database, and you need a destination column name for the output of the resulting blob and file path string. This transform also has to be configured using the Advanced Editor — something you've only briefly looked at in earlier chapters. The Advanced Editor is not intuitive, nor wizard-like in appearance, hence the name "Advanced," which you will incidentally be once you figure it out. In the editor, you won't have the ability to merge two incoming column sources into the full file path, so if your source data for the file paths have the filename separate from the file path, you should use the Merge Transforms to concatenate the columns before connecting that stream to the Import Column Transform.

Now you'll do an example where you'll import some images into your AdventureWorks2008 database. Create a new SSIS package. Transforms live in the Data Flow tab, so add a Data Flow Task to the Control Flow, and then add an Import Column Transform to the Data Flow surface. To make this easy, you're going to need to complete the following short tasks:

1. Create a directory called `c:\import\`.

2. Find a small JPEG file and copy it three times into `c:\import\images`. Change the filenames to `1.jpg`, `2.jpg`, and `3.jpg`.

3. Create a text file with the following content and save it in `c:\import\` as `filelist.txt`:

```
C:\import\1.JPG
C:\import\2.JPG
C:\import\3.JPG
```

4. Run the following SQL script in AdventureWorks2008 to create a storage location for the image files:

```
use AdventureWorks2008
Go
CREATE TABLE dbo.tblmyImages
(
    [StoredFilePath] [varchar](50) NOT NULL,
    [Document] image
)
```

5. You are going to use the `filelist.txt` file as your input stream for the files that you need to load into your database, so add a Flat File Source to your Data Flow surface and configure it to read one column from your `filelist.txt` flat file. Name the column ImageFilePath.

Take advantage of the opportunity to open up the Advanced Editor on the Flat File Transform by clicking the Show Advanced Editor link in the property window or by right-clicking the transform and selecting Advanced Editor. Look at the difference between this editor and the normal Flat File Editor. The Advanced Editor is stripped down to the core of the transform object — no custom wizards, just an interface sitting directly over the object properties themselves. It is possible to mess these properties up beyond recognition, but even in the worst case you can just drop and re-create the Transform Task. Look particularly at the Input and Output Properties of the Advanced Editor.

You didn't have to use the Advanced Editor to set up the import of the `filelist.txt` file. However, looking at the way the Advanced Editor displays the information will be really helpful when you configure the Import Column Transform. Notice that you have an External Columns (Input) and Output Columns collection with one node in each collection named "ImageFilePath." This reflects the fact that your connection describes a field called "ImageFilePath" and that this transform will simply output data with the same field name. The Column Mappings tab shows a visual representation of this mapping. If you changed the Name property value to myImageFilePath, you'd see the column mappings morph to reflect the new name. Notice also that the ID property for the one output column is 71 and its ExternalMetaDataColumnID is set to 70. Clicking the one External Column reveals that its ID property is 70. From this, you can determine that if you had to create this transform using the Advanced Editor, you would have had to add both columns and link the external source (input) to the output source. Secondly you'd notice that you can add or remove outputs, but you are limited in this editor by the transformation as to what you can do to the output. You can't, for example, apply an expression against the output to transform the data as it flows through this transform. That makes sense because this transform has a specific task. It moves data from a flat file into a stream.

Connect the Flat File Source to the Import Column Transform Task. Open the Advanced Editor for the Import Column Transform and click the Input Columns tab. The input stream for this task is the output stream for the Flat File. Select the one available column, move to the Input and Output Properties tab, and expand these nodes. This time you don't have much help. An example of this editor can be seen in Figure 5-29. The input columns collection has a column named ImageFilePath, but there are no output columns. On the Flat File Source, you could ignore some of the inputs. In the Import Column Transform, all inputs have to be re-output. In fact, if you don't map an output, you'll get the following error:

```
Validation error. Data Flow Task: Import Column [1]: The "input column
"ImageFilePath" (164)" references output column ID 0, and that column is not
found on the output.
```

Add an output column by clicking the Output Columns folder icon and click the Add Column button. Name the column myImage. Notice that the DataType property is [DT_IMAGE] by default. That is because producing image outputs is what this transform does. You can also pass DT_TEXT, DT_NTEXT, or DT_IMAGE types as outputs from this task. Your last task is to connect the input to the output. Take note of the output column's ID property for myImage. This ID will need to be updated in the FileDataColumnID property of the input column ImageFilePath. If you fail to link the output column, you'll get this error:

```
Validation error. Data Flow Task: Import Column [1]: The "output column
"myImage" (207)" is not referenced by any input column. Each output column
must be referenced by exactly one input column.
```

The Advanced Editor for each of the different transforms follows a similar layout but may have other properties available. Another property of interest in this task is Expect BOM, which you would set to True if you expect a byte-order mark at the beginning of the file path. A completed editor would resemble Figure 5-29.

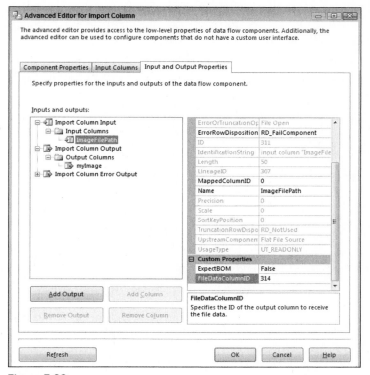

Figure 5-29

Complete this example by adding an OLE Destination to the Data Flow design surface. Connect the data from the Import Column to the OLE Destination. Configure the OLE Destination to the AdventureWorks2008 database and to the tblmyImages structure that was created for database storage. Click the Mappings setting. Notice that you have two available input columns from the Import Column Task. One is the full path and the other will be the file as DT_IMAGE type. Connect the input and destination columns to complete the transform. Go ahead and run it.

Take a look at the destination table to see the results:

```
FullFileName              Document
--------------------      ------------------------------------
C:\import\images\1.JPG    0xFFD8FFE120EE45786966000049492A00...
C:\import\images\2.JPG    0xFFD8FFE125FE45786966000049492A00...
C:\import\images\3.JPG    0xFFD8FFE1269B45786966000049492A00...
(3 row(s) affected)
```

Lookup Transform

The Lookup Transform performs what equates to an INNER JOIN on the Data Flow and a second dataset. The second dataset can be an OLE DB table or a cached file, which is loaded in the Cache Transform. After you perform the lookup, you can retrieve additional columns from the second column. If no match is found, an error will occur by default. You can later choose in the Configure Error Output button to ignore the failure (setting any additional columns retrieved from the reference table to NULL) or redirect the rows down the second non-matched green path. This is a very detailed transform and it is covered in much more detail in Chapter 7 and again in Chapter 8.

Merge Transform

The Merge Transform can merge data from two paths into a single output. The transform is useful when you wish to break out your Data Flow into a path that handles certain errors and then merge it back into the main Data Flow downstream after the errors have been handled. It's also useful if you wish to merge data from two Data Sources.

The transform is similar to the Union All Transformation, which you'll learn about in a moment, but the Merge Transform has some restrictions that may cause you to lean toward using Union All:

❑　The data must be sorted before the Merge Transform. You can do this by using the Sort Transform prior to the merge or by specifying an ORDER BY clause in the source connection.

❑　The metadata must be the same between both paths. For example, the CustomerID column can't be a numeric column in one path and a character column in another path.

❑　If you have more than two paths, you should choose the Union All Transformation.

To configure the transform, ensure that the data is sorted exactly the same on both paths and drag the path onto the transform. You'll be asked if the path you'd like to merge is Merge Input 1 or 2. If this is the first path you're connecting to the transform, select Merge Input 1. Next, connect the second path into the transform. The transformation will automatically configure itself. Essentially, it will map each of the columns to the column from the other path, and you have the choice to ignore a certain column's data.

Merge Join

One of the overriding themes of SSIS is that you shouldn't have to write any code to create your transformation. One case to prove this is the Merge Join Transformation. This transformation will merge the output of two inputs and perform an INNER or OUTER Join on the data. An example of where this would be useful is if you have a front-end web system in one data stream that has a review of a product in it, and you have an inventory product system in another data stream with the product data. You could merge the two data inputs together and output the review and product information into a single path.

If both inputs are in the same database, it would be faster to perform a join at the OLE DB Source level instead of using a transformation through TSQL. This transformation is useful when you have two different Data Sources you wish to merge, or when you don't want to write your own join code.

To configure the Merge Join Transformation, connect your two inputs into the Merge Join Transform, and then select what represents the right and left join as you connect each input. Open the Merge Join Transformation Editor and verify the linkage between the two tables. You can see an example of this in Figure 5-30. You can right-click the arrow to delete a linkage or drag a column from the left input onto the right input to create a new linkage if one is missing. Lastly, check each of the columns you want to be passed as output to the path and select the type of join you wish to make (LEFT, INNER, or FULL).

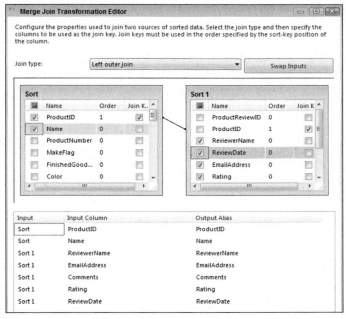

Figure 5-30

Multicast

The Multicast Transform, as the name implies, can send a single data input to multiple output paths easily. You may want to use this transformation to send a path to multiple destinations sliced in different ways. To configure the transform, simply connect the transform to your input, and then drag the output path from the Multicast Transform onto your next destination or transform. After you connect the Multicast Transform to your first destination or transform, you can keep connecting it to other transforms or destinations. There is nothing to configure in the Multicast Transformation Editor other than the names of the outputs.

> *The Multicast Transformation is similar to the Split Transform in that both transformations send data to multiple outputs. The Multicast will send all the rows from the path, whereas the Split will conditionally send part of the data to the path.*

OLE DB Command

The OLE DB Command Transform is a component designed to execute a SQL statement for each row in an input stream. This task is analogous to an ADO Command object being created, prepared, and executed for each row of a result set. The input stream provides the data for parameters that can be set into the SQL statement that is either an in-line statement or a stored procedure call. We don't know about you, but just hearing the "for each row" phrase in the context of SQL makes us think of another phrase — "performance degradation." This involves firing an update, insert, or delete statement, prepared or unprepared some unknown number of times. This doesn't mean there aren't any good reasons to use this transformation — you'll actually be doing a few in this chapter. Just understand the impact and think about your use of this transformation. Pay specific attention to the volume of input rows that will be fed into it. Weigh the performance and scalability aspects during your design phases against a solution that would cache the stream into a temporary table and use set-based logic instead.

To use the OLE DB Command Transform Task, you basically need to determine how to set up the connection where the SQL statement will be run, provide the SQL statement to be executed, and configure the mapping of any parameters in the input stream to the SQL statement. Take a look at the settings for the OLE DB Command Transformation by opening its editor. The OLE DB Command Transform is another component that uses the Advanced Editor. There are four tabs in the editor:

❑   **Connection Manager:** Allows the selection of an OLE DB Connection. This connection is where the SQL statement will be executed. This doesn't have to be the same connection that is used to provide the input stream.

❑   **Component Properties:** Here you can set the SQL Command statement to be executed in the SQLCommand property and set the amount of time to allow for a timeout in the CommandTimeout property in seconds. The property works the same way as the ADO Command object. The value for the CommandTimeout of 0 indicates no time-out. You can also name the task and provide a description in this tab.

❑   **Column Mappings:** This tab will display columns available in the input stream and the destination columns, which will be the parameters available in the SQL command. You can map the columns by clicking a column in the input columns and dragging it onto the matching destination parameter. It is a one-to-one mapping, so if you need to use a value for two parameters, you'll need use a Derived Column Transform to duplicate the column in the input stream prior to configuring the columns in this transform.

❑   **Input and Output Properties:** Most of the time you'll be able to map your parameters in the Column Mappings tab. However, if the OLE DB provider doesn't provide support for deriving parameter information (parameter refreshing), you'll have to come here to manually set up your output columns using specific parameter names and DBParamInfoFlags.

The easiest way to learn this task is by example. Suppose you have a requirement to process a small daily volume of validated, electronically sent deposit entries and to run them through logic to create deposit entries in your accounting database. You also have to build payment transactions that will need to be reviewed by accounting personnel using the accounting software, which applies the money to each customer's account. Fortunately, you don't need to know how to create deposit transactions or payment transactions. You've been given two stored procedures that will do the work of building the transactions, so you'll use them in the example.

1. Create an SSIS package named "OLE DB Command." Add a Data Flow Component to the Control Flow.

2. Create a text file containing the following entries and save it to `c:\Projects\ole db eft data.txt`. You can also download this file from www.wrox.com.

```
CustomerID,DepositAmt,DepositDate,Invoice
XY-111-222,$100.00,07/13/2005,222-063105
XX-Z11-232,$1000.00,07/13/2005,232-063105
XX-Y88-233,$555.00,07/13/2005,233-053105
```

3. Run the following SQL script to create the simulated stored procedures in your AdventureWorks2008 database (this script can also be downloaded from www.wrox.com).

```
USE ADVENTUREWORKS2008
GO
CREATE PROC usp_DepositTrans_Add (
            @CUSTOMERID varchar(10),
            @DEPOSITAMT money,
            @DEPOSITDATE smalldatetime,
            @INVOICE  varchar(15))

AS


     ---THIS IS A DUMMY PROCEDURE FOR DEMO PURPOSES
GO
CREATE PROC usp_PaymentTrans_Add (
            @CUSTOMERID varchar(10),
            @DEPOSITAMT money,
            @DEPOSITDATE smalldatetime,
            @INVOICE  varchar(15))

AS


     --THIS IS A DUMMY PROCEDURE FOR DEMO PURPOSES
```

4. Add a Flat File Source to your Data Flow to consume the comma-delimited text file `c:\projects\ole db eft file.txt`.

5. Add an OLE DB Command Transform Task to the Data Flow design surface. Connect the output of the Flat File Source to the OLE DB Command Transform.

6. Configure the OLE DB Command Transform Task to a connection to AdventureWorks2008. Update the SQLCommand property for the transform to add a deposit for each input row by setting the property to `usp_DepositTrans_Add ?, ?, ?, ?`. Each of the "?" marks stand in place of a parameter. Click Refresh to pull the parameters from the proc. The completed tab should look like Figure 5-31.

Figure 5-31

7. In the Column Mappings tab, map each column in the input columns collection to a column in the destination columns collection. This should look like Figure 5-32.

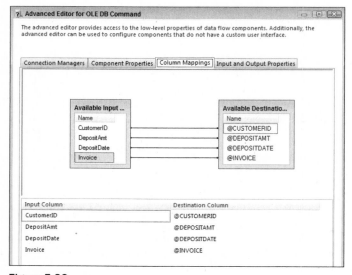

Figure 5-32

8. Add another OLE DB Command Transform Task to the Data Flow design surface. Connect the output of the first OLE DB Command Transform to the second and then go through the same configuration as for the deposit command, but this time set the SQLCommand property to `usp_PaymentTrans_Add ?, ?, ?, ?`.

When you run this package, you'll see that three rows were processed by each OLE DB Command Transform. If the procedures were functional, they would have created three deposit and three payment transactions. In this example, you found a good reason to use this task — reusability. If you have 2,000 rows running through the transform, this stored procedure would have been executed 2,000 times. It may be more efficient to process these transactions in a SQL batch, but then you'd have to stage the data and code the batch transaction. In this example, you were able to reuse existing logic that was designed for manual or one-at-a-time data entry and bundle that into an automated SSIS package fairly quickly. The main problem with this transformation is performance.

Percentage and Row Sampling

The Percentage and Row Sampling Transformations give you the ability to take the data from the source and randomly select a subset of data. The transformation produces two outputs that you can select. One output is the data that was randomly selected, and the other is the data that was not selected. You can use this to send a subset of data to a development or test server. The most useful application of this transform is to train a data-mining model. You can use one output path to train your data-mining model, and the sampling to validate the model.

To configure the transformation, select the percentage or number of rows you wish to be sampled. As you can imagine, the Percentage Sampling Transformation allows you to select the percentage of rows, and the Row Sampling Transformation allows you to specify how many rows you wish to be outputted randomly. Next, you can optionally name each of the outputs from the transformation. The last option is to specify the seed that will randomize the data. If you select a seed and run the transformation multiple times, the same data will be outputted to the destination. If you uncheck this option, which is the default, the seed will be automatically incremented by one each at runtime, and you will see random data each time.

Pivot Transform

Do you ever get the feeling that pivot tables are the modern-day Rosetta Stone for translating data to your business owners? You store it relationally, but they ask for it in a format that you have to write a complex case statement to generate. Well, not anymore. Now you can use an SSIS transformation to generate the results. A *pivot table* is a result of cross-tabulated columns generated by summarizing data from a row format. Prior to SQL Server 2005, a pivot table could be generated only by using a SELECT...CASE statement to build summary columns based on one field in the row.

Typically a Pivot Transform is generated using the following input columns:

❑ **Pivot Column:** A pivot column is the element of input data to "pivot." The word "pivot" is another way of saying "to create a column for each unique instance of." However, this data must be under control. Think about creating columns in a table. You wouldn't create 1,000 uniquely named columns in a table. So for best results when choosing a data element to pivot, pick an element that can be run through a GROUP BY statement that will generate 15 or fewer columns. If you are dealing with dates, use something like a DATENAME function to convert to the month or day of the year.

❑ **Row Columns:** Row columns are elements of input data that act as row (not column) identifiers. Just like any GROUP BY statement, some of the data are needed to define the group (row), whereas other data are just along for the ride.

❑ **Value Columns:** These columns are aggregations for data that provide the results in the matrix between the row columns and the pivot columns.

The Pivot Transform Task can accept an input stream, use your definitions of the preceding columns, and generate a pivot table output. It helps if you are familiar with your input needs and format your data prior to this transform. Aggregate the data using GROUP BY statements. Pay special attention to sorting by row columns — this can significantly alter your results.

The Pivot Transform Task uses the Advanced Editor to set up pivot rules. To set your expectations properly, you are going to have to define each of your literal pivot columns. A common misconception, and source of confusion, is approaching the Pivot Transform with the idea that you can simply set the pivot column to pivot by the month of the purchase date column, and the transformation should automatically build 12 pivot columns with the month of the year for you. It will not. It is your task to create an output column for each month of the year. If you are using colors as your pivot column, you'll need to add an output column for every possible color. What happens if columns are set up for Blue, Green, and Yellow, and the color Red appears in the input source? The Pivot Transform Task will fail. So plan ahead and know the possible pivots that can result from your choice of a pivot column or provide for an error output for data that doesn't match your expected pivot values.

In this example, you'll use some of the AdventureWorks2008 product and transactional history to generate a quick pivot table to show product quantities sold by month. This is a typical upper-management request and you can cover all the options with this example. Adventure Works Management wants a listing of each product with the total quantity of transactions by month for the year 2003.

First identify the pivot column. The month of the year looks like the data that is driving the creation of the pivot columns. The row data columns will be the product name and the product number. The value field will be the total number of transactions for the product in a matrix by month. Now you are ready to set up the Pivot Transformation.

1. Create a new SSIS project named "Pivot Example." Add a Data Flow Task to the Control Flow design surface.

2. Add an OLE DB Source Transform to the Data Flow design surface. Configure the connection to the AdventureWorks2008 database. Set the Data Access Mode to SQL Command. Add the following SQL statement into the SQL Command text box:

```
SELECT p.[Name] as ProductName, p.ProductNumber,
       datename(mm, t.TransactionDate) as TransMonth,
       sum(t.quantity) as TotQuantity
FROM production.product p
INNER JOIN production.transactionhistory t
ON t.productid = p.productid
WHERE t.transactiondate between '01/01/03' and '12/31/03'
GROUP BY p.[name], p.productnumber, datename(mm,t.transactiondate)
ORDER BY productname, datename(mm, t.transactiondate)
```

3. Add the Pivot Transform and connect the output of the OLE DB Source to the input of the transform. Open the Advanced Editor and navigate to the Input Columns tab. In many of the transforms, you have the option of passing through some values from the input to the output. In the Pivot Transform, you have to select all the columns that will be included in the output of the Pivot. All nonselected input columns will be ignored. Select all the input columns for this example.

4. Move to the Input and Output Properties tab. There is a collection of input, output, and error outputs. Remember that the input columns are the raw data coming in. The output columns will be the pivot data coming out. Figure 5-33 shows the input columns expanded and a view of the properties for the ProductName column. There are two important properties in that property editor:

❑ The LineageID property can't be changed, but you will need to know it in order to map output columns to an input column.

❑ The PivotUsage has to be set using the following codes:

    ❑ **0:** The column is just passed through as a row attribute.

    ❑ **1:** The column is the "part of column" (BOL calls this the Set Key).

    ❑ **2:** The pivot column.

    ❑ **3:** The value column.

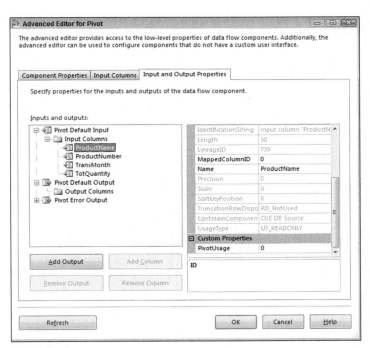

Figure 5-33

5. Set the PivotUsage properties for each of the Input Columns to match these codes:

❑ **ProductName:** 0 — A row attribute

❑ **ProductNumber:** 1 — A row identifier

❑ **TransMonth:** 2 — The pivot column

❑ **TotQuantity:** 3 — The value column

6. Expand the Output Column Node. Click the Add Column button to add a column to the output column collection. Set the name of the new output column to ProductName. Set the SourceColumn value to the LineageID of the same-named input column. Do the same thing for the ProductNumber column. Figure 5-34 shows an example of the properties that appear for the output column. There are some new properties here:

- ❑ **Comparison Flags:** Allows ignoring of case, kana type, nonspacing characters, character width, and symbols when sorting the field. The defaults use each of these settings when sorting.

- ❑ **SortKeyPosition:** Provides for custom sorting by position. Each field has a number that indicates the order by which it is sorted. A zero (0) indicates that it is nonsorted. A one (1) indicates that it is sorted.

- ❑ **PivotKeyValue:** This property is important only for the output columns that you define for the pivot column. In this column, you'll place the exact text or an expression that will resolve to the groupings that you want to appear as your pivot columns. When pivoting on colors, this value would be Blue, Green, or Red.

- ❑ **SourceColumn:** This property requires the LineageID (not the ID) of the source column. This is a "poor man's" way of connecting the input columns to the output columns.

The output columns will be generated in exactly the same order that they appear on the output columns collection. You can't move them once they are added either, so pay attention to this as you add output columns.

Figure 5-34

7. Add an output column named "January." Now for the big secret to making the whole thing work: Set the source column value to the LineageID of the TotQuantity column — *not* the TransMonth column. Remember that you are building a two-dimensional grid. The TransMonth field dictates one of the dimensions. The value in the column should be the total quantity at that dimension. Set the PivotKeyValue to "January" (without quotes). The pivot key is the literal value that will be examined in the data to determine when to put a value in a column. It is important that the incoming data sorts on this column to get consistent results. Repeat this process of creating an output column for each month of the year.

    Do not use the LineageID values that you see in any of these figures. LineageIDs are specific to your own examples.

8. To finish the example, add an OLE DB Destination. Configure to the AdventureWorks2008 connection. Connect the Pivot Default Output to the input of the OLE DB Destination. Click the New button to alter the CREATE TABLE statement to build a table named PivotTable.

9. Add a Data Viewer in the pipe between the PIVOT and OLE DB destination and run the package. You'll see the data in a pivot table in the Data Viewer as in the partial results seen in Figure 5-35.

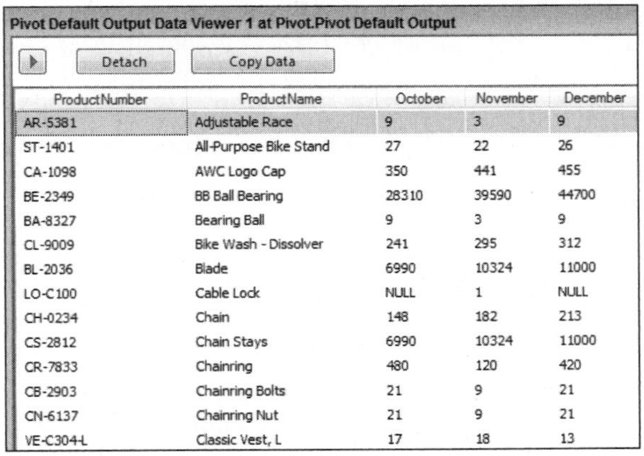

Pivot Default Output Data Viewer 1 at Pivot.Pivot Default Output

ProductNumber	ProductName	October	November	December
AR-5381	Adjustable Race	9	3	9
ST-1401	All-Purpose Bike Stand	27	22	26
CA-1098	AWC Logo Cap	350	441	455
BE-2349	BB Ball Bearing	28310	39590	44700
BA-8327	Bearing Ball	9	3	9
CL-9009	Bike Wash - Dissolver	241	295	312
BL-2036	Blade	6990	10324	11000
LO-C100	Cable Lock	NULL	1	NULL
CH-0234	Chain	148	182	213
CS-2812	Chain Stays	6990	10324	11000
CR-7833	Chainring	480	120	420
CB-2903	Chainring Bolts	21	9	21
CN-6137	Chainring Nut	21	9	21
VE-C304-L	Classic Vest, L	17	18	13

Figure 5-35

Unpivot

As you know, mainframe screens rarely conform to any normalized form. For example, a screen may show a Bill To Customer, a Ship To Customer and a Dedicated To Customer field. Typically the Data Source would store these three fields as three columns in a file [such as virtual storage access system (VSAM)]. So, when you receive an extract from the mainframe you may have three columns as shown in Figure 5-36.

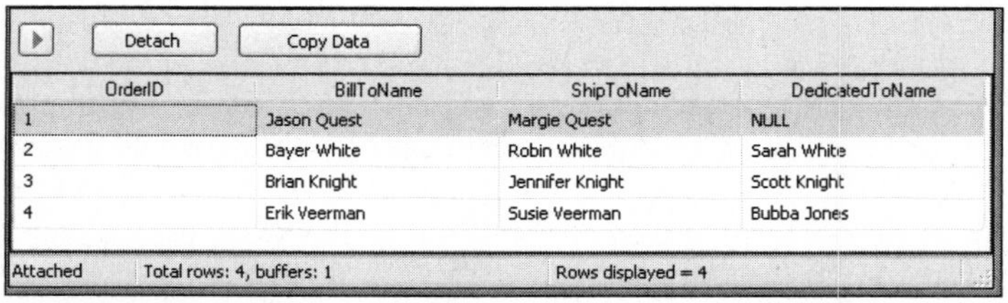

OrderID	BillToName	ShipToName	DedicatedToName
1	Jason Quest	Margie Quest	NULL
2	Bayer White	Robin White	Sarah White
3	Brian Knight	Jennifer Knight	Scott Knight
4	Erik Veerman	Susie Veerman	Bubba Jones

Attached   Total rows: 4, buffers: 1   Rows displayed = 4

Figure 5-36

Your goal is to load this file into a Customer table in SQL Server. You want a row for each customer in each column for a total of 13 rows in the Customer table as shown in the CustomerName and OrderID columns in Figure 5-37.

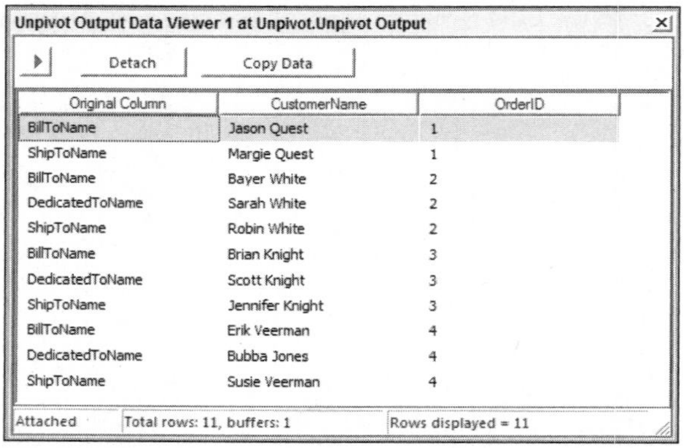

Unpivot Output Data Viewer 1 at Unpivot.Unpivot Output

Original Column	CustomerName	OrderID
BillToName	Jason Quest	1
ShipToName	Margie Quest	1
BillToName	Bayer White	2
DedicatedToName	Sarah White	2
ShipToName	Robin White	2
BillToName	Brian Knight	3
DedicatedToName	Scott Knight	3
ShipToName	Jennifer Knight	3
BillToName	Erik Veerman	4
DedicatedToName	Bubba Jones	4
ShipToName	Susie Veerman	4

Attached   Total rows: 11, buffers: 1   Rows displayed = 11

Figure 5-37

The Unpivot Transform is a way to accomplish this business requirement. In this example, you'll be shown how to use the Unpivot Transform to create rows in the Data Flow from columns and is the opposite of the Pivot Transform.

Our first step is to create a new package and drag over a new Data Flow Task onto the Control Flow. Go into the Data Flow tab to configure the task. For this example, create a Flat File Connection Manager that points to `PivotExample.csv`, which looks like Figure 5-38 and can be downloaded from www.wrox .com. Name the Connection Manager Pivot Source, and the first row is a header row. The file is comma-delimited so you will want to specify the delimiter on the Columns page.

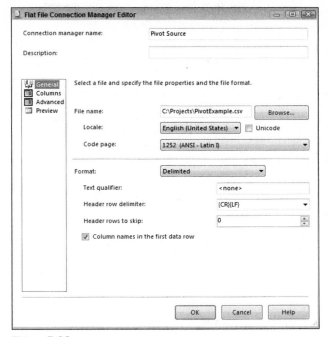

Figure 5-38

Once the Connection Manager is created, add a new Flat File Source and rename it "Mainframe Data." Point the connection to the Pivot Source Connection Manager. Ensure that all the columns are checked in the Columns page on the source and click OK to go back to the Data Flow.

The next step is the most important step. Now, you need to unpivot the data and make each column into a row in the Data Flow. You can do this by dragging an Unpivot Transform onto the Data Flow and connect it to the source. In this example, you want to unpivot the BillToName, ShipToName, and the DedicatedToName columns; and the OrderID column will just be passed through for each row. To do this, check each column you wish to unpivot as shown in Figure 5-39, and check Pass Through for the OrderID column.

As you check each column that you wish to unpivot on, the column will be added to the grid below (shown in Figure 5-39). You'll then need to type CustomerName for the Destination Column property for each row in the grid. This will write the data from each of the three columns into a single column called CustomerName. Optionally, you can also type "Original Column" for the Pivot Key Column Name property. By doing this, each row that's written by the transform will have an additional column called Original Column. This new column will state where the data came from.

Figure 5-39

The Pivot Transform will take care of columns that have NULL values. For example, if your DedicatedToName column for OrderID 1 had a NULL value as shown in Figure 5-36, that column will not be written as a row. You may wish to handle empty string values though, which will create blank rows in the Data Flow. To throw these records out, you can use a Conditional Split Transform. In this transform, you can create one condition for your good data that you wish to keep with the following code, which only brings rows with actual data:

```
ISNULL(CustomerName) ==  FALSE  && TRIM(CustomerName) != ""
```

The else condition handles empty string and NULL customers and in this example is called NULL Customer. After this, you're ready to send the data to the destination of your choice. The simplest example is to send the data to a new SQL Server table in the AdventureWorks2008 database.

Execute the package, and you'll see that the Valid Customer output goes to the customer table, and the NULL data condition just gets thrown out. You could also place a data viewer prior to the OLE DB Destination to see the data interactively.

Row Count

The Row Count Transformation provides the ability to count rows in a stream that is directed to its input source. This transformation must place that count into a variable that could be used in the Control Flow for inserting into an audit table, for example. This transformation is useful for tasks that require knowing "How many?" It is especially valuable since you don't physically have to commit stream data to a physical table to retrieve the count, and it can act as a destination, terminating your data stream. If you need to know how many rows are split during the Conditional Split Transformation, direct the output of each side of the split to a separate Row Count Transformation. Each Row Count Transformation is designed for an input stream and will output a row count into a Long (integer) or compatible data type. You can then use this variable to log information into storage, to build e-mail messages, or to conditionally run steps in your packages.

This transformation uses the Advanced Editor. As you recall, you used this editor in the Import Columns section of this chapter. Configuring this transformation is much easier though. All you really need to provide in terms of configuration is the name of the variable to store the count of the input stream.

You will now simulate a situation where you have a conditional step in a package that should run only if an input stream row count is evaluated to have a row count greater than zero. You could use this type of logic to implement conditional execution of any task, but for simplicity, you'll conditionally execute a SQL statement.

1. Create an SSIS package named Row Count Example. Add a Data Flow Task to the Control Flow design surface.

2. In the Control Flow tab, add a variable named MyRowCount. Ensure that the variable is package scoped and of type Int32. If you don't know how to add a variable, select Variable from the SSIS menu and click the Add Variable button.

3. Create a Connection Manager that connects to the AdventureWorks2008 database. Add an OLE DB Data Source to the Data Flow design surface. Configure the source to point to your AdventureWorks2008 database's Connection Manager and the table [ErrorLog].

4. Add a Row Count Transformation Task to the Data Flow tab. Open the Advanced Editor. Select the variable named User::MyRowCount as the VariableName property. Your editor should resemble Figure 5-40.

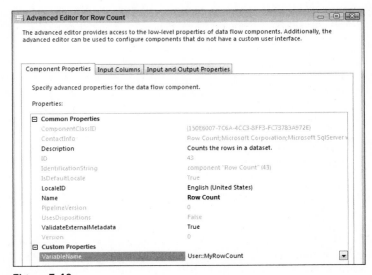

Figure 5-40

5. Return to the Control Flow tab and add a Script Task. This task is not really going to perform any action. It will be used to show the conditional ability to perform steps based on the value returned by the Row Count Transformation.

6. Connect the Data Flow Task to the Script Task.

7. Right-click the arrow connecting the Data Flow and Script Tasks. Select the Edit menu. In the Precedence Constraint Editor, change the Evaluation Operation to Expression. Set the Expression to @MyRowCount>0.

When you run the package, you'll see that the Script Task is not executed. If you are curious, insert a row into the [ErrorLog] table and rerun the package or change the source table that has data. You'll see that the Script Task will turn green, indicating that it was executed as shown in Figure 5-41.

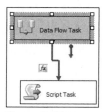

Figure 5-41

Script Component

The Script Component Transform allows you to write custom scripts as transforms, sources, or destinations. Some of the things you can do with this transform include the following:

❑ Create a custom transform that would use a .NET assembly to validate credit card numbers or mailing addresses.

❑ Validate data and skip records that don't seem reasonable. For example, you can use it in a human resource recruitment system to pull out candidates that don't match the salary requirement at a job code level.

❑ Write a custom component to integrate with a third-party vendor.

Scripts used as sources can support multiple outputs, and you have the option of precompiling the scripts for runtime efficiency. You learn much more about the Scripting Component Transform in Chapter 9.

Slowly Changing Dimension

The Slowly Changing Dimension (SCD) Transform provides a great head start in helping to solve a common, classic changing-dimension problem that occurs in the outer edge of your data model — the dimension or lookup tables. The changing-dimension issue in online transaction and analytical processing database designs is too big to cover in this chapter, but a little background may be necessary to help you understand the value of service the SCD Transformation provides.

A dimension table contains a set of discrete values with a description and often other measurable attributes such as price, weight, or sales territory. The classic problem is what to do in your dimension data when an attribute in a row changes, particularly when you are loading data automatically through an ETL process. This transform can shave days off of your development time in relation to creating the load manually through TSQL. Loading data warehouses is covered in Chapter 10.

Sort

The Sort Transformation is an asynchronous transform that allows you to sort data based on any column in the path. This will probably be one of the top ten transformations you use on a regular basis because some other transforms require sorted data. To configure the transform, open the Sort Transformation Editor once it's connected to the path and check the column that you wish to sort by. Then, uncheck any column you don't want passed through to the path from the Pass Through column. By default, every column will be passed through the pipeline. You can see this in Figure 5-42, where the user is sorting by the Name column and passing all other columns in the path as output.

In the bottom grid, you can specify the alias that you wish to output and whether you're going to sort in ascending or descending order. The Sort Order column shows which column will be sorted on first, second, third, and so on. You can optionally check the Remove Rows with Duplicate Sort Values option to "Remove rows that have duplicate sort values." This is a great way to do rudimentary de-duplication of your data. If a second value comes in that matches your same sort key, it is ignored and the row is dropped.

It's important to note that this transform is an asynchronous transform and will slow down your Data Flow immensely. Use these only when you have to and sparingly.

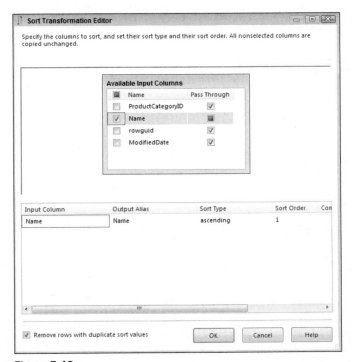

Figure 5-42

185

As was mentioned previously, you should avoid using the Sort Transform when you can due to speed. However, some transforms like the Merge Join require the data be sorted. If you place an ORDER BY statement in the OLE DB Source, SSIS is not aware of the ORDER BY statement because it could just have easily been in a stored procedure.

If you have an ORDER BY clause in your TSQL statement in the OLE DB Source or the ADO.NET Source, you can notify SSIS that the data is already sorted, alleviating the need for the Sort Transform in the Advanced Editor. After ordering the data in your SQL statement, right-click the source and select Advanced Editor. Go to the Input and Output Properties and select the OLE DB Source Output. In the Properties pane, change the IsSorted property to True.

Then, under Output Columns, select the column you are ordering on in your SQL statement, and change the SortKeyPosition to 1 if you're only sorting by a single column ascending as shown in Figure 5-43. If you have multiple columns, you could change this SortKeyPosition value to the column position in the ORDER BY statement starting at 1. A value of -1 would sort the data in descending order.

Figure 5-43

Term Extraction

If you have done some word and phrase analysis on websites for better search engine placement, you will be familiar with the job that this transformation Task performs. The Term Extraction Transformation is a tool to mine free-flowing text for word and phrase frequency. You can feed any text-based input stream into the transformation and it will output two columns: a text phrase and a statistical value for the phrase relative to the total input stream. The statistical values or scores that can be calculated can be as simple as a count of the frequency of the words and phrases, or they can be a little more complicated as the result of a formula named TFIDF score. The TFIDF acronym stands for Term Frequency and Inverse Document Frequency, and it is a formula designed to balance the frequency of the distinct words and phrases relative to the total text sampled. If you're interested, here's the formula:

```
TDIDF (of a term or phrase) = (frequency of term) * log((# rows in sample)/
(# rows with term or phrase))
```

The results generated by the Term Extraction Transformation are based on internal algorithms and statistical models that are encapsulated in the component. You can't alter or gain any insight into this logic by examining the code. However, some of the core rules for how the logic breaks apart the text to determine word and phrase boundaries are documented in Books Online. What you can do is tweak some external settings and make adjustments to the extraction behavior by examining the resulting output. Since text extraction is domain-specific, the transform also provides the ability to store terms and phrases that you have predetermined are noisy or insignificant in your final results. You can then automatically remove these items from future extractions. Within just a few testing iterations, you can have the transform producing meaningful results.

Before you write this transformation off as a cool utility that you'll never use, consider this: How useful would it be to query into something like a customer service memo field stored in your data warehouse and generate some statistics about the comments that are being made? This is the type of use for which the Term Extraction Transform is perfectly suited. The trick to understanding how to use the component is to remember that it has one input. That input must be either a NULL-terminated ANSI (DT_WSTR) or Unicode (DT_NTEXT) string. If your input stream is not one of these two types, you can use the Data Conversion Transform to convert it. Since this transformation can best be learned by playing around with all the settings, put this transform to work on exactly what we proposed before — mining some customer service memo fields.

You have a set of comment fields from a customer service database for an appliance manufacturer. In this field, the customer service representative will record a note that summarizes the contact with the customer. For simplicity's sake, you'll create these comment fields in a text file and analyze them in the Term Extraction Transformation.

1. Create the customer service text file using the following text (download this file from www.wrox.com). Save it as c:\projects\custsvc.txt.

    ```
    Ice maker in freezer stopped working model XX-YY3
    Door to refrigerator is coming off model XX-1
    Ice maker is making a funny noise XX-YY3
    Handle on fridge falling off model XX-Z1
    Freezer is not getting cold enough XX-1
    Ice maker grinding sound fridge XX-YY3
    Customer asking how to get the ice maker to work model XX-YY3
    Customer complaining about dent in side panel model XX-Z1
    Dent in model XX-Z1
    Customer wants to exchange model XX-Z1 because of dent in door
    Handle is wiggling model XX-Z1
    ```

2. Create a new SSIS package. Add a Data Flow Task to the Control Flow design surface.

3. Create a Flat File connection to c:\projects\custsvc.txt. Change the output column named in the Advanced tab to CustSvcNote. Change OutputColumnWidth to 100 to account for the length of the field.

4. Add a Flat File Source to the Data Flow design surface. Configure the source to use the Flat File connection.

5. Since the Flat File Source output is string (DT_STR), you'll need to convert the string to either the DT_WSTR or DT_NTEXT data type. Add a Data Conversion Transform to the Data Flow design surface and connect the output of the Flat File Source. Set the Input Column to CustSvcNote, the Output Alias to ConvCustSvcNote, and the Data Type to Unicode string [DT_WSTR]. Click OK to save.

6. Add a Term Extraction Transform to the Data Flow design surface. Connect the output of the Data Conversion Transform to its input. Open the Term Extraction Editor. Figure 5-44 shows the available input columns from the input stream and the two default-named output columns. You can change the named output columns if you wish. Only one input column can be chosen. Click the column ConvCustSvcNote, since this is the column that is converted to a Unicode string. If you click the unconverted column, you'll see a validation error like the following:

The input column can only have DT_WSTR or DT_NTEXT as its data type.

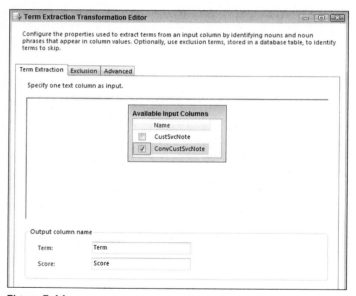

Figure 5-44

7. Even though we're not going to set these tabs, the Exclusion tab would allow you to specify noise words for the Term Extraction to ignore. The Advanced tab allows you to control how many times the word must appear before you output it as evidence. Close the Term Extraction Editor. Ignore the cautionary warnings about rows sent to error outputs. You didn't configure an error location for bad rows to be saved, but it's not necessary for this example.

8. Add an OLE DB Destination to the Data Flow. Connect the output of the Term Extraction Task to the OLE DB Destination. Configure the OLE DB Destination to use your AdventureWorks2008 connection.

9. Click the New button to configure the Name of Table or View property. A window will come up with a CREATE TABLE DDL statement. Notice that the data types are a Unicode text field and a double. Alter the statement to read:

```
CREATE TABLE [TermResults] (
    [Term] NVARCHAR(128),
    [Score] DOUBLE PRECISION
)
```

10. When you click OK, the new table TermResults will be created in the AdventureWorks2008 database. Click the Mappings tab to confirm the mapping between the Term Extract outputs of Term and Score to the table [TermResults].

11. Add a Data Viewer by right-clicking the Data Flow between the Term Extract Transform and the OLE DB Destination. Set the type to grid and accept defaults.

12. Run the package.

The package will stop on the Data Viewer that is shown in Figure 5-45 to allow you to view the results of the Term Extract Transform. You should see a list of terms and an associated score for each word. Since you just accepted all of the Term Extraction settings, the default score is a simple count of frequency. Stop the package, open the Term Extraction Transformation Editor, and view the Advanced tab.

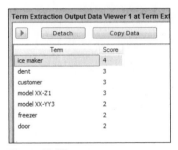

Figure 5-45

The Advanced tab allows for some configuration of the task and can be divided into four categories:

❑ **Term Type:** Settings that control how the input stream should be broken into bits called *tokens*. The Noun Term Type will focus the transform on nouns only, Noun Phrases will extract noun phrases, and Noun and Noun Phrases will extract both.

❑ **Score Type:** Choose between analyzing words by frequency or by a weighted frequency.

❑ **Parameters:** Frequency threshold is the minimum number of times a word or phrase must appear in tokens. Maximum length of term is the maximum number of words that should be combined together for evaluation.

❑ **Options:** Check this option to consider case-sensitivity or leave unchecked to disregard.

This is where the work really starts. How you set the transform up really affects the results you'll see. Figure 5-46 shows an example of the results using each of the different Term Type (noun) settings combined with the different score types [Tascam Digital Interface (TDIF)].

Figure 5-46

One of the unusual things to notice is that the term "model XX-Z1" shows a frequency score of 3 when the Term Type option is set to "Both," even though you can physically count five instances of this phrase in the customer service data. However, the term "XX-Z1" is counted with the correct frequency when you break the source text into nouns only. This demonstrates that the statistical models are sensitive to where and how noun phrases are used. As a consequence, the tagging of noun phrases may not be completely accurate.

At the moment, using a combination of these statistics, you can report that customer service is logging a high percentage of calls concerning the terms "model," "model XX-Z1," "model XX-YY3," "ice maker," "dent," and "customer." An assumption can be made that there may be some issues with models XX-Z1 and XX-YY3 that your client needs to look into.

In evaluating this data, you may determine that some words over time are just not of interest to the analysis. In this example, the words "model" and "customer" really serve no purpose but to dampen the scores for other words. To remove these words from your analysis, take advantage of the exclusion features in the Term Extraction Transform by adding these words to a table with a single Unicode NULL-terminated string column.

To really make sense of that word list, you need to add some human intervention and the next transform — Term Lookup.

Term Lookup

The Term Lookup Transform uses the same algorithms and statistical models as the Term Extraction Transform to break up an incoming stream into noun or noun phrase tokens, but it is designed to compare those tokens to a stored word list and output a matching list of terms and phrases with simple frequency counts. Now a strategy for working with both term-based transforms should become clear. Periodically use the Term Extraction Transform to mine the text data and to generate lists of statistical phrases. Store these phrases in a word list, along with phrases that you think the term extraction process should identify. Remove the phrases that you don't want identified. Use the Term Lookup Transform to reprocess the text input to generate your final statistics. This way, you are generating statistics on known phrases of importance. A real-world application of this would be to pull out all the customer service notes that had a given set of terms or that mention a competitor's name.

You can use results from the Term Extraction example by removing the word "model" from the [TermExclusions] table for future Term Extractions. You would then want to review all of the terms stored in the [TermResults] table, sort them out, remove the duplicates, and add back terms that make sense to your subject matter experts reading the text. Since you want to generate some statistics about which model numbers are generating customer service calls, but you don't want to restrict your extractions to only the occurrences of the model number in conjunction with the word "model," remove phrases combining the word "model" and the model number. The final [TermResults] table looks like a dictionary and should look something like the following:

```
term
------------
dent
door
freezer
ice
ice maker
maker
XX-1
XX-YY3
XX-Z1
```

Take a copy of the package you built in the Extraction example, but exchange the Term Extraction Transform for a Term Lookup Transform and change the OLE Destination to output to a table [TermReport].

Open the Term Lookup Editor. It should look similar to Figure 5-47. In the Reference Table tab, change the Reference Table Name option to TermResults. In the Term Lookup tab, map the ConvCustSvrNote column to the Term column on the right. Check the ConvCustSvrNote as a pass-through column. There are three basic tabs used to set up this task (in the Term Lookup tab):

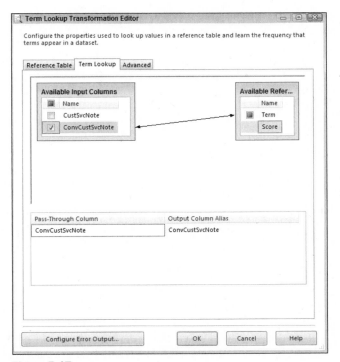

Figure 5-47

❑ **Reference Table:** This is where you will configure the connection to the reference table. The Term Lookup Task should be used to validate each tokenized term that it finds in the input stream.

❑ **Term Lookup:** After selecting the lookup table, you will map the field from the input stream to the reference table for matching.

❑ **Advanced:** This tab has one setting to check if the matching is case-sensitive.

The results of running this package will be a list of phrases that you are expecting from your stored word list. A sample of the first six rows is displayed in the following code. Notice that this result set doesn't summarize the findings. You are just given a blow-by-blow report on the number of terms in the word list that were found for each row of the customer service notes. In this text sample, it is just a coincidence that each term appears only once in each note.

```
Term            Frequency   ConvCustSvcNote
------------    ---------   -------------------------------------------------
freezer             1       ice maker in freezer stopped working model XX-YY3
ice maker           1       ice maker in freezer stopped working model XX-YY3
XX-YY3              1       ice maker in freezer stopped working model XX-YY3
door                1       door to refrigerator is coming off model XX-1
XX-1                1       door to refrigerator is coming off model XX-1
ice maker           1       ice maker is making a funny noise XX-YY3
(Only first six rows of resultset are displayed)
```

To complete the report, add an Aggregate Transform between the Term Lookup Transform and the OLE DB Destination Transform. Set up the Aggregate Transform to ignore the ConvCustSvcNote column, group by the Term column, and summarize the Frequency Column. Connect the Aggregate Transform to the OLE DB Destination and remap the columns in the OLE DB Transform.

Although this is a very rudimentary example, you will start to see the possibilities of using SSIS for very raw and unstructured Data Sources like this customer service comment data. In a short period of time, you have pulled some meaningful results from the data. Already you can provide the intelligence that model XX-Z1 is generating 45% of your sample calls and that 36% of your customer calls are related to the ice maker. Pretty cool results from what is considered unstructured data. This transform is often used for advanced text mining.

Union All

The Union All Transform works much the same way as the Merge Transform, but it does not require the data be sorted. It takes the outputs from multiple sources or transforms and combines them into a single result set. For example, in Figure 5-48, the user combines the data from three Data Conversion Transforms into a single output using the Union All Transform, and then sends the single result set into the Term Lookup Transform.

To configure the transform, connect the first source or transformation to the Union All Transform, and then continue to connect the other sources or transforms to it until you are complete. You can optionally open the Union All Editor to make sure the columns map correctly, but SSIS will take care of that for you automatically. The transform fixes minor metadata issues. For example, if you have one input that is a 20-character string and another that is 50 characters, the output of this from the Union All Transform will be the longer 50-character column. You will only need to open the Union All Editor if the column names from one of the transforms that feed the Union All Transform have a different column name.

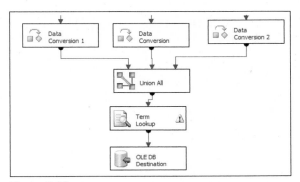

Figure 5-48

Data Flow Example

Now you can practice what you've learned in this chapter and pull together some of the transforms and connections to create a small ETL process. This process will pull transactional data from the AdventureWorks2008 database and then massage the data by aggregating, sorting, and calculating new columns. This extract may be used by another vendor or an internal organization.

1.   Create a new package and rename it `AdventureWorks2008Extract.dtsx`. Start by dragging a Data Flow Task onto the Control Flow. Double-click the task to go to the Data Flow tab.

2.   In the Data Flow tab, drag an OLE DB Source onto the design pane. Right-click the source and rename it TransactionHistory. Double-click it to open the editor. Click the New button next to the OLE DB Connection Manager drop-down box. The connection to the AdventureWorks2008 database may already be in the Data Connections list on the left. If it is, select it, and click OK. If it's not there yet, click New to add a new connection to the AdventureWorks2008 database on any server.

3.   When you click OK, you'll be taken back to the OLE DB Source Editor. Ensure that the Data Access Mode option is set to "Table or View." Select the [Production].[TransactionHistoryArchive] table from the "Name of the table" drop-down box, as shown in Figure 5-49.

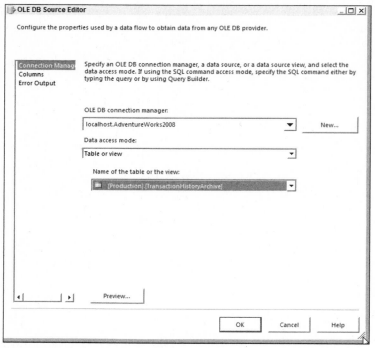

Figure 5-49

4. Go to the Columns page (shown in Figure 5-50) and uncheck every column except for ProductID, Quantity, and ActualCost. Click OK to exit the editor.

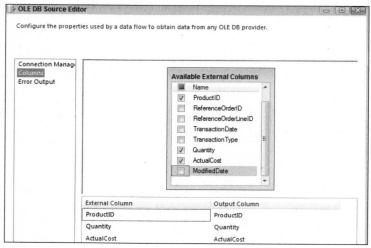

Figure 5-50

5. Drag a Derived Column Transform onto the Data Flow, right-click it, and select Rename. Rename the transform "Calculate Total Cost." Click the TransactionHistory OLE DB Source and drag the green arrow (the data path) onto the Derived Column Transform.

6. Double-click the Derived Column Transform to open the editor (shown in Figure 5-51). For the Expression column, type the following code or drag and drop the column names from the upper-left box: **[Quantity]* [ActualCost]**. The Derived Column should have the <add as a new column> option selected, and type **TotalCost** for the Derived Column Name option. Click OK to exit the editor.

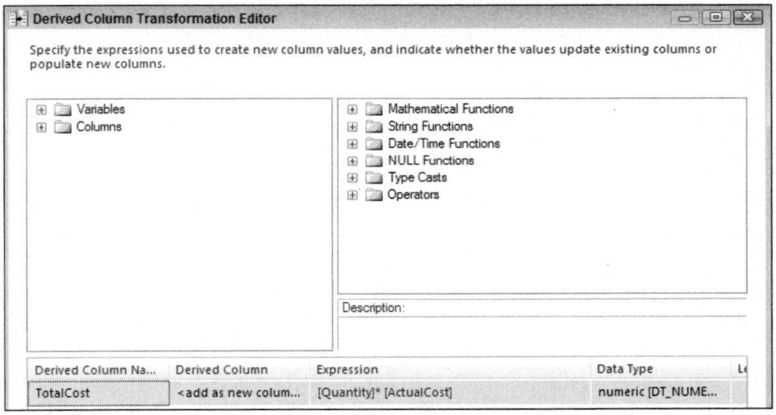

Figure 5-51

7. Drag an Aggregate Transform onto the Data Flow and rename it "Aggregate Data." Drag the green arrow from the Derived Column Transform onto this transform. Double-click the Aggregate Transform to open the editor (shown in Figure 5-52). Select the ProductID column and note that it is transposed into the bottom section. The ProductID column should have Group By for the Operation column. Next, check the Quantity and TotalCost columns and set the operation of both of these columns to Sum. Click OK to exit the editor.

Figure 5-52

8. Drag a Sort Transform onto the Data Flow and rename it "Sort by ProductID." Connect the Aggregate Transform to this transform by the green arrow as in the preceding step. Double-click the Sort Transform to configure it in the editor. You can sort by the most popular products, by checking the Quantity column and selecting Descending for the Sort Type drop-down box. Click OK to exit the editor.

9. You've now done enough massaging of the data and are ready to export the data to a flat file that can be consumed by another vendor. Drag a Flat File Destination onto the Data Flow. Connect it to the Sort Transform by using the green arrow as you saw in the last few steps. Rename the Flat File Destination "Vendor Extract."

10. Double-click the destination to open the Flat File Destination Editor. You're going to output the data to a new Connection Manager, so click New. When prompted for the Flat File Format, select Delimited. Name the Connection Manager "Vendor Extract" also, and type whatever description you'd like. If you have the directory, point the File Name option to `C:\Projects\VendorExtract.csv` (make sure this directory is created before proceeding). Check the Column Names in the First Data Row option. Your final screen should look like Figure 5-53. Click OK to go back to the Flat File Destination Editor.

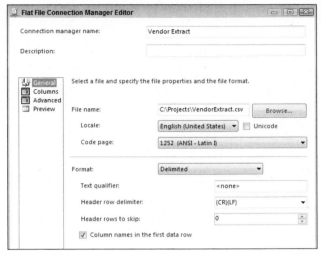

Figure 5-53

11. Go to the Mappings page and make sure that each column in the Inputs table is mapped to the Destination table. Click OK to exit the editor and go back to the Data Flow.

Now, your first larger ETL package is complete! This package is very typical of what you'll be doing day-to-day inside of SSIS, and you will see this expanded on greatly, in Chapter 8. Execute the package and you should see the rows flow through the Data Flow as shown in Figure 5-54. Note that as the data flows from transform to transform you can see how many records were passed through the transform.

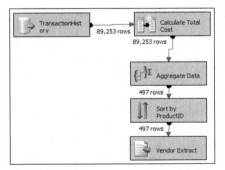

Figure 5-54

Summary

In this chapter, you learned about containers and transformations. Containers allow you as an SSIS developer to group tasks or loop through a series of tasks. Transformations allow you to change the data from a source or another transform and pass the results as output to a destination or another transformation in the path. In the next chapter, you learn how to use the SSIS expression language that is used throughout many of the transforms and tasks.

6

Using Expressions and Variables

If you have used SSIS or DTS packages for any involved ETL process, you have inevitably encountered the need to have dynamic capabilities. A *dynamic package* can reconfigure itself at runtime to do things like run certain steps conditionally, to create a series of auto-generated filenames for export, or to retrieve and set send-to addresses on an alert email from a data table. The paradigm shifted radically on how to do this as SQL Server evolved from DTS to the current SSIS packages and frankly, expressions was one of the features that was under-represented in the Books Online. As a result, the concept of expressions was a topic of many inquires as developers and architects began rolling out SSIS projects in their development shops.

This chapter is our attempt to remedy the confusion and get you up to speed on expressions. Here we will consolidate the common questions, answers, and best practices about expressions that we've been hearing about and explaining since the first release of SSIS. The good news is that expressions are easy to use and impressively powerful. The even better news is that Microsoft has now supplemented the Books Online with a hefty section on expressions. As you read this chapter you will gain an understanding not only about how expressions work, but you'll also gain some insight to how you can use expressions now on your current SSIS project.

The Paradigm

The model in DTS for realizing values and stuffing them into properties of a package was largely a "push" paradigm. The need for dynamic capabilities was important. The first versions of DTS required that you use an ActiveX Script Task to accomplish this dynamic capability. First, you'd create a value, and then use the ActiveX Script Task to navigate and set the property in the DTS model programmatically. Later when SQL Server 2000 arrived, the Dynamic Property task appeared and made the task of pushing the values into the model a little easier. The Dynamic Property task gathered the DTS package model into one user-navigable interface where individual properties could be set. Typically, you'd still need to retrieve the value with the ActiveX script, but instead of navigating the package model, all you had to do was stuff the value into an intermediate variable for the Dynamic Property task to retrieve.

If you implemented only the first method of dynamically configuring DTS packages, then the SSIS model is almost the opposite paradigm and can take some getting used to. If you have used the dynamic property model in DTS, you'll find the "variable-value-parking" aspect a familiar place to start understanding expressions in SSIS. Figure 6-1 provides a graphical description of the new expression paradigm in SSIS. SSIS uses a "pull" paradigm where a property in the task or transform objects is set either directly to an expression or to a variable that is resolved from an expression. When the package is run, the value of the expression is pulled into the property as each task or transform is accessed.

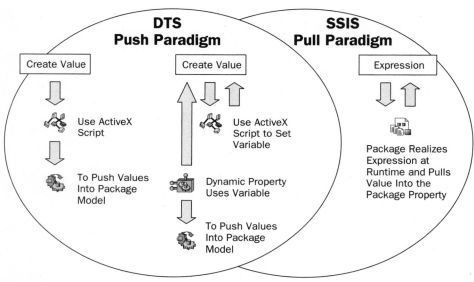

Figure 6-1

Expression Overview

Expressions are the key to understanding how to create dynamic packages in SSIS. One way to think about expressions is by comparing them to the familiar model of a spreadsheet cell in a program like Microsoft Excel. A spreadsheet cell can hold a literal value, a reference to another cell on the spreadsheet, or functions ranging from simple to complex arrangements. In each instance, the result is a resolved value displayed in the cell. Figure 6-2 shows these same capabilities of the expressions, which can hold literal values, identifiers available to the operation (references to variables or columns), or functions (built-in or user-defined). The difference in the SSIS world is that these values can be substituted directly into properties of the package model and provide powerful and dynamic workflow and operational functionalities.

Similarity of Expressions to Microsoft Excel Cells

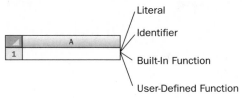

Figure 6-2

Variable Overview

Variables fit into the SSIS package development process similarly to the way they were used for DTS packages. Principally, they are used for "variable parking," in other words, they provide a method for objects in a package to communicate between themselves. The communication is always in two steps as demonstrated in Figure 6-3. First, a process either initializes the value of a variable from the package configuration or changes the variable value directly. This is represented by the package configurations and arrows from each of the tasks and transforms directed at the variable. Once the variable has been set by any of these, then the tasks and transforms can retrieve the value of the variable to use within SSIS or be restored back into the package configuration for future retrieval.

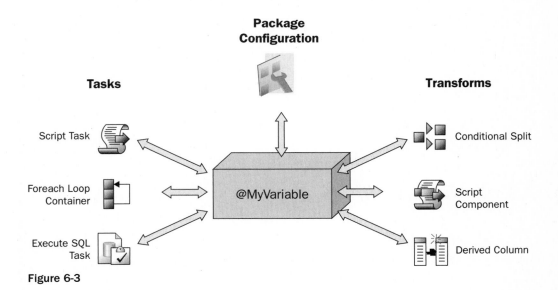

Figure 6-3

If these visual analogies explaining how expressions and variables fit into the SSIS picture make sense, then you are almost ready to dig into the details of how to build an expression. First, let's look at some of the details about data types and variables that cause most of the issues for SSIS package developers.

Understanding Data Types

In DTS package development, you only had to consider data types loosely, and even then only when you declared global variables. In the DTS Visual Basic Script Task, all variables were variants. A variant was used because it is a data type that can represent virtually any data. In fact, you could not even define a variable with a defined type in DTS or you'd get an error. This led to many ambiguous pieces of code, and as a result, there was a lot of implicit conversion going on within DTS packages.

In SSIS, you simply have to pay attention to the data types, whether the data is coming from your Data Flow, being stored in variables, or being included in expressions. You have to pay attention because the syntax checker will complain to your utter frustration about incompatible data types when you are building expressions. If something in your Data Flow allows incompatible data types, your packages will raise either warnings or errors (if implicit conversions are made). This will happen even if the conversion is between Unicode and non-Unicode character sets. Even comparison operations are subject to either hard or soft errors during implicit conversion. Bad data type decisions can have a serious impact on performance. This seemingly simple topic causes significant grief for those SSIS developers that don't spend the time to get a handle on the specifics. Use this section to get a quick brain dump about resolutions to common data-type conversion issues, starting first with a primer on SSIS data types.

SSIS Data Types

If you research the topic of data types for SSIS in the Books Online, you'll first notice that the data types are named much differently than similar types found in .NET or TSQL. This nomenclature is troublesome for most. The following table provides a matrix between SSIS data types and a typical SQL Server set of data types. You'll need this to interpret between data stream contents and data types in an expression. The .NET Managed types are important only if you are using script component, CLR, or .NET-based coding to manipulate your Data Flows.

The following table is just for SQL Server. To do a similar analysis for your own data source, look at the mapping files that can be found in this directory: `C:\Program Files\Microsoft SQL Server\100\DTS\MappingFiles\`. If you're familiar with OLE DB data types, you'll understand these SSIS data type enumerations, because they are similar. However, there is more going on than just naming differences. First, SSIS supports some data types that may not be familiar at all, nor are they applicable to SQL Server, namely most of the unsigned integer types and a few of the date types. You'll also notice the availability of the separate date-only (`DT_DBDATE`) and time-only (`DT_DBTIME`) types that were previously only available for RDMS databases like DB2 and ORACLE. With the introduction of similar data types in the SQL Server engine, they are now applicable in SSIS. Finally, notice the arrow " ⇨ " in the table, which indicates that these data types are converted to other SSIS Data Types in Data Flow operations that may be opportunities for performance enhancements.

SSIS Data Type	SQL Server Data Type	.NET Managed Type
DT_WSTR	nvarchar, nchar	System.String
DT_STR ⇨ DT_WSTR	varchar, char	
DT_TEXT ⇨ DT_WSTR	text	
DT_NTEXT ⇨ DT_WSTR	ntext, sql_variant, xml	
DT_BYTES	binary, varbinary	Array of System.Byte
DT_IMAGE ⇨ DT_BYTES	timestamp, image	
DT_DBTIMESTAMP	smalldatetime, datetime	System.DateTime
DT_DBTIMESTAMP2 ⇨ DT_DBTIMESTAMP	datetime	
DT_DBDATE ⇨ DT_DBTIMESTAMP	date	
DT_DATE ⇨ DT_DBTIMESTAMP		
DT_FILETIME ⇨ DT_DBTIMESTAMP		
DT_DBDATETIMESTAMPOFFSET	datetimeoffset	
DT_TIME2	time	System.TimeSpan
DT_TIME ⇨ DT_TIME2		
DT_NUMERIC	numeric	System.Decimal
DT_DECIMAL ⇨ DT_NUMERIC	decimal	
DT_CY ⇨ DT_NUMERIC	numeric, decimal	
DT_GUID	uniqueidentifier	System.Guid
DT_I1		System.SByte,
DT_I2	smallint	System.Int16,
DT_I4	int	System.Int32,
DT_I8	bigint	System.Int64
DT_BOOL ⇨ DT_I4	Bit	System.Boolean
DT_R4	real	System.Single,
DT_R8	float	System.Double
DT_U1	tinyint	System.Byte,
DT_U2		System.UInt16,
DT_U4		System.UInt32,
DT_U8		System.UInt64

Additional Date and Time Type Support

The latest version of SQL Server includes new data types for separate date and time values and an additional time zone–based data type compliant to the ISO 8601 standard. SSIS has always had these data type enumerations for the other RDMS sources, but now these can also be used for SQL Server as well. You'll also notice the availability of the latest additions of DT_DBTIMESTAMP2 and DT_DBTIME2 added for more precision, and DT_DBTIMESTAMPOFFSET added for the new ISO DateTimeOffset SQL Server data type.

A common issue that we see in SSIS packages is the improper selection of an SSIS date data type. For some reason DT_DBDATE and DT_DATE seem to be common selections for date types in Data Flow transforms. Improper use of these types can result in overflow errors or the removal of the time element from the date values. The idea is that SSIS data types provide a larger net for processing incoming values than you may have in your destination data source. It is your responsibility to manage the downcasting or conversion operations. Make sure you are familiar with the data type mappings in the mapping file for your data source and destination and the specific conversion issues with each type. A good start would be the date/time types, because there are many rules for conversions evidenced by the large section in the Books Online. You can find these conversion rules for date/time data types under the topic index "data types [Integration Services]" subsection "listed."

Wrong Data Types and Sizes Can Affect Performance

If you've been working with SSIS for a while, you might have realized that it is much faster than DTS used to be, but that it can also use some serious memory resources and sometimes can even be slower than you'd expect. That's because most of the work of the Data Flow transforms is done in memory. This can be good because it eliminates the most time-consuming IO operations. However, because SSIS uses memory buffers to accomplish this, the number of rows that can be loaded into a buffer is directly related to the width of the row. The narrower the row, the more rows that can be processed. If you are defining the data types of a large input source, pick your data types carefully, so that you are not using the default 50 characters per column for a text file, or the suggested data types of the Connection Manager when you do not need this extra safety cushion. Also, be aware that there are some tradeoffs for selecting specific data types if this requires any conversion as the data is being loaded into the buffers.

Data conversion is a fact of life, and you'll have to pay for it somewhere in the ETL process. These general guidelines can give you a start:

❏ Convert only when necessary. There is no need to convert all columns from a data source that are going to be dropped from the data stream. Each conversion costs something.

❏ Convert to the closest type for your destination source using the mapping files. If a value is converted to a non-supported data type, you'll have to incur an additional conversion internal to SSIS to the mapped data type.

❏ Convert using the closest size and precision. There is no need to import all columns as 50-character data columns if you are working with a fixed or reliable file format with columns that don't require as much space.

❏ Evaluate the option to convert after the fact. Don't forget that SSIS is still an ETL tool and sometimes it is more efficient to stage the data and convert the data using set-based methods.

The bottom line is that data type issues can be critical in high-volume scenarios, so plan with these guidelines in mind.

Unicode and Non-Unicode Conversion Issues

One of the things that you might not be used to in ETL package development is the default use of Unicode data types in SSIS packages. Not only is this the default import behavior, but all of the string functions in SSIS expect Unicode strings as input. Unicode is a great protective selection for handling data from import files with special characters. However, if you're not used to using this character set, this creates some unnecessary confusion. At the very least, using Unicode requires an additional step that is frequently missed, resulting in errors. For a typical demonstration, create a package that imports an Excel Data Source into a table defined with non-Unicode fields or download the samples from www.wrox.com. Excel data is imported as Unicode by default, so the mapping step in the destination transform complains that the data is not compatible, as you can see in Figure 6-4.

Note that you may experience some data being replaced by NULLs when importing Excel files using the Excel Connection Manager. This typically occurs when numeric and text data is stored within one column. One solution is to update the extended properties section of the connect string to look like this:
`Extended Properties="EXCEL 8.0;HDR=YES;IMEX=1".`

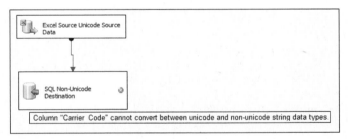

Figure 6-4

At first, you may think that all you need to do is change the source data type to match the non-Unicode destination. Using the SQL conversion table as a guide, change the column type in the advanced editor to DT_STR to match the destination SQL Server varchar data type. Now you'll find that the same error from Figure 6-4 is occurring on both the source and the destination transforms. As we discussed earlier in this section, SSIS requires purposeful conversion and casting operations. To complete the task, you only need to add a data conversion transform to convert the DT_WSTR and DT_R8 data types to DT_STR and DT_CY. The conversion transform should look similar to Figure 6-5.

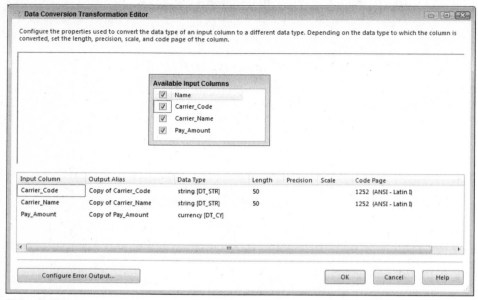

Figure 6-5

Notice in this data conversion transform that the data types and lengths are changed to truncate and convert the incoming string to match the destination source. Also, notice the Code Page setting that auto-defaults to 1252 for ANSI Latin 1. The Code Page setting depends on the source of the Unicode data you are working with. If you are working with international data sources, this may need to be changed to interpret incoming Unicode data correctly.

This type casting operation is a good, simple example of the difference between how SSIS and DTS packages handle data of differing types. However, within expressions it is not necessary to bring in the conversion transform to cast between different types. You can simply use casting operators to change the data types within the expression. The next section goes over this in more detail.

Casting in SSIS Expressions

If you want to experience poking your eye out, forget to put a casting operator in your expression Data Flow formulas. In the DTS environment, you could indiscriminately move `varchar` data from one server into another server's `nvarchar` field. However, if the servers had different code pages, corruption of the data could occur. SSIS is much more declarative about data type issues than DTS was. SSIS requires casting, which is simply, explicitly defining the data type for a value or expression.

You can run into some frustrating issues if you don't do it, but it is not always intuitive that casting is needed. For example, the result of any string function defaults to the Unicode `string` type. If you are attempting to store that value in a non-Unicode column, you are going to need a cast. If you are storing the value in a variable, you don't need to cast. (That's because the data types in variable definitions only allow Unicode; more about that later in the section "Defining Variables.") The good news is that casting is easy. In the expression language, this is going to look just like a .NET primitive cast. The new data type is provided in parentheses right next to the value to be converted. A simple example is casting a 2-byte signed integer to a 4-byte signed integer.

```
(DT_I4)32
```

Not all the casting operators are this simple. Some require additional parameters when specific precision, lengths, or code pages have to be considered to perform the operation. These operators are listed in the following table:

Casting Operator	Additional Parameters
DT_STR(<<length>>, <<code_page>>)	length — Final string length code_page — Unicode character set
DT_WSTR(<<length>>)	length — Final string length
DT_NUMERIC(<<precision>>, <<scale>>)	precision — Max number of digits scale — Number of digits after decimal
DT_DECIMAL(<<scale>>)	scale — Number of digits after decimal
DT_BYTES(<<length>>)	length — Number of final bytes
DT_TEXT(<<code_page>>)	code_page — Unicode character set

One place where casting causes the most visible trouble is during comparison operations and logical expressions. Remember that all operands in comparison operations must evaluate to a compatible data type. The same rules apply for complex or compound logical expressions. In this case, the entire expression must return a consistent data type, which may require casting of sections of the expression that may not readily appear to need casting. This is similar to the issue that you have in TSQL programming when you attempt to use a number in a where clause for a numeric column, or when using a case statement that needs to return columns of different types. In the where predicate, both the condition and the column must be convertible into a compatible type. For the case statement, each column must be cast to the same variant data type. We'll get into examples where you'll need to pay attention to casting when using comparison and logical expressions, later in this chapter, after we discuss a little more about the expression language.

The other place casting can create an invisible issue is when truncation of data occurs during casting of data. For example, casting Unicode double-byte data to non-Unicode data can result in lost characters. Significant digits can be lost in forced casting from unsigned to signed types or within types like 32-bit integers to 16-bit integers. These errors underscore the importance of wiring up the error outputs in the Data Flow Components that have them. Before we get there, let's look at variables and see how they are used in dynamic SSIS package development.

Using Variables

Variables are the glue holding dynamic package development together. As discussed earlier, variables are used to park and retrieve values between package components. They are no different than variables in any programming environment. Variables in SSIS packages are scoped, or can be accessed, within either the package level or to a specific package component. One major difference within variable definitions and expressions is that the available data types in variables are only a subset of the data types available in the rest of the SSIS environment.

Defining Variables

Variables can be created, deleted, renamed, and have their data types changed as long as the package is in design mode. Once the package is compiled and in runtime mode, the variable definition is locked; only the value of the variable can change. This is by design, so that the package is more declarative and type-safe. Creating a new variable is done through a designer that defines the scope of the variable depending upon how it is accessed. Variables can be scoped to either the package or to a specific component in the package. If the variable is scoped at a component level, only the component or its subcomponents have access to the variable. These important tips can keep you out of trouble when dealing with variables:

❏   Variables are case-sensitive. When you refer to a variable in a script task or in an expression, pay attention to the case of the name. Different shops have their own rules, but typically, variables are named using camel-case style.

❏   Variables can hide other variable values higher in the hierarchy. It is a good practice not to name variables similarly. This is a standard readability programming issue. If you have one variable outside a task and one inside the task, name them using identifiers like "inner" or "outer" to keep them separated.

Variables can be created by right-clicking the design surface of the package where you need a variable. The Variables window allows for creating, editing, and deleting variables. Figure 6-6 shows an example of two variables created within the Data Flow Task and Package scope levels.

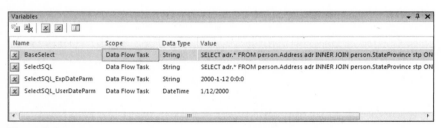

Figure 6-6

However, the Variables window does not expose all the capabilities of the variables. By selecting a variable and pressing F4, the Properties window for the SelectSQL variable is displayed, as shown in Figure 6-7.

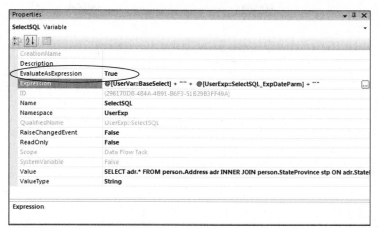

Figure 6-7

The reason for displaying the Properties window for the SelectSQL variable is to point out the EvaluateAsExpression and Expression properties. The value of a variable can either be a literal value, or can be defined dynamically. By setting the EvaluateAsExpression property to True, the variable takes on a dynamic quality that is defined by the expression provided in the Expression property. The SelectSQL variable is actually holding the result of a formula that concatenates the string value of the base select statement stored in the BaseSelect variable and a user-provided date parameter. The point often missed by beginning SSIS developers is that these variables can be used to store expressions that can be reused throughout the package. Instead of re-creating the expression all over the package, an expression can be created in a variable and then plugged in where needed. This greatly improves package maintainability by centralizing the expression definition. We'll create an example of an expression-based variable later in this chapter.

Variables can also be set programmatically using the script tasks. Refer to Chapter 9 for examples on how this is accomplished.

Variable Data Types

You may have noticed that the data types that are available for variable definition are a little different than the SSIS variables that were discussed earlier in this chapter. For example, the value type for string variable storage is String instead of DT_WSTR or DT_STR. Admittedly, this is confusing. Why does SSIS use what looks like a generalized managed type in the variable definition and yet a more specific set of data types in the Data Flows? The answer lies in the implementation of variables within the SSIS engine. Variables can be set from outside of the package, so variables are implemented in SSIS as COM variants. This allows the SSIS engine to use some late binding to resolve to the variable value within the package. However, note that this variant data type is not available anywhere within your control as an SSIS programmer. Variants are only an internal implementation in SSIS unlike DTS. Use the following table to help map the variable data types to SSIS Data Flow data types:

Variable Data Type	SSIS Data Type	Description
Boolean	DT_BOOL	Boolean value. Either True or False. Be careful setting these data types in code because the expression language and .NET languages define these differently.
Byte	DT_UI1	A 1-byte unsigned int. (Note this is not a byte array.)
Char	DT_UI2	A single character.
DateTime	DT_DBTIMESTAMP	A datetime structure that has spots for year, month, hour, minute, second, and fractional seconds.
DBNull	N/A	A declarative NULL value.
Double	DT_R8	A double-precision, floating-point value.
Int16	DT_I2	A 2-byte signed integer.
Int32	DT_I4	A 4-byte signed integer.
Int64	DT_I8	An 8-byte signed integer.
Object	N/A	An object reference. Typically used to store datasets or large object structures.
SByte	DTI1	A 1-byte, signed integer.
Single	DT_R4	A single-precision, floating-point value.
String	DT_WSTR	Unicode string value.
UInt32	DT_UI4	A 4-byte unsigned integer.
UInt64	DT_UI8	An 8-byte unsigned integer.

For most of the data types, there is ample representation. Typically, the only significant issues with variable data types center around the date/time and string data types. The only choices are the higher capacity data types. This is not a big deal from a storage perspective, because variable declaration is rather finite. You won't have too many variables defined in a package. If a package requires a string data type, one of the things from this table to point out again is that the default data type for strings is the Unicode version, and if you shove values into a variable of the string data type you'll need to convert for non-Unicode values.

This seems like a lot of preliminary information to go over before diving into creating an expression, but with at least a basic understanding of these core concepts, you will avoid most of the typical issues that we've seen SSIS developers encounter. Now let's use this knowledge to dive into the expression language and then into some sample uses of expressions in SSIS.

Working with Expressions

The language used to build expressions can be a bit disorienting at first. If you are used to using the ActiveX Script Task, then you'll be dealing with a difference similar to switching between using Visual Basic, C#, and sometimes TSQL, but all in the same language. The key to being proficient in building expressions is in understanding that the syntax of this new scripting language really is a combination of all these different languages.

C#-Like? Close, but Not Completely

Why not write the expression language in TSQL or in a .NET-compliant language? The marketing reason is that expressions should reflect the multi-platform capability of being able to operate on more than just SQL Server databases. Remember that expressions can be used on data from other RDMS sources, like Oracle, DB2, and even data from XML files. However, the technical explanation is that the SSIS and SQL Server core engines are written in native code, so any extension of the expression language to use .NET functions would incur the performance impact of loading the CLR and the memory management systems. The expression language without .NET integration can be more optimized for the custom memory management required for pumping large row sets through Data Flow operations. As the SSIS product matures, you'll see the SSIS team add more expression enhancements to expand on the existing functions. Meanwhile, let's look at some of the pitfalls of using the expression language.

The expression language is marketed as having a heavily C#-like syntax, and for the most part that is true. However, you can't just put on your C# hat and start working because there are some peculiarities mixed into the scripting language. The language is heavily C#-like when it comes to using logical and comparison operators, but leans toward a Visual Basic flavor and sometimes a little TSQL for functions. For example, notice that the following common operators are undeniably from a C# lineage:

Expression Operator	Description
||	Logical OR operation
&&	Logical AND operation
==	Comparison of two expressions to determine if equivalent
!=	Comparison of two expressions to determine inequality
? :	Conditional operator

The logical operators are syntactical changes if you are converting from DTS Visual Basic script. The conditional operator may be new to you, but it is especially important for creating compound expressions. In earlier releases of SSIS, the availability of this operator wasn't readily intuitive. If you aren't used to this C-style ternary operator, it is equivalent to similar `IF..THEN` or `IIF(<Condition>, <True Action>, <False Action>)` constructs.

The following functions look more like Visual Basic script or TSQL language functions than C#:

Expression Function	Description	C# Equivalent
POWER()	Raise numeric to a power.	Pow()
LOWER()	Convert to lowercase.	ToLower()
GETDATE()	Return current date.	Now()

This makes things interesting because you can't just plug in a C# function without checking to make sure there isn't an SSIS expression function to perform the same operation that is named differently. However, if you make this type of mistake, don't worry. Either the expression turns red, or you'll immediately get a descriptive error instructing you that the function is not recognized upon attempting to save. A quick look in the Books Online can help resolve these types of function syntax differences.

In some instances, the function you are looking for can be drastically different and cause some frustration. For example, if you are used to coding in C#, it may not be intuitive to look for the GETDATE() function to return the current date. The GETDATE() function is typically something one would expect from a TSQL language construct. Thankfully, it performs as a TSQL function should to return the current date. This is not always the case. Some functions look like TSQL functions but work in ways that are not the same:

Expression Function	Description	Difference
DATEPART()	Parses date part from a date.	Requires quotes on date part.
ISNULL()	Tests an expression for NULL.	Doesn't allow for default value.

This departure from the TSQL standard can leave you scratching your head when the expression doesn't compile. The biggest complaint about this function is that you have to use composite DATEPART() functions to get to any date part other than month, day, or year. This is a common task for naming files for archiving. The ISNULL() function also doesn't work like the TSQL function at all. It returns either true or false to test a value for existence of NULL. You can't substitute a default value as you would in TSQL.

These slight variations in the expression language between full-scale implementations of TSQL, C#, or Visual Basic syntaxes do cause some initial confusion and frustration at first, but these differences are minor in the grand scheme of things. Later in this chapter, you'll find a list of expressions that you can cut and paste to emulate many of the functions that are not immediately available in the expression language.

The Expression Builder

Several locations in the SSIS development environment allow the creation of an expression. In the Variables window or within any property expression editor, ultimately the expression is created within a UI called the Expression Builder. This UI maintains easy references to variables both system- and user-based as well as access to expression functions and operators. The most important feature of the Expression Builder is that you can test an expression to see the evaluated value by clicking an Evaluate Expression button. This is especially helpful as you learn the syntax of the expression language. By dragging and dropping variables and operators onto the expression workspace, you can see how to format expressions properly. Inside Data Flow Components, typically a specific expression builder includes additional elements related to the Data Flow. In Figure 6-8, you can see that the UI on the far right for the derived column transformation includes a column folder to allow expressions to be built with data from the Data Flow.

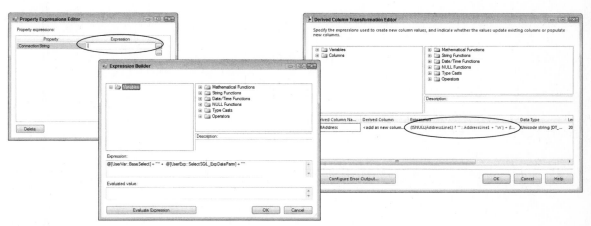

Figure 6-8

The only downside in the Data Flow Component versions of the expression builder is that you don't have the option to see the results of evaluating the expression to see if you've got the expression coded properly. The reason is that you can't see the data from the Data Flow, because this information would not be realizable without running the package.

This brings up a point about maintainability. If you have an involved expression that can be realized independent of data from the data stream, you should build the expression outside of the Data Flow Component and simply plug it in as a variable. However, there are certain instances where you have no choice but to build the expression at the Data Flow Component level. In this case, one of the best practices that we recommend is to create one variable at the package level called MyExpressionTest. This variable gives you a quick jumping off point to build up and test expressions to make sure you've got the syntax coded correctly. Simply access the variable property window and click the ellipsis beside the expression property, and the Expression Builder pops up. Use this technique to experiment with some of the basic syntax of the expression language in the next section.

Syntax Basics

Building an expression in SSIS requires an understanding of the syntax details of the expression language. Each of the following sections dive into an aspect of the expression syntax and explore the typical issues encountered with the topic with solutions.

Equivalence Operator

This operator is a binary operator used to compare two values. This operator seems to create some problems for SSIS developers not used to using the double equal sign syntax (==). Forgetting to use the double equal sign in a comparison operation can produce head-scratching results. Take for an example a precedence operation that tests a variable value to see if the value is equal to True, but the expression is written with a regular equal sign. Imagine that the variable is set by a previous script task that checks to see if there is a file available to process.

```
@MyBooleanValue = True
```

The expression is evaluated and the expression @MyBooleanValue is assigned the value of True. This overwrites any previous value for the variable. The precedence constraint succeeds, the value is true, and the tasks continue to run with a green light. If you aren't used to using the double equal sign syntax, this will bite you, and this is the reason we've discussed this operator by itself at the front of the syntax section.

String Concatenation

There are many uses for building strings within an expression. Strings are built to represent a SQL statement that can be executed against a database, to provide information in the body of an email message, or to build file paths for file processing. Building strings is one of those core things that you have to be able to do for any development task. In SSIS the concatenation operator is the "+" sign. Here is an example that you can quickly put together in the expression builder and test:

```
"The Server [" + LOWER( @[System::MachineName]) + "] is running this package"
```

This returns the string:

```
The Server [myserver] is running this package
```

If you need to build a string for a file path, use the concatenation operator to build the fully qualified path with the addition of an escape character to add the backslashes. See the later section on string literals for all the common escape characters that you'll need for string building. A file path expression would look like this:

```
"c:\\mysourcefiles\\" + @myFolder + "\\" + @myFile
```

Note that strings are built using double quotes (" ") not single quotes (' ') as you might see in TSQL. The only things to worry about here are keeping the strings all Unicode or all non-Unicode and not exceeding the limitation of 4000 characters on an expression. (Note that data types can be 8000 characters if you are building a Data Flow expression for a non-Unicode data type). The length limitation applies to the expression before and after all substitutions have been made. One of the issues that we've seen is that the expression is just under the limit, but during certain instances, the expression exceeds the boundaries of the limit, and the task fails. If you find that a task is exceeding this limit, and you are executing a SQL task, then it's time to think about creating a stored procedure to perform this work. Otherwise, you'll be out of luck, since this is the limit for an expression size.

Line Continuation

There two reasons to use line continuation characters in SSIS expressions. One is to make the expression easier to troubleshoot later, and the other is to format output for email or diagnostic use. Unfortunately, the expression language does not support the use of comments, but you can use the line hard returns to help the expression look more organized. In the expression builder, simply press the Enter key to have your expression displayed with the carriage-return-line-feed character sequence. This formatting is maintained even after you save the expression. To format output of the expression language, use the C-like escape character \n. Here's an example of using it with a simple expression:

```
"My Line breaks here\nAnd then here\n; )"
```

This returns the string:

```
My Line breaks here
And then here
; )
```

Note that it was not necessary to show the expression in code form in one line. The expression could be written out on multiple lines to ease the viewing of the expression in design time. The output would remain the same.

Literals

Literals are hard-coded information that you must provide when building expressions. SSIS expressions have three types of literals: numeric, string, and Boolean.

Numeric Literals

A numeric literal is simply a fixed number. Typically, a number will be assigned to a variable or used in an expression. SSIS has the same issues with numeric literals that you do in C# or Java — you can't just implicitly define numeric literals. Well, that's not completely true; SSIS does interpret numeric values with a few default rules, but the point is that the rules are probably not what you might expect. A value of 12 would be interpreted as the default data type of DT_UI4, or the 4-byte unsigned integer. This might be what you want to happen, but if the value were changed to 3000000000 during the evaluation process, an error similar to this will generate:

```
The literal "3000000000" is too large to fit into type DT_UI4. The magnitude of the
literal overflows the type.
```

SSIS operates on literals using logic similar to the underlying .NET CLR. Numeric literals are checked to see if they contain a decimal point. If they do not, the literal is cast using the unsigned integer DT_UI4 data type. If there is a decimal point, the literal is cast as a DT_NUMERIC. To override these rules, a suffix must be appended to the numeric literal. The suffix enables a declarative way to define the literal. The following are examples of suffixes that can be used on numeric literals:

Suffix	Description	Example
L or l	Indicates that the numeric literal should be interpreted as the long version of either the DT_UI8 or DT_R8 value types depending upon whether a decimal is present.	3000000000L $\Rightarrow$ DT_I8 3.14159265L $\Rightarrow$ DT_R8
U or u	Indicates that the numeric literal should represent the unsigned data type.	3000000000UL $\Rightarrow$ DT_UI8
F or f	Indicates the numeric literal represents a float value.	100.55f $\Rightarrow$ DT_R4
E or e	Indicates the numeric literal represents scientific notation. Note: Expects at least one digit scientific notation followed by float or long suffix.	6.626×10^{-34} J/s $\Rightarrow$ 6.626E-34F $\Rightarrow$ DT_R8 6.626E won't work. If you don't have a digit then format like this: 6.626E+0L or 6.626E+0f

Knowing these suffixes and rules, the previous example can be altered to 3000000000L, and the expression can be validated.

String Literals

When building strings, there are times when you'll need to supply special characters in the string. For example, Postgres database sources require the use of quoted column and table names. The key here is to understand the escape sequences that are understood by the expression syntax parser. The escape sequence for the double quote symbol is \". A sample expression generated SQL statement might look like this:

```
"Select \"myData\" from \"owner\".\"myTable\""
```

This expression would generate this string:

```
Select "myData" from "owner"."myTable"
```

Other common literals that you may need are listed in this table:

Suffix	Description	Example

\n	New Line or Carriage Feed Line Return	`"Print this on one line\nThis on another"`
		 `Print this on one line`
		 `This on another`

\t	Tab character	`"Print\twith\ttab\tseparation"` `Print    with    tab    separation`
\"	Double-quotation mark character	`"\"Hey!"\"` `"Hey!"`
\\	Backslash	`"c:\\myfile.txt"` `c:\myfile.txt`

There are a few other string escape sequences supported, but you'll find that the elements in this table list the most frequently used. The backslash escape sequences come in handy when building file and path strings. The double-quote escape sequence is more often used to interact with data sources that require quoted identifiers. This escape sequence is also used in combination with the remaining new line and tab characters to format strings for logging or other reporting purposes.

Boolean Literals

The Boolean literals of `True` and `False` don't have to be capitalized, nor are they case sensitive at all. Boolean expressions are shortcut versions of the logical operators. To drive certain package functionality conditionally based on whether the package is running in an off-line mode, you could write an expression in a variable using an artificial on or off type switch mechanism like this:

```
@[System::OfflineMode]==True ? 1 : 0   (Not Recommended)
```

The idea would be to use the results of this operation to determine whether a precedence constraint should operate. The precedence operator would retest the expression to see if the value was 1 or 0. This is an awfully long way to do something. How much easier is it to just create an expression in a variable called `MyPrecedenceBool` that looks like this:

```
@[System::OfflineMode]==False
```

Then all you have to do is plug the expression into the precedence editor like Figure 6-9.

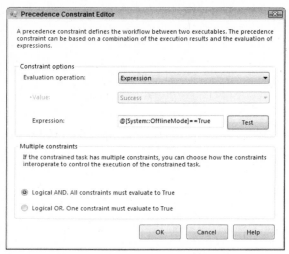

Figure 6-9

Note that using the literal is recommended over using any numeric values for evaluation. Programming any expression to evaluate numeric versions of Boolean values is dangerous and should not be a part of your SSIS techniques.

Referencing Variables

Referencing variables is easy when using the expression builder. Drag and drop variables onto the expression builder to format the variable into the expression properly. Notice that the format of the variable automatically dropped into the expression is preceded with an @ symbol followed by the namespace, a C++-like scope resolution operator, and then the variable name:

```
@[namespace::variablename]
```

Technically, if the variable is not repeated in multiple namespaces and there are no special characters (including spaces) in the variable name, you could get away with referring to the variable using a short identifier like @variablename or just using the variable name. However, this type of lazy variable referencing can get you into trouble later. We recommend that you stick with the fully qualified way of referencing variables in all SSIS expressions.

Typically, where folks have issues with variable references is in the Precedence Constraint Editor, as seen in Figure 6-9. This is most likely because there is no expression builder to help build the expression, and the whole thing has to be typed in. This is where the tip of creating the dummy variable MyExpressionTester comes in handy. You can create an expression within this dummy variable expression builder, and then simply cut-and-paste the value into the Precedence Constraint Editor.

Referencing Columns

Columns can be referenced in expressions, but only within a Data Flow Transformation Component. This makes sense. Creating a global expression to reference a value in a Data Flow is the equivalent of trying to use a single variable to capture a value of a set-based processing operation. Even a variable expression, defined at the same level or scope of a Data Flow Transformation, should not be able to reference a single column in the Data Flow under constant change. However, from within specific transformations like the Derived Column Transform, the expression builder can reference a column because from within the transform, operations occur at a row level. Expressions within a data transform can access column identifiers to allow point-and-click building of expressions. There are a few things to remember when referencing columns in expressions:

❑ Data flow column names must follow the SSIS standards for special characters.

❑ Column names must be uniquely named or qualified within a Data Flow.

❑ Columns can be referred to using lineage identifiers.

A common issue with building expressions referencing columns in a Data Flow has less to do with the expression language than the names of the columns themselves. This is particularly true when dealing with Microsoft Excel or Access data where columns can be found with non-standard naming conventions. SSIS requires that columns being used in an expression either start with a valid Unicode letter or with an underscore (_). Any other special characters require qualification of the column to use within an expression with the exception of bracket characters.

Brackets ([or]) are the designators for SSIS to qualify a column name. Qualification of column names is required if the name contains special characters — including spaces. Because bracket characters are column name qualifiers, any column with brackets in the name must be renamed to use in an expression. Change the column name inside of the Data Flow Source Component. This doesn't require changing the column name back in the originating source. Column names also must be qualified when two or more columns in a Data Flow have the same name to avoid ambiguous references. The following are examples of columns that needed qualification:

Column Name	Qualified Column Name	Description
My Column	[My Column]	Column names can't contain spaces.
File#	[File#]	Column names can't contain special characters.
@DomainName	[@DomainName]	
Enrolled?	[Enrolled?]	
Source1 ID	[Source1].[ID]	Column names can't have the same name within a Data Flow.
Source2 ID	[Source2].[ID]	

Another way to refer to columns that is unique to SSIS package development is by lineage number. A lineage number is something that SSIS assigns to each input and output as it is added to a transform component in a package. The lineage number is quickly replaced by the real column name once the expression is syntax compiled. To find the lineage number for a column, look at any advanced editor dialog box and find the column in the input column properties under LineageID.

Boolean Expressions

Boolean expressions of course evaluate to either `true` or `false`. These expressions in their simplest implementation are used in precedence constraints as gatekeepers to determine whether or not an operation should occur. Within Data Flow operations, Boolean expressions are typically employed in the conditional split transform to determine whether a row in a Data Flow is directed to another transform.

A Boolean expression to determine whether a Control Flow step would run only on Friday would require code to parse the day of the week from the current date and compare to the 6th day like this:

```
DATEPART( "dw", GETDATE() )  == 6
```

This is a useful Boolean expression for end of the week activities. To control tasks that run on the first day of the month, use an expression like this:

```
DATEPART ("dd", GETDATE() ) == 1
```

This expression validates as true only when the first day of the month occurs. Boolean expressions don't have to be this singular. Compound expressions can be built to test a variety of conditions. Here is an example where three conditions must all evaluate to `true` for the expression to return a true value:

```
BatchAmount == DepositAmount && @Not_Previously_Deposited == True && BatchAmount >
0.00
```

The `@Not_Previously_Deposited` argument in this expression is a variable; the other arguments represent columns in a Data Flow. Of course, an expression can just as easily evaluate alternate conditions, like this:

```
(BatchAmount > 0.00 || BatchAmount < 0.00) && @Not_Previously_Deposited == True
```

In this case, the `BatchAmount` must not be equal to $0.00. An alternative way to express the same thing is using the inequality operator:

```
(BatchAmount != 0.00) && @Not_Previously_Deposited == True
```

Don't get tripped up with these simple examples. They were defined for packages where the Data Flow was pumped in from data sources with known column data types, so there was no need to take extra precautions with casting conversions. If you are dealing with Data Flow from less reliable data sources, or if you know that two columns have different data types, then take extra casting precautions with your expression formulas like this expression:

```
(DT_CY)BatchAmount == (DT_CY)DepositAmount && @Not_Previously_Deposited == True &&
(DT_CY)BatchAmount > (DT_CY)0.00
```

The Boolean expression examples here are generally the style of expressions that are used to enable dynamic SSIS package operations. We did not cover the conditional, date/time, and string-based Boolean expressions, which are covered in the following sections. String expression development requires a little more information about how to handle a NULL or missing value, which is covered in the next section. Look for some examples of these Boolean expressions put to work at the end of this chapter.

Dealing with NULLs

In SSIS, variables can't really ever be set to NULL. Instead, there are default values that each variable data type maintains when there is an absence of a value. For strings, the default value is an empty string instead of the default of NULL that you might be used to in database development. However, in Data Flow operations and transforms there most certainly can be NULL values. This creates problems when variables are intermixed within Data Flow Transformations. This mixture occurs either within a Script Task or within an Expression. If a value in the Data Flow needs to be set to NULL or even tested for a NULL value, this is another matter altogether and can be accomplished rather easily with the ISNULL() expression function and the NULL(type) casting functions. Just understand that variables are going to behave a little differently.

NULLs and Variables

The issue with not being able to set variables to NULL values has to do with the COM object variant implementation of variables in the SSIS engine. Regardless of the technical issue, if you are testing a variable for an absence of value, you have to decide ahead of time what value you are going to use to represent the equivalent of a NULL value, so that you can test for it accurately. For example, the DateTime variable data type defaults to 12/30/1899 if you purposely set it to NULL. You can test this out yourself by creating a DateTime variable and setting it equal to an expression defined using the casting function NULL(DT_DBTIMESTAMP).

It helps to get a handle on the default value for the SSIS variable data types. You can find them in this table:

Variable Data Type	Default Value
Boolean	False
Byte	0
Char	0
DateTime	12/30/1899
DBNull	(Can't test in an expression)
Double	0
Int16	0
Int32	0
Int64	0
Object	(Can't test in an expression)
SByte	0
Single	0
String	"" (empty string)
UInt32	0
UInt64	0

Using this table of default values, the following expression could be used in a precedence operation after testing for the absence of a value in a string variable MyNullStringVar:

```
@[User::MyNullStringVar]==""
```

If the value of the user variable is an empty string, the expression evaluates to a TRUE value and the step will be executed.

A frequent logic error that SSIS developers make is to use a variable to set a value from an expression that will be used within a multiple instance looping structure. If the value is not reset in a way that clean retesting can be done, the value of the variable will remain the same for the life of the package. No error will be raised, but the package may not perform multiple iterations as expected. Make sure a variable is reset to enable retesting if the test is performed multiple times. This may require additional variables to cache intermediate results.

NULLs in Data Flow

Using the NULL function in the Data Flow Transforms are a different matter. Values in a Data Flow can be NULL. Here you can use the expression function to test for NULL values in the data stream. The trouble usually stems from either a misunderstanding of how the ISNULL() function works, or what to do after a NULL value is found. First, the ISNULL() expression function tests the expression in the parentheses for the value of NULL. It does not make a substitution if a NULL value is found like the same-named function does in TSQL. To emulate the TSQL function ISNULL() build an SSIS expression in a Data Flow like this:

```
IsNull(DATA_COLUMN) ? YOUR_DEFAULT_VALUE : DATA_COLUMN
```

If you wanted instead to set a column to NULL based on some attribute of the data in the incoming data stream, the logical structure is similar. First, provide the testing expression followed by the actions to take if the test is true or false. Here is a function that sets a data column in a Data Flow to NULL if the first character starts with "A":

```
SUBSTRING([MyColumn] , 1, 1)=="A" ? NULL(DT_WSTR, 255) : [MyColumn]
```

A typical issue that occurs when handling NULLs doesn't actually have anything to do with NULL values themselves, but more with string expressions. When creating data streams to punch back into RDMS data destinations, you will often want to send back a column with NULL values when a test on the data can't be completed. The logic is to either send the column data back or replace the column data with a NULL value. For most data types, this works by sending the results of the NULL function for the data type desired. For some reason this works differently when you want to save non-Unicode data with a NULL value. You'd expect the following expression to work, but it doesn't:

```
SUBSTRING([MyColumn] , 1, 1)=="A" ?
NULL(DT_STR, 255, 1252) : [MyColumn]        (This doesn't work in SSIS)
```

This won't work because of an issue with how the SSIS handles NULL values for the non-Unicode string type as parameters. The only way to fix this is to cast the NULL function like this:

```
SUBSTRING([MyColumn] , 1, 1)=="A" ?
(DT_STR, 255, 1252)NULL(DT_STR, 255, 1252) : [MyColumn]
```

This section should clear up the common issues dealing with NULL values, especially as they relate to strings. There are still some tricks to learn about dealing with strings that we'll deal with next.

String Functions

Handling strings in SSIS expressions is different from dealing with string data in SQL Server. The previous section discussed some of the differences with handling NULL values. You also have to pay attention to the Unicode and non-Unicode strings. If a package is moving data between multiple Unicode string sources, you have to pay attention to the code pages between the strings. If you are comparing strings, you also have to pay attention to string padding, trimming, and issues with data truncations. Handling strings is a little more involved than it used to be with DTS, but there are really only a few things to remember to get going.

Expression functions return Unicode string results. If you are writing an expression to return the uppercase version of a varchar-type column of data, the result will be a Unicode column with all capital letters. The string function Upper() returns a Unicode string. In fact, SSIS sets all string operations to return a Unicode string. This can be clearly seen with a demonstration expression in the Derived Column Transform in Figure 6-10.

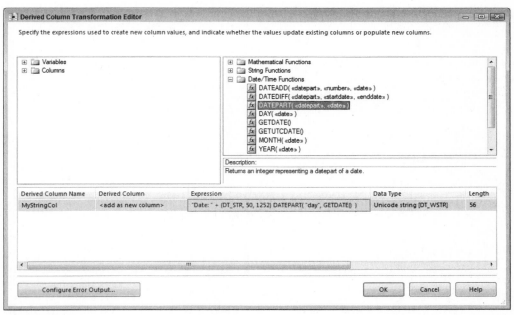

Figure 6-10

Here you are just adding a string column that includes the concatenation of a date value. The function is using a DatePart() function where the results are cast to a non-Unicode string, but the default data type chosen in the editor is a Unicode string data type. This can be overridden of course, but it is something to watch for, as you develop packages. On one hand, if the data type is reverted to non-Unicode, then the string has to be converted for each further operation. On the other hand, if the value is left as a Unicode string and the end result is to persist in a non-Unicode format, then at some point it has to be converted to a non-Unicode value. The rule that usually works out is to leave the strings converted as Unicode and convert back to non-Unicode if required during persistence. This of course depends upon whether there is a concern about using Unicode data.

Comparing strings requires that you get the two strings into the same padding length and case. The comparison is case- and padding-sensitive. Expressions should use the concatenation operator (+) to get the strings into the same padding style. Typically, this type of work is done when putting together date strings with an expected type of padding like this:

```
SUBSTRING("0" + @Day, 1, 2) + "/" + SUBSTRING("0" + @Month, 1, 2) + "/" +
SUBSTRING("00" + @Year, 1, 2)
```

This type of zero padding ensures that the values in both variables are in the same format for comparison purposes. By padding both sides of the comparison, you can ensure the proper equality check:

```
SUBSTRING("0" + @Day, 1, 2) + "/" + SUBSTRING("0" + @Month, 1, 2) + "/" +
SUBSTRING("00" + @Year, 1, 2) == SUBSTRING("0" + @FileDay, 1, 2) + "/" +
SUBSTRING("0" + @FileMonth, 1, 2) + "/" + SUBSTRING("00" + @FileYear, 1, 2)
```

The same type of padding operation can be used to fill in spaces between two values:

```
SUBSTRING(@Val1 + "     ", 1, 5) + SUBSTRING(@Val2 + "     ", 1, 5)  +
SUBSTRING(@Val3 + "     ", 1, 5)
```

Typically, space padding is used for formatting output, but could be used for comparisons. More often than not, spaces are removed from strings for comparison purposes. To remove spaces from strings in expressions, use the trim functions: LTrim(), RTrim(), and Trim(). These functions are self-explanatory, and they enable comparisons for strings that have leading and trailing spaces. Comparing these strings: "Canterbury" and "Canterbury " return a false unless the expression is written like this:

```
Trim("Canterbury") == Trim("Canterbury ")
```

This expression returns true because the significant spaces are declaratively removed. Be careful of these extra spaces in string expressions as well. Spaces are counted in all string functions. This can result in extra character counts for trailing spaces when using the LEN() function and can affect carefully counted SUBSTRING() functions that are not expecting leading spaces. If these issues are of importance, employ a Derived Column Transform to trim these columns early in the Data Flow process.

Conditional Expressions

You use the conditional expression operator to build logical evaluation expressions in the format of an IF..THEN logical structure:

```
Boolean_expression ? expression_if_true : expression_if_false
```

The first part of the operator requires a Boolean expression that will be tested for a true or false return value. If the Boolean expression returns true, then the first expression after the ternary operator (?) will be evaluated and returned as the final result of the conditional expression. If the Boolean expression returns false, then the expression after the separation operator (:) will be evaluated and returned. One rule is that both expressions as operands must adhere to this set of data type rules:

❑   Both operands must be numeric data types that can be implicitly converted.

❑   Both operands must be string data types of either Unicode or non-Unicode. Each operand can evaluate to separate types — except for the issue of setting explicit NULL values. In this case, the NULL value for DT_STR non-Unicode NULL values must be cast.

❑ Both operands must be date data types. The result if more than one data type is represented in the operands is a DT_DBTIMESTAMP data type.

❑ Both operands for a text data type must have the same code pages.

If any of these rules are broken, or the compiler detects incompatible data types, you will have to supply explicit casting operators on one or both of the operands to get the condition expression to evaluate. This is more of an issue as the conditional expression gets compounded and nested. A typical troubleshooting issue is looking at an incompatible data type message resulting from a comparison deep into a compound conditional expression. This can be a result of a column that has changed to an incompatible data type, or from a literal that has been provided without a suffix consistent with the rest of the expression. The best way to test the expression is to copy it into Notepad and test each piece of the expression until the offending portion is located.

Casting issues can also create false positives. Casting truncation can be seen in this example of a Boolean expression comparing the new datetimestampoffset and a date value.

```
(DT_DBDATE) "2008-01-31 20:34:52.123 -3:30" == (DT_DBDATE)"2008-01-31"
```

Casting converts the expression (DT_DBDATE) "2008-01-31 20:34:52.123 -3:30" to "2008-01-31" making the whole expression evaluate to true. Date and time conversion issues are one example of casting issues, but can also occur on any data type that allows forced conversion.

Date Time Functions

Date and time functions seem to cause more than a little confusion for new SSIS developers. In most instances, the syntax is just different, and that is causing the issue. As mentioned earlier, the DatePart() function is a perfect example of this. TSQL programmers will need to double quote the date part portion of the function, or they will see an error similar to this:

```
The expression contains unrecognized token "dd". If "dd" is a variable then it
should be expressed as "@dd". The specific token is not valid. If the token is
intended to be a variable name, it should be prefixed with the @ symbol.
```

The fix is simple: put double quotation marks around the date part. A properly formatted DatePart() expression should look like this:

```
DATEPART( "dd", GETDATE() )
```

Note that this expression would return the value of the day of the month, for example, 31 if the date was January 31, 2008. A common mistake is to expect this to be the day of the week. You can accomplish that task by changing the date part in the expression like this:

```
DATEPART( "dw", GETDATE() )
```

These are just minor adjustments to the SSIS expression language, but can create some frustration. Another example can be found during attempts to reference the date values in an expression. If you're used to MS Access date literals, you may be tempted to attempt something like this:

```
"SELECT * FROM myTable WHERE myDate >= " + #01/31/2008#  (DOESN'T WORK IN SSIS)
```

This won't work in SSIS. The # signs are used for a different purpose. If the string is going to be interpreted by SQL Server, just use the single quote around the date like this:

```
"SELECT * FROM MYTABLE WHERE MYDATE >= '" + "01/31/2008" + "'"
```

If the string is just going to be printed, there is no need for the single quotes. Alternatively, to plug in a date value from a variable, the expression would look like this:

```
"SELECT * FROM MYTABLE WHERE MYDATE >= '" +
(DT_WSTR, 255)@[System::ContainerStartTime] + "'"
```

Notice that the value of the date variable must be cast to match the default Unicode data type for all expression strings of DT_WSTR. The issue of simply casting a date to a string is the fact that you get all the date, and that doesn't translate into what you may want to use as a query parameter. This is clearer if the preceding expression is resolved:

```
SELECT * FROM MYTABLE WHERE MYDATE >= '02/22/2008 2:28:40 PM'
```

If the attempt is truly to only see results after 2:28:40 PM, then this query will run as expected. If items from earlier in the day are also expected, then you need to do some work to parse out the values from the variable value. If the intent is just to return rows for the date that the package is running, it is much easier to create the expression like this (with your proper date style of course):

```
"SELECT * FROM MYTABLE WHERE MYDATE >= CONVERT(nvarchar(10), getdate(), 101)"
```

This method allows SQL Server to do the work of substituting the current date from the server into the query predicate. However, if you need to parse a string from a date value in an expression, take apart one of the following formulas in this section to save you a bit of time:

Description	Expression

Convert file name with embedded date into the date time type format MM/dd/yyyy HH:mm:ss.
 	
File name format: yyyyMMddHHmmss
	`SUBSTRING(@[User::FileName],5,2) + "/" +`
	`SUBSTRING(@[User::FileName],7,2) + "/" +`
	`SUBSTRING(@[User::FileName],1,4) + " " +`
	`SUBSTRING(@[User::FileName],9,2) + ":" +`
	`SUBSTRING(@[User::FileName],11,2) + ":" +`
	`SUBSTRING(@[User::FileName],13,2)`

Convert a date time variable to a file name format of: yyyyMMddHHmmss	`(DT_WSTR,4)YEAR(GETDATE())+ RIGHT("0" +`
	`(DT_WSTR,2)MONTH(GETDATE()), 2)+ RIGHT("0" +`
	`(DT_WSTR,2)DAY( GETDATE()), 2)+ RIGHT("0"+`
	`(DT_WSTR,2)DATEPART("hh", GETDATE()), 2)+ RIGHT("0"+`
	`(DT_WSTR,2)DATEPART("mi", GETDATE()), 2)+ RIGHT("0"+`
	`(DT_WSTR,2)DATEPART("ss", GETDATE()), 2)`

In this section, we have covered most of the major syntactical issues with the expression language. The issues that have caused SSIS programmers the most trouble should not be a problem for you. Now let's create some expressions and walk through inserting them into SSIS packages to put them to work.

Using Expressions in SSIS Packages

Creating an expression requires understanding the syntax of the SSIS expression language. As discussed in the previous section, this expression language is part C#, part Visual Basic script, and sometimes some flavor of TSQL mixed in. Once you can code in the expression language, you are ready to put the expressions to work. Here we'll show you how expressions can be used in SSIS package development, with some typical examples that you can use in your package development tasks. The following packages can be downloaded in their entirety by going to www.wrox.com.

Using Variables as Expressions

Earlier in this chapter, we discussed using expressions in variables. A good example of using this in a practical way is to handle the task of processing files in a directory. The task should be familiar to all. A directory must be polled for files of a specific extension. If a file is found, it is processed, and then copied into a final, archival storage directory. An easy way to do this is to hardcode the source and destination paths along with the file extension into the Foreach Loop and File System Tasks. However, if you need to use a failover server, you'll have to go through the package and change all these settings manually. It is much easier to use variables that allow these properties to be set, and then use expressions to create the destination directory and file names. When the server changes, then only the user variables need to change to adjust to the change. The basic steps for such an SSIS package can be gleaned from Figure 6-11.

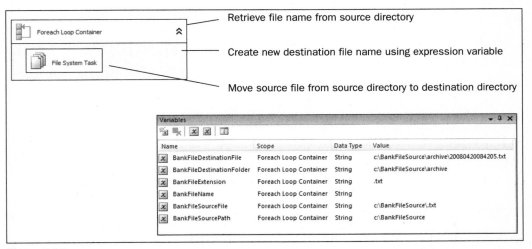

Figure 6-11

One of the things to notice in the list of variable definitions is the Namespace column. One downside to the Variables window is that you can't tell whether a variable is an expression variable or a variable that can be manipulated as a setting variable. The Namespace column provides a nice way to separate variables. In this case the namespace UserExp indicates that the variable is a user expression-based variable. The namespace UserVar indicates that the variable is defined by the user.

For this package the Foreach Loop Container Collection tab is set by an expression to retrieve the folder (or directory) from the variable BankFileSourcePath. This variable is statically defined either from configuration processes or manually by an administrator. This tells the Foreach Loop where to start looking for files. To enumerate files of a specific extension, an expression sets the Files (or FileSpec) property to the value of the variable BankFileExtension, which is also a static variable. Nothing real complicated here except that the properties of the Foreach Loop are set by expressions instead of hard-coded. The container looks like Figure 6-12.

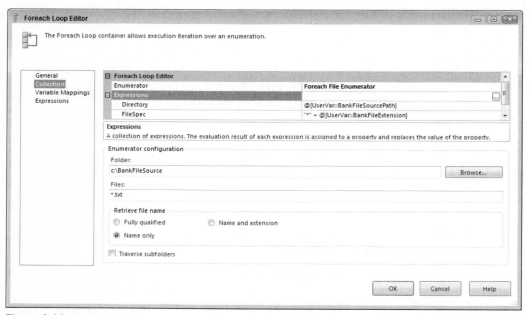

Figure 6-12

Notice that here the Foreach task is retrieving the filename only. This value is stored in the variable BankFileName. This is not shown in Figure 6-12, but would be shown in the Variable Mappings tab. With the raw filename, no extension, and no path, some variables set up as expressions can be used to create a destination file that is named using the current date. First, you need a destination location. The source folder is known, so use this folder as a starting point to create a subfolder called "archive" by creating a variable named BankFileDestinationFolder that has the property EvaluateAsExpression set to True and defined by this expression:

```
@[UserVar::BankFileSourcePath] + "\\archive"
```

You need the escape sequence to properly build a string path. Now build a variable named BankFileDestinationFile that will use this BankFileDestinationFolder value along with a date-based expression to put together a unique destination filename. The expression would look like this:

```
@[UserExp::BankFileDestinationFolder] + "\\" + (DT_WSTR,4)YEAR(GETDATE())
+ RIGHT("0" + (DT_WSTR,2)MONTH(GETDATE()), 2)
+ RIGHT("0" + (DT_WSTR,2)DAY( GETDATE()), 2)
+ RIGHT("0" + (DT_WSTR,2)DATEPART("hh", GETDATE()), 2)
+ RIGHT("0" + (DT_WSTR,2)DATEPART("mi", GETDATE()), 2)
+ RIGHT("0" + (DT_WSTR,2)DATEPART("ss", GETDATE()), 2)
 +  @[UserVar::BankFileExtension]
```

When evaluated, this results in a destination filename that looks like c:\BankFileSource\Archive\ 20080101154006.txt when the bank file destination folder is c:\BankFileSource\Archive. By using variables that evaluate to the value of an expression, combined with information set statically from administrator and environmental variables like the current date and time, you can create packages with dynamic capabilities.

Another best practice is to use expression-based variables to define common logic that you'll use throughout your SSIS package. If in the preceding example, you wanted to use this date-based string in other places within your package, define the date portion of that expression in a separate variable called DateTimeExpression. Then the expression for the BankFileDestinationFolder variable could be simplified to look like this.

```
@[UserExp::BankFileDestinationFolder] + "\\" + @[UserExp::DateTimeExpression]
 +  @[UserVar::BankFileExtension]
```

The power in separating logic like this is that an expression need not be buried in multiple places within an SSIS package. This makes maintenance for SSIS packages much easier and more manageable.

Using Expressions in Properties of Connections

Another simple example of using expressions is to dynamically change or set properties of an SSIS component. One of the common uses of this technique is to create a dynamic connection to allow packages to be altered by external or internal means. In this example, we'll assume an environment where all logins are duplicated across environments. This means you only need to change the server name to make connections to other servers. To start, create a variable named SourceServerNamedInstance that can be used to store the server name that the package should connect to for source data. Then drop a connection into the Connection Managers' section of the SSIS package, and press F4, or right-click and select Properties to get to the Properties window for the connection object. The Properties window should like Figure 6-13.

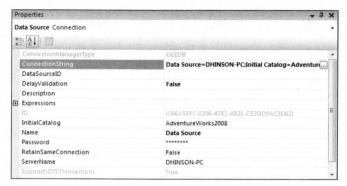

Figure 6-13

The secret here is the Expressions collection property. If you click this property as is shown in Figure 6-13, an ellipsis will display. Clicking that button will bring up the Property Expressions Editor shown in Figure 6-14, which will allow you to see the properties that can be set to an expression and ultimately do so in the expression builder.

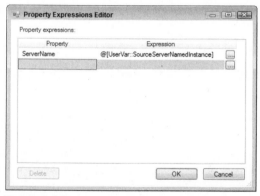

Figure 6-14

This example completes the demonstration by setting the property of the ServerName to the expression that is simply the value of the SourceServerNamedInstance variable. Here we only affected one property in the connection string, but this is not required. The entire connection string, as you may have noticed in the Property drop-down, is available to be set by a string-based expression. This same technique can be used to set any connection property in the Data Flow Components as well to dynamically alter the flat file and MS Excel-based connections. A common use is to set the connection source for a Data Flow Component to a variable-based incoming filename. You can see an example of this type of expression usage in Chapter 23.

Using Expressions in Control Flow Tasks

A common example of expressions being used in Control Flow Tasks is to create SQL statements dynamically that are run by the Execute SQL Task. The Execute SQL Task has a property called SQLStatement that can be set to a file connection, a variable, or direct input. Instead of creating parameterized SQL statements that are subject to error and OLE provider interpretation, try building the SQL statement using an expression and putting the whole SQL statement into the SQLStatement property. We'll do an example like this using a DELETE statement that should run at the start of a package to delete any data from a staging table that has the same RunJobID (a theoretical identifier for a unique SSIS data load).

To start, create one variable for the DELETE statement that doesn't include the dynamic portion of the SQL statement. A variable named DeleteSQL of type String would be set to a value of the string:

```
DELETE FROM tblStaging WHERE RunJobId =
```

Create another variable named DeleteSQL_RunJobId with the data type of Int32 to hold the value of a variable RunJobId. This value could be set elsewhere in the SSIS package.

In the ExecuteSQLTask bring up the editor and make sure that the SQLSourceType is set to DirectInput. You could also set this value to use a variable if you built the SQL statement in its entirety within an expression-based variable. In this example, we'll build the expression in the task component. To get there, click the Expressions tab of the editor and you'll see the Expressions collections property. Click the ellipses to access the Property Expressions Editor and build the SQL statement using the two variables that you defined. Make sure you use the casting operator to build the string like this:

```
@[UserVar::DeleteSQL] +  (DT_WSTR, 8) @[UserVar::DeleteSQL_RunJobId]
```

The completed ExecuteSQL Task Property Expressions Editor will look like Figure 6-15.

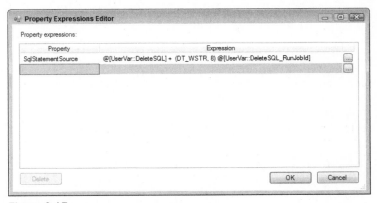

Figure 6-15

When the package is run, the expression will combine the values from both the variables and construct a complete SQL statement that will be inserted into the property SqlStatementSource for the ExecuteSQL task. This technique is more modular and works more consistently across the different OLE DB providers for dynamic query formation and execution than hard-coding the SQL statement. With this method it is possible to later define and then reconstruct your core SQL using initialization configurations. It is also a neat technique to show off how to use expressions and variables.

Using Expressions in Control Flow Precedence

Controlling the flow of SSIS packages is one of the key strengths of dynamic package development. Between each Control Flow Component is a precedence constraint that can have expressions attached to it for evaluation purposes. You can visually identify the precedence constraint as the blue arrow that connects two Control Flow Components. During runtime, as one Control Flow Component completes, the precedence constraint is evaluated to determine if the flow can continue to the next component. One common scenario is a single package that may have two separate sequence operations that need to occur based on some external factor. For example, on even days one set of tasks is run, and on odd days another separate set of tasks is run. A visual example of this type of package logic can be seen in Figure 6-16.

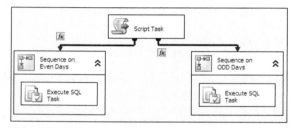

Figure 6-16

This is an easy task to perform by using an expression in a precedence constraint. To set this up define a Boolean variable as an expression called GateKeeperSequence. Make sure the variable is in a namespace UserExp to indicate that this variable is an expression-based variable. Set the expression to this formula:

```
DATEPART( "dd", GetDate() ) % 2
```

This expression takes the current day of the month and uses the modulus operator to leave the remainder as a result. Use this value to test in the precedence constraint to determine which sequence to run in the package. The sequence on even days should be run if the GateKeeperSequence returns 0 as a result, indicating that the current day of the month is evenly divisible by two. Right-click the precedence constraint and select edit to get to the editor and set it up to look like Figure 6-17.

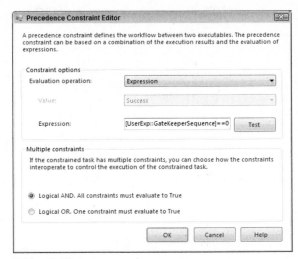

Figure 6-17

The expression @[UserExp::GateKeeperSequence]==0 is a Boolean expression that is testing the results of the first expression to see if the value is equal to zero. The second sequence should only execute if the current day is an odd day. The second precedence constraint would need an expression that looks like this:

```
@[UserExp::GateKeeperSequence]!=0
```

By factoring the first expression into a separate expression-based variable, you can reuse the same expression in both precedence constraints. This improves the readability and maintenance of your SSIS packages. With this example, you can see how a package can have sections that are conditionally executed. This same technique can also be employed to run Data Flows or other Control Flow Components conditionally using Boolean expressions. Refer back to the section on Boolean expressions if you need to review some other examples.

Using Expressions in Data Flow

Although you can set properties on some of the Data Flow Transforms, a typical use of an expression in a Data Flow Component is to alter a WHERE clause on a source component. In this example, you'll alter the SQL in a source component using a supplied date as a variable to pull out address information from the AdventureWorks database. Then you'll use a Data Flow expression to build a derived column to build a one-column data column that can be used for address labels.

To start, set up these variables at the Data Flow Scope Level:

Variable Name	Data Type	Namespace	Description
BaseSelect	String	UserVar	Contains base Select statement
SelectSQL_UserDateParm	DateTime	UserVar	Contains supplied date parm
SelectSQL	String	UserExp	Derived SQL to execute
SelectSQL_ExpDateParm	String	UserExp	Safe Date Expression

Notice that the namespaces for the BaseSelect and SelectSQL_UserDateParm variables are using a namespace UserVar. Namespaces are provided by the SSIS developer. We use them because it makes it clear which variables are expression-based and which are not. The UserVar namespace variables contain values that are provided by a user or external source. Provide these values for the following variables:

Variable Name	Value
BaseSelect	SELECT AddressLine1, AddressLine2, City,StateProvinceCode, PostalCode FROM person.Address adr INNER JOIN person.StateProvince stp ON adr.StateProvinceId = stp.StateProvinceId WHERE adr.ModifiedDate >=
SelectSQL_UserDateParm	1/12/2000

Note that you'll need to put the value from the BaseSelect variable into one continuous line to get it all into the variable. Make sure all of the string gets into the variable value before continuing.

The remaining variables will need to be set up as expression-based variables. At this point, you should be proficient at this. Set the EvaluateAsExpression property to True and prepare to add the expressions to each. Ultimately, you need a SQL string that contains the date from the SelectSQL_UserDateParm, but using dates in strings by just casting the date to a string can produce potentially unreliable results — especially if you are given the string in one culture and you are querying data stored in another collation. This is why the extra expression variable SelectSQL_ExpDateParm exists. This expression is a safe-date expression and looks like this:

```
(DT_WSTR, 4) DATEPART("yyyy", @[UserVar::SelectSQL_UserDateParm]) + "-" +
(DT_WSTR, 4) DATEPART("mm", @[UserVar::SelectSQL_UserDateParm]) + "-" +
(DT_WSTR, 4) DATEPART("dd", @[UserVar::SelectSQL_UserDateParm]) + " " +
(DT_WSTR, 4) DATEPART("hh", @[UserVar::SelectSQL_UserDateParm]) + ":" +
(DT_WSTR, 4) DATEPART("mi", @[UserVar::SelectSQL_UserDateParm]) + ":" +
(DT_WSTR, 4) DATEPART("ss", @[UserVar::SelectSQL_UserDateParm])
```

The expression parses out all the pieces of the date and creates an ISO-formatted date in a string format that can now be appended to the base SELECT SQL string. This is done in the last expression-based variable SelectSQL. The expression looks like this:

```
@[UserVar::BaseSelect] + "'" + @[UserExp::SelectSQL_ExpDateParm] + "'"
```

With all the pieces to create the SQL statement in place, all you need to do is apply the expression in a data source component. Drop an OLE Source component connected to the AdventureWorks database on the Data Flow surface, and set the Data Access Mode to retrieve the data as a SQL Command from a Variable. Set the variable name to the SelectSQL variable. The OLE DB Source Editor should look like Figure 6-18.

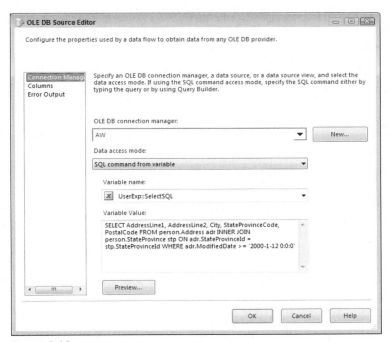

Figure 6-18

Click the Preview button to look at the data pulled with the current value of the variable SelectSQL_ UserDateParm. Change the value and check to see that the data changes as expected. Now the OLE DB source will contain the same columns, but the predicate can be easily and safely changed with a date parameter that is safe across cultures.

Now the final task is to create a one-column output that combines the address fields. Add a Derived Column Transform to the Data Flow and add a new column of type WSTR, length of 2000, named FullAddress. This column will need an expression that combines the columns of the address to build a one-column output. Remember that we are dealing with Data Flow data here, so it is possible to realize a NULL value in the data stream. If you simply concatenate every column and a NULL value exists anywhere, the entire string will evaluate to NULL. Further, we don't want to have addresses that have blank lines in the body, so we only want to add a newline character conditionally after addresses that aren't NULL. Because the data tables involved can only contain NULL values in the two address fields, the final expression looks like this:

```
(ISNULL(AddressLine1) ? "" : AddressLine1 + "\n") +
(ISNULL(AddressLine2) ? "" : AddressLine2 + "\n") +
 City + ", " + StateProvinceCode + " " + PostalCode
```

The Derived Column Transform should look similar to Figure 6-19.

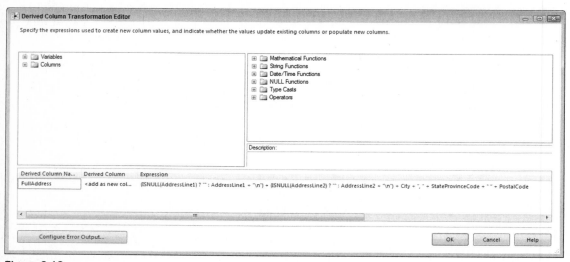

Figure 6-19

Running this example will create the one-output column of a combined address field that can be dynamically configured by a date parameter with a conditional Address2 line, depending upon whether the data exists. Using expressions to solve problems like this makes SSIS development seem almost too easy.

Summary

In this chapter, we started out with the mission of filling a gap in your understanding about expressions. The concept of expressions was a topic that got lost in the shuffle in the conversion from DTS to SSIS. Clearly, this feature is powerful; it enables dynamic package development in an efficient way and gets you out of the code and into getting work done. But expressions can be frustrating if you don't pay attention to the data types and whether you are working with data in variables or in the Data Flow. This chapter has been all about getting those "gotchas" out front and explained what we and other SSIS developers have experienced so that you don't have to experience them. Along the way, we consolidated the common questions, answers, and best practices we've learned about using expressions and made them available for you in one chapter.

In several places, we discussed setting variables programmatically and using scripting tasks and transforms to further the SSIS dynamic package capabilities. There are still places where expressions don't fit the bill and scripting tasks can be used to save the day. In the next chapter, you explore the scripting tasks both in the control and Data Flow roles and expand your SSIS capabilities.

7

Joining Data

In the simplest ETL scenarios, you use an SSIS pipeline to extract data from a single source table and populate the corresponding destination table. In practice, though, you usually won't see such trivial scenarios: The more common ETL scenarios will require you to access two or more Data Sources simultaneously and merge their results together into a single destination structure. For instance, you may have a normalized source system that uses three or more tables to represent the product catalog, whereas the destination represents the same information using a single de-normalized table (perhaps as part of a data warehouse schema). In this case you would need to join the multiple source tables together in order to present a unified structure to the destination table.

In the relational world, such requirements are easily met by employing a relational join operation. However, in the ETL world you may not be so fortunate that the tables to be joined live in the same physical database, same brand of database, same server, or in the worst cases even same physical location (all of which typically render the relational join method useless). In fact, one common scenario is where data from a legacy source system is staged in flat text files, which then need to be joined to dimensional data residing in a SQL Server data warehouse.

So the ETL system needs to be able to join data in a similar way to relational systems, but should not be constrained to having the source data live in the same physical database. SQL Server Integration Services provides several methods for performing such joins, ranging from support in native components through to custom methods implemented in TSQL or managed code.

This chapter explores the various options for performing joins, and contrasts when and which method you should use for various circumstances. After reading this chapter you should gain insight into how to optimize the various join operations in your ETL solution, and understand the design, performance, and resource tradeoffs therein.

The Lookup Component

The Lookup Component in SQL Server Integration Services allows you to perform the equivalent of relational inner and outer hash-joins. The main difference is that the operations occur outside the realm of the database engine. Typically you would use this component within the context of an integration process, such as the ETL layer that populates a data warehouse from source systems. For example, you may want to populate a table by joining data from two separate source systems on different database platforms.

The component can only join two datasets at a time, so in order to join three or more datasets you would need to chain multiple Lookup Components together. Compare this to relational join semantics where in a similar fashion you join two tables at a time, and compose multiple such operations to join three or more tables.

The transform is written to behave in a synchronous manner in that it does not block the pipeline while it is doing its work — at the same time that new rows are entering the Transformation Component, rows that have already been dealt with are leaving through one of several outputs. However, there is a catch here; in certain caching modes (discussed later) the component will initially block the package's execution for a period of time while it charges its internal caches.

The component provides several modes of operation that allow you to trade off performance and resource usage. In full-cache mode, one of the tables you are joining is loaded in its entirety into memory, and then the rows from the other table are flowed through the pipeline one buffer at a time and the selected join operation is performed. At the other end of the scale, there is no up-front caching done and each incoming row in the pipeline is compared one at a time to a specified relational table. There are modes in between these two extents, which we will explore later in this chapter (see the "Full-Cache Mode," "Partial-Cache Mode," and "No-Cache Mode" sections).

Of course, some rows will join successfully and some rows will not be joined — for example, you may have a customer who has made no purchases and thus their identifier in the customer table would have no matches in the sales table. SSIS supports this by having multiple outputs on the Lookup Component; in the simplest (default/legacy) configuration you would have one output for matched rows and a separate output for non-matched and error rows. This functionality allows you to build robust (error tolerant) processes that, for instance, might direct non-matched rows to a compensating area of the ETL that inserts a default value for the missing attributes (such as Unknown) and then merges the matched and non-matched streams back together again.

The Cache Connection Manager (CCM) is a separate component that is essential when creating advanced lookup operations. The CCM allows you to populate the Lookup cache from an arbitrary source; for instance, you can load the cache from a relational query, a text file, or a Web service. You can also use the CCM to persist the Lookup cache across iterations of a looping operation. You can still use the Lookup Component without explicitly using the CCM, however you would then lose the resource and performance gains in doing so.

The Merge Join Component

The Merge Join Component in SQL Server Integration Services allows you to perform an inner or outer join in a streaming fashion. This component behaves in a synchronous manner (although it's actually partially blocking, but that is not relevant right now) in that it does not perform the same up-front caching operations that block the Data Flow. The component accepts two sorted input streams, and outputs a single stream that combines the chosen columns into a single structure. It is not possible to configure a separate non-matched output.

The Merge Join Component is different from the Lookup Component in that it does not support OLE DB or ADO.NET connections to the reference dataset; both tables to be joined have to be streamed in via an input pipeline. Furthermore, both datasets have to be sorted and the sorting has to be by the same set of columns in exactly the same order, which can create some overhead upstream.

Merge Join typically uses less memory than the Lookup Component, because it only maintains the required few rows in memory to support joining the two streams. However, it does not support short circuit execution in that both pipelines need to stream their entire contents before the component considers its work done. For example, if the first input has five rows, and the second input has one million rows, and it so happens that the first five rows immediately join successfully, the component will still stream the other 999,995 rows from the second input even though they cannot possibly be joined anymore. This makes sense in left-join scenarios; however, the architectural reasons for this being the case in inner-join scenarios is beyond the scope of this chapter.

Contrasting to the Relational Join

Though the methods and syntax you employ in the relational and SSIS worlds may differ, joining multiple row sets together using congruent keys achieves the same desired result. In the relational database world the equivalent of a lookup is accomplished by joining two or more tables together using declarative syntax that executes in a set-based manner. The operation remains close to the data at all times; there is typically no need to move the data out-of-process with respect to the database engine (except when joining across databases, though this is usually a non-optimal operation). When joining tables within the same database, the engine can take advantage of multiple different internal algorithms, knowledge of table statistics, cardinality, temporary storage, cost-based plans, and the benefit of many years of ongoing research and code optimization. Operations can still complete in a resource-constrained environment because the platform has many intrinsic functions and operators that simplify multi-step operations, such as implicit parallelism, paging, sorting, and hashing.

In a cost-based optimization database system, the end-user experience is typically transparent; the declarative SQL syntax (calculus) abstracts the underlying relational machinations (algebra) such that the user may not in fact know how the problem was solved by the engine (thus; query plans). In other words, the engine has the ability to transform a problem statement as defined by the user into an internal form that can be optimized into one of many solution sets — transparently. The end-user experience is usually synchronous and non-blocking; results are materialized in a streaming manner with the engine effecting the highest degree of parallelism possible.

The operation is atomic in that once a join is specified, the operation either completes or fails in total — there are no sub-steps that can succeed or fail in a way the user would experience independently. Furthermore, it is not possible to receive two result sets from the query at the same time — for instance, if we specified a left join, then we could not direct the matches to go one direction and the non-matches somewhere else.

Advanced algorithms allow efficient caching of multiple joins using the same tables — for instance, round-robin read-ahead allows separate TSQL statements (using the same base tables) to utilize the same caches.

Here's a relational query that joins two tables from the AdventureWorksDW2008 database together. Notice how we only join two tables at a time, using declarative syntax, with particular attention being paid to specification of the join columns:

```
select sc.EnglishProductSubcategoryName, p.EnglishProductName
from dbo.DimProductSubcategory sc
inner join dbo.DimProduct p
on sc.ProductSubcategoryKey = p.ProductSubcategoryKey;
```

For reference purposes, Figure 7-1 shows the plan that SQL Server chooses to execute this join.

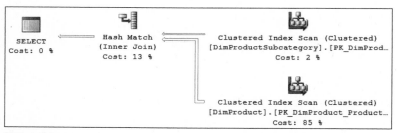

Figure 7-1

In SSIS the data is usually joined using a Lookup Transform on a buffered basis. The Merge Join Transform can also be used, though it was designed to solve a different class of patterns. The calculus/algebra for these components is deterministic; the configuration that the user supplies is directly utilized by the engine — in other words, there is no opportunity for the platform to make any intelligent choices based on statistics, cost, cardinality, or count. Furthermore, the data is loaded into out-of-process buffers (with respect to the database engine) and is then treated on a row-by-row manner; so because this moves the data away from the source we expect that performance and scale are affected.

The end-user experience is synchronous, though in the case of some modes of the Lookup Component the process is blocked while the cache loads in its entirety. Execution is non-atomic in that one of multiple phases of the process can succeed or fail independently. Furthermore, we can direct successful matches to flow out the Lookup Component to one consumer, the non-matches to flow to a separate consumer, and the errors to a third.

Resource usage and performance compete: In Lookup's full-cache mode — which is typically fastest — the cache is acquired, and then remains in memory until the process (package) terminates, and there are no implicit operators (sorting, hashing, and paging) to balance resource usage. In no-cache or partial-cache modes the resource usage is initially lower because the cache is charged on the fly; however, overall performance might be lower. The operation is explicitly parallel; individual packages scale-out, if and only if the developer intentionally created multiple pipelines and manually segmented the data.

There is no opportunity for the Lookup Component to implicitly perform in an SMP (or scale-out) manner. The same applies to the Merge Join Component — on suitable hardware it will run on a separate thread to other components, but it will not utilize multiple threads within itself.

Figure 7-2 shows an SSIS package that uses a Lookup Component to demonstrate the same functionality as the previous SQL statement. Notice how the Product table is pipelined directly into the Lookup Component, but the SubCategory table is referenced using properties on the component itself. It is interesting to compare this package with the query plan generated by SQL Server for the previous SQL query. Notice how, in this case, SQL Server chose to utilize a hash join operation, which happens to coincide with the mechanics underlying the Lookup Component when used in full-cache mode. The explicit design chosen by the developer in SSIS corresponds almost exactly to the plan chosen by SQL Server to generate the same result set.

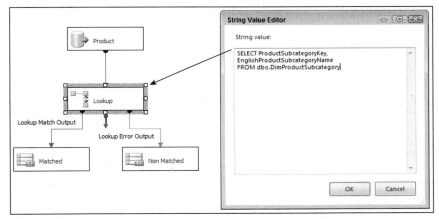

Figure 7-2

Figure 7-3 shows the same functionality; this time built using a Merge Join Component. Notice how similar this looks to the SQL Server plan (though in truth the execution semantics are quite different).

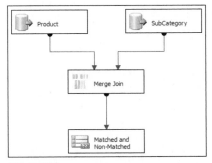

Figure 7-3

New Lookup Features

In previous versions of the product, the Lookup Component could use only source data for its cache from specific OLE DB connections, and the cache could be populated by using only a SQL query. The current version of the Lookup Component allows you to populate the cache using a separate pipeline in either the same or a different package. You can use source data from just about anywhere.

Previously you needed to reload the cache every time it was used. For example, if you had two pipelines in the same package that each required the same reference dataset, each Lookup Component would load its own copy of the cache separately. Now you can persist the cache to virtual memory or to permanent file storage. This means that within the same package, multiple Lookup Components can share the same cache, and the cache does not need to be re-loaded during each iteration of a looping operation. You can persist the cache to a file and share it with other packages. The cache file format is optimized for speed, and can be orders of magnitude faster than reloading the reference dataset from the original relational source.

The Lookup Component also provides the miss-cache feature. In scenarios where the component is configured to perform the lookups directly against the database, the miss-cache feature enables you to optimize the performance by optionally loading into cache the rows without matching entries in the reference dataset. For example, if the component receives the value 123 in the incoming pipeline, but there are no matching entries in the reference dataset, the component will not try to find that value in the reference dataset again. In other words, the component "remembers" which values it did *not* find before. You can also specify how much memory the miss-cache should use (expressed as a percentage of the total cache limit, by default 20%). This reduces a redundant and expensive trip to the database. The miss-cache feature alone can contribute up to a 40% performance improvement in some scenarios.

In the previous version of the component, you only had two outputs — one for matched rows and another that combined non-matches and errors. However, the latter output caused much consternation with SSIS users — it is often the case that a non-match is not an error and is in fact expected, so the new component has one output for non-matches and a separate output for true errors (such as truncations). Note that the old combined output is still available as an option for backwards compatibility.

For troubleshooting any issues you may have with SSIS, you can create a memory dump of the SSIS solution while it is running. To create a dump on demand, in a command prompt window run `dtutil.exe /dump processid`. The processid is the PID of dtexec or dtsdebughost that is executing the package — you can find the PID by opening up Windows Task Manager. Running this command will pause the package mid-execution, generate a mini-memory dump, and then resume package execution.

Building the Basic Package

To simplify explaining the operation of the Lookup Component in the next few sections, here is a typical ETL problem that we will use to discuss several solutions using the components configured in various modes.

The AdventureWorks2008 database is a typical OLTP store for a bicycle retailer, and AdventureWorksDW2008 is a database that contains the corresponding de-normalized data warehouse structures. We will use both these databases as well as some secondary data to represent a real-world ETL scenario. (If you do not have the databases, download them from www.codeplex.com.)

The core operation we will focus on is to extract fact data from the source system; in this scenario we will not yet be loading data into the warehouse itself. Obviously you do not want to do one without the other, but it makes it easier to understand the solution if we tackle a smaller subset of the problem by itself.

We will extract sales order (fact) data from AdventureWorks2008, and later on we will load it into AdventureWorksDW2008, performing multiple joins along the way. The order information in AdventureWorks2008 is represented by two main tables: SalesOrderHeader and SalesOrderDetail. We need to join these two tables first.

The SalesOrderHeader table has many columns that in the real world would be interesting, but for this exercise let's scope down the columns to just the necessary few. Likewise, the SalesOrderDetail table has many useful columns but we will use just a few of them. Here are the table structure and first five rows of data for these two structures:

SalesOrderID	OrderDate	CustomerID
43659	2001-07-01	676
43660	2001-07-01	117
43661	2001-07-01	442
43662	2001-07-01	227
43663	2001-07-01	510

SalesOrderID	SalesOrderDetailID	ProductID	OrderQty	UnitPrice	LineTotal
43659	1	776	1	2024.9940	2024.994000
43659	2	777	3	2024.9940	6074.982000
43659	3	778	1	2024.9940	2024.994000
43659	4	771	1	2039.9940	2039.994000
43659	5	772	1	2039.9940	2039.994000

As you can see, we need to join these two tables together because one table contains the order header information and the other contains the order details. Figure 7-4 is a conceptual view of what the join would look like.

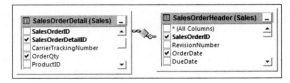

Figure 7-4

However, this does not get us all the way there. The CustomerID column is a surrogate key that is specific to the source system, and the very definition of surrogate keys dictates that no other system — including the data warehouse — should have any knowledge of them. So in order to populate the warehouse we need to get the original business (natural) key. Thus, we must join the SalesOrderHeader table (Sales.SalesOrderHeader) to the Customer table (Sales.Customer) in order to find the customer business key called AccountNumber. So our conceptual join now looks like Figure 7-5.

Figure 7-5

Similarly for Product, we need to add the Product table (Production.Product) to this join in order to derive the natural key called ProductNumber, as shown in Figure 7-6.

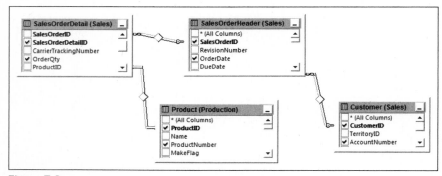

Figure 7-6

Creating the Basic Package

Refer to Figure 7-7. Create a new SSIS package that contains an OLE DB Connection Manager called AdventureWorks that points to the AdventureWorks2008 database, and a single empty Data Flow Task.

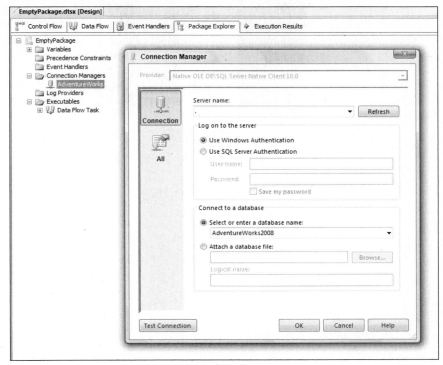

Figure 7-7

Using a Relational Join in the Source

The easiest and most obvious solution in this particular scenario is to use a relational join to extract the data. In other words, we can build a package that has a single source (let's use an OLE DB Source Component) and set the query string in the source to utilize relational joins.

Drop an OLE DB Source Component on the Data Flow design surface, hook it up to the AdventureWorks Connection Manager, and set its query string as follows:

```
select
    --columns from Sales.SalesOrderHeader
    oh.SalesOrderID, oh.OrderDate, oh.CustomerID,
    --columns from Sales.Customer
    c.AccountNumber,
    --columns from Sales.SalesOrderDetail
    od.SalesOrderDetailID, od.ProductID, od.OrderQty, od.UnitPrice, od.LineTotal,
    --columns from Production.Product
    p.ProductNumber
from Sales.SalesOrderHeader as oh
inner join Sales.Customer as c on (oh.CustomerID = c.CustomerID)
left join Sales.SalesOrderDetail as od on (oh.SalesOrderID = od.SalesOrderID)
inner join Production.Product as p on (od.ProductID = p.ProductID);
```

Note that you can either type this query in by hand, or use the Build Query button in the user interface of the OLE DB Source Component to construct it visually. Click the Preview button and make sure that it executes correctly (see Figure 7-8).

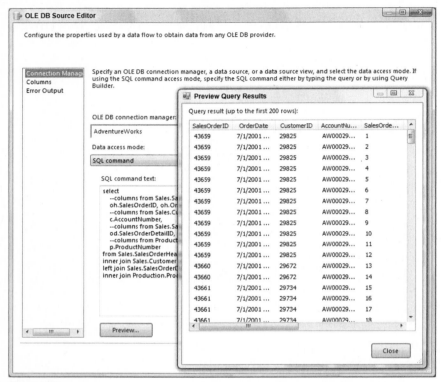

Figure 7-8

For seasoned SQL developers the query should be fairly intuitive — the only thing worth calling out is that we used a left join between the order header and order details tables because it is conceivable that an order header could exist without any corresponding details. If we had used an inner join here, we would have lost all such rows exhibiting this behavior. On the contrary, we have used inner joins everywhere else because an order header cannot exist without an associated customer, and a details row cannot exist without an associated product. In business terms we always have a customer to whom we will sell zero or (hopefully) more products.

Close the preview dialog; hit OK on the OLE DB Source Editor UI, and then hook up the Source Component to a Union All Component as shown in Figure 7-9, which serves as a temporary destination. Create a Data Viewer Grid on the pipeline in order to watch the data travel through the system. Execute the package in debug mode and notice how we get our required results in the Data Viewer window.

The Union All Component has nothing to do with this specific solution; it serves simply as a clever trick to get a temporary trash destination so that we don't have to physically land the data in a database or file. In a real solution this hack would serve no purpose, and you would need to replace it with a real destination. Note that you could also use some of the other asynchronous components or the Row Count Component for the same purpose, though in the latter case you would need to also create a temporary variable to hold the count value. In some cases the SSIS engine is smart enough to realize that the trash destination is doing nothing useful and will remove it from the execution image. If this happens you can use a Flat File Destination to write the data to a temporary file.

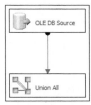

Figure 7-9

Using the Merge Join Component

Another way we could perform the join is to use Merge Join Components. In this specific scenario this does not make much sense because the database will likely perform the most optimal joins because all the data resides in one place. However, we can imagine a system where the four tables we are joining reside in more than one location; perhaps the sales and customer data is in SQL Server, and the product data is in a flat file, which is dumped nightly from a mainframe. Let's build a package to emulate such a scenario:

1. Start again with the basic package (as shown in Figure 7-7) and proceed as follows. Because we do not have any actual text files as sources, let's create them inside the same package and then utilize them as need be. Note that a real solution would not require this step; we just need to do this, so that we can emulate a scenario more complex than our own.

2. Name the empty Data Flow Task "DFT Create Text Files." Inside this task create a pipeline that selects the required columns from the Product table in the AdventureWorks2008 database and writes the data to a text file. Here is the SQL statement you will need:

```
select ProductID, ProductNumber
from Production.Product;
```

3. Configure the Flat File Destination Component to write to a location of your choice on your local hard drive, and make sure you select the delimited option and specify column headers when configuring the destination options, as shown in Figure 7-10. Name the flat file Product.txt.

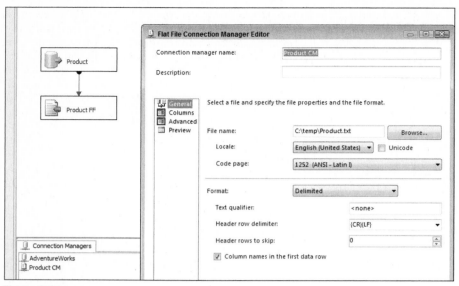

Figure 7-10

4. Execute the package; you should now have a text file containing the Product data. Now create a second Data Flow Task and rename it "DFT Extract Source." Hook up the first and second Data Flow Tasks so that they execute serially as shown in Figure 7-11. Inside the second (new) Data Flow Task, you'll use the Lookup and Merge Join solutions to gain the same result as you did previously.

Figure 7-11

When using the Lookup Component, the rule of thumb is that you want to make sure that the largest table (usually a fact table) gets streamed into the component, and the smallest table (usually a dimension table) gets cached. The reason for this is that the table that gets cached will block the flow while it is loaded into memory, and you thus want to make sure it is as small as possible. In our case the tables are all small, but imagine that the order header and details data is the largest, so we don't want to incur the overhead of caching it. Thus, you can use a Merge Join Component instead of a Lookup to achieve the same result, without the overhead of caching a large amount of data.

The simplest solution we have to retrieve the relational data would be to join the order header and order details tables directly in the Source Component (in a similar manner to that shown earlier). However, let's rather follow a more complex route in order to illustrate some of the other options we have available:

1. Drop an OLE DB Source Component on the design surface of the second Data Flow Task and name it SRC Order Header. Hook it up to the AdventureWorks Connection Manager and use the following statement as the query:

```
select SalesOrderID, OrderDate, CustomerID
from Sales.SalesOrderHeader;
```

Of course you could have just chosen the Table or View option in the source UI, or alternatively utilized a select * *query, and perhaps even deselected specific columns in the Columns tab of the UI. However, these are all bad practices and will usually lead to degraded performance. It is imperative that, where possible, you specify the exact columns you require in the select clause. Furthermore you should use a predicate (*where *clause) to limit the number of rows returned to just the ones you need.*

2. Check that the query executes OK by using the Preview button, then hook up a Sort Component downstream of the source you have just created. Open the editor for the Sort Component and choose to sort the data by the SalesOrderID column, as shown in Figure 7-12. The reason we do this is that we plan to use a Merge Join Component later, and it requires sorted input streams. (Note that the Lookup Component does not require sorted inputs.)

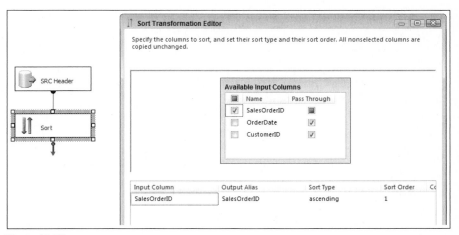

Figure 7-12

3. The next step is to retrieve the SalesOrderDetails data. Drop another OLE DB Source on the design surface, name it SRC Details, and set its query as follows. Notice how in this case you have included an ORDER BY clause directly in the SQL select statement. This is more efficient than the way you sorted the order header data, because SQL Server can sort it for you before passing it out-of-process to SSIS. Once again, we use different methods to illustrate the various options available:

```
select SalesOrderID, SalesOrderDetailID, ProductID, OrderQty, UnitPrice, LineTotal
from Sales.SalesOrderDetail
order by SalesOrderID, SalesOrderDetailID, ProductID;
```

4. Now drop a Merge Join Component on the surface and connect the outputs from the last two components to it. Specify the input coming from SRC Header (via the Sort Component) to be the left input, and the input coming from SRC Details to be the right input. You need to do this because, as discussed previously, we want to use a left join in order to keep rows from the header that do not have corresponding detail records.

After connecting both inputs, try to open the editor for the Merge Join Component; you should receive an error stating that "The IsSorted property must be set to True on both sources of this transformation." The reason we get this error is because the Merge Join Component requires inputs that are sorted exactly the same way. However, we did ensure this by using a Sort Component on one stream and an explicit TSQL ORDER BY clause on the other stream, so what's going on? Well the simple answer is that the OLE DB Source Component works in a pass-through manner, and so it does not know or care that the ORDER BY clause was specified in the second SQL query statement. By using the Sort Component we forced SSIS to perform the sort, and so in that case it is fully aware of the ordering.

In order to remedy this situation, we have to tell the Source Component that its input data is pre-sorted. Be very careful when doing this — by specifying the sort order in the following way you are asking the system to trust that you know what you are talking about and that the data is in fact sorted. If the data is not sorted, or it is sorted in a different manner to what you specified, then your package can act unpredictably, which could lead to data integrity issues and loss.

1. Refer to Figure 7-13. Right-click the SRC Details Component and choose Show Advanced Editor. Go to the Input and Output Properties tab and click the Root Node for the default output (not the error output). In the property grid on the right-hand side you should see a property called IsSorted. Change this to True.

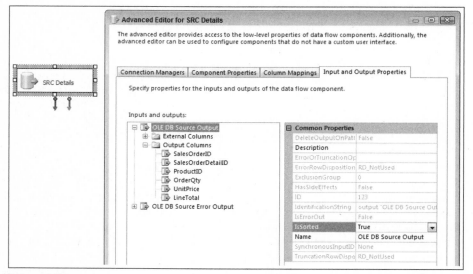

Figure 7-13

2. The preceding step told the component that the data is pre-sorted, but it did not tell it in what order. So the next step is to select the columns that are being sorted on, and assign them values as follows: If the column is not sorted, the value should be zero. If the column is sorted in ascending order, the value should be positive. If the column is sorted in descending order, the value should be negative. The absolute value of the number should correspond to the column's position in the order list. For instance, if the query was sorted as follows, "SalesOrderID ascending, ProductID descending," then we would assign the value 1 to SalesOrderID and the value -2 to ProductID, with all other columns being 0.

3. Expand the Output Columns Node under the same default Output Node, then select the SalesOrderID column. In the property grid set the SortKeyPosition value to 1, as shown in Figure 7-14.

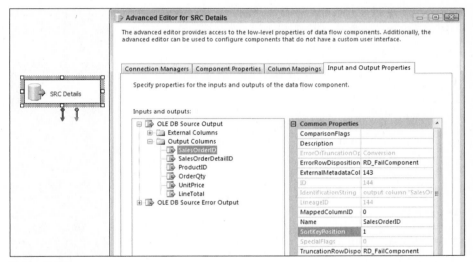

Figure 7-14

4. Close the dialog and try again to open the Merge Join UI; this time you should be successful. By default the component works in inner join mode, but you can change that very easily by selecting (in our case) Left Outer Join from the drop-down at the top of the dialog. You can also choose a Full Outer Join, which would perform a Cartesian join of all the data, though depending on the size of the source data this will have a high memory overhead. See Figure 7-15.

    If you had made a mistake earlier while specifying which input was the left and which was the right, you can click the Swap Inputs button to switch their places. The component will automatically figure out which columns you are joining on based on their sort orders; if it had somehow got it wrong, or there were more columns you needed to join on, you can drag a column from the left to the right in order to specify more join criteria. However, the component will refuse any column combinations that are not part of the ordering criteria.

5. Finally, drop a Union All Component on the surface and connect the output of the Merge Join Component to it. Place a Data Viewer Grid on the output path of the Merge Join Component and execute the package. Have a look at the results in the grid viewer. You should see that the data has been joined as required.

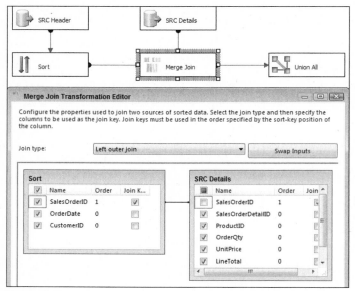

Figure 7-15

Merge Join is a useful component to use when memory limits or data sizes restrict you from using a Lookup Component. However, it requires that both input streams are sorted — which may be challenging to do with large datasets — and by design it does not provide any way of caching either dataset. The next section examines the Lookup Component and shows how it can help us solve join problems in a different way.

Using the Lookup Component

The Lookup Component solves join issues in a different manner than the Merge Join Component. The Lookup Component typically caches one of the datasets in memory, and then compares each row arriving from the other dataset in its input pipeline against the cache. The caching mechanism is highly configurable, providing a variety of different options in order to balance the performance and resource utilization of the process.

Full-Cache Mode

The first caching mode we will examine is full-cache mode, whereby the Lookup Component stores all the rows resulting from a specified query in memory. The benefit of this mode is that Lookups against the in-memory cache are very fast — often an order of magnitude or more, relative to a database lookup.

Continuing with the example package we built in the previous section (Merge Join), we will extend the existing package in order to join the other tables we require. You have got the related values from the order header and order detail tables but you still need to map the natural keys from the Product and Customer tables. You could use Merge Join Components again, but let's investigate how the Lookup Component can help us here:

1. Open the package you created in the previous step. Remove the Union All Component. Drop a Lookup Component on the surface, name it LKP Customer, and connect the output of the Merge Join Component to it. Open the editor of the Lookup Component.

2. Select Full-Cache Mode, specifying an OLE DB Connection Manager. There is also an option to specify a Cache Connection Manager (CCM) but we won't use this just yet — see later on in this chapter for details on how to use the CCM. (After you have learned about the CCM, later on you can come back and try to use it here instead of the OLE DB Connection Manager.)

3. Click the Connection tab and select the AdventureWorks connection, and then use the following SQL query:

```
select CustomerID, AccountNumber
from Sales.Customer;
```

4. Preview the results to make sure everything is set up OK, then click the Columns tab. Drag the CustomerID column from the left-hand table over to the CustomerID column on the right; this should create a linkage between these two columns, which tells the component that this column is used to perform the join. Click the checkbox next to the AccountNumber column on the right, which tells the component that you want to bring back the AccountNumber values from the Customer table for each row it compares. Note that it is not necessary to retrieve the CustomerID values from the right-hand side because we already have them from the input columns. The editor should now look like Figure 7-16.

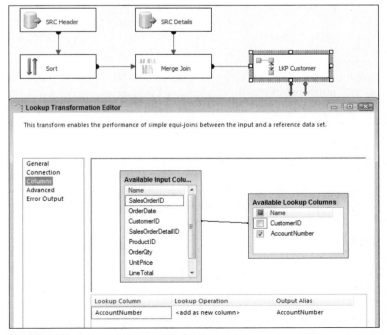

Figure 7-16

5. Click OK on the dialog, hook up a "trash" Union All Component (as shown in Figure 7-9; choose Lookup Match Output on the dialog that gets raised when you do this). Create a Data Viewer Grid on the match output path of the Lookup Component and execute the package (you could also attach a data viewer on the no-match output and error output if needed). You should see results similar to Figure 7-17. Notice how we have all the columns from the order and details data, as well as the selected column from the Customer.

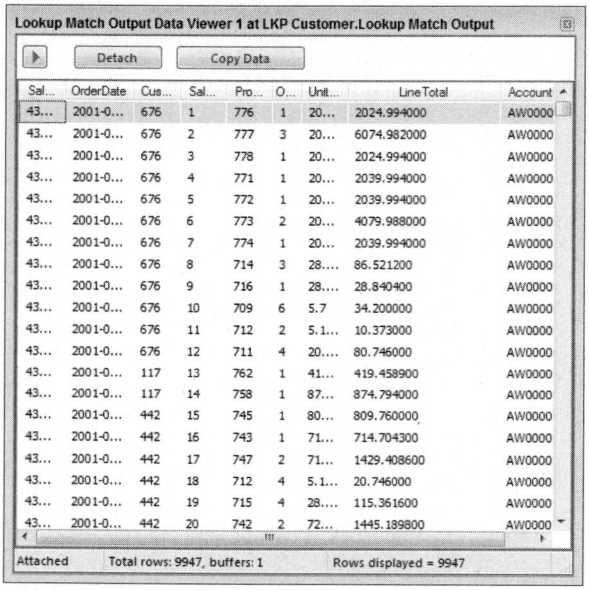
Lookup Match Output Data Viewer 1 at LKP Customer.Lookup Match Output

Detach | Copy Data

Sal...	OrderDate	Cus...	Sal...	Pro...	O...	Unit...	LineTotal	Account
43...	2001-0...	676	1	776	1	20...	2024.994000	AW0000
43...	2001-0...	676	2	777	3	20...	6074.982000	AW0000
43...	2001-0...	676	3	778	1	20...	2024.994000	AW0000
43...	2001-0...	676	4	771	1	20...	2039.994000	AW0000
43...	2001-0...	676	5	772	1	20...	2039.994000	AW0000
43...	2001-0...	676	6	773	2	20...	4079.988000	AW0000
43...	2001-0...	676	7	774	1	20...	2039.994000	AW0000
43...	2001-0...	676	8	714	3	28....	86.521200	AW0000
43...	2001-0...	676	9	716	1	28....	28.840400	AW0000
43...	2001-0...	676	10	709	6	5.7	34.200000	AW0000
43...	2001-0...	676	11	712	2	5.1...	10.373000	AW0000
43...	2001-0...	676	12	711	4	20....	80.746000	AW0000
43...	2001-0...	117	13	762	1	41...	419.458900	AW0000
43...	2001-0...	117	14	758	1	87...	874.794000	AW0000
43...	2001-0...	442	15	745	1	80...	809.760000	AW0000
43...	2001-0...	442	16	743	1	71...	714.704300	AW0000
43...	2001-0...	442	17	747	2	71...	1429.408600	AW0000
43...	2001-0...	442	18	712	4	5.1...	20.746000	AW0000
43...	2001-0...	442	19	715	4	28....	115.361600	AW0000
43...	2001-0...	442	20	742	2	72...	1445.189800	AW0000

Attached | Total rows: 9947, buffers: 1 | Rows displayed = 9947

Figure 7-17

Because the Customer table is so small and the package runs so fast, you may not have noticed what happened here. As part of the pre-execution phase of the component, the Lookup Component went and fetched all the rows from the Customer table using the query we specified (because the Lookup was configured to execute in Full-Cache mode). In this case there are only twenty thousand or so rows, so this happens very quickly. Imagine that there were many more rows, perhaps two million. In this case you would likely see a delay between executing the package and seeing any data actually travelling down the second pipeline.

Figure 7-18 is a decision tree that demonstrates how the full-cache mode operates at runtime. Note that the Lookup Component can be configured to send found and not-found rows to the same output, but the illustration assumes they are going to different outputs. In either case, the basic algorithm is the same.

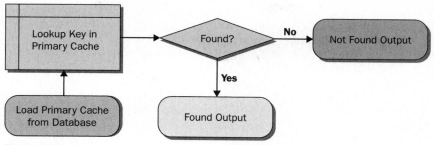

Figure 7-18

Have a look at the Progress tab on the SSIS design surface (Figure 7-19) and see how long the data took to be loaded into the in-memory cache. In larger datasets this number will be much larger and could even take longer than the execution of the primary functionality!

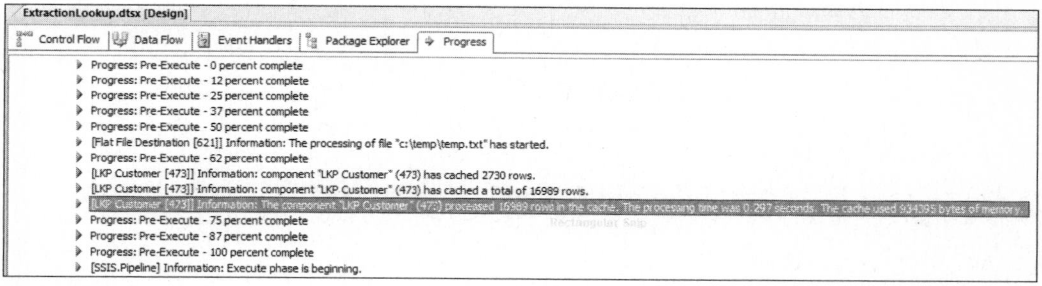

Figure 7-19

If during development and testing you want to emulate a long-running query, use the TSQL `waitfor` *statement in the query in the following manner. Remember to remove the Data Viewer first though, because it will block synchronous execution of the pipeline.*

```
waitfor delay '00:00:059'; --Wait 5 seconds before returning any rows
select CustomerID, AccountNumber
from Sales.Customer;
```

After fetching all the rows from the specified source, the Lookup Component caches them in memory in a special hash structure. The package then continues execution; as each input row enters the Lookup Component, the specified key values are compared to the in-memory hash values, and, if a match is found, the specified return values are added to the output stream.

No-Cache Mode

So what happens if the reference table (the Customer table in this case) is too large to cache all at once in the system's memory? In that case we have several options available; we can choose to cache nothing, or we can choose to cache only some of the data. Let's explore the first option: no-cache mode.

In no-cache mode the Lookup Component is configured almost exactly the same; the main difference is that at execution time the reference table is not loaded into the hash structure. Instead, as each input row flows through the Lookup Component, the component sends a request to the reference table in the database server to ask for a match. As you would expect, this can have a high performance overhead on the system, so use this mode with care.

Depending on the size of the reference data, this mode is usually the slowest, though it scales to the largest number of reference rows. It is also useful for systems where the reference data is highly volatile, where any form of caching would render the results stale and erroneous.

Figure 7-20 illustrates the decision tree that the component uses during runtime. Once again, the diagram assumes that separate outputs are configured for found and not-found rows, though the algorithm would be the same if all rows were sent to a single output.

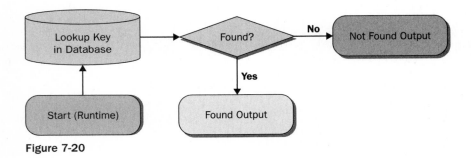

Figure 7-20

Here are the steps to build a package that uses no-cache mode:

1. Instead of building a brand new package to try out the no-cache mode, use the package you built in the previous section ("Full-Cache Mode"). Open the editor for the Lookup Component and on the first tab (General), choose the No-Cache option. In this mode you also have the ability to customize (optimize) the query that SSIS will submit to the relational engine. To do this, click the Advanced tab and check the Modify the SQL Statement checkbox. In this case the auto-generated statement is close enough to optimal, so we won't touch it. (If you have any problems reconfiguring the Lookup component, then delete the component, drop a new Lookup on the design surface, and reconnect and configure it from scratch.)

2. Execute the package and you should see that it takes slightly longer to execute than before, but the results should be the same.

The tradeoff you make between the caching modes is mostly to do with performance versus resource utilization. Full-cache mode can potentially use a lot of memory to hold the reference rows in memory, but it is usually the fastest because lookup operations do not require a trip to the database. No-cache mode, on the other hand, requires next to no memory, but is slower because it requires a database call for every lookup. This is not a bad thing; your reference table may be volatile (the data may be changing often) and so you may want to use no-cache mode to make sure you always have the latest version of each row.

Next we will look at partial-cache mode, which offers you the benefits of both full-cache and no-cache modes.

Partial-Cache Mode

The partial-cache mode gives you a middle ground between the no-cache and full-cache options. In this mode the component only caches the most-recently used data within the memory boundaries specified. As soon as the cache grows too big, the least-used cache data is thrown away.

When the package starts then, much like the no-cache mode, no data is preloaded into the Lookup cache. As each input row enters the component, it uses the specified key(s) to attempt to find a matching record in the reference table using the specified query. If a match is found, both the key and lookup values are added to the local cache on a just-in-time basis. If that same key enters the Lookup Component again, it can retrieve the matching value from the local cache instead of the reference table, thereby saving the expense and time incurred of re-querying the database.

For example, in our scenario the input stream may contain a CustomerID of 123. The first time the component sees this value, it goes to the database and tries to find it using the specified query. If it finds the value, it retrieves the AccountNumber and then adds the CustomerID/AccountNumber combination to its local cache. If Customer 123 comes through again later, the component will retrieve the AccountNumber directly from the local cache instead of going to the database.

If, however, the key is not found in the local cache, the component will check the database to see if it exists there. Note that the key may not be in the local cache for several reasons; maybe it is the first time it was seen, maybe it was previously in the local cache but was evicted due to memory pressure, or finally, it could have been seen before but was also not found in the database.

For example, if CustomerID 456 enters the component, it will check the local cache for the value and, assuming it is not found, it will then check the database. Assuming it finds it in the database, it will add 456 to its local cache. The next time CustomerID 456 enters the component, it can retrieve the value directly from its local cache without going to the database. However, it could also be the case that memory pressure caused this key/value to be dropped from the local cache, in which case the component will incur another database call.

If CustomerID 789 is not found in the local cache, and it is also not subsequently found in the reference table, the component will treat the row as a non-match, and will send it down the output you have chosen for non-matched rows (typically the no-match or error output). Every time that CustomerID 789 enters the component it will go through these same set of operations. If you have a high degree of expected misses in your Lookup scenario, this latter behavior — though proper and expected — can be a cause of long execution times because database calls are expensive relative to a local cache check.

The partial-cache mode provides another caching feature called the miss cache. If you use the partial-cache and miss-cache options together, you can get further performance gains. You can request that the component remembers values that it did not previously find in the reference table and thus will not incur the expense of looking for them again. This feature goes a long way to solving the performance issues discussed in the previous paragraph, because ideally every key is looked for once — and only once — in the reference table. The component remembers keys it did not find before and does not attempt to find them again.

To configure this mode, follow these steps (refer to Figure 7-21):

1. Open the Lookup editor, and in the General tab select the Partial Cache option. In the Advanced tab specify the upper memory boundaries for the cache and edit the SQL statement as necessary. Note that both 32-bit and 64-bit boundaries are available because the package may be built and tested on a 32-bit platform but deployed to a 64-bit platform, which has more memory. Providing both options makes it simple to configure the component's behavior on the different platforms.

2. If you want to use the miss-cache feature, configure what percentage of the total cache memory you want to use for this secondary cache (say, 25%).

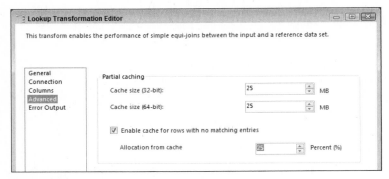

Figure 7-21

Figure 7-22 is a decision tree that demonstrates how the Lookup Component operates at runtime when using the partial-cache and miss-cache options. Note that some of the steps are conceptual, and in reality, are implemented using a more optimal design. As per the decision trees shown for the other modes, this illustration assumes separate outputs are used for the found and not-found rows.

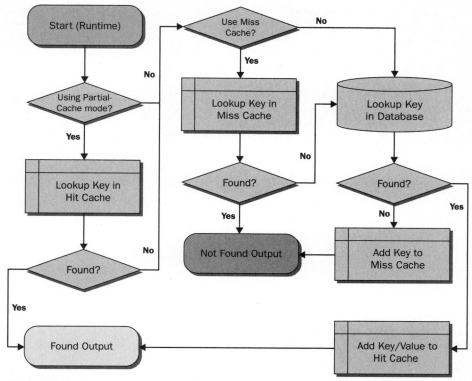

Figure 7-22

Multiple Outputs

You now have the Lookup Component working, and you have investigated different ways of optimizing its performance while using fewer or more resources. But you may not have seen how to utilize some of the other features in the component, such as the different outputs that are available.

Continue using the same package you built in the previous sections:

1. Reset the Lookup Component so that it works in full-cache mode. It so happens that our data is clean and thus every row finds a match, but we can emulate rows not being found by playing quick and dirty with the Lookup query string. This is a useful trick to use at design time in order to test the robustness and behavior of your Lookup Components. Change the query statement in the Lookup Component as follows:

```
select CustomerID, AccountNumber
from Sales.Customer
where CustomerID % 7 <> 0; --Remove 1/7 of the rows
```

2. Run the package again, and this time you should see that it fails to execute fully because the cache contains 1/7th fewer rows than before, so some of the incoming keys will not find a match, as shown in Figure 7-23. Because the default error behavior of the component is to fail on any non-match or error condition such as truncation, the Lookup halts as expected.

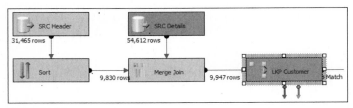

Figure 7-23

Try some of the other output options. Open the Lookup editor and on the drop-down listbox in the General tab choose how you want the Lookup Component to behave when it does not manage to find a matching join entry:

❑ Fail Component should already be selected. This is the default behavior, which will cause the component to raise an exception and halt execution if a non-matching row is found or a row causes an error such as a data truncation.

❑ Ignore Failure sends any non-matched rows as well as rows that cause errors down the same output as the matched rows, but the lookup values (in this case AccountNumber) will be set to null. You should be able to see this in the Data Viewer Grid; several of the AccountNumbers will have null values.

❑ Redirect Rows to Error Output is provided for backwards compatibility with SQL Server 2005 and causes the component to send both non-matched and error-causing rows down the same error (red) output.

❑ Redirect Rows to No Match Output causes errors to flow down the error (red) output, and no-match rows to flow down the no-match output.

3. Choose Ignore Failure and execute the package. The results should look like Figure 7-24. You can see that the number of incoming rows on the Lookup Component matches the number of rows coming out of its match output, even though 1/7th of the rows were not actually matched. This is because the rows failed to find a match, but because you configured the Ignore Failure option, the component did not stop execution.

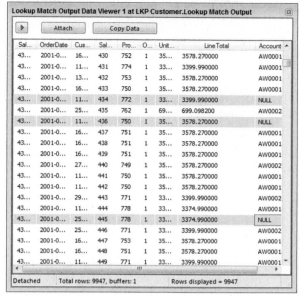

Lookup Match Output Data Viewer 1 at LKP Customer.Lookup Match Output

Attach		Copy Data						

Sal...	OrderDate	Cus...	Sal...	Pro...	O...	Unit...	Line Total	Account ▲
43...	2001-0...	16...	430	752	1	35...	3578.270000	AW0001
43...	2001-0...	11...	431	774	1	33...	3399.990000	AW0001
43...	2001-0...	13...	432	753	1	35...	3578.270000	AW0001
43...	2001-0...	16...	433	750	1	35...	3578.270000	AW0001
43...	2001-0...	11...	434	772	1	33...	3399.990000	NULL
43...	2001-0...	25...	435	762	1	69...	699.098200	AW0002
43...	2001-0...	11...	436	750	1	35...	3578.270000	NULL
43...	2001-0...	16...	437	751	1	35...	3578.270000	AW0001
43...	2001-0...	16...	438	751	1	35...	3578.270000	AW0001
43...	2001-0...	16...	439	751	1	35...	3578.270000	AW0001
43...	2001-0...	27...	440	749	1	35...	3578.270000	AW0002
43...	2001-0...	11...	441	750	1	35...	3578.270000	AW0001
43...	2001-0...	11...	442	750	1	35...	3578.270000	AW0001
43...	2001-0...	29...	443	771	1	33...	3399.990000	AW0002
43...	2001-0...	11...	444	778	1	33...	3374.990000	AW0001
43...	2001-0...	25...	445	778	1	33...	3374.990000	NULL
43...	2001-0...	25...	446	771	1	33...	3399.990000	AW0002
43...	2001-0...	16...	447	753	1	35...	3578.270000	AW0001
43...	2001-0...	16...	448	751	1	35...	3578.270000	AW0001
43...	2001-0...	11...	449	771	1	33...	3399.990000	AW0001

Detached | Total rows: 9947, buffers: 1 | Rows displayed = 9947

Figure 7-24

4. Open up the Lookup Component and this time select "Redirect rows to error output." In order to make this option work you will need a second trash destination on the error output of the Lookup Component as shown in Figure 7-25. When you execute the package using this mode, the found rows will be sent down the match output, and unlike the previous modes, not-found rows will not be ignored or cause the component to fail but will instead be sent down the error output.

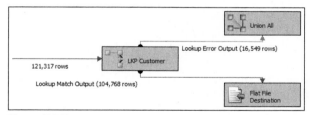

Union All

Lookup Error Output (16,549 rows)

121,317 rows

LKP Customer

Lookup Match Output (104,768 rows)

Flat File Destination

Figure 7-25

5. Finally, test the "Redirect rows to no match output" mode. You will need a total of three trash destinations for this to work as shown in Figure 7-26.

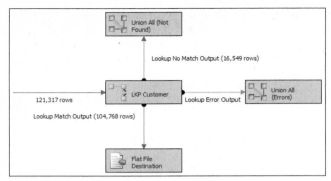

Figure 7-26

In all cases, add Data Viewer Grids to all the outputs, execute the package, and have a look at the results. The outputs should not contain any errors such as truncations, though there should be many non-matched rows.

So how exactly are these outputs useful; what can we do with them to make our packages more robust? In most cases the answer is that the errors or non-matched rows can be piped off to a different area of the package where the values can be logged or fixed as per the business requirements. For example, one common solution is for all missing rows to be tagged with an Unknown member value. In our scenario all non-matched rows might have their AccountNumber set to 0000. These fixed values are then joined back into the main Data Flow and treated the same from there on as the rows that did find a match. Let's configure our package to do this:

1. Refer to Figure 7-27. Open the Lookup editor and on the General tab choose to "Redirect rows to no match output" option. Click the Error Output tab and configure the AccountNumber column to have the value Fail Component under the Truncation column. This combination of settings means that we want a no-match output, but we don't want an error output; instead we will just fail if we get any errors. In the real world you may want to have an error output that you can use to log values to an error table, but for our scenario let's keep it a little simpler.

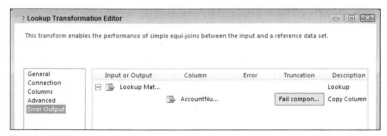

Figure 7-27

2. Drop a Derived Column Component on the design surface and connect the no-match output to it. Open up the Derived Column editor and add a new column in the grid called AccountNumber that uses the following expression (see Chapter 6 for more details):

```
(DT_STR,10,1252)"0000"
```

The Derived Column Component dialog editor should now look something like Figure 7-28.

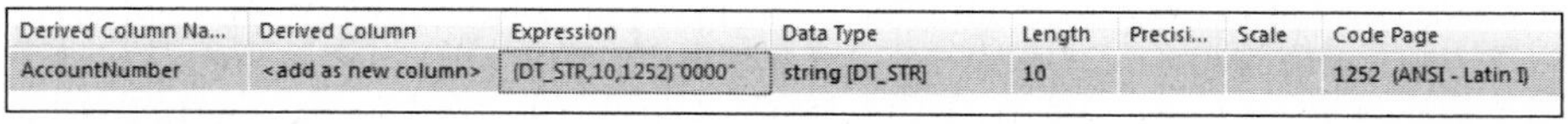

Derived Column Na...	Derived Column	Expression	Data Type	Length	Precisi...	Scale	Code Page
AccountNumber	<add as new column>	(DT_STR,10,1252)"0000"	string [DT_STR]	10			1252 (ANSI - Latin I)

Figure 7-28

Close the Derived Column editor, and drop a Union All Component on the surface. Connect both the matched output from the Lookup Component and the default output from the Derived Column into the Union All Component. Connect the Union All Component to your trash destination and then execute the package, as usual utilizing a Data Viewer Grid on the final output. The package and results should look something like Figure 7-29.

The output should show AccountNumbers for most of the values, with 0000 being emitted for those keys that are not present in the reference query (in our case because we artificially removed them).

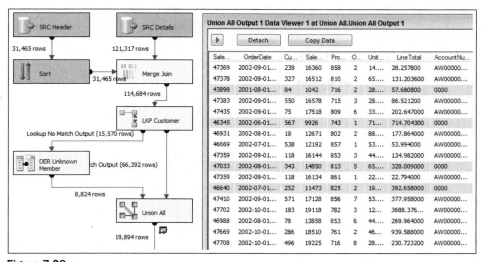

Figure 7-29

Expressionable Properties

If you ever build packages where the reference table you require is not known at design-time, this feature will be useful for you. Instead of using a static query in the Lookup Component, you can use an expression, which can dynamically construct the query string, or it could load the query string using SSIS configurations.

Figure 7-30 shows an example of using an expression within a Lookup Component. Expressions on Data Flow Components can be accessed from the property page of the Data Flow Task itself. See Chapter 6 for more details.

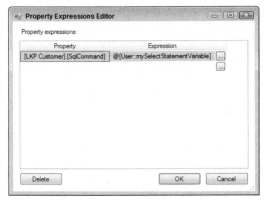

Figure 7-30

Cascaded Lookup Operations

Sometimes a single lookup operation may require several Lookup Components to get the job done. This may sound counterintuitive at first, but by using multiple Lookup Components, you can achieve a higher degree of performance without incurring the associated memory costs and processing times.

Imagine you have a large list of products that ideally you would like to load into one Lookup. You consider using full-cache mode; however, due to the sheer number of rows, you either run out of memory when trying to load the cache, or the cache loading phase takes so long that it becomes impractical (for instance, the package takes 15 minutes to execute, but 6 minutes of that time was spent just loading the Lookup cache). So you consider no-cache but the expense of all those database calls makes the solution too slow. Finally you consider partial-cache, but once again the expense of the initial database calls (before the internal cache is populated with enough data to be useful) is too high.

The solution to this problem is based on a critical assumption; the assumption being that there is a subset of reference rows (in this case product rows) that are statistically likely to be found in most, if not all data loads. For instance, if the business is a consumer goods chain, then there are likely to be a high proportion of sales transactions for people who buy milk. Similarly, there will be many transactions for sales of bread, cheese, beer, and baby diapers. On the contrary, there will be a relatively low number of sales for expensive wines. Some of these effects may be seasonal — more suntan lotion sold in summer, and more heaters sold in winter. This same assumption applies to other dimensions besides product — for instance, a company specializing in direct sales may know historically which customers (or customer segments or loyalty members) have responded to specific campaigns. A bank might know which accounts (or account types) have the most activity at specific times of the month.

This statistical property does not hold true for all datasets, but if it does, then you may derive great benefit from this pattern. If it doesn't you may still find this section useful in order to help you think about the different ways of approaching a problem and solving it with SSIS.

So how do you use this knowledge to build your solution? Using the consumer goods example, if you know that it is the middle of winter and you are not going to be selling much suntan lotion, then why load the suntan products in the Lookup Component? Rather, load just the high-frequency items like milk, bread, and cheese. Because you know you will see those items often, you want to put them in a Lookup Component configured in full-cache mode. If your product table has, say, 1 million items, then you could load the top 20% of them (in terms of frequency/popularity) into this first Lookup. That way you don't spend too much time loading the cache (because it is only 200,000 rows and not 1,000,000), and by the same reasoning, you don't use as much memory.

Of course in any statistical approach there will always be outliers — for instance, in the previous example suntan lotion will still be sold in winter to people going on holiday to sunnier places. So if any lookups fail on the first full-cache lookup, you need a second Lookup that operates in partial-cache mode to pick up the strays. The second Lookup would be configured in partial-cache mode (as detailed in the partial cache section earlier in this chapter), which means it would make database calls in the event that the item was not found in its dynamically growing internal cache. The first Lookup's not-found output would be connected to the second Lookup's input, and both of the Lookups would have their found outputs combined using a Union All Transform in order to send all the matches downstream. Figure 7-31 shows what such a package might look like.

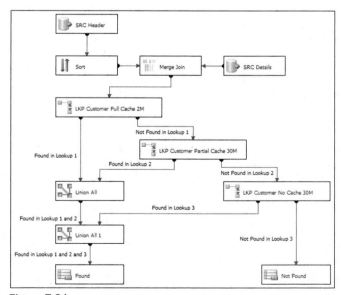

Figure 7-31

The benefit of this approach is that at the expense of a little more development time you now have a system that performs efficiently for the most common lookups, and fails over to a slower mode for those items that are not so common. That means that the lookup operation will be extremely efficient for most of your data, which typically results in an overall decrease in processing time.

In other words, you have used the Pareto principle (80/20 rule) to improve the solution. The first (full-cache) lookup stores 20% of the reference (in this case product) rows and hopefully succeeds in answering 80% of the lookup requests. For the 20% of lookups that fail, they are redirected to — and serviced by — the partial-cache lookup, which operates against the other 80% of data. Because you can constrain the size of the partial cache, you can ensure you don't run into any memory limitations — at the extreme you could even use a no-cache Lookup instead of, or in addition to, the partial-cache Lookup.

The final piece to this puzzle is how you identify up-front which items occur the most frequently in your domain. If the business does not already keep track of this information, you can derive it by collecting statistics within your packages and saving the results to a temporary location. For instance, each time you load your sales data, you could aggregate the number of sales for each item and write the results to a new table you have created for that purpose. The next time you load the product Lookup Component, you join the full product table to the statistics table and only return rows where the aggregate count is above a certain threshold. You can also use the Data Mining functionality in SQL Server to derive this information, though the details of that are beyond the scope of this chapter.

Cache Connection Manager and Transform

The Cache Connection Manager (CCM) and Cache Transform allow you to load the Lookup cache from any source. The Cache Connection Manager is the more critical of the two — it holds a reference to the internal memory cache and can both read and write the cache to a disk-based file. In fact the Lookup Component internally uses the CCM as its caching mechanism.

Like other Connection Managers in SSIS, the CCM is instantiated in the Connection Managers pane of the package design surface. You can also create new CCMs from the Cache Transform editor and Lookup Transform editor. At design time the CCM contains no data, so at runtime you need to populate it. You can do this in one of two ways:

1. You can create a separate Data Flow Task to extract data from any source and load the data into a Cache Transform as shown in Figure 7-32. You then configure the Cache Transform to write the data to the CCM. Optionally, you can configure the same CCM to write the data to a cache file (usually with the extension .caw) on disk. When you execute the package the Source Component will send the rows down the pipeline into the input of the Cache Transform. The Cache Transform will call the CCM and the CCM will load the data into a local memory cache. If configured, the CCM will also save the cache to disk so you can use it again later. This method gives you the ability to create persisted caches that you can share with other users, solutions, and packages.

2. Alternatively, you can open up the CCM editor and directly specify the filename of an existing cache file (.caw file). This option requires that you (or someone else) already created a cache file for you to reuse. At execution time the CCM loads the cache directly from disk and populates its internal memory structures.

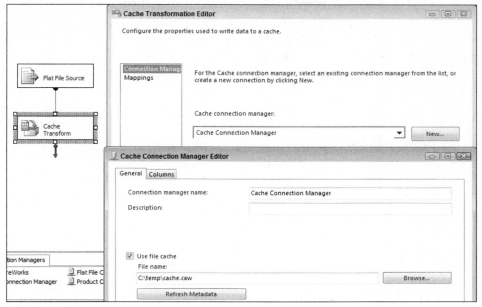

Figure 7-32

When you configure a CCM, it allows you to specify which columns of the input dataset will be used as index fields, and which columns will be used as reference fields. This is a necessary step — the CCM needs to know up-front which columns you will be joining on, so that it can create internal index structures to optimize the process. See Figure 7-33.

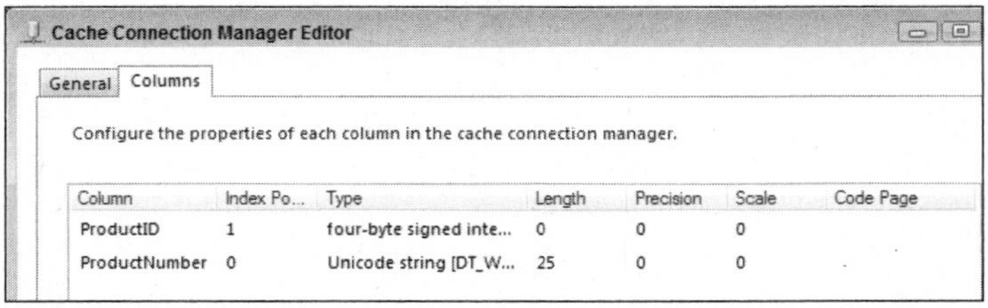

Figure 7-33

Whichever way you created the CCM, when you execute the package, the CCM will contain an in-memory representation of the data you specified. That means that the cache is now immediately available for use by the Lookup Component. Note that the Lookup Component is the only component that uses the caching aspects of the CCM; however, the Raw File Source can also read .caw files, which can be useful for debugging.

If you are using the Lookup Component in full-cache mode, you can load the cache using the CCM (instead of specifying a SQL query as described earlier in this chapter). To use the CCM option, open up the Lookup Component and select Full Cache and Cache Connection Manager in the general pane of the editor as shown in Figure 7-34. Then you can either select an existing CCM, or you can create a new one. You can now continue configuring the Lookup Component in the same way you would if you had used a SQL query. The only difference is that in the Columns tab, you can only join on columns that you had earlier specified as index columns in the CCM editor.

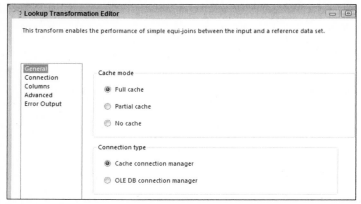

Figure 7-34

There are several benefits that the CCM gives you. First of all you can reuse caches that you had previously saved to file (in the same or a different package). For instance, you can load a CCM using the customer table and then save the cache to a .caw file on disk. Every other package that needs to do a lookup against customers can then use a Lookup Component configured in full-cache/CCM mode, with the CCM pointing at the .caw file you created.

Second, reading data from a .caw file is generally faster than reading from OLE DB, so your packages should run faster. Of course, the .caw file is an offline copy of your source data, so it could get stale and so should be reloaded every so often. Note that you can use an expression for the CCM filename, which means that you can dynamically load specific files at runtime.

Third, the CCM allows you to reuse caches across loop iterations. If you use a Lookup Component in full-cache/OLE DB mode within an SSIS Loop Container, the cache will be reloaded on every iteration of the loop. This may be your intended design, but if not, then it is difficult to mitigate the performance overhead. However, if you used a Lookup configured in full-cache/CCM mode, the CCM would be persistent across loop iterations and once again, your overall package performance should improve.

Summary

This chapter explored the different ways of joining data. Relational databases are highly efficient at joining data within their own stores; however, you may not be fortunate enough to have all your data living in the same database. SSIS allows you to perform these joins outside the database, though there are many different options for doing so, each with different performance and resource-usage characteristics.

The Merge Join Component can join large volumes of data without much memory impact; however, it has certain requirements, such as sorted input columns that may be difficult to meet. The Lookup Component is very flexible and supports multiple different modes of operation. The Cache Connection Manager adds more flexibility to the Lookup by allowing caches to be explicitly shared across packages and maintained across loop iterations. In large-scale deployments there are many different patterns that can be used to optimize performance, one of them being cascaded Lookups.

As with all SSIS solutions, there are no hard and fast rules that apply to all situations, so don't be afraid to experiment. If you run into any performance issues when trying to join data, try out a few of the other options presented in this chapter, and hopefully you will find one that makes a difference.

8

Creating an End-to-End Package

Now that you've learned about all the basic tasks and transforms in SSIS, you can jump into some practical applications for SSIS. You'll first start with a normal transformation of data from a series of flat files into SQL Server. Next you'll add some complexity to a process by archiving the files automatically. The last example will show you how to make a package that handles basic errors and makes the package more dynamic. As you run through the tutorials, remember to save your package and to a lesser degree your project on a regular basis often to avoid any loss of work.

Basic Transformation Tutorial

As you can imagine, the primary reason that people use SSIS is to read the data from a source and write it to a destination after it's potentially transformed. This tutorial walks you through a common scenario where you want to copy data from a Flat File Source to a SQL Server table without massaging the data. Don't worry; things will get much more complex later in your next package, and the next package will build on this example.

Start the tutorial by going online to the website for this book and downloading the sample extract that contains zip code information about cities. The zip code extract was retrieved from public record data from the 1990 census and has been filtered down to just Florida cities to save on your download time. You'll use this in the next tutorial as well, so it's very important not to skip this first tutorial. You can download the sample extract file called ZipCodeExtract.csv from this book's web page at www.wrox.com. Place the file into a directory called C:\Projects.

Open Business Information Development Studio (BIDS) and select File ⇨ New ⇨ Project. Then select Integration Services Project as your project type. Type **ProSSISChapter8** as the project name, and accept the rest of the defaults (as shown in Figure 8-1). You can place the project anywhere on your computer and the default location will be under the My Documents\Visual Studio 2008\ Projects folder.

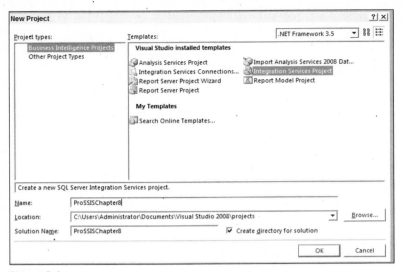

Figure 8-1

The project will be created, and you'll see a default `Package.dtsx` package file in the Solution Explorer. Right-click the `Package.dtsx` file in the Solution Explorer and select Rename. Rename the file `ZipLoad.dtsx`. When you're asked if you'd like to rename the package object as well, click Yes. If the package isn't opened yet, double-click it to open it in the Package Designer.

Creating Connections

Now that you have the package ready to begin, you need to create a shared connection that can be used across multiple packages. In the Solution Explorer, right-click Data Sources and select New Data Source. This opens the Data Source Wizard. Select the "Create a Data Source based on an existing or new connection" radio box and click New, which opens the window to create a new Connection Manager.

> *There are many ways you could have created the connection. For example, you could have created it as you're creating each source and destination. Once you're more experienced with the tool, you'll find what works best for you.*

Your first Connection Manager for this example will be to SQL Server, so select Native OLE DB\ SQL Native Client 10.0. For the Server Name option, type the name of your SQL Server and enter the authentication mode that is necessary for you to read and write to the database as shown in Figure 8-2. Lastly, select the AdventureWorks2008 database and click OK. If you don't have the AdventureWorks2008 database, you can pick any other user database on the server. You can optionally test the connection. You will then have a Data Source in the Data Source box that should be selected. Click Next and name the Data Source AdventureWorks2008.

You'll use other connections as well, but for those, you'll create connections that will be local to the package only and not shared. With the ZipLoad package open, right-click in the Connection Managers box below and select New Connection from Data Source. You should see the AdventureWorks2008 Data Source you created earlier. Select that Data Source and click OK. Once the Connection Manager is created, right-click it and rename it AdventureWorks2008 if it's not already named that. This is, of course, optional and just keeps us all on the same page.

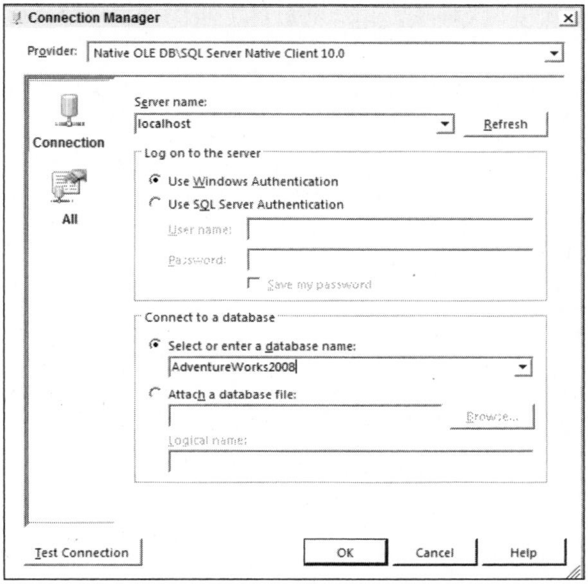

Figure 8-2

Next, create a Flat File connection and point it to the `ZipCode.txt` file in your `C:\Projects` directory. Right-click in the Connection Manager area of Package Designer, and select New Flat File Connection. Name the connection ZipCode Extract, and type any description you like. Point the File Name option to `C:\Projects\ZipCodeExtract.csv` or browse to the correct location by clicking Browse. If you can't find the file, ensure that the CSV filter is selected and that you're not just looking for `*.txt` files, which is the default.

You need to set the Format drop-down box to Delimited with <none> set for the Text Qualifier option, which are both the default options. The Text Qualifier option allows you to specify that character data is wrapped in quotes or some type of qualifier. This helps you when you have a file that is delimited by commas, and you also have commas inside some of the text data that you do not wish to separate by. Setting a Text Qualifier will ignore those commas inside the text data. Lastly, check the "Column names in the first data row" option. This states that your first row contains the column names for the file.

You can go to the Columns page to view a preview of the first 101 rows and set the row and column delimiters. The defaults are generally fine for this screen. The Row Delimiter option should be set to {CR}{LF}, which means that a carriage return and line feed separates each row. The Column Delimiter option should have carried over from the first page and will again be set to "Comma {,}". In some extracts that you may receive, the header record may be different from the data records, and the configurations won't be exactly the same as in the example.

The Advanced page is where you can specify the data types for each of the three columns. The default for this type of data is a 50-character string, which is excessive in this case. Click Suggest Types to comb through the data and find the best data type fit for the data. This will open the Suggest Column Types dialog box, where you should accept the default options and click OK.

You can now see that the data types in the Advanced page have changed for each column. One column in particular was incorrectly changed. When combing through the first 100 records, the Suggest Column Types dialog box selected a "four-byte signed integer [DT_I4]" for the zip code column but your suggest button may select a smaller data type based on the data. While this would work for the data extract you have, it won't work once you get to some states that have zip codes that begin with a zero in the northeast United States. Change this column to a string by selecting string [DT_STR] from the DataType drop-down box, and change the length of the column to 5 by changing the OutputColumnWidth option (shown in Figure 8-3). The last configuration change is to change the TextQualified option to False and click OK.

Figure 8-3

Creating the Tasks

With the first few connections created, you can go ahead and create your first task. In this tutorial, you'll have only a single task, which will be the Data Flow Task. In the Toolbox, drag the Data Flow Task over to the design pane in the Control Flow tab. Next, right-click the task and select Rename to rename the task "Load ZipCode Info."

Creating the Data Flow

Now comes the more detailed portion of almost all of your packages and where you will generally spend 70 percent of your time as an SSIS developer. Double-click the Data Flow Task to drill into the Data Flow. This will automatically take you to the Data Flow tab. You'll see that "Load ZipCode Info" was transposed to the Data Flow Task drop-down box. If you had more than this one Data Flow Task, then more would appear as options in the drop-down box.

Drag and drop a Flat File Source onto the Data Flow design pane, and then rename it "Florida ZipCode File" in the Properties window. All the rename instructions in these tutorials are optional, but they will keep you on the same page and make your operational people happier because they'll understand what's failing. Open the "Florida ZipCode File" Source and point it to the Connection Manager called ZipCode Extract. It should automatically be pointing to the flat file Connection Manager, since there's only a single one to point to. Go to the Columns page and take notice of the columns that you'll be outputting to the path. You've now configured the source, and you can click OK.

Next, drag and drop an OLE DB Destination onto the design pane and rename it AdventureWorks2008. Select the "Florida ZipCode File" Source, then connect the path (green arrow) from the "Florida ZipCode File" Source to the AdventureWorks2008. Double-click the destination and select AdventureWorks2008 from the Connection Manager drop-down box. For the "Name of the Table or View" option, click the New button next to the drop-down box. This is how you can create a table inside BIDS without having to go back to SQL Server Management Studio. The default DDL for creating the table will use the destination's name (AdventureWorks2008), and the data types may not be exactly what you'd like. This DDL will create the necessary table and can be changed, as shown here:

```
CREATE TABLE [AdventureWorks2008] (
    [StateFIPCode] smallint,
    [ZipCode] varchar(5),
    [StateAbbr] varchar(2),
    [City] varchar(16),
    [Longitude] real,
    [Latitude] real,
    [Population] int,
    [AllocationPercentage] real
)
```

Suppose this won't do for your picky DBA, who is concerned about performance. In this case, you should rename the table ZipCode (taking out the brackets) and change each column's data type to a more suitable size and type as shown with the ZipCode and StateAbbr columns:

```
CREATE TABLE [ZipCode] (
    [StateFIPCode] smallint,
    [ZipCode] char(5),
    [StateAbbr] char(2),
    [City] varchar(16),
    [Longitude] real,
    [Latitude] real,
    [Population] int,
    [AllocationPercentage] real
)
```

Once you have completed changing the DDL, click OK and the table name will be transposed into the Table drop-down box. Finally, go to the Mapping page to ensure that the inputs are mapped to the outputs correctly. SSIS attempts to map the columns based on name, and in this case, since you just created the table with the same column names, it should be a direct match, as shown in Figure 8-4.

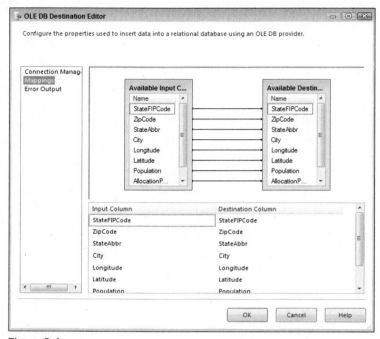

Figure 8-4

Once you've confirmed that the mappings look like Figure 8-4, click OK.

Completing the Package

With the basic framework of the package now constructed, you need to add one more task into the Control Flow tab to ensure that you can run this package multiple times. To do this, click the Control Flow tab and drag an Execute SQL Task over to the design pane. Rename the task "Purge ZipCode Table." Double-click the task and select AdventureWorks2008 from the Connection drop-down box. Finally, type the following query for the SQLStatement option (you can also click the ellipsis button and enter the query):

```
TRUNCATE TABLE ZipCode
```

Click OK to complete the task configuration. Connect the task as a parent to the "Load ZipCode Info" Task. To do this, click the "Purge ZipCode Table" Task and drag the green arrow onto the "Load ZipCode Info" Task.

Saving the Package

Your first package is now complete. Go ahead and save the package by clicking the Save icon in the top menu or by selecting File ⇨ Save Selected Items. It's important to note here that by clicking Save, you're saving the .DTSX file to the project, but you have not saved it to the server yet. To do that, you'll have to deploy the solution or package. We'll cover that in the last section of this chapter. SSIS also does not version control your packages independently. To version control your packages, you'll need to integrate a solution like Visual Source Safe into SSIS, as shown in Chapter 15.

Executing the Package

With the package complete, you can attempt to execute it. Do this by selecting the green arrow in the upper menu. You can also right-click the ZipCode.dtsx package file in the Solution Explorer and select Execute Package. Get in the habit of executing your packages this way instead of clicking the green Go button. The reason for this will be apparent in Chapter 22 when we build deployment utilities. The package will take a few moments to validate, and then it will execute.

You can see the progress under the Progress tab or in the Output window. In the Control Flow tab, you'll see the two tasks go from yellow to green (hopefully). If both turn green, then the package execution was successful. If your package failed, you can look in the Output window to see why. The Output window should be open by default, but in case it's not, you can open it by clicking View ⇨ Other Windows ⇨ Output. You can also see a graphical version of the Output window in the Progress tab (it can also be called the Execution Results tab if your package is stopped).

You can go to the Data Flow tab to see how many records were copied over. You can see the Data Flow tab in Figure 8-5. Notice the number of records displayed in the path as SSIS moves from transform to transform.

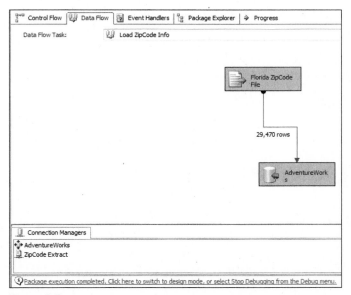

Figure 8-5

By default, when you execute a package, you'll be placed in debug mode. Changes you make in this mode will not be made available until you run the package again. You will also not be able to add new tasks or enter some editors. To break out of this mode, click the square Stop icon or click Debug ⇨ Stop Debugging.

Typical Mainframe ETL with Data Scrubbing

With the basic ETL out of the way, you will now jump into a more complex SSIS package that attempts to scrub data. You can start this scenario by downloading the `010305c.dat` public data file from the website for this book into a directory called `C:\Projects`. This file contains public record data from the Department of State of Florida.

In this scenario, you run a credit card company that's interested in marketing to newly formed domestic corporations in Florida. You want to prepare a data extract each day for the marketing department to perform a mail merge and perform a bulk mailing. Yes, your company is an old-fashioned, snail-mail spammer. Luckily the Department of State for Florida has an interesting extract you can use to empower your marketing department.

The business goals of this package are as follows:

❑ Create a package that finds the files in the `C:\Projects` directory and loads the file into your relational database.

❑ Archive the file after you load it to prevent it from being loaded twice.

❑ The package must self-heal. If a column is missing data, the data should be added automatically.

❑ If the package encounters an error in its attempt to self-heal, output the row to an error queue.

❑ You must audit the fact you loaded the file and how many rows you loaded.

Start a new package in your existing ProSSISChapter8 BIDS project from the first tutorial. Right-click the project in the Solution Explorer and select Add ⇨ New Item. From the New Item dialog box, choose "New SSIS Package." This will create `Package1.dtsx`, or some numeric variation on that name. Rename the file `CorporationLoad.dtsx`, and the package object should also be renamed. Double-click the package to open it.

Just like the last package you created, right-click in the Connection Managers area and select New Connection from the Data Source. Then select the AdventureWorks2008 shared data connection. You now have two packages using the same shared connection. If you were to change the password in the shared connection, it would change the password for both packages next time you owned them.

Next, create a new Flat File Connection Manager just as you did in the last tutorial. When the configuration screen opens, call the connection "Corporation Extract" in the General page. Type any description you'd like. For this Connection Manager, you're going to configure the file slightly differently. Click Browse and point to the `C:\Projects\010305c.dat` file (keep in mind that the default file filter is `*.txt` so you may have to type ***.*** in order to see the file). You should also change the Text Qualifier option to a single double-quote ("). Check the "Column names in the first data row" option. The final configuration should resemble Figure 8-6. Go to the Columns page to confirm that the column delimiter is Comma Delimited.

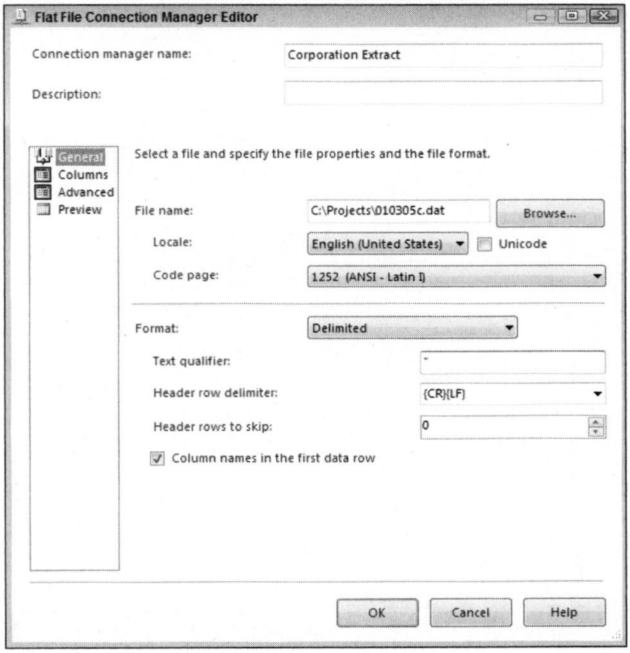

Figure 8-6

Next, go to the Advanced tab. By default, each of the columns are set to a 50-character [DT_STR] column. This will cause issues though with this file, because there are several columns that contain more than 100 characters of data and would cause you to receive a truncation error. Finally, you'll want to change the AddressLine1 and AddressLine2 columns to String [DT_STR] that is 150 characters wide, as shown in Figure 8-7. After you've properly set these two columns, click OK to save the Connection Manager.

Figure 8-7

Creating the Data Flow

With the mundane work of creating the connections now out of the way, you can go ahead and create the fun transformation. As you did in the last package, you must first create a Data Flow Task by dragging it from the Toolbox. Name this task "Load Corporate Data." Double-click the task to go to the Data Flow tab.

Drag and drop a Flat File Source onto the design pane and rename it "Uncleansed Corporate Data." Double-click the source and select Corporation Extract as your Connection Manager that you'll be using. Click OK to close the screen. You'll add the destination and transformation in a moment after the scenario is expanded a bit.

Handling Dirty Data

Before you go deeper into this scenario, you should take a time-out to look more closely at this data. As you were creating the connection, a very observant person (I did not notice this until it was too late) may have noticed that some of the important data that you'll need is missing. For example, the city and state are missing from some of the records.

To fix this for the marketing department, you'll use some of the transforms that were discussed in the last few chapters to send the good records down one path and the bad records down a different path. You will then attempt to cleanse the bad records and then send those back through the main path. There may be some records you can't cleanse (such as corporations with foreign postal codes) that you'll just have to write to an error log and deal with at a later date.

First, standardize the postal code to a five-digit format. Currently, some have five digits and some have the full 10-digit zip code with a dash (five digits, a dash, and four more digits). Some are nine-digit zip codes without the dash. To standardize the zip code, you use the Derived Column transform. Drag the transform over from the Toolbox and rename it "Standardize Zip Code."

Connect the source to the transformation and double-click the transform to configure it. Expand the Columns tree in the upper-left corner, find [ZipCode], and drag it onto Expression column in the grid below. This will pre-fill some of the information for you in the derived columns grid area. You now need to create an expression that will take the various zip code formats in the [ZipCode] output column and output only the first five characters. One way of doing this is with the SUBSTRING function. If you choose to solve the business problem with that method, the code would look like this:

```
SUBSTRING([ZipCode],1,5)
```

This code should be typed into the Expression column in the grid. Next, select that the derived column will replace the existing ZipCode output by selecting that option from the Derived Column drop-down box. You can see what the options should resemble in Figure 8-8. Once you've completed the transformation, click OK.

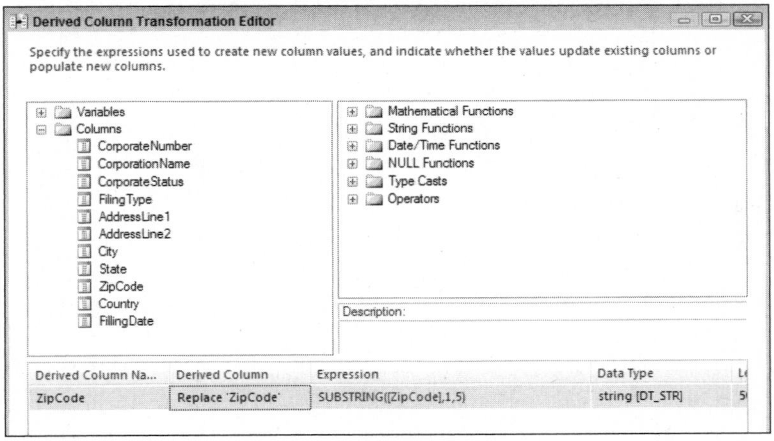

Figure 8-8

The Conditional Split Transformation

Now that you've standardized the data slightly, drag and drop the Conditional Split Transformation onto the design pane and connect the green arrow from the Derived Column Transform called "Standardize Zip Code" to the Conditional Split. Rename the transform "Find Bad Records." The Conditional Split Transformation will enable you to push certain bad records into a data-cleansing process.

To cleanse the data that has no city or state, you'll write a condition that says that any row that is missing a city or state will be moved to a cleansing path in the Data Flow. Double-click the Conditional Split Transform after you have connected it from the Derived Column Transform to edit the transformation.

Create a condition called "Missing State or City" by typing its name in the Output Name column. You will now need to write an expression that looks for empty records. One method of doing this is to use the LTRIM function. The two vertical bars (|) in the following code are the same as a logical OR in your code. Two & operators would represent a logical AND condition. You can read much more about the expression language in Chapter 6. The following code will check for a blank Column 6 or Column 7:

```
LTRIM([State]) == "" || LTRIM([City]) == ""
```

The last thing you'll need to do is give a name to the default output if the coded condition is not met. Call that output "Good Data," as shown in Figure 8-9. The default output is the name of the output that will contain the data that did not meet your conditions. Click OK to close the editor.

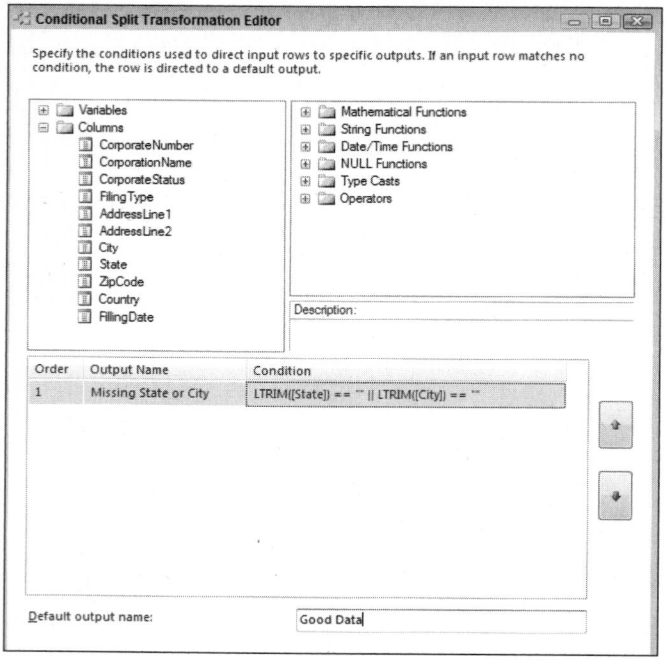

Figure 8-9

If you have multiple cases, always place conditions that you feel will capture most of the records at the top of the list because the list is read top to bottom and you don't want to evaluate records more times than is needed.

The Lookup Transformation

Next, drag and drop the Lookup Transformation onto the design pane. When you connect to it from the Conditional Split Transformation, you'll see the Input Output Selection dialog box (shown in Figure 8-10). Select "Missing State or City" and click OK. This will send any bad records to the Lookup Transformation from the Conditional Split. Rename the Lookup Transformation "Fix Bad Records."

Figure 8-10

The Lookup Transformation allows you to map a city and state to the rows that are missing that information by looking the record up against the ZipCode table you loaded earlier. Open up the transformation editor for the Lookup Transform, and in the General page, ensure that the Full Cache property is set, and that you have the OLE DB Connection Manager property set for the Connection Type. Change the "No Matching Entries" drop-down box to "Redirect rows to no match output" as shown in Figure 8-11.

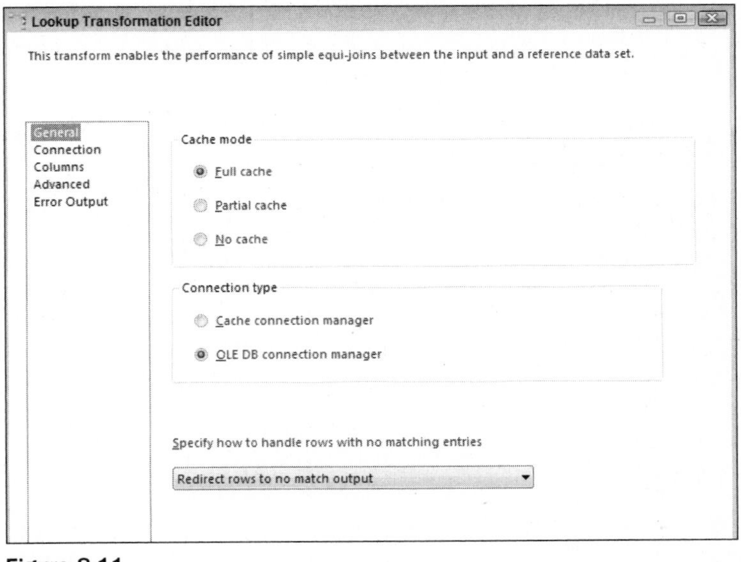

Figure 8-11

In the Connection page, select AdventureWorks2008 as the Connection Manager that contains your Lookup table. Select ZipCode from the Use Table or View drop-down box. Next, go to the Columns page and drag ZipCode from the left Available Input Columns to the right ZipCode column in the Available Lookup Columns table. This will create an arrow between the two tables as shown in Figure 8-12. Then, check the StateAbbr and City columns that you wish to output. This will transfer their information to the bottom grid. Change the Add as New Column option to Replace for the given column name as well. Select that you wish for these columns to replace the existing City and State. The final configuration should look like Figure 8-12. Click OK to exit the transform editor. There are many more options here, but you should stick with the basics for the time being. With the configuration you just did, the potentially blank or bad city and state columns will be populated from the ZipCode table.

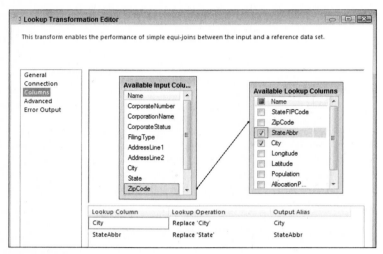

Figure 8-12

The Union All Transformation

Now that your dirty data is cleansed, go ahead and send the sanitized data back into the main data path by using a Union All Transformation. Drag and drop the Union All Transform onto the design pane and connect the "Fix Bad Records" Lookup Transform and the "Find Bad Records" Conditional Split Transform onto the Union All Transform. When you drag the green line from the Lookup Transform, you'll be prompted to define which output you want to send to the Union All Transform. Select the Lookup Match Output. There is nothing more to configure with the Union All Transformation.

Finalizing

The last step in the Data Flow is to send the data to an OLE DB Destination. Drag the OLE DB Destination to the design pane and rename it "Mail Merge Table." Connect the Union All Transform to the destination. Double-click the destination and select AdventureWorks2008 from the Connection Manager drop-down box. For the Use a Table or View option, select the New button next to the drop-down box. The default DDL for creating the table will use the destination's name (AdventureWorks2008), and the data types may not be exactly what you'd like, as shown here:

```
CREATE TABLE [Mail Merge Table] (
    [CorporateNumber] varchar(50),
    [CorporationName] varchar(50),
    [CorporateStatus] varchar(50),
    [FilingType] varchar(50),
```

```
    [AddressLine1] varchar(150),
    [AddressLine2] varchar(150),
    [City] varchar(50),
    [State] varchar(50),
    [ZipCode] varchar(50),
    [Country] varchar(50),
    [FilingDate] varchar(50)
)
```

Go ahead and change the schema to something a bit more useful. Change the table name and each column to a more logical name like the following. By making these changes the destination may show warnings about truncation after you click OK. These warnings can be ignored for the purpose of this example.

```
CREATE TABLE MarketingCorporation(
    CorporateNumber varchar(12),
    CorporationName varchar(48),
    FilingStatus char(1),
    FilingType char(4),
    AddressLine1 varchar(150),
    AddressLine2 varchar(50),
    City varchar(28),
    State char(2),
    ZipCode varchar(10),
    Country char(2),
    FilingDate varchar(10) NULL
)
```

You may have to map some of the columns this time because the column names are different. Go to the Mappings page and map each column to its new name. Click OK to close the editor.

Handling More Bad Data

The unpolished package is essentially complete, but it has one fatal flaw that you're about to discover. Go ahead and execute the package. If you do this, you can see (shown in Figure 8-13), for example, that in the `010305c.dat` file, four records were sent to be cleansed by the Lookup Transformation. Of those, only two had the potential to be cleansed. The other two records were for companies outside the country and could not be located in the Lookup Transform that contained only Florida zip codes. These two records were essentially lost because we specified in the Lookup Transform to redirect the rows that did not match to a "no match output" (shown in Figure 8-11) but we have not set up a destination for the "no match output" to go. You may remember that the business requirement was to only send marketing a list of domestic addresses for their mail merge product. They didn't care about the international addresses because you didn't have a business presence in those countries.

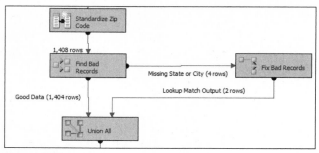

Figure 8-13

In our example, you want to send those two rows to an error queue for further investigation by a business analyst, and to be cleaned out manually. To do this properly, you'll audit each record that fails the match and create an ErrorQueue table on the SQL Server. Drag over the Audit Transformation from your Toolbox. Rename the Audit Transformation "Add Auditing Info" and connect the remaining green arrow coming out of the "Fix Bad Records" Transform to the Audit Transform.

With the Lookup problems now being handled, double-click the Audit Transform to configure that transformation. Go ahead and add two additional columns to the output. Select Task Name and Package Name from the drop-down boxes in the Audit Type column. This will transpose a default Output Column Name. Take out the spaces in each output column name, as shown in Figure 8-14, to make it easier to query later. You'll want to output this auditing information because you may have multiple packages and tasks loading data into the corporation table, and you'll want to track which package actually originated the error. Click OK to close.

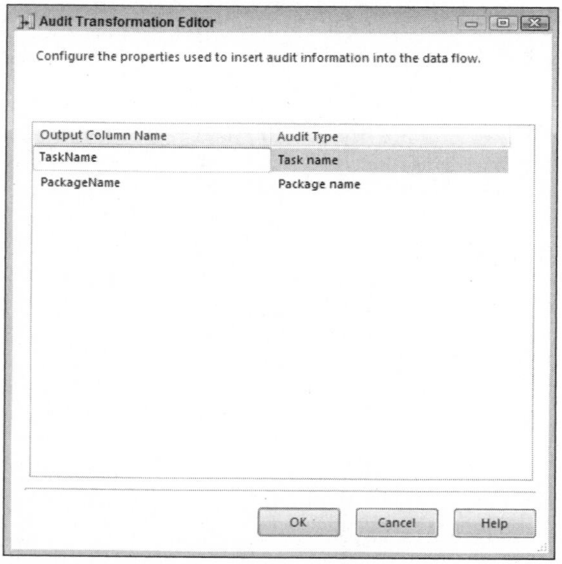

Figure 8-14

The last thing you need to do to polish up the package is to send the bad rows to the SQL Server ErrorQueue table. Drag another OLE DB Destination over to the design pane and connect the Audit Transformation to it. Rename the destination "Error Queue." Double-click the destination and select AdventureWorks2008 as the Connection Manager, and click New to add the ErrorQueue table. Name the table "ErrorQueue" and follow a similar schema to the one shown here:

```
CREATE TABLE [ErrorQueue] (
    [CorporateNumber] varchar(50),
    [CorporationName] varchar(50),
    [CorporateStatus] varchar(50),
    [FilingType] varchar(50),
    [AddressLine1] varchar(150),
    [AddressLine2] varchar(150),
    [City] varchar(50),
    [StateAbbr] varchar(50),
    [ZipCode] varchar(50),
    [Country] varchar(50),
    [FilingDate] varchar(50),
    [TaskName] nvarchar(19),
    [PackageName] nvarchar(15)
)
```

In error queue tables like the one just illustrated, be very generous when defining the schema. In other words, you don't want to create another transformation error trying to write into the error queue table. Instead, you may want to define everything as a varchar column and give more space than is actually needed.

You may have to map some of the columns this time due to the column names being different. Go to the Mappings page and map each column to its new name. Click OK to close the editor.

You are now ready to re-execute the package. This time, in my data file, four records needed to be fixed, and two of those were sent to the error queue. The final package would look something like the one shown in Figure 8-15 when executed.

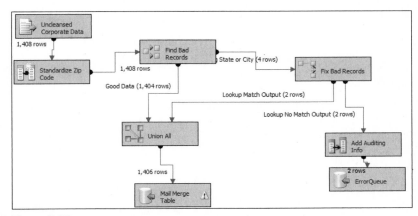

Figure 8-15

Looping and the Dynamic Task

You've come a long way in this chapter to creating a self-healing package, but it's not terribly reusable yet. Your next task in the business requirements is to configure the package so that it reads a directory for any .DAT file and performs the previous tasks to that collection of files. To simulate this example, go ahead and copy the rest of the *.DAT files from the Wrox website from the file FloridaDOS.zip and unzip them into C:\Projects.

Looping

Your first task is to loop through any set of .DAT files in the C:\Projects folder and load them into your database just as you did with the single file. To meet this business requirement, you'll need to use the Foreach Loop Container. Go to the Control Flow tab in the same package that you've been working in, and drag the container onto the design pane. Then, drag the "Load Corporate Data" Data Flow Task onto the container. Rename the container "Loop Through Files."

Double-click the container to configure it. Go to the Collection page and select Foreach File Enumerator from the Enumerator drop-down box. Next, specify that the folder will be C:\Projects and that the files will have the *.DAT extension, as shown in Figure 8-16.

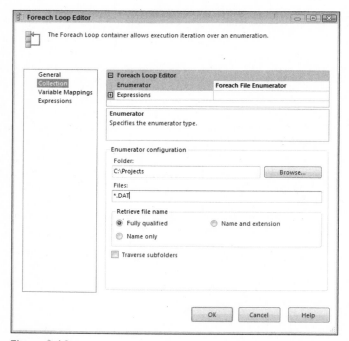

Figure 8-16

You need to now map the variables to the results of the Foreach File Enumeration. Go to the Variable Mappings page inside the Foreach Loop Editor and select <New Variable . . . > from the Variable column drop-down box. This will open the Add Variable dialog box. For the container, you'll remain at the package level. You could assign the scope of the variable to the container, but you should keep things simple for this example. Name the variable "ExtractFileName" in the Name option and click OK, leaving the rest of the options at their default settings.

You will then see the User::ExtractFileName variable in the Variable column and the number 0 in the Index option. Since the Foreach File Enumerator option has only one column, you'll only see an index of 0 for this column. If you used a different enumerator option, you would have the ability to enter a number for each column that was returned from the enumerator. Click OK to leave the Foreach Loop editor.

Making the Package Dynamic

Now with the loop created, you need to set the filename in the Corporation Extract Connection Manager to be equal to the filename that the enumerator retrieves dynamically. To meet this business requirement, right-click the Corporation Extract Connection Manager and select Properties (note that you're clicking on Properties, not on Edit as you've done in the past). In the Properties pane for this Connection Manager, click the ellipsis button next to the Expressions option.

By clicking the ellipsis button, you open the Property Expressions Editor. Select ConnectionString from the Property drop-down box, as shown in Figure 8-17. You can either type in **@[User::ExtractFileName]** in the Expression column, or click the ellipsis button, and then drag and drop the variable into the expression window. By typing **@[User::ExtractFileName]**, you are setting the filename in the Connection Manager to be equal to the current value of the ExtractFileName variable that you set in the Foreach Loop earlier. Click OK to exit the Property Expression Editor. You'll now see in the Property window that there is a single expression by clicking the plus sign.

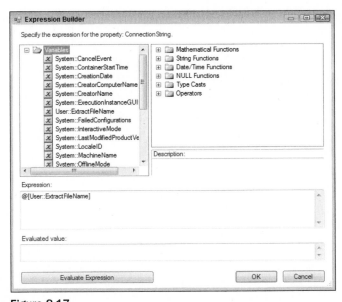

Figure 8-17

As it stands right now, each time the loop finds a `.DAT` file in the `C:\Projects` directory, it will set the `ExtractFileName` variable to that path and filename. Then, the Connection Manager will use that variable as its filename and run the Data Flow Task one time for each file it finds. You now have a reusable package that can be run against any file in the format you designated earlier.

The only missing technical solution to complete is the archiving of the files after you load them. Before you begin solving that problem, manually create an archive directory under `C:\Projects` called `C:\Projects\Archive`. Right-click in the Connection Manager window and select New File Connection. Select Existing Folder for the Usage Type, and point the file to the `C:\Projects\Archive` directory. Click OK and rename the newly created Connection Manager "archive."

Next, drag a File System Task into the "Loop Through Files" Container and connect the container to the "Load Corporate Data" Data Flow Task with an On Success constraint (the green arrow should be attached to the File System Task). Rename that task "Archive File."

Double-click the "Archive File" File System Task to open the editor (shown in Figure 8-18). Set the Operation drop-down box to Move File. Next, specify that the Destination Connection not be a variable and that it be set to the archive Connection Manager that you just created. Also select True for the OverwriteDestination option, which will overwrite the file if it already is in the archive folder. The SourceConnection drop-down box should be set to the "Corporation Extract" Connection Manager that you created a long time ago. Essentially, what you're configuring is that the file that was pulled earlier from the loop will be moved to whatever directory and filename is in the Archive File Connection Manager. Click OK to close the editor.

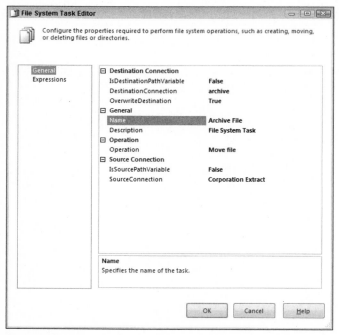

Figure 8-18

Your complete package should now be ready to execute. Go ahead and save the package first before you execute it. If you successfully implemented the solution, your Control Flow should look something like Figure 8-19 when executed. When you execute the package, you'll see the Control Flow items flash green once for each .DAT file in the directory. For the package to run again, you must copy the files back into the working directory out of the archive folder.

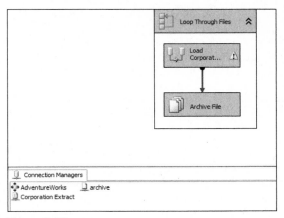

Figure 8-19

Summary

This chapter focused on driving home the basic SSIS transforms, tasks, and containers. You performed a basic ETL procedure, and then expanded the ETL to self-heal when bad data arrived from your data supplier. You then set the package to loop through a directory, find each .DAT file, and load it into the database. The finale was archiving the file automatically after it was loaded. With this type of package now complete, you could throw any .DAT file that matched the format you configured, and it will load with reasonable certainty. In the upcoming chapter, you'll dive into Script Task and Component extensively.

9

Scripting in SSIS

With the introduction of C#, and the embedding of the new Visual Studio Tools for Applications into SSIS, you can't think of using the Script Task and Script Component as scripting anymore; now it's all-out programming. In the early days of DTS-based SQL Server ETL processing, the ActiveX Script Task allowed you to embed programmatic logic and became the Swiss-Army knife of package development. Typically, you'd code logic into these Script Tasks to control the execution and logic flow within a package or to perform some specialized business validation.

Scripting in SSIS has completely evolved from these simple ActiveX roots. You've still got a Swiss-Army knife hidden in here, but there is a separation of functionality from previous uses of ActiveX scripting into three new concepts: the Scripting Task, the Scripting Component, and Expressions. Expressions are completely new to SSIS and replace the old methodology of manipulating variables or properties within the package model. The other two Scripting Components provide access into a new scripting development environment using Microsoft Visual Studio Tools for Applications (VSTA). This change finally allows SSIS developers to script logic into packages using Visual Basic 2008 *or* Visual C# 2008 .NET code.

In this chapter, you learn all about these new scripting options and learn how to exploit them in your package development tasks to control execution flow, perform custom transformations, manage variables, and provide runtime feedback.

Scripting?

If you think of scripting as having to compile at runtime and unstructured or unmanaged coding languages, then this is not scripting. If you think scripting means small bits of code in specialized places to execute specific tasks, then yes, it's scripting. The current scripting abilities have come a long way from their predecessors in DTS, and even the earlier versions of SSIS. Whether you're a grizzled veteran of DTS, or if SSIS is your first exposure to SQL Server ETL development, it is helpful to understand the historical landscape of the Scripting Components, and why there is now a separation by functional usage. We'll examine this and open up the new scripting IDE environment to walk though the mechanics of applying programmatic logic into these components — including how to add your own classes and compiled assemblies.

The ActiveX Task in the past was useful no doubt, but it was primitive. The task allowed coding in only the two ActiveX-based scripting languages, VB and J script, with no IntelliSense help. However, if you look around at historical DTS package development (or if you've had to convert any to SSIS) you'll find some significant creative work going on in these tasks. Digging into what developers were doing, the functional activities can be broken up into these categories:

❑   Retrieving or setting the value of package variables

❑   Retrieving or setting properties within the package

❑   Applying business logic to validate or format data streams

❑   Controlling workflow in a package

❑   Performing miscellaneous tasks not supported by existing package components

Retrieving and setting the value of variables and package properties was so prevalent in DTS that the SSIS team decided to create a completely different feature to allow this to be less of a programmatic task. The expressions editor, in SSIS, allows package components to be easily altered by setting component properties to an expression, or variable that represents an expression. This concept is a maturation and replacement of the Dynamic Property Component that was a part of DTS development. See Chapter 6 for information on how to use expressions and variables; they are out of scope for this chapter.

The Data Pump Task in DTS was limited. Delimited data or supported sources could be mapped, but outside of these narrow constraints, you were on your own. Because of this, you can find DTS packages that performed all the ETL steps written purely in ActiveX script. In ActiveX Script Tasks, you could connect to Data Sources via ADO, parse and manipulate the data, and push it into destination sources. In SSIS, this need was replaced and expanded with the Data Flow Container that allows this type of activity to be visually represented. However, to perform the ad-hoc data messaging functionality, scripting is still needed, so the Script Component was added. The primary role of the Scripting Component is to extend the Data Flow capabilities and allow programmatic data manipulation within the context of the data stream. However, it can do more as you'll learn later.

To continue to enable the numerous miscellaneous tasks that are needed in ETL development, the ActiveX Script Task has been replaced with the Script Task, which can be used only in the Control Flow design surface. In this task, all the various things that you could do with the ActiveX Task can be replicated, but within the managed code framework of .NET.

Today, you'll also still find the ActiveX Script Task in the BIDS environment. However, this is only to support backward compatibility and even then for only some of the more simple uses. You can get some of the functionality that used to work in DTS, but not everything converts over. For one, setting package properties, which was prevalent in DTS development, is no longer allowed in SSIS. If you are currently using this task, we recommend you get it into one of these new Scripting Components as soon as possible, since no one knows how long the ActiveX Task will be supported.

The initial versions of SSIS Script Components stopped half-way down a path of complete replacement of the older Visual Basic for Applications (VBA) implementation that had previously been used for scripting to a .NET environment. One downside for many was that only the VB language was supported.

The latest versions of these Script Components host the new Visual Studio Tools for Applications (VSTA) environment, which is the replacement for the Visual Basic for Applications (VBA) implementation. VSTA is essentially a scaled-down version of Visual Studio that can be added to an application that allows coding extensions using managed code and .NET languages. Even though SSIS packages are built inside of VS, when you are in the context of a Script Task or Component, you are actually coding in the VSTA environment that is, in fact a mini-project within the package. The new VSTA IDE provides IntelliSense, full edit-and-continue capabilities, as well as the ability to code in either VB or C#. The IDE is available when you edit script and looks like Visual Studio. You can now even access some of the .NET assemblies and even use web references. Earlier versions of SSIS required the creation of a proxy class to use a Web service.

Getting Started in SSIS Scripting

The new Script Task and Script Component, combined with the addition of VSTA to the BIDS environment, has really opened up the possibilities when it comes to script-based ETL development in SSIS. However, you may find it confusing at first to know when to use which component and what things can be done in each. Although two have the word "script" in the names, they have different usages, and even coding tasks such as variable retrieval are different in each. You need to know when to use which component and how to do similar tasks in each. First, to keep them all straight, here's a matrix to explain when to use each component:

Component	When to Use
ActiveX Script Task	Use only if you are in the middle of converting a DTS package to SSIS. This component should not be used in new development.
Script Task	Use this task when you need to program logic that either controls package execution or performs a task of retrieving or setting variables within a package during runtime.
Script Component	Use this component when pumping data using the Data Flow Task. Here you can apply programmatic logic to massage data in the pipeline.
Expressions	Use expressions to set task and component properties or variables during runtime. See Chapter 6 for more detail.

To get a good look at the scripting model, we'll walk through a TextBox "Hello World" coding project in SSIS. Although this is not a typical example of ETL programming, we'll use this as a start to understanding the scripting paradigm in SSIS with a basic Script Task. Then we'll look at specific applications of each Scripting Component.

Selecting the Scripting Language

One of the new capabilities of SSIS using the VSTA environment is the addition of the C# scripting language to the existing VB coding option. To see where you can make this choice, drop a Script Task onto the Control Flow design surface. Right-click the Script Task and click Edit from the drop-down menu. The first thing you'll notice is the availability of the Microsoft Visual C# option in the ScriptLanguage property of the task available in both the Script Task and Component. Figure 9-1 shows these options in the Script Task Editor.

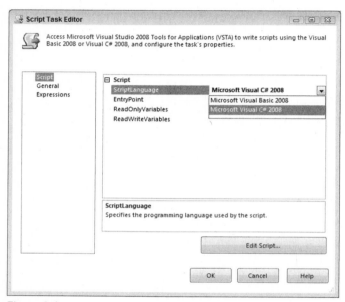

Figure 9-1

Once you click the Edit Script button, you'll be locked into the script language that you chose and won't be able to change it without deleting and recreating the Script Task. This is because each Script Component contains its own internal Visual Studio project in VB or C#. You can create separate Script Tasks where each one uses a different language within a package. However, having Script Tasks in both languages is not recommended because this makes maintenance of the package a more complex issue. The developer maintaining the package would have to be competent in both languages.

Using the VSTA Scripting IDE

To add programmatic code to a Script Task or Component, access its editor by right-clicking the component and selecting the Edit option from the drop-down menu. While the Script Task and Script Component editors look completely different, they both have a common way to access the development IDE for scripting. In Figure 9-2, notice the same Edit Script button that is in both editors.

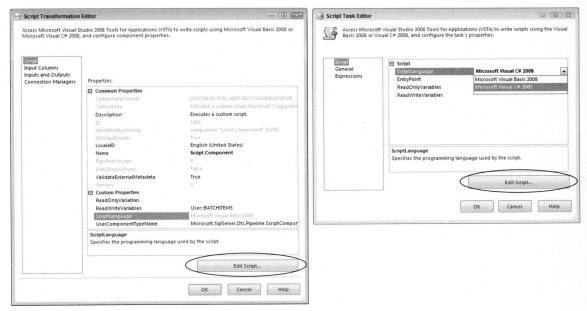

Figure 9-2

The button labeled Edit Script provides access into the scripting IDE. Once in the IDE, notice that it really looks and feels just like Visual Studio. Figure 9-3 shows an example of how this IDE looks after opening up the Script Task Component for the C# scripting language.

The previous Visual Studio 2005 VBA implementation of the scripting IDE presented the coding IDE like the Macro VBA environment in Excel. If you are still using this older environment, the same look can be achieved by navigating to the View menu option and selecting the Project Explorer and Property windows. Arrange them on the right side of the IDE to make the 2005 BIDS scripting IDE look almost like the new Visual Studio work environment.

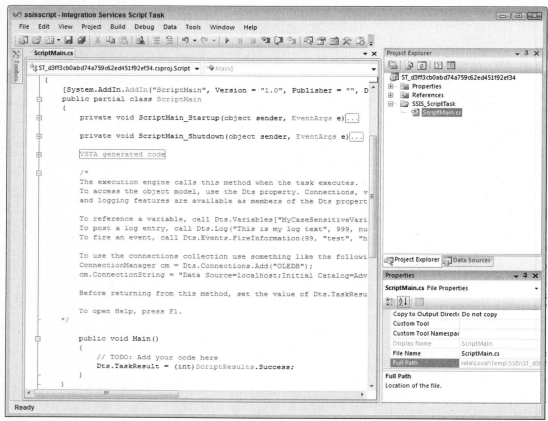

Figure 9-3

The code window on the left side of the IDE contains the code for the item selected in the Project Explorer on the top-right window. The Project Explorer shows the structure for the project that is being used within the Scripting Task. A complete .NET project is created for each Script Task or Component, and is temporarily written to a project file on the local drive where it can be altered in the Visual Studio IDE. This persistence of the project is the reason that once you pick a scripting language, and generate code in the project within, you'll be locked into that language for that Scripting Component. Notice in Figure 9-3 that a project has been created with the namespace of ST_d3ff3cb0abd74a759o62ed451f92ef34. The path to this temporary project can also be seen under the property Full Path for the ScriptMain class shown in Figure 9-2. However, you can't open up this project directly, nor need you worry about the project during deployment. These project files are extracted from stored DTS Package metadata similar to the way the SQL CLR objects are stored as metadata in SQL Server. With the project created and opened, it is ready for coding.

Example: Hello World

In the IDE, the Script Task only contains a class named ScriptMain. If you open a Script Component, you'll see more classes to support the component and the data buffer. We'll discuss what these additional classes do a little later in the chapter during the examination of the Script Component. Both components use a public class named `ScriptMain`, but the filename you see in the Project Explorer will be either `ScriptMain` or `Main` to host a public entry-point function. The function name is different for the Script Task than the Script Component because the interfaces and purposes are different. In the entry-point functions, `Main()` for the Script Task, you'll either put all the code you want to execute, or you can call into separately defined functions or classes either in or out of process. However, if you want to change the entry-point function for some reason in the Script Task only, type the name of the entry-point function in the property called EntryPoint on the Script page of the editor. (Alternatively, you could change the name of the entry point at runtime using an expression.)

In the VSTA co-generated class `ScriptMain`, you'll also see a set of assembly references already added to your project and namespaces set up in the class. Depending upon whether you chose VB or C# as your scripting language, you'll see either:

```
C#
Using System
Using System.Data
Using Microsoft.SqlServer.Dts.Runtime.VSTAProxy;
Using System.Windows.Forms;
```

Or:

```
VB
Imports System
Imports System.Data
Imports System.Math
Imports Microsoft.SqlServer.Dts.Runtime.VSTAProxy
```

These assemblies are needed to provide base functionality as a jump start to your coding. The remainder of the class includes VSTA co-generated methods for startup and shutdown operations, and finally the entry-point `Main()` function shown here in both languages:

```
C#
public void Main()
{
    // TODO: Add your code here
    Dts.TaskResult = (int)ScriptResults.Success
}

VB
Public Sub Main()
    '
    ' Add your code here
    '
    Dts.TaskResult = ScriptResults.Success
End Sub
```

This `Main()` function is a good example of one of the differences between the Script Task and the Script Component. A Script Task must return a result to notify the runtime of whether the script completed successfully or not. This result is that the `Dts.TaskResult` property is being set to indicate to the package that the task completed successfully. The Script Component does not have to do this, since it runs in the context of a data pump with many rows. There are other differences pertaining to each component that we'll discuss separately later in the chapter.

To get a message box to pop up with the phrase "Hello, World!" you need access to a class called `MessageBox` in a namespace called `System.Windows.Forms`. This namespace can either be called directly by the complete name, or the namespace can be added after the `Microsoft.SqlServer.Dts.Runtime` namespace to shorten the coding required in the class. Both of these methods are shown in the following code to insert the `MessageBox` code into the `Main()` function:

```
C#
using System.Windows.Forms
. . .
MessageBox.Show("Hello World!");
Or
System.Windows.Forms.MessageBox.Show("Hello World!");

VB
Imports System.Windows.Forms
. . .
MessageBox.Show("Hello World!")
Or
System.Windows.Forms.MessageBox.Show("Hello World!")
```

After you have added this code, get in the habit now of building the project when you are finished with the coding. The Build option is directly on the menu when you are coding. Previous versions of SSIS gave you the opportunity to run in precompile or compiled modes. SSIS now will automatically compile your code prior to executing the package in the runtime. Compiling gives you an opportunity to see what the errors are before the package finds them. Once the build is successful, close the IDE, the editor, and right-click and execute the Script Task. A pop-up message box should appear with the words "Hello World!" like Figure 9-4.

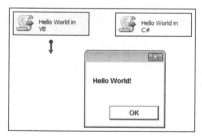

Figure 9-4

Adding Code and Classes

Using modal message boxes is obviously not the type of typical coding we want to do in production SSIS package development. Message boxes are synchronous and block until a click event is received, so they can stop a production job dead in its tracks. However, this is a basic technique to demonstrate the capabilities in the new scripting environments before getting into some of the details of passing values in and out using variables. We also don't want to always put the main blocks of code in the `Main()` function. With just a little more work, we can get some code reuse from previously written code using some cut-and-paste development techniques. At the very least, code can be structured in a less-procedural way. Consider a common task of generating a unique filename to give an archived file.

Typically, the filename might be generated by appending a prefix and an extension to something variable like a datetime value.

These functions can be added within the `ScriptMain` class bodies to look like this:

```csharp
C#
Public partial class ScriptMain
{
    . . .
    public void Main()
    {
        System.Windows.Forms.MessageBox.Show(GetFileName("bankfile", "txt"));
        Dts.TaskResult = (int)ScriptResults.Success;
    }

    public string GetFileName(string Prefix, string Extension)
    {
        return Prefix + DateTime.Now.ToString("yyyyMMddhhmmss") +
                "." + Extension;
    }
}
```

```vb
VB
Partial Class ScriptMain
    . . .
    Public Sub Main()
        System.Windows.Forms.MessageBox.Show(GetFileName("bankfile", "txt"))
        Dts.TaskResult = ScriptResults.Success
    End Sub

    Public Function GetFileName(ByVal Prefix As String, _
                                ByVal Extension As String) As String
        GetFileName = Prefix + DateTime.Now.ToString("yyyyMMddhhmmss") + _
                    "." + Extension
    End Function
End Class
```

Instead of all the code residing in the `Main()` function, we can separate and organize SSIS scripting using structured programming techniques. In this example, the `GetFileName` function builds the filename and then returns the value in the message box, as shown in Figure 9-5.

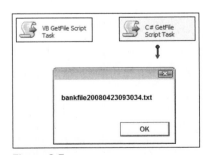

Figure 9-5

But copying code and pasting it into multiple Script Components is pretty cheesy. If you have preexisting compiled code, shouldn't you be able to reuse this code without finding the original source for the copy-and-paste operation? You can, with some qualification.

Using Managed Assemblies

The capability to reuse code written in other languages is the hallmark of COM and its successor, .NET. While you can only write SSIS scripts using Visual Basic.NET and C#, you can reuse assemblies that are part of the .NET core assemblies or any assembly created using a .NET-compliant language, including C#, J#, and even Delphi, but there are some qualifications. These are rather important so we'll state them like this:

❑ For a managed assembly to be used in an Integration Service, you must install the assembly in the Global Assembly Cache (GAC).

❑ Additionally, all dependent or referenced assemblies must also be registered in the GAC. This implies that the assembly must be strongly named.

❑ For development purposes only, VSTA can use managed assemblies anywhere on the local machine.

If you think about this it makes sense, but within SSIS, it might seem confusing at first. On one hand, a sub-project is created for the Script Component, but it is absorbed into the metadata of the package. In this case, you don't have to worry about deployment of individual script projects. However, when you use an external assembly, it does not get absorbed into the package metadata and here you *do* have to worry about deployment of the assembly. So where do you deploy the assembly you want to use? Since DTS packages can be deployed within SQL Server, the most universal place to find the assembly would be in the GAC.

If you are using any of the standard .NET assemblies, they are already loaded and stored in the GAC and the .NET Framework folders. As long as you are using the same framework for your development and production locations, using standard .NET assemblies requires no additional work. To use a standard .NET assembly in your script, you must reference it. To add a reference to a scripting project, you must be in the VSTA environment for editing your script code — not the SSIS package itself. Right-click the References Node in the Project Explorer, or go to the Project menu and select the Add Reference option. The standard .NET Add Reference window will appear as shown in Figure 9-6.

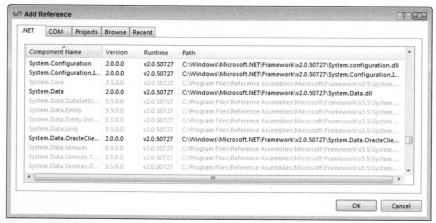

Figure 9-6

Select the assemblies from the list that you wish to reference and click the OK button to add the references to your project. Now you can use any objects located in the referenced assemblies by either directly referencing the full assembly or by adding the namespaces to your ScriptMain classes for shorter references. References can also be removed by right-clicking the reference in the References Node of the Project Explorer. (The References Node is hidden in the VB project. Click the menu option Project ⇨ Show All Files to make this node visible.) Expand the References Node to see all the references in your project. Right-click a reference and select the Remove option to remove it from the project.

Example: Using Custom .NET Assemblies

Although using standard .NET assemblies is interesting, being able to use already compiled .NET assemblies really opens up the capabilities of your SSIS development. Using code already developed and compiled means not having to copy-and-paste into each Script Task or Component and allows you to reuse code already developed and tested. To show an example of how this works, you'll create an external custom .NET library that can validate a postal code and see how to integrate this simple validator into a Script Task. (To do this, you'll need the standard class library templates that are part of Visual Studio. If you only installed BIDS, these templates are not installed by default.) You can also download the precompiled versions of these classes as well as any code from this chapter at www.wrox.com.

To start, open up a standard class library project in the language of your choice, and create a standard utility class in the project that looks something like this:

```
C#
using System;
using System.Text.RegularExpressions;
namespace ssistestlib
{
    public static class DataUtilities
    {
        public static bool isValidUSPostalCode(string PostalCode)
        {
            return Regex.IsMatch(PostalCode, "^[0-9]{5}(-[0-9]{4})?$");
        }
    }
}
VB
Imports System.Text.RegularExpressions

Public Class DataUtilities
    Public Shared Function isValidUSPostalCode
                            (ByVal PostalCode As String) As Boolean
        isValidUSPostalCode = Regex.IsMatch(PostalCode,
                                "^[0-9]{5}(-[0-9]{4})?$")
    End Function
End Class
```

Since you are creating projects for both languages, the projects (and assemblies) are named SSISUtilityLib_VB and SSISUtilityLib_Csharp. Notice the use of *static* or *shared* methods. This is not required, but is useful because you are simulating the development of what could later be a utility library loaded with many stateless data validation functions. A static or shared method allows the utility functions to be called without instantiating the class for each evaluation.

Now sign the assembly by right-clicking the project to access the Properties menu option. In the Signing tab, there is an option to select Sign the assembly, as shown in Figure 9-7. Click New on the drop-down and name the assembly to get a strong name key added to the assembly.

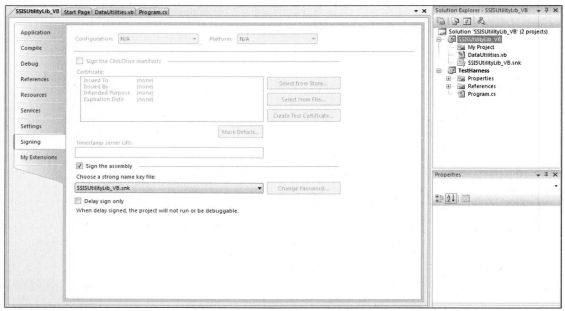

Figure 9-7

In this example, the VB version of the SSISUtilityLib project is being signed. Now, the assembly can be compiled by clicking the Build option in the Visual Studio menu and the in-process DLL will be built with a strong name to allow it to be registered in the GAC.

On the target development machine, go to the command-line prompt from the Visual Studio Tools menu to register your assembly with a command like this:

```
C:\Program Files\Microsoft Visual Studio 9.0\VC>gacutil /I
c:\ssis\scripts\SSISUtilityLib_VB\SSISUtilityLib_VB\bin\debug\
SSISUtilityLib_VB.dll
```

Note that you may have to run the command line as administrator or have the User Access Control feature of Vista turned off to register the assembly.

If you are running on a production machine, you'll also need to copy the assembly into the appropriate .NET Framework directory so that you can use the assembly in the Visual Studio IDE. Use the Microsoft .NET Framework 2.0 Configuration wizard task to Manage the Assembly Cache. Select Add an Assembly to the Assembly Cache to copy an assembly file into the global cache.

To use the compiled assembly in an SSIS package, open a new SSIS package and add a new Script Task onto the Control Flow surface. Select the scripting language you wish and click Edit Script. You'll need to right-click the Project Explorer Node for references and find the reference for SSISUtilityLib_VB.dll or SSISUtilityLib_CSharp.dll depending upon which one you built. (Remember that you may have to use the menu option Project ⇨ Show All Files in the VB projects to see the References Node.) If you've registered the assembly in the GAC, you'll be able to find it in the .NET tab. If you are in a development environment, you can simply browse to the .dll to select.

Add the namespace into the ScriptMain class. Then add these namespaces to the ScriptMain class:

```
C#
using SSISUtilityLib_CSharp;
```

```
VB
Imports SSISUtilityLib_VB
Imports System.Windows.Forms
```

Note that the SSIS C# Script Task in the sample packages that you'll see if you download the chapter materials from www.wrox.com use the C# version of the utility library. However, this is not required. The compiled .NET class libraries may be intermixed within the SSIS Script Task or Components regardless of the scripting language you choose. All that is left is to code a call to the utility function into the Main() function like this:

```
C#
public void Main()
{
    string postalCode = "12345-1111";
    string msg = string.Format(
            "Validating PostalCode {0}\nResult..{1}", postalCode,
                        DataUtilities.isValidUSPostalCode(postalCode));
    MessageBox.Show(msg);
    Dts.TaskResult = (int)ScriptResults.Success;
}
```

```
VB
Public Sub Main()
    Dim postalCode As String = "12345-1111"
    Dim msg As String = String.Format("Validating PostalCode {0}" +
            vbCrLf + "Result..{1}", postalCode,
            DataUtilities.isValidUSPostalCode(postalCode))
    MessageBox.Show(msg)
    Dts.TaskResult = ScriptResults.Success
End Sub
```

Compile the Script Task and execute it. The result should be a message box displaying a string to validate the postal code 12345-1111. The postal code format is validated by the DataUtility function IsValidUSPostalCode. There was no need to copy the function in the script project. The logic of validating the format of a U.S. Postal code is stored in the shared DataUtility function and can easily be used in both Script Tasks and Components with minimal coding and maximum consistency. The only downside to this is that there is now an external dependency in the SSIS package upon this assembly. If the assembly changes version numbers, you'll need to open and recompile all the script projects for each SSIS package using this. Otherwise, you could get an error if you aren't following backward compatibility guidelines to ensure that existing interfaces are not broken. If you have a set of well-tested business functions that rarely change, using external assemblies may be a good idea for your SSIS development.

Using the Script Task

Now that you've gotten a good overview of the scripting environment in SSIS, it's time to dig into one of the Scripting Components and give it a spin. We used the Script Task heavily to demonstrate how the SSIS scripting environment works with Visual Studio and during the execution of a package. Generally, anything that you can script in the .NET managed environment that should run once per package or code loop belongs in the Script Task. Script Tasks are extremely useful and end up being the general-purpose utility component similar to the role ActiveX Tasks performed for DTS package development.

Configuring the Script Task Editor

Earlier we looked at the Script Task Editor to point out that there are now two selections available for the scripting language. Let's look at that editor again and go over the other details. Drop a Script Task on the Control Flow surface and display the editor you see in Figure 9-8.

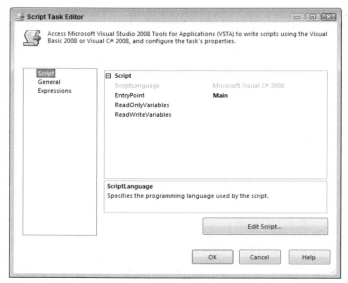

Figure 9-8

Here are the four properties on the Script tab that you can use to configure the Script Task:

❑ **ScriptLanguage:** This property defines the .NET language that will be used for the script. As demonstrated earlier, VB and C# are now both supported.

❑ **EntryPoint:** This is the name of the class that must contain a public `Main()` method that will be called inside your script to begin execution.

❑ **ReadOnlyVariables:** This property enumerates a case-sensitive, comma-separated list of SSIS variables that you will allow explicit rights to be read by the Script Task.

❑ **ReadWriteVariables:** This property enumerates a case-sensitive, comma-separated list of SSIS variables that you are allowing to be read from and written to by the Script Task.

Missing from the first release of SSIS is a property that allowed the option to precompile script code into binary code before execution. In the latest version of SSIS, all scripts are precompiled by default. This is part of the performance improvements made to reduce the overhead of loading the language engine when running a package.

The second tab, labeled General, contains the properties for the task name and description. The latest version of SSIS moves this tab down since it is not accessed as frequently as the Script tab.

The final page available on the left of this dialog is the Expression tab. The Expression tab provides access to the properties that can be set using an expression or expression-based variable. See Chapter 6 for how to use expressions and variables. Practically, changing the ScriptLanguage at runtime is not really possible, nor desired. The most common property manipulated by an expression is the Disable property that is used to bypass the task.

Once the script language is set and the script accessed, a project file with a class named ScriptMain and a default entry point named Main() is created. An example of the Main() function is provided here without the supporting class:

```
C#
public void Main()
{
    // TODO: Add your code here
    Dts.TaskResult = (int)ScriptResults.Success;
}

VB
Public Sub Main()
    Dts.TaskResult = ScriptResults.Failure
End Try
```

The code provided automatically includes the statement to set the TaskResult of the Dts object to the enumerated value for Success. The Script Task itself is a task in the collection of tasks for the package. Setting the TaskResult property of the task sets the return value for the Script Task and tells the package whether the end result was a success or failure.

By now, you've probably noticed all the references to DTS. What is this object and what can you do with it? We'll answer this question in the next section, as you peel back the details on the DTS object.

The Script Task Dts Object

The Dts object is actually a property on your package that is an instance of the Microsoft.SqlServer .Dts.Tasks.ScriptTask.ScriptObjectModel. The Dts object provides a window into the package in which your script executes. While you can't change properties of the DTS as it executes, the Dts object has seven properties and one method that allow you to interact with the package. The following is an explanation of these members:

❑ Connections: A collection of Connection Managers defined in the package. You can use these connections in your script to retrieve any extra data you may need.

❑ Events: A collection of events that are defined for the package. You can use this interface to fire off these predefined events and any custom events.

❑ ExecutionValue: A read-write property that allows you to specify additional information about your task's execution using a user-defined object. This can be any information you want.

❑ TaskResult: This property allows you to return the Success or Failure status of your Script Task to the package. This is the main way of communicating processing status or Controlling Flow in your package. This property must be set before exiting your script.

❑ Transaction: Obtains the transaction associated with the container in which your script is running.

❑ VariableDispenser: Gets the VariableDispenser object that you can use to retrieve variables when using the Script Task.

❑ Variables: A collection of all the variables that are available to any script. This is used by default in the Script Component.

❑ Log: This method allows you to write to any log providers that have been enabled.

DTS developers are sometimes locked into the fact that the Script Task can no longer alter an executing package, but in truth, between the additions of the expressions and the Dts object, you can do almost everything you could want to with the executing package. The method is just different. In the next few sections, we'll go through some of the more common things that the Active Script Task can be employed to accomplish.

Accessing Variables in the Script Task

Variables and expressions are an important feature of the SSIS roadmap. We aren't talking about scripting variables, but rather package variables that serve as intermediate communication mediums between your Script Task and the rest of your package. As discussed in Chapter 6, variables are used to drive the runtime changes within a package by allowing properties to infer their values at runtime from variables, which can be static or defined through the expression language.

The common method of using variables is to send them into a Script Task as decision-making elements or to drive downstream decisions by setting the value of the variable in the script based on some business rules. The VariableDispenser object provides methods for locking variables for read-only or read-write access and then retrieving them. Initially this was the standard way of accessing variables in scripts. The reason for the explicit locking mechanism is to allow control in the Script Task to keep two processes from competing for accessing and changing a variable.

To retrieve a variable using the VariableDispenser object, you would have to deal with the implementation details of locking semantics, and write code like the following:

```
C#
Variables vars = null;
String myval = null;
Dts.VariableDispenser.LockForRead("User::SomeStringVariable")
Dts.VariableDispenser.GetVariables(ref vars)
Myval = vars[0].Value;
vars.Unlock();   //Needed to unlock the variables
System.Windows.Forms.MessageBox.Show(myval);

VB
Dim vars As Variables
Dim myval As String
Dts.VariableDispenser.LockForRead("User::SomeStringVariable")
Dts.VariableDispenser.GetVariables(vars)
myval = vars(0).Value
vars.Unlock()   'Needed to unlock the variables
MsgBox(myval)
```

The downside to this method is that it was easy to forget to unlock the variables in an efficient way and as a result, a variable could be locked and rendered unavailable downstream in the package.

However, this type of control is not always required. Sometimes you simply want the variables that you are using in a Script Task to be locked when you are reading and writing, and not have to worry about the locking implementation details. Luckily, a much easier abstraction was created to add a `Variables` collection on the `Dts` object, and the `ReadOnlyVariables` and `ReadWriteVariables` properties for the Script Task were introduced. The only constraint is that you have to define upfront which variables going into the Script Task can be read and not written to, and which ones can be read and writable.

The `ReadOnlyVariables` and `ReadWriteVariables` properties tell the Script Task which variables to lock and how. The `Variables` collection in the `Dts` object then gets populated with these variables. The code to retrieve a variable then becomes much simpler, and the complexities of locking are abstracted, so you only have to worry about one line of code to read a variable:

```
C#
Dts.Variables["User::SomeStringVariable"].Value;
or
Dts.Variables[0].Value;

VB
Dts.Variables("User::SomeStringVariable").Value
Or
Dts.Variables(0).Value
```

Using the ordinal position of the variable in the Variables collection is the safest method if you are unsure of how to name the variable in your script. Just remember that the variables are ordered from the editor left to right, starting in the `ReadOnlyVariables` and then down to the `ReadWriteVariables`, also moving left to right. Now, if you choose to use the named variable, you are safer to use the fully qualified variable name like `User::SomeStringVariable`. Attempting to read a variable from the Variables collection that hasn't been specified in one of the variable properties of the task will throw an exception. Likewise, attempting to write to a variable not included in the `ReadWriteVariables` property also throws an exception. The biggest frustration for new SSIS developers writing VB script is dealing with this error message:

```
Error: 0xc0914054 at VB Script Task: Failed to lock variable
"SomestringVariable" for read access with error 0xc0910001 "The variable
cannot be found. This occurs when an attempt is made to retrieve a variable
from the Variables collection on a container during execution of the package,
and the variable is not there. The variable name may have changed or the
variable is not being created."
```

The resolution is simple. Either the variable name listed in the Script Task Editor or the variable name in the script doesn't match, so one must be changed to match the other. It is more confusing for the VB developers because this language is not case-sensitive. However, the SSIS variables are case-sensitive, even within the VB script.

Although Visual Basic.NET is not case-sensitive, SSIS variables are.

Another issue that happens occasionally is that more than one variable with the same name can be created with different scopes. When this happens, you have to make sure you explicitly refer to the variable by the fully qualified variable name. One of the latest helpful features of SSIS is a pop-up UI that allows the selection of the variables. Figure 9-9 is an example of this UI that allows the selection of user-defined variables.

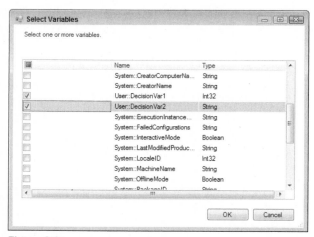

Figure 9-9

The best part is that the Script Task property for the ReadOnlyVariables or ReadWriteVariables is auto-filled with the fully qualified names: User::DecisionVar1 and User::DecisionVar2. This reduces most of the common issues with passing variables into the Script Task. All this information will now come in handy as we run through an example using the Script Task and variables to control SSIS package flow.

Example: Using Script Task Variables to Control Package Flow

In this example, we'll set up a Script Task that uses two variables to determine which one of two branches of Control Flow logic should be taken when the package executes. First, create a new SSIS package and set up these three variables:

Variable	Type	Value
DecisionIntVar	Int32	32
DecisionStrVar	String	txt
HappyPathEnum	Int32	0

Then drop three Script Tasks on the Control Flow design surface so that the package looks like Figure 9-10.

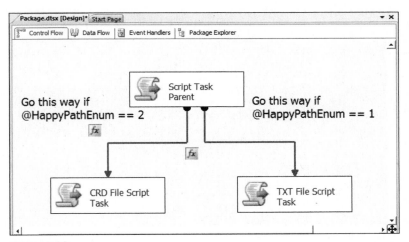

Figure 9-10

What we want to do is feed the two variables (DecisionIntVar and DecisionStrVar) that represent the number of rows determined to be in a file and the file extension into the Script Task through these variables. Assume that these values have been set by yet another process. Logic in the Script Task will determine whether the package should execute the CRD File Path Script Task or the TXT File Script Task. The control of the package is handled by the other external variable named HappyPathEnum. If the value of this variable is equal to 1, then the TXT File Script Task will be executed. If the value of the variable is equal to 2, then the CRD File Path Script Task will be executed. Open up the main Script Task Editor to set up the properties. It should look like Figure 9-11.

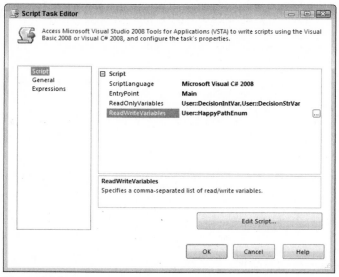

Figure 9-11

Set the Script Language and then use the ellipsis button to bring up the variable selection UI that we discussed and demonstrated in Figure 9-9. Select the variables for the ReadOnlyVariables and ReadWriteVariables separately if you are using the variable selection UI. You can also type these variables in, but remember that the variable names are case-sensitive. It is noteworthy to stop and point out the ordinal positions of these variables for this example. You can see the ordinal positions superimposed onto the editor in Figure 9-12.

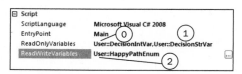

Figure 9-12

We'll keep this script simple for demonstration purposes. The most important parts are the retrieving and setting of the variables. This code uses the named references for the variables but the code lines like this:

```
C#
int rowCnt = (int)Dts.Variables["User::DecisionIntVar"].Value;

VB
Dim rowCnt As Integer = Dts.Variables("User::DecisionIntVar").Value
```

Could easily be replaced with ordinal-based references like this:

```
C#
int rowCnt = (int)Dts.Variables[0].Value;

VB
Dim rowCnt As Integer = Dts.Variables(0).Value
```

The setting of variables uses the same syntax but reverses the assignment. The code that should be pasted into the `Main()` function of the `ScriptMain` class will evaluate the two variables and set the `HappyPathEnum` variable:

```
C#
//Retrieving the value of Variables
int rowCnt = (int)Dts.Variables["User::DecisionIntVar"].Value;
string fileExt = (string)Dts.Variables["User::DecisionStrVar"].Value;

if (fileExt.Equals("txt") && rowCnt > 0)
{
    Dts.Variables["User::HappyPathEnum"].Value = 1;
}
else if (fileExt.Equals("crd") && rowCnt > 0)
{
    Dts.Variables["User::HappyPathEnum"].Value = 2;
}
Dts.TaskResult = (int)ScriptResults.Success;

VB
'Retrieving the value of Variables
Dim rowCnt As Integer = Dts.Variables("User::DecisionIntVar").Value
Dim fileExt As String = Dts.Variables("User::DecisionStrVar").Value

If (fileExt.Equals("txt") And rowCnt > 0) Then
    Dts.Variables(2).Value = 1
    Dts.Variables("User::HappyPathEnum").Value = 1
ElseIf (fileExt.Equals("crd") And rowCnt > 0) Then
    Dts.Variables(2).Value = 2
    Dts.Variables("User::HappyPathEnum").Value = 2
End If
Dts.TaskResult = ScriptResults.Success
```

To alter the flow of the package, set the two precedence constraints in the package hierarchy to be based on a successful completion of the previous Script Task and an Expression that tests the expected values of the `HappyPathEnum` variable. This precedence defines that the Control Flow should only go in a direction if the value of an expression tests true. Set the precedence between each Script Task to one of these expressions:

```
@HappyPathEnum == 1
Or
@HappyPathEnum == 2
```

313

A sample of the precedence between the Script Task and the TXT File Script Task should look like Figure 9-13.

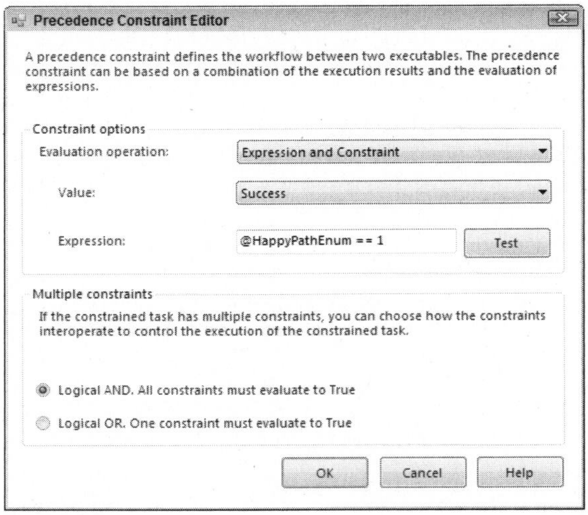

Figure 9-13

Now, to give the package something to do, simply retrieve the value of the set variable in each child Script Task to provide visual proof that the HappyPathEnum variable was properly set. Add this code into the Main() function of each child Script Task (make sure you set the message to display TXT or CRD for each associated Script Task):

```
C#
int ival = (int)Dts.Variables[0].Value;
string msg = string.Format("TXT File Found\nHappyPathEnum Value = {0}",
                    Dts.Variables[0].Value.ToString());

System.Windows.Forms.MessageBox.Show(msg);
Dts.TaskResult = (int)ScriptResults.Success;

VB
 Dim ival As Integer = Dts.Variables(0).Value
 Dim msg As String = _
 String.Format("TXT File Found" + vbCrLf + "HappyPathEnum Value = {0}",
                    Dts.Variables(0).Value.ToString())

System.Windows.Forms.MessageBox.Show(msg)
Dts.TaskResult = ScriptResults.Success
```

To see how this works, set the value of the User::DecisionIntVar variable to a positive integer number value, and the User::DecisionStrVar variable to either txt or crd, and watch the package switch from one Control Flow to the other. If you provide a value other than txt or crd (even "txt" with quotes will cause this), the package will not run either leg, which is as designed. This is a simple example that you can refer back to as your packages get more complicated, and you are referring to or updating variables within the Script Tasks. Later, we'll look at the Script Component that accesses variables in a slightly different way.

Connecting to Data Sources in a Script Task

A common use of an ActiveX Script Task in DTS packages was to grab a connection to various Data Sources for decision-making data from Excel files, INI files, flat files, or even databases like Oracle or Access. This capability provided ways to get to other Data Sources for configuring the packages, or to retrieve or output data for things we didn't have a direct connection object to use. In SSIS, with the Scripting Task, you can still make connections using any of the .NET libraries directly, or you can use connections that are defined in a package. Connections in SSIS are abstractions for connection strings that can be copied, passed around, and configured more easily than the ADO, script-based version in DTS.

The Connections collection hangs off of the DTS object in the Script Task. To retrieve a connection you call the `AcquireConnection` method on a specific named (or ordinal position) connection in the collection. The only thing you really should know ahead of time is what type of connection you are going to be retrieving, because you'll need to cast the returned connection to the proper connection type. In .NET, connections are not generic like the ADO model. Examples of concrete connections are `SqlConnection`, `OleDb.Connection`, `OdbcConnection`, and the `OracleConnection` Managers that connect using SqlClient, OLE DB, ODBC, and even Oracle data access libraries respectively. There are some things you can do to query the Connection Manager to determine what is in the connection string or if it supports transactions, but you shouldn't expect to use one connection in SSIS for everything, especially with the added Connection Managers for FTP, HTTP, and WMI.

Assuming that you're up to speed on the different types of connections covered earlier in this book, let's look at how you can use them in everyday SSIS package tasks.

Example: Retrieving Data into Variables from a Database

Although SSIS provides configurable abilities to set package-level values, there are use-cases that require you to retrieve actionable values from a database that can be used for package Control Flow or other functional purposes. One example would be some variable aspect of the application that may change, like an email address for events to use for notification. In this example, you'll retrieve a log file path for a package at runtime using a connection within a Script Task. The database that contains the settings for the log file path stores this data using the package ID. You'll first need a table in the AdventureWorks2008 database called `SSIS_SETTING`. Create the table with three fields, `PACKAGE_ID`, `SETTING`, and `VALUE`, or use this script:

```
CREATE TABLE [dbo].[SSIS_SETTING](
  [PACKAGE_ID] [uniqueidentifier] NOT NULL,
  [SETTING] [nvarchar](2080) NOT NULL,
  [VALUE] [nvarchar](2080) NOT NULL
) ON [PRIMARY]
GO
INSERT INTO SSIS_SETTING
SELECT '{INSERT YOUR PACKAGE ID HERE}', 'LOGFILEPATH', 'c:\myLogFile.txt'
```

Then create an SSIS package with one ADO.NET Connection Manager to the AdventureWorks database called `local.aw` and add a package-level variable named `LOGFILEPATH` of type `String`. Add a Script Task to the project and send in two variables: the ReadOnly `System::PackageID` and a ReadWrite variable User::LOGFILEPATH. Click the Edit Script button to open the Script project and add the namespace to System.Data.SqlClient in the top of the class. Then add the following code to the Main() method:

```csharp
C#
public void Main()
{
    string myPackageId = Dts.Variables["System::PackageID"].Value.ToString();
    string myValue = string.Empty;
    string cmdString = "SELECT VALUE FROM SSIS_SETTING " +
            "WHERE PACKAGE_ID= @PACKAGEID And SETTING= @SETTINGID";

    try
    {
        SqlConnection mySqlConn =
                (SqlConnection)Dts.Connections[0].AcquireConnection(null);
        mySqlConn = new SqlConnection(mySqlConn.ConnectionString);
        mySqlConn.Open();
        SqlCommand cmd = new SqlCommand();
        cmd.CommandText = cmdString;
        SqlParameter parm = new SqlParameter("@PACKAGEID",
                    SqlDbType.UniqueIdentifier);
        parm.Value = new Guid(myPackageId);
        cmd.Parameters.Add(parm);
        parm = new SqlParameter("@SETTINGID", SqlDbType.NVarChar);
        parm.Value = "LOGFILEPATH";
        cmd.Parameters.Add(parm);
        cmd.Connection = mySqlConn;
        cmd.CommandText = cmdString;
        SqlDataReader reader = cmd.ExecuteReader();
        while (reader.Read())
        {
            myValue = reader["value"].ToString();
        }

        Dts.Variables["User::LOGFILEPATH"].Value = myValue;

        reader.Close();
        mySqlConn.Close();
        mySqlConn.Dispose();
    }
    catch
    {
        Dts.TaskResult = (int)ScriptResults.Failure;
        throw;
    }

    System.Windows.Forms.MessageBox.Show(myValue);
    Dts.TaskResult = (int)ScriptResults.Success;
}

VB
Public Sub Main()
    Dim myPackageId As String = _
```

```
                         Dts.Variables("System::PackageID").Value.ToString()
        Dim myValue As String = String.Empty
        Dim cmdString As String = "SELECT VALUE FROM SSIS_SETTING " + _
                    "WHERE PACKAGE_ID= @PACKAGEID And SETTING= @SETTINGID"
        Try
            Dim mySqlConn As SqlClient.SqlConnection
            mySqlConn = DirectCast(Dts.Connections(0).AcquireConnection(Nothing), _
                        SqlClient.SqlConnection)
            mySqlConn = New SqlClient.SqlConnection(mySqlConn.ConnectionString)
            mySqlConn.Open()
            Dim cmd = New SqlClient.SqlCommand()
            cmd.CommandText = cmdString
            Dim parm As New SqlClient.SqlParameter("@PACKAGEID", _
                        SqlDbType.UniqueIdentifier)
            parm.Value = New Guid(myPackageId)
            cmd.Parameters.Add(parm)
            parm = New SqlClient.SqlParameter("@SETTINGID", SqlDbType.NVarChar)
            parm.Value = "LOGFILEPATH"
            cmd.Parameters.Add(parm)
            cmd.Connection = mySqlConn
            cmd.CommandText = cmdString
            Dim reader As SqlClient.SqlDataReader = cmd.ExecuteReader()
            Do While (reader.Read())
                myValue = reader("value").ToString()
            Loop
            Dts.Variables("User::LOGFILEPATH").Value = myValue
            reader.Close()
            mySqlConn.Close()
            mySqlConn.Dispose()
        Catch ex As Exception
            Dts.TaskResult = ScriptResults.Failure
            Throw
        End Try

        System.Windows.Forms.MessageBox.Show(myValue)
        Dts.TaskResult = ScriptResults.Success
    End Sub
```

In this code, the package ID is passed into the Script Task as a read-only variable and is used to build a TSQL statement to retrieve the value of the LOGFILEPATH setting from the SSIS_SETTING table. The AcquireConnection method creates an instance of a connection to the local AdventureWorks database managed by the Connection Manager and allows other SqlClient objects to access the Data Source. The retrieved setting from the SSIS_SETTING table is then stored in the writable variable LOGFILEPATH. This is a basic example, but you use this exact same technique to retrieve a recordset into an object variable that can be iterated within your package as well.

Example: Saving Data to an XML File

Another common requirement is to generate data of a certain output format. When the output is a common format like Flat File, Excel, CSV, or other database format, you can simply pump the data stream into one of the Data Flow Destinations. If you want to save data to an XML file, the structure is not homogeneous, and not as easy to transform from a column-based data stream into an XML structure without some logic or structure around it. This is where the Script Task comes in handy.

The easiest way to get data into an XML file is to load and save the contents of a dataset using the method WriteXML on the dataset. With a new Script Task in a package with an ADO.NET connection to AdventureWorks2008, add a reference to the System.Xml.dll, then add the namespaces for System.Data.SqlClient, System.IO, and System.Xml. Then code the following into the Script Task to open a connection and get all the SSIS_SETTING rows and store as XML.

See the previous example for the DDL to create this table in the AdventureWorks2008 database.

```csharp
C#
public void Main()
{
    SqlConnection sqlConn;
    string cmdString = "SELECT * FROM SSIS_SETTING ";
    try
    {
        sqlConn =
(SqlConnection)(Dts.Connections["local.aw"]).AcquireConnection(Dts.Transaction
);
        sqlConn = new SqlConnection(sqlConn.ConnectionString);
        sqlConn.Open();
        SqlCommand cmd = new SqlCommand(cmdString, sqlConn);
        SqlDataAdapter da = new SqlDataAdapter(cmd);
        DataSet ds = new DataSet();
        da.Fill(ds);
        ds.WriteXml(new
System.IO.StreamWriter("C:\\SSIS\\scripts\\ScriptDataIntoXMLFile\\
myPackageSettings.xml"));
        sqlConn.Close();
    }
    catch
    {
        Dts.TaskResult = (int)ScriptResults.Failure;
        throw;
    }
    Dts.TaskResult = (int)ScriptResults.Success;
}

VB
Public Sub Main()
    Dim sqlConn As New SqlConnection
    Dim cmdString As String = "SELECT * FROM SSIS_SETTING "
    Try
        sqlConn =
DirectCast(Dts.Connections("local.aw").AcquireConnection(Dts.Transaction),
SqlConnection)
        sqlConn = New SqlConnection(sqlConn.ConnectionString)
        sqlConn.Open()
        Dim cmd = New SqlCommand(cmdString, sqlConn)
        Dim da = New SqlDataAdapter(cmd)
        Dim ds = New DataSet
        da.Fill(ds)
        ds.WriteXml(New
StreamWriter("C:\\SSIS\\scripts\\ScriptDataIntoXMLFile\\myPackageSettings.xml"
))
```

```
            sqlConn.Close()
      Catch
            Dts.TaskResult = ScriptResults.Failure
            Throw
      End Try
      Dts.TaskResult = ScriptResults.Success
End Sub
```

The results are in XML, and there is not much to this file, except that it is in XML format.

```
<NewDataSet>
  <Table>
    <PACKAGE_ID>a5cf0c2f-8d85-42eb-91b9-cbd1fd47e5b1</PACKAGE_ID>
    <SETTING>LOGFILEPATH</SETTING>
    <VALUE>C:\SSIS\scripts\ScriptDataIntoVariable\myLogFile.txt</VALUE>
  </Table>
</NewDataSet>
```

If you need more control of the data you are exporting, or you need to serialize data, you'll need to use the Script Task in a different way. See the next example for some tips on how to do this.

Example: Serializing Data to XML

In the last example, you looked at simply dumping a recordset into an XML format by loading data into a dataset and using the `WriteToXML` method to dump the XML out to a file stream. If you need more control over the format or the data is hierarchical, using .NET XML object-based serialization can be helpful. Imagine implementations that pull data from flat-file mainframe dumps and fill fully hierarchical object models. Alternatively, imagine serializing data into an object structure to pop an entry into an MSMQ application queue. This is easy to do using some of the same concepts. Create another package with a connection to the AdventureWorks2008 database; add a Script Task with a reference to the `System.Data.SqlClient` namespace. Use the data from the previous example and create a class structure within your `ScriptMain` to hold the values for each row of settings that looks like this:

```
C#
[Serializable()]
public class SSISSetting
{
    public string PackageId { get; set; }
    public string Setting { get; set; }
    public string Value { get; set; }
}

VB
<Serializable()> Public Class SSISSetting
    Private m_PackageId As String
    Private m_Setting As String
    Private m_Value As String

    Public Property PackageId() As String
        Get
            PackageId = m_PackageId
        End Get
```

```
            Set(ByVal Value As String)
                m_PackageId = Value
            End Set
        End Property
        Public Property Setting() As String
            Get
                PackageId = m_Setting
            End Get
            Set(ByVal Value As String)
                m_Setting = Value
            End Set
        End Property
        Public Property Value() As String
            Get
                Value = m_Value
            End Get
            Set(ByVal Value As String)
                m_Value = Value
            End Set
        End Property
    End Class
```

This class will be used to fill based on the dataset like we had in the last example. It is still a flat model, but more complex class structures would have collections within the class. An example would be a student object with a collection of classes, or an invoice with a collection of line items. To persist this type of data you'll need to traverse multiple paths to fill the model. Once the model is filled, the rest is easy. First, add the namespaces System.Xml.Serialization, System.Collections.Generic, System.IO, and System.Data.SqlClient into your Script Task project. Then a simple example with the SSIS_ SETTING table would look like this:

```
C#
public void Main()
{
    SqlConnection sqlConn;
    string cmdString = "SELECT * FROM SSIS_SETTING ";

    try
    {
        sqlConn =
(SqlConnection)(Dts
.Connections["local.aw"]).AcquireConnection(Dts.Transaction);
        sqlConn = new SqlConnection(sqlConn.ConnectionString);
        sqlConn.Open();
        SqlCommand cmd = new SqlCommand(cmdString, sqlConn);
        SqlDataReader dR = cmd.ExecuteReader();
        List<SSISSetting> arrayListSettings = new List<SSISSetting>();

        while (dR.Read())
        {
            SSISSetting oSet = new SSISSetting();
            oSet.PackageId = dR["PACKAGE_ID"].ToString();
```

```
            oSet.Setting = dR["SETTING"].ToString();
            oSet.Value = dR["VALUE"].ToString();
            arrayListSettings.Add(oSet);
        }

        StreamWriter outfile = new
StreamWriter("C:\\SSIS\\scripts\\ScriptDataintoSerializableObject\\myObjectXml
Settings.xml");

        XmlSerializer ser = new XmlSerializer(typeof(List<SSISSetting>));
        ser.Serialize(outfile, arrayListSettings);
        outfile.Close();
        outfile.Dispose();
        sqlConn.Close();
    }
    catch
    {
        Dts.TaskResult = (int)ScriptResults.Failure;
        throw;
    }
    Dts.TaskResult = (int)ScriptResults.Success;
}

VB
Public Sub Main()
    Dim sqlConn As SqlConnection
    Dim cmdString As String = "SELECT * FROM SSIS_SETTING "

    Try
        sqlConn =
DirectCast(Dts.Connections("local.aw").AcquireConnection(Dts.Transaction),
            SqlConnection)
        sqlConn = New SqlConnection(sqlConn.ConnectionString)
        sqlConn.Open()
        Dim cmd As SqlCommand = New SqlCommand(cmdString, sqlConn)
        Dim dR As SqlDataReader = cmd.ExecuteReader()
        Dim arrayListSettings As New List(Of SSISSetting)
        Do While (dR.Read())
            Dim oSet As New SSISSetting()

            oSet.PackageId = dR("PACKAGE_ID").ToString()
            oSet.Setting = dR("PACKAGE_ID").ToString()
            oSet.Value = dR("PACKAGE_ID").ToString()
            arrayListSettings.Add(oSet)
        Loop

        Dim outfile As New
StreamWriter("C:\\SSIS\\scripts\\ScriptDataintoSerializableObject\\myObjectXml
Settings.xml")
        Dim ser As New XmlSerializer(GetType(List(Of SSISSetting)))

        ser.Serialize(outfile, arrayListSettings)
        outfile.Close()
        outfile.Dispose()
```

```
            sqlConn.Close()
        Catch
            Dts.TaskResult = ScriptResults.Failure
            Throw
        End Try

        Dts.TaskResult = ScriptResults.Success
    End Sub
```

The `StreamWriter` here just gets an IO stream from the file system to use for data output. The `XmlSerializer` does the heavy lifting and converts the data from the object format into an XML format. The only trick here is to understand how to deal with the `Generic List` or the collection of all the `SSISSetting` objects. This is handled by using the override where you can add the specific types to the serializer along with the `List`. The resulting XML payload will now look like this:

```
<?xml version="1.0" encoding="utf-8"?>
<ArrayOfSSISSetting xmlns:xsi="http://www.w3.org/2001/XMLSchema-instance"
xmlns:xsd="http://www.w3.org/2001/XMLSchema">
  <SSISSetting>
    <PackageId>34050406-2e0f-423a-8af3-1ec95399a6c2</PackageId>
    <Setting>34050406-2e0f-423a-8af3-1ec95399a6c2</Setting>
    <Value>34050406-2e0f-423a-8af3-1ec95399a6c2</Value>
  </SSISSetting>
</ArrayOfSSISSetting>
```

Although the XML content looks a little bit different than dumping the content of the recordset directly to XML as we did in the earlier example, it is optimized for object serialization. This is the type of content that you could push into application queues or share with external applications.

Raising an Event in a Script Task

All existing SSIS Tasks and Components raise events that can be captured and displayed by the Execution Results tab by default. Optionally these events can also be captured and logged into SSIS logging or event handlers. Event handlers are Control Flows that you set up and define to respond to specific events. They are literally Control Flow workflows within a package and give you the advantage of customizing the diagnostic information that the packages can provide at runtime.

If you have done any Windows GUI programming, you will be familiar with events. An *event* is simply a message sent from some object saying that something just happened or is about to happen. To raise or *fire* an event with a Script Task, you use the `Events` property of the `Dts` object. The `Events` property on the `Dts` object is really an instance of the `IDTSComponentEvents` interface. This interface specifies seven methods for firing events:

❑ `FireBreakpointHit`: This method supports the SQL Server infrastructure and is not intended to be used directly in code.

❑ `FireError`: Fires an event when an error occurs.

❑ `FireInformation`: Fires an event with information. You can fire this event when you want some set of information to be logged, possibly for auditing later.

❑   `FireProgress`: Fires an event when a certain progress level has been met.

❑   `FireQueryCancel`: Fires an event to determine if package execution should stop.

❑   `FireWarning`: Fires an event that is less serious than an error, but more than just information.

❑   `FireCustomEvent`: Fires a custom defined event.

In SSIS, any events you fire will be written to all enabled log handlers that are set to log that event. Logging allows you to see what happened with your script when you're not there to watch it run. This is useful for troubleshooting and auditing purposes, as you'll see in the following example.

Example: Raise Some Events

The default event handler at design time is the Execution Results tab at the top of your package in the BIDS design environment. The simplest way to use the events is to fire off some sample events and see them in this Execution Results tab. To do this create a new package with a Script Task and add the System variable `System::TaskName` as a Read-Only variable. Then add the following code to the `Main()` function:

```csharp
C#
public void Main()
{
    string taskName =
        Dts.Variables["System::TaskName"].Value.ToString();
    bool retVal = false;

    Dts.Events.FireInformation(0, taskName,
        String.Format("Starting Loop Operation at {0} ",
        DateTime.Now.ToString("MM/dd/yyyy hh:mm:ss")), "", 0,
        ref retVal);

    for(int i=0; i <= 10; i++)
    {
        Dts.Events.FireProgress(String.Format("Loop in iteration {0}", i),
                i * 10, 0, 10, taskName, ref retVal);
    }

    Dts.Events.FireInformation(0, taskName,
        String.Format("Completion Loop Operation at {0} ",
        DateTime.Now.ToString("mm/dd/yyyy hh:mm:ss")), "", 0,
        ref retVal);

    Dts.Events.FireWarning(1, taskName,
        "This is a warning we want to pay attention to...",
        "", 0);
    Dts.Events.FireWarning(2, taskName,
        "This is a warning for debugging only...",
```

```
            "", 0);

        Dts.Events.FireError(0, taskName,
            "If we had an error it would be here", "", 0);
    }


    VB
Public Sub Main()
    Dim i As Integer = 0
    Dim taskName As String =
            Dts.Variables("System::TaskName").Value.ToString()
    Dim retVal As Boolean = False

    Dts.Events.FireInformation(0, taskName, _
        String.Format("Starting Loop Operation at {0} ", _
        DateTime.Now.ToString("MM/dd/yyyy hh:mm:ss")), "", 0, _
        True)

    For i = 0 To 10
        Dts.Events.FireProgress( _
            String.Format("Loop in iteration {0}", i), _
            i * 10, 0, 10, taskName, True)
    Next

    Dts.Events.FireInformation(0, taskName, _
        String.Format("Completion Loop Operation at {0} ", _
        DateTime.Now.ToString("mm/dd/yyyy hh:mm:ss")), "", 0, False)

    Dts.Events.FireWarning(1, taskName, _
        "This is a warning we want to pay attention to...", _
        "", 0)
    Dts.Events.FireWarning(2, taskName, _
        "This is a warning for debugging only...", _
        "", 0)

    Dts.Events.FireError(0, taskName, _
        "If we had an error it would be here", "", 0)
End Sub
```

This code will perform a simple loop operation and demonstrate firing the information, progress, warning, and error events. If you run the package, you'll be able to view the information embedded in these fire event statements in the Execution Results tab in Figure 9-14. Note that raising the error event results in the Script Task failure. You may comment out the `FireError` event to see the task complete successfully.

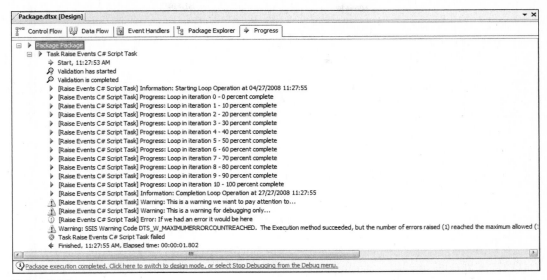

Figure 9-14

All the statements prefixed with the string [Script Task] were generated using these events fired from the Script Task. We'll leave it with you to comment out the Dts.Events.FireError method calls to demonstrate to yourself that the task can complete successfully for warnings and informational events. Note that with the firing of an error you can also force the task to generate a custom error with an error code and description. In fact, each of the events has a placeholder as the first parameter to store a custom information code. Continue to the next example to see how you can create an error handler to respond to the warning events that are fired from this Script Task.

Example: Respond to an Event

If you have already created a package for the Raise Some Events example, navigate to the Event Handlers tab. Event handlers are separate Control Flows that can be executed in response to an event. In the Raise Some Events example, you generated two Warning events. One had an information code of one (1) and the other had the value of two (2). You are going to add an event handler to respond to those warning events and add some logic to respond to the event if the information code is equal to one (1). Select the executable of Script Task and select the event handler of OnWarning. Then click the hot link that states:

```
Click here to create an 'OnWarning' event handler for executable 'Script Task'
```

This will create a Control Flow surface where you can drop SSIS Control Tasks onto the surface that will execute if an OnWarning event is thrown from the Script Task you added to the package earlier. Drop a new Script Task into the Event Handler Control Flow surface and name it OnWarning Script Task. Your designer should look like Figure 9-15.

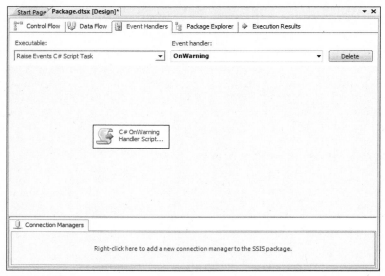

Figure 9-15

To retrieve the information code sent in the `Dts.Events.FireWarning` method call, add two system-level variables `System::ErrorCode, System::ErrorDescription` to the Read-Only Variables collection of the OnWarning Script Task. These variables will contain the values of the `InformationCode` and `Description` parameters in the `Dts.Events()` methods. You can then retrieve and evaluate these values when an event is raised by adding the following code:

```csharp
C#
        long lWarningCode = long.Parse(Dts.Variables[0].Value.ToString());
        String sMsg = string.Empty;
        if(lWarningCode == 1)
        {
            sMsg = String.Format(
                "Would do something with this warning:\n{0}: {1}",
                lWarningCode.ToString(), Dts.Variables(1).ToString());
            System.Windows.Forms.MessageBox.Show(sMsg);
        }
        Dts.TaskResult = (int)ScriptResults.Success;
```

```vbnet
VB
    Dim lWarningCode As Long = _
            Long.Parse(Dts.Variables(0).Value.ToString())
    Dim sMsg As String
    If lWarningCode = 1 Then
        sMsg = String.Format("Would do something with this warning: " _
                + vbCrLf + "{0}: {1}", _
        lWarningCode.ToString(), Dts.Variables(1).ToString())
        System.Windows.Forms.MessageBox.Show(sMsg)
    End If
    Dts.TaskResult = ScriptResults.Success
```

The code checks the value of the first parameter, which is the value of the `System::ErrorCode` and the value raised in the `Dts.Events.FireWarning` method. If the value is equivalent to one (1), an action is taken to show a message box. This action could just as well be logging an entry to a database, or sending an email. If you rerun the package now, you'll see that the first `FireWarning` event will be handled in your event handler and generate a message box warning. The second `FireWarning` event will also be captured by the event handler, but no response is made. You can see the event handler counter in the Progress or Execution Results tab is incremented to two (2). Raising events in the Script Tasks are great ways to get good diagnostic information without resorting to MessageBoxes in your packages. See Chapter 17 for much more detail about this type of development in SSIS.

Example: Logging Event Information

Scripts can also be used to log custom event information. To configure the previous example events SSIS package to log event information, go to SSIS ⇨ Logging in the Business Intelligence Designer Studio. The Configure SSIS Logs dialog will appear. Select "SSIS log provider for XML files" in the Provider Type drop-down and click Add. Click the column named Configuration and then select <New Connection> from the list to create an XML File Editor. For Usage type, select Create File and specify a path to a filename similar to `c:\ssis\scripts\raisingevents\myLogFile.xml`. (This would be something you'd use an expression or package configuration to set during runtime.) Click OK to close the File Connection Manager Editor dialog box. Your screen should look something like Figure 9-16.

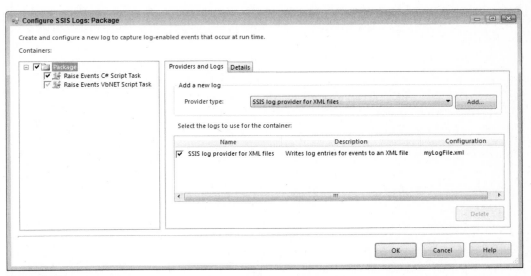

Figure 9-16

Now click the Package Node to start selecting what tasks in the package should log to the new provider, and check the box next to the provider name so that the log will be used. In the Details tab, select the `OnWarning` events specifically to log. You can choose to log any of the available event types to the providers by also selecting them in the Details tab. Now your provider configuration should look like Figure 9-17.

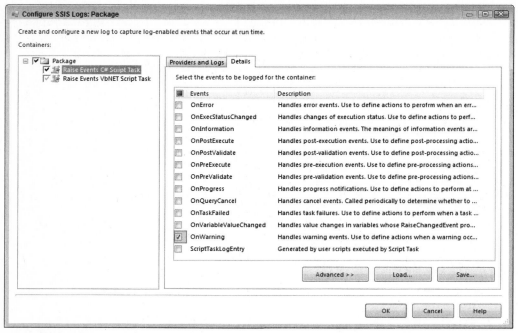

Figure 9-17

You can also go to the Advanced tab for each selected event to control exactly what properties of the event get logged as well. If you run the package again, the file specified in the logging provider will be created with content similar to the following:

```
<record>
    <event>OnWarning</event>
    <message>This is a warning we want to pay attention to...</message>
    <computer>MYCOMPUTER</computer>
    <operator>MYCOMPUTER\ADMIN</operator>
    <source>Package</source>
    <sourceid>{D86FF397-6C9B-4AD9-BACF-B4D41AC89ECB}</sourceid>
    <executionid>{8B6F6392-1818-4EE5-87BF-EDCB5DC37ACB}</executionid>
    <starttime>1/22/2008 9:30:08 PM</starttime>
    <endtime>1/22/2008 9:30:08 PM</endtime>
    <datacode>2</datacode>
    <databytes>0x</databytes>
</record>
```

You'll have other events in the file, such as Package Start and Package End, but the preceding code snippet focuses on the event that your code fired. This record contains the basic information on the event including the message, event execution time, and the computer and user that raised the event.

Using the Script Task to raise an event is just one way to get more diagnostic information into your SSIS log files. Read on to get a brief look at generating simple log entries.

Writing a Log Entry in a Script Task

Within a Script Task, the Log method of the Dts object writes a message to all enabled log providers. The Log method is simple and has but three arguments:

❑ messageText: The message to log

❑ dataCode: A field for logging a message code

❑ dataBytes: A field for logging binary data

The Log method is similar to the FireInformation method of the Events property, but it is easier to use and more efficient — you also do not need to create a specialized event handler to respond to the method call. All you need to do is set up a log provider within the package. In the previous section, you learned about how to add a log provider to a package. The following code logs a simple message with some binary data to all available log providers. This is quite useful for troubleshooting and auditing purposes. You can write out information at important steps in your script and even print out variable values to help you track down a problem.

Example: Script a Log Entry

You can see an example of how to script a log entry by adding a few lines of code to the package in the previous examples that you used to raise events. First add these lines to the appropriate Script Task that matches the language you chose in the previous example:

```
C#
Byte[] myByteArray[] = new byte[0];
Dts.Log("Called procedure: usp_Upsert with return code 4", 0, myByteArray);


VB
Dim myByteArray(0) As Byte
Dts.Log("Called procedure: usp_Upsert with return code 4", 0, myByteArray)
```

Then, select the events for the ScriptTaskLogEntry event in the Details tab of the logging configuration. This tells the SSIS package logger to expect to log any custom logging instructions like you just coded. Then run the package. You'll see a set of additional logging instructions that look like this:

```
<record>
    <event>User:ScriptTaskLogEntry</event>
    <message>Called Procedure: usp_Upsert with return code 4</message>
    <computer>MYCOMPUTER</computer>
    <operator>MYCOMPUTER\ADMIN</operator>
    <source>Raise Events C# Script Task</source>
    <sourceid>{CE53C1BB-7757-47FF-B173-E6088DA0A2A3}</sourceid>
    <executionid>{B7828A35-C236-451E-99DE-F679CF808D91}</executionid>
    <starttime>4/27/2008 2:54:04 PM</starttime>
    <endtime>4/27/2008 2:54:04 PM</endtime>
    <datacode>0</datacode>
    <databytes>0x</databytes>
</record>
```

As you can see, the Script Task is highly flexible with the introduction of the .NET-based VSTA capabilities. As far as controlling package flow or one-off activities, the Script Task has clearly taken over the role of the DTS ActiveX Script Component. However, the Script Task doesn't do all things well. If you want to apply programmatic logic to data in the data pump portion or Data Flow in an SSIS package, then you need to continue and add to your knowledge of scripting in SSIS and the Script Component.

Using the Script Component

The Script Component provides another area where programming logic can be applied in an SSIS package. This component can only be used in the Data Flow portion of an SSIS package and allows programmatic tasks to occur in the data stream. Anything you can do in .NET at a stream level can be done in this task. Connect to an HTTP Source to create a stream, parse through an existing stream, or send a stream to a custom destination. This component exists to provide, consume, or transform data using .NET code. To differentiate the different uses of the Script Component, when you create one you have to choose one of the following three types:

❑ **Source Type Component:** The role of this Script Component is to provide data to your Data Flow Task. You can define outputs and their types and use script code to populate them. An example would be reading in a complex file format, possibly XML or something that requires custom coding to read, like HTTP or RSS Sources.

❑ **Destination Type Component:** This type of Script Component consumes data much like an Excel or Flat File Destination. This component is the end of the line for the data in your data pump or stream. Here you'll typically put the data into a dataset variable to pass back to the Control Flow for further processing or send the stream to custom output destinations not supported in SSIS by a control. Examples of these output destinations can be Web service calls, custom XML formats, and multi-record formats for mainframe systems. You can even programmatically connect and send a stream to a printer object.

❑ **Transformation Type Component:** This type of Script Component can perform custom transformations on data. It consumes input columns and produces output columns. You would use the component when one of the built-in transformations just isn't flexible enough.

In this section, you'll get up to speed on all the specifics of the Script Component, starting first with an explanation of the differences between the Script Task and Component and then looking at the coding differences in the two models. In the end, you'll get an example of each implementation type of the Script Component to put all of this information to use.

Differences from a Script Task

You might ask, "Why are there two controls for the Script Task and Script Component?" Well, underneath the SSIS architecture there are really two different implementations of how the VSTA environment is used for performance. The Script Task is only going to be called once within a Control Flow, unless it is in a looping control. The Script Component has to be higher octane because it is going to be called per row of data in the data stream. You are also in the context of being able to access the data buffers directly, so there is a slight overhead in learning the differences between these two tasks.

When you are working with these two controls, the bottom line for you is that there are slightly different ways of doing the same types of things in each. This section of the chapter cycles back through some of the things you did with the Script Task and points out the differences. First, let's look at the differences in configuring the editor, then what changes when performing programmatic tasks such as accessing variables, using connections, raising events, and logging. Finally, we'll look at an example from an overall perspective.

Configuring the Script Component Editor

You'll notice the differences starting with the task editor. Adding a Script Component to the Data Flow designer brings up the editor shown in Figure 9-18, requesting the component type.

You must first add a Data Flow Task to a package to be able to add the Script Component.

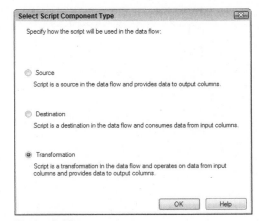

Figure 9-18

Selecting one of these choices changes the way the editor displays to configure the control. Essentially, you are choosing whether the control has input buffers, output buffers, or both. Figure 9-19 shows an example of the transformation Script Control that has both buffers.

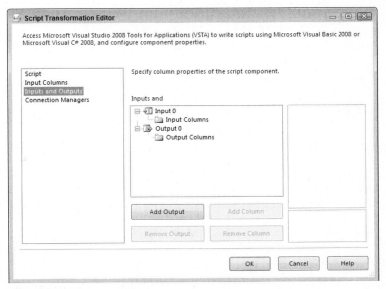

Figure 9-19

In the source version of the Script Component, the input buffers would not be available; the opposite is true of the destination version. You are responsible for defining these buffers by providing the set of typed columns for either the input or outputs. If the data is being fed into the component, the editor can reflect on the stream and set these up for you. Otherwise, you'll have to define them yourself. You can do this programmatically in the code, or ahead of time using the editor. Just select the input or output columns collection on the UI, and click the Add Column button to add a column as shown in Figure 9-20.

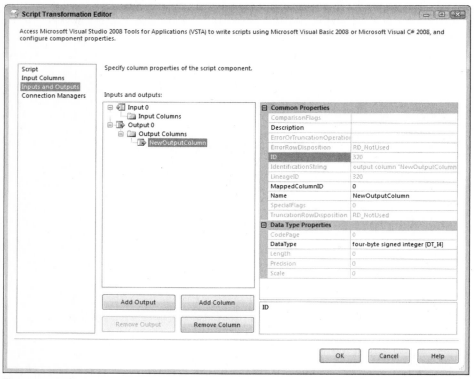

Figure 9-20

A helpful tip is to select the Output Columns Node on the tree view, so that the new column gets added to the bottom of the collection. Once you add a column, you can't move it up or down. Once you add the column, you'll need to set the Data Type, Length, Precision, and Scale. For details about the SSIS data types, see Chapter 6.

When you access the scripting environment, you'll notice some additional differences between the Script Component and the Script Task. Namely, that there are some new classes added to the Project Explorer, as seen in Figure 9-21.

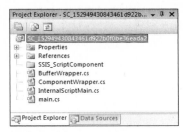

Figure 9-21

The class that is used to host custom code is named differently from the Script Task. The class name changed from `ScriptMain` to simply being called `main`. Internally there are also some changes. The main change is that there is not only one entry point method like there was in the Script Task. The methods you'll see in the `main` class depend upon the Script Component type. At least three of the following methods are typically coded and can be used as entry points in the Script Component:

❑ `PreExecute` is used for preprocessing tasks like creating expensive connections or file streams.

❑ `PostExecute` is used for cleanup tasks or setting variables at the completion of each processed row.

❑ `CreateNewOutputRows` is the method to manage the output buffers.

❑ `Input0 _ProcessInputRow` is the method to manage anything coming from the input buffers.

The remaining classes are generated automatically based on your input and output columns when you enter into the script environment, so don't make any changes to these, or they will be overwritten when you reenter the script environment.

One inconsistency that can occur within the Script Component Editor and the generation of the `BufferWrapper` class is that you can name columns in the editor that use keywords or are otherwise invalid when the `BufferWrapper` class is generated. An example would be an output column named `125K_AMOUNT`. If you create such a column, you'll get an error in the `BufferWrapper` class stating:

```
Invalid Token 125 in class, struct, or interface member declaration
```

Don't be tempted to change the property in the buffer class to something like `_125K_AMOUNT`, because this property will be rebuilt the next time you edit the script. Change the name of the output column to `_125K_AMOUNT`, and the buffer class will change automatically. The biggest difference that you need to pay attention to with the Script Component is that if you make *any* changes to this editor, you'll need to open up the Script environment so that all these base classes can be generated.

Last, but not least, you'll notice a Connections Managers tab that was not available in the Script Task Editor. This allows you to name specifically the connections that you want to be able to access within the Script Component. Although it is not required that you name these connections up front, it is extremely helpful if you do. You'll see why later, when you connect to a Data Source. Figure 9-22 shows an example of an Oracle connection added to a Script Component.

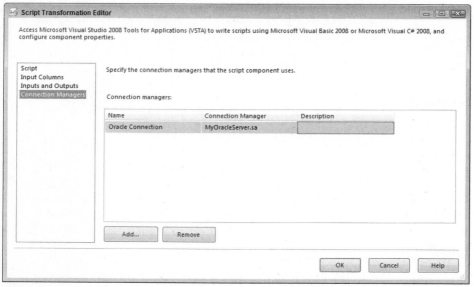

Figure 9-22

Now that you understand the differences in the Script Task and Component from a setup perspective, we'll look at how the coding is a little different. We'll start first with how you'll need to access package variables.

Accessing Variables in a Script Component

The same concepts behind accessing variables apply to the Script Component. You can either send the variables in to the control by adding them to the ReadOnlyVariables or ReadWriteVariables properties of the editor. You can also choose not to specify them up front and just use the variable dispenser within your Script Task to access, lock, and manipulate variables within the Script Component. We'd recommend that you use the properties in the editor for this component. The reason why is that the variables provided in the editor are added to the auto-generated base class variables collection as strongly typed variables. In this control, adding variables to the editor not only removes the need to lock and unlock the variables, but you get the added benefit of not having to remember the variable name within the component. Here's an example of setting the variable VALIDATION_ERRORS within a Script Component:

```
C#
this.Variables.VALIDATION_ERRORS = 1;
VB
me.Variables.VALIDATION_ERRORS = 1
```

As you can see this is much easier to use because the variable names are available in IntelliSense, and this is more maintainable because of the checking at compile time. However, if you have instances where you don't want to have to add a variable to each Script Component task, you can still use the variable dispenser in this component. It is located on the base class and can be accessed using the base class and not the DTS object. Other than these changes, the variable examples in the Script Task section of this chapter are still applicable. The remaining tasks of connecting to Data Sources, raising events, and logging will follow similar patterns. The methods of performing the tasks are more strongly named and this makes sense because we don't need any late-binding (or runtime type checking) within a high-performing Data Stream Task.

Connecting to Data Sources in a Script Component

Typically, you'll see connections being used in Source types of the Script Component, because in these types of Data Flow Tasks, the mission is to create data stream. The origination of that data is usually another external source. If you had a defined SSIS Source Component, it would be used and you wouldn't need the Script Component to connect to it.

In the latest version of SSIS, the coding has been greatly simplified. You can instantiate a specific Connection Manager and simply assign it the reference to a connection in the component's collection. Using the connections collection in the Script Component is very similar to the variables collection. The collection of strongly typed Connection Managers is created every time the script editor is opened. Again, this is helpful because you don't have to remember the names, and you get compile-time verification and checking. If you have a package with an OLE DB Connection Manager named `myOracleServer` and add it to the Script Component with the name `OracleConnection`, you'll have access to the connection using this code:

```
C#
ConnectionManagerOleDb oracleConnection =
       (ConnectionManagerOleDb)base.Connections.OracleConnection;


VB
Dim oracleConn as ConnectionManagerOleDb
oracleConn = Connections.OracleConnection
```

Raising Events

For the Script Task, we've already looked at the ability of SSIS to raise events and demonstrated with examples, scripting capabilities that manage how the package can respond to these events. These same capabilities exist in the Script Components, although you do need to consider that Script Components run in a data pipeline or stream, so the potential for repeated calls is highly likely. You should fire events sparingly within a Script Component that is generating or processing data in the pipeline to reduce overhead and increase performance. The methods are essentially the same, but without the static DTS object. Here is the code to raise an informational event in a Script Component:

```
C#
Boolean myBool=false;
this.ComponentMetaData.FireInformation(0, "myScriptComponent",
               "Removed non-ASCII Character", "", 0, ref myBool);
VB
Dim myBool As Boolean
Me.ComponentMetaData.FireInformation(0, "myScriptComponent", _
               "Removed non-ASCII Character", "", 0, myBool)
```

Either version of code will generate an event in the Progress Tab that looks like this:

```
[myScriptComponent] Information: Removed non-ASCII Character
```

Raising an event is preferred to logging because of the ability to develop a separate workflow for handling the event, but there are some instances when logging may be preferred. We'll look into logging for the Script Component in the next section.

Logging

Like the Script Task, the logging in the Script Component writes a message to all enabled log providers. It has the same interface as the Script Task, but it is exposed on the base class. Remember that Script Components run in a data pipeline or stream, so the potential for repeated calls is highly likely. Follow the same rules as with raising events and log sparingly within a Script Component that is generating or processing data in the pipeline to reduce overhead and increase performance. If you need to log a message within a Data Flow, you can improve performance by logging only in the PostExecute method, so that the results are only logged once.

Example: Script a Log Entry

This example shows how to log one informational entry to the log file providers at the end of a Data Flow Task. To use this code create a package with a Data Flow Task and add a Script Component as a source with one output column named NewOutputColumn. Create these integer variables as private variables to the main.cs class: validationBadChars, validationLength, and validationInvalidFormat. Then add this code to the CreateNewOutputRows() method in the main.cs class:

```csharp
C#
    int validationLengthErrors = 0;
    int validationCharErrors = 0;
    int validationFormatErrors = 0;

    //..in the CreateNewOutputRows() Method
    string validationMsg =
    string.Format("Validation Errors:\nBad Chars {0}\nInvalid Length " +
            "{1}\nInvalid Format {2}",
            validationCharErrors, validationLengthErrors,
            validationFormatErrors);
    this.Log(validationMsg, 0, new byte[0]);

    //This is how to add rows to the outputrows Output0Buffer collection.
    Output0Buffer.AddRow();
    Output0Buffer.AddNewOutputColumn = 1;

VB
    Dim validationLengthErrors As Integer = 0
    Dim validationCharErrors As Integer = 0
    Dim validationFormatErrors As Integer = 0

    '..in the CreateNewOutputRows() Method
    Dim validationMsg As String
    validationMsg = String.Format("Validation Errors:" + _
```

```
                    vbCrLf + "Bad Chars {0}" + _
                    vbCrLf + "Invalid Length {1}" + _
                    vbCrLf + "Invalid Format {2}", _
                    validationCharErrors, validationLengthErrors, _
                    validationFormatErrors)
        Dim myByteArray(0) As Byte
        Me.Log(validationMsg, 0, myByteArray)
        Output0Buffer.AddRow()
        Output0Buffer.AddNewOutputColumn = 1
```

For this sample to produce a log entry, remember you will have to set up a logging provider using menu option SSIS ⇨ Logging. Make sure you specifically select the Data Flow Task in which the Script Component is hosted within SSIS and the logging events specifically for the Script Component. Running the package will produce logging similar to this:

```
User:ScriptComponentLogEntry,MYPC,MYPC\ADMIN,"CSharp Basic Logging Script
Component" (1),{00000001-0000-0000-0000-000000000000},{3651D743-D7F6-43F8-
8DE2-F7B40423CC28},4/27/2008 10:38:56 PM,4/27/2008 10:38:56 PM,0,0x,
Validation Errors:
Bad Chars 0
Invalid Length  0
Invalid Format 0
OnPipelinePostPrimeOutput, MYPC,MYPC\ADMIN,Data Flow Task,{D2118DFD-DAEE-470B-
9AC3-9B01DFAA993E},{3651D743-D7F6-43F8-8DE2-F7B40423CC28},4/27/2008 10:38:55
PM,4/27/2008 10:38:55 PM,0,0x,A component has returned from its PrimeOutput
call. : 1 : CSharp Basic Logging Script Component
```

Example: Data Validation

The Script Component takes a little longer runway to get up to speed on how to use it and to get a handle on how it is different from the Script Task. Now it's time to take a look at a more comprehensive example and get the bigger picture of how this component can be used in your everyday package development.

A typical use of the Script Component is to validate data within a Data Flow. In this example, the data is contact information from a custom application that did not validate data entry, so assume the data quality is poor. However, the destination database has a strict set of requirements for the data. Your task is to validate the contact data from the Flat File Source and separate valid from invalid records into two streams: the good stream and the error stream. The good records can continue to another Data Flow; the questionable records will be sent to an error table for manual cleansing.

Create the contacts table with the following script:

```
CREATE TABLE [dbo].[Contacts](
    [ContactID] [int] IDENTITY(1,1) NOT NULL,
    [FirstName] [varchar](50) NOT NULL,
    [LastName] [varchar](50) NOT NULL,
    [City] [varchar](25) NOT NULL,
    [State] [varchar](15) NOT NULL,
    [Zip] [char](11) NULL
) ON [PRIMARY]
```

The error queue table is virtually identical except that here there are no strict requirements and we've added a column to capture the rejection reason. All data fields are nullable and set to the maximum known size:

```
CREATE TABLE dbo.ContactsErrorQueue
(
  ContactErrorID int NOT NULL IDENTITY (1, 1),
  FirstName varchar(50) NULL,
  LastName varchar(50) NULL,
  City varchar(50) NULL,
  State varchar(50) NULL,
  Zip varchar(50) NULL,
  RejectReason varchar(50) NULL
)  ON [PRIMARY]
```

Finally, the incoming data format is fixed-width and is defined as follows:

Field	Starting Position	New Field Name
First Name	1	FirstName
Last Name	11	LastName
City	26	City
State	44	State
Zip	52	Zip

The data file provided as a test sample looks like this:

```
Jason     Gerard      Jacksonville    FL        32276-1911
Joseph    McClung     JACKSONVILLE    FLORIDA   322763939
Andrei    Ranga       Jax             fl        32276
Chad      Crisostomo  Orlando         FL        32746
Andrew    Ranger      Jax             fl
```

Create a sample of this data file or download a copy from www.wrox.com. Create a new package and add a Data Flow Task. Click on the Data Flow design surface and add a Connection Manager to the Connection Managers tab. Name the Connection Manager "Contacts Mainframe Extract," browse to the data file, and set the file format to Ragged Right. Flat files with spaces at the end of the specifications are typically difficult to process in some ETL platforms. The Ragged Right option in SSIS provides a way to handle these easily without having to run the file through a Script Task to put a character into a consistent spot, or having the origination system reformat their extract files. Use the Columns tab to visually define the columns. Flip to the Advanced tab to define each of the column names, types, and widths to match the copy book data definition and the new database field name. (You may need to delete an unused column if this is added by the designer.) The designer at this point looks like Figure 9-23.

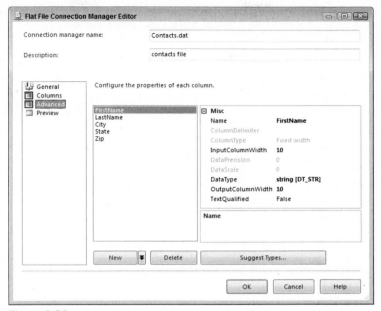

Figure 9-23

This data is all string-based, so we are hiding a complexity here. Typically, there is some data that you may want to define with strong types. Make the decision about whether you want to do that here in the Connection Manager, or later using a derived column depending upon how confident you are in the source of the data. If the Data Source is completely unreliable, import data using Unicode strings and use your Data Flow Tasks to validate the data. Then move good data into a strong data type using the Derived Column Transform.

On the Data Flow surface, drag a Flat File Source to the Data Flow editor pane. Edit the Flat File Source and set the Connection Manager to the Contract Mainframe Extract Connection Manager. This sets up the origination of the data to stream into the Data Flow Task. Check the box labeled "Retain null values from the source as null values in the Data Flow." This new feature allows the consistent testing of null values later. This hiding of null values was one of the problems with earlier versions of SSIS. Now, add a Script Component to the Data Flow. When you drop the Script Component, you will be prompted to pick the type of component to create. Select Transformation and click OK. Connect the output of the Flat File Source to the Script Component to pipe the data into this component where we can program some validation on the data.

Open up the Script Component and set the ScriptLanguage to the language of your choice. On the Input Columns tab, you will notice that Input Name is a drop-down with the name Input 0. It is possible to have more than one source pointed to this Script Component. If you had this situation, this drop-down would allow you to individually configure the inputs and select the columns from each input. For this example, select all the input columns. Set the Usage Type for the State and Zip columns to ReadWrite. The reason will be clear later.

Select the Inputs and Outputs tab to see the collection of inputs and outputs and the input columns defined previously. Here you can create additional input and output buffers and columns within each. Expand all the nodes and add these two output columns:

Column Name	Type	Size
Good Flag	DT_BOOL	N/A
RejectReason	DT_STR	50

You'll use the flag to separate the data from the data stream. The reject reason will be useful to the person who'll have to perform any manual work on the data later. The designer with all nodes expanded should look like Figure 9-24.

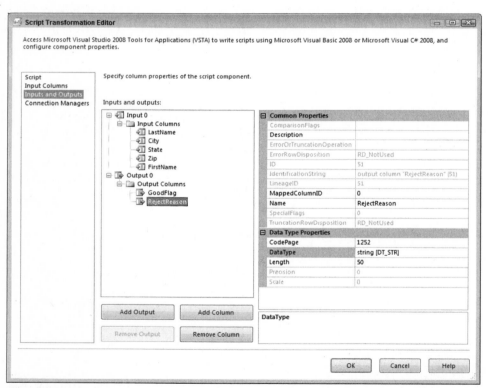

Figure 9-24

Back on the Script tab, click the Edit Script button to enter the VSTA scripting IDE. In the main class, the rules for validation need to be programmatically applied to each data row. In the Input0_ ProcessInputRow method that was co-generated by SSIS using the Script Component designer, add the rules for data validation, which are:

❏   All fields are required except for the zip code.

❏   The zip code must be in the format #####-#### or ##### and a numeric digit from 0 through 9. If the zip code is valid for the first five characters, but the whole string is not, strip the trailing records and use the first five.

❏   The state must be two uppercase characters.

Here's the overall plan: The contents of the file will be sent into the Script Component. This is where programmatic control will be applied to each row processed. The incoming row has three data fields that need to be validated to determine that all necessary data is present. The State and Zip columns need to be validated additionally by rule and even to be cleaned up if possible. The need to fix the data in the stream is why the Zip and State column usage types had to be set to ReadWrite in the designer earlier.

To aid in accomplishing these rules, the data will be validated using regular expressions. Regular expressions are a powerful utility that should be in every developer's tool belt. They allow you to perform powerful string matching and replacement routines. You can find an excellent tutorial on regular expressions at http://www.regular-expressions.info. The regular expressions for matching the data are here:

Regular Expression	Validation Description
^\d{5}([\-]\d{4})?$	Matches a five-digit or nine-digit zip code with dash
\b([A-Z]{2})\b	Ensures that the state is only two capital characters

To use the regular expression library, add the .NET System.Text.RegularExpressions namespace to the top of the main class. For performance reasons, create the instances of the RegEx class to validate the ZipCode and the State in the PreExecute() method of the Script Component. This method and the private instances of the Regex classes should look like this:

```csharp
C#
    private Regex zipRegex;
    private Regex stateRegex;
    public override void PreExecute()
    {
        base.PreExecute();
        zipRegex = new Regex("^\\d{5}([\\-]\\d{4})?$", RegexOptions.None);
        stateRegex = new Regex("\\b([A-Z]{2})\\b", RegexOptions.None);
    }
```

```vbnet
VB
    Private zipRegex As Regex
    Private stateRegex As Regex

    Public Overrides Sub PreExecute()
        MyBase.PreExecute()
        zipRegex = New Regex("^\d{5}([\-]\d{4})?$", RegexOptions.None)
        stateRegex = New Regex("\b([A-Z]{2})\b", RegexOptions.None)
    End Sub
```

To break up the tasks, create two new private functions to validate the ZipCode and State. Using byRef arguments for the reason and the ZipCode enables the data to be cleaned and the encapsulated logic to return both a true/false as well as the reason. The ZipCode validation functions should look like this:

```csharp
C#
private bool ZipIsValid(ref string zip, ref string reason)
    {
        zip = zip.Trim();
        if (zipRegex.IsMatch(zip))
        {
            return true;
        }
        else
        {
            if (zip.Length > 5)
            {
                zip = zip.Substring(0, 5);
                if (zipRegex.IsMatch(zip))
                {
                    return true;
                }
                else
                {
                    reason = "Zip larger than 5 Chars, " +
                                "Retested at 5 Chars and Failed";
                    return false;
                }
            }
            else
            {
                reason = "Zip Failed Initial Format Rule";
                return false;
            }
        }
    }
```

```vbnet
VB
    Private Function ZipIsValid(ByRef zip As String, _
                ByRef reason As String) As Boolean
        zip = zip.Trim()
        If (zipRegex.IsMatch(zip)) Then
            Return True
        Else
            If (zip.Length > 5) Then
                zip = zip.Substring(0, 5)
                If (zipRegex.IsMatch(zip)) Then
                    Return True
                Else
                    reason = "Zip larger than 5 Chars, " + _
                        "Retested at 5 Chars and Failed"
                    Return False
                End If
            Else
```

```
                reason = "Zip Failed Initial Format Rule"
                Return False
            End If
        End If
    End Function
```

The state validation functions look like this:

```
C#
    private bool StateIsValid(ref string state, ref string reason)
    {
        state = state.Trim().ToUpper();
        if (stateRegex.IsMatch(state))
        {
            return true;
        }
        else
        {
            reason = "Failed State Validation";
            return false;
        }
    }
```

```
VB
    Private Function StateIsValid(ByRef state As String, _
    ByRef reason As String) As Boolean
        state = state.Trim().ToUpper()
        If (stateRegex.IsMatch(state)) Then
            Return True
        Else
            reason = "Failed State Validation"
            Return False
        End If
    End Function
```

Now, to put it all together add the driver method `Input0_ProcessInputRow()` that is fired upon each row of the flat file:

```
C#
    public override void Input0_ProcessInputRow(Input0Buffer Row)
    {
        Row.GoodFlag = false;
        string myZip = string.Empty;
        string myState = string.Empty;
        string reason = string.Empty;

        if (!Row.FirstName_IsNull && !Row.LastName_IsNull &&
            !Row.City_IsNull && !Row.State_IsNull && !Row.Zip_IsNull)
        {
            myZip = Row.Zip;
            myState = Row.State;
            if (ZipIsValid(ref myZip, ref reason) &&
                    StateIsValid(ref myState, ref reason))
```

```
            {
                Row.Zip = myZip;
                Row.State = myState;
                Row.GoodFlag = true;
            }
            else
            {
                Row.RejectReason = reason;
            }
        }
        else
        {
            Row.RejectReason = "All Required Fields not completed";
        }
    }
```

```
VB
    Public Overrides Sub Input0_ProcessInputRow(ByVal Row As Input0Buffer)
        Dim myZip As String = String.Empty
        Dim myState As String = String.Empty
        Dim reason As String = String.Empty

        If (Row.FirstName_IsNull = False And _
            Row.LastName_IsNull = False And _
            Row.City_IsNull = False And _
            Row.State_IsNull = False And _
            Row.Zip_IsNull = False) Then
            myZip = Row.Zip
            myState = Row.State
            If (ZipIsValid(myZip, reason) And _
                    StateIsValid(myState, reason)) Then
                Row.Zip = myZip
                Row.State = myState
                Row.GoodFlag = True
            Else
                Row.RejectReason = reason
            End If
        Else
            Row.RejectReason = "All Required Fields not completed"
        End If
    End Sub
```

Notice that all fields are checked for null values using a property on the Row class that is the field name and an additional tag _IsNull. This is a property code generated by SSIS when you set up the input and output columns on the Script Component. Properties like Zip_IsNull explicitly allow the checking of a null value without encountering a Null Exception. This is handy as the property returns true if the particular column is NULL.

Next, if the Zip column is not NULL, its value is matched against the regular expression to see if it's in the correct format. If it is, the value is assigned back to the Zip column as a cleaned data element. If the value of the Zip column doesn't match the regular expression, the script checks to see if it is at least five characters long. If true, then the first five characters are retested for a valid `ZipCode` pattern. Non-matching values result in a GoodFlag in the output columns being set to `False`.

The state is trimmed of any leading or trailing white space, and then converted to uppercase and matched against the regular expression. The expression simply checks to see if it's two uppercase letters between A and Z. If it is, the GoodFlag is set to `True` and the state value is updated; otherwise, the GoodFlag is set to `False`.

To send the data to the appropriate table based on the GoodFlag, you must use the Conditional Split Task. Add this task to the Data Flow designer and connect the output of the Script Component Task to the Conditional Split Transformation. Edit the Conditional Split Transformation, and add an output named `Good` with the condition `GoodFlag == FALSE` and another output named `Bad` with the condition `GoodFlag == TRUE`. This separates the data rows coming out of the Script Component Task into two separate streams. Another way to do this is only define one stream and let the default stream be the other condition, but it seems more explicit to create streams for both conditions. The Conditional Split Transform Editor should look like Figure 9-25.

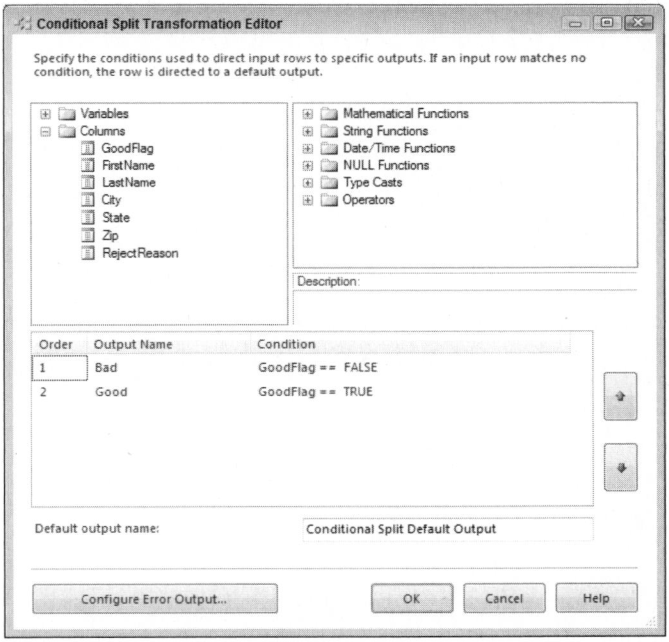

Figure 9-25

Add an OLE Connection Manager that uses the database you created for the Contacts and ContactsErrorQueue tables. Add two SQL Server Destinations to the Data Flow designer. One, named Good Destination, should point to the Contacts table; the other, to the ContactsErrorQueue table. Drag the Good output of the Conditional Split Task to the Good Destination. Set the output stream named

Good to the destination. Then open the Mappings tab in the destination to map the input stream to the columns in the Contacts table. Repeat this for the other Bad output of the Conditional Split Task to the Bad Destination.

Your final Data Flow should look something like Figure 9-26. If you run this package with the Contacts.dat file described at the top of the use-case, three contacts will validate, and two will fail with these rejection reasons:

```
Failed State Validation
Joseph     McClung        JACKSONVILLE      FLORIDA 322763939

Zip Failed Initial Format Rule
Andrew     Ranger         Jax               fl
```

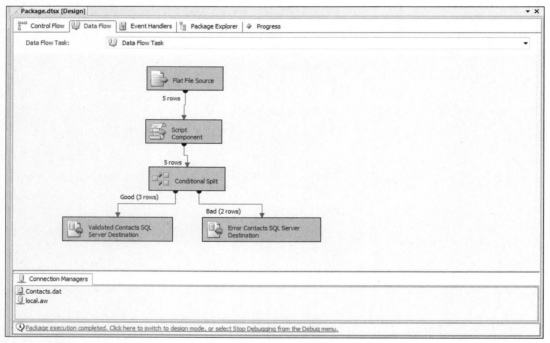

Figure 9-26

At this point, you've gotten a good overview of how scripting works in SSIS and the difference between the Script Task and the Scripting Component, but as with any programming environment, you need to know how to troubleshoot and debug your code to get all of this to work. We'll look at some of the common coding tasks in the next section that you'll need to allow for more advanced SSIS scripting development.

Essential Coding, Debugging, and Troubleshooting Techniques

We have been all over the new VSTA development environment and have introduced you to the addition of C# that moves SSIS development into the managed code arena. Now, we need to circle up and dig into some of the techniques of hardening our code for unexpected issues that occur during runtime and look at some of the techniques of troubleshooting SSIS packages. There are some differences between the Script Task and the Script Component for some of these techniques that we'll highlight here, now that you are familiar with both.

Structured Exception Handling

Structured Exception Handling (SEH) allows you to catch specific errors as they occur and perform any appropriate action needed. In many cases, you just want to log the error and stop execution, but there are some instances where you may want to try a different plan of action, depending on the error.

Here is an example of exception handling in SSIS scripting code in both languages:

```
C#
public void Main()
{
    try
    {
        string fileText = string.Empty;
        fileText = System.IO.File.ReadAllText("c:\\data.csv");
    }
    catch (System.IO.FileNotFoundException ex)
    {
        //Log Error Here
        //MessageBox here for demo purposes only
        System.Windows.Forms.MessageBox.Show(ex.ToString());
        Dts.TaskResult = (int)ScriptResults.Failure;
    }
    Dts.TaskResult = (int)ScriptResults.Success;
}


VB
Public Sub Main()
    Try
        Dim fileText As String
        fileText = FileIO.FileSystem.ReadAllText("C:\data.csv")
    Catch ex As System.IO.FileNotFoundException
        'Log Error Here
        'MessageBox here for demo purposes only
        System.Windows.Forms.MessageBox.Show(ex.ToString())
        Dts.TaskResult = ScriptResults.Failure
        Return
    End Try
    Dts.TaskResult = ScriptResults.Success
End Sub
```

This trivial example attempts to read the contents of the file at C:\data.csv into a string variable. This code makes some assumptions that might not be true. An obvious assumption is that the file exists. That is why this code was placed in a Try block. It is trying to perform an action that has the potential for failure. If the file isn't there, a System.IO.FileNotFoundException is thrown. A Try block marks a section of code that contains function calls with potentially known exceptions. In this case, the FileSystem ReadAllText function has the potential to throw a concrete exception.

The Catch block is the error handler for this specific exception. You would probably want to add some code to log the error inside the Catch block. For now, we've sent the exception to the message box as a string so that it can be viewed. See later in the chapter under each Script object type for the method to perform logging of this type. This code obviously originates from a Scripting Task since it returns a result. The result is set to Failure, and the script is exited with the Return statement if the exception occurs. If the file is found, no exception is thrown, and the next line of code is executed. In this case, it would go to the line that sets the TaskResult to the value of the Success enum, right after the End Try statement.

If an exception is not caught, the exception propagates up the call stack until an appropriate handler is found. If none is found, the exception stops execution. You can have as many Catch blocks associated with a Try block as you wish. When an exception is raised, the Catch blocks are walked from top to bottom until an appropriate one is found that fits the context of the exception. Only the first block that matches will be executed. Execution does not fall through to the next block, so it's important to place the most specific Catch block first and descend to the least specific. A Catch block specified with no filter will catch all exceptions. Typically, the coarsest Catch block is listed last. The previous code was written to anticipate the error of a file not being found, so not only does the developer have an opportunity to add some recovery code, but the framework assumes that you'll handle the details of the error itself. If the same code only contained a generic Catch statement, the error would simply be written to the package output. To see what this looks like replace the Catch statement in the preceding code snippet with these:

```
C#
Catch()

VB
Catch
```

Then the error would simply be written to the package output like this:

```
SSIS package "Package.dtsx" starting.
Error: 0x1 at VB Script Task: System.Reflection.TargetInvocationException,
mscorlib
System.IO.FileNotFoundException, mscorlib

System.Reflection.TargetInvocationException: Exception has been thrown by the
target of an invocation. ---> System.IO.FileNotFoundException: Could not find
file 'C:\data.csv'.
File name: 'C:\data.csv'
    at System.IO.__Error.WinIOError(Int32 errorCode, String maybeFullPath)
    at System.IO.FileStream.Init(String path, FileMode mode, FileAccess access,
Int32 rights, Boolean useRights, FileShare share, Int32 bufferSize,
FileOptions options, SECURITY_ATTRIBUTES secAttrs, String msgPath, Boolean
bFromProxy)
...
Task failed: VB Script Task
SSIS package "Package.dtsx" finished: Success.
```

The full stack is cut off for brevity and to point out that the task status shows that it failed.

Another feature of SEH is the `Finally` block. The `Finally` block exists inside a `Try` block and executes after any code in the `Try` block and any `Catch` blocks that were entered. Code in the `Finally` block is always executed, regardless of what happens in the `Try` block and in any `Catch` blocks. You would put code to dispose of any resources, such as open files or database connections, in the `Finally` block. Following is an example of using the `Finally` block to free up a connection resource:

```csharp
C#
public void OpenConnection(string myConStr)
{
    SqlConnection con = new SqlConnection(myConStr);
    try
    {
        con.Open();
        //do stuff with con
    }
    catch (SqlException ex)
    {
        //log error here
    }
    finally
    {
        if (con != null)
        {
            con.Dispose();
        }
    }
}
```

```vb
VB
Public Sub OpenConnection(myConStr as String)
    Dim con As SqlConnection = New SqlConnection(myConStr)
    Try
        con.Open()
        'do stuff with con
    Catch ex As SqlException
        'Log Error Here
        Dts.TaskResult = Dts.Results.Failure
        Return
    Finally
        If Not con Is Nothing Then con.Dispose()
    End Try
End Sub
```

In this example, the `Finally` block is hit regardless of whether the connection is open or not. A logical `If` statement checks to see if the connection is open and closes it to conserve resources. Typically you want to follow this pattern if you are doing anything resource intensive like using the `System.IO` or `System.Data` assemblies.

For a full explanation of the Try/Catch/Finally structure in Visual Basic.NET, see the language reference in MSDN or Books Online.

Script Debugging and Troubleshooting

Debugging is an important new feature of scripting in SSIS. You can still use the technique of popping up a message box function to see the value of variables, but there are more sophisticated techniques that will help you pinpoint the problem. Using the Visual Studio for Applications environment, you now have the ability to set breakpoints, examine variables, and even evaluate expressions interactively.

Breakpoints

Breakpoints allow you to flag a line of code where execution pauses while debugging. Breakpoints are invaluable in determining what's going on inside your code. They allow you to step into your code and see what happens as it executes. Unfortunately, breakpoints only work inside of Script Tasks.

You can set a breakpoint in several ways. One way is to click in the gray margin at the left of the text editor at the line where you wish to stop execution. Another way is to move the cursor to the line you wish to break on and hit F9. Yet another way is to select Debug ➪ Toggle Breakpoint.

To continue execution from a breakpoint, press F10 to step to the next line or F5 to run all the way through to the next breakpoint.

When you have a breakpoint set on a line, the line gets a red highlight like the one shown in Figure 9-27.

Figure 9-27

When a Script Task has a breakpoint set somewhere in the code, it will have a red dot on it similar to the one in Figure 9-28.

Figure 9-28

Row Count and Data Viewers

Previously, you looked at using the Visual Studio for Applications environment to debug a Script Task using breakpoints and other tools. Unfortunately, you do not have the ability to debug the Script Component using this environment. Any breakpoints that you set will be ignored. Instead, you must resort to inspecting the data stream using the Row Count Component or a Data Viewer.

The Row Count Component is very straightforward; it simply states how many rows passed through it. The Data Viewer is a much better way to debug your component, however. To add a Data Viewer, select the connector arrow, leaving the component that you want to see data for. In the previous example, this would be the connector from the Script Component to the Conditional Split Task. Right-click this connection and select Data Viewers. The Data Flow Path Editor will pop up. Click Add to add the Data Viewer. On the Configure Data Viewer screen, select Grid as the type. Click the Grid tab and make sure all the columns you wish to see are in the Displayed Columns list. Close out this window and the Data Path Flow Editor window by clicking OK. Figure 9-29 shows the Data Path Flow Editor with a Data Viewer configured on Output 0.

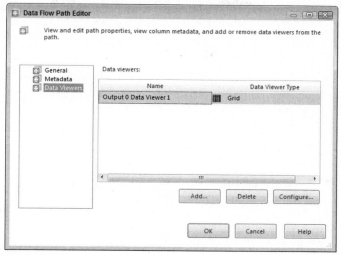

Figure 9-29

Now when you run this package again, you will get a Data Viewer window after the Script Component has executed. This view will show the data output by the Script Component. Figure 9-30 shows an example. Click the Play button to continue package execution, or simply close the window.

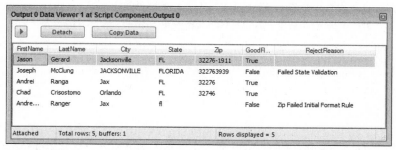

Figure 9-30

While using the Data Viewer certainly helps with debugging, it is no replacement for being able to step into the code. An alternative is to use the `FireInformation` event on the `ComponentMetaData` class in the Script Component. It is like the message box, but without the modal effect.

Autos, Locals, and Watches

The Visual Studio environment provides you with some powerful views into what is happening with the execution of your code. These views consist of three windows known as the Autos window, Locals window, and Watch window. These windows share a similar layout and display the value of expressions and variables, though each has a distinct method determining what data to display.

The Locals window displays variables that are local to the current statement, as well as three statements behind and in front of the current statement. For a running example, the Locals window would appear, as in Figure 9-31.

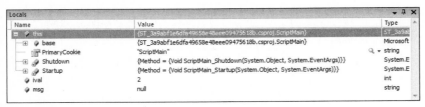

Figure 9-31

Watches are another very important feature of debugging. Watches allow you to specify a variable to watch. You can set up a watch to break execution when a variable's value changes or some other condition is met. This will allow you to see exactly when something is happening, such as a variable that has an unexpected value.

To add a watch, select the variable you want to watch inside the script, right-click it, and select Add Watch. This will add an entry to the Watch window.

You can also use the Quick Watch window, accessible from the Debug menu, or through the Ctrl+Alt+Q key combination. The Quick Watch window is shown in Figure 9-32 in the middle of a breakpoint, and you can see the value of `ival` as it is being assigned the variable value of 2.

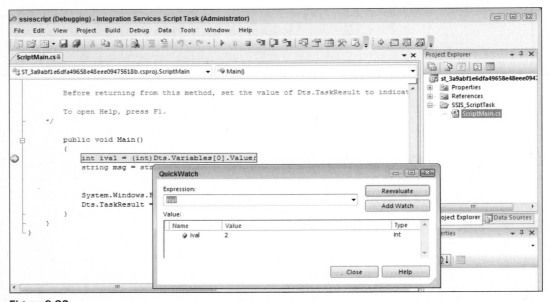

Figure 9-32

This window allows you to evaluate an expression at runtime and see the result in the window. You can then click the Add Watch button to move it to the Watch window.

The Immediate Window

The Immediate window allows you to evaluate expressions, execute procedures, and print out variable values. It is really a mode of the Command window, which allows you to issue commands to the IDE. Unfortunately, this too is only useful when you are within a breakpoint and this can only be done within a Script Task.

If you can't find the Immediate window, but see the Command window, just type the command immed *and press Enter.*

The Immediate window is very useful while testing. You can see the outcome of several different scenarios. Suppose you have an object obj of type MyType. MyType declares a method called DoMyStuff() that takes a single integer as an argument. Using the Immediate window, you could pass different values into the DoMyStuff() method and see the results. To evaluate an expression in the Immediate window and see its results, you must start the command with a question mark (?):

```
?obj.DoMyStuff(2)
"Hello"
```

Commands are terminated by pressing the Enter key. The results of the execution are printed on the next line. In this case, calling DoMyStuff() with a value of 2 returns the string "Hello."

You can also use the Immediate window to change the value of variables. If you have a variable defined in your script and you want to change its value, perhaps for negative error testing, you can use this window, as shown in Figure 9-33.

```
Immediate Window
?greeting
"Hello, World!"

greeting = "Goodbye, Cruel World!"
"Goodbye, Cruel World!"
```

Figure 9-33

In this case, the value of the variable greeting is printed out on the line directly below the expression. After the value is printed, it is changed to "Goodbye Cruel World." The value is then queried again, and the new value is printed. If you are in a Script Task and need to get additional information, this is a useful way to do it.

Summary

In this chapter, you learned about the available scripting options in SSIS from the beginning with DTS and the use of ActiveX scripts to the new versions of SSIS that support managed code development and a robust IDE development environment. You used the new Visual Studio Tools for Applications IDE to develop some basic Script Tasks. Then, to see how all this fits together in SSIS, we dove right in to using the Script Tasks to retrieve data into variables, save data into external XML files, and used some .NET serialization techniques that can allow custom serialization into MSMQ queues or Web services. To understand how to leverage existing code libraries, you even created a utility class, registered it into the GAC, and accessed it in an SSIS script to validate data.

SSIS scripting is powerful, but it has been difficult for some to differentiate between when to use a Script Task and when a Script Component is appropriate. You have been all over both of these in detail in this chapter and can now use these with confidence in your daily development.

Experiment with the scripting features of SSIS using the examples in this chapter, and you will find all kinds of uses for them. Don't forget to review the chapter on expressions to learn about the capabilities of controlling properties within the SSIS model at runtime. Now we are going to take what we've learned so far about the SSIS toolset capability from Control Flow and Data Flow Tasks, to Expressions and Scripting Tasks and Components and put them to work. Read on to the next chapter for a breakdown on the techniques you need to do a typical job of loading a data warehouse using SSIS services.

Loading a Data Warehouse

10

Among the various applications of SQL Server Integration Services (SSIS), the most common is loading a data warehouse. SSIS provides the ETL features and functionality to efficiently handle many of the tasks required when dealing with transactional source data that will be extracted and loaded into a data mart, data warehouse, or even an operational data store (ODS), including the capabilities to then process data from the relational data warehouse into the SQL Server Analysis Services (SSAS) cubes.

Soup to nuts, SSIS provides the core foundation of data processing from your source, to staging, to your data mart, and onto your cubes (and beyond!). Figure 10-1 highlights a common architecture of a business intelligence (BI) solution.

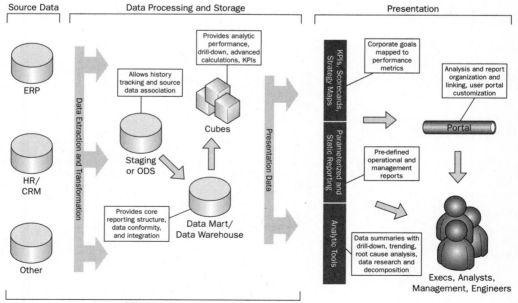

Figure 10-1

The presentation layer on the right side of Figure 10-1 shows the main purpose of the BI solution, which is to provide business users (from the top to the bottom of an organization) meaningful data that they can take actionable steps from. Underlying the presentation data are the back-end structures and processes that make it possible for data to become meaningful and visible to the right people.

ETL is a large part of this back-end process because its responsibility is to move and restructure the data between the data tiers of the BI architecture. This involves many steps, as you will see, from data profiling, to data extraction, dimension table loading, fact table processing, and SSAS processing. This chapter will set you on course to architecting and designing an ETL process for data warehouse and business intelligence ETL.

In fact, SSIS contains several tasks and transformations out-of-the-box to get you well on your way to a stable and straightforward ETL process. Some of these components include the Data Profiling Task, the Slowly Changing Dimension Transformation, and the Analysis Services Execute DDL Task. The tutorials in this chapter all coordinate together to demonstrate the processing required for the Sales Quota Fact table and SSAS measure group, which includes the ETL required for the Employee dimension.

Data Profiling

In the end, data warehousing and BI is about reporting and analytics, and the first key to reaching that objective is understanding the source data, because that has immeasurable impact on how you design the structures and build the ETL.

Data profiling is the process of analyzing the source data to better understand what condition the data is in, in terms of cleanliness, patterns, number of nulls, and so on. In fact, you probably have done data profiling before with scripts and spreadsheets, but perhaps you didn't realize that it was called data profiling.

SSIS 2008 includes a new Control Flow Task called the Data Profiling Task. This task is reviewed in Chapter 3 but let's drill into some more details on how to leverage it for data warehouse ETL.

Initial Execution of the Data Profiling Task

It is important to know that the Data Profiling Task is not like the other tasks in SSIS because it is not intended to be run over and over again through a scheduled operation. Think about SSIS being the wrapper for this tool. You use the SSIS framework to configure and run the Data Profiling Task, and then you observe the results through the separate data profile viewer. The output of the Data Profiling Task will be used to help you in your development and design of the ETL and dimensional structures in your solution. Periodically, you may want to re-run the Data Profile Task to see how the data has changed, but the package you develop will not include the task in the overall recurring ETL process.

Let's begin!

1. Start out by opening BIDS and creating a new SSIS project called Data Warehouse ETL. You will use this project throughout this chapter.

2. In the Solution Explorer, Rename `package.dtsx` as `Profile_Employee_Data.dtsx`.

3. The Data Profiling Task requires an ADO.NET connection to the source database (as opposed to an OLE DB connection). Therefore, create a new ADO.NET connection in the Connection Managers window by right-clicking and choosing New ADO.NET Connection, and then click the New button on the ADO.NET Connection Managers' window.

4. Create a connection to your local machine or where the AdventureWorks2008 sample database is installed, as shown in Figure 10-2.

Figure 10-2

5. Save the connection information and return to the SSIS package designer.

6. Drag a Data Profiling Task from the Toolbox onto the Control Flow and double-click the new task to open up the Data Profiling Task Editor.

7. The Data Profiling Task includes a wizard that will create your profiling scenario quickly, therefore click the Quick Profile Button on the General tab.

8. In the Single Table Quick Table Form, choose the AdventureWorks2008 connection, and in the Table Or View drop-down, select the [Sales].[vSalesPerson] view from the list. Enable all the checkboxes in the Compute list and change the Functional Dependency Profile to use 2 columns as determinant columns as shown in Figure 10-3.

Figure 10-3

9. Select OK to save the changes, which will populate the Requests list in the Data Profiling Task Editor as shown in Figure 10-4. Chapter 3 describes each of these different request types, and you will see the purpose and output of a few of these when we run the viewer.

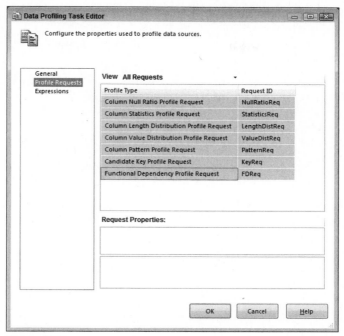

Figure 10-4

10. Return to the General tab of the editor and in the Destination property box, choose New File Connection. This is where you will define the XML file where the profile output is stored (the results of the Data Profiling Task when it is run).

11. In the File Connection Manager Editor, change the Usage type drop-down to "Create file" and enter **C:\Employee_Profile.xml** in the File text box. Select OK to save your changes to the connection and OK to save your changes in the Data Profiling Task Editor.

12. Now, it is time to execute this simple package. Run the package in BIDS, which will initiate several queries against the source table or view (in this case, a view). Since this view only returns a few rows, the Data Profiling Task will execute rather quickly, but with large tables, this may take several minutes (or longer if your table has millions of rows and you are performing several profiling tests at once).

The results of the profile are stored in the `Employee_Profile.xml` file, which we will now review with the Data Profile Viewer tool.

Reviewing the Results of the Data Profiling Task

Despite what some business users expect, data cannot be magically generated, no matter how creative you are with data cleansing. For example, if you are requested to build a Sales target analysis that uses employee data, and are asked to build into the analysis a Sales Territory Group, but the source column only has 50% of the data even populated for this, the business user needs to rethink the value of the data or fix the source. This is a simple example for the purpose of the tutorials in this chapter, but consider a more complicated example or a larger table.

The point is that data comes in all different qualities. Some data is simply missing, other data has typos, sometimes a column has so many different discrete values that it is hard to analyze, and so on. The purpose of doing data profiling is to understand the source for two reasons. First, it allows you to review the data with the business user, which can affect change, and second, it provides you the insight you need when developing your ETL operations.

Now that you have run the Data Profiling Task, your next objective is to evaluate the results.

1. Observing the output requires using the Data Profile Viewer. This utility is found in the Integration Services sub-directory for Microsoft SQL Server 2008 (Start Button ⇨ All Programs).

2. Open the `Employee_Profile.xml` file created earlier by clicking the Open button and navigating to the C:\ drive (or the location where the file was saved), highlighting the file, and clicking Open again.

3. In the Profiles navigation tree drill, first click on the table icon on the top left to put the tree viewer into "Column View." Second, drill down into the details by expanding the Data Sources, server (local), Databases, AdventureWorks2008, Tables, [Sales].[vSalesPerson], and Columns objects as shown in Figure 10-5.

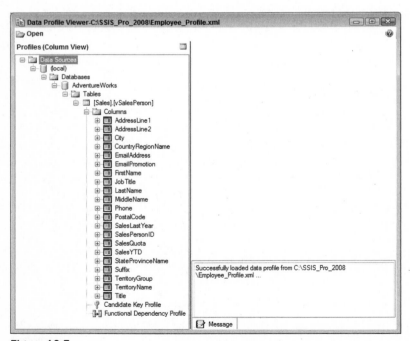

Figure 10-5

4. The first profiling output to observe is the Candidate Key Profile, so click this item under the Columns list, which will open the results in the viewer on the right. You will see that the Data Profiling Task has identified seven columns that are unique across the entire table (with 100% uniqueness) as shown in Figure 10-6.

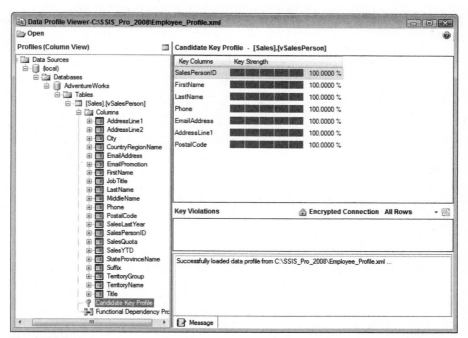

Figure 10-6

Given the small size of this table, all of these columns are unique, but with larger tables, you will see fewer columns and less than 100% uniqueness, with the ability to see the exceptions or Key Violations. What column looks to be the right candidate key for this table? Wait until the next section and you will see how these results affect your ETL.

5. Next, click the Functional Dependency Profile object on the left and observe the results. This shows the relationship between values in multiple columns. There are two columns shown, a Determinant Column(s) and Dependant Column. The question is, for every unique value (or combination) in the Determinant Column, is there only one unique value in the Dependant Column. Observe the output. What is the relationship between these combinations of columns: TerritoryGroup and TerritoryName, StateProvinceName and CountryRegionName. Wait until the next section and you will see how these results affect your ETL.

6. Next, in the profile tree, expand the TerritoryName column and highlight the Column Length Distribution, and then in the distribution profile on the right, double-click the length distribution of 6, as shown in Figure 10-7.

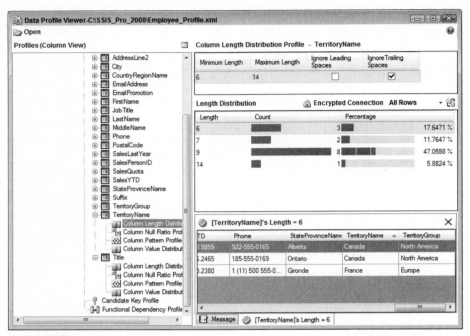

Figure 10-7

The column length distribution shows the number of rows by length, with the data browser on the bottom right of Figure 10-7 showing the actual. What are the maximum and minimum lengths of values for the column?

7. Under TerritoryName in the profile browser, select the Column Null Ratio Profile and then double-click the row in the profile viewer on the right to view the detail rows, as shown in Figure 10-8.

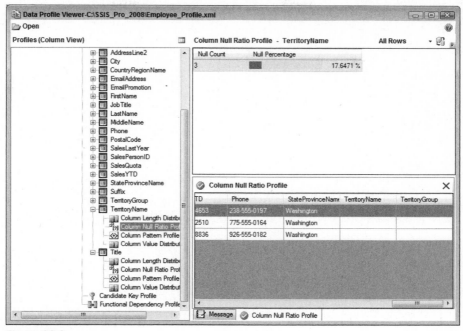

Figure 10-8

The Column Null Ratio shows what percentage of rows in the entire table have NULL values. This is valuable for ETL considerations because it spells out when NULL handling is required for the ETL process, which is one of the most common transformation processes.

8. Next, select the Column Value Distribution Profile on the left under the Territory Name and observe the output in the results viewer. How many unique values are there in the entire table? How many values are only used one time in the table?

9. In the left navigation pane, expand the Phone column and then click the Column Pattern Profile. Double-click the first pattern number 1 in the list on the right as shown in Figure 10-9.

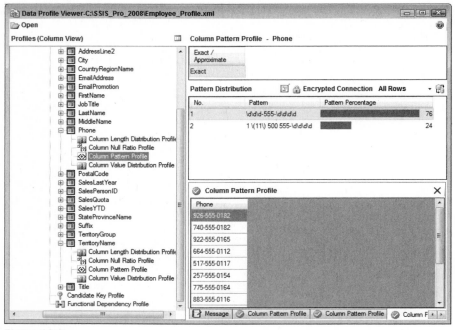

Figure 10-9

The Column Pattern Profile uses the regular expression syntax to display what pattern or range of patterns that the data in the column contain. Notice that for the Phone Number column, two patterns emerge. The first is for phone numbers that are in the syntax ###-555-####, which is translated to \d\d\d-555-\d\d\d\d in regular expression syntax. The other pattern begins with 1 \(11\) 500 555- and ends with four variable numbers.

10. The final data profiling type to review is the Column Statistics Profile. This is only applicable to data types related to numbers (integer, float, decimal, numeric) and dates (dates only allow minimum and maximum calculations). In the Profiles tree view on the left of the Data Profile Viewer, expand the SalesYTD column and then click the Column Statistics Profile. Four results are calculated across the spread of values in the numeric column:

a. **Minimum:** The lowest number value in the set of column values

b. **Maximum:** The highest number value in the set of column values

c. **Mean:** The average of values value in the set of column values

d. **Standard Deviation:** The average variance between the values and the mean

The Column Statistics Profile is very valuable for fact table source evaluation, since the measures in a fact table are almost always numeric based, with a few exceptions.

Overall, the output of the Data Profiling Task has helped to identify the quality and range of values in the source. This naturally leads into using the output results to formulate the ETL design.

Turning Data Profile Results into Actionable ETL Steps

The typical first step in evaluating source data is to check the existence of source key columns and referential completeness between source tables or files. Two of the data profiling outputs can help in this effort:

❑ The Candidate Key Profile will provide the columns (or combination of columns) with the highest uniqueness. It is crucial to identify a candidate key (or composite key) that is 100% unique, because when you load your dimension and fact tables, you need to know how to identify a new or existing source record. In the preceding example, shown in Figure 10-6, several columns meet the criteria. The natural selection from this list is the SalesPersonID column.

❑ The Column NULL Ratio is another important output of the Data Profiling Task. This can be used to verify that foreign keys in the source table have completeness, especially if the primary key to foreign key relationships will be used to relate a dimension table to a fact or a dimension table and another dimension table. Of course this isn't verifying that the primary to foreign key values line up, but this will give you an initial understanding of referential data completeness.

As just mentioned, the Column NULL Ratio can be used for an initial review of foreign keys in source tables or files. The Column NULL Ratio is an excellent output, because it can be used for almost every destination column type, such as dimension attributes, keys, and measures. Any time you have a column that has NULLs, you will most likely have to deal with the NULLs and replace them with unknowns or perform some data cleansing to handle them.

In the example shown in Figure 10-8, the Territory Name has approximately a 17% NULL ratio. In your dimension model destination, this is a problem, because the Employee dimension has a foreign surrogate key to the Sales Territory dimension. Since there isn't completeness in the Sales Territory, you don't have a reference to the dimension. This is an actionable item that you will need to address in the dimension ETL section later.

Another useful output of the Data Profiling Task is the column length and statistics presented. Data type optimization is important to define; when you have a large inefficient source column where most of the space is not used [such as a char(1000)] you will want to scale back the data type to a reasonable length. Use the Column Length Distribution as shown in Figure 10-7.

The Column Statistics can be helpful in defining the data type of your measures. Optimization of data types in fact tables is more important than dimensions, so consider the source column's max and min to determine what data type to use for your measure. The wider a fact table is, the slower it will perform because fewer rows will fit in the server's memory for query execution, and the more disk space it will take up on the server.

Once you have evaluated your source data, the next step is to develop your data extraction, the E of ETL.

Data Extraction

Data extraction applies to many types of ETL, beyond just data warehouse and BI data processing. In fact, several chapters in this book deal with data extraction for various needs, such as incremental extraction, change data capture, and dealing with various sources. Refer to the following chapters to plan out your SSIS data extraction:

❑   Chapter 5 takes an initial look at the Source adapters in the Data Flow that will be used for your extraction.

❑   Chapter 11 deals with using the SQL Server relational engine for performing change data capture.

❑   Chapter 12 is a look at heterogeneous, or non-SQL Server sources for data extraction.

The balance of this chapter deals with the core of data warehouse ETL, which is dimension and fact table loading, SSAS object processing, and ETL coordination.

Dimension Table Loading

Dimension transformation and loading is about tracking the current and sometime history of associated attributes in a dimension table. Figure 10-10 shows the dimensions related to the Sales Quota Fact table in the AdventureWorksDW2008 database. The objective of this section is to process data from the source tables into the dimension tables.

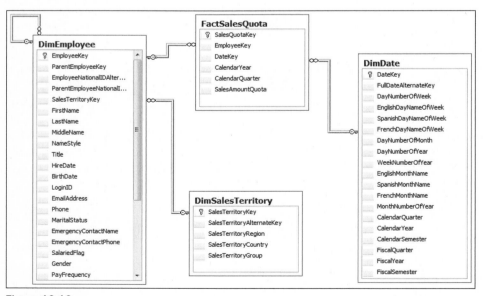

Figure 10-10

In this example, you will notice that each dimension (DimEmployee, DimSalesTerritory, and DimTime) has a surrogate key named *Dimension*Key, as well as a candidate key named *Dimension*AlternateKey. The surrogate key is the most important concept in data warehousing because it allows the tracking of change history and optimizes the structures for performance. See *The Data Warehouse Toolkit*, by Ralph Kimball and Margy Ross (Wiley, 2002) for a detailed review of the use and purpose of surrogate keys. Surrogate keys are often auto-incrementing identity columns that are contained in the source table.

Dimension ETL has several objectives, each of which are reviewed in the tutorial steps to load the DimSalesTerritory and DimEmployee tables, including:

❑ Identifying the source keys that uniquely identify a source record and that will map to the alternate key

❑ Performing any Data Transformations to align the source data to the dimension structures

❑ Handling the different change types for each source column and adding or updating dimension records

SSIS includes a built-in transformation called the Slowly Changing Dimension (SCD) Transformation to assist in the process. This is not the only transformation that you can use to load a dimension table, but you will use it in these tutorial steps to accomplish dimension loading. The SCD also has some drawbacks, which are reviewed at the end of this section.

Loading a Simple Dimension Table

Many dimension tables are like the Sales Territory dimension in that they only contain a few columns, and history tracking is not required for any of the attributes. In this example, the DimSalesTerritory is sourced from the [Sales].[SalesTerritory] table, and any source changes to any of the three columns will be updated in the dimension table. These columns are referred to as changing dimension attributes, because the values can change.

1. To begin creating the ETL for the DimSalesTerritory table, return to your SSIS project created in the first tutorial and create a new package named ETL_DimSalesTerritory.dtsx.

2. Since you will be extracting data from the AdventureWorks2008 database and loading data into the AdventureWorksDW2008 databases, create two OLE DB connections in your package to these databases named AdventureWorks2008 and AdventureWorksDW2008, respectively. Refer to Chapter 2 for help on defining the connections.

3. Drag a new Data Flow Task from the Toolbox onto the Control Flow and navigate to the Data Flow designer.

4. Drag an OLE DB Source adapter into the Data Flow and double-click the new source to open the editor. Configure the OLE DB Connection Manager drop-down to use the AdventureWorks2008 database and leave the data access mode selection as "Table or view." In the "Name of the table or the view" drop-down, choose the [Sales].[SalesTerritory] as shown in Figure 10-11.

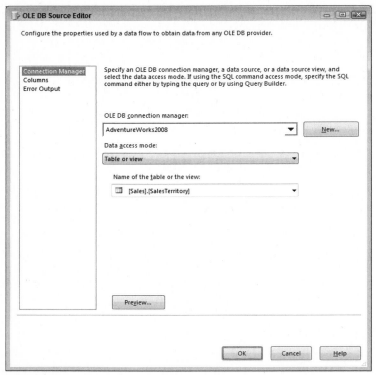

Figure 10-11

5. On the Columns property page, change the Output Column value for the TerritoryID column to SalesTerritoryAlternateKey, change the Name column to SalesTerritoryRegion, and change the Output Column for the Group column to SalesTerritoryGroup. Also, uncheck all the columns under SalesTerritoryGroup because they are not needed for the DimSalesTerritory table, as shown in Figure 10-12.

Figure 10-12

6. Select OK to save your changes and then drag a Lookup Transformation onto the Data Flow and connect the green data path from the OLE DB Source onto the Lookup.

7. Edit the Lookup Transformation and on the General property page, leave the Cache mode set at Full cache, and leave the Connection type as "OLE DB Connection Manager" as shown in Figure 10-13.

Figure 10-13

8. On the Connection property page, set the OLE DB Connection Manager drop-down to the AdventureWorks2008 connection. Change the "Use a table or a view" drop-down to [Person].[CountryRegion].

9. On the Columns property page, drag the CountryRegionCode from the available Input Columns list to the matching column in the Available Lookup Columns list, then select the checkbox next to the Name column in the same column list. Rename the Output Alias of the Name column to SalesTerritoryCountry as shown in Figure 10-14.

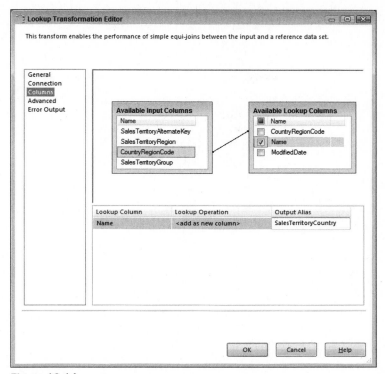

Figure 10-14

10. Select OK in the Lookup Transformation Editor to save your changes.

At this point in the process, you have performed some simple initial steps to align the source data up with the destination dimension table. The next steps are the core of the dimension processing and use the SCD Transformation.

11. Next, drag a Slowly Changing Dimension Transformation from the Toolbox onto the Data Flow and connect the green data path output from the Lookup onto the Slowly Changing Dimension Component. When you drop the path onto the SCD, you will be prompted to select the output of the Lookup. Choose the Lookup Match Output from the drop-down and then click OK.

12. To invoke the SCD wizard, double-click the transformation, which will open up a splash screen for the wizard. Proceed to the second screen by clicking Next.

13. The first input of the wizard is to identify the dimension table that the source data relates to. Therefore choose the AdventureWorksDW2008 as the Connection Manager and then choose [dbo].[DimSalesTerritory] as the table or view, which will automatically display the dimension table's columns in the list as shown in Figure 10-15. For the SalesTerritoryAlternateKey, change the Key Type to Business key.

Figure 10-15

a. The first purpose of the screen in Figure 10-15 is to identify the candidate key (or business key) from the dimension table and what it matches with from the input. This will be used to identify row matches between the source and destination.

b. The second purpose is to match columns from the source to attributes in the dimension table, which will be used on the next screen of the wizard to identify the change tracking type. Notice that the columns are automatically matched between the source input and the destination dimension because they have the same name and data type. On other scenarios, you may have to manually perform the match.

14. On the next screen of the SCD wizard, you will need to identify what type of change each matching column is identified as. It has already been mentioned that all the columns are changing attributes for the DimSalesTerritory dimension; therefore, select all the columns and choose the "Changing attribute" Change Type from the drop-down lists, as shown in Figure 10-16.

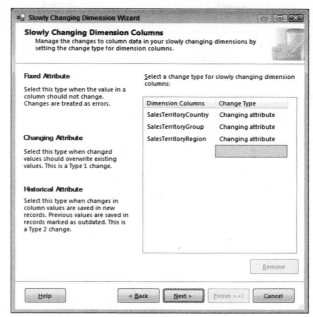

Figure 10-16

Three options exist for the Change Types: Changing attribute, Historical attribute, and Fixed attribute. As has already been mentioned, a Changing attribute is updated if the source value changes. For the Historical attribute, when a change happens, a new record is generated and the old record preserves the history of the change. More on this will be reviewed when we walk through the DimEmployee dimension ETL. Finally, a Fixed attribute is when no changes should happen, and the ETL should either ignore the change or break.

15. The next screen titled Fixed and Changing Attribute Options prompts you to choose which records you want to update when a source value changes. The "Fixed attributes" option is grayed out because no Fixed attributes were selected on the prior screen. Under the "Changing attributes" option, you can choose to update the changing attribute column for all the records that match the same candidate key, or you can choose to just update the most recent one. It doesn't matter in this case, because there will only be one record per candidate key value, because there are no historical attributes that would cause a new record. Leave this box unchecked and proceed to the next screen.

16. The Inferred Dimension Members screen is about handling placeholder records that were added during the fact table load, because a dimension member didn't exist when the fact load was run. Inferred members will be reviewed in the DimEmployee dimension ETL, but the screen is shown in Figure 10-17.

Figure 10-17

17. Given the simplicity of the Sales Territory dimension, this concludes the wizard, and on the last screen you merely confirm the settings that you had configured. Select Finish to complete the wizard.

The net result of the SCD wizard is that it will automatically generate for you several downstream transformations, pre-configured to handle the change types based on the candidate keys you selected. Figure 10-18 shows the completed Data Flow with the SCD Transformation.

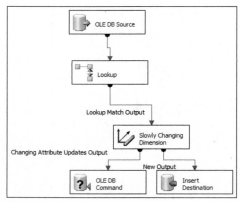

Figure 10-18

Since this dimension is simple, there are only two outputs. One output is called New Output, which will insert new dimension records if the candidate key identified from the source does not have a match in the dimension. The second output, called Changing Attribute Updates Output, is for when you have a match across the candidate keys and one of the changing attributes does not match between the source input and the dimension table. This OLE DB command uses an UPDATE statement to perform the operation.

Loading a Complex Dimension Table

Dimension ETL often requires complicated logic that makes the dimension project tasks take the longest for design, development, and testing. This is due to change requirements for various attributes within a dimension such as tracking history, updating inferred member records, and so on. Furthermore, with larger or more complicated dimensions, the data preparation tasks often require more logic and transformations before the history is even handled in the dimension table itself.

Preparing the Data

To exemplify a more complicated dimension ETL process, you will now create a package for the DimEmployee table. This package will deal with some missing data as already identified in your data profiling research earlier.

1. In the SSIS project, create a new package called ETL_DimEmployee.dtsx and add two OLE DB Connection Managers for AdventureWorks2008 and AdventureWorksDW2008, as you did in the DimSalesTerritory package.

2. Create a Data Flow Task and add an OLE DB Source adapter to the Data Flow.

3. Configure the OLE DB Source adapter to connect to the AdventureWorks2008 connection and change the data access mode to SQL command. Finally enter the following SQL code in the SQL command text window. These changes are shown in Figure 10-19.

```sql
SELECT
    e.NationalIDNumber as EmployeeNationalIDAlternateKey
, manager.NationalIDNumber as ParentEmployeeNationalIDAlternateKey
, s.FirstName, s.LastName, s.MiddleName, e.JobTitle as Title
, e.HireDate, e.BirthDate, e.LoginID, s.EmailAddress
, s.PhoneNumber as Phone, e.MaritalStatus, e.SalariedFlag
, e.Gender, e.VacationHours, e.SickLeaveHours, e.CurrentFlag
, s.CountryRegionName as SalesTerritoryCountry
, s.TerritoryGroup as SalesTerritoryGroup
, s.TerritoryName as SalesTerritoryRegion
, s.StateProvinceName
FROM [Sales].[vSalesPerson] s
    INNER JOIN [HumanResources].[Employee] e
    ON e.[BusinessEntityID] = s.[BusinessEntityID]
    LEFT OUTER JOIN HumanResources.Employee manager
    ON (e.OrganizationNode.GetAncestor(1)) = manager.[OrganizationNode]
```

Figure 10-19

4. Select OK to save the changes to the OLE DB Source adapter.

5. Next, drag a Lookup Transformation to the Data Flow and connect the green data path output from the OLE DB source to the Lookup. Name the Lookup Sales Territory.

6. Double-click the Lookup Transformation to bring up the Lookup editor. On the General page, change the drop-down named "Specify how to handle rows with no matching entries" to "Redirect rows to no match output." Leave the Cache mode as Full cache and Connection type as OLE DB Connection Manager.

7. On the Connection property page, change the OLE DB connection to AdventureWorksDW2008 and then select [dbo].[DimSalesTerritory] in the drop-down below called "Use a table or a view."

8. On the Columns property page, join the SalesTerritoryCountry, SalesTerritoryGroup, and SalesTerritoryRegion columns between the input columns and lookup columns as shown in Figure 10-20. In addition, select the checkbox next to SalesTerritoryKey in the lookup columns to return this column to the Data Flow.

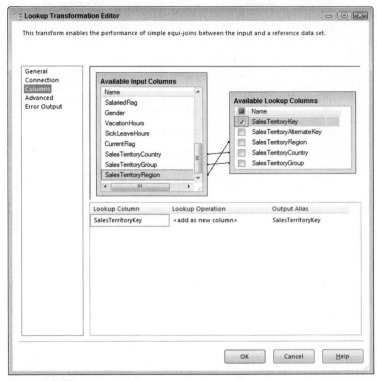

Figure 10-20

At this point, recall from your data profiling that some of the sales territory columns in the source have NULL values. Also recall that TerritoryGroup and TerritoryName have a functional relationship of one-to-many. In fact, assume that you have conferred with the business, and they confirmed that you can look at the StateProvinceName and CountryRegionName, and if another salesperson has the same combination of values, you can use their SalesTerritory information.

9. To handle the missing SalesTerritories with the preceding requirements, add a second Lookup Transformation to the Data Flow, and name it Get Missing Territories. Then connect the green path output of the Sales Territory Lookup to this new lookup. You will be prompted to choose the Output; select Lookup No Match Output from the drop-down list as shown in Figure 10-21.

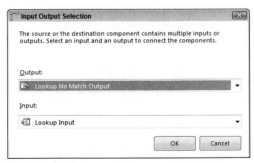

Figure 10-21

10. Edit the new lookup and configure the OLE DB Source adapter to connect to the AdventureWorks2008 connection. Then change the data access mode to SQL command. Enter the following SQL code in the SQL command text window:

```
SELECT DISTINCT
CountryRegionName as SalesTerritoryCountry
, TerritoryGroup as SalesTerritoryGroup
, TerritoryName as SalesTerritoryRegion
, StateProvinceName
FROM [Sales].[vSalesPerson]
WHERE TerritoryName IS NOT NULL
```

11. On the Columns property page, join the SalesTerritoryCountry and StateProvinceName between the input and lookup columns list and then check the checkboxes next to SalesTerritoryGroup and SalesTerritoryRegion on the lookup list. Append the word New to the OutputAlias, as shown in Figure 10-22.

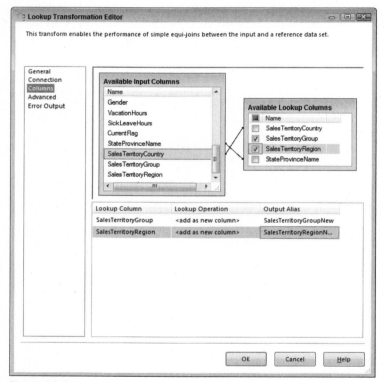

Figure 10-22

12. Next, you will re-create the SalesTerritory Lookup from the prior steps to get the SalesTerritoryKey for the records that originally had missing data.

13. Add a new Lookup to the Data Flow named Reacquire SalesTerritory and connect the output of the Get Missing Territories Lookup (use the Lookup Match Output when prompted). Edit the Lookup and on the General tab, leave the Cache mode as Full cache and Connection type as OLE DB Connection Manager.

14. On the Connections page, specify the AdventureWorksDW2008 Connection Manager and change the "Use a table or a view" to [dbo].[DimSalesTerritory].

15. On the Columns property page (shown in Figure 10-23), match the columns between the input and lookup table, making sure that you use the "New" Region and Group column. Match across SalesTerritoryCountry, SalesTerritoryGroupNew, and SalesTerritoryRegionNew. Also return the SalesTerritory Key and name its Output Alias as SalesTerritoryKeyNew.

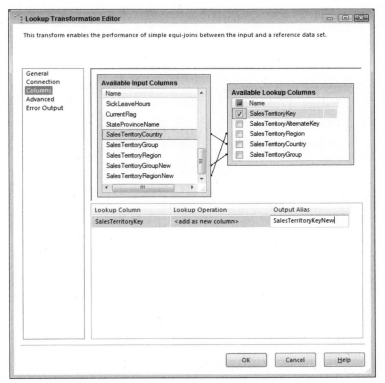

Figure 10-23

16. Select OK to save your Lookup changes and then drag a Union All Transformation onto the Data Flow. Connect two inputs into the Union All Transformation:

a. The Lookup Match Output from the original Sales Territory Lookup

b. The Lookup Match Output from the Reacquire SalesTerritory (from steps 13–15 above)

17. Edit the Union All Transformation, and locate the SalesTerritoryKey column. Change the <ignore> value in the drop-down for the input coming from second lookup to use the SalesTerritoryNew column. This is shown in Figure 10-24.

Figure 10-24

18. Select OK to save your changes to the Union All. At this point, your Data Flow will look similar to the one pictured in Figure 10-25.

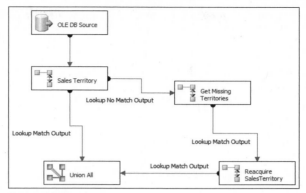

Figure 10-25

These steps are an example of how to handle one data preparation task. When you go to prepare data for your dimension, chances are you will need to perform several steps to get it ready for the dimension data changes.

You can use many of the other SSIS transformations for this purpose, described in the rest of the book. A couple of examples include using the Derived Column to convert NULLs to Unknowns and the Fuzzy Lookup and Grouping to cleanse dirty data.

Handling Complicated Dimension Changes with the SCD Transformation

Now, you are ready to use the SCD wizard again; only for the DimEmployee table, you will need to handle different change types and inferred members.

1. Continue with the Data Flow development and add a Slowly Changing Dimension Transformation to the Data Flow and connect the data path output of the Union All to the SCD Transformation. Then double-click the SCD Transformation to launch the SCD wizard.

2. On the Select a Dimension Table and Keys page, choose the AdventureWorksDW2008 Connection Manager and the [dbo].[DimEmployee] table.

  a. In this example, not all the columns have been extracted from the source, and other destination columns are related to the dimension change management; therefore, not all the columns will automatically be matched between the input columns and the dimension columns.

  b. Find the EmployeeNationalIDAlternateKey and change the Key Type to Business Key.

  c. Select Next.

3. Next, on the Slowly Changing Dimension Columns page, make the following Change Type designations as shown in Figure 10-26:

   a. **Fixed Attributes:** BirthDate, HireDate

   b. **Changing Attributes:** CurrentFlag, EmailAddress, FirstName, Gender, LastName, LoginID, MaritalStatus, MiddleName, Phone, SickLeaveHours, Title, VacationHours

   c. **Historical Attributes:** ParentEmployeeNationalIDAlternateKey, SalariedFlag, SalesTerritoryKey

Figure 10-26

4. On the Fixed and Changing Attribute Options page, uncheck the checkbox under the Fixed attributes label. The result of this is that when a value changes for a column identified as a fixed attribute, the change will be ignored, and the old value in the dimension will not be updated. If you had checked this box, the package would fail.

5. On the same page, check the box for Changing attributes. As described earlier, this will ensure that all the records (current and historical) will get updated when a change happens to a changing attribute.

6. Shown in Figure 10-27, you will now be prompted to configure the Historical Attribute Options. The SCD Transformation needs to know how to identify the current record when a single business key has multiple values (recall, when a historical attribute changes, a new copy of the record is created). Two options are available: The first is where a single column is used to identify the record. The better choice is a start and end date. The DimEmployee table has a StartDate and EndDate column; therefore, use the second configuration option button and set the "Start date column" to StartDate, and the "End date column" to EndDate. Finally, set the "Variable to set date values" drop-down to System::StartTime.

Figure 10-27

7. Assume for this example that you may have missing dimension records when processing the fact table, and when this happens, a new inferred member is added to the dimension. Therefore, on the Inferred Dimension Members page, leave the "Enable inferred member support" checked. The SCD Transformation needs to know when a dimension member is an inferred member. The best choice is to have a column that identified the record as inferred; however, the DimEmployee table does not have a column for this purpose. Therefore leave the "All columns with a change type are null" option selected as shown in Figure 10-28.

Figure 10-28

8. This concludes the wizard settings. Click the Finish button so that the SCD can build the downstream transformations needed based on the configurations. Your Data Flow will now look similar to the one shown in Figure 10-29.

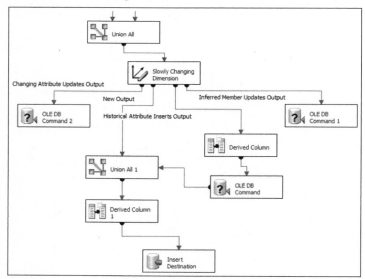

Figure 10-29

As you can see, when dealing with historical attribute changes and inferred members, the output of the SCD Transformation is more complicated with updates, unions, and derived calculations. One of the positive values of the SCD wizard is the rapid development of dimension ETL. Handling changing attributes, new members, historical attributes, inferred members, and fixed attributes is a complicated objective that usually takes hours to code, but with the SCD wizard, you can accomplish this in minutes.

Before looking at some drawbacks and alternatives to the SCD, here are the outputs and how they work, moving from left to right in Figure 10-29:

❑ **Changing Attribute Updates Output:** The changing attribute output records are records where at least one of the attributes that was identified as a changing attribute goes through a change. This update statement is handled by an OLE DB Command Transformation with the code shown here:

```
UPDATE [dbo].[DimEmployee]
SET [CurrentFlag] = ?,[EmailAddress] = ?,[FirstName] = ?,[Gender] = ?,[LastName] =
?,[LoginID] = ?,[MaritalStatus] = ?,[MiddleName] = ?,[Phone] = ?,[SickLeaveHours] =
?,[Title] = ?,[VacationHours] = ?
WHERE [EmployeeNationalIDAlternateKey] = ?
```

The question marks (?) in the code are mapped to input columns sent down from the SCD. Note that the last question mark is mapped to the business key, which will ensure all the records are updated. If you had unchecked the changing attribute checkbox in Step 4 of the preceding list, then the current identifier would have been included and only the latest record would have changed.

❑ **New Output:** New output records are simply new members that are added to the dimension. If the business key doesn't exist in the dimension table, then the SCD will send the row out this output. Eventually these rows are inserted with the Insert Destination shown in Figure 10-29 (which is an OLE DB Destination). The Derived Column 1 Transformation shown in Figure 10-30 is to add the new StartDate of the record, which is required for the metadata management.

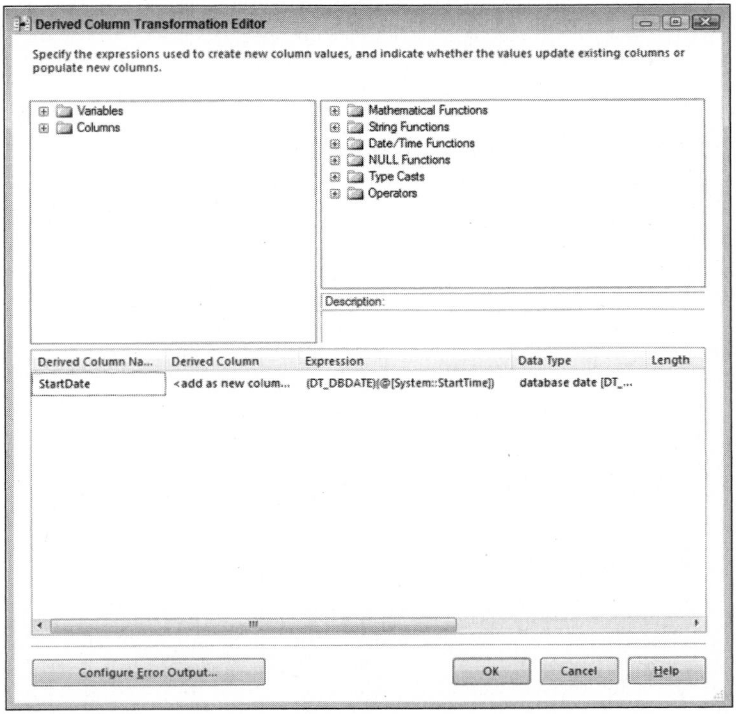

Figure 10-30

This dimension has a unique situation, because it has both a StartDate column as well as a Status column. The values for the Status column are Current and <NULL>, therefore you should add a second Derived Column to this transformation called Status and force a "Current" value in it. You will also need to include it in the destination mapping.

❑ **Historical Attribute Inserts Output:** The historical output is for any attributes that you marked as historical and underwent a change. Therefore you need to add a new row to the dimension table. Handling historical changes requires two general steps:

    ❑ Updating the old record with the EndDate (and NULL Status). This is done through a Derived Column Transformation that defines the EndDate as the `System::StartTime` variable and an OLE DB command that runs an update statement with the following code:

```
UPDATE [dbo].[DimEmployee]
SET [EndDate] = ?
, [Status] = NULL
WHERE [EmployeeNationalIDAlternateKey] = ?
AND [EndDate] IS NULL
```

        This update statement was altered to add setting the Status column to NULL because of the requirement mentioned in the new output. Also, note that the `[EndDate] IS NULL` is included in the `WHERE` clause because this identifies that the record is the latest record.

    ❑ Inserting the new version of the dimension record. This is handled by a Union All Transformation to the new outputs. Since both require inserts, this can be handled in one destination. Also note that the Derived Column shown earlier in Figure 10-30 is applicable to the historical output.

❑ **Inferred Member Updates Output:** Handling inferred members is done through two parts of the ETL. During the fact load when the dimension member is missing, an inferred member is inserted. Second, during the dimension load, if one of the missing inferred members shows up in the dimension source, then the attributes need to get updated in the dimension table. The following update statement is used in the OLE DB Command 1 Transformation:

```
UPDATE [dbo].[DimEmployee]
SET [BirthDate] = ?,[CurrentFlag] = ?,[EmailAddress] = ?,[FirstName] =
?,[Gender] = ?,[HireDate] = ?,[LastName] = ?,[LoginID] =
?,[MaritalStatus] = ?,[MiddleName] =
?,[ParentEmployeeNationalIDAlternateKey] = ?,[Phone] = ?,[SalariedFlag] =
?,[SalesTerritoryKey] = ?,[SickLeaveHours] = ?, [Title] =
?,[VacationHours] = ?
WHERE [EmployeeNationalIDAlternateKey] = ?
```

What is the difference between this update statement and the update statement used for the changing attribute output? The difference is that this one includes updates of the changing attributes, the historical attributes, and the fixed attributes. In other words, because you are updating this as an inferred member, all the attributes are updated, not just the changing attributes.

❑ **Fixed Attribute Output (not used by default):** The fixed attribute output is not used by default by the SCD wizard, however, it is an additional output that can be used in your Data Flow. For example, you may want to audit the records where a fixed attribute has changed. To use it, you can simply take the green output path from the SCD Transformation and drag it to a Destination adapter where your fixed attribute records are stored for review. You will need to choose the Fixed Attribute Output when prompted by adding the new path.

❑ **Unchanged Output (not used by default):** Another output not used by the SCD by default is the Unchanged Output. As your dimensions are being processed, chances are that most of your dimension records do not undergo any changes. Therefore, the records do not need to be sent out for any of the prior outputs. However, you may wish to audit the number of records that are unchanged. You can do this by adding a Row Count Transformation and then dragging a new green data path from the SCD onto the Row Count Transformation and choosing the Unchanged Output when prompted by adding the new path.

Considerations and Alternates to the SCD Transformation

As you can see, the SCD boasts powerful rapid development and is a great tool for most of your dimension ETL needs. It also helps to simplify and standardize your dimension ETL processing. However, the SCD is not always the right SSIS choice to handling your dimension ETL.

Some of the drawbacks include:

❑ For each row in the input, a new lookup is sent to the relational engine to see if changes have happened. In other words, the dimension table is not cached in memory. That is expensive! If you have tens of thousands of dimension source records or more, this can be a limiting feature of the SCD.

❑ For each row in the source that needs to be updated, a new update statement is sent to the dimension table (and updates are used by the changing output, historical output, and inferred member output). If you have a lot of updates happening every time your dimension package runs, this will cause your package to run slow.

❑ The Insert Destination is not set to fast-load. This is because deadlocks can occur between the updates and the inserts. When the insert runs, each row is added one at a time, which can be very expensive.

❑ The SCD works well for historical, changing, and fixed dimension attributes, and as you saw, changes can be made to the downstream transformations. However, if you open up the SCD wizard again and make a change to any part of the wizard, you will automatically lose your changes.

Consider some of these approaches to optimize your SCD package:

❑ Create an index on your dimension table for the business key, followed by the current row identifier (like the EndDate). If a clustered index does not already exist, create this index as a clustered index, because this will prevent a query plan lookup from getting the underlying row. This will help the lookup that happens in the SCD as well as all of the updates.

❑ The row-by-row updates can be changed to set-based updates. To do this, you will need to change the OLE DB command to a Destination adapter to stage the records to a temporary table, then in the Control Flow, add an Execute SQL Task to perform the set-based update.

❑ If you remove all the OLE DB command transformations, then you can also change the Insert Destination to use fast load and essentially bulk insert the data, rather than performing row-at-a-time inserts.

Overall, these alterations may provide you enough performance improvements that you can continue to use the SCD Transformation effectively; however, if you still need an alternate approach, try building the same SCD process through the use of other built-in SSIS transformations such as these:

❑ The Lookup Transformation and the Merger Join Transformation can be used to cache the dimension table data. This will greatly improve performance because then only a single select statement will run against the dimension table, rather than potentially thousands.

❑ The Derived Column Transformation and the Script Component can be used to evaluate which columns have changed, and then the rows can be sent out to multiple outputs. Essentially this would mimic the change evaluation engine inside of the SCD.

❑ After the data is cached and evaluated, you can use the same SCD output structure to handle the changes and inserts, with the consideration to use set-based updates.

Fact Table Loading

Fact table loading is often simpler than dimension ETL, because a fact table usually just involves inserts and, occasionally, updates. When dealing with large volumes, you may need to handle partition inserts and deal with updates in a different way.

In general, fact table loading involves a few common tasks:

❑ Preparing your source data to be at the same grain as your fact table, including having the dimension business keys and measures in the source data

❑ Acquiring the dimension surrogate keys for any related dimension

❑ Identifying new records for the fact table (and potentially updates)

The Sales Quota fact table is relatively straightforward and will give you a good start to developing your fact table ETL.

1. In your SSIS project for this chapter, create a new package and rename it `ETL_FactSalesQuota.dtsx`.

2. Just like the other packages you developed in this chapter, add two OLE DB Connection Managers to the AdventureWorks2008 and the AdventureWorksDW2008 databases.

3. Create a new Data Flow Task and add an OLE DB Source adapter. Name it Sales Quota Source. Configure the OLE DB Source adapter to connect to the AdventureWorks2008 Connection Manager, and change the data access mode to SQL Command as shown in Figure 10-31. Add the following code to the SQL command text window:

```
SELECT QuotaDate, SalesQuota, NationalIDNumber as EmployeeNationalIDAlternateKey
  FROM Sales.SalesPersonQuotaHistory
 INNER JOIN HumanResources.Employee
    ON SalesPersonQuotaHistory.BusinessEntityID = Employee.BusinessEntityID
```

Figure 10-31

4. Next, your objective is to acquire the surrogate keys from the dimension tables. You will use a Lookup Transformation for this purpose. Drag a Lookup Transformation onto the Data Flow and connect the green data path output of the OLE DB Source adapter onto the Lookup Transformation. Rename the Lookup as Employee Key.

5. Double-click the Employee Key Transformation to bring up the Lookup Editor. On the General property page, leave the Cache mode set to Full cache and the Connection type set as OLE DB Connection Manager.

6. On the Connection property page, change the OLE DB Connection Manager drop-down to AdventureWorksDW2008 and enter the following code as shown in Figure 10-32:

```
SELECT EmployeeKey, EmployeeNationalIDAlternateKey
FROM DimEmployee
WHERE EndDate IS NULL
```

Including the EndDate IS NULL filter will ensure that the most current dimension record surrogate key is acquired in the Lookup.

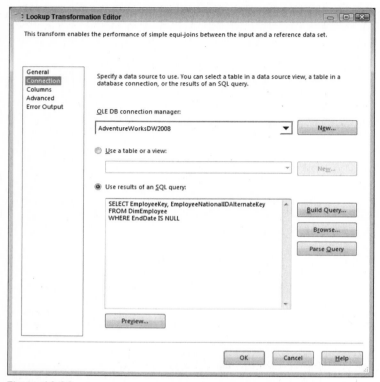

Figure 10-32

7. Change to the Columns property page, and map the EmployeeNationalIDAlternateKey from the input columns to the lookup columns. Then select the checkbox next to the EmployeeKey of the Lookup, as shown in Figure 10-33.

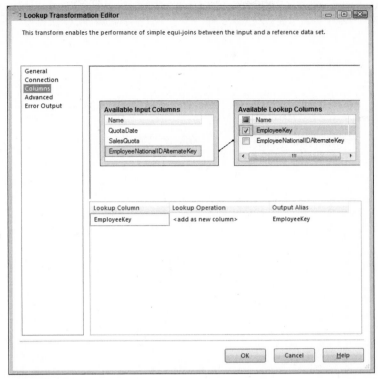

Figure 10-33

8. Select OK to save your changes to the Lookup Transformation.

9. For the DateKey, a Lookup is not needed because the DateKey is a smart key, meaning that the key is based on the date itself in YYYYMMDD format. Therefore you will use a Derived column to calculate the Date Key for the fact table. Add a Derived Column Transformation to the Data Flow and connect the green data path output of the Employee Lookup to the Derived Column Transformation. When prompted, choose the Lookup Match Output from the Lookup Transformation. Name the Derived Column as Date Keys.

10. Double-click the Derived Column Transformation and add these three new Derived Column columns with their associated expressions as shown in Figure 10-34:

   ❑ DateKey: `YEAR([QuotaDate])*10000 + MONTH([QuotaDate])*100 + DAY([QuotaDate])`

   ❑ CalendarYear: `(DT_I2) YEAR([QuotaDate])`

   ❑ CalendarQuarter: `(DT_UI1) DATEPART("q",[QuotaDate])`

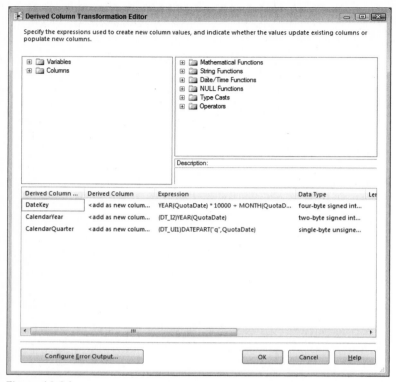

Figure 10-34

At this point in your Data Flow, you will have the data ready for the fact table. If your data has already been incrementally extracted, so that you are only getting new rows, you can use an OLE DB Destination to insert it right into the fact table. Assume for this tutorial that you need to identify which records are new and which records are updates, and handle them appropriately. Follow these steps to accomplish fact updates and inserts.

A Merge Join will be used to match source input records to the actual fact table records, but before you add the Merge Join, you will need to add a Sort to the source records (a requirement of the Merge Join) and also extract the fact data into the Data Flow.

11. Add a Sort Transformation to the Data Flow and connect the green data path output from the Derived Column Transformation onto the Sort Transformation. Double-click the Sort Transformation to bring up the Sort Transformation Editor and sort the input data by the following columns: EmployeeKey, CalendarYear, CalendarQuarter, as shown in Figure 10-35. The CalendarYear and CalendarQuarter are important columns for this fact table because they identify the level of detail that the fact table is associated with the date dimension. This is called the *date grain*.

Figure 10-35

Figure 10-36 shows what your Data Flow should look like at this point.

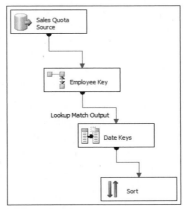

Figure 10-36

12. Next, add a new OLE DB Source adapter to the Data Flow and name it Sales Quota Fact. Configure the OLE DB Source to use the AdventureWorksDW2008 Connection Manager and use the following SQL command:

```
SELECT EmployeeKey, CalendarYear
, CalendarQuarter, SalesAmountQuota
FROM dbo.FactSalesQuota
ORDER BY 1,2,3
```

13. Because we are using an ORDER BY statement in the query (sorting by the first 3 columns in order), we need to configure the OLE DB Source adapter to know that the data is entering the Data Flow sorted. First, select OK to save the changes to the OLE DB Source, and then right-click the Sales Quota Fact adapter and choose Show Advanced Editor.

14. On the Input and Output Properties tab, click the OLE DB Source Output object in the left window and in the right window, change the IsSorted property to True as shown in Figure 10-37.

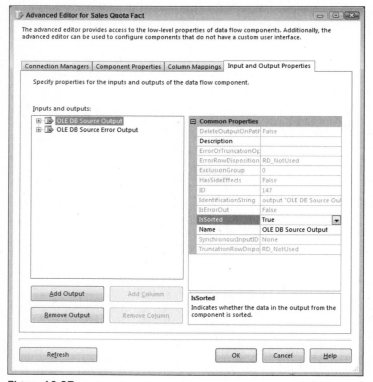

Figure 10-37

15. Next, expand the OLE DB Source Output on the left and then expand the Output Columns folder. Make the following changes to the Output Column properties:

a. Select the EmployeeKey column and change its SortKeyPosition to 1 as shown in Figure 10-38.

b. Select the CalendarYear column and change its SortKeyPosition to 2.

c. Select the CalendarQuarter column and change its SortKeyPosition to 3.

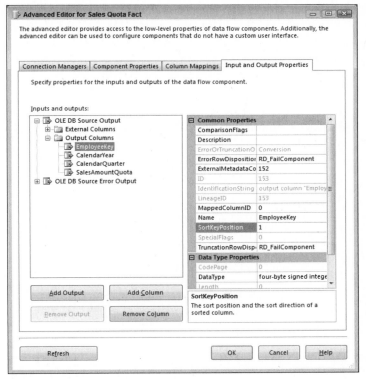

Figure 10-38

d. Select OK to save the changes to the advanced properties.

16. Next, add a Merge Join Transformation to the Data Flow. First, connect the green data path output from the Sort Transformation onto the Merge Join. When prompted, choose the input option named Merge Join Left Input. Then connect the green data path output from the Sales Quota Fact Source onto the Merge Join.

17. Double-click the Merge Join Transformation to open its editor. You will see that the EmployeeKey, CalendarYear, and CalendarQuarter columns are already joined between inputs. Make the following changes as shown in Figure 10-39:

a. Change the Join type drop-down to a Left outer join.

b. Check the SalesQuota, EmployeeKey, DateKey, CalendarYear, and CalendarQuarter columns from the Sort input list.

c. Check the SalesAmountQuota from the Sales Quota Fact column list and then change the Output Alias for this column to be SalesAmountQuota_Fact.

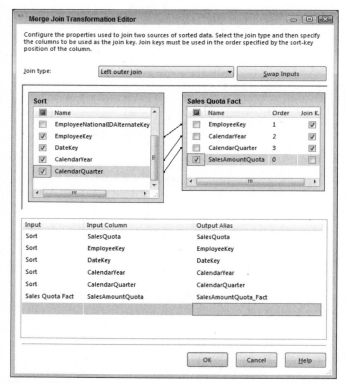

Figure 10-39

18. Select OK to save your Merge Join configuration.

19. Your next objective is to identify which records are new quotas and which are changed sales quotas. A conditional split will be used to accomplish this task; therefore, drag a Conditional Split Transformation onto the Data Flow and connect the green data path output from the Merge Join Transformation onto the Conditional Split. Rename the Conditional Split as Identify Inserts and Updates.

20. Double-click the Conditional Split to open the editor and make the following changes as shown in Figure 10-40:

a. Add a new condition named New Fact Records with the following condition: `ISNULL([SalesAmountQuota_Fact])`. If the measure from the fact is null, it indicates that the fact record does not exist for the employee and date combination.

b. Add a second condition named Fact Updates with the following condition: `[SalesQuota] != [SalesAmountQuota_Fact]`

c. Change the default output name to No Changes.

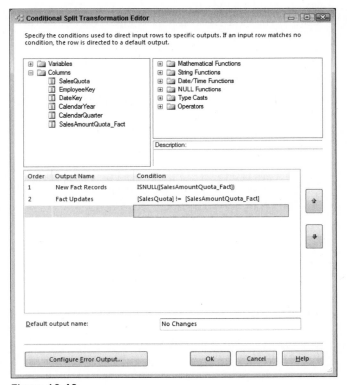

Figure 10-40

21. Select OK to save the changes to the Conditional Split.

22. Add an OLE DB Destination adapter to the Data Flow named Fact Inserts. Drag the green data path output from the Conditional Split Transformation onto the OLE DB Destination. When prompted to choose an output from the Conditional Split, choose the New Fact Records output.

23. Double-click the Fact Inserts Destination and change the OLE DB Connection Manager to AdventureWorksDW2008. In the "Name of the table or the view" drop-down, choose the [dbo].[FactSalesQuota] table.

24. Switch to the Mappings property page and match up the SalesQuota column from the input column list to the SalesAmountQuota in the available destinations column list, as shown in Figure 10-41. The other columns (EmployeeKey, DateKey, CalendarYear, and CalendarQuarter) should already match. Select OK to save your changes to the OLE DB Destination.

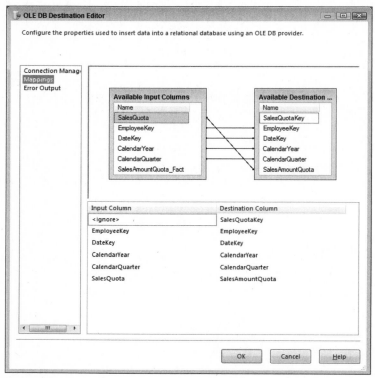

Figure 10-41

25. Next, you will need to handle the fact table updates. Drag an OLE DB Command Transformation to the Data Flow and rename it Fact Updates. Drag the green data path output from the Conditional Split onto the Fact Updates Transformation, and when prompted, choose the Fact Update output from the Conditional Split.

26. Double-click the OLE DB Command Transformation and change the Connection Manager drop-down to AdventureWorksDW2008. On the Component Properties tab, add the following code to the SQLCommand property (make sure you click the ellipsis button to open up an editor window):

```
UPDATE dbo.FactSalesQuota
SET SalesAmountQuota = ?
WHERE EmployeeKey = ?
AND CalendarYear = ?
AND CalendarQuarter = ?
```

27. Switch to the Column Mappings tab and map the SalesQuota to Param_0, Employee_Key to Param_1, CalendarYear to Param_2, and CalendarQuarter to Param_3 as shown in Figure 10-42.

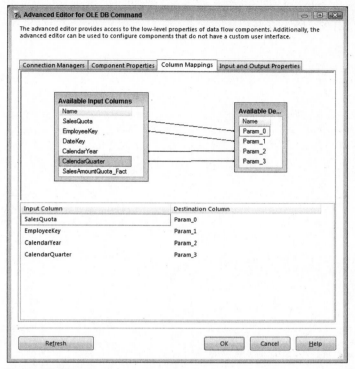

Figure 10-42

28. Select OK to save your changes to the OLE DB Command update. Your fact table ETL for the FactSalesQuota is complete, and should look similar to Figure 10-43.

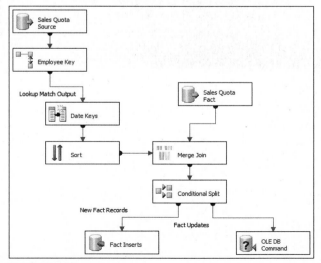

Figure 10-43

Here are some final considerations for fact table ETL:

❑ A Merge Join was used in this case to help identify which records were updates or inserts, based on matching the source to the fact table. Refer to the Chapter 7 to see other alternatives to associating the source to fact table.

❑ For the inserts and updates, you may want to leverage the relational engine to handle either the insert or update at the same time. With SQL Server 2008, a MERGE statement now exists that will perform either an insert or update depending on whether the record exists. See Chapter 11 on how to use this feature.

❑ Another alternative to the OLE DB Command fact table updates is to use a set-based update. The OLE DB command works well and is easy for small data volumes; however, your situation may not allow row-at-a-time updates. Consider staging the updates to a table and then performing a set-based update (through a multi-row SQL UPDATE statement) by joining the staging table to the fact table and updating the sales quota that way.

❑ Inserts are another area of improvement considerations. Fact tables often have millions of rows in them, and therefore you should look at how to optimize the inserts. Consider dropping the indexes, loading the fact table, and then re-creating the indexes. This is often a lot faster. See Chapter 14 for ideas on how to tune the inserts.

❑ If you have partitions in place, you can insert the data right into the partitioned fact table, however, when you are dealing with high volumes, the overhead that the relational engine has to undergo may inhibit performance. You should consider in these situations to switch the current partition out in order to load it separately, then you can switch it back into the partitioned table.

Inferred members are another challenge for fact table ETL. How do you handle a missing dimension key? One approach includes scanning the fact table source for missing keys and adding the inferred member dimension records before the fact table ETL runs. An alternative is to redirect the missing row when the lookup doesn't have a match, then add the dimension key during the ETL, followed by bringing back the row into the ETL through a Union All. One final approach is to handle the inferred members after the fact table ETL finishes. You would need to stage the records that have missing keys, add the inferred members, and then re-process the staged records into the fact table.

As you can see, fact tables have some unique challenges, but overall can be handled effectively with SSIS. Now that you have loaded both your dimensions and fact tables, the next step is to then process your SSAS cubes, if SSAS is part of your data warehouse or business intelligence project.

SSAS Processing

Processing SSAS objects in SSIS can be as easy as using the Analysis Services Processing Task. However, if your SSAS cubes require adding or processing specific partitions or changing names of cubes or servers, then you will need to consider other approaches. In fact, many, if not most solutions require using other processing methods.

The primary ways to process SSAS dimensions and cubes through SSIS include:

❑ **The Analysis Services Processing Task:** which can be defined with a unique list of dimensions and partitions to process. However, this task does not allow modifications of the objects through expressions or configurations.

❑ **The Analysis Services Execute DDL Task:** which can process dimensions and partitions through XMLA scripts. The advantage of this task is the ability to make the script dynamic by changing the script contents before it is executed.

❑ **The Script Task:** which can use the API for SSAS, which is called AMO (or Analysis Management Objects). With AMO, you can create objects, copy objects, process objects, and so on.

❑ **The Execute Process Task:** which can run `ascmd.exe`, which is the SSAS command-line tool that can run XMLA, MDX, and DMX queries. The advantage of the `ascmd.exe` tool is the ability to pass in parameters to a script that is run.

To demonstrate the use of some of these approaches, this next tutorial will use the Analysis Services Processing Task to process the dimensions related to the sales quotas and then the Analysis Services Execute DDL Task to handle the processing of the partitions.

Before beginning these steps, create a new partition in SSAS for the Sales Targets Measure called Sales_Quotas_2008. This is for demonstration purposes. An XMLA script has been created and included in the downloadable content at www.wrox.com for this chapter called `Sales_Quotas_2008.xmla`.

1. In your SSIS project for this chapter, create a new package and rename it to `SSAS_SalesTargets.dtsx`.

2. Right-click in the Connection Managers window and choose New Analysis Services Connection. Then in the Add Analysis Services Connection Manager window, click the Edit button to bring up the connection properties, as shown in Figure 10-44.

   a. Specify your server in the "Server or file name" text box (such as localhost if you are running SSAS on the same machine)

   b. Change the "Log on to the server" option to Use Windows NT Integrated Security.

   c. In the Initial catalog drop-down box, choose the Adventure Works SSAS database which by default is named the Adventure Works DW 2008 database. You may need to install the sample SSAS solution, which is available from www.codeplex.com.

Figure 10-44

d. Select OK to save your changes to the Connection Manager, and then OK in the Add Analysis Services Connection Manager window.

e. Finally, rename the connection that is in the SSIS Connection Managers window to AdventureWorksAS.

3. To create the dimension processing, drag an Analysis Services Processing Task from the Toolbox onto the Control Flow and rename the task as Process Dimensions.

4. Double-click the Process Dimensions Task to bring up the editor and navigate to the Processing Settings property page.

a. Confirm that the Analysis Services Connection Manager drop-down is set to AdventureWorksAS.

b. Click the Add button to open up the Add Analysis Services Object window. As shown in Figure 10-45, check the Date, Employee, and Sales Territory dimensions, and then click OK to save your changes.

c. For each dimension, change the Process Options drop-down to say Process Default, which will either perform a dimension update or, if the dimension has never been processed, it will fully process the dimension.

d. Click the Change Settings button and in the Change Settings editor, click the Parallel selection option under the Processing Order properties. Click OK to save your settings. Your SSAS processing task should look like Figure 10-46.

e. Select OK to save your changes to the Analysis Services Processing Task.

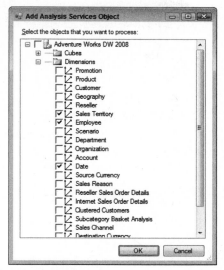

Figure 10-45

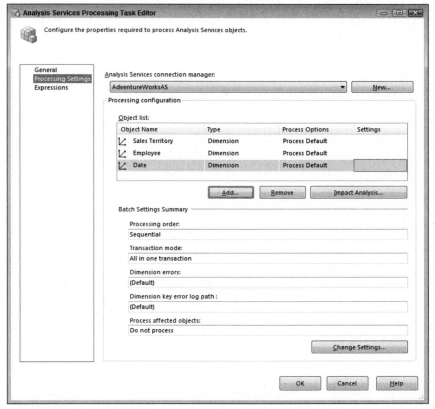

Figure 10-46

5. Before continuing, you will create an SSIS package variable that will designate the XMLA partition for processing. Name the SSIS variable as Sales_Quota_Partition and define the variable as a String data type with "Fact Sales Quota" entered as the value.

6. Next, drag an Analysis Services Execute DDL Task onto the Data Flow and drag the green precedence constraint from the SSAS Processing Task onto the SSAS Execute DDL Task. Rename the Execute DDL Task as Process Partition.

   a. Edit the Process Partition Task and navigate to the DDL property page.

   b. Change the Connection property to AdventureWorksAS and leave the SourceType as Direct Input, as shown in Figure 10-47.

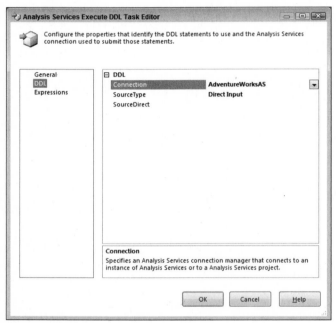

Figure 10-47

   c. Change to the Expressions property page of the editor and click in the Expressions property in the right window. Click in the ellipsis on the right side of the text box, which will open up the Property Expressions Editor. Choose the Source property in the drop-down box as shown in Figure 10-48.

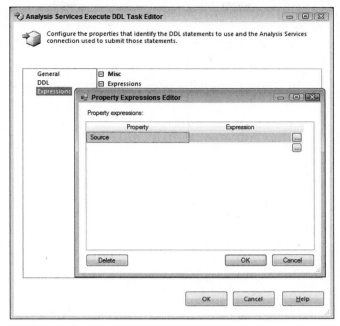

Figure 10-48

d. Next, you will add the XMLA code that will execute when the package is run. The expressions will dynamically update the code when this task executes. Click the ellipsis on the right side of the Source property as shown in Figure 10-48 to open the Expression Builder.

e. Enter the following code in the Expression text box, which is also shown in Figure 10-49:

```
"<Batch xmlns=\"http://schemas.microsoft.com/analysisservices/2003/engine\">
  <Parallel>
    <Process xmlns:xsd=\"http://www.w3.org/2001/XMLSchema\"
xmlns:xsi=\"http://www.w3.org/2001/XMLSchema-instance\"
xmlns:ddl2=\"http://schemas.microsoft.com/analysisservices/2003/engine/2\"
xmlns:ddl2_2=\"http://schemas.microsoft.com/analysisservices/2003/engine/2/2\"
xmlns:ddl100_100=\"http://schemas.microsoft.com/analysisservices/2008/engine/100/10
0\">
      <Object>
        <DatabaseID>Adventure Works DW</DatabaseID>
        <CubeID>Adventure Works DW</CubeID>
        <MeasureGroupID>Fact Sales Quota</MeasureGroupID>
        <PartitionID>"
+ @[User::Sales_Quota_Partition]
+ "</PartitionID>
      </Object>
      <Type>ProcessFull</Type>
      <WriteBackTableCreation>UseExisting</WriteBackTableCreation>
    </Process>
  </Parallel>
</Batch>"
```

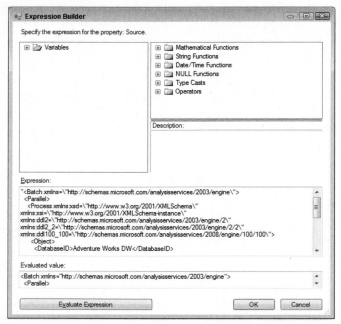

Figure 10-49

f. This code generates the XMLA, and includes the Sales_Quota_Partition variable. The good news is that you don't need to know XMLA; you can use SSMS to generate it for you.

To automatically generate the XMLA code that will process a Sales Quota partition, open up SSMS and connect to SSAS. Expand the Databases folder, then the Adventure Works SSAS database, then the Cubes folder; then expand the Adventure Works cube, and finally expand the Sales Targets measure group. Right-click the Sales Quota partition and choose Process as shown in Figure 10-50.

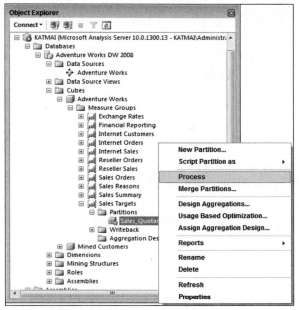

Figure 10-50

The processing tool in SSMS looks very similar to the SSAS processing task in SSIS shown previously in Figure 10-46, except that the SSMS processing tool has a Script button near the title bar. Click the Script button.

The XML code generated by SSMS is the basis for the SSIS expression just used. The differences include: double quotes surrounding the code, all the double quotes in the code have a backslash "\" in front of them (this is needed by the expression language, since a double quote is reserved), and the <PartitionID> tag's value is replaced by the Sales_Quota_Partition value.

   g.   Click OK in the open windows to save your changes.

7.   Finally, the Process Partition Task will show an error because there is no code entered into the DDL property. The code is generated at runtime through the expression. To disable this error, highlight the task and pull open the property window in BIDS. Change the DelayValidation property to True and the error will disappear.

8.   The SSIS package that you have just developed should look similar to Figure 10-51.

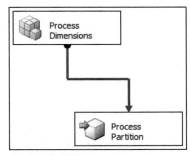

Figure 10-51

If you were to fully work out the development of this package, you would likely have a couple more tasks involved in the process. First, the current partition is entered in the variable, but what you haven't done yet is put the code in place to update this variable when the package is run. This would be the first task and could either be an Execute SQL Task to pull the value for the current partition from a configuration table or the system date into the variable, or you could use a Script Task to populate the variable.

Second, if you have a larger solution with many partitions that are at the weekly or monthly grain, you would need a task that created a new partition, as needed, before the partition was run. This could either be an Execute DDL Task similar to the one you just created for the processing task, or you could use a Script Task and leveraged AMO to create or copy an existing partition to a new partition.

As you can see, processing SSAS objects in SSIS can require a few simple steps, or it may require several more complex steps depending on the processing needs of your SSAS solution.

Master ETL Package

Putting it all together is perhaps the easiest part of the ETL process because it simply involves using SSIS to coordinate the execution of the packages in the order that they require.

The best practice to do this is to use a master package that executes the child packages leveraging the Execute Package Task. The determination of precedence is a matter of understanding the overall ETL as well as the primary to foreign key relationships in the tables.

The steps to use the Execute Package Task vary, depending on whether you will be referencing packages stored in the file system, or whether you've deployed your packages to a server.

For packages that are stored in SQL Server, follow these steps after you have created a new package in your SSIS project:

1. First, in the Connection Managers window, create a new OLE DB connection to the MSDB database on the server where you deployed your packages. Name the connection MSDB Package Store so that its purpose is clear.

2. Drag an Execute Package Task from the Toolbox onto the Control Flow.

3. Double-click the Execute Package Task to bring up the task editor.

4. Navigate to the Package property page and confirm that the Location property is set to SQL Server. For the Connection property, choose the MSDB Package Store created in the first step.

5. For the PackageName property, click the ellipsis on the right side of the properties checkbox. In the Select Package window, choose the ETL package that you deployed to the SSIS service. Select OK to save your changes, and return to the Execute Package Task Editor, as shown in Figure 10-52.

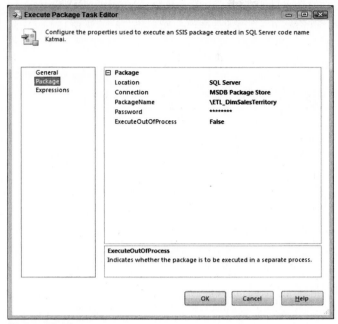

Figure 10-52

6. Select OK to save your changes to complete the configuration of one of the Execute Package Tasks in the master ETL package.

When you use packages stored in SQL Server, they will all share the same connection, but the PackageName property will be a reference to the package within the MSDB database. For packages that are stored in the file system, each package referenced by an Execute Package Task will have a separate connection. Follow these steps to configure the Execute Package Task if you will store your packages in the file system:

1. Drag an Execute Package Task from the Toolbox into the Control Flow.

2. Double-click the Execute Package Task to open the task editor.

3. On the Package property page, change the Location property to File System and then in the Connection drop-down, choose <New connection> from the list. Browse to the package you are configuring to execute as shown in Figure 10-53, and then click OK to save your package connection.

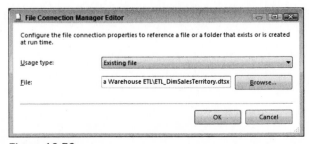

Figure 10-53

4. Your Execute Package Task will look like the one pictured in Figure 10-54. Also notice that a new connection has been created in the Connection Managers window referencing your package. For each new package you reference in the file system, a new connection will appear.

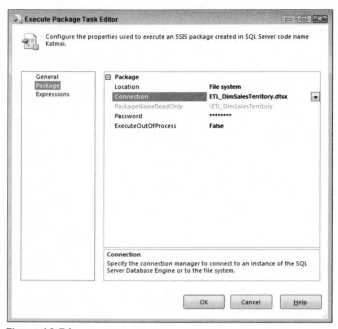

Figure 10-54

Typically, a data warehouse ETL first involves executing a staging process. Second, the ETL packages for the dimension tables are executed, followed by the fact table ETL and concluding with the cube processing. The master package for the examples in this chapter is shown in Figure 10-55.

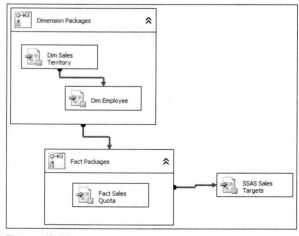

Figure 10-55

The related packages are grouped with Sequence Containers to help visualize the processing order. In this case, the Dim Sales Territory package needs to be run before the Dim Employee package because of the foreign key reference in the DimEmployee table. Larger solutions will have multiple dimension and fact packages.

When you deploy your master packages between servers, your Execute Package Task connections (either the MSDB connection or each package connection) can just be a part of your connection configurations. Therefore when your master package is deployed, the references can be updated through SSIS configurations.

Summary

Moving from start to finish in a data warehouse ETL effort requires a lot of planning and research. Your research should include both data profiling as well as interviews with the business users to understand how they will be using the dimension attributes, so that you can identify the different attribute change types.

The development of your dimension and fact packages will require some thoughtful considerations on how to most efficiently perform inserts and updates, especially considering data changes and missing members. And finally, don't leave your SSAS processing packages to the last minute . You may be surprised at the time it may take to develop a flexible package that can dynamically handle selective partition processing and creation.

In the next chapter, you will consider when and how to use the SQL Server relational engine during your ETL SSIS development.

11

Using the Relational Engine

There's an old adage that says when you're holding a hammer, everything else looks like a nail. When you use SSIS to build a solution, make sure that you are using the right tool for every problem you tackle. SSIS will be excellent for some jobs, and SQL Server will shine at other tasks. When used in concert, the combination of the two can be powerful.

This chapter discusses other features in the SQL Server arsenal that can help you build robust and high-performance ETL solutions. The SQL Server relational engine has many features that were designed with data loading in mind, and as such the engine and SSIS form a perfect marriage to extract, load, and transform your data. In SQL Server 2008 some of the new relational features were built in direct consultation with the SSIS team.

This chapter assumes you are using SQL Server 2008 as the source system, though many of the same principles will apply to earlier versions of SQL Server and to other relational database systems too. You should also have the SQL Server 2008 versions of AdventureWorks and AdventureWorksDW installed; these are available from www.codeplex.com.

The easiest way to look at how the relational engine can help you design ETL solutions is to segment the topic into the three basic stages of ETL: extraction, transformation, and loading. Because the domain of transformation is mostly within SSIS itself, there is not much to say there about the relational engine, so the scope of interest will be narrowed down to extraction and loading.

Data Extraction

Even if a data warehouse solution starts off simple — using one or two sources — it can rapidly become more complex once the users start realizing the value of the solution and request data from additional business applications to be included in the process. More data increases the complexity of the solution, but it also increases the execution time of the ETL. Storage is certainly cheap today, but the size and amount of data is growing exponentially. If you have a fixed batch window of time in which you can load the data, it is essential to minimize the expense of all the operations. This section looks at ways of lowering the cost of extraction, and how you can use those methods within SSIS.

SELECT * Is Bad

The SSIS OLE DB Source and ADO.NET Source adapters allow you to select a table name that you want to load, which makes for a simple development experience, but terrible runtime performance. What happens at runtime is that the component issues a SELECT * FROM <table> command to SQL Server, which obediently returns every single column and row from the table.

This is a problem for several reasons:

❑ **CPU and I/O Cost:** You typically only need a subset of the columns from the source table, and every extra column you ask for incurs processing overhead in all the subsystems it has to travel through in order to get to the destination. If the database is on a different server, then the layers include NTFS (the file system), the SQL Server storage engine, the query processor, TDS (tabular data stream, SQL Server's data protocol), TCP/IP, OLE DB, the SSIS Source adapter, and finally the SSIS pipeline (and there are probably a few other layers we skipped). So even if you are only extracting one redundant integer column of data from the source, once you multiply that cost by the number of rows and processing overhead it quickly adds up. Saving just 5% on processing time can still help you reach your batch window target.

❑ **Robustness:** If the source table has 10 columns today and your package requests all the data in a SELECT * manner, then if tomorrow the DBA adds another column to the source table, your package could break. Suddenly the package gets an extra column that it doesn't know what to do with, and things could go awry.

❑ **Intentional design:** For maintenance, security, and self-documentation reasons the required columns should be explicitly specified.

❑ **DBA 101:** If you are still not convinced, find any seasoned DBA, and they are likely to launch into a tirade of why SELECT * is the root of all evil.

As Figure 11-1 shows, the Source adapters also give you the option of using checkboxes to select or deselect the columns that you require, but the problem with this approach is that the filtering occurs client-side. In other words, all the columns are brought across (incurring all that I/O overhead), and then the deselected columns are thrown away once they get to SSIS.

Figure 11-1

So what is the preferred way to extract data using these adapters? The simple answer is to forget that the table option exists, and instead only use the query option. Also forget that the column checkboxes exist. For rapid development and prototyping these options are useful, but for deployed solutions you should type in a query. SSIS makes it simple to do this by providing a query builder in both the OLE DB and ADO.NET Source adapters, which allows you to construct a query in a visual manner, as shown in Figure 11-2.

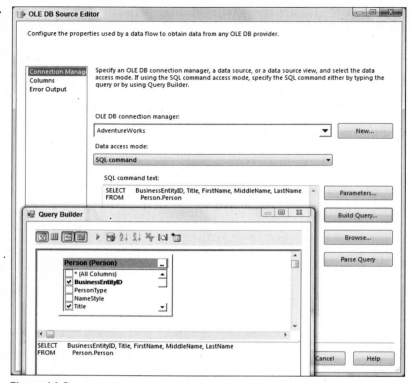

Figure 11-2

WHERE Is Your Friend

As an ancillary to the previous tenet, the WHERE clause (also called the query predicate) is one of the most useful tools you can use to increase performance. Once again, the table option in the Source adapters does not allow you to narrow down the set of columns, but specifically to this section it also does not allow you to limit the number of rows. If all you really need are the rows from the source system that are tagged with yesterday's date, then why stream every single other row over the wire just to throw them away once they get to SSIS? Instead, use a query with a WHERE clause to limit the number of rows being returned. Once again, the less data you request, the less processing and I/O is required, and thus the faster your solution will be.

```
--BAD programming practice (returns 11 columns, 121,000 rows)
SELECT * FROM Sales.SalesOrderDetail;

--BETTER programming practice (returns 6 columns, 121,000 rows)
SELECT SalesOrderID, SalesOrderDetailID, OrderQty,
       ProductID, UnitPrice, UnitPriceDiscount
FROM Sales.SalesOrderDetail;
```

```
--BEST programming practice (returns 6 columns, 357 rows)
SELECT SalesOrderID, SalesOrderDetailID, OrderQty,
       ProductID, UnitPrice, UnitPriceDiscount
FROM Sales.SalesOrderDetail
WHERE ModifiedDate = '2001-07-01';
```

In case it is not clear, Figure 11-3 shows how you would use this SELECT statement (and the other queries discussed next) in the context of SSIS. Drop an OLE DB or ADO.NET Source adapter onto the package design surface, point it at the source database (which is AdventureWorks2008 in this case), select the "query" option, and plug in the preceding query.

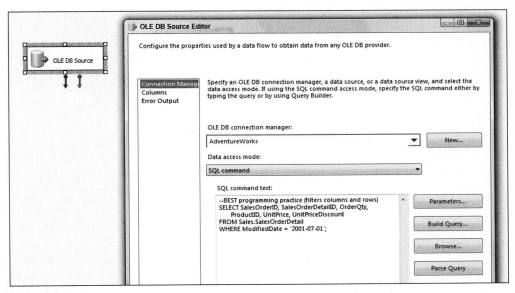

Figure 11-3

Transform during Extract

The basic message here is to do some of your transformations while you are extracting. This is not a viable approach for every single transformation you intend doing — especially if your ETL solution is used for compliance reasons, and you want to specifically log any errors in the data — but it does make sense for primitive operations, such as trimming whitespace, converting magic numbers to NULLs, sharpening data types, and even something as simple as providing a friendlier column name.

A "magic number" is a value used to represent the "unknown" or NULL value in some systems. This is generally considered bad database design practice; however, it is necessary in some systems that do not have the concept of a NULL state. For instance, you may be using a source database where the data steward could not assign the value "Unknown" or NULL to (say) a date column, so instead the operators plugged in "1999/12/31," not expecting that one day the "magic number" would suddenly gain meaning!

The practice of converting data values to the smallest type that can adequately represent them is called "data sharpening." In one of the following examples you convert a DECIMAL(37,0) value to BIT because the column only ever contains the values 0 or 1, because it is more efficient to store and process the data in its smallest (sharpest) representation.

Many data issues can be cleaned up as you're extracting the data, before it even gets to SSIS. This does not mean you physically fix the data in the source system (though that would be an ideal solution); it just means that you write a query smart enough to fix some basic problems and project the clean view to the data consumer. Why pull dirty data from SQL Server if you know you are immediately going to fix it up in SSIS; rather, fix it up "on-the-fly" so SSIS gets it clean in the first place.

By following this advice you can offload the simple clean-up work to the SQL Server database engine, and because it is very efficient at doing such a task, this can improve your ETL performance as well as lowering the package complexity. A drawback of this approach is that data quality issues in your source systems are further hidden from the business, and hidden things tend to not get fixed!

To demonstrate this concept, imagine you are pulling data from the following source schema. Don't regard the problems demonstrated in this example as simply being illustrative; the issues reflect some real-world issues that the authors have seen.

Column Name	Data Type	Examples	Notes
CUSTOMER_ID	Decimal(8,0)	1, 2, 3	The values in this column are integers (4 bytes), but the source is declared as a decimal, which takes 5 bytes of storage per value.
CUSTOMER_NAME	Varchar(100)	"Northwind Traders__", "_XXX", "_Adventure Works", "_", "Acme Apples", "____", ""	The problem with this column is that where the customer name has not been provided, a blank string "" or "XXX" is used instead of NULL. There are also many leading and trailing blanks in the values (represented by "_" in the examples)
ACTIVE_IND	Decimal(38,0)	1, 0, 1, 1, 0	Whether by intention or mistake, this simple True/False value is represented by a 17-byte decimal!
LOAD_DATE	DateTime	"2000/1/1", "1972/05/27", "9999/12/31"	The only problem in this column is that unknown dates are represented using a magic number; in this case "9999-12-31". In some systems dates are represented using text fields, which means that the dates can be invalid or ambiguous.

If you retrieve the native data into SSIS from the source just described, it will obediently generate the corresponding pipeline structures to represent this data, including the multi-byte decimal ACTIVE_IND column that will only ever contain the values 1 or 0. Depending on the number of rows in the source, there is a large processing and storage overhead in allowing this default behavior. All the data issues described previously will be brought through to SSIS, and you will have to fix them there. Of course, that may be your intent but you could make your life easier by dealing with them as early as possible.

Here is the default query that you might design:

```
--Old query
SELECT
    CUSTOMER_ID, CUSTOMER_NAME, ACTIVE_IND
FROM
    dbo.Customers;
```

Here is how you can improve the robustness, performance, and intention of the query. In the spirit of the "right tool for the right job" you clean the data right inside the query so that SSIS gets it in a cleaner state. Once again, you can use this query in an SSIS Source Component instead of using the table method or plugging in a default SELECT * query.

```
--New query:
SELECT
    --Convert to INT and alias using a friendlier name
    CONVERT(INT, CUSTOMER_ID)                       AS CustomerID
    --Trim whitespace, convert empty strings to NULL and alias
    ,NULLIF(LTRIM(RTRIM(CUSTOMER_NAME)), '')        AS CustomerName
    --Convert to BIT and alias
    ,CONVERT(BIT, ACTIVE_IND)                       AS IsActive
    ,CASE
        --Convert magic dates to NULL
        WHEN LOAD_DATE = '9999-12-31' THEN NULL
        --Convert date to smart surrogate integer of form YYYYMMDD
        ELSE CONVERT(INT, (CONVERT(NVARCHAR(8), LOAD_DATE, 112)))
    END AS LoadDateID --Alias using friendly name
FROM
    dbo.Customers
WHERE --Of course, we should always use a WHERE clause
    LOAD_DATE = GETDATE();
```

Let's look at what you have done here:

❑   First of all you have sharpened the CUSTOMER_ID column from a 5-byte decimal to a 4-byte integer. You did not do this conversion in the source database itself; you just converted its external projection. You also gave the column a friendlier name that your ETL developers many find easier to read and remember.

❑   Next you trimmed all the leading and trailing whitespace from the CUSTOMER_NAME column. If the column value was originally an empty string (or if after trimming it ended up being an empty string), then you convert it to NULL. Once again you give it a friendlier alias.

❑ You sharpened the ACTIVE_IND column to a Boolean (BIT) column and give it a name that is simpler to understand — it may not be obvious that _IND means Indicator.

❑ The LOAD_DATE conversion takes some explaining:

   ❑ First you want to convert all magic numbers to a true NULL representation. You could do this using the NULLIF() function in SQL Server, but it is better in this case to use a CASE statement so that the code is easier to understand. Be careful that you do not blindly convert all magic numbers — for instance in scientific applications, the date "9999-12-31" might actually have meaning.

   ❑ Next you converted any real (non-magic) dates to an integer representation of the form YYYYMMDD. In standard data warehouse practice it is often the case that a date column is converted to an integer representation for use as a "smart" surrogate key. Such practice is covered in many standard data warehouse design books, so we will not expound on the subject here. (Truth be told, you would probably not follow such practice in a dimension such as DimCustomer, so this example is simply a convenient vehicle to illustrate the point.)

❑ Finally, you added a WHERE clause in order to limit the number of rows.

So what benefit did you gain? Well because you did this conversion in the source extraction query, SSIS will receive the data in a cleaner state than it was originally. Of course there are bound to be other data quality issues that SSIS will need to deal with, but at least you can get the trivial ones out of the way while improving basic performance at the same time. As far as SSIS is concerned, when it sets up the pipeline column structure, it will use the names and types represented by the query. For instance, it will believe the IsActive column is (and always has been) a BIT — it doesn't waste any time or space by treating it as a 17-byte DECIMAL. When you execute the package, the data will be transformed inside the SQL engine and SSIS will consume it in the normal manner (albeit more efficiently because it's cleaner and sharper).

You also gave the columns friendlier names that your ETL developers may find more intuitive. This adds nothing to the performance, but it costs little and makes your packages easier to understand and maintain.

Many ANDs Make Light Work

OK, that is a bad pun. But it's also relevant. What this tenet says is that you should let the SQL engine combine different datasets for you where it makes sense. In technical terms, this means do any relevant JOINs, UNIONS, sub-queries, and so on directly in the extraction query.

That does not mean you should use relational semantics to join rows from the source system to the destination system or across heterogeneous systems (even though that might be possible) because that will lead to tightly coupled and fragile ETL design. Instead, this means that if you have two or more tables in the same source database that you are intending to join using SSIS, then JOIN or UNION those tables together as part of the SELECT clause.

For example, you may want to extract data from two tables — SalesQ1 and SalesQ2 — in the same database. You could use two separate SSIS Source adapters, extract each table separately, then combine the two data streams in SSIS using a Union All Component. But a simpler way would be to use a single Source adapter that uses a relational UNION ALL operator to combine the two tables directly:

```
--Extraction query using UNION ALL
SELECT --Get data from Sales Q1
    SalesOrderID,
    SubTotal
FROM
    Sales.SalesQ1

UNION ALL --Combine Sales Q1 and Sales Q2

SELECT --Get data from Sales Q2
    SalesOrderID,
    SubTotal
FROM
    Sales.SalesQ2
```

Here is another example. In this case, you need information from both the Product and the Subcategory table. Instead of retrieving both tables separately into SSIS and joining them there, you issued a single query to SQL and asked it to JOIN the two tables for you. See Chapter 7 for more information.

```
--Extraction query using a JOIN
SELECT
    p.ProductID,
    p.[Name]        AS ProductName,
    p.Color         AS ProductColor,
    sc.ProductSubcategoryID,
    sc.[Name]       AS SubcategoryName
FROM
    Production.Product AS p
INNER JOIN --JOIN
    Production.ProductSubcategory AS sc
ON p.ProductSubcategoryID = sc.ProductSubcategoryID;
```

SORT in the Database

SQL Server has intimate knowledge of the data stored in its tables, and as such it is highly efficient at operations such as sorting — especially because it has indexes to help it do the job. While SSIS allows you to sort data in the pipeline, you will find that for large datasets SQL Server is more proficient. As an example, you may need to retrieve data from a table, then immediately sort it so that a Merge Join Transformation can use it (the Merge Join Component requires pre-sorted inputs). You could sort the data in SSIS by using the Sort Transformation, but depending on your package design you may also be able to sort the data directly during extraction in the SELECT clause. Here is an example:

```
--Extraction query using a JOIN and a ORDER BY
SELECT
    p.ProductID,
    p.[Name]        AS ProductName,
    p.Color         AS ProductColor,
    sc.ProductSubcategoryID,
    sc.[Name]       AS SubcategoryName
FROM
    Production.Product AS p
INNER JOIN --JOIN
    Production.ProductSubcategory AS sc
ON p.ProductSubcategoryID = sc.ProductSubcategoryID
ORDER BY --SORT
    p.ProductID,
    sc.ProductSubcategoryID;
```

In this case, you are asking SQL Server to pre-sort the data, so that it arrives in SSIS already sorted. Because SQL Server is more efficient at sorting large datasets than SSIS, this may give you a good performance boost. See Chapter 7 for more information on why this is useful.

Note that the SSIS OLE DB and ADO.NET Source adapters submit queries to SQL Server in a pass-through manner — meaning that they do not parse the query in any useful way themselves. The ramification is that the Source adapters may not know that the data is coming back sorted. To work around this problem you need to tell the Source adapters that the data is ordered. Right-click the Source adapter and choose Show Advanced Editor. Go to the Input and Output Properties tab and click the root node for the default output (not the error output). In the property grid on the right-hand side you should see a property called IsSorted. Change this to True.

Setting the IsSorted property to true just tells the component that the data is pre-sorted, but it does not tell it in what order. So the next step is to select the columns that are being sorted on, and assign them values as follows: If the column is not sorted, the value should be zero. If the column is sorted in ascending order, the value should be positive. If the column is sorted in descending order, the value should be negative. The absolute value of the number should correspond to the column's position in the order list. For instance, if the query was sorted with ColumnA ascending, ColumnB descending, then you would assign the value 1 to ColumnA and the value -2 to ColumnB, with all other columns being set to 0. Be very careful when doing this — by specifying the sort order, you are by contract telling the system to trust that you know what you are talking about, and that the data is in fact sorted. If the data is not sorted, or it is sorted in a different manner to that you specified, then your package can act unpredictably, which could lead to data and integrity losses.

In Figure 11-4, the data is sorted by the SalesOrderID field. Expand the Output Columns Node under the default output node, and then select the SalesOrderID column. In the property grid set the SortKeyPosition value to 1. Now the Source adapter is aware that the query is returning a sorted dataset, and furthermore it knows exactly which columns are used for the sorting.

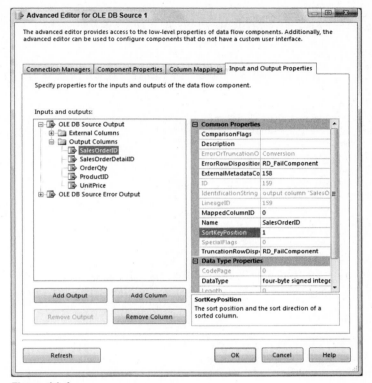

Figure 11-4

Modularize

If you find you have common queries that you keep using, then try and encapsulate those queries in the source system. This statement is based on ideal situations; in the real world you may not be allowed to touch the source system, but if you can, then here is the benefit. All you are doing is creating views, procedures, and functions that read the data — you are not writing any data changes into the source. Once the (perhaps complex) queries are encapsulated in the source, your queries can be used in multiple packages by multiple ETL developers. Here is an example:

```
USE SourceSystemDatabase;
GO

CREATE PROCEDURE dbo.up_DimCustomerExtract(@date DATETIME)
-- Test harness (also the query statement you'd use in the SSIS source adapter):
-- EXEC dbo.up_DimCustomerExtract '2004-12-20';
AS BEGIN
    SET NOCOUNT ON;

    SELECT
        --Convert to INT and alias using a friendlier name
```

```
            CONVERT(INT, CUSTOMER_ID)                   AS CustomerID
        --Trim whitespace, convert empty strings to NULL and alias
        ,NULLIF(LTRIM(RTRIM(CUSTOMER_NAME)), '')        AS CustomerName
        --Convert to BIT and use friendly alias
        ,CONVERT(BIT, ACTIVE_IND)                        AS IsActive
        ,CASE
            --Convert magic dates to NULL
            WHEN LOAD_DATE = '9999-12-31' THEN NULL
            --Convert date to smart surrogate INT of form YYYYMMDD
            ELSE CONVERT(INT, (CONVERT(NVARCHAR(8), LOAD_DATE, 112)))
        END AS LoadDateID --Alias using friendly name
    FROM
        dbo.Customers
    WHERE --Filter rows using input parameter
        LOAD_DATE = @date;

    SET NOCOUNT OFF;
END; --proc
GO
```

To use this stored procedure from SSIS, you would simply call it from within an OLE DB or ADO.NET Source adapter. The example shows a static value for the data parameter, but in your solution you would use a variable or expression instead, so that you could call the procedure using different date values. See Chapter 6 for more details.

```
EXEC dbo.up_DimCustomerExtract '2004-12-20';
```

Here are some notes on the benefits you have gained here:

❑   In this case you have encapsulated the query in a stored procedure, though you could have encased it in a user-defined function or view just as easily. A side benefit is that this complex query definition is not hidden away in the depths of the SSIS package — you can easily access it using SQL Server.

❑   The benefit of a function or procedure is that you can simply pass a parameter to the module (in this case @date) in order to filter the data (study the WHERE clause in the preceding code). Note, however, that SSIS Source adapters have difficulty parsing parameters in functions, so you may need to use a procedure instead (which SSIS has no problems with), or you can build a dynamic query in SSIS to call the function (see Chapter 6 for more information).

❑   If the logic of this query changes — perhaps you need to filter in a different way, or maybe you need to point the query at an alternative set of tables — then you can simply change the definition in one place, and all the callers of the function will get the benefit. However, there is a risk here too — if you change the query by (say) removing a column, then the packages consuming the function might break, because they are suddenly missing a column they previously expected. Make sure any such query updates go through a formal change management process in order to mitigate this risk.

SQL Server Does Text Files Too

It is a common pattern for source systems to export nightly batches of data into text files, and for the ETL solution to pick up those batches and process them. This is typically done using a Flat File Source adapter in SSIS, and in general you will find SSIS is the best tool for the job. However, in some cases you may want to treat the text file as a relational source and sort it, join it, or perform calculations on it in the manner described in the previous tenets. Because the text file lives on disk, and it is a file not a database, this is not possible — or is it?

SQL Server includes a table-valued function called OPENROWSET that is an ad hoc method of connecting and accessing remote data using OLE DB from within the SQL engine. In this context, you can use it to access text data, using the OPENROWSET(BULK...) variation of the function.

> *Note that the use of the* OPENROWSET *and* OPENQUERY *statements has security ramifications, so they should be used with care in a controlled environment. If you want to test this functionality, you may need to enable the functions in the SQL Server Surface Area Configuration Tool. Alternatively, use the TSQL configuration function as shown in the following code. Remember to turn this functionality off again after testing it (unless you have adequately mitigated any security risks). See Books Online for more information.*

```
sp_configure 'show advanced options', 1; --Show advanced configuration options
--Switch on OPENROWSET functionality
GO
RECONFIGURE;
GO

sp_configure 'Ad Hoc Distributed Queries', 1; --Switch on specific functionality
GO
RECONFIGURE;
GO

sp_configure 'show advanced options', 0; --Remember to hide advanced options
GO
RECONFIGURE;
GO
```

The SQL Server documentation has loads of information on how to use these two functions, but here is a basic example to demonstrate the concepts. First create a text file with the following data in it. Use a comma to separate each column value. Save the text file using the name BulkImport.txt in a folder of your choice.

```
1,AdventureWorks
2,Acme Apples Inc
3,Northwind Traders
```

Next create a format file that will help SQL Server understand how your custom flat file is laid out. You can create the format file manually or you can get SQL Server to generate it for you: Create a table in the database where you want to use the format file (you can delete the table later; it is just a shortcut to build the format file). Execute the following statement in SQL Server Management Studio — for this example we are using the AdventureWorks2008 database to create the table, but you can use any database because you will delete the table afterwards. The table schema should match the layout of the file.

```
--Create temporary table to define the flat file schema
USE AdventureWorks2008
GO

CREATE TABLE BulkImport(ID INT, CustomerName NVARCHAR(50));
```

Next open up a command prompt, navigate to the folder where you saved the `BulkImport.txt` file and type the following command, replacing "AdventureWorks2008" with the database where you created the BulkImport table:

```
bcp AdventureWorks2008..BulkImport format nul -c -t, -x -f BulkImport.fmt -T
```

If you look in the folder where you created the data file, you should now have another file called `BulkImport.fmt`. This is an XML file that describes the column schema of your flat file — well actually it describes the column schema of the table you created, but hopefully you created the table schema to match the file. Here is what the format file should look like:

```
<?xml version="1.0"?>
<BCPFORMAT xmlns="http://schemas.microsoft.com/sqlserver/2004/bulkload/format"
xmlns:xsi="http://www.w3.org/2001/XMLSchema-instance">
 <RECORD>
  <FIELD ID="1" xsi:type="CharTerm" TERMINATOR="," MAX_LENGTH="12"/>
  <FIELD ID="2" xsi:type="CharTerm" TERMINATOR="\r\n" MAX_LENGTH="100"
    COLLATION="SQL_Latin1_General_CP1_CI_AS"/>
 </RECORD>
 <ROW>
  <COLUMN SOURCE="1" NAME="ID" xsi:type="SQLINT"/>
  <COLUMN SOURCE="2" NAME="CustomerName" xsi:type="SQLNVARCHAR"/>
 </ROW>
</BCPFORMAT>
```

Remember to delete the temporary table (BulkImport) you created because you don't need it anymore. If you have done everything right, you should now be able to use the text file in the context of a relational query. Type the following query into SQL Server Management Studio, replacing the file paths with the exact folder path and names of the two files you created:

```
--Select data from a text file as if it was a table
SELECT
    T.* --SELECT * used for illustration purposes only
FROM OPENROWSET( --This is the magic function
    BULK 'D:\Data\BulkImport.txt', --Path to data file
    FORMATFILE = 'D:\Data\BulkImport.fmt' --Path to format file
) AS T; --Command requires a table alias
```

When you execute this command you should get back rows in the same format as if they had come from a relational table. To prove that SQL Server is treating this result set in the same manner it would treat any relational data, try using the results in the context of more complex operations such as sorting:

```
--Selecting from a text file and sorting the results
SELECT
    T.OrgID, --Not using SELECT * anymore
    T.OrgName
FROM OPENROWSET(
    BULK 'D:\Data\BulkImport.txt',
```

```
        FORMATFILE = 'D:\Data\BulkImport.fmt'
) AS T(OrgID, OrgName) --For fun, give the columns different aliases
ORDER BY T.OrgName DESC; --Sort the results in descending order
```

New in SQL Server 2008 is the ability to declare if and how the text file is pre-sorted. If the system that produced the text file did so in a sorted manner, then you can inform SQL Server of that fact. Note that this is a contract by you, the developer, to SQL Server. SQL Server will use something called a streaming assertion when reading the text file to double-check your claims, but there are cases where this can really help with performance. Later on you will see how this ordering contract helps with the MERGE operator, but here's a simple example to demonstrate the savings.

Run the following query; note how you are asking for the data to be sorted by OrgID this time. Also note that you have asked SQL Server to show you the query plan that it uses to run the query:

```
SET STATISTICS PROFILE ON; --Show query plan

SELECT
    T.OrgID,
    T.OrgName
FROM OPENROWSET(
    BULK 'D:\Data\BulkImport.txt',
    FORMATFILE = 'D:\Data\BulkImport.fmt'
) AS T(OrgID, OrgName)
ORDER BY T.OrgID ASC; --Sort the results by OrgID
```

Have a look at the query plan that SQL Server generates. The query plan shows the internal operations SQL Server has to perform to generate the results. Of particular interest note the second operation, which is a SORT:

```
SELECT     <...snipped...>
  |--Sort(ORDER BY:([BULK].[OrgID] ASC))
       |--Remote Scan(OBJECT:(STREAM))
```

This is obvious and expected; you asked SQL Server to sort the data and it does as requested. Well here's the trick — in this case the text file happened to be pre-sorted by OrgID anyway, so the sort you requested was actually redundant. (Have a look at the text data file; the ID values increase monotonically from 1 to 3.)

Let's prove that fact. Type the same query into SQL again, but this time use the OPENROWSET(...ORDER) clause:

```
SET STATISTICS PROFILE ON; --Show query plan

SELECT
    T.OrgID,
    T.OrgName
FROM OPENROWSET(
    BULK 'D:\Data\BulkImport.txt',
    FORMATFILE = 'D:\Data\BulkImport.fmt',
    ORDER (OrgID ASC) --Declare the text file is already sorted by OrgID
) AS T(OrgID, OrgName)
ORDER BY T.OrgID ASC; --Sort the results by OrgID
```

Once again you have asked for the data to be sorted, but you have also contractually declared that the source file is already pre-sorted. Have a look at the new query plan. Here's the interesting result; even though you asked SQL Server to sort the result in the final ORDER BY clause, it didn't bother doing so because you told it (and it confirmed) that the file was already ordered as such:

```
SELECT    <...snipped...>
  |--Assert <...snipped...>
      |--Sequence Project(<...snipped...>)
          |--Segment
              |--Remote Scan(OBJECT:(STREAM))
```

As you can see, there is no SORT operation in the plan. There are other operators, but they are just assertions that are very cheap and are checking the contract you specified is true. For instance, if a row arrived that was not ordered in the fashion you declared, the statement would fail. The streaming assertion check is cheaper than a redundant sort operation, and it's good logic to have in place in case you got the ordering wrong, or the source system one day starts outputting data in a different order than you expected.

So after all that, why is this useful to SSIS? Here are a few examples:

❑ You may intend loading a text file in SSIS and then immediately joining it to a relational table. Now you could do all that within one SELECT statement, using a single OLE DB or ADO.NET Source Component.

❑ Some of the SSIS Components expect sorted inputs (for instance the Merge Join Component). Assuming the source is a text file, instead of sorting the data in SSIS you can sort it in SQL Server. If the text file happens to be pre-sorted you can declare it as such and save even more time and expense.

❑ The Lookup Component in SQL Server 2005 could only populate its cache from relational tables. Now you can populate it with data from text files too. In SQL Server 2008 the Lookup Component can populate data from almost anywhere (see Chapter 7), but this still may prove a useful technique in some scenarios.

Be careful when using this technique. If the source data file changes in structure (for instance, a column is dropped), and you don't keep the format file in sync, then the query will fail. If the format file gets deleted or corrupted, the query will also fail. However, if you can protect against these kinds of issues, this technique can be a boon to your development efforts.

Use Set-Based Logic

The premise here is simple; avoid any use of cursors like the plague. Cursors are nearly always avoidable, and they should only be used as a final resort. Try out the following features and see if they can help you build efficient TSQL operations:

❑ Common Table Expressions allow you to modularize sub-sections of your queries, and also support recursive constructs so you can, for instance, retrieve a self-linked (parent-child) organizational hierarchy using a single SQL statement.

❑ Table valued parameters allow you to pass arrays into stored procedures as variables. This means that you can program your stored procedure logic using the equivalent of dynamic arrays.

❑ UNION is now joined by its close cousins, INTERSECT and EXCEPT, which complete the primitive set of operations you need to perform set arithmetic. UNION joins two rowsets together, INTERSECT finds their common members, and EXCEPT finds the members that are present in one rowset but not the other.

Here is an example where you can bring all these ideas together. The example scenario is that you have two tables of data, both representing customers. The challenge is to group the data into three subsets: one set containing the customers that exist in the first table only, the second set containing customers that exist in the second table only, and the third set containing the customers that exist in both the tables. The specific example illustrates the power and elegance of common table expressions (CTEs) and the set-arithmetic statements. If you remember Venn diagrams from school, then what we are trying to achieve is the relational equivalent of the diagram shown in Figure 11-5.

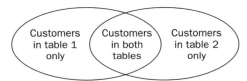

Figure 11-5

Following is a single statement that will partition the data as required. This statement is not meant to convey good programming practice, because it is not the most optimal or concise query you could write to derive these results. It is simply meant to demonstrate the manner in which these constructs can be used. By studying the verbose form you may appreciate the elegance, composability, and self-documenting nature of the syntax.

For convenience you will use related tables from AdventureWorks2008 and AdventureWorksDW2008. Note how you use multiple CTE structures to generate intermediate results (though the query optimizer is smart enough to not execute the statements separately). Also notice the use of UNION, EXCEPT, and INTERSECT to derive specific results:

```
WITH SourceRows AS ( --CTE containing all source rows
    SELECT BusinessEntityID AS ContactID
    FROM AdventureWorks2008.Person.Person
),
DestinationRows(ContactID) AS ( --CTE containing all destination rows
    SELECT CONVERT(INT, RIGHT(CustomerAlternateKey, 8))
    FROM AdventureWorksDW2008.dbo.DimCustomer
),
RowsInSourceOnly AS ( --CTE: rows where ContactID is in source only
    SELECT ContactID FROM SourceRows --select from previous CTE
    EXCEPT --EXCEPT means 'subtract'
    SELECT ContactID FROM DestinationRows --select from previous CTE
),
RowsInSourceAndDestination AS( --CTE: ContactID in both source & destination
    SELECT ContactID FROM SourceRows
    INTERSECT --INTERSECT means 'find the overlap'
```

```
        SELECT ContactID FROM DestinationRows
),
RowsInDestinationOnly AS ( --CTE: ContactID in destination only
     SELECT ContactID FROM DestinationRows
     EXCEPT --Simply doing the EXCEPT the other way around
     SELECT ContactID FROM SourceRows
),
RowLocation(ContactID, Location) AS ( --Final CTE
     SELECT ContactID, 'Source Only' FROM RowsInSourceOnly
     UNION ALL --UNION means 'add'
     SELECT ContactID, 'Both' FROM RowsInSourceAndDestination
     UNION ALL
     SELECT ContactID, 'Destination Only' FROM RowsInDestinationOnly
)
SELECT * FROM RowLocation --Generate final result
ORDER BY ContactID;
```

Here is a sample of the results:

```
ContactID    Location
-----------  ----------------
10998        Source Only
10999        Source Only
11000        Both
. . .
19977        Both
19978        Destination Only
19979        Destination Only
```

SQL Server provides many powerful tools to use in your data extraction arsenal. Learn about them and then start using the SQL engine and SSIS in concert to deliver optimal extraction routines. The list presented previously is not exhaustive; there are many other similar techniques you can use to improve the value of the solutions you deliver.

SQL Server 2008 Change Data Capture

Even though this topic is still concerned with extraction, it is important enough that it deserves a section of its own. Note that Change Data Capture (CDC) is covered extensively in Books Online (by the actual developer of CDC), and demonstrated in more detail in the related www.codeplex.com samples.

If you are running nightly batches for your ETL, you want to make sure you are only processing the most recent data — for instance, just the data from the preceding day's operations. You do not want to go back and process every transaction from the last five years during each night's batch. However, that's the ideal world, and sometimes the source system is not able to tell you which rows belong to the time window you need.

This problem space is typically called Change Data Capture, or CDC. The term refers to the fact that you want to capture just the changed data from the source system within a specified window of time.

The changes may include inserts, updates, and deletes, and the required window of time may vary anything from "give me the changes from the last few minutes" all the way through to "give me all the changes for the last day/week/and so on." The key requisite to CDC solutions is that they need to identify the rows that were affected since a specific, granular point in time.

There are some common techniques to handle this problem, such as:

❑ Adding new date/time columns to the source system. This is usually not feasible, either because it is a legacy system and no one knows how to add new functionality, or it is possible but the risk and change management cost is too high, or simply because the DBA or data steward won't let you! On some systems, such as ERP applications, this change is impossible due to the sheer number and size of tables and the prohibitive cost thereof.

❑ Adding triggers to the source system. Such triggers may watch for any data changes and then write an audit record to a separate logging table that the ETL then uses as a source. Though this is less invasive than the previous method, the same challenges apply. An issue here is that every database operation now incurs more I/O cost — when a row is inserted or updated the original table is updated, and then the new log table is updated too in a synchronous manner. This can lead to decreased performance in the application.

❑ Complex queries. It is academically possible to write long complex queries that compare every source row/column to every destination column; but practically speaking this is usually not an alternative because the development and performance costs are too high.

❑ Dump and reload. Sometimes there is no way around the problem, and you are forced to delete and recopy the complete set of data every night. For small datasets, this may not be a problem, but once you start getting into the terabyte range you are in trouble. This is the worst possible situation and one of the biggest drivers for non-intrusive low-impact CDC solutions.

❑ Third-party solutions. There are software vendors that specialize in CDC solutions for many different databases and applications. This is a good option to look into, because the vendors have the experience and expertise to build robust and high-performance tools.

❑ There are other solutions besides the ones mentioned, such as using queues and application events, but some of these are non-generic and tightly coupled.

❑ Last, but not least — and the subject of this section in the chapter — is new functionality in SQL Server 2008 called Change Data Capture, which provides CDC right out-of-the-box. This technology is delivered by the SQL Replication team, but was designed in concert with the SSIS team. Note that there is another new similarly named technology in SQL Server 2008 called Change Tracking, which is a synchronous technique that could also be used in some CDC scenarios.

Benefits of SQL Server 2008 CDC

Here are some of the benefits that SQL Server 2008 CDC (hereafter referred to as CDC) provides you:

❑ **Low impact:** You do not need to change your source schema tables in order to support CDC. Other techniques for change data capture, such as triggers and replication, require that you add new columns (such as timestamps and GUIDs) to the tables you are interested in tracking. With CDC, you can be up and running immediately without changing the schema. Obviously your source system needs to be hosted on SQL Server 2008 in order to take advantage of the CDC functionality.

❑ **Low overhead:** The CDC process is a job that runs asynchronously in the background, and reads the changes off the SQL Server transaction log. What this means in plain English is that unlike triggers, any updates to the source data do not incur a synchronous write to a logging table. Rather, the writes are delayed until the server is idle, or the writes can be delayed until a time that you specify (for instance 2 A.M. every morning).

❑ **Granular configuration:** The CDC process allows you to configure the feature on a per-table basis, which means it is not an all-or-nothing proposition. You can try it out on one table, and once you iron out any issues, you can slowly start using it on more tables.

❑ **High fidelity capture:** The technology flags which rows were inserted, updated, and deleted. It can also tell you exactly which columns changed during updates. Other auditing details such as the event timestamp, as well as the specific transaction ID are also provided.

❑ **High fidelity requests:** The CDC infrastructure allows you to make very granular requests to the CDC store, so that you can find out exactly when certain operations occurred. For instance, you can ask for changes within any batch window ranging from a few minutes (near real time) through to hours, days, weeks, or more. You can ask for the final aggregated image of the rows, and you can ask for the intermediate changes too.

❑ **Ease of use:** The APIs that you use to request the data are based on the same SQL semantics you are already used to — SELECT statements, user-defined functions, and stored procedures.

❑ **Resilient to change:** The replication team built the technology with change management in mind, meaning that if you set up CDC to work on a certain table, and someone adds or deletes a column in that table, the process is robust enough in most cases to continue running while you make the appropriate fixes. This means that you don't lose data (and you don't lose sleep!).

❑ **Transactional consistency:** The operations enable you to request changes in a transactionally consistent manner. For instance, if two tables in the source were updated within the context of the same source transaction, you have the means to establish that fact and retrieve the related changes together.

The purpose of this section is not to delve into every last detail of CDC; rather the goal is to explore how to use CDC in the context of SSIS and ETL in general. For more in-depth details on the technology and considerations around planning, security, operations, and administration, please see Books Online and other resources on www.microsoft.com/sql. There are also samples on www.codeplex.com that use SQL and SSIS together to deliver a CDC solution.

Preparation

There are a few steps you need to take to get CDC working. Once again, CDC is intended for sources that reside on a SQL Server 2008 database. If your data resides on an earlier version of SQL Server or another vendor's solution, unless you migrate the data, this solution is probably not for you. However, you may still want to test the waters and see what benefits you can gain from the functionality — in which case find yourself a test server and follow these same steps.

> *CDC is also only available on certain editions of SQL Server, namely SQL Server 2008 Enterprise, Developer, and Evaluation editions.*

First, the DBA or a member of the SQL sysadmin fixed server role needs to enable CDC on the SQL Server 2008 database. This is a very important point; there should be a clear separation of roles and duties, and open dialog between the DBA and the ETL developer. The ETL developer may be tempted to turn CDC on for every single table, but that is a bad idea. Although CDC has low overhead, it does not have zero overhead. The DBA, on the other hand, may be protective of their data store and not want anyone to touch it.

Whether the DBA and the ETL developer are different individuals or the same person, the respective parties should consider the pros and cons of the solution from all angles. Books Online has more details on these considerations, so once again let's forge ahead with the understanding that much of this may be prototypical.

The rest of this topic will assume that you are using AdventureWorks2008 on a SQL Server 2008 installation. Here is how to enable the functionality at a database level:

```
USE AdventureWorks2008;
GO


--Enable CDC on the database
EXEC sys.sp_cdc_enable_db;
GO


--Check CDC is enabled on the database
SELECT name, is_cdc_enabled
FROM sys.databases WHERE database_id = DB_ID();
```

When you flip this switch at the database level, SQL Server sets up some of the required infrastructure that you will need later. For instance, it creates a database schema called cdc as well as the appropriate security, functions, and procedures.

The next step is to ensure that SQL Server Agent is running on the same server you just enabled CDC on. Agent allows you to schedule when the CDC process will crawl the database logs and write entries to the capture instance tables (also known as shadow tables; we will use the two terms interchangeably). If these terms make no sense to you right now, don't worry; they will later. The important thing to do at this point is to use SQL Server 2008 Configuration Manager to ensure that Agent is running. Once again, because this chapter is not focused on the deep technical details of CDC itself, but rather on how to use its functionality within the context of ETL, you will need to visit Books Online if you are not sure how to get Agent running.

Next, you can enable CDC functionality on the tables of your choice. Run the following command in order to enable CDC on the HumanResources.Employee table:

```
USE AdventureWorks2008;
GO


--Enable CDC on a specific table
EXECUTE sys.sp_cdc_enable_table
     @source_schema = N'HumanResources'
    ,@source_name = N'Employee'
    ,@role_name = N'cdc_Admin'
    ,@capture_instance = N'HumanResources_Employee'
    ,@supports_net_changes = 1;
```

The `supports_net_changes` option allows you to retrieve only the final image of a row, even if it was updated multiple times within the time window you specified. If there were no problems then you should see the following message displayed in the output of the query editor:

```
Job 'cdc.AdventureWorks2008_capture' started successfully.
Job 'cdc.AdventureWorks2008_cleanup' started successfully.
```

If you want to verify that CDC is enabled for any particular table, you can issue a command of the following form:

```
--Check CDC is enabled on the table
SELECT [name], is_tracked_by_cdc FROM sys.tables
WHERE [object_id] = OBJECT_ID(N'HumanResources.Employee');

--Alternatively, use the built-in CDC help procedure
EXECUTE sys.sp_cdc_help_change_data_capture
    @source_schema = N'HumanResources',
    @source_name = N'Employee';
GO
```

Well done. If all has gone well, the CDC process is now alive and well and watching the source table for any changes.

You used the default configuration for setting up CDC on a table, but there are optional parameters that allow you much more power. For instance, you can configure exactly which columns should and shouldn't be tracked, the filegroup where the shadow table should live, and enable other modes. For now, simple is good, so the next step is to have a look at what SQL Server has done for you.

Capture Instance Tables

Capture Instance tables are also known as shadow tables and change tables; these are the tables that SQL Server creates behind the scenes to help the magic of CDC happen. Here is how the CDC process works:

1. The end user makes a data change in the source system table you are tracking. SQL Server writes the changes to the database log, and it then writes the changes to the database. Note that SQL Server always does the log-write (and always has) regardless of whether or not CDC is enabled — in other words the database log is not a new feature of CDC, but CDC makes good use of it.

2. There is a process that runs on server idle time, or on a scheduled interval (controlled by SQL Server Agent) that reads the changes back out of the log and writes them to a separate change tracking (shadow) table with a special schema. In other words, the user wrote the change to the database; the change was implicitly written to the SQL log; the CDC process read it back out the log and wrote it to a separate table. Why not write it to the second table in the first place? The reason is that synchronous writes are impactful to the source system; the user may experience slow application performance if their update caused two separate writes to two separate tables. By using an asynchronous log reader, the DBA can amortize the writes to the shadow table over a longer period. Of course, you may decide to schedule the Agent job to run on a highly frequent basis, in which case the experience may be almost synchronous, but that is an ETL implementation decision. Normally the log reader will run during idle time or when the users are not using the system, so there is little to no application performance overhead.

3. The ETL process then reads the data out of the change table and uses it to populate the destination. We will get to this section later; for now let's continue to study the SQL change tables.

Note that there is a default schedule that prunes the data in the change tables to keep the contents down to three days worth of data, in order to prevent the amount of CDC data from becoming unwieldy. You should change this default configuration to suit your specific needs.

When you enabled CDC on the HumanResources.Employee table, SQL used a default naming convention to create a shadow table in the same database called cdc.HumanResources_Employee_CT. The table has the same schema as the source table, but it also has several extra metadata columns that CDC needs to do its magic. Issue the following command to see what the shadow table looks like. There should be no rows in the table right now, so you will get back an empty result set.

```
SELECT * FROM cdc.HumanResources_Employee_CT;
```

Here is a brief overview of the main metadata columns. The __$start_lsn and __$seqval columns identify the original transaction and order that the operations occurred in. These are important values — the API (which we will look at later) operates purely in terms of the LSNs (commit log sequence numbers). But you can easily map date/time values to and from LSNs to make things simpler.

The __$operation column shows the source operation that caused the change (1 = delete, 2 = insert, 3 = update (before image), 4 = update (after image), and 5 = merge).

The __$update_mask column contains a bit mask to tell you which specific columns changed during an update. It tells you what columns changed on a row-by-row basis; however, the mask is just a bitmap, so you need to map the ordinal position of each bit to the column name that it represents. CDC provides functions such as sys.fn_cdc_has_column_changed to help you make sense of these masks.

OK, now for the exciting part. Make a data change in the source table and then have a look at the shadow table again to see what happened. To keep it simple, update one specific field on the source table using the following command. Remember that the process runs asynchronously, so you may have to wait a few seconds before the changes appear in the shadow table. So after running the following statement, wait a few seconds and then run the preceding SELECT statement again.

```
--Make an update to the source table
UPDATE HumanResources.Employee
    SET HireDate = DATEADD(day, 1, HireDate)
WHERE BusinessEntityID IN (1, 2, 3);
```

Instead of waiting for the asynchronous log reader process to occur, you can also force the process to happen on demand by issuing the command:

```
--Force CDC log crawl
EXEC sys.sp_cdc_start_job;
```

The shadow table should contain two rows for every source row you updated. Why two rows, when you only performed one update per row? The reason is that for updates, the change table contains the before and after images of the affected rows. Now try inserting or deleting a row in the source and have a look at what rows get added to the shadow table.

The CDC API

The previous section was just academic background on what is happening; you don't actually need all this knowledge in order to apply the solution to the problem at hand. CDC provides a set of functions and procedures that abstract away the details of the technology and make it very simple to use. When you enabled CDC on the table, SQL automatically generated several function wrappers for you so that you can query the shadow table with ease. Here is an example:

```
USE AdventureWorks2008;
GO

--Let's check for all changes since the same time yesterday
DECLARE @begin_time AS DATETIME = GETDATE() - 1;
--Let's check for changes up to right now
DECLARE @end_time AS DATETIME = GETDATE();

--Map the time intervals to a CDC query range (using LSNs)
DECLARE @from_lsn AS BINARY(10)
    = sys.fn_cdc_map_time_to_lsn('smallest greater than or equal', @begin_time);
DECLARE @to_lsn AS BINARY(10)
    = sys.fn_cdc_map_time_to_lsn('largest less than or equal', @end_time);

--Validate @from_lsn using the minimum LSN available in the capture instance
DECLARE @min_lsn AS BINARY(10)
    = sys.fn_cdc_get_min_lsn('HumanResources_Employee');
IF @from_lsn < @min_lsn SET @from_lsn = @min_lsn;

--Return the NET changes that occurred within the specified time
SELECT * FROM
    cdc.fn_cdc_get_net_changes_HumanResources_Employee(@from_lsn, @to_lsn,
      N'all with mask');
```

The CDC functions only understand LSNs. So the first thing you do is to map the date/time values to LSN numbers, being careful to check the minimum and maximum extents. You then call a wrapper function for the table called `cdc.fn_cdc_get_net_changes_<table name>()`, which returns the rows that have changed. You specify `all with mask`, which means that the __$update_mask column is populated to tell you which columns changed. If you don't need the mask, just specify `all`, because calculating the mask is expensive. The `all` and `all with mask` options both populate the __$operation column accordingly.

If you had used the parameter value `all with merge`, the same results would come back, but the __$operation flag would only contain either 1 (delete) or 5 (merge). This is useful if you only need to know whether the row was deleted or changed, but do not care what the specific change was. This option is computationally cheaper for SQL to execute. If you use the TSQL MERGE operator (discussed later in this chapter) in combination with CDC, then this option makes the most sense, because you can leave it up to MERGE to figure out whether to insert, update, or delete the destination row.

The function you used in this example returns the net changes for the table — meaning that if any specific row had multiple updates applied against it in the source system, the result you would get back would be the net combined result of those changes. For instance, if someone inserted a row and then later on (within the same batch window) updated that same row twice, the function would return a row marked as Inserted (__$operation =2), but the data columns would reflect the latest values after the second update. Net changes are most likely what you will use for loading your warehouse, because they give you the final image of the row at the end of the specified window, and do not encumber you with any interim values the row might have had. For some near-real-time scenarios, and applications such as auditing and compliance tracking, you may require the interim values too.

Instead of asking for only the net changes to the source table, you can also ask for the granular (interim) changes. To do this you use another function that DC automatically generated for you, in this case called `cdc.fn_cdc_get_all_changes_<table name>()`. Here is an example of using the update mask and the all-changes mode together:

```
USE AdventureWorks2008;
GO

--First update another column besides the HireDate so we can
--test the difference in behavior
UPDATE HumanResources.Employee
    SET VacationHours = VacationHours + 1
WHERE BusinessEntityID IN (3, 4, 5);

WAITFOR DELAY '00:00:10'; --Wait 10s to let the log reader catch up

--Map times to LSNs as we did previously
DECLARE @begin_time AS DATETIME = GETDATE() - 1;
DECLARE @end_time AS DATETIME = GETDATE();
DECLARE @from_lsn AS BINARY(10)
  = sys.fn_cdc_map_time_to_lsn('smallest greater than or equal', @begin_time);
DECLARE @to_lsn AS BINARY(10)
  = sys.fn_cdc_map_time_to_lsn('largest less than or equal', @end_time);
DECLARE @min_lsn AS BINARY(10)
  = sys.fn_cdc_get_min_lsn('HumanResources_Employee');
IF @from_lsn < @min_lsn SET @from_lsn = @min_lsn;

--Get the ordinal position(s) of the column(s) we want to track
DECLARE @hiredate_ord INT
  = sys.fn_cdc_get_column_ordinal(N'HumanResources_Employee', N'HireDate');
DECLARE @vac_hr_ord INT
  = sys.fn_cdc_get_column_ordinal(N'HumanResources_Employee', N'VacationHours');

--Return ALL the changes and a flag to tell us if the HireDate changed
SELECT
    BusinessEntityID,
    --Boolean value to indicate whether hire date was changed
    sys.fn_cdc_is_bit_set(@hiredate_ord, __$update_mask) AS [HireDateChg],
    --Boolean value to indicate whether vacation hours was changed in the source
    sys.fn_cdc_is_bit_set(@vac_hr_ord, __$update_mask) AS [VacHoursChg]
FROM
    cdc.fn_cdc_get_all_changes_HumanResources_Employee(@from_lsn, @to_lsn, N'all');
```

This call should return every row from the shadow table without aggregating them into a net-changes view. This is useful if your destination system needs to track everything that happened to a source table, including interim values. It includes two BIT fields that indicate whether specific columns were changed.

If you want to disable CDC on a table, use a command of the following form. Be careful though; this command will drop the shadow table and any data it contains.

```
EXECUTE sys.sp_cdc_disable_table
    @source_schema = N'HumanResources',
    @source_name = N'Employee',
    @capture_instance = N'HumanResources_Employee';
```

Using CDC from within SSIS

Knowing the row operation and which columns changed on a row-by-row basis helps you build robust and efficient ETL solutions. Your SSIS packages can use the CDC output to make informed decisions on which rows are new and thus need to be inserted, which rows are updated and thus need to be updated in the destination, and which rows need to be deleted (less common in data warehouses).

After setting up the infrastructure described in the previous sections, you can use the same function calls directly from within the SSIS Source adapters. Alternatively you can wrap the logic up in a stored procedure that you can call from SSIS. Here is a basic implementation of a stored procedure to demonstrate the concept:

```
USE AdventureWorks2008;
GO

CREATE PROCEDURE dbo.CDC_GetHREmployee(@begin_time DATETIME, @end_time DATETIME)
AS BEGIN
    SET NOCOUNT ON;

    --Map the time intervals to a CDC query range (using LSNs)
    DECLARE @from_lsn AS BINARY(10)
      = sys.fn_cdc_map_time_to_lsn('smallest greater than or equal', @begin_time);
    DECLARE @to_lsn AS BINARY(10)
      = sys.fn_cdc_map_time_to_lsn('largest less than or equal', @end_time);
    DECLARE @min_lsn AS BINARY(10)
      = sys.fn_cdc_get_min_lsn('HumanResources_Employee');
    IF @from_lsn < @min_lsn SET @from_lsn = @min_lsn;

    --Get the ordinal position(s) of the column(s) we want to track
    DECLARE @hiredate_ord INT
      = sys.fn_cdc_get_column_ordinal(N'HumanResources_Employee',N'HireDate');
    DECLARE @vac_hr_ord INT
      = sys.fn_cdc_get_column_ordinal(N'HumanResources_Employee',N'VacationHours');

    --Return ALL changes & flags to tell us if HireDate & VacationHours changed
    SELECT
        BusinessEntityID,
        BirthDate,
        HireDate,
        VacationHours,
        sys.fn_cdc_is_bit_set(@hiredate_ord, __$update_mask) AS [HireDtChg],
```

```
        sys.fn_cdc_is_bit_set(@vac_hr_ord, __$update_mask) AS [VacHoursChg],
        __$operation AS [_Operation] --Include the operation type
    FROM
        cdc.fn_cdc_get_net_changes_HumanResources_Employee(@from_lsn, @to_lsn,
         N'all with mask');

    SET NOCOUNT OFF;
END; --proc
GO
```

You can test that the procedure works as expected using a command like this:

```
--Try calling the procedure
DECLARE @begin_time AS DATETIME = GETDATE() - 1;
DECLARE @end_time AS DATETIME = GETDATE();

EXEC dbo.CDC_GetHREmployee @begin_time, @end_time;
```

One of the big advantages of CDC is that it provides enough information for you to easily develop slowly changing dimension logic in your packages. For rows that are flagged as updates, you can use the update mask functionality within a Conditional Split Transformation to send rows that qualify as SCD-2 updates down a different branch to those that qualify as SCD-1 updates.

Let's build a package to use these concepts. Imagine you want to build a solution whereby all updates are SCD-1 (inline update) unless the HireDate value changed, in which case the row should be treated as an SCD-2 (insert). Open up BIDS, and create a new package. Create a new variable called StartTime and set its type to DateTime with a default value of yesterday's date or earlier. Create another variable called EndTime also of type DateTime and set its default value to tomorrow's date or later, all as shown in Figure 11-6.

You are purposefully choosing an extremely wide date range in order to ensure you get all the rows. These variables represent the start and end time of the batch window, so later on you can try changing them to shorter ranges and seeing what happens. In a real solution, you should set the value of these dates according to the current date and the required batch window.

Figure 11-6

Next you need to create a new Data Flow Task and in it set up an OLE DB Source Component, pointing it at the AdventureWorks2008 database. Choose query mode, and in the query pane enter the following text:

```
EXEC dbo.CDC_GetHREmployee ?, ?
```

This statement tells the Source adapter to call the procedure called `CDC_GetHREmployee` in the AdventureWorks2008 database, and pass the procedure two parameters. Click the Parameters button and map the two parameters to the `StartTime` and `EndTime` variables, as shown in Figure 11-7. Remember to also rename the default parameter names to match those in the stored procedure.

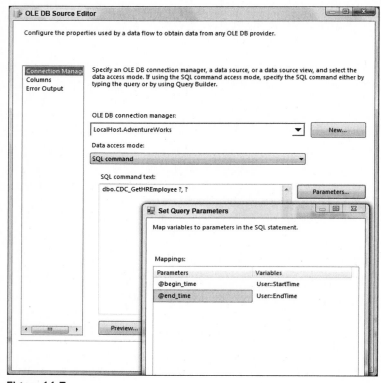

Figure 11-7

Click OK twice to close the edit screens and go back to the package editor. Drop a Conditional Split Transformation on the design surface and connect the Source Component to it. Open the Conditional Split Editor and enter the following conditions:

Order	Output Name	Condition
1	DeleteOutput	_Operation == 1
2	InsertOutput	_Operation == 2
3	SCD2Output	_Operation == 4 && HireDtChg
4	SCD1Output	_Operation == 4

Name the default output "ElseOutput". You will not actually write the data to the destination because the focus of this section is on extraction; instead you will just count the number of rows going down each branch. You can imagine that a real package would do something more useful with each set of rows.

Create five new variables in the package called (say) rc1, rc2, rc3, rc4, and rc5, and make them all of type Int32. Drop five Row Count Components on the package and connect each of the five outputs of the Conditional Split to the Row Count Components one at a time. Open up each Row Count Component and associate each one with a different one of the variables you just created.

Using SQL Server Management Studio, try adding new rows into the source table in the database, delete other rows, and make some updates. Execute the package and note how many rows flow down each input. If you had inserted or deleted any rows in the source table, you should see them flow down the insert and delete paths. The updates flow down the SCD2 branch if and only if the hire date changed. All other updates flow down the SCD1 branch. You can put a Data Viewer grid on some of the paths to see what data flows through them, as shown in Figure 11-8.

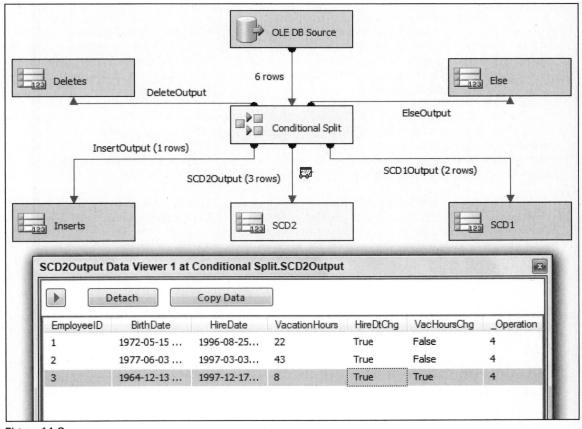

Figure 11-8

CDC gives you powerful capabilities to track changes in your source system without requiring any schema changes. It runs in an asynchronous manner and so incurs minimal operational overhead on the source. Once you get the basics right, it is simple to configure and use within SSIS — and most importantly it allows you to build elegant, robust, and high-performance ETL solutions that load only the delta.

Data Loading

The next major section focuses on data loading. Many of the same techniques presented in the data extraction section apply here too, so the focus will be on areas that have not been covered before.

Database Snapshots

Database snapshots were introduced in SQL Server 2005 as a way to persist the state of a database at a specific point in time. The underlying technology is referred to as copy-on-first-write, which is a fancy way of saying that once you create the database snapshot, it is relatively cheap to maintain because it only tracks things that have changed since the database snapshot was created. Once you have created a database snapshot you can change the primary database in any way, for instance changing rows, creating indexes, and dropping tables. If at any stage you want to revert all your changes back to when you created the database snapshot, you can do that very easily by doing a database restore using the database snapshot as the media source.

In concept, the technology sounds very similar to backup and restore; the key difference being that this is a completely online operation, and depending on your data loads, the operations can be near instantaneous. This is because when you create the snapshot, it is a metadata operation only — you do not physically "back up" any data. When you "restore" the database from the snapshot you do not restore all the data; rather you restore only what has changed in the interim period.

This technique proves very useful in ETL when you want to prototype any data changes. You can create a package that makes any data changes you like, confident in the knowledge that you can easily roll back the database to a clean state in a short amount of time. Of course you could achieve the same goals using backup and restore (or transactional semantics), but those methods typically have more overhead and/or take more time. Snapshots may also be a useful tool in operational ETL; you can imagine a scenario whereby a snapshot is taken before an ETL load and then if there are any problems, the data changes can be easily rolled back.

There is a performance overhead to using snapshots, because you can think of them as a "live" backup. Any activity on the source database incurs activity on the snapshot database, because the first change to any database page causes that page to be copied to the database snapshot. Any further changes to the same page do not cause further copy operations. You will need to test the performance overhead in the solutions you create, though you should expect to see an overhead of anywhere from 5% to 20%.

Because you are writing data to the destination database in this section, it is useful to create a database snapshot so you can roll back your changes very easily. Run this complete script:

```
--Use a snapshot to make it simple to rollback the DML
USE master;
GO

--To create a snapshot we need to close all other connections on the DB
ALTER DATABASE [AdventureWorksDW2008] SET SINGLE_USER WITH ROLLBACK IMMEDIATE;
ALTER DATABASE [AdventureWorksDW2008] SET MULTI_USER;

--Check if there is already a snapshot on this DB
IF EXISTS (SELECT [name] FROM sys.databases
  WHERE [name] = N'AdventureWorksDW2008_Snapshot') BEGIN
    --If so RESTORE the database from the snapshot
    RESTORE DATABASE AdventureWorksDW2008
    FROM DATABASE_SNAPSHOT = N'AdventureWorksDW2008_Snapshot';

    --If there were no errors, drop the snapshot
    IF @@error = 0 DROP DATABASE [AdventureWorksDW2008_Snapshot];
END; --if

--OK, let's create a new snapshot on the DB
CREATE DATABASE [AdventureWorksDW2008_Snapshot] ON (
    NAME = N'AdventureWorksDW2008_Data',
    --Make sure you specify a valid location for the snapshot file here
    FILENAME = N'D:\Data\AdventureWorksDW2008_Data.ss')
AS SNAPSHOT OF [AdventureWorksDW2008];
GO
```

The script should only take a couple of seconds to run. What it does is to create a database file in the specified folder that it tagged as being a snapshot of the AdventureWorksDW2008 database. You can run the following command to list all the database snapshots on the server:

```
--List database snapshots
SELECT
    d.[name] AS DatabaseName,
    s.[name] AS SnapshotName
FROM sys.databases AS s
INNER JOIN sys.databases AS d
ON (s.source_database_id = d.database_id);
```

You should now have a snapshot called "AdventureWorksDW2008_Snapshot". This snapshot is your "live backup" of AdventureWorksDW2008. Once you have ensured that the database snapshot is in place, test the snapshot functionality by changing some data or metadata in AdventureWorksDW2008. For instance, you can create a new table in the database and insert a few rows:

```
--Create a new table and add some rows
USE AdventureWorksDW2008;
GO

CREATE TABLE dbo.TableToTestSnapshot(ID INT);
GO
INSERT INTO dbo.TableToTestSnapshot(ID) SELECT 1 UNION SELECT 2 UNION SELECT 3;
```

You can confirm the table is present in the database by running this statement. You should get back three rows:

```
--Confirm the table exists and has rows
SELECT * FROM dbo.TableToTestSnapshot;
```

Now you can test the snapshot rollback functionality. Imagine that the change you made to the database was much more impactful than just creating a new table (perhaps you dropped the complete sales transaction table, for instance) and you now want to roll the changes back. Execute the same script that you used to originally create the snapshot; you will notice that the script includes a check to make sure the snapshot exists, and then, if so, it issues a RESTORE ... FROM DATABASE_SNAPSHOT command.

After running the script, try running the SELECT command again that returned the three rows. You should get an error saying the table "TableToTestSnapshot" does not exist. This is good news; the database has been restored to its previous state! Of course this same logic applies whether you had created a table or dropped one, added or deleted rows, or just about any other operation. And the really cool benefit is that it should only have taken a couple of seconds to run this "live restore."

As part of the original snapshot script, the database was rolled back but the script should also have created a new snapshot in the old one's place. Make sure the snapshot is present before continuing with the next sections, because you want to make it simple to roll back any changes you make.

The MERGE Operator

If your source data table is conveniently partitioned into data you want to insert, data you want to delete, and data you want to update, then it is simple to use the INSERT, UPDATE, and DELETE statements to perform the respective operations. However, it is often the case that the data is not presented to you in this format. More often than not you have a source system with a range of data that needs to be loaded, but you have no way of distinguishing which rows should be applied in which way. The source contains a mix of new, updated, and unchanged rows, and may even have some tombstone structures to represent deleted rows too.

One way you can solve this problem is to build logic that compares each incoming row with the destination table, using the likes of Lookup Transforms. See Chapter 7 for more information. Another way to do this would be to use CDC (discussed previously in this chapter) to tell you explicitly which rows and columns were changed, and in what way.

There are many other ways of doing this too, but if none of these methods are suitable then there is a new alternative in SQL Server 2008, which comes in the form of an operator called MERGE (also known in some circles as "upsert" due to its mixed Update/Insert behavior).

The MERGE statement is similar in usage to the INSERT, UPDATE, and DELETE statements; however, it is more useful in that it can perform all three of their duties within the same operation. Here is pseudocode to represent how it works; after this you will delve into the real syntax and try some examples:

```
MERGE INTO Destination
Using these semantics:
{
    <all actions optional>
    If a row in the Destination matches a row in the Source then: UPDATE
```

```
        If a row exists in the Source but not in the Destination then: INSERT
        If a row exists in the Destination but not in the Source then: DELETE
}
FROM Source;
```

As you can see, you are able to issue a single statement to SQL Server and it is able to figure out on a row-by-row basis which rows should be INSERTED, UPDATED, and DELETED in the destination. This can provide a huge time savings over doing it the old way; issuing two or three separate statements to achieve the same goal. Note that SQL Server is not just cleverly rewriting the MERGE query back into INSERT and UPDATE statements behind the scenes; instead this functionality is a DML primitive deep within the SQL core engine, and as such it is highly efficient.

Now you are going to apply this knowledge to a real set of tables. In the extraction section of this chapter you used customer data from AdventureWorks2008 and compared it to data in AdventureWorksDW2008. There were some rows that occurred in both of the tables, some rows that were only in the source, and some rows that were only in the destination. You will now use MERGE to synchronize the rows from AdventureWorks2008 to AdventureWorksDW2008 so that both tables contain the same data.

This is not a real-world scenario because you would not typically write rows directly from the source to the destination without cleaning and shaping the data in an ETL tool like SSIS, but for the sake of convenience the example is an illustrative way of demonstrating the concepts.

First you need to add a new column to the destination table just so you can see what happens after you run the statement. This is not something you would need to do in the real solution.

```
USE AdventureWorksDW2008;
GO

--Add a column to the destination table to help us track what happened
--You would not do this in a real solution, this just helps the example
ALTER TABLE dbo.DimCustomer ADD Operation NVARCHAR(10);
GO
```

Now you can run the MERGE statement. The code is commented to explain what it does. The destination data is updated from the source in the manner specified by the various options. There are blank lines between each main section of the command to improve readability; however, this should not detract from the fact that this is a single statement:

```
USE AdventureWorksDW2008;
GO

--Merge rows from source into the destintion
MERGE

--Define the destination table
INTO AdventureWorksDW2008.dbo.DimCustomer AS [Dest] --Friendly alias

--Define the source query
USING (
```

```
    SELECT
        BusinessEntityID AS ContactID,
        --Convert key into destination format
        N'AW' + RIGHT(N'0000000'
            + CONVERT(NVARCHAR(10), BusinessEntityID), 8) AS
CustomerAlternateKey,
        --Keep example simple by using just a few data columns
        FirstName,
        LastName
    FROM AdventureWorks2008.Person.Person
) AS [Source] --Friendly alias

--Define the join criteria (how SQL matches source/destination rows)
ON [Dest].CustomerAlternateKey = [Source].CustomerAlternateKey

--If the same key is found in both the source & destination...
WHEN MATCHED
--For *illustration* purposes, only update every second row...
AND ContactID % 2 = 0
    --Then update data values in the destination
    THEN UPDATE SET
        [Dest].FirstName = [Source].FirstName,
        [Dest].LastName = [Source].LastName,
        [Dest].Operation = N'Updated'
    --Note: <WHERE ContactID = ...> clause is implicit

--If a key is in the source but not in the destination...
WHEN NOT MATCHED BY TARGET
    --Then insert row into the destination
    THEN INSERT
    (
        GeographyKey, CustomerAlternateKey, FirstName,
        LastName, DateFirstPurchase, Operation
    )
    VALUES
    (
        1, [Source].CustomerAlternateKey, [Source].FirstName,
        [Source].LastName, GETDATE(), N'Inserted'
    )

--If a key is in the destination but not in the source...
WHEN NOT MATCHED BY SOURCE
    --Then do something relevant, say, flagging a status field
    THEN UPDATE SET
        [Dest].Operation = N'Deleted';
    --Note: <WHERE ContactID = ...> clause is implicit

    --Alternatively we could have deleted the destination row
    --but in AdventureWorksDW2008 that would fail due to FK constraints
--WHEN NOT MATCHED BY SOURCE THEN DELETE;
GO
```

After running the statement you should get a message in the query output pane telling you how many rows were affected:

```
(23789 row(s) affected)
```

You can now check the results of the operation by looking at the data in the destination table. If you scroll through the results you should see each row's Operation column populated with the operation that was applied to it:

```
--Have a look at the results
SELECT CustomerAlternateKey, DateFirstPurchase, Operation
FROM AdventureWorksDW2008.dbo.DimCustomer;
```

Here is a subset of the results. For clarity, the different groups of rows have been separated in this book by blank lines:

```
CustomerAlternateKey DateFirstPurchase         Operation
-------------------- ------------------------- ----------
AW00019975           2002-04-11 00:00:00.000   NULL
AW00019976           2003-11-27 00:00:00.000   Updated
AW00019977           2002-04-26 00:00:00.000   NULL

AW00019978           2002-04-20 00:00:00.000   Deleted
AW00019979           2002-04-22 00:00:00.000   Deleted

AW00008000           2008-02-24 20:48:12.010   Inserted
AW00005229           2008-02-24 20:48:12.010   Inserted
AW00001809           2008-02-24 20:48:12.010   Inserted
```

As you can see, a single MERGE statement has inserted, updated, and deleted rows in the destination in the context of just one operation. The reason that some of the updates show a NULL operation is that for illustration purposes a predicate was used in the WHEN MATCHED section to only UPDATE every second row.

Note that the source query can retrieve data from a different database (as per the example), and furthermore it can even retrieve data using the OPENROWSET() function you read about earlier. However, note that MERGE requires that the source data stream is sorted on the join key; SQL will automatically sort the source data for you if required so make sure that the appropriate indexes are in place for a more optimal experience.

If the source query happens to be of the form OPENROWSET(BULK...) — in other words, you are reading from a text file — then make sure you have specified any intrinsic sort order that the text file may already have. If the text file is already sorted in the same manner as the order required for MERGE (or you can ask the source extract system to do so), then SQL is smart enough to not incur a redundant sort operation.

The MERGE operator is a very powerful technique for improving mixed-operation data loads, but how do you use it in the context of SSIS?

If you do not have the benefit of change data capture (CDC, discussed previously in this chapter) and the data sizes are too large to use the Lookup Component in an efficient manner (see Chapter 7), then you may have to extract your data from the source, clean and shape it in SSIS, and then dump the results to a staging table in SQL Server. From the staging table, you now need to apply the rows against the true destination table. You could certainly do this using two or three separate INSERT, UPDATE, and DELETE statements; with each statement JOINing the staging table and the destination table together in order to compare the respective row and column values. But you can now use a MERGE statement instead. The MERGE operation is more efficient than running the separate statements, and it is also more intentional and elegant to develop and maintain.

Make sure you execute the original snapshot script again in order to undo the changes you made in the destination database.

Summary

There are many other opportunities for using SQL in concert with SSIS in your ETL solution. The ideas presented in this chapter are not exhaustive; there are many other ways to increase your return on investment using the Microsoft data platform. Every time you find a way of using a tool optimized for the task at hand, you can lower your costs and improve your efficiencies. There are tasks that SSIS is much better at doing than the SQL engine, but the opposite statement applies too. Make sure you think about which tool will provide you the best solution when building ETL solutions; the best solutions may utilize a combination of the complete SQL Server business intelligence stack.

12

Accessing Heterogeneous Data

In Chapter 11 you discovered how to incrementally extract data from sources with SSIS. In this chapter, you learn about importing and working with data from heterogeneous, or non–SQL Server, sources. In today's enterprise environments, data may exist in many diverse systems, such as mainframes, Oracle, DB2, Office documents, XML, or flat files, to name just a few. The data may be generated within the company, or it may be delivered through the Internet from a trading partner. Whether you need to import data from a spreadsheet to initially populate a table in a new database application, pull data from other sources for your data warehouse, or rely on a Web service to grab up-to-the-minute information, accessing heterogeneous data is probably a big part of your job.

You can load data into SQL Server using SSIS from any ODBC-compliant or OLE DB-compliant source. Many ODBC drivers and OLE DB providers are supplied by Microsoft for sources like Excel, Access, DB2, FoxPro, Sybase, Oracle, and dBase. Others are available from database vendors. A variety of Data Source Components are found in SSIS. These include Excel, Flat File, XML, ADO.NET (which is used to connect to .NET Sources), OLE DB (which allows connections to many different types of data), and Raw File (which is a special source used to read data that has been previously exported to a Raw File Destination). If the supplied Data Sources do not meet your needs, you can also create custom Data Sources.

This chapter walks you through accessing data from several of the most common sources. Each one is relatively easy to work with, but each is configured a bit differently:

❑ **Excel and MS Access** (versions 2007 and earlier): Excel is often used as a quick way to store data because spreadsheets are easy to set up and use. Access applications are frequently upsized to SQL Server as the size of the database and number of users increase.

❑ **Oracle:** Even companies running their businesses on Oracle or another of SQL Server's competitors sometimes make use of SQL Server for its cost-effective reporting and business intelligence solutions.

❑ **XML and Web Services:** XML and Web services (which is XML delivered through HTTP) are standards that allow very diverse systems to share data. The XML Data Source allows you to work with XML as you would almost any other source of data.

❑ **Flat Files:** Beyond just standard delimited files, SSIS can parse flat files of various types and code page encoding, which allow files to be received from and exported to different operating systems and non-Windows based systems, which reduce the need to convert flat files before or after working with them in SSIS.

❑ **ODBC:** Many organizations maintain older systems that use legacy ODBC providers for data access. Because of the complexities and cost of migrating systems to newer versions, ODBC is still a common source.

❑ **Other Heterogeneous Sources:** The sources listed so far are the most common; however, this only touches upon the extent of Data Sources that SSIS can access. The last section of this chapter provides you resources and generalities when you are trying to access other sources such as Teradata, SAP, DB2, or Sybase.

Excel and Access

SSIS deals with Excel and Access data in a similar fashion because they use the same underlying provider technology for data access. For Microsoft Office 2003 and earlier, the data storage technology is called the JET Engine, which stands for Join Engine Technology; therefore, when you access these legacy releases of Excel or Access, you will be using the JET OLE DB Provider.

Since the release of Office 2007, a new office engine was introduced called ACE that is essentially a newer version of the JET but that supports the new file formats of Excel and Access. ACE stands for Access Engine and is used for Office 2007 and later. You will find it under the name "Microsoft Office 12.0 Access Database Engine OLE DB Provider" in the OLE DB provider list. Therefore, when connecting to Access or Excel in these versions, you will use the ACE OLE DB Provider.

Later in this section you will see how to connect to both Access and Excel for both the JET and ACE engines.

Limited 64-Bit Support

As of the release of SQL Server 2008 and this book, 64-bit providers do not exist for either the JET or ACE engines (either the X64 or IA64 64-bit versions). However, there are still ways to work with the 32-bit version of the JET and ACE providers even if you are working on a 64-bit machine.

To be sure, SSIS can run natively on a 64-bit machine (just like it can on a 32-bit machine). This means that when the operating system is running the X64 version of Windows Server 2003, Windows Vista, or Windows Server 2008, you are able to natively install and run SQL Server in the X64 architecture (an IA64 Itanium build is also available from Microsoft support). The limitation is that some of the data access providers (like ACE and JET) will not work when a package is run natively in this environment. Instead, you will need to run the package in a 32-bit emulation mode on the same server.

When you install SSIS with the native X64 installation bits, you will also get the 32-bit runtime executables that can be used to run packages that need access to 32-bit drivers not supported in the

64-bit environment. When working on a 64-bit machine, you can run packages in 32-bit emulation mode through the BIDS design environment and through the 32-bit version of DTExec. Here are the details:

❑ **Business Intelligence Development Studio:** By default, when you are in a native 64-bit environment and you run a package, you are running the package in 64-bit mode. However, you can change this behavior by modifying the properties of your SSIS project. Figure 12-1 shows the Run64bitRuntime property on the Debugging property page. When you set this to False, the package will run in 32-bit emulation mode even though the machine is a 64-bit.

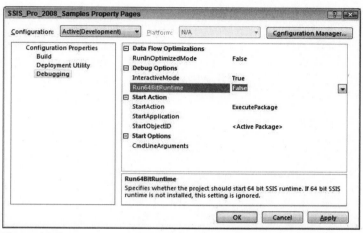

Figure 12-1

❑ **32-bit version of DTExec:** By default, a 64-bit installation of SSIS will reference the 64-bit version of DTExec, usually found in the `C:\Program Files\Microsoft SQL Server\90\DTS\Binn` folder. However a 32-bit version will also be included in `C:\Program Files (X86)\Microsoft SQL Server\90\DTS\Binn`, and you can reference that directly if you want a package to run in 32-bit emulation mode in order to access the ACE and JET providers.

Be careful to make sure not to run all your packages in 32-bit emulation mode when running on a 64-bit machine, just the ones that need 32-bit support. The 32-bit emulation mode will limit the memory accessibility and the performance. The best approach is to modularize your packages so you limit the need for the 32-bit support.

Refer to the following article for an in-depth discussion of the 64-bit support in SSIS: `http://ssis.wik.is/64-bit_Story`.

Working with Excel Files

Excel is a common source and destination because it is often the favorite "database" software of many people without database expertise (especially in your accounting department!). SQL Server Integration Services has Data Flow Source and Destination Components made just for Excel that ease the connection setup, whether connecting to Excel 2003 or earlier, or to Excel 2007 or later (the JET and ACE providers).

You can be sure that these components will be used in many SSIS packages, because data is often imported from Excel files into a SQL Server database or exported into Excel for many high-level tasks such as sales forecasting. Because Excel is so easy to work with, it is common to find inconsistencies in the data. For example, while possible to implement, it is less likely for an Excel workbook to have lookup lists or data type enforcement in place. It's often possible for the person entering data to type a note in a cell where a date should go. Of course, cleansing the data is part of the ETL process, but it may be even more of a challenge when importing from Excel.

In this section, you look at both exporting to and importing from Excel as the AdventureWorks staff performs their annual inventory.

Access

MS Access is the database of choice for countless individual users and small workgroups. It has many great features and wizards that enable a small application or prototype to be quickly developed. Often, when an application has outgrown its humble Access origins, discussions of moving the data to SQL Server emerge. Many times, the client will be rewritten as a web or desktop application using VB.NET or another language. Sometimes the plan will be to link to the SQL Server tables, utilizing the existing Access front-end. Unfortunately, if the original application was poorly designed, moving the data to SQL Server will not improve performance.

> *Designing an application with a SQL back-end and Access front-end that performs well is beyond the scope of this book. To learn more about creating Access applications where SQL Server hosts the data, read* Expert One-on-One Microsoft Access Application Development *by Helen Feddema. (Wrox, 2004.)*

Also, keep in mind that Access select queries will be imported into SQL Server as tables. Any queries that must be ported to the SQL Server database will have to be rewritten. Many select queries can be rewritten as views. Update, append, delete, create table, and parameterized select queries can be rewritten as stored procedures if you need to move them to the SQL Server database. There may also be VBA (Visual Basic for Applications) functions used in queries. You may want to rewrite them as CLR User Defined Functions in SQL Server. What you do depends on the requirements for your application or solution, and that discussion could fill up a whole book in itself.

Importing Access tables is similar to importing Excel worksheets. It is very easy to accomplish using the Import and Export Wizard and, if you have several tables to import at once, that's probably the way to go. See Chapter 2 for detailed instructions on how to use the wizard. In this section you learn how to import data from Access by building an SSIS package along with a few tips specific to Access.

Understanding Access Security

Connecting to an Access database is usually quite simple. If Access security has been enabled on the database, it gets a bit more complicated. Before you learn how to import from Access, take a quick look at how Access security works.

The simplest way to "secure" an Access database is to set a Database Password. This is done by opening the database in exclusive mode and then entering a password in the Set Database Password dialog box found at Tools ⇨ MA Security ⇨ MA Set Database Password. After that, the password must be supplied by anyone who opens the database, including your SSIS package.

The other method involves associating a database with a Workgroup Information file (system.mdw), setting up groups and users, and configuring permissions. Users attempting to open the database authenticate against the workgroup file. Access provides a wizard that can be used to set up groups and permissions, simplifying the process.

A default Workgroup file is specified in the registry for the user. If more than one individual shares the same database, usually a Workgroup Information file is stored on the network. Either that file can be the default workgroup file for the user or it can be used only for a specific database. If it is for the specific database, the path to the workgroup file must be specified as a startup command-line argument in a shortcut provided to the user. A user name and password can also be included in the command, like this:

```
"C:\Program Files\Microsoft Office\Office11\MSACCESS.EXE"
    "C:\SSIS_Pro_2008\SSIS_Pro_12_Samples\Northwind.mdb" /wrkgrp
"C:\SSIS_Pro_2008\SSIS_Pro_12_Samples\system.mdw"
    /user [user] /pwd [password]
```

If the Access database does not have security enabled, all users actually open the database as the Admin user with a blank password. That enables the user to create, modify, and own all of the Access objects without even being aware that security, albeit not much security, is being used in the background. Creating a non-blank Admin password effectively enables security.

The Admin account is the same account no matter which Workgroup Information file is used, and it is a member of the Admins group by default. It seems counterintuitive, but moving the Admin account to a group with no object permissions and removing it from the Admins group is an Access security best practice. This keeps anyone with a copy of Access, who opens the file using the Admin account from a different Workgroup file, from viewing or modifying data. Before taking the rights away from Admin, another account must be added to the Admins group.

If you would like to learn more about how to set up Access security, refer to Microsoft Access Help for more information.

Configuring an Access Connection Manager

Once the Connection Manager is configured properly, importing from Access is simple. First, look at the steps required to set up the Connection Manager:

1. Create a new SSIS package and create a new Connection Manager by right-clicking in the Connection Managers' section of the design area of the screen.

2. Select New OLE DB Connection to bring up the Configure OLE DB Connection Manager dialog box.

3. Click New to open the Connection Manager. In the Provider drop-down list, choose one of the following access provider types:

❑ Microsoft Jet 4.0 OLE DB Provider (for Access 2003 and earlier)

❑ Microsoft Office 12.0 Access Database Engine OLE DB Provider (for Access 2007 and later)

4. Click OK after making your selection.

5. The Connection Manager dialog box changes to an Access-specific dialog. Browse to the Access database file to set the Database File Name property. You are using the Northwind MS Access sample database for this example.

6. By default, the database user name will be Admin with a blank password. If security has been enabled for the Access database, a valid user name and password must be entered. Enter the password on the All pane in the Security section. The user Password property is also available in the properties window. Check the "Save my password" option. Additionally, the path to the Workgroup Information File (`system.mdw`) must be set in the ODBC:System Database property, also found by clicking the All tab.

7. If, on the other hand, a database password has been set, enter the database password in the Password property on the Connection pane. This also sets the ODBC:Database Password property found on the All tab.

8. If both a database password and user security have been set up, enter both passwords on the All pane. In the Security section, enter the user password and enter the database password for the Jet OLEDB:New Database Password property (see Figure 12-2). Check the "Save my password" option. Be sure to test the connection and click OK to save the properties.

Figure 12-2

Importing from Access

Once you have the Connection Manager created, follow these steps to import from Access:

1. Using the project you created in the last section with the Access Connection Manager already configured, add a Data Flow Task to the Control Flow design area.

2. Click the Data Flow tab to view the Data Flow design area. Add an OLE DB Source Component and name it Customers.

3. Double-click the Customers icon to open the OLE DB Source Editor. Set the OLE DB Connection Manager property to the Connection Manager that you created in the last section.

4. Select Table or View from the "Data access mode" drop-down list. Choose the Customers table from the list under "Name of the table or the view" (see Figure 12-3).

5. Click Columns on the left where you can choose which columns to import and change the output names if you need to.

6. Click OK to accept the configuration.

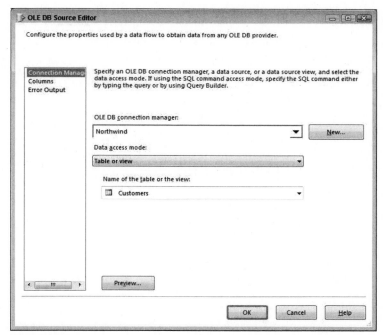

Figure 12-3

7. Create a Connection Manager pointing to AdventureWorks2008.

8. Create an OLE DB Destination Component and name it NW_Customers. Drag the connection (green arrow) from the Customers Source Component to the NW_Customers Destination Component.

9. Double-click the Destination Component to bring up the OLE DB Destination Editor and configure it to use the AdventureWorks2008 Connection Manager.

10. You can choose an existing table or you can click New to create a new table as the Data Destination. If you click New, you will notice that the Create Table designer does not script any keys, constraints, defaults, or indexes from Access. It makes its best guess as to the data types, which may not be the right ones for your solution. When building a package to be used in a production system, you will probably want to design and create the SQL Server tables in advance.

A tool that could save some time when porting Access tables to SQL is the Access Upsizing Wizard. This can be found in the Tools ⇨ Database Utilities menu of Access. This tool will enable you to upload the table and attributes along with, or without, the data. You still need to review the data types and the index names that the wizard creates, but it could save you quite a bit of time over the manual process.

11. For now, click New to bring up the table definition (see Figure 12-4). Notice that the table name is the same as the Destination Component, so change the name to NW_Customers if you did not name the OLE DB Destination as instructed previously.

12. Click OK to create the new table.

13. Click Mappings on the left to map the source and destination columns.

14. Click OK to accept the configuration.

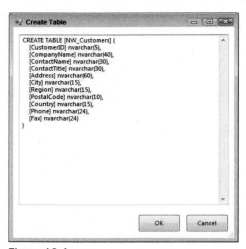

Figure 12-4

15. Run the package. All of the Northwind customers should now be listed in the SQL Server table. Check this by clicking New Query in the Microsoft SQL Server Management Studio. Run the following query to see the results (see Figure 12-5):

```
USE AdventureWorks2008
GO
SELECT * FROM NW_Customers
```

Figure 12-5

16. Empty the table to prepare for the next example by running this query:

```
TRUNCATE TABLE NW_CUSTOMERS
```

Using a Parameter

Another interesting feature is the ability to pass a parameter from a package variable to a SQL command.

In Access, you can create a query that prompts the user for parameters at runtime. You can import most Access select queries as tables, but data from an Access parameter query cannot be imported using SSIS.

1. Using the package you started in the last section, create a variable to hold the parameter value.

2. Move back to the Control Flow tab and right-click the design area.

3. Choose Variables and add a variable by clicking the Add Variable icon. Name it CustomerID. Change the Data Type to String. Give it a value of ANTON (see Figure 12-6). Close the Variables window and navigate back to the Data Flow tab.

Figure 12-6

The design area or component that is selected determines the scope of the variable when it is created. The scope can be set to the package if it is created right after clicking the Control Flow design area. You can also set the scope to a Control Flow Task, Data Flow Component, or Event Handler Task.

4. Double-click the Customers Component to bring up the OLE DB Source Editor and change the data access mode to SQL Command. A SQL Command text box and some buttons appear. You can click the Build Query button to bring up a designer to help build the command or click

Browse to open a file with the command you want to use. For this example, type in the following SQL statement (see Figure 12-7):

```
SELECT CustomerID, CompanyName, ContactName, ContactTitle,
    Address, City, Region, PostalCode, Country, Phone, Fax
FROM Customers
WHERE (CustomerID = ?)
```

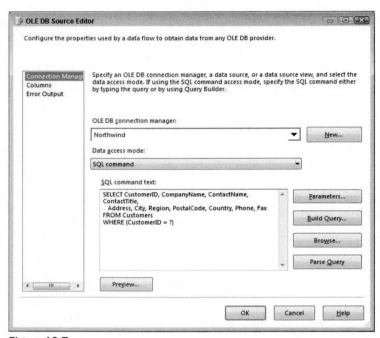

Figure 12-7

5.   The ? symbol is used as the placeholder for the parameter in the query. Map the parameters to variables in the package by clicking the Parameters button. Choose User::CustomerID from the Variables list and click OK (see Figure 12-8).

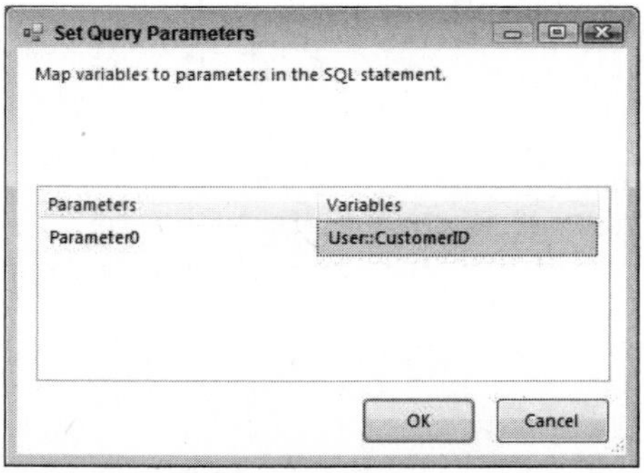

Figure 12-8

Variables in SSIS belong to a namespace. By default, there are two namespaces, User and System. Variables that you create belong to the User namespace. You can also create additional namespaces.

Note that you cannot preview the data after setting up the parameter because the package must be running to load the value into the parameter.

6.   Click OK to accept the new configuration and run the package. This time, only one record will be imported (see Figure 12-9).

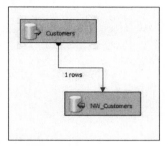

Figure 12-9

You can also go back to SQL Server Management Studio to view the results:

```
USE AdventureWorks2008
GO
SELECT * FROM NW_Customers
```

If you wish to use multiple parameters in your SQL command, use multiple question marks (?) in the query and map them in order to the parameters in the parameter mapping. To do this you would set up a second package-level variable for CompanyName and set the value to Island Trading. Change the query in the Customers Component to the following:

```
SELECT CustomerID, CompanyName, ContactName,
    ContactTitle, Address, City, Region,
    PostalCode, Country, Phone, Fax
FROM Customers
WHERE (CustomerID = ?) OR
    (CompanyName = ?)
```

Now the Parameters dialog box will show the two parameters. Associate each parameter with the appropriate variable (see Figure 12-10).

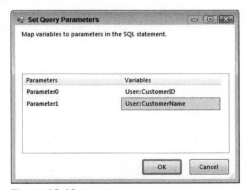

Figure 12-10

Importing data from Access is a simple process as long as Access security has not been enabled. Often, porting an Access application to SQL Server is the desired result. Make sure you have a good book or resource to help ensure success.

Now you'll see just how easy it is to import from Oracle, as long as you do a bit of configuration first.

Oracle

Because of SQL Server's world-class reporting and business intelligence tools, more and more shops running Oracle rely on SQL Server for their reporting needs. Luckily, importing data from Oracle is much like importing from other sources, such as a text file or another SQL Server instance. In this section, you learn how to access data from a sample Oracle database.

Oracle Client Setup

Connecting to Oracle in SSIS is a two-step process. First you have to install the Oracle client software, and then you use the OLE DB provider in SSIS to connect to Oracle.

To be sure, the Microsoft Data Access Components (MDAC) that come with the operating system include an OLE DB provider for Oracle. This is the Microsoft-written OLE DB provider to access an Oracle Source System. However, even though the OLE DB provider is installed, you cannot use it until you install a second component called the Oracle client software from Oracle. In fact, when you install the Oracle client software, Oracle has also written an OLE DB provider that can be used to access an Oracle Source. The OLE DB providers have subtle differences, which are referenced later.

Installing the Oracle Client Software

Installing the Oracle client software involves first locating the right Oracle client software from the Oracle website. This is found on the Oracle support website. To get there, first go to the main Oracle home page at http://www.oracle.com/ and then click the support link.

You will be looking for a link titled "Download Oracle Software." As you are well aware, there are several versions of Oracle (currently Oracle 8i, 9i, 10g, 11g), and each has a different version of the Oracle client. Some of them are backward compatible; however, it is always best to go with the version that you are connecting to.

If you use the Instant Client, be sure to install the Basic and ODBC packages. Since you will be connecting from SSIS, you need to choose the Microsoft Windows (32-bit, X64, or Itanium; Itanium is only available for 10g) links for the specific version. Be sure you look for the Client, such as "Oracle Database 11g Release 1 Client" or "Oracle Database 10g Client Release 2." It is best to install the full client software in order to make sure you have the right components needed for the OLE DB providers.

Configuring the Oracle Client Software

Once you download and install the right client for both the version of Oracle you will be connecting to and the right platform of Windows you are running, the final step will be configuring it to reference the Oracle servers. You will probably need help from your Oracle DBA or the support team of the Oracle application to configure this. The two options are: an Oracle name server or manually configuring a TNS file. The TNS file is more common and is found in the Oracle install directory under the network\ADMIN folder. This is called the Oracle Home directory. The Oracle client uses the Windows environment variables %Path% and %ORACLE_HOME% to find the location to the client files. Either replace the default TNS file with one provided by an Oracle admin, or create a new entry in it to connect to the Oracle server.

A typical TNS entry looks like this:

```
[Reference name] =
  (DESCRIPTION =
    (ADDRESS_LIST =
      (ADDRESS = (PROTOCOL = TCP)(HOST = [Server])(PORT = [Port Number]))
    )
    (CONNECT_DATA =
      (SID = [Oracle SID Name])
    )
  )
```

Replace the brackets with valid entries. The [Reference Name] will be used in SSIS to connect to the Oracle server through the provider.

64-Bit Considerations

As mentioned, after you install the Oracle client software, you can then use the OLE DB provider for Oracle in SSIS to extract data from an Oracle Source or to send data to an Oracle Destination. These procedures are described next. However, if you are working on a 64-bit server, either Itanium or X64, you may need to make some additional configurations.

First of all, if you want to connect to Oracle with a native 64-bit connection, you will have to use the Oracle-written OLE DB provider for Oracle because the Microsoft-written OLE DB driver for Oracle is only available in a 32-bit mode. Be sure you also install the right 64-bit Oracle client (Itanium IA64 or X64) if you want to use connect in native 64-bit mode. Although it is probably obvious to you, it bears mentioning that even though you may have X64 hardware, in order to leverage it in 64-bit mode, the operating system must be installed with the X64 version.

Furthermore, even though you may be working on a 64-bit server, you can still use the 32-bit provider through the 32-bit Windows emulation mode. Review the 64-bit details in the "Excel and Access" section earlier in this chapter for details on how to work with packages in 32-bit mode when you are on a 64-bit machine. You will need to use the 32-bit version of DTExec for package execution and when working in BIDS, you will need to change the Run64bitRuntime property of the project to False.

Importing Oracle Data

In this example, the alias, ORCL, is used to connect to an Oracle database named orcl. Your Oracle administrator can provide more information on how to set up your tnsnames.ora file to point to a test or production database in your environment. The following tnsnames file entry is being used for the subsequent steps:

```
ORCL =
  (DESCRIPTION =
    (ADDRESS = (PROTOCOL = TCP)(HOST = VPC-XP)(PORT = 1521))
    (CONNECT_DATA =
      (SERVER = DEDICATED)
      (SERVICE_NAME = orcl)
    )
  )
```

To extract data from an Oracle server, perform the following steps. These assume that you have installed the Oracle client and configured a tnsnames file or an Oracle names server.

1. Create a new Integration Services project using BIDS.

2. Add a Data Flow Task to the design area. On the Data Flow tab, add an OLE DB Source. Name the OLE DB Source Oracle.

3. In the Connection Managers area, right-click and choose New OLE DB Connection to open the Configure OLE DB Connection Manager dialog.

4. Click New to open the Connection Manager dialog. Select Microsoft OLE DB Provider for Oracle from the list of providers and click OK.

5. Type the alias from your tnsnames.ora file for the Server Name.

6. Type in the user name and password and check "Save my password" (see Figure 12-11). This example illustrates connecting to the widely available scott sample database schema. The user name is scott with a password of tiger. Verify the credentials with your Oracle administrator. You will probably want to test the connection to make sure that everything is configured properly. Click OK to accept the configuration.

Figure 12-11

7. In the custom properties section of the Oracle Component's property dialog, change the AlwaysUseDefaultCodePage property to True.

8. Open the OLE DB Source Editor by double-clicking the Oracle Source Component. With the Connection Manager tab selected, choose the Connection Manager pointing to the Oracle database.

9. Select "Table or view" from the "Data access mode" drop-down. Click the drop-down list under "Name of the table or the view" to see a list of the available tables. Choose the `"Scott"."Dept"` table from the list.

10. Select the Columns tab to see a list of the columns in the table.

11. Click Preview to see sample data from the Oracle table. At this point, you can add a Data Destination Component to import the data into SQL Server or another OLE DB Destination. This is demonstrated several times elsewhere in the chapter, so you won't look at it again here.

Importing Oracle data is very straightforward, but there are a few things to watch out for. The current Microsoft ODBC driver and Microsoft-written OLE DB provider for Oracle were designed for Oracle 7. At the time of this writing, Oracle 11g is the latest version available. Specific functionality and data types that were implemented after the 7 release will probably not work as expected. See Microsoft's Knowledge Base article 244661 for more information. If you want to take advantage of newer Oracle features, you should consider using the Oracle-written OLE DB provider for Oracle, which will be installed with the Oracle client software.

Now that you have seen how to import data from several sources using SSIS, you'll take a look at using the XML features.

XML and Web Services

Although not a common source for large volumes of data, XML is an integral technology standard in the realm of data. This section considers XML from a couple of different perspectives. First of all, you will work with the Web Service Task to interact with a public Web service. Secondly, you will use the XML Source adapter to extract data from an XML document embedded in a file. In one of the Web service examples, you will also use the XML Task to read the XML file.

Configuring the Web Service Task

In very simple terms, a Web service is to the web as a function is to a code module. It accepts a message in XML, including arguments, and returns the answer in XML. The thing about XML technology is that it allows computer systems that are completely foreign to each other to communicate in this common language. When using Web services, this transfer of XML data occurs across the enterprise or across the Internet using the HTTP protocol. Many Web services — for example, stock-tickers and movie listings — are freely available for anyone's use. Some Web services, of course, are private or require a fee. Probably the most useful application is to allow orders or other data to be exchanged easily by corporate partners, or to receive information from either a service that you pay for or a public service that is exposed for free on the Internet. In the following examples, you'll learn how to use a Web service to get the weather forecast of a U.S. ZIP code by subscribing to a public Web service and you will learn how to use the Web Service Task to perform currency conversion.

Weather by ZIP Code Example

In this example, you learn how to use a Web service to retrieve data.

1. To begin, create a new package and create an HTTP Connection by right-clicking in the Connection Managers' pane and choosing New Connection.

2. Choose HTTP and click Add to bring up the HTTP Connection Manager Editor. Type **http://www.webservicex.net/WeatherForecast.asmx?wsdl** as the Server URL (see Figure 12-12). In this case, you'll use a publicly available Web service so you won't have to worry about any credentials or certificates. If you must supply proxy information to browse the web, fill that in on the Proxy tab.

3. Before continuing, click the Test Connection button, and then click OK to accept the Connection Manager.

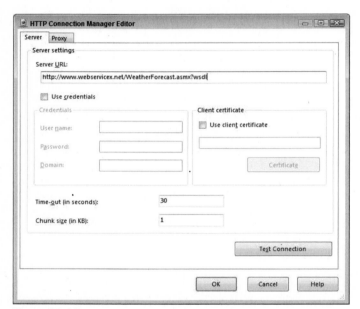

Figure 12-12

4. Next, add a Web Service Task from the Toolbox to the Control Flow workspace.

5. Double-click the Web Service Task to bring up the Web Service Task Editor. Select the General pane. Make sure that the HttpConnection property is set to the HTTP connection you created in the last step.

6. In order for a Web service to be accessed by a client, a Web Service Definition Language (WSDL) file must be available that describes how the Web service works — that is, the methods available and the parameters that the Web service expects. The Web Service Task provides a way to automatically download this file.

In the WSDLFile property, enter the fully qualified path `c:\weather.wsdl` where you want the WSDL file to be created (see Figure 12-13).

7. Set the OverwriteWSDLFile property to True and then click Download WSDL to create the file. If you are interested, you can open the file with Internet Explorer to learn more about its XML structure.

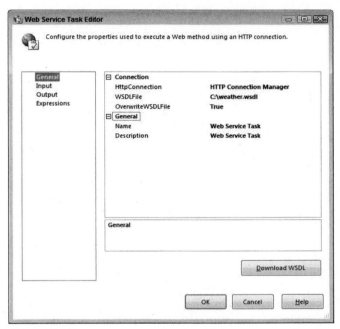

Figure 12-13

By downloading the WSDL file, the Web Service Task now knows the Web service definition.

8. Select the Input pane of the Web Service Task Editor and then, next to the Service property, open the drop-down list and you will have one service to choose from, called WeatherForecast.

9. After selecting the WeatherForecast service, click in the Method property and choose the GetWeatherByZipCode option.

10. Web services are not limited to providing just one method. If multiple methods are provided, you'll see all of them listed. Notice that another option exists called GetWeatherByPlaceName, which you would use if you wanted to enter a city instead of a ZIP code. Once the GetWeatherByZipCode method is selected, a list of arguments appears. In this case, a `ZipCode` property is presented. Enter a ZIP code of a location in a U.S. city (such as 30303 for Atlanta, or if you live in the U.S., try entering your own ZIP code). See Figure 12-14.

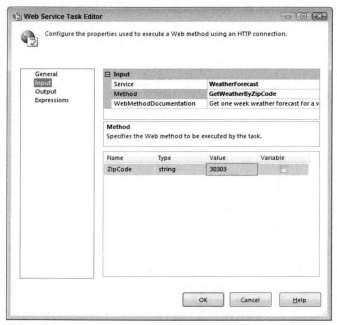

Figure 12-14

11. Now that everything is set up to invoke the Web service, you need to tell the Web Service Task what to do with the result. Switch to the Output property page of the Web Service Task Editor. Choose File Connection in the drop-down of the OutputType property. You can also store the output in a variable to be referenced later in the package.

12. In the File property, open the drop-down list and choose <new connection>.

13. When you are presented with the File Connection Manager Editor, change the Usage type property to "Create file" and change the File property to c:\weatheroutput.xml as Figure 12-15 shows.

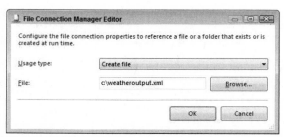

Figure 12-15

14. Select OK in the File Connection Manager Editor and OK in the Web Service Task Editor to finish configuring the SSIS package.

Now you're ready to run the package. After executing the package, wait for the Web Service Task to complete successfully. If all went well, use Internet Explorer to open the XML file that was returned by the Web service (`c:\weatheroutput.xml`) and see the weather forecast for the ZIP code. It will look something like this:

```
<?xml version="1.0" encoding="utf-16" ?>
 <WeatherForecasts xmlns:xsi="http://www.w3.org/2001/XMLSchema-instance"
xmlns:xsd="http://www.w3.org/2001/XMLSchema">
   <Latitude xmlns="http://www.webservicex.net">33.93777</Latitude>
   <Longitude xmlns="http://www.webservicex.net">84.2716446</Longitude>
   <AllocationFactor
xmlns="http://www.webservicex.net">0.002473</AllocationFactor>
   <FipsCode xmlns="http://www.webservicex.net">13</FipsCode>
   <PlaceName xmlns="http://www.webservicex.net">ATLANTA</PlaceName>
   <StateCode xmlns="http://www.webservicex.net">GA</StateCode>
-  <Details xmlns="http://www.webservicex.net">
-  <WeatherData>
   <Day>Monday, March 31, 2008</Day>
  <WeatherImage>http://www.nws.noaa.gov/weather/images/fcicons/nfew.jpg
</WeatherImage>
   <MaxTemperatureF>61</MaxTemperatureF>
   <MinTemperatureF>35</MinTemperatureF>
   <MaxTemperatureC>16</MaxTemperatureC>
   <MinTemperatureC>2</MinTemperatureC>
   </WeatherData>
   </Details>
   </WeatherForecasts>
```

The Currency Conversion Example

In this second example, you learn how to use a Web service to get back a value that can be used in the package to perform a calculation. You'll use the value with the Derived Column Transformation, to convert a price list to another currency.

1. Begin by creating a new SSIS package. This example will require three variables. To set up the variables, make sure that the Control Flow tab is selected. If the Variables window is not visible, right-click in the design area and select Variables. Set up the three variables as in the following table. At this time, you do not need to have initial values.

Name	Scope	Data Type
XMLAnswer	Package	String
Answer	Package	String
ConversionRate	Package	Double

2. Add a Connection Manager pointing to the AdventureWorks2008 database.

3.   Add a second connection; this time create an HTTP Connection Manager and set the Server URL to `http://www.webservicex.net/CurrencyConvertor.asmx?wsdl`.

Note that this Web service was valid at the time of this writing, but the authors cannot guarantee its future availability.

4.   Drag a Web Service Task to the design area and double-click the task to open the Web Service Task Editor. Set the HTTPConnection property to the Connection Manager you just created.

5.   Type in a location to store the WSDLFile such as **c:\CurrencyConversion.wsdl** and then click the Download WSDL button as you did in the last example to download the WSDL file.

6.   Click Input to see the Web service properties. Select CurrencyConvertor in the Service property and ConversionRate as the Method.

7.   Two parameters will display, FromCurrency and ToCurrency. Set FromCurrency equal to USD and ToCurrency equal to EUR (see Figure 12-16).

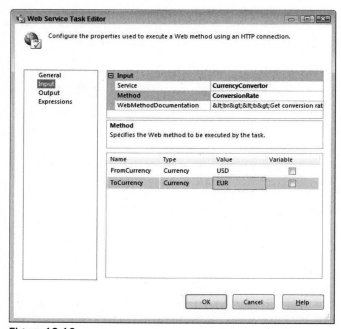

Figure 12-16

8.   Click Output and set the OutputType to Variable.

9. The variable name to use is User::XMLAnswer (see Figure 12-17). Click OK to accept the configuration.

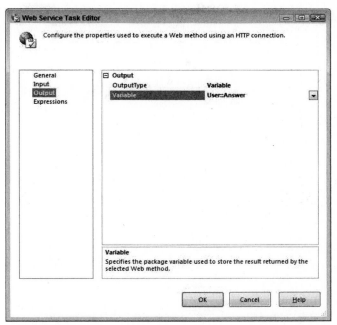

Figure 12-17

At this point, you may be interested in viewing the XML that it returned from the Web service. You can save the XML in a file instead of a variable. Then, after running the task, examine the file. Or, you can set a breakpoint on the task and view the variable at runtime. See Chapter 17 to learn more about breakpoints and debugging.

The value of the XML returned will look something like this:

```
<?xml version="1.0" encoding="utf-8">
<double>0.836</double>
```

10. Since (for the sake of the example) you just need the number and not the XML, add an XML Task to the designer to evaluate the XML.

11. Drag the precedence constraint from the Web Service Task to the XML Task, and then open the XML Task Editor by double-clicking the XML Task.

12. Change the OperationType to XPATH. The properties available will change to include those specific for the XPATH operation. Set the properties to match those in the following table:

Section	Property	Value
Input	OperationType	XPATH
	SourceType	Variable
	Source	User:XMLAnswer
Output	SaveOperationResult	True
Operation Result	OverwriteDestination	True
	Destination	User::Answer
	DestinationType	Variable
Second Operand	SecondOperandType	Direct Input
	SecondOperand	/
Xpath Options	PutResultInOneNode	False
	XpathOperation	Values

The XPATH query language is beyond the scope of this book and, luckily, this XML is very simple with only a root element that can be accessed by using the slash character (/). Values are returned from the query as a list with a one-character unprintable row delimiter. In this case, only one value is returned, but it still has the row delimiter that you can't use.

There are a couple of options here. You could save the value to a file, then import using a File Source Component into a SQL Server table, and finally use the Execute SQL Task to assign the value to a variable. But, in this example, you will get a chance to use the Script Task to eliminate the extra character.

1. Add a Script Task to the design area and drag the precedence constraint from the XML Task to the Script Task.

2. Open the Script Task Editor and select the Script pane.

3. In order for the Script Task to access the package variables, they must be listed in the ReadOnlyVariables or ReadWriteVariables properties (as appropriate whether you will be updating the variable value in the script) in a semicolon-delimited list. Enter **User::Answer** in the ReadOnlyVariable property and **User::ConversionRate** in the ReadWriteVariables property (see Figure 12-18).

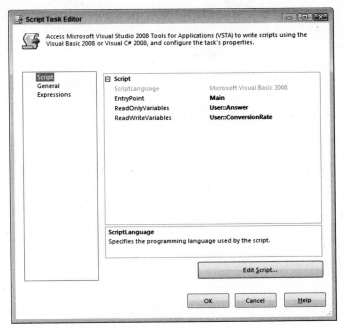

Figure 12-18

4. Click Design Script to open the code window. A Microsoft Visual Studio Tools For Applications environment opens. The script will save the value returned from the Web service call to a variable. One character will be removed from the end of the value, leaving only the conversion factor. This will then be converted to a double and saved in the `ConversionRate` variable for use in a later step.

5. Replace `Sub Main` with the following code:

```
Public Sub Main()
    Dim strConversion As String
    strConversion = Dts.Variables("User::Answer").Value.ToString
    strConversion = strConversion.Remove(strConversion.Length -1,1)
    Dts.Variables("User::ConversionRate").Value = CType(strConversion,Double)
    Dts.TaskResult = Dts.Results.Success
End Sub
```

6. Close the scripting environment, and then click OK to accept the Script Task configuration.

7. Add a Data Flow Task to the design area and connect the Script Task to the Data Flow Task. The Control Flow area should resemble what you see in Figure 12-19.

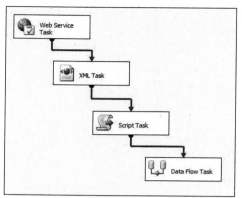

Figure 12-19

8. Move to the Data Flow tab and add a Connection Manager pointing to the AdventureWorks2008 database, if you did not do so when getting started with this example.

9. Drag an OLE DB Source Component to the design area.

10. Open the OLE DB Source Editor and set the OLE DB Connection Manager property to the AdventureWorks2008 connection. Change the data access mode property to SQL Command. Type the following query in the command window:

```
SELECT ProductID, ListPrice
FROM Production.Product
WHERE ListPrice > 0
```

11. Click OK to accept the properties.

12. Add a Derived Column Transform to the design area.

13. Drag the Data Flow Path from the OLE DB Source to the Derived Column Component.

14. Double-click to open the Derived Column Transformation Editor dialog box. Variables, columns, and functions are available for easily building an expression. Add a Derived Column called EuroListPrice. In the Expression field type:

```
ListPrice * @[User::ConversionRate]
```

15. The Data Type should be a decimal with a scale of 2. Click OK to accept the properties (see Figure 12-20).

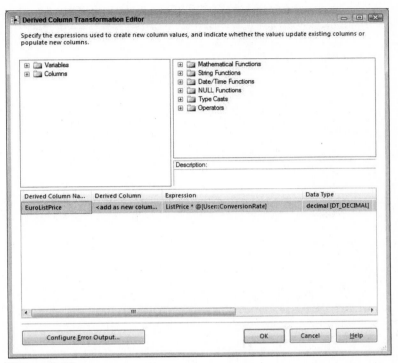

Figure 12-20

16. Add a Flat File Destination Component to the Data Flow design area. Drag the Data Flow Path from the Derived Column Component to the Flat File Destination Component.

17. Bring up the Flat File Destination Editor and click New to open the Flat File Format dialog.

18. Choose Delimited and click OK (see Figure 12-21).

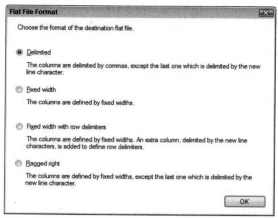

Figure 12-21

19. The Flat File Connection Manager Editor will open. Browse to or type in the path to a file. Here you can modify the file format and other properties if required (see Figure 12-22). Check "Column names in the first data row."

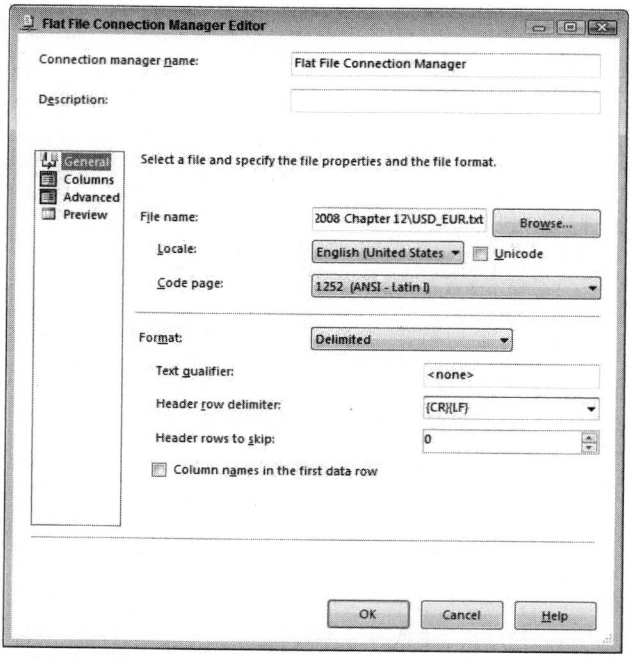

Figure 12-22

20. Click OK to dismiss the Flat File Connection Manager Editor dialog box. You should now be back at the Flat File Destination Editor.

21. Click Mappings and then click OK. The Data Flow design area should resemble what you see in Figure 12-23.

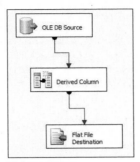

Figure 12-23

22. Run the package and then open the file that you defined in the last step. You should see a list of products along with the list price and the list price converted to Euros (see Figure 12-24).

```
USD_EUR.txt - Notepad

File  Edit  Format  View  Help
ProductID,ListPrice,EuroListPrice
514,133.34,110.83
515,147.14,122.3
516,196.92,163.67
517,133.34,110.83
518,147.14,122.3
519,196.92,163.67
520,133.34,110.83
521,147.14,122.3
522,196.92,163.67
680,1431.5,1189.86
706,1431.5,1189.86
707,34.99,29.08
708,34.99,29.08
709,9.5,7.89
710,9.5,7.89
711,34.99,29.08
712,8.99,7.47
713,49.99,41.55
714,49.99,41.55
```

Figure 12-24

Many free Web services are available for you to try. See www.xmethods.net for a list of services, some of which are free. In the next section, you learn how to import an XML file into relational tables.

Working with XML Data as a Source

SQL Server provides many ways to work with XML. The XML Source adapter is yet another jewel in the SSIS treasure chest. It enables you to import an XML file directly into relational tables if that is what you need to do. In this example, you import an RSS (Really Simple Syndication) file from the web.

The way that the XML Source adapter works in SSIS is that you first connect to an XML file, and then you need to provide the XSD definition of the XML structure, so that SSIS can read the file and correctly interpret the XML elements and attribute structure. Don't have an XSD? No problem, SSIS can self-generate the XSD from right within the XML Source adapter. There is no guarantee that the generated XSD will work with another XML file coming from the same source, which is why it is better to have an XSD definition that is provided by the XML Source that will universally apply to the related files that are used by SSIS.

1. Create a new Integration Services package to get started.

2. Add a Data Flow Task to the Control Flow design area and then click the Data Flow tab to view the Data Flow design area.

3. Add an XML Source and name it SQLNews.

4. Double-click the SQLNews Component to open the XML Source Editor.

5. Make sure that the Connections Manager property page is selected on the left.

6. Select XML File Location for the data access mode. For the XML location property, type in the following address:

```
http://www.sqlservercentral.com/sscrss.xml
```

If you click the Browse button, a regular File Open dialog box opens. It is not obvious at first that you can use a URL address instead of a file on disk.

The XML file must be defined with an XML Schema Definition (XSD), which describes the elements in the XML file. Some XML files have an in-line XSD, which you can determine by opening the file and looking for xsd tags. There are many resources and tutorials available on the web if you would like to learn more about XML schemas. If the file you are importing has an in-line schema, make sure that "Use inline schema" is checked. If an XSD file is available, you can enter the path in the XSD location property (see Figure 12-25). In this case, you will create the XSD file right in the Source adapter.

1. Click Generate XSD and put the file in a directory on your machine (such as `c:\sscrss.xsd`). Once the file is generated, you can open the file with Internet Explorer to view it if you are interested in learning more.

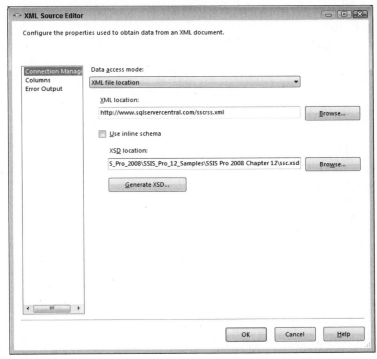

Figure 12-25

2. Now that the SQLNews Component understands the XML file, click Columns. You will notice a drop-down box next to "Output name" listing channel and item (see Figure 12-26).

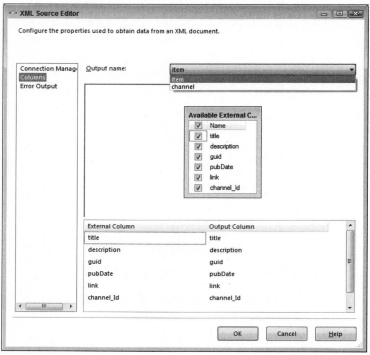

Figure 12-26

Even though the XML document is one file, it represents two tables with a one-to-many relationship. If you browse to `www.sqlservercentral.com/sscrss.xml`, you'll see a channel, which describes the source of the information, usually news, and several items, or articles, defined. One note of caution here: If you are importing into tables with primary/foreign key constraints, there is no guarantee that the parent rows will be inserted before the child rows. Be sure to keep that in mind as you design your XML solution.

The properties of the channel and item tags match the columns displayed in the XML Source Editor. At this point, you can choose which fields you are interested in importing and change the output names if required. The way that the XML Source adapter works is that all the output name selections will be available as downstream paths. When you use an output path from the XML Source adapter, you will be able to choose which output you want to use.

1. Create a new Connection Manager pointing to the AdventureWorks2008 database or to another test database.

2. Add an OLE DB Destination Component to the design area and name it Channel.

3. Drag the Data Flow Path (green arrow) from the XML Source to Channel. Because the XML data represents two tables, an Input Output Selection box opens (see Figure 12-27). Choose Channel in the Output drop-down and click OK.

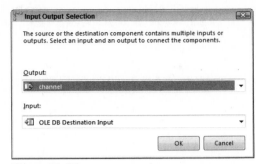

Figure 12-27

4. Double-click the Channel icon to bring up the OLE DB Destination Editor. Make sure that the OLE DB Connection Manager property is set to point to your sample database.

5. Next to Use Table or View, click New. A window with a table definition will pop up. Click OK to create the table. Click Mappings and then click OK to accept the configuration.

6. Add a second OLE DB Destination Component and name it NewsItem.

7. Drag a Data Flow Path (green arrow) from the XML Source to the NewsItem Component. This time, the designer will automatically set up the connection to use the Item table.

8. Double-click the NewsItem Destination Component and verify that the Connection Manager property is set to the test database.

9. Click the New button next to "Name of the table or the view" to see a Create Table statement. Notice that the description field is only 255 characters. Modify the statement, increasing the number of characters to 2000, and click OK to create the table (see Figure 12-28). Click Mappings to view and set the mappings, and then click OK to accept the configuration.

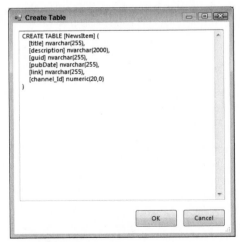

Figure 12-28

10. Add one more OLE DB Destination Component and name it Errors. Drag a red Data Flow Path from the XML Source to the Errors Component. An Input Output Selection dialog box opens. Select Item Error Output (Error Output) in the Output option (see Figure 12-29) and click OK.

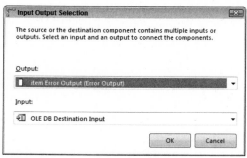

Figure 12-29

11. The Configure Error Output dialog box will then open. In the Truncation property of the Description row, change the value to Redirect row (see Figure 12-30) and click OK.

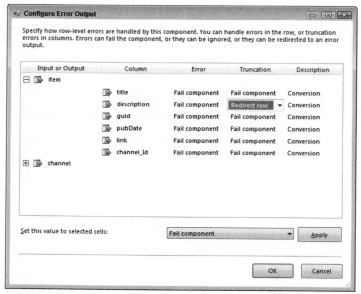

Figure 12-30

12. Double-click the OLE DB Destination that you named Errors and make sure it is pointing to the test database. Click New next to "Name of the table or the view," and OK to create an Errors table. Click Mappings to accept the mappings and then click OK to save the configuration. The Data Flow design area should now resemble Figure 12-31.

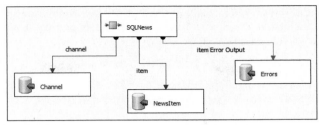

Figure 12-31

Run the package. If it completed successfully, some of the rows will be added to the NewsItem table. Any row with a description over 2000 characters long will end up in the Errors table.

Flat Files

Flat files are one of the more common sources to work with because data in the flat files is easy to read and create by most RDBMS systems and ETL tools. The challenges in working with flat files deal with handling data in a format where data types are not enforced, and also in data that is structured in challenging ways. You may also run into files that are encoded into a different code page than ASCII, such as a UNIX encoding.

SSIS can handle various formats of flat files with varying code pages. The only challenging data is unstructured data, but this can also be handled in SSIS, though not with the Flat File Source adapter, but rather through a Script Component that is acting as a source. Refer to Chapter 9 for a primer on using the Script Component.

Loading Flat Files

Loading flat files from SSIS is a lot more straightforward than extracting data from a flat file. The reason is that when you are loading data into a flat file from an SSIS Data Flow, SSIS already knows the specific data types and column lengths. Extracting data is harder because flat files do not contain information about the data types of the column nor the structure of the file. This first example begins by using SSIS to create and load a flat file.

1. Create a new SSIS package with a Data Flow Task.

2. From the Toolbox, drag an OLE DB Source adapter onto the Data Flow and configure it to connect to AdventureWorks2008 database.

3. Change the data access mode to SQL Command and type in the following SQL statement in the text window:

```
SELECT Name, ProductNumber, ListPrice
FROM [Production].[Product]
```

481

4. Switch to the Columns property page of the OLE DB Source Editor and change the column selection to only include ProductID, Name, ProductNumber, ListPrice, and Size (these should be the only columns that are checked).

5. Select OK to save your changes to the OLE DB Source adapter.

6. Add a Flat File Destination adapter to the Data Flow (be sure to use the Flat File Destination and not the Source!) and connect the green data path from the OLE DB Source to the Flat File Destination.

7. Double-click the Flat File Destination to open the editor.

8. Select New next to the Flat File Connection Manager drop-down, which will open up a new window named Flat File Format (see Figure 12-32). Choose Fixed Width and select OK, which will open up the Flat File Connection Manager Editor.

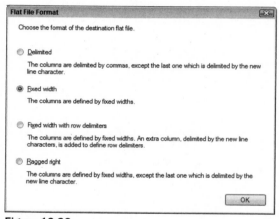

Figure 12-32

Creating and configuring a Flat File Connection Manager is easier to create from within a Destination adapter that already understands the data, than by adding a Flat File Connection Manager directly in the Connection Managers' window.

As Figure 12-32 shows, there are several options for the format of the flat file. The options for the Flat File are described right in the selection window.

9. At this point, in the Flat File Connection Manager Editor, name your connection Products Flat File Destination, and pick a location and name for your file and enter it in the Filename window, such as **c:\products.txt**.

10. Open the Code Page drop-down list and observe the dozens of supported code pages from ANSI 1252 to IBM EBCDIC to UTF to MAC. Any of these can be selected if you intend to send the file to another machine that will consume the data in a different format. Change the Code page to 65001 (UTF-8), which should be the last one on the list.

11. Switch to the Advanced property page on the left, which will show a list of the columns that the Flat File Destination adapter received from the upstream transformation (in this case the Source adapter). Select OK to save the Flat File Connection Manager properties.

12. Finally, in the Flat File Destination Editor, click the Mappings property page on the left, which will by default map the input columns to the columns created in the destination file.

Note that in the Flat File Destination Editor, on the Connection Manager tab, there is a checkbox called "Overwrite data in the file" as Figure 12-33 shows. When this is checked, the file will be cleared before data is loaded in the Data Flow. If this is unchecked, then data will be appended to the file.

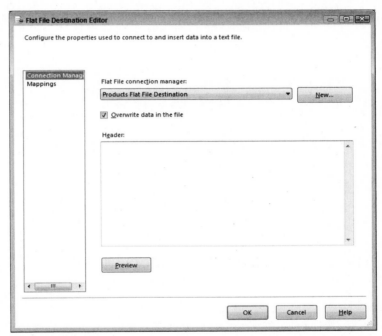

Figure 12-33

13. Leave "Overwrite data in the file" checked and select OK to save the Flat File Destination properties.

Run this simple package, which will create the flat file and overwrite any data that previously existed.

Extracting Data from Flat Files

Now that you have created and loaded a flat file, the next task is to understand how to extract data from a flat file. Of course, when you are working in your work environment, the first step in extracting data from a flat file is to make sure you have access to the file and you somewhat understand how the data is structured.

In this example, you will be working with a fixed-width file created in the prior example, encoded in UTF-8 code page format. The file contains a list of AdventureWorks2008 products.

1. Create a new SSIS package and a new Data Flow Task within the package.

2. Drag the Flat File Source adapter from the Toolbox onto the Data Flow workspace and then double-click the Flat File Source to open the flat file editor.

3. Connecting to a flat file requires using a package connection. Therefore, in the Flat File Source Editor, click the New button next to the Flat File Connection Manager drop-down, which will open up the Flat File Connection Manager Editor.

4. Name the connection Products File Source in the "Connection manager name" text box.

5. Click the Browse button and find the `products.txt` file that you created in the last exercise (such as `c:\products.txt`).

6. Change the Code page to 65001 (UTF-8).

7. Change the Format drop-down to the Fixed-width selection option.

8. Switch to the Columns property page and note that because this file is a fixed-width file, you need to set the column widths. Click on the red line and drag it to the right until the fields line up based on rows and columns as Figure 12-34 shows (it is easier if your window is maximized, and alternately, you can just change the Row width property to 102).

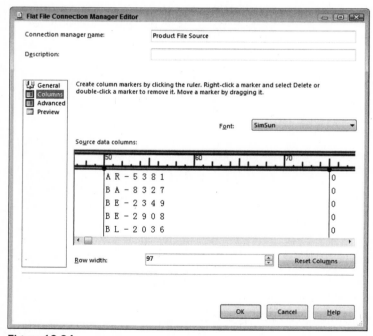

Figure 12-34

9. Next, you will need to identify the fixed-width columns by clicking in the text space right before each column starts as Figure 12-34 shows. You will need to do this for every column.

10. Click the Advanced property page tab and then click the Suggest Types button, which will open up the Suggest Column Types window. Click OK to have SSIS scan the file and then suggest data types for the file.

11. While you are still in the Advanced Editor, you should see Column 0 through Column 2. Click Column 0 and in the properties in the right window, change the Name property to ProductName.

12. Click on Column 2 and change its Name to ProductNumber.

13. For Column 2, change the Name property to ListPrice and change the DataType drop-down to [DT_CY] as Figure 12-35 shows.

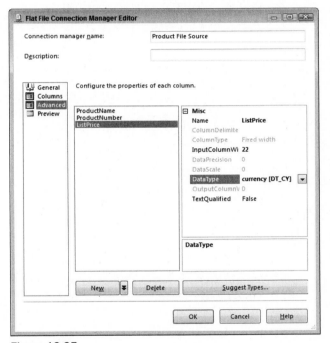

Figure 12-35

14. Select OK to save the Flat File Connection Manager properties.

15. While still in the Flat File Source Editor, select the Columns tab, and verify that all the columns are checked in the Available External Columns list.

16. Select OK to save the properties.

17. Next from the Data Flow Toolbox, drag a Multicast Transformation to the Data Flow workspace and connect the green data path from the Flat File Source adapter to the multicast.

At this point, you would usually create downstream transformations or a destination. For the purpose of example, run the package and observe how the flat file data is extracted into the Data Flow. Nothing is done with it, but it demonstrated how to extract data from a flat file.

ODBC

ODBC stands for Open Database Connectivity and is a legacy connection standard for passing data between systems. However, it is still widely used today for access to RDBMS systems that do not have an OLE DB provider.

Just like the standard OLE DB providers, ODBC is part of the Windows operating system installed by the MDAC (Microsoft Data Access Components) when the operating system gets installed. However, ODBC works differently than the OLE DB providers in that you will need to set up the connection information through an applet in the Administrative Tools called Data Sources (ODBC). The OLE DB connections, on the other hand, are managed directly by the applications and not by the OS. There are some similarities in connecting to Oracle because for Oracle connections, you need to have the configuration managed external to SSIS as well.

For SSIS, the ODBC connectivity is handled through the ADO.NET Source and ADO.NET Destination adapters. Therefore, the process to get access to an ODBC Source or Destination is to first configure the connection in the Data Sources (ODBC) applet and then reference the ODBC connection through an ADO.NET connection in SSIS.

The following example uses public domain data from a DBF Source file, which can be accessed through an ODBC connection. The file is a set of records containing a list of U.S. cities and their properties and is available for download with this book's examples in a file called `ci15au07.dbf`. Use the following steps to connect to an ODBC-based source:

1. Within the machine that you are working on, open up the Administrative Tools folder found in the Control Panel list. Then open up the Data Sources (ODBC) application from this list of administrative programs. Figure 12-36 shows the ODBC Data Source Administrator tool.

Figure 12-36

2. Switch to the System DSN tab, where you will create the ODBC reference (so it is accessible to all users) and click Add.

3. In the Create New Data Source window, scroll down and choose the Microsoft dBase Driver (not the Microsoft Access dBase Driver) and select Finish.

4. In the ODBC dBase Setup window, change the Data Source Name to US_Cities and uncheck the Use Current Directory checkbox.

5. Click the Select Directory button and navigate to the folder where the `ci15au07.dbf` file is located (provided with the book's online files). Select OK to save the directory path. Figure 12-37 shows the ODBC dBASE Setup window (in this case, the `.dbf` file is located at the root of the c:\ drive).

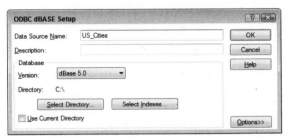

Figure 12-37

6. Select OK in the ODBC dBASE Setup window and OK in the ODBC Data Sources Administrator to save the US Cities DBF reference.

7. Create a new package in SSIS and a new Data Flow.

8. Drag an ADO.NET Source adapter from the Toolbox into the Data Flow workspace and double-click the ADO.NET Source to open its editor.

9. In the ADO.NET Source Editor, click on the New button next to the ADO.NET Connection Manager window.

10. Select the New button again when the Configure ADO.NET Connection Manager window opens.

11. The Connection Manager window will allow you to reference the DBF file through an ODBC connection. Change the Provider drop-down list to the .Net providers\Odbc Data Provider, and in the "Use user or system Data Source name," select US_Cities from the list as Figure 12-38 shows.

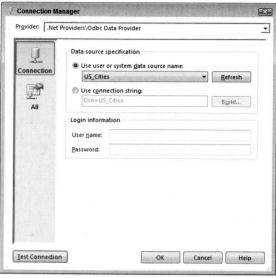

Figure 12-38

12. Select OK in the Connection Manager window and OK in the Configure ADO.NET Connection Manager window, which will return you to the ADO.NET Source Editor with the US_Cities connection selected.

13. In the "Name of the table or the view" drop-down list, choose the ci15au07 table in the list. Figure 12-39 shows the ADO.NET Source Editor window.

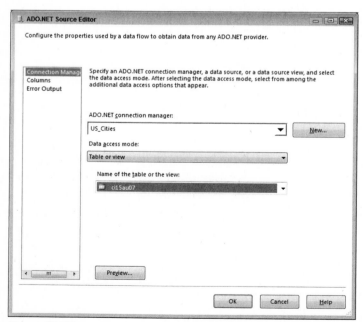

Figure 12-39

14. Click the Columns property page tab to bring up a list of the columns available in this file.

15. Select OK to save the changes of the ADO.NET Source adapter.

16. To demonstrate loading this ODBC Source to a destination table, drag an OLE DB Destination adapter and connect the green data path from the ADO NET Source to the OLE DB Destination adapter.

17. Configure the OLE DB Destination to load the data to a new table in one of the sample databases.

After you run this new package, use SSMS to open the table you just loaded and observe the loaded results.

If you have a need to load data to an ODBC Destination, the process is very similar, only you will be using the ADO NET Destination adapter to perform this operation.

Other Heterogeneous Sources

Beyond the heterogeneous data already discussed, you may come across other non-SQL Server systems that you need access to. Examples of this include DB2 or Teradata or applications like SAP or Peoplesoft, or even decision support systems (DSS). A general approach in connecting to these is to first search for an OLE DB provider, so that you can then use the OLE DB adapters in the Data Flow to extract and load data to the system.

A great resource for other sources and information about connectivity is the SSIS wiki, `http://ssis .wik.is/Data_Sources`.

If you need to connect to an IBM DB2 system, an OLE DB provider is available from the Microsoft website, `http://msdn2.microsoft.com/en-us/library/Aa213281.aspx`. This provider was originally used in the Host Integration Server but has been made available for broad use.

If an OLE DB provider is not available from Microsoft, you can always check the company that owns the system to see if they provide a free OLE DB or ODBC driver. Be aware that sometimes it is not in their interest to make it easy to connect to their systems, so even if they do have a provider, it may be slow. Alternatively, some software companies sell providers. The following is a list of companies to research that can assist in expanding your connectivity options:

❑ Data Direct (`http://www.datadirect.com/`) sells data connection providers (ODBC and OLE DB) that can be installed on Windows operating systems. Some of the connections include Sybase, IBM DB2, Teradata, Informix, and Lotus Notes.

❑ ETI (`http://www.eti.com`) offers data integration, some of which are specifically created for SSIS use. These include SAS, SAP, Teradata, Sybase, DB2, and others.

❑ Persistent Systems (`http://www.persistentsys.com/`) has a high-performance Oracle Destination adapter for SSIS if you are looking to bulk load data into Oracle. Performance numbers show over 100 time performance gains as compared to the OLE DB Destination.

Some systems may only have programmatic APIs that you can only connect to the data programmatically. In these cases, you can also use the Script Component as a source and leverage the system API. See Chapter 9 for more information about leveraging the Script Component.

Summary

SSIS includes the ability to connect to a variety of Data Sources for extraction and loading, but getting there may take a little bit of configuring. Data connects can sometimes be tricky for the simple reason that they require the coordination of third-party software and SSIS adapters. But the good news is that most sources are accessible in SSIS whether through the standard built-in providers or through external providers that can be installed on your SSIS server.

So far this book has covered the basic techniques of building SSIS packages. You now have enough knowledge to put all the pieces together and build a more complex package. The next chapter focuses on how to guarantee that your SSIS packages will scale and work reliably.

Reliability and Scalability

Reliability and scalability are goals for all your systems, yet they may seem like a strange combination for a chapter. Often, though, there are direct links, as you will see. Errors and the unexpected conditions that precipitate them are the most obvious threats to a reliable process. There are several features of SQL Server 2008 Integration Services that allow you to handle these situations with grace and integrity, keeping the data moving and systems running. Error outputs and checkpoints are the two features you will focus on in this chapter, and they highlight to you how these can be used in the context of reliability. The implementation of these methods can also have a direct effect on package performance, and therefore scalability, and you will learn how to take into account these considerations for your package and process design. The ability to provide checkpoints does not natively extend inside the Data Flow, but there are methods you can apply to achieve this. The methods can then be transferred almost directly into the context of scalability, allowing you to partition packages and improve both reliability and scalability at the same time. All of these methods can be combined, and while there is no perfect answer, you will look at the options and acquire the necessary information to make informed choices for your own SSIS implementations.

Restarting Packages

Everyone has been there — one of your Data Transformation Services (DTS) packages failed overnight, and you now have to completely rerun the package. This is particularly painful if some of the processes inside the package are expensive in terms of resources or time. In DTS, the ability to restart a package from where it left off did not exist, and picking apart a package to run just those tasks that failed was tedious and error-prone. There have been a variety of exotic solutions demonstrated, such as a post-execution process that goes into the package and re-creates the package from the failed step onward. Although this worked, it required someone with a detailed knowledge of the DTS object model, which most production DBAs did not have. If your process takes data from a production SQL Server that has a very small window of ETL opportunity, you can almost guarantee that the DBA is not going to be pleased when you tell him you need to run the extract again and that it may impact his users.

For this reason, the introduction of "Package Restartability" or checkpoints in SQL Server 2005 was manna from heaven. In this chapter, you are going to learn everything you need to know to make this happen in your SSIS packages.

Checkpoints are the foundation for restarting packages in SSIS, and they work by writing state information to a file after each task completes. This file can then be used to determine which tasks have run and which failed. More detail about these files is provided in the "Inside the Checkpoint File" section. To ensure that the checkpoint file is created correctly, there are three package properties and one task property that you must set, and they can be found on the property pages of the package and task. The package properties are as follows:

❑ **CheckpointFilename:** This is the filename of the checkpoint file, which must be provided. There are no specific conventions or requirements for the filename.

❑ **CheckpointUsage:** There are three values, which describe how a checkpoint file is used during package execution:

　❑ **Never:** The package will not use a checkpoint file and therefore will never restart.

　❑ **If Exists:** If a checkpoint file exists in the place you specified for the `CheckpointFilename` property, then it will be used, and the package will restart according to the checkpoints written.

　❑ **Always:** The package will always use a checkpoint file to restart, and if one does not exist, the package will fail.

❑ **SaveCheckpoints:** This is a simple Boolean to indicate whether checkpoints are to be written. Obviously this must be set to true for this scenario.

The one property you have to set on the task is FailPackageOnFailure. This must be set for each task or container that you want to be the point for a checkpoint and restart. If you do not set this property to true and the task fails, no file will be written, and the next time you invoke the package, it will start from the beginning again. You'll see an example of this happening later.

As you know, SSIS packages are broken down into Control Flow and Data Flow. Checkpoints only happen at the Control Flow; it is not possible to checkpoint transformations or restart inside a Data Flow. The Data Flow Task can be a checkpoint, but it is treated as any other task. Implementing your own checkpoint and restart feature for data is described later in the chapter.

Remember also that if nothing fails in your package, no file will be generated. You'll have a look later at the generated file itself and try to make some sense out of it, but for now, you need to know that the file will contain all the information needed by the package when it is restarted, to behave like nothing untoward had interrupted it. That's enough information to be able to make a start with using checkpoints in your packages, so now you can proceed with some examples.

Simple Control Flow

The basic idea of this first example package is that you have three Execute SQL Tasks, as shown in Figure 13-1.

Figure 13-1

The second of those tasks, aptly named "2," is set to fail with a divide-by-zero error, as you can see in the Task Editor, shown in Figure 13-2.

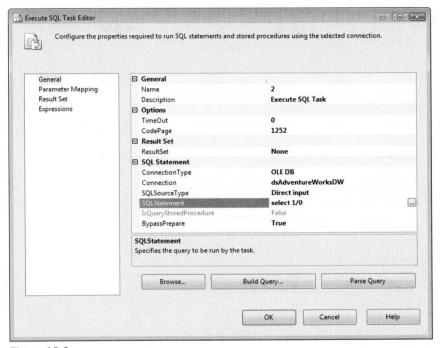

Figure 13-2

The task labeled "1" is expensive, so you want to make sure that you don't need to execute it twice, if it finishes and something else in the package fails. You now need to set up the package to use checkpoints and the task itself. First, set the properties of the package that you read about earlier, as shown in Figure 13-3.

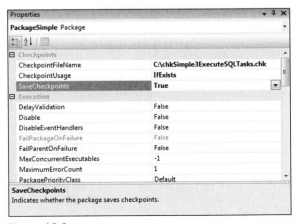

Figure 13-3

Now you need to set the properties of the task to use checkpoints, as you saw earlier (see Figure 13-4). Change the FailPackageOnFailure property to True.

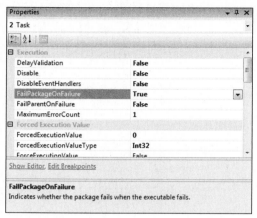

Figure 13-4

Now you can execute the package. The expected outcome is shown in Figure 13-5 — the first task completes successfully (green), but the second task fails (red). Since the printing of this book is in black and white, you will not be able to see the distinct colors here, but you should notice that the tasks contain different shades of gray.

Figure 13-5

If you had created this package in DTS, you would have had to write some logic to cope with the failure in order to not have to execute task 1 again. Because you are working in SSIS and have set the package up properly, you can rely on checkpoints. When the package failed, the error output window said something like this:

```
SSIS package "PackageSimple.dtsx" starting.
Information: 0x40016045 at PackageSimple: The package will be saving checkpoints to
file "C:\chkSimple3ExecuteSQLTasks.chk" during execution. The package is configured
to save checkpoints.
Information: 0x40016047 at 1: Checkpoint file "C:\chkSimple3ExecuteSQLTasks.chk"
was updated to record completion of this container.
Error: 0xC002F210 at 2, Execute SQL Task: Executing the query "select 1/0" failed
with the following error: "Divide by zero error encountered.". Possible failure
reasons: Problems with the query, "ResultSet" property not set correctly,
parameters not set correctly, or connection not established correctly.
Task failed: 2
Warning: 0x80014058 at PackageSimple: This task or container has failed, but
because FailPackageOnFailure property is FALSE, the package will continue. This
warning is posted when the SaveCheckpoints property of the package is set to TRUE
and the task or container fails.
SSIS package "PackageSimple.dtsx" finished: Failure.
```

As you can see, the output window says that a checkpoint file was written. If you look at the file system, you can see that this is true, as shown in Figure 13-6. You'll have a look inside the file later when you have a few more things of interest in there, but for the moment, just know that the package now knows what happened and where.

Figure 13-6

Now you need to fix the problem by removing the divide-by-zero issue with the second task and run the package again. Figure 13-7 shows what happens when you do that.

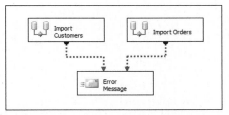

Figure 13-7

Task 2 was executed again and then task 3. Task 1 was oblivious to the package running again.

Earlier you saw that the task you want to be the site for a checkpoint must have the FailPackageOnFailure property set to true, otherwise no file will be written, and when the package executes again it will start from the beginning. Here is how that works. Set task 2 to not use checkpoints by setting this property to false, as shown in Figure 13-8.

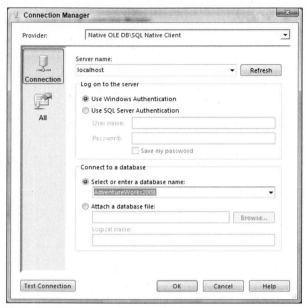

Figure 13-8

Execute the package once again, setting up task 2 to fail with a divide-by-zero error. No checkpoint file is written, as you expected. This means that after you've fixed the error in the task and rerun the package, the results look like Figure 13-9 (all tasks are green), which may or may not be what you want.

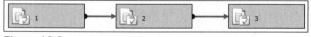

Figure 13-9

This example has been a very simple one and has simply involved three tasks joined by workflow. Hopefully this has given you an idea about restartability in packages; the examples that follow will be more complicated and involved than this one.

Containers within Containers and Checkpoints

Containers and transactions have an effect on checkpoints. You'll demonstrate that in this example and change some properties and settings while you're at it. First, create a package using Sequence Containers and Checkpoints. In this package you have two sequence containers, which themselves contain Execute SQL Tasks, as you can see in Figure 13-10.

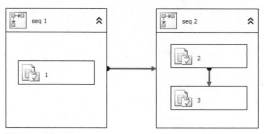

Figure 13-10

Make sure the package has all the settings necessary to use checkpoints, as in the previous example. On the initial run-through of this package, the only container that you want to be the site for a checkpoint is task 3, so set the FailPackageOnFailure property of task 3 to true. Figure 13-11 shows what happens when you deliberately set this task to fail, perhaps with a divide-by-zero error; see the earlier example to see how to do that.

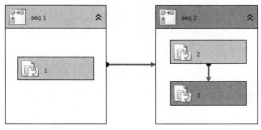

Figure 13-11

As expected, task 3 has failed, and the sequence container, seq2, has also failed because of this. If you now fix the problem with task 3 and re-execute the package, you will see results similar to those shown in Figure 13-12.

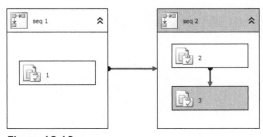

Figure 13-12

So there's no real difference here from the earlier example except that the sequence container "seq 2" is also colored green. Now you'll change the setup of the package to see the behavior change dramatically. What you're going to do is make the sequence container "seq 2" transacted. That means you're going to wrap "seq 2" and its child containers in a transaction. Change the properties of the "seq 2" container to look like Figure 13-13. Set the TransactionOption property to Required.

Figure 13-13

The "seq 2" container has its TransactionOption property set to Required, which means that it will start its own transaction. Now open the two child Execute SQL Tasks and set their TransactionOption properties to Supported, as shown in Figure 13-14, so that they will join a transaction if one exists.

Figure 13-14

Now execute the package again. On the first run-through, the package fails as before at task 3. The difference comes when you fix the problem with task 3 and re-execute the package. The result looks like Figure 13-15.

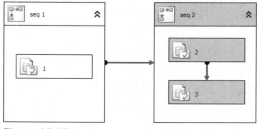

Figure 13-15

498

As you can see, because the container was transacted, the fact that task 3 failed is not recorded in the checkpoint file. The fact that the sequence container failed is recorded instead; hence the sequence container is re-executed in its entirety when the package is rerun.

Variations on a Theme

You may have noticed another property in the task property pages next to the FailPackageOnFailure property — the FailParentOnFailure property. In the previous example, the "seq 2" container is the parent to the two Execute SQL Tasks 2 and 3. You'll run through a few variations of the parent/child relationship here so that you can see the differences. In each example, you will force a failure on the first run-through; you will correct whatever problem there is and then run the package through a second time.

Failing the Parent, Not the Package

What happens then if instead of setting the FailPackageOnFailure property of task 3 to true, you set the FailParentOnFailure property to true? After fixing the issue, on the re-execution of the package the whole package will be run again. Why? Because no checkpoint file has been written.

Remember that if you want a checkpoint file to be written, the task that fails must have the FailPackageOnFailure property set to true; otherwise no file is written.

Failing the Parent and the Package

In this variation, you still have a transacted sequence container, and you still have task 3's FailParentOnFailure property set to true. What you also have is the "seq 2" sequence container's FailPackageOnFailure property set to true. Figure 13-16 shows what happens on the rerun of the package after a failure.

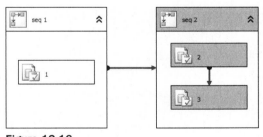

Figure 13-16

As you can see, the sequence container executes in its entirety, and the output window from the package confirms that you used a checkpoint file and that you started a transaction:

```
SSIS package "PackageContainerFailures.dtsx" starting.
Information: 0x40016046 at PackageContainerFailures: The package restarted from
checkpoint file " C:\Restartability\CheckPoint Files\ContainerTest.chp ". The
package was configured to restart from checkpoint.
Information: 0x40016045 at PackageContainerFailures: The package will be saving
checkpoints to file "C:\Restartability\CheckPoint Files\ContainerTest.chp" during
execution. The package is configured to save checkpoints.
Information: 0x4001100A at seq 2: Starting distributed transaction for this
container.
Information: 0x4001100B at seq 2: Committing distributed transaction started by
this container.
SSIS package "PackageContainerFailures.dtsx" finished: Success.
```

Failing the Task with No Transaction

Remove the transactions from your package and simply run through this package again, getting it to fail the first time around at task 3; fix the problem and then re-execute the package. Remember that task 3 has its FailParentOnFailure property set to true, and the "seq 2" sequence container has its FailPackageOnFailure set to true. The outcome, shown in Figure 13-17, is not exactly what you expected. The sequence container has executed but nothing within has. The usage case for this scenario at the time of this writing escapes us.

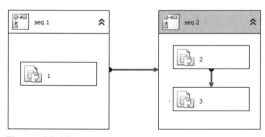

Figure 13-17

Failing the Package, Not the Sequence

You may think that if the tasks 2 and 3 have the sequence container as a parent, then the package itself must be the parent of the sequence container. If this is the case, would setting FailParentOnFailure on the sequence container not be the same as setting FailPackageOnFailure on the same container? The quick answer is no. If you try this option, you will see no checkpoint file being written, and by now you know what that means. The message here is that if you want a checkpoint file to be written, then make sure that the place you want to set as a restart point has FailPackageOnFailure set to true.

Inside the Checkpoint File

Earlier we mentioned that you would look inside the file and see what is actually inside, once you had more things to put in there. In the package shown in Figure 13-18, although you have only three tasks, you also have a variable value being changed. The purpose of this package is to show you what kind of information is stored in a checkpoint file. To add a variable, simply click the designer while in Workflow and choose Variables from the SSIS menu.

Figure 13-18

To alter the value of a variable using the Script Task, you add the variable name to the ReadWriteVariables section on the Script Task's editor. You then need to add some script to change the value. The following is that script:

```
public void Main()
{
    Dts.Variables["v1"].Value = 2;
    Dts.TaskResult = (int)ScriptResults.Success;
}
```

Now, cause the package to fail as shown in Figure 13-19.

Figure 13-19

Instead of spending too much time figuring out an elaborate way to make your task or container fail, you can simply set the ForceExecutionResult on the task or container to Failure.

Inside the generated checkpoint file, you should find something like this:

```
<DTS:Checkpoint xmlns:DTS="www.microsoft.com/SqlServer/Dts"
DTS:PackageID="{5B59AB20-8B19-4C58-8021-6296A2F57158}"><DTS:Variables
DTS:ContID="{5B59AB20-8B19-4C58-8021-6296A2F57158}">
<DTS:Variable><DTS:Property DTS:Name="Expression"></DTS:Property><DTS:Property
DTS:Name="EvaluateAsExpression">0</DTS:Property><DTS:Property
DTS:Name="Namespace">User</DTS:Property><DTS:Property
DTS:Name="ReadOnly">0</DTS:Property><DTS:Property
DTS:Name="RaiseChangedEvent">0</DTS:Property><DTS:VariableValue
DTS:DataType="3">2</DTS:VariableValue><DTS:Property
DTS:Name="ObjectName">v1</DTS:Property><DTS:Property DTS:Name="DTSID">
{A28969A0-0633-4D43-9325-DF54B30EBF2D}</DTS:Property><DTS:Property
DTS:Name="Description">This is the variable being
changed</DTS:Property><DTS:Property
DTS:Name="CreationName"></DTS:Property></DTS:Variable></DTS:Variables>
<DTS:Container DTS:ContID="{5BE98D21-AE77-4278-9784-BEE4D9115967}" DTS:Result="0"
DTS:PrecedenceMap=""/><DTS:Container DTS:ContID="{87431A77-CB01-4AFF-8A18-
0CB89209DD26}" DTS:Result="0" DTS:PrecedenceMap="Y"/></DTS:Checkpoint>
```

The file is better broken down into the constituent parts. The first part tells you about the package to which this file applies:

```
<DTS:Checkpoint xmlns:DTS="www.microsoft.com/SqlServer/Dts"
DTS:PackageID="{5B59AB20-8B19-4C58-8021-6296A2F57158}">
```

The next section of the file, the longest part, details the package variable that you were manipulating:

```
<DTS:Variables DTS:ContID="{5B59AB20-8B19-4C58-8021-6296A2F57158}">
<DTS:Variable><DTS:Property DTS:Name="Expression"></DTS:Property><DTS:Property
DTS:Name="EvaluateAsExpression">0</DTS:Property><DTS:Property
DTS:Name="Namespace">User</DTS:Property><DTS:Property
DTS:Name="ReadOnly">0</DTS:Property><DTS:Property
DTS:Name="RaiseChangedEvent">0</DTS:Property><DTS:VariableValue
DTS:DataType="3">2</DTS:VariableValue><DTS:Property
DTS:Name="ObjectName">v1</DTS:Property><DTS:Property DTS:Name="DTSID">
{A28969A0-0633-4D43-9325-DF54B30EBF2D}</DTS:Property><DTS:Property
DTS:Name="Description">This is the variable being
changed</DTS:Property><DTS:Property
DTS:Name="CreationName"></DTS:Property></DTS:Variable></DTS:Variables>
```

One of the most important things this part of the file tells you is that the last value assigned to the variable, v1, was 2. When the package re-executes, it is this value that will be used.

The final part of the file tells you about the tasks in the package and what their outcomes were. It only tells you about the two tasks that succeeded and not the one that failed:

```
<DTS:Container DTS:ContID="{5BE98D21-AE77-4278-9784-BEE4D9115967}" DTS:Result="0"
DTS:PrecedenceMap=""/><DTS:Container DTS:ContID="{87431A77-CB01-4AFF-8A18-
0CB89209DD26}" DTS:Result="0" DTS:PrecedenceMap="Y"/></DTS:Checkpoint >
```

The first container mentioned is the "Set v1 value to 2" Task:

```
<DTS:Container DTS:ContID="{5BE98D21-AE77-4278-9784-BEE4D9115967}" DTS:Result="0"
DTS:PrecedenceMap=""/>
```

The next and final task to be mentioned is the "Set v1 value to 1" Task:

```
DTS:Container DTS:ContID="{87431A77-CB01-4AFF-8A18-0CB89209DD26}" DTS:Result="0"
DTS:PrecedenceMap="Y"/></DTS:Checkpoint >
```

That concludes your whirlwind tour of package restartability in SSIS. Hopefully, you will get something out of it, because using the features will save you hours of reloading time.

Package Transactions

In this part of the chapter, you see how you can use transactions within your packages to handle data consistency. There are two types of transactions available in an SSIS package:

❑ **Distributed Transaction Coordinator (DTC) Transactions:** One or more transactions that require a DTC and can span connections, tasks, and packages

❑ **Native Transaction:** A transaction at a SQL Server engine level, using a single connection managed through using TSQL transaction commands

Here is how Books Online defines MSDTC: "The Microsoft Distributed Transaction Coordinator (MS DTC) allows applications to extend transactions across two or more instances of SQL Server. It also allows applications to participate in transactions managed by transaction managers that comply with the X/Open DTP XA standard."

You will learn how to use them by going through four examples in detail. Each example builds on the previous example, except for the last one:

❑ **Single Package:** Single transaction using DTC

❑ **Single Package:** Multiple transactions using DTC

❑ **Two Packages:** One transaction using DTC

❑ **Single Package:** One transaction using a native transaction in SQL Server

For transactions to happen in a package and for tasks to join them, you need to set a few properties at both the package and the task level. As you go through the examples, you will see the finer print of what this means, but the following table will get you started with understanding the possible settings for the TransactionOption property.

Property Value	Description
Supported	If a transaction already exists at the parent, the container will join the transaction.
Not Supported	The container will not join a transaction, if one is present.
Required	The container will start a transaction if the parent has not; otherwise it will join the parent transaction.

So armed with these facts, you can get right into the thick of things and look at the first example.

Single Package, Single Transaction

To start the first example, create the simple package shown in Figure 13-20.

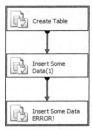

Figure 13-20

This package is quite basic in that all it does is create a table and insert some data into the table, and then the final task will deliberately fail. The first task contains the following as the code to be executed:

```
CREATE TABLE dbo.T1(col1 int)
```

The second task inserts some data into the table you just created:

```
INSERT dbo.T1(col1) VALUES(1)
```

To make the final task fail, you may want to try executing from this task a statement like the following:

```
INSERT dbo.T1(col1) VALUES('A')
```

Run the package with no transactions in place and see what happens. The results should look like Figure 13-21: The first two tasks succeed, and the third fails.

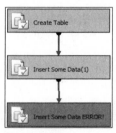

Figure 13-21

If you go to your database, you should see that the table was created and the data inserted, as shown in Figure 13-22.

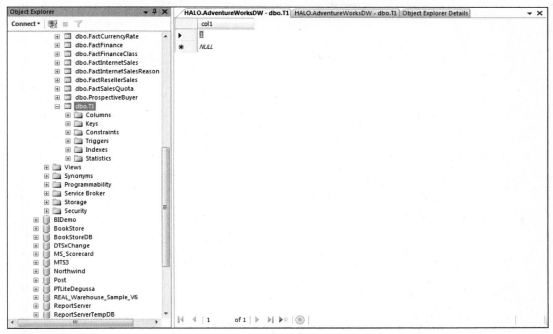

Figure 13-22

Now you want to make sure that the table will not be created if anything in the package fails. Drop the table and start again. The first thing you want to do is to tell the package to start a transaction that the tasks can join. You do that by setting the properties of the package as shown in Figure 13-23. Set the TransactionOption property to Required.

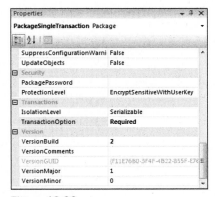

Figure 13-23

You now need to tell the tasks in the package to join this transaction, by setting their TransactionOption properties to "Supported," as shown in Figure 13-24. As an option for setting the properties of all these tasks quickly, select all the tasks and set the TransactionOption property to the desired value. This technique will allow you to set the properties on all the tasks at once.

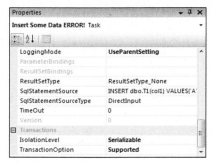

Figure 13-24

Now when you re-execute the package, a DTC transaction will be started by the package, all the tasks will join, and because of the failure in the last task, the work in the package will be undone. A good way to see that a DTC transaction was started is to look at the output window:

```
SSIS package "Transactions .dtsx" starting.
Information: 0x4001100A at Transactions: Starting distributed transaction for this
container.
Task failed: Insert Some Data ERROR !!!
Information: 0x4001100C at Insert Some Data ERROR !!!: Aborting the current
distributed transaction.
Information: 0x4001100B at Transactions: Committing distributed transaction started
by this container.
Warning: 0x8004D019 at Transactions: The transaction has already been aborted.
SSIS package "Transactions .dtsx" finished: Failure.
```

Single Package, Multiple Transactions

The aim of this second package is to be able to have two transactions running in the same package at the same time. Create the package as shown in Figure 13-25. If you're not feeling creative, you can use the same statements in the tasks as you used in the previous example.

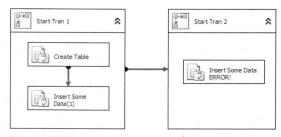

Figure 13-25

The package contains two sequence containers, each containing its own child tasks. The "Start Tran 1" Container begins a transaction, and the child tasks will join the transaction. The "Start Tran 2" Container also starts a transaction of its own, and its child task will join that transaction. As you can see, the task in "Start Tran 2" will deliberately fail. The "CREATE TABLE" Task creates a table into which all the other child tasks of both sequence containers will insert. The idea here is that after this package has run, the table will be created and the data inserted by the "Insert Some Data(1)" Task will be in the table even though the task in "Start Tran 2" fails. This could be useful when you have logical grouping of data manipulation routines to perform, and they either all succeed or none of them do. The following table details the tasks and containers in the package along with the package itself and the setting of their TransactionOption properties.

Task/Container	TransactionOption Property Value
Package	Supported
"Start Tran 1"	Required
CREATE TABLE	Supported
Insert Some Data(1)	Supported
"Start Tran 2"	Required
Insert Some Data ERROR !!!	Supported

After you execute the package, the results should look like Figure 13-26. The first container succeeded, but the second one failed because its child task failed.

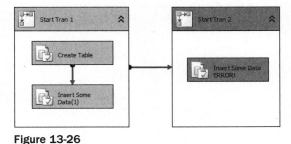

Figure 13-26

If you now look in the database, you will see that the table was created and a row inserted. To prove that two transactions were instantiated, take another look at the output window:

```
SSIS package "Multiple transactions same Package.dtsx" starting.
Information: 0x4001100A at Start Tran 1: Starting distributed transaction for this
container.
Information: 0x4001100B at Start Tran 1: Committing distributed transaction started
by this container.
Information: 0x4001100A at Start Tran 2: Starting distributed transaction for this
container.
Error: 0xC00291D7 at ERROR !!!, Execute SQL Task: No connection manager is
specified.
Error: 0xC0024107 at ERROR !!!: There were errors during task validation.
Information: 0x4001100C at ERROR !!!: Aborting the current distributed transaction.
Warning: 0x80019002 at Start Tran 2: The Execution method succeeded, but the number
of errors raised (3) reached the maximum allowed (1); resulting in failure. This
occurs when the number of errors reaches the number specified in MaximumErrorCount.
Change the MaximumErrorCount or fix the errors.
Information: 0x4001100C at Start Tran 2: Aborting the current distributed
transaction.
Warning: 0x80019002 at Multiple transactions same Package: The Execution method
succeeded, but the number of errors raised (3) reached the maximum allowed (1);
resulting in failure. This occurs when the number of errors reaches the number
specified in MaximumErrorCount. Change the MaximumErrorCount or fix the errors.
SSIS package "Multiple transactions same Package.dtsx" finished: Failure.
```

Two Packages, One Transaction

This example consists of two packages: "Caller" and "Called." What you want to do is to have a transaction span multiple packages. You'll have the Caller package create a table and then call a child package using an Execute Package Task, Called, which itself will create a table and insert some data. You will then introduce an error in the Caller package that will cause it to fail. The result should be that the work done in both of the packages is undone. Figure 13-27 shows the "Caller" package.

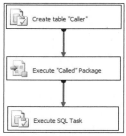

Figure 13-27

Figure 13-28 shows the "Called" package.

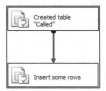

Figure 13-28

As before, you will need to set the TransactionOption properties on the tasks and containers, using the values in the following table:

Task/Container	TransactionOption Property Value
"Caller" Package	Required
CREATE TABLE "Caller"	Supported
EXECUTE "Called" Package	Supported
Make Things Fail	Supported
"Called" Package	Supported
Created Table "Called"	Supported
Insert Some Rows	Supported

The point to note here is that the child package "Called" becomes nothing more than another task. The parent of the "Called" package is the Execute Package Task in the "Caller" package. Because the Execute Package Task is in a transaction, and the Called package also has its TransactionOption set to Supported, it will join the transaction in the parent package.

If you change the TransactionOption property on the Execute Package Task in the "Caller" package to Not Supported, when the final task in the "Caller" package fails, the work in the "Called" package will not be undone. To see how to change the option, please refer back to Figure 13-24.

Single Package Using a Native Transaction in SQL Server

This example differs from the others in that you are going to use the transaction-handling abilities of SQL Server and not those of MSDTC. Although the example is short, it does demonstrate the fact that transactions can be used in packages that are not MSDTC transactions. Native SQL transactions will allow you a finer level of granularity when deciding what data gets rolled back and committed, but they are possible only against SQL Server. The package for this example is shown in Figure 13-29.

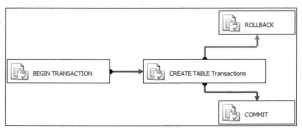

Figure 13-29

Although you cannot see it because the book is in black and white, the workflow line coming from the "CREATE TABLE Transactions" Task to the "Rollback" Task is red, indicating failure.

The following table lists the contents of the SQLStatement property for each of the Execute SQL Tasks:

Task	SQLStatement Property Value
BEGIN TRANSACTION	BEGIN TRANSACTION
CREATE TABLE Transactions	CREATE TABLE dbo.Transactions(col1 int)
ROLLBACK	ROLLBACK TRANSACTION
COMMIT	COMMIT TRANSACTION

The key to making the package use the native transaction capabilities in SQL Server is to have all the tasks use the same Connection Manager. In addition to this, you must make sure that the RetainSameConnection property on the Connection Manager is set to True, as shown in Figure 13-30.

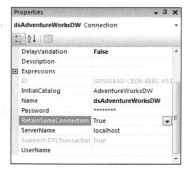

Figure 13-30

When the package is executed, SQL Server will fire up a transaction and either commit or rollback that transaction at the end of the package. You will now have a look at that happening on SQL Server by using Profiler, as shown in Figure 13-31. Profiler is really useful in situations like this. Here you simply want to prove that a transaction was started and that it either finished successfully or failed. You could also use it when firing SSIS packages to make sure that what you think you are executing is what you are actually executing.

EventClass	TextData	ApplicationName	NTUserName	LoginName	CPU
SQL:BatchStarting	BEGIN TRANSACTION	Microsoft SQ...	Darren	HALO\D...	
SQL:BatchCompleted	BEGIN TRANSACTION	Microsoft SQ...	Darren	HALO\D...	0
Audit Logout		Microsoft SQ...	Darren	HALO\D...	16
Audit Login	-- network protocol: LPC set quoted_identifier on set a...	Microsoft SQ...	Darren	HALO\D...	
SQL:BatchStarting	exec [sys].sp_oledb_ro_usrname	Microsoft SQ...	Darren	HALO\D...	
SQL:BatchCompleted	exec [sys].sp_oledb_ro_usrname	Microsoft SQ...	Darren	HALO\D...	0
SQL:BatchStarting	select collationname(0x0904D00034)	Microsoft SQ...	Darren	HALO\D...	
SQL:BatchCompleted	select collationname(0x0904D00034)	Microsoft SQ...	Darren	HALO\D...	0
SQL:BatchStarting	CREATE TABLE dbo.Transactions(col1 int)	Microsoft SQ...	Darren	HALO\D...	
SQL:BatchCompleted	CREATE TABLE dbo.Transactions(col1 int)	Microsoft SQ...	Darren	HALO\D...	0
Audit Logout		Microsoft SQ...	Darren	HALO\D...	0
Audit Login	-- network protocol: LPC set quoted_identifier on set a...	Microsoft SQ...	Darren	HALO\D...	
SQL:BatchStarting	exec [sys].sp_oledb_ro_usrname	Microsoft SQ...	Darren	HALO\D...	
SQL:BatchCompleted	exec [sys].sp_oledb_ro_usrname	Microsoft SQ...	Darren	HALO\D...	0
SQL:BatchStarting	select collationname(0x0904D00034)	Microsoft SQ...	Darren	HALO\D...	
SQL:BatchCompleted	select collationname(0x0904D00034)	Microsoft SQ...	Darren	HALO\D...	0
SQL:BatchStarting	COMMIT TRANSACTION	Microsoft SQ...	Darren	HALO\D...	
SQL:BatchCompleted	COMMIT TRANSACTION	Microsoft SQ...	Darren	HALO\D...	0
Audit Logout		Microsoft SQ...	Darren	HALO\D...	0

Figure 13-31

That ends your whistle-stop look at transactions within SSIS packages, and hopefully you can take something away from this section and use it in your packages.

Error Outputs

Error outputs can obviously be used to improve reliability, but they also have an important part to play for scalability as well. From a reliability perspective, they are a critical feature for coping with bad data. An appropriately configured component will direct failing rows down the error output as opposed to the main output. These rows are now removed from the main Data Flow path and may then receive additional treatment and cleansing to enable them to be recovered and merged back into the main flow. They can be explicitly merged, such as with a Union Transform, or implicitly through a second adapter directed at the final destination. Alternatively they could be discarded. Rows are rarely discarded totally; more often they will be logged and dealt with at a later point in time.

The capability to recover rows is perhaps the most useful course of action. If a data item is missing in the source extract but required in the final destination, the error flow path can be used to fix this. If the data item is available from a secondary system, then a lookup could be used. If the data item is not available elsewhere, then perhaps a default value can be used instead.

In other situations, the data may be out of range for the process or destination. If the data causes an integrity violation, then the failed data could be used to populate the constraining reference with new values and then the data itself could be successfully processed. If a data type conflict occurs, then maybe a simple truncation would suffice, or an additional set of logic could be applied to try and detect the real value, such as with data time values held in strings. The data could then be converted into the required format.

When assumptions or fixes have been made to data in this way, it is best practice to always mark rows as having been manipulated, so that if additional information becomes available later, they can be targeted directly. In addition, whenever an assumption is made, it should be clearly identified as such to the end user.

All of the scenarios described here revolve around trying to recover from poor data, within the pipeline and the current session, allowing processing to continue, and ideally fixing the problem such that data is recovered. This is a new concept when compared with DTS and several other products, but the ability to fix errors in real time is a very valuable option that you should always consider when building solutions.

The obvious question that then occurs is this: Why not include the additional transformations used to correct and cleanse the data in the main Data Flow path, so that any problems are dealt with before they cause an error? This would mean that all data flowed down a single path and the overall Data Flow design may appear simpler, with no branching and merging flows. This is where the scalability factor should come into your solution design. Ideally, you would always build the simplest Data Flow possible, using as few transformations as possible. The less work you perform, the greater the performance and therefore scalability.

Figure 13-32 illustrates a simple Data Flow used to load some data. In this contrived scenario, some of the rows will be missing values for SpecialtyCode and ConsultantCode. The source data contains text descriptions as well, so these are being used to perform a lookup to retrieve the missing values. The initial design logic goes that you evaluate the column for NULL values in a Conditional Split Transform. Bad rows are directed to an alternate output that connects to the Lookup Transform. Once the lookup has populated the missing value, the rows are then fed back into the main pipeline through the Union All Transform. The same pattern is followed for the SpecialtyCode and ConsultantCode columns, ensuring that the final insert through the OLE DB Destination has all good data. This is the base design for solving your problem, and it follows the procedural logic quite closely.

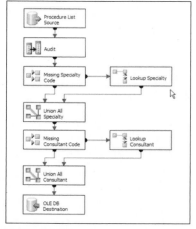

Figure 13-32

Figure 13-33 shows two alternative Data Flow designs, presented side by side for easy comparison. In the first design, you disregard any existing data in the SpecialtyCode and ConsultantCode columns and populate them entirely through the lookup. Although this may seem like wasted effort, the overall design is simpler, and in testing it was slightly faster compared to the more complicated design in Figure 13-32. This was with a test dataset that had a bad row ratio of 1 in 3, that is, one row in three had missing values. If the ratio dropped to 1 in 6 for the bad rows, then the two methods performed the same.

The second design assumes that all data is good until proven otherwise, so you insert directly into the destination. Rows that fail due to the missing values pass down the error output, "OLE DB Destination Error Output," and are then processed through the two lookups. The choice between the two designs is whether you fix all rows or only those that fail. Using the 1 in 3 bad rows test data, fixing only the failed rows was 20% faster than fixing all rows. When the bad row ratio dropped to 1 in 6, the performance gain also dropped, to only 10%.

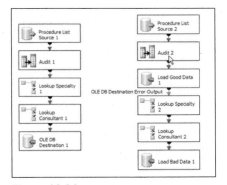

Figure 13-33

As demonstrated by the previous examples, the decision on where to include the corrective transformations is based on the ratio of good rows to bad rows, when compared with how much work is required to validate the quality of the data. The cost of fixing the data should be excluded if possible, as that will be required regardless of the design, but often the two are inseparable.

The performance characteristics of the corrective transforms should also be considered. In the preceding examples, you used lookups, which are inherently expensive transforms. The test data and lookup reference data included only six distinct values to minimize the impact on the overall testing. Lookups with more distinct values, and higher cardinality, will be more expensive, as the caching becomes less effective and itself will consume more resources.

In summary, the more expensive the verification, the more bad rows you require to justify adding the validation and fix to the main flow. For fewer bad rows, or a more expensive validation procedure, you have increased justification for keeping the main flow simple and for using the error flow to perform the fix-up work.

The overall number of rows should also influence your design, because any advantages or disadvantages will be amplified with a greater number of rows, regardless of the ratio. For a smaller number of rows, the fixed costs may outweigh the implied benefits, as any component has a cost to manage at runtime, so a more complicated Data Flow may not be worthwhile with fewer overall rows.

This concept of using error flows versus the main flow to correct data quality issues and related errors is not confined to those outputs that implement the error output explicitly. You can apply the same logic manually, primarily through the use of the Conditional Split Transformation, as in the first example, Figure 13-32. You can perform a simple test to detect any potential issues and direct rows of differing quality down different outputs. Where expensive operations are required, your goal is to ensure that as few rows as possible follow this path, and that the majority of the rows follow cheaper, and usually simpler, routes to their destination.

Finally, do not be put off by the name of an error output; they are not things to be avoided at all costs. Component developers often take advantage of the rich underlying pipeline architecture, using error outputs as a simple way of indicating the result of a transformation for a given row. They do not affect the overall success or failure state of a package, so don't be put off from using them.

You should be aware that the performance figures quoted here are for indicative purposes only. They illustrate the differences in the methods described but should not be taken as literal values that you can expect to reproduce, unless you're using exactly the same design, data, and environment. The key point is that testing such scenarios should be a routine part of your development practice.

Scaling Out

You are no doubt already familiar with the term *scaling out*, and of course the concept can be applied to SSIS systems. Although there are no magic switches here, there are several interesting features of SSIS, and you will see how they can be applied. Following this combined theme, you will learn how these strategies benefit reliability as well.

Architectural Improvements

The development team at Microsoft has made two important improvements in the Integration Services engine in regards to performance and scalability. The first improvement is in the Lookup Transformation in the Data Flow. The second improvement is within the Transformation Data Pipeline itself. These improvements represent an enormous leap from the previous version of SQL Server. So drastic are these improvements that recent benchmarks are boasting a 1 terabyte load in less than 30 minutes.

> *This benchmark test is documented by Microsoft at the following URL:*
> `http://www.microsoft.com/sqlserver/2008/en/us/benchmarks.aspx`.

Lookup Transformation Improvements

The most notable improvement in the Lookup Transformation is in the way it caches data and the options available to optimize that configuration. The new Data Sources available to this transformation now include pure in-memory cache and persistent file storage (also called persisted cache). Both of these options require the transformation to be configured to use the full-cache option, however. A new Connection Manager called the Cache Connection Manager governs these two types of caching options.

Caching operations in the new Lookup Transformation provide three modes to choose from (full, partial, or none). Using the fulls-cache mode, the lookup set will be stored in its entirety and will load before the lookup operation actually runs, but will not repopulate on every subsequent lookup operation. A partial cache will only store matched lookups, and no-cache will repopulate the cache every time. Of course you can also manually configure the size of the cache to store, measured in megabytes.

Persistent file storage is another very exciting caching feature in that it will store your cache in a file that can been reused across other packages. Talk about reusability! To add to the excitement, the cache can now be loaded from a variety of sources including text files, XML files, or even Web services. Basically, any source can now be used to populate the cache in Integration Services 2008. Lastly, partial-cache mode is enhanced with a new cache option called miss-cache, in which items being processed for lookup that do not have a match will be cached, so that they will not be retried in future lookup operations. All these features translate into scalability and performance gains that make this new version a real winner.

Data Pipeline Improvements

The Data Pipeline, as the work-horse of the data processing engine, has been the main target by the Integration Services development team for improvement in regards to scalability and performance. In 2008, the Data Pipeline architecture has been re-written to provide a fully multi-threaded engine for true parallelism. This improvement allows most pipelines to scale better without the manual tweaking that was required in 2005. This is perhaps the greatest improvement in the area of scalability.

Scale Out Memory Pressures

By design, the pipeline processing takes place almost exclusively in memory. This makes for faster data movement and transformations, and a design goal should always be to make a single pass over your data. In this way, you eliminate the time-consuming staging and the costs of reading and writing the same data several times. The potential disadvantage of this is that for large amounts of data and complicated sets of transformations, you need a large amount of memory, and it needs to be the right type of memory for optimum performance.

The virtual memory space for 32-bit Windows operating systems is limited to 2 GB by default. Although you can increase this amount through the use of the /3GB switch applied in the boot.ini file, this often falls short of the total memory available today. This limit is applied per process, which for your purposes means a single package during execution, so by partitioning a process across multiple packages, you can ensure that each of the smaller packages is its own process and therefore takes advantage of the full 2–3 GB virtual space independently. The most common method of chaining packages together to form a consolidated process is through the Execute Package Task, in which case it is imperative that you set the child package to execute out of process. You must set the ExecuteOutOfProcess property to true to allow this to happen.

It is worth noting that unlike the SQL Server database engine, SSIS does not support Advanced Windowing Extensions (AWE), so scaling out to multiple packages across processes is the only way to take advantage of larger amounts of memory. If you have a very large memory requirement, then you should consider a 64-bit system for hosting these processes.

For more a more detailed explanation of how SSIS uses memory, and the in-memory buffer structure used to move data through the pipeline, see Chapter 14.

Scale Out by Staging Data

Staging of data is very much on the decline; after all, why incur the cost of writing to and reading from a staging area, when you can perform all the processing in memory with a single pass of data? With the inclusion of the Dimension and Partition Processing Destinations, you no longer need a physical Data Source to populate your SQL Server Analysis Services (SSAS) cubes — yet another reason for the decline of staging or even the traditional data warehouse. Although this is still a contentious subject for many, the issue here is this: Should you use staging during the SSIS processing flow? Although it may not be technically required to achieve the overall goal, there are still some very good reasons why you may want to, coming from both the scalability and reliability perspectives.

For this discussion, staging could also be described as partitioning. The process could be implemented within a single Data Flow, but for one or more of the reasons described next, it may be subdivided into multiple Data Flows. These smaller units could be within a single package, or they may be distributed through several as discussed next. The staged data will be used only by another Data Flow and does not need to be accessed directly through regular interfaces. For this reason, the ideal choices for the source and destinations are the raw file adapters. This could be described as vertical partitioning, but you could also overlay a level of horizontal partitioning, as by executing multiple instances of a package in parallel.

Raw file adapters allow you to persist the native buffer structures to disk. The in-memory buffer structure is simply dumped to and from the file, without any translation or processing as found in all other adapters, making these the fastest adapters for staging data. You can take advantage of this to artificially force a memory checkpoint to be written to disk, allowing you to span multiple Data Flow Tasks and packages. Staging environments and raw files are also discussed later on in Chapter 14, but some specific examples will be illustrated here.

The key use for raw files is that by splitting a Data Flow into at least two individual tasks, the primary task can end with a raw file destination, and the secondary task can begin with a raw file source. The buffer structure is exactly the same between the two tasks, so the split can be considered irrelevant from an overall flow perspective, but it provides perfect preservation between the two.

Data Flow Restart

As covered previously, the checkpoint feature provides the ability to restart a package from the point of failure, but it does not extend inside a Data Flow. However, if you divide a Data Flow into one or more individual tasks, each linked together by raw files, you immediately gain the ability to restart the combined flow. Through the correct use of native checkpoints at the (Data Flow) task level, this process becomes very simple to manage.

The choice of where to divide a flow is subjective, but two common choices would be immediately after extraction and immediately after transformation, prior to load.

The post-extraction point offers several key benefits. Many source systems are remote, so extraction may take place over suboptimal network links and can be the slowest part of the process. By staging immediately after the extraction, you do not have to repeat this slow step in the event of a failure and restart. There may also be an impact on the source system during the extraction, and very often this must take place during a fixed time window when utilization is low. In this case, it may be unacceptable to repeat the extract in the event of a failure, until the next time window, usually the following night.

Staging post-transformation simply ensures that the transformation is not wasted if the destination system is unavailable.

You may wish to include additional staging points mid-transformation. These would usually be located after particularly expensive operations and before those that you suspect are at risk to fail. Although you can plan for problems, and the use of error outputs described previously should allow you to handle many situations, you can still expect the unexpected and plan a staging point with this in mind. The goal remains the ability to restart as close to the failure point as possible and to reduce the cost of any reprocessing required.

Figure 13-34 shows an example data load process that you may wish to partition into multiple tasks to take advantage of Data Flow restart.

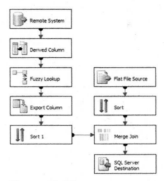

Figure 13-34

For this scenario, the OLE DB Source connects to a remote SQL Server over a slow network link. Due to the time taken for this data extraction and the impact on the source system, it is not acceptable to repeat the extract if the subsequent processing fails for any reason. For this reason, you choose to stage data through a raw file immediately after the Source Component. The resulting Data Flow layout is shown in Figure 13-35. This is a Data Flow Task.

Figure 13-35

The Flat File Source data is accessed across the LAN, and it needs to be captured before it is overwritten. The sort operation is also particularly expensive due to the volume of data. For this reason, you choose to stage the data after the sort is complete. The resulting Data Flow is shown in Figure 13-36.

Figure 13-36

Finally, you use a third Data Flow Task to consume the two staging raw files and complete the process. This is shown in Figure 13-37.

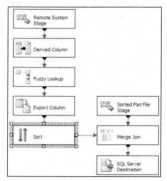

Figure 13-37

Following this example, a single Data Flow has been divided into three separate tasks. For the purposes of restarting a failed process, you would use a single package and implement checkpoints on each of the three Data Flow Tasks.

Scale across Machines

In a similar manner to the Data Flow restart just discussed, you can also use raw file adapters to partition the Data Flow. By separating tasks into different packages, you can run packages across machines. This may be advantageous if a specific machine has properties not shared with others. Perhaps the machine capable of performing the extract is situated in a different network segment from the machine best suited for processing the data, and direct access is unavailable between the main processing machine and the source. The extract could be performed, and the main processing machine would then retrieve the raw data to continue the process. These situations will be organizational restrictions rather than decisions driven by the design architecture.

The more compelling story for scaling across machines is to use horizontal partitioning. A simple scenario would utilize two packages. The first package would extract data from the source system, and through the Conditional Split you produce two or more exclusive subsets of the data and write this to individual raw files. Each raw file would contain some of the rows from the extract, as determined by the expression used in the Conditional Split. The most common horizontal partition scheme is time-based, but any method could be used here. The goal is to subdivide the total extract into manageable chunks, so for example if a sequential row number is already available in the source, this would be ideal, or one could be applied. See the T-SQL ROW_NUMBER function. Similarly a Row Number Transformation could be used to apply the numbering, which could then be used by the split, or the numbering and splitting could be delivered through a Script Component.

With a sorted dataset, each raw file may be written in sequence, completing in order, before moving on to the next one. While this may seem uneven and inefficient, it is assumed that the time delay between completion of the first and final destinations is inconsequential compared to the savings achieved by the subsequent parallel processing.

Once the partitioned raw files are complete, they are consumed by the second package, which performs the transformation and load aspects of the processing. Each file is processed by an instance of the package running on a separate machine. This way, you can scale across machines and perform expensive transformations in parallel. For a smaller-scale implementation, where the previously described 32-bit virtual memory constraints apply, you could parallel process on a single machine, such that each package instance would be a separate thread, allowed its own allocation of virtual memory space.

For destinations that are partitioned themselves, such as a SQL Server data warehouse with table partitions or a partitioned view model, or Analysis Services partitions, it may also make sense to match the partition schema to that of the destination, such that each package addresses a single table or partition.

Figure 13-38 shows a sample package that for the purposes of this example you will partition horizontally.

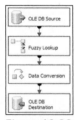

Figure 13-38

In this scenario, the Fuzzy Lookup is processing names against a very large reference set, and this is taking too long. To introduce some parallel processing, you decide to partition on the first letter of a name field. It is deemed stable enough for matches to be within the same letter, although in a real-world scenario this may not always be true. You use a Conditional Split Transformation to produce the two raw files partitioned from A to M and from N to Z. This primer package is illustrated in Figure 13-39.

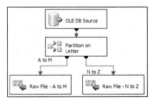

Figure 13-39

Ideally you would then have two instances of the second package, Figure 13-39, running in parallel on two separate machines. However, you need to ensure that the lookup data is filtered on name to match the raw file. Not all Pipeline Component properties are exposed as expressions, allowing you to dynamically control them, so you would need two versions of the package, identical except for a different Reference table name property in the Fuzzy Lookup, as shown in Figure 13-40. In preparation, you would create two views, one for names A to M and the other for names N to Z to match the two raw files. The two package versions would each use the view to match the raw file they will process.

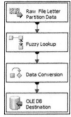

Figure 13-40

For any design that uses raw files, the additional I/O cost must be evaluated against the processing performance gains, but for large-scale implementations it offers a convenient way of ensuring consistency within the overall flow and incurs no translation penalty associated with other storage formats.

Summary

In this chapter, you looked at some of the obvious SSIS features provided to help you build reliable and scalable solutions, such as checkpoints and transactions. You also learned about some practices you can apply, such as Data Flow restarts and scaling across machines; although these may not be explicit features, they are nonetheless very powerful techniques that can be implemented in your package designs.

14

Understanding and Tuning the Data Flow Engine

This chapter dives under the hood of SSIS to consider the architecture of the engine and its components, and then best practices for design and optimization including the following concepts:

- ❑ Control Flow and Data Flow comparison
- ❑ Data Flow Transformation types
- ❑ Data Flow buffer architecture and execution trees
- ❑ Monitoring Data Flow execution
- ❑ Data Flow design practices
- ❑ Tuning the Data Flow engine
- ❑ Performance monitoring

The initial part of this chapter is more abstract and theoretical, but we'll then move into the practical and tangible. In the concluding sections, you will take the knowledge you have developed here and bring it to application, considering a methodology to optimization and looking at a few real-world scenarios.

The SSIS Engine

Before learning about buffers, asynchronous components, and execution trees, consider this analogy — traffic management. Have you ever driven in a big city and wondered how the traffic system works? It's remarkable to consider how the traffic lights are all coordinated in a city. In Manhattan, for example, a taxi drive can take you from midtown to downtown in minutes — in part because the lights are timed in a rolling fashion to maintain efficiency. The heavy fine assessed to anyone who "locks the box" (remains in the intersection after the light turns red) demonstrates how detrimental it is to interfere with the synchronization of such a complex traffic grid.

Contrast the efficiency of Manhattan with the gridlock and delay that result from a poorly designed traffic system. Everyone has been there before — sitting at a red light for minutes despite the absence of traffic on the intersecting streets, and then after the light changes, you find yourself at the next intersection in the same scenario! Even in a light-traffic environment, progress is impeded by poor coordination and inefficient design.

Bringing this back around to SSIS, in some ways the engine is similar to the grid management of a big city because the SSIS engine coordinates server resources and Data Flow for efficient information processing. Part of the process to make a package execution efficient requires your involvement. In turn, this requires knowing how the SSIS engine works and some important particulars of components and properties that affect the data processing. That is the purpose of this chapter: to provide the groundwork of understanding SSIS that will lead to better and more efficient design.

Understanding the SSIS Data Flow and Control Flow

From an architectural perspective, the difference between SSIS Data Flow and Control Flow is important. One aspect that will help illustrate the distinction is to look at them from the perspective of how the components are handled. In the Control Flow, the *task* is the smallest unit of work, and tasks require completion (success, failure, or just completion) before the subsequent tasks are handled. In the Data Flow, the *transformation* is the basic component; however, a transformation functions very differently from a task. Instead of one transformation necessarily waiting for associated transformations before work can be done, the transformations work together to process and manage data.

Comparing and Contrasting the Data Flow and Control Flow

Although the Control Flow looks very similar to the Data Flow with processing objects (tasks and transformations) and green and red connectors that bridge them, there is a world of difference between them. The Control Flow, for example, does not manage or pass data between components; rather it functions as a task coordinator with isolated units of work. Here are some of the Control Flow concepts:

❑ Workflow orchestration

❑ Process-oriented

❑ Serial or parallel tasks execution

❑ Synchronous processing

As highlighted, the Control Flow Tasks can be designed to execute both serially and in parallel — in fact, more often than not there will be aspects of both. A Control Flow Task can branch off into multiple tasks that are performed in parallel as well as a single next step that is performed essentially in serial from the first. To show this, Figure 14-1 is a very simple Control Flow process where the tasks are connected in a linear fashion. The execution of this package shows that the components are serialized — only a single task is executing at a time.

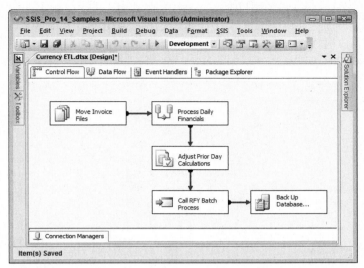

Figure 14-1

The Data Flow, on the other hand, can branch, split, and merge, providing parallel processing, but the concept is different from the Control Flow. Even though there may be a set of connected linear transformations, you cannot necessarily call the process serial, because the transformations in most cases will be running at the same time, handling subsets of the data in parallel. Here are some of the unique aspects of the Data Flow:

❑ Information-oriented

❑ Data correlation and transformation

❑ Coordinated processing

❑ Streaming in nature

❑ Sources and destinations

Similar to the Control Flow shown in Figure 14-1, Figure 14-2 models a simple Data Flow where the components are connected one after the other. The difference between the Data Flow in Figure 14-2 and the Control Flow in Figure 14-1 is that only a single task is executing in the linear flow. In the Data Flow, however, all the transformations are doing work at the same time. In other words, the first batch of Data Flowing in from the source may be in the final destination step (Currency Rate Destination), while at the same time data is still flowing in from the source.

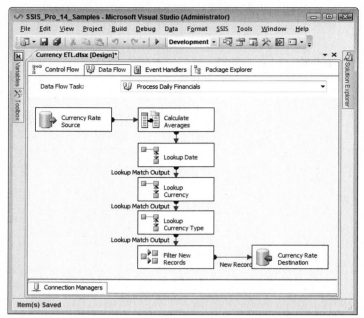

Figure 14-2

Multiple components are running at the same time because the Data Flow Transformations are working together in a coordinated streaming fashion, and the data is being transformed in groups as it is passed down from the source to the subsequent transformations.

SSIS Package Execution Times from Package Start to Package Finish

Since a Data Flow is merely a type of Control Flow Task, and there can be more than one Data Flow embedded in a package, the total time it takes to execute a package is measured from the execution of the first Control Flow Task or Tasks through the completion of the last task being executed, regardless of whether the components executing are Data Flow Transformations or Control Flow Tasks. This may sound obvious, but it is worth mentioning, because when designing a package, maximizing the parallel processing where appropriate (with due regard to your server resources) will help optimize the flow and reduce the overall processing time.

The package in Figure 14-3 has several tasks executing a variety of processes and using precedence constraints in a way that demonstrates parallel execution of tasks. The last task, Back Up Database, is the only task that does not execute in parallel because it has to wait for the execution of all the other tasks.

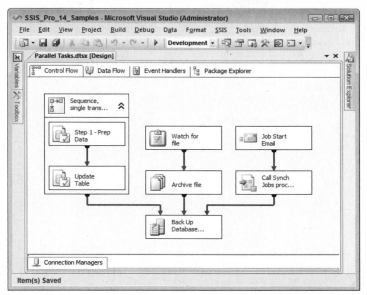

Figure 14-3

Because the Control Flow has been designed with parallelization, the overlap in tasks allows the execution of the package to complete faster than it would if the steps were executed in a serial manner as earlier shown in Figure 14-1.

Handling Workflows with the Control Flow

Both of the components of the Control Flow have been discussed in Chapter 3 as well as the different types of precedence constraints. Since the Control Flow contains standard workflow concepts that are common to most scheduling and ETL tools, the rest of this chapter will focus on the Data Flow; however, a brief look at the Control Flow parallelization and processing is warranted.

The Control Flow, as has already been mentioned, can be designed to execute tasks in parallel or serial, or a combination of the two. Tasks also are *synchronous* in nature, meaning that the task requires completion before handing off an operation to another process. While it is possible to design a Control Flow that contains tasks that are not connected with constraints to other tasks, the tasks are still synchronously tied to the execution of the package. Said in another way, a package cannot kick off the execution of a task and then complete execution while the task is still executing. Rather, the SSIS execution thread for the task is synchronously tied to the task's execution and will not release until the task completes successfully or fails.

The synchronous nature of tasks should not be confused with the synchronous and asynchronous nature of transformations in the Data Flow. The concepts are slightly different. In the Data Flow, a transformation's synchronicity is a matter of communication (how data is passed between transformations) rather than the process orientation of the Control Flow.

SSIS allows the maximum number of parallel tasks that execute to be set on a package-by-package basis. This setting, called the MaxConcurrentExecutables, is a property of the Control Flow. Click in a blank space on the Control Flow, and then pull up the Properties window. Figure 14-4 shows the property, which is settable to a whole number.

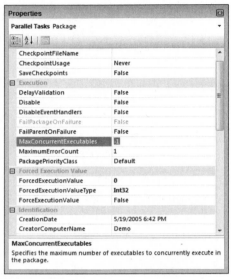

Figure 14-4

The default setting is -1, indicating to SSIS to add 2 to the number of processors and use that value for the number of tasks to execute in parallel. For example, if the server has four processors and the default value is used, SSIS will allow up to six tasks to be executed in parallel. Furthermore, if the number of possible parallel executing tasks (based on Control Flow design) is more than the number of allowable parallel tasks ("allowable" as specified by the MaxConcurrentExecutables setting), then some of the Control Flow Tasks will have to wait to execute until parallel threads are available.

Some tasks require more server resources than others, so the package Concurrency should not be tied directly to the number of processors that your server contains. Rather, task workload should be evaluated across the tasks. For example, if your package contains a Data Flow, then most likely it will consume more server resources than the other tasks. In fact, each Data Flow can be set up to use multiple threads during execution, a property that is described in more detail in the Data Flow section that follows.

Data Processing in the Data Flow

The Data Flow is the core data processing factory of SSIS packages, where the primary data is handled, managed, transformed, integrated, and cleansed. Think of the Data Flow as a pipeline for data. A house, for example, has a primary water source, which is branched to all the different outlets in the house.

If a faucet is turned on, water will flow out the faucet, while at the same time water is coming in from the source. If all the water outlets in a house are turned off, then the pressure backs up to the source to where it will no longer flow into the house until the pressure is relieved. On the contrary, if all the water outlets in the house are opened at once, then the source pressure may not be able to keep up with the flow of water and the pressure coming out of the faucets will be weaker. Of course, don't try this at home; it may produce other problems!

The Data Flow is appropriately named because the data equates to the water in the plumbing analogy. The Data Flows from the Data Sources through the transformations to the Data Destinations. In addition to the flowing concept, there are similarities to the Data Flow pressure within the pipeline. For example, while a Data Source may be able to stream 10,000 rows per second, if a downstream transformation consumes too much server resources, it could apply backward pressure on the source and reduce the number of rows coming from the source. Essentially, this creates a bottleneck that may need to be addressed to optimize the flow. In order to understand and apply design principles in a Data Flow, an in-depth discussion of the Data Flow architecture is merited. Understanding several Data Flow concepts will give you a fuller perspective of what is going on under the hood of an executing package. Each of these are addressed over the next few pages:

- ❏ Data buffer architecture
- ❏ Transformation types
- ❏ Transformation communication
- ❏ Execution trees

After your review of the architecture, your analysis will shift to monitoring packages in order to determine how the Data Flow engine is handling data processing.

Memory Buffer Architecture

The Data Flow manages data in groups of data called *buffers*. A buffer is merely memory that is allocated for the use of storing rows and columns of data where transformations are applied. This means that as data is being extracted from sources into the engine, it is put into these pre-allocated memory buffers. Buffers are dynamically sized based on row width (the cumulative number of bytes in a row) and other package and server criteria. A buffer, for example, may include 9000 rows of data with a few columns of data. Figure 14-5 shows a few groupings of buffers.

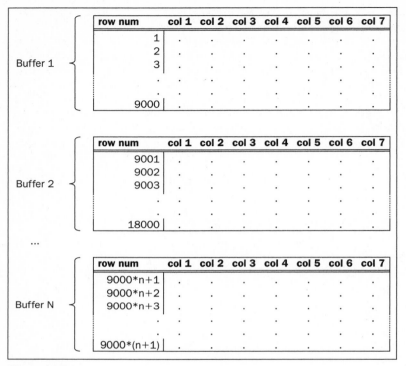

Figure 14-5

Although it is easy to picture data being passed down from transformation to transformation in the Data Flow similar to the flow of water in the pipeline analogy, this is not a complete picture of what is going on behind the scenes. Instead of data being passed down through the transformations, groups of transformations pass over the buffers of data and make in-place changes as defined by the transformations. Think of how much more efficient this process is than if the data were copied from one buffer to the next every time a transformation specified a change in the data! To be sure, there are times when the buffers are copied and other times when the buffers are held up in cache by transformations. The understanding of how and when this happens will help determine the right design to optimize your solution.

The understanding of how memory buffers are managed requires knowing something about the different types of Data Flow Components — transformations and adapters.

Types of Transformations

The adapters and the transformations in the Data Flow have certain characteristics that group each into different categories. The base-level differences between them are the way they communicate with each other, and how and when data is handed off from one transformation to another. Evaluating transformations on two fronts will provide the background you need to understand how the buffers are managed:

- ❑ **Blocking nature:** non-blocking (sometimes called streaming), semi-blocking, blocking
- ❑ **Communication mechanism:** synchronous and asynchronous

In reality, these classifications are related, but from a practical standpoint, discussing them separately provides some context to data management in the Data Flow.

Non-Blocking, Semi-Blocking, and Blocking

The most obvious distinction between transformations is their blocking nature. All transformations fall into one of three categories: non-blocking, semi-blocking, or blocking. These terms describe whether data in a transformation is passed downstream in the pipeline immediately, in increments, or after all the data is fully received.

The blocking nature of a transformation is related to what a transformation is designed to accomplish. Since the Data Flow engine just invokes the transformations without knowing what they internally do, there are no properties of the transformation that discretely identify this nature. However, when we look at the communication between transformations in the next section (the synchronous and asynchronous communication), we can identify how the engine will manage transformations one to another.

Non-Blocking Transformations, Streaming and Row-Based

Most of the SSIS Transformations are non-blocking. This means that the transformation logic that is applied in the transformation does not impede the data from moving on to the next transformation after the transformation logic is applied to the row. Two categories of non-blocking transformations exist: streaming and row-based. The difference is whether the SSIS Transformation can use internal information and processes to handle its work or whether the transformation has to call an external process to retrieve information it needs for the work. Some transformations can be categorized as streaming or row-based depending on their configuration, which are indicated in the list below.

Streaming transformations are usually able to apply transformation logic quickly, using pre-cached data and processing calculations within the row being worked on. In these transformations, it is usually the case that a transformation will not slip behind the rate of the data being fed to it. These transformations focus their resources on the CPUs, which in most cases is not the bottleneck of an ETL system. Therefore, they are classified as streaming. The following transformations stream the data from transformation to transformation in the Data Flow:

- ❑ Audit
- ❑ Character Map
- ❑ Conditional Split
- ❑ Copy Column

❑ Data Conversion

❑ Derived Column

❑ Lookup (with a full-cache setting)

❑ Multicast

❑ Percent Sampling

❑ Row Count

❑ Script Component (provided the script is not configured with an asynchronous output, which will be discussed later)

❑ Union All (the Union All acts like a streaming transformation but is actually a semi-blocking transformation because it communicates asynchronously, which we will consider in the next section)

The second grouping of non-blocking transformations is identified as *row-based*. These transformations are still non-blocking in the sense that the data can flow immediately to the next transformation after the transformation logic is applied to the buffer. The row-based description indicates that the rows flowing through the transformation are acted on one-by-one with a requirement to interact with an outside process such as a database, file, or component. Given their row-based processes, in most cases these transformations may not be able to keep up with the rate at which the data is fed to them, and the buffers are held up until each row is processed. The following transformations are classified as row-based:

❑ Export Column

❑ Import Column

❑ Lookup (with a no-cache or partial-cache setting)

❑ OLE DB Command

❑ Script Component (where the script interacts with an external component)

❑ Slowly Changing Dimension (each row is looked up against the dimension in the database)

Figure 14-6 shows a Data Flow composed of only streaming transformations. If you look at the row counts in the design UI, you will notice that the transformations are passing rows downstream in the pipeline as soon as the transformation logic is completed. Streaming transformations do not have to wait for other operations in order for the rows being processed to be passed downstream.

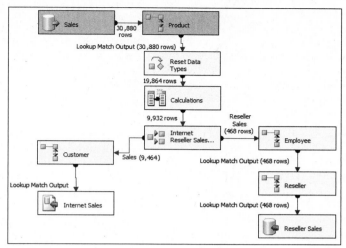

Figure 14-6

Also, notice in Figure 14-6 that data is inserted into the destination even while transformation logic is still being applied to some of the earlier transformations. This very simple Data Flow is handling a high volume of data with minimal resources, such as memory usage, because of the streaming nature of the Transformation Components used.

Semi-Blocking Transformations

The next category of Transformation Components are the ones that hold up records in the Data Flow for a period of time before allowing the memory buffers to be passed downstream. These are typically called semi-blocking transformations, given their nature. Only a few out-of-the-box transformations are semi-blocking in nature:

- ❑ Data Mining Query
- ❑ Merge
- ❑ Merge Join
- ❑ Pivot
- ❑ Term Lookup
- ❑ Unpivot
- ❑ Union All (Also included in the streaming transformations list, but under the covers, the Union All is semi-blocking.)

The Merge and Merge Join Transformations are described in detail in Chapter 5 and Chapter 7, but in relation to the semi-blocking nature of these components, note that they require the sources to be sorted on the matching keys of the merge. Both of these transformations function by waiting for key matches from both sides of the merge (or join), and when the matching sorted keys from both sides pass through the transformations, the records can then be sent downstream while the next set of keys is handled. Figure 14-7 shows how a Merge Join within a Data Flow will partially hold up the processing of the rows until the matches are made.

Typically the row count upstream of the Merge Join is much higher than the row count just below the Merge Join, because the Merge Join waits for the sorted key matches as they flow in from both sides of the merge. Buffers are being released downstream, just not in a streaming fashion as in the non-blocking Transformation Components. You may also be wondering why there is not a Sort Transformation on the right-side source of the Merge Join despite the fact that the transformations require the sources to be sorted. This is because the source data was pre-sorted and the Source adapter was configured to recognize that Data Flowing into the Data Flow was already sorted. Chapter 7 describes how to set the IsSorted property of a source.

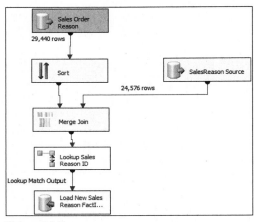

Figure 14-7

Semi-blocking transformations require a little more server resources since the buffers will need to stay in memory until the right data is received.

Blocking Transformations

The final category of the transformation types is the actual blocking transformations. For one reason or another, these components require a complete review of the upstream data before releasing any row downstream to the connected transformations and destinations. The list is also smaller than the list of non-blocking transformations because of the limited logic applications that require all the rows. Here is the list of the blocking transformations:

❑ Aggregate

❑ Fuzzy Grouping

❑ Fuzzy Lookup

❑ Row Sampling

❑ Sort

❑ Term Extraction

❑ Script Component (when configured to receive all rows before sending any downstream)

The two widely used examples of the blocking transformations are the Sort and Aggregate Transforms; each of these requires the entire dataset before handing off the data to the next transform. For example, in order to have an accurate average, all the records need to be held up by the Aggregate Transform. Similarly, to sort data in a flow, all the data needs to be available to the Sort Transformation before the component will know the order in which to release records downstream. Figure 14-8 shows a Data Flow that contains an Aggregate Transformation. The screen capture of this process shows that the entire source has already been brought into the Data Flow, but no rows have been released downstream while the transformation is determining the order.

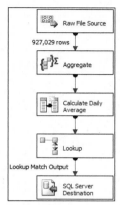

Figure 14-8

With a Blocking Component in the Data Flow, as you can see in Figure 14-8, the data is no longer streaming through the Data Flow, and there will not be a time when data can be inserted into the destination while data is being extracted from the source.

Blocking transformations are more resource-intensive for several reasons. First, since all the data is being held up, either the server must use a lot of memory to store the data or, in the case where the server does not have enough memory, a process of file staging happens, which requires the IO overhead of staging the data to disk temporarily. The second reason these transformations are intensive is that they usually put a heavy burden on the processor to perform the work of data aggregation, sorting, or fuzzy matching.

Synchronous and Asynchronous Transformation Outputs

Another important differentiation between transformations is how transformations that are connected to one another by a path communicate with one another. While closely related to the discussion on the blocking nature of transformations, *synchronous* and *asynchronous* refer more to the relationship between the input and Output Component connections and buffers.

Some transformations have an Advanced Editor window, which, among other things, drills into specific column-level properties of the transformations' input and output columns and is useful in explaining the difference between synchronous and asynchronous outputs. Figure 14-9 shows the Advanced Editor of the Sort Transformation, highlighting the Input and Output Properties tab. This particular transformation has a Sort Input and Sort Output group with a set of columns associated with each.

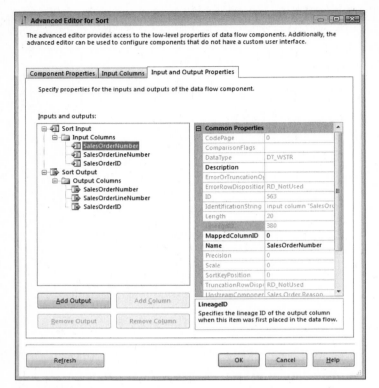

Figure 14-9

When a column is highlighted, the advanced properties of that column are displayed on the right, as Figure 14-9 shows. The advanced properties include such things as the data type of the column, the description, and so on. One important property to note is the `LineageID`. This is the integer pointer to the column within the buffers. Every column used in the Data Flow has at least one `LineageID` in the Data Flow. A column can have more than one `LineageID` as it passes through the Data Flow based on the types of transformation outputs (synchronous or asynchronous) that a column goes through in the Data Flow.

Asynchronous Transformation Outputs

It is easier to begin with the *asynchronous* definition because it leads into a comparison of the two kinds of transformation outputs, *synchronous* and asynchronous. A transformation output is asynchronous if the buffers used in the input are different from the buffers used in the output. In other words, many of the transformations cannot perform the specified operation and at the same time preserve the buffers (the number of rows or the order of the rows), so a copy of the data must be made to accomplish the desired effect.

The Aggregate Transformation, for example, may output only a fraction of the number of rows coming into it, or when the Merge Join Transformation has to marry two datasets together, the resulting number of rows will not be equivalent to the number of input rows. In both cases, the buffers are received, the processing is handled, and new buffers are created.

The Advanced Editor of the Sort shown earlier in Figure 14-9 highlights an input column. One of the properties of the input column is the LineageID. Notice that in this transformation, all the input columns are duplicated in the output columns list. In fact, as Figure 14-10 shows, the output column highlighted for the same input has a different LineageID.

The LineageIDs are different for the same column because the Sort Transformation output is asynchronous, and the data buffers in the input are not the same buffers in the output; therefore a new column identifier is needed for the output. In the preceding examples, the input LineageID is 380, while in the output column, the LineageID is 566.

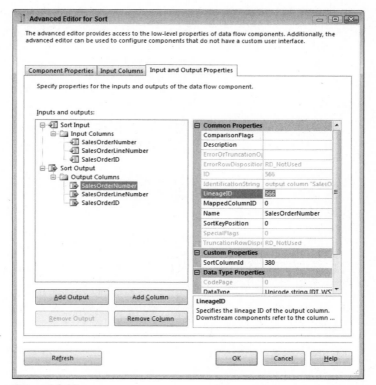

Figure 14-10

A list doesn't need to be included here, because all of the semi-blocking and blocking transformations already listed have asynchronous outputs by definition — none of them can pass input buffers on downstream because the data is held up for processing and reorganized.

One of the SSIS engine components is called the buffer manager. For asynchronous component outputs, the buffer manager is busy at work, decommissioning buffers for use elsewhere (in sources or other asynchronous outputs) and reassigning new buffers to the data coming out of the transformation. The buffer manager also schedules processor threads to components as threads are needed.

Synchronous Transformation Outputs

A synchronous transformation is one where the buffers are immediately handed off to the next downstream transformation at the completion of the transformation logic. This may sound like the definition given for streaming transformations, and it should, since there is almost complete overlap between streaming transformations and synchronous transformations. The word *buffers* was intentionally used in the definition of synchronous outputs, because the important point is that the same buffers received by the transformation input are passed out the output. Regarding the LineageIDs of the columns, they remain the same as the data is passed through the synchronous output, without a need to duplicate the buffers and assign a new LineageID as discussed previously in the asynchronous transformation output section.

Figure 14-11 shows the Advanced Editor of a synchronous component output, the Derived Column Transformation. There is a big difference between the advanced Input and Output properties of the Derived Column compared with the Sort (shown in Figure 14-9 and Figure 14-10). As you saw, all of the columns in the Sort's input and output are duplicated, while Figure 14-11 shows that the Derived Column Transformation contains only output columns.

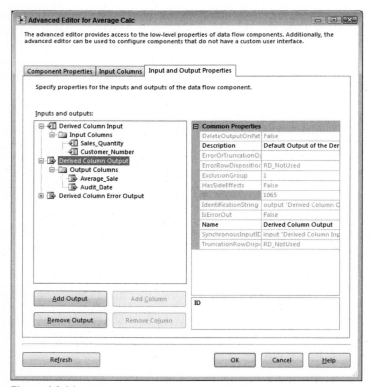

Figure 14-11

The rest of the columns are not included in the input or output list because they are not directly used by the transformation, and because the Derived Column Transformation output is synchronous. In other words, the columns coming from the upstream component flow through the Derived Column Transformation (in this example) and are available to the next downstream component.

> *A transformation is not limited to a single synchronous output. Both the Multicast and the Conditional Split can have multiple outputs, but all the outputs are synchronous.*

With the exception of the Union All, all of the non-blocking transformations listed in the previous section also have synchronous outputs. The Union All, while it functions like a streaming transformation, is really an asynchronous transformation. Given the complexity of unioning multiple sources together and keeping track of all the pointers to the right data from the different source inputs, the Union All instead copies the upstream data to new buffers as it receives them and passes the new buffers off to the downstream transformations.

> *Synchronous transformation outputs preserve the sort order of incoming data, while some of the asynchronous transformations do not. The Sort, Merge, and Merge Join asynchronous components of course have sorted outputs because of their nature, but the Union All, for example, does not.*

A definitive way to identify synchronous versus asynchronous components is to look at the SynchronousInputID property of the Column Output properties. If this value is 0, the component output is asynchronous, but if this property is set to a value greater than 0, the transformation output is synchronous to the input whose ID matches the SynchronousInputID value. Figure 14-11 shows the Derived Column Transformation with a value of 1065, indicating that the Derived Column Transformation output is synchronous and tied to the single Derived Column input.

Finally, a transformation output can be synchronous with only one of its inputs. This is why the Union All is asynchronous; its output cannot be synchronous with all inputs.

Source and Destination Adapters

Source and Destination adapters are integral to the Data Flow, and therefore merit brief consideration in this chapter. In fact, because of their differences in functionality, sources and destinations are therefore classified differently.

First of all, in looking at the advanced properties of a Source adapter, the source will have the same list of external columns and output columns. The external columns come directly from the source and are copied into the Data Flow buffers and subsequently assigned LineageIDs. While the external source columns do not have LineageIDs, the process is effectively the same as an asynchronous component output. Source adapters require buffers to be allocated where the incoming data can be grouped and managed for the downstream transformations to perform work against.

Destination adapters, on the other hand, function as synchronous components, since their buffers are de-allocated and data is loaded into the destinations. In the advanced properties of the destination adapter (as shown in Figure 14-12), an External Column list is also shown, which represents the destination columns used in the load. Notice that there is no primary Output Container (besides the Error Output) for the Destination adapter, since the buffers do not flow through the component, but rather are committed to a destination adapter as a final step in the Data Flow.

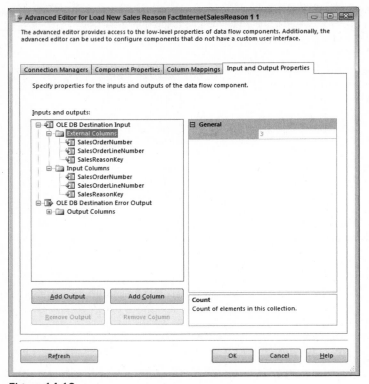

Figure 14-12

Advanced Data Flow Execution Concepts

The discussion of transformation types and how outputs handle buffers leads into a more advanced discussion of how the SSIS coordinates and manages the overall Data Flow processing. This section will take and apply the discussion of synchronous and asynchronous transformations and tie them together to provide the bigger picture of a package execution.

Relevant to this discussion is a more detailed understanding of buffer management within an executing package based on how the package is designed.

Execution Trees

In one sense, you have already looked at execution trees, although they weren't explicitly referred to by this name. An execution tree is the logical grouping of Data Flow Components (transformations and adapters) based on their synchronous relationship to one another. Groupings are delineated by asynchronous component outputs that indicate the completion of one execution tree and the start of the next.

Figure 14-13 shows a moderately complex Data Flow that uses multiple components with asynchronous outputs.

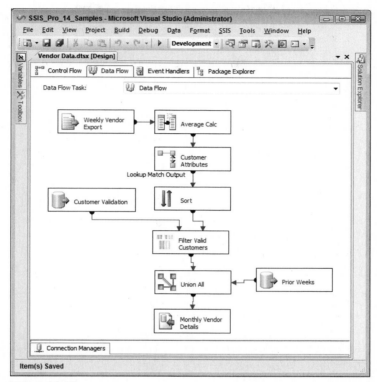

Figure 14-13

You will recall that components with asynchronous outputs use different input buffers. The input participates in the upstream execution tree, while the asynchronous output begins the next execution tree. In light of this, the execution trees for Figure 14-13 start at the Source adapters and are then completed, and a new execution tree begins at every asynchronous transformation. The example in Figure 14-14 has six execution trees.

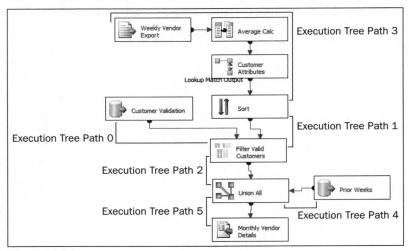

Figure 14-14

Execution trees are base 0, meaning you count them starting with a 0. In the next section, you will see how the pipeline logging identifies them. Although the execution trees seem out of order, you have used the explicit order given by the pipeline logging.

In the next section, you will address ways to log and track the execution trees within a Data Flow, but for now the discussion will emphasize a few principles of what happens in an execution tree.

As previously explained, the input and output buffers in a transformation with asynchronous outputs are different because the buffer data grouping cannot be preserved in both count, order, and columns. Rows within the input buffers may merge with other buffers, creating more (or fewer) rows in the output buffers than in either of the source buffers. Or input buffers may contain data that needs to be sorted or aggregated, which also fails to preserve the order or row count.

When SSIS executes a package, the buffer manager defines different buffer profiles based on the execution trees within a package. All the buffers used for a particular execution tree are identical in definition. When defining the buffer profile for each execution tree, the SSIS buffer manager looks at all the transformations used in the execution tree and includes every column in the buffer that is needed at any point within the execution tree. If you focus on execution tree path #3 in Figure 14-14, you'll see that it contains a Source adapter, a Derived Column Transformation, and a Lookup. Without looking at the source properties, the following list defines the four columns that the Source adapter is using from the source:

- ❑ CurrencyCode

- ❑ CurrencyRate

- ❑ AverageRate

- ❑ EndofDayRate

A quick look at the Derived Column Transformation in Figure 14-15 shows that two more columns are being added to the Data Flow: Average_Sale and Audit_Date.

Figure 14-15

And finally, the Lookup Transformation adds another three columns to the Data Flow, as Figure 14-16 highlights.

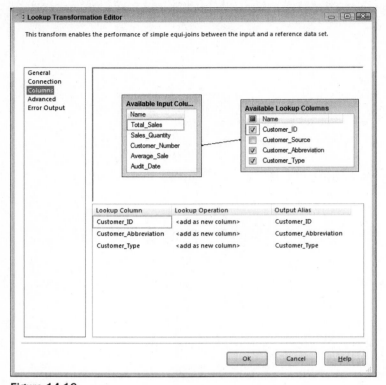

Figure 14-16

Added together, the columns used in these three components total nine. This means that the buffers used in this execution tree will have nine columns allocated, even though some of the columns are not used in the initial transformations or adapter. Optimization of a Data Flow can be compared with optimizing a relational table, where the smaller the width and number of columns, the more that can fit into a Data Flow buffer. This has some performance implications, and the next section will look in more detail at optimizing buffers.

When a buffer is used in an execution tree and reaches the transformation input of the asynchronous component (the last step in the execution tree), the data is subsequently not needed since it has been passed off to a new execution tree and a new set of buffers. At this point, the buffer manager can use the allocated buffer for other purposes in the Data Flow.

> It is important to call out that SSIS 2008 differs from SSIS 2005 in how the processor threads are assigned to execution trees. In SSIS 2005, each execution tree only received a single processor thread, and therefore a large execution tree may have generated a processor bottleneck even without the processors being fully utilized. However, with SSIS 2008, the process thread scheduler can assign more than one thread to a single execution tree if threads are available and if the execution tree requires intense processor utilization. To be sure, each transformation can receive a single thread, so if an execution tree only has two components that participate, then the execution tree can have a max of two threads.

One advanced property of the Data Flow is the `EngineThreads` property. In the Control Flow, when a Data Flow Task is highlighted, this property appears in the property window list, as Figure 14-17 shows.

It is important to modify the `EngineThreads` property of the Data Flow so that the execution trees are not sharing process threads, and extra threads are available for large or complex execution trees. Furthermore, all the execution trees in a package share the number of processor threads allocated in the `EngineThreads` property of the Data Flow. A single thread or multiple threads are assigned to an execution tree based on availability of threads and complexity of the execution tree.

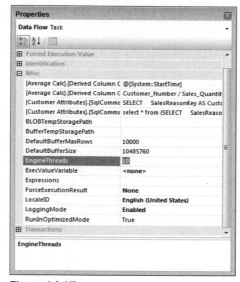

Figure 14-17

In the last section of this chapter, you will see how the number of threads available in a Data Flow is allocated to the execution trees. The value for `EngineThreads` does not include the threads allocated for the number of sources in a Data Flow, which are automatically allocated separate threads.

Monitoring Data Flow Execution

Built into the SSIS logging is the ability to monitor specific pipeline events related to execution trees. This can be very useful in understanding your Data Flow and how the engine is managing buffers and execution.

Pipeline logging events are available in the Logging features of SSIS. An overview of the general SSIS logging is provided in Chapter 9, but for this discussion, you will focus on only the specific pipeline events that relate to the execution tree discussion. Two specific pipeline execution events are available to capture during the processing:

❑   PipelineExecutionPlan

❑   PipelineExecutionTrees

To capture the event, create a new log entry through the logging designer window under the SSIS menu Logging option. The pipeline events are available only when your Data Flow is selected in the tree menu navigator of the package executable navigator, as Figure 14-18 shows.

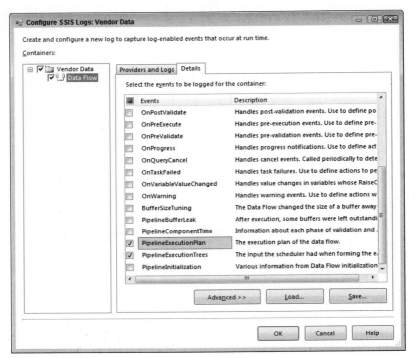

Figure 14-18

On the Details tab of the Configure SSIS Logs window, shown in Figure 14-18, the two execution information log events just listed are available to capture. When the package is run, these events can be tracked to the selected log provider as defined. However, during development, it is useful to see these events when testing and designing a package. SSIS includes a way to see these events in the Business Intelligence Development Studio as a separate window. The Log Events window can be pulled up either from the SSIS menu by selecting "Log Events" or through the View menu, listed under the Other Windows submenu. As is standard, this window can float or be docked in the designer.

When the package is executed in design-time through the interface, the log events selected will be displayed in the Log Events window. For each Data Flow, there will be one event returned for the PipelineExecutionPlan event and one for the PipelineExecutionTrees event, as shown in Figure 14-19. These log details have been captured from the sample Data Flow used in Figure 14-13 and Figure 14-14.

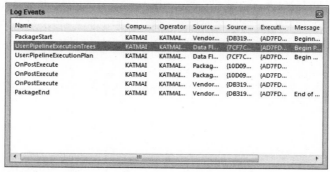

Figure 14-19

Note that all pipeline events selected in the Logging configuration are included in the Log window. To capture the details for a more readable view of the Message column, simply right-click the log entry and copy, which will put the event message into the clipboard. A more detailed analysis of the message text is discussed in the following section.

Pipeline Execution Tree Log Details

The execution tree log event describes the grouping of transformation inputs and outputs that participate in each execution tree. Each execution tree is numbered for readability. The following text comes from the message column of the PipelineExecutionTrees log entry:

```
Begin Path 0
   output "OLE DB Source Output" (582); component "Customer Validation" (573)
   input "Merge Join Right Input" (686); component "Filter Valid Customers"
        (684)
End Path 0

Begin Path 1
   output "Sort Output" (554); component "Sort" (552)
   input "Merge Join Left Input" (685); component "Filter Valid Customers"
        (684)
End Path 1

Begin Path 2
   output "Merge Join Output" (687); component "Filter Valid Customers" (684)
   input "Union All Input 1" (1530); component "Union All" (1529)
End Path 2

Begin Path 3
   output "Flat File Source Output" (878); component "Weekly Vendor Export"
        (877)
   input "Derived Column Input" (1064); component "Average Calc" (1063)
   output "Derived Column Output" (1065); component "Average Calc" (1063)
   input "Lookup Input" (276); component "Customer Attributes" (266)
```

```
        output "Lookup Match Output" (280); component "Customer Attributes" (266)
        input "Sort Input" (553); component "Sort" (552)
    End Path 3

    Begin Path 4
        output "OLE DB Source Output" (1524); component "Prior Weeks" (1514)
        input "Union All Input 2" (1542); component "Union All" (1529)
    End Path 4

    Begin Path 5
        output "Union All Output 1" (1531); component "Union All" (1529)
        input "SQL Server Destination Input" (813); component "Monthly Vendor
          Details" (800)
    End Path 5
```

In the log output, each execution tree evaluated by the engine is listed with a `begin path` and an `end path`, with the transformation input and outputs that participate in the execution tree. Some execution trees may have several synchronous component outputs participating in the grouping, while others may be composed of only an input and output between two asynchronous components. The listing of the execution trees is base 0, so the total number of execution trees for your Data Flow will be the numeral of the last execution tree plus one. In this example, there are six execution trees. A quick way to identify synchronous and asynchronous transformation outputs in your Data Flow is to review this log. Any transformation where both the inputs and outputs are contained within one execution tree is synchronous. Contrarily, any transformation where one or more inputs are separated from the outputs in different execution trees therefore has asynchronous outputs.

Pipeline Execution Plan Log Details

The second type of log detail that applies to the discussion of execution trees and execution threads is the PipelineExecutionPlan. This particular log detail dives one step deeper into the SSIS engine process for a Data Flow by identifying the threads that will be allocated and used during the process. The following text comes from the message column of the PipelineExecutionPlan log output:

```
Begin output plan
    Begin transform plan
        Call PrimeOutput on component "Sort" (552)
            for output "Sort Output" (554)
        Call PrimeOutput on component "Filter Valid Customers" (684)
            for output "Merge Join Output" (687)
        Call PrimeOutput on component "Union All" (1529)
            for output "Union All Output 1" (1531)
    End transform plan

    Begin source plan
        Call PrimeOutput on component "Customer Validation" (573)
            for output "OLE DB Source Output" (582)
        Call PrimeOutput on component "Weekly Vendor Export" (877)
            for output "Flat File Source Output" (878)
```

```
        Call PrimeOutput on component "Prior Weeks" (1514)
            for output "OLE DB Source Output" (1524)
    End source plan
End output plan

Begin path plan
    Begin Path Plan 0
        Call ProcessInput on component "Filter Valid Customers" (684)
            for input "Merge Join Right Input" (686)
    End Path Plan 0

    Begin Path Plan 1
        Call ProcessInput on component "Filter Valid Customers" (684)
            for input "Merge Join Left Input" (685)
    End Path Plan 1

    Begin Path Plan 2
        Call ProcessInput on component "Union All" (1529)
            for input "Union All Input 1" (1530)
    End Path Plan 2

    Begin Path Plan 3
        Call ProcessInput on component "Average Calc" (1063)
            for input "Derived Column Input" (1064)
        Create new row view for output "Derived Column Output" (1065)
        Call ProcessInput on component "Customer Attributes" (266)
            for input "Lookup Input" (276)
        Create new row view for output "Lookup Match Output" (280)
        Call ProcessInput on component "Sort" (552)
            for input "Sort Input" (553)
    End Path Plan 3

    Begin Path Plan 4
        Call ProcessInput on component "Union All" (1529)
            for input "Union All Input 2" (1542)
    End Path Plan 4

    Begin Path Plan 5
        Call ProcessInput on component "Monthly Vendor Details" (800)
            for input "SQL Server Destination Input" (813)
    End Path Plan 5

    End path plan
```

This text is a little more difficult to decipher. A few pointers will help determine some details of the pipeline execution plan. First of all, execution plan is identified by three types, source plan, transform plan, and path plan. The Source Plan and Transform Plan are allocated for the Source adapters and outputs of the asynchronous components. The Path Plan defines how the execution trees are broken up into subtrees for processor thread assignments. Each plan matches up with the plans reviewed in the execution tree details in the previous section. The Subpath Plan shows when an execution tree has a subtree for threading parallelization.

By using the two pipeline log entries just described, you can now better understand how the engine is processing your data. In any system, the road to applying design principles first requires a level of understanding.

SSIS Data Flow Design and Tuning

Now that you have the background of how the Data Flow engine works, it will now be easier to understand the design principles and tuning practices for creating Data Flows.

Designing a data-processing solution requires more than just sending the source data into a black-box transformation engine with outputs that push the data into the destination. And of course, system requirements will dictate the final design of the process, including but not limited to the following:

❑   Source and destination system impact

❑   Processing time windows and performance

❑   Destination system state consistency

❑   Hard and soft exception handling and restartability needs

❑   Environment architecture model, distributed hardware, or scaled-up servers

❑   Solution architecture requirements, such as flexibility of change or OEM targeted solutions

❑   Modular and configurable solution needs

❑   Manageability and administration requirements

In reviewing this list, you can quickly map several of these to what you have learned about SSIS already. In most cases, a good architecture will leverage the built-in functionality of the tool, which in the end reduces administration and support requirements. The tool selection process, if it is not completed before a solution is developed, should include a consideration of the system requirements and functionality of the available products.

Data Flow Design Practices

There are three main design practices that you should constantly have in mind when designing packages:

❑   Limit synchronicity

❑   Reduce staging and disk IO

❑   Reduce the reliance on an RDBMS

When looking to limit synchronicity, what you should be conscious of is processes that need to complete before the next process begins. For example, if you run a long INSERT TSQL statement that takes one half hour to complete, and then run an UPDATE statement that updates the same table, the UPDATE statement cannot run until the INSERT script finishes. These processes are synchronous. It would be better to design a Data Flow that handles the same logic as the INSERT statement and also combines the

UPDATE logic at the same time (without using a SQL UPDATE); then you are not only taking advantage of the SSIS Data Flow, but you are making the logic asynchronous. You can seriously reduce overall process times by taking this approach.

Reducing disk IO is about minimizing the staging requirements in your ETL process. Disk IO is often the biggest bottleneck in an ETL job because the nature bulk operations is about moving a lot of data, and when you add staging data to a database, that data ultimately needs to be saved to the disk drives. Instead, reduce your need on staging tables and leverage the Data Flow for those same operations; then you will decrease the disk overhead of the process and achieve better scalability. The Data Flow primarily uses memory, and memory is a lot faster to access than disks, so you will gain significant improvements of speed. Not only that, but when you stage data to a table, you are doubling the disk IO of the data, because you are both inserting and then selecting back out of the table.

Keep in mind that solution requirements often drive design decisions, and there are situations where staging or the RDBMS are useful in data processing. Some of these are discussed in this section. Your goal, though, is to rethink your design paradigms with SSIS.

Reducing the RDBMS reliance is similar to reducing staging environments, but it also means reducing the logic you place on the DDBMS to perform operations like grouping and data cleansing. This will not only reduce the impact on your RDBMS, but when using production databases, it will alleviate the load and make room for more critical RDBMS operations.

These three principles are worked out further in the next section by discussing ways to leverage the Data Flow for your ETL operations.

Leveraging the Data Flow

For sure, the biggest value that SSIS brings is the power of the Data Flow. Not to minimize the out-of-the-box functionality of restartability, configurations, logging, event handlers, or other Control Flow Tasks; the primary goal of the engine is to "integrate," and the Data Flow is the key to realizing that goal. Accomplishing data-processing logic through Data Flow Transformations brings performance and flexibility.

Most data architects come from DBA backgrounds, which means that the first thing that comes to their minds when trying to solve a data integration, processing, or cleansing scenario is to use an RDBMS, such as SQL Server. People gravitate to areas they are comfortable with, so this is a natural response. When your comfort in SQL is combined with an easy-to-use and low-cost product like DTS, which in many ways relies on relational databases, the result is a widely adopted tool.

Moving to SSIS in some ways requires thinking in different terms — Data Flow terms. In previous chapters, you looked at the different Data Flow Transformations, so the focus in this section will be on applying some of those components into design decisions and translating the SQL-based designs into Data Flow processes.

The three architecture best practices relate directly to the value that the Data Flow provides:

❑ **Limit synchronicity:** By bringing more of the processing logic into the Data Flow, the natural result is fewer process-oriented steps that require completion before moving on. In the previous chapter, you looked at the general streaming nature of the Data Flow. This translates to reduced overall processing times.

❑ **Reduce staging and expensive IO operations:** The Data Flow performs most operations in memory (with occasional use of temp folders and some interaction with external systems). Whenever processing happens on data that resides in RAM, processing is more efficient. Disk IO operations rely on the performance of the drives, the throughput of the IO channels, and the overhead of the operating system to write and read information to the disk. With high volumes or bursting scenarios typical with data processing and ETL, disk IO is often a bottleneck.

❑ **Reduce reliance on RDBMS:** Relational engines are powerful tools to use, and the point here is not to detract from their appropriate uses to store and manage data. By using the Data Flow to cleanse and join data rather than the RDBMS, the result is reduced impact on the relational system, which frees it up for other functions that may be higher priority. Reading data from a database is generally less expensive than performing complex joins or complicated queries. In addition, related to the first bullet, all RDBMS operations are synchronous. Set-based operations, while they are very useful and optimized in a relational database system, still require that the operation be complete before the data is available for other purposes. The Data Flow, on the other hand, can process joins and lookups and other cleansing steps in parallel while the data is flowing through the pipeline. However, it is important to note that an RDBMS engine can be leveraged in certain ways; for example, if a table has the right indexes, you can use an ORDER BY, which may be faster than an SSIS Sort Transformation.

Data Integration and Correlation

The Data Flow provides the means to combine data from different source objects completely independent of the connection source where the data originates. The most obvious benefit of this is the ability to perform in-memory correlation operations against heterogeneous data without having to stage the data. Said in another way, with SSIS, you can extract data from a flat file and join it to data from a database table inside the Data Flow, without first having to stage the flat file to a table and then perform a SQL Join operation. This can be valuable even when the data is coming from the same source, such as a relational database engine; source data extractions are more efficient without complex or expensive joins, and data can usually begin to flow into the Data Flow immediately. In addition, single table SELECT statements provide less impact to the source systems than do pulls where join logic is applied. Certainly there are situations where joining data in the source system may be useful and efficient; in many cases, however, focusing on data integration within the Data Flow will yield better performance. When different source systems are involved, the requirement to stage the data is reduced.

Several of the built-in transformations can perform data correlation similar to how a database would handle joins and other more complex data relationship logic. The following transformations provide data association for more than one Data Source:

❑ Lookup

❑ Merge Join

❑ Merge

❑ Union All

❑ Fuzzy Lookup

❑ Term Lookup

❑ Term Extract

Chapter 7 dives into leveraging the joining capabilities of SSIS, a great reference for designing your SSIS Data Flows.

Furthermore, beyond the built-in capabilities of SSIS, custom adapters and transformations allow more complex or unique scenarios to be handled. This is discussed in Chapter 18.

Data Cleansing and Transformation

The second major area of consideration where you can apply the Data Flow is data cleansing. Cleansing data involves managing missing values; correcting out-of-date, incomplete, or miskeyed data; converting values to standard data types; changing data grain or filtering data subsets; and de-duplicating redundant data. Consistency is the goal of data cleansing whether the Data Source is a single system or multiple disparate sources.

Many of the Data Flow Components provide data-cleansing capabilities or can participate in a data-cleansing process. Some of the more explicit transformations usable for this process include the following:

- ❑ Aggregate
- ❑ Character Map
- ❑ Conditional Split
- ❑ Data Conversion
- ❑ Derived Column
- ❑ Fuzzy Grouping
- ❑ Fuzzy Lookup
- ❑ Pivot
- ❑ Script Component
- ❑ Sort (with de-duplicating capabilities)
- ❑ Unpivot

Each of these transformations, or a combination of them, can handle many data-cleansing scenarios. A few of the transformations provide compelling data-cleansing features that even go beyond the capabilities of many relational engines. This makes use of the Data Flow. For example, the Fuzzy Lookup and Fuzzy Grouping (de-duplication) provide cleansing of dirty data by comparing data similarity within certain defined ranges. Pivot and Unpivot have the ability to transform data coming in by pivoting rows to columns or vice versa. Also, the Script Transformation offers very powerful data-cleansing capabilities with the full features of VB.NET embedded; it is highlighted in detail in Chapter 9. Since the goal of this chapter is to highlight and discuss the application of SSIS, the example will focus on a couple of common examples of data cleansing using the Derived Column Transformation and the Aggregate Transformation. These two transformations have particular relevance in how data cleansing can be accomplished in the Data Flow in comparison with common query logic.

As Chapter 5 demonstrates, the Derived Column Transformation's capabilities allow the ability to replace column values coming through the Data Flow. One of the more common data-cleansing scenarios that the Derived Column Transformation can accomplish is to replace [blank] and NULL values extracted from various sources. Using the expression language, described in detail in Chapter 6, a check of values could be performed for both cases described. Figure 14-20 shows the Derived Column using the "Replace" column option on the SalesTerritoryAlternateKey column coming through this transformation.

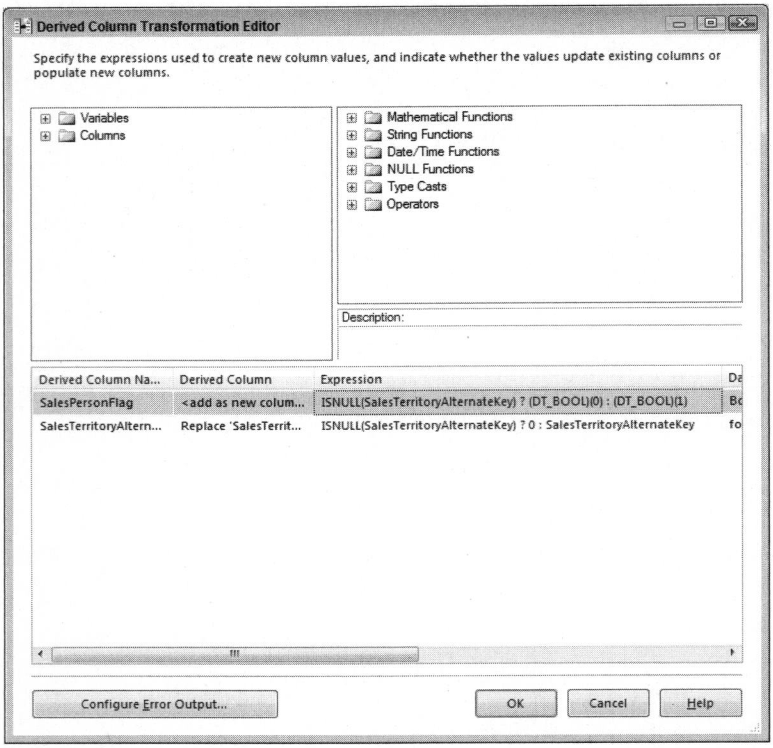

Figure 14-20

The following expression code is used to cleanse the [AddressLine1] input column in the example:

```
ISNULL(SalesTerritoryAlternateKey) ? 0 : SalesTerritoryAlternateKey
```

The expression checks to see if the SalesTerritoryAlternateKey is NULL. If the input column value is NULL, the expression returns a 0; otherwise the actual column value is used. The expression uses a few of the different functions available in the language, particularly the conditional case expression (<Boolean> ? <True> : <false>).

The second valuable transformation to highlight is the Aggregate. The Aggregate Transformation brings GROUP BY logic to the Data Flow, but you can have multiple groups of aggregates with different outputs, and different aggregations defined for each group. Many Data Transformation scenarios require changing the grain or the level of detail from the source to the destination, and in most situations the requirement is to roll up the data to higher levels of detail than what the source system makes available.

In Figure 14-21, the Aggregate Transformation takes the input, and groups by source date column, and applies aggregations across three other input columns.

Figure 14-21

Although not pictured, the Aggregate Transformation can also provide multiple groupings with different outputs per grouping. This means if one grouping should be by SalesOrderID and another by OrderDate, they both can be accomplished in the same Aggregate Component. The Advanced button will enable multiple groups and outputs.

Staging Environments

A word must be mentioned about the appropriate use of staging environments. To this point in the chapter, the emphasis has been on thinking in Data Flow terms by moving core data process logic into the Data Flow. And in most cases, this will yield high-performance results, especially when the timeliness of moving the data from point A to point B is the highest priority, such as near real-time or tight-processing-window scenarios. Doing this also mitigates some management overhead, limiting interim database usage.

A few situations merit staging environments and are worth mentioning for consideration:

❑ **Restartability:** The built-in checkpoint logic of SSIS revolves around the Control Flow. What this means is that a failure in the Data Flow will not persist the data state. Rather, when the package is restarted, the Data Flow will restart from the beginning. The implications affect design if the source system is in flux and an error in the Data Flow causes a processing window to be missed. By landing the raw data first, the chance for data errors is minimized, and in the event of a failure during the load process, the package can be restarted from the staged data.

❑ **Processing Windows and Precedence:** Certain requirements may dictate that the various source extraction windows do not line up with each other or with the data load window for the destination. In these scenarios, it would be necessary to stage the data for a period of time until the full data set is available or the destination database load window has been reached.

❑ **Source Back Pressure:** At times, the Data Flow Transformations may apply back pressure on the source extractions. This would happen when the flow of data coming in is faster than the performance of the transformations to handle the data processing in the pipeline. The back pressure created would slow down the extraction on the source system, and if the requirement is to extract the data in the fastest time with the least impact, then staging the raw data extract may help eliminate the back pressure.

❑ **Data Flow Optimization:** Staging certain elements, such as business keys, can actually provide valuable data to optimize the primary Data Flow. For example, if the Lookup Source query can be filtered based on a set of keys that was pre-staged, this may allow overall gains in processing times by reducing the time it takes to load the Lookup plus the amount of memory needed for the operation. A second example is the use of staging to perform set-based table updates. Updates in a large system are often the source of system bottlenecks, and since SSIS cannot perform set-based updates in the Data Flow, one consideration is to stage tables that can be used in a later Execute SQL Task for a set-based update, which may provide a more efficient process.

Staged data can also prove useful in data validation and error handling. Given some of the uses of staging, is there a way to accomplish data staging but still retain the performance gain by leveraging the Data Flow? Yes. One emphasis that has been suggested is the reduction of synchronous processing in the Control Flow. In regard to data staging, the most natural thought when you have to introduce a staging environment is to first pick up the data from the source and land it to a staging environment, and then pick the data back up from the staging environment and apply the transformation logic to it. What about landing the raw data to a staging environment at the same time that the transformations are applied? Figure 14-22 shows a Data Flow designed with a staging table that does not require the data to reside in the table before the transformation logic is applied.

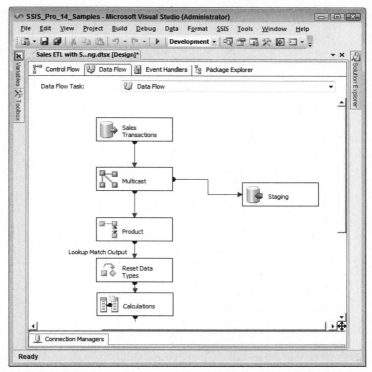

Figure 14-22

The Multicast Transformation in this example is taking the raw source data and allowing it to stream down to the core Data Flow, while at the same time the raw source data is being staged to a table. The data within the table is now available to query for data validation and checking purposes; in addition, it provides a snapshot of the source system that can then be used for reprocessing when needed. Although the data is landed to staging, two differences distinguish this example from a model that first stages data, and then uses the staged data as a source. First, as has been mentioned, the process is no longer synchronous; data can move from point A to point B in many cases in the time it takes simply to extract the data from A. Second, the staging process requires only a single pass on the staging table (for the writes) rather than the IO overhead of a second pass that reads the data from the staging. If your restartibility requirements and source systems allow, this approach may provide the best of both worlds — leveraging the Data Flow but providing the value of a stage environment.

Optimizing Package Processing

There are a few techniques you can apply when you're streamlining packages for performance. This section covers how to apply certain optimization techniques to achieve better throughput.

Optimizing Buffers, Execution Trees, and Engine Threads

If you recall earlier in this chapter, for each execution tree in a Data Flow, a different buffer profile is used. This means that downstream execution trees may require different columns based on what is added or subtracted in the Data Flow. You also saw that the performance of a buffer within a Data Flow is directly related to the row width of the buffer. Narrow buffers can hold more rows, and therefore the throughput will be higher.

Some columns that are used in an execution tree may not be needed downstream. For example, if an input column to a Lookup Transformation is used as the key match to the reference table, this column may not be needed after the Lookup, and therefore should be removed before the next execution tree. SSIS does a good job of providing warnings when columns exist in an execution tree but are not used in any downstream transformation or destination adapter. Figure 14-23 highlights the Progress tab within a package where column usage has not been optimized in the Data Flow. Each warning, highlighted with a yellow exclamation point, indicates the existence of a column not used later in downstream components, and which therefore should be removed from the pipeline after initial use.

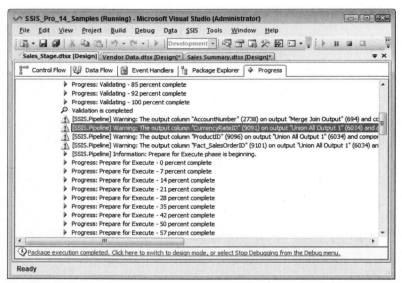

Figure 14-23

The warning text describes the optimization technique well:

```
[SSIS.Pipeline] Warning: The output column "CurrencyRateID" (9091) on
output "Union All Output 1" (6034) and component "Union All" (6032) is
not subsequently used in the Data Flow Task. Removing this unused
output column can increase Data Flow Task performance.
```

Any asynchronous component whose input closes out an execution tree will have the option of removing columns in the output. You would normally do this through the edit dialog box of the transformation, but you can also do it in the Advanced Editor if the component provides an advanced properties window. For example, in the Union All Transformation, you can highlight a row in the editor and delete it with the Delete keyboard key. This will ensure that the column is not used in the next execution tree.

A second optimization technique in this area revolves around optimizing the processor utilization by adding the available use of more execution threads for the Data Flow. As was highlighted in the last chapter, increasing the `EngineThreads` Data Flow property to a value greater than the number of execution trees plus the number of Source Components will ensure that SSIS has enough threads to use.

Careful Use of Row-Based Transformations

Row-based transforms, as described earlier in this chapter, are non-blocking transformations, but they exhibit the functionality of interacting with an outside system (for example, a database or file system) on a row-by-row basis. Compared with other non-blocking transformations, these transformations are slower because of this nature. The other type of non-blocking transformation, streaming, can use internal cache or provide calculations using other columns or variables readily available to the Data Flow, making them perform very fast. Given the nature of row-based transformations, their usage should be cautious and calculated.

Of course, some row-based transformations have critical functionality, so this caution needs to be balanced with data-processing requirements. For example, the Export and Import Column Transformation can read and write from files to columns, which is a very valuable tool, but has the obvious overhead of the IO activity with the file system.

Another useful row-based transformation is the OLE DB Command Transformation, which can use input column values and execute parameterized queries against a database, row by row. The interaction with the database, although it can be optimized, still requires overhead to process. Figure 14-24 shows a SQL Server Trace run against a database that is receiving updates from an OLE DB Command Transformation.

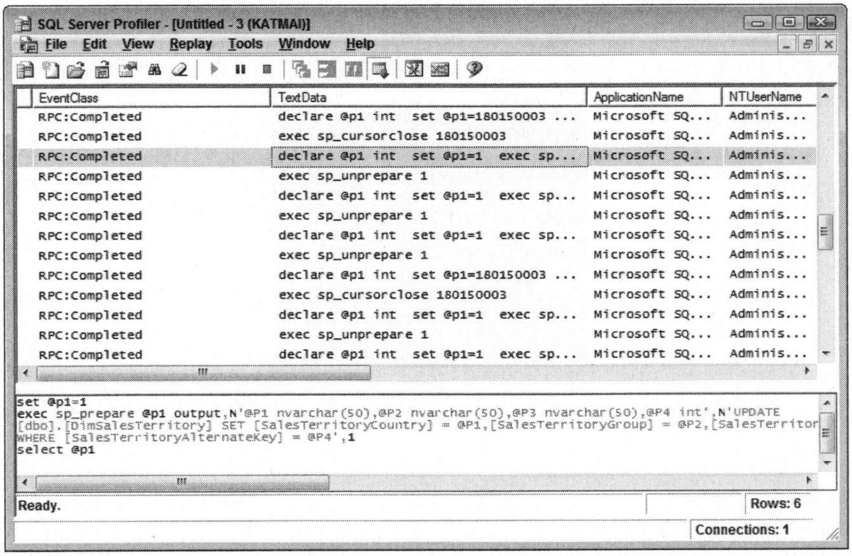

Figure 14-24

This is only a snapshot, but for each row that goes through the OLE DB Command Transformation, a separate UPDATE statement is issued against the database. Taking into consideration the duration, reads, and writes, the aggregated impact of thousands of rows will cause Data Flow latency at the transformation.

For this scenario, one alternative is to leverage set-based processes within databases. In order to do this, the data will need to be staged during the Data Flow, and you will need to add a secondary Execute SQL Task to the Control Flow that runs the set-based update statement. The result may actually reduce the overall processing time when compared with the original OLE DB Command approach. This alternative approach is not meant to diminish the usefulness of the OLE DB Command but rather to provide an example of optimizing the Data Flow for higher-volume scenarios that may require optimization.

Understand Blocking Transformation Impacts

A blocking transformation requires the complete set of records cached from the input before it can release records downstream. Earlier in the chapter, we showed you a list of about a dozen transformations that meet this criterion. The most common examples are the Sort and Aggregate Transformations.

Blocking transformations are intensive because they require caching all the upstream input data, and they also may require more intensive processor usage based on their functionality. When not enough RAM is available in the system, the blocking transformations may also require temporary disk storage. You need to be aware of these limitations when you're working to optimize a Data Flow. The point of mentioning the nature of blocking transformations is not to minimize their usefulness but rather to advise that in some situations they are very useful and perform much better than alternative approaches. Rather, the intention here is to use these transformations in the right places and know the resource impact.

Since sorting data is a common requirement, one optimization technique is valuable to mention. Source data that can be sorted in the adapter through an ORDER BY statement (if the right indexes are in the source table) or presorted in a flat file does not require the use of a Sort Transformation. As long as the data is physically sorted in the right order when coming into the Data Flow, the Source adapter can be configured to indicate that the data is sorted and which columns are sorted in what order. Figure 14-25 shows the Advanced Editor of a Source adapter with the Source Output folder highlighted. The first step is to set the IsSorted property to True, as seen on the right-hand properties screen.

Figure 14-25

The second requirement is to indicate which columns are sorted. To do this, open the Source Output folder and then the Output Columns subfolder. This will open the list of columns that the adapter will send out into the pipeline. To set the sort column order and direction, highlight the first column that is sorted. The example in Figure 14-26 uses the presorted `SalesOrderID` column, which is highlighted in the figure.

Figure 14-26

The `SortKeyPosition` should be set for the columns used in sorting. For the first column that is sorted, set the `SortKeyPosition` to a 1 or -1. A -1 indicates that the column is sorted in descending order. Continue to the next sorted column, if applicable, and set the value to a 2 or -2, and subsequently continue for all sorted columns. It is important to note that when sort columns include character-based columns, make sure the collation in SQL matches the SSIS collation. Otherwise you may get wrong results.

Troubleshooting Data Flow Performance Bottlenecks

A great approach for identifying bottlenecks within a specific Data Flow is to make a copy of your Data Flow and begin decomposing your Data Flow by replacing components out with a placeholder transformation. In other words, take a copy of your Data Flow and run it without any changes. This will give you a baseline of the execution time of the package.

Next, remove all the Destination adapters, and replace them with the Multicast Transformation (the Multicast is a great placeholder transformation as it can act as a destination without any outputs and has no overhead). Figure 14-27 represents a modified package where the Destination adapters have been replaced with Multicast Transformations.

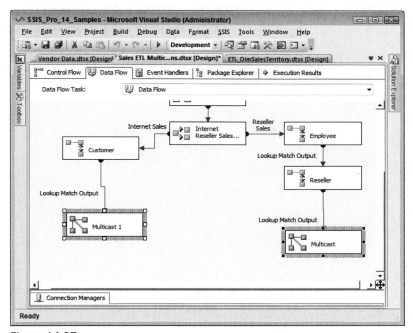

Figure 14-27

Run this modified Data Flow and evaluate your execution time. Is it a lot faster? If so, you've identified your problem — it's one or more of your destinations.

If your package without the destinations still runs the same, then your performance bottleneck is a source or one of the transformations. The next most common issue is the source, so this time, delete all your transformations and replace them with Multicast Transformations, as Figure 14-28 shows.

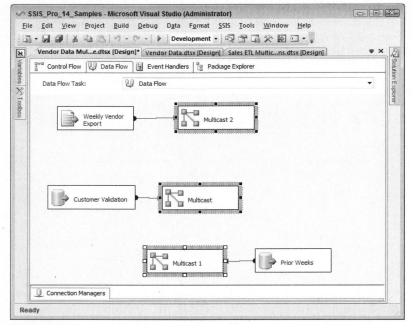

Figure 14-28

Now, run your package. If the execution time is just as slow as the first run, then you can be sure that the performance issue is one or more of the sources. If the performance is a lot faster, then you have a performance issue with one of the transformations.

This generalized approach can be applied over an over until you figure out where the issue lies. In other words, go back to your original copy of the Data Flow and start keep replacing transformations out until you have identified the transformation that causes the biggest slowdown. It may be the case that you have more than one transformation or adapter that is the culprit, but with this approach you will know where to focus your redesign or reconfiguration efforts.

Pipeline Performance Monitoring

Earlier in this chapter, one of the things you looked at was the built-in Pipeline logging functionality and how it could help you understand what SSIS was doing behind the scenes when running a package with one or more Data Flows. Another tool available to SSIS is the Windows operating system tool called Performance Monitor (PerfMon for short), which is available to local administrators in the machine's Administrative Tools. When SSIS is installed on a machine, a set of counters is added that allows the tracking of the Data Flow's performance.

As Figure 14-29 shows, the Pipeline counters can be used when selecting the SQLServer:SSIS Pipeline 10.0 object.

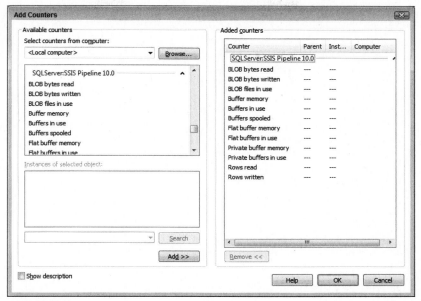

Figure 14-29

The following counters are available in the SQLServer:SSIS Pipeline object within PerfMon. Descriptions of these counters are provided next:

- ❑ BLOB bytes read
- ❑ BLOB bytes written
- ❑ BLOB files in use
- ❑ Buffer memory
- ❑ Buffers in use
- ❑ Buffers spooled
- ❑ Flat buffer memory
- ❑ Flat buffers in use
- ❑ Private buffers in use
- ❑ Rows read
- ❑ Rows written

The BLOB counters (Binary Large Objects, such as images) help identify the volume of the BLOB data types flowing through the Data Flow. Since handling large binary columns can be a huge drain on the available memory, understanding how your Data Flow is handling BLOB data types becomes important. Remember that BLOB data can be introduced to the Data Flow not only by Source adapters but also by the Import (and Export) Column Transformations.

Since buffers are the mechanism that the Data Flow uses to process all data, the buffer-related counters provide the most valuable information to seeing how much and where memory is being used in the Data Flow. The Buffer Memory and Buffers in Use counters are the high-level counters that provide totals for the server, both memory use and total buffer count. Essentially, the Buffer Memory counter shows the total memory being used by SSIS and can be compared with the amount of available system memory to know if SSIS processing is bottlenecked by the available physical memory. Furthermore, the Buffers Spooled counter provides even more indication of resource limitations on your server. It shows the number of buffers temporarily written to disk if enough system memory is not available. Anything greater than zero shows that your Data Flow is having to use temporary disk storage to accomplish its work, which comes with an IO impact and overhead.

In regard to the buffer details, two types of buffers exist, flat and private. Flat buffers are the primary Data Flow buffers used when a Source adapter sends data into the Data Flow. Synchronous transformation outputs pass the flat buffers to the next component, and asynchronous outputs use reprovisioned or new flat buffers to be passed to the next transformation. On the other hand, some transformations require different buffers, called *private buffers*, which are not received from upstream transformations or passed on to downstream transformations. Instead, they are the private cache of data that a transformation uses to perform its operation. Three primary examples of private buffer use are found in the Aggregate, Sort, and Lookup Transformations, which use private buffers to cache data that is used for calculations and matching. These transformations still use flat buffers for data being received and passed, but they also use private buffers to manage and cache supplemental data used in the transformation. The flat and private buffer counters show the breakdown of these usages and help identify where buffers are being used and to what extent.

The last counters in the Pipeline counters list simply show the number of rows handled in the Data Flow, whether Rows Read or Rows Written. These numbers are aggregates of the rows processed since the counters were started.

When reviewing these counters, remember that they are an aggregate of all the SSIS packages and embedded Data Flows running on your server. If you are attempting to isolate performance impacts of specific Data Flows or packages, run these by themselves and capture the Pipeline counters for review.

The Pipeline counters can be tracked in the UI of Performance Monitor in real time or captured at a recurring interval for later evaluation. Figure 14-30 shows the Pipeline counters tracked during the execution of Figure 14-22.

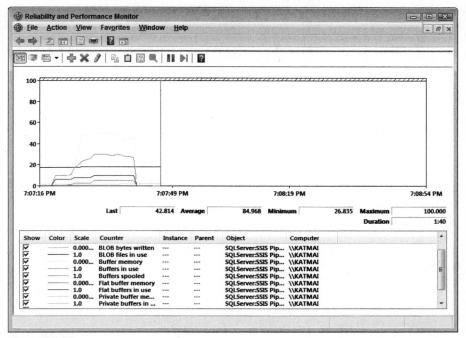

Figure 14-30

Notice that the buffer usage scales up and then drops, and that the plateau lines occur during the database commit process, when SSIS has completed its processes and is waiting on the database to commit the insert transaction. When the package is complete, the buffers are released and the buffer counters drop to zero, while the row count buffers remain stable, since they represent the aggregate rows processed since the PerfMon was started.

Summary

The flexibility of SSIS brings more design options and, in turn, requires you to give more attention to establishing the architecture. As you've seen in this chapter, understanding and leveraging the Data Flow in SSIS reduces processing time, eases management, and opens the door to scalability. Therefore, choose the right architecture up front, and it will ease the design burden and give overall gains to your solution.

Once you have established a model for scalability, the reduced development time of SSIS will allow attention to be given to optimization, where fine-tuning the pipeline and process will make every second count.

Source Control and Software Development Life Cycle

Software Development Life Cycles play an important role in any type of application development. Many SQL Server database administrators and ETL developers have little experience with Microsoft Source Control tools because the tools themselves have been less than "database project-friendly." Microsoft has responded with a more reliable version of Visual SourceSafe and a new source control architecture called Team System.

In addition, many SQL Server DBAs have not been involved with Software Development Life Cycles (SDLCs) beyond executing scripts attached to change control documentation. Legislation around the world has changed the role of the SQL Server DBA in the enterprise because of new requirements for tracking changes. Regarding Software Development Life Cycles, DBAs now must participate in ever-earlier phases of the project development.

In addition, SQL Server DBAs — especially SSIS developers — will realize greater productivity and development cycle fault tolerance as they employ source-controlled development practices. These practices produce code that is auditable, an added benefit in the current corporate climate.

This chapter provides an overview of some of the available features in Microsoft's new offerings. It includes a brief description of how to store a project in Visual SourceSafe and a detailed walkthrough that describes creating a Team Project — using Visual Studio Team System — for SSIS. In practice, Team Projects will most likely be created by someone else in the software development enterprise.

> *A more detailed examination of Team System is beyond the scope of this book but can be found in* Professional Software Testing with Visual Studio 2005 Team System: Tools for Software Developers and Test Engineers *by Tom Arnold, Dominic Hopton, Andy Leonard, and Mike Frost. (Wrox, 2007).*

Because the line between database administrator and software developer has blurred and blended over the years, the Team Project walkthrough is built in Visual Studio 2008. In the Team Project walkthrough, you are going to put together a project that uses the source control and collaboration functionality provided by Visual Studio Team System to demonstrate working with the tool and complying with your SDLC process.

This chapter also contains information about debugging and breakpoints — highlighting features new to database administrators and ETL developers in SSIS.

Included is a discussion regarding development and testing with an emphasis on agile development methodology, which is very well suited for SSIS development because of the methodology's ability to adapt to changes — a common occurrence in ETL development.

The chapter concludes with a discussion about managing package deployment.

Introduction to Software Development Life Cycles

Software Development Life Cycles (or SDLCs) are a systematic approach to each component of application development — from the initial idea to a functioning production application. A *step* (or *phase*) is a unit of related work in an SDLC. A *methodology* is a collection of SDLC steps in action, applied to a project. *Artifacts* are the recorded output from steps.

For example, the first step of an SDLC is Analysis. The methodology requires a requirements document as an Analysis artifact.

Software Development Life Cycles: A Brief History

Software Development Life Cycles have existed in some form or other since the first software applications were developed. The true beginning of what is now termed "software" is debatable. For our purposes, the topic is confined to binary operations based on Boolean algebra.

In 1854, mathematician George Boole published *An Investigation of the Laws of Thought, on which are founded the Mathematical Theories of Logic and Probabilities*. This work became the foundation of what is now called Boolean algebra. Some 80 years later, Claude Shannon applied Boole's theories to computing machines of Shannon's era. Shannon later went to work for Bell Labs.

Another Bell Labs employee, Dr. Walter Shewhart, was tasked with quality control. Perhaps the pinnacle of Dr. Shewhart's work is statistical process control (SPC). Most quality control and continuous improvement philosophies in practice today utilize SPC. Dr. Shewhart's work produced a precursor to Software Development Life Cycles, a methodology defined by four principles: Plan, Do, Study, and Act (PDSA).

Dr. Shewhart's ideas influenced many at Bell Labs, making an accurate and formal trace of the history difficult. Suffice it to say that Dr. Shewhart's ideas regarding quality spread throughout many industries; one industry influenced was the software industry.

Types of Software Development Life Cycles

SQL Server Integration Services provides integrated support for many SDLC methodologies. This chapter touches on a few of them. In general, SDLCs can be placed into one of two categories: waterfall and iterative.

Waterfall SDLCs

The first formal Software Development Life Cycles are sequential or linear. That is, they begin with one step and proceed through subsequent steps until reaching a final step. A typical example of linear methodology steps is the following:

❑ **Analysis:** Review the business needs and develop requirements.

❑ **Design:** Develop a plan to meet the business requirements with a software solution.

❑ **Development:** Build the software solution.

❑ **Implementation:** Install and configure the software solution.

❑ **Maintenance:** Address software issues identified after implementation.

These methodologies are referred to as *waterfall* methodologies because information and software "fall" one-way from plateau to plateau (step to step).

Waterfall methodology has lots of appeal for project managers. It is easier to determine the status and completeness of a linear project: It's either in analysis, in development, in implementation, or in maintenance.

A potential downside to the waterfall methodology is that the analysis and design steps are traditionally completed in a single pass at the beginning of the project. This does not allow much flexibility should business needs change after the project starts. In addition, the development and implementation steps are expected to be defined prior to any coding.

Iterative SDLCs

Iterative methodology begins with the premise that it's impossible to know all requirements for a successful application before development starts. Conversely, iterative development holds that software is best developed within the context of knowledge gained during earlier development of the project. Development therefore consists of several small, limited-scope, feature-based iterations that deliver a product ever closer to the customer's vision.

The following are examples of iterative SDLCs:

❑ **Spiral:** Typified by ever-expanding scope in hopes of identifying large design flaws as soon as possible.

❑ **Agile:** A collection of methodologies fall into this category, including Scrum, Feature-Driven Development, Extreme Programming, Test-Driven Design, and others.

❑ **Microsoft Solutions Framework:** Microsoft's own practice gleaned from a sampling of best practices from different methodologies.

What happens if, hypothetically, an iteration fails to produce the desired functionality? The developer or DBA must remove the changes of the last iteration from the code and begin again. This is much easier to accomplish if the developer or DBA has stored a copy of the previous version someplace safe, hence the need for *source control*.

Source control is defined as preserving the software source code in a format that allows recovery to a previous state of development or version, and it is a basic tenet of all iterative Software Development Life Cycles.

Versioning and Source Code Control

SQL Server 2008 and SQL Server Integration Services (SSIS) integrate with source control products such as Microsoft Visual SourceSafe (VSS) and the Visual Studio Team System. Visual SourceSafe is Microsoft's basic stand-alone source control product. Visual Studio Team System is part of Microsoft's Team Foundation Server, a suite of SDLC management tools — which includes a source control engine.

Microsoft Visual SourceSafe

Visual SourceSafe 2005, which ships with the Visual Studio developer product suites, works with both Visual Studio 2005 and Visual Studio 2008. It boasts improved stability, performance, access, and capacity. In this section, you'll create a project in SQL Server Business Intelligence Development Studio (BIDS) and use it to demonstrate integrated source control with Microsoft Visual SourceSafe.

After installing Visual SourceSafe 2005, be sure to install the update for using Visual SourceSafe 2005 with Visual Studio 2008 and the SQL Server Business Intelligence Development Studio. The update is available from `http://msdn2.microsoft.com/en-us/vstudio/aa718670.aspx`.

To configure SSIS source control integration with Microsoft Visual SourceSafe 2005, open the SQL Server Business Intelligence Development Studio. You don't need to connect to an instance of SQL Server to configure integrated source control.

To configure Visual SourceSafe as your SSIS source control, click Tools ⇨ Options. Click Source Control and select Microsoft Visual SourceSafe. Expand the Source Control Node and click Environment for detailed configuration, as shown in Figure 15-1.

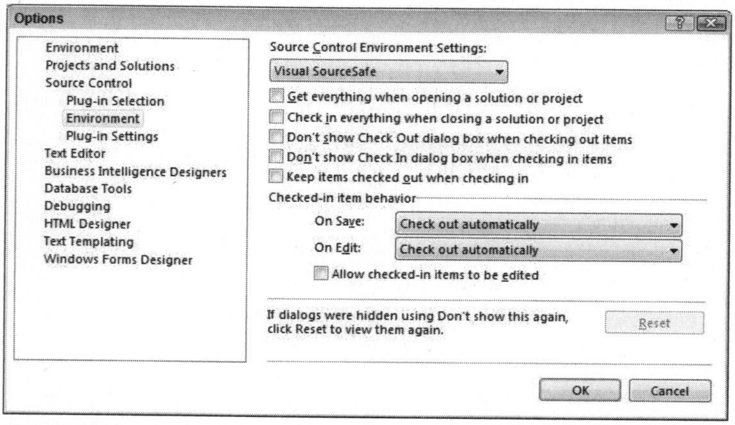

Figure 15-1

The Source Control Environment Settings drop-down list contains three options that represent source control environment roles: Visual SourceSafe, Independent Developer, and Custom.

The Custom role is automatically selected if you begin customizing the source control behaviors in the environment. The following options are available for customization:

- **Get everything when opening a solution or project:**
  - **Checked:** Retrieves all solution or project files from source control when a solution or project is opened.
  - **Not checked:** You must manually retrieve files from source control.

- **Check in everything when closing a solution or project:**
  - **Checked:** Automatically checks in all files related to a solution or project on close.
  - **Not checked:** Does not automatically check in all files related to a solution or project on close.

- **Don't show Check Out dialog box when checking out items:**
  - **Checked:** Hides Check Out dialog box when checking out items.
  - **Not checked:** Displays Check Out dialog box when checking out items.

- **Don't show Check In dialog box when checking in items:**
  - **Checked:** Hides Check In dialog box when checking in items.
  - **Not checked:** Displays Check In dialog box when checking in items.

- **Keep items checked out when checking in:**
  - **Checked:** Allows you to continue editing items that have been checked into source control.
  - **Not checked:** You must manually check out the file before editing it.

- **Checked-in item behavior on Save:**
  - **Prompt for checkout:** You are prompted to check out the files after each Save.
  - **Check out automatically:** Files are checked out automatically when you Save.
  - **Save as:** When Save is clicked, a Save As dialog box appears.

- **Checked-in item behavior on Edit:**
  - **Prompt for checkout:** You are prompted to check out the files when you begin editing.
  - **Prompt for exclusive checkouts:** You are prompted to exclusively check out the files when you begin editing.
  - **Check out automatically:** Files are checked out automatically when you begin editing.
  - **Do nothing:** When you begin editing, SQL Server Management Studio does nothing.

❏ **Allow checked-in items to be edited:**

  ❏ **Checked:** When you begin editing a checked-in file, the Checkout on Edit dialog box appears. This option allows you to check out the file or continue editing without checking out the file.

  This is not a best practice. The only situation where this has any useful application is if you intend to save the contents as a new file. If this is the case, it is recommended that you open the existing source-controlled version, save it as the other file, and then make your edits.

  ❏ **Not checked:** Edits to checked-in items are not allowed.

The following predefined roles, and their settings, are available:

❏ **Visual SourceSafe:** A generic role with the following settings:

  ❏ **Keep items checked out when checking in:** Not checked.

  ❏ **Checked-in item behavior on Save:** Check out automatically.

  ❏ **Checked-in item behavior on Edit:** Check out automatically.

  ❏ **Allow checked-in items to be edited:** Not checked.

❏ **Independent Developer:** A role defined for stand-alone development with the following settings:

  ❏ **Keep items checked out when checking in:** Checked.

  ❏ **Checked-in item behavior on Save:** Check out automatically.

  ❏ **Checked-in item behavior on Edit:** Check out automatically.

  ❏ **Allow checked-in items to be edited:** Not checked.

Check out automatically is the default behavior for checked-in items when saving or editing a project. By not requiring developers to manually check out code, this feature alone saves hours of development time.

One of the options for Source Control (or the Plug-in Selection) is Microsoft Visual SourceSafe (Internet). You can configure Visual SourceSafe for remote access through an intranet or the Internet. This allows you to store source files off-site. A detailed description is beyond the scope of this book, but you can learn more by browsing the "How to: Enable the Internet Service for Remote Access" topic in the Microsoft Visual SourceSafe Documentation.

For the purposes of this demo, select Visual SourceSafe from the Source Control Environment Settings drop-down list and configure source control options as shown in Figure 15-1. This SourceSafe walkthrough assumes that you have installed Visual SourceSafe 2005 on your local machine and the Visual Studio 2008 update.

1. Open the SQL Server Business Intelligence Development Studio. Because BIDS uses the Visual Studio Integrated Development Environment (IDE), opening SQL Server Business Intelligence Development Studio will open Visual Studio 2008.

2. When the BIDS IDE opens, click File ⇨ New ⇨ Project to start a new project. Enter a project name in the New Project dialog box. For now, **do not** check the Add to Source Control checkbox as shown in Figure 15-2.

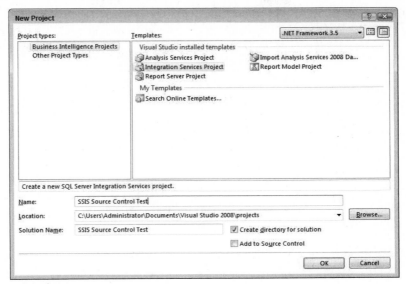

Figure 15-2

3. Click OK to proceed, and a new project is created in the BIDS IDE.

4. Add the project to Microsoft Visual SourceSafe by right-clicking the project name in the Solution Explorer and selecting Add to Source Control.

5. If you are connecting for the first time to Visual SourceSafe 2005, a wizard will walk you through the creation of a new SourceSafe database. If you have an existing database, proceed to Step 6.

   a. The first screen of the wizard will prompt you to choose an existing SourceSafe database or create a new one. Select the "Create a new database" option and click Next.

   b. The location of the SourceSafe files can be on a local drive, or on a windows share. If you have an available share, enter it here. To test the use of SourceSafe, enter a path to the local C: drive such as `C:\VSS_Files` as shown in Figure 15-3.

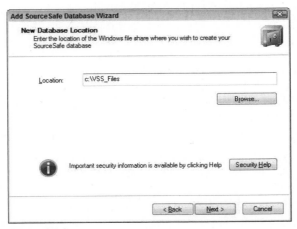

Figure 15-3

c. On the next screen of the wizard, you will be prompted to give the VSS database connection a name. Enter a name such as "SSIS Project Source Control" and click Next.

d. On the next screen you will need to choose the Team Version Control Model. You must choose the Lock-Modify-Unlock Model as shown in Figure 15-4. The Copy-Modify-Merge model will corrupt your packages in SSIS.

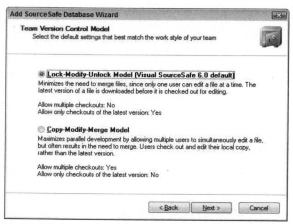

Figure 15-4

e. To complete the wizard, click Next and then Finish.

6. In order to add your project to SourceSafe, you will need to log into the Visual SourceSafe database. You will therefore be prompted to log in to Microsoft Visual SourceSafe. Enter your credentials and click OK as shown in Figure 15-5.

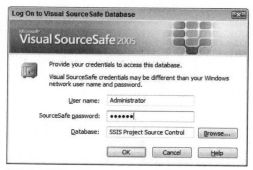

Figure 15-5

7. The final screen is to specify the root of the solution. The Add to SourceSafe dialog box appears, as shown in Figure 15-6. SSIS Source Control Test.root is the default VSS project name assigned to your project. Accept the default by clicking OK.

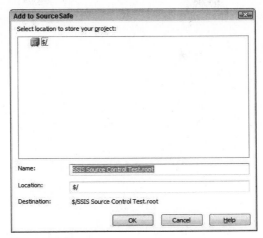

Figure 15-6

8. Because an SSIS Source Control Test project does not currently exist in your instance of Visual SourceSafe, you will be prompted to create a project. Click Yes on the dialog box.

After successfully creating a VSS project to maintain your source code, you are returned to the BIDS development environment. Notice the source control "lock" icons beside your project and Package file as shown in Figure 15-7. The lock icons indicate that the objects are checked in.

Figure 15-7

To test SourceSafe integration with your new SSIS project, manually check out `Package.dtsx` for editing by right-clicking `Package.dtsx` in the Solution Explorer and clicking Check Out for Edit. The Check Out for Edit dialog box appears, as shown in Figure 15-8. You can enter a comment to identify why you are checking out the package. This is a good location for change control documentation references, or at a minimum, good notes.

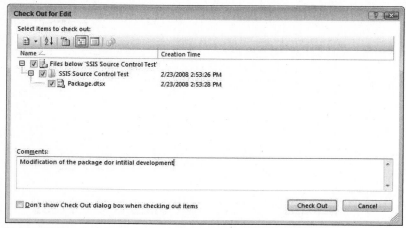

Figure 15-8

Click Check Out to start the checkout process. If a copy of the package already exists in your local project files, then a Microsoft Visual SourceSafe dialog box will appear, prompting you overwrite your local file or keep your changes. Select the "Replace Your Local File with this Version from SourceSafe?" option and check the Apply to All Items checkbox. Click OK to begin editing. The Solution Explorer icon beside the `Package.dtsx` item will change to a red check mark to indicate that the item is checked out exclusively to you, as shown in Figure 15-9.

Figure 15-9

When you are ready to check in your packages, follow these brief steps:

1. Click View ⇨ Pending Checkins to open the Pending Checkins window. The Pending Checkins window displays checked-out files awaiting check-in, as shown in Figure 15-10.

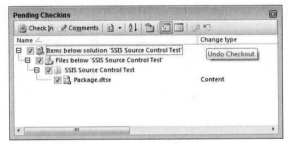

Figure 15-10

2. Click the Comments button to add any notes to your check-in operation. Again, this is an excellent place to add change control documentation references and bug fixes. Click the Check In button to check your code back into source control. The Source Control confirmation dialog box appears.

3. If you check the Don't Show this Dialog Box Again (Always Check In) checkbox, you will not see this dialog box on check-in operations. Click the Check In button to continue. Note that the Pending Checkins window is now empty, as no items are checked out for the project.

   Now that the package is checked in, recall that the On Edit property back in Figure 15-1 is set to "Check out automatically."

4. Observe the `Package.dtsx` item in the Solution Explorer as you drag a Data Flow Task onto the Control Flow workspace. What happened? A red check mark appears beside the `Package.dtsx` item. This is the "automatic checkout on edit" feature in action. The Pending Checkins window will now contain the `Package.dtsx` item, as well as its parent items.

In the next set of steps, you will create a simple package and during your package development, you will occasionally make comments in the source control and periodically check in your package. At the end of the package development, you will roll back the changes to the prior version that was checked in and branch the development to a second version of the package.

1. Continue the package construction by right-clicking the Connection Managers' workspace just below the Control Flow workspace. Click New ADO.NET Connection to launch the Configure ADO.NET Connection Manager. Click the New button to open the Connection Manager editor. Type or select a server name in the Server Name drop-down list. Select "Use Windows Authentication" to log on to the server, and select AdventureWorks2008 in the Database Name drop-down list, as shown in Figure 15-11.

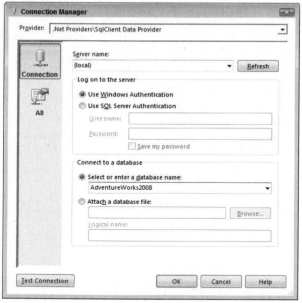

Figure 15-11

2. Click OK to continue, and OK again to choose the ADO.NET Connection Manager just created.

3. Double-click the Data Flow Task on the Control Flow workspace to edit it. Drag an ADO.NET Source onto the Data Flow workspace and double-click it to edit.

4. In the "Name of the table or the view" drop-down, choose the Purchasing.vVendor database view from the list and click OK.

5. Save your package, and then open the Pending Checkins window by clicking View ⇨ Pending Checkins. Click the Comments button and enter **Added Connection and ADO.NET source** in the Comment text box as shown in Figure 15-12.

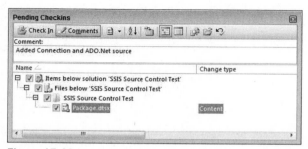

Figure 15-12

6. Click the Check In button to add current changes to source control.

7. Continue editing the package by dragging a Flat File Destination onto the Data Flow workspace. Drag the ADO.NET Source output (represented by a green arrow) from the ADO.NET Source to the Flat File Destination.

8. Double-click the Flat File Destination to edit. Click the New button beside the Flat File Connection Manager drop-down list.

9. The Flat File Format dialog box will appear; select Delimited and click OK. The Flat File Connection Manager appears. Enter **File 1** in the Connection Manager Name text box. Click the Browse button beside the File Name text box and enter **C:\File1.txt** in the File Name text box. Click Open to continue.

10. Check the "Column names in the first data row" checkbox and accept the remaining defaults as shown in Figure 15-13.

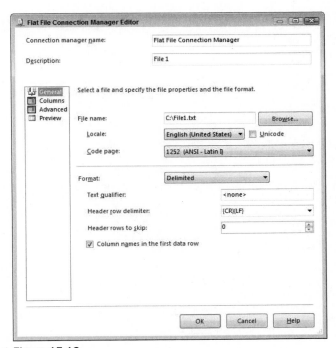

Figure 15-13

11. Click OK to close the Flat File Connection Manager Editor. This returns you to the Flat File Destination Editor. Click the Mappings item from the list on the left to configure column mappings for the connection.

12. Click OK to close the Flat File Destination Editor, and then save your package changes.

13. Next, click View ⇨ Pending Checkins to view the Pending Checkins window. Enter **Added File1.txt destination** in the Comments text box and click the Check In button.

14. You now have a functional version of a package in source control. Click the Play button (or press F5) to execute the package. After some validation completes, confirm that your package will execute in BIDS.

Note that the `Package.dtsx` *item is read-only, as it is now saved in VSS.*

15. Click the Stop button (or press Shift+F5) to stop the debugger and then close the package.

You will now roll back to an earlier version of the package:

1. To begin the rollback, click File ⇨ Source Control ⇨ Launch Microsoft Visual SourceSafe. Navigate to the SSISDemo1 folder containing `Package.dtsx` as shown in Figure 15-14.

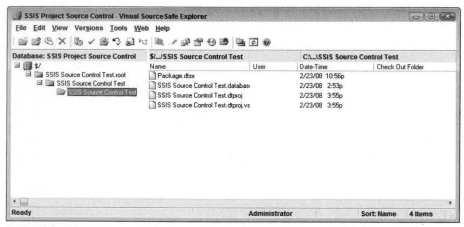

Figure 15-14

2. View the history of the project by clicking Tools ⇨ Show History (or Ctrl+H). The Project History Options dialog box displays as shown in Figure 15-15.

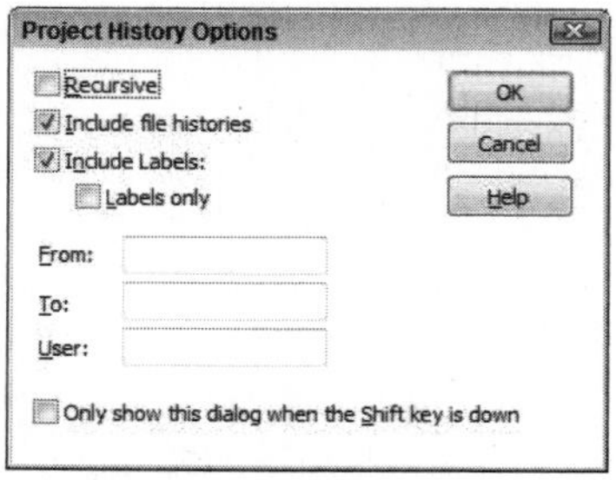

Figure 15-15

3. For the purposes of this demo, click the OK button to accept the defaults. The History of Project dialog box appears, showing all source control activity and items, as shown in Figure 15-16.

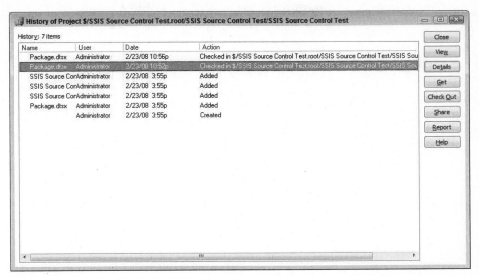

Figure 15-16

4. `Package.dtsx` will be shown multiple times in the list. Highlight the second newest and click the Details button on the right, which will open up the History Details window as shown in Figure 15-17.

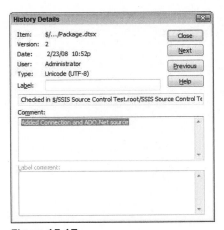

Figure 15-17

5. Confirm that the Comment text area displays the **Added Connection and ADO.Net source** version of the package and click Close to return to the History window.

6. With the same package selected, click the Get button. A dialog box asking if you wish to get the entire project with this version displays. Click the Yes button, and another dialog box will prompt you for the location of the project files, as shown in Figure 15-18.

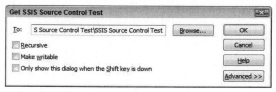

Figure 15-18

7. Clicking the OK button restores the previous version of code over your existing version. After clicking the OK button, return to the SQL Server Business Intelligence Development Studio environment. A prompt to reload displays as shown in Figure 15-19.

Figure 15-19

8. Click the Yes to All button to reload all files in the project. Click the Data Flow tab to observe that the Flat File Destination and File1 Connection Manager are no longer part of this project, as shown in Figure 15-20. They have been removed from the project due to your version rollback from source control.

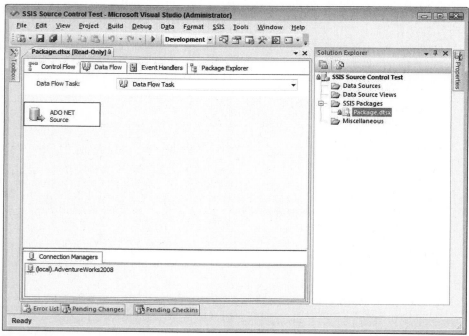

Figure 15-20

9. Add another Flat File Destination to the Data Flow workspace. Configure this Flat File Destination exactly like the first, except change the file and Connection Manager names from File1 to File2 as shown in Figure 15-21.

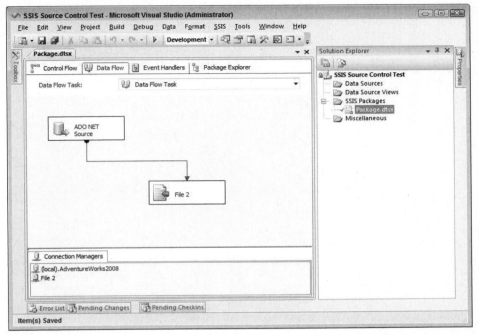

Figure 15-21

10. Open the Pending Checkins window and add the following comment: **Rolled back and added File2.txt destination**. Click the Check In button to store this version in source control.

11. Execute the package by clicking the Play button. Verify that C:\File2.txt is created and populated with Vendor data from the AdventureWorks2008 database.

12. Return to Visual SourceSafe and if the package is checked in, right-click the package and choose Check Out.

13. Next, pull up the history of Package.dtsx by right-clicking the package within the Solution Explorer and choosing View History. The version history of Package 1 is shown in Figure 15-22. Highlight the second version of the package in the list and click the Get button.

Figure 15-22

14. Click OK when the location confirmation dialog box displays and return to the BIDS environment. You will also be prompted on what to do with the existing file, as shown in Figure 15-23. Choose Replace to overwrite the current version in BIDS with the old version.

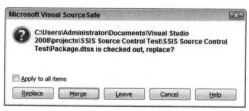

Figure 15-23

15. Click the Data Flow Task tab and confirm that you now see the original working version of the package. The File1 Connection Manager and Flat File Destination should now reflect this status, as shown in Figure 15-24.

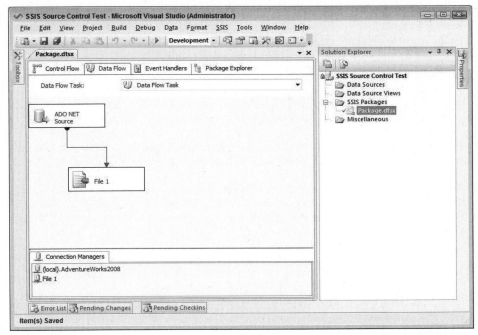

Figure 15-24

This example has provided a rudimentary procedure for manually accomplishing *branching* — a topic that is covered in the next section.

Visual SourceSafe is a familiar source control tool to many with application development experience. For this reason, it has been updated and integrated into the 2008 integrated Visual Studio development environments.

The next section provides a brief introduction to Microsoft's new source control (and so much more) server and client tools known collectively as Visual Studio Team System.

Team Foundation Server, Team System, and SSIS

With the coordinated release of Visual Studio 2005, Microsoft introduced Team System and Team Foundation Server — a powerful enterprise Software Development Life Cycle suite and project management repository consisting of collaborative services, integrated functionality, and an extensible application programming interface (API). Team System seamlessly integrates software development, project management, testing, and source control into the Visual Studio IDE, both Visual Studio 2005 and Visual Studio 2008.

Using Team System with BIDS and SSIS requires that you have a Visual Studio Team System 2008 on your network and have installed the Team Explorer 2008 on your development machine.

❑ Visual Studio Team System 2008 (VSTS) can be purchased for use, but during your evaluation period, Microsoft has provided a Virtual PC that you can download and use. The trial virtual PC image is available from `http://download.microsoft.com`. Search for VSTS 2008 Trial. The examples in this section use the same trial version of VSTS.

❑ Visual Studio Team Explorer 2008 is the client tool that integrates with Visual Studio and allows you to connect to the Team System server and explore the development items as well as work with the source control environment built into VSTS. The source control used by VSTS is not a version of Visual SourceSafe, but rather a more robust source control environment.

After satisfying the preceding requirements, follow these steps to use the VSTS source control. In the next section, you will also see how to create bugs and work items in the VSTS Team Explorer.

1. To configure Team Foundation Server as your SSIS source control, open up BIDS (or close any existing open projects) and click Tools ⇨ Options. Choose Source Control and select Visual Studio Team Foundation Server. Expand the Source Control Node for detailed configuration, as shown in Figure 15-25.

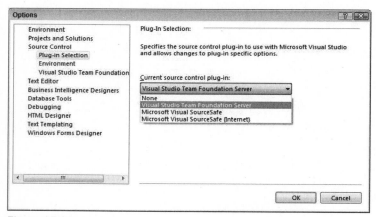

Figure 15-25

This section discusses the relationship between Team System and SQL Server Integration Services. The walkthrough is shown using Business Intelligence Developer Studio (BIDS). If the SQL Server 2008 client tools are installed or Visual Studio 2008 is installed, opening BIDS will open Visual Studio 2008. If Team System is specified as the source controller for either environment, the environment, upon opening, will attempt to connect to a Team Foundation Server.

2. Once Visual Studio 2008 is configured to use Visual Studio Team Foundation Server as the source control, press Ctrl+\, Ctrl+M, or click the Team Explorer tab to view the Team System properties (or choose Team Explorer under the View menu).

3. In the Team Explorer window, click the Add Existing Team Project icon (as shown in Figure 15-26) to connect to the Team System server.

Figure 15-26

4. Click the Servers' button to browse for a Team Foundation Server (or select an existing TF Server from the drop-down list if the server has already been added). In the Add/Remove Team Foundation Server window, click Add to add a new server. Figure 15-27 shows the tfsrtm08 trial version server added to the list.

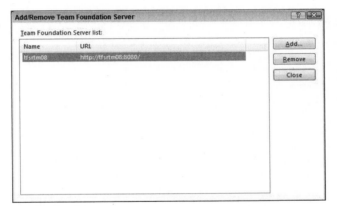

Figure 15-27

5. After adding the server, close the server list window and choose the new server from the drop-down list. Click OK to save your server selection changes.

6. Once you've connected to the Team Foundation Server, open the Team Explorer and click the New Team Project icon, or right-click the Team Foundation Server and click New Team Project. The New Team Project Wizard starts. Enter a name (such as SSIS VSTS Project) and optional description for the new team project, and click Next to continue. Select a Process Template on the next step of the New Team Project Wizard, as shown in Figure 15-28.

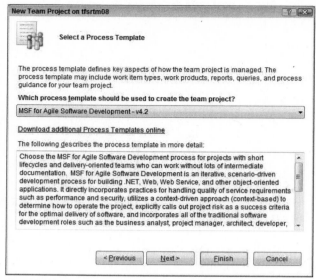

Figure 15-28

7. Click Next to continue. A great feature of the Visual Studio Team System product is the automatic creation of a project management website using Windows SharePoint Services and Reporting Services.

8. Click Next to proceed and enter a Team Project Portal title and description in the next step of the wizard as shown in Figure 15-29, and click Next to continue.

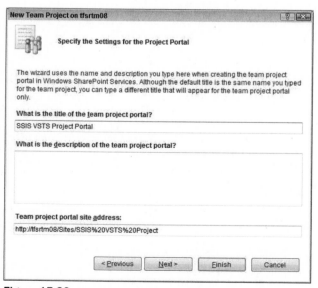

Figure 15-29

9. In the next step of the wizard, you'll initialize source control. Confirm that the "Create an empty source control folder" option is selected, and click Next to continue.

10. The confirmation dialog box displays a summary of selections made. Click Finish to set up the new Team Project. A new Team Project is defined according to the configuration you specified. Creation status is indicated by a progress bar as setup scripts execute. If all goes as expected, the wizard will display a Team Project Created dialog box as shown in Figure 15-30.

At this point, you have created a Team System Container for your SSIS projects. A Team Project is similar to a Visual Studio solution, in that you can add several SSIS projects (or any other type of project) to it.

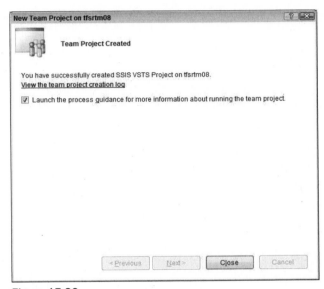

Figure 15-30

If this is your first Team Project, leave the "Launch the process guidance for more information about running the team project" checkbox as shown in Figure 15-30 and click the Close button to complete the New Team Project Wizard.

The View Process Guidance Page is checked by default. Team System provides a great overview of the process in the Process Guidance page as shown in Figure 15-31. These pages provide a wealth of information, useful to beginners and the experienced alike.

"Why create a Team Project," you ask? The short answer is, "The practice of database development is changing." Team development is becoming practical, even required for DBAs, in software shops of all sizes. It is no longer confined to the enterprise with dozens or hundreds of developers.

Team System provides a mechanism for DBAs to utilize team-based methodologies, perhaps for the first time. The Team Project is the heart of Team System's framework for the database developer.

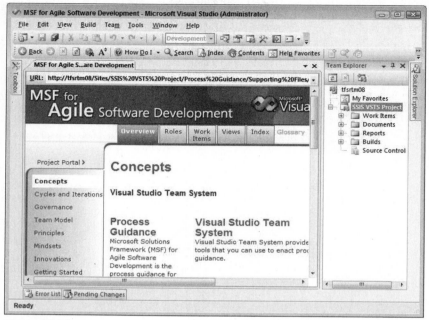

Figure 15-31

MSF Agile and SSIS

MSF Agile is an iterative methodology template included with Team System. In a typical agile software project, a time- and scope-limited project — called an *iteration* — is defined by collaboration with the customer. Deliverables are established, but they may be de-scoped in the interests of delivering a completed feature-set at the end of the iteration. An important aspect of agile iterations is that features slip, but timelines do not slip. In other words, if the team realizes that all features cannot be developed to completion during the time allotted, the time is not extended, and features that *cannot* be developed to completion are removed from the feature-set.

> *Agile methodologies are very suitable to SSIS and BI development projects because they allow more flexible changes so the end solution is suited to the user's need and is adopted.*

No one uses a single methodology alone. There are facets of waterfall thinking in any iterative project. In practice, your methodology is a function of the constraints of the development environment imposed by regulatory concerns, personal style, and results.

Once an MSF Agile Team Project hierarchy has been successfully created, the following sub-items are available under the project in Team Explorer (see Figure 15-32):

❑ Work Items

❑ Documents

❑ Reports

❑ Team Builds

❑ Source Control

Figure 15-32

Take a moment now to examine some sub-items.

Work Items

In MSF Agile projects, work items consist of Tasks, Bugs, Scenarios, and Quality of Service Requirements. Bugs are self-explanatory — they are deficiencies or defects in the code or performance of the application. Scenarios map to requirements and are akin to Use Cases in practice. Quality of Service (QoS) Requirements include acceptable performance under attack or stress. QoS includes scalability and security. Tasks are a catchall category for work items that includes features yet to be developed.

To create a Work Item, right-click the Work Item folder, select Add Work Item, and choose one of the work item types. Figure 15-33 shows the work item Bug template, which allows bugs to be tracked and handled for your SSIS project.

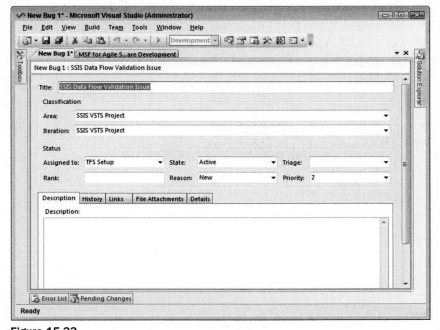

Figure 15-33

Documents

The MSF Agile template includes several document templates to get you started with project documentation. Included are the following:

- ❑ **Development:** Microsoft Project templates for development and testing efforts
- ❑ **Process Guidance:** An HTML document that describes the MSF Agile process
- ❑ **Project Management:** An Excel template containing a project "to do" list as well as an issues and triage spreadsheet
- ❑ **Requirements:** Listing requirements for validation scenarios and a Quality of Service (QoS) Requirements list
- ❑ **Security:** Document sample defining the security plan for functional areas in the solution
- ❑ **Shared Documents:** A repository for miscellaneous project documents
- ❑ **Test:** Test plans for unit and integration testing

Reports

The MSF Agile template contains several built-in Reporting Services project status reports. These reports are accessible directly from Reporting Services or from the Project Portal (SharePoint Portal Services) website.

The Reporting Services home page contains links to several reports as shown in Figure 15-34.

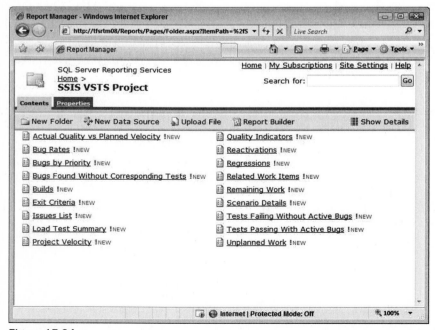

Figure 15-34

The reports are formatted in a style sheet that complements the SharePoint Portal website. The Remaining Work report is shown in Figure 15-35.

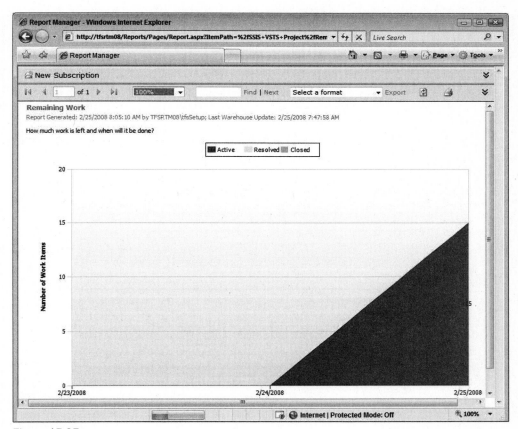

Figure 15-35

The Remaining Work report is part of the larger reporting solution provided by the Project Portal. The Project Portal provides a nice interface for the development team, but project managers are the target audience. The Project Portal can also serve to inform business stakeholders of project status.

To navigate to the Project Portal home page, right-click the Team Project in the Team Explorer and click Show Project Portal.

The Project Portal

The Project Portal (see Figure 15-36) is implemented in SharePoint Portal Services and contains several helpful portals, including the following:

❑ Main Menu

❑ Announcements

❑ Links

❑ Reports (Bug Rates, Builds, and Quality Indicators)

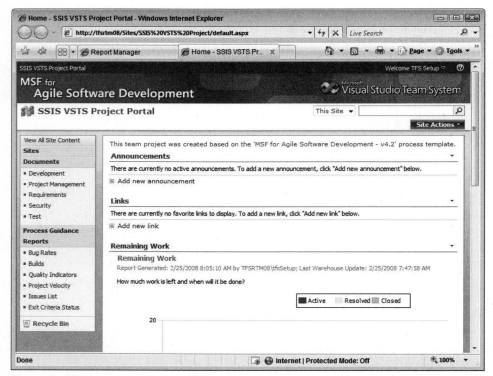

Figure 15-36

Putting It to Work

In this section, you'll create a small SSIS package to demonstrate some fundamental Team System features.

1. To begin, create a new SSIS project in BIDS by clicking File ➪ New ➪ Project. From the Project Types tree view, select Business Intelligence Projects. From the Templates list view, select Integration Services Project. Do not check the Add to Source Control checkbox. Enter **SSIS VSTS Integration Example** as the project name in the Name text box as shown in Figure 15-37.

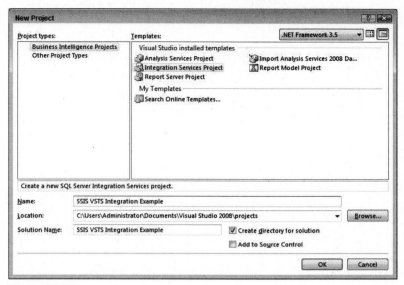

Figure 15-37

2. Click OK to create the new project. Drag a Data Flow Task onto the Control Flow workspace.

3. Right-click in the Connection Managers tab and select New OLE DB Connection to add a database connection. Click the New button to create a new OLE DB Connection.

4. Select your local server from the Server Name drop-down list. Configure the connection for Windows or SQL Server authentication. Select AdventureWorks2008 as the database name. You can click the Test Connection button to test connectivity configuration. Click OK to close the Connection Manager dialog, and OK again to continue.

5. Double-click the Data Flow Task to edit. Drag an OLE DB Source onto the Data Flow workspace. Double-click the OLE DB Source to edit.

6. In the OLE DB Source Editor window, select the AdventureWorks2008 connection in the OLE DB Connection Manager drop-down list. Select Table or View in the Data Access Mode drop-down list. Select [Sales].[vStoreWithDemographics] in the "Name of the table or the view" drop-down list. Click OK to continue.

7. Drag an Aggregate Transformation onto the Data Flow workspace. Connect the output of the OLE DB Source to the Aggregate Transformation by dragging the green arrow from the Source to the Transformation. From the Available Input Columns table, select StateProvinceName, SquareFeet, and AnnualSales. In the grid below, ensure that the operation for StateProvinceName is Group by, the operation for SquareFeet is Average, and the operation for AnnualSales is Sum as shown in Figure 15-38.

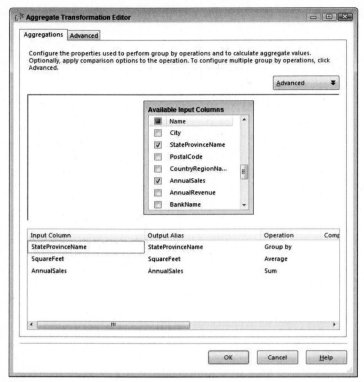

Figure 15-38

8. Click OK to close the Aggregate editor, and drag an OLE DB Source Output (denoted by the green arrow) from the OLE DB Source to the Aggregate.

Drag an Excel Destination onto the Data Flow workspace and connect the Aggregate output to it. Double-click the Excel Destination to open the Excel Destination Editor. Click the New button beside the OLE DB Connection Manager drop-down list to create a new Excel connection object. Enter **c:\SSIS_output.xls** in the Excel file path text box. Click OK to continue.

9. You can create an Excel spreadsheet in this step. If you enter the desired name of a spreadsheet that does not yet exist, the Excel Destination Editor will not be able to locate a worksheet name. The "No tables or views could be loaded" message to this effect will appear in the Name of Excel Worksheet drop-down list.

10. To create a worksheet, click the New button beside the Name of the Excel Sheet drop-down list. A Create Table dialog box will appear. Click OK to accept the defaults and create the worksheet and Excel workbook.

11. Click Mappings in the Excel Destination Editor to configure column-to-data mappings. Accept the defaults by clicking OK.

12. Click File ⇨ Save All to save your work.

Now that you have created a simple SSIS package, you will use this package to test out the Team System functionality with SSIS.

Version and Source Control with Team System

The objective in this section is to walk you through integrating your SSIS project and package with Team System source control and versioning functionality.

1. To add your SSIS project to the Team Project, open the Solution Explorer, right-click the project, and click Add to Source Control.

2. The Add Solution SSIS VSTS Integration Example to Source Control dialog box appears containing a list of Team Projects. Select the SSIS VSTS Project you created earlier, as shown in Figure 15-39.

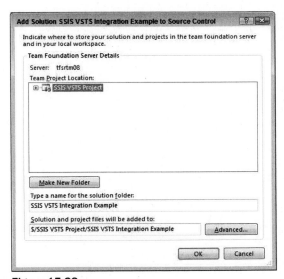

Figure 15-39

3. Click OK to continue. You have successfully created a Team Project and an SSIS project. The Team Project contains version control information — even now.

4. Click View ⇨ Other Windows ⇨ Pending Changes to view the current source control status for the SSIS project, as shown in Figure 15-40.

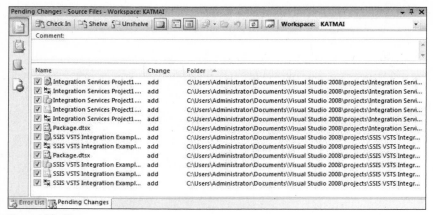

Figure 15-40

The Change column indicates that the files are currently in an Add status. This means the files are not yet source-controlled but are ready to be added to source control.

5. Click the Check In button to add the current SSIS VSTS Integration Example project to the SSIS VSTS Project's source control. This clears the Pending Checkin list. Editing the SSIS VSTS Integration Example project will cause the affected files to reappear in the Pending Checkin list.

Any change to the SSIS VSTS Integration Example project is now tracked against the source-controlled version maintained by the SSIS VSTS Project. Seemingly insignificant changes count: For instance, moving any of the items in the Data Flow workspace is considered an edit to the package item and is tracked.

The default behavior for source control in Visual Studio is that checked-in items are automatically checked out when edited.

6. You can view the current status of all Team Projects on your Team Foundation Server in the Source Control Explorer. To access the Source Control Explorer, double-click Source Control in the Team Explorer or click View ⇨ Other Windows ⇨ Source Control Explorer as shown in Figure 15-41.

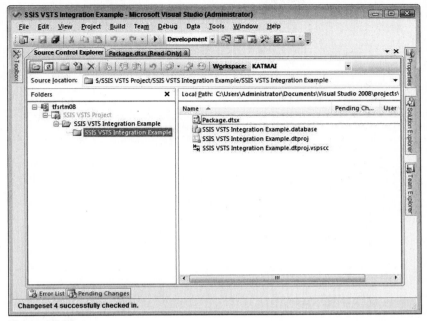

Figure 15-41

This next example will now implement a larger change to demonstrate practical source control management before moving into some advanced source control functionality.

1. In your SSIS project, add an Execute SQL Task to the Control Flow workspace. Configure the task by setting the Connection Type to OLE DB, the Connection to your AdventureWorks2008 connection, and the SQLSourceType to Direct input. Set the SQL Statement to the following:

```
if not exists(select * from sysobjects where id = object_id('Log')
and ObjectProperty(id, 'IsUserTable') = 1)
begin
    CREATE TABLE Log (
      LogDateTime datetime NOT NULL,
      LogLocation VarChar(50) NOT NULL,
      LogEvent VarChar(50) NOT NULL,
      LogDetails VarChar(1000) NULL,
      LogCount Int NULL
    ) ON [Primary]
    ALTER TABLE Log ADD CONSTRAINT DF_Log_LogDateTime DEFAULT (getdate()) FOR
         LogDateTime
  end

INSERT INTO Log
(LogLocation, LogEvent, LogDetails, LogCount)
VALUES('SSISDemo', 'DataFlow', 'Completed', '1st Run')
```

2. It is always a good practice to check your SQL before execution. Do so by clicking the Parse Query button and correct the SQL if necessary. Then click OK to continue.

3. Connect the Data Flow Task to the Execute SQL Task by dragging the output (green arrow) of the Data Flow Task over to the Execute SQL Task.

4. Save your changes by clicking the Save button on the toolbar. You now have updated your SSIS project and saved the changes to disk, but you have not committed the changes to source control. You can verify this in the Pending Changes window by clicking View ⇨ Other Windows ⇨ Pending Changes as shown in the lower window in Figure 15-42.

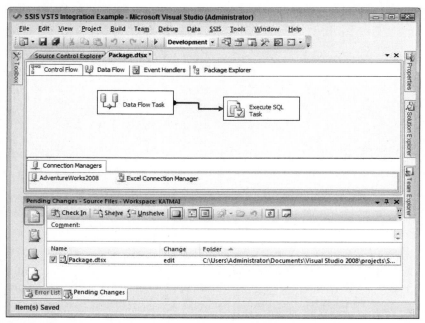

Figure 15-42

5. The Change column indicates that Package.dtsx is in an Edit status. This means that changes to the existing source-controlled Package.dtsx file have been detected. Click the Check In button to publish your changes to source control.

The next section introduces shelving and unshelving changes, using the code in its current state.

Shelving and Unshelving

Shelving is a new concept in Microsoft source control technology since the release of VSTS. It allows you to preserve a snapshot of the current source state on the server for later retrieval and resumed development. You can also shelve code and pass it to another developer as part of a workload reassignment. In automated nightly build environments, shelving provides a means to preserve semi-complete code in a source control system without fully checking it into the build.

1. Shelving a package requires that you have a pending check-in. If there are no packages pending a check-in, first make a change to the package such as moving the Data Flow Task. To shelve code, click the Shelve button on the Pending Checkin toolbar. The Shelve dialog box appears, as shown in Figure 15-43.

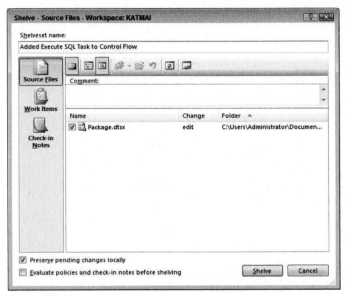

Figure 15-43

The "Preserve pending changes locally" checkbox allows you to choose between rolling back or keeping the edits since the last source code check-in. Checking the checkbox will keep the changes. Unchecking the checkbox will roll changes back to the last source-controlled version.

The rollback will effectively "undo" all changes — even changes saved to disk.

2. Leave the "Preserve pending changes locally" checkbox checked and click Shelve to proceed.

The shelving process has stored the code changes for later use, and you or other developers on your team can resume the development process from the point of the original code check-in before the modified version was shelved. At some point you may need to go back and unshelve the code. This can be handled with the following steps, but before unshelving, you need to have all pending code checked in.

1. To unshelve code, click the Unshelve button on the Pending Checkin toolbar. You'll see the dialog box shown in Figure 15-44.

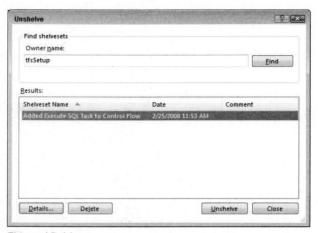

Figure 15-44

2. Click Unshelve to proceed with unshelving. The Unshelve Details Wizard opens, providing options for unshelving metadata and preserving the shelve set on the server.

Also note that an administrator or the user who created the shelving can now delete the shelved files after the code is checked back in.

Unshelving code with conflicts will roll the project back to its state at the time of shelving. For this reason, you may wish to consider shelving your current version of the code prior to unshelving a previous version.

If you are prompted to reload objects in your Visual Studio project, respond by clicking Yes or Yes to All. Your current version will be rolled back to the shelve set version.

Branching

The ability to *branch* code provides a mechanism to preserve the current state of a SSIS project *and* modify it in some fashion. Think of it as driving a stake in the sod of project space marking the status of the current change set as "good."

To branch, open Source Control Explorer by clicking View ⇨ Other Windows ⇨ Source Control Explorer. Right-click the project name you wish to branch and click Branch from the context menu, which brings up the Branch dialog box shown in Figure 15-45. Select a name for the branched project and enter it into the To text box. Note the option to lock the new branch — thus preserving it indefinitely from accidental modification. You can further secure the branched code by including the option to not create local working copies for the new branch.

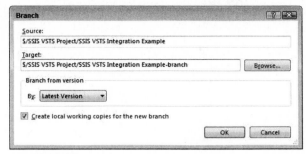

Figure 15-45

Merging

Merging is the inverse operation for branching. It involves recombining code that has been modified with a branch that has not been modified. A merge operation requires that the code has first been changed and checked-in. Follow these steps to merge two branches:

1. To merge projects, open Source Control Explorer. Right-click the name of the branched project containing the changes and click Merge.

2. The project you right-clicked in the previous step should appear in the Source Branch text box of the Version Control Merge Wizard. Select the Target branch (the branch containing no changes) from the Target Branch drop-down, as shown in Figure 15-46. Note the options to merge all or selected changes from the Source branch into the Target branch. Click Next to proceed.

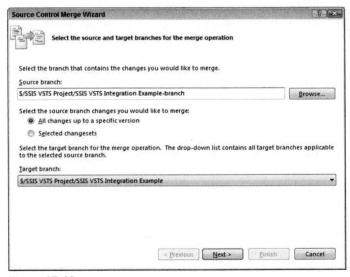

Figure 15-46

3. The Source Control Merge Wizard allows users to select the version criteria during merge. The options include Latest Version (default), Workspace, Label, Date, and Change Set. Click Finish to proceed.

If the Version Control Merge Wizard encounters errors while attempting the merge, the Resolve Conflicts dialog box is displayed. Click Auto-Merge All to attempt an automatic merge. Click Resolve to manually merge branches.

When all conflicts have been resolved, the Resolve Conflicts dialog will reflect this condition.

You should never merge the XML code within a package file from different versions. This could corrupt the file. Therefore when merging projects, always merge the list of objects but not the files themselves.

Labeling (Striping) Source Versions

Labeling provides a means to mark (or "stripe") a version of the code. Generally, labeling is the last step performed in a source-controlled version of code — marking the version as complete. Additional changes require a branch.

1. To label a version, open Source Control Explorer. Right-click the project and click Apply Label. Enter a name for the Label and optional comment. Click the Add button to select files or project(s) to be labeled as shown in Figure 15-47.

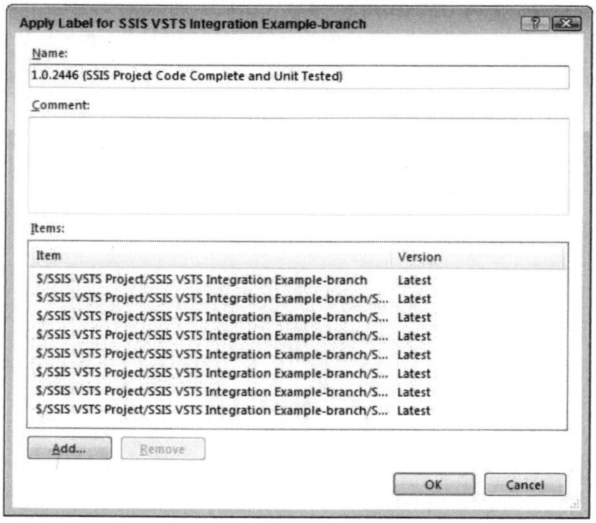

Figure 15-47

2. Click OK to complete labeling.

Much has been debated about when to shelve, branch, or label. The following advice is recommended to standardize your SSIS development process:

❏ **Shelve:** When your code is not code complete. In other words, if your code isn't ready for the nightly or weekly build, shelve it for now.

❏ **Branch:** When you need to add functionality and features to an application that can be considered complete in some form. Some shops will have you branch if the code can be successfully built; others will insist on no branching unless the code can be labeled.

❏ **Label:** When you wish to mark a version of the application as "complete." In practice, labels *are* the version; for instance "1.2.0.2406."

Code Deployment and Promotion from Development to Test to Production

SQL Server Integration Services is decoupled from the SQL Server engine. Packages are developed in either Business Intelligence Development Studio or Visual Studio. Because of this, code promotion is addressed in different ways.

After packages are developed, they exist in XML files with a `.dtsx` file extension. The packages can then be deployed to the file system of a test or production server, or they can be deployed to a SQL Server database where they can reside in the MSDB database.

The Deployment Wizard

You will now look at one method for migrating a package created in Visual Studio into an instance of SQL Server using the Deployment Wizard.

1. In Solution Explorer, right-click the project and click Properties to display the project Property Pages. Click Deployment Utility beneath Configuration Properties and set CreateDeploymentUtility to True, as shown in Figure 15-48.

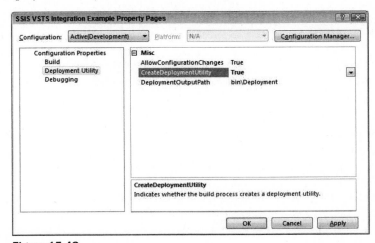

Figure 15-48

2. Click OK to close the Property Pages.

3. Build the solution in Visual Studio (or Business BIDS) by clicking Build ⇨ the Build Solution (or Build [Solution Name]).

4. A \Deployment folder is created in the project \bin directory if you accepted the Configuration Property defaults in a previous step. The Deployment folder contains the package .dtsx files (one per package in the project) and a file of type SSISDeploymentManifest (one per project). To deploy the package, right-click the SSISDeploymentManifest file and click Deploy to start the Package Installation Wizard.

   The Package Installation Wizard allows you to install an SSIS package to an instance of SQL Server (which is managed by the Integration Services service) or to a File System location. For SQL Server or File System installations, a folder is created (the default directory is in %Program Files%) to hold support files only or support and package .dtsx files, respectively — as shown in Figure 15-49.

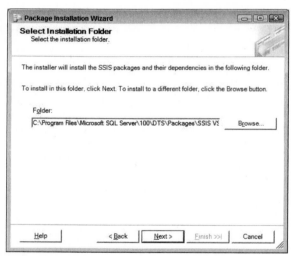

Figure 15-49

5. After you select the installation location, click Next to continue.

6. A confirmation screen displays; click Next to continue. A summary displays showing the location of the files installed; click Finish to complete the installation.

Import a Package

Another method for migrating a code-complete package is to import it directly into an instance of Integration Services on a target server, as follows:

1. To import a package into SQL Server (through the Integration Services service) open Microsoft SQL Server Management Studio and connect to an instance of Integration Services on the destination SQL Server.

2. In the Integration Services tree view, expand the Stored Packages item. There are two sub-items listed beneath Stored Packages: File System and MSDB. The package may be imported into either (or both — with the same name, if desired). Right-click File System or MSDB and click Import Package to begin the import.

3. Select a Package location (SQL Server, File System, or SSIS Package Store). Choosing File System disables the Server text box and Authentication controls. Select File System.

4. Click the ellipsis beside the Package Path text box and navigate to the .dtsx file of the package you desire to import as shown in Figure 15-50. Enter a Package name in the appropriate text box and click OK to import the package.

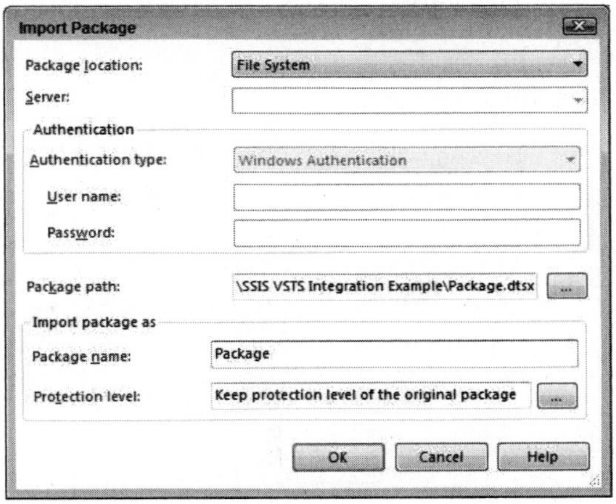

Figure 15-50

Once a package is imported into an instance of SQL Server Integration Services, it may be exported to another instance of SQL Server, File System, or SSIS Package Store via the Export Package functionality as shown in Figure 15-51.

To start the export, right-click the Package name and click Export Package.

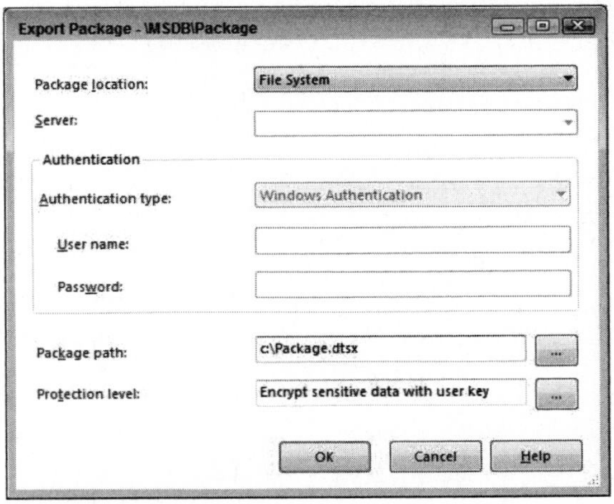

Figure 15-51

607

Export functionality can be used to promote SSIS packages from development to test to production environments.

Summary

You now have a clearer picture of the Software Development Life Cycle of SSIS projects. In this chapter, you learned how to use Visual Studio to add SSIS projects to Microsoft Visual SourceSafe. You also learned how to do the following:

- ❏ Create a Team Project in Team System
- ❏ Add an SSIS project to the Team Project
- ❏ Manage and report project status
- ❏ Control the SSIS source code

Finally, you have more experience with code promotion — deploying an SSIS package from Development to an Integration Services server, as well as exporting a package to another Integration Services server.

You also know more about software development methodologies and about how Team Foundation Server allows you to customize Team System to clearly reflect your methodology of choice.

16

DTS 2000 Migration

By now, you are probably pretty familiar with various basic aspects of SSIS. In earlier chapters, you've studied the new SSIS interface, the new object model, internal design, and how to write SSIS packages.

In SQL Server 2008, you can easily run SQL Server 2000 DTS packages in the 2008 environment. In a future release of SQL Server however, DTS will be officially deprecated and not supported. In this chapter, you look at how to migrate DTS 2000 packages to SSIS and, if necessary, how to run DTS 2000 packages under SSIS.

Managing DTS 2000 Packages within SQL Server Management Studio

Later in this chapter, we discuss how to migrate your DTS packages to SSIS, but for some companies, that isn't an option for a number of months until the migration project is approved. As a temporary solution, you can choose to run DTS 2000 packages under SSIS, if you have the Data Transformation Services 2000 runtime installed or run the package from within the SQL Server 2008 Management Studio using the SQL Server 2000 DTS runtime engine.

To edit packages in SQL Server 2008, you'll first need to install a component of the SQL Server 2005 (yes, SQL Server 2005) Feature Pack. The SQL Server Feature Pack is a series of optional installations that can enhance your SQL Server experience like an OLE DB Provider for DB2 or in our case the SQL Server 2000 DTS Designer Components. If you do not have this one component installed, you will receive the following error when you try to open DTS packages in Management Studio:

```
SQL Server 2000 DTS Designer Components are required to edit DTS packages.
Install the special Web download, "SQL Server 2000 DTS Designer Components" to
use this feature. (Microsoft.SqlServer.DtsObjectExplorerUI)
```

To open a DTS package in Management Studio that is stored in SQL Server's MSDB database, connect to the database engine and select the package in the Management ➪ Legacy ➪ Data Transformation Services tree. This will open the DTS Designer that you're already familiar with. You can also right-click Data Transformation Services and select Open Package to open a COM-structured package (.dts). If you right-click the DTS folder and select Import Package, you can import the package from the file system into the MSDB database of your SQL Server 2008 instance.

Once the package is open, you can edit the package just like you did in SQL Server 2000. The main missing feature you will see is that you cannot create a new package in Management Studio. To create a new package, you'll have to open an existing DTS package, delete all the tasks, and then click Save As to the new package name.

Running DTS 2000 Packages under SSIS

You can also run DTS packages in SSIS by using the Execute DTS Package Task. Though you can do this, the package becomes difficult to manage because you have to manage two runtimes and logging mechanisms. To try an example on how to do this: First, download the two sample DTS packages from www.wrox.com. Then, create a blank SSIS package called DTSExample.dtsx. In the Control Flow, drag on an Execute DTS 2000 Package Task.

In the task, set the StorageLocation property to Structured Storage File. Then, point the File property to the DTS package you downloaded from the Wiley website as shown in Figure 16-1. For the PackageName property, select the most recent version of the package. The PackagePassword and PackageID properties will automatically be updated.

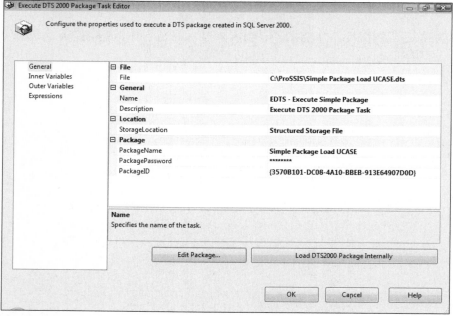

Figure 16-1

You can then click the Load DTS2000 Package Internally button to embed the package inside the SSIS package so that you will no longer have to manage the package externally. If the DTS Designer Components are installed, you can click Edit Package to open the Package Designer to make changes to the package. Don't make any changes to the package at this time. Close the DTS 2000 Package Designer if it's open, and then click OK. You will be at the design surface of the Control Flow tab, with the package showing, as shown in Figure 16-2.

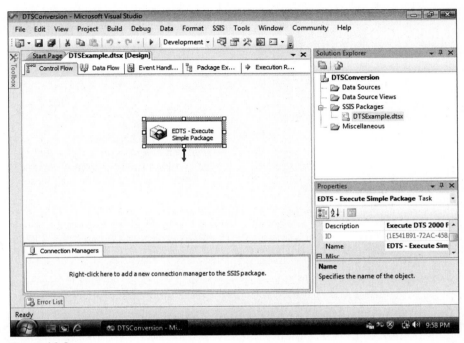

Figure 16-2

Test-run this package and it will be successful. If for any reason it is not, read the error message to find out what went wrong and make modifications accordingly.

Migrating DTS 2000 Packages to SSIS

Microsoft provides the DTS Migration Wizard to facilitate the process of transferring your DTS 2000 packages to SSIS. The DTS Migration Wizard analyzes your current DTS 2000 package and tries to map its tasks, components, global variables, and workflow constraints to their equivalent parts, where applicable, in SSIS.

The bad news is that because SSIS is totally reengineered, it is not possible to migrate all packages that you can create in DTS 2000. The Migration Wizard provides a best-effort attempt. If your package cannot be migrated using the wizard, you will have to upgrade it manually. In fact, for those packages, you probably want to use manual upgrade anyway so that you can take full advantage of the enhanced functions and capabilities. From personal experience of migrating thousands of packages, we've seen anywhere between a 35 and 50 percent success rate using the wizard. We qualify a successful package migration as a package that migrates with no intervention needed. To be clear, all of your DTS packages will migrate to SSIS but there's a strong chance that they will not work in SSIS once migrated. Here are a few of the components in DTS and the chance that they will migrate with no issues to SSIS, based on our conversion experience.

DTS Object	Migration Success to SSIS
Execute SQL Task	95%
Transform Data Task	50%
ActiveX Script Task	10% (depending on what objects are in the task)
OLAP Tasks	0%
Flat File Source	25%
OLE DB Source	75%

The Transform Data Task may not migrate if any ActiveX scripting is inside of it. People would typically use ActiveX script inside a Transform Data Task in order to apply business rules to the data as it moves through the task. If the task cannot migrate to SSIS, it will instead migrate to an Execute DTS Package Task and embed that one DTS task inside the task.

The ActiveX Script Task in general will always migrate to an ActiveX Script Task in SSIS but there's a fair chance it won't work once you click the Execute button. Whether the task works depends on what type of code you're doing inside of the task. The DTS object model and the SSIS object model are substantially different, and some items may not work. If, however, you're using a WMI object inside the script, the ActiveX Script Task will function in SSIS. In addition to that, the ActiveX Script Task will be decommissioned in a future release of SQL Server and need to be replaced anyway.

The Flat File Source will always migrate to SSIS as well, but may require additional work once you migrate. For example, if you have a flat file that does not map all of its columns to the destination in the Transform Data Task, the migrated task in SSIS could potentially send the data to the wrong destination column, which would be a horrible bug in your new package. It will be critically important to test each of these and all converted packages after migration because of flaws like this in the wizard.

In this section, you will see how to use the Migration Wizard to upgrade two sample DTS 2000 packages. You can download the two sample packages from www.wrox.com. The packages are identical with one small exception, which is discussed momentarily. They will create a sample table in the TempDB database to load with an Execute SQL Task and then send data into the table using a Transform Data Task. The package, which is shown in Figure 16-3, has a series of global variables to dynamically configure the package. The main global variables set the server name (strServerName) and the location of the flat file (strFileName). The dynamic nature of the package is done through the Dynamic Properties Task.

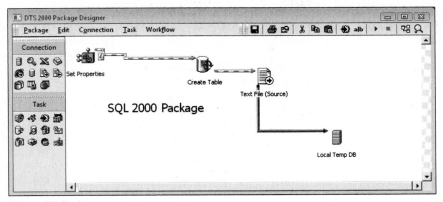

Figure 16-3

The Simple Package Load UCASE.dts package is slightly special, even though from all outward appearances it looks identical to the Simple Package Load.dts package. The difference between the two packages is that the Simple Package Load UCASE.dts package contains a small ActiveX script inside the Transform Data Task (shown in Figure 16-4). To see the script, go to the Transform Data Task and double-click the line between the StateAbbr columns in the Transformations tab.

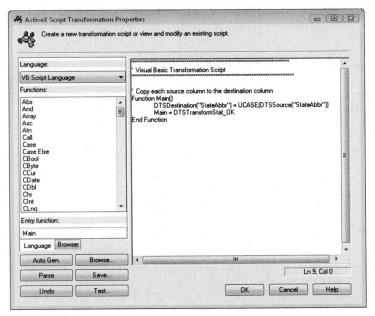

Figure 16-4

The reason this package is included in the example packages is to show you how differently this package is treated by the Package Migration Wizard. Any package that contains even the simplest ActiveX script inside a transformation like this will not be properly migrated. Instead this logic will be broken into its own Execute DTS 2000 Package Task in SSIS.

Using the Package Migration Wizard

You can invoke the Package Migration Wizard from multiple places. Depending on where you invoke the wizard from, the migrated package destination location will be different. For example, if you invoke the wizard from BIDS, it will assume that you want to migrate DTS 2000 packages into an SSIS package file (.dtsx). If the wizard is invoked from Management Studio, it will assume that you want to migrate the package into the MSDB database on a server you define. Following are ways you can use to invoke the Package Migration Wizard:

❑ From SQL Server Management Studio, connect to the database engine, and you can invoke the Package Migration Wizard by using the right-click context menu of the Data Transformation Services Node under the Management ⇨ Legacy Node in the Object Explorer.

❑ From BIDS, right-click SSIS Packages in Solution Explorer with the SSIS project open and pick Migrate DTS 2000 Package.

❑ From a DOS prompt, type **DTSMigrationWizard** to invoke the wizard. By default, the binary DTSMigrationWizard.exe resides at C:\Program Files\Microsoft SQL Server\10\DTS\ Binn folder. This may be different in your environment if you customized your SQL Server 2008 installation.

Because BIDS is the home where you create and edit your SSIS packages, you'll use BIDS to see step-by-step how you can migrate the package you created in the previous section. If you migrate the packages using Management Studio, your packages will be deployed right in the MSDB database, and you won't be able edit the package easily.

To start this example, place the sample file (ZipCodeExtract.csv) in the C:\Projects\ Pro SSIS 2008 directory. Invoke the Package Migration Wizard from BIDS by right-clicking the SSIS Packages Node and selecting Migrate DTS 2000 Package. You will see a welcome window from the wizard. Click Next to continue.

In the next page, shown in Figure 16-5, you choose the source type and location. In this case, you can assume that your package is stored in a .DTS package file (Structured Storage File). If you choose this option, you can only migrate a single package at a time. After you select Structured Storage File, point to the location where your file is located (C:\Projects\Pro SSIS 2008\Simple Package Load.dts in my case). If you select Microsoft SQL Server, you can migrate all the packages on that instance to SSIS. Click Next.

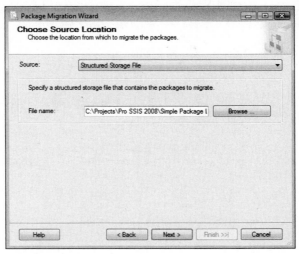

Figure 16-5

The next page of the wizard asks you to pick the destination location of the package you are migrating, as shown in Figure 16-6. As mentioned earlier, because the wizard is invoked within BIDS, it assumes that you want the package in a .dtsx file format. You can see from the figure that the Destination drop-down list box is grayed out and the default selection is DTSX File. If you want to migrate the package to a database server, invoke the package from the command line instead. In this case, you can pick the C:\Projects\Pro SSIS 2008 directory as the destination folder. Click Next.

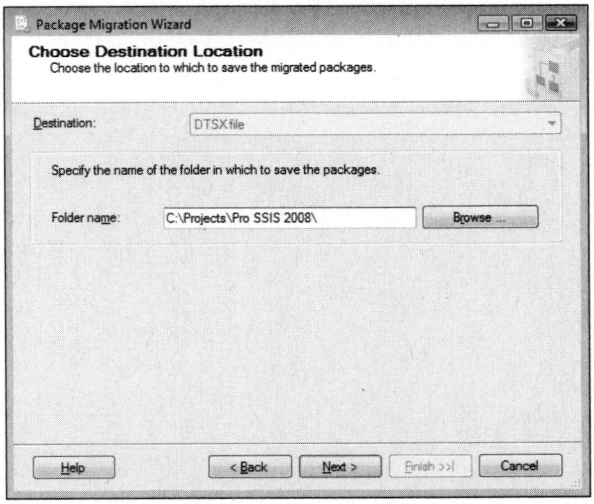

Figure 16-6

In the next step, the wizard lists the packages available on the source server that can be migrated, as shown in Figure 16-7. Because we're migrating from a structured file (.dts), there's only one package, Simple Package Load, which you downloaded earlier. Check the box next to the package name. Note that it even gives you the choice of migrating previous versions of the package. You can also change the name of the SSIS package that will be created as well. Click Next.

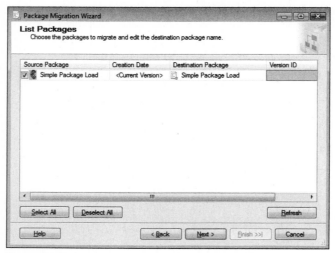

Figure 16-7

The wizard then asks you to provide a log file location, as shown in Figure 16-8. The log file will log the migration process. This information will be valuable if the migration is unsuccessful, because the migration process can take a large amount of time in some cases if you're migrating a larger number of packages. For example, a test case of migrating 50 mildly complex packages took 40 minutes, and by optionally creating a log, you can walk away from the process and read the log when you come back. You will use the C:\Projects\Pro SSIS 2008\MigrationLog.log file for this example. Click Next.

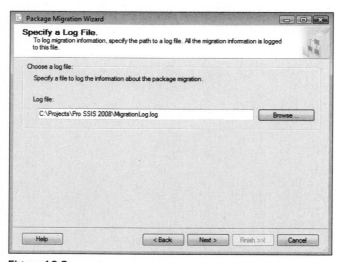

Figure 16-8

You now will see a summary screen of this migration-related information, as shown in Figure 16-9. You can scan over, and go back and change settings, if desired. Otherwise, click Finish to migrate the package now.

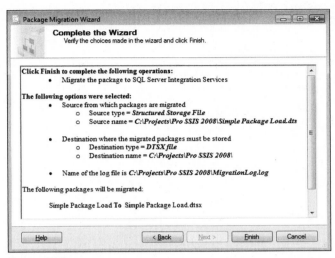

Figure 16-9

The migration process starts; you will see its progress in real time. After it is done, you can click the Report button to view the migration report. In this case, your package has migrated successfully, as shown in Figure 16-10. Click Close to finish the Package Migration Wizard and be returned back to the BIDS environment where you can edit the package. If for any reason the migration is not successful, the error will be in the final report. Based on the error message, you will be able to fix what is wrong to continue.

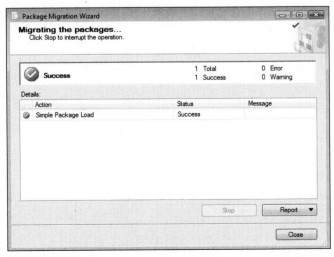

Figure 16-10

With the package now migrated, you will want to complete the migration final touches in BIDS and test it there. The converted package looks like Figure 16-11. Earlier on, you'll recall that the package had two global variables that were used by the Dynamic Properties Task to set the connection properties of the server name and the flat file connection string. In SSIS, there is no equivalent task, so the Dynamic Properties has now become a non-functional Script Task.

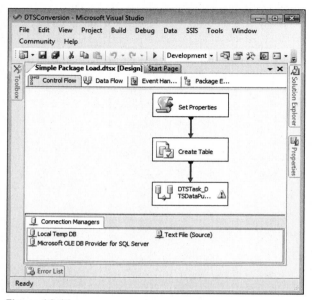

Figure 16-11

Inside the Script Task, you'll see that all the code is commented out and essentially acts as a placeholder to remind you to convert the logic to expressions. The script will show you all the properties that the variables were setting previously. You will replace this logic with SSIS expressions.

To map the first connection to the variable, left-click the Text File (Source) Connection Manager and in the Properties window, click the ellipsis button next to the Expressions property. This opens the Properties Expression Editor. Select the ConnectionString property and click the ellipsis button in the Expression column. This opens the Expression Builder screen, which aids in writing expressions. Drag the strFileName variable from the Variables tree in the top-left pane as shown in Figure 16-12 and click OK twice.

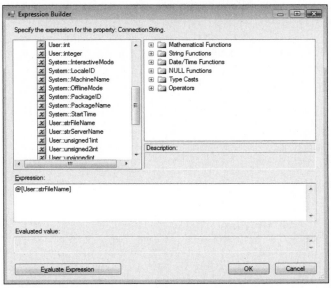

Figure 16-12

Repeat the same process over again for the Local TempDB Connection Manager. This time, you'll set the ServerName property to the strServerName variable. After you have this process complete, you can remove the Script Task in your package. You're now ready to execute the package.

After you're able to see the first package working, you can migrate the second package, Simple Package Load UCASE.dts, which has the ActiveX script inside of the Transform Data Task. This time you'll see that because of the ActiveX script, one piece of the package is migrated into an Execute DTS 2000 Package Task renamed Load ZipCodes (shown in Figure 16-13). To truly migrate this package to SSIS, you would want to remove this task and rebuild the logic for that one section from scratch.

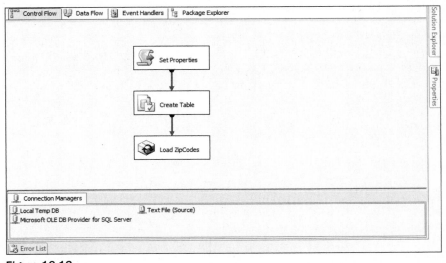

Figure 16-13

Third-Party Migration Solution

DTS xChange (http://www.dtsxchange.com) is a solution offered by a Microsoft partner, Pragmatic Works Software, which migrates DTS packages to SSIS while applying a series of best practices rules to the packages. The solution is broken into three pillars:

❑ **Profile:** DTS xChange Profiler helps you estimate your migration project in hours and dollar cost whether you choose to use an automation tool or not.

❑ **Convert:** DTS xChange will migrate your packages, applying rules to each DTS package as it migrates them to enforce best practices.

❑ **Monitor:** The SSIS Performance Warehouse is a software development kit (SDK) to help you get the most out of your new SSIS environment. It contains a series of reports and a data warehouse to monitor your SSIS package execution.

The DTS xChange Profiler feature allows you to profile how large of a migration effort you have to completely migrate to SSIS in terms of dollars and hours. The process allows you to specify how long you believe each type of task will take you to migrate, whether you choose to use DTS xChange or manually re-engineer the package. Then, a report is generated with the migration cost in terms of dollars and hours to migrate each package and the total cost in man-hours.

The core component to DTS xChange is the actual migration of the packages. Prior to migrating the packages, you can choose between a dozen best practice rules that Pragmatic Works has implemented over thousands of packages for its customers. These rules will enable you to truly capture the full benefit of SSIS and realize some of your investment in the new platform. DTS xChange will also migrate many of the tasks that the built-in Migration Wizard cannot migrate, like Dynamic Properties Tasks. Some of these best practice rules can also be applied to new packages you create in the SSIS environment by using a separate tool called SSIS Wiz by Pragmatic Works.

Migration of hundreds of packages is a fast process with DTS xChange. As packages migrate, they are also validated to ensure that the package will work in production once you click the Start button. The program will check to ensure that files exists, table names that you think are there have actually been deployed, and that your credentials will also work in the package.

The last component of DTS xChange is a reporting and analytics component called the SSIS Performance Warehouse. This component is a software development kit (SDK) that will send auditing information about your package runtime and statistics into a data warehouse for future inspection. There is also a series of reports and cubes that goes on top of the data warehouse for easy viewing.

You can download DTS xChange from http://www.DTSxChange.com, and the demo version can migrate up to five packages for free, and profile your entire environment.

Summary

In this chapter, you learned about DTS 2000 package migration, and about running DTS 2000 packages within SSIS. Eventually, you will have to migrate all your DTS 2000 packages into SSIS packages. If you have many packages and they are fairly complex, you can choose to install the DTS 2000 runtime and continue running them within SSIS. You can start migrating smaller and simpler packages with the Migration Wizard. As you gain more experience, you can start to tackle more complex packages. As mentioned earlier, you will probably have to rethink how the old package was designed and then redesign it using SSIS's enhanced functionality. This way, you will be able to fully take advantage of the richer functionality, and better performance and scalability provided by SSIS.

Error and Event Handling

SQL Server Integration Services provides some valuable features to enable you to control the workflow of your SSIS packages at a very granular level. Functionality that you might expect to be available only by scripting can often be accomplished by setting a few properties of a component. In addition, SSIS comes with powerful error-handling capabilities, the ability to log detailed information as the package runs, and debugging functionality that speeds up troubleshooting and design.

This chapter walks you through controlling the package workflow, beginning at the highest level using precedence constraints and then drilling down to event handling. You'll see how trappable events play a role in breakpoints, and how to perform exception handling for bad data in the Data Flow. Finally, you learn how these features can be used for troubleshooting, debugging, and enabling you to build robust SSIS packages.

Precedence Constraint

Precedence constraints are the green, red, and blue connectors in the Control Flow that can be used to handle error conditions and the workflow of a package.

Be aware, precedence constraints look a lot like data paths in the Data Flow, but they are much different. On the one hand, precedence constraints define what tasks should be executed in which order; on the other hand, Data Flow paths define what transformations and destinations data should be routed to. Data Flow paths deal with moving data; precedence constraints deal with workflow handling.

Precedence Constraint Basics

The main purpose of precedence constraints is to control when tasks and containers should run in relation to one another. This revolves around whether tasks are successful (green) or fail (red) or whether they just complete (blue for success or failure). Precedence constraints can be more granularly controlled through advanced properties, which are addressed in the next section.

Figure 17-1 shows a typical example. If the Initial Data Flow Task completes successfully, the Success Data Flow Task will execute. A green arrow (on the left) points to the Success Data Flow Task. If the Initial Data Flow Task fails, the Failure Send Mail Task executes, sending notification of the failure. A red arrow (in the middle) points to the Failure Send Mail Task. No matter what happens, the Completion Script Task will always execute. A blue arrow (on the right) points to the Completion Script Task.

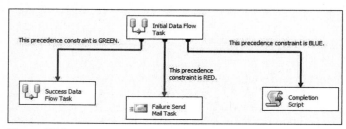

Figure 17-1

By default, the precedence constraint will be a green arrow designating success. To change how the precedence constraint is evaluated, you can right-click the arrow and choose a different outcome from the pop-up menu, as shown in Figure 17-2.

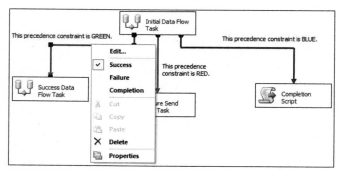

Figure 17-2

Tasks may also be combined into groups by using containers, and with this design the workflow can be controlled by the success or failure of the container. For example, a package may have several Data Flow Tasks that can run in parallel, each loading data from a different source. All of these must complete successfully before continuing on to the next step. These tasks can be added to a Sequence Container, and the precedence constraint can be drawn from the container to the next step. Figure 17-3 is an example showing how a Sequence Container might be used. After the Initialization Script runs, the Import Data Container executes. Within it, three Data Flow processes run in parallel. A failure of any of the Data Flow Tasks will cause the Import Data Container to fail, and the failure message will be sent. If all three complete successfully, the Clean Up Script will run.

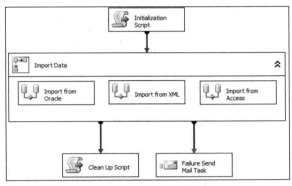

Figure 17-3

Advanced Precedence Constraints and Expressions

Beyond the basics, precedence constraints can also be configured to evaluate Boolean expressions and be combined with other precedence constraints through a logical OR evaluation. The advanced precedence constraints are defined through the Precedence Constraint Editor, which Figure 17-4 shows. To pull up the editor, either double-click the precedence constraint arrow or right-click the arrow and choose Edit.

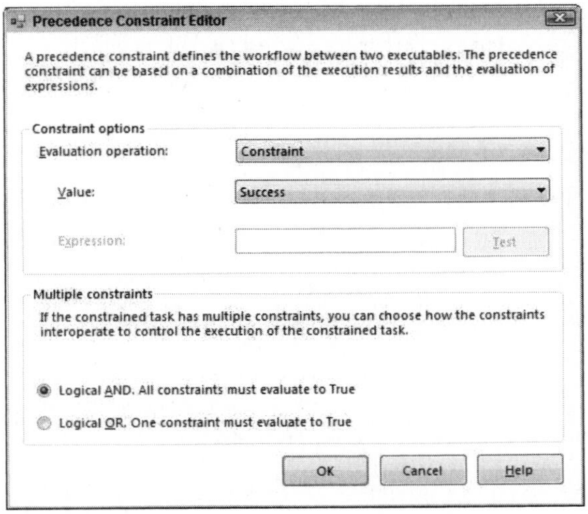

Figure 17-4

Using Boolean Expressions with Precedence Constraints

With the editor, the workflow within a package can be controlled by using Boolean expressions in place of, or in addition to, the outcome of the initial task or container. Any expression that can be evaluated to True or False can be used. For example, the value of a variable that changes as the package executes can be compared to a constant. If the comparison resolves to True, the connected task will execute. The way a precedence constraint is evaluated can be based on both the outcome of the initial task and an expression. This allows the SSIS developer to finely tune the workflow of a package. The following table shows the four Evaluation Operation options contained in the drop-down box for configuring a precedence constraint:

Evaluation Operation	Definition
Constraint	The execution result is applied to the constraint (success, failure, or completion) without the use of an expression.
Expression	Any expression that evaluates to True or False is used to evaluate the constraint without the consideration of the execution result.
Expression AND Constraint	*Both* the specified execution result *and* an expression condition must be satisfied for the constraint to allow the next task to run.
Expression OR Constraint	*Either* the specified execution result *or* an expression condition must be satisfied for the constraint to allow the next task to run.

There you can choose which type of Evaluation Operation to use and set the value of the constraint and/ or supply the expression.

In the following example, you simulate flipping a coin to learn more about using expressions with precedence constraints. First, create a new table to hold the results. Connect to a test database in SQL Server Management Studio and run this script:

```
CREATE TABLE CoinToss (
    Heads INT NULL,
    Tails INT NULL )
GO
INSERT INTO CoinToss SELECT 0,0
```

1.   Start a new SSIS project in BIDS.

2.   Create a Connection Manager pointing to the test database where the CoinToss table was created. The steps for creating a Connection Manager are covered in Chapter 3.

3.   Add an Execute SQL Task to the Control Flow design area.

4.   Change the name of the task to Clear Results.

5.   Double-click the Clear Results Task to open the Execute SQL Task Editor.

6.   Set the Connection property to point to the Connection Manager that you just created and then type the following code in the SQLStatement field:

```
UPDATE CoinToss
SET Tails = 0, Heads = 0
```

7. Click OK to accept the configuration and dismiss the dialog box.

8. Right-click the Control Flow design area and select Variables from the pop-up menu to open the Variables window.

9. Create a new package-level variable called Result. Set the Data Type to Int32.

10. Add a For Loop Container to the design area. You will use the container to simulate flipping the coin a given number of times, so name it Coin Toss Simulator.

11. Drag the Precedence Constraint from the Clear Results Task to the Coin Toss Simulator.

12. Select the Coin Toss Simulator and open the Variables window.

13. Add a variable called Count, with a Data Type of Int32. In this case, the variable will only be used by the For Loop and the scope will be Coin Toss Simulator.

14. Double-click the Coin Toss Simulator Container to open the For Loop Editor.

15. Set the properties as in the following table and click OK.

Property	Value
InitExpression	@Count = 0
EvalExpression	@Count < 100
AssignExpression	@Count = @Count + 1

This should look familiar to you if you have programmed in almost any language: The For loop will execute 100 times.

16. Drag a Script Task into the Coin Toss Simulator. Because the Coin Toss Simulator is a container, you can drag other tasks into it. Name the Script Task "Toss."

17. Double-click Toss to open the Script Task Editor. In the Script pane, ReadWriteVariables section, type in **User::Result**. The script will have access only to variables set up in this way.

18. Click Design Script to open the Visual Studio design environment. Each time this script runs, it will randomly set the Result variable equal to a one or a two. Replace Sub Main with this code:

```
Public Sub Main()
    Randomize()
    Dts.Variables("User::Result").Value = CInt(Int((2 * Rnd()) + 1))
    Dts.TaskResult = ScriptResults.Success
End Sub
```

19. Close the script design area and click OK to accept the changes.

20. Drag two Execute SQL Tasks into the Coin Toss Simulator Container. Name one Heads and the other Tails.

21. Connect the Coin Toss Script Task to each of the Execute SQL Tasks.

22. Double-click the Precedence Constraint pointing to Heads to bring up the Precedence Constraint Editor.

23. Change the Evaluation Operation from Constraint to Expression. The Expression text box will now become available. Type the following into the Expression property:

```
@Result == 1
```

24. Click OK. The precedence constraint will change from green to blue, meaning completion, and will have an *fx* symbol next to it specifying that the precedence uses an expression. Figure 17-5 shows the Precedence Constraint Editor with an expression set.

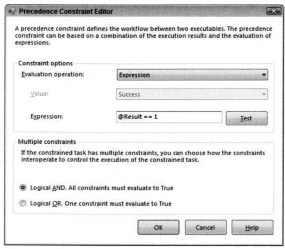

Figure 17-5

When evaluating two values in an SSIS Boolean expression, you will need to use two equals, signs (==). This indicates that the expression will return TRUE or FALSE depending on whether the values are equal. NULL values do not evaluate, so be sure to check to make sure that both sides of the == will return an actual value. The only time you will use a single equals sign is when you are using an SSIS expression to set the value of a variable, such as when using a For Loop Container.

25. To continue with the example, next open the properties of the precedence constraint that is connected to the Tails Task. Change the Evaluation Operation from Constraint to Expression. Type this in the Expression property:

```
@Result == 2
```

26. Click OK to accept the properties. At this point, the package should resemble Figure 17-6.

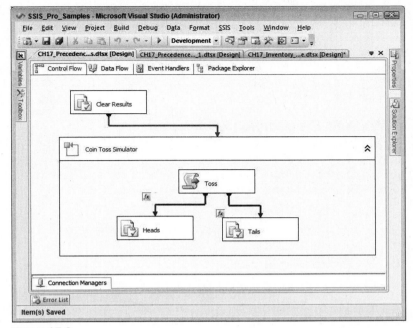

Figure 17-6

Just a couple more details and you'll be ready to run the package!

27. Double-click Heads to open the Execute SQL Task Editor. In the Connection property, set the value to the test database Connection Manager. Type this in the SQLStatement property to increment the count in the CoinToss table:

```
UPDATE CoinToss SET Heads = Heads + 1
```

28. Click OK to accept the changes. Bring up the Execute SQL Task Editor for the Tails object. Set the Connection property to the test database Connection Manager. Type this code in the SQLStatement property:

```
UPDATE CoinToss SET Tails = Tails + 1
```

29. Click OK to accept the configuration and run the package.

As the package runs, you can see that sometimes Heads will execute, and sometimes Tails will execute. Once the package execution completes, return to SQL Server Management Studio to view the results by running this query:

```
SELECT * FROM CoinToss
```

Out of 100 coin tosses, Heads should have come up approximately 50 times.

This simple example demonstrates how to use an expression to control the package workflow instead of or combined with the outcome of a task. In a business application, maybe the precedence constraint could be used to ensure that the number of rows affected by a previous step is less than a certain value. Or possibly, a task should execute only if it is a particular day of the week. Any variable within scope can be used, and several functions and operators are available to build the expression. Any valid expression will work as long as it evaluates to True or False. See Chapter 6 to learn more about building and using expressions.

Working with Multiple Precedence Constraints

In your package workflow, you can have multiple precedence constraints pointing to the same task. By default, the conditions of *both must be True* to enable execution of the constrained task. You also have the option of running a task if at *least one of the conditions is True* by setting the Multiple Constraint property to "Logical OR. One constraint must evaluate to True" (see Figure 17-7).

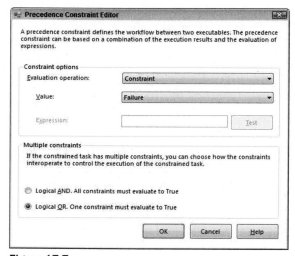

Figure 17-7

The solid arrows change to dotted arrows when the Logical OR option is chosen. Figure 17-8 shows how the Send Mail Task will execute if either of the Data Flow Tasks fails. In this example, both precedence constraints are configured to fail but the Logical OR has been set instead of the Logical AND. Because the Logical OR has been turned on, the precedence constraints are dashed lines. Figure 17-8 shows the Import Customers Data Flow is successful (green), but the Import Orders failed (red). Because one of the Data Flows is red, the Error Message Send Mail Task is executing. If both Data Flows had been successful, the Error Message Task would not have run.

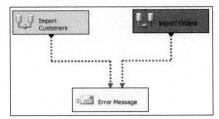

Figure 17-8

Let's take a look at another example where an expression is evaluated in addition to using multiple constraints. In this workflow we are loading data from a series of files that exist on a network drive into a SQL database. The business rules require that no file will be allowed to be loaded into the database more than once, and the files must be archived, whether they have been loaded previously or not. Figure 17-9 shows the workflow with the required business rules implemented.

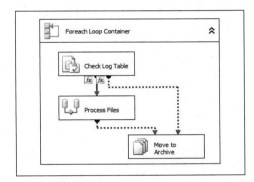

Figure 17-9

In this workflow, a Foreach Loop Container will be used to loop through the files you want to load into the database. With each iteration of the loop, the filename will be assigned to a variable, which will then be used in the next task (the Execute SQL Task) to determine if it has been previously loaded. The Execute SQL Task called Check Log Table will use the variable that holds the current filename as an input parameter to a SQL statement to determine if it does in fact exist in the table. The result of the query will return either a 1 or a 0, to be stored in a variable that is called User::blnFlag. This task is pivotal in that it will be the basis for the evaluation within the precedence constraints. Double-clicking the precedence constraint connecting the Check Log Table Execute SQL Task and the Process Files Data Flow Task will display the dialog as shown in Figure 17-10.

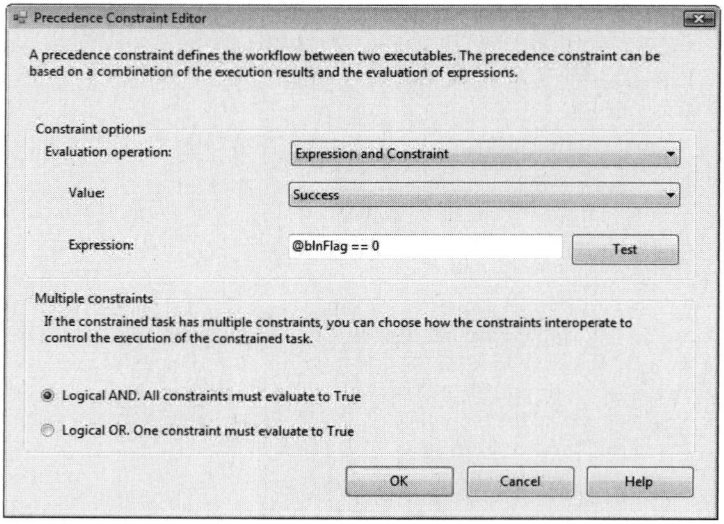

Figure 17-10

The properties of the precedence constraint in Figure 17-10 are set to allow the workflow to pass through to the next task (the Process Files Data Flow Task) if the previous step succeeded and the expression has evaluated to true. What this constraint is essentially asking is: "Was the previous step successful and is this a new file that has not been previously loaded?" Now that you have determined the business rule behind that constraint, double-click the "dotted" precedence constraint that connects the Check Log Table Execute SQL Task and the Move to Archive File System Task. The dialog presented for this constraint is shown in Figure 17-11

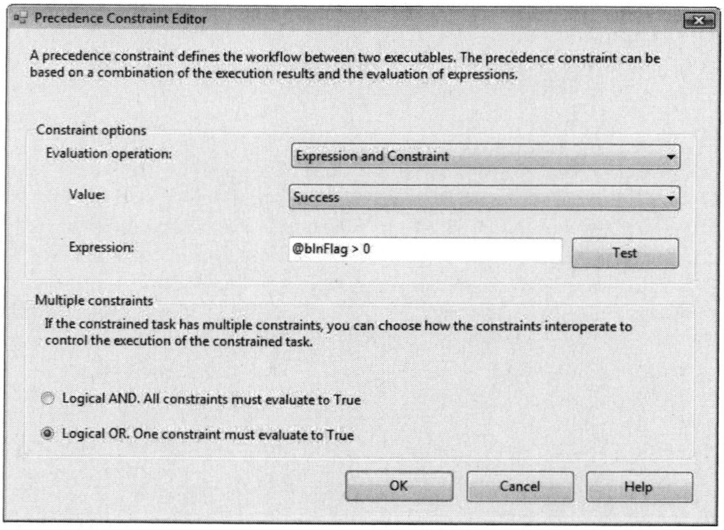

Figure 17-11

The properties of the precedence constraint in Figure 17-11 are representing a couple of pieces of business rule logic. First, the evaluation operation is set to Expression and Constraint. Second, the

Expression is testing whether your variable @blnFlag is greater than 0. The interpretation of this expression is asking: "Has the current file been previously loaded?" Lastly, the Logical OR radio button is selected to facilitate an "OR" condition between your two precedence constraints. In plain English, the properties that are defined for the two precedence constraints will allow the file to be processed and archived if it hasn't been previously loaded OR to just archive the file.

By using precedence constraints, you control the order of events within a package. After a task or container executes, and depending on how the precedence constraint between the two components was evaluated, the second task or container runs. With all of these options, you can control the workflow of your package at a very granular level. The great thing about precedence constraints in SSIS is that they afford you the flexibility to implement complex business rules like the scenario previously demonstrated. Drilling down a bit more, you will now learn another way to control package execution: event handling.

Event Handling

Each task and container raises events as it runs, such as an OnError event, among several others that are discussed shortly. SSIS allows you to trap and handle these events by setting up workflows that will run when particular events fire. This functionality in SSIS is called event handlers.

Event handlers are set up by navigating to the Event Handlers tab in the SSIS package design environment. Figure 17-9 shows the Event Handler tab right next to the Control Flow and Data Flow tabs that you have worked with up to now. The Event Handler design area is just like the Control Flow area — you can use the same component types and do anything that is possible at the Control Flow level. Once several event handlers have been added to a package, the workflow could get very complicated and difficult to understand if you had to view it all at once, so separating event handlers from the Control Flow makes sense.

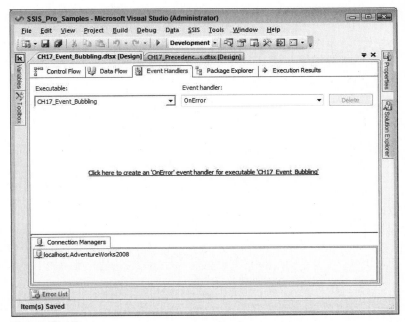

Figure 17-12

It is important, however, to make sure your packages are well designed and documented because an event handler that was set up and then forgotten could be the source of a hard-to-troubleshoot problem within the package.

As you can see in Figure 17-12, the event handler functionality is driven by two drop-down menus. The first, Executable, is used to set which task or container in the package the event handler is associated with. The highest level executable is the package itself, followed by the tasks and containers contained in the Control Flow.

The second drop-down, called Event Handler, defines what event the event handler will listen for in the defined executable. Events are described next.

Events

As the package and each task or container executes, a dozen different events are raised. You can capture the events by adding event handlers that will run when the event fires. The OnError event may be the event most frequently handled, but some of the other events will be useful in complex ETL packages. Events can also be used to set breakpoints and control logging, which are all covered later in the chapter.

The following table shows a list of all of the events:

Event	Description
OnError	This event is raised whenever an error occurs. You can use this event to capture errors instead of using the failure precedence constraint to redirect the workflow.
OnExecStatusChanged	Each time the execution status changes on a task or container, this event fires.
OnInformation	During the validation and execution events of the tasks and containers, this event reports information. This is the information displayed in the Progress tab.
OnPostExecute	Just after task or container execution completes, this event fires. You could use this event to clean up work tables or delete no-longer-needed files.
OnPostValidate	This event fires after validation of the task is complete.
OnPreExecute	Just before a task or container runs, this event fires. This event could be used to check the value of a variable before the task executes.
OnPreValidate	Before validation of a task begins, this event fires.
OnProgress	As measurable progress is made, this event fires. The information about the progress of an event can be viewed in the Progress tab.
OnQueryCancel	This event is raised when an executable checks to see if it should stop or continue running.

Event	Description
OnTaskFailed	It's possible for a task or container to fail without actual errors. You can trap that condition with this event.
OnVariableValueChanged	Any time a variable value changes, this event fires. Setting the RaiseChangeEvent property to False prevents this event from firing. This event will be very useful when debugging a package.
OnWarning	Warnings are less critical than errors. This event fires when a warning occurs. Warnings are displayed in the Progress tab.

Inventory Example

This example demonstrates how to use event handlers by setting up a simulation that checks the inventory status of some random products from AdventureWorks. For this example, you begin by setting up a new SSIS package that performs several steps, next you define an OnError event handler event to fire when an error occurs, and finally, you use the OnPreExecute event to capture execution details of the package.

1. Run this script in SQL Server Management Studio against the AdventureWorks2008 database to create the tables and a stored procedure used in the example:

```
USE AdventureWorks2008
GO
CREATE TABLE InventoryCheck (
    ProductID INT )
GO
CREATE TABLE InventoryWarning (
    ProductID INT, ReorderQuantity INT )
GO
CREATE TABLE MissingProductID (
    ProductID INT )
GO
CREATE PROC usp_GetReorderQuantity @ProductID INT,
    @ReorderQuantity INT OUTPUT AS
    IF NOT EXISTS(SELECT ProductID FROM Production.ProductInventory
            WHERE ProductID = @ProductID) BEGIN
        RAISERROR('InvalidID',16,1)
        RETURN 1
    END

    SELECT @ReorderQuantity = SafetyStockLevel - SUM(Quantity)
    FROM Production.Product AS p
    INNER JOIN Production.ProductInventory AS i
    ON p.ProductID = i.ProductID
    WHERE p.ProductID = @ProductID
    GROUP BY p.ProductID, SafetyStockLevel
    RETURN 0
GO
```

2. Create a new SSIS package.

3. Add a Connection Manager pointing to the AdventureWorks2008 database using the ADO.NET provider. This example uses the Execute SQL Task with parameters. The parameters work differently depending on which provider is being used. For example, parameters used with the OLE DB provider are numerically named starting with zero. Parameters used with ADO.NET providers use names beginning with the @ symbol.

4. Set up the variables in the following table. (Click the Control Flow area right before opening the Variables window so that the scope of the variables will be at the Package level.)

Name	Scope	Data Type	Value
Count	Package	Int32	0
ProductID	Package	Int32	0
ReorderQuantity	Package	Int32	0

5. Drag a Sequence Container to the Control Flow design area and name it Inventory Check. You can use a Sequence Container to group tasks, treating the tasks as a unit in the workflow of the package. In this case, you will use it to experiment with the event handlers. Set the MaximumErrorCount property of Inventory Check to 9999 in the Property window. This example will raise errors by design, and setting the MaximumErrorCount property will allow the simulation to continue running after the errors fire.

6. Drag an Execute SQL Task into the Inventory Check Container, and name it Empty Tables. Double-click the task to open the Execute SQL Task Editor. First change the ConnectionType property to ADO.NET. Set the Connection property to the Connection Manager pointing to AdventureWorks2008. Click the ellipsis button next to the SQLStatement property and type the following into the Enter SQL Query window:

```
DELETE FROM MissingProductID
DELETE FROM InventoryWarning
DELETE FROM InventoryCheck
```

7. Click OK to accept the statements and OK once more to accept the Execute SQL Task Editor changes.

8. Drag a For Loop Container into the Inventory Check Container, and name it Inventory Query Simulator. Double-click the Inventory Query Simulator and fill in the properties as shown in the following table:

Property	Value
InitExpression	@Count =1
EvalExpression	@Count <= 50
AssignExpression	@Count = @Count + 1

9. Click OK to accept the configuration.

10. Set the `MaximumErrorCount` property of the Inventory Query Simulator to 9999 in the Properties window.

11. Drag a precedence constraint from the Empty Tables Task to the Inventory Query Simulator.

12. Drag a Script Task into the Inventory Query Simulator Container, and name it Generate ProductID.

13. Double-click to open the Script Task Editor. Select the Script pane. Set the `ReadWriteVariables` property to `User::ProductID`, as shown in Figure 17-13.

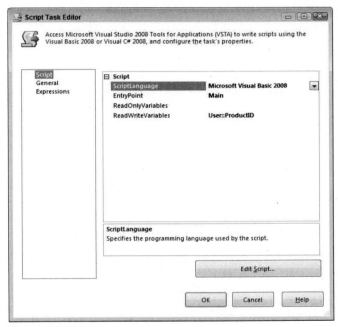

Figure 17-13

14. Check the ScriptLanguage property. If this property is set to Microsoft Visual C# 2008, change the drop-down to Microsoft Visual Basic 2008.

15. Next, click Edit Script to open the Visual Studio design environment. You will use this Script Task to generate a random ProductID. Replace `Sub Main` with the following code:

```
Public Sub Main()
    Randomize()
    Dts.Variables("User::ProductID").Value = CInt(Int((900 * Rnd()) + 1))
    Dts.TaskResult = ScriptResults.Success
End Sub
```

16. Close the Visual Studio script design environment and then click OK to accept the changes to the Script Task.

17. Add an Execute SQL Task to the Inventory Query Simulator and name it Check Inventory Level.

18. Drag a Precedence Constraint from Generate ProductID to Check Inventory Level.

19. Double-click the Check Inventory Level Task to open the Execute SQL Task Editor.

20. Set the ConnectionType property to ADO.NET.

21. Find the Connection Manager for the AdventureWorks2008 database in the list of connections and change the SQLStatement property to usp_GetReorderQuantity. Next change the IsQueryStoredProcedure to True. This task will call the usp_GetReorderQuantity with the two parameters. The ResultSet property should be set to None since you are using an output parameter to get the ReorderQuantity value from the stored procedure. The General pane of the Execute SQL Task Editor should resemble Figure 17-14.

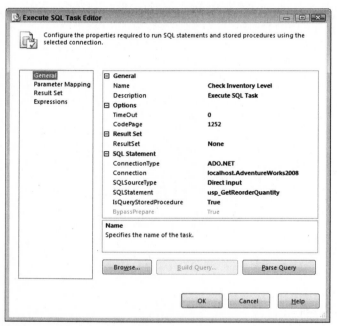

Figure 17-14

22. On the Parameter Mapping pane, set up the parameters as in the following table:

Variable Name	Direction	Data Type	Parameter Name
User::ProductID	Input	LONG	@ProductID
User::ReorderQuantity	Output	LONG	@ReorderQuantity

23. Click OK to accept the configuration. As described earlier, set the `MaximumErrorCount` property of the Check Inventory Level Task to 9999 using the Properties window.

24. Add another Execute SQL Task and name it Insert Warning. This task will be used to insert a row into the InventoryWarning table whenever the current inventory is less than the established reorder point for a particular product. Connect Check Inventory Level to Insert Warning.

25. Double-click the Precedence Constraint and set the Evaluation operation property to Expression and Constraint.

26. Set the Expression property to `@ReorderQuantity > 0` and leave the Value property at Success (see Figure 17-15).

27. Click OK to accept the changes to the precedence constraint.

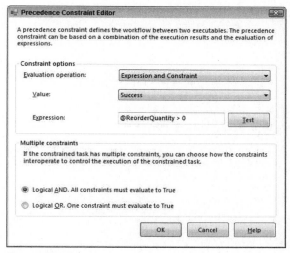

Figure 17-15

28. Double-click the Insert Warning Task and set the ConnectionType to ADO.NET.

29. Choose the AdventureWorks2008 Connection Manager from the Connection list, and click the ellipsis next to SQLStatement, and type this into the Enter SQL Query dialog box:

```
INSERT INTO InventoryWarning (ProductID, ReorderQuantity)
SELECT @ProductID, @ReorderQuantity
```

30. Click OK to accept the command. On the Parameter Mapping pane, set up two parameters, as shown in the following table. In this case they will both be input parameters.

Variable Name	Direction	Data Type	Parameter Name
User::ProductID	Input	LONG	@ProductID
User::ReorderQuantity	Input	LONG	@ReorderQuantity

31. Click OK to accept the configuration. The package should now resemble Figure 17-16.

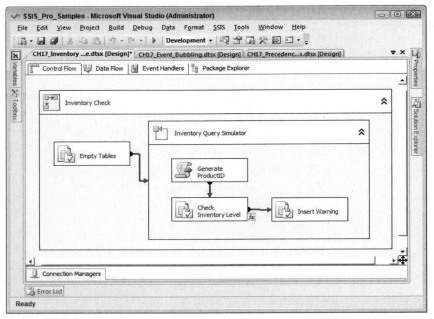

Figure 17-16

When you run the package, sometimes the Check Inventory Level Task will fail. The Generate ProductID script will not always come up with a valid ProductID. When that happens, the stored procedure will raise an error and cause the Check Inventory Level Task to fail. Because the `FailParentOnFailure` and `FailPackageOnFailure` properties are set to `False` by default, and the `MaximumErrorCount` property is set to 9999 on the task and parent containers, the package will continue to run through the simulation even after a failure of this task.

You will notice that once the Check Inventory Level Task fails, it will turn red, but the simulation will continue running and the loop will cause the color to change between red and green. A great way to view what is going on as the package runs is to click the Progress tab. This is also a fantastic troubleshooting tool, with detailed information about each step. Once the package completes and debugging is stopped, you can continue to view the information on the Execution Results tab.

After running the package, you can view the results by querying the InventoryWarning table to see the rows that were inserted when the `User::ReorderQuantity` variable was greater than 0. Run this query in SQL Server Management Studio:

```
SELECT * FROM InventoryWarning
```

Using the OnError Event Handler Event

The package you just created is almost guaranteed to generate some errors at the Check Inventory Level Task every time it runs. You could add a task connected to the Check Inventory Level with the Precedence Constraint set to Failure, but in this case you will create an event handler to add a row to the MissingProductID table each time the Check Inventory Level Task fails.

1. Click the Event Handlers tab. Because you can have a large number of event handlers in a package, you must select the object and the event from the drop-down lists.

2. Click the Executable drop-down to see the package objects in a hierarchy. The Package has a child, Inventory Check, which has children Empty Tables, Inventory Query Simulator, and so on (see Figure 17-17).

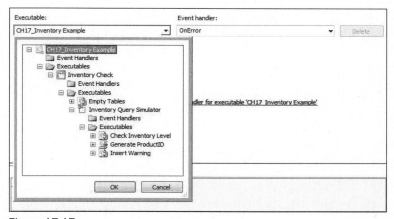

Figure 17-17

3. Select Check Inventory Level and click OK to close the list.

4. Choose OnError in the Event Handler list if it isn't there by default. You must click the link "Click here to create an 'OnExecute' event handler for executable 'Check Inventory Level'" to create the new event handler. The screen will change to a design area very much like the Control Flow tab. You can now drag any Control Flow Level Task or Container to the design area. In this case you will add an Execute SQL Task that adds a row to the MissingProductID table whenever the Check Inventory Level Task fails.

5. Event handlers can be as simple or as complex as you need them to be. All functionality available at the Control Flow level is available at the Event Handler level, including the ability to add an event handler to an event handler.

6. Drag an Execute SQL Task to the Event Handler design area and name it Insert Missing ProductID.

7. Double-click the task to bring up the Execute SQL Task Editor.

8. Change the Connection Type to ADO.NET.

9. Choose the AdventureWorks2008 Connection Manager from the Connection list. Click the ellipsis next to the SQLStatement property to open the Enter SQL Query dialog box. Type the following statement:

```
INSERT INTO MissingProductID (ProductID) SELECT @ProductID
```

10. Click OK to accept the query and then switch to the Parameter Mapping pane. Add one parameter with the properties shown in the following table:

Variable Name	Direction	Data Type	Parameter Name
User::ProductID	Input	LONG	@ProductID

11. Click OK to accept the configuration.

Now, when you run the package, the new event handler will fire whenever the Check Inventory Level Task raises an error. You can query the MissingProductID table to see the results by running this query in SQL Server Management Studio:

```
SELECT * from MissingProductID
```

Using the OnPreExecute Event Handler Event

Suppose you would like to keep a record of all the ProductID numbers that were tested. To do this, complete the following steps:

1. Add another event handler to the Check Inventory Level Task. With Check Inventory Level selected in the Executable list, select OnPreExecute under Event Handler.

2. Click the link to create the handler.

3. Add an Execute SQL Task to the Event Handler design area and name it Record ProductID.

4. Double-click to open the Execute SQL Task Editor.

5. Change the ConnectionType property to ADO.NET.

6. Select the AdventureWorks2008 Connection Manager from the Connection list.

7. Add this statement to the SQLStatement property by typing in the Property text box or using the Enter SQL Query dialog box:

```
INSERT INTO InventoryCheck (ProductID) SELECT @ProductID
```

8. Add one parameter, `@ProductID`, on the Parameter Mapping pane with exactly the same properties as the one added to the `OnError` event task, as the following table shows.

Variable Name	Direction	Data Type	Parameter Name
User::ProductID	Input	LONG	@ProductID

9. Click OK to accept the configuration and run the package.

Once execution of the package has completed, go back to SQL Server Management Studio to see the results by running the following queries:

```
SELECT * FROM InventoryCheck
SELECT * FROM MissingProductID
SELECT * FROM InventoryWarning
```

The InventoryCheck table should have one row for each ProductID that was generated. This row was entered at the Check Inventory Level `OnPreExecute` event, in other words, before the task actually executed. The MissingProductID table should have several rows, one for each ProductID that caused the `usp_GetReorderQuantity` to raise an error. These rows were added at the Check Inventory Level `OnError` event. Finally, the InventoryWarning table will have some rows if the inventory level of any of the products was low. These rows were added at the Control Flow level.

Event Handler Inheritance

Events handlers defined at executables will inherit the events of their children. This means that if you have a container and the container had an event handler `OnError` event defined on it, then if a child task that exists in the container errors, the event handler of the container will fire. This is sometimes referred to as the event "bubbling" or traveling up from child task to parent container. As mentioned already, the highest level executable is the package itself. Therefore if you define an event handler event at the package level, then whenever that event occurs in the package, the event handler will fire.
To demonstrate this with the example inventory package, you'll move the `OnError` event handler from the task to a parent container.

1. Using the package created in the previous section, navigate to the Check Inventory Level `OnError` event handler.

2. Select the Insert Missing Product ID Task, then right-click and select Copy from the pop-up window.

3. Create an `OnError` event handler for the Inventory Check Container.

4. Right-click the design area of the new event handler and select Paste.

5. Go back to the Check Inventory Level `OnError` event and click the Delete button to completely remove the original event handler.

Run your package again. You will see that the errors are now trapped at the Inventory Check Container level by viewing the error handler as the package runs. The `OnError` event bubbled up from the task to the For Loop Container to the Inventory Check Container.

What would happen if you had an `OnError` event handler on both the Check Inventory Level Task and the Sequence Container? Surprisingly, both will fire when an error is raised at the Check Inventory Level Task. This could cause some unexpected results. For example, suppose you had an error handler at the parent container to perform a particular task, such as sending an email message. An error in a child container that you expected to be handled at that level would also cause the parent's `OnError` handler to execute. To prevent this from happening, you can set a system variable, `Propagate`, to False at the child task's Error Handler level. To demonstrate this, add the `OnError` event handler back to the Check Inventory Level Task.

1. Once again, create an event handler for the Check Inventory Level `OnError` event. You can copy and paste the Insert Missing Product ID Task from the Inventory Check `OnError` event handler.

2. While still working in the Check Inventory Level `OnError` Event design area, click the design area and open the Variables window. If the system variables are not visible, click the gray X box to display them (see Figure 17-18). Make sure that the `Propagate` property is set to True, the default.

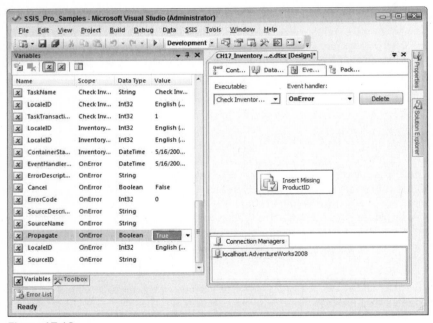

Figure 17-18

3. Run the package. While the package is running, navigate to each of the error handlers to watch as they execute. You will notice that both `OnError` events will fire and the MissingProductID table will end up with two rows for every invalid ProductID.

4. After execution of the package is complete, change the Propagate property to False by using the Variables window. Now only the Check Inventory Level `OnError` event handler will execute. The `OnError` event will no longer bubble to the parent containers.

5. Run the package again. This time, you should find the expected behavior; the error will be handled only at the Check Inventory Level Task.

When the Propagate *property is set to* False *on an* OnEvent *handler, you no longer need to modify the* MaximumErrorCount *property of the parent containers from the default setting of 1 to keep the package running after the error.*

Breakpoints

Many programmers use breakpoints to debug programs, viewing the value of variables and following the flow of the logic as they step through the source code. SSIS allows you to set breakpoints on the package or any Control Flow Level Task or Container. You can also set breakpoints in Script Task code just like most programming environments.

Using the Inventory Example package created in a previous section, follow these steps to enable and use breakpoints:

1. Right-click the Inventory Query Simulator (For Loop) Container, and choose Edit Breakpoints from the pop-up menu. The Set Breakpoints dialog box opens. A list of possible events where a breakpoint can be set is displayed, as shown in Figure 17-19.

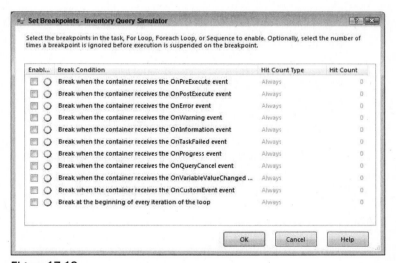

Figure 17-19

2. Enable the last item, "Break at the beginning of every iteration of the loop," which is available only for looping containers. Under Hit Count Type, you can choose Always, Hit Count Equals, Hit Count Greater Than or Equal To, or Hit Count Multiple. The last item will suspend execution when the hit count is equal to a multiple of the value set for Hit Count. For example, setting the Hit Count Type to Hit Count Multiple and the Hit Count to 5 will cause the execution to be suspended every fifth time through the loop.

3. Go ahead and set the type to Hit Count Multiple and the Hit Count to 5 as in Figure 17-20.

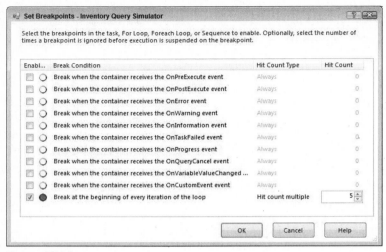

Figure 17-20

4. Click OK. The container will now have a red circle in its top-right corner specifying that a breakpoint has been set (see Figure 17-21).

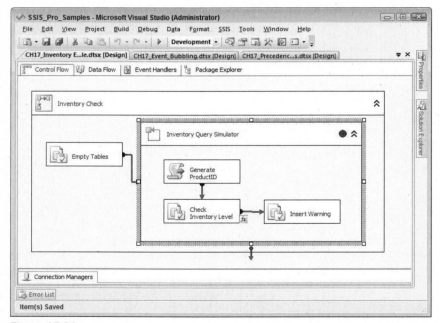

Figure 17-21

5. Run the package.

When the Hit Count reaches 5, the execution will stop and the red dot will change to a red circle with an arrow. You can now view the values of the variables in the Locals window. If the Locals window is not visible, open it from Debug ⇨ Windows ⇨ Locals. Expand Variables, and look for the User variables that were set up for the package (see Figure 17-22). User::Count should have a value of 5. If the value of a variable cannot be completely viewed in the window, such as a long string, you can mouse over to see the entire value in a tooltip.

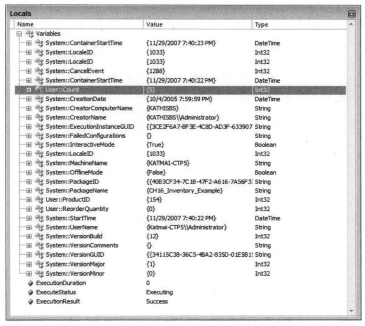

Figure 17-22

Restart the package and it will run until the Hit Count reaches 10.

There are also watch windows to make it easier to view the variables you are interested in viewing. Open the Locals watch window from Debug ⇨ Windows ⇨ Watch ⇨ WatchLocals. In the first row of the Watch 1 window, type User::Count in the Name field (see Figure 17-23). You can view the values of all system and user variables from the Locals window. You can also add variables to the watch windows by right-clicking the variables you want to in the Locals window (Figure 17-22) and choosing Add Watch.

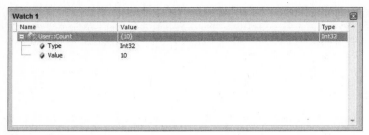

Figure 17-23

Another very cool feature is the ability to change the value of variables on the fly. In the watch window, expand User::Count. Right-click and choose Edit Value. Change the value to 40 and restart the package. The next time the execution is suspended, the value should be at 45. The value of some system variables may also be interesting to view and change. For example, you might modify the value of a task property as the package executes. You can use breakpoints and the watch windows to view the value to make sure it is what you expected or change the value manually to correct it.

An additional debugging window may also help troubleshoot packages, known as the Call Stack window. This window shows a list of the tasks that have executed up to the breakpoint. This could be very useful when trying to figure out a very complex workflow.

The ability to set breakpoints on the tasks and containers will save you lots of time while troubleshooting your packages. Data Viewers are similar to breakpoints, but they are used to view data as the package executes. See Chapter 5 for more information on how you can use Data Viewers in your packages.

Error Rows

Error rows have been briefly touched upon in several chapters including Chapter 5, "The Data Flow," Chapter 12, "Accessing Heterogeneous Data," and Chapter 14, "Understanding and Tuning the Data Flow Engine." However, a chapter on SSIS error and event handling would only be partially complete without a further discussion on handling errors.

Error rows are dealt with in the Data Flow through the use of the Error Row Configuration properties. These properties tell the Data Flow Components what to do when a row fails an operation, such as a data conversion or a missing lookup or a truncation. The properties are found in sources, transformations, and destinations, depending on whether an error can occur.

The basic error properties window allows errors to be handled in one of three ways: failure of the Data Flow Task, ignoring the failure, or redirecting the row. Furthermore, truncation errors can be handled separately than conversion errors. Figure 17-24 shows the Error Output property page of an OLE DB Source adapter.

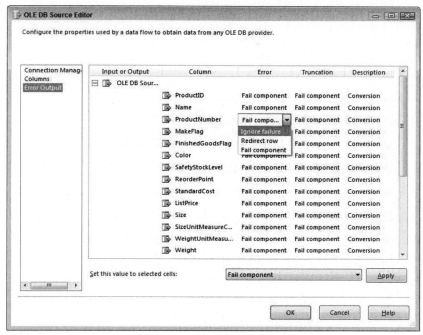

Figure 17-24

Figure 17-24 also shows the drop-down selection of the ProductNumber column that defines how the SSIS Data Flow engine should handle an error row for the selected column. The following table clarifies the implications of the error handling section:

Error Handler	Description
Fail Component	When Fail Component is chosen for a column or the component and an error occurs (such as a conversion from a source to the Data Flow Pipeline), the Data Flow will stop and fail, and any OnError events will fire for the Data Flow Task.
Redirect Row	If a row reaches an error for any column marked to be redirected, the entire row is sent out the red error path output and the Data Flow will not fail. If the red error path output is not used, then the row will get tossed out of the Data Flow.
Ignore Failure	Ignore Failure simply means that the error will be ignored. If the error is in a source or transformation such as a conversion or a missing lookup record, then the error column values will be set to NULL. If the error is a truncation, then the value will be sent downstream just with the partially truncated value. Beware that when you are dealing with destinations, an ignore failure for a truncation or other error will ignore the entire row, not just the error column.

When Redirect Row is selected for any column (error or truncation), be aware that when the Redirect Row condition is met, the entire row will be redirected out the red error path output.

As an example of how to use the error row handling, create a new package in BIDS with an OLE DB connection to the AdventureWorks2008 database.

1. Create a Data Flow Task in the package and navigate to the Data Flow designer.

2. Drag an OLE DB Source adapter to the Data Flow and configure it to use the AdventureWorks2008 connection as the Connection Manager. In the "Name of the table or the view" drop-down, choose the [Production].[Product] table from the list.

3. Drag a Data Conversion Transformation onto the Data Flow region, and then connect the OLE DB Source adapter to the Data Conversion.

4. Edit the Data Conversion Component and add a new row based on the input column Size. Name the output alias Size_Numeric and configure the new data type to be numeric [DT_Numeric] as Figure 17-25 shows.

Figure 17-25

The Data Conversion Transformation will create a new column in the Data Flow called Size_Numeric with a numeric data type, but the original Size column will still remain with the WSTR length 5 data type.

5. Within the Data Conversion Transformation, click the Configure Error Output button in the bottom-left corner of the transformation, which will bring up the Configure Error Output window. Because there is only one column defined in the Data Conversion Transformation, you will only see one column to change the error settings for.

6. Change the Error value to Redirect Row for the Size_Numeric column as Figure 17-26 demonstrates.

Figure 17-26

7. Return to the Data Flow by selecting OK in both the Configure Error Output and the Data Conversion Transformation Editor. You will see that the Data Conversion Transformation now has a yellow exclamation mark on it, indicating that an error row was configured to be redirected, but the red error path has not yet been used.

8. Drag a Derived Column Transformation to the Data Flow and then connect the red error path from the Data Conversion onto the new Derived Column Transformation. When you do this, the Configure Error Output window will automatically pop up for the Data Conversion Transformation. This is an alternate method to set the error handling for a failure. Click OK to return to the Data Flow.

9. Edit the Derived Column Transformation and add a new column named Size_Numeric. For the Expression type, type in the following code to add a 0 value to the records that failed the conversion in the prior transformation: (DT_NUMERIC,18,0) 0

10. After saving the Derived Column Transformation, drag a Union All Transformation to the Data Flow and then connect both the green data path output from the Data Conversion Transformation and the green data path output from the Derived Column Transformation to the Union All Transformation. Double-click the Union All Transformation to bring up its editor and scroll down to the bottom of the column list. Multi select both the ErrorCode and ErrorColumn columns, and then hit the Delete key on your keyboard. Click OK to save the changes.

11. Before running your package to test it, add a Multicast Transformation to the Data Flow connected to the output of the Union All. A Multicast is usable as a placeholder transformation

as you are developing and testing your package. Run your package, and observe the results. Your Data Flow execution will look similar to Figure 17-27.

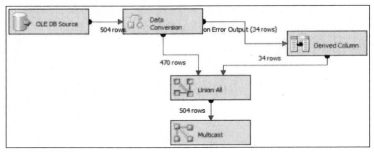

Figure 17-27

Note that some of the rows are sent to the Derived Column Transformation, but are brought back together with the main Data Flow rows through the Union All Transformation. At this point you have not added a destination, so the next step in this example will be to land the data to a new destination table, where you can also handle errors.

12. Stop the package execution and replace the Multicast with an OLE DB Destination adapter.

13. Edit the OLE DB Destination and confirm that the AdventureWorks2008 connection is listed in the OLE DB Connection Manager drop-down and change the data access mode to "Table or view."

14. To create a new destination table, click the New button next to the "Name of the table or the view" drop-down box. Change the name of the table to [Updated_Products] and also change the data type of the [Name] column to nvarchar(21) Select OK in the Create Table window, which will run the CREATE TABLE statement in the AdventureWorks2008 database.

15. While still in the OLE DB Destination Editor, click the Mappings property page, which will by default map all the input columns form the Data Flow to the destination table columns based on name and data type. Click OK to save the changes.

In the Data Flow designer, you will notice that the Destination adapter has a yellow exclamation point on it, and when hovering over it (or displaying the error window) it indicated that there may be a truncation error for the Name column going from a length of 50 to a length of 21. To finish this example, you will now redirect the error rows to a flat file.

16. Drag a Flat File Destination adapter onto the Data Flow and connect the red error path output from the OLE DB Destination onto the Flat File Destination. When the Configure Error Output window pops up, change the Error handling drop-down to Redirect Row and click OK to save your changes.

17. Edit the Flat File Destination adapter and click the New button next to the Flat File Connection Manager drop-down. When prompted, leave the Flat File Format selected on Delimited and click OK, which will bring up the Flat File Connection Manager Editor.

18. Type **C:\Truncated_Names.txt** in the File name text box and then click OK to save the connection properties. You will be returned to the Flat File Destination Editor; to finish, click the Mappings page in the Flat File Destination Editor, which will automatically map the columns from the error path to the flat file. Click OK to close the Destination Editor.

When you run your package, your results should look like what is shown in Figure 17-28.

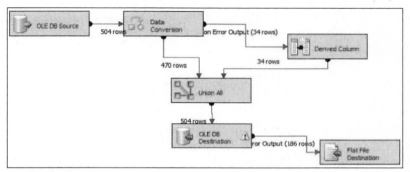

Figure 17-28

The rows with the Name column truncation were sent to the flat file. You can check your results by opening the flat file on your C:\ drive, which will show that the full names were added to the flat file. As noted earlier, if you had set the OLE DB Destination error to Ignore Failure, error rows would be ignored, not just the column value.

Logging

Logging is an important part of any data process, because logging gives administrators and developers insight into what transpired during a process, with the following benefits:

❑ Error triage to help identify as quickly as possible what was the point and cause of the failure, such as the failure of a Lookup Transformation to match a record.

❑ Root cause analysis so that a solution can be put in place to prevent a failure situation in the future.

❑ Performance metrics such as package and execution times so that negative performance trends can be observed and addressed before the performance impact causes an ETL failure.

SSIS contains built-in logging features that capture execution details about your packages. Logging enables you to record information about events you are interested in as the package runs. The logging information can be stored in a text or XML file, to a SQL Server table, to the Windows Event Log, or to a file suitable for Profiler.

Logging can be enabled for all or some tasks and containers and for all or any events. Tasks and containers can inherit the settings from parent containers. Multiple logs can be set up, and a task or event can log to any or all logs configured. You also have the ability to control which pieces of information are recorded for any event.

Logging Providers

SSIS includes several default log providers. These providers are selected in the Provider type combo box and are defined as follows:

❑ **SSIS Log Provider for Text Files:** This provider is used to store log information to a CSV file on the file system. This provider requires you to configure a File Connection object that defines the location of the file. Storing log information in a text file is the easiest way to persist a package's execution. Text files are portable, and the CSV format is a simple-to-use industry-wide standard.

❑ **SSIS Log Provider for SQL Profiler:** This provider produces a SQL Profiler trace file. The file must be specified with a `trc` file extension so that you can open it using the SQL Profiler diagnostic tool. Using SQL profiler trace files is an easy way for DBAs to view log information. Using Profiler, you could view the execution of the package step-by-step, even replaying the steps in a test environment.

❑ **SSIS Log Provider for SQL Server:** This provider sends package log events to a table in the specified SQL Server database. The database is defined using an OLE DB Connection. The first time this package is executed, a table called sysdtslog100 will be created automatically. Storing log information in a SQL Server database inherits the benefits of persisting information in a relational database system. You could easily retrieve log information for analysis across multiple package executions.

❑ **SSIS Log Provider for Windows Event Log:** This provider sends log information to the Application event store. The entries created will be under the Source name SQLISPackage. No additional configuration is required for this provider. Logging package execution to the Windows Event Log is possibly the easiest way to store log events. The Windows Event Log is easy to view and can be viewed remotely if required.

❑ **SSIS Log Provider for XML Files:** This provider stores log information in a specified XML file on the file system. The file is specified through a File Connection object. Make sure you save the file with an `xml` file extension. Logging events to XML inherits the advantages of the XML specification. XML files are very portable across systems and can be validated against a Schema definition.

Log Events

Once you have configured the log providers you wish to employ, you must define what events in the package to log. This is done in the Details tab of the Log Configuration dialog box, as shown in Figure 17-29. To enable an event to be logged, check the box next to its name. For instance, in Figure 17-29, the `OnError` event for the package has been selected to be logged. By selecting other containers on the left-hand side of the dialog box, additional events can be selected down to an individual task or Data

Flow event level. To select all events at once, check the box in the header row of the table. By selecting individual containers in the tree view on the left, you can configure the logging of events on an individual task level. By configuring logging at the task level, the special events exposed by a task can additionally be included in the log.

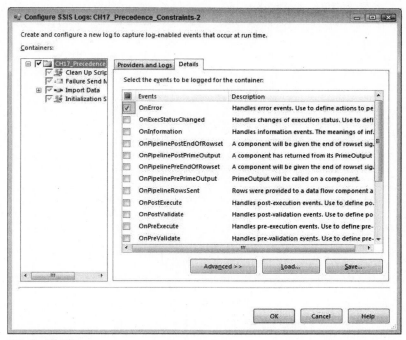

Figure 17-29

To practice working with the SSIS logging, follow these steps:

1. Open one of the packages you created earlier in this chapter or any package with several Control Flow Tasks.

2. From the menu, navigate to SSIS ➪ Logging to open the Configure SSIS Logs dialog box. To enable logging, you must first check the box next to the package name in the left pane (see Figure 17-30), in the example in Figure 17-30, the package is titled "CH17_Precedence_Constraints."

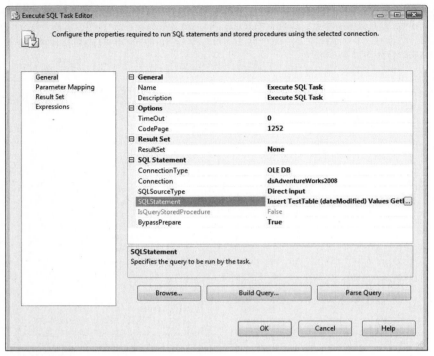

Figure 17-30

Notice that the checkboxes for the child objects in the package are grayed out. This means that they will inherit the logging properties of the package. You can click into any checkbox to un-check an object. Clicking again to check the box will allow you to set up logging properties specific for that task or container.

3. To get started, the log providers must be defined at the package level. Select package in the TreeView control on the left (the top level) so that the package is highlighted.

4. In the Provider type dropdown list, choose which type of provider you would like to configure; as an example, choose SSIS Log Provider for XML File.

5. Click Add to add the provider to the list. Click the drop-down under Configuration and choose <New Connection>. Once the File Connection Manager Editor opens, set the Usage Type property to Create File. Type **c:\SSIS_Log.xml** as the path for the XML file or click Browse to the XML file location as in Figure 17-31.

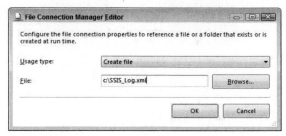

Figure 17-31

6. Click OK to accept the configuration and dismiss the dialog box. In the Configure SSIS Logs dialog box, you should now see the new log provider and its properties.

7. Check the box next to the new logging provider to enable it at the package level. At this point, you can give the log provider a descriptive name if you wish as in Figure 17-32.

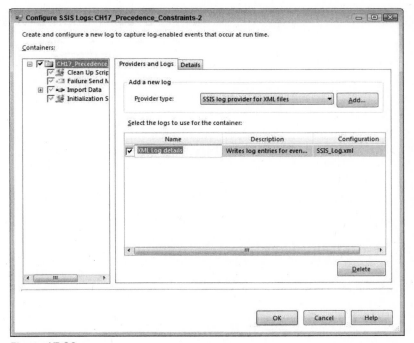

Figure 17-32

8. Click the Details tab to view a list of events that you can log. By clicking Advanced, you will also see a list of possible fields (see Figure 17-33).

9. Choose the `OnPreExecute`, `OnPostExecute`, and `OnError` events. Notice that all of the fields are automatically chosen. You can uncheck some of the fields if you don't think the information will be useful.

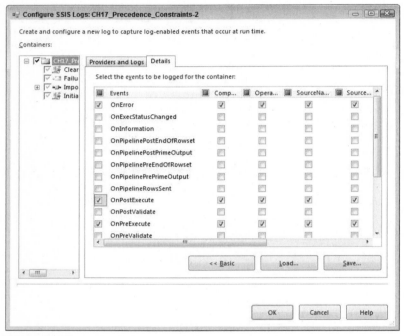

Figure 17-33

10. Move back to the Providers and Logs tab. When you checked the log provider at the package level (by checking the checkbox at the highest level in the tree view of the left pane), you enabled that log for all components in the package that are set to inherit settings from their parent container. Even if that log provider is chosen for an object that does not inherit the log settings, you can use it to select different events and fields. Once you modify the logging on a parent container, such as a For Loop Container, the child objects will now inherit from the container, not the package.

11. When you are satisfied with the logging settings, click OK to close the dialog box. If you view the Properties window of a task or container, you will find the LoggingMode property. This property can be set to UseParentSetting, Enabled, or Disabled and will match the settings you just configured.

Run the package. Once the package execution has completed, open the log file to view the XML (see Figure 17-34).

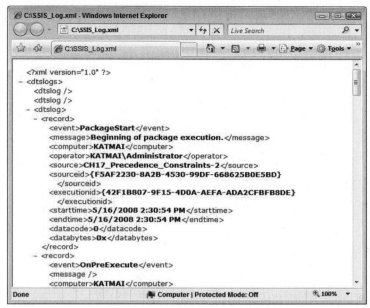

Figure 17-34

Setting up logging for a package can be as complicated or as simple as you would like. It's possible that you may want to log similar information, such as the OnError event, for all packages. You can save the settings as a template by clicking Save when on the Detail tab of the Configure SSIS Logs dialog box. Alternatively, you can load a previously saved template by clicking the Load button.

Summary

In conclusion, SSIS gives you the ability to handle errors during execution and while troubleshooting:

❑ During execution, you can handle errors gracefully by using the precedence constraints to control what tasks execute when errors occur; by using the event handlers to trap for specific events in the package at different levels and run code to perform cleanup and alerting; and by configuring the Data Flow error paths to handle data exceptions gracefully without failing the package.

❑ While troubleshooting and developing, you can use the breakpoint functionality to pause execution and monitor variable values and package state information, and you can turn on SSIS package logging to capture execution information that can give insight into the execution details such as errors, warnings, and execution times.

Now that the core features of SSIS have been covered, the final chapters focus on advanced topics, including building custom components, integrating SSIS with applications, and managing SSIS externally.

18

Programming and Extending SSIS

Once you start implementing a real-world integration solution, you may have requirements that the built-in functionality in SSIS does not meet. For instance, you may have a legacy system that has a proprietary export file format, and you need to import that data into your warehouse. You have a robust SSIS infrastructure that you have put in place that allows you to efficiently develop and manage complex ETL solutions, but how do you meld that base infrastructure with the need for customization? That's where custom component development comes into play. Out-of-the-box, Microsoft provides a huge list of components for you in SSIS; however, you can augment those base components with your own more specialized tasks.

The benefit here is not only to businesses, but to software vendors too. You may decide to build components and sell them on the web, or maybe start a community-driven effort on a site such as www.codeplex.com. Either way, the benefit you get is that your components will be built in exactly the same way that the ones that ship with SSIS are built; there is no secret sauce (besides expertise) that Microsoft adds to their components to make them behave any differently from your own. The opportunity is that you truly can "build a better mouse trap" — if you don't like the way that one of the built-in components behaves, then you can simply build your own one instead.

Building your first component may be a little challenging, but hopefully with the help of this chapter you will be able to overcome this. In this chapter you focus on the pipeline — not because it is better than any other area of programmability within SSIS, but because it will probably be the area where you have the most benefit to gain; and it does require a slightly greater level of understanding. It also allows you to see some of the really interesting things that Microsoft has done in SSIS. All forms of extensibility are well covered in the SQL Server documentation and samples, so don't forget to leverage those resources as well.

The Sample Components

Three sample components will be defined in this section to demonstrate the main component types. The Transform Component will then be expanded in Chapter 19 to include a user interface. All code samples will be available on the website for this book, which you can find at www.wrox.com.

The *pipeline*, for all intents and purposes, is the way your data moves from A to B and how it is manipulated, if at all. You can find it on the Data Flow tab of your packages after you have dropped a Data Flow Task into the Control Flow. There's no need to go into any more detail about where to find the pipeline in your package, because this has been covered elsewhere in this book.

As discussed in other chapters, Integration Services allow you to use three basic component types in the pipeline. The first component type is a Source, which retrieves data from an external location (for instance a SQL Server query, a text file, or a Web service) and transforms the input into the internal buffer format that the pipeline expects.

The Transformation-Type Component accepts buffers of data from the pipeline on one side, does something useful with the data (for instance sorting it, calculating totals, or multicasting the rows), and then pushes the rows downstream for the next component to consume.

The Destination-Type Component also accepts buffers of data from the pipeline on its input, but instead of writing the output rows to the pipeline again, it writes them to a specific external source, such as a text file or SQL Server table.

This chapter walks you through building three components; one example for each of the component types just discussed. Note that there are further classifications of components such as synchronous and asynchronous components, but this chapter will help you get the basics right. Following is a high-level description of what each sample component will do.

Component 1: Source Adapter

The Source adapter needs to be able to do quite a few things in order to be able to present the data to the downstream components in the pipeline in a format that the next component understands and is expecting. Here is a list of what the component needs to do:

❑ Accept and validate a Connection Manager. A Connection Manager is an optional component for Source adapters, since it is possible to write a Source adapter that does not require a Connection Manager. However, a Connection Manager helps to isolate the connectivity logic (such as the credentials) from the user-specific functionality (such as the query) defined in the Source adaptor. As such a Connection Manager is highly recommended.

❑ Add output columns to the component for the downstream processes.

❑ Connect to the Data Source.

❑ Get the data from the Data Source.

❑ Assign the correct parts of the data to the correct output columns.

❑ Handle any data errors.

This component is going to need to do quite a bit of work in order to present its data to the outside world. Stick with it and you'll see how easy this can be. Your aim in the Source adapter is to be able to take a file with a custom format, read it, and present its data to the downstream components.

The real-world scenario that we will cover is that there are many systems that export data in a proprietary format, which is hard to then import into another system. Let's imagine that the legacy system exports customer data in the following format:

```
<START>
Name:
Age:
Married:
Salary:
<END>
```

As you can see, this is a nonstandard format that none of the Source adapters out-of-the-box could deal with adequately. Of course, you could use a Script Component to read and parse the file using VB or C#, but then you'd need to duplicate the code in every package that needed to read this type of file. Writing a custom Source Component means that you can re-use the component in many different packages, which may save you time and maintenance compared to the scripting route.

Component 2: Transformation

The transform is where you are going to take data from a source, manipulate it, and then present the newly arranged data to the downstream components. This component performs the following tasks:

❑   Creates input columns to accept the data from upstream.

❑   Validates the data to see that it is how the component expects it.

❑   Checks the column properties because this transform will be changing them in place.

❑   Handles somebody trying to change the metadata of the transform by adding or removing inputs and/or outputs.

The scenario we will use here is that we want to create a simple data obfuscation device that will take data from the source and reverse the contents. The quirk, though, is that the column properties must be set correctly, and you can only perform this operation on certain data types.

Component 3: Destination Adapter

The Destination adapter will take the data received from the upstream component and write it to the destination. This component will need to do the following:

❑   Create an input that accepts the data.

❑   Validate that the data is correct.

❑   Accept a Connection Manager.

❑   Validate the Connection Manager (did you get the right type of Connection Manager?).

❑   Connect to the Data Source.

❑   Write data from the Data Source.

We will use the opposite scenario here to the one presented earlier. In this case we will imagine that the pipeline retrieved data from some standard source (such as SQL Server) but we now want to write the data out to a custom flat file format, perhaps as the input file for a legacy system.

The Destination adapter will basically be a reverse of the Source adapter. When it receives the input rows, it needs to create a new file with data layout resembling that of the source file.

The components you'll build are really quite simple, but the point is not their complexity, but how you use the methods in Microsoft's object model. The methods presented for tackling these tasks can be used as the basis for more complex operations.

The Pipeline Component Methods

Components are normally described as having two distinct phases: design-time and runtime. The design-time phase refers to the methods and interfaces that are called when the component is being used in a development sense. In other words, the code that is being run when the component is dragged onto the SSIS design surface, and when it is being configured. The runtime functionality refers to the calls and interfaces that are being used when the component is actually being executed, in other words when the package is being run.

When you implement a component, you *inherit* from the base class, `Microsoft.SqlServer.Dts` `.Pipeline.PipelineComponent`, and provide your own functionality by *overriding* the base methods, some of which are primarily design-time, others runtime. If you are using native code to write SSIS components, then the divide between the runtime and design-time is clearer because the functionality is implemented on different interfaces. Commentary on the methods has been divided into these two sections, but there are some exceptions, notably the connection-related methods; a section on connection time–related methods is included later on.

In programming terms, a class can inherit functionality from another class, termed the base class. If the base class provides a method, and the inheriting class wishes to change the functionality within this method, it can override the method. In effect, you replace the base method with your own. From within the overriding method, you can still access the base method, and call it explicitly if required, but any consumer of the new class will see only the overriding method.

Design-Time Functionality

The following methods are explicitly implemented for design-time, overriding the `PipelineComponent` methods, although they will usually be called from within your overriding method. Not all of the methods have been listed, because for some there is little more to say, and others have been grouped together according to their area of function, Refer to the SQL Server documentation for a complete list.

There are some methods that are described as verification methods, and these are a particularly interesting group. They provide minor functions, such as adding a column or setting a property value, and you could quite rightly think that there is little point in ever overriding them, because there isn't much value to add to the base implementation. As mentioned, these are your verification methods, and code has been added to verify that the operation about to take place within the base class is allowed. The following sections expand on the types of checks you can do, and if you want to build a robust component, these are well worth looking into.

Another very good reason to implement these methods as described is actually to reduce code. These methods will be used by both a custom user interface (UI) and the built-in component editor, or Advanced Editor. If you raise an error saying that a change is not allowed, then both user interfaces can capture this and provide feedback to the user. Although a custom UI would be expected to prevent blatantly inappropriate actions, the Advanced Editor is designed to offer all functionality, so you are protecting the integrity of your component regardless of the method used.

ProvideComponentProperties

This method is provided so you can set up your component. It is called when a component is first added to the Data Flow, and it initializes the component. It does not perform any column-level activity, because this is left to `ReinitializeMetadata`; when this method is invoked, there are generally no inputs or outputs to be manipulated anyway. The sorts of procedures you may want to set in here are:

❑ Remove existing settings, such as inputs and outputs. This allows the component to be rebuilt and can be useful when things go wrong.

❑ Add inputs and outputs, ready for column work later on in the component lifetime. You may also define custom properties on them and specify related properties, such as linking them together for synchronous behavior.

❑ Define the connection requirements. By adding an item to the RuntimeConnectionCollection, you have a placeholder prepared for the Connection Manager at runtime, as well as informing the designer of this requirement.

❑ The component may have custom properties that are configurable by a user in addition to those you get for free from Microsoft. These will hold settings other than the column-related one that affect the overall component operation or behavior.

Validate

`Validate` is called numerous times during the lifetime of the component, both at design-time and at runtime, but the most interesting work is usually the result of a design-time call. As the name suggests, it validates that the content of the component is correct and will enable you to at least run the package. If the validation encounters a problem, then the return code used is important to determine any further actions, such as calling `ReinitializeMetaData`. The base class version of `Validate` performs its own checks in the component, and you will need to extend it further in order to cover your specific needs. `Validate` *should not* be used to change the component at all; it should *only report* the problems it finds.

ReinitializeMetaData

The `ReinitializeMetaData` method is where all the building work for your component is done. You add new columns, remove invalid columns, and generally build up the columns. It is called when the `Validate` method returns VS_NEEDSNEWMETADATA. It is also your opportunity in the component to do any repairs that need to be done, particularly around invalid columns as mentioned previously.

MapInputColumn and MapOutputColumn

These methods are used to create a relationship between an input/output column and an external metadata column. An external metadata column is an offline representation of an output or input column and can be used by downstream components to create an input. For instance, you may connect your Source Component to a database table and retrieve the list of columns. However, once you disconnect from the database and edit the package in an offline manner, it may be useful for the source to "remember" the external database columns.

This functionality allows you to validate and maintain columns even when the Data Source is not available. It is not required, but it makes the user experience better. If the component declares that it will be using External Metadata (`IDTSComponentMetaData100.ValidateExternalMetadata`) then the user in the advanced UI will see upstream columns to the left and the external columns on the right; if you are validating your component against an output, you will see the checked listbox of columns.

Input and Output Verification Methods

There are several methods you can use to deal with inputs and outputs. The three functions you may need to perform are adding, deleting, and setting a custom property. The method names clearly indicate their functions:

- ❑   `InsertInput`
- ❑   `DeleteInput`
- ❑   `SetInputProperty`
- ❑   `InsertOutput`
- ❑   `DeleteOutput`
- ❑   `SetOutputProperty`

For most components, the inputs and outputs will have been configured during `ProvideComponentProperties`, so unless you expect a user to add additional inputs and outputs and fully support this, you should override these methods and fire an error to prevent this. Similarly, unless you support additions, you would also want to deny deletions by overriding the corresponding methods. Properties can be checked for validity during the `Set` methods as well.

Set Column Data Types

There are two methods used to set column data types: one for output columns and the other for external metadata columns. There is no input column equivalent, because the data types of input columns are determined by the upstream component.

- ❑   `SetOutputColumnDataTypeProperties`
- ❑   `SetExternalMetadataColumnDataTypeProperties`

These are verification methods that can be used to validate or prevent changes to a column. For example, in a Source Component, you would normally define the columns and their data types within `ReinitializeMetaData`. You could then override `SetOutputColumnDataTypeProperties`, and by comparing the method's supplied data types to the existing column, you could prevent data type changes but allow length changes.

There is quite a complex relationship between all of the parameters for these methods; please refer to SQL Server documentation for reference when using this method yourself.

PerformUpgrade

This method should allow you to take a new version of the component and update an existing version of the component on the destination machine in a transparent manner.

RegisterEvents

This method allows you to register custom events in a Pipeline Component. You can therefore have an event fire on something happening at runtime in the package. This is then eligible to be logged in the package log.

RegisterLogEntries

This method decides which of the new custom events are going to be registered and selectable in the package log.

SetComponentProperty

In the `ProvideComponentProperties` method, you told the component about any custom properties that you would like to expose to the user of the component and perhaps allow them to set. This is a verification method, and here you can check what it is that the user has entered for which custom property on the component and ensure that the values are valid.

Set Column Properties

There are three column property methods, each allowing you to set a property for the relevant column type:

- ❑   `SetInputColumnProperty`
- ❑   `SetOutputColumnProperty`
- ❑   `SetExternalMetadataColumnProperty`

These are all verification methods and should be used accordingly. For example, you may set a column property during `ReinitializeMetaData`, and to prevent a user interfering with this, you could examine the property name (or index) and throw an exception if it is a restricted property, in effect making it read-only.

Similarly, if several properties are used in conjunction with each other at runtime to provide direction on the operation to be performed, you could enumerate all column properties to ensure that those related properties exist and have suitable values. You could assign a default value if a value is not present or raise an exception depending on the exact situation.

For an external metadata column, which will be mapped to an input or output column, any property set directly on this external metadata column can be cascaded down onto the corresponding Input or Output column through this overridden function.

SetUsageType

This method deals with the columns on inputs into the component. In a nutshell, you use it to select a column and to tell the component how you will treat each column. What you see coming into this method is the Virtual Input. What this means is that it is a representation of what is available for selection to be used by your component. These are the three possible usage types for a column:

❑ DTSUsageType.UT_IGNORED: The column will not be used by the component. What happens is that you will be removing this InputColumn from the InputColumnCollection. This differs from the other two usage types, which add a reference to the InputColumn to the InputColumnCollection if it does not exist already or you may be changing its Read/Write property.

❑ DTSUsageType.UT_READONLY: The column is read-only. The column is selected, and data can be read and used within the component but cannot be modified.

❑ DTSUsageType.UT_READWRITE: The column is selected, and you can both read and write or change the data within your component.

This is another of the verification methods, and you should use it to ensure that the columns selected are valid. For example, the Reverse String sample shown later in the chapter can operate only on string columns, so you must check that the data type of the input column is DT_STR for string or DT_WSTR for Unicode strings. Similarly, the component performs an in-place change, so the usage type must be read/write. Setting it to read-only would cause problems during execution when you try to write the changed data back to the pipeline buffer. The Data Flow makes important decisions on column handling based on the read/write flag, and if the component writes to a read-only column, it will likely corrupt the data and the user will get incorrect results. Therefore you should validate the columns as they are selected to ensure that they meet the requirements for your component design.

On Path Attachment

There are three closely related path attachment methods, called when the named events occur, and the first two in particular can be used to improve the user experience:

❑ OnInputPathAttached

❑ OnOutputPathAttached

The reason these methods are here is to handle situations where, for instance, the inputs or outputs are all identical and interchangeable. Using the multicast as an example, you attach to the dangling output and another dangling output is automatically created. You detach, and the extra output is deleted.

Runtime

Runtime, also known as execution-time, is when you actually work with the data, through the pipeline buffer, with columns and rows of data. The following methods are all about preparing the component, doing the job it was designed for, and then cleaning up afterward.

PrepareForExecute

This method is rather like the `PreExecute` method described next and can be used for setting up anything in the component that you will need at runtime. The difference is that you do not have access to the Buffer Manager, so you cannot get your hands on the columns in either the output or the input at this stage. The distinction between the two is very fine apart from that, so usually you will end up using `PreExecute` exclusively, because you will need access to the Buffer Manager anyway.

PreExecute

`PreExecute` is called once and once only each time the component is run, and it is the recommendation of Microsoft that you do as much preparation as possible for the execution of your component in this method. In this case, you'll use it to enumerate the columns, reading off values and properties, calling methods to get more information, and generally preparing by gathering all the information you require in advance. For instance, you may want to save references to common properties, column indexes, and state information to a variable so that you access it efficiently once you start pumping rows through the component.

This is the earliest point in the component that you will access the component's Buffer Manager, so you have the live context of columns, as opposed to the design-time representation. The live and design-time representations of columns may not match. The design-time may contain more information that you do not need at runtime. As mentioned, you do the column preparation for your component in this method, because it is called only once per component execution, unlike some of the other runtime methods, which are called multiple times.

PrimeOutput and ProcessInput

These two methods are dealt with together because they are so closely linked that to deal with them any other way would be disjointed. These two methods are essentially how the data flows through components. Sometimes you use only one of them, and sometimes you use both. There are some rules you can follow.

In a Source adapter, the `ProcessInput` method is never called, and all of the work is done through `PrimeOutput`. In a Destination adapter, it is the opposite way around; the `PrimeOutput` method is never called, and the whole of the work is done through the `ProcessInput` method.

Things are not quite that simple with a transform. There are two types of transforms, and the type of transform you are writing will dictate which method or indeed methods your component should call. For a discussion on synchronous versus asynchronous transforms, see Chapter 5.

❑ **Synchronous:** `PrimeOutput` is not called and therefore all the work is done in the `ProcessInput` method. The buffer LineageIDs remain the same. For a detailed explanation of buffers and LineageIDs, please refer to Chapter 14.

❑ **Asynchronous:** Both methods are called here. The key difference between a synchronous and an asynchronous component is that the asynchronous component does not reuse the input buffer. The `PrimeOutput` method hands the `ProcessInput` method a buffer to fill with its data.

PostExecute

This method would be where you clean up anything that you started in PreExecute. Although it can do this, it is not limited to just that. After reading the description of the Cleanup method in just a second, you're going to wonder about the difference between that and this method. The answer is, for this release, nothing. If you want to think about this logically, then PostExecute is the opposite side of the coin to PreExecute.

Cleanup

As the method name suggests, this is called as the very last thing your component will do, and it is your chance to clean up whatever resources may be left. However, it is rarely used. Logically, then Cleanup is the opposite of PrepareForExecute.

DescribeRedirectedErrorCode

If you are using an error output and directing rows down there in case of errors, then you should expose this method to give more information about the error. When you direct a row to the error output, you specify an error code. This method will be called by the pipeline engine, passing in that error code, and it is expected to return a full error description string for the code specified. These two values are then included in the columns of the error output.

Connection Time

These two methods are called several times throughout the life cycle of a component, both at design-time and at runtime, and are used to manage connections within the component.

AcquireConnections

This method is called both at design-time and when the component executes. There is no explicit result, but the connection is normally validated and then cached in a member variable within the component for later use. At this stage, a connection should be open and ready to use.

ReleaseConnections

If you have any open connections, as set in the AcquireConnections method, then this is where they should be closed and released. If the connection was cached in a member variable, use that reference to issue any appropriate Close or Dispose methods. For some connections, such as a File Connection Manager, this may not be relevant as all that was returned was a file path string, but if you took this a stage further and opened a text stream or similar on the file, it should now be closed.

Building the Components

Now you can move on to actually building the components. These components are simple and demonstrate the most commonly used methods when building your own components. They also help give you an idea of what the composition of a component resembles, the order in which things happen, and which method is meant to do what. They will not implement all the available methods. The components have been built and they can be extended, so why not download them and give them a go? If you happen to break them, simply revert back to a previous good copy. No programmer gets things right the first time, so having the component break is part of the experience. (Or at least that's what programmers tell themselves at two o'clock in the morning when they are still trying to figure out why the thing isn't doing what they asked.) The component classes are covered in the next sections. You will then be shown how to make sure your component appears in the correct folder, what to put in the `AssemblyInfo` file, how it gets registered in the GAC, and how to sign the assembly. This is common to all three components, so it is dealt with as one topic.

Preparation

In this section of the chapter, you'll go through the steps that are common to all the Pipeline Components. These are the basic sets of things you need to do before you fly into coding.

Start by opening Visual Studio 2008, and create a new project, a Class Library project, as shown in Figure 18-1.

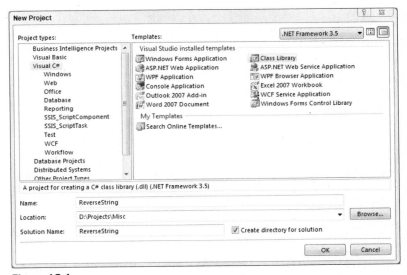

Figure 18-1

Now select the Add References option from the Project menu, and select the following assemblies, which are also illustrated in Figure 18-2:

- ❏ `Microsoft.SqlServer.DTSPipelineWrap`

- ❏ `Microsoft.Sqlserver.DTSRuntimeWrap`

- ❏ `Microsoft.Sqlserver.ManagedDTS`

- ❏ `Microsoft.SqlServer.PipelineHost`

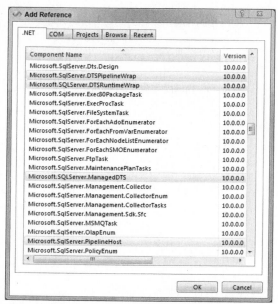

Figure 18-2

Once you have those set up, you can start to add the `using` directives. These directives tell the compiler which libraries you are going to use. These are the directives you will need:

```
#region Using directives

using System;
using System.Collections.Generic;
using System.Text;
using System.Globalization;
using System.Runtime.InteropServices;
using Microsoft.SqlServer.Dts.Pipeline;
using Microsoft.SqlServer.Dts.Pipeline.Wrapper;
using Microsoft.SqlServer.Dts.Runtime.Wrapper;
using Microsoft.SqlServer.Dts.Runtime;

#endregion
```

The first stage in building a component is to inherit from the `PipelineComponent` base class and to decorate the class with `DtsPipelineComponent`. From this point on, you are officially working on a Pipeline Component.

```
namespace Konesans.Dts.Pipeline.ReverseString
{
    [DtsPipelineComponent(
        DisplayName = "ReverseString",
        ComponentType = ComponentType.Transform,
        IconResource =  "Konesans.Dts.Pipeline.ReverseString.ReverseString.ico")]
    public class ReverseString : PipelineComponent
    {
        ...
```

The `DtsPipelineComponent` attribute supplies design-time information about your component, and the first key property here is `ComponentType`. The three options — Source, Destination, or Transformation — reflect the three tabs within the SSIS designer Toolbox. This option determines which tab or grouping of components your component belongs to. The display name should be self-explanatory, and the `IconResource` is the reference to the icon in your project that will be shown to the user in both the Toolbox and when the component is dropped onto the Package Designer. This part of the code will be revisited later in the chapter when the attribute for the User Interface, which you'll be building later, is added.

Now type the following in the code window:

```
public override
```

Once you hit the spacebar after the word "override," you'll see a list of all the methods on the base class. You are now free to type away to your heart's content and develop the component.

We cover development of the components a little later, but for now let's focus on how you deploy it into the SSIS environment once it is ready. The component will need to be built and it also needs a few other things to happen to it. If you are a seasoned developer, then this section will probably be old hat to you, but it's important for everybody to understand what needs to happen for the components to work. This is what needs to be covered:

- ❑ Provide a strong name key for signing the assembly.
- ❑ Set the build output location to the `PipelineComponents` folder.
- ❑ Use a post-build event to install the assembly into the global assembly cache (GAC).
- ❑ Set assembly-level attributes in the `AssemblyInfo.cs` file.

SSIS needs the GAC because it can execute in designer or agent, with different directories. Strong names are a consequence of this requirement. The `PipelineComponents` folder allows the designer to discover the component and put it in the Toolbox. Assembly-level stuff is a consequence of the fact that the strong name, with version, is persisted in the package, making all your packages break if you rebuild the component unless you stop incrementing the version.

You can start by looking at how you sign the project. Right-click your C# project and choose Properties from the context menu. You are not going to look at all of the tabs on the left-hand side of the screen, but you are going to look at the ones that are relevant to what you're doing here. Figure 18-3 shows the Application tab.

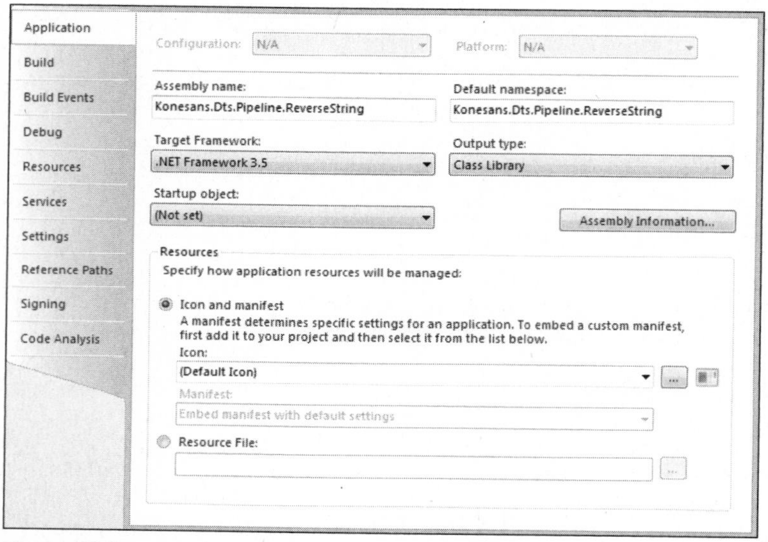

Figure 18-3

In this tab, the only thing you really need to do is change the assembly name to be the same as your default namespace.

On the Build tab, shown in Figure 18-4, you need to be concerned with the output path box toward the bottom of the dialog box. This tells the project that when it builds, the output should be placed in a certain folder. On a 32bit (x86) PC, this folder is usually located here:

```
C:\Program Files\Microsoft SQL Server\100\DTS\PipelineComponents
```

Note that if you have 64bit (x64) environment then you should explicitly choose the 32bit location:

```
C:\Program Files (x86)\Microsoft SQL Server\100\DTS\PipelineComponents
```

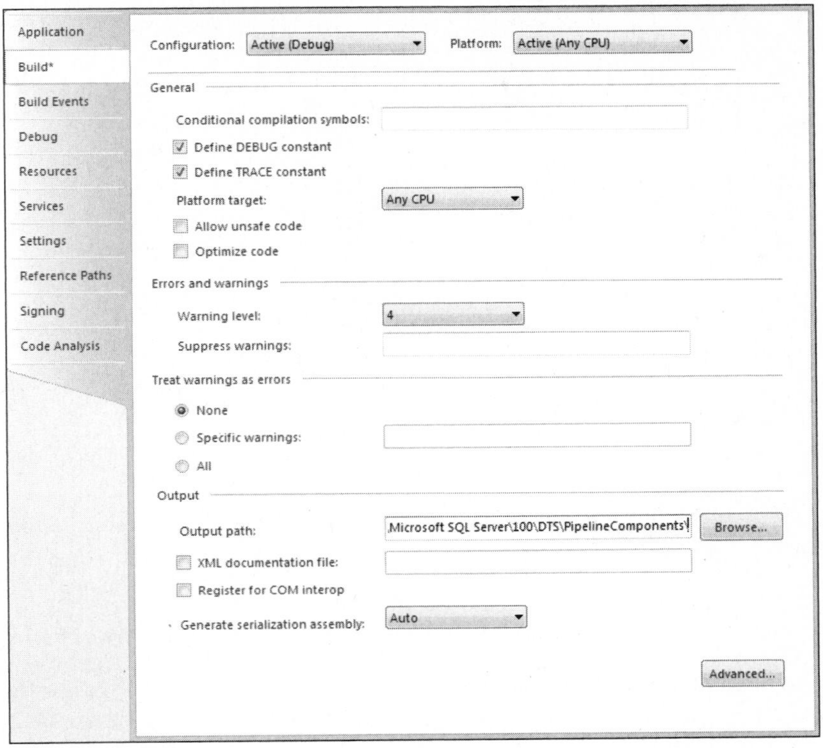

Figure 18-4

For the designer to use a component it must be placed in a defined folder, and for the runtime engine to work correctly, it must be placed in the global assembly cache. So setting the build location and installing into the GAC are both required steps, which you can do manually, but it makes for faster development if you do it as part of the build process.

Click the Build Events tab and then in the "Post-build command line" enter the commands that will automatically do these tasks. An example build event command is shown as follows and also illustrated in Figure 18-5. Be sure to include the double quotes in the path statements. If this exact command doesn't work in your development environment then do a search for gacutil.exe on your hard drive, and use its path in the manner shown here:

```
"C:\Program Files\Microsoft SDKs\Windows\v6.0A\Bin\gacutil" /if "$(TargetPath)"
```

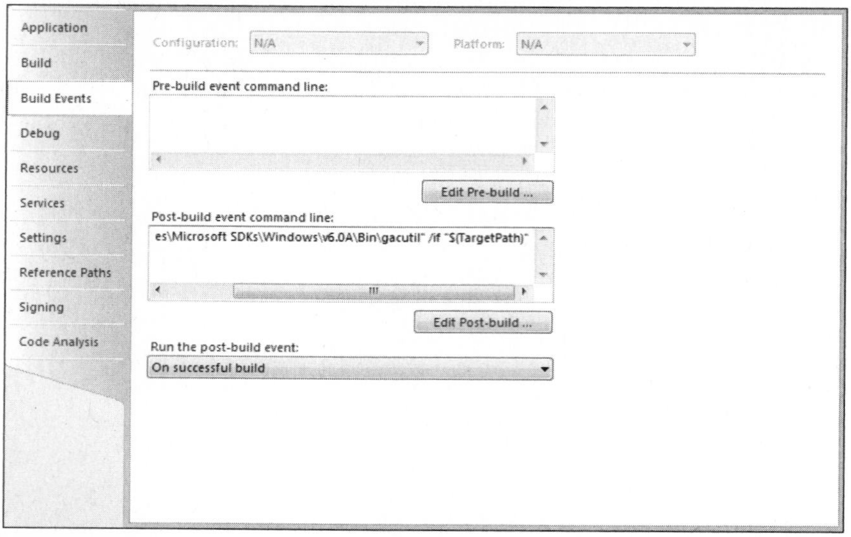

Figure 18-5

What happens when you compile the code is that Visual Studio will expand the macros shown in the preceding code into real paths, for instance the first command shown will expand into the following statement, and Visual Studio will then execute the statement. Since you have declared the statement in the Post-build event, then, after compiling the code, the statement will run automatically and will place the new library (dll) into the global assembly cache (GAC).

```
"C:\Program Files\Microsoft SDKs\Windows\v6.0A\Bin\gacutil" /if
"C:\Program Files\Microsoft SQL
    Server\100\DTS\PipelineComponents\ReverseString.dll"
```

Because the assembly is to be installed in the GAC, you also need to sign the assembly using a strong name key, which can be specified and created from the Signing page, as shown in Figure 18-6.

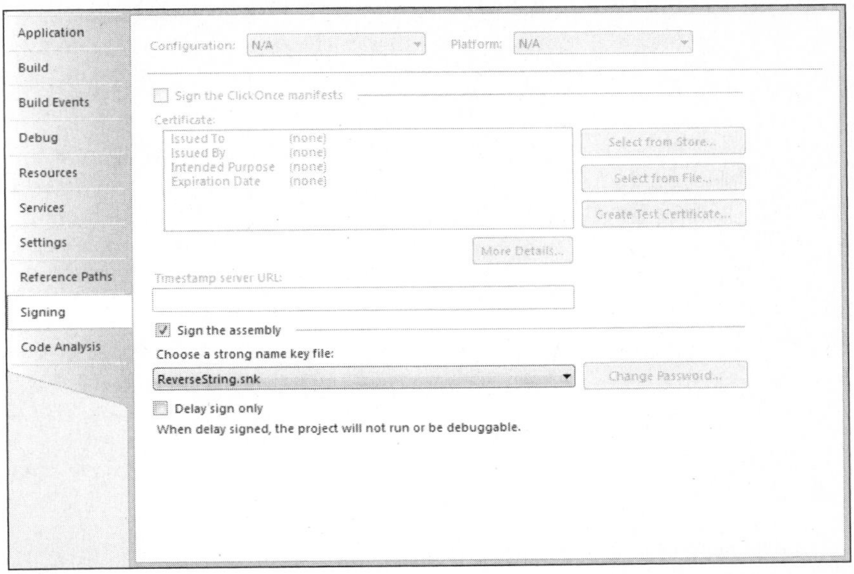

Figure 18-6

That is it as far as the project's properties are concerned, so now you can move on to looking at the `AssemblyInfo` file. While most assembly attributes can be set through the Assembly Information dialog box, available from the Application tab of Project Properties, shown previously in Figure 18-3, you require some additional settings. Shown next is the `AssemblyInfo.cs` file for the example project, which can be found under the `Properties` folder within the Solution Explorer of Visual Studio:

```
#region Using directives
using System;
using System.Security.Permissions;
using System.Reflection;
using System.Runtime.CompilerServices;
using System.Runtime.InteropServices;

#endregion

[assembly: AssemblyTitle("ReverseString")]
[assembly: AssemblyDescription("Reversing String Transformation for SQL Server
Integration Services")]
[assembly: AssemblyConfiguration("")]
[assembly: AssemblyProduct("Reverse String Transformation")]
[assembly: AssemblyTrademark("")]
[assembly: AssemblyCulture("")]

[assembly: AssemblyVersion("2.0.0.0")]
[assembly: AssemblyFileVersion("2.0.0.0")]
[assembly: CLSCompliant(true)]
[assembly: PermissionSet(SecurityAction.RequestMinimum)]
[assembly: ComVisible(false)]
```

The first section of attributes listed represents primarily information, and you would change these to reflect your component and company, for example. The `AssemblyCulture` should be left blank unless you are experienced at working with localized assemblies and understand the implications of any change.

The `AssemblyVersion` attribute is also worth noting; as the version is fixed, it does not use the asterisk token to generate an automatically incrementing build number. The assembly version forms part of the fully qualified assembly name, which is how a package references a component under the covers. So if you changed the version for every build, you would have to rebuild your packages for every new version of the component. So that you can differentiate between versions, you should use `AssemblyFileVersion`, although you will need to manually update this.

The other attribute worth special note is `CLSCompliant`. Best practice dictates that the .NET classes and assemblies conform to the Command Language Specification (CLS), and compliance should be marked at the assembly level. Individual items of noncompliant code can then be decorated with the `CLSCompliant` attribute, marked as `false`. The completed samples all include this, and you can also refer to SQL Server documentation for guidance, as well as following the simple compiler warnings that are raised when this condition is not met.

Here is an example of how to deal with a method being noncompliant in your component:

```
[CLSCompliant(false)]
public override DTSValidationStatus Validate()
{
...
```

Building the Source Component

As mentioned earlier, the Source adapter needs to be able to retrieve information from a file and present the data to the downstream component. The file is not your standard-looking file. The format is strange but consistent. When you design the Destination adapter, you will write the contents of an upstream component to a file in a very similar format. After you have read this chapter, you may want to take the Source adapter and alter it slightly so that it can read a file produced by the sample Destination adapter.

The very first method to look at is `ProvideComponentProperties`. This gets called almost as soon as you drop the component onto the designer. Here is the method in full before you begin to break it down:

```
public override void ProvideComponentProperties()
{
    ComponentMetaData.RuntimeConnectionCollection.RemoveAll();
    RemoveAllInputsOutputsAndCustomProperties();

    ComponentMetaData.Name = "Professional SSIS Source Adapter";
    ComponentMetaData.Description = "Our first Source Adapter";

    IDTSRuntimeConnection100 rtc =
        ComponentMetaData.RuntimeConnectionCollection.New();
    rtc.Name = "File To Read";
    rtc.Description = "This is the file from which we want to read";
```

```
    IDTSOutput100 output = ComponentMetaData.OutputCollection.New();
    output.Name = "Component Output";
    output.Description = "This is what downstream Components will see";

    output.ExternalMetadataColumnCollection.IsUsed = true;
}
```

Now you can break down some of this code.

```
ComponentMetaData.RuntimeConnectionCollection.RemoveAll();
RemoveAllInputsOutputsAndCustomProperties();
```

The very first thing this code does is remove any runtime connections in the component, which you'll be adding back soon. You can also remove inputs, outputs, and custom properties. Basically your component is now a clean slate. This is not strictly required for this example; however, it's advantageous to follow this convention, because it prevents any unexpected situations that may arise in more complicated components.

```
ComponentMetaData.Name = "Professional SSIS Source Adapter";
ComponentMetaData.Description = "Our first Source Adapter";
ComponentMetaData.ContactInfo = "www.Konesans.com";
```

These three lines of code simply help to identify your component when you look in the property pages after adding it to the designer. The only property here that may not be obvious is ContactInfo, which simply identifies to the user the developer of the component. If a component throws a fatal error during loading or saving, for example — areas not influenced by the user-controlled settings — then the designer will show the contact information for support purposes.

```
IDTSRuntimeConnection100 rtc = ComponentMetaData.RuntimeConnectionCollection.New();
rtc.Name = "File To Read";
rtc.Description = "This is the file from which we want to read";
```

Your component needs a runtime connection from which you can read and get the data. You removed any existing connections earlier in the method, so here is where you add it back. Simply give it a name and a description.

```
IDTSOutput100 output = ComponentMetaData.OutputCollection.New();
output.Name = "Component Output";
output.Description = "This is what downstream Components will see";
```

The way downstream components will see the data is to present it to them from an output in this component. In other words, the output is the vehicle that the component will use to present data from the input file to the next component downstream. Here you add a new output to the output collection and give it a name and a description. The final part of this component is to use ExternalMetadataColumns, which will allow you to view the structure of the Data Source with no connection.

```
output.ExternalMetadataColumnCollection.IsUsed = true;
```

Here, you tell the output you created earlier that it will use ExternalMetaData columns.

The next method to look at is the `AcquireConnections` method. In this method, you want to make sure that you have a runtime connection available and that it is the correct type. You then want to retrieve the filename from the file itself. Here is the method in full:

```
public override void AcquireConnections(object transaction)
{

    if (ComponentMetaData.RuntimeConnectionCollection["File To
Read"].ConnectionManager != null)
    {
        ConnectionManager cm =
                Microsoft.SqlServer.Dts.Runtime.DtsConvert.GetWrapper(
                ComponentMetaData.RuntimeConnectionCollection["File To Read"].
                ConnectionManager);

        if (cm.CreationName != "FILE")
        {
            throw new Exception("The Connection Manager is not a FILE Connection
                              Manager");
        }
        else
        {
            fil = (Microsoft.SqlServer.Dts.Runtime.DTSFileConnectionUsageType)
                  cm.Properties["FileUsageType"].GetValue(cm);

            if (_fil != DTSFileConnectionUsageType.FileExists)
            {
                throw new Exception("The type of FILE connection manager must be an
                                  Existing File");
            }
            else
            {
                _filename = ComponentMetaData.RuntimeConnectionCollection["File To
                            Read"].ConnectionManager.AcquireConnection(transaction).
                            ToString();
                if (_filename == null || _filename.Length == 0)
                {
                    throw new Exception("Nothing returned when grabbing the filename");
                }
            }
        }
    }
}
```

This method covers a lot of ground and is really quite interesting. The first thing you want to do is find out if you can get a Connection Manager from the runtime connection collection of the component. The runtime connection was defined during `ProvideComponentProperties` earlier. If it is null, then the user has not provided a runtime connection.

```
if (ComponentMetaData.RuntimeConnectionCollection["File To Read"].ConnectionManager
!= null)
```

The next line of code is quite cool. What it does is convert the native Connection Manager object to a managed Connection Manager. You need the managed Connection Manager to find out what type it is and the properties.

```
ConnectionManager cm =
Microsoft.SqlServer.Dts.Runtime.DtsConvert.ToConnectionManager(
ComponentMetaData.RuntimeConnectionCollection["File To Read"].ConnectionManager);
```

Once you have the managed Connection Manager, you can start to look at some of its properties and make sure that it is what you want. All Connection Managers have a CreationName property. For this component, you want to make sure that the CreationName property is FILE, as highlighted here:

```
if (cm.CreationName != "FILE")
```

If the CreationName is not FILE, then you send an exception back to the component:

```
throw new Exception("The type of FILE connection manager must be an Existing
File");
```

You've established that a connection has been specified and that it is the right type. The problem with the FILE Connection Manager is that it can still have the wrong usage mode specified. To find out if it has the right mode, you will have to look at another of its properties, the FileUsageType property. This can return to you one of four values, defined by the DTSFileConnectionUsageType enumeration:

❏   DTSFileConnectionUsageType.CreateFile: The file does not yet exist and will be created by the component. If the file does exist, then you can raise an error, although you may also accept this and overwrite the file. Use this type for components that create new files. This mode is more useful for Destination Components, not sources.

❏   DTSFileConnectionUsageType.FileExists: The file exists, and you would be expected to raise an error if this is not the case.

❏   DTSFileConnectionUsageType.CreateFolder: The folder does not yet exist and will be created by the component. If the folder does exist, then you can decide how to handle this situation as with CreateFile earlier. Also more useful for destinations.

❏   DTSFileConnectionUsageType.FolderExists: The folder exists, and you would be expected to raise an error if this is not the case.

The type you want to check for in your component is DTSFileConnectionUsageType.FileExists and you do that like this, throwing an exception if the type is not what you want:

```
fil = (Microsoft.SqlServer.Dts.Runtime.DTSFileConnectionUsageType)cm.Properties
["FileUsageType"].GetValue(cm);

if (_fil != Microsoft.SqlServer.Dts.Runtime.DTSFileConnectionUsageType.FileExists)
{...}
```

You're nearly done checking your Connection Manager now. At this point, you need the filename so you can retrieve the file later on when you need to read it for data. You do that like this:

```
_filename = ComponentMetaData.RuntimeConnectionCollection
["File To Read"].ConnectionManager.AcquireConnection(transaction).ToString();
```

That concludes the `AcquireConnections` method, so you can now move straight on to the `Validate` method:

```
[CLSCompliant(false)]
public override DTSValidationStatus Validate()
{
    bool pbCancel = false;

    IDTSOutput100 output = ComponentMetaData.OutputCollection["Component Output"];

    if (ComponentMetaData.InputCollection.Count != 0)
    {
        ComponentMetaData.FireError(0, ComponentMetaData.Name, "Unexpected input
                found. Source components do not support inputs.", "", 0, out pbCancel);
        return DTSValidationStatus.VS_ISCORRUPT;
    }

    if (ComponentMetaData.RuntimeConnectionCollection["File To Read"].
                                                ConnectionManager == null)
    {
        ComponentMetaData.FireError(0, "Validate", "No Connection Manager
                                            Specified.", "", 0, out pbCancel);
        return DTSValidationStatus.VS_ISBROKEN;
    }

    // Check for Output Columns, if not then force ReinitializeMetaData
    if (ComponentMetaData.OutputCollection["Component
        Output"].OutputColumnCollection.Count == 0)
    {
        ComponentMetaData.FireError(0, "Validate", "No output columns specified.
                    Making call to ReinitializeMetaData.", "", 0, out pbCancel);
        return DTSValidationStatus.VS_NEEDSNEWMETADATA;
    }

    //What about if we have output columns but we have no ExternalMetaData
    // columns?  Maybe somebody removed them through code.

    if (DoesEachOutputColumnHaveAMetaDataColumnAndDoDatatypesMatch(output.ID)
            == false)
    {
        ComponentMetaData.FireError(0, "Validate", "Output columns and metadata
                columns are out of sync.  Making call to ReinitializeMetaData.", "",
                0, out pbCancel);
        return DTSValidationStatus.VS_NEEDSNEWMETADATA;
    }
    return base.Validate();
}
```

The first thing this method does is check for an input. If it has an input, it raises an error back to the component using the `FireError` method and returns `DTSValidationStatus.VS_ISCORRUPT`. This is a Source adapter, and there is no place for an input. Since the data rows enter the component from the file, there is no need for a buffer input that would receive data from an upstream component.

```
if (ComponentMetaData.InputCollection.Count != 0)
```

The next thing you do is check that the user has specified a Connection Manager for your component. If not, then you return back to the user a message indicating that a Connection Manager is required. Again, you do this through the `FireError` method. If there is no Connection Manager specified, then you tell the component it is broken. Remember that you do the validation of any Connection Manager that is specified in `AcquireConnections()`.

```
if (ComponentMetaData.RuntimeConnectionCollection["File To Read"].ConnectionManager
== null)
{
    ComponentMetaData.FireError(0, "Validate", "No Connection Manager Specified.",
"", 0, out pbCancel);
    return DTSValidationStatus.VS_ISBROKEN;
}
```

The next thing to do is check to see if the output has any columns. On the initial drop onto the designer, the output will have no columns. If this is the case, the `Validate()` method will return `DTSValidationStatus.VS_NEEDSNEWMETADATA`, which in turn calls `ReinitializeMetaData`. You will see later what happens in that method.

```
if (ComponentMetaData.OutputCollection["Component
Output"].OutputColumnCollection.Count == 0)
{
    ComponentMetaData.FireError(0, "Validate", "No output columns specified.  Making
                        call to ReinitializeMetaData.", "", 0, out pbCancel);
    return DTSValidationStatus.VS_NEEDSNEWMETADATA;
}
```

So if the output has output columns, then one of the things you want to check for is whether the output columns have an `ExternalMetaDataColumn` associated with them. You'll recall that in `ProvideComponentProperties`, it was stated that you would use an `ExternalMetadataColumnCollection`. So for each output column, you need to make sure that there is an equivalent external metadata column, and that the data type properties also match.

```
if (DoesEachOutputColumnHaveAMetaDataColumnAndDoDatatypesMatch(output.ID) == false)
{
    ComponentMetaData.FireError(0, "Validate", "Output columns and metadata columns
                    are out of sync.  Making call to ReinitializeMetaData.", "",
                    0, out pbCancel);
    return DTSValidationStatus.VS_NEEDSNEWMETADATA;
}
```

The next method is a function that we use to validate some properties of the component. This is not a method provided by Microsoft that we are overriding; rather it is completely custom code used to help us do some common work — which is why such functions are sometimes called helper methods. This rather long-named helper method, `DoesEachOutputColumnHaveAMetaDataColumnAndDoDatatypesMatch`, accepts as a parameter the ID of an output, so you pass in the output's ID. There are two things that this method has to do. First, it has to check that each output column has an `ExternalMetadataColumn` associated with it, and second, it has to make sure that the two columns have the same column data type properties. Here is the method in full:

```
private bool DoesEachOutputColumnHaveAMetaDataColumnAndDoDatatypesMatch(int
outputID)
{

    IDTSOutput100 output =
                    ComponentMetaData.OutputCollection.GetObjectByID(outputID);
    IDTSExternalMetadataColumn100 mdc;
    bool rtnVal = true;

    foreach (IDTSOutputColumn100 col in output.OutputColumnCollection)
    {

        if (col.ExternalMetadataColumnID == 0)
        {
            rtnVal = false;
        }
        else
        {
            mdc = output.ExternalMetadataColumnCollection.GetObjectByID
             (col.ExternalMetadataColumnID);

            if (mdc.DataType != col.DataType || mdc.Length != col.Length ||
                    mdc.Precision != col.Precision || mdc.Scale != col.Scale ||
                    mdc.CodePage != col.CodePage)
            {
                rtnVal = false;
            }
        }
    }
    return rtnVal;
}
```

The first thing this method does is to translate the ID passed in as a parameter to the method into an output.

```
IDTSOutput100 output = ComponentMetaData.OutputCollection.GetObjectByID(outputID);
```

Once you have that, the code loops over the output columns in that output and asks if the `ExternalMetadataColumnID` associated with that output column has a value of 0 (that is, there is no value). If the code finds an instance of a value, then it sets the return value from the method to be false.

```
foreach (IDTSOutputColumn100 col in output.OutputColumnCollection)
{

    if (col.ExternalMetadataColumnID == 0)
    {
        rtnVal = false;
    }
...
```

If all output columns have a nonzero `ExternalMetadataColumnID`, then you move on to the second test:

```
mdc = output.ExternalMetadataColumnCollection.GetObjectByID
    (col.ExternalMetadataColumnID);

if (mdc.DataType != col.DataType || mdc.Length != col.Length || mdc.Precision !=
    col.Precision || mdc.Scale != col.Scale || mdc.CodePage != col.CodePage)
{
    rtnVal = false;
}
```

In this part of the method, you are checking that all attributes of the output column's data type match those of the corresponding `ExternalMetadataColumn`. If they do not, then again you return false from the method, which causes the `Validate()` method to call `ReinitializeMetaData`. Notice how you are using the ID over a Name, since names can be changed by the end user.

`ReinitializeMetaData` is where a lot of the work happens in most components. In this component, it will fix up the output columns and the `ExternalMetadataColumns`. Here's the method:

```
public override void ReinitializeMetaData()
{
    IDTSOutput100 _profoutput = ComponentMetaData.OutputCollection["Component
                                                                    Output"];

    if (_profoutput.ExternalMetadataColumnCollection.Count > 0)
    {
        _profoutput.ExternalMetadataColumnCollection.RemoveAll();
    }

    if (_profoutput.OutputColumnCollection.Count > 0)
    {
        _profoutput.OutputColumnCollection.RemoveAll();
    }

    CreateOutputAndMetaDataColumns(_profoutput);

}
```

This is a really simple way of doing things. Basically, you are going to remove all the `ExternalMetaDataColumns` and then remove the output columns. You will then add them back using the `CreateOutputAndMetaDataColumns` helper method.

As an exercise, you may want to see if you can work out which columns actually need fixing, instead of just dropping and re-creating them all.

`CreateOutputAndMetaDataColumns` is a helper method that creates the output's output columns and the `ExternalMetaData` columns to go with them. This implementation is very rigid, and it presumes that the file you get will be in one format only:

```
private void CreateOutputAndMetaDataColumns(IDTSOutput100 output)
{
    IDTSOutputColumn100 outName = output.OutputColumnCollection.New();
    outName.Name = "Name";
    outName.Description = "The Name value retrieved from File";
    outName.SetDataTypeProperties(DataType.DT_STR, 50, 0, 0, 1252);
    CreateExternalMetaDataColumn(output.ExternalMetadataColumnCollection, outName);

    IDTSOutputColumn100 outAge = output.OutputColumnCollection.New();
    outAge.Name = "Age";
    outAge.Description = "The Age value retrieved from File";
    outAge.SetDataTypeProperties(DataType.DT_I4, 0, 0, 0, 0);

    //Create an external metadata column to go alongside with it
    CreateExternalMetaDataColumn(output.ExternalMetadataColumnCollection, outAge);

    IDTSOutputColumn100 outMarried = output.OutputColumnCollection.New();
    outMarried.Name = "Married";
    outMarried.Description = "The Married value retrieved from File";
    outMarried.SetDataTypeProperties(DataType.DT_BOOL, 0, 0, 0, 0);

    //Create an external metadata column to go alongside with it
    CreateExternalMetaDataColumn(output.ExternalMetadataColumnCollection,
        outMarried);

    IDTSOutputColumn100 outSalary = output.OutputColumnCollection.New();
    outSalary.Name = "Salary";
    outSalary.Description = "The Salary value retrieved from File";
    outSalary.SetDataTypeProperties(DataType.DT_DECIMAL, 0, 0, 10, 0);

    //Create an external metadata column to go alongside with it
    CreateExternalMetaDataColumn(output.ExternalMetadataColumnCollection,
        outSalary);
}
```

This code follows the same path for every column you want to create, so you'll just look at one example here, because the rest are variations of the same code. In `CreateOutputAndMetaDataColumns`, you first need to create an output column and add it to the `OutputColumnCollection` of the output, which is a parameter to the method. You give the column a name, a description, and a data type along with details about the data type.

`SetDataTypeProperties` takes the name, the length, the precision, the scale, and the code page of that data type. A list of what is required for these fields can be found in Books Online.

```
IDTSOutputColumn100 outName = output.OutputColumnCollection.New();
outName.Name = "Name";
outName.Description = "The Name value retrieved from File";
outName.SetDataTypeProperties(DataType.DT_STR, 50, 0, 0, 1252);
```

Note that if you decided to use Unicode data, which does not require a code page, then the same call would have looked like this:

```
outName.SetDataTypeProperties(DataType.DT_WSTR, 50, 0, 0, 0);
```

You now look to create an `ExternalMetaDataColumn` for the `OutputColumn`, and you do that by calling the helper method called `CreateExternalMetaDataColumn`. This method takes as parameters the `ExternalMetaDataColumnCollection` of the output and the `Column` for which you want to create an `ExternalMetaDataColumn`:

```
CreateExternalMetaDataColumn(output.ExternalMetadataColumnCollection, outName);
```

The first thing you do in the method is create a new `ExternalMetaDataColumn` in the `ExternalMetaDataColumnCollection` that was passed as a parameter. You then map the properties of the output column that was passed as a parameter to the new `ExternalMetaDataColumn`. Finally, you create the relationship between the two by assigning the ID of the `ExternalMetaDataColumn` to the `ExternalMetadataColumnID` property of the output column.

```
IDTSExternalMetadataColumn100 eColumn = externalCollection.New();
eColumn.Name = column.Name;
eColumn.DataType = column.DataType;
eColumn.Precision = column.Precision;
eColumn.Length = column.Length;
eColumn.Scale = column.Scale;
eColumn.CodePage = column.CodePage;
column.ExternalMetadataColumnID = eColumn.ID;
```

At this point, the base class will call the `MapOutputColumn` method. You can choose to override this method to decide if you want to allow the mapping to occur, but in this case you should choose to leave the base class to simply carry on.

Now you will move on to looking at the runtime methods. `PreExecute` is the usual place to start for most components, but it is done slightly differently here. Normally you would enumerate the output columns and enter them into a struct, so you could easily retrieve them later. For illustration purposes, you're not going to do that here (but you do this in the Destination adapter, so you could port what you do there into this adapter as well). The only method you are interested in with this adapter is `PrimeOutput`. Here is the method in full:

```
public override void PrimeOutput(int outputs, int[] outputIDs, PipelineBuffer[]
buffers)
{
    ParseTheFileAndAddToBuffer(_filename, buffers[0]);
    buffers[0].SetEndOfRowset();
}
```

On the face of this method, it looks really easy, but as you can see, all the work is being done by the helper called `ParseTheFileAndAddToBuffer` method. To that procedure, you need to pass the filename you retrieved in `AcquireConnections`, and the buffer is `buffers[0]`, because there is only one buffer and the collection is zero-based. You'll look at the `ParseTheFileAndAddToBuffer` method in a moment, but the last thing you do in this method is call `SetEndOfRowset` on the buffer. This basically tells the downstream component that there are no more rows to be had from the adapter. Now you will look at the `ParseTheFileAndAddToBuffer` method in a bit more detail:

```
private void ParseTheFileAndAddToBuffer(string filename, PipelineBuffer buffer)
{
    TextReader tr = File.OpenText(filename);
    IDTSOutput100 output = ComponentMetaData.OutputCollection["Component Output"];
    IDTSOutputColumnCollection100 cols = output.OutputColumnCollection;
    IDTSOutputColumn100 col;

    string s = tr.ReadLine();
    int i = 0;

    while (s != null)
    {
        if (s.StartsWith("<START>"))
            buffer.AddRow();

        if (s.StartsWith("Name:"))
        {
            col = cols["Name"];
            i = BufferManager.FindColumnByLineageID(output.Buffer, col.LineageID);
            string value = s.Substring(5);
            buffer.SetString(i, value);
        }

        if (s.StartsWith("Age:"))
        {
            col = cols["Age"];
            i = BufferManager.FindColumnByLineageID(output.Buffer, col.LineageID);
            Int32 value;
            if (s.Substring(4).Trim() == "")
                value = 0;
            else
                value = Convert.ToInt32(s.Substring(4).Trim());

            buffer.SetInt32(i, value);
        }

        if (s.StartsWith("Married:"))
        {
            col = cols["Married"];
            bool value;
            i = BufferManager.FindColumnByLineageID(output.Buffer, col.LineageID);
            if (s.Substring(8).Trim() == "")
                value = true;
            else
                value = s.Substring(8).Trim() != "1" ? false : true;

            buffer.SetBoolean(i, value);
        }
```

```
        if (s.StartsWith("Salary:"))
        {
           col = cols["Salary"];
           Decimal value;
           i = BufferManager.FindColumnByLineageID(output.Buffer, col.LineageID);

           if (s.Substring(7).Trim() == "")
               value = 0M;
           else
               value = Convert.ToDecimal(s.Substring(8).Trim());

           buffer.SetDecimal(i, value);
        }
        s = tr.ReadLine();
    }
    tr.Close();
}
```

Because this is not a lesson in C# programming, we will simply describe the points relevant to SSIS programming in this component. You start off by getting references to the output columns collection in the component:

```
IDTSOutput100 output = ComponentMetaData.OutputCollection["Component Output"];
IDTSOutputColumnCollection100 cols = output.OutputColumnCollection;
IDTSOutputColumn100 col;
```

The IDTSOutputColumn100 object will be used when you need a reference to particular columns. Now the problem with the file is that the columns in the file are actually in rows, and so you need to pivot them into columns. First we read a single line from the file using this code:

```
string s = tr.ReadLine();
```

For this specific source file format, the way to identify that you need to add a new row to the buffer is if when reading a line of text from the file it begins with the word <START>. You do that in this code here (remember that the variable s is assigned a line of text from the file):

```
if(s.StartsWith("<START>"))
    buffer.AddRow();
```

As you can see, you have added a row to the buffer, but the row is empty with no data in it yet. As you read lines in the file, you test the start of each line. This is important because you need to know this in order to be able to grab the right column from the output columns collection and assign it the value from the text file. The first column name you test for is the "Name" column:

```
if (s.StartsWith("Name:"))
{
    col = cols["Name"];
    i = BufferManager.FindColumnByLineageID(output.Buffer, col.LineageID);

    string value = s.Substring(5);
    buffer.SetString(i, value);
}
```

The first thing you do here is to check what the row begins with. In the preceding example, it is "Name:". Next, you set the IDTSColumn100 variable column to reference the Name column in the OutputColumnCollection. You need to be able to locate the column in the buffer, and to do this you need to look at the Buffer Manager. This has a method called FindColumnByLineageID, which returns the integer location of the column. You need this to assign a value to the column.

To this method, you pass the output's buffer and the column's LineageID. Once you have that, you can use the SetString method on the buffer object to assign a value to the column by passing in the Buffer column index and the value you want to set the column to. Now you no longer have an empty row; it has one column populated with a real data value.

You pretty much do the same with all the columns you want to set values for. The only variation is the method you call on the buffer object. The buffer object has a set<datatype> method for each of the possible data types. In this component, you need a SetInt32, a SetBoolean, and a SetDecimal method. They do not differ in structure from the SetString method at all. You can also set the value in a non type-safe manner by using buffer[i] := value, though as a best practice this is not advised.

You can now compile the project, and assuming there are no syntax errors, the project should output the .dll in the specified folder, and register it in the GAC. We discuss how you integrate the component into SSIS later on.

Building the Transform Component

In this section, you build the transform that is going to take data from the upstream Source adapter. After reversing the strings, it will pass the data to the downstream component. In this example, the downstream component will be the Destination adapter, which you'll be writing right after you're done with the transform. The component will need a few things prepared earlier in order to execute efficiently during its lifetime.

```
private ColumnInfo[] _inputColumnInfos;

const string ErrorInvalidUsageType = "Invalid UsageType for column '{0}'";
const string ErrorInvalidDataType = "Invalid DataType for column '{0}'";

CLSCompliant(false)]
public struct ColumnInfo
{
    public int bufferColumnIndex;
    public DTSRowDisposition columnDisposition;
    public int lineageID;
}
```

The structure or struct that you create here, called ColumnInfo, is something you use in various guises time and time again in your components. It is really useful for storing details about columns that you will need later in the component. In this component, you will store the BufferColumnIndex, which is basically where the column is in the buffer, so that you can retrieve the data. You'll store how the user wants the row to be treated in an error, and you'll also store the column's LineageID, which helps to retrieve the column from the InputColumnCollection.

Logically, it would make sense to code the component beginning with the design-time, followed by the runtime. The very first thing that happens when your component is dropped into the SSIS Package Designer surface is that it will make a call to `ProvideComponentProperties`. In this component, you want to set up an input and an output, and you also need to tell your component how it is going to handle data — as in whether it is a synchronous or an asynchronous transformation, as discussed earlier in the chapter. Just as you did with the Source adapter, we'll look at the whole method first and then examine parts of the method in greater detail. Here is the method in full:

```
public override void ProvideComponentProperties()
{
    ComponentMetaData.UsesDispositions = true;

    ReverseStringInput = ComponentMetaData.InputCollection.New();
    ReverseStringInput.Name = "RSin";

    ReverseStringInput.ErrorRowDisposition = DTSRowDisposition.RD_FailComponent;

    ReverseStringOutput = ComponentMetaData.OutputCollection.New();
    ReverseStringOutput.Name = "RSout";

    ReverseStringOutput.SynchronousInputID = ReverseStringInput.ID;

    ReverseStringOutput.ExclusionGroup = 1;

    AddErrorOutput("RSErrors", ReverseStringInput.ID,
                   ReverseStringOutput.ExclusionGroup);


}
```

Now to break it down. The very first thing you do is to tell the component to use dispositions:

```
ComponentMetaData.UsesDispositions = true;
```

In this case, this tells your component that it can expect an error output. Now you move on to adding an input to the component:

```
// Add a new Input, and name it.
ReverseStringInput = ComponentMetaData.InputCollection.New();
ReverseStringInput.Name = "RSin";

// If an error occurs during data movement, then the component will fail.
ReverseStringInput.ErrorRowDisposition = DTSRowDisposition.RD_FailComponent;

// Add a new Output, and name it.
ReverseStringOutput = ComponentMetaData.OutputCollection.New();
ReverseStringOutput.Name = "RSout";

// Link the Input and Output together for a synchronous behavior
ReverseStringOutput.SynchronousInputID = ReverseStringInput.ID;
```

This isn't too different from adding the input, except that you tell the component that this is a synchronous component by setting the `SynchronousInputID` on the output to the ID of the input you created earlier. If you were creating an asynchronous component, you would set the `SynchronousInputID` of the output to be 0, like this:

```
ReverseStringOutput.SynchronousInputID = 0
```

This tells SSIS to create a buffer for the output that is separate from the input buffer. This is not an asynchronous component, though; you will revisit some of the subtle differences later.

```
AddErrorOutput("RSErrors",
ReverseStringInput.ID,ReverseStringOutput.ExclusionGroup);

ReverseStringOutput.ExclusionGroup = 1;
```

`AddErrorOutput` creates a new output on the component and tags it as being an error output by setting the `IsErrorOut` property to true. To the method, you pass the name of the error output you want, the input's `ID` property, and the output's `ExclusionGroup`. An `ExclusionGroup` is needed when two outputs use the same synchronous input. Setting the exclusion group allows you to direct rows to the correct output later in the component using `DirectRow`.

That's it for `ProvideComponentProperties`. Now you'll move on to the `Validate` method. As mentioned earlier, this method is called on numerous occasions, and it is your opportunity within the component to check whether what has been specified by the user is allowable by the component.

Here is your completed `Validate` method:

```
[CLSCompliant(false)]
public override DTSValidationStatus Validate()
{
    bool Cancel;

    if (ComponentMetaData.AreInputColumnsValid == false)
        return DTSValidationStatus.VS_NEEDSNEWMETADATA;

    foreach (IDTSInputColumn100 inputColumn in
            ComponentMetaData.InputCollection[0].InputColumnCollection)
    {
        if (inputColumn.UsageType != DTSUsageType.UT_READWRITE)
        {
            ComponentMetaData.FireError(0, inputColumn.IdentificationString,
                    String.Format(ErrorInvalidUsageType, inputColumn.Name), "",
                    0, out Cancel);
            return DTSValidationStatus.VS_ISBROKEN;
        }

        if (inputColumn.DataType != DataType.DT_STR && inputColumn.DataType !=
                                            DataType.DT_WSTR)
        {
```

```
            ComponentMetaData.FireError(0, inputColumn.IdentificationString,
                        String.Format(ErrorInvalidDataType, inputColumn.Name), "",
                        0, out Cancel);
            return DTSValidationStatus.VS_ISBROKEN;
        }
    }

    return base.Validate();
}
```

This method will return a validation status to indicate the overall result and may cause subsequent methods to be called. Refer to the SQL Server documentation for a complete list of values (see DTSValidationStatus).

Now to break down the Validate method. A user can easily add and take away an input from the component at any stage and add it back. It may be the same one, or it may be a different one, presenting the component with an issue. When an input is added, the component will store the LineageIDs of the Input columns. If that input is removed and another is added, those LineageIDs may have changed because something like the query used to generate those columns may have changed; therefore you are presented with different columns, so you need to check to see if that has happened, and if it has, invalidated the LineageIDs. If it has, the component will call ReinitializeMetaData.

```
if (ComponentMetaData.AreInputColumnsValid == false)
{ return DTSValidationStatus.VS_NEEDSNEWMETADATA; }
```

The next thing you should check for is that each of the columns in the InputColumnCollection chosen for the component has been set to READ WRITE. This is because you will be altering them in place — in other words, you will read a string from a column, reverse it, then write it back over the old string. If they are not set to READ WRITE, you need to feed that back by returning VS_ISBROKEN. You can invoke the FireError method on the component, which will result in a red cross on the component along with tooltip text indicating the exact error.

```
if (RSincol.UsageType != DTSUsageType.UT_READWRITE)
{
    ComponentMetaData.FireError(0, inputColumn.IdentificationString,
                        String.Format(ErrorInvalidUsageType, inputColumn.Name), "",
                        0, out Cancel);
    return DTSValidationStatus.VS_ISBROKEN;
}
```

The last thing you do in Validate is to check that the columns selected for the component have the correct data types:

```
if (inputColumn.DataType != DataType.DT_STR && inputColumn.DataType !=
                                        DataType.DT_WSTR)
...
```

If the data type of the column is not one of those in the list, you again fire an error and set the return value to VS_ISBROKEN.

Now you will look at the workhorse method of so many of your components: ReinitializeMetaData. Here is the method in full:

```
public override void ReinitializeMetaData()
{
    if (!ComponentMetaData.AreInputColumnsValid)
    {
        ComponentMetaData.RemoveInvalidInputColumns();
    }

    base.ReinitializeMetaData();
}
```

Remember back in the Validate method mentioned earlier that if Validate returns VS_NEEDSNEWMETADATA, then the component internally would automatically call ReinitializeMetaData. The only time you do that for this component is when you have detected that the LineageIDs of the input columns are not quite as expected, that is to say, they do not exist on any upstream column and you want to remove them.

```
if (!ComponentMetaData.AreInputColumnsValid)
{
    ComponentMetaData.RemoveInvalidInputColumns();
}
```

You finish off by calling the base class's ReinitializeMetaData method as well. This method really can become the workhorse of your component. You can perform all kinds of triage on your component here and try to rescue the component from an aberrant user.

The SetUsageType method is called when the user is manipulating how the column on the input will be used by the component. In this component, this method validates the data type of the column and whether the user has set the column to be the correct usage type. The method returns an IDTSInputColumn, and this is the column being manipulated.

```
[CLSCompliant(false)]
public override IDTSInputColumn100 SetUsageType(int inputID, IDTSVirtualInput100
virtualInput, int lineageID, DTSUsageType usageType)
{
    IDTSVirtualInputColumn100 virtualInputColumn =
        virtualInput.VirtualInputColumnCollection.GetVirtualInputColumnByLineageID(
        lineageID);

    if (usageType == DTSUsageType.UT_READONLY)
        throw new Exception(String.Format(ErrorInvalidUsageType,
            virtualInputColumn.Name));

    if (usageType == DTSUsageType.UT_READWRITE)
    {
        if (virtualInputColumn.DataType != DataType.DT_STR &&
            virtualInputColumn.DataType != DataType.DT_WSTR)
```

```
      {
          throw new Exception(String.Format(ErrorInvalidDataType,
              virtualInputColumn.Name));
      }
   }

   return base.SetUsageType(inputID, virtualInput, lineageID, usageType);
}
```

The first thing the method does is get a reference to the column being changed, from the virtual input, which is the list of all upstream columns available.

You then perform the tests to ensure the column is suitable, before proceeding with the request through the base class. In this case, you want to ensure that the user only picks columns of type string. Note that this method looks a lot like the `Validate` method. The only real difference is that the `Validate` method obviously returned a different object but also reported errors back to the component. `Validate` uses the `FireError` method, but `SetUsageType` throws an exception; in `SetUsageType` you are checking against the `VirtualInput`, and in `Validate()` you check against the `Input100`. (We used to use `FireError` in here also, but we found that it wasn't as predictable on what got bubbled back to the user, and we were advised that the correct way would be to throw a new exception.) These are important, because this is one of the key verification methods you can use, allowing you to validate in real time the change that is made to your component and prevent it if necessary.

The `InsertOutput` method is the next design-time method you'll be looking at, and it is called when a user attempts to add an output to the component. In your component, you want to prohibit that, so if the user tries to add an output, you should throw an exception telling them it is not allowed.

```
[CLSCompliant(false)]
public override IDTSOutput100 InsertOutput(DTSInsertPlacement insertPlacement, int
outputID)
{
    throw new Exception("You cannot insert an output (" +
        outputID.ToString() + ")");
}
```

You do the same when the user tries to add an input to your component in the `InsertInput` method:

```
[CLSCompliant(false)]
public override IDTSInput100 InsertInput(DTSInsertPlacement insertPlacement, int
inputID)
{
    throw new Exception("You cannot insert an output (" +
        outputID.ToString() + ")");
}
```

Notice again how in both methods you throw an exception in order to tell the user that what they requested is not allowed.

If the component were asynchronous, you would need to add columns to the output yourself. You have a choice of methods in which to do this. If you want to add an output column for every input column selected, then the `SetUsageType` method is probably the best place to do that. This is something about which Books Online agrees. Another method for doing this might be the `OnInputPathAttached`.

The final two methods you'll look at for the design-time methods are the opposite of the previous two. Instead of users trying to add an output or an input to your component, they are trying to remove one of them. You do not want to allow this either, so you can use the DeleteOutput and the DeleteInput methods to tell them. Here are the methods as implemented in your component.

First the DeleteInput method:

```
[CLSCompliant(false)]
public override void DeleteInput(int inputID)
{
    throw new Exception("You cannot delete an input");
}
```

Now the DeleteOutput method:

```
[CLSCompliant(false)]
public override void DeleteOutput(int outputID)
{
    throw new Exception("You cannot delete an ouput");
}
```

That concludes the code for the design-time part of your Transformation Component. Now you will move on to the runtime methods.

The first runtime method you'll be using is the PreExecute method. As mentioned earlier, this is called once in your component's life, and it is where you typically do most of your setup using the state-holding struct mentioned at the top of this section. It is the first opportunity you get to access the Buffer Manager, providing access to columns within the buffer, which you will need in ProcessInput as well. Keep in mind that you will not be getting a call to PrimeOutput, because this is a synchronous component, and PrimeOutput is not called in a synchronous component. Here is the PreExecute method in full:

```
public override void PreExecute()
{
    // Prepare array of column information. Processing requires
    // lineageID so we can do this once in advance.

    IDTSInput100 input = ComponentMetaData.InputCollection[0];
    _inputColumnInfos = new ColumnInfo[input.InputColumnCollection.Count];

    for (int x = 0; x < input.InputColumnCollection.Count; x++)
    {
        IDTSInputColumn100 column = input.InputColumnCollection[x];
        _inputColumnInfos[x] = new ColumnInfo();
        _inputColumnInfos[x].bufferColumnIndex =
            BufferManager.FindColumnByLineageID(input.Buffer, column.LineageID);
        _inputColumnInfos[x].columnDisposition = column.ErrorRowDisposition;
        _inputColumnInfos[x].lineageID = column.LineageID;
    }
}
```

The first thing this method does is get a reference to the input collection. The collection is zero-based, and because you have only one input, you have used the indexer and not the name, though you could have used the name as well.

```
IDTSInput100 input = ComponentMetaData.InputCollection[0];
```

At the start of this section was a list of the things your component would need later. This included a struct that you were told you would use in various guises, and it also included an array of these structs. You now need to size the array, which you do next by setting the size of the array to the count of columns in the InputColumnCollection for your component:

```
_inputColumnInfos = new ColumnInfo[input.InputColumnCollection.Count];
```

Now you loop through the columns in the InputColumnCollection. For each of the columns, you create a new instance of a column and a new instance of the struct:

```
IDTSInputColumn100 column = input.InputColumnCollection[x];
_inputColumnInfos[x] = new ColumnInfo();
```

You then read from the column the details you require and store them in the ColumnInfo object. The first thing you want to retrieve is the location of the column in the buffer. You cannot simply do this by the order that you added them to the buffer. Though this would probably work, it is likely to catch you out at some point. You can find the column in the buffer by the use of a method called FindColumnByLineageID on the BufferManager object. This method takes the buffer and the LineageID of the column that you wish to find as arguments:

```
_inputColumnInfos[x].bufferColumnIndex =
BufferManager.FindColumnByLineageID(input.Buffer, column.LineageID);
```

You now need only two more details about the input column: the LineageID and the ErrorRowDisposition. Remember, ErrorRowDisposition tells the component how to treat an error.

```
_inputColumnInfos[x].columnDisposition = column.ErrorRowDisposition;
_inputColumnInfos[x].lineageID = column.LineageID;
```

When you start to build your own components, you will see that this method really becomes useful. You can use it to initialize any counters you may need or to open connections to Data Sources as well as anything else you think of.

The final method you are going to be looking at for this component is ProcessInput. Remember, this is a synchronous transform as dictated in ProvideComponentProperties, and this is the method in which the data is moved and manipulated. This method contains a lot of information that will help you understand the buffer and what to do with the columns in it when you receive them. It is called once for every buffer passed.

Here is the method in full:

```
public override void ProcessInput(int inputID, PipelineBuffer buffer)
{
    int errorOutputID = -1;
    int errorOutputIndex = -1;
    int GoodOutputId = -1;

    IDTSInput100 inp = ComponentMetaData.InputCollection.GetObjectByID(inputID);

    #region Output IDs
    GetErrorOutputInfo(ref errorOutputID, ref errorOutputIndex);
    // There is an error output defined
    errorOutputID = ComponentMetaData.OutputCollection["RSErrors"].ID;
    GoodOutputId = ComponentMetaData.OutputCollection["ReverseStringOutput"].ID;
    #endregion

    while (buffer.NextRow())
    {
        // Check if we have columns to process
        if (_inputColumnInfos.Length == 0)
        {
            // We do not have to have columns. This is a Sync component so the
            // rows will flow through regardless. Could expand Validate to check
            // for columns in the InputColumnCollection
            buffer.DirectRow(GoodOutputId);
        }
        else
        {
            try
            {
                for (int x = 0; x < _inputColumnInfos.Length; x++)
                {
                    ColumnInfo columnInfo = _inputColumnInfos[x];

                    if (!buffer.IsNull(columnInfo.bufferColumnIndex))
                    {
                        // Get value as character array
                        char[] chars =
                            buffer.GetString(columnInfo.bufferColumnIndex)
                            .ToString().ToCharArray();

                        // Reverse order of characters in array
                        Array.Reverse(chars);

                        // Reassemble reversed value as string
                        string s = new string(chars);

                        // Set output value in buffer
                        buffer.SetString(columnInfo.bufferColumnIndex, s);
                    }
                }
                buffer.DirectRow(GoodOutputId);
            }
```

```
        catch(Exception ex)
        {
            switch (inp.ErrorRowDisposition)
            {
                case DTSRowDisposition.RD_RedirectRow:
                    buffer.DirectErrorRow(errorOutputID, 0, buffer.CurrentRow);
                    break;
                case DTSRowDisposition.RD_FailComponent:
                    throw new Exception("Error processing " + ex.Message);
                case DTSRowDisposition.RD_IgnoreFailure:
                    buffer.DirectRow(GoodOutputId);
                    break;
            }
        }
    }
  }
}
```

There is a lot going on in this method, so we'll break it down to make it more manageable. The first thing you want to do is find out from the component the location of the error output, as shown here:

```
int errorOutputID = -1;
int errorOutputIndex = -1;
int GoodOutputId = -1;
#region Output IDs
GetErrorOutputInfo(ref errorOutputID, ref errorOutputIndex);

errorOutputID = ComponentMetaData.OutputCollection["RSErrors"].ID;
GoodOutputId = ComponentMetaData.OutputCollection["ReverseStringOutput"].ID;
#endregion
```

The method `GetErrorOutput` returns the output ID and the Index of the error output. Remember that you defined the error output in `ProvideComponentProperties`.

Because you could have many inputs to a component, you want to isolate the input for this component. You can do that by finding the output that is passed in to the method:

```
IDTSInput100 inp = ComponentMetaData.InputCollection.GetObjectByID(inputID);
```

You need this because you want to know what to do with the row if you encounter an issue. You gave a default value for the `ErrorRowDisposition` property of the input in `ProvideComponentProperties`, but this can be overridden in the UI.

The next thing you want to do is check that the upstream buffer has not called `SetEndOfRowset`, which would mean that it has no more rows to send after the current buffer; however, the current buffer might still contain rows. You then loop through the rows in the buffer like this:

```
while (buffer.NextRow())
...
```

You then check to see if the user asked for any columns to be manipulated. Remember, this is a synchronous component, so all columns and rows are going to flow through even if you do not specify any columns for this component. Therefore, you tell the component that if there are no input columns selected, the row should be passed to the normal output. You do this by looking at the size of the array that holds the collection of `ColumnInfo` struct objects:

```
if (_inputColumnInfos.Length == 0)
{
    buffer.DirectRow(GoodOutputId);
}
```

If the length of the array is not zero, the user has asked the component to perform an operation on the column. In turn, you need to grab each of the `ColumnInfo` objects from the array so you can look at the data. Here you begin your loop through the columns, and for each column you create a new instance of the `ColumnInfo` struct:

```
for (int x = 0; x < _inputColumnInfos.Length; x++)
{
    ColumnInfo columnInfo = _inputColumnInfos[x];
...
```

You now have a reference to that column and are ready to start manipulating it. You first convert the column's data into an array of chars:

```
char[] chars =
buffer.GetString(columnInfo.bufferColumnIndex).ToString().ToCharArray();
```

The interesting part of this line is the method `GetString()` on the buffer object. It returns the string data of the column and accepts as an argument the index of the column in the buffer. This is really easy, because you stored that reference earlier in the `PreExecute` method.

Now that you have the char array, you can perform some operations on the data. In this case, you want to reverse the string. This code is not particular to SSIS, and it a trivial example of string manipulation, but you can imagine doing something more useful here such an encryption, cleaning or formatting.

```
Array.Reverse(chars);
string s = new string(chars);
```

Now you will move on to where you reassign the changed data back to the column using the `SetString()` method on the buffer:

```
buffer.SetString(columnInfo.bufferColumnIndex, s);
```

Again this method takes as one of the arguments the index of the column in the buffer. It also takes the string you want to assign to that column. You can see now why it was important to make sure that this column was read/write. If there was no error, you point the row to the good output buffer:

```
buffer.DirectRow(GoodOutputId);
```

If you encounter an error, you want to redirect this row to the correct output or alternatively throw an error. You do that in the `catch` block like this:

```
catch(Exception ex)
{
    switch (inp.ErrorRowDisposition)
    {

        case DTSRowDisposition.RD_RedirectRow:
            buffer.DirectErrorRow(errorOutputID, 0, buffer.CurrentRow);
            break;
        case DTSRowDisposition.RD_FailComponent:
            throw new Exception("Error processing " + ex.Message);
        case DTSRowDisposition.RD_IgnoreFailure:
            buffer.DirectRow(GoodOutputId);
            break;
    }
}
```

The code is pretty self-explanatory. If the input was configured by the user to redirect the row to the error output, then you do that. If it was told to either fail the component, or the user did not specify anything, then you throw an exception. Otherwise the component is asked to just ignore the errors and allow the error row to flow down the normal output.

Now how would this have looked had it been an asynchronous transform? You would get a buffer from both `PrimeOutput` and `ProcessInput`. The `ProcessInput` method would contain the data and structure that came into the component, and `PrimeOutput` would contain the structure that the component expects to pass on. The trick here is to get the data from one buffer into the other. Here is one way you can approach it.

At the class level, create a variable of type `PipelineBuffer`, something like this:

```
PipelineBuffer _pipelinebuffer;
```

Now in `PrimeOutput`, assign the output buffer to this buffer:

```
public override void PrimeOutput(int outputs, int[] outputIDs, PipelineBuffer[]
buffers)
{
    _pipelinebuffer = buffers[0];
}
```

You now have a cached version of the buffer from `PrimeOutput`, and you can go straight over to `ProcessInput` and use it. Books Online has a great example of doing this in an asynchronous component: navigate to "asynchronous outputs."

> *Do not be afraid to look through Books Online. Microsoft has done a fantastic job of including content that helps with good, solid examples. Also search for the SSIS component samples on* msdn.microsoft.com.

Building the Destination Adapter

The requirement for the Destination adapter is that it accepts an input from an upstream component of any description and converts it to a format similar to that seen in the Source adapter. The component will use a FILE Connection Manager, and as you have seen in earlier components, this involves a significant amount of validation. You also need to validate whether the component is structurally correct, and if it isn't, you need to correct things. The first thing you always need to do is declare some variables that will be used throughout the component. You also need to create the very valuable state-information struct that is going to store the details of the columns, which will be needed in PreExecute and ProcessInput.

```
#region Variables
private ArrayList _columnInfos = new ArrayList();
private Microsoft.SqlServer.Dts.Runtime.DTSFileConnectionUsageType _fil;
private string _filename;
FileStream _fs;
StreamWriter _sw;
#endregion
```

You should quickly run through the meaning of these variables and when they will be needed. The _columnInfos variable will be used to store ColumnInfo objects, which describe the columns in the InputColumnCollection. The _fil variable will be used to validate the type of FILE Connection Manager the user has assigned to your component. _filename stores the name of the file that is retrieved from the FILE Connection Manager. The final two variables, _fs and _sw, are used when you write to the text file in ProcessInput. Now take a look at the ColumnInfo struct:

```
#region ColumnInfo
private struct ColumnInfo
{
    public int BufferColumnIndex;
    public string ColumnName;
}
#endregion
```

The struct will be used to store the index number of the column in the buffer and also to store the name of the column.

You will now move on to looking at the ProvideComponentProperties method, which is where you set up the component and prepare it for use by an SSIS package, as in the other two components. Here's the method in full:

```
public override void ProvideComponentProperties()
{
    ComponentMetaData.RuntimeConnectionCollection.RemoveAll();
    RemoveAllInputsOutputsAndCustomProperties();

    ComponentMetaData.Name = "Professional SSIS Destination Adapter";
    ComponentMetaData.Description = "Our first Destination Adapter";
    ComponentMetaData.ContactInfo = "www.Konesans.com";

    IDTSRuntimeConnection100 rtc =
                ComponentMetaData.RuntimeConnectionCollection.New();
    rtc.Name = "File To Write";
```

```
        rtc.Description = "This is the file to which we want to write";

        IDTSInput100 input = ComponentMetaData.InputCollection.New();
        input.Name = "Component Input";
        input.Description = "This is what we see from the upstream component";
        input.HasSideEffects = true;
    }
```

The first part of the method gets rid of any runtime Connection Managers that the component may have and removes any custom properties, inputs, and outputs that the component has. This makes the component a clean slate to which you can now add back anything it may need.

```
ComponentMetaData.RuntimeConnectionCollection.RemoveAll();
RemoveAllInputsOutputsAndCustomProperties();
```

The component requires one connection, as defined as follows:

```
IDTSRuntimeConnection100 rtc = ComponentMetaData.RuntimeConnectionCollection.New();
rtc.Name = "File To Write";
rtc.Description = "This is the file to which we want to write";
```

This piece of code gives the user the opportunity to specify a Connection Manager for the component. This will be the file to which you write the data from upstream.

```
IDTSInput100 input = ComponentMetaData.InputCollection.New();
input.Name = "Component Input";
input.Description = "This is what we see from the upstream component";
```

The next thing you do is add back the input. This is what the upstream component will connect to, and through which you will receive the data from the previous component. Now you need to make sure that the IDTSInput100 object of the component remains in the execution plan, regardless of whether it is attached, by making the HasSideEffects property true. What this means is that at runtime the SSIS execution engine is smart enough to "prune" components from the package that are not actually doing any work. You need to explicitly tell SSIS that this component is doing work (external file writes) by setting this property.

```
input.HasSideEffects = true;
```

Having finished with the ProvideComponentProperties method, you now move on to the AcquireConnections method. This method is not really any different from the AcquireConnections method you saw in the Source adapter; the method is shown in full but is not described in detail. If you need to get the line-by-line details of what's happening, you can look back to the Source adapter. The tasks this method accomplishes are the following:

❑   Check that the user has supplied a Connection Manager to the component.

❑   Check that the Connection Manager is a FILE Connection Manager.

❑   Make sure that the FILE Connection Manager has a FileUsageType property value of DTSFileConnectionUsageType.CreateFile. (This is different from the Source, which required an existing file.)

❑   Get the filename from the Connection Manager.

```
public override void AcquireConnections(object transaction)
{
    bool pbCancel = false;

    if (ComponentMetaData.RuntimeConnectionCollection["File To
Write"].ConnectionManager != null)
    {
        ConnectionManager cm =
                Microsoft.SqlServer.Dts.Runtime.DtsConvert.GetWrapper(
                ComponentMetaData.RuntimeConnectionCollection["File To Write"]
                .ConnectionManager);

        if (cm.CreationName != "FILE")
        {
            ComponentMetaData.FireError(0, "Acquire Connections", "The Connection
                Manager is not a FILE Connection Manager", "", 0, out pbCancel);
            throw new Exception("The Connection Manager is not a FILE Connection
                            Manager");
        }
        else
        {
            _fil = (DTSFileConnectionUsageType)cm.Properties["FileUsageType"]
                    .GetValue(cm);

            if (_fil != DTSFileConnectionUsageType.CreateFile)
            {
                ComponentMetaData.FireError(0, "Acquire Connections",
                    "The type of FILE connection manager must be Create File", "",
                    0, out pbCancel);
                throw new Exception("The type of FILE connection manager must be
                                Create File");

            }
            else
            {
                _filename = ComponentMetaData.RuntimeConnectionCollection
                    ["File To Read"].ConnectionManager.AcquireConnection(transaction)
                    .ToString();

                if (_filename == null || _filename.Length == 0)
                {
                    ComponentMetaData.FireError(0, "Acquire Connections", "Nothing
                        returned when grabbing the filename", "", 0, out pbCancel);
                    throw new Exception("Nothing returned when grabbing the filename");
                }
            }
        }
    }
}
```

There is a lot of ground covered in the AcquireConnections method. A lot of this code is covered again in the Validate method, which you will visit now. The Validate method is also concerned that the input to the component is correct, and if it isn't, you'll try to fix what is wrong by calling ReinitializeMetaData. Here is the Validate method:

```
[CLSCompliant(false)]
public override DTSValidationStatus Validate()
{
    bool pbCancel = false;

    if (ComponentMetaData.OutputCollection.Count != 0)
    {
        ComponentMetaData.FireError(0, ComponentMetaData.Name, "Unexpected Output
                    Found. Destination components do not support outputs.", "",
                    0, out pbCancel);
        return DTSValidationStatus.VS_ISCORRUPT;
    }

    if (ComponentMetaData.RuntimeConnectionCollection["File To Write"]
            .ConnectionManager == null)
    {
        ComponentMetaData.FireError(0, "Validate", "No Connection Manager returned",
                            "", 0, out pbCancel);
        return DTSValidationStatus.VS_ISCORRUPT;
    }

    if (ComponentMetaData.AreInputColumnsValid == false)
    {
        ComponentMetaData.InputCollection["Component Input"]
                    .InputColumnCollection.RemoveAll();
        return DTSValidationStatus.VS_NEEDSNEWMETADATA;
    }

    return base.Validate();
}
```

The first check you do in the method is to make sure that the component has no outputs:

```
bool pbCancel = false;

if (ComponentMetaData.OutputCollection.Count != 0)
{
    ComponentMetaData.FireError(0, ComponentMetaData.Name, "Unexpected Output found.
            Destination components do not support outputs.", "", 0, out pbCancel);
    return DTSValidationStatus.VS_ISCORRUPT;
}
```

You now want to check to make sure the user specified a Connection Manager. Remember that you are only validating the fact that a Connection Manager is specified, not whether it is a valid type. The extensive checking of the Connection Manager is done in `AcquireConnections()`.

```
if (ComponentMetaData.RuntimeConnectionCollection["File To
Write"].ConnectionManager == null)
{
    ComponentMetaData.FireError(0, "Validate", "No Connection Manager returned", "",
                        0, out pbCancel);
    return DTSValidationStatus.VS_ISCORRUPT;
}
```

The final thing you do in this method is to check that the input columns are valid. *Valid* in this instance means that the columns in the input collection reference existing columns in the upstream component. If this is not the case, you call the trusty `ReinitializeMetaData` method.

```
if (ComponentMetaData.AreInputColumnsValid == false)
{
    ComponentMetaData.InputCollection["Component Input"]
                .InputColumnCollection.RemoveAll();
    return DTSValidationStatus.VS_NEEDSNEWMETADATA;
}
```

The return value `DTSValidationStatus.VS_NEEDSNEWMETADATA` means that the component will now call `ReinitializeMetaData` to try to sort out the problems with the component. Here is that method in full:

```
public override void ReinitializeMetaData()
{
    IDTSInput100 _profinput = ComponentMetaData.InputCollection["Component Input"];
    _profinput.InputColumnCollection.RemoveAll();
    IDTSVirtualInput100 vInput = _profinput.GetVirtualInput();
    foreach (IDTSVirtualInputColumn100 vCol in vInput.VirtualInputColumnCollection)
    {
        this.SetUsageType(_profinput.ID, vInput, vCol.LineageID,
                    DTSUsageType.UT_READONLY);

    }
}
```

You will notice that the columns are blown away in `ReinitializeMetaData` *and built again from scratch. A better solution is to test what the invalid columns are and try to fix them. If you cannot fix them, you could remove them, and then the user could reselect at leisure. Books Online has an example of doing this.*

The `IDTSVirtualInput` and `IDTSVirtualInputColumnCollection` in this component need a little explanation. There is a subtle difference between these two objects and their input equivalents. The "virtual" objects are what your component could have as inputs — that is to say, they are upstream inputs and columns that present themselves as available to your component. The inputs themselves are what you have chosen for your component to have as inputs from the virtual object. In the `Reinitialize` method, you start by removing all existing input columns:

```
IDTSInput100 _profinput = ComponentMetaData.InputCollection["Component Input"];
_profinput.InputColumnCollection.RemoveAll();
```

You then get a reference to the input's virtual input:

```
IDTSVirtualInput100 vInput = _profinput.GetVirtualInput();
```

Now that you have the virtual input, you can add an input column to the component for every virtual input column you find:

```
foreach (IDTSVirtualInputColumn100 vCol in vInput.VirtualInputColumnCollection)
{
    this.SetUsageType(_profinput.ID, vInput, vCol.LineageID,
                      DTSUsageType.UT_READONLY);
}
```

The `SetUsageType` method simply adds an input column to the input column collection of the component, or removes it depending on what your UsageType value is. When a user adds a connector from an upstream component that contains its output to this component and attaches it to this component's input, then the `OnInputAttached` is called. This method has been overridden in the component herein:

```
public override void OnInputPathAttached(int inputID)
{
    IDTSInput100 input = ComponentMetaData.InputCollection.GetObjectByID(inputID);
    IDTSVirtualInput100 vInput = input.GetVirtualInput();
    foreach (IDTSVirtualInputColumn100 vCol in vInput.VirtualInputColumnCollection)
    {
        this.SetUsageType(inputID, vInput, vCol.LineageID, DTSUsageType.UT_READONLY);
    }
}
```

This method is the same as the `ReinitializeMetaData` method except that you do not need to remove the input columns from the collection. This is because if the input is not mapped to the output of an upstream component, there can be no input columns.

You have now finished with the design-time methods for your component and can now move on to look at the runtime methods. You are going to be looking at only two methods: `PreExecute` and `ProcessInput`.

`PreExecute` is executed once and once only in this component, so you want to do as much preparation work as you can in this method. It is also the first opportunity in the component to access the Buffer Manager, which contains the columns. In this component, you use it for two things: getting the information about the component's input columns and storing essential details about them.

```
public override void PreExecute()
{
    IDTSInput100 input = ComponentMetaData.InputCollection["Component Input"];

    foreach (IDTSInputColumn100 inCol in input.InputColumnCollection)
    {
        ColumnInfo ci = new ColumnInfo();
        ci.BufferColumnIndex = BufferManager.FindColumnByLineageID(input.Buffer,
                                   inCol.LineageID);
        ci.ColumnName = inCol.Name;
        _columnInfos.Add(ci);
    }

    // Open the file
    _fs = new FileStream(_filename, FileMode.OpenOrCreate, FileAccess.Write);
    _sw = new StreamWriter(_fs);
}
```

First, you get a reference to the component's input:

```
IDTSInput100 input = ComponentMetaData.InputCollection["Component Input"];
```

You now loop through the input's `InputColumnCollection`:

```
foreach (IDTSInputColumn100 inCol in input.InputColumnCollection)
{
```

For each input column you find, you need to create a new instance of the `ColumnInfo` struct. You then assign to the struct, values you can retrieve from the input column itself, as well as the Buffer Manager. You assign these values to the struct and finally add them to the array that is holding all the `ColumnInfo` objects:

```
ColumnInfo ci = new ColumnInfo();
ci.BufferColumnIndex = BufferManager.FindColumnByLineageID(input.Buffer,
                       inCol.LineageID);
ci.ColumnName = inCol.Name;
_columnInfos.Add(ci);
```

Doing things this way will allow you to move more quickly through the `ProcessInput` method. The last thing you do in the `PreExecute` method is to get a reference to the file you want to write to:

```
_fs = new FileStream(_filename, FileMode.OpenOrCreate, FileAccess.Write);
_sw = new StreamWriter(_fs);
```

You will use this in the next method, `ProcessInput`. `ProcessInput` is where you are going to keep reading the rows that are coming from the upstream component. While there are rows, you will write those values to a file. This is a very simplistic view of what needs to be done, so you should have a look at how to make that happen.

```
public override void ProcessInput(int inputID, PipelineBuffer buffer)
{
    while (buffer.NextRow())
    {
        _sw.WriteLine("<START>");
        for (int i = 0; i < _columnInfos.Count; i++)
        {
            ColumnInfo ci = (ColumnInfo)_columnInfos[i];

            if (buffer.IsNull(ci.BufferColumnIndex))
            {
                _sw.WriteLine(ci.ColumnName + ":");
            }
            else
            {
                _sw.WriteLine(ci.ColumnName + ":" +
                    buffer[ci.BufferColumnIndex].ToString());
            }
        }
        _sw.WriteLine("<END>");
    }
    if (buffer.EndOfRowset) _sw.Close();
}
```

The first thing you do is check that there are still rows in the buffer:

```
while (buffer.NextRow())
{
...
```

You now need to loop through the array that is holding the collection of ColumnInfo objects that were populated in the preExecute method:

```
for (int i = 0; i < _columnInfos.Count; i++)
```

For each iteration, you create a new instance of the ColumnInfo object:

```
ColumnInfo ci = (ColumnInfo)_columnInfos[i];
```

You now need to retrieve from the buffer object the value of the column whose index you will pass in from the ColumnInfo object. If the value is not null, you write the value of the column and the column name to the text file. If the value is null, you write just the column name to the text file. Again, because you took the time to store these details in a ColumnInfo object earlier, the retrieval of these properties is easy.

```
if (buffer.IsNull(ci.BufferColumnIndex))
{
    _sw.WriteLine(ci.ColumnName + ":");
}
else
{
    _sw.WriteLine(ci.ColumnName + ":" + buffer[ci.BufferColumnIndex].ToString());
}
```

Finally you check if the upstream component has called SetEndOfRowset; if so, you close the file stream:

```
if (buffer.EndOfRowset) _sw.Close();
```

That concludes your look at the Destination adapter. You are now going to look at how you get SSIS to recognize your components and what properties you need to assign to your components.

Using the Components

In this section you install the components you have created into the SSIS design environment so you can use them to build packages. You then learn how to debug the components so you can troubleshoot any coding issues in them.

Installing the Components

To add a component to the SSIS Toolbox, open BIDS and then create or open an SSIS solution. Create a new Data Flow Task and then double-click it in order to enter the Data Flow panel. Right-click on the Toolbox and select Choose Items from the context menu. When the Choose Toolbox Items dialog box appears, click the SSIS Data Flow Items tab and scroll down until you see the component. Check your new component and click OK. When you go back to the Toolbox, you should see your new component.

Debugging Components

Debugging components is a really great feature of SSIS. If you are a Visual Studio .NET developer, you should easily recognize the interface. If you're not familiar with Visual Studio, hopefully this section will allow you to become proficient in debugging your components.

There are two phases for debugging. The design-time can be debugged only while you're developing your package, so it makes sense that you will need to use BIDS to do this. The second experience, which is the runtime experience, is slightly different. You can still use BIDS, though, and when your package runs, the component will stop at breakpoints you designate. You need to set up a few things first, though. You can also use DTExec to fire the package straight from Visual Studio. The latter method saves you the cost of invoking another instance of Visual Studio.

The component you are going to debug is the Reverse String Transform.

Design-Time

You will now jump straight in and start to debug the component at design-time. Open the Visual Studio Reverse String C# project and set a C# breakpoint at ProvideComponentProperties (SSIS also has breakpoints, they are discussed further in Chapter 17). Now create a new SSIS project in BIDS. In the package, add a Data Flow Task and double-click it. If your component is not in the Toolbox already, add it now.

You need to create a full pipeline in this package because you'll be using it later on when you debug the runtime, so get an OLE DB or ADO.NET Connection Manager and point it to the AdventureWorks2008 database. Now add an OLE DB or ADO.NET Source adapter to the design surface and configure it to use the Connection Manager you just created. Point the source to one of the tables in AdventureWorks2008 — perhaps Person.Person — and select the columns you want to use.

It's now time to add your new components to the designer. However, before you do that, you need to tell the component's design project to attach to the devenv.exe process you're working in, so that it can receive the component's methods being fired. The way you do that is as follows. In the Visual Studio Reverse String C# project, select Debug ⇨ Attach to Process. The Attach to Process dialog box opens (see Figure 18-7), which allows you to choose what you want to debug as well as which process.

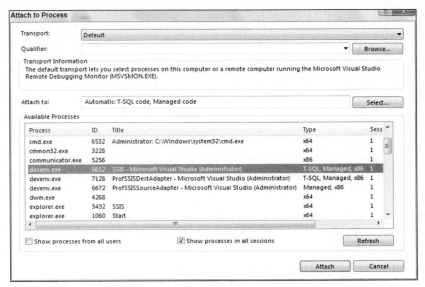

Figure 18-7

The process you're interested in is the package you're currently building. This shows up in the Available Processes list as Integration Services Project 1 – Microsoft Visual Studio (the name you see may differ). You can see just above this window a small box containing the words "Managed Code." This tells the debugger what you want to debug in the component. There are a number of options available, and if you click the Select button to the right of the label, you'll be able to see them. They are Managed, Native, and Script.

Highlight the process for your package and click Attach. If you look down now at the status bar in your component's design project, you should see a variety of debug symbols being loaded. Go back to the SSIS package and drop the ReverseString Transform onto the design surface. Because one of the very first things a component does when it gets dropped into a package is call `ProvideComponentProperties`, you should immediately see your component break into the code in its design project, as shown in Figure 18-8.

```
    Ctor

    #region Design Time

    #region ProvideComponentProperties
    public override void ProvideComponentProperties()
    {
        // Perform component setup operations
        ComponentMetaData.RuntimeConnectionCollection.RemoveAll();
        RemoveAllInputsOutputsAndCustomProperties();

        ComponentMetaData.UsesDispositions = true;

        // Add Input
        IDTSInput100 input = ComponentMetaData.InputCollection.New();
        input.Name = "ReverseStringInput";
        input.ErrorRowDisposition = DTSRowDisposition.RD_FailComponent;

        // Add Output
        IDTSOutput100 output = ComponentMetaData.OutputCollection.New();
        output.Name = "ReverseStringOutput";
        output.SynchronousInputID = input.ID; // (Synchronous Transform)
        output.ExclusionGroup = 1;
```

Figure 18-8

As you can see, the breakpoint on `ProvideComponentProperties` in the component's design project has been hit. This is indicated by a yellow arrow inside the breakpoint red circle. You are now free to debug the component as you would with any other piece of managed code in Visual Studio.NET. If you're familiar with debugging, a number of windows appear at this point at the bottom of the IDE, things like "Locals," "Autos," and "Call Stack." These can help you get to the root of any debugging problems, but you do not need to use them now.

To leave debugging mode, go back into Visual Studio and on the menu choose Debug ⇨ Stop Debugging.

Building the Complete Package

Since the package already has a source and Transformation Component on it, you just need to add a destination. First make sure you have configured the ReverseString Transform to reverse some of the columns by double-clicking it and selected the required columns in the custom UI (or the Advanced UI if you have not built the custom UI yet, which is discussed in Chapter 19).

In the SSIS Connections pane, create a new File Connection Manager, setting the Usage Type to Create File. Enter a filename in a location of your choice, and then close the Connection Manager dialog.

Drop the Destination Component you have just built onto the design surface and connect the output of the ReverseString Transform to the input of the destination. Open the destination's editor and on the first tab of the Advanced Editor, set the "File to Write" property value to the name of the connection you just created. Flip over to the Input Columns tab in the editor, and select which columns you want to write to the output file.

Runtime Debugging

As promised, in this section you are going to look at two ways of debugging. As with design-time debugging, the first is through the BIDS designer. The other is by using DTExec and the package properties. Using BIDS is similar to the design-time method with a subtle variation.

You should now have a complete pipeline with the ReverseString Transform in the middle. If you don't, quickly make up a pipeline like in Figure 18-9.

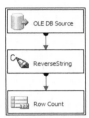

Figure 18-9

Instead of a real destination that writes to a file or database, it is often useful to write to a so-called trash destination. You can use a Row Count Transformation or Union All Transformation for this purpose.

You then need to add a breakpoint to the Data Flow Task that is hit when the Data Flow Task hits the OnPreExecute event. You need to do this so that you can attach your debugger to the correct process at runtime. Right-click the Data Flow Task itself and select Edit Breakpoints. The Set Breakpoints dialog box will appear, as shown in Figure 18-10.

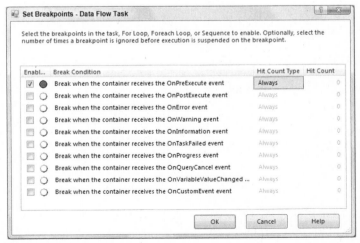

Figure 18-10

You are now ready to execute your package. Press F5 to start executing the SSIS package, and allow the breakpoint in the Data Flow Task to be hit. When you hit the breakpoint, switch back to the component's design process and follow the steps detailed earlier when debugging the design-time in order to get to the screen where you chose what process to debug.

When you execute a package in the designer, it is not really the designer that is doing the work. It hands off the execution to a process called DtsDebugHost.exe. This is the package that you want to attach to, as shown in Figure 18-11. You will probably see two of these processes listed, the one you want has "Managed" listed under the Type column (don't attach to the process showing "x86" as the Type).

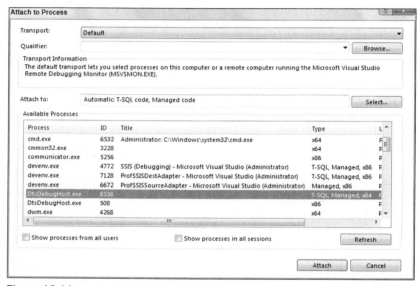

Figure 18-11

Click Attach and watch the debug symbols being loaded by the project. Before returning to the SSIS package, you need to set a breakpoint on one of the runtime methods used by your component, such as PreExecute. Now return to the SSIS project and press F5 again. This will release the package from its suspended state and allow the package to flow on. Now when the ReverseString Component hits its PreExecute method, you should be able to debug what it is doing. In Figure 18-12, the user is checking to make sure that the LineageID of a column is being retrieved correctly and is ready to be used in the ProcessInput method that follows.

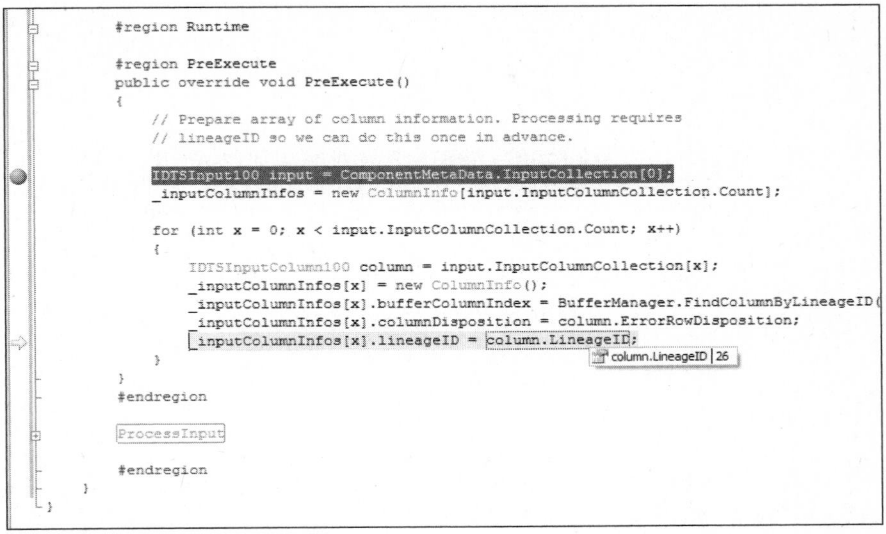
#region Runtime
#region PreExecute
public override void PreExecute()
{
// Prepare array of column information. Processing requires
// lineageID so we can do this once in advance.
IDTSInput100 input = ComponentMetaData.InputCollection[0];
_inputColumnInfos = new ColumnInfo[input.InputColumnCollection.Count];
for (int x = 0; x < input.InputColumnCollection.Count; x++)
{
IDTSInputColumn100 column = input.InputColumnCollection[x];
_inputColumnInfos[x] = new ColumnInfo();
_inputColumnInfos[x].bufferColumnIndex = BufferManager.FindColumnByLineageID(
_inputColumnInfos[x].columnDisposition = column.ErrorRowDisposition;
_inputColumnInfos[x].lineageID = column.LineageID;
column.LineageID | 26
}
}
#endregion
ProcessInput
#endregion
}
}

Figure 18-12

That concludes your look at the first method for debugging the runtime. The second method involves BIDS indirectly because you need to create a package like this one that you can call later. After that, you do not need BIDS at all. You do, however, still need the component's design project open. Open your Visual Studio Reverse String C# project's properties and look at the Debug tab on the left, which should look similar to Figure 18-13.

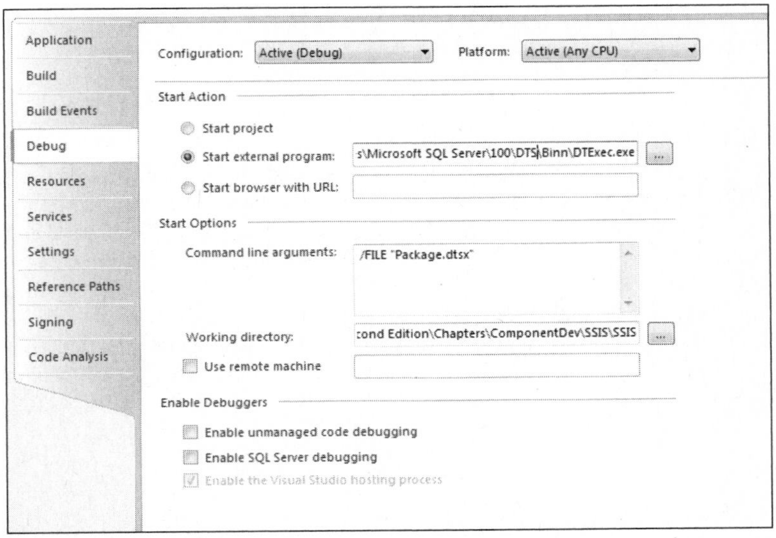
Application
Build
Build Events
Debug
Resources
Services
Settings
Reference Paths
Signing
Code Analysis
Configuration: Active (Debug)
Platform: Active (Any CPU)
Start Action
Start project
Start external program: s\Microsoft SQL Server\100\DTS\Binn\DTExec.exe
Start browser with URL:
Start Options
Command line arguments: /FILE "Package.dtsx"
Working directory: cond Edition\Chapters\ComponentDev\SSIS\SSIS
Use remote machine
Enable Debuggers
Enable unmanaged code debugging
Enable SQL Server debugging
Enable the Visual Studio hosting process

Figure 18-13

As you can see, you have said that you want to start an external program to debug. That program is DTExec, which is the new and more powerful version of DTSRun. On the command line, you will pass a parameter /FILE to DTExec. This tells DTExec the name and location of the package you just built. Make sure the file path to your package is valid. Make sure you still have a C# breakpoint set on PreExecute, and press F5 in your project. A DOS window will appear and you will see some messages fly past, which are the same messages you would see in the designer. Eventually you will get to your breakpoint, and it will break in exactly the same way as it did when you were using BIDS. So, why might you use one over the other? The most obvious answer is speed. It is much faster to get to where you want to debug your component using DTExec than it is doing the same in BIDS. The other advantage is that you do not need to have two tools open at the same time. You can focus on your component's design project and not have to worry about BIDS at all.

Upgrading to SQL 2008

If you already built components in SQL 2005 and you want to use them in SQL 2008, you will have to update the code and recompile them. This is because Microsoft updated the interface names and some of the underlying functionality. However, this is not a difficult problem — simply open your old project in Visual Studio 2005 or Visual Studio 2008 and do a search and replace to rename the interfaces from IDTS*90 to IDTS*100. There are also one or two methods that have changed; however, the compiler will warn you of any problems.

You will also have to update the project references. In the Solution Explorer, open the References Node and delete any references showing an error icon. Add back the references discussed earlier in this chapter (such as Microsoft.SqlServer.DTSPipelineWrap), making sure to select the ones marked as version 10.0 (SQL Server 2008), not the ones marked version 9.0 (SQL Server 2005).

Everything should now compile, and you should be able to run your components in the SQL 2008 BIDS environment.

Summary

In this chapter, you have built Pipeline Components. Although designing your own components isn't exactly like falling off a log, once you get a handle on what methods do what, when they are called, and what you can possibly use them for, you can certainly create new components with only a moderate amount of knowledge in programming. Once you have the basic patterns right, it is simple to develop your second, third, and tenth components. The components you have designed are certainly very simple in nature, but hopefully this chapter will give you the confidence to experiment with some of your own unique requirements. In Chapter 19, you learn how to create custom user interfaces for your components. While this is not a necessary step (since SSIS provides a default UI for custom components) it can make your components more user-friendly, especially if they are tricky to configure.

19

Adding a User Interface to Your Component

Now that you've learned how to extend the pipeline with your own custom components, the next step is to improve the user experience and efficiency, by adding a user interface. This will be demonstrated using the ReverseString example from the previous chapter.

Pipeline Components do not require the developer to provide a user interface, because the components ship with a default interface called the Advanced Editor. Although this saves time and resources, the overall user experience can be poor. It can increase the package development time and requires the user to have an intimate knowledge of the component to be able to correctly set the required columns and properties. It is also dangerous and open to data integrity problems, because the more complex the configuration required, the more acute the lack of suitable prompts and real-time validation becomes, making configuration tedious and error-prone. For complex components with multiple inputs, the Advanced Editor will not be suitable. For simple components, however, the built-in Advanced Editor, as used by several stock components, is perfectly acceptable. If you want to add that extra style and guidance for the end user, though, this chapter is for you.

You will learn how to add a user interface to a component and look in detail at each of the stages. You will then be able to apply these techniques to your own components. It is worth noting that this chapter deals exclusively with managed components.

Three Key Steps

There are three steps in adding a user interface (UI) to any component, and each will be examined in detail. However, it is essential that you build the actual component first; get the functionality working properly, iron out any problems, tweak the performance, and make sure it installs properly. Once those core tasks are complete, you can add the polish to the solution by designing the UI. If you try to build anything other than a simple UI at the same time you are building the component, you may find it creates overhead in keeping the two projects working well in tandem.

With that said, here's a summary of each of the three key UI steps.

The first step is to add a class that implements the IDtsComponentUI interface. This defines the methods needed for the designer to interact with your user interface class. This class is not the visible UI itself; rather it provides a way for the designer to ask for what it needs when it needs it, as well as exposing several methods that allow you to hook into the life cycle of your UI. For example, you have a New method, which is called when a component is first added to a package, and an Edit method, called when you open an existing component inside your package. The interface will be expanded on in the following paragraphs.

The second step is to actually build the visible interface, normally a Windows Form. The form is invoked from the IDtsComponentUI.Edit method, and by customizing the constructor, you can pass through references to the base component and supporting services. The form then displays details such as component properties or data-handling options including inputs, outputs, and columns within each.

The final stage is to update the component itself to tell the designer that you have provided a user interface and where to find it, or specifically where to find the IDtsComponentUI implementation. You do this through the UITypeName property of the DtsPipelineComponent attribute, which decorates the component, your existing PipelineComponent inheriting class. The UITypeName is the fully qualified name of the class implementing your user interface, allowing the designer to find the assembly and class to invoke the user interface when required through the interface methods mentioned previously.

In summary, you need a known interface with which the designer can interact, and a form that you display to the user through the relevant interface method, and the component needs to advertise that it has a user interface and offer instructions of where to find the UI when required.

Building the User Interface

Now that the key stages have been explained, you can examine each of them in detail. This guidance makes very few assumptions, explaining all the actions required; so as long as you can open Visual Studio on your own, you should be able to follow these steps, and perhaps, more importantly, understand why.

Adding the Project

If you followed the example in the previous chapter, you currently have an existing solution in Visual Studio 2008 that contains the Pipeline Component project (ReverseString). Therefore, your first step is to add a new Class Library project to host the UI, as shown in Figure 19-1. Although the UI can be implemented within the Pipeline Component project, for performance reasons this is not the recommended approach. Because SSIS has distinct runtime versus design-time elements, the combination of the two functions leads to a larger assembly, which requires more memory and consequently lower runtime performance. When you deploy your components in production, the component UI would never be shown, so it is important that your components can operate without a UI. To support this use, the core component code should not have any dependencies on UI code. The separate-project design practice also allows for easier code development and maintenance, reducing confusion and conflicts within the areas of code.

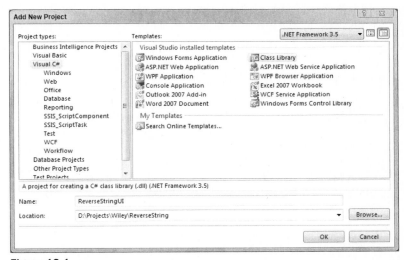

Figure 19-1

Starting with the empty project, the first task is to configure any project properties, so you need to set the Assembly Name and Default Namespace to be consistent with your development practices, as shown in Figure 19-2.

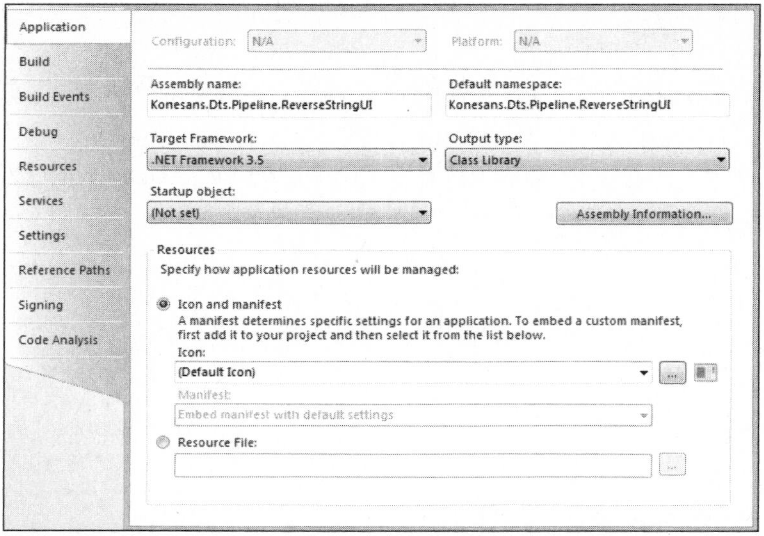

Figure 19-2

The user interface assembly does not need to be placed in a defined location like tasks and components (`%Program Files%\Microsoft SQL Server\100\DTS\PipelineComponents` or `%Program Files%\Microsoft SQL Server\100\DTS\Tasks`), but it does need to be installed within the global assembly cache (GAC). So within the project properties, you can leave the build output path location as the default value, but for ease of development you can add a post-build event command on the Build Events page, as shown in Figure 19-3. Refer to Chapter 18 for more details on what this command should look like.

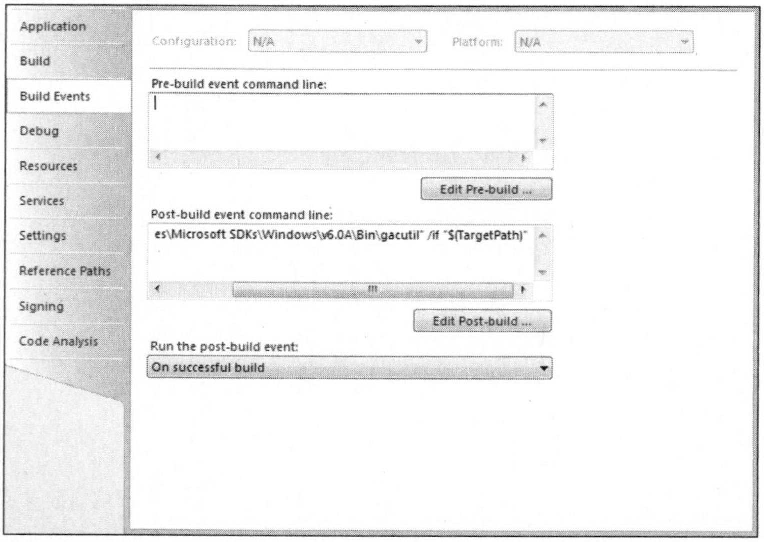

Figure 19-3

Because the assembly will be installed in the GAC, you will need to sign the assembly using a strong name key, which can be configured from the Signing page, as shown in Figure 19-4. For more information about strong names and their importance in .NET, see "Security Briefs: Strong Names and Security in the .NET Framework":

```
http://msdn.microsoft.com/en-us/library/aa302416.aspx
```

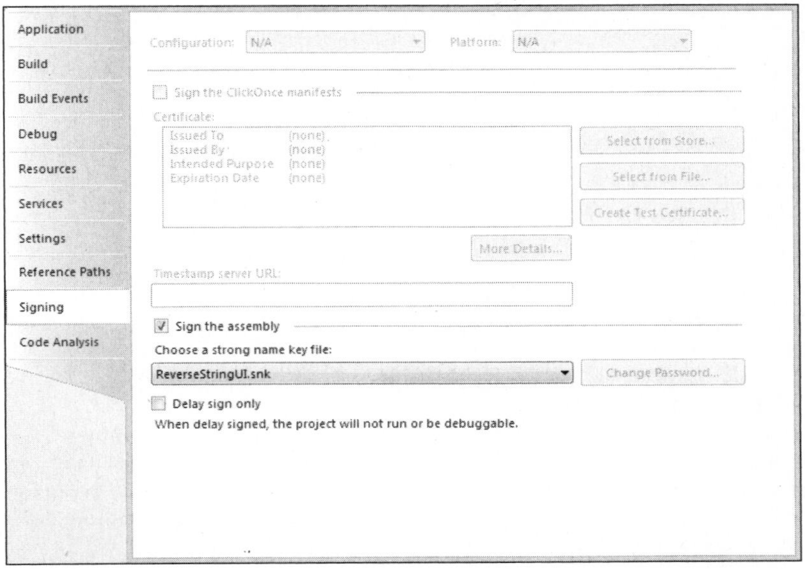

Figure 19-4

Although most assembly attributes can now be set through the Assembly Information dialog box accessed from the Application page of Project Properties, you still next need to manually edit AssemblyInfo.cs, adding the CLSCompliant attribute, as described in Chapter 18 and as shown here:

```
#region Using directives
using System;
using System.Security.Permissions;
using System.Reflection;
using System.Runtime.CompilerServices;
using System.Runtime.InteropServices;
#endregion

[assembly: AssemblyTitle("ReverseStringUI")]
[assembly: AssemblyDescription("Reversing String Transformation UI for SQL Server
Integration Services")]
[assembly: AssemblyConfiguration("")]
[assembly: AssemblyProduct("Reverse String Transformation")]
[assembly: AssemblyTrademark("")]
[assembly: AssemblyCulture("")]
```

```
[assembly: AssemblyVersion("2.0.0.0")]
[assembly: AssemblyFileVersion("2.0.0.0")]
[assembly: CLSCompliant(true)]
[assembly: PermissionSet(SecurityAction.RequestMinimum)]
[assembly: ComVisible(false)]
```

The AssemblyVersion *will form part of the* UITypeName *property described later in the chapter; therefore, it is important that this is not allowed to auto-increment using the * token, because this will break the linkage between the component and its user interface.*

You also require a Windows Form to actually display your component's interface to the user in addition to the default class you have in your project, so one can be added at this stage.

The final preparatory task is to add some additional references to your project. The recommended three are listed here:

❑ Microsoft.SqlServer.Dts.Design

❑ Microsoft.SqlServer.DTSPipelineWrap

❑ Microsoft.SQLServer.ManagedDTS

Implementing IDtsComponentUI

You now have the empty framework for the UI assembly, and you can start coding. The first step is to implement the Microsoft.SqlServer.Dts.Pipeline.Design IDtsComponentUI interface. Using the default class in the project, you can add the interface declaration and take advantage of the new Visual Studio context menu features, as well as use the Implement Interface command to quickly generate the five method stubs, saving you from manually typing them out.

The methods are documented in detail in the following sections; however, it is useful to understand the scenarios in which each method is called, highlighting how the Initialize method is usually called before the real action method:

❑ **Adding a new component to the package:**

    ❑ Initialize

    ❑ New

❑ **Editing the component, either through a double-click or by selecting Edit from the context menu:**

    ❑ Initialize

    ❑ Edit

❑ **Deleting the component, through the Delete key or by selecting Delete from the context menu:**

    ❑ Delete

You will now look at the methods in more detail and examine how they are implemented in the example.

IDtsComponentUI.Delete

The `Delete` method is called when a component is deleted from the SSIS designer. It allows you to perform any cleaning operations that may be required or warn users of the consequences. This is not normally required, because the consequences should be fairly obvious, but the opportunity is available.

For this example, simply remove the placeholder exception, leaving an empty method.

IDtsComponentUI.Help

The `Help` method has not been implemented in SQL Server 2008. For this example, simply remove the placeholder exception. The method will not be called, but this should prevent any surprises in case of a service pack introducing the functionality, although this is unlikely.

IDtsComponentUI.New

The `New` method is called when a component is first added to your package through the SSIS designer. Use this method to display a user interface specific to configuring the component for the first time, such as a wizard to help configure the component, or an option dialog box that gathers some information that will influence the overall use of the component. The Script Transformation uses this method to display a dialog box asking you to specify the type, source, destination, or transformation.

The `New` method is not widely used, because configuration of the component usually requires you to have wired up the Data Flow paths for the component. In addition, most people start by laying out the package and adding most or all of the components together, allowing them to visualize and validate their overall Data Flow design, before configuring each component in detail, but in specialized circumstances you have this option.

For this example, simply remove the placeholder exception, leaving an empty method.

IDtsComponentUI.Initialize

`Initialize` is the first method to be called when adding or editing a component, and although you do not actually perform any actions at this stage, the parameters provided are normally stored in private member variables for later use. At a minimum, you will store the `IDTSComponentMetaData100` reference, because a UI will always need to interact with the underlying component, and this is done through the `IDTSComponentMetaData100` reference.

For components that use connections or variables, you would also store a reference to `IServiceProvider`. This allows you to access useful services, like the connection service (`IDtsConnectionService`) and the variable service (`IDtsVariableService`). These designer services allow you to create new connections and variables, respectively. For connections, the service will invoke the Connection Manager user interface, provided by the connection author, and for variables you use the dialog box built into the SSIS designer. This is a good example of how Microsoft has made life easier for component developers, offering access to these services, saving you time and effort. There are two other services available, the `IErrorCollectionService` for retrieving error and warning event messages, and `IDtsClipboardService`, which allows component developers to determine if a component was created by a copy-and-paste operation.

In the ReverseString example, these services are not required, but you would follow the same pattern as you do with `IDTSComponentMetaData100` here.

```
private IDTSComponentMetaData100 _dtsComponentMetaData;

[CLSCompliant(false)]
public void Initialize(IDTSComponentMetaData100 dtsComponentMetadata,
IServiceProvider serviceProvider)
{
// Store ComponentMetaData for later use
_dtsComponentMetaData = dtsComponentMetadata;
}
```

IDtsComponentUI.Edit

The `Edit` method is called by the designer when you edit the component, and this is the place where you actually display the visible window or form of the user interface component. The purpose of the `Edit` method is to display the form, passing through any references you need, stored in private variables during `Initialize`. The `Edit` method also has a Boolean return value that notifies the designer whether changes have been made.

This is perhaps one of the most useful features of the component UI pattern, as it allows you to make changes directly to the component, but they are persisted only if the return value is true. In other words, the users can make as many changes as they want in the custom UI, but none of those changes are saved into the component unless the return value is true. You get commit or rollback functionality for free, rather than having to write additional code to cache changes within the UI, and only apply them when a user clicks the OK button.

It also allows you to benefit from validation routines you have written into the component itself. For example, the `ReverseString.SetUsageType` method checks data types and the `UsageType` property for the column being selected, because this component supports only string types. Putting the validation into the component, rather than the UI, ensures that if a user bypasses your UI and uses the built-in Advanced Editor or the Visual Studio Properties instead, the same validation takes place.

Therefore, your UI should focus on the display side and leave as much validation as possible to the component. Inevitably, some validation will be implemented in the UI, but always bear in mind that you can use the existing component code in a modularized manner, saving time and simplifying maintenance through reuse.

For ease of implementation, you can use the `DialogResult` functionality of the form to indicate the return value for the form. This is illustrated in the example implementation of `Edit`:

```
public bool Edit(IWin32Window parentWindow, Variables variables, Connections
connections)
{
    try
    {
        // Create UI form and display
        ReverseStringUIForm ui = new ReverseStringUIForm(_dtsComponentMetaData);
        DialogResult result = ui.ShowDialog(parentWindow);

        // Set return value to represent DialogResult. This tells the
    // managed wrapper to persist any changes made
        // on the component input and/or output, or properties.
        if (result == DialogResult.OK)
        {
```

```
        return true;
    }
}
catch (Exception ex)
{
    MessageBox.Show(ex.ToString());
}
return false;
}
```

The `Edit` method also provides references to the `Variables` and `Connections` collections. You can use these collections to list the available variables and connections. The `Variables` collection is already limited to those in scope for the current Data Flow Task.

If your component uses connections or variables, you would modify the form constructor to accept these, as well as the `System.IServiceProvider` reference you captured during `Initialize`. This allows you to offer the option of selecting an existing item or creating a new one as required. These are not required for the Reverse String Component, but an example of an `Edit` method implementation using them is shown here:

```
public bool Edit(IWin32Window parentWindow, Variables variables, Connections
connections)
{
    try
    {
        TraceSourceUIForm ui = new TraceSourceUIForm(_dtsComponentMetaData,
            variables, connections, _serviceProvider);
        DialogResult result = ui.ShowDialog(parentWindow);
        if (result == DialogResult.OK)
        {
            return true;
        }
    }
    catch (Exception ex)
    {
        Konesans.Dts.Design.ExceptionDialog.Show(ex);
    }
    return false;
}
```

Setting the UITypeName

This section deals with changes to the Reverse String Component itself, rather than the user interface project. This is listed as the last of the three key steps for providing a user interface, but it is generally done fairly early on, because once it's complete, you can actually test your UI in the designer itself.

You need to tell the designer that your component has a user interface, in effect overriding the Advanced Editor dialog box provided by default. To do this, set the `UITypeName` property of the

`DtsPipelineComponentAttribute`, which already decorates the component class in the transformation project. The required format of the property value is as follows:

```
<Full Class Name>,
<Assembly Name>,
Version=<Version>,
PublicKeyToken=<Token>
```

You may recognize the format as being very similar to an assembly strong name, because apart from the additional `<Full Class Name>` *at the beginning, it is the assembly strong name. Using the strong name, the designer can find and load the assembly, and then using the class name, it knows exactly where to go for its entry point, the* `IDTSComponentUI` *implementation.*

Setting this property often causes developers problems, but if you know where to look, it is quite easy:

```
...
namespace Konesans.Dts.Pipeline.ReverseStringUI
{
    public class ReverseStringUI : IDtsComponentUI
    {
...
```

This code snippet from the main UI class file shows the namespace and the class name, so the first token on the `UITypeName` is `Konesans.Dts.Pipeline.ReverseStringUI.ReverseStringUI`.

The remainder is just the strong name of the assembly. The simplest way to obtain this is to compile the project, and if you set the post-build events as described previously, your assembly will have been installed in the GAC. Open the assembly viewer (`C:\WINDOWS\assembly`) and locate your assembly. The tooltip for an assembly will show the string name, as shown in Figure 19-5.

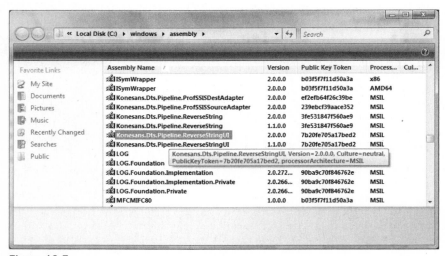

Figure 19-5

The individual tokens are shown again in the Properties dialog box, and there you can highlight the text for copy-and-paste operations to save typing mistakes, particularly with the public key token.

If you make a mistake in setting this property, you will get an error such as this one when you to use the component UI:

```
Could not load file or assembly 'Konesans.Dts.Pipeline.TrashDestination,
Version=2.0.0.0, Culture=neutral, PublicKeyToken=b8351fe7752642cc' or one of its
dependencies. The system cannot find the file specified. (mscorlib)
```

The completed attribute for the `ReverseString` Component, referencing the `ReverseStringUI` assembly, is illustrated as follows:

```
[DtsPipelineComponent(
   DisplayName = "ReverseString",
   ComponentType = ComponentType.Transform,
   IconResource = "Konesans.Dts.Pipeline.ReverseString.ReverseString.ico",
   UITypeName = "Konesans.Dts.Pipeline.ReverseStringUI.ReverseStringUI,
   Konesans.Dts.Pipeline.ReverseStringUI, Version=2.0.0.0, Culture=neutral,
 PublicKeyToken=7b20fe705a17bed2")]
public class ReverseString : PipelineComponent
...
```

Building the Form

The final stage of the development is to build the form itself, allowing it to capture the user input and apply the selections to the component. You are about to start building the form, but before you do, review the following summary of the progress so far.

You have implemented `IDTSComponentUI`, providing the methods required by the designer to support a custom user interface. The `IDTSComponentUI.Edit` method is used to display the form, passing through a reference to the base component (`IDTSComponentMetaData100`). This was gained using the `IDTSComponentUI.Initialize` method and stored in a private class-level variable.

Finally, you have updated the component itself to include the `UITypeName` property for the `DtsPipelineComponentAttribute`. This allows the designer to detect and then find your user interface class, thereby calling the `IDTSComponentUI` methods you have now implemented, leading to the display of the form.

The sample form for the user interface is shown in Figure 19-6.

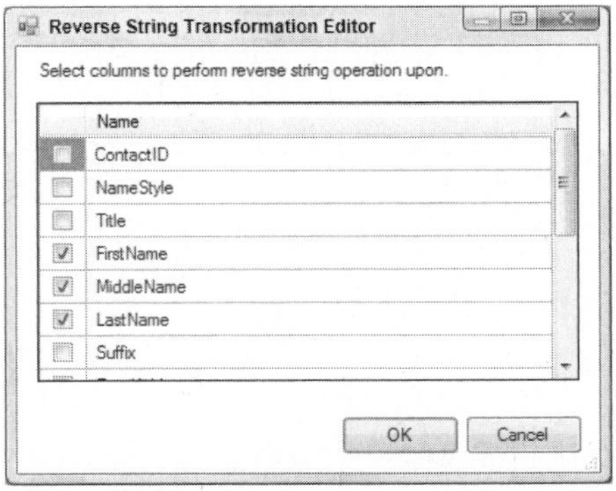

Figure 19-6

Form Constructor

As previously mentioned, the default form constructor is modified to accept the references you will need, such as the component and support objects, variables, and connections. For this example, you just have the component reference, IDTSComponentMetaData100. You should store these constructor parameters in private member variables for later use elsewhere in the form, as well as using them directly in the constructor itself.

The commit and rollback feature discussed in the "IDtsComponentUI.Edit" section has one specific requirement. Any changes made must be done through a wrapper class, rather than applied directly to the IDTSComponentMetaData100 reference. This wrapper, the IDTSDesigntimeComponent100 design-time interface, is created within the constructor and stored in a private member variable for later use.

Changes can be made directly to IDTSComponentMetaData100, but they will be permanent, so even if you return false from IDtsComponentUI.Edit, the changes will persist. Users like recognizable and intuitive user interfaces, and the ability to recover from a mistake using the Cancel button is one of those design patterns that all users have been grateful for on numerous occasions. Writing code to implement this yourself would be a considerable amount of work, so make sure you issue changes only through the design-time interface.

The complete form constructor is shown as follows, including the call to the SetInputVirtualInputColumns method, covered later in the chapter:

```
private IDTSComponentMetaData100 _dtsComponentMetaData;
private IDTSDesigntimeComponent100 _designTimeComponent;
private IDTSInput100 _input;

public ReverseStringUIForm(IDTSComponentMetaData100 dtsComponentMetaData)
{
    InitializeComponent();

    // Store constructor parameters for later
    _dtsComponentMetaData = dtsComponentMetaData;

    // Get design-time interface for changes and validation
    _designTimeComponent = _dtsComponentMetaData.Instantiate();

    // Get Input
    _input = _dtsComponentMetaData.InputCollection[0];

    // Set any form controls that host component properties or connections here
    // None required for ReverseString component

    // Populate DataGridView with columns
    SetInputVirtualInputColumns();
}
```

Column Display

Once all of the constructor parameters have been stored and the initial preparation is complete, you can begin to interrogate the component and other objects that may have been supplied on the constructor to populate the form controls.

The Reverse String Transformation will operate on any column the user selects, so the user interface will simply consist of a way to allow columns to be selected. For this example, you should use a `DataGridView` control. Using the control designer, you'll pre-configure two columns: a checkbox column for the selection state (`DataGridViewCheckBoxColumn`) and a text column for the column name (`DataGridViewTextBoxColumn`). The individual form controls are not covered in detail; rather the focus will be on their use and interaction with the component, because the choice of control is entirely up to you as the user interface developer. To see exactly how the controls have been configured, review the completed project available at www.wrox.com.

Because you allow users to select columns, the initial requirement is to enumerate the columns and determine their current selection state. To find out how to do this, you need to understand the architecture of a component in relation to data movement. For a simple synchronous transformation such as this one, you have a single input. The input has a collection of input columns, which at runtime hold the data provided in the pipeline buffer, so the transformation itself operates on these columns.

> *For more detail on pipeline architecture, see Chapter 14.*

In the Reverse String Component, the presence of an input column means that the user wants the operation to be performed on that column. By default, the input will contain no columns, because no columns have been selected for transformation. To select a column, you set the column usage type to something other than `DTSUsageType.UT_IGNORED`. For this component, because you do an in-place transformation on the column value, you require both read and write access as indicated by `DTSUsageType.UT_READWRITE`. This allows you to read the column value and reverse it before writing it back into the buffer.

> *It is important that you select only columns that are required for any transformation and minimize excess columns through all stages of the pipeline for performance reasons. The designer will display a warning like this when it detects unused columns:*
>
> ```
> [DTS.Pipeline] Warning: The output column "ProductPrice" (36) on output "OLE DB
> Source Output" (10) and component "Products" (1) is not subsequently used in the
> Data Flow task. Removing this unused output column can increase Data Flow task
> performance.
> ```

Because the input column collection is empty by default, you actually work on the virtual input column collection instead. The virtual input represents all the upstream columns available to the transformation, allowing you to enumerate columns, as well as interrogating the virtual input column's `UsageType` property.

Calling `GetVirtualInput` to get the collection of virtual columns is a potentially expensive operation, depending on the number of upstream columns. You should therefore call it only once, and cache the result for later use in other methods. You should also be aware that since a virtual input is very much a snapshot of current state, it can become invalid. Simple changes to the current component do not affect the virtual columns, but deeper changes like `ReinitializeMetaData` can invalidate it. You should therefore plan the lifetime of the cached reference and periodically refresh it after major changes.

The use of the virtual input and the column usage type is the basis for the `SetInputVirtualInputColumns` helper method included in the form. This populates the `DataGridView` with a list of columns and their current selection state. This method is the final call in the form constructor and completes the initialization of the form. As a separate exercise you may wish to augment this procedure with logic to hide (or grey-out) non-string columns, so that the user does not inadvertently try to reverse numeric values.

```
private void SetInputVirtualInputColumns()
{

    _virtualInput = _input.GetVirtualInput();

    IDTSVirtualInputColumnCollection100 virtualInputColumnCollection =
        _virtualInput.VirtualInputColumnCollection;

    IDTSInputColumnCollection100 inputColumns = _input.InputColumnCollection;

    int columnCount = virtualInputColumnCollection.Count;
    for (int i = 0; i < columnCount; i++)
    {
        IDTSVirtualInputColumn100 virtualColumn = virtualInputColumnCollection[i];
        int row;

        if (virtualColumn.UsageType == DTSUsageType.UT_READONLY ||
            virtualColumn.UsageType == DTSUsageType.UT_READWRITE)
        {
            row = this.dgColumns.Rows.Add(   new object[]
                { CheckState.Checked, " " + virtualColumn.Name });
        }
        else
        {
            row = this.dgColumns.Rows.Add(new object[]
                { CheckState.Unchecked, " " + virtualColumn.Name });
        }

        this.dgColumns.Rows[rowIndex].Tag = i;

        DataGridViewCheckBoxCell cell =
              (DataGridViewCheckBoxCell)dgColumns.Rows[row].Cells[0];
        cell.ThreeState = false;
    }
}
```

The pipeline engine is implemented in native code for performance, so calls to pipeline objects normally use a wrapper class and incur the overhead of COM Interop. You should therefore minimize such calls through efficient coding practices. In the preceding example, the count from the virtual input column collection is retrieved only once, as opposed to being interrogated within the `for` loop test itself.

Column Selection

The next stage of the user interface is to react to user input and reflect any changes back to the component. In this example, the only choice offered is the selection of columns, made through the `DataGridView`, as captured through the `CellContentClick` event. You use this event rather than one of the others available such as `CellValueChanged`, because this is raised immediately and you can give timely feedback to the user.

Through the `DataGridViewCellEventArgs`, you can obtain the row and column indices for the cell. This is first used to validate that the row exists and that the column is the first column, because this column contains the checkboxes used for managing selection. You then use the virtual input again and set the usage type as indicated by the checkbox or cell value.

Because the example component includes validation within the overridden `SetUsageType` method, you need to ensure that you catch any exceptions thrown, and can react and feedback to the component user as shown here:

```
private void dgColumns_CellContentClick(object sender, DataGridViewCellEventArgs e)
{
    if (e.ColumnIndex == 0 && e.RowIndex >= 0)
    {
        // Get current value and flip boolean to get new value
        bool newValue = !Convert.ToBoolean(dgColumns.CurrentCell.Value);

        // Get the virtual column to work with
        IDTSVirtualInputColumn100 virtualColumn =
            _virtualInput.VirtualInputColumnCollection[e.RowIndex];

        try
        {
            // Set the column UsageType to indicate the column is selected or not
            if (newValue)
                _designTimeComponent.SetUsageType(_input.ID, _virtualInput,
                    virtualColumn.LineageID, DTSUsageType.UT_READWRITE);
            else
                _designTimeComponent.SetUsageType(_input.ID, _virtualInput,
                    virtualColumn.LineageID, DTSUsageType.UT_IGNORED);
        }
        catch(Exception ex)
        {
            // Catch any error from base class SetUsageType here.
            // Display simple error message from exception
            MessageBox.Show(ex.Message, "Invalid Column", MessageBoxButtons.OK,
                MessageBoxIcon.Error);

            // Rollback UI selection
            dgColumns.CancelEdit();
        }
    }
}
```

To complete the description of the user interface example, there are two button controls on the form, named OK and Cancel, each with their respective `DialogResult` property values set. By using the dialog results in this way, you do not need any event handler bound to the `click` event, and no additional code is required to close the form. The dialog result is then used within `IDTSComponentUI` `.Edit` to commit or roll back any changes made to the component wrapper, as shown previously.

This concludes the example, and if you have been building as you read, all that remains is to compile the project. If you configured the build events that were described at the beginning, the assemblies should be in the correct locations ready for use.

You will need to start a new instance of Visual Studio and open an SSIS project. Before you can use the component, it needs to be added to the Toolbox. To add a component to the Toolbox, right-click the

Toolbox and select Choose Items from the context menu. When the Choose Toolbox Items dialog appears, click the SSIS Data Flow Items tab and scroll down until you see the component. Check your new component and click OK. When you go back to the Toolbox, you should see your new component. Another method is to select Reset Toolbox from the context menu instead.

The completed example is available for download from www.wrox.com.

Further Development

The simple component that was used lacks some of the other features you may require. For example, components can use runtime connections or have properties. These would generally be represented through additional form controls, and their values would be interrogated, and controls initialized in the form constructor. You will now look at these other methods in greater detail.

Runtime Connections

As previously discussed, components can use connections, and the System.IServiceProvider from IDtsComponentUI.Initialize, and the Connections collection from IDtsComponentUI.Edit, allow you to provide meaningful UI functions around them. Examples have been given of passing these as far as the form constructor, so now you will be shown what you then do with them. This example shows a modified constructor that accepts the additional connection-related parameters, performs some basic initialization, and stores them for later use. You would perform any column- or property-related work as shown in the previous examples, but for clarity none is included here. The final task is to initialize the connection-related control.

For this example, you will presume that the component accepts one connection, which would have been defined in the ProvidedComponentProperties method of the component. You will use a ComboBox control to offer the selection options, as well as the ability to create a new connection through the IDtsConnectionService. The component expects an ADO.NET SqlClient connection, so the list will be restricted to this, and the current connection, if any, will be preselected in the list. The preparatory work for this is all shown here:

```
private IDTSComponentMetaData100 _dtsComponentMetaData;
private IDTSDesigntimeComponent100 _designTimeComponent;
private IDtsConnectionService _dtsConnectionService;
private Microsoft.SqlServer.Dts.Runtime.Connections _connections;

// Constant to define the type of connection we support and wish to work with.
private const string Connection_Type =
    "ADO.NET:System.Data.SqlClient.SqlConnection, System.Data, Version=2.0.0.0,
    Culture=neutral, PublicKeyToken=b77a5c561934e089";

public ConnectionDemoUIForm(IDTSComponentMetaData100 dtsComponentMetaData,
            IServiceProvider serviceProvider, Connections connections)
{
    InitializeComponent();

    // Store constructor parameters for later.
    _dtsComponentMetaData = dtsComponentMetaData;
    _connections = connections;
```

```
        // Get IDtsConnectionService and store.
        IDtsConnectionService dtsConnectionService =
            serviceProvider.GetService(typeof(IDtsConnectionService))
            as IDtsConnectionService;
        _dtsConnectionService = dtsConnectionService;

        // Get design-time interface for changes and validation.
        _designTimeComponent = _dtsComponentMetaData.Instantiate();

        // Perform any other actions, such as column population or
        // component property work.

        // Get Connections collection, and get name of currently selected connection.
        string connectionName = "";
        if (_dtsComponentMetaData.RuntimeConnectionCollection[0] != null)
        {
            IDTSRuntimeConnection100 runtimeConnection =
                _dtsComponentMetaData.RuntimeConnectionCollection[0];
            if (runtimeConnection != null
                && runtimeConnection.ConnectionManagerID.Length > 0
                && _connections.Contains(runtimeConnection.ConnectionManagerID))
            {
                connectionName = _connections[runtimeConnection.ConnectionManagerID].Name;
            }
        }

        // Populate connections combo.
        PopulateConnectionsCombo(this.cmbSqlConnections, Connection_Type,
           connectionName);
    }
```

The final command in the constructor is to call your helper function, `PopulateConnectionsCombo`, to populate the combo box. The parameters for this are quite simple: the combo box to populate, the type of connection you wish to list, and the name of the currently selected connection. Using these three items, you can successfully populate the combo as shown here:

```
    private void PopulateConnectionsCombo(ComboBox comboBox,
        string connectionType, string selectedItem)
    {
        // Prepare combo box by clearing, and adding the new connection item.
        comboBox.Items.Clear();
        comboBox.Items.Add("<New connection...>");

        // Enumerate connections, but for type supported.
        foreach (ConnectionManager connectionManager in
           _dtsConnectionService.GetConnectionsOfType(connectionType))
        {
            comboBox.Items.Add(connectionManager.Name);
        }

        // Set currently selected connection
        comboBox.SelectedItem = selectedItem;
    }
```

The ADO.NET connection is slightly different from most connections in that it has what can be thought of as subtypes. Because you need a specific subtype, the `System.Data.SqlClient.SqlConnection`, you need to use the full name of the connection, as opposed to the shorter creation name moniker, ADO.NET, which you may see elsewhere and which is the pattern used for other simpler types of Connection Managers.

If you have any problems with this sample code, perhaps because you have different versions of SQL Server on the same box, then change the relevant line of the preceding code to the following. This alternative code lists any Connection Manager in the combo.

```
// Enumerate connections, but for any connection type.
   foreach (ConnectionManager connectionManager in
      _dtsConnectionService.GetConnections())
   {
      comboBox.Items.Add(connectionManager.Name);
   }
```

Now that you have populated the combo box, you need to handle the selection of an existing connection or the creation of a new connection. When you author a Connection Manager yourself, you can provide a user interface by implementing the `IDtsConnectionManagerUI`, which is analogous to the way you have implemented `IDtsComponentUI` to provide a user interface for your component. The connection service will then display this user interface when you call the `CreateConnection` method.

The following example is the event handler for the connections combo box, which supports new connections and existing connections, and ensures that the selection is passed down to the component:

```
private void cmbSqlConnections_SelectedValueChanged(object sender, EventArgs e)
{
   ComboBox comboBox = (ComboBox)sender;

   // Check for index 0 and <New Item...>
   if (comboxBox.SelectedIndex == 0)
   {
      // Use connection service to create a new connection.
      ArrayList newConns = _dtsConnectionService.CreateConnection(Connection_Type);
      if (newConns.Count > 0)
      {
         // A new connection has been created, so populate and select
         ConnectionManager newConn = (ConnectionManager)newConns[0];
         PopulateConnectionsCombo(comboBox, Connection_Type, newConn.Name);
      }
      else
      {
         // Create connection has been cancelled
         comboxBox.SelectedIndex = -1;
      }
   }

   // An connection has been selected. Verify it exists and update component.
   if (_connections.Contains(comboxBox.Text))
   {
      // Get the selected connection
      ConnectionManager connectionManager = _connections[comboxBox.Text];
```

```
        // Save selected connection
    _dtsComponentMetaData.RuntimeConnectionCollection[0].ConnectionManagerID =
        _connections[comboxBox.Text].ID;
    _dtsComponentMetaData.RuntimeConnectionCollection[0].ConnectionManager =
        DtsConvert.ToConnectionManager100(_connections[comboxBox.Text]);
    }
}
```

By following the examples shown here, you can manage connections from within your user interface, allowing the user to create a new connection or select an existing one, and ensure that the selection is persisted through to the component's RuntimeConnectionCollection, thereby setting the connection.

You can also use variables within your UI. Normally the selected variable is stored in a component property, so by combining the property access code from the Component Properties section and following the pattern for Runtime Connections, substituting the IDtsVariableService instead, you can see how this can be done.

Component Properties

As an example of displaying and setting component-level properties, you may have a string property that is displayed in a simple text box control and an enumeration value that is used to set the selected index for a combo box control. The following example assumes that the two component properties, StringProp and EnumProp, have been defined in the overridden ProvideComponentProperties method of your component class. You would then extend the form constructor to include some code to retrieve the property values and display them in the form controls. This assumes that you have added two new form controls, a TextBox control called MyStringTextBox, and a ComboBox called MyEnumValComboBox. An example of the additional form constructor code is shown here:

```
MyStringTextBox.Text =
_dtsComponentMetaData.CustomPropertyCollection["StringProp"].Value.ToString();

MyEnumValComboBox.SelectedIndex =
Convert.ToInt32(_dtsComponentMetaData.CustomPropertyCollection["EnumProp"].Value);
```

The appropriate events for each control would then be used to set the property value of the component, ensuring that this is done through the design-time interface. A variety of events could be used to capture the value change within the Windows Form control, and this may depend on the level of validation you wish to apply within the form, or if you wish to rely solely on validation routines within an overridden SetComponentProperty method in your component class. Capturing these within the control's validating event would then allow you to cancel the change in the form, as well as displaying information to the user. A simple example is shown here for the two properties:

```
private void MyStringTextBox_Validating(object sender, CancelEventArgs e)
{
    // Set the property, and capture any validation errors
    // thrown in SetComponentProperty
    try
    {
      _designTimeComponent.SetComponentProperty("StringProp",
            MyStringTextBox.Text);
```

```
      }
   catch(Exception ex)
   {
      // Display exception message
      MessageBox.Show(ex.Message);

      // Cancel event due to error
      e.Cancel = true;
   }
}

private void MyEnumValComboBox_SelectedIndexChanged(object sender, EventArgs e)
{
   try
   {
      _designTimeComponent.SetComponentProperty("EnumProp ",
         ((ComboBox)sender).SelectedIndex);
   }
   catch(Exception ex)
   {
      // Display exception message
      MessageBox.Show(ex.Message);

      // Cancel event due to error
      e.Cancel = true;
   }
}
```

Providing an overridden SetComponentProperty is a common requirement. The most obvious reason
is that component properties are stored through the object type, but you may require a specific type,
such as integer, so the type validation code would be included in SetComponentProperty. A simple
example of this is shown here, where the property named IntProp is validated to ensure that it is an
integer:

```
public override IDTSCustomProperty100 SetComponentProperty(string propertyName,
object propertyValue)
{
   int result;
   if (propertyName == "IntProp" &&
      int.TryParse(propertyValue.ToString(), out result) == false)
   {
      bool cancel;
      ComponentMetaData.FireError(0, ComponentMetaData.Name, "The IntProp property
         is required to be a valid integer.", "", 0, out cancel);
      throw new ArgumentException("The value you have specified for IntProp is not
         a numeric value");
   }

   return base.SetComponentProperty(propertyName, propertyValue);
}
```

You build on this example and learn how to handle the exceptions and events in the following section.

Handling Errors and Warnings

The previous example and the column selection method in the main example, both demonstrated how you can catch exceptions thrown from the base component when you apply settings. Although it is recommended that you use managed exceptions for this type of validation and feedback, you may also wish to use the component events such as `FireError` or `FireWarning`. Usually, these would be called immediately prior to the exception and used to provide additional information in support of the exception. Alternatively, you could use them to provide the detail and only throw the exception as a means of indicating that an event has been raised. To capture the event information, you can use the `IErrorCollectionService`. This service can be obtained through `System.IServiceProvider`, and the preparatory handling is identical to that of `IDtsConnectionService` as illustrated in the previous example. For the following examples, you will assume that a class-level variable containing the `IErrorCollectionService` has been declared, `_errorCollectionService`, and populated through in the form constructor.

The following example demonstrates how you can use the `GetErrorMessage` method of the `IErrorCollectionService` to retrieve details of an event. This will also include details of any exception thrown as well. The validating method of a text box control is illustrated, and `SetComponentProperty` is based on the overridden example shown previously, to validate that the property value is an integer:

```
private void txtIntPropMessage_Validating(object sender, CancelEventArgs e)
{
    // Clear any existing errors in preparation for setting property
    _errorCollectionService.ClearErrors();

    try
    {
        // Set property through IDTSDesigntimeComponent100
        _designTimeComponent.SetComponentProperty("IntProp",
            this.txtIntPropMessage.Text);
    }
    catch
    {
        // Display message
        MessageBox.Show(_errorCollectionService.GetErrorMessage());

    // Cancel event due to error
    e.Cancel = true;
    }
}
```

If a non-integer value is entered, the following message is displayed:

```
Error at Data Flow Task [ReverseString]: The IntProp property is required to be a
valid integer.
Error at Data Flow Task [ReverseString [84]]: System.ArgumentException: The value
you have specified for IntProp is not a numeric value
    at Konesans.Dts.Pipeline.ReverseString.ReverseString.SetComponentProperty(String
propertyName, Object propertyValue)
    at
Microsoft.SqlServer.Dts.Pipeline.ManagedComponentHost.HostSetComponentProperty(
IDTSDesigntimeComponent100 wrapper, String propertyName, Object propertyValue)
```

This second example demonstrates the GetErrors method and how to enumerate through the errors captured by the service individually:

```
private void txtIntPropErrors_Validating(object sender, CancelEventArgs e)
{
    // Clear any existing errors in preparation for setting property
    _errorCollectionService.ClearErrors();

    try
    {
        // Set property through IDTSDesigntimeComponent100
        _designTimeComponent.SetComponentProperty("IntProp",
            this.txtIntPropErrors.Text);
    }
    catch
    {
        // Get ICollection of IComponentErrorInfo and cast into
        // IList for accessibility
        IList<IComponentErrorInfo> errors =
            _errorCollectionService.GetErrors() as IList<IComponentErrorInfo>;

        // Loop through errors and process into message
        string message = "";
        for (int i = 0; i < errors.Count; i++)
        {
            IComponentErrorInfo errorInfo = errors[i] as IComponentErrorInfo;
            message += "Level: " + errorInfo.Level.ToString() + Environment.NewLine +
                "Description : " + Environment.NewLine + errorInfo.Description
                + Environment.NewLine + Environment.NewLine;
        }

        // Display message
        MessageBox.Show(message);

        // Cancel event due to error
        e.Cancel = true;
    }
}
```

If a non-integer value is entered, the following message is displayed:

```
Level: Error
Description :
The IntProp property is required to be a valid integer.

Level: Error
Description :
System.ArgumentException: The value you have specified for IntProp is not a numeric
value
    at Konesans.Dts.Pipeline.ReverseString.ReverseString.SetComponentProperty(String
propertyName, Object propertyValue)
    at
Microsoft.SqlServer.Dts.Pipeline.ManagedComponentHost.HostSetComponentProperty(
IDTSDesigntimeComponent100 wrapper, String propertyName, Object propertyValue)
```

As you can see, both the event and exception information are available through the `IErrorCollectionService`. You can also see the use of the `Level` property in this example, which may be useful for differentiating between errors and warnings. For a complete list of `IComponentErrorInfo` properties, please refer to the SQL Server documentation.

Column Properties

When you require column-level information, beyond the selection state of a column, it is best practice to store this as a custom property on the column. This applies to all column types. An example of this can be seen with the stock Character Map Transform. If you select a column and perform an in-place operation, such as the Lowercase operation, this is stored as a custom property on that input column. To confirm this, select a column as described and view the component through the Advanced Editor (to open the Advanced Editor, right-click the Character Map Transform and select Show Advanced Editor). If you then navigate to the Input and expand to select the column, you will see a custom property called `MapFlags`. This stores the operation enumeration, as shown in Figure 19-7.

Figure 19-7

If your component uses custom column properties in this way, these are perhaps the best candidates for a custom user interface. Using the Advanced Editor to navigate columns and set properties correctly carries a much higher risk of error and is more time-consuming for the user than a well-designed user interface. Unfortunately this does raise the complexity of the user interface somewhat, particularly from the Windows Forms programming perspective, as the effective use of form controls is what will determine the success of such a UI. However, if you are still reading this chapter, you will probably be comfortable with such challenges.

To persist these column-level properties, simply call the appropriate `SetColumnTypeProperty` method on the design-time interface, `IDTSDesigntimeComponent100`. Obviously, you want to make sure that you previously created the actual properties. For example, in the following code, a property is being set on an input column:

```
_designTimeComponent.SetInputColumnProperty(_input.ID, inputColumn.ID,
    "PropertyName", propertyValue);
```

Other Considerations

Any good user interface should be designed with usability, accessibility, localization, and other such principles in mind. That means that the user interface should not require a mouse to be configured — the user should be able to navigate using just the keyboard just as easily. Descriptions should be clear, and strings and controls should be tested to ensure that any resizing operation does not truncate them. If the component is intended to be sold to customers, localization (and globalization) may be something you want to think about — there is a lot of information on `msdn.microsoft.com` on these topics, but as a start you want to make sure that string literals live in resource files, and right-to-left language users are not confused by the interface.

Test the component and make sure it does not crash when receiving invalid input, any error messages are descriptive, and exception recovery is graceful. Also keep in mind that users may intentionally or mistakenly use the default UI (Advanced Editor) for the component and corrupt the state that may otherwise have been protected by your UI. If the component is designed right, the validation is modularized and shared by the component and its UI; however, if this is not possible, then try to ensure that the UI does not break if the metadata is corrupt.

Remember that both the component and its UI may need to be deployed together to other machines (depending on their intended use). If this is the case, consider building an installation script to place the files in the right folders and install them in the GAC as necessary.

Summary

You will now hopefully have a good understanding of what is required to implement your own custom user interface for a Pipeline Component. We hope that you have understood how to apply this guidance for yourself and, perhaps more importantly, why certain practices are to be followed, allowing you to go on and confidently develop your own components. This functionality allows you to really exploit the power and extensibility of SQL Server Integration Services.

External Management and WMI Task Implementation

Throughout this book, you've been exposed to different ways to manage the development and administration of SSIS packages using the Visual Studio IDE and the SQL Server Management Studio. This chapter expands on those operations by providing an overview of the ways in which you perform these same management and administration functions programmatically through managed code. You learn how to perform package management operations using the managed `Application` and `Package` classes exposed in the dynamic-linked library `Microsoft.SQLServer.ManagedDTS.dll` by the .NET `Microsoft.SqlServer.Dts.Runtime` namespace.

The second half of this chapter details the capabilities of the WMI Data Reader Task and the WMI Event Watcher Task. These tasks provide access to system information via the Windows Management Interface model, better known as WMI. Through a query-based language called WQL, similar to SQL in structure and syntax, you can obtain information about a wide variety of system resources to assist you in your SQL Server administrative responsibilities. With WMI, you can mine system-based metrics to look for hardware and operating system trends. In SSIS, using WMI, you can also work more proactively to monitor a Windows-based system for notable events that occur in the system, and even trigger responsive actions.

External Management of SSIS with Managed Code

The SSIS development team has exposed a robust architecture to manage SSIS through managed code. Managed code in this case refers to the use of the .NET Framework Common Language Runtime that hosts code written in C# or VB.NET.

Through a rich object model, you can customize your applications to control almost every aspect of managing an SSIS package. This section attempts to provide a brief overview of the SSIS programming model as it applies to externally managing SSIS packages.

Setting Up a Test SSIS Package for Demonstration Purposes

For this chapter, we'll be using a test SSIS package created purely for demonstration purposes. Note that all the code in this chapter can be downloaded from www.wrox.com. The package you will set up for this chapter is designed specifically to highlight some of the capabilities of using the managed code libraries. To start, create a new directory structure for this chapter under c:\ssis\ called extmgt. Then create a new SSIS package under a subdirectory called testSSISpackage.

The package needs two variables, both are strings, but one is an expression-based variable. Set up the variables using this table:

Variable Name	Type	Value	Expression?
myExpression	String	@System::PackageName	Yes
myVariable	String	Hello World	No

Now drop two Script Tasks on the Control Flow surface and set the ReadOnlyVariables property to the myVariable variable. For the first Script Task, set the script language to C# and set the code like this:

```
C#
    public void Main()
     {
         bool ret = false;
         Dts.Events.FireInformation(0, "TestPackage",
             "Running C# Script Task to Display Message " +
             Dts.Variables[0].Value.ToString(), "", 0, ref ret);

         Dts.TaskResult = (int)ScriptResults.Success;
     }
```

Do the exact same thing for the other Script Task, except set the language to VB.NET, and the code like this:

```
VB
    Public Sub Main()
        Dim ret As Boolean = False
        Dts.Events.FireInformation(0, "TestPackage", _
            "Running VB.NET Script Task to Display Message " + _
            Dts.Variables(0).Value.ToString(), "", 0, ret)

        Dts.TaskResult = ScriptResults.Success
    End Sub
```

Test the package to make sure that everything is working correctly. You should see results that look like Figure 20-1.

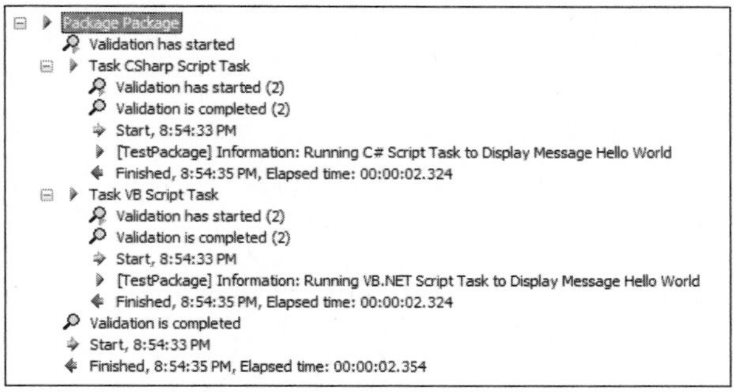

Figure 20-1

Now that you have a working test package, we can use it to highlight the management capabilities of the DTS runtime managed code library.

The DTS Runtime Managed Code Library

To continue with the external management examples in this chapter, you need to have SQL Server installed (with SDK). You'll also need the Visual Studio project templates for developing Console and Web applications. The code will be simple enough to follow along, and as always you can download the code for this chapter from www.wrox.com. If you have installed the SQL Server SDK, you will find a DLL registered in the global assembly cache named `Microsoft.SQLServer.ManagedDTS.dll`. In this DLL is a namespace called `Microsoft.SqlServer.Dts.Runtime`. To access the classes in this namespace, you must first create a project in Visual Studio and then add a reference to the namespace for `Microsoft.SQLServer.ManagedDTS.dll`. To keep from having to type the full namespace reference, you'll want to add either an `Imports` or `Using` statement to include the namespace in your code classes like this:

```
C#
using Microsoft.SqlServer.Dts.Runtime;
VB
Imports Microsoft.SqlServer.Dts.Runtime
```

Once the reference is added to your project, you can investigate the encapsulated classes using the Object Browser. (Ctrl+Alt+J or View ⇨ Object Browser). The most important classes for external management of SSIS packages are the `Application` and `Package` objects. You'll work with these classes and their methods in many of the examples in this chapter.

The `Application` object is the core class that exposes methods used to connect to and interface with an SSIS service instance. The following are typical management operations that can be performed using this class:

❑ Load, save, and delete SSIS packages on the Windows files system, SQL Server, or Integration Services repository.

❑ Construct and execute packages either from a storage facility or in memory.

❑ Add, remove, and rename folders in SQL Server or Integration Services repository folders.

❑ Control package permissions stored within a SQL Server.

❑ Obtain state information and status regarding the execution of packages in SQL Server or the SSIS package repository.

The `Package` object represents an instance of a single SSIS package. Although this object exposes many methods that allow you to control every aspect of a package, this chapter will only deal with functionality that applies to maintenance-type operations. Here are the maintenance-based operations that the `Package` object exposes:

❑ Configure Log Providers.

❑ Manage Package Configurations.

❑ Manage Connection Managers in SQL Server and Integration Services.

Now that you have an overview of the managed class library for DTS runtime, let's dig deeper into each of the primary classes and get into some useful examples.

Application Object Maintenance Operations

SSIS packages can be stored on either the Windows file system, the SSIS package store, or within SQL Server. The methods of the `Application` object allow you to manage SSIS packages in each of these storage scenarios including management of packages in other server instances. Once the package is loaded or constructed in the `Application` object, it may be run or executed. The flexibility to store, load, and run packages in separate machine spaces expands the scaling capabilities of SSIS packages.

The convention that the SSIS team chose to employ in naming the methods on this `Application` class is to use `DtsServer` in their names when the operation applies to packages in the SSIS package store, and `SqlServer` in their names when storage is in SQL Server. If you don't see either in the method name, typically, this will mean that the operation is for packages stored in the file system.

In terms of the operations that the application object supports, you'll find methods for general package, folder, and role maintenance.

Package Maintenance Operations

The `Application` object exposes the following methods to manage packages in the Windows file system, the SSIS package store, and SQL Server database instance:

- ❑ `LoadPackage`: Loads a package from the file system.

- ❑ `LoadFromDtsServer`: Loads a package from the specified SSIS package store.

- ❑ `LoadFromSqlServer`: Loads a package to the specified SQL Server instance.

- ❑ `LoadFromSqlServer2`: Loads a package to the specified SQL Server instance by supplying a valid connection object.

- ❑ `SaveToXML`: Saves a package object to the file system with a `dtsx` file extension.

- ❑ `SaveToDtsServer`: Saves a package to the SSIS package store.

- ❑ `SaveToSqlServer`: Saves a package to the specified SQL Server instance.

- ❑ `SaveToSqlServerAs`: Saves a package as a different name to the specified SQL Server instance.

- ❑ `RemoveFromDtsServer`: Removes a package from the SSIS package store.

- ❑ `RemoveFromSqlServer`: Removes a package from the specified SQL Server instance.

- ❑ `ExistsOnDtsServer`: Indicates whether a specified package already exists in the SSIS package store at the specified path.

- ❑ `ExistsOnSqlServer`: Indicates whether a specified package already exists on a specified SQL Server.

Now armed with the basic capabilities of the application class, let's get some real-world examples put together. First, you'll put together an example that examines the variables in a package, and then we'll look at how you can programmatically deploy packages to a DTS package store.

A Package Maintenance Example

At the most basic level you need to understand how to access a package programmatically to examine the internals. This is where the `Package` object class is used. This class mirrors the structure of the SSIS packages and allows them to be loaded into a navigable object model. Once the package is deep copied into this `Package` structure, you can look at anything in the package. The following C# code snippet is just a partial demonstration of how to load your demonstration package into a `Package` object variable from the file system. Notice that because the package exists on the file system, you are using the `LoadPackage` method of the application object instead of the methods that apply to DTS or SQL Server package stores. Note that this snippet assumes you have the references to `Microsoft.SQLServer.ManagedDTS.dll`.

```
C#
using Microsoft.SqlServer.Dts.Runtime;
public void LoadPackage()
{
    Application dtsApp = new Application();
    string TestPackageFullPath =
      "C:\\SSIS\\extmgt\\TestSSISPackage\\TestSSISPackage\\Package.dtsx";
```

```
        Package pac =  dtsApp.LoadPackage(TestPackageFullPath, null);
        . . .
}

VB
Imports Microsoft.SqlServer.Dts.Runtime
Public Sub LoadPackage()
    Dim dtsApp as new Application()
    Dim TestPackageFullPath as String = _
        "C:\\SSIS\\extmgt\\TestSSISPackage\\TestSSISPackage\\Package.dtsx"
    Dim package As Package = dtsApp.LoadPackage(TestPackageFullPath, Nothing)
    . . .
End Sub
```

Once the application class is created and the `package` object is loaded, you can interrogate the package object to perform many different tasks. A useful example involves examining the variables within a package. You can do this easily by iterating the variables collection to look for user variables or system variables. The following code snippet is in the form of a function that you can add to your solution to perform this task:

```
C#
        private static void DisplayFilePackageVariables(string FullPath,
                                        bool ShowOnlyUserVariables)
        {
            Application app = new Application();
            Package package = app.LoadPackage(FullPath, null);
            string sMsg = "Variable:[{0}] Type:{1} Default Value:{2}
                        IsExpression?:{3}\n";

            foreach(Variable var in package.Variables)
            {
                if ((var.Namespace != "System") &&
                    ShowOnlyUserVariables) ||
                    !ShowOnlyUserVariables)
                {
                    Console.WriteLine(String.Format(sMsg, var.Name,
                                var.DataType.ToString(),
                                var.Value.ToString(),
                                var.EvaluateAsExpression.ToString()));
                }
            }
        }

VB
    Private Sub DisplayFilePackageVariables(ByVal FullPath As String, ByVal
                ShowOnlyUserVariables As Boolean)
        Dim app As New Application()
        Dim package As Package = app.LoadPackage(FullPath, Nothing)
        Dim sMsg As String
        sMsg = "Variable:[{0}] Type:{1} Default Value:{2} IsExpression?:{3}"
                + vbCrLf
```

```
        For Each Variable In package.Variables
            If ((Variable.Namespace <> "System" And _
                    ShowOnlyUserVariables = True) Or _
                    ShowOnlyUserVariables = False) Then

                Console.WriteLine(String.Format(sMsg, Variable.Name, _
                                    Variable.DataType.ToString(), _
                                    Variable.Value.ToString(), _
                                    Variable.EvaluateAsExpression.ToString()))
            End If
        Next
    End Sub
```

If you run this code using the full file path of the demonstration SSIS package and set the option to show only the user variables, the console results will look like Figure 20-2.

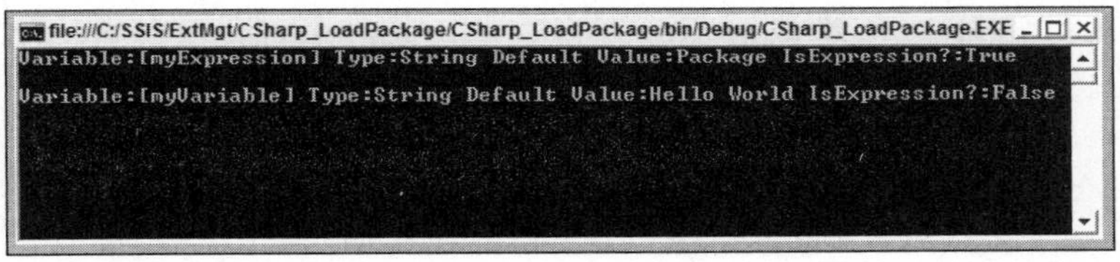

Figure 20-2

You can see in the console that this correctly shows the two user variables that you set up earlier in the Test SSIS package at the start of this chapter. The results also correctly show that the myExpression variable is an expression-based variable using the EvaluateAsExpression property. The power of the application and package objects don't stop there. You can also move packages from one store to another as you'll see in this next example.

A Package Transfer Example

The application object also contains methods that allow you to move SSIS packages from one storage facility to another. These are very useful for doing things like moving all existing packages on a server to a file storage location while you rebuild a server, or moving all existing packages from one server to another. A great use of these methods is to allow the development of programs for auto-deployment of new SSIS packages.

Once an SSIS package has been deeply copied or loaded into the package object, method calls on the application object can save them into a storage medium. You can load and save from any medium giving you the capability to move the package. The next code snippet is a well-named function that will move SSIS packages from a file to a DTS storage location. To be able to move a package from the file system, you need the full file path to the dtsx file. You also need the DTS storage information details like the server name, the folder on the server, and the resulting package name. Before we go any further, let's look at the DTS package store on your server.

The DTS package store is kept in the Integration Server. You log into the Integration Server using the SSMS tool the same way you would SQL Server, but choose the Integration Server instance instead of SQL Server. The integration server environment has a different node structure that looks like Figure 20-3.

Figure 20-3

Notice here that the server MyPC has two different connections in the SSMS console. The first is to the SQL Server services, and the second is to the Integration Services. Underneath the Integration Services Node, you'll see two nodes, one for the packages that are currently running, and the second for packages that are stored. We'll look at the running packages later in the complete package management example; for now, we are focusing on the stored packages. In the Stored Packages Node, you'll see one node for the File System and one node for the MSDB database. To get the Integration Services to look like Figure 20-3, we loaded two sample packages created in Chapter 3 using the techniques from Chapter 22 both as file packages and as DTS stored packages.

Regardless of which node you choose to store the package, you can set up folders to allow you to organize the packages into function areas. In Figure 20-3, the folders MyFilePackages and MySSPackages were created prior to loading the packages into them. The MyFilePackages folder represents packages that are running under the Integration Service, but are deployed (or stored) in the file system. The MySSPackage folder represents packages that are loaded and run from the MSDB database. In the next section, we demonstrate how to create these folders programmatically. You could just as easily have organized these packages by business function, to make it easier to quickly find the packages that affect your accounting and operational areas.

The next code snippet demonstrates how to take the Demonstration SSIS package you created at the beginning of this chapter and move it into the MSDB database on this server. First, the code obtains a reference to a package object in the file system and loads the package into the package object model. Then the package is saved into the DTS store under the MySSPackages folder.

```csharp
C#
    private static void TransferPackageFromFileToDtsServer(
                        string FullFilePath,
                        string DTSServerPath,
                        string Server,
                        string SavePackageAsName)
    {
        Application app = new Application();
        Package package = app.LoadPackage(FullFilePath, null);

        if (app.FolderExistsOnDtsServer(DTSServerPath, Server))
```

```
        {
            if (!DTSServerPath.EndsWith("\\"))
            {
                DTSServerPath = DTSServerPath + "\\";
            }

            Console.WriteLine("Transferring Package " +
                                package.Name.ToString()
                            + "\n");
            app.SaveToDtsServer(package, null, DTSServerPath +
                            SavePackageAsName, Server);
        }
    }

VB
    private sub TransferPackageFromFileToDtsServer( _
                            ByVal FullFilePath As String, _
                            ByVal DTSServerPath As String, _
                            ByVal Server As String, _
                            ByVal SavePackageAsName As String)

        Dim app As New Application()
        Dim package = app.LoadPackage(FullFilePath, Nothing)

        If app.ExistsOnDtsServer(DTSServerPath, Server) Then
            If (DTSServerPath.EndsWith("\") = False) Then
                DTSServerPath = DTSServerPath + "\"
            End If
        End If

        Console.WriteLine("Transfering Package " + _
                        package.Name.ToString() + vbCrLf)
        app.SaveToDtsServer(package, Nothing, DTSServerPath + _
                        SavePackageAsName, Server)
    End Sub
```

On both sides, the package needs to be referred to with the complete path. The helper function allows the package to be specifically named and removes that implementation detail from the caller. If you run this function against the demonstration SSIS package using this code (after substituting your server for MyPC), the package will be copied to the DTS store:

```
C#
TransferPackageFromFileToDtsServer(TestPackageFullPath, "msdb\\MySSPackages",
"MyPC", "MyTestPackage");

VB
TransferPackageFromFileToDtsServer(TestPackageFullPath, "msdb\MySSPackages", _
"MyPC", "MyTestPackage")
```

If you refresh the nodes in the Integration Server, you'll now see the SSIS demonstration package stored under the MySSPackages Node using the name MyTestPackage. The Integration Server Node should now look like Figure 20-4.

Figure 20-4

Using this example and building other well-named methods, you can move packages from the DTS store to the file system, or from the file system to the SQL Server store, or even from server to server. One of the things we skipped over to show this example was the creation of the folder structures in your SQL Server or DTS storage location. Let's look at this in the next section.

Package Folder Maintenance

On either the DTS or SQL Server package repositories, you can perform all the management operations of creating, renaming, or deleting folder structures as well as testing for the existence of an expected folder. To manage storage folders on either the DTS or SQL Server package storage locations, you'll need to use one of the following methods of the `Application` object:

- ❏ `CreateFolderOnDtsServer`: Creates a new folder in the "Stored Packages" Node of the application object's server.

- ❏ `CreateFolderOnSqlServer`: Creates a new folder in the specified server's "Stored Packages" Node using the specified user name and password.

- ❏ `RemoveFolderFromDtsServer`: Removes the specified folder from the application object's server.

- ❏ `RemoveFolderFromSqlServer`: Removes the specified folder from the specified server using the supplied user name and password.

- ❏ `RenameFolderOnDtsServer`: Renames the specified folder on the application object's server.

- ❏ `RenameFolderOnSqlServer`: Renames the specified folder on the specified server using the supplied user name and password.

- ❏ `FolderExistsOnDtsServer`: Determines if the specified folder currently exists on the application object's server.

- ❏ `FolderExistsOnSqlServer`: Determines if the specified folder currently exists on the specified server using the supplied user name and password.

To exhibit the use of folder maintenance operations, the following examples show how to employ a few of these methods. Look at these code snippets that can be used to create a folder in the DTS SSIS package store:

```
C#
private static void CreateDtsStoreFolder(string ParentDTSFolder,
                                    string NewDTSFolder,
                                    string Server)
{
    Application app = new Application();
    app.CreateFolderOnDtsServer(ParentDTSFolder, NewDTSFolder, Server);

    if (!ParentDTSFolder.EndsWith("\\"))
    {
        ParentDTSFolder = ParentDTSFolder + "\\";
    }

    if(app.FolderExistsOnDtsServer(ParentDTSFolder + NewDTSFolder, Server))
    {
        Console.WriteLine(String.Format("New Folder {0} was created on {1}",
                NewDTSFolder, Server));
    }
}

VB
Private Sub CreateDtsStoreFolder(ByVal ParentDTSFolder As String, _
                                ByVal NewDTSFolder As String, _
                                ByVal Server As String)
    Dim app As New Application()
    app.CreateFolderOnDtsServer(ParentDTSFolder, NewDTSFolder, Server)
    If (ParentDTSFolder.EndsWith("\") = False) Then
        ParentDTSFolder = ParentDTSFolder + "\"
    End If
    If app.FolderExistsOnDtsServer( _
                ParentDTSFolder + NewDTSFolder, Server) Then
        Console.WriteLine(String.Format("New Folder {0} was created on {1}", _
                NewDTSFolder, Server))
    End If
End Sub
```

In this example, you'll notice that the method for creating the folder and then the method for checking to see whether the folder exists have both been used. Because there are separate methods for this depending upon the SSIS package store, you'll notice that this method is also strongly named. If you run this code using the existing Integration Server folder we've been working with so far, "msdb\ MySSPackages," and pass in "MyOpsPackages" as the NewDTSFolder, then you'll see the folder created as in Figure 20-5. You'll be able to see the folder under the MySSPackages folder.

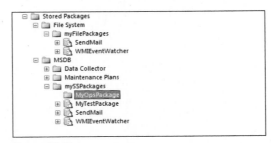

Figure 20-5

Folder maintenance allows you to automate your setup processes when moving packages from one storage location to another. The DTS runtime also enables changing package roles.

Package Role Maintenance

The `Application` object exposes methods that allow for SQL Server roles to be referenced and then assigned to SSIS packages. These methods are valid only for packages stored in the SQL Server package store.

- ❑ `GetPackageRoles`: This method takes two string parameters that return the assigned reader role and writer role for the package.

- ❑ `SetPackageRoles`: This method sets the reader role and writer role for a package.

Packages installed on an Integration Instance or SQL Server Instance can be assigned roles. The roles in the Integration Instance are slightly different than the SQL Server roles. Roles allow the assignment of read or write access to users or processes that will execute the packages. Read access gives the user the ability to view and run the package. To be able to modify the package, a user must have been assigned write access. To detail this capability, the following code snippet assigns a role to a package and then checks to ensure that the assignment is in effect:

```csharp
C#
private static void AssignRoleReadWriteAccessToPackage(string Server,
                string PackagePath, string RoleToAssign)
{
    Application app = new Application();
    app.LoadFromDtsServer(PackagePath, Server, null);
    string readerRole = string.Empty;
    string writerRole = string.Empty;
    string msg = "Role {0} has Reader Role of {1} and Writer Role of {2} on
                package {3}";

    app.SetPackageRoles(Server, PackagePath, RoleToAssign, RoleToAssign);
    app.GetPackageRoles(Server, PackagePath, out readerRole, out writerRole);

    Console.WriteLine(String.Format(msg, RoleToAssign, readerRole,
                writerRole, PackagePath));
    Console.Read();
}

VB
Private Sub AssignRoleReadWriteAccessToPackage(ByVal Server As String, _
                                    ByVal PackagePath As String, _
                                    ByVal RoleToAssign As String)
    Dim app As New Application()
    app.LoadFromDtsServer(PackagePath, Server, Nothing)
    Dim readerRole As String = String.Empty
    Dim writerRole As String = String.Empty
    Dim msg As String = "Role {0} has Reader Role of {1} and Writer Role of
                    {2} on package {3}"

    app.SetPackageRoles(Server, PackagePath, RoleToAssign, RoleToAssign)
```

```
      app.GetPackageRoles(Server, PackagePath, readerRole, writerRole)

      Console.WriteLine(String.Format(msg, RoleToAssign, readerRole, _
            writerRole, PackagePath))
      Console.Read()
   End Sub
End Sub
```

Running this code using the role of db_ssisltduser changes the default role assignments on the package to the specific role that you have designated. Figure 20-6 shows how the package role assignments will change.

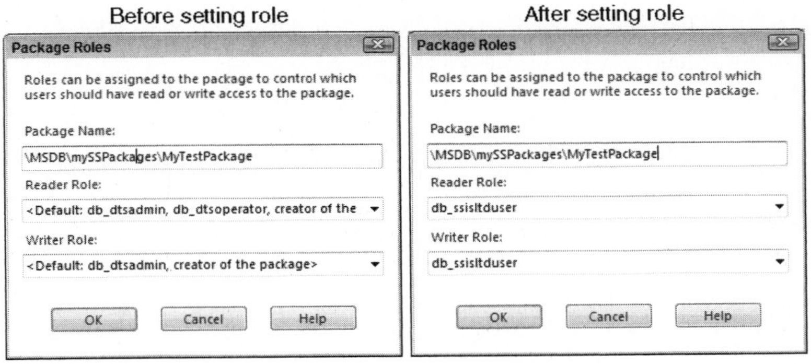

Figure 20-6

Notice that the default roles are removed, so one thing you'll want to do is coding for all the roles when you update the roles. Besides changing roles on packages, sometimes you just want to monitor packages. The next section demonstrates how to do this programmatically using the DTS runtime.

Package Monitoring

The `Application` class exposes a method to enumerate all the packages that are currently being executed on an SSIS server. By accessing a running package, you can view some general properties of the package's execution status and can even stop a package's execution status. The methods that can be used are:

❑   `GetRunningPackages`: Returns a `RunningPackages` object that enumerates all the packages currently running on a server.

❑   `RunningPackages`: A collection of `RunningPackage` objects.

❑   `RunningPackage`: An informational object that includes such information as package start time and current running duration.

The following code uses the `GetRunningPackage` object to enumerate information about each running package, such as the package's start time and running duration. You can see the Running Packages folder back in Figure 20-3 of this chapter. This folder shows the current running packages using the SSMS console. Another way to do this programmatically is to use this code:

```csharp
C#
private static void GetRunningPackageInformation(string Server)
{
    Application app = new Application();
    RunningPackages runPkgs = app.GetRunningPackages(Server);

    Console.WriteLine("Running Packages Count is {0}", runPkgs.Count);
    foreach(RunningPackage pkg in runPkgs)
    {
        Console.WriteLine("Instance ID: {0}", pkg.InstanceID);
        Console.WriteLine("Package ID: {0}", pkg.PackageID);
        Console.WriteLine("Package Name: {0}", pkg.PackageName);
        Console.WriteLine("User Name Running Package: {0}", pkg.UserName);
        Console.WriteLine("Execution Start Time: {0}",
                pkg.ExecutionStartTime.ToString());
        Console.WriteLine("Execution Duration: {0} secs",
                pkg.ExecutionDuration.ToString());
    }
}
```

```vb
VB
Private Sub GetRunningPackageInformation(ByVal Server As String)
    Dim app As New Application()
    Dim runPkgs As RunningPackages = app.GetRunningPackages(Server)

    Console.WriteLine("Running Packages Count is {0}", runPkgs.Count)
    For Each RunningPackage In runPkgs
        Console.WriteLine("Instance ID: {0}", RunningPackage.InstanceID)
        Console.WriteLine("Package ID: {0}", RunningPackage.PackageID)
        Console.WriteLine("Package Name: {0}", RunningPackage.PackageName)
        Console.WriteLine("User Name Running Package: {0}", _
                RunningPackage.UserName)
        Console.WriteLine("Execution Start Time: {0}", _
                RunningPackage.ExecutionStartTime.ToString())
        Console.WriteLine("Execution Duration: {0} secs", _
                RunningPackage.ExecutionDuration.ToString())
    Next
End Sub
```

To see this in action, run your SSIS package, and then run this code to see any package that is currently running. This type of code can be useful to monitor your server to see if any packages are running prior to shutting down the server. You may have a need to get an inventory of the packages on a server. In this case, you'll want to review the next section, which shows you how to do this programmatically.

Package Listing

When you just want to get an inventory of the packages that exist in a particular SSIS storage location, DTS runtime has a solution for this as well. The `PackageInfos` collection of the `Application` object returns an enumeration of all the packages stored in an SSIS package store. This is useful for taking an inventory of all the packages that exist on a server. Here is the code that will do this for a DTS package store:

```csharp
C#
private static void IterateDTSStorePackagesAndPrintInfo(string Path,
                string Server)
{
    Application app = new Application();
    string sMsg = "Package [{0}] found. " +
      "Version {1}.{2}.{3} " +
        "Creation Date {2}\n";

    Console.WriteLine("Enumerating packages on Server [" + Server + "]");
    Console.WriteLine("Folder = " + Path);

    if(app.FolderExistsOnDtsServer(Path, Server))
    {
    Console.WriteLine("Folder Verified\n");
    PackageInfos pInfos = app.GetDtsServerPackageInfos(Path, Server);
    foreach(PackageInfo pInfo in pInfos)
        {
        Console.WriteLine(String.Format(sMsg, pInfo.Name,
                pInfo.VersionMajor.ToString(),
                pInfo.VersionMinor.ToString(),
                pInfo.VersionBuild.ToString(),
                pInfo.CreationDate.ToLongDateString().ToString()));
        }
    }
    else
    {
    Console.WriteLine("Folder Not Found");
    }
}

VB
Private Sub IterateDTSStorePackagesAndPrintInfo(ByVal Path As String, _
                            ByVal Server As String)
    Dim app As New Application()
    Dim pInfos As PackageInfos
    Dim pInfo As PackageInfo
    Dim sFolder As String = "msdb\mySSPackages"
    Dim sMsg As String = String.Empty
    sMsg = "Package [{0}] found. " + _
          "Version {1}.{2}.{3} " + _
          "Creation Date {2}" + vbCrLf

    Console.WriteLine("Enumerating packages on Server [" + Server + "]")
    Console.WriteLine("Folder = " + Path)
```

```
      If (app.FolderExistsOnDtsServer(Path, Server)) Then
          Console.WriteLine("Folder Verified" + vbCrLf)
          pInfos = app.GetDtsServerPackageInfos(Path, Server)
          For Each pInfo In pInfos
              Console.WriteLine(String.Format(sMsg, pInfo.Name, _
                      pInfo.VersionMajor.ToString(), _
                      pInfo.VersionMinor.ToString(), _
                      pInfo.VersionBuild.ToString(), _
                      pInfo.CreationDate.ToLongDateString))
          Next
      Else
          Console.WriteLine("Folder Not Found")
      End If
End Sub
```

Call this code against your Integration Server like this:

```
C#
IterateDTSStorePackagesAndPrintInfo("msdb\\mySSPackages", ".")
VB
IterateDTSStorePackagesAndPrintInfo("msdb\mySSPackages", ".")
```

The result is that the code will stream information about the packages stored on the server instance like Figure 20-7.

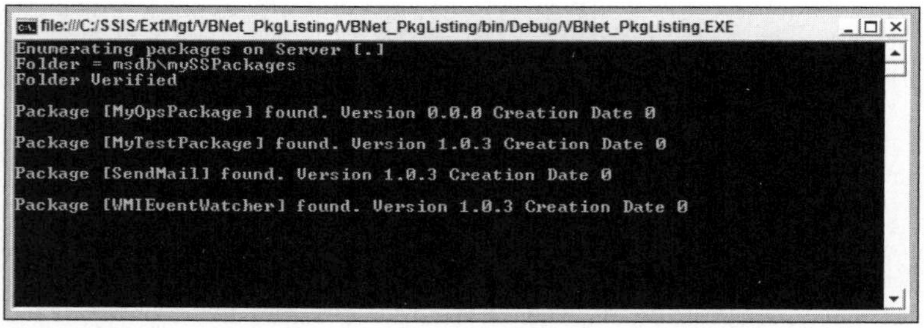

Figure 20-7

This is only the tip of the iceberg when it comes to what you can do with the DTS runtime libraries. To get an idea of what you can do using this library, in the next section you build a simple UI that will enable you to use some of the code techniques described so far.

A Package Management Example

The following example demonstrates how to incorporate package management operations in a web-based application. This example demonstrates how to enumerate the folder structure of a SQL Server SSIS package store, enumerate the packages that are contained in a selected folder, and allows you to execute a package from the web page itself. In this chapter, we'll demonstrate with a C# version of the project. However, you can download a VB.NET version of the project as well as the source you'll see in this chapter from www.wrox.com.

To start, first create a new web project in Visual Studio. Launch Visual Studio and select File ⇨ New ⇨ Web Site. In the New Web Site dialog (see Figure 20-8), choose Visual C# or Visual Basic as the language. Leave the rest of the fields as they are.

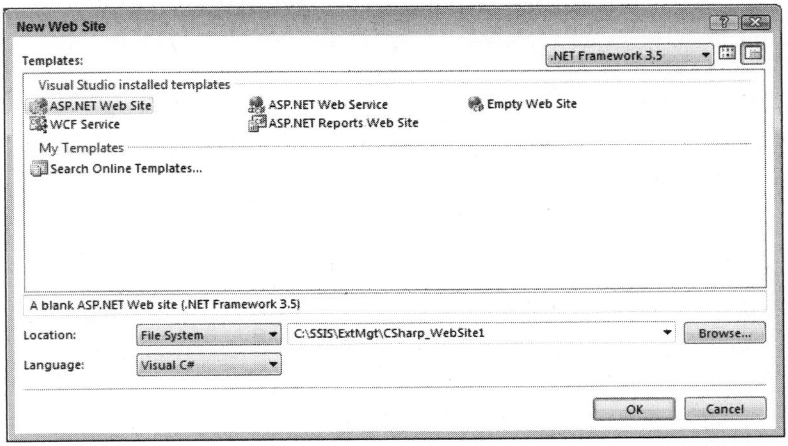

Figure 20-8

Click the OK button and the Web Site project will be initialized. By default, the `Default.aspx` page is created and displayed automatically. Now you'll start building the page that will display the information you want. First, you must add the web controls to the page.

To do this, select the Design view from the bottom-left corner of the `Default.aspx` tab. This puts the interface into graphics designer mode. From the Toolbox on the left-hand side of the window, drag a TreeView control onto the page. The TreeView control is in the Navigation group of the Toolbox. Now drag a GridView control onto the page. The GridView is located in the Data group of the Toolbox. And finally drag over a Button control from the Toolbox. The Button control can be found in the Standard group. Click the Button control and in the Properties tab change the Text property to the word "Refresh."

Now you need to add some supporting HTML in the source view of the page to configure the columns of the GridView control. To do so, click the Source button on the bottom left of the `Default.aspx` page tab. This switches the view to show you the HTML code that defines this page. Add the following HTML code between the `<asp:GridView1>` elements. The `<asp:BoundField>` elements you're adding configure the GridView to display three data columns and a button column. You could do this through the Design interface, but this is a bit quicker for your purposes:

```
<Columns>
    <asp:BoundField DataField="PackageName" HeaderText="Name" />
    <asp:BoundField DataField="PackageFolder" HeaderText="Folder" />
    <asp:BoundField DataField="Status" HeaderText="Status" />
    <asp:ButtonField Text="Execute"  ButtonType=Button/>
</Columns>
```

The page should now look like Figure 20-9.

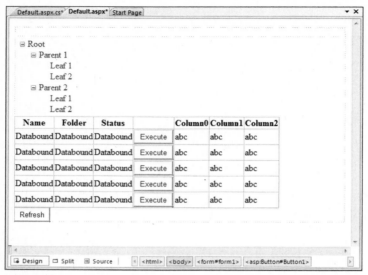

Figure 20-9

Before you leave this screen, you need to create a few event handlers on these controls. To do this, select the TreeView control. Go to the Properties tab in the bottom right of the Visual Studio IDE. On the toolbar of the Properties window, select the lightning bolt symbol that signifies the Events view. The Events view allows you to configure what event handlers you will need to handle for this page. With the TreeView selected and the Events view shown in the Properties window, double-click in the `SelectedNodeChanged` event in the Behavior group. Notice that the `Default.aspx.cs` code-behind page is automatically loaded, and the event handler code for the `SelectedNodeChanged` event is automatically created. Switch back to the `Default.apsx` tab and do the same thing for the TreeView Load event. Now repeat the same process for the GridView `RowCommand` event and the Button `Click` events. To view a description of what these events do, you can search for the event name in the Help screen.

The full HTML code of the page should now look something like this:

```
<%@ Page Language="C#" AutoEventWireup="true"  CodeFile="Default.aspx.cs"
Inherits="_Default2" %>

<!DOCTYPE html PUBLIC "-//W3C//DTD XHTML 1.1//EN"
"http://www.w3.org/TR/xhtml11/DTD/xhtml11.dtd">

<html xmlns="http://www.w3.org/1999/xhtml" >
<head runat="server">
    <title>Untitled Page</title>
</head>
<body>
```

```
    <form id="form1" runat="server">
    <div>
        <asp:TreeView ID="TreeView1" runat="server" ShowLines="True"
            OnLoad="TreeView1_Load" OnSelectedNodeChanged=
            "TreeView1_SelectedNodeChanged">

        </asp:TreeView>
        <br />
        <asp:GridView ID="GridView1" runat="server" AutoGenerateColumns=False
            OnRowCommand="GridView1_RowCommand" >
            <Columns>
                <asp:BoundField DataField="PackageName" HeaderText="Name" />
                <asp:BoundField DataField="PackageFolder" HeaderText="Folder"
                    />
                <asp:BoundField DataField="Status" HeaderText="Status" />
                <asp:ButtonField Text="Execute"  ButtonType=Button/>
            </Columns>
        </asp:GridView>
         <br />
        <asp:Button ID="Button1" runat="server" OnClick="Button1_Click"
                    Text="Refresh" /></div>
    </form>
</body>
</html>
```

Now you need to start adding the code behind the page that makes this page work. For this example, you will be creating a few custom classes to support code you will be writing in the code-behind page of the Web Form. First, you need to add two new class files. To do this, select File ⇨ New ⇨ File from the main menu. In the Add New File dialog box that appears, select a new Class object and name it `PackageGroup.cs`. The `PackageGroup` object will be used to wrap a `PackageInfo` object and enhance its functionality. Next, add another Class object and call this one `PackageGroupCollection.cs`. Notice that these two files have been added to the App_Code directory of the solution. In Visual Studio, your code external modules are stored in the App_Code directory. Add a reference in your project to the `Microsoft.SQLServer.ManagedDTS.dll`. Next, open the `PackageGroup.cs` file and add the following code to the file. You can overwrite the code that was automatically generated with this code.

```
using System;
using System.Data;
using System.Configuration;
using System.Web;
using System.Web.Security;
using System.Web.UI;
using System.Web.UI.WebControls;
using System.Web.UI.WebControls.WebParts;
using System.Web.UI.HtmlControls;
using Microsoft.SqlServer.Dts.Runtime;

/// <summary>
/// Summary description for PackageGroup
/// </summary>
///
```

```csharp
public class PackageGroup
{
  Application dtsapp;

  public PackageGroup(PackageInfo packageInfo, string server)
  {
    dtsapp= new Application();
    _packageinfo = packageInfo;
    _server = server;
  }

  private PackageInfo _packageinfo;
  private string _server;

  public string PackageName
  {
    get { return _packageinfo.Name;}
  }

  public string PackageFolder
  {
    get{return _packageinfo.Folder;}
  }

  public string Status
  {
    get { return GetPackageStatus(); }
  }

  public void ExecPackage()
  {
    Package p = dtsapp.LoadFromSqlServer(string.Concat(_packageinfo.Folder +
               "\\" + _packageinfo.Name) , _server, null, null, null);
    p.Execute();
  }

  private string GetPackageStatus()
  {
    RunningPackages rps= dtsapp.GetRunningPackages(_server);
    foreach( RunningPackage rp in rps)
    {
      if (rp.PackageID == new Guid(_packageinfo.PackageGuid))
      {
        return "Executing";
      }
    }
    return "Sleeping";
  }
}
```

As you can see, this object wraps a `PackageInfo` object. You could just link the `PackageInfo` objects to the GridView, but this method codes a wrapper with additional functionality to determine a package's execution status and execute a package. The `ExecutePackage` method can be called to execute the package, and the `GetPackageStatus` method searches the currently running packages on the server and returns an execution status to the calling object.

To store information about multiple packages, you need to roll all the `PackageGroup` objects you create into a collection object. To do this, you created a strongly typed collection class called `PackageGroupCollection` to house very concrete `PackageGroup` objects. Open the `PackageGroupCollection` file and add the following code. Once again, you can overwrite the code that was automatically created when the file was created with this example code.

```csharp
using System;
using System.Data;
using System.Configuration;
using System.Web;
using System.Web.Security;
using System.Web.UI;
using System.Web.UI.WebControls;
using System.Web.UI.WebControls.WebParts;
using System.Web.UI.HtmlControls;

/// <summary>
/// Summary description for PackageGroupCollection
/// </summary>
///
public class PackageGroupCollection : System.Collections.CollectionBase
{
  public PackageGroupCollection()
  {
  }

  public void Add(PackageGroup aPackageGroup)
  {
    List.Add(aPackageGroup);
  }

  public void Remove(int index)
  {
    if (index > Count - 1 || index < 0)
    {
      throw new Exception("Index not valid!");
    }
    else
```

```
      {
        List.RemoveAt(index);
      }
    }

    public PackageGroup Item(int Index)
    {
      return (PackageGroup)List[Index];
    }
}
```

This class simply inherits from the `System.CollectionBase` class to implement a basic `IList` interface. To learn more about strongly typed collections and the `CollectionBase` class, search the Help files. Next you will add the code-behind page of the `Default.aspx` page. Select the `Default.aspx.cs` tab and add the following code to this page:

```
using System;
using System.Data;
using System.Data.SqlClient;
using System.Configuration;
using System.Web;
using System.Web.Security;
using System.Web.UI;
using System.Web.UI.WebControls;
using System.Web.UI.WebControls.WebParts;
using System.Web.UI.HtmlControls;
using System.Threading;
using Microsoft.SqlServer.Dts.Runtime;

public partial class _Default : System.Web.UI.Page
{
  Application dtsapp;
  PackageGroupCollection pgc;

  protected void Page_Load(object sender, EventArgs e)
  {
    //Initialize Application object
    dtsapp = new Application();
  }

  protected void TreeView1_Load(object sender, EventArgs e)
  {
    //Clear TreeView and Load root node
    //Load the SqlServer SSIS folder structure into tree view and show all
    //nodes
    TreeView1.Nodes.Clear();
    TreeView1.Nodes.Add(new TreeNode("MSDB", @"\"));
    LoadTreeView(dtsapp.GetPackageInfos(@"\", "localhost", null, null));
    TreeView1.ExpandAll();
  }

  protected void TreeView1_SelectedNodeChanged(object sender, EventArgs e)
  {
```

```csharp
    //Build Collection of PackageGroups
  pgc = BuildPackageGroupCollection(dtsapp.GetPackageInfos(
        TreeView1.SelectedNode.ValuePath.Replace('/', '\\'),
        "localhost", null, null));
  //Rebind the GridView to load Package Group Collection
  LoadGridView(pgc);
  //Store the Package Group Collection is Session State
  Session.Add("pgc", pgc);
}

protected void GridView1_RowCommand(object sender,
                                    GridViewCommandEventArgs e)
{
  if (((Button)e.CommandSource).Text.ToString() == "Execute")
  {
    pgc = (PackageGroupCollection)Session["pgc"];
    PackageGroup pg = pgc.Item(Convert.ToInt32(e.CommandArgument));
    Thread oThread = new System.Threading.Thread(new
                    System.Threading.ThreadStart(pg.ExecPackage));
    oThread.Start();
    LoadGridView(pgc);
  }
}

protected void LoadTreeView(PackageInfos pis)
{
  foreach (PackageInfo p in pis)
  {
    if (p.Flags == DTSPackageInfoFlags.Folder)
    {
      TreeNode n = TreeView1.FindNode(p.Folder);
      n.ChildNodes.Add(new TreeNode(p.Name));
      LoadTreeView(dtsapp.GetPackageInfos(p.Folder + '/' + p.Name,
                "localhost", null, null));
    }
  }
}

protected void LoadGridView(PackageGroupCollection pgc)
{
  GridView1.DataSource = pgc;
  GridView1.DataBind();
}

protected PackageGroupCollection BuildPackageGroupCollection(PackageInfos
      packageInfos)
{
  PackageGroupCollection pgc = new PackageGroupCollection();
  foreach (PackageInfo p in packageInfos)
  {
    if (p.Flags == DTSPackageInfoFlags.Package)
    {
```

```
            PackageGroup pg = new PackageGroup(p, "localhost");
            pgc.Add(pg);
        }
    }
    return pgc;
}


protected void Button1_Click(object sender, EventArgs e)
{
    LoadGridView((PackageGroupCollection)Session["pgc"]);
}
}
```

The preceding code handles the execution of the page request. First is the Page_Load method that is run every time the asp worker process loads the page to be processed. In this method, an Application object is loaded for use during the processing of the page.

When the page is processed, there are several additional methods that are called. The TreeView_Load method is called. This method in turn calls the LoadTreeView method that accepts a PackageInfos collection. This collection of PackageInfo objects is processed one by one, and the information is loaded into the TreeView according to the hierarchy of the SQL Server SSIS package folders. When the page is first loaded, just the TreeView is displayed. By selecting a folder in the TreeView, the page is posted back to the server, and the TreeView1_SelectedNodeChanged method is called. This method calls another method in this page called BuildPackageGroupCollection, which accepts a PackageInfos collection. The PackageInfos collection is processed to look for valid package objects only. To determine this, the PackageInfo class exposes a Flag property that identifies the PackageInfo object as a Folder or a Package object. Once the collection is built, the LoadGridView method is called to link the PackageGroupCollection to the GridView. In the LoadGridView method, the collection is bound to the GridView object. This action automatically loads all the objects in the PackageGroupCollection into the GridView.

So how does the GridView know which columns to display? Remember back in the beginning of this example when you added the <asp:BoundColumn> elements to the GridView object. Notice that the DataField attributes are set to the properties of the PackageGroup objects in the PackageGroupCollection object. So in your walk-through of the code, the page is basically finished processing and the results would be displayed to the user in the web page. So try it and inspect what you have so far. Go ahead and build and then run the project. Figure 20-10 shows a sample of what you may see when you run the web page. Your results may vary depending on the folders and packages you have configured in your server.

You'll need to click on the MySSPackages Node to see the packages in the grid.

So now take a look at how the status field and Execute button work. When the GridView is loaded with PackageGroup objects, the status property of the PackageGroup class is called. Look in the PackageGroup.cs file and you will see that when the status property is called, a collection of RunningPackages is created. By iterating through all the RunningPackage objects, if the GUID of the package in question matches the GUID of a running package, a result of Executing is returned to the GridView. Otherwise, the Sleeping status result is returned. The Execute button works in a similar fashion.

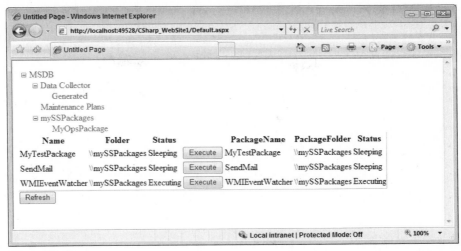

Figure 20-10

When the Execute button is clicked, the `GridView1_RowCommand` method is called in the page's code-behind file. This method re-instantiates the `PackageGroup` object from the page's viewstate cache. When found, the package is executed by calling the `Execute` method of the `PackageGroup` object. Notice that this call is being done in a newly created thread. By design, a web page is processed synchronously. This means that if the package was executed in the same thread, the `Execute` method would not return until the package was finished executing. So by starting the package in a new thread, the page can return, and the status of the package can be displayed in the GridView. So give it a try. Make sure your package runs long enough for you to refresh the web page and see the status value change.

That's just a basic implementation of some of the functionality exposed by the `Microsoft.SqlServer` `.Dts.Runtime` namespace to manage your SSIS packages through managed code. You saw how to obtain a collection of `PackageInfo` objects and how to leverage the functionality of the objects in an application. In addition, you learned how to run a package and determine which packages are currently running. Obviously, this is a simple application and could stand to be greatly improved with error handling and additional functionality. For example, you could add functionality to cancel a package's execution, load or delete package files to SQL Server through the website, or modify the code to support the viewing of packages in the SSIS file storage hierarchy.

Package Log Providers

Log providers are used to define the destination for the log information that is generated when a package executes. For instance, if you require a record of the execution of your package, a log provider could persist the events and actions that had transpired into a log file, recording not only the execution but also, if required, the values and results of the execution. Defining what should be logged during a package's execution is a two-step process. First, you must define which log providers to use. You can define multiple providers in a single package. The second step is to define what information should be sent to the defined log providers.

To demonstrate how you would do this using the UI, configure logging for the test SSIS package by selecting select SSIS ⇨ Logging from the menu. The Configure SSIS Logs dialog box that is displayed shows all the containers that currently exist in the package. The first step is completed by configuring SSIS Log Providers on the Providers and Logs tab, shown in Figure 20-11.

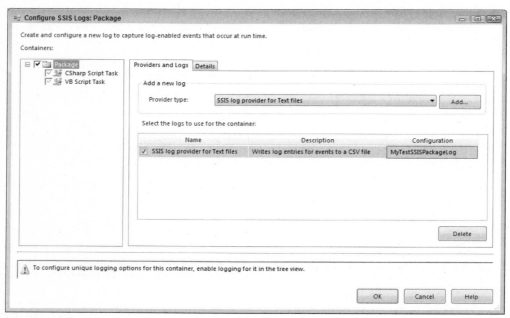

Figure 20-11

SQL Server Integration Services includes several default log providers. These providers are selected in the Provider Type combo box and are defined as follows:

- ❑ **SSIS Log Provider for Text Files:** This provider is used to store log information to a CSV file on the file system. This provider requires you to configure a File Connection object that defines the location of the file. Storing log information in a text file is the easiest way to persist a package's execution. Text files are portable and the CSV format is a simple-to-use industry-wide standard.

- ❑ **SSIS Log Provider for SQL Profiler:** This provider produces a SQL Provider trace file. The file must be specified with a `trc` file extension so that you can open it using the SQL Profiler diagnostic tool. Using SQL Profiler trace files is an easy way for DBAs to view log information. Using Profiler, you could view the execution of the package step-by-step, even replaying the steps in a test environment.

- ❑ **SSIS Log Provider for SQL Server:** This provider sends package log events to a table in the specified SQL Server database. The database is defined using an OLE DB Connection. The first time this package is executed, a table called sysssislog will be created automatically. Storing log information in a SQL Server database inherits the benefits of persisting information in a relational database system. You could easily retrieve log information for analysis across multiple package executions.

❑ **SSIS Log Provider for Windows Event Log:** This provider sends log information to the Application event store. The entries created will be under the Source name SQLISPackage. No additional configuration is required for this provider. Logging package execution to the Windows Event Log is possibly the easiest way to store log events. The Windows Event Log is easy to view and can be viewed remotely if required.

❑ **SSIS Log Provider for XML Files:** This provider stores log information in a specified XML file on the file system. The file is specified through a File Connection object. Make sure you save the file with an `xml` file extension. Logging events to XML inherits the advantages of the XML specification. XML files are very portable across systems and can be validated against a Schema definition.

Specifying Events to Log

Once you have configured the log providers you wish to employ, you must define what events in the package to log. This is done in the Details tab of Log Configuration dialog box, as shown in Figure 20-12. To enable an event to be logged, check the box next to its name. For instance, in Figure 20-12, the OnError event for the package has been selected to be logged. By selecting other containers on the left-hand side of the dialog box, additional events can be selected down to an individual task or Data Flow event level. To select all events at once, check the box in the header row of the table. By selecting individual containers in the tree view on the left, you can configure the logging of events on an individual task level. By configuring logging at the task level, the special events exposed by a task can additionally be included in the log.

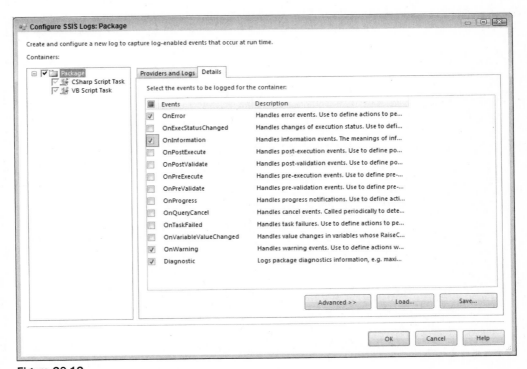

Figure 20-12

This is the way to set up a log file using the UI. To learn how to examine log providers programmatically, continue on to the next section.

Programming to Log Providers

The `package` object exposes the `LogProviders` collection object, which contains the configured log providers in a package. The `LogProvider` object encapsulates a provider's configuration information.

The `LogProvider` object exposes the following key properties:

- ❑ `Name`: A descriptive name for the log provider.

- ❑ `ConfigString`: The name of a valid `Connection` object within the package that contains information on how to connect to the destination store.

- ❑ `CreationName`: The `ProgID` of the log provider. This value is used in the creation of log providers dynamically.

- ❑ `Description`: Describes the type of provider and optionally the destination to which it points.

The next two examples enumerate all the log providers that have been configured in a package and write the results to the console window. To get extra mileage out of these examples, the C# version loads the package from a file and the VB.NET version loads the package from an Integration Server:

```
C#
private static void GetPackageLogsForPackage(string PackagePath)
{
    Application dtsapp = new Application();
    Package p = dtsapp.LoadPackage(PackagePath, null);
    Console.WriteLine("Executing Package {0}", PackagePath);
    p.Execute();

    Console.WriteLine("Package Execution Complete");
    Console.WriteLine("LogProviders");
    LogProviders logProviders = p.LogProviders;
    Console.WriteLine("LogProviders Count: {0}", logProviders.Count);
    LogProviderEnumerator logProvidersEnum = logProviders.GetEnumerator();

    while (logProvidersEnum.MoveNext())
    {
        LogProvider logProv = logProvidersEnum.Current;
        Console.WriteLine("ConfigString:    {0}", logProv.ConfigString);
        Console.WriteLine("CreationName     {0}", logProv.CreationName);
        Console.WriteLine("DelayValidation {0}", logProv.DelayValidation);
        Console.WriteLine("Description      {0}", logProv.Description);
        Console.WriteLine("HostType         {0}", logProv.HostType);
        Console.WriteLine("ID               {0}", logProv.ID);
        Console.WriteLine("InnerObject      {0}", logProv.InnerObject);
        Console.WriteLine("Name             {0}", logProv.Name);
        Console.WriteLine("-----------------");
    }
}
```

```
}
```

```vb
VB
Private Sub GetPackageLogsForPackage(ByVal PackagePath As String, ByVal Server _
                                     As String)
    Dim app As New Application()
    Dim p As Package = app.LoadFromDtsServer(PackagePath, Server, Nothing)
    Console.WriteLine("Executing Package {0}", PackagePath)
    p.Execute()

    Console.WriteLine("Package Execution Complete")
    Console.WriteLine("LogProviders")
    Dim logProviders As LogProviders = p.LogProviders()
    Console.WriteLine("LogProviders Count: {0}", logProviders.Count)

    Dim logProvidersEnum As LogProviderEnumerator = _
                 logProviders.GetEnumerator()

    While (logProvidersEnum.MoveNext())
        Dim logProv As LogProvider = logProvidersEnum.Current
        Console.WriteLine("ConfigString:    {0}", logProv.ConfigString)
        Console.WriteLine("CreationName     {0}", logProv.CreationName)
        Console.WriteLine("DelayValidation  {0}", logProv.DelayValidation)
        Console.WriteLine("Description      {0}", logProv.Description)
        Console.WriteLine("HostType         {0}", logProv.HostType)
        Console.WriteLine("ID               {0}", logProv.ID)
        Console.WriteLine("InnerObject      {0}", logProv.InnerObject)
        Console.WriteLine("Name             {0}", logProv.Name)
        Console.WriteLine("-----------------")
    End While
End Sub
```

You can of course dynamically configure a package's log providers. To do so, a valid connection must initially be created to support the communications to the database. In the following code, you'll see that first a package is loaded into memory. Then the connection is created for the mytext.xml file and named. This name is used later as the ConfigString for the log provider to connect the output to the file Connection Manager.

```csharp
C#
public static void CreatePackageLogProvider(string PackagePath, string Server)
{
    Application dtsapp = new Application();
    Package p = dtsapp.LoadFromDtsServer(PackagePath, Server, null);

    ConnectionManager myConnMgr = p.Connections.Add("FILE");
    myConnMgr.Name = "mytest.xml";
    myConnMgr.ConnectionString = "c:\\ssis\\mytest.xml";

    LogProvider logProvider = p.LogProviders.Add("DTS.LogProviderXMLFile.2");
    logProvider.ConfigString = "mytest.xml";

    p.LoggingOptions.SelectedLogProviders.Add(logProvider);
    p.LoggingOptions.EventFilterKind = DTSEventFilterKind.Inclusion;
```

```
        p.LoggingOptions.EventFilter = new string[] { "OnError", "OnWarning",
            "OnInformation" };
        p.LoggingMode = DTSLoggingMode.Enabled;
        logProvider.OpenLog();
        p.Execute();
}


VB
Public Sub CreatePackageLogProvider(ByVal PackagePath As String, ByVal Server
                                As String)
    Dim dtsapp As New Application()
    Dim p As Package = dtsapp.LoadFromDtsServer(PackagePath, Server, Nothing)

    Dim myConnMgr As ConnectionManager = p.Connections.Add("FILE")
    myConnMgr.Name = "mytest.xml"
    myConnMgr.ConnectionString = "c:\ssis\mytest.xml"

    Dim logProvider As LogProvider =
            p.LogProviders.Add("DTS.LogProviderXMLFile.2")
    logProvider.ConfigString = "mytest.xml"
    p.LoggingOptions.SelectedLogProviders.Add(logProvider)
    p.LoggingOptions.EventFilterKind = DTSEventFilterKind.Inclusion
    p.LoggingOptions.EventFilter = New String() {"OnError", "OnWarning",
        "OnInformation"}
    p.LoggingMode = DTSLoggingMode.Enabled
    logProvider.OpenLog()
    p.Execute()
End Sub
```

Next, the log provider is instantiated by passing the `ProgID` of the provider you wish to create. The following is a list of the `ProgIDs` for each type of log provider available:

Notice that the ProgIDs have changed from SSIS 2005 with the switch from "1" to "2".

❑ **Text File Log Provider:** `DTS.LogProviderTextFile.2`

❑ **SQL Profiler Log Provider:** `DTS.LogProviderSQLProfiler.2`

❑ **SQL Server Log Provider:** `DTS.LogProviderSQLServer.2`

❑ **Windows Event Log Provider:** `DTS.LogProviderEventLog.2`

❑ **XML File Log Provider:** `DTS.LogProviderXMLFile.2`

Package Configurations

Package configurations are a flexible method of dynamically configuring a package at runtime. This allows you a high degree of flexibility in the execution of SSIS packages. This allows you to design the package to run in different environments without having to modify the package file itself. When a package is written, not all operational parameters may be known, such as the location of a file or the value of a variable. By supplying this information at runtime, the user does not have to hard-code these values into a package. When a package is run, the values stored in the specified configuration store are loaded for use during the package's execution. The configuration capabilities of SSIS support the storage of data in five different data stores. The following list describes each type of data store and its capabilities:

- ❑ **XML File Configuration:** The XML File Configuration option stores package information in an XML file on the file system. This configuration provider lets you store multiple configuration settings in a single file. As an alternative to hard-coding the path to the XML file, the path can be stored in a user-defined environment variable. This option allows you to modify the XML file easily and distribute the configuration easily with the package.

- ❑ **Environment Variable:** The Environment Variable option allows you to store a configuration value in an environment variable. This option will only allow you to save a single configuration parameter. By specifying an environment variable that is available on each machine the package will run on, you can be sure that the package configuration will be valid for each environment. Also, the setup of the environment variable can be done once during initial setup of package's environment.

- ❑ **Registry Entry:** The Registry Entry option allows you to store a configuration value in a registry value. Only a single value can be specified. Optionally, you can specify an environment variable that contains a registry key where the value is stored. Configuration entries in the registry are a secure and reliable way to store configuration values.

- ❑ **Parent Package Variable:** The Parent Package Variable option allows you to specify a fully qualified variable in a different package as the source for the configuration value. Only a single value can be stored in a specified configuration store. This is a good way to link packages and pass values between packages at runtime. If one package depends on the results from another package, this option is perfect.

- ❑ **SQL Server:** The SQL Server option creates an SSIS Configuration table in a database that you specify. Because this table could hold the configurations for multiple packages, a configuration filter value should be specified to allow the system to return the correct configuration values. This option allows you to specify multiple configuration values that will be stored under the filter name specified. Optionally, you can specify the database, table, and filter in an environment variable in the following format:

```
<database connection>;<configuration table>;<filter>;
```

For example:

```
VSTSB2.WroxTestDB;[dbo].[SSIS Configurations];Package1;
```

Creating a Configuration

To create a configuration for a package, select the menu options SSIS ⇨ Package Configurations. In the dialog that is displayed, select the "Enable package configurations" checkbox. From here, you must define which package configuration provider to use. This can be accomplished through the Package Configuration Wizard that is started when you click the Add button.

On the first page of the wizard, shown in Figure 20-13, you must decide which configuration provider you wish to use to store the configuration information. For this example, choose the XML File Configuration option. Now specify the path where the configuration file will reside. Having a standard location to store your configuration files will help ensure that as a package is moved from environment to environment, the links to the configuration will not be broken. If the path to the configuration is not standard, you can store the path to the configuration file in an environment variable and reference the environment variable in the package wizard. Remember, if you have recently added the environment variable to your system, you may need to reboot for it to be available for use in your package.

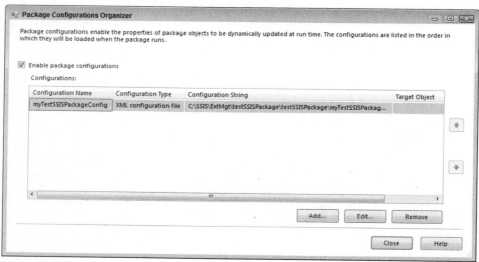

Figure 20-13

Once you've chosen a configuration storage provider, the next step is to specify the properties to save in the configuration store, as shown in Figure 20-14. You can either select a single value from the property tree view or select multiple values at one time. Because you selected the XML File Configuration provider, you can select multiple values to store.

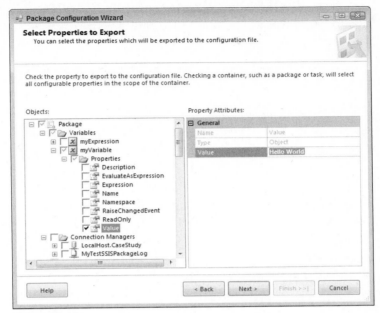

Figure 20-14

Notice that not only can you store default values to load at the time the package is executed, but you can also load entire object definitions at runtime. This is useful if you just want to load a variable's value or actually specify an entire variable configuration at runtime. This would be useful if you wanted to configure the actual properties of a variable. Almost every aspect of a package can be persisted to a configuration store. These include package properties, configured values in defined tasks, configuration information for log providers, and Connection Manager information. About the only thing you can't store in a package configuration store is specific data about the package configurations.

Once finished, the package configuration information is stored in the package. When the package is executed, the configuration providers will load the values from the specified data stores and substitute the values found for the default values saved in the package.

Programming the Configuration Object

You can also programmatically configure a package's configuration through the Configuration object. This is useful if you would like to configure a package through managed code as shown at the beginning of this chapter. All package configurations can be accessed through the Configurations collection of the package object.

The Configuration object exposes functionality to dynamically configure a package's configuration settings. This allows you to programmatically configure a package based on the environment in which it will run. Because a package can contain multiple configuration sources, you can discover all the configurations in a package by enumerating the configuration objects in the Configuration object.

Configuration Object

The Configuration object exposes the following members:

❏ ConfigurationString: The path describing where the physical configuration store is located.

❏ ConfigurationType: Sets the configuration provider to be used to interface to the configuration data store. The configuration type is referenced in from the DTSConfigurationType enumeration. Note that a DTSConfigurationType that starts with an "I" denotes that the configurationstring is stored in an environment variable.

❏ Name: The unique name for the configuration object in the package.

❏ PackagePath: Defines the path of the actual data that is being accessed.

The following example details how to add an existing configuration store to a package. First, the EnableConfiguration property is set to true. Then, an empty configuration object is added to the package. The configuration object is then set to the Config File type, which directs the configuration to expect a valid dtsconfig file to be specified in the configurationstring property. Finally, the path to the configuration information is supplied and the package's path is stored. The package is then saved, thus persisting the configuration setup to the package file.

```csharp
C#
private static void CreatePackageConfig(string PackagePath)
{
    Application app = new Application();
    Package pkg = app.LoadPackage(PackagePath, null);
    Variable var = pkg.Variables.Add("myConfigVar", false, "", "Test");
    string packagePathToVariable = var.GetPackagePath();

    pkg.EnableConfigurations = true;

    Configuration config = pkg.Configurations.Add();
    config.ConfigurationString = "ConfigureMyConfigVar";
    config.ConfigurationType = DTSConfigurationType.EnvVariable;
    config.Name = "ConfigureMyConfigVar";
    config.PackagePath = packagePathToVariable;
    app.SaveToXml(@"C:\SSIS\extmgt\TestSSISPackage\TestSSISPackage\" +
                "myTestSSISPackageConfig.xml", pkg, null);
    Console.WriteLine("Configuration Created and Saved");
}
```

```vbnet
VB
Private Sub CreatePackageConfig(ByVal PackagePath As String)
    Dim app As New Application()
    Dim pkg As Package = app.LoadPackage(PackagePath, Nothing)

    Dim var As Variable = pkg.Variables.Add("myConfigVar", False, "", "Test")
    Dim packagePathToVariable As String = var.GetPackagePath()

    pkg.EnableConfigurations = True
```

```
        Dim config As Configuration = pkg.Configurations.Add()
        config.ConfigurationString = "ConfigureMyConfigVar"
        config.ConfigurationType = DTSConfigurationType.EnvVariable
        config.Name = "ConfigureMyConfigVar"
        config.PackagePath = packagePathToVariable
        app.SaveToXml("C:\SSIS\extmgt\TestSSISPackage\TestSSISPackage\" _ _
                    myTestSSISPackageConfig.xml", _
                 pkg, Nothing)
        Console.WriteLine("Configuration Created and Saved")
    End Sub
```

If you run this code against the Test SSIS package for this chapter, you'll see a new
`myTestSSISPackageConfig.xml` file in the TestSSISPackage directory with the additional variable that
was added and a configuration for the variable.

This section has described how you can use the DTS runtime code library to perform many of your
mundane administrative tasks programmatically. Let's look now at another feature of SSIS that you can
use in your administrative Toolbox — the WMI.

Windows Management Instrumentation Tasks

SSIS includes two special tasks that allow you to query system information and monitor system events.
These tasks are the WMI Data Reader Task and the WMI Event Watcher Task. These tasks are especially
useful for system management tasks, as you will discover with examples later in this chapter. WMI uses
a specialized query language known as WQL, which is similar to SQL, to obtain information about a
Windows system. There are many features and capabilities of WMI. We won't be able to cover all of
them, but here are a few common uses:

❑   You can get information on files and directories, such as file size, or enumerate the files in a
     folder. You can also monitor the file system for events, such as whether a file has been modified
     recently. This could be required in a package if your package is importing data from a CSV or
     XML file. A change in the file could trigger tasks to fire in your package.

❑   You can find out if an application is currently running. In addition, you can find out how much
     memory that application is using or how much processor time it has used. This would be useful
     if your package needed to know if a companion process was running before creating some sort
     of output result.

❑   You can obtain information about users in Active Directory, such as whether a user is active or if
     they have certain permissions on a resource. This would be useful in a package if information
     about a user or machine on the network is required for your package's execution.

❑   You can control services that are running on a computer system and actually start and stop them
     as required. This would be useful if your package needed to stop a service during a data
     transfer.

This is just a small sample of the information you can glean from a computer system. You can obtain
information not only on the current system but also on remote systems. As you can see, this gives you

access to a great deal of information that could be used in the execution of an SSIS package. For example, you could determine if enough disk space existed on a drive before copying a backup file from a remote system to the current system. You could also monitor a file for updates and automatically import the changes into a database table. Later in this chapter you see how to actually implement these two examples.

WMI Reader Task Explained

The WMI Data Reader Task has the following parameters that must be configured properly for the task object to work:

- ❑ `WmiConnection`: A configured WMI Connection Object.

- ❑ `WqlQuerySourceType`: This setting specifies where the WQL query is referenced. The query can be manually typed in or can be stored in a file or a variable.

- ❑ `WqlQuerySource`: This field sets the actual source of the WQL Query Source selected in the `WqlQuerySourceType`.

- ❑ `OutputType`: This parameter sets the structure that the results of the WQL query are stored in when executed.

- ❑ `Overwrite Destination`: This parameter determines if the previous results are retained or overwritten when the task is executed.

- ❑ `Destination Type`: This allows you to specify how the results will be stored.

- ❑ `Destination`: This parameter allows you to specify the location of the destination type.

To start configuration of the WMI Data Reader Task, you must first create a WMI Connection Manager object. The WMI Connection Manager specifies the WMI namespace that the query will run against. The WMI class used in the query must be contained within that namespace. The standard namespace for most machines is the `\root\cimv2` namespace. This namespace contains the majority of WMI classes that can be called to get system information. The connection object specifies the target computer system that the query will be run against. By default, the SSIS WMI Connection points to the localhost machine, but remote systems can be specified as well by using the NetBIOS, IP address, or DNS name of the remote machine. Because security is always an issue, the WMI Connection Object specifies the user that the query will be run against. Whether it is Windows Authentication or a specified user, the user must have permissions to query the WMI repository on the system for it to work.

Next, the WQL query must be designed. Because WMI is so expansive a subject, this chapter couldn't possibly start to explain the intricacies of the model. We suggest that you locate a good book on WMI scripting to learn the details of how WMI works. Another resource for free WMI tools is the MSDN downloads site. Two applications that are helpful for WQL query generation are the Scriptomatic V2 application, which allows you to browse the classes in WMI namespace and generate WMI queries in several different scripting formats, and the WMI Administrative tools package. This package includes several sample apps to enumerate the classes in various namespaces and monitor WMI filter events, among other useful features. These two tools can help you derive WMI queries quickly and easily.

Once you have figured out the structure of your query, you must decide into which object type to store your query results. The WMI Data Reader Task Object gives you basically two choices, a String or a Data Table. Either object can be stored in a user-defined variable or in a file on the file system. When storing the result in a user-defined variable, the variable must be defined as a String data type or Object data type. This means that when you're obtaining numeric information from the system, you must convert the resultant string to the appropriate data type for use in a mathematical expression. The file transfer example will suggest one way to accomplish this transformation, but this is not the only way. When storing a Data Table to file, the result is a basic comma-separated file with the properties listed in the first row and the actual values returned in the second row.

WMI Data Reader Example

The best way to explain the WMI Data Reader Task is to see an example of it in action. The idea of this example is to query the file system for the size of a database file and for the amount of free space on a drive. With this information, you can then determine if the drive has enough space to handle the new file. For simplicity, this example will copy from directories on the same drive. At the end of the example, you will learn how to modify the WMI queries to query the same information from remote systems.

To set up this example, you must first create a file you would like to copy. This example uses a backup of the AdventureWorks2008 database (but any large file will do). If you don't know how to create a backup of the AdventureWorks2008 database, you can create any large file or use a file from one of many examples in this book. If you do use the AdventureWorks2008 backup, it will tie into the WMI Event Watcher Task example later in this chapter. As always, you can also download the complete samples for this chapter from www.wrox.com.

Now, open a new Integration Services Project and call it WMI_DataReader. Drag a new WMI Data Reader Task object from the Toolbox to the Control Flow page of the package. First, give this task a unique name; call it "WMI Data Reader Task - Read Free Space on C." Now, right-click the task and select Edit from the pop-up menu to bring up the WMI Data Reader Task Editor. Click the WMI Options tab to render the editor as shown in Figure 20-15.

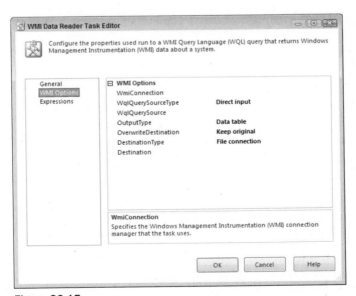

Figure 20-15

Click in the WmiConnection parameter field and select the button to the right. Select <New WMI Connection ...> from the drop-down list. The dialog box shown in Figure 20-16 will be displayed.

Figure 20-16

Give the new WMI connection a name and enter a description. Here's where you can also enter the computer system you wish to query. Leave the server name set to the default of \\LocalHost to query the local computer, and leave the default namespace as \root\cimv2. The setting of cimv2 is the main WMI repository that contains the core WMI classes to access information on the system. Finally, check the box to use Windows Authentication or enter a user name and password that has rights to query the CIM repository on this computer. Click the Test button to verify the settings, and then click OK to close the dialog box. This will complete the WMI connection and add it automatically to the WMIConnection property in the editor.

Back in the WMI Data Reader Task Editor dialog box, leave the WqlQuerySourceType as DirectInput. Next, select the WqlQuerySource field and click the ellipsis button on the right-hand side. In the dialog box that appears, enter the following WQL query in the WqlQuerySource window:

```
SELECT FreeSpace FROM Win32_LogicalDisk Where DeviceID ='C:'
```

This query will return the amount of free space that exists on drive C. Next, change the OutputType to Property Value and leave the OverwriteDestination field set to Overwrite Destination. Set the DestinationType property to Variable. Click in the Destination field and choose the ellipsis button to the right and select <New variable...>. In the Add Variable dialog box that appears (shown in Figure 20-17), enter FreeSpaceOnC in the Name field, set the data type to string, and give the variable a default of zero. Leave the rest of the fields at their default values and click OK to close the dialog box. We'll explain the string data type in a minute.

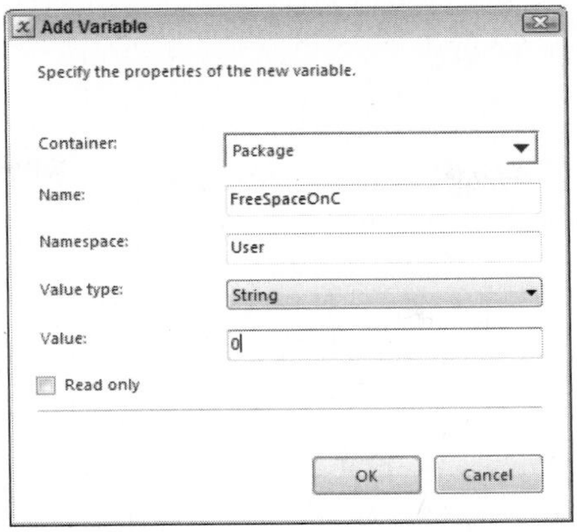

Figure 20-17

Now, you'll add another WMI Data Reader Task and configure it to return the size of the AdventureWorks2008 backup file. Call this task "WMI Data Reader Task - Read DB File Size." Open the WMI Data Reader Task dialog box for this new task. Click in the WMI Connector field and choose the WMI Connection Manager connection. Because the CIM class you will be using to obtain the file size of the backup file is in the same CIM namespace, you can reuse the same WMI Connection Object.

Leave the WqlQuerySourceType as DirectInput. Now, click the SqlQuerySource field and click the ellipsis to the right to open the query editor dialog box. Enter the following query:

```
Select FileSize FROM CIM_Datafile WHERE Name =
"C:\\SSIS\\EXTMGT\\WMI_DataReader\\AdventureWorks2008.bak"
```

In the OutputType field, choose Property Value. In the DestinationType, choose Variable, and then click in the Destination field and choose <New variable...>. Call the new variable DBBackupFileSize, with a data type of string and an initial value set to zero (0).

That's all there is to configuring the tasks themselves. Hook them together so that you can add some logic to handle the data the WQL query will return. It was stated previously that the WMI Data Reader could only write to strings and Data Table objects. Well, when a string is returned, it has several extraneous characters at the end that will cause a data conversion from String to Integer to fail. You can see these characters by setting a breakpoint on the PostExecute event of one of the WMI Data Reader Tasks and running the package. When the task turns green, go to the Variables tab and look at the data in the two user-defined variables. The value looks like this: "FileSize\r\n45516800\r\n".

To massage this data into a usable form suitable for conversion to an Integer data type, you will create a Script Task to strip the extra characters from the string, leaving just numeric digits in the string. To start, click the Event Handler tab of the package. In the Executables drop-down box, choose the WMI Data Reader Task called "WMI Data Reader Task - Read Free Space on C." Now select the OnPostExecute event handler and click the hyperlink in the middle of the page to create the event. Drag a Script Task object from the Toolbox and drag it onto the page. Change the name of the object to "FileSizeOnC Data Massage." Right-click the task and select Edit from the pop-up menu. On the left-hand side of the Script Editor dialog box, choose the Script page. In the ReadWriteVariables property, select the variable User:: FreeSpaceOnC. This will give you read/write access to the variable from within the VB.NET script.

Now, click the Edit Script button in the bottom-right corner of the window. In the Script Host editor that appears, add the following code immediately after the start of the Main subroutine:

```
C#
string s = System.Convert.ToString(Dts.Variables["User::FreeSpaceOnC"].Value);
s = System.Text.RegularExpressions.Regex.Replace(s, "\\D", "");
Dts.Variables["User::FreeSpaceOnC"].Value = Int64.Parse(s);

VB
Dim s As String
s = CType(Dts.Variables("User::FreeSpaceOnC").Value, String)
s = System.Text.RegularExpressions.Regex.Replace(s, "\\D", "")
Dts.Variables("User::FreeSpaceOnC").Value = Int64.Parse(s).ToString()
```

As you can see, this code parses the string and uses the `RegularExpressions` library to strip the characters from the returned value. Then the cleaned up string is cast to return an Int64 value as a string. In short, this code will strip all the extraneous characters from the string and return a numerical result into the same variable. The result is that the contents of the string are ready to be used in a mathematical expression. To finish, close the Script Host windows and hit OK to close the Script Task Editor dialog box. Repeat this same setup for the ReadDBFileSize Task, making sure to change the variable references to the appropriate variable names.

You're now in the home stretch of this example. The final steps to complete are to set up the file transfer and add the precedence constraint that will ensure that you have enough space on the drive before you initiate the transfer. First drag a File System Task onto the Control Flow page. Name this task "Copy Db File." Right-click the task and click Edit in the pop-up menu. In the File System Task Editor, set the following properties as shown in Figure 20-18.

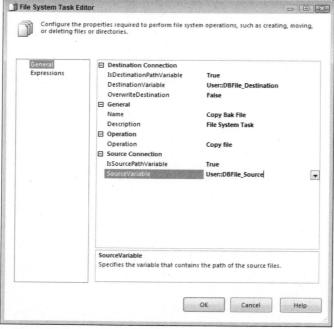

Figure 20-18

In the Source and Destination variable fields, create two variables called `DBFile_Source` and `DBFile_Destination` as string variables. In the default field of the `DBFile_Source` variable, enter the full path to the AdventureWorks2008 backup file. If you are using the file structure from the download files, this will be `c:\ssis\extmgt\WMI_DataReader\AdventureWorks2008.bak`. In the `DBFile_Destination` variable, enter the back up folder or `c:\ssis\extmgt\WMI_DataReader\Backup`. Click OK to close the dialog box. If you are not using the download sample files, make sure you create the directory in which you intend to back up the file. The File System Task will not create the directory automatically.

The final step is to link these tasks with precedence constraints. Link the tasks as shown in Figure 20-19.

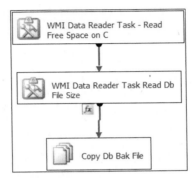

Figure 20-19

After adding the links, right-click the constraint between the Read DB File Size Task and the Copy Db File Task. Click the Edit option in the pop-up menu to open the Precedence Constraint Editor. Set the Evaluation option to Expression and Constraint and then enter the following line of code in the Expression field:

```
(DT_I8)@FreeSpaceOnC > (DT_I8)@DBBackupFileSize
```

As you can see, this is where the massaging of the data in the Script Task pays off. If you had not stripped the extraneous characters from the string, then the cast from String data type to the Integer data type would fail. Click OK to close the Precedence Constraint Editor dialog box.

Now you are ready for the moment of truth: running the package. If all went well, all the tasks should green up and the file should have been copied to the backup directory. That is assuming you had enough space available on the drive.

We mentioned earlier about ways you could improve this example. It seems a waste that you have to hard-code the WQL query with the path to the file being checked for size, especially since the path to the file is already stored in the `DBFile_Source` variable. One option is to build the WQL query on the fly with a Script Task. This would allow you to construct the path in the WQL in the proper format, namely changing the single backslash in the path to double backslashes. Also, in a more advanced scenario, the file could be located on another computer system. This could easily be handled by creating a separate WMI Connection Object pointing to the second system and assigning it to the WmiConnection property in the WMI Data Reader Task - Read DB File Size Task. For remote machines use the NetBIOS name, the IP address, or the DNS name in the ServerName property instead of the \\localhost default setting.

WMI Event Watcher Task

As outlined earlier, not only can WMI obtain information about a computer system, but it can also monitor that system for certain events to occur. This capability could allow you to monitor the file system for a change in a file or monitor the Windows system for the start of an application. The WMI Event Watch Task has the following options to configure:

❑ WmiConnection: This is a configured WMI Connection Manager.

❑ WqlQuerySourceType: This setting specifies where the WQL query is referenced. The query can be manually typed in or can be stored in a file or a variable.

❑ WqlQuerySource: This field sets the actual source of the WQL Query Source selected in the WqlQuerySourceType.

❑ ActionAtEvent: This option sets the actions that are to occur when the WMI event being monitored occurs. This option has two settings, Log the Event and Fire the SSIS Event, or just Log the Event.

❑ AfterEvent: This field is used to determine what should happen after the WMI event occurs. This setting could be Return with Success, Return with Failure, or Watch for the Event Again.

❑ ActionAtTimeout: This defines the action that should be taken if the task times-out waiting for the WMI event to occur. This could be Log the Time-Out and Fire the SSIS event, or just Log the Time-Out.

❑ AfterTimeout: This defines the action that should be taken after the task times-out. This option sets what should happen after the ActionAtTimeout occurs. This could be Return with Failure, Return with Success, or Watch for the Event Again.

❑ NumberOfEvents: This option specifies how many events must occur before the specified action is taken.

❑ Timeout: This sets how long the task should wait, in seconds, before the specified time-out action is taken. A setting of zero (0) denotes that the task will never time-out.

The WMI Event Watcher Task is similar to the WMI Data Reader Task in that the basic query setup is the same in both cases. You must define a WMI Connection Object and create a WMI query to monitor for an event. The specific options available in this task define how the task will react when the event occurs.

There are two basic types of actions: What should happen when the event actually occurs, and what should happen if the event does not occur within a specified time. Both these actions can either log the event to the package log or, in addition to logging the event, fire an event that can be used to perform additional specified tasks. Also, both actions can dictate what happens after the event occurs or the task times out. These after-events can be to pass to subsequent tasks a success or failure of the WMI Event Watcher Task or simply to continue to monitor for the event to occur again.

WMI Event Watcher Task Example

In the WMI Data Reader example, you used WMI to check the size of a file before you copied it to the drive. You'd most likely perform this type of task after some other process had created the backup of the database. In some cases, you can execute the package manually when you are ready to perform the actions in the package. However, if you need certain tasks to be performed in response to an event like the backup file being created, then use the WMI Event Watcher Task. This task can monitor any system event including the creation of a file like the backup file we used in the WMI reader example. In this example, you'll use the WMI Event Watcher Task to look for the file, and then kick off the WMI Data Reader package created earlier. You could also use this example to look for incoming data files that need to be processed. There is an example of this use of the WMI Task in Chapter 3.

To use this task to determine when the backup has completed from our first WMI example, create a new SSIS package called WMI Event Watcher Package. Now add a WMI Event Watcher Task to the Control Flow page of the package. Name this task "WMI Event Watcher Task - Monitor DB File." Right-click the task and select Edit from the pop-up menu. You are now presented with the WMI Event Watcher Task Editor. Select WMI Option from the listbox and configure the properties as outlined in the following.

First, create a `WmiConnection` pointing to the machine where the backup file would normally be created. In this example that will be in the root directory of the WMI_DataReader project. You can use the same connection properties as outlined in the previous example. Next, enter the WqlQuerySource that will monitor the file system for changes to the `AdventureWorks2008.bak` file.

```
Select * from __InstanceModificationEvent within 30 where targetinstance isa
"CIM_DataFile" and targetinstance.name =
"C:\\SSIS\\extmgt\\WMI_DataReader\\AdventureWorks2008.bak"
```

As you can see, this query monitors the `AdventureWorks2008.bak` file for changes every 30 seconds.

The rest of the properties are specific to the WMI Event Watcher task. Set the ActionAtEvent property to Log the Event and Fire the SSIS Event. As you'll see in a moment, this event will be used to launch the "Db Data File Copy" package created in the previous example. Next, set the AfterEvent property to Watch for this Event Again. This setting will essentially set up a monitoring loop that will perpetually monitor the file for changes as long as the package is running. Because you do not care if the task times out, leave the time-out settings at their default values. The editor should look like Figure 20-20. Click the OK button to close the dialog box.

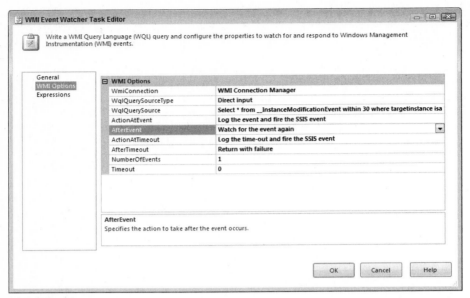

Figure 20-20

Now that the task is configured, you need to configure the event handler that will be fired when a file change is detected. Click the Event Handler tab and select the WMI Event Watcher Task - Monitor DB File in the executable combo box, and then the WMIEventWatcherEventOccurred in the Event Handlers combo box. Click the hyperlink in the middle of the page to create this event. Now drag an Execute Package Task from the Toolbox to the event page. Rename this task as Execute WMI Data Reader Package. The Execute Package Task event handler should look like Figure 20-21.

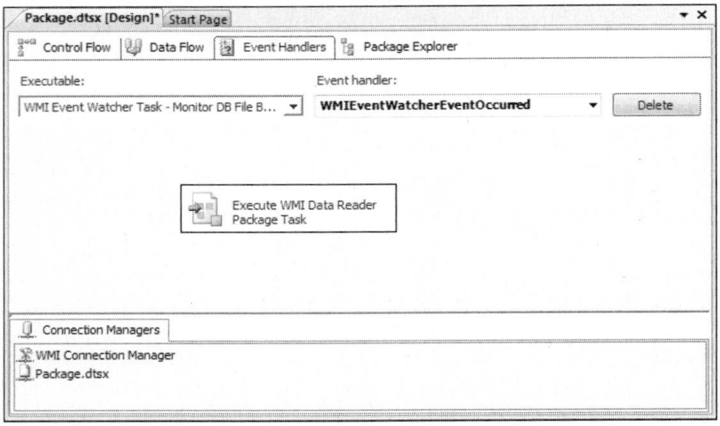

Figure 20-21

Right-click the task and select Edit from the pop-up menu. In the execute Package Task Editor dialog box, click the Package item in the listbox. For this example, you will be referencing the package via the file system, but in real life you would probably be calling a package that had been deployed to a SQL Server instance. For demonstration purposes, the WMI Data Reader Package file will be referenced so that you can see the package execute in the Visual Studio IDE. So in the Location property, choose File System. In the Connection property, create a new file connection pointing to the WMI Data Reader Package.dtsx file. Leave the rest of the properties at their default values. The Execute Package editor should look like Figure 20-22. Click OK to finish configuration of this example.

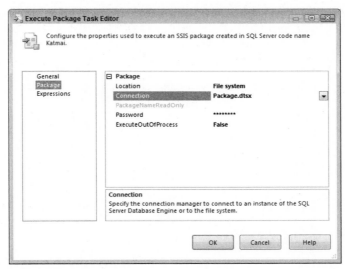

Figure 20-22

Now test out your new package by first removing the AdventureWorks2008.bak backup file from the c:\ssis\extmgt\WMI_DataReader directory. Then run the WMI Event Watcher Package. The WMI Event Watcher Task should turn yellow. The WMI Event Watcher is now monitoring the file location where it expects to find the AdventureWorks2008.bak file for changes. Now copy the AdventureWorks2008.bak file into the root WMI_DataReader directory to simulate the SQL Server process of creating a backup of the AdventureWorks2008 database. In fact, you can also test this package by going into SSMS and creating a backup in this root directory. At some point during the backup process, you should see the WMI Data Reader Package kick off and copy the backup file to the c:\ssis\extmgt\WMI_DataReader\Backup directory.

When the copy is complete, the package will continue to monitor the backup file for change. So when the next backup is found in the root WMI_DataReader directory, the package will initiate another file copy of the backup. The package is responding to WMI events that will detect the change to the directory to copy the file. As you can see, these WMI features are an extremely powerful capability that SSIS does a great job of abstracting for you in these WMI Tasks.

Summary

This chapter has provided you with the basic information to manage and administer your SSIS packages. You were exposed to the DTS runtime libraries. You have seen how easy it is to manipulate package information, make changes programmatically, and transfer packages between your environments. You've also seen how to create and maintain package configurations to customize packages at runtime. In addition, you've seen how to configure log providers, which allow you to apply logging to existing packages at runtime for diagnostic purposes.

In the second half of the chapter, you saw how to use the WMI Reader Task and WMI Event Watcher Task in your packages. Using these two tasks, you discovered how you can gain access to a huge amount of system information to use in your packages. With the WMI Event Watcher, you learned how to monitor the system for events to occur and perform actions in your SSIS package in response. With both the DTS runtime libraries and the WMI Tasks, you should be able to enhance your system administration capabilities working with SSIS. Later in Chapter 22, you'll learn more about Administering SSIS packages, but next you'll be looking at some examples of using SSIS in external applications.

21

Using SSIS with External Applications

SQL Server 2008 Integration Services accepts data from nearly any source and presents output, including ADO.NET datasets and SSIS data readers that are consumable by external applications. These features allow SSIS to sink and source external applications with ease. In this chapter, you take a look at three examples of external applications that utilize SSIS. This chapter is not intended to exhaust all possible combinations of external interface with SSIS, but rather to provide a sampling of some available functionality.

SSIS is flexible and configurable, so there are many ways to approach interaction with external applications. This book is rife with examples, including the following:

❑ **Sources and Destinations:** Implicit objects inside SSIS that provide connectivity to Data Sources and Destinations. New in 2008 are two new sources called the ADO.NET Source and the Performance Counters Source. The ADO.NET Source uses the .NET provider to access the data being sourced. The Performance Counters Source extracts performance measures from the operating system. There are also two new destinations added in 2008, one being the ADO.NET Destination, which loads data using the .NET provider, and the SQL Server Compact Edition Destination, which loads data into, well, the Compact Edition of SQL Server.

❑ **Scripting:** Arguably provides the most flexibility when interacting with external applications. Similar to Integration Services 2005, the Script Component still comes in three flavors: Source, Destination, or Transformation. The exciting enhancement in this version is the option to use C# as well as VB.NET. The .NET Framework version for developing in this component is 3.5. We know plenty of developers will cheer about this enhancement! See Chapter 9 for an example and more information.

Because interface scenarios can vary, it is difficult to define best practices. That said, generally accepted software development practices apply, including the following:

❑ **Employ a methodology:** Chapter 15 provides an introduction to Software Development Life Cycles (SDLCs). A development methodology is not a prescribed recipe; it is a framework that assists you in creating the proper recipe for your software development project.

❑ **Debug:** Execute your SSIS package in debug mode in either the Business Intelligence Developer Studio or the Visual Studio Integrated Development Environment (IDE). You may also find that using breakpoints in conjunction with the watch window helps greatly during your development cycle and is a highly recommended best practice. Another great tip is to group similar tasks in containers (preferably a Sequence Container) and execute just the container you choose to test. This technique will allow you to do unit-type testing without having to run the entire package to avoid the "all or nothing" approach to package development.

❑ **Test:** Whenever possible, obtain a sample of actual ("live") data and execute your package against this data. This will ensure that the business logic implemented in your packages are fine-tuned and will validate the correctness of your package logic. In the absence of access to a copy of live data, populate tables with dummy data based on the business rules embedded in the tables of the production data, and execute your package against them. When populating your tables with dummy data, it is very important that you fully understand the semantics of the production data and be sure to mirror those as accurately as possible. This will prevent you from developing logic that may work on test data, but raises problems during production.

In the first example, SSIS will read data from a Microsoft Office InfoPath document and perform a Sorting Transform on the data and write the data out to a flat file for the destination. The key concept behind this exercise is to demonstrate how Integration Services can easily source and transform data from an XML document.

InfoPath Documents

This example demonstrates the ability of SSIS to interact with an external Microsoft Office application, namely InfoPath

> *Microsoft InfoPath is a desktop forms client that provides a rich interface to XML-based documents. For more information about Microsoft InfoPath, see* Professional InfoPath 2003 *by Ian Williams and Pierre Greborio (Wiley, 2004).*

Using a document created from the Timecard template supplied with InfoPath 2003, you will import portions of data stored in an InfoPath document and output the results to a comma-delimited flat file.

Portions of imported data in this demonstration appear disconnected in the Data Flow Task. This example demonstrates an SSIS method to join disconnected data. This example also covers some troubleshooting.

Many thanks to Wenyang Hu for permission to reuse some elegant XSL!

Create a new Integration Services project in SSIS. Drag an XML Task onto the Control Flow. Double-click the XML Task to open the editor. Configure the XML Task as follows:

- ❑ **Operation Type:** XSLT.
- ❑ **Source Type:** File Connection.
- ❑ **Source:** New File Connection. Configure the New File Connection as follows:
  - ❑ **Usage Type:** Existing File.
  - ❑ **File:** Click Browse to locate and select an InfoPath timecard directory and file. The timecard file may be generated using the InfoPath 2003 Timecard template, or you can get the `Timecard_ARay.xml` file from the Resources available for this book at www.wrox.com.
- ❑ **Save Operation Result:** True.
- ❑ **Overwrite Destination:** True.
- ❑ **Destination Type:** File Connection.
- ❑ **Destination:** New File Connection. Configure the New File Connection as follows:
  - ❑ **Usage Type:** Create File.
  - ❑ **File:** Use the same InfoPath directory containing the Timecard files. Filename: `TimecardResult.xml`.
- ❑ **Second Operand Type:** File Connection.
- ❑ **Second Operand:** New File Connection. Configure the New File Connection as follows:
  - ❑ **Usage Type:** Existing File.
  - ❑ **File:** `SSISInfoPath.xsl` (Wenyang Hu's XSL file — see Resources).

Why transform the Timecard XML file? Because the SSIS XML Task does not support multiple namespaces.

When you're done, the Task Editor should look like Figure 21-1. Click OK to proceed.

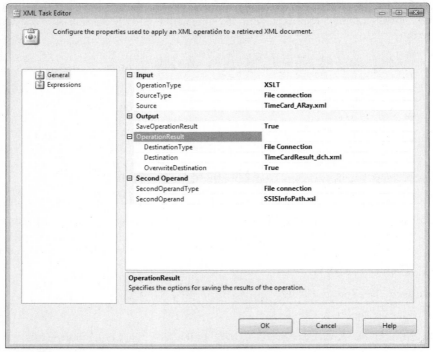

Figure 21-1

Now take a brief look at some XML Task properties before moving on.

The top property of the task, OperationType, determines the remaining properties. The XML Task Editor changes to present different properties for different OperationTypes. There are six OperationTypes:

❑ **Diff:** Creates a *Diffgram* (an XML document consisting of the differences between two XML documents) XML document from the differences between the XML defined in the Source property and the XML defined in the SecondOperand property.

❑ **Merge:** Adds XML defined in the SecondOperand property to the XML defined in the Source property. This operation type is useful if you are continuously adding XML fragments to a master XML document, for example.

❑ **Patch:** Adds a Diffgram defined in the SecondOperand property to the XML defined in the Source property. This operation can occur after another Diff operation is executed in a previous XML Task, for example.

❏ **Validate:** Validates the XML defined in the `Source` property by the XML Schema Definition (XSD) or Document Type Definition (DTD) defined in the `SecondOperand` property.

❏ **XPath:** Specifies an XPath query in the `SecondOperand` property executed against the XML defined in the `Source` property to evaluate or aggregate or to return a node or value list. The XPath operation is useful when you are only interested in certain portions of your XML document. For more information about using XPath, see *XPath 2.0 Programmer's Reference, 3rd Edition,* by Michael Kay (Wiley, 2004).

❏ **XSLT:** Applies XML Stylesheet Language (XSL) documents defined in the `SecondOperand` property to the XML defined in the `Source` property. An XSLT document essentially acts like a template for rendering or transforming your XML documents in a form more suitable for end-user consumption. For more information about XSLT, see *XSLT 2.0 Programmer's Reference, 3rd Edition,* by Michael Kay (Wiley, 2004).

The `OperationResult` property defines the output of the XML Task. The `DestinationType` property can be set to File Connection or Variable, requiring a corresponding Connection Manager or Variable, respectively, to be assigned to the `Destination` property.

To generate the `TimecardResult.xml` file, you must execute this task.

This is also a good development practice: Create a task and then test it before moving on. You may find that you cannot accomplish what you wish with this type of task, and this discovery may impact downstream development decisions.

Right-click the XML Task and click Execute Task. You may receive a validation error in the Errors window — especially on the first execution of the task. If everything is configured properly, however, the task will succeed and the `TimecardResult.xml` file will be created in the Timecards directory.

Drag a Data Flow Task onto the Control Flow. Connect the XML Task to the Data Flow Task using the available precedence constraint (the green arrow on the XML Task). Double-click the Data Flow Task to proceed. Drag an XML Source onto the Data Flow and double-click it to edit. Browse to the location of `TimecardResult.xml` — generated in a previous step — to configure the XML Location parameter. Click the Generate XSD button to automatically generate a schema definition for the file (this is such a time-saver!) as shown in Figure 21-2. Click OK to proceed.

If you receive the error "Unable to infer the XSD from the XML file. The XML contains multiple namespaces" while stepping through this example, make sure you are using the `SSISInfoPath.xsl` file supplied in Resources. If you are adapting this example, make sure your transformation eliminates multiple namespaces from your source XML.

Drag a Merge Join Transform onto the Data Flow. Merge Joins, discussed in Chapter 5, are designed to join rows of data from disparate sources. This example uses them to join disconnected data from the same source: the same XML file. The desired result is one row from the file containing the employee name and information about the work week.

This merge could be accomplished many other ways; this is an example of the flexibility of SSIS.

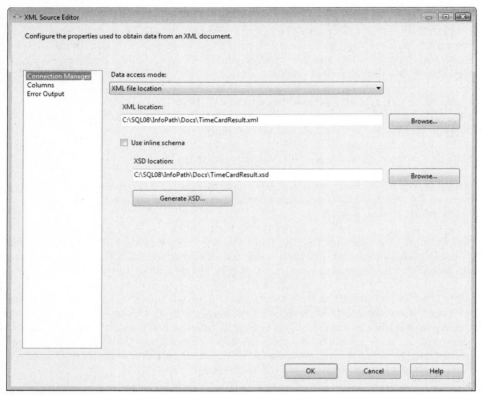

Figure 21-2

In order to join the disconnected data, the Merge Join needs a field upon which to join. To create this field, drag two Derived Column Transformations onto the Data Flow. Connect the XML Source to one of the Derived Column Transformations. Select timecard_employee_name from the Output drop-down list on the Input Output Selection dialog box. Connect the XML Source to the other Derived Column Transformation, and select Week as the Derived Column input. Double-click each Derived Column in turn to open their respective editors. Configure the same Derived Column for each as follows (as shown in Figure 21-3):

- ❑ **Derived Column:** <add as new column>
- ❑ **Derived Column Name:** JoinID
- ❑ **Expression:** 1
- ❑ **Data Type:** 4-byte signed integer [DT_I4]

Notice that the value for the Expression property is a literal number (1). This may look a bit confusing because you may expect a snippet of code to be placed there. In this case, you are simply providing the value in place of an actual expression.

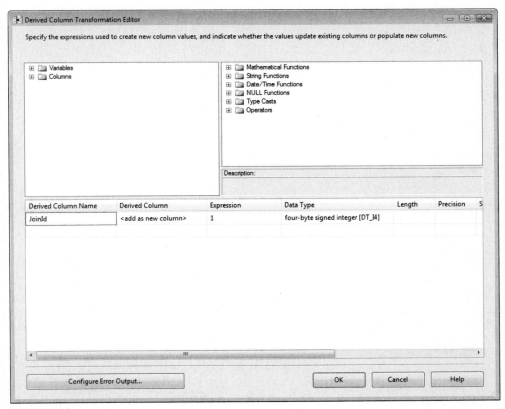

Figure 21-3

Click OK to proceed. You can now connect the outputs of the Derived Column Transformations to the Merge Join Transformation, except for one thing: The Merge Join requires the input data to be sorted. So drag and drop two Sort Transformations onto the Data Flow. Connect the output of each Derived Column Transformation to a respective Sort Transformation. Double-click each Sort Transformation to configure it. Select the JoinID for each Sort, allowing all other columns to pass through the transformation, as shown in Figure 21-4.

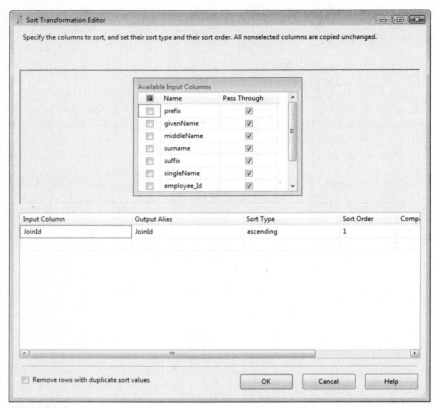

Figure 21-4

Connect the outputs of each Sort to the Merge Join Transformation. Assign the output of the first Sort Transformation to the Merge Join. When prompted, select Merge Join Left Input as the input for the first Sort output — the second will connect by default to the remaining available input. Double-click the Merge Join Transformation to edit it. Make sure that Inner Join is selected in the Join Type drop-down list, and that the Join Key checkbox for each JoinID field is checked in the Available Columns tables. Check the Select checkbox for the JoinID columns in the join, as well as other columns you wish to add to the pipeline as shown in Figure 21-5. By checking the columns you wish to add, the pipeline will allow these columns to be included as input columns in the Flat File Destination in the next step. Click OK to close the editor.

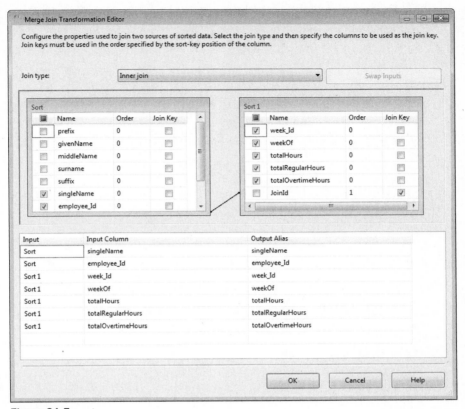

Figure 21-5

Add a Flat File Destination to the Data Flow and connect the Merge Join to it. Double-click the Flat File Destination to configure it. Click the new Flat File Connector to configure a new file destination named TimeCardOutput. Select Delimited as the Flat File Type. The Flat File Connection will be created, and the Flat File Connection Manager Editor will display. Click Browse to choose a filename and enter `TimecardOutput.csv`. Click OK to return to the Flat File Destination Editor. Click the Mappings item to generate the column mappings as shown in Figure 21-6, and then click OK to close the editor.

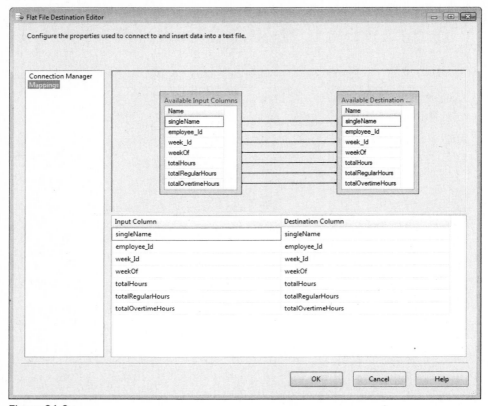

Figure 21-6

Right-click each Sort output, respectively, and click Data Viewers. Make sure Data Viewers is selected in the left pane of the Data Flow Path Editor, and then click the Add button. Accept the default name of the Data Viewer and make sure Grid is selected on the General tab of the Configure Data Viewer Wizard. Click OK to add a Data Viewer to the Sort output. Add another Grid Data Viewer to the output of the Merge Join. Test the Data Flow by clicking the Play button and observing the results. View the line item produced in the Data Viewer in Figure 21-7.

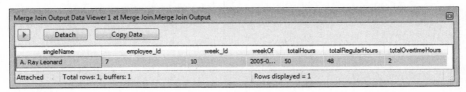

Figure 21-7

This example demonstrated some techniques for importing and filtering a subset of data from an XML document. You used an InfoPath-generated XML document as the source, but the approach to the solution is valid for loading any XML document into SSIS.

ASP.NET Applications

The first example in this chapter demonstrated the XML Task in SSIS, which adds flexibility to SSIS by providing a mechanism for working with XML data. In the first example, an InfoPath document was consumed by the XML Task. This example demonstrates the capability of SSIS to interact with custom external applications by interfacing with a simple ASP.NET application.

This example application is written in C# 2005 and displays the output from an SSIS package in an ASP.NET GridView control. Thanks to Ashvini Sharma and Ranjeeta Nanda for technical support!

In BIDS, create a new Integration Services project. Drag a Data Flow Task onto the Control Flow and double-click it to open the Data Flow tab. Drag an OLE DB Source onto the Data Flow and double-click to edit. Configure the OLE DB Source as follows (shown in Figures 21-8 and 21-9):

The AdventureWorks database no longer comes with the SQL Server install in 2008, but can be downloaded separately from the CodePlex site located here: `http://www.codeplex.com/MSFTDBProdSamples`.

- ❑ **OLE DB Connection Manager:** Click New to open the Configure OLE DB Connection Manager dialog box, and then click New to open the Connection Manager dialog box. Configure the connection as follows:
    - ❑ **Server Name:** [Your server name]
    - ❑ **Log on to the server:** Use Windows Authentication
    - ❑ **Select or enter a database name:** AdventureWorks2008
- ❑ Click the Test Connection button to confirm connectivity, as shown in Figure 21-8, and then click OK to proceed.
- ❑ **Data Access Mode:** SQL Command
- ❑ **SQL Command Text:**

```
SELECT Title, FileName FROM Production.[Document]
```

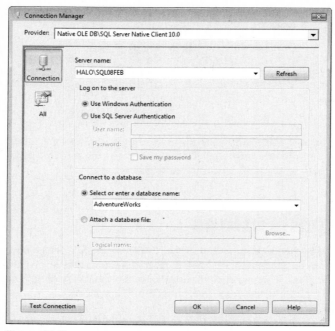

Figure 21-8

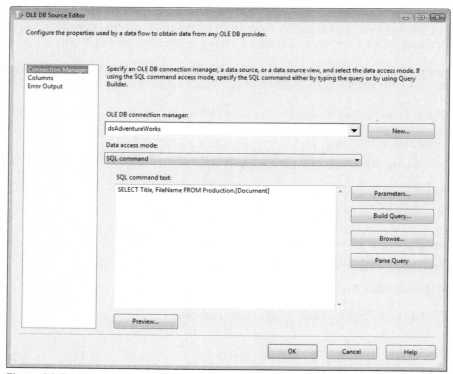

Figure 21-9

Select the fields you wish to return by clicking Columns in the listbox and checking the Title and Filename checkboxes. Click OK to close the editor.

Drag a DataReader Destination onto the Data Flow and supply a meaningful name. The naming convention is important when referencing this component from your ASP.NET page. The DataReader Destination name will be used to set the CommandName property when using the SqlClient .NET namespace in the code-behind. Connect the output of the OLE DB Source to the DataReader Destination and double-click the DataReader Destination to begin editing. Click the Input Columns tab on the Advanced Editor for the DataReaderDest dialog. Select the Title and Filename fields (selected earlier in the OLE DB Source) for the DataReader and click OK to close the editor. Test the SSIS functionality before proceeding.

Open a new instance of Visual Studio to create a new Web Site or add a new Web Site to your current SSIS project by selecting File ⇨ Add ⇨ New Web Site Name the Web project ASP_Feed_Web. Set the Location to File System and select C# as the Language as shown in Figure 21-10.

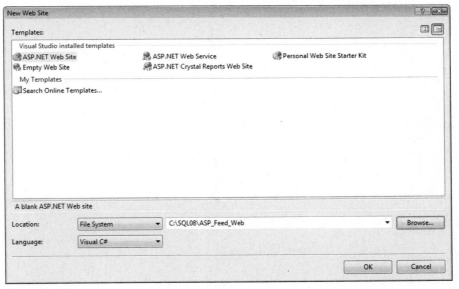

Figure 21-10

Now that you have created a new project, you need to include a couple of .NET class libraries that will first connect to the SSIS package you just created and secondly display the data in a GridView ASP.NET control. You include these class libraries by adding a "Reference" to the project. In Solution Explorer, right-click the Web Site project and click Add Reference. If `Microsoft.SqlServer.Dts.DtsClient` appears in the list of References on the .NET tab, double-click it to add a reference to the project. If not, click the Browse tab and navigate to `%Program Files%\Microsoft SQL Server\100\DTS\Binn\ Microsoft.SqlServer.Dts.DtsClient.dll` and click OK.

The DTSClient DLL contains interfaces to SSIS connection and command objects. See Books Online and MSDN for more information about this library.

Right-click the `Default.aspx` object and click View Designer. The ASP.NET control you will use to display the data from the SSIS package is called a *GridView*. It will display the data in a table-like format and render the column names automatically by default. Drag a GridView control from the Toolbox onto the web page. Double-click the page to open the code viewer. Add the following code at the top of the page:

```
using System.Data.SqlClient;
using Microsoft.SqlServer.Dts.DtsClient;
```

In the `Page_Load` subroutine, add the following line of code, replacing [your package directory] with the actual name of the directory containing your SSIS package:

```
connectToSSISPackage("[your package directory]\Package.dtsx")
```

Add the following function to the `_Default` partial class:

```
protected void connectoToSSISPackage(string packagePath)
{
    // Create the DTS connection object
    DtsConnection oConn = new DtsConnection();

    // Set the ConnectionString Property to the path of the package
    oConn.ConnectionString = String.Format("-f {0}", packagePath);

    // Open the Connection to the package
    oConn.Open();

    // Create a new DTSCommand object
    DtsCommand oCmd = new DtsCommand(oConn);

    // Set the CommandText Property to the Name of the Data Reader Task in
    // your SSIS package
    oCmd.CommandText = "DataReaderDest";

    // Declare a DataReader variable
    IDataReader dr;

    // Create a new DataSet object
    DataSet ds = new DataSet();

    // Execute the Command object calling the SSIS package
    // and return a DataReader object
    dr = oCmd.ExecuteReader(CommandBehavior.Default);

    // Load the DataReader object into the DataSet
```

```
        ds.Load(dr, LoadOption.OverwriteChanges,
            dr.GetSchemaTable().TableName);

        // Set the GridView's DataSource property to the DataSet
        grid1.DataSource = ds;

        // Bind the data to the GridView
        grid1.DataBind();

        // Close the Connection
        oConn.Close();

    }

    protected void Page_Load(object sender, EventArgs e)
    {
        connectoToSSISPackage(@"C:\SQL08\ASPSSIS\ASPSSIS\DataReaderASP.dtsx");
    }
```

The `connectToSSISPackage` function receives a path to an SSIS package through the "path" argument. As a reminder, the "path" argument is the fully qualified path and filename of the location of the SSIS package on your local file system. A new SSIS connection (of `DTSConnection` type) called oConn is created, which will connect to the SSIS package specified in the "path" argument of the method.

> *If your environment does not recognize the `DTSConnection` data type, make sure you have a reference properly defined and have included the `Imports Microsoft.SqlServer.Dts.DtsClient` statement at the beginning of your code.*

The path argument is the connection string for the SSIS connection. After the SSIS connection is opened, a new SSIS command (of `DTSCommand` type) is created and assigned to the SSIS connection. The `CommandText` property of the SSIS command object is set to the *name* of the DataReader Destination in the SSIS package.

Next, a DataReader object is defined and populated with the results of the SSIS command's execution. A dataset is created and filled with the DataReader's data. The GridView's DataSource property is assigned to the dataset and the GridView is refreshed with a call to `DataBind`. Finally, the SSIS connection is closed.

Click the Play button to test. A list of document names and file paths should populate the grid as shown in Figure 21-11.

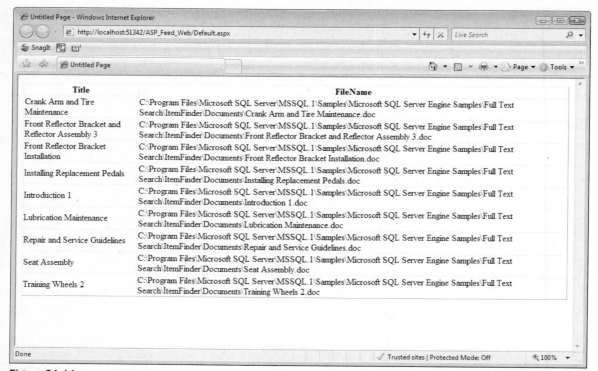

Figure 21-11

This example demonstrates a simple yet powerful feature of SSIS — the ability to expose output directly to ASP.NET applications. The DataReader Destination provides a flexible interface for SSIS package output.

Winform .NET Applications

The previous example in this chapter showed you how to consume data in an ASP.NET GridView control through a DataReader in an external SSIS package. In a sense, the SSIS package was supplying the data in a "push" format using the DataReader Destination. What if you wanted to interact with your packages in a more dynamic way? What if your requirement was to supply information to your package at runtime through a user interface? This next example shows you how to do just that.

This example includes two new projects, an Integration Services project and a Visual C# Windows Application. Special thanks to Nayan Patel for technical support.

The goal of this exercise is to dynamically set a variable inside an SSIS package from a Windows interface and execute the package. The package itself will take the value of the variable and insert it into a table, which you will have to create.

Open SQL Server Management Studio and create a new table in the AdventureWorks2008 database called SSIStest. The following is the defined structure for the table:

Column Name	DataType
id	int (set as an identity column)
description	varchar(50)

Save the table and name it SSIStest.

Create a new Integration Services project in BIDS. Rename the default starter package to Package1.dtsx. Create a new Data Source and point to the AdventureWorks2008 database. You will also need to create a Connection Manager as well. Right-click in the Connection Manager pane and choose New Connection From Data Source. Select the dsAdventureWorks2008 Data Source and click OK.

You now need to create a package-level variable that will be used by the Windows interface to be set dynamically. Click in the designer so that you can be sure you are at the package level. Right-click in the designer and select Variables. In the Variables pane, click the icon to create a new variable. The new variable will be defined as shown here:

Name	Scope	Datatype	Value
myvar	Package1	String	oldvalue

Drag an Execute SQL Task from the Toolbox onto the designer. Double-click the task to configure its properties as shown in Figure 21-12.

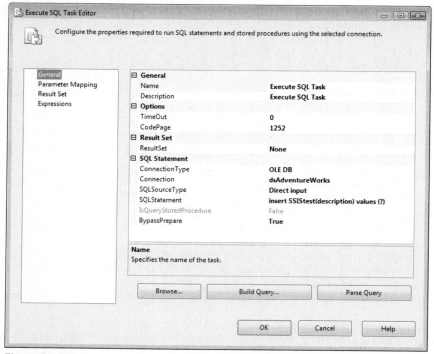

Figure 21-12

Set the Connection to the dsAdventureWorks Connection Manager. Type the following query into the SQLStatement property:

```
Insert SSIStest (description) values (?)
```

The question mark in the query will be the placeholder for the input parameter. Click the Parameter Mapping menu item and configure the parameter as shown in Figure 21-13:

Variable Name	Direction	Data Type	Parameter Name	Value
User::myvar	Input	VARCHAR	0	old_value

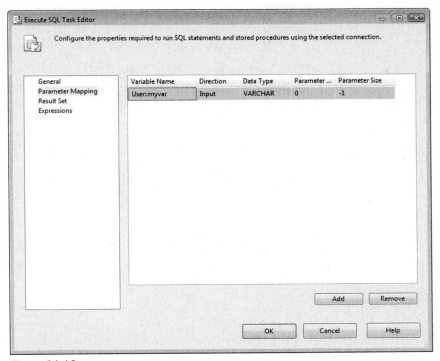

Figure 21-13

Click OK when you're finished to return to the designer. Save your project and make a special note where the package resides on the file system. When you create the user interface to interact with this package, you will need to point to the package located on the file system like you did in the previous exercise.

In Visual Studio 2005, create a new Visual C# Windows Application Project. Once the project is open, a reference to a .NET class library is necessary to interact with the Integration Services package. Right-click the References folder and select Add Reference as displayed in Figure 21-14. Under the .NET tab find and select the `Microsoft.SQLServer.ManagedDTS` reference (Figure 21-15) from the list and click OK. You're now ready to start designing the interface to this project.

Figure 21-14

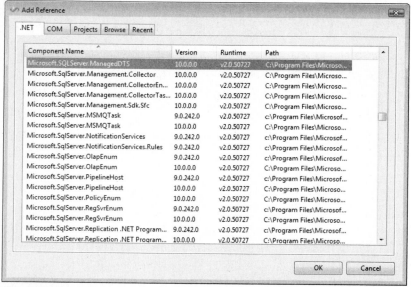

Figure 21-15

Drag a TextBox control and a Button control on the form designer like displayed in Figure 21-16. The look and feel of the UI is not important here; we are mostly concerned about the functionality behind the scenes, so don't be too concerned about the appearance at this point.

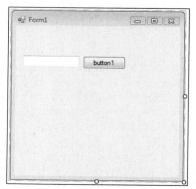

Figure 21-16

The TextBox you placed on the form will allow the user to enter a value that you will use to dynamically set the variable in the package. The Button control will actually execute the operation. Double-click the Button control to open the code window and stub out the `Click` event for that control.

Before you get started writing the code, you need to add a reference to another class library. At the very top of your code, type the following reference:

```
using SSIS_Runtime = Microsoft.SqlServer.Dts.Runtime;
```

The `SSIS_Runtime` declaration is an alias to the .NET reference. This coding technique comes in handy when referencing long namespaces as well as definitively using the intended classes during development.

In the `Form1` class, you will create the `ExecutePackage` method. This method will create the necessary objects to load your package, set the variable at runtime, and then execute the package. Type the following lines of code into the class file:

```
public void ExecutePackage()
{
    // Create a string variable to hold the location of our SSIS package
        string strPackagePath = @"C:\Documents and Settings\Administrator\My
Documents\Visual Studio 2008\Projects\Integration Services Project2\Integration
Services Project2\Package1.dtsx";

    // Create a new Application class object
    SSIS_Runtime.Application oApp = new SSIS_Runtime.Application();

    // Create a new Package class object
    SSIS_Runtime.Package oPackage = new SSIS_Runtime.Package();

    // Load the SSIS package
    oPackage = oApp.LoadPackage(strPackagePath, null);

    // Set the myvar variable in the package to the value of the textbox
    oPackage.Variables["myvar"].Value = textBox1.Text.Trim();

    // Execute the package
    oPackage.Execute();
}
```

Now that the `ExecutePackage` method has been created, you need to call this method once the button on your form is clicked. In the `Click` event method for your button type the following piece of code:

```
private void button1_Click(object sender, EventArgs e)
{
    ExecutePackage();
}
```

That's it! If you don't happen to see the `button1_Click` method stubbed out already for you, switch to the designer and double-click the button. This action will create the `Click` event method and allow you to provide the actual implementation.

Now run the project. You will then be presented with the form that you just created. Enter a bit of text into the textbox and click the button. Open Management Studio and expand the AdventureWorks2008 database. Start a new query and type the following line of SQL:

```
Select * From SSIStest
```

You should now see a new record in the table with the text you entered through the Windows application. This simple, yet powerful example demonstrates how you can dynamically set properties in an Integration Services package programmatically. This can be useful in a variety of ways if your environment requires frequent changes to SSIS packages at the time of execution, such as variables, task properties, and even Data Sources.

Summary

This chapter presented three examples that demonstrate how SSIS relates to external applications — as both a source to external applications and a method for reading external sources.

The examples covered three interfaces with external applications:

❑　An InfoPath 2003 Data Source

❑　An output to ASP.NET

❑　A dynamic property assignment through a Winform application

In these three examples, only one used the database — and that was a source of sample data. SSIS is designed to interface with the world beyond SQL Server — what's more, this enterprise development tool ships with this functionality "off the shelf."

The good folks at Microsoft have delivered a powerful enterprise development solution that reaches well beyond the SQL Server database.

Learn more by participating in the Developer Community. A good place to start is the Microsoft TechNet website for SQL Server at: http://technet.microsoft.com/en-us/sqlserver/bb671048
.aspx?wt.svl=leftnav.

22

Administering SSIS

So you have a set of packages and are ready to run the package in production. This chapter focuses on how to administer packages after you've deployed them to production. Specifically, we cover how to configure, deploy, and then administer the SSIS service. We also cover how to create a stand-alone ETL server and some of the command-line utilities you can use to make your job easier. After this chapter, you'll be able to create a package that will not require any effort to migrate from development to production after the first deployment.

Package Configuration

Now that you have a set of packages complete, the challenge is trying to migrate those packages to your testing environment or production without having to manually configure the packages for that environment. For example, your production server may not have the same directory to pull extract files from or the same user name to use to connect to the database. Configuration files help you make the migrations seamless and the configuration automated to reduce your risk of errors. In this section and the next, you'll see two different methods for configuration. One is to create a configuration repository and the other is to create your own repository, which mimics configuration files but gives you more flexibility.

The SSIS Package Configuration option allows you to write any SSIS property for the package, connection, container, variable, or any task into an XML file or a table, for example, and then read the setting at runtime. You could deploy the configuration file to multiple servers and point the setting inside the file to a new SQL Server database on the second server, and when the package runs, it will shift its connection to the new database automatically. They also come in handy later when you deploy the packages to production using the deployment utility.

Let's do a quick example to show you the strengths and weaknesses of package configurations. In this example, you're going to create a simple package with a Script Task that will pop up a message with the configuration value instead of its normal, hard-coded value. You'll then create multiple configuration files and you'll see which configuration file wins.

First, create a new package called `ConfigFiles.dtsx`. Drag over a new Script Task onto the Control Flow tab in the newly created package and name the task Popup Value. Next, create a new string variable called `strMessage` that is scoped to the package and not the Script Task. Seed a default value of "Hard Coded Value" for the string variable.

Double-click the Script Task to configure it. In the Script page, type **strMessage** for the ReadOnlyVariables property. Change the ScriptLanguage property to Microsoft Visual Basic 2008. Click Edit Script to add your code to the task. Double-click the `ScriptMain.vb` file in the Project Explorer window if it's not already open. The code you're going to add will pop up the value from the `strMessage` variable by using the following code in the `Main()` subroutine:

```
Public Sub Main()
    '
    ' Add your code here
    MsgBox(Dts.Variables("strMessage").Value)
    Dts.TaskResult = ScriptResults.Success
End Sub
```

For more information about the Script Task, see Chapter 9. Close the task. If you execute the package at this point, you should see the pop-up dialog box that states "Hard Coded Value". If you see that value, you're now ready to set this variable from a configuration file instead.

Select Package Configurations from the SSIS menu, or by right-clicking in the background of the Control Flow tab. This opens the Package Configurations Organizer where you will create and arrange the priority of your package configurations. Click Enable Package Configurations to enable this feature.

To add your first package configuration, click Add. This will take you to the Package Configuration Wizard. You can set your package configuration to use an XML file, SQL Server table, environment variable, registry setting, or to read a variable from a parent package. Most people choose to use XML files or a SQL Server table. XML files are generally easier to implement because the files will be portable and easy to transport from environment to environment. In this example, you'll use an XML file. Type **c:\Projects\configuration.xml** for the Configuration File name property. The default extension for the configuration XML files is `.dtsConfig`, but we prefer to use an XML extension so it is easily registered to most XML editors.

You can even make the path and filename of the XML file dynamic by reading it from an environment variable. Otherwise, the file must be in the `C:\Projects` folder on each server that you wish to deploy the package to, which may not be allowed in your production environment. You can also change this later during deployment, but that is discussed in a moment in the "Deployment Utility" section.

Click Next to go to the Properties to Export screen in the wizard. If the `c:\Projects\configuration.xml` file had already existed on your server, you would be prompted whether you wish to reuse the existing file or overwrite the file. If you had chosen to reuse an existing file, the next screen would be the final summary screen. This option is fantastic if you wish to have all of your packages in your project reuse the same configuration file, but to do this the property names have to exactly match.

Back in the Properties to Export screen, you can check any property that you wish to have read from the configuration file. In this case, you want to drill down to Variables ⇨ strMessage ⇨ Properties and finally check the Value option (as shown in Figure 22-1). Click Next to proceed to the next screen.

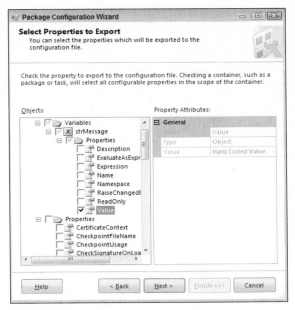

Figure 22-1

You are then taken to the summary screen where you should name the configuration "Variable File" and click Finish, which takes you back to the Package Configurations Organizer. Click Close to exit the organizer and execute the package. If you run the package again, you'll notice that the popup should still have the same old message. The configuration file now has been created after you close the wizard.

Open the `configuration.xml` file in your favorite XML editor or Notepad, and replace the old variable value of "Hard Coded Value" with a new value of "Config File Changed Value" as shown below in the following code. The other pieces of the configuration file contain lots of metadata about who created the configuration file and from what package.

```
<?xml version="1.0" ?>
- <DTSConfiguration>
- <DTSConfigurationHeading>
  <DTSConfigurationFileInfo GeneratedBy="pragmaticpc\pragmaticworks"
GeneratedFromPackageName="ConfigFiles" GeneratedFromPackageID=
"{75B381D2-1617-4A4C-8F57-D61A14CFB379}" GeneratedDate="3/5/2008 10:54:48 PM" />
  </DTSConfigurationHeading>
- <Configuration ConfiguredType="Property"
Path="\Package.Variables[User::strMessage].Properties[Value]" ValueType="String">
  <ConfiguredValue>Hard Coded Value</ConfiguredValue>
  </Configuration>
  </DTSConfiguration>
```

When you execute the package again, notice this time the message has changed.

You can also create multiple configuration files. For example, you may want a configuration file that contains your corporate logging database for all of your packages to use and then another configuration file for the individual package. As you add more package configurations, they stack onto each other in the Configurations Organizer screen. At runtime, if there is a conflict between two configurations, the last configuration on the bottom will win.

To demonstrate this, create one additional configuration. This time, when you're asked for the configuration type, select SQL Server. For the Connection property, select New and point the connection to the AdventureWorks database, which will create a Connection Manager. Lastly, click New for the Configuration Table property. The table can be called whatever you'd like as long as you have the core four columns. Name the table `ctrlConfigurations`, as shown in the following script:

```
CREATE TABLE [dbo].[ctrlConfigurations]
(
    ConfigurationFilter NVARCHAR(255) NOT NULL,
    ConfiguredValue NVARCHAR(255) NULL,
    PackagePath NVARCHAR(255) NOT NULL,
    ConfiguredValueType NVARCHAR(20) NOT NULL
)
```

Type **Development** for the Configuration Filter. When the package reads from the `ctrlConfigurations` table, it will read all the properties where the ConfigurationFilter column is equal to "Development," as shown in Figure 22-2. Typically, you'd want to have this filter set to either the package name or group of packages that you wish to share the same configuration settings. This is because all configurations in SQL Server are stored in the same table.

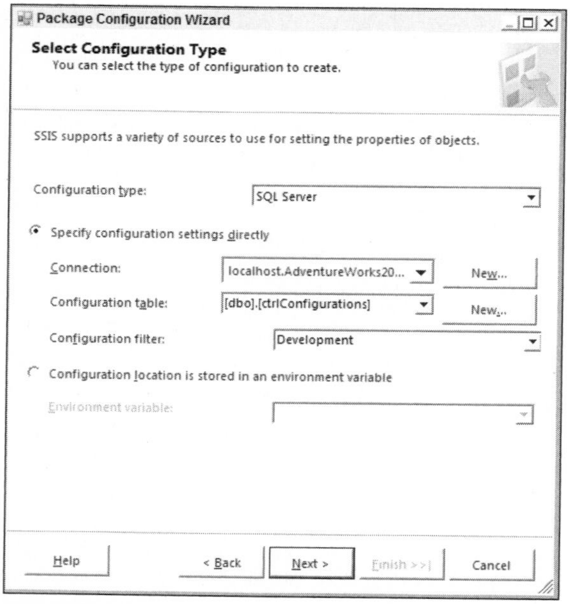

Figure 22-2

Click Next to go to the next screen and name this configuration "SQL Server Config". You should now have two package configurations as shown in Figure 22-3. Set the variable's value by going to the ctrlConfigurations table in the AdventureWorks2008 database and setting the ConfiguredValue column to "SQL Server Config Value" as shown in the following query:

```
Update ctrlConfigurations
SET ConfiguredValue = 'SQL Server Config Value'
   where ConfiguredValue = 'Hard Coded Value'
```

When you execute the package, notice that now the value that pops up is "SQL Server Config Value". This is because there were two configurations that set the same variable but the one at the bottom (see Figure 22-3) will set the value last.

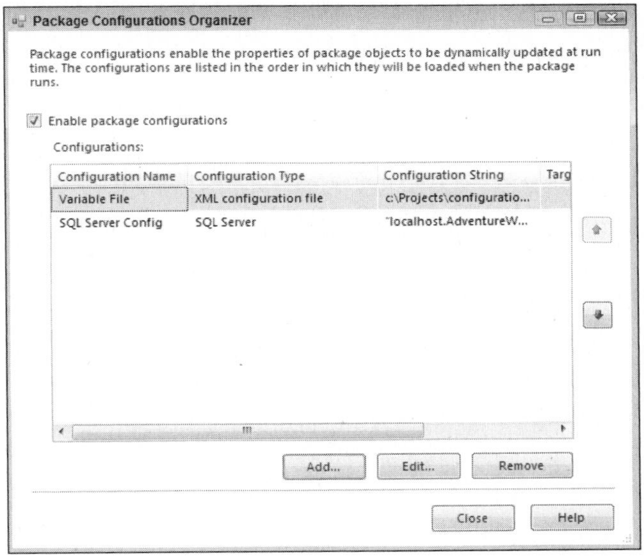

Figure 22-3

Package configuration files make it easy to migrate a package from environment to environment. For the most part, it's going to be easier to store your configurations in the SQL Server because you can write some sort of front-end to modify the settings, and you can create reports to view the settings. The main problem with package configurations is that data is not encrypted, so you should not store anything that should be secure inside package configurations.

There are a few methodologies you can employ when you use configuration files. One is to group all the like configuration properties together into files or with filters if you choose to store the settings in a table. The other option, which many prefer, is to store each property in its own file or with its own filter. If you choose the latter option, it's higher maintenance in creating your package because you may have to create dozens of files, but it allows you to pick which settings you'd like and reuse the settings over and over again.

Deployment Utility

In SSIS, you can create a deployment utility that will help a user install your project of packages and any dependencies. This deployment utility is like creating a program like InstallShield, and is perfect for times where you want to pass a set of packages to a customer or a production DBA that may not know how to install SSIS packages the manual way. When you create a deployment utility, all the files that are necessary to install the project are copied into a centralized directory, and an .SSISDeploymentManifest file is created for the installer to run, which opens the Package Installation Wizard.

Creating the Deployment Manifest

To create a deployment utility, simply right-click the SSIS project in BIDS and select Properties. In the Property Pages dialog box, go to the Deployment Utility page and change the CreateDeploymentUtility property to True, as shown in Figure 22-4. This is set to False by default. The AllowConfigurationChanges property is a key setting as well, and when set to True will prompt the installer if he'd like to change any settings that may be exposed via a configuration file at installation time. The DeploymentOutputPath property shows you where the deployment utility will be outputted to underneath the project folder.

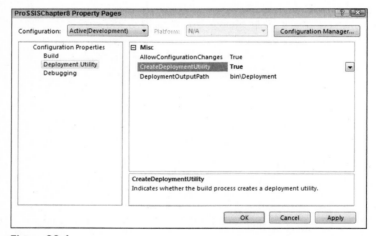

Figure 22-4

Next, under the Build menu, select Build <Project Name>, where <Project Name> represents your project's name. This will open each package and build the package. If there are any errors in the package, then you will see them at this point. As it builds the project, each package, and the project's .SSISDeploymentManifest file, is validated then outputted into the \bin\deployment directory under your project's folder.

After building the deployment utility, you will want to change the CreateDeploymentUtility to False again. Otherwise, each time you click the Play button to execute the package, each package will be validated and executed, which may take an enormous amount of time for a large project.

The Package Deployment Wizard

Now that you have created a deployment .SSISDeploymentManifest file, you're now ready to send the contents of the <project location>\bin\deployment folder to the installation person. The installation person would then need to copy the contents of the folder to the server he wishes to deploy to and double-click the .SSISDeploymentManifest file. The installer could also run it remotely, but it is preferred to run it on the same server as the target deployment server to simplify the installation. You can also modify the .SSISDeploymentManifest file in your favorite XML editor to modify which packages are deployed.

After skipping over the introduction screen, you are asked where you want to deploy the packages, as shown in Figure 22-5. You can either choose a File System Deployment or a SQL Server Deployment. A File System Deployment just copies the files to a directory on the server. A SQL Server Deployment stores the packages in the msdb database on the target server. Later in this chapter (in the "File System or the MSDB Deployment" section), we cover the pros and cons to each option here but for the time being, just select the SQL Server Deployment. You can also have the wizard validate each package after you install the package. This ensures the package that was delivered to you is valid on your machine, including the Data Sources.

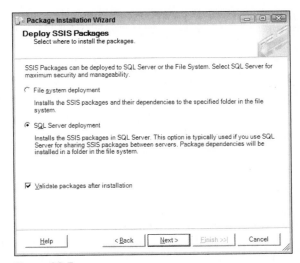

Figure 22-5

If you're following this example, select SQL Server Deployment and click Next. If you select SQL Server Deployment, the next screen prompts you for which SQL Server 2008 instance you wish to deploy the packages. Additionally type "/" (without the quotes) for the Package Path property. This specifies that the packages will be installed into the root path. If you had selected a File System Deployment, the next screen prompts you for which file path you wish for the packages to be deployed. The last option in the SQL Server Deployment screen is to specify if you wish to rely on the SQL Server for protecting the package by encrypting the package. This is the preferred option and will change the ProtectionLevel package property to ServerStorage as it installs each package. We talk more about the ProtectionLevel property later in this chapter.

Even though you have selected a SQL Server Deployment, there may still be files that must be deployed like configuration files and readme files. The next screen prompts you for where you'd like to put these files. Generally, they'll go under a folder named after the project under the `C:\Program Files\ Microsoft SQL Server\100\DTS\Packages` folder.

After you click Next, the packages will be installed in the package store on the server. After the packages are installed, if the developer selected True to the AllowConfigurationChanges in BIDS (shown in Figure 22-6), then you will receive an additional screen giving you, as an installer, a chance to edit the values in the configuration file at deployment time. This can be seen in Figure 22-4, and you can pull down the drop-down box to see multiple configuration files. Unfortunately, it does not show which packages these files are tied to.

Figure 22-6

The only other additional screen you would see is a popup if there was a user password on any package.

After the packages have been deployed, they are validated, as shown in Figure 22-7. If there is a problem, you would see it in the Packages Validation screen, and you can redeploy once the problem is corrected. The last screen is a summary screen to complete the wizard.

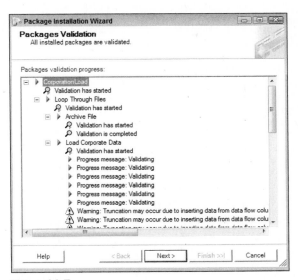

Figure 22-7

There are other ways to deploy packages that we'll show later in this chapter, but this is a great way to deploy packages in bulk. If you wish to deploy a package in Management Studio, as you'll see later in this chapter, you have to do it one package at a time. The file system, however, is much easier. With this method of storage, you can just copy the `.dtsx` and supporting files manually into a directory that's being monitored by the SSIS service, and the packages will be seen from Management Studio immediately.

The main thing to remember about the deployment utility is that when it is used, every package and project dependencies are deployed. If you do not want to deploy this many packages, you can edit the `.SSISDeploymentManifest` file in a text editor to remove any extra files you do not wish to migrate. Some find it useful to create a project in the same project solution that contains a subset of the packages that they wish to deploy, if this is too aggressive for them.

If you did want to edit the .SSISDeploymentManifest XML file before sending the folder to a client, you could just remove one of the <Package> lines as shown in the following XML example. You can also see in the file who created the deployment tool for you and when, in the header of the XML. This information will be useful for tracking down who to ask questions to later if the project doesn't install appropriately. If you do not wish to deploy a configuration file with the wizard, you can remove the <ConfigurationFile> line in order to prevent the configuration file from overwriting the older that may already be on the server file.

```xml
<?xml version="1.0" ?>
<DTSDeploymentManifest GeneratedBy="BRIANKNIGHT\bknight"
GeneratedFromProjectName="Pro SSIS"
GeneratedDate="2008-01-15T23:39:54.7343750-05:00"
AllowConfigurationChanges="true">
  <Package>EventHandler.dtsx</Package>
  <Package>Package1.dtsx</Package>
  <Package>Restartability.dtsx</Package>
  <Package>ConfigFiles.dtsx</Package>
  <Package>Chapter1.dtsx</Package>
  <Package>RawFile.dtsx</Package>
  <Package>DBSnapshots.dtsx</Package>
  <Package>Logging.dtsx</Package>
  <Package>FileWatcher.dtsx</Package>
  <Package>ConfigRepository.dtsx</Package>
  <ConfigurationFile>configuration.xml</ConfigurationFile>
</DTSDeploymentManifest>
```

The Package Store

When you deploy your packages, they are stored into what is called the SSIS Package Store. The Package Store in some cases will actually physically store the package, such as the msdb database option. If you're using file system storage, the Package Store just keeps a pointer to the top-level directory and just enumerates through the packages stored underneath that directory. In order to connect to the Package Store, the SSIS Service must be running. This service is called SQL Server Integration Services, or MSDTSServer100. There is only one instance of the service per machine or per set of clustered machines.

You can configure the SSIS service in the Services applet in Control Panel ⇨ Administrative Tools. Double-click SQL Server Integration Services. As you can see, the service is set to automatically start by default, and starts under the NT AUTHORITY\NetworkService account. In the Recovery tab, you may decide that you want the service to automatically start up again in the event of a failure. In the Recovery tab, you can specify how to react if the service fails the first, second, and subsequent times. As you can see in Figure 22-8, the service has been changed to restart if a failure occurs two times. The failure count is also reset after 2 days in this figure.

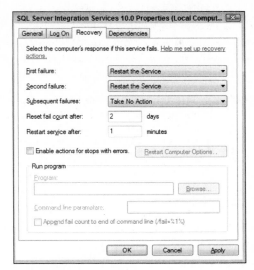

Figure 22-8

While you can run and stop packages programmatically without the service, the service makes running packages more manageable. For example, if you have the service run the package, it tracks that the package is executing and people with the proper permission can interrogate the service, to find out which packages are running. Those that are in the Windows Administrators group can stop all running packages. Otherwise, you can only stop packages that you have started. It can also aid in importing and exporting packages into the Package Store. We cover other uses for the service throughout this chapter, but one last great use for the service is to enable you to create a centralized ETL server to handle the execution of your packages throughout your enterprise.

The MSDTSServer100 service is configured through an XML file that is located by default in the following path: `C:\Program Files\Microsoft SQL Server\100\DTS\Binn\MsDtsSrvr.ini.xml`. This path will vary if you're in a cluster. If you cannot find the path, go to the HKEY_LOCAL_MACHINE\SOFTWARE\Microsoft\Microsoft SQL Server\100\SSIS\ServiceConfigFile registry key in the registry. By default, the XML file should look like the following file:

```
<?xml version="1.0" encoding="utf-8" ?>
- <DtsServiceConfiguration xmlns:xsd="http://www.w3.org/2001/XMLSchema"
xmlns:xsi="http://www.w3.org/2001/XMLSchema-instance">
  <StopExecutingPackagesOnShutdown>true</StopExecutingPackagesOnShutdown>
- <TopLevelFolders>
- <Folder xsi:type="SqlServerFolder">
  <Name>MSDB</Name>
  <ServerName>.</ServerName>
  </Folder>
- <Folder xsi:type="FileSystemFolder">
  <Name>File System</Name>
  <StorePath>..\Packages</StorePath>
  </Folder>
  </TopLevelFolders>
  </DtsServiceConfiguration>
```

There isn't a lot to really configure in this file, but it does have some interesting uses. The first configuration line tells the packages how to react if the service is stopped. By default, packages that the service is running will stop if the service stops or fails over. You could also configure the packages to continue to run until they complete after the service is stopped by changing the StopExecutingPackagesOnShutdown property to False as shown here:

```
<StopExecutingPackagesOnShutdown>false</StopExecutingPackagesOnShutdown>
```

The next configuration sections are the most important. They specify which paths and servers the MSDTSServer100 service will read from. Whenever the service starts, it reads this file to determine where the packages are stored. In the default file, you will have a single entry for a SQL Server that looks like the following SqlServerFolder example:

```
<Folder xsi:type="SqlServerFolder">
<Name>MSDB</Name>
<ServerName>.</ServerName>
</Folder>
```

The <Name> line represents how the name will appear in Management Studio for this set of packages. The <ServerName> line represents where the connection will point to. There is a problem, however: If your SQL Server is on a named instance, this file will still point to the default non-named instance (.). If you do have a named instance, simply replace the period with your instance name.

The next section shows you where your File System packages will be stored. The <StorePath> property shows the folder where all packages will be enumerated from. The default path is C:\program files\ microsoft sql server\100\dts\Packages, which is represented as ..\Packages in the default code that follows. The part of the statement goes one directory below the SSIS service file and then into the Packages folder.

```
<Folder xsi:type="FileSystemFolder">
<Name>File System</Name>
<StorePath>..\Packages</StorePath>
</Folder>
```

Everything in the Packages folder, and below that folder, will be enumerated. You can create subdirectories under this folder and they will immediately show up in Management Studio without having to modify the service's configuration file. Each time you make a change to the MsDtsSrvr.ini .xml file, you must stop and start the MSDTSServer100 service.

Creating a Central SSIS Server

Many enterprise companies have so many packages, they decide to separate the service from SQL Server and place it on its own server. When you do this, you must still license the server just as if it's running SQL Server. The advantage of this is that your SSIS packages will not suffocate the SQL Server's memory during a large load, and you have a central spot to manage. The disadvantage of this is that now you must license the server separately and you add an added layer of complexity when you're debugging packages. When you do this you create a fantastic way to easily scale packages by adding more memory to your central server, but you also create an added performance hit because all remote data must be copied over the network before entering the Data Flow buffer.

To create a centralized SSIS hub, you must only modify the `MsDtsSrvr.ini.xml` file and restart the service. The service can read a UNC path like `\\ServerName\Share`, and it can point to multiple remote servers. In the below example, the service will enumerate packages from three servers, one that is local and another that is a named instance. After restarting the service, you will see a total of six folders to expand in Management Studio. We cover the Management Studio aspect of SSIS in much more detail later in this chapter.

```xml
<?xml version="1.0" encoding="utf-8" ?>
<DtsServiceConfiguration xmlns:xsd="http://www.w3.org/2001/XMLSchema"
xmlns:xsi="http://www.w3.org/2001/XMLSchema-instance">
  <StopExecutingPackagesOnShutdown>true</StopExecutingPackagesOnShutdown>
 <TopLevelFolders>
 <Folder xsi:type="SqlServerFolder">
  <Name>Server A MSDB</Name>
  <ServerName>localhost</ServerName>
  </Folder>
  <Name>Server B MSDB</Name>
  <ServerName>SQLServerB</ServerName>
  </Folder>
  <Name>Server C MSDB</Name>
  <ServerName>SQLServerC\NamedInstance</ServerName>
  </Folder>
<Folder xsi:type="FileSystemFolder">
  <Name>Server A File System</Name>
  <StorePath>P:\Packages</StorePath>
  </Folder>
<Folder xsi:type="FileSystemFolder">
  <Name>Server B File System</Name>
  <StorePath>\\SQLServerB\Packages</StorePath>
  </Folder>
<Folder xsi:type="FileSystemFolder">
  <Name>Server C File System</Name>
  <StorePath>\\SQLServerC\Packages</StorePath>
  </Folder>
  </TopLevelFolders>
  </DtsServiceConfiguration>
```

Your next issue is how to schedule packages when using a centralized SSIS hub like this example. You can schedule your packages through SQL Server Agent or through a scheduling system like Task Scheduler from Windows. Because you're already paying for a license of SQL Server, it's better to install SQL Server on your server and use Agent since it gives you much more flexibility, as you will see in a later section. Keep in mind that packages run from the machine that executes the package. So if you have a package stored on Server A but execute it from Server B, it will use Server B's resource. You can also store configuration tables and logging tables on this SQL Server to centralize its processing as well. Both scheduling mechanisms are covered in a later section in this chapter.

Clustering SSIS

The unfortunate news is that SSIS is not a clustered service by default. Microsoft does not recommend that you cluster SSIS, because it could lead to unpredictable results. For example, if you place SSIS in the same Cluster Group as SQL Server, and if SQL Server were to fail over, it would cause SSIS to fail over as well. Even though it does not cluster in the main SQL Server setup, it can still be clustered manually through a series of relatively easy steps. If you feel you must cluster SSIS, this section walks you through those steps, but makes the assumption that you already know how to use Windows clustering and know the basic clustering architecture. Essentially, the steps to setting up SSIS as a clustered service are:

1. Install SSIS on the other nodes that can own the service.

2. Create a new cluster group (optionally).

3. If you created a new group, create a virtual IP, name, and drive as clustered resources.

4. Copy over the `MsDtsSrvr.ini.xml` file to the clustered drive.

5. Modify the `MsDtsSrvr.ini.xml` file to change the location of the packages.

6. Change the registry setting to point to the `MsDtsSrvr.ini.xml` file.

7. Cluster the MSDTSServer100 service as a generic service.

First, we must discuss a minor decision you'll have to make prior to clustering. You can choose to cluster the MSDTSServer100 service in the main SQL Server cluster group for a given instance or you can create its own cluster group. You will find that while it's easier to piggyback the main SQL Server service, it adds complexity to management.

The SSIS service only has a single instance in the entire Windows cluster. If you have a four-instance SQL Server cluster, where would you place the SSIS service then? This is one reason why it makes the most sense to move the SSIS service into its own group. The main reason, though, is a manageability one. If you decide that you need to fail over the SSIS service to another node, you would have to fail over the SQL Server as well if they shared a cluster group, which would cause an outage. Moving the SSIS service into its own cluster group ensures that only the SSIS service fails over and does not cause a wider outage.

Placing the service in its own group comes at a price, though. The service will now need a virtual IP address, its own drive, and a name on the network. Once you have those requirements, you're all ready to go ahead and cluster. If you decided to place SSIS into its own group, you would not need the drive, IP, or name.

The first step to cluster is to install SSIS on all nodes in the Windows cluster. If you installed SSIS as part of your SQL Server install, you'll see that SSIS installed only on the primary node. You'll now need to install it manually on the other nodes in the cluster. Make sure you make the installation simple and install SSIS on the same folder on each node.

If you want to have the SSIS service in a different group as the database engine, you'll first have to create a new group called SSIS in Cluster Administrator for the purpose of this example (although it can be called something else). This group will need to be shared by whichever nodes you would like to participate in the cluster. Then, add to the group a physical drive that is clustered, an IP address, and a network name. The IP address and network name are virtual names and IPs.

From whichever node owns the SSIS group, copy the `MsDtsSrvr.ini.xml` file to the clustered physical drive that's in the SSIS cluster group. We generally create a directory called `<Clustered Drive Letter>\SSISSetup` to place the file. Make a note of wherever you placed the file for a later configuration step. You'll also want to create a folder called Packages on the same clustered drive for your packages to be stored. This directory will store any packages and configuration files that will be stored on the file system instead of the msdb database.

Next, open the Registry editing tool and change the HKEY_LOCAL_MACHINE\SOFTWARE\ Microsoft\Microsoft SQL Server\100\SSIS\ServiceConfigFile key to point to the new location (including the filename) for the `MsDtsSrvr.ini.xml` file. Make sure you backup the registry before making this change.

After this change, you're now ready to cluster the MSDTSServer100 service. Open Cluster Administrator again and right-click the SSIS cluster group (if you're creating it in its own group) and select New ⇨ Resource. This will open the Resource Wizard, which clusters nearly any service in Windows. On the first screen type **Integration Services** for the name of the clustered resource and select Generic Service. This name is a logical name that is only going to be meaningful to the administrator and you.

Next, on the Possible Owner screen, add any node that you wish to potentially own the SSIS service. On the Dependencies page, add the group's Network Name, IP Address, and Drive as dependencies. This will ensure that the SSIS service will not come online before the name and drives are online. Also, if the drive fails, the SSIS service will also fail.

The next screen is the Generic Service Parameters, where you will want to type **MSDTSServer100** for the service to cluster. The last screen in the wizard is the Registry Replication screen, where you will want to ensure that the SOFTWARE\Microsoft\Microsoft SQL Server\100\SSIS\ServiceConfigFile key is replicated. If a change is made to this registry key, it will be replicated to all other nodes. After you finish the wizard, the SSIS service will be almost ready to come online and be clustered.

The final step is to move any packages that were stored on the file system over to the clustered drive in the `Packages` folder. The next time you open Management Studio, you should be able to see all the packages and folders. You'll also need to edit the `MsDtsSrvr.ini.xml` file to change the SQL Server to point to SQL Server's virtual name and not the physical name, which will allow failovers of the database engine. In the same file, you will need to change the path in the StorePath to point to the `<Clustered Drive>:\Packages` folder you created earlier as well. After this, you're ready to bring the service online in Cluster Administrator.

Now that your SSIS service is clustered, you will no longer connect to the physical machine name to manage the packages in Management Studio. You will now connect to the network name that you created in Cluster Administrator. If you added SSIS as a clustered resource in the same group as SQL Server, you would connect to the SQL Server's virtual network name.

File System or the MSDB Deployment

As was discussed earlier, there are two places you can store your packages: on the file system or in the msdb database. During development, packages are all stored as .DTSX files on the file system or in your source control system. Each storage option has its own pros and cons, and which option you choose will be based on what is more important to you. We cover these pros and cons in much depth in this section but to summarize, the following table gives you a high-level idea of which storage option is best, based on what functionality you're most interested in. Just because a given storage option is not checked, does not mean it doesn't have that functionality. The ones checked are just most optimized for the given functionality.

Functionality	Best in File System	Best in MSDB
Security		@@ch
Backup and recovery	@@ch	
Deployment	@@ch	
Troubleshooting	@@ch	
Availability	@@ch	
Execution Speed	@@ch	@@ch

If security concerns you greatly, you may want to consider placing your packages in the msdb database. To secure your packages on the file system, you could have multiple layers of security by using the Windows Active Directory security on the folder on the file system where the packages are at. You could also then place a password on the packages to keep users who may have administrator rights to your machine from executing the package. This does add extra complexity to your package deployments in some cases. If you store your packages in the msdb database, you can assign package roles to each package to designate who can see or execute the package. The packages can also be encrypted in the msdb database, which strengthens your security even more. We cover this in much more depth later in this chapter.

Backup and recovery is simpler when you store your packages in the msdb database. If you store your packages in the msdb database, then you must only wrap the msdb database into your regular maintenance plan to back up all the packages. As packages are added, they are wrapped into the maintenance plan. The problem with this is that you cannot restore a single package using this mechanism. You'd have to restore all the packages to a point in time, and that would also restore the jobs and history. The other option is a file system backup, which would just use your favorite backup software to backup the folders and files. However, you must rely on your Backup Operator to do this for you, which makes some uneasy. You could at that point restore individual packages to a point in time. In reality, you may just go ahead and redeploy the packages from SourceSafe if you couldn't retrieve a backup file.

File system deployments are much simpler but less sophisticated. To deploy packages onto the file system, you must only copy them into the directory for the package store. You can create subdirectories under the parent directory to subdivide it easily. You can also copy a single package over easily as well, in case you need to make a package change. To import a package into the package store using the msdb database, you must use Management Studio (or a command-line tool called dtutil.exe) and import them package by package. To do a bulk migration, you could use the deployment utility we discussed in the last chapter.

Along the same lines as deployment is troubleshooting. If something were to go bump in the night and you wanted to see if the packages in production were the same release as the packages you thought you had deployed, you only need to copy the files down to your machine and perform a comparison using SourceSafe or another similar tool. If the files were stored in the msdb database, you would have to right-click each package in Management Studio and select Export. If the same packages were stored in the file system, you must only copy the files to your machine.

Availability of your packages is always on the top of the list for DBAs. If you store the packages in the msdb database and the database engine goes down, the packages are unavailable. If they were stored in the file system, then your packages would be available for execution. Of course, if the database engine is down, then probably one of your key Data Sources would also be down at the time.

The good news is no matter what storage option you choose, the performance will be the same. As you can see, there are many pros and cons to each storage option and neither overwhelmingly wins. The main reason that we choose to use the file system generally is for simplicity of deployment.

Management Studio

In SSIS, there's delineation between development and administration. This makes the development model much more like developing a regular C# program. In a web application, you would never make a code change to the C# application on the production server. Instead, if you wanted to make a change, you would check it out of Source Control, make the change, and then redeploy. The same C# model applies to SSIS.

When you open Management Studio, select the Connect drop-down box in the Object Explorer window and select Integration Services. Once you connect, you will see all the different stores that are available for you to explore. Figure 22-9 shows the results of the configuration change we made to the MsDtsSrvr.ini.xml file. As you can see, there are two stores that this SSIS service is controlling.

A connection to that store isn't made until you expand one of the folders as shown with the File System store in Figure 22-9 (your list of packages may vary from mine). At that point, you may experience a timeout if you're trying to connect to an msdb database that isn't online, or where the server is offline. Otherwise, when you expand the folder, you will see a list of folders and packages that are stored in that particular store.

Figure 22-9

You can also access all the packages that are running, if you're an Administrator, or packages that you started under the Running Packages folder. From here, you can stop packages that are running too long by right-clicking the package and selecting Stop. You can also right-click the folder and select Reports ⇨ General to see a report of all the packages running and for how long. In Figure 22-10, you can see that there are two instantiations of the Package1 package. Both were executed by the Administrator account, and the Execution duration is the amount of milliseconds since the start time.

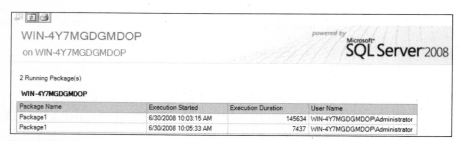

Package Name	Execution Started	Execution Duration	User Name
Package1	6/30/2008 10:03:15 AM	145634	WIN-4Y7MGDGMDOP\Administrator
Package1	6/30/2008 10:05:33 AM	7437	WIN-4Y7MGDGMDOP\Administrator

Figure 22-10

You can right-click any item or folder in the tree to produce item-specific reports. At a package level, you can see all the details for the package that the designer has exposed in BIDS. At the folder level, you can see all the packages in the folder and their build numbers.

Running Packages with DTExecUI

The primary way to execute a package is with DTExecUI.exe. This utility is a graphical wrapper for DTExec.exe, and provides an easier way to produce the necessary switches to execute the package. Nearly all the same tabs and options you see in DTExecUI.exe will be available also when you schedule the package. The quickest way to open the utility is from within Management Studio. To open it from there, right-click any package that you wish to execute and select Run. You can also open the utility by selecting Start ⇨ Run and typing **DTExecui.exe**.

Before we begin with this utility, it's important to note that it's a 32-bit utility. The utility will run on a 64-bit machine; however, it will wrap the 32-bit version of DTExec.exe. In a later section of this chapter, we cover some tricks to use to run the package in 64-bit mode.

When you right-click a package in Management Studio and select Run, the first screen in DTExecUI is filled out for you automatically. This page, shown in Figure 22-11, points to the package you wish to execute and where the package is located. If you select the Package Store to connect to from the Package Source drop-down box, you'll be able to see all the packages stored on the server no matter where they are stored. Your other options are SQL Server or the File System. With the SQL Server option, you will only see packages stored in the msdb of that server that you name. The File System option allows you to point to a .dtsx file to execute.

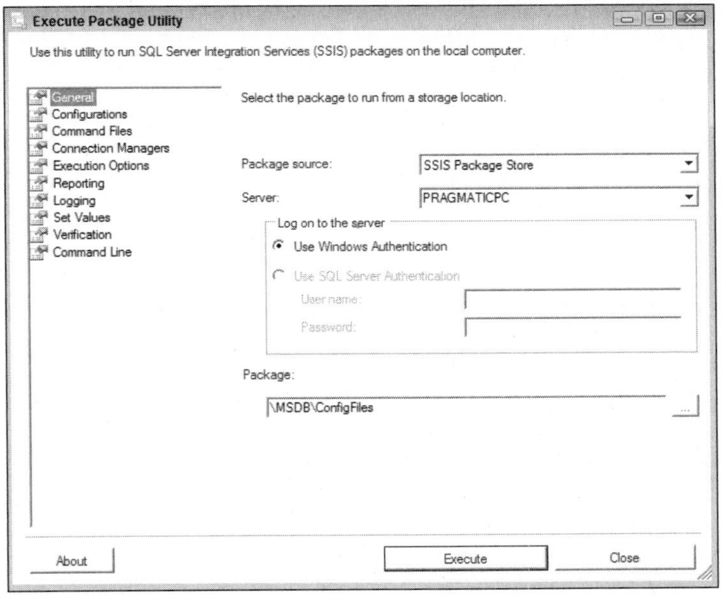

Figure 22-11

The next page in the Execute Package Utility is the Configurations page. In this page, you can select additional configuration files that you wish to use for this execution of the package. If you do not select an additional configuration file, any configuration files that are already on the server will be used. You will not be able to see existing configuration files that are being used in the package.

The Command Files page provides links to files that contain a series of additional switches you can use during execution. Remember, this tool wraps DTExec, which is a command-line utility. With a command file, you can place part of the standard DTExec switches in a file and the reuse them over and over again for every package.

The Connection Managers page shows the power of Connection Managers. This page allows you to change the Connection Manager settings at runtime to a different setting than what the developer had originally intended. For example, perhaps you'd like to move the destination connection for a package to a production server instead of a QA server (shown in Figure 22-12). Another typical example is when you don't have the same drive structure in production as they had in development and you need to move the Connection Manager to a different directory.

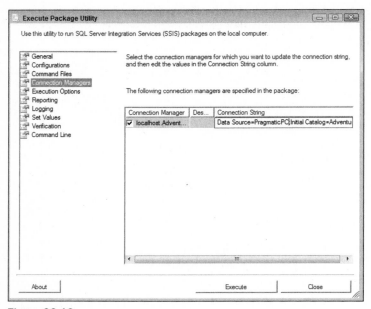

Figure 22-12

The Execution Options page (shown in Figure 22-13) gives you advanced settings for the package execution. For example, you can force the package to fail upon the first package warning, which would normally be ignored. You can also simply validate the package without executing the package. An especially powerful setting in this page is the Maximum Concurrent Executables option. This option simply controls how many concurrent tasks will run in parallel. Often times, you may migrate the package to a different environment with less processors and it could cause performance issues until you lower this setting. The setting of -1 means that two tasks plus the number of CPUs will run concurrently. The last set of options on this page allows you to enable checkpoints on the package, if they are not already enabled, by checking the Enable Package Checkpoints option and specifying a name.

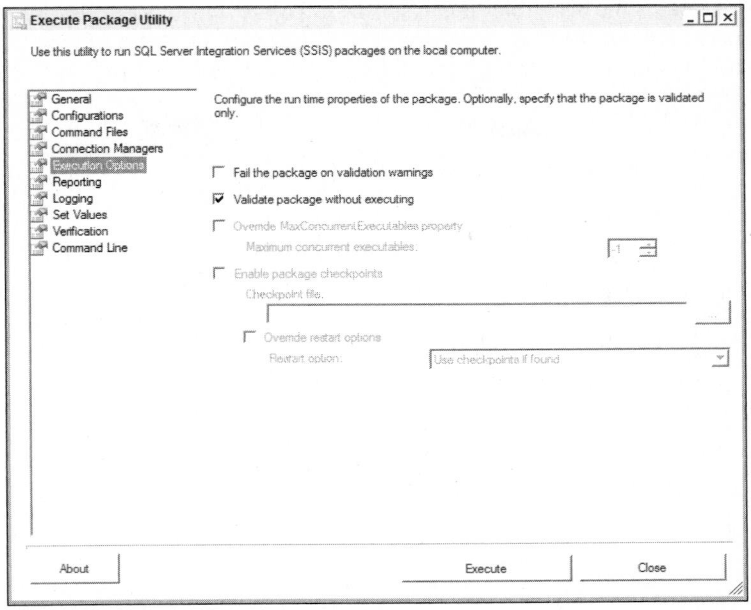

Figure 22-13

The Reporting page (shown in Figure 22-14) controls what type of detail will be shown in the console. The default option is Verbose, which may be too detailed for you. You may decide that you'd rather only show Errors and Warnings, which would perform slightly better than the verbose message. You can also control which columns will show in the console.

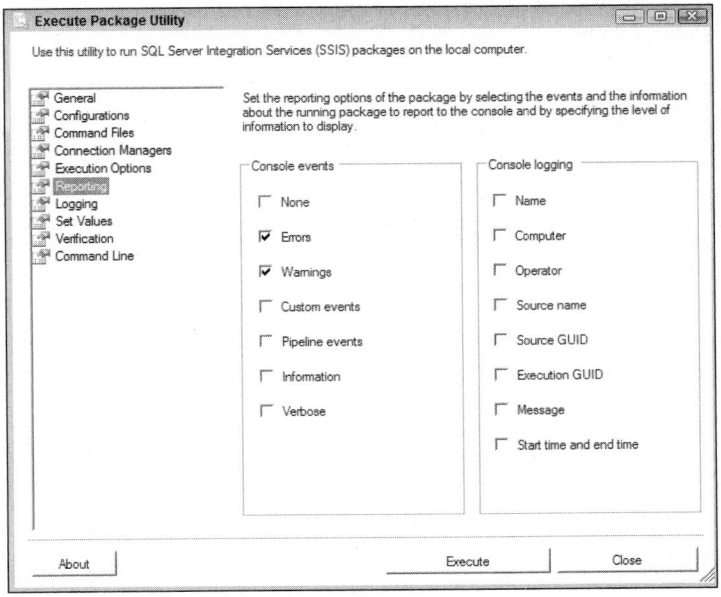

Figure 22-14

Another powerful page is the Set Values page (shown in Figure 22-15). This page allows you to override nearly any property you wish by typing the property path for the property. The most common use for this would be to set the value of a variable. To do this, you would use a property path that looked like this: \Package.Variables[VariableName].Value, then type the value for the variable in the next column. This page is also a way to work around some properties that can't be set through expressions. With those properties, you generally can access them through the property path.

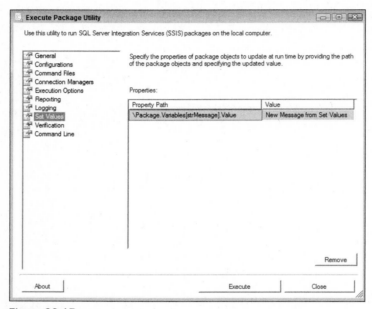

Figure 22-15

In the Verification page (shown in Figure 22-16), you can ensure that you only execute packages that meet your criteria. For example, you may want to make sure you only execute signed packages or packages of a certain build number. This may be handy for Sarbanes-Oxley compliance, where you must guarantee you don't execute a rogue package.

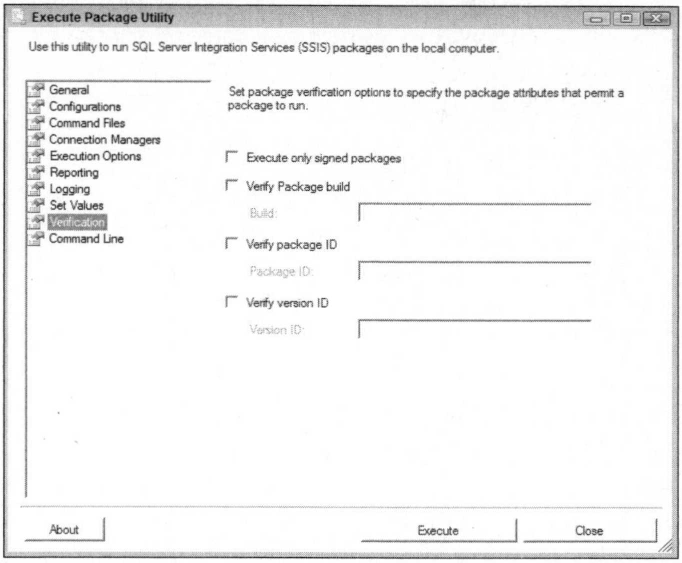

Figure 22-16

The Command Line page (shown in Figure 22-17) is one of the most important ones. This page shows you the exact DTExec.exe command that will be executing. You can also edit the command here as well. After the command is how you'd like it, you can copy and paste it in a command prompt after the command DTexec.exe. We cover DTexec.exe in a later section, but this page can save you from having to learn how to use that utility. It is also sometimes the only way execute the package in 64-bit mode.

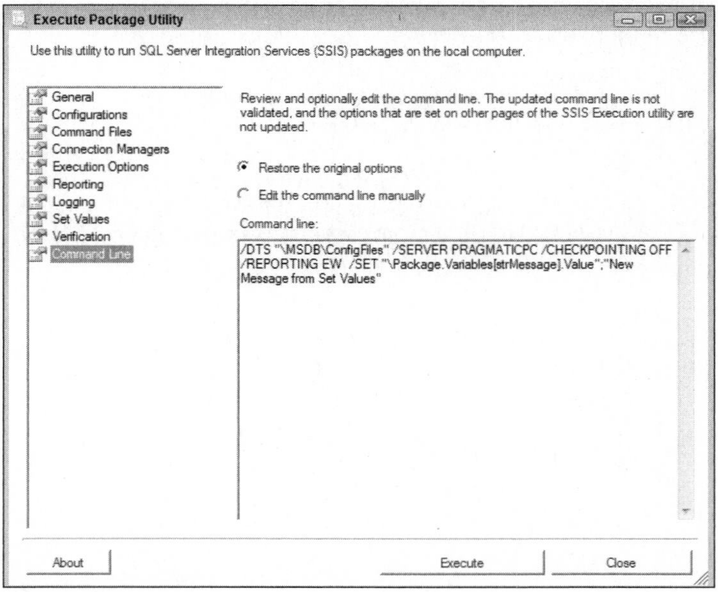

Figure 22-17

You can also execute the package by clicking the Execute button at any time from any page. After you click the Execute button, you will see the Package Execution Progress window, which will show you any warnings, errors, and informational messages, as shown in Figure 22-18. You'll only see a fraction of the message in some cases and you can hover over the message to see the full message.

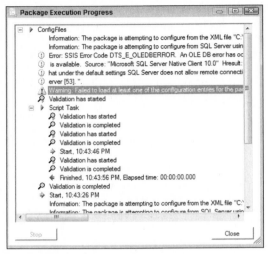

Figure 22-18

Security

The only login option for connecting to the SSIS service is to use your Active Directory account. Once you connect, you'll only see packages that you are allowed to see. This protection is accomplished based on package roles. Package roles are only available on packages stored in the msdb database. Packages stored on the file system must be protected with a password.

Package roles can be accessed in Management Studio by right-clicking a package that you wish to protect and selecting Package Roles. The Package Role dialog box shown in Figure 22-19 allows you to choose the MSDB role that will be in the writer role and reader role. The writer role can perform administration-type functions like overwrite a package with a new version, delete a package, manage security, and stop the package from running. The reader role can execute and view the package. The role can also export the package from Management Studio.

Figure 22-19

Package roles use database roles from the msdb database. By default, people who are in the db_ dtsadmin, db_dtsoperator database roles or the creator of the package can be a reader. The writer role is held by members of the db_dtsadmin database role, or the creator of the package by default. When you select the drop-down box in the Package Roles dialog box, you can change the package role from the default one to another customized role from the msdb database.

You may want to customize a group of people as the only ones who can execute the accounting set of packages. Let's do a quick example together to secure a package to a role called Accounting for the writer and reader package role. First, open Management Studio and connect to your development or local database engine instance. Then, expand System Databases ⇨ msdb ⇨ Security and right-click Roles, selecting New Role. This opens the New Database Role dialog box (shown in Figure 22-20). You will of course need the appropriate security to create a new database role.

Name the role AccountingRole and make your own login a member of the role by clicking the Add button. Additionally, make your own user an owner of the role. You may have to add your login as a user to the msdb database prior to adding the role if it's not there already.

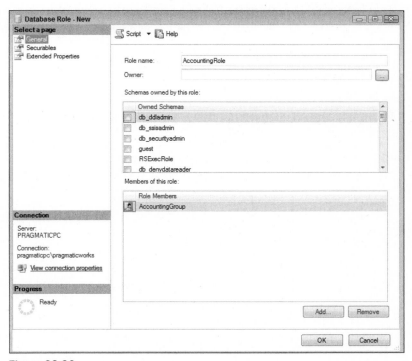

Figure 22-20

You're now ready to tie this role to a package. In Management Studio, connect to Integration Services. Right-click any package stored in the msdb database and select Package Role to secure the package. For the writer and reader roles, select the newly created AccountingRole role and click OK. Now, packages of the AccountingRole role will be able to perform actions to the package. If you're a member of the sysadmin role for the server, you will be able to perform all functions in SSIS like execute and update any package and bypass the package role.

If your packages are stored on the file system, you must set a package password on the package to truly secure it. You can also enforce security as well, by protecting the directory with Windows Active Directory security on the file or folder where your packages are stored. To set a package password in BIDS, you can set the ProtectionLevel property to EncryptSensitiveWithPassword and type a password for the PackagePassword property. You can also set a package password using a utility called DTutil.exe, which we cover in a later section in this chapter.

To connect to a package store, the SSIS service must be started on the given server. Additionally, you must have TCP/IP port 135 open between your machine and the server. This is a common port used for DCOM, and many network administrators will not have this open by default. You'll also need to have the SQL Server database engine port open (generally TCP/IP port 1433) to connect to the package store in the msdb database.

Command-Line Utilities

We've spent the bulk of this chapter focusing on the GUI tools you can use to administer SSIS. There are also a series of tools that you can use from a command line that act as a Swiss Army knife to an SSIS administrator. The two tools that you'll use are DTExec.exe and DTUtil.exe. DTExec is a tool you'll use to execute your packages from a command line, and DTUtil.exe can help you migrate a package or change the security of a package, just to name a few of its functions.

DTExec

You've already seen the power of DTExecUI for executing your packages. That tool wraps the command-line utility DTExec. A shortcut here is to use DTExecUI to create the command for you. You can see the full list of switches for this utility by typing:

```
dtexec.exe /?
```

For example, to execute a package that is stored in the msdb database on your localhost, you could use the following command. This command is more verbose than is required. In reality, you only need to type the /DTS and /SERVER switches to find and execute the package.

```
DTExec.exe /DTS "\MSDB\DBSnapshots" /SERVER localhost /MAXCONCURRENT " -1 "
/CHECKPOINTING OFF  /REPORTING V
```

In Windows Task Manager, you can kill the instantiation of DTExec in order to stop a runaway package that refuses to stop through normal means.

DTUtil

One of the best undiscovered command-line tools in your administrator kit is DTUtil.exe. This is also a good tool for developers as well. The tool performs a number of functions, including moving packages, renumbering the PackageID, re-encrypting a package, and digitally signing a package. To see everything this tool can do, you can type the following command from a command prompt:

```
DTUtil.exe /?
```

Essentially, this tool can be used to do many of the things that you do in Management Studio and to a lesser extent, BIDS. The next few sections show you a few creative ways to use DTUtil.exe.

Re-Encrypting All Packages in a Directory

By default, SSIS files in development are encrypted to prevent an unauthorized person from seeing your SSIS package. The type of encryption is seamless behind the scenes, and is at a workstation and user level. Earlier in development you can set the ProtectionLevel property to EncryptSensitiveWithUserKey (default option) to lock down password information in Connection Managers. You can also set a password on the package by changing the ProtectionLevel property to EncryptSensitiveWithPassword.

By default, if you were to send a package that you're developing to another developer on your team, he would not be able to open it. The same would apply if you logged in with a different user. You would receive the following error:

```
There were errors while the package was being loaded.
The package might be corrupted.
See the Error List for details.
```

The error is very misleading. In truth, you can't open the package because the originating user encrypted the package whether on purpose or not. To fix this, the owner of the package can open the package and select a different option in the Properties pane (like a package password) for the ProtectionLevel option. The default option is EncryptSensitiveWithUserKey. To protect the entire package with a password, select the EncryptAllWithPassword option.

An option that we like is that an SSIS designer encrypts all packages with the default option, and when he's ready to send to production, he can develop a batch file to loop through a directory's .dtsx file and set a password. The batch file would use DTUtil.exe and look like this:

```
for %%f in (*.dtsx) do Dtutil.exe /file %%f /encrypt file;%%f;3;newpassword
```

This would loop through each .dtsx file in your directory and assign the password of newpassword. The production support group could then use the same batch file to reset the password to a production password. The number 3 prior to the word newpassword sets the ProtectionLevel property of the package to EncryptAllWithPassword.

Handling a Corrupt Package

Occasionally when you copy objects in and out of a container, you may corrupt a given task in the package. In that example, you can't delete the task or move it outside the container or link it in the container. This doesn't happen often, but when you suspect you have a corrupt package or object, you can use DTUtil.exe to re-generate the package's XML. To do this, you can use the -I switch to generate a new PackageID and regenerate the XML, like this:

```
DTUtil.exe -I -File dbsnapshots.dtsx
```

Once you do this, the package may look different when you open it because the XML has been regenerated. For example, some of your containers may be smaller than original and placed in areas they weren't originally in. You can also use this command to generate a new PackageID when the developer copied and pasted the package in BIDS.

You can also create a batch file to loop through the directory and regenerate the ID for every package in the directory. The batch file will loop through every .dtsx file and execute DTUtil.exe. The batch file would look like this:

```
for %%f in (*.dtsx) do dtutil.exe /I /FILE "%%f"
```

Scheduling a Package

The primary way to schedule packages in SSIS is with SQL Server Agent, which ships with the SQL Server database engine. If you don't have a database engine in your environment, then you must use something like Task Scheduler, which ships with Windows. Scheduling a package with SQL Server Agent is much simpler and gives you much more flexibility.

The first step to scheduling a package is to connect to the database engine. Ensure that the SQL Server Agent service is started. Right-click Jobs under the SQL Server Agent tree and select New Job. The New Job dialog box will open.

In the General page, type the name of your job as **Execute Package**. In the Steps page, click New, which opens the New Job Step dialog box. Type **Execute Sample Package** for the Step Name property in the General page as shown in Figure 22-21. Then, select SQL Server Integration Services Package as the type of step. For the time being, use the default SQL Agent Service Account as the Run As account. This means that the account that starts SQL Server Agent will execute the package, and sources and destinations in your package will use Windows Authentication with that account if they're set up to use Windows Authentication.

For the Package Source, select the SSIS Package Store and point to a valid SSIS service location. Pick any test package that won't have production impact by clicking the ellipsis button. When you click the ellipsis button, you'll see all the folders in the package store, and whether they are in the msdb database on the file system.

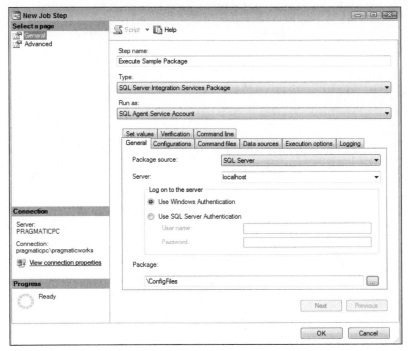

Figure 22-21

The rest of the options resemble exactly what you saw earlier in DTExecUI.exe, with the exception of the Reporting tab because there is no console to report to from a job. You can also optionally go to the Advanced page to set the Include Step Output in History to get more information about the job when it succeeds or fails. Click OK to go back to the New Job dialog box. You can then go to the Schedules page to configure when you'd like the job to run. Click OK again to go back to the main Management Studio interface.

With the job now scheduled, right-click the newly created job and select Start Job at Step. You will then see a status box open that starts the job. After you see a success, it does not mean the job passed or failed. Instead it just means that the job was started successfully. You can right-click the job and select View History to see if it was successful. This opens the Log File Viewer, which shows you each execution of the package. You can drill into each execution to see more details about the step below. The information this step gives you is adequate to help you diagnose a problem, but you may need package logs to truly diagnose the problem.

Proxy Accounts

A classic problem in SSIS and DTS is that a package may work in the design environment but not work once scheduled. Typically, this is because you have connections that use Windows Authentication. At design time, the package uses your credentials, and when you schedule the package, it uses the SQL Server Agent service account by default. This account may not have access to a file share or database server that is necessary to successfully run the package. Proxy accounts in SQL Server 2008 allow you to circumvent this problem.

With a proxy account, you can assign a job to use an account other than the SQL Server Agent account, as shown in Figure 22-22. Creating a proxy account is a two-step process. First, you must create a credential that will allow a user to use an Active Directory account that is not their own, Then, you specify how that account may be used.

To first create a credential, open Management Studio and right-click Credentials under the Security tree and select New Credential (shown in Figure 22-22). For this example, you'll create a credential called Admin Access. The credential will allow users to temporarily gain administrator access. For the Identity property, type the name of an administrator account or an account with higher rights. Lastly, type the password for the Windows account, and click OK.

As you can imagine, because you're typing a password here, be careful of your company's password expiry policies. Credential accounts should be treated as service accounts.

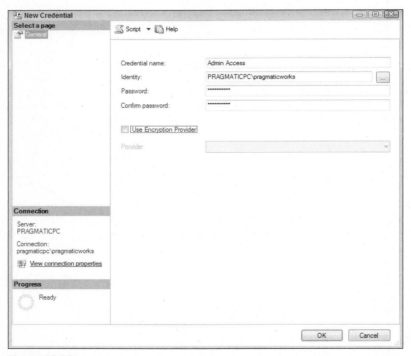

Figure 22-22

The next step is to specify how the credential can be used. Under the SQL Server Agent tree, right-click Proxies and select New Proxy, which opens the New Proxy Account dialog box (shown in Figure 22-23). Type **Admin Access Proxy** for the Proxy Name property, and **Admin Access** as the Credential Name. Check SQL Server Integration Services Package for the subsystem type allowed to use this proxy.

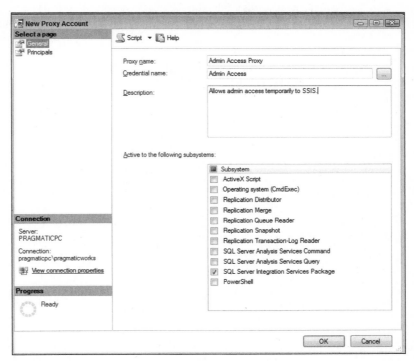

Figure 22-23

Optionally, you can go to the Principals page in the New Proxy Account dialog box to state which roles or accounts can use your proxy from SSIS. You can explicitly grant server roles, specific logins, or members of given msdb roles rights to your proxy. Click Add to grant rights to the proxy one at a time.

You can now click OK to save the proxy. Now if you create a new SSIS job step as was shown earlier, you'll be able to use the new proxy by selecting the Admin Access Proxy from the Run As drop-down box. Any connections that use Windows Authentication will then use the proxy account instead of the standard account.

64-Bit Issues

As we mentioned before, DTExecUI.exe is a 32-bit application. Because of this, whenever you execute a package from DTExecUI.exe, it will execute in 32-bit mode and potentially take longer to execute than if you were executing it on your development machine. Much of this is because data must be marshaled back and forth between 32-bit mode and 64-bit mode. To get around this problem, you can go to the

Command Line page of this tool and copy the command out of the window, and paste it into a command prompt, prefixing `dtexec.exe` in front of it.

DTExec comes in two flavors: 32-bit and 64-bit. The 32-bit version is stored in the `\Program Files (x86)` directory and the 64-bit version is stored in the main `\Program Files` directory. Occasionally, we have seen issues where the environment variables have issues and point to the wrong `C:\Program Files\Microsoft SQL Server\100\DTS\Binn\` directory. You can fix this issue by right-clicking My Computer from your desktop and selecting Properties. Go to the Advanced tab and select Environment Variables. From the System Variables window, select the Path variable and click Edit. In that window, you will see the path to the Binn directory. Ensure here that the path is set to `\Program Files` and not `\Program Files (x86)`, and click OK. After that, you can go to a command prompt, type **DTExec**, and know that you're executing the 64-bit version (the version is of DTExec shown in the first few lines of executing a package). It's important to note that this only applies to 64-bit machines.

A particularly annoying quirk is that (at the time of this publication) there is no MDAC driver for the 64-bit architecture. The impact of this is that you can't execute packages in 64-bit mode if they refer to anything that uses Jet in particular (Access and Excel). If you need to do this, you can execute the package using the 32-bit version of DTExec.exe. Another option in BIDS is to right-click the project, select Properties, and set the Run64BitRuntime to false in the Debugging page. This will set packages inside the project to run in 32-bit mode when debugging.

We've listed a few quirks of the 64-bit architecture and SSIS here, but the benefits are incredible. Keep in mind that SSIS is very memory intensive. If you're able to scale up the memory on demand with a 64-bit architecture, there's a truly compelling reason to upgrade. Even though tools like DTExecUI are not 64-bit ready, packages that are scheduled will run under 64-bit mode. If you wish for a package to run under 32-bit mode, you'll have to schedule the step to run the 32-bit DTExec from the scheduled job by going to the runtime option in the Execution Options tab in SQL Server Agent.

Performance Counters

There are a few key performance counters to watch when you're trying to monitor performance of your SSIS package. These counters will greatly help you troubleshoot, if you have memory contention or if you need to tweak your SSIS settings. Inside the System Monitor (also known to old-school administrators as perfmon) is a Performance Object called SQLServer: SSIS Pipeline. There are quite a few other objects as well but they're not useful enough to describe here.

If you're trying to benchmark how many rows are being read and written, you can use the Rows Read and Rows Written counters. These counters show you the number of rows since you starting monitoring the packages. It sums all rows in total across all packages, and does not allow you to narrow down to a single package.

The most important counters are the buffer counters. The Buffer Memory counter shows you the amount of memory, in total, being used by all the packages. The Buffers In Use shows you how many buffers are actually in use. The critical counter here, though, is Buffers Spooled. This shows you how many buffers have been written from memory to disk. This is critical for the performance of your system. If you have buffers being spooled, you have a potential memory contention, and you may want to consider increasing the memory or changing your buffer settings in your package. We talked more about this in Chapter 14 but for the time being, know that you should never see this number creep above a 5, if not 0.

Summary

In this chapter, you've been shown how to administer SQL Server Integration Services. We showed you how to run and schedule your packages from Management Studio or how to use some of the more advanced command-line tools to perform the same functions. Lastly, you were shown some of the key performance counters in SSIS to watch for performance issues. In the next chapter, you will see a case study to tie the entire book's concepts together.

23

Case Study: A Programmatic Example

Typically a book like this has to cover so much material that there is not enough space to really dig into some of the typical issues that you run into when you put the book down and start putting together your first solution. You end up coming back to the book to flip through all of the one-off examples, but they just don't seem to provide any insight or applicability to your current project or deadline. The case study is your best chance to get specific, to get into the ring, to take a business issue and run with it. Hopefully you'll be the beneficiary of this.

You will use the SSIS environment to solve a payment processing problem with payment data of varying levels of quality that has to be validated against corporate billing records. This example is a little different from the typical data-warehouse-type ETL case study; it's a little more programmatic. Not to say that there is not any ETL. You'll need to import three heterogeneous data formats, but the interesting part is the use of the SSIS Data Flow Transforms that allow for the development of smart validation and matching programming logic. This will all combine into a solid learning opportunity that showcases the real capabilities of SSIS.

What You Will Take Away

The principal advantages of this case study are multiple opportunities to highlight specific techniques and use-cases that you can take away and add to your SSIS toolkit. Specifically, you'll get examples of:

❑ How to use expressions in variables to create uniquely named files.

❑ How to use expressions in package properties.

❑ How to use expressions in variables to dynamically configure OLD DB Connections.

❑ How to set variables from Control Flow Script Tasks and Data Flow Script Components.

❏   How to retrieve and set variables in Control Flow with Execute SQL Task with Output Parameters and result sets for both OLE DB and .NET Connections.

❏   How to create conditional workflows with expressions and precedence constraints.

❏   How to retrieve Currency amounts from a database into a Double variable data type within an Execute SQL Control Flow.

❏   How to retrieve row counts using Aggregate Count and Row Count Transforms.

❏   How to iterate through a set of XML files and import using the Data Flow XML Source.

❏   How to use the Import Column Transform to save complete files into a database.

❏   How to create a parent package to manage child packages.

❏   How to use the Lookup and Fuzzy Lookup Transforms to match data elements.

If any of these takeaways sound like a problem that you are dealing with, then dive in and let's get started.

Background

Company ABC is a small benefits company that sells several niche products to other small business owners. They offer these products directly to the employees of the small businesses, but the employers are billed, not the employees. Company ABC considers the employers to be their customers and creates monthly invoices for the employee-selected services. Each invoice contains an invoice number for reference purposes. Company ABC's customers deduct the cost of the products from the employee paychecks. These payments are then submitted back to Company ABC in a lump sum, but because of timing issues and ever-changing worker populations, the payment doesn't always match the billed amount. Customers have the option of paying invoices using one of the following payment methods:

❏   Pay by using PayPal or an email payment service. These services directly credit a corporate bank account and typically provide a small description of the service being paid, the amount, and an email address or other type of surrogate user identity. These entries are downloaded daily from an online bank account and are available within an OLE DB–compliant Data Source.

❏   Pay by check. The customer sends a copy of the invoice and a check in the mail to a special address that is serviced by a bank. The invoice could match fully, partially, or not even be provided with the payment. The bank credits the account for each check received and provides an output file containing as much data as practicable from the supporting material to help the company identify and apply the payment. A payment that is serviced like this is commonly known as a *lockbox*.

❏   Pay by wire. Payments can be made by direct debit of customer bank accounts or direct credit to the corporate account. These payments are known as wires. This type of payment entry provided through a large bank or an automated clearinghouse is also known as ACH processing.

Business Problem

Just working with the low-quality payment data involves a significant amount of manual lookup to match payments to customers and invoices. Because Company ABC is growing, the volume of payments is exceeding their capacity to continue to process payments manually. If the invoice number was always received with the payment, an automated process could easily identify the customer from the invoice and make some decisions about the payment by comparing the paid and billed amounts. So far, attempts at automating even the paper invoice through the mail have failed because customers don't always send in copies of invoices, or they resend in old, outdated invoices. Using a bank lockbox has helped ease the burden of getting the deposits processed, but the bank makes mistakes too, truncating and transposing customer name or invoice data. Opening up the company to wires and PayPal accounts has really complicated matters, because very little corroborating data is provided in these transactions.

Approximately 60% of the incoming payments can't be automatically identified using a strict compare of invoice number and payment amount. The good news is that they can almost all be manually identified by a small group of subject matter experts (SMEs) who really understand the process and know how to use the corporate data. The bad news is that once a customer and invoice are identified by the SMEs, the method of making the match is not recorded. The next month the process of identification starts all over again. Company ABC needs a way to wade as far as possible through the payments automatically to take the place of the SMEs. This process should match items by invoice number, name, and email address with some measurable certainty and leave only the most troublesome payments for research activity. They need a solution that runs continuously to meet the demands of a 24-hour turnaround standard for their industry.

Solution Summary

Company ABC has made the need to resolve this payment-processing hurdle their top priority. They already have a custom software application that gives users the ability to break the bulk payments down to an employee level, but the application requires that the customer and invoice be identified. The solution is to use SSIS to develop a package that can process data from these heterogeneous Data Sources. This solution should require no human intervention on items that can be identified as paid-as-billed items. The solution should be as "smart" as possible and be able to identify bank items that have been manually identified before. Items that can't be identified will still need to be processed manually, but it is expected that this number should drop 20 to 40 percent.

In preparation for the design of the SSIS package, specification documents for the two input files, ACH and Lockbox, have been gathered. Each file provided by the bank contains a batch of multiple payment transactions. These files can be sent by either the bank or ACH clearinghouse to specific folders. The process should be able to access these folders and continuously look for new files to process. When a file is located in the input folder, it needs to be validated for proper format, for previous processing, so a file is not processed more than once, and for each payment to summarize and balance to the total deposit. Files not meeting these criteria will be rejected. Once a file is verified, each payment in the file should be examined for matches to existing invoices. If no match is found, the data should be examined against previously matched data. Matched data will flow into a completed queue to be broken into employee-level charges by another piece of software. Unmatched data will flow into a working queue that will require user intervention. Successful customer matches will be stored for future matching. Finally, statistics will be created for the input for reporting purposes. Figure 23-1 is a diagram of the business solution.

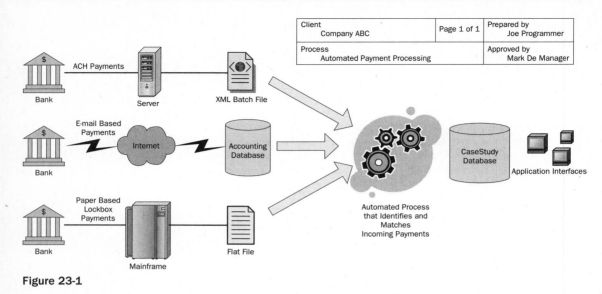

Client		Page 1 of 1	Prepared by
Company ABC			Joe Programmer
Process			Approved by
Automated Payment Processing			Mark De Manager

Figure 23-1

Solution Architecture

Before you jump into building this integration service, we should lay out the big picture of what we are to accomplish. You have two sets of tasks: first, to import files of three different formats, to validate the data, and to load them into your data structures; and second, to process the payments to find customer and invoice matches. Figure 23-2 shows a design where the importing logic is divided into three packages, each one specific to the type of file that you need to process. We've learned that breaking SSIS packages into service-oriented units simplifies the maintenance and troubleshooting, so we'll demonstrate this method here. Another benefit of this architecture is that it makes it easier for you to choose just one of these three packages to create and still follow along with the case study. Don't worry about creating these packages at this point; just get the big picture about where we are going. You can either create the packages for this solution one at a time, as you walk through the case study instructions, or alternatively, download the complete solution from www.wrox.com.

Because the main job of the first core task is to load, it makes sense to name the three separate packages: CaseStudy_Load_Bank, CaseStudy_Load_ACH, and CaseStudy_Load_Email, respectively. This allows us to separate the load processes from the identification processes. The identification logic to apply to each transaction in the payment data is universal, so it makes sense to put this logic into a separate package. You can name this package CaseStudy_Process. This will make the final package, named CaseStudy_Driver, the master package that will coordinate the running of each of these processes using precedence constraints.

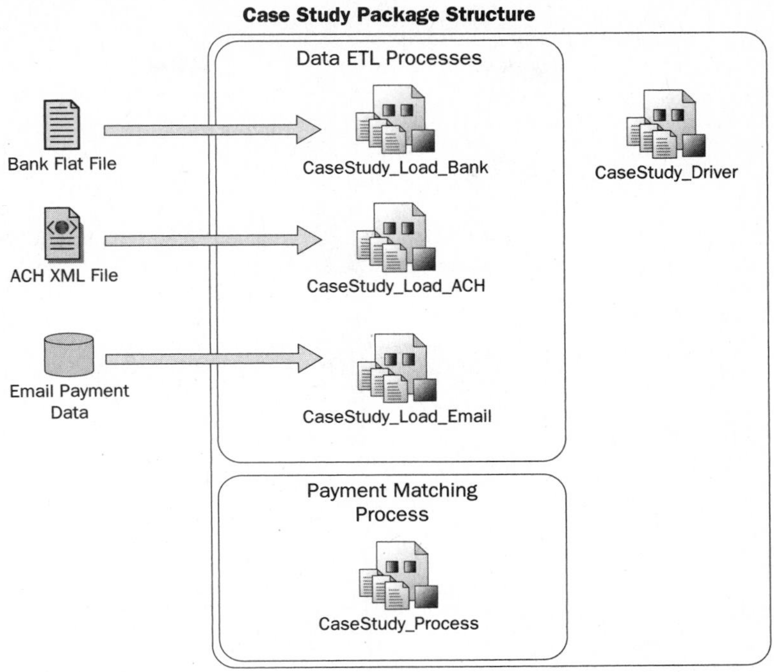

Case Study Package Structure

Figure 23-2

When you are building packages that have external dependencies on things such as file hierarchies, it is a good idea to programmatically validate the locations for existence before processing. You'll check for default paths and create them if they don't exist. If files for the Lockbox or ACH processes exist, you should read the files, parse the transaction information, validate totals against a control record in the file, and then persist the information from the file into permanent storage. The toughest part of this processing logic is that the validation routines have to validate file formats, proper data types, and file balances and check for file duplication. When processing any flat file from an external source, be aware of how that import file was generated, and what you might find in it. Don't be surprised to find that some systems allow a date of 02/30/2008 or amount fields with data like .0023E2.

The downloaded bank transactions for the PayPal or E-Pay transactions will be easier to process — at least from an import standpoint. You only need to read information from a table in another OLE DB–compliant Data Source. You'll be creating a batch from the transactions, so balancing also shouldn't be an issue. The hardest part will be identifying these payments, because usually only an amount and an email address are embedded in the transaction. All this information can be summarized in a flowchart like the one in Figure 23-3.

Chapter 23: Case Study: A Programmatic Example

In the CaseStudy_Process package, you are required to complete a matching process of the payment information to find customers and invoices. You'll first attempt a high-confidence match using an exact match to the invoice number. If a match is not made, you'll move to a fuzzy lookup on the invoice number. If a match is still not made, you'll keep moving down to lower-confidence-level matches until you can retrieve an invoice or at least customer identification. Transactions identifiable only by customer will be checked against available invoices for a match within a billed-to-paid tolerance of 5 percent. Transactions that simply don't have enough certainty to be identified will be left at this point to subject-matter experts, who will individually review and research the transactions to identify the customer or refund the payment. Research can be saved via software outside this SSIS project into the CustomerLookup table. A summary flowchart for the CaseStudy_Process package is shown in Figure 23-4.

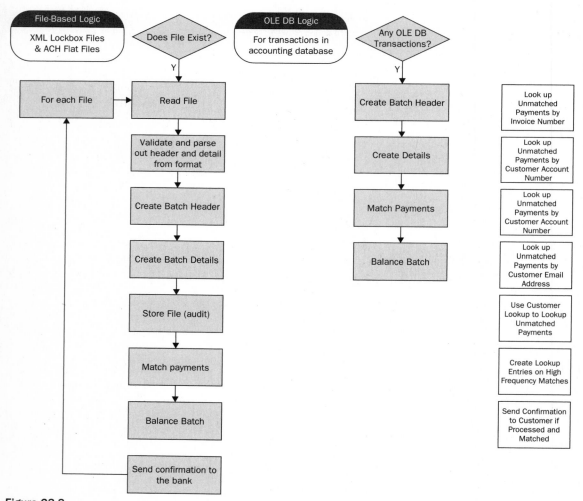

Figure 23-3

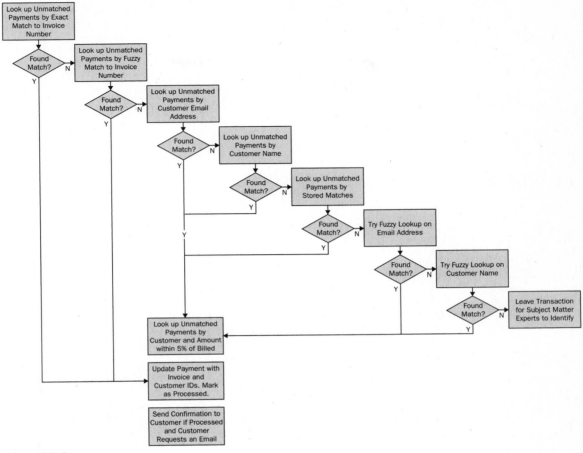

Figure 23-4

Naming Conventions and Tips

There's nothing like opening up a package that fails in production and seeing tasks named Execute SQL Task, Execute SQL Task1, and Execute SQL Task2. What do they do? There is also something to be said when there is so much annotation that it is a nightmare to maintain. The balance depends on your philosophy and your team, but for now, the following rules seem to make sense in your SSIS development processes:

❑ Name the package. Name it something other than package.dtsx. This matters later when you deploy the packages.

❑ Name packages with ETL verb extensions: <Package Name>_Extract, <Package Name>_ Transform, or <Package Name>_Load. The extension _Process seems to be explicit enough for those packages that don't fall into the other three categories.

❑ Provide some brief annotation about what the package does, where it gets inputs and outputs, and what to do if it fails. Can it be rerun again? Is it part of a larger set of packages? Should it be restarted on checkpoints?

❑ Add short descriptive words to SSIS tasks and transforms, but don't alter the name altogether. For example, change an Execute SQL Task to Execute SQL Task to Retrieve Invoice ID. Use the description field on the object to provide the detailed information. (You'll see this info in a tooltip when the mouse hovers over the object.) It is important to document, but completely changing the name of an Execute SQL Task to Retrieve Invoice ID obscures information about the "how" that is embedded with the knowledge that the task is an Execute SQL Task. You could of course learn the pictures or use abbreviations, but our stance is that you need to worry about the guy coming behind you, who has to maintain your package.

Additional SSIS Tips Before You Start a Large Project

This whole solution has many parts, so don't get overwhelmed if you are creating them from scratch or attempting to troubleshoot something. Here are some additional tips for this Case Study and SSIS package development in general:

❑ Packages save themselves when you run them, so just be aware.

❑ Packages don't save themselves as you are working, so save periodically as you work on these large development packages. There is a nice recovery feature that sometimes will save you — don't depend on it.

❑ Data Viewers are your friends. They are like grid message boxes. Add them in temporarily to see what is in your transformation stream.

❑ Default data types aren't your friend. If your tables don't use Unicode text fields, watch your settings when you are adding columns or source data.

❑ If you are at a point where you want to experiment, either use source control, or stop and save a copy of the SSIS project directory for the package you are working on. Experiment with the copy until you figure out what is wrong. Go back to the original project folder, make your corrections, and continue. There is no undo in SSIS after you run the package if you aren't using source control.

❑ Disable tasks or groups of tasks as you work through large packages to focus only on specific functional areas until they work. To disable a task, right-click it and select Disable from the pop-up menu. (Note, however, that you can't disable a transform in the Data Flow.)

Data Architecture

This section details the Data Sources both in SQL Server and in the format of each of the input files. First, create default locations to simulate your receiving area for the external files, and then you'll take a closer look at each of the input files that are part of the business requirements. All the sample data and complete set of scripts for this step can be downloaded from www.wrox.com. When you unzip the sample files for this chapter to your c:\ drive, a directory structure will be created starting with the parent directory c:\CaseStudy. Underneath are folders containing Database Scripts, sample import files, and all of the packages. There are two downloads for this chapter, one where all Script Tasks are done in VB.NET, and another for C#, so you can follow along with the .NET language of your choice.

You'll need to run the database scripts to create a database called CaseStudy, the table structures, procs and other database objects, and specific customer and invoice data. The downloaded zip file also puts all the sample import files into the directories so that you can follow along. So if you like, you can follow along and piece this solution together, or download the packages and explore.

File Storage Location Setup

Create a base directory or use the download files at www.wrox.com to store the file-based imports to this project. Throughout the case study, the base location will be referred to as C:\casestudy\. In the base directory, you'll need two subdirectories: ACH\ and LOCKBOX\. You will use these locations to store the files you'll create in the next few sections.

Bank ACH Payments

Customers make payments within their own banks or electronic payment systems to Company ABC through an automated clearinghouse. The automated clearinghouse bundles up all the payments for the day and sends one XML file through an encrypted VPN connection to an encrypted folder. The bank wires contain only a minimum amount of information at the transactional level. Each XML file does contain a header row with a unique ID that identifies the file transmission. The header also contains a total deposit amount and a transaction count that can be used to further verify the file transmission. Each transactional detail row represents a deposit and contains two date fields: the date the deposit item was received, and the date the deposit item was posted to Company ABC's deposit account. Each payment contains the amount of the deposit and a free-form field that could contain the customer's name on a bank account, an email address, or anything the customer adds to the wire. More commonly, the description contains the name on the customer's bank account — which is often very different from the name in Company ABC's customer data. To make the sample ACH file, and for each file in this example, you'll need to re-create these files manually or download the files from this book's page at www.wrox.com. The bank ACH file looks like the following:

```
<BATCH>
<HEADER><ID>AAS22119289</ID>
<TOTALDEPOSIT>180553.00</TOTALDEPOSIT>
<DEPOSITDATE>07/15/2008</DEPOSITDATE>
<TOTALTRANS>6</TOTALTRANS>
</HEADER>
<DETAIL><AMOUNT>23318.00</AMOUNT>
<DESC>Complete Enterprises</DESC>
<RECEIVEDDATE>07/15/2008</RECEIVEDDATE>
<POSTEDDATE>07/15/2008</POSTEDDATE></DETAIL>
<DETAIL><AMOUNT>37054.00</AMOUNT>
<DESC>Premier Sport</DESC>
<RECEIVEDDATE>07/15/2008</RECEIVEDDATE>
<POSTEDDATE>07/15/2008</POSTEDDATE></DETAIL>
<DETAIL><AMOUNT>34953.00</AMOUNT>
<DESC>Intl Sports Association</DESC>
<RECEIVEDDATE>07/15/2008</RECEIVEDDATE>
<POSTEDDATE>07/15/2008</POSTEDDATE></DETAIL>
<DETAIL><AMOUNT>22660.00</AMOUNT>
<DESC>Arthur Datum</DESC>
```

```
<RECEIVEDDATE>07/15/2008</RECEIVEDDATE>
<POSTEDDATE>07/15/2008</POSTEDDATE></DETAIL>
<DETAIL><AMOUNT>24759.00</AMOUNT>
<DESC>Northwind Traders</DESC>
<RECEIVEDDATE>07/15/2008</RECEIVEDDATE>
<POSTEDDATE>07/15/2008</POSTEDDATE></DETAIL>
<DETAIL><AMOUNT>37809.00</AMOUNT>
<DESC>Wood Fitness</DESC>
<RECEIVEDDATE>07/15/2008</RECEIVEDDATE>
<POSTEDDATE>07/15/2008</POSTEDDATE></DETAIL>
</BATCH>
```

Lockbox Files

Company ABC has starting using a lockbox service that their bank provides for a nominal fee. This service images all check and invoice stubs sent to a specific address that the bank monitors. The bank provides a data file containing the following data attributes for each deposit item: the amount, a reference number for the invoice, and an image key that can be used to review the images of the item online. The terms of the service dictate that if the bank can't determine the invoice number because of legibility issues or if the invoice is not sent in with the deposit item, either a customer account number or a customer name might be used in place of the invoice number. Periodically during the day, the bank will batch a series of payments into one file containing a header that includes a batch number, the posted deposit date for all deposit items, and an expected total for the batch.

The structure of the file from the bank is as follows:

```
HEADER:
TYPE            1A          TYPE OF LINE H-HEADER
POSTDATE        6A          DATE DEPOSIT POSTED
FILLER          1A          SPACE(1)
BATCHID         12A         UNIQUE BATCH NBR

DETAIL (TYPE I):
TYPE            1A          TYPE OF LINE I-INVOICE
IMGID           10A         IMAGE LOOK UP ID (2-6 IS ID)
DESC            25A         INVOICE OR DESC INFO

DETAIL (TYPE C)
TYPE            1A          TYPE OF LINE C-CHECK
IMGID           10A         IMAGE LOOK UP ID (2-6 IS ID)
DESC            8S 2        CHECK AMOUNT
```

Download or create, using the following data, a file named `c:\casestudy\lockbox\samplelockbox`
`.txt` to simulate the Lockbox transmission in this example:

```
H080108 B1239-99Z-99 0058730760
I4001010003 181INTERNAT
C4001010004   01844400
I4002020005 151METROSPOOO1
C4002020006   02331800
```

```
I4003030009 MAGIC CYCLES
C4003030010   02697000
I4004040013 LINDELL
C4004040014   02131800
I4005040017 151GMASKI0001
C4005040019   01938800
```

PayPal or Direct Credits to Corporate Account

Company ABC has started a pilot program to allow customers to make payments using PayPal and other similar online electronic payment services. Customers like this option because it is easy to use. However, these payments are difficult to process for the Accounting group, because not all email addresses have been collected for the customers, and that is the most common description on the transactions. Accounting personnel have to do some research in their CRM solution to determine who the customer is and to release the deposit to the payment systems. Once they've matched the customer to the transaction description (email address), they would like to be able to save the matching criteria as data to be used in future processing. Currently the accounting department uses a data synch process in their accounting software to download these transactions directly from a special bank account, periodically, during the day. This information is available through a read-only view in the database called [vCorpDirectAcctTrans]. Figure 23-5 shows the structure of this view.

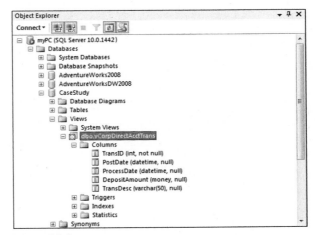

Figure 23-5

Case Study Database Model

The case study database model (see Figure 23-6) is limited to only the information relevant to the case study. The core entities are the following:

❑   **Customer:** An entity that utilizes products and services from Company ABC. To keep it simple, only the customer name, account number, and email address attributes are represented in the table.

❑   **Invoice:** A monthly listing of total billed products and services for each customer. Each invoice is represented by a unique invoice number. Invoice details are not shown in the case study data model for simplicity.

❑ **BankBatch:** Any set of transactions from a bank or deposit institution that is combined. Auditable information expected for the exchange of monetary data is a major part of this entity. Files, or batches, of transactions must be validated in terms of the number of transaction lines, and most importantly, by amount. Care must be taken not to load a batch more than once. Recording the bank batch number or BankBatchNbr field and comparing incoming batches should allow you to keep this from happening.

❑ **BankBatchDetail:** Each bank batch will be composed of many transactions that break down into essentially a check and an invoice. You could receive as much as both pieces of information or as little as none of this information. For auditing purposes, you should record exactly what you received from the input source. You'll also store in this table logically determined foreign keys for the customer and invoice dimension.

❑ **CustomerLookUp:** This lookup table will be populated by your SSIS package and an external application. This will allow users to store matching information to identify customers for future processing. This will allow the data import processes to "learn" good matches from bad data.

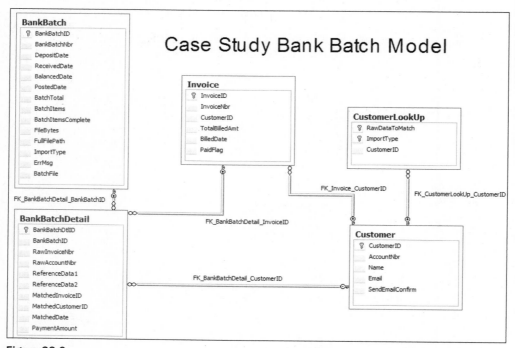

Figure 23-6

Database Setup

To get started, you need to set up the database named CaseStudy. The database and all objects in it will become the basis for your solution to this business issue. Of course, as mentioned earlier, all input files and scripts are available from the www.wrox.com website. This database is not a consistent data model in the strictest sense. There are places where NVARCHAR and VARCHAR data fields are being used for demonstration purposes, and we'll point these out as you work through this case study. Working with

NVARCHAR and VARCHAR fields was mentioned as one of the difficulties that new SSIS developers struggled with, so you'll get to experience how to deal with this issue in this case study. There are two ways to create a new database. Use the Microsoft SQL Server Management Studio to connect to a server or database engine of your choice. On the Databases Node, right-click and select the pop-up menu option New Database. In the New Database editor, provide the database name as CaseStudy. Click OK to accept the other defaults. The second easy option is to run the following SQL script in a new query editor:

```
USE [master]
GO
CREATE DATABASE [CaseStudy] ON  PRIMARY
( NAME = N'CaseStudy', FILENAME = N'C:\Program Files\Microsoft SQL
Server\MSSQL10.MSSQLSERVER\MSSQL\DATA\CaseStudy.mdf' , SIZE = 3072KB , MAXSIZE =
    UNLIMITED,
FILEGROWTH = 1024KB )
 LOG ON
( NAME = N'CaseStudy_log', FILENAME = N'C:\Program Files\Microsoft SQL
Server\MSSQL10.MSSQLSERVER\MSSQL\DATA\CaseStudy_log.ldf' , SIZE = 1024KB , MAXSIZE =
    2048GB ,
FILEGROWTH = 10%)
 COLLATE Latin1_General_CI_AI
GO
EXEC dbo.sp_dbcmptlevel @dbname=N'CaseStudy', @new_cmptlevel=90
GO
```

Customer

The Customer table can be created in the Microsoft SQL Server Management Studio. Click the New Query button in the toolbar to open a New Query window. Run the following SQL statement in the window:

```
use casestudy
GO
CREATE TABLE [dbo].[Customer](
  [CustomerID] [int] IDENTITY(1,1) NOT NULL,
  [AccountNbr] [char](15) NOT NULL,
  [Name] [varchar](50)    NOT NULL,
  [Email] [varchar](50)    NULL,
  [SendEmailConfirm] [bit] NOT NULL CONSTRAINT [DF_Customer_SendEmailConfirm]
DEFAULT ((0)),
 CONSTRAINT [PK_Customer] PRIMARY KEY CLUSTERED
(
  [CustomerID] ASC
) ON [PRIMARY]
) ON [PRIMARY]
```

To fill the table with potential customers, we'll manufacture some data using the AdventureWorks2008 database. Don't worry; you don't have to have AW installed. Use the script "Step 2. Create Customer Table and Data.sql" from the downloaded zip file to populate the Customer table. This script doesn't need access to the AW database to load the customer data into the database using a script. Here is a partial listing of the full script:

```
--NOTE: THIS IS ONLY A PARTIAL LISTING
--THERE ARE 104 CUSTOMERS TO ENTER. EITHER DOWNLOAD THE FULL SCRIPT OR
--FOLLOW ALONG TO GENERATE THE CUSTOMER DATA FROM ADVENTUREWORKS2008 DATA
INSERT INTO CaseStudy..Customer(AccountNbr, [Name], email, SendEmailConfirm)
SELECT 'INTERNAT0001', 'International', 'GAchong@International.com',1
INSERT INTO CaseStudy..Customer(AccountNbr, [Name], email, SendEmailConfirm)
SELECT 'ELECTRON0002', 'Electronic Bike Repair & Supplies', 'CAbel@msn.com',1
INSERT INTO CaseStudy..Customer(AccountNbr, [Name], email, SendEmailConfirm)
SELECT 'PREMIER0001', 'Premier Sport, Inc.', NULL, 0
INSERT INTO CaseStudy..Customer(AccountNbr, [Name], email, SendEmailConfirm)
SELECT 'COMFORT0001', 'Comfort Road Bicycles', NULL, 0
```

If you are curious, the queries that generated this data from the AW database are commented out at the bottom of the script file.

Invoice

To create the Invoice table, run the following SQL statement:

```
USE [CaseStudy]
GO
CREATE TABLE [dbo].[Invoice](
  [InvoiceID] [int] IDENTITY(1,1) NOT NULL,
  [InvoiceNbr] [varchar](50) NOT NULL,
  [CustomerID] [int] NOT NULL,
  [TotalBilledAmt] [money] NOT NULL,
  [BilledDate] [datetime] NOT NULL,
  [PaidFlag] [smallint] NOT NULL CONSTRAINT [DF_Invoice_PaidFlag]  DEFAULT
((0)),
 CONSTRAINT [PK_Invoice] PRIMARY KEY CLUSTERED
(
  [InvoiceID] ASC
) ON [PRIMARY]
) ON [PRIMARY]
GO
ALTER TABLE [dbo].[Invoice]  WITH NOCHECK ADD  CONSTRAINT
[FK_Invoice_CustomerID]
FOREIGN KEY([CustomerID])
REFERENCES [dbo].[Customer] ([CustomerID])
GO
ALTER TABLE [dbo].[Invoice] CHECK CONSTRAINT [FK_Invoice_CustomerID]
```

You will use the Customer table to generate three months' worth of invoice data. In doing so, you are creating invoice numbers with the customer account number embedded in the invoice number. Companies commonly do this because it provides an extra piece of identification as a cross-check in an environment where there is very limited data. Use the following SQL snippet to simulate and create a set of invoice entries or use the downloaded script "Step 3. Create Invoice Table and Data.sql" to load this data in statically:

```
INSERT INTO Invoice(InvoiceNbr, CustomerID, TotalBilledAmt, BilledDate,
PaidFlag)
SELECT  InvoiceNbr = '151' + Accountnbr,
        CustomerID,
        TotalBilledAmt = cast(131 * (ascii(left(name, 1)) +
ascii(substring(name,
                        2, 1))) as money),
        BilledDate = '06/01/2008 00:00:00',
        PaidFlag = 0
FROM customer
UNION
SELECT  InvoiceNbr = '181' + Accountnbr,
        CustomerID,
        TotalBilledAmt = case
            when left(Accountnbr, 1) in ('A', 'B', 'C', 'D', 'E', 'F', 'G')
            then cast(131 * (ascii(left(name, 1)) + ascii(substring(name,
                                                    2, 1)))

                as money)
            else
                cast(191 * (ascii(left(name, 1)) + ascii(substring(name,
                                                    2, 1)))

                as money)
            end,
        BilledDate = '07/01/2008 00:00:00',
        PaidFlag = 0
FROM customer
UNION
SELECT  InvoiceNbr = '212' + Accountnbr,
        CustomerID,
        TotalBilledAmt = case
            when left(Accountnbr, 1) in ('A', 'F', 'G')
            then cast(132 * (ascii(left(name, 1)) + ascii(substring(name, 2,
                                                    1)))

                as money)
            else
                cast(155 * (ascii(left(name, 1)) + ascii(substring(name, 2,
                                                    1)))

                as money)
            end,
        BilledDate = '08/01/2008 00:00:00',
        PaidFlag = 0
FROM customer
GO
UPDATE invoice set totalbilledamt = 18444.00
WHERE invoicenbr = '151INTERNAT0002' and totalbilledamt = 23973
```

CustomerLookUp

The CustomerLookUp table will be used to store resolutions of bad customer identification data that continues to be sent through the accounting feeds. Data that the auto-processes can't match would be matched manually, and the bad data string for an existing customer can be stored for each import type for future matching purposes. The structure can be created using the following SQL script:

```
USE [CaseStudy]
GO
CREATE TABLE [dbo].[CustomerLookUp](
  [RawDataToMatch] [varchar](50) NOT NULL,
  [ImportType] [char](10) NOT NULL,
  [CustomerID] [int] NOT NULL,
 CONSTRAINT [PK_CustomerLookUp] PRIMARY KEY CLUSTERED
(
  [RawDataToMatch] ASC,
  [ImportType] ASC
) ON [PRIMARY]
) ON [PRIMARY]
GO
ALTER TABLE [dbo].[CustomerLookUp]  WITH NOCHECK ADD  CONSTRAINT
[FK_CustomerLookUp_CustomerID] FOREIGN KEY([CustomerID])
REFERENCES [dbo].[Customer] ([CustomerID])
GO
ALTER TABLE [dbo].[CustomerLookUp] CHECK CONSTRAINT [FK_CustomerLookUp_CustomerID]
```

BankBatch

The BankBatch table will not only store the summary data from the batch file but also store the file itself in the BatchFile field. This table can be created using the following SQL statement:

```
USE [CaseStudy]
GO
CREATE TABLE [dbo].[BankBatch](
  [BankBatchID] [int] IDENTITY(1,1) NOT NULL,
  [BankBatchNbr] [nvarchar](50) NULL,
  [DepositDate] [datetime] NULL,
  [ReceivedDate] [datetime] NULL,
  [BalancedDate] [datetime] NULL,
  [PostedDate] [datetime] NULL,
  [BatchTotal] [money] NULL,
  [BatchItems] [int] NULL,
  [BatchItemsComplete] [int] NULL,
  [FileBytes] [int] NULL,
  [FullFilePath] [nvarchar](1080) NULL,
  [ImportType] [char](10) NULL,
  [ErrMsg] [varchar](1080) NULL,
  [BatchFile] [ntext] NULL,
 CONSTRAINT [PK_BankBatch] PRIMARY KEY CLUSTERED
(
  [BankBatchID] ASC
)WITH (PAD_INDEX  = OFF, STATISTICS_NORECOMPUTE  = OFF,
  IGNORE_DUP_KEY = OFF, ALLOW_ROW_LOCKS  = ON,
```

```
     ALLOW_PAGE_LOCKS  = ON) ON [PRIMARY]
) ON [PRIMARY] TEXTIMAGE_ON [PRIMARY]
GO
CREATE NONCLUSTERED INDEX [IX_BatchNumber_ImportType] ON [dbo].[BankBatch]
(
    [BankBatchNbr] ASC,
    [ImportType] ASC
)
GO
```

BankBatchDetail

The detail to the BankBatch table can be created using the following SQL script:

```
USE [CaseStudy]
GO
CREATE TABLE [dbo].[BankBatchDetail](
    [BankBatchDtlID] [int] IDENTITY(1,1) NOT NULL,
    [BankBatchID] [int] NOT NULL,
    [RawInvoiceNbr] [nvarchar](50) NULL,
    [RawAccountNbr] [nvarchar](50) NULL,
    [ReferenceData1] [nvarchar](50) NULL,
    [ReferenceData2] [nvarchar](50) NULL,
    [MatchedInvoiceID] [int] NULL,
    [MatchedCustomerID] [int] NULL,
    [MatchedDate] [datetime] NULL,
    [PaymentAmount] [money] NULL,
 CONSTRAINT [PK_BankBatchDtlID] PRIMARY KEY CLUSTERED
(
    [BankBatchDtlID] ASC
) ON [PRIMARY]
) ON [PRIMARY]

ALTER TABLE [dbo].[BankBatchDetail]  WITH NOCHECK ADD  CONSTRAINT
[FK_BankBatchDetail_BankBatchID] FOREIGN KEY([BankBatchID])
REFERENCES [dbo].[BankBatch] ([BankBatchID])
GO
ALTER TABLE [dbo].[BankBatchDetail] CHECK CONSTRAINT
[FK_BankBatchDetail_BankBatchID]
GO
ALTER TABLE [dbo].[BankBatchDetail]  WITH CHECK ADD  CONSTRAINT
[FK_BankBatchDetail_CustomerID] FOREIGN KEY([MatchedCustomerID])
REFERENCES [dbo].[Customer] ([CustomerID])
GO
ALTER TABLE [dbo].[BankBatchDetail]  WITH CHECK ADD  CONSTRAINT
[FK_BankBatchDetail_InvoiceID] FOREIGN KEY([MatchedInvoiceID])
REFERENCES [dbo].[Invoice] ([InvoiceID])
```

Corporate Ledger Data

To simulate a view into your Direct Credits to the Corporate Account, you need to create the GLAccountData structure and your view [vCorpDirectAcctTrans]. Run the following SQL to create the physical table:

```
USE [CaseStudy]
GO
CREATE TABLE [dbo].[GLAccountData](
  [TransID] [int] IDENTITY(1,1) NOT NULL,
  [PostDate] [datetime] NULL,
  [ProcessDate] [datetime] NULL,
  [DepositAmount] [money] NULL,
  [TransDesc] [varchar](50) NULL,
  [GLAccount] [char](10) NULL,
 CONSTRAINT [PK_GLAccountData] PRIMARY KEY CLUSTERED
(
  [TransID] ASC
) ON [PRIMARY]
) ON [PRIMARY]
```

Run the following SQL to create the logical view to this data:

```
USE [CaseStudy]
GO
CREATE VIEW dbo.vCorpDirectAcctTrans
AS
SELECT     TransID, PostDate, ProcessDate, DepositAmount, TransDesc
FROM        dbo.GLAccountData
```

Run this SQL batch to load the GLAccountData with some sample deposit transactions from the direct-pay customers:

```
INSERT INTO GLACCOUNTDATA(postdate, processdate, depositamount, transdesc,
glaccount)
SELECT '08/09/08', '08/10/08', 22794.00, 'PAYPAL*MBlack@Marsh.com', 'BANK'
UNION
SELECT '08/09/08', '08/10/08', 21484.00, 'PAYPAL*JBrown@CapitalCycles.com',
'BANK'
UNION
SELECT '08/09/08', '08/10/08', 22008.00, 'PAYPAL*DBlanco@msn.com', 'BANK'
UNION
SELECT '08/09/08', '08/10/08', 22794.00, 'PAYPAL*CBooth@MagicCycle', 'BANK'
UNION
SELECT '08/09/08', '08/10/08', 22401.00, 'PAYPAL*ABaltazar@msn.com', 'BANK'
```

ErrorDetail

There are some great new logging options in SSIS, and in this Case Study we'll log detailed errors that can occur at the column level when processing. This table will allow you to store that information, and by storing the Execution ID, you can later join the custom-logged error detail with the step-level error information logged during package execution.

```
USE [CaseStudy]
GO
CREATE TABLE [dbo].[ErrorDetail](
  [ExecutionID] [nchar](38) NOT NULL,
  [ErrorEvent] [nchar](20) NULL,
  [ErrorCode] [int] NULL,
  [ErrorColumn] [int] NULL,
  [ErrorDesc] [nvarchar](1048) NULL,
  [ErrorDate] [datetime] NULL,
  [RawData] [varchar](2048) NULL
) ON [PRIMARY]
```

Stored Procedure to Add Batches

Because we are in a rigorous-enterprise financial processing environment, separating the logic that performs basic data insert and core matching logic provides advantages for audit purposes and allows for the process of creating new batches to be more modular. The other advantage to using stored procedures is to deliver higher performance. A stored procedure allows all the TSQL logic to be placed in one place and can be optimized by the Query Optimizer. A stored procedure can also be placed under separate execution rights and managed separately, instead of embedding the TSQL into and applying the rights to the package itself. This first stored procedure will be used to add a new bank batch to the payment processing system. Run the script to add it to Case Study database:

```
Use CaseStudy
GO
CREATE PROC usp_BankBatch_Add(
  @BankBatchID int OUTPUT,
  @BankBatchNbr nvarchar(50)=NULL,
  @DepositDate datetime=NULL,
  @ReceivedDate datetime=NULL,
  @BatchTotal money=NULL,
  @BatchItems int=NULL,
  @FileBytes int=NULL,
  @FullFilePath nvarchar(100)=NULL,
  @ImportType char(10)
)
AS
  /*=========================================================
   PROC: usp_BankBatch_Add
   PURPOSE: To Add BankBatch Header Basic info
            and to validate that the batch is new.
   OUTPUT: Will return BankBatchID if new or 0 if exists
   HISTORY: 04/01/08 Created
   ========================================================*/
  SET NOCOUNT ON
  If @ReceivedDate is null
    SET @ReceivedDate = getdate()

  IF LEN(@BankBatchNbr) <= 1 OR Exists(Select top 1 *
       FROM BankBatch
       WHERE BankBatchNbr = @BankBatchNbr
       AND ImportType = @ImportType)
     BEGIN
```

```
                SET @BANKBATCHID = 0
                RETURN -1
            END
    ELSE
        BEGIN
            INSERT INTO BankBatch(BankBatchNbr, DepositDate, ReceivedDate,
                                  BatchTotal, BatchItems, FileBytes, FullFilePath,
                                  ImportType)
            SELECT UPPER(@BankBatchNbr), @DepositDate, @ReceivedDate,
                        @BatchTotal, @BatchItems, @FileBytes,
                        UPPER(@FullFilePath),
                        UPPER(@ImportType)

            SET @BANKBATCHID = Scope_Identity()
        END

    SET NOCOUNT OFF

GO
```

Stored Procedure to Update a Batch with Invoice and Customer Id

This stored procedure will be used to update a payment with a matching invoice or customer identification number relating back to the dimension tables. Run the script to add this procedure to CaseStudy:

```
CREATE PROC dbo.usp_BankBatchDetail_Match(
            @BankBatchDtlID int,
            @InvoiceID int=NULL,
            @CustomerID int=NULL)
AS
    /*================================================
    PROC: usp_BankBatchDetail_Match
    PURPOSE: To update as paid an incoming payment
            with matched invoice and customerid
    HISTORY: 04/01/08 Created
    ================================================
    */

    SET NOCOUNT ON

    --UPDATE BANKBATCH DETAIL WITH INVOICE AND CUSTOMERID
    --NOTE: IF EITHER IS NULL THEN DON'T UPDATE
    --MATCHED DATE. THIS WILL PUSH THE ITEM INTO A SUBJECT-
    --MATTER-EXPERT'S QUEUE TO IDENTIFY.
    UPDATE BankBatchDetail
    SET MatchedInvoiceID = @InvoiceID,
        MatchedCustomerID = @CustomerID,
        MatchedDate = case when @InvoiceID is NULL or @CustomerID is NULL then
                        NULL
                        else getdate() end
    WHERE BankBatchDtlID = @BankBatchDtlID

    SET NOCOUNT OFF
```

Stored Procedure to Balance a Batch

This stored procedure is used to examine all payments in a batch and to mark the batch as complete when all payments have been identified with an invoice and a customer. Again, we are using a stored procedure for all the reasons explained previously for auditing, modularity, and performance:

```
GO
CREATE PROC usp_BankBatch_Balance
AS
  /*============================================================
   PROC: usp_BankBatch_Balance
   PURPOSE: To update batchdetails when they are matched
            Then keep BankBatches balanced by matching all
            line items
   ============================================================
  */
  UPDATE bankbatchdetail
  SET MatchedDate = GetDate()
  where (matchedinvoiceid is not null
  and matchedcustomerid is not null)
  and  (matchedinvoiceid <> 0
  and matchedcustomerid <> 0)

  UPDATE BANKBATCH
  SET BatchItemsComplete = BatchItems - b.NotComplete
  FROM BANKBATCH A
  INNER JOIN (
  select bankbatchid, count(*) as NotComplete
  from bankbatchdetail
  where
  (matchedinvoiceid is null
  OR matchedcustomerid is null
  OR matcheddate is null)
  group by bankbatchid
  ) B
  on A.BankBatchID = B.BankBatchID

  UPDATE BankBatch
  SET BalancedDate = getdate()
  WHERE BalancedDate IS NULL
  and BatchItems = BatchItemsComplete
```

Case Study Load Packages

The import integration process, as discussed earlier, will contain three distinct packages (of the four) that need to be built. To keep this from becoming a 100-step process, you'll put each together separately, and then within each package we'll break up the setup into several sections: Package Setup and File System Tasks, Control Flow Processing, Data Flow Validation, and Data Flow ETL. Each step will be explained in detail the first time, and as things become repetitive, we'll drop some detail on the screenshots, so you'll pick up some speed. You can also walk through just one of these load packages and then download the complete solution from www.wrox.com to see and explore the final result.

Bank File Load Package

The bank-batch load package will be set up to look in specific file directories for Lockbox flat files. External dependencies like file folders can be a headache during package deployment if you hard-code them, because you'll have to remember to have them set up *identically* in each environment. Instead, you are going to build-in the ability of your package to get these paths from variables and build them as needed. You can then use configuration files to set up the package in each environment without any further intervention. However, you could still have some issues if the directories that you provide are not created, so you need to consider this as you set up the precedence and control of flow in your package. It means adding a few extra steps, but it will allow your package to adjust during initial deployment and any future changes to these file locations.

Bank File Package and Variable Setup Tasks

To get started, you need to create a new SSIS project. Create a package named CaseStudy_Load_Bank in `c:\casestudy\casestudy_load_bank\`. When the project is built, go to the Solution Explorer and click the `Package.dtsx` file. In the Property window, find the Name property and change the name from package.dtsx to casestudy_load_Bank.dtsx. Answer Yes to change the name of the package object as well.

Use the menu SSIS ⇨ Variables to access the Variables editor and add the variables as shown in the following table. We are using all-caps here because variables are case-sensitive and while you are new to SSIS, this keeps you from some frustration if you are not used to case sensitivity. Variable names with all-caps are not required for SSIS package development. Most of these values will be set automatically to default values within each load package, so values are here to aid in understanding with the exception of LBBASEFILEPATH. This variable value can be set manually, but most likely would be set in a configuration file for the package. Because all the other file paths and filenames for processed files are based on this variable, the package can be easily configured for different server environments.

Variable Name	Scope	Data Type	Value
BANKBATCHID	CaseStudy_Loa..	Int32	0
BANKBATCHNBR	CaseStudy_Loa..	String	
BATCHITEMS	CaseStudy_Loa..	Int64	0
BATCHTOTAL	CaseStudy_Loa..	Double	0
DEPOSITDATE	CaseStudy_Loa..	DateTime	12/30/1899
FILEBYTES	CaseStudy_Loa..	Int64	0
LBBASEFILEPATH	CaseStudy_Loa..	String	c:\casestudy\lockbox
LBCURRENTFILE	CaseStudy_Loa..	String	c:\casestudy\lockbox\ samplelockbox.txt
LBERRORFILE	CaseStudy_Loa..	String	
LBERRORFILEPATH	CaseStudy_Loa..	String	
LBIMPORTTYPE	CaseStudy_Loa..	String	LOCKBOX
LBPROCESSEDFILE	CaseStudy_Loa..	String	
LBPROCESSEDFILEPATH	CaseStudy_Loa..	String	
OLEDBCONNECTSTRING	CaseStudy_Loa..	String	Data Source=.Initial; Catalog=CaseStudy; Provider=SQLNCLI10.1; Integrated Security=SSPI; Auto Translate=False;

Because the File System Tasks only allow the source and destination properties to be set to variables — not expressions derived from variable values — you are going to have to create a few variables that "go the other way" and instead are derived from expressions.

The variables @LBPROCESSEDFILEPATH and @LBERRORFILEPATH need to retrieve their values relative to the base file paths. For example, the variable @LBPROCESSEDFILEPATH should be set up relative to the base Lockbox file path in a subdirectory called processed\. To do this, you'll use an expression to generate the value of the variable. Click the variable in the Variables Editor. In the Property window, set the EvaluateAsExpression property to True. In the Expression property, add the expression to match Figure 23-7. The \\ is required as an escape sequence for the backslash in the Expressions Editor. Set both variables up to be evaluated as expressions the same way. Notice in the Variables Editor, and as shown in Figure 23-8, the values change immediately.

For Variable Name	Set Expression To
LBERRORFILEPATH	@LBBASEFILEPATH + "\\error"
LBPROCESSEDFILEPATH	@LBBASEFILEPATH + "\\processed"

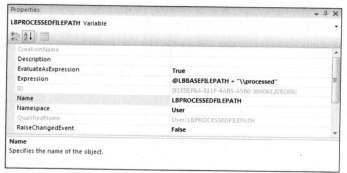

Figure 23-7

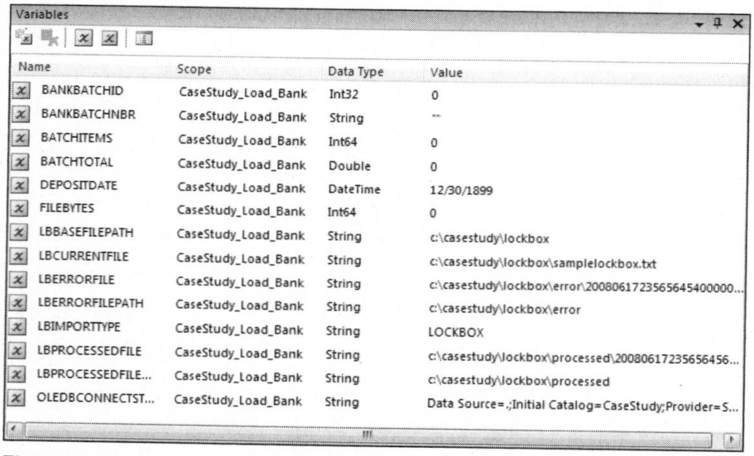

Figure 23-8

The variables for specific processed and error versions of the current file being processed need to retrieve a unique value that can be used to rename the file into its respective destination file path. Set up the @LBERRORFILE and @LBPROCESSEDFILE variables to be evaluated using expressions similar to the following formula:

```
@LBERRORFILEPATH + "\\" + REPLACE(REPLACE(REPLACE(REPLACE((DT_WSTR,
50)GETUTCDATE(),"-",""),"  ", ""),".", ""),":", "") + (DT_WSTR, 50)@FILEBYTES +
".txt"
```

This formula will generate a name similar to 2008081605520801600000000.txt for the file to be moved into an off-line storage area.

In the Connection Managers tab, add an OLE DB Connection to connect to the CaseStudy database. Name the connection CaseStudy.OLEDB. You'll use this connection for all control and Data Flow activities that interact with the database. To enable this connection to be configurable during runtime, set the connect string property of the connection to the variable @OLEDBCONNECTSTRING using the Expressions collection on the Connection Properties window. Notice earlier that this variable was set to the default instance using this connection string value:

```
Data Source=.;Initial Catalog=CaseStudy;Provider=SQLNCLI10.1;Integrated
Security=SSPI;Auto Translate=False;
```

You may need to specifically name your server instance instead of using the "." identifier. Figure 23-9 shows how the connection should appear when complete.

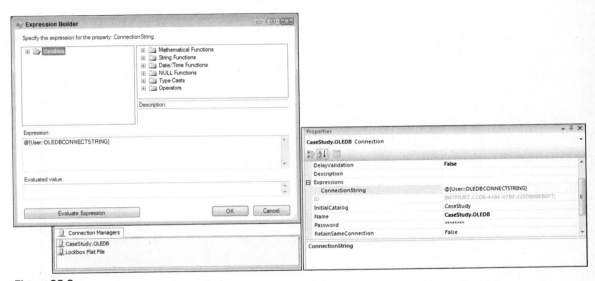

Figure 23-9

Finally, add a New Flat File Connection in the Connection Managers tab. Configure the properties in the following table on the connection. You'll notice that instead of parsing out each individual column in the file, here you are bringing the whole 80-character line into the data stream so that you can parse out each data element later. The reason for doing this is that the lockbox flat file will attempt to cast parsed text values into specific data types, resulting in import errors if there are unexpected non-ASCII characters or non-valid elements like 00000000 for dates. By bringing in the whole line, you'll be able to parse and test each element allowing for more control in your ETL process. This is the preferred ETL technique if the data quality is found to be poor or inconsistent, or if you are not using a staging table.

Property	Setting
Name	Lockbox Flat File
Description	Flat File for Lockbox processing
File Name	c:\casestudy\lockbox\samplelockbox.txt
Format	Ragged right
Advanced:OutputColumnWidth	80
Advanced:DataType	string[DT_STR]
Advanced:Name	line (case is important)

The only problem with the previous step is that you had to set a filename to a literal in order to set up the connection. However, at runtime you'll want to retrieve the filename that you'll be processing from your variable LBCURRENTFILE. Save the Flat File Connection, and then access the expressions collection in the Properties tab. Use the expression editor just like you did for the OLE DB Connection to set the ConnectionString property to @LBCURRENTFILE.

At this point, you should be looking at a package named CaseStudy_Load_Bank with two connections and a bunch of variables. In the next section, you'll start adding the Control Flow.

Bank File Control Flow Processing

You want the CaseStudy_Load_Bank package to process these flat files streaming in from the bank, but before you start, you need to ensure that the directories needed for your load package exist. You'll use a File System Task to do this because it can perform the operation of checking for and creating a directory. One nifty thing that it will do by default is to create all the subdirectories in the hierarchy down to the last subdirectory when you create a directory. This is why you'll set up a File System Task to check for and create a directory using lowest subdirectory path values — LBPROCESSEDFILEPATH and LBERRORFILEPATH. You won't need to create a path explicitly for the variable LBBASEFILEPATH. You'll get this for free, when you check for and create the subdirectories. We'll use this to get started on laying out the Control Flow for our package.

Bank File Control Flow File Loop

Add two File System Tasks to the Control Flow design surface of the package, one for checking and adding the lockbox processed file path, and another for the lockbox error-file path. These two paths are where the package will move incoming lockbox files depending upon how they are processed. Change the name and description properties to the following:

Name	Description
File System Task Folder LB Processed Folder	Ensures that the LB Processed Folder exists
File System Task Folder LB Error Folder	Ensures that the LB Error Folder exists

For each File System Task set the following properties.

Property	Setting
Operation	Create Directory
UseDirectoryIfExists	True
IsSourcePathVariable	True
SourceVariable	Choose the corresponding variable for each task. (Notice how easy this is when the task is named properly?)

Now connect the two lockbox File System Tasks together by setting a precedence constraint between the File System Task Folder LB Processed Folder Task and the File System Task Folder LB Error Folder Task. The precedence constraint should automatically be set to Success. If you run the package now, you should see a file hierarchy created on your machine resembling Figure 23-10.

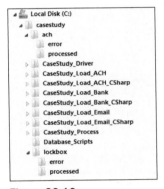

Figure 23-10

Drop a Sequence Container on the Control Flow design surface. Change the Name property to Sequence of Lockbox Processing. Connect the precedence from the last Lockbox File System Task to the Sequence Container so that the Sequence Container is not executed unless the File System Task completes successfully.

Add a Foreach Loop Container inside the Sequence Container. Change the Name property to For Each Lockbox File. The Foreach Loop is expecting a literal path to poll. You want the loop to rely on a variable, so you'll have to use an expression. This task object is a little confusing because there are actually two sets of expression collections: One set in the left tab is for the container; the second set appears only when the Collections tab is selected. The second set of expressions is the collection of properties for the Foreach Enumerator. It is this second set of expressions that you want to alter. Click the ellipsis to the right of this Expressions collection.

In the Expressions Editor, the property folder doesn't exist with this name. Unfortunately, it is named Directory. Select the Directory property and set its value to the variable LBBASEFILEPATH. Evaluate the expression to ensure that it matches the base lockbox path. Close the Expressions Editor. Set the property

Files to "*.txt". Leave the Retrieve File value as Name Fully Qualified. The collections tab of the Foreach Loop Container should look like Figure 23-11.

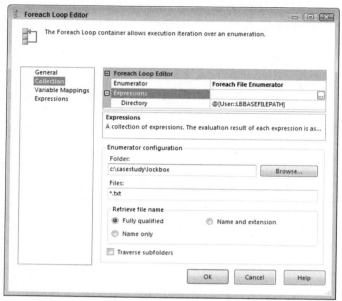

Figure 23-11

@LBBASEFILEPATH *and* @[User::LBBASEFILEPATH] *are the same thing since they are both in the same namespace.*

To store the name of the file you are processing into a variable, click the Variable Mappings tab on the left side of the Foreach Loop Container. Select the variable named LBCURRENTFILE to retrieve the value of the Foreach Loop for each file found. Leave the index on the variable mapping set to zero (0). This represents the first position in a files collection or the filename returned by the loop. Click OK to complete this task.

Bank File Control Flow Retrieval of File Properties

One of the things you have to save into the BankBatch data table is the filename and the number of bytes in the file. The Foreach Loop Task did the work of storing the filename into the variable LBCURRENTFILE. Now with the filename it would be easy to retrieve the file size using a Script Task and some VB.NET or C# code, and then set the value of the variable. We also need to reset the value of some of the other variables, so this will be a good spot to add this logic as well. For some detailed explanation of setting variables within Script Tasks, see Chapter 9.

Getting back to the Control Flow of the Bank File package, add a Script Task within the Foreach Loop. Change the name to "Script LB File Size into Variable." Provide the variable LBCURRENTFILE for the ReadOnlyVariables property. Select the variables BANKBATCHID, BANKBATCHNBR, BATCHITEMS,

BATCHTOTAL, DEPOSITDATE, and FILEBYTES from the drop-down list of variables for the ReadWriteVariables property. Note if you choose to hand-key variables into this property that when passing variables into the Script Task, the @ sign should not be used, but you can fully qualify the variables with the namespace like User::BATCHITEMS.

Select the Script language of your preference. Click the Edit Script button. This opens up the .NET development environment. Add either an Imports or using reference to the System.IO namespace depending upon your selected .NET language and update the script to pull the file bytes from the filename provided in the DTS object Variables collection. First pull in a reference to the System.IO library by adding the last reference you see in this code:

```
C#
using System;
using System.Data;
using Microsoft.SqlServer.Dts.Runtime;
using System.IO;   //<--Added Input/Output library


VB
Imports System
Imports System.Data
Imports System.Math
Imports Microsoft.SqlServer.Dts.Runtime
Imports System.IO '<--Added Input/Output library
```

Then add a VB Sub or C# void function to reset the variables that you can call in the Script Task Main() function. This separation is only to encourage code separation instead of large procedural code typically found in the Main() function. Note that the conversion of default values is explicit. This is required. Simply assigning the value of 0 to one of these variables would not cast properly.

```
C#
    public void ResetVariables()
    {
        //Resets variables
        Dts.Variables["BANKBATCHID"].Value = System.Convert.ToInt32(0);
        Dts.Variables["BANKBATCHNBR"].Value = "";
        Dts.Variables["BATCHITEMS"].Value = System.Convert.ToInt64(0);
        Dts.Variables["BATCHTOTAL"].Value = System.Convert.ToDouble(0);
        Dts.Variables["DEPOSITDATE"].Value = DateTime.MinValue;
        Dts.Variables["FILEBYTES"].Value = System.Convert.ToInt64(0);
    }
VB
    Public Sub ResetVariables()
        'Resets variables
        Dts.Variables("BANKBATCHID").Value = System.Convert.ToInt32(0)
        Dts.Variables("BANKBATCHNBR").Value = ""
        Dts.Variables("BATCHITEMS").Value = System.Convert.ToInt64(0)
        Dts.Variables("BATCHTOTAL").Value = System.Convert.ToDouble(0)
        Dts.Variables("DEPOSITDATE").Value = DateTime.MinValue
        Dts.Variables("FILEBYTES").Value = System.Convert.ToInt64(0)
    End Sub
```

Then replace the `Main()` function within the Script Task with this one:

```
C#
public void Main()
{
    //'**
    //'SCRIPT
    //'PURPOSE: To take file bytes and save to global variable
    //'==============================================================
    Int64 lDefault = 0;
    Boolean bVal;

    try
    {
        //Reset Variables
        ResetVariables();

        //Use .Net IO Library to examine file bytes
        FileInfo oFile = new
                FileInfo(Dts.Variables["LBCURRENTFILE"].Value.ToString());
        Dts.Variables["FILEBYTES"].Value = oFile.Length;
        Dts.Events.FireInformation(0, "Script Task to Vars", _
            "File Bytes Found:" +
         Dts.Variables["FILEBYTES"].Value.ToString(), "", 0, ref bVal);
        //Alternative Troubleshooter
        //System.Windows.Forms.MessageBox.Show("File Bytes Found:" +
        //Dts.Variables["FILEBYTES"].Value.ToString());

        Dts.TaskResult = (int)ScriptResults.Success;
    }
    catch(Exception ex)
    {
        Dts.Events.FireError(0, "Script Task To Vars", ex.ToString(),
                "", 0);
        Dts.Variables["FILEBYTES"].Value = lDefault;
        Dts.TaskResult = (int)ScriptResults.Failure;
    }
}

VB
Public Sub Main()
'**
'SCRIPT
'PURPOSE: To take file bytes and save to global variable
'==============================================================
    Dim oFile As FileInfo
    Dim lDefault As Int64
    Dim bVal As Boolean
    lDefault = 0
    Try
        'Reset Variables
        ResetVariables()

        'Use .Net IO Library to examine file bytes
```

```
        oFile = New FileInfo(Dts.Variables("LBCURRENTFILE").Value.ToString)
        Dts.Variables("FILEBYTES").Value = oFile.Length
        Dts.Events.FireInformation(0, "Script Task to Vars", _
                "File Bytes Found:" +
                Dts.Variables("FILEBYTES").Value.ToString(), _
                "", 0, bVal)
        'Alternative Troubleshooter
        'System.Windows.Forms.MessageBox.Show("File Bytes Found:" _
        '      + Dts.Variables("FILEBYTES").Value.ToString())
        Dts.TaskResult = ScriptResults.Success
    Catch ex As Exception
        Dts.Events.FireError(0, "Script Task To Vars", ex.ToString(), "", 0)
        Dts.Variables("FILEBYTES").Value = lDefault
        Dts.TaskResult = ScriptResults.Failure
    End Try
End Sub
```

Now close the Script editor and save this task. Clicking OK to save is important. If you open up the script after you edit and have not saved the task, then your earlier script changes are lost. While we are mentioning tips, another good practice in SSIS is to code and test smaller units of work. Back to the code, you'll notice the use of the FireInformation method in the script. This method will stream an informational entry into the Execution Results tab containing the value of file bytes found in the file to process.

At this point, you would know the filename and file size. The Foreach Loop stored the filename into a variable. The Script Task retrieved the file size and stored the data into the FILEBYTES variable. You still need to figure out whether you have seen this file before. A unique batch number by import type is embedded in the header of the file. There are a few ways to retrieve that information. One way is to use the System.IO library in the Script Task you just created to open up and examine the file header row. Another way is to use a Data Flow Task to open up and examine the file. Although you could do the same thing in the Script Task, the Data Flow Task allows you to turn the file into a stream to examine the contents easily. It also provides the added advantage of failure upon encountering a bad format at a column level. You can then alter your Control Flow to push this file to the error folder.

To finish out the retrieval Control Flow for now, add a Data Flow Task. Connect the successful completion of the Script Task to this task. Change the Name property to "Data Flow Lockbox Validate File and Header Info." This task will parse out the batch header information into variables, validate the data contents, and then perform a lookup for a similar batch. An existing BankBatchID will be returned in the BankBatchID variable. You'll come back and configure the Data Flow in the next section, "Bank File Data Flow Validation." Disable the Data Flow Task for now by right-clicking the task and selecting Disable in the pop-up menu. (Follow the same steps later and select Enable to re-enable the task.)

You should save the entire package and run it to make sure everything is working so far.

Bank File Control Flow Batch Creation

The last task for the bank-file Control Flow is to lay out the workflow to validate that key values are in the Batch file and that Batch has not already been processed. This ultimately will be determined by the Data Flow Task that you added, but have not yet completed. For now, you know that if certain basic elements in the batch file, such as the batch number, are missing or the batch amount is zero, then the package should move the file to the error folder.

To enable moving the file, add a File System Task named "File System Task Error Folder." Instead of choosing a move file operation in the File System Task, select the option to rename the file. This may not be intuitive, but to move the file you need the filename stored separately. Because the variable @LBERRORFILE is a full file path and a unique filename, it is easier to move the file by simply renaming it. The File System Task properties should be set to the values shown in the following table:

Property	Value
IsDestinationPathVariable	True
Destination Variable	User::LBERRORFILE
OverwriteDestination	True
Name	File System Task Error Folder
Description	Moves bad files to an error folder
Operation	Rename File
IsSourcePathVariable	True
SourceVariable	User::LBCURRENTFILE

The File System Task here will complain if the value for User::LBCurrentFile *is empty or if it doesn't have a default value, so make sure you set this up initially as described in the earlier setup section.*

To connect the Data Flow and File System Task together, add a precedence constraint that looks for the existence of a Bank Batch Id and amount. On the constraint, select the Multiple constraint option of Logical OR and set the Evaluation Operation to Expression OR Constraint. Set the Value to Failure and the Expression to:

```
@BANKBATCHID!=0 || @BATCHTOTAL == 0.00
```

If either Data Flow fails, the Data Flow found an existing BankBatchId, or there is no valid amount in the amount spot in the bank file, the precedence constraint will send the workflow to the File System Task that will archive the file in the error folder.

Now if the elements are all present, and there is no existing bank batch by batch number, the batch needs to be persisted to the database. To do this, add an Execute SQL Task. This task will use a stored procedure, usp_BankBatch_Add, to add the parsed information in the Lockbox file as a row in the BankBatch table to represent a new batch file. The procedure usp_BankBatch_Add will return the new BankBatchId if it could be successfully added. Because you are using an OLE DB Connection Manager, set up Execute SQL Task properties like this:

Property	Value
Name	Execute SQL task to add Bank Batch Hdr
ConnectionType	OLE DB
Connection	CaseStudy.OLEDB
SQLStatement	EXEC dbo.usp_BankBatch_Add ? OUTPUT, ?, ?, ?, ?, ?, ?, ?, ?
IsQueryStoredProcedure	(Will be greyed out)

When you use the OLE DB provider, the parameters have to be marked as ? because of the different provider implementations of handling parameters. Map the input parameters to the procedure parameters on the Parameter Mappings tab. You'll notice that the OLE DB provider uses more generic variable mapping than what you'll do later with the ADO.NET provider. The finished Execute SQL Task editor should look like Figure 23-12.

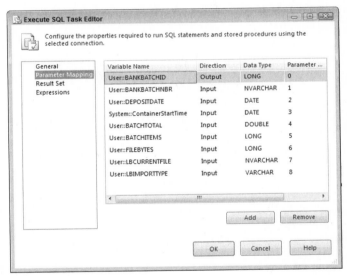

Figure 23-12

If this Execute SQL Task doesn't return a new BankBatchId indicating that the batch header has been persisted, you don't want any other tasks connected to it to be executed. Furthermore, the offending file needs to be moved into an error folder to be examined because something is wrong. Create another precedence constraint between the Execute SQL Task and the File System Task Error Folder. The Control Flow should take this path if either the Execute SQL Task fails or the BankBatchId is zero (0). Set up the Precedence Constraint Editor to look like Figure 23-13.

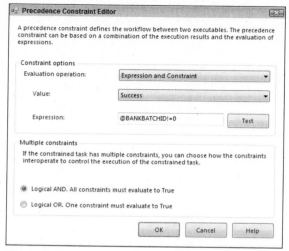

Figure 23-13

Add a second new Data Flow Task to the Foreach Loop. Change the name property to Data Flow Lockbox Detail Data Load. You'll come back later to configure the Data Flow in the next section. Connect the successful completion of the Execute SQL Task to this task. Add an expression to check for a nonzero BankBatchID, and set the constraint to apply when there is a successful completion and an evaluation of the constraint as true between the Execute SQL Task and this new Data Flow Task.

Now if the Data Flow Lockbox Detail Data Load fails to extract, transform, and load the batch details, you've still got an issue. Add a simple Failure constraint between the Data Flow Lockbox Detail Data Load and the previously created File System Task Error Folder.

If the file is processed successfully in the Data Flow Lockbox Detail Data Load, you need to move it to the "processed" folder. Add another new File System Task and connect it to the successful completion of the second Data Flow Task. Set up this task just like the Error Folder File System Task but point everything to the processed folder.

Property	Value
IsDestinationPathVariable	True
Destination Variable	User::LBPROCESSEDFILE
OverwriteDestination	True
Name	File System Task Processed Folder
Description	Moves completed files to an error folder
Operation	Rename File
IsSourcePathVariable	True
SourceVariable	User::LBCURRENTFILE

You now have the basic structure set up for the Bank File Lockbox Control Flow. You still need to go back and build your transforms in the Data Flow Tasks, but we'll get to that in the next sections. If you are following along, go ahead and save the package at this point. If you want to test the package, you can set up the variables and test the different workflows. Just remember to watch the movement of the sample file into the processed and error folders, and make sure you put it back after each run. The CaseStudy_ Load_Bank package at this point should look like Figure 23-14.

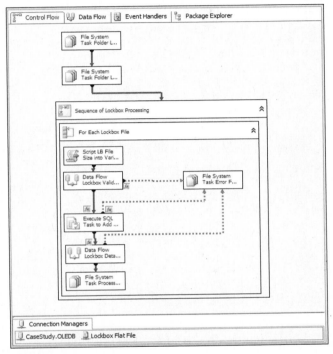

Figure 23-14

Bank File Data Flow Validation

In this section of the package, you are going to fill in the details of the Data Flow Container for validating the Lockbox file. The strategy will be to open up the Lockbox file and retrieve information from the header to pass back to the Control Flow via variables. You'll use a Flat File Connection to read the file, a Conditional Split Transform to separate out the header and the check lines, derived columns to parse out the header line, and an Aggregate Count Transform to count the check transactions. You'll use Script Component Transforms to pull this information from the transformation stream and store it in your variables to return them back to the Control Flow. You'll recall that the Control Flow decides whether the file is good or not, and either moves the file into an error or a processed folder.

Bank File Data Flow Parsing and Error Handling

To use the Flat File Connection you defined earlier in the Data Flow, add a Flat File Source to the Data Flow design surface. Select the Flat File Connection created in the previous step named Lockbox Flat File. Name this transform source Flat File Lockbox.

One of the main purposes of this Data Flow is to perform an extraction of the header information and then perform a lookup on the batch number. You will use the Lookup Transformation for this task, and one of the "gotchas" to using this task is that it is case-sensitive. Because at this point your source contains all the data in a single column, it makes sense to go ahead and run the data through a transform that can convert the data to uppercase in one step. Add a Character Map Transform to the Data Flow. It should be connected to the output of the Flat File Source and be configured to perform an in-line change to the incoming data. Select the incoming column named "line" and set the Destination to In-Place Change. Set the operation type to Uppercase and leave the output alias as "line." Save the Character Map Transform.

The Lockbox file contains three types of data formats: header, invoice, and check. At this stage, you are trying to determine whether this batch has been previously processed, so you only need the information from the header and a count of the check transactions. To split the one-column flat file input, add a Conditional Split Transform to the Data Flow. Set up the transform to use the leftmost character of the input stream to split the line into two outputs: Header and Check. The transform should look like Figure 23-15.

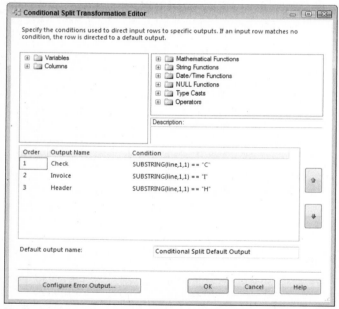

Figure 23-15

Add a Derived Column Task to the Data Flow. Name it Derived Columns from Header. Connect to the Header output of the Conditional Split. This task is where the individual data elements are parsed from the line into the data fields they represent. With the Derived Column Task, you also get the conversion utilities as an added benefit. Because the import stream is a string type, this is where you have to think ahead on your conversions. Downstream, if you ultimately want to add a row to the BankBatch table, the Batch Number you extract from this input stream must be converted into a Unicode variable text field. If you parse the text string into the data type of [DT_WSTR] at this stage, you will match the destination field. Paying attention to data types early will save you many headaches further into the package. Set up the derived columns to match Figure 23-16.

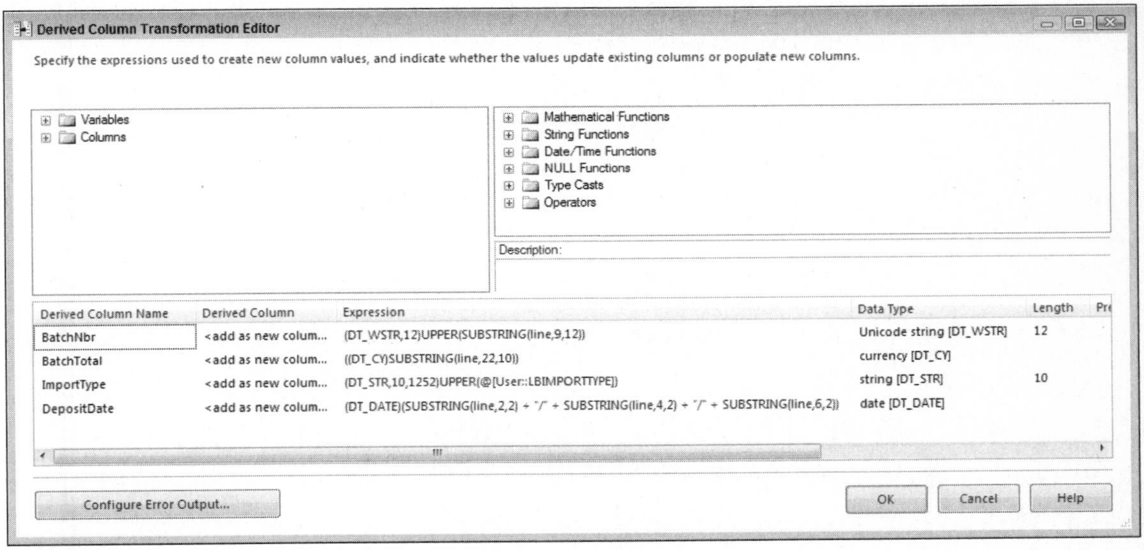

Figure 23-16

Wait a minute! These explicit castings of string data could be disastrous. What if the bank provides some bad data in the Batch Total field? Good question. If you just left the default error handling in place, the package would fail. You don't want that to happen; you just want to reject the file. To do that, you need the Control Flow to recognize that something is wrong and divert the file to the error folder. Notice that we said Control Flow — not Data Flow. This is why the precedence and constraint you set up between this Data Flow Task and the Execute SQL Task to add a Bank Batch header is set up to reject the file if the Data Flow Task fails.

To make sure this happens, click the Configure Error Output button, and make sure that for each derived column the component is set to fail and redirect row if there are any errors in creating the columns. See Figure 23-17 for the completed error output.

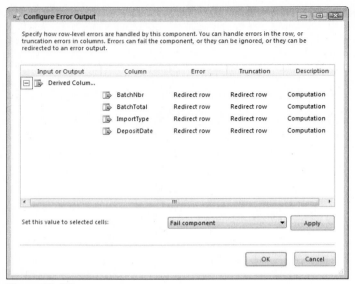

Figure 23-17

There are many different options for handling errors in SSIS. In this Data Flow, if there is an error parsing the lockbox header, it is probably an invalid format-type error, so you want to be able to capture information about that error in that column, so the file can be fixed and resubmitted. To do this, add a Script Component Task to make use of the error stream you created from the Derived Column Task. Set it up as a transformation. The error stream currently contains your raw data, an error code, and a column number for each error generated. You can use the Script Component to add the error description to your stream, and then in another Transform Task you can log the information into your [ErrorDetail] table. Connect the error output of the Derived Column Task to the Script Component Task to capture the original input stream. Name this task Script Component Get Error Desc. Open the Script Transformation Editor and select all the input columns on the Input Columns tab. Then, in the Inputs and Outputs tab, expand the Output0 collection and add an output column (not an output) named ErrorDesc. Set the type to [DT_WSTR] with a length of 1048. Open up the design environment for the Script Component. Change your `ProcessInputRow()` method to the following:

```csharp
C#
    public override void Input0_ProcessInputRow(Input0Buffer Row)
    {
        //'Script
        //'Purpose: To retrieve the error description to write to error log
        Row.ErrorDesc = ComponentMetaData.GetErrorDescription(Row.ErrorCode);
    }
```

```vb
VB
    Public Overrides Sub Input0_ProcessInputRow(ByVal Row As Input0Buffer)
        'SCRIPT
        'PURPOSE: To retrieve the error description to write to error log
        Row.ErrorDesc= ComponentMetaData.GetErrorDescription(Row.ErrorCode)
    End Sub
```

Close the Script Editor and then the Script Transformation Editor. Now add a Derived Column Transform and name it Derived Column System Variables. Along with the detailed error message, it will be helpful to add other information like the ExecutionInstanceGUID to log in to your custom ErrorDetail table. The ExecutionInstanceGUID is a unique ID given to each run of an SSIS package that will allow you to combine your custom error logging with other package error logging to give you a complete picture of what occurred when a package failed. Create the Derived Columns shown in Figure 23-18.

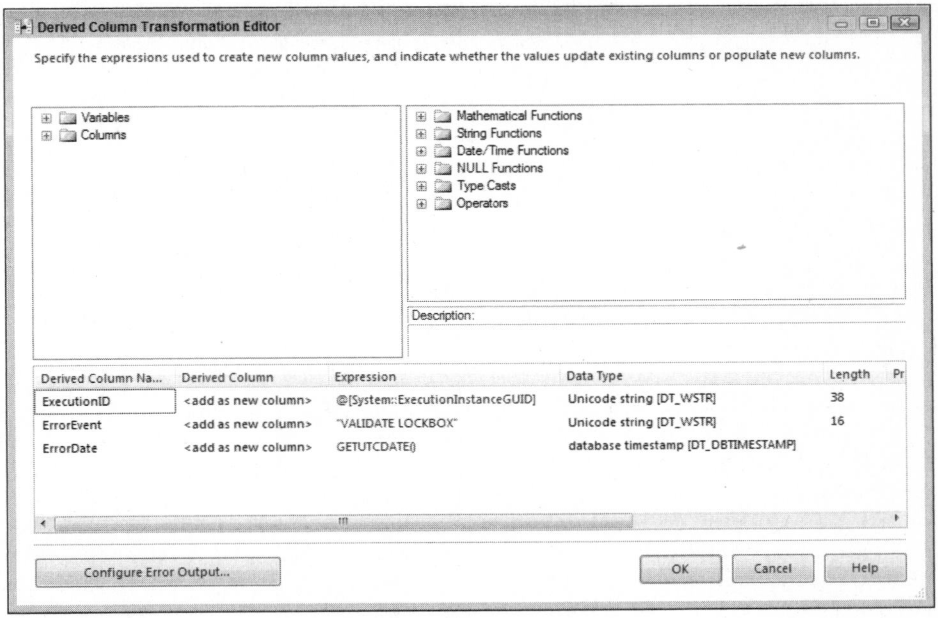

Figure 23-18

Add an OLE DB Destination to save this data into the ErrorDetail table. Name the transform "OLE DB Destination Error Log." Set up the OLE DB Connection and the name of the table to ErrorDetail. Map the columns. Most input columns should match the destination columns in the table. Map the column [Line] to the [RawData] column. Now you've handled the worst-case scenario of bad batch header data. Not only do you store the error of a bad conversion or batch header, but the flow of data will now stop at this transform. This leaves the value of the BankBatchID to the default of 0, which will cause the Control Flow to divert the file to the error folder — just what you want.

Bank File Data Flow Validation

Now, if all the data elements of the Bank Batch file parse correctly, the "Derived Columns from Header" Transform should contain data that was successfully converted to proper data types. You now have to determine if the BatchNbr parsed from the file has already been processed. This can be accomplished by checking to see if it matches any existing BatchNbr in the BankBatch table by import type. Add a Lookup Transformation Task to the flow of the Derived Column. Change the name to Lookup BankBatchID. Connect the CaseStudy.OLEDB connection. In the Reference tab, select BankBatch table. The Lookup Transform is case sensitive, and this is why the derived column converted the contents to uppercase.

In the Columns tab, connect the BatchNbr input column to the BankBatchNbr column. Connect the ImportType input column to the ImportType column. This is the equivalent of running a query against the BankBatch table looking for a matching row ImportType and BatchNbr for each row in the input stream. In the grid, add a lookup column BankBatchID by selecting the field in the lookup table. The result of the lookup will be either a NULL value or a retrieved BankBatchID. Because you are expecting the Lookup Task to return no matches, use the Configure Error Output to set the error output for the lookup to Ignore Failure. Figure 23-19 shows an example of the mapping to retrieve the BankBatchId as a new column.

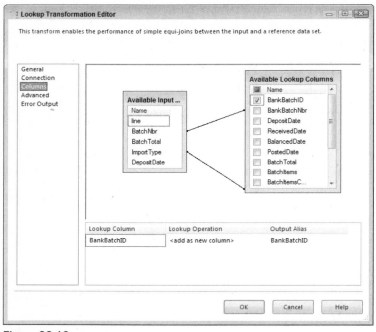

Figure 23-19

To handle the NULL situation and other validations, add a new Script Component Task to the Data Flow and connect to the successful output stream of the Lookup Task as a destination. Name this task Script Component to Store Variables. In this task, select the columns Line, BankBatchID, BatchNbr, BatchTotal, ImportType, and DepositDate from the input stream. They will be added automatically as input columns and will be available in a row object. Add the matching variables to the ReadWriteVariable property: BANKBATCHID, BANKBATCHNBR, DEPOSITDATE, BATCHTOTAL. Remember, variables are case-sensitive and must be passed as a comma-delimited list. (Thank the SSIS team for the ability to select variables!)

In the Script Component, use the row object to retrieve the values that are in the input row stream. Because you are processing the header row, you'll have only one row to process. Accessing the row values is not a problem. However, saving the value to a package variable is not allowed when processing at a row level. You can only access package variables in the PostExecute event stub. To retrieve the values, use variables to capture the values in the row-level event, and then update the package variables in the PostExecute event. If you have a need to retrieve information from your Data

Flow into variables, as in this example, this technique will be really useful to you. To continue with this example, replace the Script Component script with the following code:

```csharp
C#
using System;
using System.Data;
using Microsoft.SqlServer.Dts.Pipeline.Wrapper;
using Microsoft.SqlServer.Dts.Runtime.Wrapper;

[Microsoft.SqlServer.Dts.Pipeline.SSISScriptComponentEntryPointAttribute]
public class ScriptMain : UserComponent
{

    public int LocalBankBatchId = 0;
    public double LocalBatchTotal = 0;
    public string LocalBatchNbr = "";
    public DateTime LocalDepositDate  = DateTime.MinValue;
    public bool bVal;

    public override void PreExecute()
    {
        base.PreExecute();
        /*
          Add your code here for preprocessing or remove if not needed
        */
    }

    public override void PostExecute()
    {
        //'SCRIPT
        //'PURPOSE: To set SSIS variables with values retrieved earlier
        //'============================================================
        try
        {
            //'Attempt to accept the values
            Variables.BANKBATCHID = LocalBankBatchId;
            Variables.BANKBATCHNBR = LocalBatchNbr;
            Variables.DEPOSITDATE = LocalDepositDate;
            Variables.BATCHTOTAL = LocalBatchTotal;
        }
        catch(Exception ex)
        {
            //'If any failure occurs fail the file
            Variables.BANKBATCHID = System.Convert.ToInt32(0);
            Variables.BATCHTOTAL = System.Convert.ToDouble(0);
            ComponentMetaData.FireError(0, "", ex.Message, "", 1, out bVal);
        }
        base.PostExecute();
    }

}
```

```csharp
public override void Input0_ProcessInputRow(Input0Buffer Row)
{
    string Msg = string.Empty;
    try
    {
        //'If there is no header metadata then mark for failure
        if( Row.DepositDate_IsNull == true ||
            Row.BatchTotal_IsNull == true ||
              (double)Row.BatchTotal == 0D )
        {
            LocalBankBatchId = 0;
            LocalBatchTotal = 0D;
        }
        else
        {
            //'Retrieve the data from the stream
            if( Row.BankBatchID_IsNull )
            {
                LocalBankBatchId = 0;
            }
            else
            {
                LocalBankBatchId = Row.BankBatchID;
            }
            LocalBatchNbr = Row.BatchNbr;
            LocalDepositDate = Row.DepositDate;
            LocalBatchTotal = (double)Row.BatchTotal
                            / System.Convert.ToDouble(100);
        }
        Msg = String.Format("Variables: BankBatchId={0}, " +
            "BatchTotal={1}, BatchNbr=[{2}]", LocalBankBatchId,
            LocalBatchTotal, LocalBatchNbr);
        ComponentMetaData.FireInformation((int)0, ComponentMetaData.Name,
            Msg, "", (int)0, ref bVal);
    }
    catch(Exception ex)
    {
        ComponentMetaData.FireError(0, "", ex.Message, "", 1, out bVal);
    }
}

}


VB
Imports System
Imports System.Data
Imports System.Math
Imports Microsoft.SqlServer.Dts.Pipeline.Wrapper
Imports Microsoft.SqlServer.Dts.Runtime.Wrapper
```

```vbnet
<Microsoft.SqlServer.Dts.Pipeline.SSISScriptComponentEntryPointAttribute> _
<CLSCompliant(False)> _
Public Class ScriptMain
    Inherits UserComponent
    Public LocalBankBatchId As Integer = 0
    Public LocalBatchTotal As Double = 0
    Public LocalBatchNbr As String = ""
    Public LocalDepositDate As Date = Date.MinValue
    Public bVal As Boolean

    Public Overrides Sub PreExecute()
        MyBase.PreExecute()
    End Sub

    Public Overrides Sub PostExecute()
        'SCRIPT
        'PURPOSE: To set SSIS variables with values retrieved earlier
        '============================================================
        Try
            'Attempt to accept the values
            Variables.BANKBATCHID = LocalBankBatchId
            Variables.BANKBATCHNBR = LocalBatchNbr
            Variables.DEPOSITDATE = LocalDepositDate
            Variables.BATCHTOTAL = LocalBatchTotal
        Catch ex As Exception
            'If any failure occurs fail the file
            Variables.BANKBATCHID = 0
            Variables.BATCHTOTAL = 0
            ComponentMetaData.FireError(0, "", ex.Message, "", 1, bVal)
        End Try

        MyBase.PostExecute()
    End Sub

    Public Overrides Sub Input0_ProcessInputRow(ByVal Row As Input0Buffer)
        'SCRIPT
        'PURPOSE: This sub will fire for each row processed
        '         since we only have one header row we only
        '         this sub will fire only one time.
        '         Store values in variables
        '============================================================
        Dim Msg As String
        Try
            'If there is no header metadata then mark for failure
            If Row.DepositDate_IsNull = True Or _
                Row.BatchTotal_IsNull = True Or _
                    Row.BatchTotal = 0D Then
                LocalBankBatchId = 0
                LocalBatchTotal = 0D
```

```
                Else
                    'Retrieve the data from the stream
                    If Row.BankBatchID_IsNull Then
                        LocalBankBatchId = 0
                    Else
                        LocalBankBatchId = Row.BankBatchID
                    End If
                    LocalBatchNbr = Row.BatchNbr
                    LocalDepositDate = Row.DepositDate
                    LocalBatchTotal = Row.BatchTotal / CDbl(100)
                End If
                Msg = String.Format("Variables: BankBatchId={0}, " + _
                    "BatchTotal={1}, BatchNbr=[{2}]", LocalBankBatchId, _
                    LocalBatchTotal, LocalBatchNbr)
                ComponentMetaData.FireInformation(0, ComponentMetaData.Name, _
                    Msg, "", 0, bVal)
            Catch ex As Exception
                ComponentMetaData.FireError(0, "", ex.Message, "", 1, bVal)
            End Try
        End Sub
    End Class
```

A few things to note that are going on in this Script Task: First, the NULL possibility is being checked and converted to a 0 to adhere to the Control Flow rules you've already set up. Notice as well, that the BatchTotal is being converted from an implied to an explicit decimal with the calculation `Row.BatchTotal / CDbl(100)`. This could have occurred in the Derived Column Transform as well. There are many different ways to approach these validations. Another technique, if the data quality is extremely poor, would be to have the Derived Column Transform only return string data, and then this same Script Transform could validate, cast, and return very specific information about data quality.

Bank File Data Flow Capturing Total Batch Items

The last variable that you need to retrieve is the number of transactions in the lockbox batch. Recall earlier that the data stream for the lockbox file was split into the header and detail lines. Now you are really only interested in the check lines in the file. Add an Aggregation Transformation to the Conditional Split Transform to count the rows in the separated (Check) output detail data stream. Name the transform "Aggregate Check Count." Select the line column from the input columns. Set the Output Alias to BatchItems. Set the operation to Count. This will count the number of checks and put that count into your Data Flow. The component should look like Figure 23-20. Now you just need to save the count of the checks into a variable.

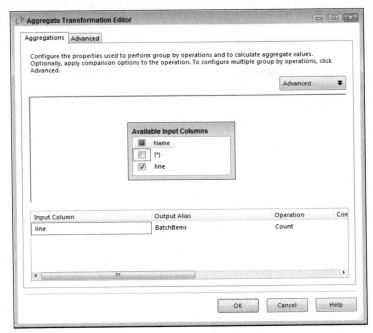

Figure 23-20

Add a Destination Script Component Task named "Script Component Capture BatchItem" to the Data Flow and attach the Aggregate output. Select the BatchItems column from the input stream to feed into the component. Add the variable BATCHITEMS to the ReadWriteVariables property. A common issue at this point is that the type returned by the Aggregate output is a Unicode Long data type. That's why your BatchItems variable was preset to INT64. Add the following script to the task in the ProcessInputRow stub:

```
C#
[Microsoft.SqlServer.Dts.Pipeline.SSISScriptComponentEntryPointAttribute]
public class ScriptMain : UserComponent
{
    public Int64 LocalBatchItems = 0;
    public override void PostExecute()
    {
        //'Script
        //'Purpose: To Set Value of variable unavailable for writing
        //'          in processInputRow method
        Variables.BATCHITEMS = LocalBatchItems;
        base.PostExecute();
    }

    public override void Input0_ProcessInputRow(Input0Buffer Row)
    {
```

```
        //'Script
        //'Purpose: To retrieve the count of rows to process
        bool bval = false;
        try
        {
            if (Row.BatchItems_IsNull)
            {
                LocalBatchItems = (Int64)0;
            }
            else
            {
                LocalBatchItems = (Int64)Row.BatchItems;
            }
        }
        catch (Exception ex)
        {
            LocalBatchItems = (Int64)0;
            this.ComponentMetaData.FireError((int)0,
                ComponentMetaData.Name.ToString(),
                ex.ToString(), "", (int)0, out bval);
        }
    }
}
```

```
VB
Public Class ScriptMain
    Inherits UserComponent
    Public LocalBatchItems As Int64
    Public Overrides Sub Input0_ProcessInputRow(ByVal Row As Input0Buffer)
        '**
        'SCRIPT
        'PURPOSE: Attempt to save the value of batch items
        '          from aggregation to local variables b/c we
        '          can't set DTS Variables in this sub
        Try
            If Row.BatchItems_IsNull = True Then
                LocalBatchItems = 0
            Else
                LocalBatchItems = Row.BatchItems
            End If
        Catch ex As Exception
            LocalBatchItems = 0
        End Try
    End Sub
    Public Overrides Sub PostExecute()
        '**
        'SCRIPT
        'PURPOSE: Sets the value of DTS variables to
        '          local values
        Variables.BATCHITEMS = LocalBatchItems
        MyBase.PostExecute()
    End Sub
End Class
```

This will complete the Bank FileData Flow Validation, which should at this point look like Figure 23-21. Now you can enable the Data Flow Lockbox Validate File and Header Info in the Control Flow and disable the Execute SQL Task (to keep from inserting a new batch) to run a test of the package. Remember that the only purpose of this Data Flow is to determine whether the file is properly formatted, and whether it is indeed a new file to process. All it will do is open the file and parse the information from the file. Play around with the header of the file and put in invalid data such as "02/31/08". You should see the transformation move through the error section of the Data Flow and store a row in the ErrorDetail table. The text file will then be moved into the error folder in the `c:\casestudy\lockbox\error` directory.

This Data Flow is by no means complete and ready for production. The batch lines making up the detail should also be validated for proper data types using the same techniques in this step. Essentially the default BANKBATCHID is set to fail prior to this set of transformations. If the transformation flows completely to the Script Component and stores the batch header information, it will be considered a success. If not, this step will be considered suspect, and the file will be rejected. This should give you a good idea of what you can do without having to stage the data before processing it.

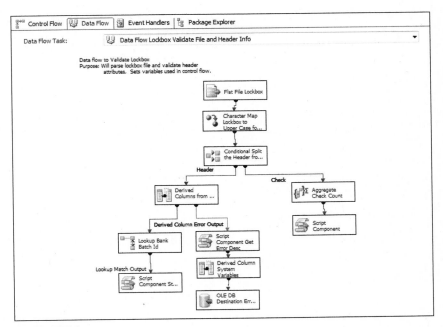

Figure 23-21

Bank File Data Flow Detail Processing ETL

Once you've validated your file, loading the detail data into the BankBatchDetail table will be rather simple. You have all the header-related information. The Execute SQL Task will create a row in the BankBatch table to store the batch, and you'll store the primary key in the BANKBATCHID variable. You now need to re-examine the text file in another Data Flow and process the detail transactions. Your strategy will be to separate the bank batch file again into two parts, the header and detail. The difference in this Data Flow is that you'll need to split the detail into two parts: a part containing individual payment invoice information, and a part containing check lines from the batch file. After validating the contents, you will recombine the two rows into one. That will give you the ability to do a straight insert using one row into the BankBatchDetail table.

Processing the Bank File Check and Invoice Detail Lines

At this point, you should be a little more familiar with setting up Flat File, Character Map, Lookup, Conditional Split, Script, and Derived Column Transforms. We'll forego some of the details to move through setting up this Data Flow. To start, enable the Data Flow Lockbox Detail Data Load Task in the Control Flow. Double-click it to expose the Data Flow design surface. Add a Flat File Source onto the design surface, and set it up to use the Lockbox Flat File Connection for the Lockbox Flat File that you set up in the first validation Data Flow. Name it "Flat File Lockbox Source."

Because the lookup transactions are case-sensitive, it is better to add a Character Map Transform to convert the stream to uppercase while all the data is in one column. Name the Character Map, and set the operation to Uppercase and the destination to In-place.

Add a Conditional Split Transform similar to what you did earlier when validating the batch file. This time you'll split the file into each of its parts: the header, check, and invoice lines. Set up the transform to use the leftmost character of the input stream to split the line into three outputs: Header, Check, and Invoice, based on the characters "H," "C," and "I," respectively.

Add two Derived Column Transforms to the Data Flow. Attach one to the Checks output of the Conditional Split Transform. Name it Derived Column Check. Attach the other to the Invoice output of the Conditional Split Transform. Name it Derived Column Invoice. Don't worry about the header portion for the moment. Using the business specs, create the following new columns to parse out of each line type (note two different Derived Column Components).

Transform	Derived Column	Expression	Data Type
Invoice	RawInvoiceNbr	trim(substring(line,13,len([line])-13))	[DT_WSTR] 50
Invoice	MatchingKey	trim(substring(line,2,4))	[DT_WSTR] 50
Invoice	ReferenceData1	trim(substring(line,2,10))	[DT_WSTR] 50
Check	PaymentAmount	((DT_NUMERIC,11,2)SUBSTRING([line],15,8) / (DT_NUMERIC,11,2)100.00)	[DT_CY]
Check	MatchingKey	trim(substring(line,2,4))	[DT_WSTR] 50
Check	ReferenceData2	trim(substring(line,2,10))	[DT_WSTR] 50

Notice that here you don't need the use of an UPPER() expression to make sure that all these parsed values are uppercase for the future Lookup Task. The CharacterMap Component has already converted the string to all uppercase. Also, notice that there is an auto conversion to DT_WSTR when you are importing a text source. This is worth mentioning here because the default data types and lengths are inferred from the field from the import source. If you were saving this data to a non-Unicode data field, it can be annoying that your settings will be overwritten if you change anything in the expression. However, if you don't get the data type right here, you'll need to add a Data Conversion Transform to convert the data into a compatible format, or the SSIS validation engines will complain — and may not compile. The other thing to notice here is the use of TRIM statements. In flat file data, the columns are tightly defined, but that doesn't mean the data within them lines up exactly to these columns. Use the TRIM statements to remove leading and trailing spaces that will affect your lookup processes downstream.

Now at this point, you've got two output streams: one from the invoice lines and one from the check lines. You want to put them back together into one row. Any transformation you use is going to require that you sort these outputs and then find something in common to join them together. To put them together, you have to have some data that matches between the outputs. Luckily, the bank provides the matching information, and you parsed it out in the Derived Column Task. The column name shared by both outputs that contains the same data is ReferenceData1. Look at a two-line sample from the Lockbox file. Columns two through six (2–6) contain the string 4001, which is defined in your business specs as the lookup key that ties the transaction together. (The entire sequence 4001010003 refers to an image system lookup ID.)

```
I4001010003 181INTERNAT
C4001010004   01844400
```

Add two new Sort Transformations to the Data Flow and connect one to each Derived Column output. Select the field MatchingKey in both sorts and sort ascending. Select all columns for pass-through, except for the Line column. You will no longer use the line data, so there is no need to continue to drag this data through your transformation process. Now you are ready to merge the outputs.

Add a Merge Join Transformation to connect the two outputs to the component. In the editor, select the RawInvoiceNbr and ReferenceNbr1 columns from the Invoice sort stream. Select the PaymentAmount and ReferenceData2 columns from the Check sort stream. There is no need to bring the Matching Key data forward because that information is embedded in the ReferenceData fields. Make sure the JOIN type is set to INNER Join.

This stream is now one row per check and invoice combination. You are almost ready to insert the data into the BankBatchDetail table. All you need now is the Foreign Key for the BankBatch table. Earlier you stored this information in a global variable. To merge this into your stream, add a Derived Column Task and add the variable BANKBATCHID to the stream. (You could have done this earlier in either the check or invoice processing steps as well.) You automatically get all the other fields in the Data Flow as pass-through.

Add an OLE DB Destination and connect to the CaseStudy.OLEDB connection. Connect the transform and select the table BankBatchDetail. Map the columns from the output to the BankBatchDetail table where the column names match. We still have a little left to do, but the core of the Bank File Data Flow is shown in Figure 23-22.

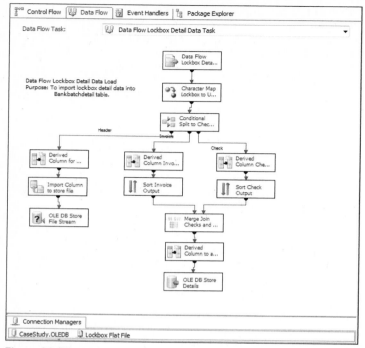

Figure 23-22

Saving a Bank File Snapshot in the Database

You still have one task left to do before closing out this Data Flow, and that is saving a snapshot of the file contents into the BankBatch row. Everything else you are doing in this Data Flow is saving data at the payment or detail level. Saving the entire file contents for audit purposes is a batch-level task. To do this, you'll need to create a separate stream that will use the Header portion of the Conditional stream you split off early in the Data Flow. Start by adding a Derived Column Task connecting to the header-based output; this pushes the identification elements down to a later OLE DB Transform that will update the batch. Add the following columns to the Derived Column Task:

Derived Column	Expression	Data Type
LBCurrentFile	@[User::LBCURRENTFILE]	[DT_WSTR] 100
BankBatchID	@[User::BANKBATCHID]	[DT_I4]

Add an Import Column Transformation and connect it to this Header Derived Column Transform. On the Input Columns tab, select the field that contains the file path in the stream: LBCurrentFile. Then go to the Advanced Input Output property tab and expand the Import Column Input and Import Column Output Nodes. Add an output column to the Output Column Node called FileStreamToStore. Set the DataType property to [DT_NTEXT]. The editor should look similar to Figure 23-23, but the LineageIDs may be different. Note the LineageID and set the property name FileDataColumnID in the LBCurrentFile Input Column to that LineageID. Using Figure 23-23, the ID would be 437.

Add an OLE DB Command Transform to the output of the Header Derived Column Transform. Set the OLE DB Connection to CaseStudy.OLEDB. Then set the SQL Command to `Update BankBatch Set BatchFile = ? where BankBatchID = ?` and click Refresh. In the Mappings tab, connect the FileStreamToStore to the Destination Column Param_0, which is the [BatchFile] field in the BankBatch table. Connect the BankBatchID to the Destination column Param_1. Click Refresh and save.

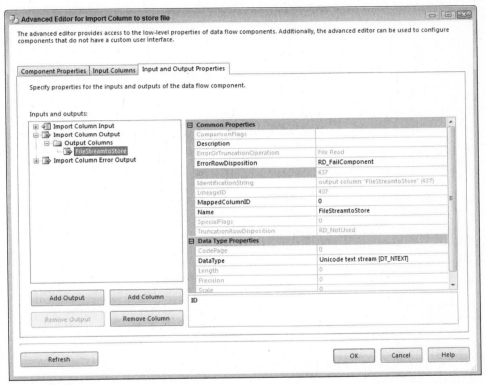

Figure 23-23

This completes the Data Flow Task. The task will parse and save the lockbox detail file into your BankBatchDetail data table. The entire Data Flow should look similar to Figure 23-22. Now would be a good time to save the package. If you've run the package up to this point, check to see that a lockbox sample file exists in the `c:\casestudy\lockbox\` folder. Enable the Execute SQL Task and run the package to watch it execute.

To run the test file through multiple times, you'll need to reset the database by deleting the contents of the BankBatch and BatchBatchDetail tables between runs. Otherwise, in subsequent runs, the package will fail upon finding that the file has been previously processed. Use this script to reset the database for multiple runs:

```
DELETE FROM BANKBATCHDETAIL
DELETE FROM BANKBATCH
```

This completes the first third of the ETL processes for the Lockbox Bank Batch payment method. You will next start to build the two remaining processing options. One is for ACH (which involves processing an XML file) and the other for email payments that are stored in a database. You can skip ahead to the Case Study Process package if you want to complete the processing of this Lockbox Bank Batch file or continue to build the other payment processing methods.

ACH Load Package

In the business specs, you have to process ACH files that represent the payment wire detail. The approach to this problem will resemble closely what you did for the Lockbox, but the XML file format that is sent for this payment method adds more data consistency and a few new processing tricks. Again, you can also walk through and create this ACH load package or download the complete solution from www.wrox.com to see and explore the final result.

ACH Package Setup and File System Tasks

To get started, you need to create a new SSIS package named CaseStudy_Load_ACH in c:\casestudy\ casestudy_load_ACH\. When the project is built, go to the Solution Explorer and click the Package .dtsx file. In the Property window, find the Name property and change the name from package.dtsx to casestudy_load_ACH.dtsx. Answer Yes to change the name of the package object as well.

Use the menu SSIS ⇨ Variables to access the Variables editor and add the variables as shown in the following table:

Variable Name	Scope	Data Type	Value
BANKBATCHID	CaseStudy_Loa..	Int32	0
BANKBATCHNBR	CaseStudy_Loa..	String	
BATCHITEMS	CaseStudy_Loa..	Int64	0
BATCHTOTAL	CaseStudy_Loa..	Double	0
DEPOSITDATE	CaseStudy_Loa..	DateTime	12/30/1899
FILEBYTES	CaseStudy_Loa..	Int64	0
ACHBASEFILEPATH	CaseStudy_Loa..	String	c:\casestudy\ach
ACHCURRENTFILE	CaseStudy_Loa..	String	c:\casestudy\ach\sampleach.xml
ACHERRORFILE	CaseStudy_Loa..	String	
ACHERRORFILEPATH	CaseStudy_Loa..	String	
ACHIMPORTTYPE	CaseStudy_Loa..	String	ACH
ACHPROCESSEDFILE	CaseStudy_Loa..	String	
ACHPROCESSEDFILEPATH	CaseStudy_Loa..	String	

The variables @ACHPROCESSEDFILEPATH and @ACHERRORFILEPATH need to retrieve their values relative to the base file paths. For example, the variable @ACHPROCESSEDFILEPATH should be set up relative to the base Lockbox file path in a subdirectory called processed\. To do this, you'll use an expression to generate the value of the variable. Click the variable in the Variables Editor. In the Property window, set the property EvaluateAsExpression to True. Set these variables up to be evaluated as expressions like this:

For Variable Name	Set Expression To
ACHERRORFILEPATH	@ACHBASEFILEPATH + "\\error"
ACHPROCESSEDFILEPATH	@ACHBASEFILEPATH + "\\processed"

The variables for specific processed and error versions of the current file being processed need to retrieve a unique value that can be used to rename the file into its respective destination file path. Set the @ACHERRORFILE and @ACHPROCESSEDFILE variables up to be evaluated using expressions similar to the following formula:

```
@ACHERRORFILEPATH + "\\" + REPLACE(REPLACE(REPLACE(REPLACE((DT_WSTR,
50)GETUTCDATE(),"-",""), " ", ""),".", ""),":", "") + (DT_WSTR, 50)@FILEBYTES +
".txt"
```

This formula will generate a name similar to 200808160552080160000000.xml for the file to be moved into an off-line storage area.

In the Connection Managers tab, add an OLE DB Connection to connect to the CaseStudy database. Name the connection CaseStudy.OLEDB. This package won't use a dynamic connection like the Bank File package to simplify the example, but feel free to work this out on your own. We do want to add an additional connection to the package, just to show the difference between using OLE DB and ADO.NET in the Execute SQL Tasks, so add an ADO.NET Connection that also connects to the CaseStudy database. Name this connection CaseStudy.ADO.NET.

ACH Control Flow Processing

Just like the CaseStudy_Load_Bank package in the previous example, you need to be able to process many files that are coming in from an ACH institution, but this time the file format is XML. You'll also notice that there is no XML connector. This presents a new twist that we'll have to resolve in the Data Flow Tasks later. Otherwise, the basic structure of this package is the same as the Bank File Load Package.

ACH Control Flow Loop

Add two File System Tasks to the Control Flow design surface of the package. One task will be used for checking and adding the ACH processed file path and another for the ACH error-file path. These two paths are where the package will move incoming lockbox files depending upon how they are processed. Change the name and description properties to the following:

Name	Description
File System Task Folder ACH Processed Folder	Ensures that the ACH Processed Folder exists
File System Task Folder ACH Error Folder	Ensures that the ACH Error Folder exists

For each File System Task, set the following properties:

Property	Setting
Operation	Create Directory
UseDirectoryIfExists	True
IsSourcePathVariable	True
SourceVariable	Choose the corresponding variable for each task.

Stack the two File System Tasks on top of one another. The precedence constraint should automatically be set to Success.

Drop a Sequence Container on the Control Flow design surface. Change the Name property to "Sequence of ACH Processing." Connect the precedence from the last Lockbox File Systems Task to the Sequence Container, so that the Sequence Container is not executed unless the File Systems Task completes successfully. Minimize the Sequence Loop to give yourself more room to work.

Add a Foreach Loop Container inside the Sequence Container. Change the Name property to "For Each ACH File." The Foreach Loop is expecting a literal path to poll. You want the loop to rely on a variable, so you'll have to use an expression. You did this same thing for the bank file package. Go back and review if you are unsure. On the Foreach Loop you need to set the Directory property to an expression that gets its value from the variable ACHBASEFILEPATH. However, if you use the Expressions Tab in the editor, you will not see a property called Directory. On this task, you'll find the properties for the Enumerator in the Collection tab at the top of the dialog. You can see this in Figure 23-24. Here you'll find the Directory property and call set is to the variable ACHBASEFILEPATH. Evaluate the expression to ensure that it matches the base ACH path. Set the property files to "*.xml". Leave the Retrieve File value as Name Fully Qualified. The Collection tab of the Foreach Loop Container should look like Figure 23-24.

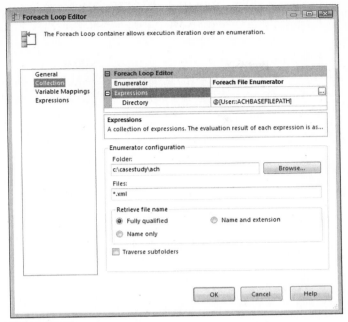

Figure 23-24

To store the name of the file you are processing into a variable, click the Variable Mappings tab on the left side of the Foreach Loop Container. Select the variable named ACHCURRENTFILE to retrieve the value of the Foreach Loop for each file found. Leave the index on the variable mapping set to zero (0). This represents the first position in a files collection or the filename returned by the loop. Click OK to complete this task.

ACH Control Flow Retrieval of XML File Size

Just like the Bank Batch file, you need to examine the file to retrieve the number of complete bytes. Like you did before, the variables will need to be reset. The additional issue with processing XML files is that while you can iterate through a set of XML files, you don't have a control source that you can set with a variable. The closest thing to it is the Data Flow XML Source Component, but the filename can't be set.

The workaround that you'll employ is to set up the XML Source with a fixed filename. You'll do that later, but in this stage, you need to change the name of the iterated file to the filename that will be plugged into the XML Source later. You'll be able to change the name of each current file in the iterations to the fixed filename easily inside a Script Task while checking the file size. To get started, add a Script Task within the Foreach Loop. Change the name to "Script ACH File Size into Variable." Provide the variable ACHBASEFILEPATH for the ReadOnlyVariables property. Provide the variables BANKBATCHID, BANKBATCHNBR, BATCHITEMS, BATCHTOTAL, DEPOSITDATE, FILEBYTES, and now ACHCURRENTFILE into the ReadWriteVariables property.

Select the script language of your preference. Click the Edit Script button. This opens up the .NET development environment. Add an Imports or Using reference to the System.IO namespace and update the script to pull the file bytes from the filename provided in the DTS object Variables collection. First, pull in a reference to the `System.IO` library by adding the last reference you see in this code:

```
C#
using System;
using System.Data;
using Microsoft.SqlServer.Dts.Runtime;
using System.IO; //'<--Added Input/Output library

VB
Imports System
Imports System.Data
Imports System.Math
Imports Microsoft.SqlServer.Dts.Runtime
Imports System.IO '<--Added Input/Output library
```

Then add a VB `Sub` or C# `void` function to reset the variables that you can call in the Script Task `Main()` function:

```
C#
    public void ResetVariables()
    {
        //Resets variables
        Dts.Variables["BANKBATCHID"].Value = System.Convert.ToInt32(0);
        Dts.Variables["BANKBATCHNBR"].Value = "";
        Dts.Variables["BATCHITEMS"].Value = System.Convert.ToInt64(0);
        Dts.Variables["BATCHTOTAL"].Value = System.Convert.ToDouble(0);
        Dts.Variables["DEPOSITDATE"].Value = DateTime.MinValue;
        Dts.Variables["FILEBYTES"].Value = System.Convert.ToInt64(0);
    }
VB
    Public Sub ResetVariables()
        'Resets variables
        Dts.Variables("BANKBATCHID").Value = System.Convert.ToInt32(0)
        Dts.Variables("BANKBATCHNBR").Value = ""
        Dts.Variables("BATCHITEMS").Value = System.Convert.ToInt64(0)
        Dts.Variables("BATCHTOTAL").Value = System.Convert.ToDouble(0)
        Dts.Variables("DEPOSITDATE").Value = DateTime.MinValue
        Dts.Variables("FILEBYTES").Value = System.Convert.ToInt64(0)
    End Sub
```

Then replace the `Main()` function within the Script Task with this one:

```
C#
        public void Main()
        {
            //'**
            //'SCRIPT
            //'PURPOSE: To take file bytes and save to global variable
            //'============================================================
            Int64 ldefault = 0;
            string sNewFile = string.Empty;
            try
```

```
            {
                //'Reset Variables
                ResetVariables();

                //'Retrieve File Byte Info
                FileInfo oFile = new
FileInfo(Dts.Variables["User::ACHCURRENTFILE"].Value.ToString());
                //'Because XML Source can't be set by expression
                //'Use Current file name and change to fixed
                //'SampleACH.xml
                sNewFile = Dts.Variables["User::ACHBASEFILEPATH"].Value +
                        "\\SampleACH.xml";
                oFile.MoveTo(sNewFile);
                Dts.Variables["User::ACHCURRENTFILE"].Value = sNewFile;
                Dts.Variables["User::FILEBYTES"].Value = oFile.Length;

                //'Dts.Events.FireInformation(0, "Script Task to Vars", _
                //'    "File Bytes Found:" +
                // Dts.Variables("FILEBYTES").Value.ToString(), "", 0, bVal)
                System.Windows.Forms.MessageBox.Show("File Bytes Found:" +
                        Dts.Variables["FILEBYTES"].Value.ToString());
                Dts.TaskResult = (int)ScriptResults.Success;
            }
            catch (Exception ex)
            {
                Dts.Events.FireError(0, "Script Task To Vars",
                    ex.ToString(), "", 0);
                Dts.Variables["FILEBYTES"].Value = ldefault;
                Dts.TaskResult = (int)ScriptResults.Failure;
            }
        }

VB
    Public Sub Main()
        '**
        'SCRIPT
        'PURPOSE: To take file bytes and save to global variable
        '================================================================
        Dim oFile As FileInfo
        Dim lDefault As Int64
        Dim sNewFile As String
        lDefault = 0
        Try
            'Reset Variables
            ResetVariables()

            'Retrieve File Byte Info
            oFile = New
FileInfo(Dts.Variables("User::ACHCURRENTFILE").Value.ToString)
            'Because XML Source can't be set by expression
            'Use Current file name and change to fixed
            'SampleACH.xml
```

```
            sNewFile = Dts.Variables("User::ACHBASEFILEPATH").Value + _
                "\SampleACH.xml"
            oFile.MoveTo(sNewFile)
            Dts.Variables("User::ACHCURRENTFILE").Value = sNewFile
            Dts.Variables("User::FILEBYTES").Value = oFile.Length

            'Dts.Events.FireInformation(0, "Script Task to Vars", _
            ' "File Bytes Found:" + _
            'Dts.Variables("FILEBYTES").Value.ToString(), "", 0, bVal)

            System.Windows.Forms.MessageBox.Show("File Bytes Found:" + _
                Dts.Variables("FILEBYTES").Value.ToString())
            Dts.TaskResult = ScriptResults.Success
        Catch ex As Exception
            Dts.Events.FireError(0, "Script Task To Vars", ex.ToString(), _
                "", 0)
            Dts.Variables("FILEBYTES").Value = lDefault
            Dts.TaskResult = ScriptResults.Failure
        End Try
    End Sub
```

Notice here that the filename sent into the Script Task is used to retrieve the file bytes, but then the file is renamed to a static name SampleACH.xml. The name changing is happening in this code:

```
C#:   oFile.MoveTo(sNewFile);
VB:   oFile.MoveTo(sNewFile)
```

The variable is also updated so that the rest of the process, including the Data Flow XML Source, will continue to operate on the same fixed filename.

To finish out the retrieval Control Flow for now, add a Data Flow Task. Connect the successful completion of the Script Task to this task. Change the Name property to "Data Flow ACH Validate File and Header Info." You'll come back and configure the Data Flow in the previous section, "Bank File Data Flow Validation." Disable the task for now. You should save the entire package and run to make sure everything is working so far.

ACH Control Flow Batch Creation

The last task for the bank-file Control Flow is to lay out the workflow that validates the existence of key values in the Batch file and that the Batch itself has not already been processed. To enable moving the file if there is a problem, add a File System Task named File System Task Error Folder. Instead of choosing a move file operation in the File System Task, select the option to rename the file. The File System Task properties should be set to the values shown in the following table:

Property	Value
IsDestinationPathVariable	True
Destination Variable	User::ACHERRORFILE
OverwriteDestination	True
Name	File System Task Error Folder
Description	Moves bad files to an error folder
Operation	Rename File
IsSourcePathVariable	True
SourceVariable	User::ACHCURRENTFILE

The File System Task here will complain if the value for User::ACHCurrentFile is empty or if it doesn't have a default value, so make sure you set this up initially as described in the earlier set up section.

To connect the Data Flow and File System Task together, add a precedence constraint that looks for the existence of a Bank Batch Id and amount. On the constraint, select the Multiple Constraint option of Logical AND and set the Evaluation Operation to Expression And Constraint. Set the Value to Failure and the Expression to:

```
@BANKBATCHID!=0
```

If the Data Flow fails, or the Data Flow found an existing BankBatchId, the precedence constraint will send the workflow to the File System Task that will archive the file in the error folder.

Now if the elements are all present, and there is no existing bank batch by batch number, the batch needs to be persisted to the database. To do this add an Execute SQL Task. This task will use a stored procedure, usp_BankBatch_Add, to add the parsed information in the Lockbox file as a row in the BankBatch table to represent a new batch file. The procedure usp_BankBatch_Add will return the new BankBatchId if it could be successfully added. This time we'll use an ADO.NET Connection Manager to see the difference between using the OLE DB Connection Manager; set Execute SQL Task properties up like this:

Property	Value
Name	Execute SQL task to add Bank Batch Hdr
ConnectionType	ADO.NET
Connection	CaseStudy.ADO.NET
SQLStatement	`EXEC usp_BankBatch_Add @BankBatchID OUTPUT, @BankBatchNbr, @DepositDate, @ReceivedDate, @BatchTotal, @BatchItems, @FileBytes, @FullFilePath, @ImportType`
IsQueryStoredProcedure	False

Because you are using an ADO.NET provider now, you'll notice that the parameter data types more closely match the types of the variables. The finished Execute SQL Task Editor parameter mappings should look like Figure 23-25.

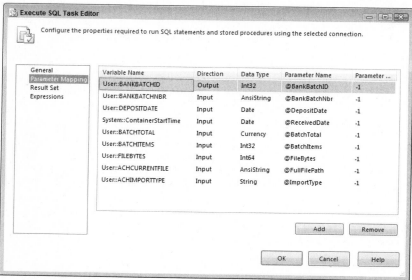

Figure 23-25

If the Execute SQL Task finds an existing BankBatchID or fails, you also need to move the file into an error folder. Connect the Execute SQL Task to the File System Error Folder Task failure precedence and constraint conditions — except change the expression to apply when the BankBatchID does not equal zero (0) OR if the Data Flow Task fails. Set the Evaluation Operation to Expression OR Constraint. Set the Value to Failure and the Expression to @BANKBATCHID == 0. Select the Multiple Constraint property to the option of Logical OR.

Add a second new Data Flow Task to the Foreach Loop. Change the name property to Data Flow ACH Detail Data Load. You'll come back later to configure the Data Flow in the next section. Connect the successful completion of the Execute SQL Task to this task. Add an expression to check for a nonzero BankBatchID, and set the constraint to successful completion between the Execute SQL Task and this new Data Flow Task.

If the Data Flow Lockbox Detail Data Load fails to extract, transform, and load the batch details, you've still got an issue. Add a simple Failure constraint between the Data Flow Lockbox Detail Data Load and the previously created File System Task Error Folder. (You could also use the Event Handler control surfaces to create actions or workflows to occur upon failures.)

If the file is processed successfully in the Data Flow Lockbox Detail Data Load, you need to move it to the "processed" folder. Add another new File System Task and connect it to the successful completion of the second Data Flow Task. Set up this task just like the Error Folder File System Task but point everything to the processed folder.

Property	Value
IsDestinationPathVariable	True
Destination Variable	User::ACHPROCESSEDFILE
OverwriteDestination	True
Name	File System Task Processed Folder
Description	Moves completed files to an error folder
Operation	Rename File
IsSourcePathVariable	True
SourceVariable	User::ACHCURRENTFILE

You now have the basic structure set up for the ACH File Lockbox Control Flow. You still need to go back and build your transforms in the Data Flow Tasks. You'll get to that in the next sections. If you are following along, go ahead and save the package at this point. If you want to test the package, you can set up the variables and test the different workflows. Just remember to watch the movement of the sample file into the processed and error folders and make sure you put it back after each run. The CaseStudy_Load_ACH package at this point should look like Figure 23-26.

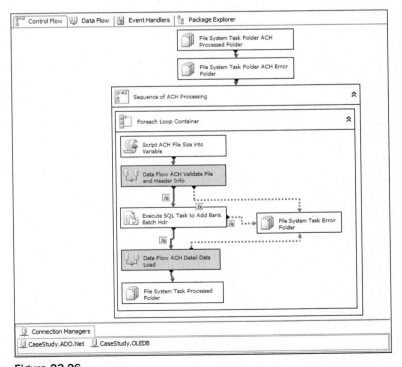

Figure 23-26

To test the progress so far, disable the Execute SQL Task so that a batch row won't be created. Disable the Lockbox Sequence Container, so it won't be run. Save, and then execute the package to ensure that everything so far is set up properly.

ACH Data Flow Validation

In this section of the package, you are going to fill in the details for the ACH Data Flow Container. The strategy will be to open up the ACH file, retrieve information from the header, and pass the information back to the Control Flow via variables. You'll use an XML Data Source combined with an XSD file that you'll create and edit to read the file. Because the data is structured and hierarchical, you don't have the parsing tasks that are associated with flat files. However, you can still have bad data in the structure, so you'll have to validate the file. You'll use a lookup on the header to look for matches by batch number, and a Script Component will pull this information from the transformation stream and send it back into your Control Flow for evaluation and further processing.

ACH Data Flow Parsing and Error Handling

Start by enabling the ACH Validate File and Header Info Data Flow. Click the task to enter the Data Flow. Add an XML Source to the Data Flow. In the XML Source Editor, set the XML Location to the fixed name of the sample ACH file `SampleAch.xml` in the `c:\casestudy\ach\` directory. You should immediately see the message shown in Figure 23-27. This message is acknowledging that an XML formatted file has been selected, but the task needs schema information from the XSD file to set up data types and sizes. Because you don't have an XSD file, you'll use a utility provided with this component to generate one.

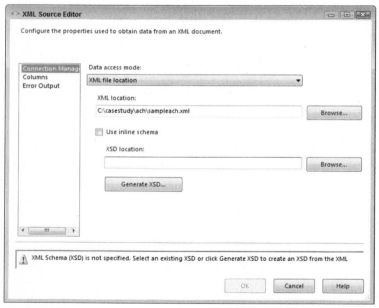

Figure 23-27

Provide the XML source with a path to build the XSD as `c:\casestudy\ach\ach.xsd`. Then click the Generate XSD button to create the file. Unfortunately, the XSD generator is not perfect, so if you use this tool, you'll need to manually validate the XSD file. Here's where error-handling strategy and design come into play. You can set up the XSD with all text fields, and the file will always parse successfully. However, you will have to type-check all the fields yourself. If you strongly type your XSD as we are recommending here, the task could fail, and you won't get a chance to make any programmatic decisions. Another thing to note is that the automatically generated XSD is based on the available data in the XML file, so in the case of your header, which has only one row, it doesn't have much data to review to pick data types. That's why the XSD type designation for the BATCHITEMS variable is incorrect. Open up the XSD in Notepad and change the XSD type designation from xs:UnsignedByte to xs:UnsignedInt. Now you match the data type of your global BATCHITEMS variable.

In the XML Source Component, go to the Error Output tab. For both header and detail output and for every column and every error type, set the action to Redirect Row. Because you are dealing with an ACH file, the effect of truncating numbers and dates is a big deal. If you have a truncation or date issue, you want the file to fail, and redirecting the output will allow you to record what went wrong and then end the current Data Flow Task that exists solely to validate the incoming file.

In the same way as the lockbox, if you do get row errors, you would like to gather as much information about the error to assist in the troubleshooting process. The XML Source has two error outputs, Header and Detail, so you'll have twice as much work to do. Create two Script Component Tasks as transformations like you did to capture errors in the Lockbox Data Flow for each of the error outputs from the XML Source. Select the ErrorCode and ErrorColumn columns from the input. Create a new Output Column named ErrorDesc of type Unicode string [DT_WSTR] and size 1048. Open up the design environment for the Script Component. Change your ProcessInputRow event code to the following:

```csharp
C#
    public override void Input0_ProcessInputRow(Input0Buffer Row)
    {
        //'Script
        //'Purpose: To retrieve the error description to write to error log
        Row.ErrorDesc = ComponentMetaData.GetErrorDescription(Row.ErrorCode);
    }
```

```vb
VB
    Public Overrides Sub Input0_ProcessInputRow(ByVal Row As Input0Buffer)
        'SCRIPT
        'PURPOSE: To retrieve the error description to write to error log
        '==================================================================
        Row.ErrorDesc= ComponentMetaData.GetErrorDescription(Row.ErrorCode)
    End Sub
```

Add two Derived Column Transforms with the following derived columns. Connect them to the output of the two Script Component Transformations.

Derived Column	Expression	DataType
ExecutionID	@[System::ExecutionInstanceGUID]	DT_WSTR 38
ErrorEvent	"ACH"	DT_WSTR 20
ErrorDate	@[System::ContainerStartTime]	DT_DATE

For the Detail output only, add the following derived column:

RawData	(DT_STR, 1028, 1252) ErrorDesc	DT_STR 1048

Now add two OLE DB Destination Components and connect them to the output of the Derived Columns mapping the fields to the table ErrorDetail, exactly as you did for the Lockbox Data Flow. Map the converted [rawdata] field to the [rawdata] field for the detail output. Map the ID field of the header output to the output [rawdata] field. The error handling of the bad XML file should look like Figure 23-28.

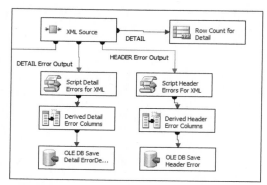

Figure 23-28

ACH Data Flow Validation

If the XML data is good, you want to perform a lookup on the batch number. If you recall, the Lookup Transform is case-sensitive, but unlike the flat file where you could convert the whole line to uppercase, here you'll have to convert each field of importance. Add a Character Map Transform Task and convert the Header output ID field (a batch number) to uppercase as an in-place change.

You also need a value in your stream to allow a lookup on import type. Batch numbers are only guaranteed to be unique by this type, and it is stored in the global variables. Add a Derived Column Transform to add a column ImportType to your output stream. Because the [ImportType] field in the BankBatch table is of type CHAR(10), add the derived column as a type string [DT_STR] of size 10. Also add a casting transform to specifically cast the ID column in place to a Unicode [DT_WSTR] string of size 50.

Now you should be ready to add the Lookup Transform to the Data Flow. Set the OLE DB Connection to CaseStudy.OLEDB. This time you'll set the Lookup to the results of the following query instead of the table directly. Using only what you need is generally more efficient depending upon the table size and index structures. The SQL statement should look like this:

```
SELECT BANKBATCHID, UPPER(BANKBATCHNBR) AS BANKBATCHNBR, UPPER(IMPORTTYPE) AS
IMPORTTYPE
FROM BANKBATCH
ORDER BY BANKBATCHNBR
```

In the Columns tab, link the Input Column ID to the Lookup column of BankBatchNbr. Link the ImportType columns. Add BankBatchID as the Lookup column with an output alias of BANKBATCHID. Because you are expecting that you will not get a match on the lookup and that this is indeed a new file, use the Configure Error output button and set the Lookup step to Ignore Failure on the Lookup Output.

Add a Script Component Task as a destination to capture the successful end of your transformation Data Flow. Connect it to the Lookup output. Open the editor and select all the available input columns. Add the following global variables as ReadWriteVariables: BANKBATCHNBR, BANKBATCHID, BATCHTOTAL, BATCHITEMS, DEPOSITDATE. Insert the following code to store the variables:

```csharp
C#
public class ScriptMain : UserComponent
{
    public int LocalBankBatchId = 0;
    public double LocalBatchTotal = 0;
    public string LocalBatchNbr = string.Empty;
    public DateTime LocalDepositDate = DateTime.MinValue;

    public override void PreExecute()
    {
        base.PreExecute();
    }

    public override void PostExecute()
    {
        bool bVal = false;
        //'SCRIPT
        //'PURPOSE: To set SSIS variables with values retrieved earlier
        //'=========================================================
        try
        {
            //'Attempt to accept the values
            Variables.BANKBATCHID = LocalBankBatchId;
            Variables.BANKBATCHNBR = LocalBatchNbr;
            Variables.DEPOSITDATE = LocalDepositDate;
            Variables.BATCHTOTAL = LocalBatchTotal;
        }
        catch (Exception ex)
        {
            //'If any failure occurs fail the file
            Variables.BANKBATCHID = 0;
            Variables.BATCHTOTAL = 0;
            ComponentMetaData.FireError(0, "", ex.Message, "", 1, out bVal);
        }
        base.PostExecute();
    }

    public override void Input0_ProcessInputRow(Input0Buffer Row)
    {
        //'SCRIPT
        //'Purpose: Pull Information from Header row and set variables
        bool bVal = false;
```

```
                  string Msg = string.Empty;
                  try
                  {
                      //'If there is no header metadata then mark for failure
                      if(Row.DEPOSITDATE_IsNull ||
                          Row.TOTALDEPOSIT_IsNull ||
                          System.Convert.ToDouble(Row.TOTALDEPOSIT) == 0D)
                      {
                          LocalBankBatchId = 0;
                          LocalBatchTotal = Convert.ToDouble(0D);
                      }
                      else
                      {
                          //'Retrieve the data from the stream
                          if (Row.BankBatchID_IsNull)
                          {
                              LocalBankBatchId = 0;
                          }
                          else
                          {
                              LocalBankBatchId = Row.BankBatchID;
                          }
                          LocalBatchNbr = Row.ID;
                          LocalDepositDate = Convert.ToDateTime(Row.DEPOSITDATE);
                          LocalBatchTotal = Convert.ToDouble(Row.TOTALDEPOSIT);
                      }
                      Msg = String.Format("Variables: BankBatchId={0}, " +
                          "BatchTotal={1}, BatchNbr=[{2}]", LocalBankBatchId,
                          LocalBatchTotal, LocalBatchNbr);
                      ComponentMetaData.FireInformation(0, ComponentMetaData.Name,
                          Msg, "", 0, ref bVal);
                  }
                  catch(Exception ex)
                  {
                      ComponentMetaData.FireError((int)0, ComponentMetaData.Name,
                          ex.Message.ToString(), "", 1, out bVal);
                  }
              }

VB
Public Class ScriptMain
    Inherits UserComponent
    Public LocalBankBatchId As Integer = 0
    Public LocalBatchTotal As Double = 0
    Public LocalBatchNbr As String = ""
    Public LocalDepositDate As Date = Date.MinValue

    Public Overrides Sub PreExecute()
        MyBase.PreExecute()
    End Sub

    Public Overrides Sub PostExecute()
        Dim bVal As Boolean
```

```vb
        MyBase.PostExecute()
        'SCRIPT
        'PURPOSE: To set SSIS variables with values retrieved earlier
        '==============================================================
        Try
            'Attempt to accept the values
            Variables.BANKBATCHID = LocalBankBatchId
            Variables.BANKBATCHNBR = LocalBatchNbr
            Variables.DEPOSITDATE = LocalDepositDate
            Variables.BATCHTOTAL = LocalBatchTotal
        Catch ex As Exception
            'If any failure occurs fail the file
            Variables.BANKBATCHID = 0
            Variables.BATCHTOTAL = 0
            ComponentMetaData.FireError(0, "", ex.Message, "", 1, bVal)
        End Try

    End Sub

    Public Overrides Sub Input0_ProcessInputRow(ByVal Row As Input0Buffer)
        'SCRIPT
        'Purpose: Pull Information from Header row and set variables
        Dim bVal As Boolean
        Dim Msg As String
        Try
            'If there is no header metadata then mark for failure
            If Row.DEPOSITDATE_IsNull = True Or _
                Row.TOTALDEPOSIT_IsNull = True Or _
                    System.Convert.ToDecimal(Row.TOTALDEPOSIT) = 0D Then
                LocalBankBatchId = 0
                LocalBatchTotal = 0D
            Else
                'Retrieve the data from the stream
                If Row.BankBatchID_IsNull Then
                    LocalBankBatchId = 0
                Else
                    LocalBankBatchId = Row.BankBatchID
                End If
                LocalBatchNbr = Row.ID
                LocalDepositDate = Row.DEPOSITDATE
                LocalBatchTotal = Row.TOTALDEPOSIT
            End If
            Msg = String.Format("Variables: BankBatchId={0}, " + _
                    " BatchTotal={1}, BatchNbr=[{2}]", LocalBankBatchId, _
                    LocalBatchTotal, LocalBatchNbr)
            ComponentMetaData.FireInformation(0, ComponentMetaData.Name, _
                    Msg, "", 0, bVal)
        Catch ex As Exception
            ComponentMetaData.FireError(0, ComponentMetaData.Name, _
                    ex.Message, "", 1, bVal)
        End Try
    End Sub
End Class
```

The ACH Validation Data Flow is now almost complete; you only have one more minor task.

ACH Data Flow Capturing Total Batch Items

The last variable that you need to retrieve is the number of transactions in the ACH file details. The XML Source automatically splits the file stream into its multiple parts. In this case the stream is split into header and detail lines. At this point you are really only interested in the check lines in the file. Instead of running an aggregate and pushing the stream into a Script Component like you did in the Lockbox package, use one of the new Row Count Data Flow Components. This component allows you to set a variable directly from an aggregate count. The configured Row Count Transform should look like Figure 23-29.

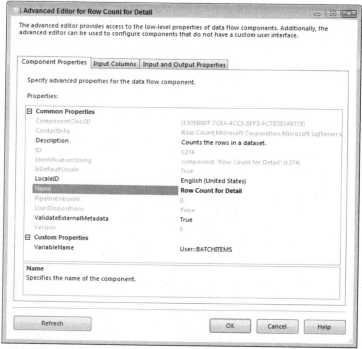

Figure 23-29

That was easier than putting the Script Component in to capture the Count(*), now wasn't it? This component is one of the latest additions to SSIS.

At this point, the Data Flow for validation purposes is complete. The final Data Flow should look like Figure 23-30. If you've still got the Lockbox Sequence Container disabled, then go ahead and run the package. Once you get it working properly, archive a copy, because you've got another Data Flow to build to import the ACH XML file. Play around with the XML file by adding bad data and malforming the structure of the file to see how the Data Flow handles it.

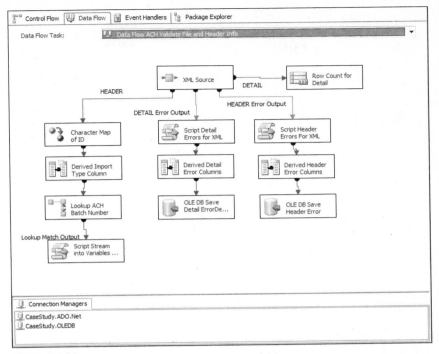

Figure 23-30

ACH Data Flow Detail Processing ETL

This section in a lot of ways mirrors the Data Flow for Lockbox Processing. Once you've validated the ACH XML file, the Control Flow will create a [BankBatch] row and start the process of importing the detail. You have all the header-related information, just as you did for the Lockbox process, and because the file has been validated, you can simply transform the data into the [BankBatchDetail] table.

Processing the ACH File

Enable the Data Flow Task named Data Flow "ACH Detail Data Load" and drill down into its design surface. Add an XML Source and set it up exactly the same as you did for the Validation Data Flow. However, this time you already have an XSD file, so just point the component to it. Leave the ErrorOutput settings to "Fail component if an error is encountered while processing the file." You'll also leave the error-handling components out in this Data Flow, although in production you should add them back in.

> *If you ran the package to test the ACH Validation section, you'll need to move the* SampleACH.XML *file back into the directory* c:\casestudy\ach\.

This time, you are concerned mainly with the detail portion of the XML data. You have the foreign key information stored in a variable, so you don't need to perform any lookups on data, but you will want to use the Lookup later on the DESC field that you are going to import to the RawInvoiceNbr field in the

CaseStudy_Processing package. Add a Character Map Transform to convert the DESC field to uppercase and replace its current value in the stream.

The only other thing you need is that foreign key stored in the variable @BANKBATCHID. Add a Derived Column Transform to add that variable to the current stream. Add another column named RAWINVOICENBR and select the [DESC] field from the Columns input collection as a string [DT_WSTR] type of length 50. This selection of string type has the result of conversion in one step.

Add an OLE DB Destination and connect to the CaseStudy.OLEDB connection. Select the [BankBatchDetail] table and map the columns in the following table:

Input Column	Destination Column
BankBatchID	BankBatchID
Amount	PaymentAmount
RawInvoiceNbr	RawInvoiceNbr

Saving the ACH File Snapshot in the Database

The final thing you need to do is save the entire XML file in the [BankBatch] table. You'll use exactly the same technique from the Lockbox process. Add a Derived Column Transform and connect to the Header output of the XML file. Add columns for the variables BANKBATCHID and ACHCURRENTFILE. Make sure the ACHCURRENTFILE column is set to [DT_WSTR] 100. Refer back to the "Bank File Data Flow Validation" section to see an example of this transform.

Add an Import Column Transform and connect to this Header Derived Column Transform. On the Input Columns tab, select the field that contains the file path in the stream: ACHCURRENTFILE. Then go to the Advanced Input Output property tab and expand the Input Column Input and Import Column Output Nodes. Add an output column to the output columns Node named FileStreamToStore. Set the DataType property to [DT_NTEXT]. The editor should look similar to Figure 23-31, but the LineageIDs may be different. Note the LineageID, and set the property named FileDataColumnID in the ACHCurrentFile Input Column to that LineageID.

Add an OLE DB Destination to the output of the Header Derived Column Transform. Set the OLE DB Connection to CaseStudy.OLEDB. Then set the SQL Command to Update BankBatch Set BatchFile = ? WHERE BANKBATCHID = ? and click Refresh. In the Mappings tab, connect the FileStreamToStore to the Destination Column Param_0, which is the [BatchFile] field in the BankBatch table. Connect the field BankBatchID to the Destination Column Param_1. Click Refresh and save.

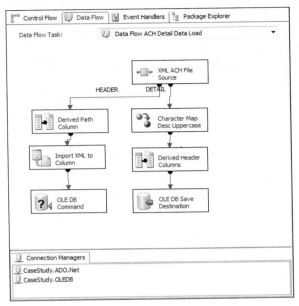

Figure 23-31

The final Data Flow for ACH processing should look similar to Figure 23-31. After you've gotten a successful run of this Data Flow, archive the package.

Email Load Package

The email payment processing is interesting. The payment transactions are stored in a relational database, so you don't have data issues. You just need to check to see if there are any to process. You also have to make sure that you haven't picked the transaction up before. In this case, you don't have a Batch, because the information is transactional, so a batch will be the set of transactions available when the package runs. To avoid picking up duplicates, you'll store the transactional primary key from the accounting system into the batch detail records as your [ReferenceData1] field. You can then use this field in your extraction to keep from pulling a transaction more than once. Again, you can also walk through and create this Email load package or download the complete solution from www.wrox.com to see and explore the final result.

Email Package Setup and File System Tasks

To get started, you need to create a new SSIS package named CaseStudy_Load_Email in c:\casestudy\ casestudy_load_Email\. When the project is built, go to the Solution Explorer and click the Package .dtsx file. In the Property window, find the Name property and change the name from package.dtsx to casestudy_load_Email.dtsx. Answer Yes to change the name of the package object as well.

Use the menu SSIS ⇨ Variables to access the Variables editor and add the variables as shown in the following table:

Variable Name	Scope	Data Type	Value
BANKBATCHID	CaseStudy_Loa..	Int32	0
BANKBATCHNBR	CaseStudy_Loa..	String	
BATCHITEMS	CaseStudy_Loa..	Int32	0
BATCHTOTAL	CaseStudy_Loa..	Double	0
DEPOSITDATE	CaseStudy_Loa..	DateTime	12/30/1899
EMAILMPORTTYPE	CaseStudy_Loa..	String	EMAIL
FILEBYTES	CaseStudy_Loa..	Int64	0

Add an OLE DB Connection to the Connection Manager that connects to the CaseStudy database. Name the connection CaseStudy.OLEDB. Create an ADO.NET Connection in the Connection Manager as well that connects to the CaseStudy database. Having connections of both types is not necessary for typical package development, but both provide opportunities to demonstrate the differences in using one or the other.

Email Control Flow Processing

Unlike the previous packages, the Email processing is a one-time interrogation of an external datastore, so there will be no looping involved. There is also no need to examine a file structure to validate data elements. This package is much easier. One interesting technique to point out in this example is the use of casting in SQL Server to be able to retrieve a monetary amount back into an SSIS `Double` variable type structure. The `Double` data type is the closest thing to a monetary variable type in SSIS.

Add a Sequence Container to the Control Flow surface named Sequence of Email Payment Processing. Then add a new Script Task named "Script to Reset Variables Task" to the Email Payment Processing Sequence Container. This task may be familiar to you as it is the same as in previous packages. Feed into the task all the variables, except the `EmailImportType`. The code will be real simple:

```csharp
C#
    Public void Main()
    {
        Dts.Variables["BANKBATCHID"].Value = System.Convert.ToInt32(0);
        Dts.Variables["BANKBATCHNBR"].Value = String.Empty;
        Dts.Variables["BATCHITEMS"].Value = System.Convert.ToInt32(0);
        Dts.Variables["BATCHTOTAL"].Value = System.Convert.ToDouble(0);
        Dts.Variables["DEPOSITDATE"].Value = DateTime.MinValue;
        Dts.Variables["FILEBYTES"].Value = System.Convert.ToInt64(0);
        Dts.TaskResult = (int)ScriptResults.Success
    }
```

```VB
VB
Public Sub Main()
    Dts.Variables("BANKBATCHID").Value = System.Convert.ToInt32(0)
    Dts.Variables("BANKBATCHNBR").Value = String.Empty
    Dts.Variables("BATCHITEMS").Value = System.Convert.ToInt32(0)
    Dts.Variables("BATCHTOTAL").Value = System.Convert.ToDouble(0)
    Dts.Variables("DEPOSITDATE").Value = DateTime.MinValue
    Dts.Variables("FILEBYTES").Value = System.Convert.ToInt64(0)
    Dts.TaskResult = ScriptResults.Success
End Sub
```

The next task is to add an Execute SQL Task named Execute SQL to Check For Trans. This task will count the number of transactions and the total amount in the accounting system not yet processed. The task will set the variables BATCHITEMS and BATCHTOTAL equal to the number and total amounts of available transactions to work. Set up the properties using the following table:

Property	Setting
ResultSet	SingleRow
ConnectionType	OLE DB
Connection	CaseStudy.OLEDB
SQLSourceType	Direct Input
SQLStatement	SELECT TranCnt, Convert(float, TotAmt) AS TotAmt FROM (SELECT count(*) as TranCnt, isnull(Sum(DepositAmount), 0) As TotAmt FROM vCorpDirectAcctTrans Corp LEFT OUTER JOIN BANKBATCHDETAIL DTL ON cast(CORP.TRANSID as varchar(50)) = DTL.REFERENCEDATA1 WHERE DTL.REFERENCEDATA1 is null) SUBQRY
ResultSet:ResultName	0
ResultSet:Variable	User::BATCHITEMS
ResultSet:ResultName	1
ResultSet:Variable	User::BATCHTOTAL

Remember from the Bank Batch file example that you have to use ordinal positions to capture results when using the OLE DB Connection. In this case, you are capturing two results. The issue that is hidden here is that SSIS only has a Double variable data type. The DepositAmount field in the BankBatch table is a SQL Server money data type. When the TSQL returns the money amount it will not bind to the SSIS Double variable, and you'll get an error that looks like this:

```
Error: 0xc232F309 at Execute SQL to check for Trans, Execute SQL Task: An
error occurred while assigning a value to variable "BATCHTOTAL": "The type of
the value being assigned to variable "User::BATCHTOTAL" differs from the
current variable type. Variables may not change type during execution.
Variable types are strict, except for variables of type Object.
```

Because the variable data types can't be altered, you have to convert the money amount into the equivalent of a double in SQL Server. In this example, the conversion to float allows the mapping to occur. Connect the Script Task to this Execute SQL Task.

Now add a new Execute SQL Task into the Sequence Container. (A tip that can save time is to copy an existing task.) Name this new Execute SQL Task "Add Email Bank Batch Hdr." This task will create the batch header for your email-based transactions using a stored procedure usp_BankBatch_Add. Set up the parameters to look like Figure 23-32.

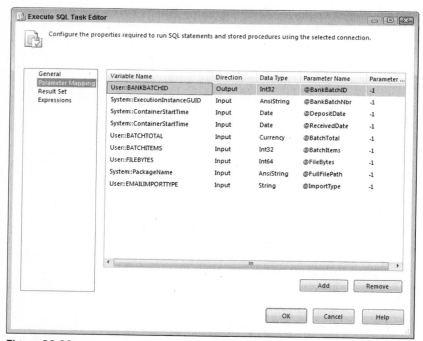

Figure 23-32

Notice here that we don't really have a unique identifier in the accounting system for the batch of transactions we are pulling, so we are using the Execution Instance GUID that is unique for every run of the package. An alternative here would be to create a variable built by an expression that resolves to a date-based attribute or a combination of date and transactional attributes, like the batch total.

Add a conditional constraint in combination with an expression between the both SQL Execute Tasks that won't allow the second SQL Task to be executed if there are no transaction items to be worked as email payments. The expression should be set to:

```
@BATCHITEMS>0
```

The last step is to add the Data Flow Task and connect it to the Execute SQL Batch Task. At the moment, the Email Control Flow Tasks should resemble Figure 23-33. Continue on to the next section before testing this Control Flow.

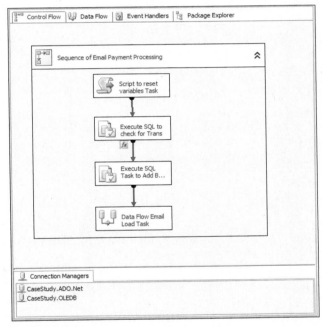

Figure 23-33

You should save the package at this point before proceeding to flesh out the Data Flow Task.

Email Data Flow Processing

If the package initiates the Email Data Flow, there must be some email-based accounting transactions in the accounting database, and the Execute SQL Task will have already created a new row with a BankBatchID from the BankBatch table for you that is stored in the BANKBATCHID variable. All you have to do is extract the data from the accounting view, add the foreign key to the data, and insert the rows into the [BankBatchDetail] table.

Start by drilling into the Data Flow Email Load Task design surface. Add an OLE DB Source to the Data Flow. Connect to the CaseStudy.OLE.DB connection and set the data access mode to "Table or view." Set the name of the table or view to the view vCorpDirectAcctTrans.

You also need to add that BankBatchID foreign key to your stream, so add a Derived Column Transform to add the BANKBATCHID variable to the stream. Connect the OLE DB Source and the Derived Column Transforms.

Look at a sample of the TransDesc data that is being brought over in Figure 23-34. To get this to match the email addresses in the Customer table, it would be better to strip off the PAYPAL* identifier. Because the BankBatchDetail file expects a nvarchar field of 50 characters, and you also need to be consistent with case-sensitivity, convert the type and case at the same time by adding an additional column named RawInvoiceNbr as a string [DT_WSTR] of 50 characters, and set the expression to the following:

```
(DT_WSTR, 50)TRIM(UPPER(REPLACE(REPLACE(TransDesc,"PAYPAL",""),"*","")))
```

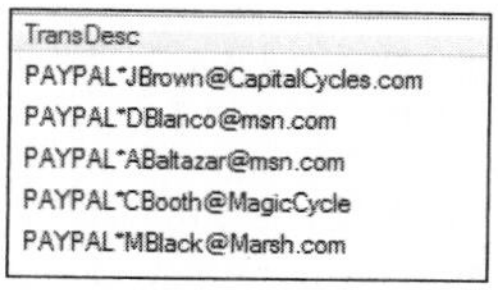

TransDesc
PAYPAL*JBrown@CapitalCycles.com
PAYPAL*DBlanco@msn.com
PAYPAL*ABaltazar@msn.com
PAYPAL*CBooth@MagicCycle
PAYPAL*MBlack@Marsh.com

Figure 23-34

Add two more columns to the Derived Column Transform to also convert the TransID and TransDesc fields to an ANSI string value. Name the columns TransIDtoString and TransDescToString. Set the Data Types to [DT_WSTR] with lengths of 50. The expressions should look like this:

```
(DT_WSTR, 50)[TransDesc]
(DT_WSTR, 50)[TransID]
```

Add an OLE DB Destination Task and connect it to the output of the Derived Column Task. Set the connection to the CaseStudy.OLEDB connection. Set the table to [BankBatchDetail]. Map the fields in the Mapping tab to those shown in the following table:

Input Field	Destination in [BankBatchDetail]
DepositAmount	PaymentAmount
<ignore>	ReferenceData2
BankBatchID	BankBatchID
RawInvoiceNbr	RawInvoiceNbr
TransIDtoString	ReferenceData1
TransDesctoString	ReferenceData2

This completes the construction of the Data Flow for the Email Load Task. The Email Load Data Flow should look like Figure 23-35.

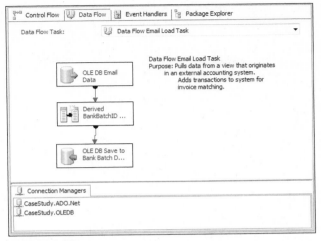

Figure 23-35

At this point all three of the payment processing packages are complete. Later we'll put all the packages together, but for now, each one can be run individually to see how the bank batch file, the XML ACH file, and the email data files are loaded into the BankBatch and BankBatchDetail tables. After testing thoroughly, and loading all the payment data, you'll be ready to go to the next section, which will use an advance Data Flow to perform much of the matching of payment information to invoices.

Testing

Test the packages by disabling all the Sequence Containers and even the Data Flow Tasks. Work your way through each of the tasks, enabling them as you go. Use this SQL script to delete rows that you may be adding to the database during repeated testing that may change the flow of logic in the Control Flow sections:

```
DELETE FROM BANKBATCHDETAIL
GO
DELETE FROM BANKBATCH
```

Case Study Invoice Matching Process

Each of the three load packages puts the data into the database. The Invoice Matching package is going to perform the magic. All this payment data from different sources with varying degrees of quality needs to be matched by invoice or customer attributes against your dimension tables of Invoice and Customer. Having it combined in one place allows this package to apply the logic of payment matching to all payments at once. If you do this right, every time the package runs, it is money in the bank for Company ABC.

The strategy for this package is to mimic the logic provided from the business specifications in Figure 23-4. You will queue all the payment transactions that are unmatched for a moment in time. Then you will run that stream of payments through a gauntlet of matching options until you break through your confidence level for matching. This design will make it easy to add further matching scenarios in the future, and will allow you to use the advanced fuzzy matching logic available today in the Integration Services.

You'll be breaking the construction of the package into these sections: Package Setup, High-Confidence Data Flow, and Medium-Confidence Data Flow.

Matching Process Control Flow

This portion of the Case Study will create the Control Flow steps that are needed to systematically review pending and unmatched payment transactions. You will set up the variables needed to store unmatched payment counts at each stage of the matching process. You will create placeholder Data Flow Tasks that will perform the matching, and then you'll send out an email to report on the statistics for the matching operations.

Matching Process Package Setup

To get started, you need to create a new SSIS package named CaseStudy_Process in `c:\casestudy\ casestudy_process\`. When the project is built, go to the Solution Explorer and click the `Package .dtsx` file. In the Property window, find the Name property and change the name from `package.dtsx` to `casestudy_process.dtsx`. Answer Yes to change the name of the package object as well.

Use the menu SSIS ⇨ Variables to access the Variables editor and add the variables as shown in the following table:

Variable Name	Scope	Data Type	Value
HIGHCONFMATCHCNTSTART	CaseStudy_Process	Int32	0
HIGHCONFMATCHCNTEND	CaseStudy_Process	Int32	0
MEDCONFMATCHCNTEND	CaseStudy_Process	Int32	0
HIGHCONFMATCHAMTSTART	CaseStudy_Process	Double	0
HIGHCONFMATCHAMTEND	CaseStudy_Process	Double	0
MEDCONFMATCHAMTEND	CaseStudy_Process	Double	0
EMAILMSG	CaseStudy_Process	String	

Add an OLE DB Connection to the Connection Manager that connects to the CaseStudy database. Name the connection CaseStudy.OLEDB.

Add an SMTP Connection to the Connection Manager that connects to a viable SMTP mail server. Name the connection Mail Server. In the SMTP Connection, provide your available SMTP server address.

The EMAILMSG variable needs to get its value from an expression. Set the variable property EvaluateAsExpression to true and then create this monster expression for the email body:

```
"COMPANY ABC\nAutomated Payment Matching Results: \n" +
"Job started with " + (DT_WSTR, 25) @HIGHCONFMATCHCNTSTART  + " payments for "
+ (DT_WSTR, 50)@HIGHCONFMATCHAMTSTART +
"\nWe received and successfully processed " +  (DT_WSTR, 25)
(@HIGHCONFMATCHCNTSTART-@HIGHCONFMATCHCNTEND) +
" payments for " + (DT_WSTR, 50) (@HIGHCONFMATCHAMTSTART-@HIGHCONFMATCHAMTEND)
+ " automatically with a High-Level of confidence." +
"\nWe processed " + (DT_WSTR, 25) (@HIGHCONFMATCHCNTEND-@MEDCONFMATCHCNTEND) +
" payments for " + (DT_WSTR, 25) (@HIGHCONFMATCHAMTEND-@MEDCONFMATCHAMTEND) +
" with a Medium-Level of confidence." +
"\n\nDo not respond to this email. This is an automated message."
```

This expression looks unwieldy, but the resulting message that the package will email will look like this:

```
COMPANY ABC
Automated Payment Matching Results:
Job started with 0 payments for 0
We received and successfully processed 0 payments for 0 automatically with a
High-Level of confidence.
We processed 0 payments for 0 with a Medium-Level of confidence.

Do not respond to this email. This is an automated message.
```

Notice in this example that the formatting escape sequence \n is used to generate a carriage return line feed, instead of the traditional way VB programmers use to concatenate the constant vbcrlf or the TSQL method of concatenating CHAR(13) + CHAR(10). The \n is just one of the many formatting escape sequences that you may want to use in expressions like this. Go back and review these in detail in Chapter 6.

Add the Matching Process Logic

The matching process logic contains three Execute SQL Tasks that will take snapshots of the total amounts and counts of available payment information to match in between two matching workflows, encapsulated in two Data Flow Containers. A final Execute SQL Task will update all batches for balances to complete the Control Flow. What you'll do to speed up the development of this Control Flow is build out the first Execute SQL Task, and then copy and paste with a few changes to make the others.

To start, add an Execute SQL Task to the Control Flow. This task needs to query the database for the pending payments and record the total number and dollar amount prior to starting the High Confidence Data Flow Task. Name the task "Execute SQL Get High Conf Stats." Connect to the OLE DB Connection. Set up two result columns like this to retrieve first an amount value into the variable and then a count that represents the unmatched payment transactions at this point.

Property	Setting
ResultSet	SingleRow
ConnectionType	OLE DB
Connection	CaseStudy.OLEDB
SQLSourceType	Direct Input
SQLStatement	SELECT convert(float, sum(paymentamount)) as TotAmt, count(*) as TotCnt FROM bankbatchdetail d INNER JOIN BANKBATCH h ON h.bankbatchid = d.bankbatchid WHERE matcheddate is null AND RawInvoiceNbr is not null AND RawInvoiceNbr <> '
ResultSet:ResultName	0
ResultSet:Variable	User:: HIGHCONFMATCHAMTSTART
ResultSet:ResultName	1
ResultSet:Variable	User:: HIGHCONFMATCHCNTSTART

Add a Data Flow Task to the Control Flow. Name the task "High Confidence Data Flow Process Task Start." Connect the Data Flow to the earlier Execute SQL Task. You'll see this task in the "Matching Process High-Confidence Data Flow" section.

Add another Execute SQL Task by copying the first Execute SQL Task "Execute SQL Get High Conf Stats." Name the task "High Confidence Data Flow Process Task End." Connect the tasks. Just change the variable mappings in the result column to HIGHCONFMATCHAMTEND and HIGHCONFMATCHCNTEND.

Add another Data Flow Task to the Control Flow. Name the task "Medium Confidence Data Flow Process Task." Connect the task to the Execute SQL Task. You'll see this task in the "Matching Process Medium-Confidence Data Flow" section.

Add another Execute SQL Task by copying the "Execute SQL Get High Conf Stats" SQL Task. Name the task "Medium Confidence Data Flow Process Task End." Connect the tasks. Change the variable mappings in the result column to MEDCONFMATCHAMTEND and MEDCONFMATCHCNTEND.

Add a new Execute SQL Task from the Toolbox. Name the task "Execute SQL to Balance by Batch." Set the OLE DB Connection. Set the SQLStatement property simply to EXEC usp_BankBatch_Balance. This procedure will update and balance batch level totals based on the payments that are processed. Neither parameter mappings nor result mappings are required.

Finally, add a Send Mail Task. Set it up to connect to the Mail Server SMTP Connection. Fill in the To, From, and Subject properties. (If you don't have access to an SMTP Connection, disable this task for testing.) Then set up the expressions to use the variable @EMAILMSG.

The completed Control Flow should look similar to Figure 23-36.

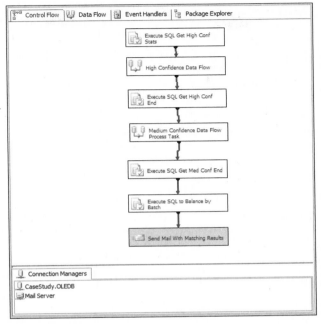

Figure 23-36

With the Control Flow of the Matching Process Case Study package all ready, you'll proceed to filling out the logic in the two Data Flow Containers you added.

Matching Process High-Confidence Data Flow

Your first level of matching should be on the data attributes that are most likely to produce the highest-quality lookup against the target Invoice table. The attribute that would provide the highest-quality lookup and confidence level when matching would be the Invoice Number. An invoice number is a manufactured identification string generated by Company ABC for each created bill. If you get a match by invoice number, you can be highly confident that payment should be applied against this invoice number.

First, you need to create a stream of items to process in your Data Flow. You'll do this by querying all pending payments that at least have some sort of data in the RawInvoiceNbr field. If there is no data in this field, the items can't be matched through an automated process until a subject-matter expert can look up the item or identify it in another way. Add an OLE DB Source to the Data Flow. Set up the following properties:

Property	Value
Connection	CaseStudy.OLEDB Connection
DataAccessMode	SQLCommand
SQLCommandText	SELECT h.ImportType, BankBatchDtlID, UPPER(RawInvoiceNbr) as RawInvoiceNbr, PaymentAmount FROM bankbatchdetail d INNER JOIN BANKBATCH h ON h.bankbatchid = d.bankbatchid WHERE matcheddate is null AND RawInvoiceNbr is not null AND RawInvoiceNbr <> ''

Notice that the [RawInvoiceNbr] field has been converted to uppercase before it is delivered into your data stream, to be consistent with the stored data and to result in more lookup matches.

Add a Sort Transform to the output of the OLE DB Source and sort the data by the [BankBatchDtlID] field in ascending order. Even though you could order the incoming data by BankBatchDtlID by adding an ORDER BY clause to the SQLCommandText property in the OLE DB Source, you still need this Sort Transform to sort the stream for a later Merge Join operation.

Add the first Lookup Transform, which is going to be a lookup by Invoice. You are going to add many of these, so we'll go over this first one in detail. For each item in the stream, you want to set up an attempt to match the information in the [RawInvoiceNbr] field from the different payment Data Sources to your real invoice number in the invoice dimension table. In other lookups, you may attempt name or email lookups. The invoice number is considered your highest-confidence match because it is a unique number generated by the billing system. If you find a match to the invoice number, you have identified the payment. Set up the following properties on the component:

Property	Value
Connection	CaseStudy.OLEDB Connection
SQL Query	SELECT InvoiceID, Convert(Nvarchar(50), UPPER(ltrim(rtrim(Invoice Nbr)))) As InvoiceNbr, CustomerID FROM INVOICE

In the Columns tab, connect the Input Column [RawInvoiceNbr] to the Lookup Column [InvoiceNbr]. If there is a match on the lookup, pull back the InvoiceID and CustomerID. This information will be in the Lookup data. Do this by adding these columns as Lookup columns to the Lookup Column Grid.

The default behavior of the Lookup Transform is to fail if there is a no-match condition. You don't want this to happen, because you expect that you aren't going to get 100 percent matches on each transform. What you'd like to be able to do is separate the matches from the non-matches, so that you only continue to look up items in the stream that are unmatched. To do that, you will use this built-in capability to "know" if a match has been made, and instead of failing the component or package, you will divert the stream to another lookup. In the Lookup Transform, use the Configure Error Output button to set up the action of a failed lookup to be Redirect Row as in Figure 23-37.

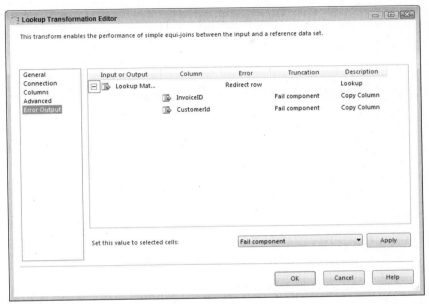

Figure 23-37

Because the invoice number can be keyed incorrectly at the bank or truncated, it may be off by only a few digits, or by using an "O" instead of a zero. Using only inner-join matching, you may miss the match, but there may still be a good chance of a match if you can use the Fuzzy Lookup. This package is also going to use a lot of Fuzzy Lookup Transforms. They all need to be set up the same way, so you'll do this one in detail and then just refer to it later.

1. Add a Fuzzy Lookup Transform to the Data Flow to the right of the Lookup Task. Connect the Error Output of the previous Invoice Lookup Transform to the Fuzzy Lookup. Set up the OLE DB Connection to CaseStudy.OLEDB.

2. Select the option to Generate a New Index with the reference table set to [Invoice]. (Later it will be more efficient to change these settings to store and then use a cached reference table.)

3. In the Columns tab, match the [RawInvoiceNbr] fields to the [InvoiceNbr] field.

4. Deselect the extra Error columns from being passed through from the input columns. These columns were added to the stream because it was diverted using the error handler. You aren't interested in these columns because a no-match is not considered an error for this transform.

5. Right-click the line between the two columns. Click Edit Relationship on the pop-up menu. Check all the comparison flags starting with Ignore.

6. Select the InvoiceID and CustomerID fields to return as the lookup values if a match can be made with the fuzzy logic.

7. In the Advanced tab, set the Similarity Threshold up to .70 for the Invoice fuzzy match. The Similarity Threshold is essentially a rated value to indicate how close of a match a source data value is to a lookup value. The closer this value is set to 1, the more exact the match must be. This setting of .70 would have been determined after heavy data profiling — that you can now also do in SSIS with the Data Profiler Task.

Because the output of the Fuzzy Lookup contains a number indicating the similarity threshold, you can use this number to separate the stream into high- and low-similarity matches. Low-similarity matches will continue through further matching attempts. High-similarity matches will be remerged with other high-similarity matches. Add a Conditional Split Task to separate the output into two streams based on the field [_Similarity], which represents a mathematical measurement of "sameness" between the [RawInvoiceNbr] provided by Company ABC's customers and the InvoiceNbr that you have on file. The splits should always be set up like Figure 23-38.

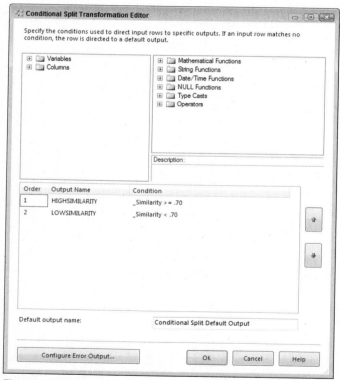

Figure 23-38

You want to merge any high-similarity matching from the Fuzzy Lookup and the previous Inner-Join Lookup Transform, but to do that, the Fuzzy Lookup output must be sorted. This step will also be repeated many times. Add a Sort Transform and select to sort the column [BankBatchDtlID] field in ascending order. The Sort Transforms do two things: They sort data, and they also allow you to remove the redundant fuzzy-data-added columns by deselecting them for pass-through. Remove references to these fields (_Similarity, Confidence, ErrorCode, and ErrorColumn) when passing data through sorts.

Add a Merge Component to the Data Flow. Connect the output of the Invoice Lookup to the High Similarity output of the Fuzzy Lookup (via the Sort Transform). In the Merge Editor you can see all the fields from both sides of the merge. Sometimes a field will come over with the value to <IGNORE> the field. Make sure you match these fields, or some of the data is going to be dropped from your stream. A merge transaction will look like Figure 23-39.

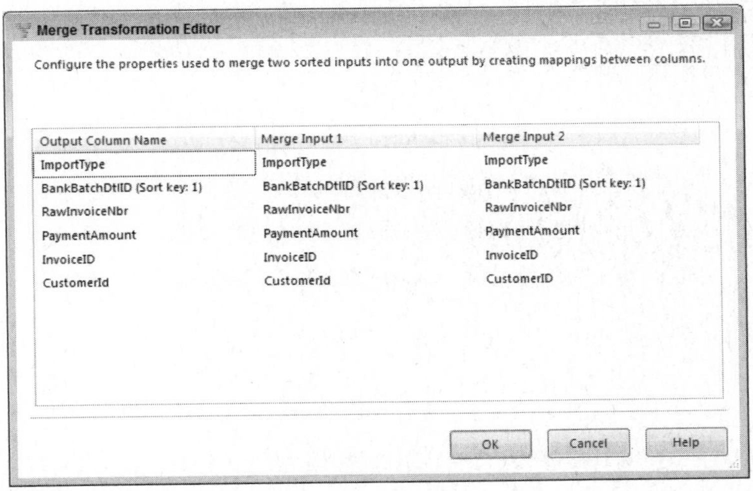

Merge Transformation Editor

Configure the properties used to merge two sorted inputs into one output by creating mappings between columns.

Output Column Name	Merge Input 1	Merge Input 2
ImportType	ImportType	ImportType
BankBatchDtlID (Sort key: 1)	BankBatchDtlID (Sort key: 1)	BankBatchDtlID (Sort key: 1)
RawInvoiceNbr	RawInvoiceNbr	RawInvoiceNbr
PaymentAmount	PaymentAmount	PaymentAmount
InvoiceID	InvoiceID	InvoiceID
CustomerId	CustomerId	CustomerID

Figure 23-39

At this point, the only items in the Merge are matched by Invoice, and you should have foreign keys for both the customer and the invoice. These keys can now be updated by executing the stored procedure usp_BankBatchDetail_Match for each of the matching items in your merged stream. Add an OLE DB command to the Data Flow and set up the OLE DB Connection. Set up the SQLCommand property as `usp_BankBatchDetail_Match ?, ?, ?`. Click Refresh to retrieve the parameters to match. Match the InvoiceID, CustomerID, and BankBatchDtlID fields from the input and output. The stored procedure will run for each row in your stream and automatically update the foreign keys. If a row is found with both invoice and customer keys, the stored procedure will also mark that transaction as complete.

This completes the High-Confidence Data Flow. At this point, your Data Flow should look like Figure 23-40. When this Data Flow returns to the Control Flow, the Execute SQL Task will recalculate the number of remaining pending transactions by count and by amount. The next step is the Medium-Confidence Data Flow.

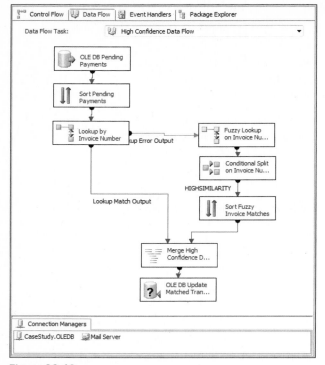

Figure 23-40

Matching Process Medium-Confidence Data Flow

The Medium-Confidence Data Flow is made up of matches using customer information. Because names and email addresses are more likely to be similar, this level of matching is not as high on the confidence-level continuum as an invoice number. Furthermore, identifying the customer is only the first step. You will still need to identify the invoice for the customer. To find the invoice, you'll attempt to match on the closest non-paid invoice by amount for the customer. All of these tasks, until you get to the end, are similar to the High-Confidence Data Flow. The only difference is that the lookups use the Customer table instead of the Invoice table. For this reason, we'll just list the basic steps. Refer to Figure 23-42 to see a picture of the final result to use as a roadmap as you put this Data Flow together.

1. Add an OLE DB Source, set up exactly the same way as for the High-Confidence Data Flow.

2. Add a Lookup to the Data Flow connecting to the OLE DB Source. Name it Email Lookup. Look for exact matches between RawInvoiceNbr and the field [Email] in the Customer table. Set the error handling to Redirect when encountering a Lookup error. Use this SQL Query:

```
Select CustomerID, CONVERT(NVARCHAR(50), UPPER(rtrim(Email))) as Email FROM
Customer WHERE Email is not null AND Email <> ''
```

3. Add another Lookup by Customer Name beside the Email Lookup. Feed it the error output of the Email Lookup. Look for exact matches between RawInvoiceNbr and the field [Name] in the Customer table. Set the error handling to Redirect when encountering a Lookup error. Use this SQL Query:

```
SELECT CustomerID, CONVERT(NVARCHAR(50), UPPER(rtrim([Name]))) as [Name] FROM
CUSTOMER WHERE [Name] is not null and [Name] <> ''
```

4. Add Sort Components to the outputs of both lookups. Place them directly under each lookup. Sort by BankBatchDtlID ascending. In the sort by name matches, don't forget to deselect the error columns.

5. Add a Merge Component to merge the two outputs of the Sorts for matches by Email and Name.

6. Add a Lookup using the CustomerLookup table next to the Name Lookup. Feed it the error output of the Customer Name Lookup. Look for exact matches between the fields [RawInvoiceNbr] and the lookup field [RawDataToMatch]. This lookup requires an additional match on the fields [ImportType] for both the input and output data. Set the error handling to Redirect. Use the table name [CustomerLookup] as the source. Look up and return the CustomerID.

7. Add a Sort to the CustomerLookup Task. Deselect the extra columns.

8. Add a Fuzzy Lookup Transform to the Data Flow. Connect it to the error output of the CustomerLookup Lookup. Connect to the Customer table, and match by RawInvoiceNbr to Email Address. Select the CustomerID for the lookup. Set the Similarity for this transform also to .70. Remove the columns for pass-through that start with lookup.

9. Add the Conditional Split Component to the output of the Fuzzy Lookup to separate the matches by similarity values above and below .70.

10. Moving to the left, add a new Merge Transform to merge the results of the email and name merge with the customer lookup matched sort results. Combine the matched results of the two sorted outputs.

11. Add a Sort to the High Similarity Results of the Fuzzy Lookup by Email. Deselect the columns that were added by the Fuzzy Lookup starting with "_". Sort by BatchDetailID.

12. Add a new Merge Task to combine the Email Fuzzy Lookup Sort to the Email, Name, and CustomerLookup merged results.

13. Add a Fuzzy Lookup Transform to the Data Flow beside the conditional split from the last Email Fuzzy Lookup. Name it Fuzzy Name Lookup. Move it to the same level to the right of the conditional lookup. Connect the Low Similarity Output from the Email Fuzzy Lookup to the new Fuzzy Name Lookup. Use the [Customer] table to look for matches matching [RawInvoiceNbr] to [Name]. Uncheck the pass-through checkbox for the input column [CustomerID] that is being fed by the Low Similarity stream. Retrieve a new lookup of CustomerID. In the Advanced tab, move the Similarity setting to .65. This time we'll accept a lower similarity setting based on previous Data Profiling.

14. Add another Conditional Split below the Fuzzy Name Lookup and split the output into High and Low Similarity, again using the .70 number.

15. Add a sort to sort the HIGHSIMILARITY output from the Conditional Split you just created. Remove the extra columns.

16. Add the last Merge Transform to merge the Sort from the high-similarity fuzzy name match with all the other matches that have been merged so far. At this point, you have captured in the output of this Merge Task all the transactions that you were not able to identify by invoice number, but that you have been able to identify by customer attributes of email or name. These are all of your medium-confidence matches. Knowing the customer might be good, but finding the payment invoice would be even better.

17. Add another Lookup Transform to the Data Flow below the last Merge Transform. Name it Lookup Invoice By Customer. Connect the output of the Merge Transform to it. Open the editor. Put the following basic SQL query in as the reference table:

```
"SELECT INVOICEID, CUSTOMERID, TotalBilledAmt FROM INVOICE"
```

In the Columns tab, link the CustomerID that you have discovered to the CustomerID in the invoice lookup table. Connect the paymentamount field to the TotalBilledAmount field. Go to the Advanced tab to update the contents of the Caching SQL statement to the following:

```
select * from (SELECT INVOICEID, CUSTOMERID, TotalBilledAmt FROM INVOICE) as
refTable  where [refTable].[CUSTOMERID] = ? and
(ABS([refTable].[TotalBilledAmt] - ?)<([RefTable].[TotalBilledAmt]*.05))
```

18. Click the Parameters button. A box for parameters will appear, as shown in Figure 23-41. Select the field PaymentAmount to substitute for Parameter1. This query looks for matches using the CustomerID field and an amount that is within 5 percent of the billed premium.

To have the result return an Invoice Number, click back on the Columns tab and select the InvoiceID field in the grid. At this stage, you don't care if you don't get a match in terms of error handling. Set the error-handling behavior to Ignore Error, and just send the data through regardless of whether it matches or not. If you have the customer ID and that's it, fine. If you have both, that's even better, but you'll send your results through regardless.

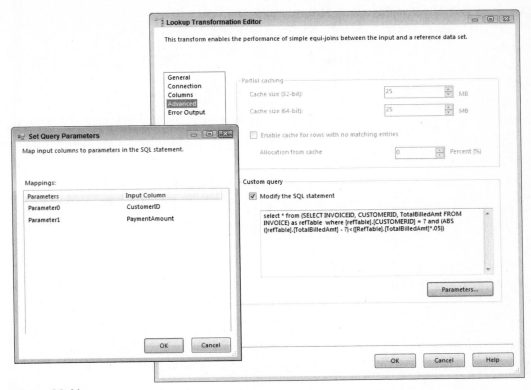

Figure 23-41

19. Add an OLE DB Command Transform to the Data Flow at the bottom. Attach a connection to the results of the last invoice lookup by amount. Set the connection to CaseStudy.OLEDB. Set the SQLCommand property to usp_BankBatchDetail_Match ?, ?, ?. Click Refresh to retrieve the parameters to match. Match the InvoiceID, CustomerID, and BankBatchDtlID fields from the input and output. The stored procedure will run for each row in your stream and automatically update the foreign keys. If a row is found with both invoice and customer keys, the stored procedure will also mark that transaction as complete.

This completes the task of building the Medium-Confidence Data Flow and the CaseStudy_Process package. The Data Flow should look similar to Figure 23-42.

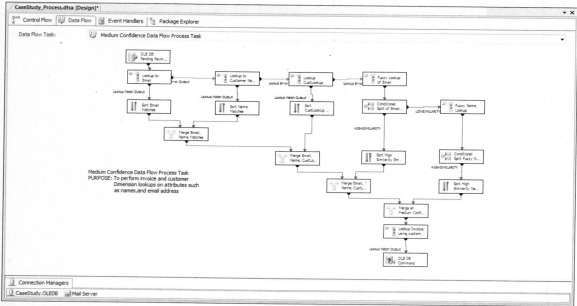

Figure 23-42

Once you have the package created and the build is successful, you are ready to run the package and review the results. Go ahead and run the CaseStudy_Process package before proceeding.

Interpreting the Results

Before you started this exercise of creating the CaseStudy_Process SSIS package, you had loaded a set of 16 payment transactions for matching into the BankBatchDetail table. By running a series of SQL statements comparing the RawInvoiceNbr with invoices and customers, you could only retrieve a maximum of 7 matches. This translates into a 44 percent match of payments to send to the payment processors without any further human interaction. The development of this package with heavy usage of Fuzzy Lookup Transforms increases your identification hit-rate to 13 out of 16 matches, or an 81 percent matching percentage. The results can be broken out as shown in the following table:

Stage in Process	# of New Matches	Match Percent
High-Confidence Invoice Match	2	12%
Med-Confidence Invoice Match	9	56%
Med-Confidence Customer Match	2	12%

As you may recall, the business expectations were to make an improvement to match all but 20 to 40 percent of every payment that comes into Company ABC. You are right at, or just under, the best percentage with your test data — and this is just a beginning. Remember that the unidentified items will be worked on by SMEs, who will store the results of their matching customer information in the CustomerLookup table. Incidentally, you used this data even though the table is empty within the Lookup CustLookup Transform in the Medium-Confidence Data Flow. As SME-provided information is stored, the Data Flow will become "smarter" in matching incoming payments by referring to this matching source as well.

Now look at the three items that weren't matched by your first run:

Item Matching Information	Payment Amount
Intl Sports Association	$ 34,953.00
JBROWN@CAPITALCYCLES.COM	$ 21,484.00
181INTERNA	$ 18,444.00

The first item looks like a customer name, and if you search in the Customer table, you'd find a similar customer named International Sport Assoc. Because it is highly likely that future payments will be remitted in the same manner, the package could store the match between the customer's actual name and the string Intl Sports Association in the CustLookup table. Look back at Step 6 of the Matching Process for Medium-Confidence Data Flow to see where this could be plugged in. If you add these entries manually to the CustLookup table and reset the bankbatch tables, when you rerun the files you'll see that future runs will match these customers.

The second item looks like a customer email address. If you can find the customer to whom this email address belongs, you can update that information directly into the Customer table to facilitate a future match. There is one customer named Capital Road Cycles that has several invoices at or around $20,000. You could also update the CustLookup table with matching data for this email address.

If you query the Invoice table using an invoice number like 181INTERNA, you find several, but they are all for an amount of $34,953.00. This payment is for $18,444.00. Because the payment is significantly different from your billed amount, someone is going to have to look at this payment to approve the processing because you can't make a reliable match based on amount. This transaction will be manually processed based on your current business rules regardless of anything you could have done. Because the matching is against an invoice number, you also don't have anything of use for your customer lookup table.

If you were to now delete all the rows from the BankBatch and BankBatchDetail tables and rerun both the CaseStudy_Load and CaseStudy_Process packages, the payment matching process now improves to 15 out of 16 matches — a whopping 94 percent match. Company ABC will be highly pleased with the capabilities that you have introduced them to with this SSIS solution.

Creating a Parent Driver Package

These packages were designed to run together in a sequence. The three packages that comprise the payment ETL processes should always run serially before the CaseStudy_Process package is attempted. Each time the CaseStudy_Process runs, additional payments will be matched to the invoices. Unidentified payments will need to be matched using an external application. However, when users have to manually identify an item, their identification can be stored either by updating the data in the dimension tables or in your lookup tables. The sample packages here would then use that information in the medium-confidence-level Data Flow on the next run of the job. To have each of these packages run in concert, create an additional package called CaseStudy_Driver that will coordinate the running of each of the child packages.

Driver Package Setup

To get started, you need to create a new SSIS package named CaseStudy_Driver in `c:\casestudy\casestudy_driver\`. When the project is built, go to the Solution Explorer and click the `Package.dtsx` file. In the Property window, find the Name property and change the name from `package.dtsx` to `casestudy_driver.dtsx`. Answer Yes to change the name of the package object as well.

Add four SSIS Package Tasks to the Control Flow work surface. Put the first three that will represent the Load packages into a Sequence Container to provide a visual indication that they are related. Connect the three Package Tasks in the Sequence Container together with a completion constraint. Then connect the Sequence Container to the last Package Task.

Name the Package Tasks CaseStudy_Load_Bank, CaseStudy_Load_ACH, CaseStudy_Load_Email, and CaseStudy_Process, respectively. Then open up each Package Task and assign the package by browsing to the package matching the name of the task. You can browse to the path of the packages that should be in the `c:\casestudy\` folder hierarchy.

The final package should look like Figure 23-43.

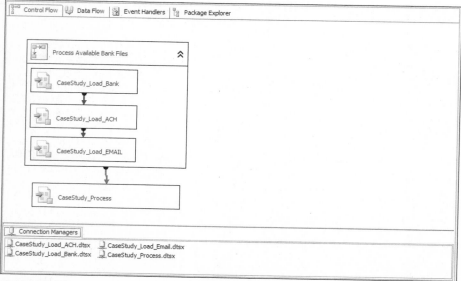

Figure 23-43

This completes the development of the Driver package. You can now reset the BankBatch tables and run the whole solution under this one package. When you do this in Visual Studio, the IDE will pop into each child solution so that you can see the Control and Data Flows within each package.

Driver Package Deployment

Developing these packages separately makes the packages easier to troubleshoot and maintain. Merging all the packages makes the solution easier to run and coordinate. This package can now be easily scheduled in the SQL Agent, where it would look like Figure 23-44.

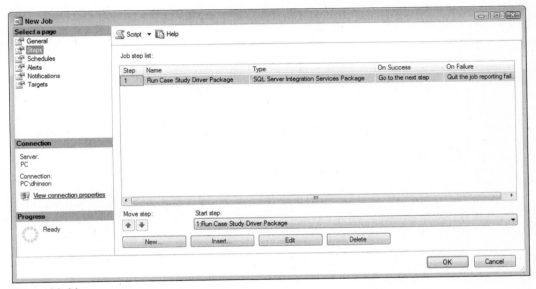

Figure 23-44

Summary

During this project, you gained some experience with most of the transforms and more than a few of the common tasks in the Toolbox. You learned firsthand that the new Data Flow is powerful, because you worked through typical staging logic in memory without having to commit the data and witnessed the results of the new Fuzzy Lookup Transformations. You saw how visual the environment is and how easy it is to understand what is going on with the stream as it is being transformed. Transforming is what you do in the Data Flow, not in the Control Flow — even though it looks like a Control Flow page.

This case study provided an in-depth look at the new capabilities of the SSIS development environment. It is a real development environment now. That is why you first started with some business requirements and worked through the exercise like a development project. You focused on the nuts and bolts of error handling, naming conventions, and some practical tips for testing. Hopefully you saw a few things that you can use to solve that problem on your desk with SSIS.

Index

S

powered by

books24x7

Programmer to Programme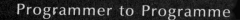

Take your library
wherever you go.

Now you can access more than 200 complete Wrox books online, wherever you happen to be! Every diagram, description, screen capture, and code sample is available with your subscription to the **Wrox Reference Library**. For answers when and where you need them, go to wrox.books24x7.com and subscribe today!

Find books on

- **ASP.NET**
- **C#/C++**
- **Database**
- **General**
- **Java**
- **Mac**
- **Microsoft Office**
- **.NET**
- **Open Source**
- **PHP/MySQL**
- **SQL Server**
- **Visual Basic**
- **Web**
- **XML**

wrox™

www.wrox.com